W9-APL-480

Frommer's®

1st
Edition

Europe

Macmillan • USA

MACMILLAN TRAVEL

A Simon & Schuster Macmillan Company
1633 Broadway
New York, NY 10019

Find us online at **http://www.mgr.com/travel** or
on America Online at Keyword: **Frommer's**

ISBN 0-02-861388-0
ISSN 1091-9511

Executive Editor: Alice Fellows
Editors: Ron Boudreau, Robin Michaelson, Kelly Regan
Production Editor: Lori Cates
Digital Cartography by Roberta Stockwell and Ortelius Design
Design by Michele Laseau

SPECIAL SALES

Bulk purchases (10+ copies) of Frommer's and selected Macmillan travel guides are
available to corporations, organizations, mail-order catalogs, institutions, and charities at
special discounts, and can be customized to suit individual needs. For more information
write to Special Sales, Macmillan General Reference, 1633 Broadway, New York, NY
10019.

Manufactured in the United States of America

Contents

3   The Czech Republic 140

by John Mastrini & Alan Crosby

4   Denmark 187

by Darwin Porter & Danforth Prince

5   England 210

by Darwin Porter & Danforth Prince

6   France   285

by Darwin Porter & Danforth Prince

7 Germany   378

by Darwin Porter & Danforth Prince

8 Greece   458

by John Bozman & Sherry Marker

List of Maps

ABOUT THE AUTHORS

Darwin Porter, a native of North Carolina, was assigned to write the very first edition of a Frommer guide devoted solely to one European country. Since then, he has written many bestselling Frommer guides to all the major European destinations. In 1982 he was joined in his research efforts across England by **Danforth Prince,** formerly of the Paris bureau of the *New York Times,* who has traveled and written extensively about Europe.

John Bozman has been traveling in and writing about Greece for many years. He is a novelist, playwright, and writer of screen plays, and has traveled extensively in Europe, Latin America, and Southeast Asia. He is co-author of *Frommer's Greece, 1st Edition,* and *Frommer's Frugal Guide to Greece* and author of *Frommer's Europe.*

Alan Crosby has lived and worked as a journalist in Prague for the last 6 years. He is co-author of *Frommer's Prague & the Best of the Czech Republic, 1st Edition.*

Richard Jones, who lives in London, conducts tours of Ireland and Britain, and leads his own walking tours in London. He is the author of *Frommer's Walking Tours: London* and *Frommer's Walking Tours: England's Favorite Cities.*

Joseph S. Lieber's grandparents emigrated from Hungary at the turn of the century, and he has lived there off and on for a number of years. A student of European history, he now lives in Boston. He is author of *Frommer's Budapest & the Best of Hungary.*

Sherry Marker's love of Greece began when she majored in classical Greek at Harvard. She has studied at the American School of Classical Studies in Athens, and studied ancient history at the University of California at Berkley. Author of a number of guides to Greece, she has published articles in the *New York Times, Travel & Leisure,* and *Hampshire Life.* She has books on a variety of subjects, including a history of London for young adults and biographies of Norman Rockwell and Edward Hopper. She is co-author of *Frommer's Greece, 1st Edition.*

John Mastrini is a former television news anchor from the United States. He has lived in Prague since 1989 where he works as a journalist and media consultant. He is co-author of *Frommer's Prague & the Best of the Czech Republic, 1st Edition.*

George McDonald is a professional travel writer who lives in Brussels, and has lived and worked in many countries around the world. He has authored a number of travel books, as well as numerous articles, and is author of *Frommer's Amsterdam* and *Frommer's Belgium, Holland & Luxembourg.*

An Invitation to the Reader

In researching this book, we discovered many wonderful places—hotels, restaurants, shops, and more. We're sure you'll find others. Please tell us about them, so we can share the information with your fellow travelers in upcoming editions. If you were disappointed with a recommendation, we'd love to know that, too. Please write to:

Frommer's Europe, 1st Edition
Macmillan Travel
1633 Broadway
New York, NY 10019

An Additional Note

Please be advised that travel information is subject to change at any time—and this is especially true of prices. We therefore suggest that you write or call ahead for confirmation when making your travel plans. The authors, editors, and publisher cannot be held responsible for the experiences of readers while traveling. Your safety is important to us, however, so we encourage you to stay alert and be aware of your surroundings. Keep a close eye on cameras, purses, and wallets, all favorite targets of thieves and pickpockets.

What the Symbols Mean

✪ Frommer's Favorites
Hotels, restaurants, attractions, and entertainment you should not miss.

⑤ Super-Special Values
Hotels and restaurants that offer great value for your money.

The following abbreviations are used for credit cards:

AE	American Express	EC	EuroCard
CB	Carte Blanche	JCB	Japan Credit Bank
DC	Diners Club	MC	MasterCard
ER	enRoute	V	Visa

Introduction: Planning a Trip to Europe

by Darwin Porter & Danforth Prince

Irresistible and intriguing, the ever-changing Europe of today has more than ever to offer the visitor. In compiling this volume for today's time-pressed traveler, we've tried to do two things: lead the traveler to Europe's famous cities, their art and architecture, and guide the traveler to all the must-see experiences that no one should miss. So though this guide has to skim the highlights, we've also tossed in offbeat destinations and adventurous suggestions to lead to surprises and delights around every corner. In other words, we've tried to capture something of the best—the very essence of Europe—into one carry-along edition.

EUROPE TODAY

The Old World is still here, more polished and refined than before, but you'll also encounter the New Europe. Change is afoot, but much of the old remains. While attempts are being made in that direction, Europe is hardly one country yet. The European Union is still an association, not yet a union, and the day hasn't quite come when you no longer need to show a passport at border crossings. But it's on the way.

A lot of other changes are coming as well, including a single European currency (*ecu*). But until all these changes are brought about, you can happily settle for the way things are at present. After all, it's still the diversity that attracts the foreign visitor. From the splendor of a Greek temple towering above the arid Sicilian landscape to the majestic peaks of the Alps, from the sound of flamenco in a Madrid tavern to the blasting of a brass band in Munich's Hofbräuhaus, from the Portuguese Algarve's beach resorts to the chilly villages of Swedish Lapland above the Arctic Circle—diversity is what it's all about. There's no other place on earth where you can experience such enormous cultural changes by driving from one mountain valley to another where you're likely to encounter not only a different language but different food and architecture as well.

If you've come to pay your respects to the past, you're on the right continent. Europe saw some of the greatest intellectual and artistic developments the world has ever known. Museums are repositories of much of this past glory. But the good news is that the continent is still in a dynamic, creative mode—artistic and cultural ferment are still very much part of the present. The dynamic European environment is all about life, innovation, entertainment, and, of course, food, as well as artistic and cultural grandeur.

Europe is also about people. Europeans have seen the best and worst of times, and a new, better educated, and more sophisticated younger generation is waiting to welcome you. They may seem a bit standoffish at first, maybe a little distrustful, but once you praise their food and drink, the beauty of a landscape, the quality of craftsmanship in a product, they may melt before your eyes and welcome you as part of the family.

We've tried to prepare this edition to help you discover where you want to go and what you want to see. This introductory chapter is designed to help you with what you'll need to know before you go—the advance-planning tools for an enjoyable trip. The greatest reward, of course, will come later when you discover Europe for yourself.

1 Visitor Information & Entry Requirements

SOURCES OF VISITOR INFORMATION   Tourist Offices   Start with the European tourist offices in the United States, Canada or England. If you live in New York or London, you're especially fortunate because often you can visit national tourist offices in person; otherwise, you must write or call for information. Many of the larger countries have offices in such cities as Los Angeles or Chicago, perhaps Miami.

If you aren't sure which country you want to visit, send for a 60-page booklet, distributed free with maps and color photos, called *Planning Your Trip to Europe.* This information-packed document is revised annually by the 26-nation European Travel Commission. Contact: European Planner, P.O. Box 1754, New York, NY 10185 (☎ **800/863-8767**).

You may also want to obtain **U.S. State Department** background bulletins. Contact the Superintendent of Documents, U.S. Government Printing Office, Washington, DC 20402 (☎ 202/783-3238). The U.S. government is also the best source of travel advisories. Contact the **U.S. Department of State's Citizen Emergency Center** (☎ 202/647-5225 or 202/647-4000 outside business hours). A similar service is provided for Britishers by the **Travel Advice Unit** (☎ 0171/270-4129 in London Mon–Fri 9:30am–4pm), a branch of the Foreign Office.

Travel Videos   A good source for these is **Small World Productions,** P.O. Box 28369, Seattle, WA 96118 (☎ **206/329-7167**), which offers 39 videos for different countries. One of the most useful of these is *Europe Through the Back Door,* although it's a bit dated (1987). The cost is $24.95, plus $4 shipping.

Another useful source is **Complete Guide to Special Interest Video** from Video Learning Library, 15838 N. 62nd St., Scottsdale, AZ 85254 (☎ **800/526-7002** or 602/596-9970). This guide, costing $19.95, plus $3.50 shipping, contains more than 10,000 travel listings. Travel videos, lasting from half an hour to 1 1/2 hours, can be rented or bought directly from the Video Learning Library.

The Internet   The Internet can provide lots of travel-related information. The danger here is overkill, as you'll quickly realize after spending time on-line trying to access the specific information you need and want.

Some commercial providers, including Prodigy, CompuServe, and America Online, offer services that can reserve by credit or charge card most of the components of your upcoming trip. You can also tune directly into the Internet databases that are provided by the tourist offices of the countries you plan to visit or the home page of the destination itself.

There are also dozens of different chat lines and newsgroups that share insights into the experiences of other travelers—but be warned that the validity of such information is open to question.

Access any legitimate web browser by initiating a search that begins with the keyword "travel" and selecting wherever you want to go after that by pointing and clicking. To place yourself in a position of receiving messages relating to travel, access the **Travel-L** list. Send an e-mail message to "listserv@mv3090.ege.edu.tr" to subscribe. When prompted for a "subject," leave the box blank; in the body of the message, type "subscribe travel-l<first name><last name>."

Travel Agents   If you decide to use a travel agent, make sure that the agent is a member of the American Society of Travel Agents (ASTA). If you get poor service from an agent, you can complain to the **ASTA Consumer Affairs Department,** 1101 King St., Alexandria, VA 22314 (☎ **703/739-2782**). You might also want to obtain a copy of a booklet, *Avoiding Travel Problems.* To do so, mail a self-addressed, stamped envelope to ASTA World Headquarters, Fulfillment Department, 1101 King St., Alexandria, VA 22314.

Newsletters & Magazines   Many travel newsletters are rip-offs and not worth your investment in them. However, there are a few good ones. Our favorite, *Travel Smart,* 40 Beechdale Rd., Dobbs Ferry, NY 10522 (☎ **800/327-3633** or 914/693-8300), is packed with money-saving tips and filled with the latest offerings in travel to Europe and other places. The introductory subscription costs $37, with a renewal rate of $44. It's issued monthly, as is the *Consumer Reports Travel Letter,* Circulation Department, P.O. Box 53629, Boulder, CO 80322 (☎ **800/234-1970**), costing $39 annually.

Oriented toward budget travel is *ITN,* a 100-page nonglossy monthly that's honest and candid, with updates on everything from discount airfares to the best B&Bs. The classifieds are particularly intriguing if you're an adventurous traveler. The cost of an annual subscription is $18 in the United States (add another $10 for other countries). A lifetime subscription costs $225. Contact **International Travel News,** 520 Calvados Ave., Sacramento, CA 95815 (☎ **800/366-9191** for credit-card subscriptions).

"Culturgrams" are written by a local of a particular country and cover the mores and manners of the country, along with addresses of sources or information. Useful maps are also included. They're issued by the **Kennedy Center Publications Office,** Brigham Young University, P.O. Box 24538, Provo, UT 84602 (☎ **800/528-6279** to order; fax 801/378-5882). Fax orders must either be prepaid or accompanied by credit/charge-card information. The cost is $3 per culturgram, with discounts granted with purchases of six or more "grams."

Travel Bookstores   If you live outside a large urban area, you can order maps or travel guides from bookstores specializing in mail- or phone-order service. Some of these are: **Book Passage,** 51 Tamal Vista Blvd., Corte Madera, CA 94925 (☎ 800/321-9785 or 415/927-0960); **The Complete Traveller,** 199 Madison Ave., New York, NY 10016 (☎ 212/685-9007); **Forsyth Travel Library,** 9154 W. 57th St. (P.O. Box 2975), Shawnee Mission, KS 66201 (☎ 800/367-7984 or 913/384-3440); and **The Traveller's Bookstore,** 22 W. 52nd St., New York, NY 10019 (☎ 800/755-8728 or 212/664-0995).

Canadians can contact **Ulysses Bookshop,** 4176 rue St-Denis, Montréal, PQ H2M5 (☎ 514/843-9447), or 101 Yorkville Ave., Toronto, ON M5R 1C1 (☎ 416/323-3609).

PASSPORTS   U.S. Citizens   A passport, needed for entry into European countries, is available at passport agencies, authorized post offices, and clerks of court— or you can write for Form DSP-11 for a new passport or Form DSP-82 to renew an old one. Contact **Passport Services,** Office of Correspondence, Department of State,

1111 19th St. NW, Washington, DC 20522. Proof of citizenship is required, including an expired passport, a certified copy of your birth certificate (must have a registrar's seal), a document of your birth abroad, or naturalized citizenship documents. Military IDs, student IDs with photo, driver's licenses, and employee identification cards are accepted as well, along with two identical recent 2- by 2-inch photos. First-time applicants age 18 and older are charged $65, plus a $10 processing fee. Persons under 18 are charged $30, plus a $10 processing fee. Children 14 and older must apply in person; otherwise parents and guardians can apply. To answer your questions, request *Your Trip Abroad* (publication #044-000-02335-1) for $1.25 from the U.S. Government Printing Office, Superintendent of Documents, P.O. Box 371954, Pittsburgh, PA 15250 (☎ **202/512-1800**). To report a passport lost or stolen, call 202/647-0518.

Canadian Citizens   Post offices, passport offices, and most travel agencies issue application forms, and citizens can also apply in person at one of 28 regional offices. To apply by mail, send an application form with proof of citizenship, two identical passport photographs, and $35 in Canadian currency to **Passport Office,** Foreign Affairs, Ottawa, ON K1A 0G3. For more information, call 800/567-6868.

VISAS   Countries covered in this guide do not require visas for U.S. or Canadian citizens unless they intend a protracted stay. The visa situation, however, is always changing, and a 20-page booklet, issued by the U.S. Department of State's Bureau of Consular Affairs, will keep you abreast of entry requirements. Send 50¢ to the **Consumer Information Center,** Department 371B, Pueblo, CO 81009. The latest information can also be obtained by calling 202/663-1225 Mon–Fri 8:30am–5pm.

DRIVING PERMITS   Although a valid U.S. state driver's license usually suffices, technically motorists need an International Driving Permit (IDP) to drive in many European countries. Your car-rental agency will advise. To play it safe, it's always wise to travel with an IDP, which can be obtained from the **American Automobile Association (AAA).** Those 18 and over can submit two 2- by 2-inch photographs and a valid U.S. state driver's license, plus a $10 fee. If you're not near a branch of the AAA, you can write for an IDP application to AAA, 1000 AAA Dr., Mail Stop 28, Heathrow, FL 32746 (☎ **407/444-4240**).

2 Money

ATMs   Plus, Cirrus, and other networks connecting automated-teller machines operate in Europe. If your bank card or credit card has been programmed with a PIN (Personal Identification Number), it's likely that you can use your card at ATMs abroad. Check to see if your PIN code must be reprogrammed for usage in Europe. Note that Discover cards are accepted only in the United States. For Cirrus locations abroad, call 800/424-7787. For Plus usage abroad, dial 800/843-7587.

CREDIT & CHARGE CARDS   Most middle-bracket and virtually all first-class and deluxe hotels and restaurants in Europe accept major credit and charge cards— American Express, Diners Club, MasterCard, and Visa. In budget establishments, it depends—many do, some don't.

Note: The exchange rate for credit/charge-card purchases is determined at the time the transaction is received at the card's headquarters—not when you incurred an expense. Based on fluctuating exchange rates, that can work either for or against you.

TRAVELER'S CHECKS   Most large banks sell traveler's checks, charging fees that average between 1% and 2% of the value of the checks you buy, although some out-of-the-way banks, in rare instances, have charged as much as 7%. If your bank wants more than a 2% commission, it sometimes pays to call the traveler's check issuers directly for the address of outlets where this commission will be lower.

Issuers sometimes have agreements with groups to sell checks commission free. For example, American Automobile Association (AAA) clubs sell American Express checks in several currencies without commission.

American Express (☎ 800/221-7282 in the U.S. and Canada) is one of the largest issuers of traveler's checks. No commission is charged to holders of certain types of American Express cards. The company issues checks denominated in U.S. and Canadian dollars, British pounds sterling, Swiss and French francs, German marks, and Dutch guilders.

Citicorp (☎ 800/645-6556 in the U.S. and Canada, or 813/623-1709, collect, from anywhere else in the world) issues checks in U.S. dollars, British pounds, and German marks.

Thomas Cook (☎ 800/223-7373 in the U.S. and Canada, or 609/987-7300, collect, from other parts of the world) issues MasterCard traveler's checks denominated in U.S. and Canadian dollars, French francs, British pounds, German marks, Dutch guilders, and Spanish pesetas.

Interpayment Services (☎ 800/221-2426 in the U.S. or Canada, or 212/858-8500, collect, from other parts of the world) sells Visa checks that are issued by a consortium of member banks and the Thomas Cook organization. Traveler's checks are denominated in U.S. and Canadian dollars, British pounds, and German marks.

Wire Services   If you find yourself out of money, a new wire service provided by American Express can help you tap willing friends and family for emergency funds. Through **MoneyGram,** 6200 S. Quebec St. (P.O. Box 5118), Englewood, CO 80155 (☎ 800/926-9400), money can be sent around the world in less than 10 minutes. Senders should call AMEX to learn the address of the closest outlet that handles MoneyGrams. Cash, credit card, or the occasional personal check (with ID) are acceptable forms of payment. AMEX's fee for the service is $10 for the first $300 with a sliding scale for larger sums. The service includes a short telex message and a 3-minute phone call from sender to recipient. The beneficiary must present a photo ID at the outlet where the money is received.

CURRENCY EXCHANGE   Although currency conversions in this guide were accurate at press time, European exchange rates fluctuate. Before going, check a national tourist office or the financial pages of your local newspaper, or else call **Thomas Cook Currency Services** (☎ 212/757-6915 in New York, or 0171/480-7226 in London).

Many hotels in Europe will not accept dollar-denominated personal checks, and if they do, they'll certainly charge for the conversion. In some cases they'll accept countersigned traveler's checks, or a credit card, but if you're prepaying a deposit on hotel reservations, it's cheaper and easier to pay with a check drawn on a European bank. This can be arranged by a currency specialist such as **Ruesch International,** 700 11th St. NW, Washington, DC 20001 (☎ 800/424-2923 or 202/408-1200). To place an order, call Ruesch and state the type and amount of the check you need. Ruesch will quote a U.S. dollar equivalent, adding a $2 fee per check as its service fee. After receiving your dollar-denominated personal check for the agreed-upon amount, Ruesch will mail you a bank draft in your currency of choice, drawn on a European bank and payable to whichever party you specified. Ruesch will also convert checks expressed in foreign currency into U.S. dollars, provide foreign currencies in cash from more than 120 countries, and sell traveler's checks payable in either dollars or any of six foreign currencies.

TIPS ABOUT CURRENCY EXCHANGE It's more expensive to purchase foreign currency in your own country than it is once you've reached your destination. Therefore, bring only enough foreign currency to last the first 24 hours or so, saving your major cash transactions until you get there. If you're facing a holiday or a weekend, then protect yourself accordingly by carrying more foreign currency.

Whenever possible, convert your currency at a bank, as invariably they give better rates than tourist offices, hotels, or travel agencies. Remember: you lose money every time you make a transaction, so it's better to convert large sums at once and avoid too frequent a service fee. Because of the vagaries of European banking, you often get more money when converting traveler's checks than you do from converting cash. Always try, if possible, to cash a traveler's check at the bank issuing it—American Express for American Express traveler's checks, for example.

Try not to "overconvert"—that is, convert more dollars into foreign currency than you'll need. When you have to convert the money back into dollars at the end of the trip, you'll lose on the exchange, as you are in fact buying dollars now instead of selling them.

VAT All European countries charge a Value-Added Tax on goods and services. Rates vary from country to country—from 15% to 25%—though the goal in EU countries is to arrive at a uniform rate of about 15%. You can get back most of the tax on purchases (but not services) that are over a designated amount (usually $50–$100) when you leave the country. Regulations vary from country to country, so inquire at the tourist office when you arrive to find out the procedure—ask what percentage of the tax will be refunded, if the refund will be given to you at the airport or train station, or mailed to you at a later date. Look for a sign posted in participating stores. Ask the storekeeper for the necessary forms, save all your receipts, and, if possible, keep the purchases in their original packages. Plan to allow an extra 30 minutes or so at the airport or train station to process the VAT-refund forms.

3 When to Go

Europe is a continent for all seasons, offering everything from a bikini beach party on the Riviera in summer to the finest skiing in the world in the Alps in winter.

Europe has a continental climate with distinct seasons, but there are great variations in temperature from one part to another. Northern Norway, for example, is plunged into Arctic darkness in winter, while in sunny Sicily the climate is temperate. Europe is north of most of the United States, so all over the continent, except in the south, summer daylight hours are somewhat longer than in the United States, while night falls earlier in the winter. Seasonal changes are generally less extreme than in the United States.

The peak travel period—when all tourist facilities are strained—lasts from mid-May to mid-September. In general, this is also the most expensive time to travel, except in Austria and Switzerland where prices are actually higher in winter during the ski season. And since Scandinavian hotels depend on business clients instead of tourists, lower prices can often be found in the fleeting summer months when business clients vacation and a smaller number of tourists take over.

Smaller crowds, relatively fair weather, and often lower prices at hotels are granted in the shoulder seasons—the months immediately before mid-May and after mid-September. Off-season (except at ski resorts) is November to Easter, with the exception in many places of Christmas and New Year's. Italy is at its most crowded during the Easter celebrations.

If you want the latest weather update for your country of choice, call 900/ WEATHER and find out the prevailing conditions. The cost is 95¢ per minute.

CLIMATE   Britain & Ireland   Everyone knows that it rains a lot in Britain and Ireland. Winters are usually rainier than summers; August and September to mid-October are often the sunniest months. Summer daytime temperatures average in the low to mid-60s Fahrenheit, dropping to the 40s on winter nights. Ireland, whose shores are bathed by the Gulf Stream, tends to have the mildest climate, and also has the most changeable weather—a dark, rainy morning can quickly turn into a sunny afternoon, and vice versa. The Scottish Lowlands have a climate similar to England's, but the Highlands are much colder, with storms and snow in winter.

Scandinavia   Summer temperatures above the Arctic Circle average in the mid-50s Fahrenheit, dropping to the mid-teens during the dark winters. In the south, summer temperatures are in the 70s Fahrenheit, dropping to the 20s in winter. Fjords are often warm enough for summer swimming, but rain is frequent. The sun shines 24 hours a day in midsummer above the Arctic Circle. Denmark's climate is relatively mild by comparison, with moderate summer temperatures and winters that can be damp and foggy, with temperatures in the mid-30s.

Northern Europe   In the Netherlands, the weather is never extreme at any time of year. Summer temperatures average around 67°F and the winter average is about 40°F. The climate is rainy, however—the driest months are February to May. Mid-April to mid-May is when the tulip fields burst into color. The climate is very similar to that in northern Germany, where summer temperatures can rise into the 70s, and winters are damp and chilly. Belgium's climate is moderate, varying from 73°F in July and August to 40°F in December and January. It does rain a lot, but the weather is at its finest in July and August.

France & Germany   The weather in Paris is approximately the same as in the U.S. Mid-Atlantic states, but like most of Europe, there's less extreme variation in temperature than in the States. In summer the temperature rarely goes beyond the mid-70s. Summers are fair and can be hot along the Riviera. Winters tend to be mild, averaging in the 40s, although it's warmer along the Riviera. Germany's climate ranges from the moderate summers and chilly, damp winters in the north to the mild summers and very cold and sunny winters of the alpine south.

Switzerland & the Alps   The alpine climate is shared by Bavaria in southern Germany, and the Austrian Tyrol and Italian Dolomites—winters are cold and bright and spring comes late, with snow flurries well into April. Summers are mild and sunny, though the alpine regions can experience dramatic changes in weather any time of year.

Central Europe   In Vienna and along the Danube Valley the climate is moderate. Summer daytime temperatures average in the 70s, falling at night to the 50s. Winter temperatures are in the 30s and 40s during the day. In Budapest, temperatures can reach 80°F in August and 30°F in January, the coldest month. Winter is damp and chilly, spring is mild, and May and June are usually wet. The best weather is in the late summer through October. In Prague and Bohemia, summer months have an average temperature of 65°F, but are the rainiest months, while January and February are usually sunny and clear, with temperatures around freezing.

Southern Europe   Summers are hot in Italy, Spain, and Greece, with temperatures in the high 80s Fahrenheit, or even higher in some parts of Spain. Along the Italian Riviera, summer and winter temperatures are mild, and except in the alpine regions,

Italian winter temperatures rarely drop below freezing. The area around Madrid is dry and arid, and summers in Spain are coolest along the Atlantic coast, with mild temperatures year-round on the Costa del Sol. Portugal, as an Atlantic seaboard country, is very rainy, but has a temperature range between 50°F and 75°F year-round. In Greece there's sunshine all year. Winters are mild, with temperatures around 50°–55°F. Hot summer temperatures are often helped by cool breezes. The best seasons to visit Greece are mid-April to June and mid-September to the end of October, when the wildflowers bloom and the tourists go home.

4 Outdoor & Adventure Vacations

BALLOONING The world's largest hot-air–balloon operator is **Buddy Bombard Balloon Adventures,** 855 Donald Ross Rd., Juno Beach, FL 33408 (☎ **800/ 862-8537** or 407/775-0039). About three dozen hot-air balloons are available, some stationed in the Loire Valley and in Burgundy in France. The 5-day/4-night tours incorporate food and wine tasting and include all meals, lodging in Relais & Châteaux hotels, sightseeing attractions, rail transfers to and from Paris, and a daily balloon ride over vineyards and fields.

Filzmoos in the Austrian Tyrol is one of the best centers for the adventure of ballooning over Austria's dramatic alpine terrain. Arrangements can be made through the **Austrian Ballooning Club,** Endressstrasse 79, Vienna A-1230 (☎ **0222/ 889-8222**), or the **Balloon Sportclub Vienna,** Mariahilferstrasse 41–43, Vienna A-1060 (☎ **0222/587-8139**).

CANOEING TOURS Between May and early July, **Journeys Beyond,** P.O. Box 7511-FF, Jackson, WY 83001 (☎ **307/733-9615**), offers guided canoe tours on two of southwestern France's most scenic rivers, the Dordogne and the Tarn. Each lasts between 5 and 8 days and includes breakfast, dinner, and overnight accommodations in riverside inns as part of the net price, which runs $1,500–$1,975 per person, double occupancy (without airfare). Canoes are equipped to carry participants' luggage inside, all paddling is downstream, and inns are adjacent to the riverbanks. No more than 12 miles are covered per day. Itineraries on the Tarn include some sections with white water.

CYCLING Cycling tours are a good way to see Europe at your own pace. Some of the best are featured by the **Cyclists' Tourist Club,** 69 Meadrow, Godalming, Surrey, England GU7 3HS (☎ **01483/417-217**). Membership charges are £25 ($40) a year for adults and £12.50 ($20) for those 17 and under. Membership includes information and suggested cycling routes through most European countries.

Holland Bicycling Tours, Inc., P.O. Box 6485, Thousand Oaks, CA 91359 (☎ **800/852-3258**), is the North American representative of a Dutch-based company that leads 8-day bicycle tours in Europe. Cycling is on well laid-out paths and quiet country roads that are flat and mostly downhill.

If you'd like more options in arranging bike tours, get a copy of the annualized December issue of *Tourfinder,* published by *Bicycle USA* magazine, costing $7. Copies are available from the League of American Bicyclists, Suite 120, 190 W. Ostend St., Baltimore, MD 21230 (☎ **410/539-3399**).

HIKING Wilderness Travel, Inc., 801 Allston Way, Berkeley, CA 94710 (☎ **800/368-2794** or 510/548-0420), specializes in walking tours, treks, and inn-to-inn hiking tours of Europe. This company also offers less strenuous walking tours.

Hiking, or "rambling" as it's called in England, is one of the most popular British activities. In England and Wales alone there are some 100,000 miles of trails and footpaths—many of them historical, such as the Pennine Way, in Yorkshire. The **Ramblers' Association,** 1–5 Wandsworth Rd., London SW8 2XX (☎ **0171/ 582-6878**), publishes an annual yearbook that costs £10.30 ($16.50) and lists some 2,500 bed-and-breakfasts near the trails.

Above the Clouds, P.O. Box 398, Worcester, MA 01602 (☎ **800/233-4499** or 508/799-4499), specializes in hiking in England. In one of its programs, you hike every day, staying at the same inn; in the second program, you hike from inn to inn, stopping at a different place every night.

English Lakeland Ramblers, 18 Stuyvesant Oval, Suite 1A, New York, NY 10009 (☎ **800/724-8801** or 212/505-1020), has designed its walking tours, which last 7– 8 days, for the average active person in reasonably good physical shape. On its tour of the English Lake District, you'll stay and have your meals in a charming 17th-century country inn near Ambleside and Windermere. There are also tours in other regions (five in the Cotswolds and five in Scotland). They also offer inn-to-inn tours and privately guided tours year-round.

Sherpa Expeditions, 131A Heston Rd., Hounslow, Middlesex, England TW5 0RD (☎ **0181/577-2717**), offers both self-guided and group treks through off-the-beaten-track regions of Europe.

For serious trekkers, the **Club Alpino Italiano,** 7 Via E. Fonseca Pimental, Milan 20127 (☎ **02/2614-1378**), publishes a guide *Rifugi Alpini* listing various huts available to hikers in the Italian Alps. The guide is comprised of two volumes, costing 95,000 lire ($60.80).

For more information about alpine trailblazing, contact **Österreichischer Alpenverein (Austrian Alpine Club),** Wilhelm-Greil-Strasse 15, Innsbruck, A-6020 (☎ **0512/595470**). Membership in this alpine club costs 460 AS ($43.70). For that, you're given a 50% reduction for overnight stays in mountain refuges in Austria.

Norwegians themselves, as well as visitors, enjoy hiking in the mountains and wilderness that make up much of their country. The **Norwegian Mountain Touring Association,** Stortingsgata, N-0125 Oslo 1 (☎ **22-83-25-50**), provides guided hikes lasting 4–12 days. Of course, hikes are for people in at least average physical condition. The cost is 4,000–11,000Kr ($616–$1,694), including meals and lodgings.

HORSEBACK RIDING   A company that can help you combine a trek through the Italian countryside with equestrian panache is **Equitour,** P.O. Box 807, Dubois, WY 82513 (☎ **800/545-0019** in the U.S. and Canada). Established in 1983 from a base in northwestern Wyoming, this company markets horseback-riding holidays throughout the world. In Italy, Equitour represents an outfit specializing in equestrian treks through Tuscany. Only English tack is used. Tours are limited to four to seven participants, and last for 8 days. The tour involves traversing most of Tuscany, spending nights in a series of farmhouses and inns. The trek costs around $1,250 per person, double occupancy, and includes all meals and accommodations, all horseback riding, and guide fees.

England is also a great country for horseback riding. **Eastern Equation** provides a relaxing and thrilling holiday for riders and nonriders of any age. Beginning through advanced riders have an opportunity to train and trail ride in bucolic environs. Contact Cross Country International, P.O. Box 1170, Millbrook, NY 12545 (☎ **800/ 828-8768**), for more details. For pony trekking in Scotland, try **Cairnhouse Riding Centre,** Blackwaterfoot, Arran (☎ **01770/860-466**).

A California-based clearinghouse for at least eight French stables is **FITS (Fun in the Saddle) Equestrian Tours,** 685 Lateen Rd., Solvang, CA 93463 (☎ **800/ 666-3487** or 805/688-9494). It can arrange cross-country treks through such regions as the Pyrénées, Périgord, Brittany, Quercy, and the Loire Valley, with overnight stops en route in colorful country inns, private homes, and farmhouses. Rides last 5–7 hours a day; routes are engineered to avoid as much traffic as possible. Luggage and daily picnic fare follow in vans. Prices run $750–$2,200 per person, all-inclusive.

WILDERNESS/ADVENTURE TRAVEL   Mountain Travel–Sobek, 6420 Fairmount Ave., El Cerrito, CA 94350 (☎ **800/227-2384** or 510/527-8100), is a wilderness specialist company, formed by a 1991 union between two of California's largest adventure-tour operators. They offer hillclimbing itineraries in Europe. Overnight accommodations are in renovated farmhouses, country inns, and an occasional monastery. The company also offers high-altitude explorations of the rocky (glacier-free) Dolomites. Varying from year to year, based on demand and the availability of guides, they're designed only for experienced mountaineers in excellent physical condition.

   Waymark Holidays, 44 Windsor Rd., Slough, Berkshire, England SLI 2EJ (☎ **01753/516-477**), which is owned by avid naturalists and mountaineers, offers walking tours through the mountains and lush alpine meadows. Their primary tour is along the Alta Via 4, the Italian "highway" that winds its way through the snow-encrusted peaks and lush green valleys of the Gran Paradiso National Park. The route is rigorous, but allows for unparalleled vistas into the mountains. The tour is 14 nights, with 2 consecutive nights spent in each hut to allow for exploration of individual peaks. The price of £675 ($1,080) includes all meals and accommodations.

   Founded in 1941, **Outward Bound** offers courses in wilderness training, incorporating healthy doses of both mountain climbing and boating under challenging conditions. Courses last from 3 days to 3 months. There are now 54 Outward Bound schools and centers throughout the world. For information on the British (the original) versions of Outward Bound, contact Outward Bound Trust, Chestnut Field, Regent Place, Rugby, Warwickshire CV21 2PJ (☎ **01788/560-423**).

5 Educational & Volunteer Vacations

ARCHEOLOGICAL DIGS   Earthwatch Boston, 680 Mount Auburn St. (P.O. Box 403), Watertown, MA 02272-9924 (☎ **617/926-8200**), and **Earthwatch Europe,** 57 Woodstock Rd., Delsyre Court, Oxford, England 0X2 6HU (☎ **01865/311-600**), offer education-packed participation in archeological digs in prime locations, such as Italy.

PROMOTING INTERNATIONAL UNDERSTANDING   The Friendship Force, 57 Forsyth St. NW, Suite 900, Atlanta, GA 30303 (☎ **404/522-9490**), fosters friendship among peoples around the world by arranging for en masse visits, usually once a year. Group bookings mean lower prices for air transportation to the host country. Each participant is required to spend 2 weeks in the host country, and 1 full week must be spent in the home of a family as a guest. Volunteers can spend the second week traveling in the host country.

   People to People, 501 E. Armour Blvd., Kansas City, MO 64109-2200 (☎ **816/531-4701**), promotes international understanding through cultural exchanges of adult professionals (in many different fields) for 2- and 3-week programs. There's also a 4-week summer high-school educational program. A summer collegiate study-abroad and internship program offers graduate and undergraduate credit opportunities. Local chapters help arrange homestays and other programs for members. Privileges include travel opportunities, newsletters, and a magazine. Annual fees are $25 for families, $15 for individuals, and $10 for students.

HOME EXCHANGES **Intervac U.S.,** P.O. Box 590504, San Francisco, CA 94159 (☎ **800/756-HOME** or 415/435-3497), is part of the largest worldwide home-exchange network, with a special emphasis on Europe. It publishes four catalogs a year, listing homes in more than 36 countries. Members contact each other directly. The cost is $65 plus postage, which includes the purchase of three of the company's catalogs (which will be mailed to you), plus the inclusion of your own listing in one of the three catalogs. A fourth catalog costs an extra $21. If you want to publish a photograph of your home, there's an additional charge of $11.

The Invented City, 41 Sutter St., Suite 1090, San Francisco, CA 94104 (☎ **800/ 788-CITY** or 415/252-1141), is another international home-exchange agency. Listings are published three times a year, in February, May, and November. A membership fee of $75 allows you to list your home, and you can also give your preferred time to travel, your occupation, and your hobbies.

EDUCATIONAL/STUDY TRAVEL The **National Registration Center for Studies Abroad (NRCSA),** 823 N. 2nd St., Milwaukee, WI 53203 (☎ **414/ 278-0631**), publishes a catalog ($2) of schools in Europe. It will register you at the school of your choice, arrange for room and board, and make airline reservations, all for no extra fee. Ask for a free copy of the newsletter. Costs run $350–$600 per week, depending on the location and the number of meals included. Rates include tuition, registration, and lodging at all schools and books, learning materials, and meals at others.

The **American Institute for Foreign Study (AIFS),** 102 Greenwich Ave., Greenwich, CT 06830 (☎ **800/727-2437** or 203/869-9090), can help you arrange study programs and summer programs, with bed and board included, and set up transportation. It can also help you arrange study programs.

The biggest organization dealing with higher education in Europe is the **Institute of International Education,** 11 E. Brooks (P.O. Box 371), Annapolis Junction, MD 20701-0371 (☎ **800/445-0443**). A few of its booklets are free, but for $36.95, plus $4 for postage, you can purchase the more definitive *Vacation Study Abroad.*

University Vacations, 10461 NW 26th St., Miami, FL 33172 (☎ **800/ 792-0100** or 305/591-1736), offers upmarket liberal arts programs at Oxford and Cambridge universities. The summer headquarters is Brasenose College, Oxford OX1 4AJ, England. Courses usually last 7–12 days and combine lectures and excursions, with dining in the intimate fellows' dining rooms. Accommodations are in private rooms with available en suite facilities in the medieval colleges. There are neither formal academic requirements nor pressures of examinations or written requirements.

A clearinghouse for information on European-based language schools is **Lingua Service Worldwide,** 216 E. 45th St., 17th Floor, New York, NY 10017 (☎ **800/ 394-LEARN** or 212/867-1225).

Courses in Italian language, fine arts, history, literature, and culture for foreign students are available at several centers in Italy, with the best-recommended headquartered in Florence. You can contact any of the following for information: The **British Institute of Florence,** Courses on Italian Language and Culture, Palazzo Lanfredini, Lungarno Guicciardini 9, 50125 Firenze (☎ **055/284031;** fax 055/ 289557); the **Centro di Lingua e Cultura Italiana per Stranieri,** Piazza Santo Spirito 4, 50134 Firenze (☎ **055/2396966;** fax 055/280800); and the **Centro Linguistico Italiano Dante Alighieri,** Via d' Bardi 12, 50125 Firenze (☎ **055/ 2342984;** fax 055/234276). The **Italian Cultural Institute** in New York (☎ **212/ 879-4242**) also has information.

The **Alliance Française,** 101 bd. Raspail, 75270 Paris CEDEX 06 (☎ **01-45-44-38-28**), a state-approved nonprofit organization, has a network of establishments in 133 countries offering French-language courses. The international school in Paris is open all year, and you can enroll for a minimum of 2 weeks. Fees tend to be reasonable, and the school offers numerous activities and services. Write for information and application forms at least 1 month before your departure. In North America, the largest branch is the Alliance Française, 2819 Ordway St. NW, Washington, DC 20008 (☎ **800/6-FRANCE**).

Salminter, Calle Toro 34–36, 37002 Salamanca (☎ **923/21-18-08**), conducts courses in conversational Spanish, with optional courses in business Spanish, translation techniques, and Spanish culture. Classes contain no more than 10 people. There are 2-week, 1-month, and 3-month sessions at seven progressive levels. The school can arrange housing with Spanish families or in furnished apartments shared with other students.

CULINARY SCHOOLS　For travelers interested in enhancing their cooking skills, culinary schools abound, especially in Italy and France. **Italian Cuisine in Florence,** Via Trieste 1, 50139 Firenze (☎ **055/480041**), provides several gourmet classes in regional as well as Nouva Cucina. Most courses are 5 days, but short workshops for larger groups are also available. The **International Cooking School of Italian Food and Wine,** 201 E. 28th St., New York, NY 10016-8538 (☎ **212/779-1921**), offers courses in Bologna, the "gastronomic capital of Italy." Owner/operator Mary Beth Clark teaches the fine art of La Cucina Tradizionale and La Cucina Nuova. Classes are conducted in English. The course includes excursions into Bologna and the surrounding region, concentrating on the fabulous markets and *ristorantes* found in the Emilia-Romagna region. Prices average around $3,000; discount packages are offered to noncooking participants.

Le Cordon Bleu, rue Léon-Delhomme 8, 75015 Paris (☎ **800/457-2433** in the U.S., or 01-53-68-22-50), was established in 1895 and is the most famous French cooking school. Its best-known courses last 10 weeks, at the end of which certificates of competence are issued. If you prefer a less intense immersion, you can opt for a 4-day workshop or even a 3-hour demonstration class. Enrollment in these is on a first-come, first-served basis and costs 220F ($44) for a demonstration and 4,590F ($918) for the 4-day workshop. Also of interest to professional chefs (or wannabes) are the 2- and 5-week courses in catering; they're offered twice a year and attract avid business hopefuls.

6 Health & Insurance

HEALTH　You'll encounter few health problems traveling in Europe. The tap water is generally safe to drink, the milk pasteurized, and health services good to superb.

Remember to bring along any prescriptions you need written in generic, not brand-name form. You can obtain a list of English-speaking doctors before you leave from the **International Association for Medical Assistance to Travelers (IAMAT),** in the United States at 417 Center St., Lewiston, NY 14092 (☎ **716/754-4883**); and in Canada at 40 Regal Rd., Guelph, ON N1K 1B5 (☎ **519/836-0102**).

If you suffer from a chronic illness or special medical condition, it's a good idea to wear a Medic Alert identification tag that will immediately alert any doctor to your condition and provide Medic Alert's 24-hour hotline phone number so that foreign doctors can obtain medical information on you. The initial membership costs $35. In addition, there's a $15 yearly fee. Contact the **Medic Alert Foundation,** 2323 Colorado Ave., Turlock, CA 95381-1009 (☎ **800/432-5378**).

The U.S. government issues a helpful 198-page book, *Health Information for the International Traveler*, available for $14. Contact the U.S. Government Printing Office, Superintendent of Documents, P.O. Box 371954, Pittsburgh, PA 15250 (☎ **202/512-1800**). Specify stock number 017-023-00195-7.

INSURANCE   Comprehensive insurance programs, covering basically everything—from trip cancellation to lost luggage, to medical coverage abroad and accidental death—are offered by the following companies:

> **Access America,** 6600 W. Broad St., Richmond, VA 23230 (☎ **800/ 284-8300**).
> **Mutual of Omaha** (Tele-Trip), Mutual of Omaha Plaza, Omaha, NE 68175 (☎ **800/228-9792**).
> **Safeware,** 2929 N. High St. (P.O. Box 02211), Columbus, OH 43202 (☎ **614/262-0559**), which also offers specific coverage for your computer.
> **Travel Guard International,** 1145 Clark St., Stevens Point, WI 54481 (☎ **800/826-1300**).
> **Travel Insured International, Inc.,** P.O. Box 280568, East Hartford, CT 06128-0568 (☎ **800/243-3174** in the U.S., or 203/528-7663 outside the U.S. between 7:45am and 7pm EST).

Remember that Medicare only covers U.S. citizens traveling in Mexico and Canada. Companies specializing in accident and medical care are

> **Healthcare Abroad (MEDEX),** ℅ Wallach & Co., 107 W. Federal St. (P.O. Box 480), Middleburg, VA 22117-0480 (☎ **800/237-6615** or 540/ 687-3166).
> **Travel Assistance International** (Worldwide Assistance Services), 1133 15th St. NW, Suite 400, Washington, DC 20005 (☎ **800/821-2828** or 202/ 331-1609).

7 Tips for Travelers with Special Needs

FOR PEOPLE WITH DISABILITIES   Before you go, there are several agencies that can provide advance-planning information. One is the **Travel Information Service** of the MossRehab Hospital in Philadelphia (☎ **215/456-9603** voice, or 215/ 456-9602 TDD), which provides assistance with travel needs to telephone callers only.

You can obtain a copy of **"Air Transportation of Handicapped Persons,"** published by the U.S. Department of Transportation. The copy is sent free by writing for Free Advisory Circular No. AC12032, Distribution Unit, U.S. Department of Transportation, Publications Division, M-4332, Washington, DC 20590.

Names and addresses of tour operators for people with disabilities can be obtained from the **Society for the Advancement of Travel for the Handicapped,** 347 Fifth Ave., New York, NY 10016 (☎ **212/447-7248**). Annual membership dues are $45, or $25 for senior citizens and students. Send a stamped, self-addressed envelope.

The **American Foundation for the Blind,** 15 W. 16th St., New York, NY 10011 (☎ **800/232-5463** to order information kits and supplies, or 212/502-7600), offers information on travel and the various requirements for the transport and border formalities for seeing-eye dogs. It also issues identification cards to those who are legally blind. Travelers with a hearing impairment can contact the **American Academy of Otolaryngology,** 1 Prince St., Alexandria, VA 22314 (☎ **703/836-4444** or 703/ 519-1585 TTY).

The **Information Center for Individuals with Disabilities,** Fort Point Place, 27–43 Wormwood St., Boston, MA 02210 (☎ 800/462-5015 or 617/727-5540), is another good source. It has lists of travel agents who specialize in tours for persons with disabilities.

For a $25 annual fee, consider joining **Mobility International USA (MIUSA),** P.O. Box 10767, Eugene, OR 97440 (☎ 541/343-1284 voice and TDD). It answers questions on various destinations and also offers discounts on the videos, publications, and programs it sponsors.

The 500-page *Travelin' Talk Directory,* P.O. Box 3534, Clarksville, TN 37043 (☎ 615/552-6670), lists outfits and people who help travelers with disabilities. It sells for $35.

For a list of travel agent specialists worldwide, consult the *Directory of Travel Agencies for the Disabled,* available from Twin Peaks Press, P.O. Box 129, Vancouver, WA 98666 (☎ 800/637-2256), costing $19.95, plus another $2 shipping.

FEDCAP Rehabilitation Services (formerly known as the Federation of the Handicapped), 154 W. 14th St., New York, NY 10011 (☎ 212/727-4200), operates summer tours to Europe and elsewhere for its members. Membership costs $4 yearly.

For people who need wheelchairs and walkers, **Flying Wheels Travel,** 143 West Bridge (P.O. Box 382), Owatoona, MN 55060 (☎ 800/535-6790 or 507/451-5005), offers escorted tours and cruises internationally.

Directions Unlimited, 720 N. Bedford Rd., Bedford Hills, NY 10507 (☎ 800/533-5343), offers tours to Europe for travelers with disabilities, especially group tours for the blind. This outfit can also arrange group tours for persons in wheelchairs.

One of the best firms that makes arrangements for travelers with disabilities is **Access Adventures,** 206 Chestnut Ridge Rd., Rochester, NY 14624 (☎ 716/889-9096), which is operated by a former physical rehabilitation counselor. Among the many travel agents working with travelers with mobility impairments is **Accessible Journeys,** 35 W. Sellers Ave., Ridley Park, PA 19078 (☎ 800/846-4537 or 610/521-0339). You can also consult **Wheelchair Journeys,** 16979 Redmond Way, Redmond, WA 98052 (☎ 206/885-2210).

FOR GAY & LESBIAN TRAVELERS   The **International Gay Travel Association (IGTA),** P.O. Box 4974, Key West, FL 33041 (☎ 305/292-0217, or 800/448-8550 for voice mail), has encouraged gay and lesbian travel worldwide since its founding in 1983. With around 1,200 member agencies, it specializes in networking travelers with the appropriate gay-friendly service organization or tour specialist. It offers a quarterly newsletter, marketing mailings, and a membership directory that's updated four times a year. Travel agents who are IGTA members will be tied into this organization's vast information resources.

A number of tour operators cater to the gay/lesbian traveler, including **Islanders/Kennedy Travels,** 183 W. 10th St., New York, NY 10014 (☎ 212/242-3220), which arranges both individual trips or group tours for gays. It also offers corporate travel plans for the lesbian or gay executive. Another agency, **Hanns Ebensten Travel,** 513 Fleming St., Key West, FL 33040 (☎ 305/294-8174), specializes in outdoor trips for men. **Adventure Bound Expeditions,** 711 Walnut St., Boulder, CO 80302 (☎ 303/449-0990), is a similar outfitter, living up to the promise of its name. Women seeking a similar outdoor adventure, including hiking and barging trips in Europe, should contact **Rainbow Adventures,** 15033 Kelly Canyon Rd., Bozeman, MT 59715 (☎ 800/804-8686).

Some other tour operators familiar with gay and lesbian travel include **RSVP Travel Productions,** 2800 University Ave. SE, Minneapolis, MN 55414 (☎ 800/328-7787); **Toto Tours,** 1326 W. Albion, Suite 3W, Chicago, IL 60626 (☎ 800/565-1241 or 312/274-8686); **Olivia,** 4400 Market St., Oakland, CA 94608 (☎ 800/631-6277); **Yellowbrick Road,** 1500 W. Balmoral Ave., Chicago, IL 60640 (☎ 800/642-2488 or 312/561-1800); and **Skylink Women's Travel,** 746 Ashland Ave., Santa Monica, CA 90405 (☎ 800/225-5759 or 310/452-0506).

A number of publications offer information about gay travel, including general information as well as listings of bars, hotels, restaurants, and places of interest. Men can pick up *Spartacus,* the international gay guide ($29.95), or *Odysseus 1997, The International Gay Travel Planner,* a guide to accommodations ($25). Both lesbians and gay men might want to pick up *Ferrari Travel Planner* ($16). These books and others are available from **Giovanni's Room,** 1145 Pine St., Philadelphia, PA 19107 (☎ 215/923-2960). In New York, contact **A Different Light Bookstore,** 151 W. 19th St., New York, NY 10011 (☎ 800/343-4002 or 212/989-4850).

Our World, 1104 N. Nova Rd., Suite 251, Daytona Beach, FL 32117 (☎ 904/441-5367), is devoted to options and bargains ($35 for 10 issues). *Out and About,* 8 W. 19th St., Suite 401, New York, NY 10011 (☎ 800/929-2268), $49 a year, aims for the more upscale gay male traveler, and has been praised by everybody from *Travel & Leisure* to the *New York Times.*

FOR SENIORS Many senior discounts are available, but some require membership in a particular association. For information before you go, obtain the free booklet *101 Tips for the Mature Traveler* from **Grand Circle Travel,** 347 Congress St., Suite 3A, Boston, MA 02210 (☎ 800/221-2610 or 617/350-7500).

SAGA International Holidays, 222 Berkeley St., Boston, MA 02116 (☎ 800/343-0273), offers quality tours for senior citizens. They prefer participants to be at least 50 years of age or older. Insurance and airfare are included in the net price of the tours, which usually last an average of 17 nights. SAGA's grand tour of Europe takes participants by deluxe motorcoach, stopping at four-star hotels. **Grand Circle Travel,** 347 Congress St., Suite 3A, Boston, MA 02210 (☎ 800/221-2610 or 617/350-7500), offers escorted tours and cruises for retired people.

The **American Association of Retired Persons (AARP),** 601 E St. NW, Washington, DC 20049 (☎ 202/434-AARP), offers discounts on car rentals and hotels.

The **National Council of Senior Citizens,** 1331 F St. NW, Washington, DC 20004 (☎ 202/347-8800), charges $12 per person or per couple for membership, which includes a monthly newsletter with travel tips. Reduced discounts on hotel and auto rentals are available.

Mature Outlook, P.O. Box 10448, Des Moines, IA 50306 (☎ 800/336-6330), is a membership program for people more than 50 years of age. For an annual fee of $14.95, members receive a bimonthly magazine and are offered discounts at ITC-member hotels, auto rentals, and restaurants, and free coupons for discounts at Sears & Roebuck Co.

One of the most dynamic organizations for senior citizens is **Elderhostel,** 75 Federal St., Boston, MA 02110 (☎ 617/426-7788), established in 1975. Elderhostel maintains an array of educational programs throughout Europe, most lasting for around 3 weeks. Airfare, hotel accommodations in student dormitories or modest inns, all meals, and tuition are included. Courses are ungraded, and are especially focused in the liberal arts. Participants must be older than 55. Write or phone for a free catalog and a list of upcoming courses and destinations.

If you're 45 or older and need a companion to share your travel, **Golden Companions,** P.O. Box 5249, Reno, NV 89513 (☎ 702/324-2227), might provide the answer. Members meet through a confidential mail network and, once they've connected, make their own travel plans. Benefits include bimonthly membership updates as well as a newsletter, *The Golden Gateways.* Membership for a full year is $94.

Partners in Travel, 11660 Chenault St., Suite 119, Los Angeles, CA 90049 (☎ 310/476-4869), publishes a newsletter semiannually with some 500 travel personals (not limited just to seniors). A $25 subscription covers the newsletter, plus a counseling service, information for travelers going alone, and a listing of some 100 tour-operator specialists.

If you'd like an extended stay abroad in the off-season at huge discounts, consult **Sun Holidays,** 7280 W. Palmetto Park Rd., Suite 301, Boca Raton, FL 33433 (☎ 800/243-2057 or 407/367-0105).

FOR SINGLES   The travel industry is largely geared toward couples, and so solo travelers often wind up paying the penalty. It pays to travel with someone, and one company that resolves this problem is **Travel Companion,** P.O. Box P-833, Amityville, NY 11701 (☎ 516/454-0880), which matches single travelers with like-minded companions. It's headed by Jens Jurgen, who charges $99 for a 6-month listing. People seeking travel companions fill out forms stating their preferences and needs and receive a listing of potential travel partners. Companions of the same or opposite sex can be requested. A bimonthly newsletter also gives numerous money-saving travel tips of special interest to solo travelers. A sample copy is available for $5. For an application and more information, contact Jens Jurgen at Travel Companion.

Since single supplements on tours can be hefty, some tour companies will arrange for you to share a room with another single traveler. A company that offers a "guaranteed-share plan" is **Cosmos** (☎ 800/221-0090); book through your travel agent or call Cosmos.

With years of experience in bringing single people together, **Club Med,** 40 W. 57th St., New York, NY 10019 (☎ 800/CLUB-MED), is a useful resource, as is **Contiki Holidays,** Suite 900, 300 Plaza Alicante, Garden Grove, CA 92640 (☎ 800/CONTIKI). The latter specializes in the 18- to 35-year-old market.

Adventure Center, 1311 63rd St., Suite 200, Emeryville, CA 94608 (☎ 510/654-4200), is sales agent for Explore World-Wide, Ltd, a London-based company that arranges packages for small groups of travelers for offbeat tours of Europe.

FOR FAMILIES   *Family Travel Times* is published 10 times a year by **TWYCH (Travel with Your Children),** 45 W. 18th St., 7th Floor, New York, NY 10011 (☎ 212/477-5524), and includes a weekly call-in service for subscribers. Subscriptions cost $55 a year. TWYCH also publishes two nitty-gritty information guides, *Skiing with Children* and *Cruising with Children* ($29 and $22, respectively). A publication list and a sample issue are available by sending $3.50 to the above address.

Families Welcome!, 21 W. Colony Place, Suite 140, Durham, NC 27705 (☎ 800/326-0724 or 919/489-2555), a travel company specializing in worry-free vacations for families, offers "City Kids" packages to certain European cities. As well as accommodations, packages can include car rentals, train and ferry passes, and special air prices, and are individually designed for each family. A welcome kit containing "insider's information" is included.

The Family Travel Guide: An Inspiring Collection of Family Friendly Vacations is a 410-page book filled with information. For a copy, mail $16.95 plus $1 for postage and handling to **Carousel Press,** P.O. Box 6061, Albany, CA 94706 (☎ 510/527-5849).

Also consider the offerings of **Club Med,** 40 W. 57th St., New York, NY 10019 (☎ **800/CLUB-MED**), which features Mini Clubs and Baby Clubs at its properties in Europe. One child under 5 for each paying adult stays free in the parents' room. Two especially family-friendly hotel chains are **Novotel** (☎ **800/221-4542**), which accepts two children free in parents' room, and **Sofitel** (☎ **800/221-4542**), which offers a free second room for children July–Aug and over the Christmas holidays.

Tour operators specializing in families traveling with children include **Rascals in Paradise,** 650 5th St., Suite 505, San Francisco, CA 94107 (☎ **800/872-7225** or 415/978-9800), and **Grandtravel,** 6900 Wisconsin Ave., Suite 706, Chevy Chase, MD 20815 (☎ **800/247-7651** or 301/986-0790), the latter featuring tours for persons traveling with grandchildren (ages 7–17).

FOR STUDENTS   Council Travel (a subsidiary of the Council on International Educational Exchange) is America's largest student, youth, and budget travel group, with more than 60 offices worldwide. The main office is at 205 E. 42nd St., New York, NY 10017 (☎ **800/226-8624** or 212/822-2600). International Student Identity Cards, issued to all bona fide students for $19, entitle holders to generous travel and other discounts. Discounted international and domestic air tickets are available. For those up to the age of 25 who are not students, but still want the youth travel discounts, CIEE issues the "GO25: International Youth Travel Card," costing $19. The card comes with a 1-year validity and a copy of "Travel Handbook: International Youth Travel Card Discounts."

Eurotrain rail passes, YHA passes, weekend packages, overland safaris, and hostel/hotel accommodations are also bookable. Council Travel sells a number of publications for young people, including *Work, Study, Travel Abroad: The Whole World Handbook; Volunteer: The Comprehensive Guide to Voluntary Service in the U.S. and Abroad;* and *Going Places: The High School Student's Guide to Study, Travel, and Adventure Abroad.*

For real budget travelers, it's worth joining **Hostelling International/IYHF (International Youth Hostel Federation).** For information, contact Hostelling Information/American Youth Hostels (HI-AYH), 733 15th St. NW, Suite 840, Washington, DC 20005 (☎ **800/444-6111** or 202/783-6161). Annual membership costs $25, $15 for seniors 55 and over, and $10 for youths under 18.

FOR VEGETARIANS   Before you go, the **Vegetarian Resource Group,** P.O. Box 1463, Baltimore, MD 21203 (☎ **410/366-8343**), can provide data about obtaining vegetarian meals or food in Europe. The **Vegan Society,** St. Leonards-on-Sea, in England (☎ **01424/427393**), publishes the *Vegan Holiday & Restaurant Guide,* obtainable in many bookstores, and the **Vegetarian Society of the United Kingdom,** at Parkdale, Dunham Road, Altrincham, Cheshire WA14 4QG (☎ **0161/9280793**), provides information helpful to the vegetarian traveler.

8 Getting There

By land or sea, the ways of getting to Europe from the United States, Canada, and the United Kingdom are varied. We'll explore some of the options in this section, and tell you many ways to save money off regular fares.

You can also consult the Consumer Union's monthly report, *Consumer Reports Travel Letter,* P.O. Box 53629, Boulder, CO 80322 (☎ **800/234-1970**). Subscriptions cost $39 annually.

BY PLANE

Most of the major airlines that fly to Europe charge approximately the same fare, but if a price war should break out over the Atlantic (and these are almost always brewing over the most popular routes), fares could change overnight, usually in the consumer's favor.

If seeking a budget fare is uppermost in your mind, the key is "advance booking"—you must be willing to purchase your tickets as far ahead as possible. Moreover, since the number of seats allocated to low-cost "advance-purchase" fares is severely limited, the early bird often (though not always) obtains the low-cost seat. Many discounts are available for passengers who can travel midweek—or midwinter—in either direction.

High season on most airline routes is usually June–Sept 6 (this could vary), both the most expensive and most crowded time to travel. If your schedule permits, you should try to plan your departure for the low or shoulder season. Shoulder season is Apr–May, Sept 7–Oct, and Dec 15–24. Low season is Nov–Dec 14 and Dec 25–Mar.

All the major carriers offer an **APEX** ticket, generally their cheapest transatlantic option. Usually such a ticket must be purchased 14–21 days in advance, and a stay in Europe must last at least 7 days but not more than 30. Changing the date of departure from North America within 21 days of departure will sometimes entail a penalty of around $150, but with some tickets, no changes of any kind are permitted.

A more flexible (but more expensive) option is the **regular economy fare.** This ticket offers the same seating and services as the APEX ticket for a shorter stay than the 7-day APEX minimum requirement. One of the most attractive side benefits of an economy-class ticket is the absolute freedom to make last-minute changes in flight dates, and unrestricted stopovers.

Business class and **first class,** although substantially more expensive, are especially useful for anyone who needs to be as rested and alert as possible upon arrival in Europe.

If you're dissatisfied with the service you've received on either a U.S. or foreign commercial airline, you can contact the consumer relations representative. To learn the name and phone number of the contact, so that you can file your complaint, you can first call the Department of Transportation's **Office of Consumer Affairs,** C-75, Washington, DC 20590 (☎ **202/366-2220**).

CONSOLIDATORS   Consolidators, also known as "bucket shops," exist in many shapes and forms. In its purest sense, a bucket shop acts as a clearinghouse for blocks of tickets that airlines discount and consign during normally slow periods of air travel.

One of the biggest consolidators is **Travac,** 989 Sixth Ave., New York, NY 10018 (☎ **800/TRAV-800** or 212/563-3303), which offers discounted seats throughout the United States to most cities in Europe on airlines that include TWA, United, and Delta. Another branch office is at 2601 E. Jefferson St., Orlando, FL 32803 (☎ 407/896-0014).

In New York, try **TFI Tours International,** 34 W. 32nd St., 12th Floor, New York, NY 10001 (☎ **800/745-8000** or 212/736-1140 in New York State). Other consolidators include **Euram Tours,** 1522 K St. NW, Suite 430, Washington, DC 20005 (☎ **800/848-6789**).

Travel Avenue, 10 S. Riverside Plaza, Suite 1404, Chicago, IL 60606 (☎ **800/333-3335** in the U.S.), is a leading agency in the Midwest. Tickets are often cheaper than those of most bucket shops, and it charges the customer a $25 fee on international tickets rather than taking the usual 10% commission from an airline; it rebates most of the charge back to the customer—hence, the lower fares. **TMI (Travel Management International),** 3617 DuPont Ave. S., Minneapolis, MN 55409 (☎ **800/245-3672**), offers a wide variety of discounts, including youth fares, student fares, and access to other kinds of air-related discounts as well.

An option for clients with flexible travel plans is available through **Airhitch,** 2472 Broadway, Suite 20, New York, NY 10025 (☎ **212/864-2000**). Prospective travelers inform Airhitch of any 5 consecutive days in which they're available to fly to Europe. Airhitch agrees to fly the passengers within those 5 days from any of three U.S. regions. Attempts will be made to fly passengers to and from cities of their choice within their region, but there are no guarantees. Typical one-way fares to Europe are $169 from the Northeast, $229 from the Midwest or Southeast, and $269 from the West Coast or Northwest.

UniTravel, 1177 N. Warson Rd., St. Louis, MO 63132 (☎ **800/325-2222**), is best for passengers who need to get to Europe on short notice—its tickets may or may not be reduced from the price a client would get if he or she had phoned the airlines directly.

One final name for our list is **1-800-FLY-4-LESS,** RFA Building, 5440 Morehouse Dr., San Diego, CA 92121 (☎ **800/359-4537**), which specializes in finding only the lowest fares. Travelers who need tickets on short notice can utilize this service to obtain low discounted fares with no advance-purchase requirements. Call for information on available consolidator airline tickets for last-minute travel.

CHARTER FLIGHTS In a strict sense, a charter flight occurs on an aircraft reserved months in advance for a one-time-only transit between two predetermined points. Before paying for a charter, check the restrictions on your ticket or contract. You may be asked to purchase a tour package and pay far in advance, and you'll pay a stiff penalty (or forfeit the ticket entirely) if you cancel. Charters are sometimes canceled when the plane doesn't fill up. In some cases, the charter-ticket seller will offer you an insurance policy in case you need to cancel for a legitimate reason (hospitalization, death in the family, whatever).

Council Charter, run by the Council on International Educational Exchange, 205 E. 42nd St., New York, NY 10017 (☎ **800/800-8222** or 212/661-1450), arranges charter seats on regularly scheduled aircraft. One of the biggest New York charter operators is **Travac,** 989 Sixth Ave., New York, NY 10018 (☎ **800/TRAV-800** in the U.S., or 212/563-3303).

Sometimes charter outfitters specialize in travel to one country, as does **Homeric Tours, Inc.** (☎ **800/223-5570** or 212/753-1100), which features tours to Greece, especially Athens and Thessalonia. For Canadians, some good charter deals are offered by **Martinair** (☎ **800/627-8462** or 407/391-1313).

REBATORS To confuse the situation even more, rebators also compete in the low-airfare market. These outfits pass along to the passenger part of their commission, although many of them assess a fee for their services. Most rebators offer discounts that run 10%–25%, plus a $25 handling charge. They're not travel agents, although they sometimes offer such similar services as land arrangements and car rentals.

Specializing in clients in the Middle East, **Travel Avenue,** Suite 1404, 10 S. Riverside Plaza, Chicago, IL 60606 (☎ **800/333-3335** or 312/876-1116), offers upfront cash rebates on every air ticket over $300 it sells. Also available are tours and cruise tickets, plus hotel reservations, usually at prices lower than if you have pre-reserved them on your own. Another major rebator is **The Smart Traveller,** 3111 SW 27th Ave. (P.O. Box 330010), Miami, FL 33133 (☎ **800/448-3338** or 305/448-3338), offering discounts on packaged tours.

AIRLINES

NORTH AMERICAN AIRLINES   North American carriers with frequent service and flights to European destinations are **Air Canada** (☎ 800/776-3000), **American Airlines** (☎ 800/624-6262), **Canadian Airlines International** (☎ 800/426-7000), **Continental Airlines** (☎ 800/231-0856), **Delta** (☎ 800/241-4141 in the U.S.), **Northwest Airlines** (☎ 800/447-4747), **TWA** (☎ 800/221-2000), **United Airlines** (☎ 800/538-2929), **USAir** (☎ 800/428-4322), and **Virgin Atlantic Airways** (☎ 800/862-8621)

EUROPEAN NATIONAL AIRLINES   In choosing an airline, remember that the national carriers of the European countries will offer the greatest number of direct flights to and within your destination, especially significant if your destination is not a major city or hub.

Austria Airlines (☎ **800/843-0002** in the U.S. and Canada) has the only direct nonstop flights into Vienna from New York and Chicago. Belgium's national carrier, **Sabena** (☎ **800/955-2000**) flies nonstop to Brussels from Boston, Chicago, New York, and Atlanta. **ČSA Czech Airlines** (☎ **800/223-2365**) is the national airline of the Czech Republic, and has the only direct flights to Prague from North America. **British Airways** (☎ **800/AIRWAYS**) offers direct flights to London, Manchester, Birmingham, and Glasgow. **Air France** (☎ **800/237-2747**) offers daily nonstop flights to Paris from several North American gateways. **Lufthansa** (☎ **800/645-3880**) is Germany's national carrier. Germany's hub is Frankfurt, but Lufthansa also has direct flights to Berlin.

Hungary's national airline is **Malev Hungarian Airlines** (☎ **800/262-5380**). Italy's national carrier, **Alitalia** (☎ **800/223-5730**), flies nonstop to both Rome and Milan from several North American cities. International flights on **Aer Lingus** (☎ **800/223-6537**) arrive at Ireland's hub, Shannon Airport. **KLM Royal Dutch Airlines** (☎ **800/374-7747**) has direct flights to Amsterdam. **TAP** (☎ **800/221-7370**), the national airline of Portugal, has some flights comanaged by Delta (see above); in making connections for Lisbon flights from gateways other than New York, it's easier to make reservations through Delta's network. The national carrier of all three Scandinavian countries is **SAS World Airlines** (☎ **800/221-2350**), with direct flights to Copenhagen, Oslo, and Stockholm. **Icelandair** (☎ **800/223-5500** in the U.S.) is another choice for connections to Scandinavian cities through its home port of Reykjavik. The national carrier of Spain, **Iberia Airlines** (☎ **800/772-4642**) offers daily nonstop service to Madrid from both New York and Miami. **Swissair** (☎ **800/221-4750** in the U.S. for reservations and information, 800/267-9477 in Canada), Switzerland's national carrier, offers service from a number of North American gateways.

BARGAIN AIRLINES   To gain a foothold in the highly competitive transatlantic market, some newer airlines often tempt the traveler with discounted rates. These include **Continental Airlines** (☎ **800/231-0856**), which in the summer of 1996 offered a $620 round-trip midweek flight from Newark International Airport outside New York City to London. Continental also flies to Madrid, Paris, Frankfurt, and Munich from Houston and Denver.

Icelandair (☎ **800/223-5500**) became famous in the 1960s for its discounted fares from the East Coast to Luxembourg. Although prices have risen considerably since then, it's still a bargain. In 1996 it offered a round-trip fare midweek to Luxembourg for $398 from New York, Baltimore/Washington, or Orlando. Seats at this fare can be reserved no earlier than 3 days before departure.

Virgin Atlantic Airways (☎ 800/862-8621) has been viewed as a bargain airline, or at least one offering good value. Typical rates (as of the summer of 1996) were $446 from such gateways as Boston, New York, and Orlando, and $608–$633 from Los Angeles.

Tower Air (☎ 800/34-TOWER or 718/553-8500 in New York State), is known for its discounted New York–Paris round-trip, costing $525 (as of the summer of 1996).

BY SHIP

OCEAN LINER   The **Cunard Line,** 555 Fifth Ave., New York, NY 10017 (☎ 800/5-CUNARD or 212/880-7500), boasts that its flagship, *Queen Elizabeth 2,* is the only five-star luxury ocean liner providing regular transatlantic service—some 18 voyages a year between April and December.

Fares are based on season and cabin grade. During the super-value season (Apr 12–May 3 and Dec 9–15), the fares for a 6-day crossing are $1,995–$9,940. During the peak season (June 6–Oct), fares for a 6-day crossing run $2,945–$12,125. These fares are per person, based on double occupancy. Passengers also pay $185 port and handling charges. Many packages are offered, and in conjunction with the ship fare, a one-way flight on the British Airways Concorde can be obtained from $495.

PACKAGE TOURS

PACKAGES   All major airlines flying to Europe sell independent vacation packages. **Continental Vacations** (☎ 800/634-555) has a 6-night trip to London from Atlanta—including round-trip airfare, accommodations in a tourist-class hotel with continental breakfast, and a 4-day London Explorer pass with unlimited bus travel—for $1,092 per person. **Delta Dream Vacations** (☎ 800/872-7786) offer fly/drive and fly/rail packages. For travelers with limited time, it features 3-day city "sprees." Other good tour operators are **United Airlines Vacation Planning Center** (☎ 800/328-7786) and **American Airlines Fly Away Vacations** (☎ 800/321-2121).

For Germany, **DER Tours,** 11933 Wilshire Blvd., Los Angeles, CA 90025 (☎ 800/782-2424 or 310/479-4411), offers discounted airfares, car rentals, hotel packages, short regional tours, and German Rail, Eurail, and other rail passes. Call for information about the **Swissair** (☎ 800/688-7947 in the U.S.) tour packages and to obtain a copy of the airline's winter brochure, *The Alpine Experience,* or its summer offerings in *Look No Further—Switzerland.*

GROUP & ESCORTED TOURS   With a good tour group, you'll know ahead of time just what your visit will cost, and you won't have to worry about your transportation, your luggage, hotel reservations, or other "nuts and bolts" requirements of travel. Consult a good travel agent for the latest offerings and advice.

American Express Vacations, P.O. Box 1525, Fort Lauderdale, FL 33302 (☎ 800/446-6234 in the U.S. and Canada), offers the most comprehensive tours to Europe. If it doesn't have a tour that covers what you want, it will arrange an individualized itinerary through specified regions for you.

Perillo Tours, 577 Chestnut Ridge Rd., Woodcliff Lake, NJ 07675-9888 (☎ 800/431-1515 in the U.S., or 201/307-1234), has sent more than a million travelers to Italy. Nine different itineraries are offered Apr–Oct, ranging from 8 to 15 days each, covering broadly different regions of the peninsula. The "Off-Season Italy" tour, offered Nov–Apr, covers three of the country's premier cities when they're likely to be less densely crowded. **Italiatour,** a company of the Alitalia Group (☎ 800/845-3365 or 212/765-2183 in New York State), offers a widely varied selection of tours through all parts of the peninsula. The company appeals to clients who don't want any semblance of a tour—their longest offering is a loosely supervised 8-night jaunt through the major art cities of Italy, with accommodations in luxury hotels. Prices begin at $1,349 per person. Airfare is included, as well as hotel accommodations (double occupancy), breakfasts, transfers between cities, some city tours, and a gondola ride in Venice. More luxurious tours are offered by **Abercrombie & Kent,** 1520 Kensington Rd., Oak Brook, IL 60521 (☎ **800/323-7308** or 708/954-2944). Overnight stays are spent in four- or five-star accommodations. Several tours are offered from Britain to Italy.

The **Kemwel Corporation** (☎ **800/666-7269**), North American agents for Swisspak (formerly Austrian Holidays), is loosely affiliated with both Austrian Airlines and Swissair. Their most popular tours include fully escorted brief overviews (5 days, 4 nights) of central European cities, including the "Imperial Capitals" tour, which visits Vienna, Prague, and Budapest; and "Alpine Panorama," which showcases Vienna, Klagenfurt, Innsbruck, and Salzburg. Air transport on Austrian Airlines can be arranged simultaneously when you book the tour, usually at favorable rates.

More far-flung touring experiences are offered by **British Airways** (☎ **800/ 262-2422**), which passes along to consumers the favorable pricing ensured by the company's huge buying power. It also offers unusual and inexpensive add-ons in London before or after a continental tour.

Travel Concepts, 62 Commonwealth Ave., Suite 3, Boston, MA 02116-3029 (☎ **617/266-8450**), specializes in art-history and cultural and winery tours to less-traveled regions of France. Tours are usually custom-designed for groups of 10 or more.

The French Experience, 370 Lexington Ave., New York, NY 10017 (☎ **212/ 986-1115**), offers fly/drive packages and prearranged package tours of various regions that can be adapted for group or individual needs, and also takes reservations for about 30 hotels in Paris and arranges short-term apartment rentals.

Bennett Tours, 270 Madison Ave., New York, NY 10016 (☎ **800/221-2420** or 212/532-5060 in New York), has land packages with experienced guides and a wide range of prices. Other reliable tour operators include **Holiday Tours of America,** 425 Madison Ave., Suite 1602, New York, NY 10017 (☎ **800/677-6454** or 212/832-8989 in New York), and **Scantours, Inc.,** 1535 6th St., Suite 205, Santa Monica, CA 90401 (☎ **800/223-7226** or 310/451-0911).

Sun Holidays, 7280 W. Palmetto Park Rd., Suite 301, Boca Raton, FL 33433 (☎ **800/422-8000** or 407/367-0105), specializes in extended vacations for senior citizens, featuring excursions to the Costa del Sol in Spain and the Algarve and Cascais/Lisbon areas of Portugal. The company also sponsors fully escorted motorcoach tours of Spain and Portugal. **Trafalgar Tours,** 11 E. 26th St., Suite 1300, New York, NY 10010 (☎ **212/689-8977**), offers two 10-day tours of southern Spain, priced according to season.

TAP Air Portugal Discovery Vacations, 399 Market St., Newark, NJ 07105 (☎ **800/247-8686**), offers theme-based tours of Portugal. If you're interested in more loosely organized tours, the company can also arrange for the use of a self-drive rental car with a preplanned itinerary.

Specialists in group motorcoach tours of Europe include **Travcoa,** P.O. Box 2630, Newport Beach, CA 92658 (☎ **800/992-2003** or 714/476-2800); **Tauck Tours,** 276 Post Rd. W., Westport, CT 06880 (☎ **800/468-2825** or 203/226-6911); **Maupintour,** P.O. Box 807, Lawrence, KS 66044 (☎ **800/255-4266** or 913/ 843-1211); **Globus,** 5301 S. Federal Circle, Littleton, CO 80123 (☎ **800/221-0090** or 303/797-2800); and **Caravan Tours,** 401 N. Michigan Ave., Chicago, IL 60611 (☎ **800/227-2826** or 312/321-9800).

TRAVEL CLUBS   After you pay an annual fee, the travel club gives you a hotline number to call to find out what discounts are available. Some of these become available a few days in advance of actual departure, sometimes as long as a week, and sometimes as much as a month. You're limited to what's available, and you have to be fairly flexible.

Moment's Notice, 7301 New Utrecht Ave., New York, NY 11228 (☎ **212/ 486-0500**), charges $25 per year for membership, which allows spur-of-the-moment participation in dozens of tours. Each offers air and land packages, which sometimes represent substantial savings over what you'd have paid through more conventional channels. Although membership is required for participation in the tours, anyone can call the company's hotline (☎ **718/234-6295**) to learn what options are available.

Membership in the **Sears Discount Travel Club,** 3033 S. Parker Rd., Suite 900, Aurora, CO 80014 (☎ **800/433-9383** in the U.S.), costs $50 and offers members a catalog (issued four times a year), maps, discounts at select hotels, and a limited guarantee that equivalent packages will not be undersold by any other travel organization. The club also offers a 5% rebate on the value of all airline tickets, tours, hotels, and car rentals purchased through it. The **Encore Travel Club,** 4501 Forbes Blvd., Lanham, MD 20706 (☎ **800/638-8976** in the U.S.), charges $49.95 a year for membership which offers up to 50% discounts at more than 4,000 hotels as well as on airfares, cruises, and car rentals through its volume-purchase plans. Membership includes a travel package outlining the company's many services, and use of a toll-free phone number for advice and information.

FLY/DRIVE TOURS   Fly/drive holidays, which combine airfare and car rental, are increasing in popularity and are a lot cheaper than booking both airfare and car rental independently.

British Airways (☎ **800/876-2200**) allows you to "Create Your Own Vacation" with its fly/drive package, embracing a number of destinations, not only in Britain and Ireland but in continental Europe as well. An itinerary can be arranged to fit your budget, with discounts at hotels as well as on the car.

CIE Tours International (☎ **800/243-8687**) has a self-drive "Go-As-You-Please Ireland" vacation, modestly priced at $39–$52 per person daily (a 7-night minimum). B&B accommodations are arranged at private homes or farmhouses. CIE Tours can also get special airfares with British Airways and Aer Lingus.

Aer Lingus (☎ **800/223-6537** or 212/557-1110) features a "Go As You Please" fly/drive package in Ireland. You're given hotel vouchers and the chance to stay at various B&Bs or farmhouses; for a higher charge you'll be booked into Best Western hotels instead of B&Bs.

The French Experience and TAP Air Portugal Discovery Vacations (see above) also offer fly/drive tours and packages.

SPECIAL-INTEREST TOURS   For music and opera lovers, **Dailey-Thorp,** 330 W. 58th St., Suite 610, New York, NY 10019-1817 (☎ **212/307-1515**), is the best in the business, and is able to purchase otherwise unavailable tickets to the Salzburg Festival, La Scala, and even, on occasion, to Bayreuth. Tours last 7–15 days and include first-class or deluxe accommodations and meals in top-rated European restaurants.

For art lovers who want to get off the beaten path, **Esplanade Tours,** 581 Boylston St., Boston, MA 02116 (☎ **800/426-5492** or 617/266-7465), the

American agent for London-based Swan Hellenic Tours, has guided tours focusing on the art and architecture of various regions of France, lasting 8–12 days. Tours include lectures, usually by Britain-based authorities.

Amateur watercolor enthusiasts can join an "Arts in the South of France" trip, sponsored by **Art Trek,** P.O. Box 807, Bolinas, CA 94924 (☎ **800/786-1830** or 415/868-9558). Tours are led by art instructors, and take place May–July, when the Mediterranean sunlight is at its intense, impressionistic best. The average cost, including airfare from the West Coast, is $4,455 per person. Each tour lasts 16 days, with half board included in accommodations based on double occupancy.

Other art and architecture tours are offered by **4th Dimension Tours,** 1150 NW 72nd Ave., Suite 250, Miami, FL 33126 (☎ **800/343-0020** or 305/477-1525); and **Smithsonian Institution's Study Tours and Seminars,** 110 Jefferson Dr. SW, Room 3045, Washington, DC 20560 (☎ **202/357-4700**).

Barge & Voyage, 140 E. 56th St., Suite 4C, New York, NY 10022 (☎ **800/438-4748**), offers barge tours, mainly in France, on luxury vessels holding 12–52 passengers with entertainment on board. **EuroCruises,** 303 W. 13th St., New York, NY 10014 (☎ **800/688-3876** or 212/691-2099), operates some 20 European-based cruise lines with some 60 ships sailing European waterways.

Those seeking a sports-oriented vacation can contact **Fishing International,** P.O. Box 2132, Santa Rosa, CA 95405 (☎ **800/950-4242**), which offers salmon- and trout-fishing packages in Norway, France, and Ireland. **Golf International,** 275 Madison Ave., New York, NY 10016 (☎ **800/833-1389** or 212/986-9176), features golf packages to Britain, France, and Ireland. **TAP Air Portugal Discovery Vacations** (☎ **800/247-8686;** see above) offers golf packages in the Algarve.

Championship Tennis Tours, 9 Antigua, Dana Point, CA 92629 (☎ **800/545-7717** or 714/661-7331), wraps together tennis packages to major events in Europe, including Wimbledon, the Italian Open, and the French Open.

9 Getting Around

BY TRAIN

If you plan a lot of rail travel, you'll do well to secure the latest copy of the *Thomas Cook European Timetable of Railroads.* This comprehensive, 500-plus-page timetable documents all of Europe's mainline passenger rail services with detail and accuracy. It's available in North America exclusively from **Forsyth Travel Library,** P.O. Box 2975, Shawnee Mission, KS 66201 (☎ **800/FORSYTH**), at a cost of $24.95 plus $4.50 postage.

For more information about traveling by train in Europe, call **Rail Europe, Inc.,** 2100 Central Ave., Suite 200, Boulder, CO 80301 (☎ **800/4-EURAIL** or 303/443-5100), but when and if you get through, don't expect the staff member to be particularly helpful or polite. Rail Europe's Rail 'N' Drive programs, arranged in co-operation with Hertz or Avis, allow you to combine driving with taking the train. Another source of information (again, if you can get through) is **German Rail/DER Tours,** 9501 W. Devon, Rosemont, IL 60018 (☎ **800/782-2424** or 708/692-6300). Like Rail Europe, this is not a particularly cooperative staff.

EURAILPASSES The **Eurailpass** permits unlimited first-class rail travel in any country in Western Europe, except Great Britain, and also includes Hungary in Eastern Europe. Here's how it works: The pass is sold only in North America. Vacationers can purchase a Eurailpass good for 15 days for $522; a pass for 21 days costs $678.

A 1-month pass costs $838, a 2-month pass goes for $1,148, and a 3-month pass runs $1,468. Children under 4 travel free, provided they don't occupy a seat (otherwise they're charged half fare); children under 12 are charged half fare.

If you're under 26, you can purchase a **Eurail Youthpass,** which entitles you to unlimited second-class travel for 15 days for $588, for 1 month for $595, and for 2 months for $798.

Simply show the pass to the ticket collector, then settle back to enjoy the scenery. Seat reservations are required on some trains. Many of the trains have *couchettes* (sleeping cars), for which an additional fee is charged. Obviously, the 2- or 3-month traveler gets the greatest economic advantages—the Eurailpass is ideal for extensive trips. Passholders can visit all of Europe's major sights, from Brittany to Sicily, then end the vacation in Norway, for example. Travelers in Europe for 15 days or 1 month have to estimate rail distance before determining if such a pass is to their benefit—to obtain full advantage of the ticket for 15 days or 1 month, you'd have to spend a great deal of time on the train.

Eurailpass holders are entitled to considerable reductions on certain buses and ferries as well. You'll get a 20% reduction on second-class accommodations from certain companies operating ferries between Naples and Palermo, and for crossings to Sardinia and Malta.

Travel agents in all towns, and railway agents in such major cities as New York, Montréal, and Los Angeles, sell all these tickets. A Eurailpass is available at the North American offices of CIT Travel Service, the French National Railroads, the German Federal Railroads, and the Swiss Federal Railways.

The **Eurail Saverpass** is a money-saving ticket that offers discounted 15 days of first-class travel all over Europe, but only if groups of three people travel constantly and continuously together between April and September, or if two people travel constantly and continuously together between October and March. The Saverpass costs $452 for 15 days.

The **Eurail Flexipass** is the most flexible option. It's valid in first class and offers the same privileges as the Eurailpass. However, it provides a certain number of travel days that can be used within a longer period of consecutive days. There are two passes: 10 days of travel within 2 months for $616 and 15 days of travel within 2 months for $812.

With many of the same qualifications and restrictions as the previously described Flexipass, the **Eurail Youth Flexipass** is sold only to travelers under age 26; it allows 10 days of travel within 2 months for $438 and 15 days of travel within 2 months for $588.

BRITRAIL PASSES   The classic **Britrail Pass** allows unlimited rail travel during an 8- or 15-day period. The 8-day pass costs $325 for travel in first class, $235 in "standard" class; the 15-day pass, $525 for first class, $365 for standard.

The **Britrail Flexipass** lets you travel anywhere on BritRail. It's particularly good for visitors who want to alternate travel days with sightseeing time in a particular city or region. One Flexipass can be used for 4 days within any 1-month period and costs $289 for travel in first class and $199 in economy; seniors pay $245 and youths 16–25 pay $160 to travel in economy class. Another Flexipass allows 8 days of travel within a month at a cost of $399 for first class and $280 for economy; a senior pass costs $339, and the youth economy-class pass costs $225.

Americans can obtain BritRail passes at **BritRail Travel International,** 1500 Broadway, New York, NY 10036 (☎ **800/677-8585** in the U.S., 800/555-2748 in Canada, or 212/575-2667 in New York).

THE SCANRAIL PASS   If your visit to Europe will be primarily in Scandinavia, the Scanrail pass may be better and cheaper for you than the Eurailpass. This pass allows its owner a predesignated number of days of free rail travel, but only within a larger time block. For example, you could choose a total of any 5 days of unlimited rail travel during a 15-day period, 10 days of rail travel in a 1-month period, or a month of unlimited rail travel. The pass, valid on all lines of the state railways of Denmark, Finland, Norway, and Sweden, offers discounts or free travel on some (but not all) of the region's ferryboat lines. The pass can be purchased only in North America, at any office of **Rail Europe** (☎ **800/848-7245**) or at **ScanAm World Tours**, 933 N.J. 23, Pompton Plains, NJ 07444 (☎ **800/545-2204**).

BY CAR

Many rental companies grant discounts to clients who reserve in advance before leaving home (usually 48 hours) through the toll-free reservations offices in the renter's home country. Rentals of a week or more are almost always less expensive than day rentals.

When you reserve a car, be sure to ask if the price includes the EU value-added tax (VAT), personal accident insurance (PAI), collision-damage waiver (CDW), and any other insurance options. If not, ask what they'll cost, because at the end of your rental they can make a big difference in your bottom line. As in the United States, the CDW and some added insurance are sometimes offered free by certain credit/ charge-card companies if you use their card to pay for the rental. Check directly with your card issuer to avoid buying unnecessary coverage.

Travel Guard International, 1145 Clark St., Stevens Point, WI 54481 (☎ **800/ 826-1300**), offers an 8-day policy for $19 that covers up to $25,000 in repairs. After 8 days, additional coverage goes for $3 per day. Avis and Hertz, among other companies, require that you purchase a theft-protection policy in Italy.

Avis (☎ **800/331-1084**) offers a "Know Before You Go" program for Americans who plan motor trips through France, Britain, and Germany. Information supplied includes gasoline prices, speed limits (in miles per hour), driver's license requirements, and other data. Avis also supplies free maps of these countries. For more information, call **800/297-4447** 24 hours a day.

Other companies with international branches are **Budget Rent-a-Car** (☎ 800/ 472-3325); **Dollar Rent-a-Car** (known as Eurodollar in Europe; ☎ 800/800-6000); **Hertz** (☎ 800/654-3001); and **National** (called Europcar abroad; ☎ 800/ 227-3876). If arrangements are made in advance, it's possible to pick up a car in one country and return it in another. There may, however, be a drop-off charge.

U.S.-based companies that specialize in European car rentals are: **Auto-Europe** (☎ 800/223-5555), **Europe by Car** (☎ 800/223-1516, 800/252-9401 in California, or 212/581-3040 in New York), **Bon Voyage by Car** (☎ 800/272-3299), and **Kemwel** (☎ 800/678-0678).

BY RV   Recreational vehicles (RVs) are called caravans in Europe. The best outfitter for RV rentals is **Bon Voyage by Car,** 5658 Sepulveda Blvd., Suite 201, Van Nuys, CA 91411 (☎ **800/272-3299**). A 10-day rental in Britain of a high-top conversion vehicle, complete with kitchen and bathroom facilities, including taxes and insurance, is $80 a day for four passengers. You must send 25% of the rental when making a reservation.

Other information about RV travel is available from the **Recreation Vehicle Industry Association,** 1896 Preston White Dr. (P.O. Box 2999), Reston, VA 22090 (☎ **703/620-6003,** ext. 311). Another good source for data is the **Family Campers and RVers Association,** 4804 Transit Rd., Building 2, Depew, NY 14043

(☎ **716/668-6242**), with an annual membership fee of $25 for individuals or an entire family. The organization provides members an international camping carnet for $10 that's good for certain discounts, as well as a helpful magazine issued 10 times a year.

MAPS   The **AAA** supplies good maps to its members. Maps can also be secured by mail or phone from **Michelin Travel Publications,** P.O. Box 19008, Greenville, SC 29602 (☎ **800/423-0485**), or from the **Hagstrom Map & Travel Center,** 57 W. 43rd St., New York, NY 10036 (☎ **212/398-1222**), where city maps begin at $7.95 and regional and country maps go for $9.95 and up.

10 For British Travelers

Citizens of member states of the European Union traveling in other EU countries need only an identity card—not a passport (although if you already possess a passport, it's always useful to carry it). Britishers who don't have a passport but want to apply for one can call the **London Passport Office** (☎ **0171/271-3000**) for details and information.

CUSTOMS   While traveling in EU countries, you can buy your wine, spirits, or cigarettes in an ordinary shop and bring home *almost* as much as you like. (H.M. Customs and Excise does not set theoretical limits.) If you're returning home from a non-EU country, or if you buy your goods in a duty-free shop, the standard allowances still apply: You're allowed to bring home 200 cigarettes and 2 liters of table wine, plus 1 liter of spirits or 2 liters of fortified wine. British Customs tends to be strict and complicated in its requirements. Get in touch with **Her Majesty's Customs and Excise Office,** New King's Beam House, 22 Upper Ground, London SE1 9PJ (☎ **0171/620-1313**), for more information.

GETTING THERE   By Plane   You can fly to the continent from 18 British airports (different destinations are served by different airports). If a special air-travel promotion is not available when you want to travel, ask about a "Eurobudget ticket," which imposes restrictions or length-of-stay requirements. An APEX ticket can also trim costs. APEX tickets must be reserved in advance, but offer a discount without the usual booking restrictions.

British Airways (☎ **0181/897-4000**) flies from a number of airports to every major European capital and many large cities on the Continent. All major national carriers in Europe offer flights to their home countries from London. When calling these national carriers, ask about special offers or package promotions.

Travel agents usually have "deals" to cut costs in getting from the U.K. to continental destinations; these could be in the form of a charter flight or some special land or air-travel promotion.

Daily **newspapers** often carry ads for companies that tout "slashed" fares to the Continent. A good source is the London magazine *Time Out.* The *Evening Standard* has a daily travel section, as well as the Sunday editions of almost any newspaper. **Trailfinders** (☎ **0171/937-5400** in London) is a consolidator that offers access to tickets on major European carriers, including British Airways.

There are many bucket shops around Victoria and Earls Court in London offering low fares. Make sure the company you deal with is a member of the IATA, ABTA, or ATOL, which are umbrella organizations that will help you out if anything goes wrong.

CEEFAX, an information service included on many home and hotel TVs, runs details of package holidays and flights to continental Europe and beyond. Just switch to your CEEFAX channel and you'll find a menu of listings that includes travel information.

Make sure you understand the bottom line on any special deal you're offered—that is, ask if all surcharges, including airport taxes and other hidden costs, are cited—before committing yourself to purchase. Also, make sure you understand what the penalties are if you're forced to cancel at the last minute.

By Train   Many different rail passes are available in the U.K. for travel in continenal Europe. Stop in at the **International Rail Centre,** Victoria Station, London SW1V 1JY (☎ **0171/834-2345**), or **Wasteels,** 121 Wilton Rd., London SW1V 1JZ (☎ **0171/834-7066**), to find the best option for the trip you're planning.

There are a number of options for travelers under age 26. **Inter-Rail and EuroYouth passes,** available only to such travelers, entitles the pass holder to unlimited second-class travel in 26 European countries. Eurotrain **"Explorer" tickets** are another option for travelers under age 26. They allow passengers to move in a leisurely fashion from London to Rome, for example, with as many stopovers en route as desired, and return by a different route. All travel must be completed within 2 months of the date of departure. Such a ticket sells for £195 round-trip. For £153 round-trip, the same route can be traveled without any stopovers for either the outbound or the return trip. Both these tickets include ferryboat transport across the Channel. **Campus Travel,** 52 Grosvenor Gardens, London SW1W OAG (☎ **0171/730-3402**), can give you prices and help you book tickets.

Wasteels, Victoria Station, opposite platform 2, London SW1V 1JY (☎ **0171/834-7066**), sells a **Rail Europe Senior Pass** for £5 that entitles the holder to discounted tickets on many European rail lines. To qualify, purchasers must be bonafide residents of the U.K., 60 years of age, and hold a British Senior Citizen rail card, which is available for £16 at any BritRail office. Wasteels's main office lies just around the corner from Victoria Station, at 122A Wilton Rd., London SW1 V1J (☎ **0171/834-6744**).

By Chunnel   The *Eurostar Express* passenger train has twice-daily service between London and both Paris and Brussels—a 3-hour trip. **Rail Europe** (☎ **800/94-CHUNNEL**) sells direct-service tickets on the *Eurostar* between London and Paris or Brussels. A round-trip ticket between Paris and London costs $344 in first class and $242 in second class. You can cut the second-class cost to $148 by making a (nonrefundable) 14-day advance purchase. You can phone for *Eurostar* reservations (☎ **01345/300003** in London, **01-44-51-06-02** in Paris, and **800/EUROSTAR** in the U.S.). *Eurostar* trains arrive and depart from Waterloo Station in London, Gare du Nord in Paris, and Central Station in Brussels.

By Ferry/Hovercraft   **Brittany Ferries** (☎ **01705/827701**) is the largest British ferry/drive outfit. It sails from the southern coast of England to five destinations in Spain and France. From Portsmouth, sailings reach St-Malo and Caen; from Poole, Cherbourg. From Plymouth, sailings go to Santander in Spain.

P&O Channel Lines (☎ **01304/242233**) operates car and passenger ferries between Portsmouth and Cherbourg (three departures a day; 5 hours each way, 7 hours at night); between Portsmouth and Le Havre, France (three a day; 5¹/₂ hours each way); and between Dover and Calais, France (25 sailings a day; 1¹/₄ hours each way).

P&O's major competitor is **Stena Sealink** (☎ **01233/647-047**), which carries both passengers and vehicles on its routes. This company is represented in North America by BritRail (☎ **800/677-8585**, or 212/575-2667 in New York). Stena Sealink offers conventional ferryboat service between Southampton and Cherbourg (one or two trips a day; 6–8 hours each way) and between Newhaven and Dieppe (four departures daily; 4 hours each way). Stena Sealink's conventional car ferries between Dover and Calais are very popular; they depart 20 times a day in both directions and take 1¹/₂ hours to make the crossing. Typical one-way fares between England and France are £24 for adults, £22 for seniors, and £14 for children.

By far the most popular route across the Channel is between Calais and Dover. **Hoverspeed** (☎ **01304/240-241**) operates at least 12 Hovercraft crossings daily (the trip takes 35 minutes). They also run a SeaCat (a catamaran propelled by jet engines) that takes slightly longer to make the crossing between Folkestone and Boulogne. The SeaCats depart about four times a day on the 55-minute voyage.

Traveling by Hovercraft or SeaCat cuts the time of your surface journey from the U.K. to the Continent. A SeaCat crossing from Folkestone to Boulogne is longer in miles but is covered faster than conventional ferryboats making the Dover–Calais crossing. Typical one-way fares are £25 per person.

Scandinavia Seaways (☎ **0171/409-6060**) offers sea links to Germany plus all the Scandinavian countries. From England, the Norway route is the most popular. Fares are reduced on so-called Flag Days. Ask about these when booking.

By Car   If you plan to take a rented car across or under the Channel, check with the rental company about license and insurance requirements before you leave. There are many "drive-on, drive-off" car-ferry services across the Channel. The most popular crossings are on Sealink's ferries, Dover and Folkestone to Calais and Boulogne.

Chunnel trains, called by the French *Le Shuttle,* carry passenger cars, charter buses, taxis, and motorcycles, a 35-minute ride (19 minutes of which are actually in the Chunnel) in bright, air-conditioned carriages. When the trip is over, you simply drive off toward your destination. Total travel time between the English and French highway system is about an hour. This car service operates 24 hours a day, 365 days a year; it runs every 15 minutes during peak travel periods and at least once an hour at night.

By Coach   With regular departures from London's Victoria Coach Station, **Eurolines** (☎ **0171/730-8235** or 01582/404511) has a comprehensive network of services to destinations throughout Europe. Coaches have reclining seats and a choice of smoking or nonsmoking areas. Return tickets are valid for up to 6 months, and passengers may leave their return date open.

Information and credit/charge-card reservations can be obtained by telephone, or passengers may book in person at Eurolines, 52 Grosvenor Gardens, Victoria, London SW1W OAU (opposite Victoria Rail Station). A round-trip ticket from London to Rome, for example, using as direct a route as possible, costs between £129 and £139, and from £87 one-way, depending on the season. Passengers under 26 pay around £10 less each way. Departures in either direction are daily. Passengers can interrupt their journey, pending available space on subsequent legs of their trip, in Paris or Milan en route.

ORGANIZED TOURS   The oldest travel agency in Britain, **Cox & Kings** (☎ **0171/873-5006**) was established in 1758 as the paymasters and transport directors for the British armed forces in India. The company continues to send travelers from Britain throughout the world, specializing in unusual, if pricey, holidays.

Far more economical are group tours offered by **Trafalgar Tours,** 15 Grosvenor Place, London SW1X 7HH (☎ **0171/235-7090**) in London, or **Trophy Tours/ Frames Rickards,** 11 Herbrand St., London WC1N 1EX (☎ **0171/637-4171**).

A phone call to the London headquarters of the **International Association of Travel Agencies (IATA)** (☎ **0181/744-9280**) can provide names and addresses of tour operators who specialize in travel relating to your particular interest.

Bicycle Tours   The best cycling tours of France and Italy are organized by **Alternative Travel Group, Ltd,** 69–71 Banbury Rd., Oxford OX2 6PE (☎ **01865/310-399**). Another good outfitter to check with is **Bike Tours,** P.O. Box 75, Bath, Avon, BA1 RX (☎ **01225/480-130**).

TIPS FOR TRAVELERS WITH SPECIAL NEEDS   Before you go, travelers with special needs may want to check with the offerings of the following organizations.

For Travelers with Disabilities   The **Royal Association for Disability and Rehabilitation (RADAR),** Unit 12, City Forum, 250 City Rd., London ECIV 8AF (☎ **0171/250-3222**), publishes three holiday "fact packs," which sell for £2 each or £5 for a set of all three. The first one provides general information, including planning and booking a holiday, insurance, finances, and useful organization and holiday providers. The second outlines transport and equipment, transportation available when going abroad, and equipment for rent. The third deals with specialized accommodations.

Another good service is the **Holiday Care Service,** Imperial Building, 2nd Floor, Victoria Road, Horley, Surrey RH6 7PZ (☎ **01293/774-535;** fax 01293/784-647), a national charity that advises on accessible accommodations for the elderly and persons with disabilities. Annual membership costs £25. Once a member, you can receive a newsletter and access to a free reservations network for hotels throughout Britain and—to a lesser degree—Europe and the rest of the world.

If you plan to fly to your European destination, contact the **Transport Users Councils,** Kingsway House, 5th Floor, 103 Kingsway, London WC2B 6QZ (☎ **0171/242-3882**), which publishes an information-packed booklet *Care in the Air.* You should also call the airline of your choice and advise the staff that you'll need assistance in boarding and disembarking.

For Singles   Solo travelers should contact **Explore World-Wide, Ltd.,** 1 Frederick St., Aldershot, Hampshire GU11 1LQ (☎ **01252/344-161**), which specializes in compiling small groups (12–20 participants) of unattached travelers for offbeat tours of parts of Europe. Children are not encouraged to participate. The company prefers to sell land packages as entities separate from airline tickets.

Another specialist for the solo traveler is **Campus Travel Group,** 52 Grosvenor Gardens, London SW1W 0AG (☎ **0171/730-3402**), offering discounted rail and charter flights. Yet another good source is **HF Holidays** (☎ **0181/905-9388**), popular with 18- to 35-year-olds interested mainly in walking tours of Europe.

For Families   The best deals for families are often package tours put together by large British travel companies. Thomsons Tour Operators, through its subsidiary, **Skytours** (☎ **0171/387-9321**), offers dozens of air/land packages to continental Europe, with free airline seats for children under 18 who accompany their parents. To qualify, parents must book airfare and hotel accommodations lasting 2 weeks or more, as far in advance as possible. Savings for families with children can be substantial.

For Students   Open 7 days a week, **Campus Travel,** 52 Grosvenor Gardens, London SW1W 0AG (☎ **0171/730-3402**), opposite Victoria Station, is Britain's leading specialist in student and youth travel worldwide. It provides a comprehensive travel service specializing in low rail, sea, and airfares, holiday breaks, and travel insurance, plus student discount cards. Whether you're booking a visit to Vienna, a skiing trip to Norway, or a round-the-world trip, the experienced staff at Campus Travel can help you.

The International Student Identity Card (ISIC) will entitle you to savings on flights, sightseeing, food, and accommodations. It sells for £5 and is well worth the cost. Always show your ISIC when booking a trip—you may not get a discount without it.

Youth hostels are the place to stay. You'll need an International Youth Hostels Association card, which you can purchase from either of London's youth hostel retail outlets: 14 Southampton St. (near Covent Garden), London WC23 7HY (☎ 0171/836-1036); or 52 Grosvenor Gardens, London SW1W OAG (☎ 0171/823-4739). They also sell all the paraphernalia a camper, hiker, or shoestring traveler might need. To apply for a membership card, take your passport and some passport-sized photos of yourself, plus a membership fee of £9. More information on membership is available from the **Youth Hostels Association of England and Wales (YHA),** 8 St. Stephen's Hill, St. Albans, Hertfordshire AL1 2DY (☎ 01727/855215).

The Youth Hostel Association puts together a *YHA Budget Accommodations Guide* (Volume 1 covers Europe and the Mediterranean; Volume 2, the rest of the world), which lists the address, phone number, and admissions policy for every youth hostel in the world. The volumes are £6.99 each, and either of them can be purchased at the retail outlets listed above. If ordering by mail, add 61p for postage in the U.K.

If you're traveling in summer, many youth hostels will be full. To avoid disappointment, it's best to book ahead.

TRAVEL INSURANCE   Most big travel agents offer their own insurance, and will try to sell you their package when you book a holiday. Think before you sign. Britain's Consumers' Association recommends that you insist on seeing the policy and reading the fine print before buying travel insurance. You should shop around for the best deals. **Columbus Travel Insurance, Ltd** (☎ 0171/375-0011 in London) sells travel insurance only to people who have been official residents of Britain for at least a year.

1

Austria

by Darwin Porter & Danforth Prince

Austria now stands at the crossroads of Europe, between the eastern and western parts of the continent, as it did in the heyday of the Austro-Hungarian Empire. Its capital, Vienna, stranded during the postwar years on the edge of Western Europe, is taking its place again as an important international city.

There's a lot to do here, from exploring historic castles and palaces to skiing on some of the world's finest alpine slopes or hiking in the Danube Valley.

1 Vienna & the Danube Valley

Vienna still retains much of the glory and grandeur of the empire's heady days. Museum treasures from all over Europe, baroque palaces through which Maria Theresa and her brood wandered, the lively music of Johann Strauss, Gustav Klimt's paintings, the concert halls, the unparalleled opera—it's all still here, as if the empire were still flourishing.

Tourism is growing as thousands arrive every year to view Vienna's great art and architecture, to feast on lavish Viennese pastries, to go exploring in the Vienna Woods, to sail down the Danube, to attend Vienna's balls, operas, and festivals, and often to listen to the "music that never stops."

Visitors today face a newer and brighter Vienna, a city with more *joie de vivre* and punch than it's had since before the war. There's also a downside: Prices are on the rise—they haven't reached the height of the Ferris wheel at the Prater, but they're climbing there.

ONLY IN VIENNA

Cruising the Danube (Donau)   Johann Strauss took a bit of poetic license in calling the Donau "The Blue Danube," as it's actually a muddy green. To take a cruise, try the legendary DDSG, Blue Danube Shipping Company, Donaureisen, Handelskai 265 (☎ **0222/727-500**), which offers mostly one-day trips from Vienna. Along the way you'll pass some of the most famous sights in eastern Austria, including Krems and Melk.

Watching the Lippizaner Stallions   Nothing evokes that heyday of imperial Vienna more than the Spanish Riding School, which specializes in "dressage," a severely disciplined art originally taught to riders in Vienna by the "master of the horse," La Guérinière, who fled here to escape the French Revolution. The stallions are a result of crossbreeding between Spanish thoroughbreds and Karst (Arabian) horses. These white horses are the finest equestrian performers on earth. Riders wear brown dress coats, with doeskin breeches and two-corner hats, and they put the horses through their incredible demonstrations, with the public admitted to watch.

Heurigen Hopping in the Vienna Woods When the *heurigen,* wine taverns that celebrate the arrival of each year's new wine or *heuriger,* place a symbolic pine branch over their doors, the Viennese rush to the taverns to drink the new wine and feast on country dishes such as local ham, bacon and lentils, and roast pork. Grinsing is the most visited area. The light, white wine, served chilled, is made from a medley of grapes harvested in the vineyards of the Wienerwald or Vienna Woods. Shaded by hazels and birches in centuries-old courtyards, often with a panoramic view of the Danube Valley, the Viennese taste the results of each new harvest, turning the occasion into a festival.

Exploring the Habsburgs' Lifestyle One of the great dynastic ruling families of Europe, the Habsburg, was based in Vienna. Even today you can see the grandeur of their former lifestyle. Their winter palace, Hofburg, was the seat of an imperial throne that once governed the Austro-Hungarian Empire. The sprawling palace complex reads like an architectural textbook—dating from 1279 with subsequent additions through the 18th century. Here they ruled until their dynasty came to an end in 1918. You can also visit their summer palace, Schönbrunn, with its 1,441 rooms. The great baroque architect, J. B. Fischer von Erlach, modeled his plans on those of Versailles.

Cycling Along the Danube The Lower Danube Cycle Track has been called a "velocipede's Valhalla." A river-bordering bike train between Vienna and Naarn links the most exciting villages and stops along the Danube. As you cycle along, you can take in the attractions, ranging from castles of yesterday to medieval towns, along with latticed vineyards adding to the scenery. You can rent bikes from the train or ferry stations, and the Vienna tourist office will provide route maps.

Strolling on the Kärntnerstrasse The center of the Inner City and the heart of Viennese life is the pedestrian-only Kärntnerstrasse (or "Carinthia Street," in English). One of Europe's liveliest shopping streets, it competes in Vienna with the Graben, which is the second major shopping center. At any time of the day or night, people can be seen parading along this merchandise-stuffed street, taking in the new window displays of fabulous merchandise. Street performers during the day are always out to amuse—vaudeville isn't dead. When you tire of all that, you can retreat to one of the cafe terraces for the best people-watching in Vienna.

A Concert by the Vienna Boys' Choir In this city steeped in musical traditions and institutions—everybody from Mozart to Johann Strauss the Elder to Richard Strauss to Wagner—one group has distinguished itself among all others. It's the Vienna Boys' Choir or *Wiener Sängerknaben,* with origins going back to the 12th century. Created by Maximilian I, the choir was attached to the Hofmusikkapelle at the Hofburg, where it still performs. The choir sings mass at the Hofburgkapelle on Sundays and holidays, except in July and August. The voices are among the purest in all of Europe, and hearing these children is reason enough to buy a ticket to Vienna.

Experiencing the Majesty of St. Stephan's Cathedral It's been suggested that without Dompfarre St. Stephan, Vienna would "lose its soul." Its vast roof is exactly

Vienna Attractions & Accommodations

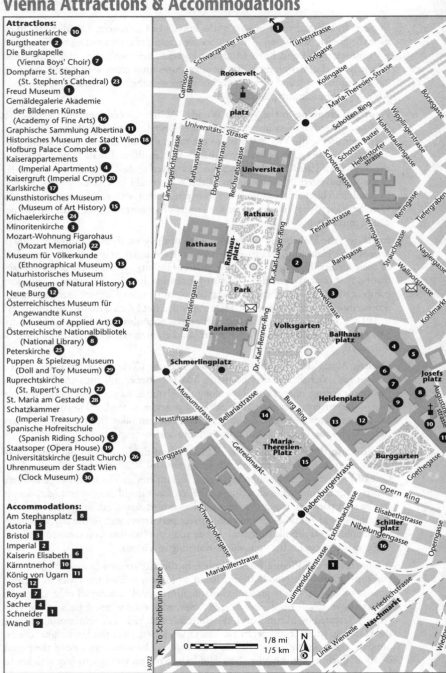

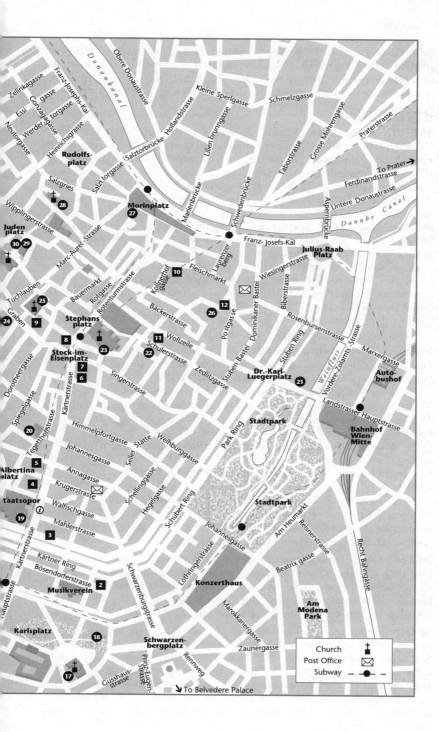

Church ✝
Post Office ✉
Subway •—•—

twice the height of its walls. The Viennese regard this monument with great affection, calling it *Der Steffl.* One of its chief treasures is the Wiener Neustadt altarpiece in carved wood, painted and gilded—found in the Virgin's Choir. In all, the cathedral is one of Europe's great gothic structures, crowned by a 450-foot steeple.

ORIENTATION

ARRIVING　By Plane　Vienna's international airport, **Wien Schwechat** (☎ 0222/7007), is about 12 miles southeast of the city center. There is regular bus service between the airport and the City Air Terminal (Wien Mitte), at the Hotel Hilton. Buses run daily every 20–60 minutes 8:50am–7:30pm, and also to accommodate flights arriving after 7:30pm. The one-way fare is 70 AS ($6.65). There's also service between the airport and two railroad stations, the Westbahnhof and the Südbahnhof, leaving the Westbahnhof every 30 minutes 5:40am-11:40pm (reaching the Südbahnhof 15 minutes later) and starting from the airport every 30 minutes 5:55am-11:50pm. The trip takes 20 to 25 minutes from the airport to the Inner City. Fares between the airport and the train station are 70 AS ($6.65) per person.

There's also train service between the airport and the Wien Nord and Wien Mitte rail stations. Trains run daily from 5:07am to 9:30pm. The trip time takes about 45 minutes, and the fare is 34 AS ($3.25). A one-way taxi ride from the airport into the Inner City is likely to cost 410 AS ($38.95).

A branch of the official Vienna Tourist Information Office in the arrival hall of the airport is open Oct–May daily 9am–10pm; June–Sept daily 9am–11pm.

By Train　Vienna has four principal rail stations, with frequent connections to all Austrian cities and towns and to all major European cities, such as Munich and Milan. For train information for all stations, call **0222/17-17.**

The **Wien Westbahnhof,** Europaplatz, is for trains arriving from western Austria, Western Europe, and many Eastern European countries. It has frequent train connections to all major Austrian cities. Trains from Salzburg pull in one per hour daily from 5:40am to 8:40pm; the trip takes 3¼ hours.

The **Wien Südbahnhof,** Südtirolerplatz, has train service to southern Austria, including the new countries of Slovenia, Croatia (formerly part of Yugoslavia), and Italy. It also has links to Graz, the capital of Styria, and to Klagenfurt, the capital of Carinthia.

Other stations include **Franz-Josef Bahnhof,** Franz-Josef-Platz, used mainly by local trains, although connections are made here to Prague and Berlin. **Wien Mitte,** Landstrasser Hauptstrasse 1, is also a terminus of local trains, plus a depot for trains to the Czech Republic and trains to Schwechat Airport.

By Bus　The **City Bus Terminal** is at the Wien Mitte rail station, Landstrasser Hauptstrasse 1. This is the arrival depot for Post buses and Bundesbuses to points all over the country, and also the arrival point for private buses from various European cities. The terminal has lockers, currency-exchange kiosks, and a ticket counter open daily 6:15am–6pm. For bus information, call **0222/711-01** daily 6am–9pm.

By Car　Vienna can be reached from all directions via major highways (called *autobahnen*) or by secondary highways. The main artery from the west is Autobahn A-1, coming in from Munich (a distance of 291 miles), Salzburg (209 miles), and Linz (116 miles). Autobahn A-2 arrives from the south, from Graz (124 miles) and Klagenfurt (192 miles). Autobahn A-4 comes in from the east, connecting with Route E-58, which runs to Bratislava and Prague. Autobahn A-22 takes traffic from the northwest, and Route E-10 connects to the cities and towns of southeastern Austria and Hungary.

VISITOR INFORMATION   The official **Vienna Tourist Information Office** is at Kärntnerstrasse 38 (☎ **0222/513-88-92**), open daily 9am–7pm. You can make room reservations here. Address postal inquiries to the Vienna Tourist Board, Obere Augartenstrasse 40, A-1025 Vienna (fax 0222/216-84-92).

CITY LAYOUT   Vienna has evolved over the years into one of the largest metropolises of central Europe, with a surface area covering 160 square miles. It has been divided into 23 districts (*bezirke*), each identified with a Roman numeral.

The size and shape of **Bezirke I,** the **Inner City,** roughly correspond to the original borders of the medieval city. Other than the Cathedral of St. Stephan, very few medieval (gothic or medieval) buildings remain—many were rebuilt in the baroque or neoclassical style, whereas others are modern replacements of buildings bombed during World War II. As Austria's commercial and cultural nerve center, the central district contains dozens of streets devoted exclusively to pedestrian traffic. The most famous of these is **Kärntnerstrasse,** which bypasses the Vienna State Opera House during its southward trajectory toward the province of Carinthia (Kärnten).

The Inner City is surrounded by the **Ringstrasse,** a circular boulevard about 2¹/₂ miles long whose construction between 1859 and 1888 was one of the most ambitious (and controversial) examples of urban restoration in the history of central Europe. Confusingly, the name of this boulevard changes many times during its encirclement of the Inner City. Names that apply to it carry the suffix -*ring:* for example, Opernring, Schottenring, Burgring, Dr.-Karl-Lueger-Ring, Stubenring, Parkring, Schubertring, and Kärntner Ring.

Surrounding the Ringstrasse are what is known as the **inner suburban districts** (Bezirkes II through IX). These contain most of the villas and palaces of Vienna's 18th-century nobility, as well as complexes of modern apartment houses and the 19th-century homes of middle-class entrepreneurs. The **outer suburban districts** contain a wide range of residential, industrial, and rural settings.

Northeast of the center, beyond the Danube Canal, is the **Second District,** with the famous amusement park, the Prater. East of the center, in the **Third District,** you'll find the art treasures and baroque setting of the Belvedere Palace. West of the center is Schönbrunn Palace.

GETTING AROUND   By Public Transportation   Vienna Transport (*Wiener Verkehrsbetriebe*), with its network of facilities covering hundreds of miles, can take you there—by U-Bahn (underground), streetcar, or bus.

Vienna has a uniform fare, allowing the same tickets to be used on all these means of transportation as well as on the **Schnelbahn (Rapid Transit)** of the Austrian Federal Railways in the Vienna area and on some connecting private bus lines.

There are no conductors on most buses and streetcars, which means that you must have the correct change, 21 AS ($2), when you get your ticket at a vending machine at the station or aboard the vehicle you choose. A ticket from the machine will be stamped with the date and time of purchase. It's wiser to buy your tickets in advance at a *tabak-trafik* (tobacconist shop) or at an advance-sales office. All advance-sales offices of Vienna Public Transport are open Mon 6am–noon, Tues–Wed 6:30am–12:30pm, Thurs–Fri 12:30–6:30pm. For location of offices, see "Discount Passes," below. Tickets purchased in advance must be stamped before you start your ride by the machine on conductorless streetcars or at the platform barriers of the underground or Stadtbahn. Once a ticket is stamped, it may be used for any one trip in one direction, including changes.

Discount Passes   The Vienna card gives you access to all public modes of transportation (subway, bus, and tram) within Vienna at a single, discounted price. For 50

AS ($4.75), you can purchase a 24-hour network pass good for a full day of public transport. A 72-hour network pass sells for 180 AS ($17.10). An 8-day strip ticket can be used for 8 separate days of travel, punched by the rail attendant each day it is used. At 265 AS ($25.20), this versatile pass is quite a bargain. A single ticket costs 17 AS ($1.60); that's also the price for two rides by a child. A child under 6 years old rides for free. A Vienna card is easy to find throughout the capital city and entitles holders to unlimited use of the city's public transportation system, as well as discounts in city museums, shops, and restaurants. You can purchase a card over the telephone with a credit card (**☎ 0222/798-44-00-28**).

Vienna Public Transport Information Centers are at the following locations: on Karlsplatz (**☎ 0222/587-31-86**), open Mon–Fri 7am–6pm and on Sat, Sun, and holidays 8:30am–4pm; on Stephansplatz (**☎ 0222/512-42-27**), open Mon–Fri 8am–6pm and on Sat–Sun 8:30am–4pm; and on Praterstern (**☎ 0222/24-93-02**), open Mon–Fri 8am–6pm and on Sat–Sun 8:30am–4pm.

By Bus & Subway You can ride directly into the Inner City on the U-Bahn (underground) U1 or on city bus no. 1A, 2A, or 3A. The underground runs daily 6am–midnight and the buses operate Mon–Sat 6am–10pm, Sun 6am–8pm.

By Taxi Taxi stands are marked by signs, or you can call for a radio cab by phoning 31-300, 60-160, 81-400, 91-091, or 40-100. Fares are indicated on an officially calibrated taxi meter. The basic fare is 26 AS ($2.45), plus 12 AS ($1.15) per kilometer. There is an extra charge of 16 AS ($1.50) for luggage carried in the trunk. For night rides after 11pm, and for trips on Sunday and holidays, the basic fee is 27 AS ($2.55), plus 14 AS ($1.35) per kilometer. For rides called on the telephone, additional charges apply.

By Car Major local car-rental agencies include **Avis,** Opernring 3–5 (☎ 0222/587-62-41); **Budget Rent-a-Car,** Hilton Air Terminal (☎ 0222/7007); and **Hertz,** Kärntner Ring 17 (☎ 0222/795-32). A 20% value-added tax is attached to rentals.

By Bicycle Vienna has more than 155 miles of marked bicycle paths within the city limits. In fact, city officials encourage bicycle riding. In July and August, many Viennese leave their cars in the garage and ride bikes. Specially marked cars of the U-Bahn will transport bicycles free during that time, but only Mon–Fri 9am–3pm and after 6:30pm until the trains stop running. On weekends in July and August, bicycles are also carried free, but only from 9am until the end of the day's run.

Bicycle-rental stores abound at such places as the Prater and along the banks of the Danube Canal, which is the favorite venue for most Viennese to go bicycling. One of the best-known shops is **Radverleih Salztorbrücke,** 1 Donaukanalpromenade near the Salztorbrüke, north of Stephansplatz (☎ **0222/535-34-22** for information), open Apr–Oct daily 10am–7pm. Bike rentals begin at about 200 AS ($19) per day.

FAST FACTS: Vienna

American Express The most convenient office is at Kärntnerstrasse 21–23 (☎ 0222/515-40-0), open Mon–Fri 9am–5:30pm, Sat 9am–noon.

Business Hours Most shops are open Mon–Fri 9am–6pm, Sat 9am–noon, 12:30pm, or 1pm. On the first Sat of every month, the custom is for shops to remain open until 4:30 or 5pm. The tradition is called *langer Samstag.*

Currency The Austrian currency is the **schilling,** written ASch, AS, ÖS, or simply S. A schilling is made up of 100 groschen (which are seldom used). Coins are minted as 5, 10, and 50 groschen, and 1, 5, 10, 20, 25, and 50 schilling. Banknotes appear as 20, 50, 100, 500, 1,000, and 5,000 schilling. At this writing $1 = 10.53 schillings, or 1 schilling = $9^{1}/_{2}$¢, and this was the rate used in this chapter.

Dentists/Doctors For dental problems during the night or on Sat and Sun, call 0222/512-20-78. If you have a medical emergency during the night, call 141 daily 7pm–7am. See also "Emergencies" and "Hospitals," below.

Drugstores Called *apotheke,* they are open Mon–Fri 8am–noon and 2–6pm, Sat 8am–noon. Each apotheke posts in its window a list of shops that take turns staying open at night and Sunday.

Embassies/Consulates The Embassy of the **United States** is at Boltzmanngasse 16, A-1090 Vienna (☎ 0222/313-39). The consular section is at Gartenbaupromenade 2–4, A-1010 Vienna (☎ 0222/313-39). Lost passports, tourist emergencies, and other matters are handled by the consular section. Both the embassy and consulate are open Mon–Fri 8:30am–noon and 1–3:30pm.

The Embassy of **Canada,** Laurenzerberg 2 (☎ 0222/531-38-30-00), is open Mon–Fri 8:30am–12:30pm and 1:30–3:30pm; the **United Kingdom,** Jauresgasse 12 (☎ 0222/713-15-75), open Mon–Fri 9:15am–noon and 2–5pm; **Australia,** Mattiellistrasse 2–4 (☎ 0222/5128-580), open Mon–Fri 8:45am–1pm and 2–5pm; and **New Zealand,** Springsiedelgasse 28 (☎ 0222/318-85-05), open Mon–Fri 8:30am–5pm.

Emergencies   Call 122 to report a fire, 133 for the police, or 144 for an ambulance.

Hospitals   The major hospital is Allgemeines Krankenhaus, Währinger Gürtel 18–20 (☎ 0222/404-00).

Lost Property   A lost-property office, Zentrales Fundamt, is maintained at Wasagasse 22 (☎ 0222/313-44-0), open Mon–Fri 8am–noon. Items found on trains are taken to the central lost-property office at the Westbahnhof. Items left on buses and streetcars are passed on to the Wasagasse office after 3 days. If you miss something as soon as you get off the bus, you can pick it up (provided it is returned) at Wiener Stadtwerke (Verkehrsbetriebe; ☎ 0222/501-30-0) without waiting 3 days.

Photographic Needs   The most central place for film and camera supplies is Foto Niedermayer, Graben 11, near Stephansplatz (☎ 0222/512-33-61).

Police   The emergency number is **133.**

Post Office   Addresses for these can be found in the telephone directory under "Post." Post offices are generally open for mail services Mon–Fri 8am–noon and 2–6pm. The central post office, the Hauptpostamt, at Barbaragasse 2 (☎ 0222/515-09-0), and most general post offices are open daily 24 hours a day.

Taxes   Vienna imposes no special city taxes, other than the national value-added tax that's tacked on to all goods and services. The tax depends on the item, but can range up to 32% on luxury goods, 20% on car rentals.

ACCOMMODATIONS
ON OR NEAR KÄRNTNERSTRASSE
Very Expensive

○ **Hotel Bristol.** Kärntner Ring 1, A-1015 Vienna. ☎ **0222/515-160.** Fax 0222/515-16-550. 137 rms, 9 suites. A/C MINIBAR TV TEL. 4,400–5,600 AS ($418–$532) double; from 11,000 AS ($1,045) suite. AE, DC, MC, V. Parking 400 AS ($38). U-Bahn: Karlsplatz. Tram: 1 or 2.

This six-story landmark is a superb choice, with a decor evoking the full power of the Habsburg Empire. When it was constructed in 1894 next to the State Opera it was in ultimate luxury style, and it's kept updated to give its guests the benefit of black-tile baths and modern conveniences. Many of the architectural embellishments rank as *objets d'art* in their own right, including the black carved marble fireplaces and the oil paintings in the salons. Bedrooms are sumptuously appointed. The club floor offers luxurious comfort, enhanced by period furnishings in the style of the hotel's *fin de siècle* architecture. The Bristol's restaurant, the Korso, is one of the best in Vienna. The modern Rôtisserie Sirk and the elegant Café Sirk are also meeting places for gourmets.

○ **Hotel Imperial.** Kärntner Ring 16, A-1015 Vienna. ☎ **800/325-3589** in the U.S., or 0222/50-110-0. Fax 0222/501-10-440. 128 rms, 32 suites. A/C MINIBAR TV TEL. 5,100–7,500 AS ($484.50–$712.50) double; from 11,000 AS ($1,045) suite. AE, DC, MC, V. Parking 450 AS ($42.75). U-Bahn: Karlsplatz.

This hotel is Vienna's grandest, lying two blocks from the State Opera and one block from the Musikverein. The hotel was built in 1869 as the private residence of the duke of Württemberg. The Italian architect Zanotti designed the massive facade with a heroic frieze carved into the triangular pediment below the roofline. It was converted into a private hotel in 1873. Everything is outlined against a background of polished red, yellow, and black marble, crystal chandeliers, Gobelin tapestries, and fine rugs. Some of the royal suites are palatial, but all rooms are soundproof and generally spacious. Courtyard rooms are more tranquil but minus the view. The elegant restaurant, Zur Majestät, has a turn-of-the-century atmosphere, antique silver, portraits of Francis Joseph, and superb service; the cuisine offers traditional Austrian dishes done with a light touch and excellent flavor.

Hotel Sacher. Philharmonikerstrasse 4, A-1010 Vienna. ☎ **0222/514-56.** Fax 0222/51-45-78-10. 116 rms, 3 suites. A/C MINIBAR TV TEL. 3,800–4,300 AS ($361–$408.50) double; from 10,800 AS ($1,026) suite. Rates include breakfast. AE, DC, MC, V. Parking 380 AS ($36.10). U-Bahn: Karlsplatz. Bus: 4A. Tram: 1, 2, 62, 65, D, or J.

Much of the glory of the Habsburgs is still evoked by the public rooms here. The decor of red velvet, crystal chandeliers, traditional wallpaper, and brocaded curtains gives a nostalgic feeling of Old Vienna. Heavy group traffic, however, is taking a toll. Although the hotel has its diehard admirers, if you're going truly grand, the Imperial and Bristol are superior. Demi-suites and chambers with drawing rooms are more expensive. The reception desk is fairly flexible about making arrangements for salons, apartments, or joining two rooms together, if it's possible to do so.

Expensive

Hotel Astoria. Kärntnerstrasse 32–34, A-1015 Vienna. ☎ **0222/515-77-0.** Fax 0222/515-77-82. 107 rms, 1 suite. MINIBAR TV TEL. 2,400 AS ($228) double; 3,800 AS ($361) suite. Rates include breakfast. AE, DC, MC, V. U-Bahn: Stephansplatz.

The Hotel Astoria is for nostalgia buffs who want to recall the grand life of the closing days of the Austro-Hungarian Empire. A first-class hotel, the Astoria has a desirable location on the shopping mall close to St. Stephan's Cathedral and the State Opera. Decorated in a slightly frayed turn-of-the-century style, the hotel offers well-appointed and traditionally decorated bedrooms. The interior rooms tend to be too dark, and singles are just too cramped. Of course, it has been renovated over the years, but the old style has been respected, and management offers a good standard at a reasonable price.

Hotel König von Ungarn. Schulerstrasse 10, A-1010 Vienna. ☎ **0222/515-84-0.** Fax 0222/515-848. 33 rms, 1 suite. A/C MINIBAR TV TEL. 2,200 AS ($209) double; 2,600 AS ($247) suite. Rates include breakfast. AE, DC, MC, V. Parking 200 AS ($19). U-Bahn: Stephansplatz.

In a choice site on a narrow street near the cathedral, this hotel has been in the business of receiving paying guests for more than four centuries, and is Vienna's oldest continuously operated accommodation. It's an evocative, intimate, and cozy retreat in an early 17th-century building, once a *pied-à-terre* for Hungarian noble families visiting the Austrian capital. Mozart reportedly lived here in 1791. The interior is filled with interesting architectural details, and the King of Hungary restaurant is one of the city's finest. Bedrooms have low-key luxury, old tradition, and modern convenience, along with some Biedermeier decorative touches.

Moderate

Hotel am Stephansplatz. Stephansplatz 9, A-1010 Vienna. ☎ **0222/534-05-0.** Fax 0222/534-05-711. 60 rms. MINIBAR TV TEL. 2,260 AS ($214.70) double. Rates include breakfast. AE, DC, MC, V. Parking 350 AS ($33.25). U-Bahn: Stephansplatz.

You'll walk out your door and face the front entrance to Vienna's cathedral if you stay in this hotel, with its unadorned facade. The location is unbeatable, although a lot of other Viennese hotels have more charm than this one and a more helpful staff. Nevertheless, the place has many winning qualities and is not overrun with group package tours. Some bedrooms contain painted reproductions of rococo furniture and red-flocked wallpaper. Most rooms, however, are rather sterile and functional, and 10 come with showers only instead of club baths. Lack of air-conditioning could be a problem here in the evening, as guests must open their windows onto Stephansplatz, which can be noisy until late at night.

✪ **Hotel Kaiserin Elisabeth.** Weihburggasse 3, A-1010 Vienna. ☎ **0222/515-260.** Fax 0222/515-267. 620 rms, 3 suites. MINIBAR TV TEL. 1,900–2,300 AS ($180.50–$218.50) double; 2,600 AS ($247) suite. Rates include buffet breakfast. AE, DC, MC, V. Parking 350 AS ($33.25). U-Bahn: Stephansplatz.

This hotel of yellow stone is conveniently located only one block from St. Stephan's. The interior offers oriental rugs on well-maintained marble or wood floors. The soundproof rooms have been considerably updated since Richard Wagner, Franz Liszt, and Edvard Grieg each spent a night here. Modern composers are still attracted to the place. Although some parts of the building date from the 14th century, you're likely to see an up-to-date decor of polished wood, clean linen, and perhaps another oriental rug in your room.

Hotel Royal. Singerstrasse 3, A-1010 Vienna. ☎ **0222/51-568.** Fax 0222/513-96-98. 80 rms, 2 suites. MINIBAR TV TEL. 1,600–2,200 AS ($152–$209) double; 2,800 AS ($266) suite. Rates include breakfast. AE, DC, MC, V. U-Bahn: Stephansplatz.

The outside of this nine-story hotel presents a restrained dignity to the older buildings around it, lying less than a block from St. Stephan's Cathedral. The lobby contains the piano where Wagner composed *Die Meistersinger von Nürnberg*. Each room is furnished differently, with some good reproductions of antiques and an occasional original. The entire facility was built in 1960 and rebuilt in 1982. Try for a room with a balcony and a view of the cathedral. Corner rooms with spacious foyers are also desirable, although those facing the street tend to be noisy.

Inexpensive

Hotel Kärntnerhof. Grashofgasse 4, A-1010 Vienna. ☎ **0222/512-19-23.** Fax 0222/513-22-28-33. 43 rms (41 with bath), 1 suite. 900 AS ($85.50) double without bath, 1,680 AS ($159.60) double with bath; 2,250 AS ($213.75) suite. Rates include breakfast. AE, DC, MC, V. Parking 180 AS ($17.10). U-Bahn: Stephansplatz.

Only a four-minute walk from the cathedral, the Kärntnerhof advertises itself as a *gutbürgerlich* family-oriented hotel. The decor of the public rooms is tastefully arranged around oriental rugs, well-upholstered chairs and couches with cabriole legs, and an occasional 19th-century portrait. The bedrooms are more up-to-date, usually with the original parquet floors and striped or patterned wallpaper set off by curtains. The private baths glisten with tile walls and floors.

✪ **Hotel Post.** Fleischmarkt 24, A-1010 Vienna. ☎ **0222/51-58-30.** Fax 0222/515-83-808. 107 rms (77 with bath). TV TEL. 820 AS ($77.90) double without bath, 1,350 AS ($128.25) double with bath; 1,060 AS ($100.70) triple without bath, 1,660 AS ($157.70) triple with bath. Rates include buffet breakfast. AE, DC, MC, V. Tram: 1 or 2.

The Hotel Post lies in the medieval slaughterhouse district, today an interesting section full of hotels and restaurants. The dignified front is constructed of gray stone, with a facade of black marble on the street level. The manager is quick to tell you that both Mozart and Haydn frequently stayed in a former inn at this address. Those composers would probably be amused to hear recordings of their music played in the coffeehouse/restaurant, Le Café/Alte Weinstube, attached to the hotel. Bedrooms are streamlined and functionally albeit simply furnished, each well maintained.

⑤ Hotel Schneider. Getreidemarkt 5, A-1060 Vienna. ☎ **0222/588-380.** Fax 0222/ 588-38-212. 71 rms. MINIBAR TV TEL. 1,600–2,160 AS ($152–$205.20) double. Rates include buffet breakfast. AE, DC, MC, V. Parking 250 AS ($23.75). U-Bahn: Karlsplatz.

This hotel stands in the center of Vienna between the State Opera and the famous Nasch Market. It's a modern five-story building with panoramic windows on the ground floor and a red-tile roof. The interior is warmly decorated in part with 19th-century antiques and comfortably upholstered chairs. Musicians, singers, actors, and other artists form part of the loyal clientele. This is one of Vienna's better small hotels, and families are especially fond of the place because 35 of the accommodations contain kitchenettes. Some units are air-conditioned.

⑤ Hotel Wandl. Petersplatz 9, A-1010 Vienna. ☎ **0222/53-45-50.** Fax 0222/53-455-77. 138 rms (134 with bath). TV TEL. 1,450 AS ($137.75) double without bath, 1,650–1,750 AS ($156.75–$166.25) double with bath. Rates include breakfast. No credit cards. Parking 300– 400 AS ($28.50–$38). U-Bahn: Stephansplatz.

Stepping into this hotel is like stepping into a piece of a family's history—it has been under the same ownership for generations. The establishment has views of the steeple of St. Stephan's from many of its windows, which often open onto small balconies with railings. The breakfast room is a high-ceilinged two-toned room with hanging chandeliers and lots of ornamented plaster; bedrooms offer the kind of spacious dimensions that went out of style 60 years ago. Some units contain minibar and TV. The hotel faces St. Peter's Church.

DINING
ON OR NEAR KÄRNTNERSTRASSE
Very Expensive

◘ Drei Husaren. Weihburggasse 4. ☎ **0222/512-10-92.** Reservations required. Main courses 255–395 AS ($24.25–$37.55); *menu dégustation* (six courses) 880 AS ($83.60); fixed-price four-course business lunch 390 AS ($37.05). AE, DC, MC, V. Daily noon–3pm and 6–11 pm. Closed mid-July to mid-Aug. U-Bahn: Stephansplatz. VIENNESE/INTERNATIONAL.

This enduring favorite serves an inventive and classic Viennese cuisine. Just off Kärntnerstrasse, the restaurant is expensive and select, with a delectable cuisine rated as the best traditional food in Vienna. To the background music of Gypsy melodies, you'll dine on freshwater salmon with pike soufflé, breast of guinea fowl, or an array of sole dishes. The chef specializes in veal, including his deliciously flavored kalbsbrücken Metternich. The place is celebrated for its repertoire of more than 35 hors d'oeuvres.

König von Ungarn (King of Hungary). Schulerstrasse 10. ☎ **0222/512-53-19.** Reservations required. Main courses 250–350 AS ($23.75–$33.25); fixed-price menu 450 AS ($42.75) at lunch, 700 AS ($66.50) at dinner. MC. Sun–Fri noon–2:30pm and 6–10:30 pm. U-Bahn: Stephansplatz. Bus: 1A. VIENNESE/INTERNATIONAL.

This beautifully decorated restaurant is inside the famous hotel of the same name, which is housed in a 16th-century building. You dine in an atmosphere of crystal, chandeliers, antiques, marble columns, and a vaulted ceiling. The service here is superb, with an appealing menu. If you're in doubt about what to order, try the tafelspitz, a savory boiled-beef specialty elegantly dispensed from a trolley. Other menu choices, which change seasonally, include a ragoût of seafish with fresh mushrooms, or tournedos with a mustard-and-horseradish sauce. Chefs balance flavors, textures, and colors to create a long-favored cuisine.

✪ Sacher Hotel Restaurant. Philharmonikerstrasse 4. ☎ **0222/514-560.** Reservations required. Main courses 250–380 AS ($23.75–$36.10); fixed-price menu 580 AS ($55.10). AE, DC, MC, V. Daily noon–2:30pm and 6–11pm. U-Bahn: Karlsplatz. AUSTRIAN/VIENNESE/INTERNATIONAL.

Long an enduring favorite—either before or after the opera—this famous restaurant has few serious detractors. Seemingly all celebrities who come to Vienna eventually are seen in the red dining room, where they're likely to order the restaurant's most famous dish, tafelspitz, the Viennese boiled-beef platter that was fit for an emperor. The chef serves it with a savory, herb-flavored sauce. Other excellent dishes include fish terrine, veal steak with morels, and rib steak with onions. For dessert, the Sacher torte enjoys world renown. It's said to have been created in 1832 by Franz Sacher while he served as Prince Metternich's apprentice.

Moderate

Dö & Co. Akademiestrasse 3. ☎ **0222/512-64-74.** Reservations recommended for one of the tables. Main courses 155–245 AS ($14.75–$23.30). AE, DC, MC, V. Mon–Fri 10:30 am–7:30 pm, Sat 9:30 am–3pm. U-Bahn: Karlsplatz. DELI.

A sophisticated delicatessen, this place is next to the State Opera. Depending on the season, the asparagus might have been flown in from Paris or Argentina, whereas the shellfish may have come from either the North Sea or the Bosphorus. The rich display of food fills sprawling rows of glass cases laden with pâtés, seafood salads, and Viennese pastries. You can take out your purchases or sit at one of the tiny, somewhat-cramped tables near the entrance.

⑤ Rotisserie Sirk. In the Hotel Bristol, Kärntnerstrasse 53. ☎ **022/515-16-552.** Reservations recommended. Main courses 200–300 AS ($19–$28.50). AE, DC, MC, V. Restaurant, daily noon–2:30pm and 6–11:30pm. Cafe, daily 10am–midnight. Closed July. U-Bahn: Karlsplatz. VIENNESE/INTERNATIONAL.

This modern restaurant is conveniently near the State Opera. The kitchen prepares conservative but flavorful meals with flair and gusto, and the Sirk offers good value, especially when compared to the higher-priced citadels around it. On the lower street level is an art nouveau cafe, complete with rich pastries, beveled glass, and big windows. A stairwell leads up to the second floor where a traditional three-course opera supper, with a varied choice of components, is offered nightly. Specialties include "3 kleine Filets" (beef, pork, and veal) served with mushrooms, spinach, and a pepper-cream sauce; roast duck crisp from the oven with red cabbage and bread dumplings; and medallions of venison in a goose-liver sauce.

Inexpensive

Augustinerkeller. Augustinerstrasse 1. ☎ **0222/533-10-26.** Main courses 110–170 AS ($10.45–$16.15); glass of wine 28–32 AS ($2.65–$3.05). AE, DC, MC, V. Daily 11am–midnight. U-Bahn: Stephansplatz. AUSTRIAN.

The Augustinerkeller, in the basement of the part of the Hofburg complex that shelters the Albertina Collection, has served wine, beer, and food since 1857, although the vaulted ceilings and sense of timelessness evoke an establishment even older than that. It has a lively group of patrons from all walks of life, and sometimes they get boisterous, especially when the *schrammel* music goes on late into the night. It's one of the best values for wine tasting in Vienna. Aside from the wine and beer, the establishment serves simple food, including roast chicken on a spit, schnitzel, and Viennese tafelspitz (boiled beef).

✪ Buffet Trzesniewski. Dorotheergasse 1. ☎ **0222/512-32-91.** Reservations not accepted. Sandwiches 8 AS (75¢); pastries 20 AS ($1.90). No credit cards. Mon–Fri 9am–7:30pm, Sat 9am–1pm. U-Bahn: Stephansplatz. SANDWICHES.

Everyone in Vienna knows about this place, from the most hurried office worker to the city's elite hostesses. Franz Kafka lived next door and used to come in for sandwiches and beer. Its current incarnation is unlike any buffet you may have seen, with six or seven cramped tables and a rapidly moving queue of clients who jostle for space next to the glass countertops. You'll indicate to the waitress the kind of sandwich you want, and if you can't read German signs, you just point. Most people come here for the delicious finger sandwiches, which include 18 combinations of cream cheese, egg and onion, salami, mushroom, herring, green and red peppers, tomatoes, lobster, and many more.

Ⓢ Figlmüller. Wollzeile 5. ☎ **0222/512-61-77.** Reservations recommended for parties of four or more. Main courses 90–198 AS ($8.55–$18.80). No credit cards. Daily 11am–10pm. Closed Aug. U-Bahn: Stephansplatz. VIENNESE.

In the Inner City, this restaurant is one of the most famous *beisels* (a typical Viennese tavern) in Vienna. A passageway leads to a site that's about 500 years old. Inside, the relaxed ambience enhances good, simple Viennese cookery, with a Wiener schnitzel that by now is legendary. It sprawls across (and off) your plate, it's so big. You'll also find an excellent selection of Viennese sausages, along with tafelspitz (boiled beef) and about 10 fresh salads. Daily specials are written on a blackboard.

Zwölf-Apostelkeller. Sonnenfelsgasse 3. ☎ **0222/512-67-77.** Main courses 70–145 AS ($6.65–$13.80). No credit cards. Daily 4:30pm–midnight. Closed July. Bus: 1A. Tram: 1, 2, 21, D, or N. VIENNESE.

Sections of this old wine tavern's walls predate 1561. Rows of wooden tables stand under vaulted ceilings, with illumination provided partially by the streetlights set into the masonry floor. This place is popular with students, partly because of its low prices and because of its proximity to St. Stephan's. It's so deep that you feel you're entering a dungeon. In addition to beer and wine, the establishment serves hearty Austrian fare. Specialties include Hungarian goulash soup, meat dumplings, and a *schlachtplatte* (hot black pudding, liverwurst, pork, and pork sausage with a hot bacon-and-cabbage salad).

NEAR FLEISCHMARKT

Moderate

Ⓢ Griechenbeisl. Fleischmarkt 11. ☎ **0222/533-19-77** or 0222/533-19-47. Reservations required. Main courses 165–225 AS ($15.70–$21.40); fixed-price menu 270–445 AS ($25.65–$42.30). AE, DC, MC, V. Daily 11am–1am (last orders at 11:30pm). Tram: N or Z. AUSTRIAN.

Griechenbeisl was established in 1450 and is still one of the leading restaurants of Vienna. It has a labyrinthine collection of dining areas on three different floors, all with low vaulted ceilings, smoky paneling, wrought-iron chandeliers, and Styrian-vested waiters who scurry around with large trays of food. As you go in, be sure to see the so-called inner sanctum, with signatures of such former patrons as Mozart, Beethoven, and Mark Twain. The food is *gutbürgerlich*—hearty, ample, and solidly bourgeois. Menu items include deer stew, both Hungarian and Viennese goulash, sauerkraut garni, and venison steak—in other words, all those favorite recipes from grandmother's kitchen.

Inexpensive

Wein-Comptoir. Bäckerstrasse 6. ☎ **0222/51-21-760.** Reservations recommended. Main courses 125–290 AS ($11.90–$27.55). AE, DC, MC, V. Mon–Sat 5pm–2am (last orders at 1am). U-Bahn: Stephansplatz. AUSTRIAN/INTERNATIONAL.

This is one of the most charming wine-tavern restaurants in the Old Town. You can visit just to sample a wide selection of wines, mostly Austrian, on the street level, or descend into the brick-vaulted cellar, where tables are arranged for meals. Here, waiters run up and down the steep steps, serving not only wine but also standard platters of Austrian and international food. Since most dishes are cooked to order, prepare yourself for a long wait. Full meals might include breast of venison in a goose-liver sauce, tafelspitz (boiled beef), or breast of pheasant with bacon.

NEAR STADTPARK
Very Expensive

⊗ Gottfried Restaurant. Untere Viaduktgasse 45 at Marxergasse 3. ☎ **0222/713-82-56.** Reservations required. Main courses 240–330 AS ($22.80–$31.35); fixed-price menu 690 AS ($65.55). AE, DC, MC, V. Tues–Sat noon–3pm and 6pm–midnight. Bus: 25A. VIENNESE.

One of the best restaurants in Vienna, the Gottfried was established in 1985 on a commercial street near the City Air Terminal. The pure-white walls and lace-covered windows are offset with ruby-colored oriental carpets, pink napery, and unglazed terra-cotta floors. This place seems to reach for new culinary heights in Vienna, and the delicately flavored, never overseasoned dishes beautifully combine tradition with innovation. Your meal might begin with potato soup with truffles or include carpaccio, a salad of lobster with fresh asparagus, a salad of wild duck, and a Provençal fish soup so rich it could almost be considered a relish.

⊗ Steirereck. Rasumofskygasse 2. ☎ **0222/713-31-68.** Reservations required. Main courses 248–350 AS ($23.55–$33.25); three-course fixed-price lunch 395 AS ($37.55); five-course fixed-price dinner 880 AS ($83.60). AE, V. Mon–Fri 10:30am–3pm and 7pm–midnight. Closed holidays. Bus: 4. Tram: N. VIENNESE/AUSTRIAN.

Steirereck means "corner of Styria," which is exactly what Heinz and Margarethe Reitbauer have created in the rustic decor of this intimate restaurant. On the Danube Canal, between Central Station and the Prater, it has been acclaimed by some Viennese as the best in the city. The Reitbauers offer both traditional Viennese dishes and "new Austrian" selections. You might begin with a caviar-semolina dumpling, roasted turbot with fennel (served as an appetizer), or the most elegant and expensive item of all, goose-liver Steirereck. Enticing main courses are asparagus with pigeon and saddle of lamb for two diners. The menu is wisely limited and well prepared, changing daily depending on the fresh produce available at the market.

Moderate

Kardos. Dominikaner Bastei 8. ☎ **0222/512-69-49.** Reservations recommended. Main courses 100–220 AS ($9.50–$20.90). AE, MC, V. Tues–Sat 11am–2:30pm and 6–11pm. U-Bahn: Schwedenplatz. HUNGARIAN/BALKAN.

This restaurant specializes in the strong flavors and mixed grills of the Great Hungarian Plain, turning out such traditional specialties as palatschinken Hortobagy, fish soup in the style of Lake Balaton, piquant little rolls known as grammel seasoned with minced pork and spices, and a choice of grilled meats. In an atmospheric cellar, the restaurant is filled with bold colors and Hungarian accessories, with a sense of Gypsy *schmaltz*. There's sometimes a strolling violinist during the winter months.

AT SCHOTTENRING
Inexpensive

⊛ Zum Schwarzen Kameel (Stiebitz). Bognergasse 5. ☎ **0222/533-81-25.** Main courses 150–280 AS ($14.25–$26.60). No credit cards. Mon–Fri 9am–8pm, Sat 9am–3pm. U-Bahn: Schottentor. Bus: 2A or 3A. INTERNATIONAL.

This restaurant has remained in the same family since 1618. A delicatessen against one of the walls sells wine, liquor, and specialty meat items, although most of the action takes place among the chic clientele in the cafe. On a Saturday morning the cafe section is packed with weekend Viennese recovering from a late night with massive doses of caffeine. The restaurant beyond the cafe, with only 11 tables, is a perfectly preserved art deco room. Specialties include herring filet Oslo, potato soup, tournedos, Roman saltimbocca, and daily fish specials.

COFFEEHOUSES & CAFES

✪ **Café Demel.** Kohlmarkt 14. ☎ **0222/533-55-16.** Daily 10am–7pm. U-Bahn: U3. Bus: 1A or 2A.

The windows of this much-venerated establishment are filled with fanciful spun-sugar creations of characters from folk legends. Perhaps Lady Godiva's 5-foot tresses will shelter a miniature village of Viennese dancers. Inside you'll find a splendidly baroque Viennese landmark of black marble tables, cream-colored embellished plaster walls, elaborate half paneling, and crystal chandeliers covered with white milk-glass globes. Dozens of different pastries are offered every day, including cream-filled horns (*gugelhupfs*). Coffee costs 45 AS ($4.30), and those tempting cakes begin at 48 AS ($4.55).

Café Dommayer. Dommayergasse 1. ☎ **0222/877-54-65.** Mon–Sat 7am–midnight. Tram: U4 (green line) to Schönbrunn.

One of the city's most atmospheric cafes, not far from Schönbrunn Palace, this is where both Johann Strausses (father and son alike) played waltzes for members of Vienna's *grande bourgeoisie*. Established in 1787 by a local writer, the cafe contains an old-world decor of Biedermeier accessories set amid silver samovars, formally dressed waiters, and a stylish and very Viennese clientele. Coffee varies in price up to 38 AS ($3.60).

Café Leopold Hawelka. Dorotheergasse 6. ☎ **0222/512-82-30.** Mon and Wed–Sat 8am–2am, Sun 4pm–2am. Closed July 12–Aug 9. U-Bahn: Stephansplatz.

Just off the Graben, this cafe was one of the most famous rendezvous points for poets, artists, and the literati in days gone by. Nowadays it's the most frequented cafe in Vienna for young people from around the world. Coffee ranges from 7 to 37 AS (65¢ to $3.50).

ATTRACTIONS

SIGHTSEEING SUGGESTIONS

If You Have 1 Day   Begin at St. Stephan's Cathedral and from there branch out for a tour of the enveloping Inner City, or Old Town. But first climb the tower of the cathedral for a panoramic view of the city (you can also take an elevator to the top). Stroll down Kärntnerstrasse, the main shopping artery, and enjoy the 11am ritual of coffee in a grand cafe, such as the Café Imperial. In the afternoon, visit Schönbrunn, seat of the Habsburg dynasty. Have dinner in a typically Viennese wine tavern.

If You Have 2 Days   On the second day, explore other major attractions of Vienna, including the Hofburg, the Imperial Crypts, and the Kunsthistorisches Museum. In the evening, attend an opera performance or some other musical event.

If You Have 3 Days   On your third day, try to work into your schedule two important performances: the Spanish Riding School (Tuesday through Saturday) and the Vienna Boys' Choir (singing at masses on Sunday). Explore the Belvedere Palace and its art galleries; stroll through the Naschmarkt, the city's major open-air market; and cap the day by a visit to one or more of Vienna's cabarets or wine bars.

If You Have 5 Days   On day 4, take a tour of the Vienna Woods and then visit Klosterneuburg Abbey, the major abbey of Austria. Return to Vienna for an evening of fun.

On day 5, "mop up" all the attractions you missed on your first four days. These might include a visit to the Albertina Graphische Sammlungen, the most important graphic-arts collection in the world; and a walk through the Stadtpark, at Parkring.

THE TOP ATTRACTIONS

The Inner City (*Innere Stadt*) is the tangle of streets from which Vienna grew in the Middle Ages. Much of your exploration will be confined to this area, encircled by the boulevards of "The Ring" and the Danube Canal. The main street of the Inner City is Kärntnerstrasse, most of which is a pedestrian mall. The heart of Vienna is Stephansplatz, the square on which St. Stephan's Cathedral sits.

The Hofburg Palace Complex

The winter palace of the Habsburgs, known for its vast, impressive courtyards, the Hofburg sits in the heart of Vienna. To reach it (you can hardly miss it), head up Kohlmarkt to Michaelerplatz 1, Burgring (☎ 0222/587-55-54). You can also take the U-Bahn to Stephansplatz, Herrengasse, or Mariahilferstrasse, or else tram no. 1, 2, D, or J to Burgring.

This complex of imperial edifices, the first of which was constructed in 1279, grew and grew as the empire did, so that today the Hofburg Palace is virtually a city within a city. The palace, which has withstood three major sieges and a great fire, is called simply *die Burg,* or "the palace," by Viennese. Of its more than 2,600 rooms, fewer than two dozen are open to the public.

✪ **Schatzkammer (Imperial Treasury).** Hofburg, Schweizerhof. ☎ **0222/533-79-31.** Admission 60 AS ($5.70) adults; 30 AS ($2.85) children, senior citizens, and students. Wed–Mon 10am–6pm.

The Schatzkammer is the greatest treasury in the world. It's divided into two sections: the Imperial Profane and the Sacerdotal Treasuries. One part displays the crown jewels and an assortment of imperial riches, and the other, of course, contains ecclesiastical treasures. The most outstanding exhibit in the Schatzkammer is the imperial crown, which dates from 962. It's so big that, even though padded, it was likely to slip down over the ears of a Habsburg at a coronation. Studded with emeralds, sapphires, diamonds, and rubies, this 1,000-year-old symbol of sovereignty is a priceless treasure. Also on display is the imperial crown worn by the Habsburg rulers from 1804 to the end of the empire. You'll see the saber of Charlemagne and the holy lance from the 9th century. Among great Schatzkammer prizes is the Burgundian Treasure seized in the 15th century, rich in vestments, oil paintings, gems, and robes.

✪ **Kaiserappartements (Imperial Apartments).** Hofburg, Schweizerhof. ☎ **0222/ 533-7570.** German-language guided tour 70 AS ($6.65); English-language tours aren't available unless you hire a freelance tour guide loitering around the entryway, or prearrange one with the Vienna Tourist Information Office. Mon–Sat 8:30am–4:30pm, Sun 8:30am–1pm.

The Hofburg complex also includes the Kaiserappartements, where the emperors and their wives and children lived, on the first floor. To reach these apartments, you enter via the rotunda of Michaelerplatz. The apartments are richly decorated with tapestries, many from Aubusson. The Imperial Silver and Porcelain Collection descends directly from the Hapsburg household and provides an insight to their court etiquette. Most of these pieces are from the 18th and 19th centuries. Leopoldinischer Trakt, or Leopold's apartments, date from the 17th century. These Imperial Apartments seem to be more closely associated with Francis Joseph than with any other emperor, because of his long reign.

۞ Die Burgkapelle (Palace Chapel). Hofburg (entrance on Schweizerhof). **☎ 0222/ 533-99-27.**

Construction of this gothic chapel began in 1447 during the reign of Emperor Frederick III, but it was subsequently massively renovated. From 1449 it was the private chapel of the royal family. Today the Burgkapelle is the home of the Hofmusikkapelle Wein, an ensemble consisting of the Vienna Boys' Choir and members of the Vienna State Opera chorus and orchestra. For concert ticket information, see "Performing Arts," below.

Neue Burg. Heldenplatz. **☎ 0222/521-770.** Admission to Hofjagd and Rüstkammer, Musikinstrumentensammlung, and Ephesos-Museum, 30 AS ($2.85) adults, 15 AS ($1.45) children. Hofjagd and Rüstkammer and Musikinstrumentensammlung and Ephesos-Museum, Wed–Mon 10am–6pm.

The last addition to the Hofburg complex was the Neue Burg, or New Château. Construction was started in 1881 and continued until work was halted in 1913. The palace was the residence of Archduke Franz Ferdinand, the nephew and heir apparent of Francis Joseph, whose assassination at Sarajevo set off the chain of events that led to World War I. The arms and armor collection is second only to that of the Metropolitan Museum of Art in New York. It's in the Hofjagd and Rüstkammer, on the second floor of the New Château. On display are crossbows, swords, helmets, and pistols, plus armor, mostly the property of the emperors and princes of the House of Habsburg. Another section, the Musikinstrumentensammlung (**☎ 0222/521-77-470**), is devoted to musical instruments, mainly from the 17th and 18th centuries, but with some from the 16th. In the Ephesos-Museum (Museum of Ephesian Sculpture), Neue Burg 1, Heldenplatz, with an entrance behind the Prince Eugene monument (**☎ 0222/521-77-0**), you'll see the Parthian monument, the most important relief frieze from Roman times ever found in Asia Minor.

Graphische Sammlung Albertina. Augustinerstrasse 1. **☎ 0222/53-483.** Admission 45 AS ($4.30) adults, 20 AS ($1.90) students, free for children under 11. Mon–Thurs 10am–4pm, Fri 10am–2pm, Sat–Sun 10am–1pm.

The development of graphic arts since the 14th century is explored at this Hofburg museum. Housing one of the world's greatest graphics collections, the museum was named for a son-in-law of Maria Theresa. The most outstanding treasure in the Albertina is the Dürer collection, although what you'll usually see are copies—the originals are shown only on special occasions. See, in particular, Dürer's *Praying Hands*, which has been reproduced throughout the world.

Augustinerkirche. Augustinerstrasse 3. **☎ 0222/533-70-99.** Guided tour, 10 AS (95¢) contribution. To arrange a visit, contact the church office, Pfarre St. Augustin, Augustinerstrasse 3, or the music office (**☎ 0222/533-69-63**).

This church was constructed in the 14th century as part of the Hofburg complex to serve as the parish church of the imperial court. In the latter part of the 18th century it was stripped of its baroque embellishments and returned to the original gothic features. The Chapel of St. George, dating from 1337, is entered from the right aisle. The royal weddings of Maria Theresa and François of Lorraine (1736), Marie Antoinette and Louis XVI of France (1770), Marie-Louise of Austria to Napoléon (1810, but by proxy—he didn't show up), and Francis Joseph and Elizabeth of Bavaria (1854) were all held here. The most convenient—and perhaps the most dramatic—time to visit the church is on Sunday at 11am, when a high mass is celebrated, with choir, soloists, and orchestra.

✪ **Spanische Hofreitschule.** Michaelerplatz 1, Hofburg. ☎ **0222/533-90-32.** Regular performances, 240–800 AS ($22.80–$76) seats, 190 AS ($18.05) standing room. Training performances with music, 240 AS ($22.80). (Children under 3 not admitted, but children 3–6 attend free with adults.) Training session, 100 AS ($9.50) adults, 20 AS ($1.90) children. Regular performances, Mar–June and Sept to mid-Dec, Sun at 10:45am, most Weds at 7pm. Training performances with music, May and Sept, Sat at 10am. Training sessions, mid-Feb to June, end of Aug to mid-Dec, Tues–Fri 10am–noon except on public holidays.

The Spanish Riding School is in the white, crystal-chandeliered ballroom in an 18th-century building of the Hofburg complex, designed by J. E. Fischer von Erlach. We always marvel at the skill and beauty of the sleek Lippizaner stallions as their adept trainers put them through their paces in a show that hasn't changed for four centuries.

Reservations for performances must be made in advance, as early as possible. Order your tickets for the Sunday and Wednesday shows in writing to Spanische Reitschule, Hofburg, A-1010 Vienna (Fax 43/1/535-01-86), or through a travel agency in Vienna. (Tickets for Saturday shows can be ordered only through a travel agency.) Tickets for training sessions with no advance reservations can be purchased at the entrance Innerer Burghof-In der Burg.

Museums

Gemäldegalerie Akademie der Bildenden Künste (Academy of Fine Arts). Schillerplatz 3. ☎ **0222/58-816.** Admission 30 AS ($2.85) adults and children. Tues and Thurs–Fri 10am–1pm, Wed 10am–1pm and 3–6pm, Sat–Sun 9am–1pm. U-Bahn: Karlsplatz.

When in Vienna, always make at least one visit to the painting gallery in the Academy of Fine Arts to see the *Last Judgment* triptych by the incomparable Hieronymus Bosch. In this work, the artist conjured up all the demons of the nether regions for a terrifying view of the suffering and sins of humankind. There are many 15th-century Dutch and Flemish paintings and several works by Lucas Cranach the Elder. The academy is noted for its 17th-century art by van Dyck, Rembrandt, Botticelli, and a host of other artists.

✪ **Kunsthistorisches Museum (Museum of Fine Arts).** Maria-Theresien-Platz, Burgring 5. ☎ **0222/521-77-0.** Admission 95 AS ($9.05) adults, 60 AS ($5.70) students and senior citizens, free for children under 11. Tues–Sun 10am–6pm. U-Bahn: Mariahilferstrasse. Tram: 52, 58, D, or J.

Across from the Hofburg Palace, this huge building houses many of the fabulous art collections gathered by the Habsburgs when they added new territories to their empire. A highlight here is a fine collection of ancient Egyptian and Greek art. The museum also has works by many of the greatest European masters, such as Velázquez and Titian.

Churches

✪ **Dompfarre St. Stephan (St. Stephan's Cathedral).** Stephansplatz 1. ☎ **0222/ 515-52.** Cathedral, free; tour of catacombs, 40 AS ($3.80), 15 AS ($1.45) children under 14. Guided tour of cathedral, 40 AS ($3.80) adults, 15 AS ($1.45) children under 14. North Tower, 40 AS ($3.80) adults, 15 AS ($1.45) children under 15; South Tower, 25 AS ($2.40) adults, 15 AS ($1.45) students, 5 AS (45¢) children under 15. Evening tours, including tour of the roof, 130 AS ($12.35) adults, 50 AS ($4.75) children under 15. Cathedral, daily 6am–10pm except times of service. Tour of catacombs, Mon–Sat at 10, 11, and 11:30am, and 2, 2:30, 3:30, 4, and 4:30pm; Sun at 2, 2:30, 3:30, 4, and 4:30pm. North Tower, daily 9am–6pm; South Tower, daily 9am–5:30pm. Guided tour of cathedral, Mon–Sat at 10:30am and 3pm; Sun 3pm. Special evening tour Sat 7pm (May–Sept). U-Bahn: Stephansplatz.

A basilica built on the site of a romanesque sanctuary, the cathedral was founded in the 12th century in what even in the Middle Ages was the town's center. Stephansdom was virtually destroyed in a 1258 fire that swept through Vienna, and toward the dawn of the 14th century the ruins of the romanesque basilica gave way to a gothic building. The cathedral suffered terribly in the Turkish siege of 1683, but then was allowed a rest from destruction until the Russian bombardments of 1945. Reopened in 1948 after restoration, the cathedral is today one of the greatest gothic structures in Europe, rich in woodcarvings, altars, sculptures, and paintings. The steeple, rising some 450 feet, has come to symbolize the very spirit of Vienna. You can climb the 343-step south tower of St. Stephan's, which dominates the Viennese skyline and offers a view of the Vienna Woods. Called *Alter Steffl* (Old Steve), the tower with its needlelike spire was built between 1350 and 1433. The North Tower (Nordturm), reached by elevator, was never finished to match the South Tower, but was crowned in the Renaissance style in 1579. You view a panoramic sweep of the city and the Danube.

ATTRACTIONS OUTSIDE THE INNER CITY

✪ **Schönbrunn Palace.** Schönbrunner Schlossstrasse. ☎ **0222/81-113.** Admission 95 AS ($9.05) adults, 40 AS ($3.80) children 6–15, free for children under 6. Apartments, Apr–Oct, daily 8:30am–5pm; Nov–Mar, daily 9am–4:30pm. U-Bahn: U4 (green line) to Schönbrunn.

A Habsburg palace of 1,441 rooms, Schönbrunn was designed and built between 1696 and 1712 by those masters of the baroque, the von Erlachs, who were ordered to create a palace whose grandeur would surpass that of Versailles. However, Austria's treasury, drained by the cost of wars, would not support the ambitious undertaking, and the original plans were never carried out.

When Maria Theresa became empress, she changed the original plans, and the Schönbrunn we see today is her conception, with its delicate rococo touches, designed for her by Austrian Nikolaus Pacassi. It was the imperial summer palace during Maria Theresa's 40-year reign, from 1740 to 1780, the scene of great ceremonial balls and lavish banquets, and the fabulous receptions held here during the Congress of Vienna.

The State Apartments are the most stunning in the palace. Much of the interior ornamentation is in $23^1/_2$-karat gold, and many porcelain tile stoves are in evidence. Of the 40 rooms that you can visit, particularly fascinating is the "Room of Millions," decorated with Indian and Persian miniatures, the grandest rococo salon in the world.

✪ **Belvedere Palace.** Prinz-Eugen-Strasse 27. ☎ **0222/795-57.** Admission 60 AS ($5.70) adults, 30 AS ($2.85) children. Tues–Sun 10am–5pm. Tram: D to Schloss Belvedere.

Belvedere Palace was designed by Johann Lukas von Hildebrandt, who was the last major Austrian baroque architect. Built as a summer home for Prince Eugene of Savoy, the Belvedere consists of two palatial buildings, the design of which foretokens the rococo. The pond reflects the sky and palace buildings, which are made up of a series of interlocking cubes. The interior is dominated by two great, flowing staircases.

Unteres Belvedere (Lower Belvedere), with its entrance at Rennweg 6A, was constructed from 1714 to 1716, and contains the Gold Salon, one of the palace's most beautiful rooms. It also houses the Barockmuseum (Museum of Baroque Art). Oberes Belvedere (Upper Belvedere) was started in 1721 and completed in 1723. It contains the Gallery of 19th- and 20th-Century Art, with an outstanding collection of the works of Gustav Klimt (1862–1918); be sure to see his extraordinary *Judith*. The Museum of Medieval Austrian Art is in the Orangery.

ORGANIZED TOURS

Wiener Rundfahrten (Vienna Sightseeing Tours), Stelzhamergasse 4–11 (☎ 0222/
712-468-30), offers many tours, ranging from a 75-minute "Vienna—Getting
Acquainted" trip to a 1-day excursion by motorcoach to Budapest costing 1,250 AS
($118.75) per person. The get-acquainted tour costs 220 AS ($20.90) for adults
and is free for children 12 and under, and is a favorite with visitors who are pressed
for time. Tours leave the State Opera daily at 10:30 and 11:45am and at 3 and
4:30pm.

"Vienna Woods—Mayerling," another popular excursion, lasting about 4 hours,
leaves from the State Opera and takes you to the towns of Perchtoldsdorf and
Modling, passing by the Höldrichsmühle, where Franz Schubert composed many of
his beloved *lieder,* going to the Abbey of Heiligenkreuz, a center of Christian culture
since medieval times. The commemorative chapel in the village of Mayerling reminds
visitors of the tragic suicide of Crown Prince Rudolph, only son of Emperor Francis
Joseph. The tour also takes you for a short walk through Baden, the spa once a favorite summer resort of the aristocracy. Tours cost 480 AS ($45.60) for adults and
160 AS ($15.20) for children.

A "Grand City Tour," which includes visits to Schönbrunn and Belvedere Palaces,
leaves the State Opera daily at 9:30am and again at 2:30pm, lasting about 3 hours
and costing 390 AS ($37.05) for adults and 160 AS ($15.20) for children.

A variation on the city tour includes an optional visit to the Spanish Riding School,
where the world-renowned Lippizaner horses are trained and showcased. This tour
is offered Tuesday through Saturday, leaving from the State Opera building at
9:30am. In addition to driving in a bus past the monuments of Vienna, with guided
commentary, the tour includes a half-hour performance by the Lippizaners on their
home turf. Adults pay 480 AS ($45.60) and children are charged 160 AS ($15.20);
children under 12 tour for free.

Information and booking for these tours is possible either through Vienna
Sightseeing Tours (see above) or through their affiliate, Elite Tours, Operngasse 4
(☎ 0222/513-22-25).

SHOPPING

The main shopping streets are in the city center (First District). Here you'll find
Kärntnerstrasse, between the State Opera and Stock-im-Eisen-Platz; the Graben, be-
tween Stock-im-Eisen-Platz and Kohlmarkt; Kohlmarkt, between the Graben and
Michaelplatz; and Rotensturmstrasse, between Stephansplatz and Kai. There are also
Mariahilferstrasse, between Babenbergerstrasse and Schönbrunn, one of the longest
streets in Vienna; Favoritenstrasse, between Südtiroler Platz and Reumannplatz; and
Landstrasser Hauptstrasse.

The state-owned **Dorotheum,** Dorotheergasse 17 (☎ 0222/515-60-0), is the
oldest auction house in Europe, dating from 1707, when it was founded by Emperor
Joseph I as an auction house where impoverished aristocrats could fairly (and
anonymously) get good value for their heirlooms. Today the Dorotheum is also the
scene of many art auctions. If you're interested in what's being auctioned off, you
give a small fee to a *sensal,* one of the licensed bidders, and he or she will bid in your
name.

The three-floor ✪ **Ö.W. (Österreichische Werkstatten),** Kärntnerstrasse 6
(☎ 0222/512-24-18), sells hundreds of handmade art objects from Austria. Leading artists and craftspeople throughout the country organized this cooperative to
showcase their wares. The location is easy to find, lying only half a minute's walk
from St. Stephan's Cathedral.

✪ **Albin Denk,** Graben 13 (☎ **0222/512-44-39**), is the oldest continuously operating porcelain store in Vienna, in business since 1702. You'll see thousands of objects from Meissen, Dresden, and other regions.

Established in 1830 by the Plankl family, ✪ **Loden Plankl,** Michaelerplatz 6 (☎ **0222/533-80-32**), is the oldest and most reputable outlet in Vienna for traditional Austrian clothing. You'll find Austrian loden coats, shoes, trousers, dirndls, jackets, lederhosen, and suits for men, women, and children. The building, located opposite the Hofburg, dates from the 17th century.

VIENNA AFTER DARK

The best source of information about what's happening on the cultural scene is *Wien Monatsprogramm,* distributed free at tourist information offices and at many hotel reception desks. *Die Presse,* the Viennese daily, publishes a special magazine in its Thursday edition outlining the major cultural events for the coming week. It's in German but might still be helpful.

THE PERFORMING ARTS

TICKETS TO THE AUSTRIAN STATE THEATERS   Tickets and information for the four state theaters—the Staatsoper and the Burgtheater (see below), the Volksoper, and the Akademietheater—can be obtained by calling a central office, ☎ **0222/51444-29-59,** Mon–Fri 8am–5pm. The major season is from September to June. For all four theaters, box-office sales are made only 1 month before each performance at the **Bundestheaterkasse,** Goethegasse 1 (☎ **0222/51-44-40**), open Mon–Fri 8am–6pm, Sat 9am–2pm, and Sun and holidays 9am–noon. Credit- and charge-card sales can be arranged by telephone within 6 days of a performance by calling **0222/513-15-13** on Mon–Fri 10am–6pm, Sat–Sun 10am–noon. Tickets for all state theater performances, including the opera, may also be obtained by writing to the Österreichischer Bundestheaterverband, Goethegasse 1, A-1010 Vienna; orders must be received at least 3 weeks in advance of the performance to be booked.

Opera & Classical Music

Music is at the heart of the cultural life in Vienna. This has been true for a couple of centuries or so, and the city continues to lure composers, musicians, and music-lovers. Vienna's opera is still the world's quintessential opera house, one of the three most important in the world. Besides the world-renowned Vienna Philharmonic, Vienna is home to three other major orchestras: the Vienna Symphony, the ÖRF Symphony Orchestra, and the Niederösterreichische Tonkünstler. The Wiener Sympohniker (Vienna Symphony) performs in the **Konzerthaus,** Lothringerstrasse 20 (☎ **0222/712-1211**), a major concert hall with three auditoriums, also the venue for chamber music and a diversity of programs.

In summer when the state theaters are closed, the Vienna Opera Festival presents performances and movie screenings of highlights from past opera seasons. The venue is the plaza in front of City Hall, and everything is free.

Staatsoper (Vienna Opera). Opernring 2. ☎ **0222/5144-29-60.** Tickets 120–2,300 AS ($11.40–$218.50). Tours two to five times daily, 40AS ($3.80) per person; tour times are posted on a board outside the entrance. U-Bahn: Karlsplatz.

When the opera was bombed into a shell in World War II, the Viennese made its restoration their top priority, despite other pressing needs, finishing it in time for the country's celebration of independence from occupying forces in 1955. With the Vienna Philharmonic in the pit and leading stars of the world on the stage, a repertoire of some 40 works is given every season. In their day, Gustav Mahler and

Richard Strauss worked here as directors. The new year usually starts off with a gala performance of *Die Fledermaus.*

Wiener Philharmoniker (Vienna Philharmonic). Boserndorferstrasse 12, Vienna 1. ☎ **0222/505-8681-32.**

The home of the prestigious Philharmonic is the **Musikverein,** when it is not traveling throughout the world. Built between 1867 and 1869, the concert hall is suitably ornate, and is the site of the famous New Year's Day concert, broadcast internationally.

✪ **Vienna Boys' Choir.** Die Burgkapelle, Hofburg (entrance on Schweizerhof). ☎ **0222/533-99-27.** Tickets, 60–280 AS ($5.70–$26.60). Masses (performances) held only Jan–June and mid-Sept until the end of Dec, Sun and holidays at 9:15am.

The famous Vienna Boys' Choir, along with singers from the opera, performs here in the palace chapel of the Hofburg (see above). Written applications for reserved seats should be sent at least 8 weeks in advance of the time you wish to attend, but send no checks or money. For reservations, write to Verwaltung der Hofmusikkapelle, Hofburg, A-1010 Vienna. If you failed to reserve in advance, you may be lucky enough to secure tickets from a block sold at the Burgkapelle box office every Friday from 3 to 5pm, but the queue starts lining up at least half an hour before that. Or you might settle for standing room (it's free).

Theater

A theater giving performances in English is Vienna's **English Theatre,** at Josefsgasse 12 (☎ **0222/402-12-60** or 0222/402-82-84).

Burgtheater (National Theater). Dr.-Karl-Lueger-Ring 2. ☎ **0222/51444-26-56.** Tickets 50–500 AS ($4.75–$47.50). Tram: 1, 2, or D.

The Burgtheater produces classical and modern plays, and even if you don't understand German, you might want to attend a performance here, especially if a familiar Shakespeare play is being given. This is one of Europe's premier repertory theaters; it is the dream of every German-speaking actor to appear here.

NIGHTCLUBS, CABARETS, BARS & CASINOS

Eden Bar. Liliengasse 2. ☎ **0222/512-74-50.** U-Bahn: Stephansplatz.

Local society figures in evening dress are often drawn to this chic rendezvous spot in Vienna. The setting is one of 19th-century grandeur. Tables and private boxes surround the dance floor, or you can find a seat at the half-moon–shaped bar. It's open nightly 10pm–4am, but if you show up much before midnight you may have the place to yourself. Drinks begin at 210 AS ($19.95).

Papa's Tapas. Schwarzenbergplatz 10. ☎ **0222/505-03-11.** Cover 50–150 AS ($4.75–$14.25), depending on the event. U-Bahn: Karlsplatz.

This place attracts rock 'n' roll fans. In a corner is the Wurlitzer Bar, with its American-made jukebox. You get all vintage '50s stuff, including Elvis. When there's no live music, the place operates as a bar, with a large beer costing 42 AS ($4). Open Mon–Thurs 8pm–2am, Fri–Sat 8pm–3:30am.

P1 Discothek. Rotgasse 9. ☎ **0222/535-99-95.** Cover 50 AS ($4.75). U-Bahn: Stephansplatz.

The leading disco of Vienna (subject to change, of course), this lively place is filled with Viennese and visitors, most in their mid-20s. In what used to be a film studio, the dance club has a spacious floor that accommodates as many as 2,000 dancers. The club was launched on the road to fame when Tina Turner made an appearance here back in 1988. Two deejays alternate nightly. Once or twice per month live music is presented. Open Sun–Thurs 9pm–4am, Fri–Sat 9pm–6am. Beer costs 45 AS ($4.30) and up.

Queen Anne. Johannesgasse 12. ☎ **0222/512-02-03.** No cover. U-Bahn: Stadtpark.

Lots of interesting people are attracted to this nightclub, the leading one in town. Patrons have included David Bowie, German playboy Gunther Sachs, the princess of Auersperg, and the '70s heavy-metal band Deep Purple. The club has a big collection of the latest Stateside and Italian records, as well as occasional musical acts ranging from Mick Jagger lookalikes to imitations of Watusi dancers. Open daily 10pm–6am. A scotch and soda goes for 95 AS ($9.05).

Esterházykeller. Haarhof 1. ☎ **0222/533-34-82.** U-Bahn: Stephansplatz.

The ancient bricks and scarred wooden tables of this famous drinking spot are permeated with the aroma of endless pints of spilled beer. An outing here isn't recommended for everyone, although to its credit no one ever feels sloppily dressed at the Esterházykeller. A promenade through this establishment's endless recesses and labyrinthine passages could provide views of the faces you may have thought appeared only in movies. Wine, a specialty, starts at 28 AS ($2.65) a glass. Open Mon–Fri 10am–10pm, Sat–Sun 4–10pm.

St. Urbani-Keller. Am Hof 12. ☎ **0222/533-91-02.** U-Bahn: Stephansplatz or Fahnenpasse.

Named after the patron saint of wine making, this cellar is one of the most historic in Vienna. Many of the artifacts inside, from the paneling in the German Romantic style to the fanciful wrought-iron lighting fixtures, were designed by one of Austria's most famous architects, Walcher von Molthein. The cellar has brick vaulting dating from the 13th century and sections of solid Roman walls you can admire while listening to the folk music at night. Open daily 6pm–1am, with hot food served until midnight. Beer begins at 39 AS ($3.70). Watch your step on the way up or down.

Casino Wien. Esterházy Palace, Kärntnerstrasse 41. ☎ **0222/512-48-36.** No cover.

For games of chance, this casino, opened in 1968, is the place to go. You can charge up to 4,000 AS ($380) on your Diners Club, MasterCard, or Visa credit card. You'll need to show your passport to get in. There are gaming tables for French and American roulette, blackjack, and chemin de fer, as well as the ever-present slot machines. Open daily 11am–3am with the tables opening at 3pm.

Gay Bars

Alfi's Goldener Spiegel, Linke Wienzeile 46 (entrance on Stiegengasse; ☎ **0222/ 56-66-08**), is one of the most popular gay havens in Vienna, attracting a lot of foreigners. Attached to the bar is a restaurant serving food at moderate prices and specializing in Wiener schnitzel. Open Wed–Mon 7pm–2am. Beer costs 38 AS ($3.60) and up.

The Alte Lampe, Heumühlgasse 13 (☎ **0222/567-34-54**), is the oldest gay bar in Vienna, established in the 1960s. Today's patrons listen to the same schmaltzy piano music that has been played here for years. Open daily 9pm–4am. A large beer costs 35 AS ($3.35).

THE HEURIGEN

These wine taverns lie on the outskirts of Vienna. Celebrated in operettas, films, and song, these gardens of vintners lie principally in Grinzing (the most popular district) or in Sievering, Neustift, Nussdorf, or Heiligenstadt.

The most-visited section, Grinzing, lies at the edge of the Vienna Woods, a 15-minute drive northwest of the center. Take tram no. 38 to Grinzing.

One of Vienna's well-known wine taverns, **Alter Klosterkeller im Passauerhof,** Cobenzigasse 9, Grinzing (☎ **0222/320-63-45**), maintains an old-fashioned ambience little changed since the turn of the century. Some of its foundations date from the 12th century. Menu specialties include such familiar fare as tafelspitz (boiled beef), roasts, and plenty of strudel. You can order a glass or bottle of wine, perhaps a meal, costing 150 AS ($14.25) and up. Drinks begin at 30 AS ($2.85). Music is played 7–11:30pm. Open March–Dec daily 4pm–midnight.

Altes Presshaus, Cobenzlgasse 15 (☎ **0222/32-23-93**), is the oldest heurige in Grinzing, with an authentic cellar you might ask to see. The interior is filled with wood paneling and antique furniture, giving the place character. The garden terrace blossoms throughout the summer. Meals cost 150 to 280 AS ($14.25 to $26.60); drinks begin at 30 AS ($2.85). Open March–Dec daily 4pm–midnight.

DAY TRIPS ALONG THE DANUBE

KLOSTERNEUBURG On the northwestern outskirts of Vienna, this old market town is the site of **Klosterneuburg Abbey (Stift Klosterneuburg),** Stiftsplatz 1 (☎ **02243/411-212**), the most historically significant abbey in Austria. It's visited not only for its history but for its art treasures, including the world-famous enamel altar of Nikolaus of Verdun, a work dating back to 1181. The monastery also boasts the largest private library in Austria, with more than 1,250 handwritten books and many antique paintings.

The Museum of the Monastery can be visited May 1–Nov 15 on Fri 2–5pm and Sat–Sun 10am–5pm. Guided tours of the monastery are possible Apr–Oct Mon–Sat every hour from 9–11am and 1:30–4:30pm; Nov–March Mon–Sat at 10 and 11am, and then every hour from 1:30–4:30pm; throughout the year, Sun and holidays at 11am and on the half hour between 1:30 and 4:30pm. For the tour and the museum, adults pay 50 AS ($4.75); students, children, and senior citizens 40 AS ($3.80).

Motorists can take Route 14 northwest of Vienna, following the south bank of the Danube. Otherwise, take the U-Bahn from the Westbahnhof heading for Heiligenstadt, where you can then board bus 239 or 341 to Klosterneuburg.

HERZOGENBURG MONASTERY Funded in the early 12th century by a German bishop from Passau, this Augustinian monastery, A-3130 Herzogenburg (☎ **02782/3315** or 3112), lies 7 miles south of Traismauer and 10 miles south of the Danube. From Vienna, head west of the city via the A-21 autobahn, following the signs to Salzburg and Linz, exiting at the signposted turnoff for Heiligenkreuz.

The present complex of buildings comprising the church and the abbey was reconstructed in the baroque style. That master of baroque, Fischer von Erlach, designed some of the complex. Outstanding is the high altar, painted by Daniel Gran, and the series of 16th-century paintings on wood. The monastery is known for its library containing more than 80,000 works.

Hour-long guided tours take visitors through the monastery daily April 1–Oct 11am and 1–5pm for an admission of 40 AS ($3.80).

KREMS In the eastern part of the Wachau on the left bank of the Danube lies Krems, a city some 1,000 years old. The city today encompasses Stein and Mautern, once separate towns. Krems is a mellow town of courtyards, old churches, and ancient houses in the heart of vineyard country, with some partially preserved town walls. Just as the Viennese flock to Grinzing and other suburbs to sample new wine

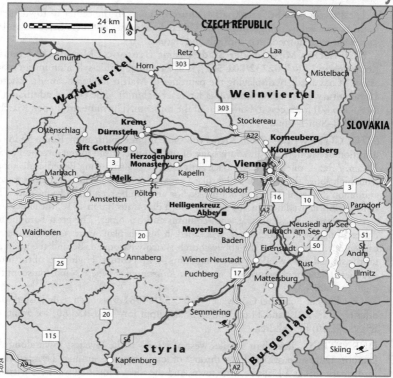

in *heurigen,* so the people of the Wachau come here to taste the vintners' products, which appear in Krems earlier in the year.

It's located 50 miles west of Vienna and 18 miles north of St. Pölten. From Vienna, drive north along the A-22 autobahn until it splits into three roads near the town of Stockerau. Once here, drive due west along Route 3, following the signs into Krems.

Trains depart from both the Wien Nord Station and from the Wien Franz-Josefs Bahnhof for Krems at intervals of 1 hour or less, beginning daily around 5am and continuing until around 8:30pm. Many are direct, although some will require a transfer in the railway junctions of Absdorf-Hippersdorf or St. Pölten. The trip takes 1 to 1¹/₂ hours. Call **0222/17-17** for schedules.

During the warm-weather months, between mid-May and late September, river cruisers owned by the DDSG-Donaureisen Shipping Line depart westward from Vienna on Saturday and Sunday at 9am en route to Passau, in Germany. They arrive upstream in Tulln around 11:45am, then continue westward to Krems, arriving there around 2:10pm. For more information, call the shipping line in Vienna (☎ **0222/727-50,** ext. 451) or the tourist office in either Tulln or Krems.

The most interesting part of Krems today is what was once the little village of Stein. Narrow streets are terraced above the river, and the single main street, Steinlanderstrasse, is flanked with houses, many from the 16th century. The **Grosser Passauerhof,** Steinlanderstrasse 76, is a gothic structure decorated with an oriel. Another house, at Steinlanderstrasse 84, which combines Byzantine and Venetian elements among other architectural influences, was once the imperial toll house.

The **Pfarrikirche St. Viet (parish church)** stands in the center of town at the Rathaus, reached by going along either Untere Landstrasse or Obere Landstrasse. It's somewhat overadorned, rich with gilt and statuary.

Historisches Museum der Stadt Krems (Historical Museum of Krems), Körnermarkt 14 (☎ **02732/801-567**), is in a restored gothic-syle Dominican monastery. It has a gallery displaying the paintings of Martin Johann Schmidt, a noted 18th-century artist better known as Kremser Schmidt. The cost of admission is 40 AS ($3.80) for access to both areas of the museum. The museum is open March–Nov Wed–Sun 1–6pm.

STIFT GÖTTWEIG From Krems you can continue south along Route 33 in the direction of Mautern on the south bank of the Danube. Head in the direction of St. Pölten. After 4 miles you'll approach Stift Göttweig, a sprawling Benedictine abbey lying high above the Danube Valley, like a gateway to the Wachau. The corner towers and onion domes of the abbey dot the skyline and can be seen for miles around. The Benedictines arrived here in 1083. Following a disastrous fire in 1718, the abbey was reconstructed in classical style, with columns and balconies. The great baroque architect, Lukas von Hildebrandt, was called in but his plans were never completely carried out. Nevertheless, the abbey church is richly baroqued. Behind the main altar the stained-glass windows are from the mid-15th century. Highlights of the tours conducted here are the emperor's rooms, or *Kaiserzimmer,* where Napoléon spent the night in 1809.

The abbey at Furth bei Göttweig (☎ **02732/85581-0**) is open daily Easter–Oct, offering tours at 10 and 11am, and 2, 3, and 4pm for 40 AS ($3.80) for adults or 25 AS ($2.40) for children.

DÜRNSTEIN Less than 5 miles west of Krems is the loveliest town along the Danube, Dürnstein, which draws throngs of tour groups in summer. Terraced vineyards mark this as a Danube wine town, and the town's fortified walls are partially preserved. The location is 50 miles west of Vienna. To reach it, motorists can take Route 3 west.

Train travel to Dürnstein from Vienna requires a transfer in Krems (see above). In Krems, trains depart approximately every 2 hours on routes that parallel the northern bank of the Danube on their way to Linz. These departures connect with trains from Vienna. They arrive in Dürnstein after only 4 miles and two stops. Call **0222/ 17-17** in Vienna for information.

About eight buses a day travel between Krems and Dürnstein, some of which coordinate with the arrival time of one of the many daily trains from Vienna. The bus trip between Krems and Dürnstein takes 20 minutes.

The **ruins of a castle fortress,** 520 feet above the town, are a link with the Crusades. Here Richard the Lion-Hearted of England was held prisoner in 1193. You can visit the ruins if you don't mind a vigorous climb (allow an hour). The castle isn't much, but the view of Dürnstein and the Wachau is more than worth the effort.

The 15th-century **pfarrkirche (parish church)** also merits a visit. The building was originally an Augustinian monastery, reconstructed in the baroque style; the church tower is the finest baroque example in the whole country.

MELK Finally, you arrive at one of the chief sightseeing goals of every pilgrim to Austria, or in the words of Empress Maria Theresa, "If I had never come here, I would have regretted it." Some 55 miles west of Vienna, reached along Autobahn A-1, on the right bank of the Danube, Melk marks the western terminus of the Wachau. It lies upstream from Krems.

One of the finest baroque buildings in the world, **Melk Abbey,** Dietmayerstrasse 1 (☎ **02752/2312**), and the stiftskirche (the abbey church) are the major attractions.

The rock-strewn bluff where the abbey now stands overlooking the river was the seat of the Babenbergs, who ruled Austria from 976 until the Habsburgs took over. A center of learning and culture, its influence spread all over Austria, a fact that is familiar to readers of the *The Name of the Rose* by Umberto Eco. Most of the design of the present abbey was by the baroque architect Jakob Prandtauer. Its marble hall, called the Marmorsaal, contains pilasters coated in red marble. Despite all this adornment, the abbey takes second place in lavish glory to the **Stiftskirche,** the golden abbey church, damaged by fire in 1947 but now almost completely restored.

Throughout the year, the abbey is open daily, with tours leaving at 15–20-minute intervals from 9am–5pm. Guides make efforts to translate into English a running commentary that is otherwise German. Adults pay 70 AS ($6.65) for guided tours and 55 AS ($5.25) for unguided tours; children 45 AS ($4.30) and 30 AS ($2.85).

2 Salzburg & Environs

A baroque city on the banks of the Salzach River, set against a mountain backdrop, Salzburg is the beautiful capital of the province of Land Salzburg. The city and the river were so named because many of the early residents earned their living in the salt mines in the region. In this "heart of the heart of Europe," Mozart was born in 1756. The composer's association with the city beefs up tourism, providing major revenue to the area.

The Old Town lies on the left bank of the river, where a monastery and bishopric were founded in 700. From that start, Salzburg grew in power and prestige, becoming an archbishopric in 798. In the heyday of the prince-archbishops, the city became known as the "German Rome." Responsible for much of its architectural grandeur are those masters of the baroque, Fischer von Erlach and Lukas von Hildebrandt.

"The City of Mozart," "Silent Night," and *The Sound of Music*—Salzburg lives essentially off its rich past. Site of the world's snobbiest summer musical festival, it is a front-ranking cultural mecca for classical music all year round. Its natural setting among alpine peaks and on both banks of the Salzach River gives it the backdrop needed to perpetuate its romantic image. Although Salzburg may have neglected the boy wonder of Europe in his time, it has paid Mozart tribute ever since the Salzburg Festival was begun in 1925 to honor its native son.

One of Europe's greatest tourist capitals, most of Salzburg's day-to-day life spins around promoting its music and its other connections. Although *The Sound of Music* was filmed way back in 1964, this Julie Andrews blockbuster has become a cult attraction and is definitely alive and well in Salzburg today, with the many Salzburgers busy making a buck off its images of Maria von Trapp and the von Trapp brood trilling "Do-Re-Mi." Ironically, Austria was the only country in the world where the musical failed when it first opened. It played for only a single week in Vienna, closing after audiences dwindled.

ONLY IN SALZBURG

Mozart's Music Everywhere It is said that somewhere at any time of the day or night in Salzburg somebody is playing the music of Johannes Chrysostomus Theophilus Wolfgang Amadeus Mozart. It might be at a festival, an open-air concert, or more romantically, an orchestra in a belle époque. Regardless, the sound of music drifting through the air of Salzburg is likely to have been created by this child prodigy during his short 35-year lifespan. Mozart during most of his life had little means of support, and regrettably he isn't around today to grow rich on the royalties—those on his 1787 Don Giovanni alone would doubtless be enough to sustain him in grand luxe style. In spite of the success of The Magic Flute late in 1791, his career ended in obscurity. Try to arrange to hear Mozart on his home turf where he knew such acclaim and so much pain. He's the biggest "rock star" of the 18th century. Where to go to hear this musical genius? A better question might be where not to go.

Cafe Sitting   A time-honored tradition in this city of art and culture. Find a cafe table on Mozartplatz and, while nibbling on your strudel, enjoy the strains of a string orchestra. The coffeehouse is an institution in Salzburg; you can sit for hour after hour over a single cup of coffee, read magazines or newspapers supplied by the cafe, or even write your memoirs. Of course, you can order coffee, too, in at least 20 or 30 different versions, everything from jet black to *weissen ohne* (with milk). Even the drinking water served with your coffee—you get two glasses side by side for some reason—is the best in Europe: It comes ice cold from the Alps.

Shopping Getreidegasse   This is the main shopping street of Salzburg, one of the liveliest in Europe. With its towering, five- and six-story Altstadt houses, it's more like a movie set. But that merchandise in the jam-packed stores is real, albeit expensive. At any time of the day or night, people can be seen parading along this merchandise-stuffed street, taking in the new window displays of fabulous things from all corners of the globe. The scene lasts well into the night.

Wandering Through Mirabell Gardens   You can live out a baroque fantasy by wandering through Fischer von Erlach's gardens on the right bank, with their classical statuary and reflecting pools. It makes you wish you'd lived in a more elegant era. These are the gardens where Julie Andrews and her seven charges *do-re-mi*-ed in *The Sound of Music*. The most enthralling section is the Dwarf's Garden, with its 12 statues of the little Danubian dwarfs. The gardens were built by the fabled archbishop, Wolf Dietrich, in 1606 as a setting for the sumptuous Mirabell Palace that he had constructed for his mistress Salome Alt and their brood of 10.

Attending a Performance of *Everyman*   This annual event, staged at the time of the Salzburg Festival near the cathedral at Domplatz, is an adaptation of Hoffmannsthal's morality play. It's been holding audiences spellbound for decades.

Touring the Hohensalzburg Fortress   For your sightseeing highlight, visit this fortress, the largest medieval fortress in central Europe, dating from 1077. The fortress towers 400 feet above the Salzach River on a rocky dolomite ledge. Once residence of the powerful archbishop rulers of Salzburg, it was also a siege-proof haven against invaders. A sinister part is the torture chamber, which once echoed with screams of unfortunate wretches. Some 100 tiny steps carry you to a lookout post for a panoramic view of Salzburg and the distant Alps.

ORIENTATION

ARRIVING   By Plane   The **Salzburg Airport,** Innsbrucker Bundesstrasse 95 (☎ **0662/8580**), lies 4 miles southwest of the city center. It has regularly scheduled air service to all Austrian airports, as well as to Frankfurt, Amsterdam, Berlin, Dresden, Düsseldorf, Hamburg, Paris, and Zurich. Major airlines serving the Salzburg Airport are Austrian Airlines (☎ **0662/85-45-11**), Lauda Air (☎ **0662/85-63-64**), Air France (☎ **0662/17-89**), and Tyrolean (☎ **0662/85-45-33**).

Salzburg

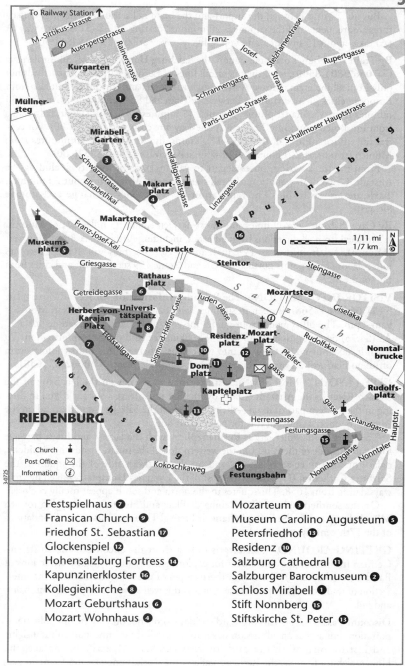

Festspielhaus **7**
Fransican Church **9**
Friedhof St. Sebastian **17**
Glockenspiel **12**
Hohensalzburg Fortress **14**
Kapunzinerkloster **16**
Kollegienkirche **8**
Mozart Geburtshaus **6**
Mozart Wohnhaus **4**

Mozarteum **3**
Museum Carolino Augusteum **5**
Petersfriedhof **13**
Residenz **10**
Salzburg Cathedral **11**
Salzburger Barockmuseum **2**
Schloss Mirabell **1**
Stift Nonnberg **15**
Stiftskirche St. Peter **13**

Bus no. 77 runs between the airport and the main rail station of Salzburg. Departures are frequent, and the trip takes 20 minutes, costing 19 AS ($1.80) one way. A taxi takes about 15 minutes, and you're likely to pay at least 125 AS ($11.90).

By Train   Salzburg's main rail station, the **Salzburg Hauptbahnhof,** Südtirolerplatz (☎ **0662/804-8500**), is on the major rail lines of Europe, with frequent arrivals not only from all the main cities of Austria, such as Vienna and Innsbruck, but also from European cities such as Munich. Between 5:05am and 8:05pm, trains arrive every 30 minutes from Vienna (trip time: 3 hours, 30 minutes). There are eight daily trains from Innsbruck (trip time: 2 hours). A one-way fare costs 336 AS ($31.90). For central rail information, call **0662/17-17.** Trains also arrive every 30 minutes from Munich (trip time: 2¹/₂ hours), a one-way ticket costing 280 AS ($26.60).

From the train station, buses depart to various parts of the city, including the Altstadt. Or you can walk from the rail station to the Altstadt in about 20 minutes. Taxis are also available. The rail station has a currency exchange and storage lockers.

By Car   Salzburg is 209 miles southwest of Vienna and 95 miles east of Munich. It's reached from all directions by good roads, including Autobahn A-8 from the west (Munich), A-1 from the east (Vienna), and A-10 from the south. Route 20 comes into Salzburg from points north and west, and Route 159 serves towns and cities from the southeast.

VISITOR INFORMATION   The **Salzburg Information Office,** at Mozartplatz 5 (☎ **0662/847568**), is open in summer daily 8am–8pm and off-season Mon–Sat 9am–6pm. The office books tour guides for you, makes hotel reservations for a 50 AS ($4.75) deposit plus a 30 AS ($2.85) booking fee, and provides information. To reach it, take bus no. 5, 6, or 51 into the center. There's also a tourist information office on Platform 2A of the Hauptbahnhof, Südtirolerplatz (☎ **0662/873638**).

CITY LAYOUT   Most of what visitors come to see lies on the left bank of the Salzach River in the **Altstadt** (Old Town). You must leave your car if you're driving in the modern part of town—the right bank of the Salzach—and descend on the Altstadt by foot, as most of it is for pedestrians only.

The heart of the inner city is **Residenzplatz,** with the largest and finest baroque fountain this side of the Alps. On the western side of the square stands the **Residenz,** palace of the prince-archbishops, and on the southern side of the square is the **Salzburg Cathedral (Dom).** To the west of the Dom lies **Domplatz,** linked by archways dating from 1658. The squares to the north and south appear totally enclosed.

On the southern side of Max-Reinhardt-Platz and Hofstallgasse, edging toward **Mönchsberg,** stands the **Festspielhaus** or Festival Theater, built on the foundations of the 17th-century court stables.

GETTING AROUND   Salzburg is only a short distance from the Austrian–German frontier, so it's convenient for exploring many of the nearby attractions of Bavaria (see chapter 7). On the northern slopes of the Alps, the city is at the intersection of traditional European trade routes and is well served today by air, autobahn, and rail.

Discount Passes   The Salzburg Card entitles visitors not only to use of public transportation, but acts as an admission ticket to the city's most important cultural sights and institutions. With the card, tourists can visit Mozart's birthplace, the Hohensalzburg fortress, the Residenz gallery, the world-famous water fountain gardens at Hellbrunn, the Baroque Museum in the Mirabell garden, and the gala rooms in the Archbishop's Residence. The card can also be used to take in sights outside of town: Hellbrunn Zoo, the open-air museum in Grossingmain, an excursion to the salt mines of the Dürnberg, or a trip in the gondola at Untersberg are but a few examples of the card's usefulness. With the card, approximately the size of a credit card, you'll receive a brochure with maps and sightseeing hints. The cards are valid for 24, 48, and 72 hours and cost 180 AS ($17.10), 260 AS ($24.70), and 350 AS ($33.25) respectively. Children up to 15 years of age receive a 50% discount. The pass can be purchased from Salzburg travel agencies, hotels, tobacconists, and municipal offices.

By Bus/Tram A quick, comfortable service is provided by city buses and trams through the center of the city from the Nonntal parking lot to Sigmundsplatz, the city-center car park. Fares are 19 AS ($1.80) for one ride for an adult, 10 AS (95¢) for children 6 to 15; those 5 and under travel free. *Be warned:* Buses stop running at 11pm.

By Taxi You'll find taxi ranks scattered at key points all over the city center and in the suburbs. The Salzburg Funktaxi-Vereinigung (radio taxis) office is at Rainerstrasse 2 (☎ **0662/8111**). To order a taxi in advance, call that number. Taxi fares start at 30 AS ($2.85).

By Car Driving a car in Salzburg is definitely not recommended. However, you'll need a car for touring around Land Salzburg, unless you have the endless time needed to rely on public transportation. Arrangements for car rentals are always best if made in advance. If not, then try **Avis** (☎ **0662/877278**) or **Hertz** (☎ **0662/876674**), both located at Ferdinand-Porsche-Strasse 7. Both offices do business Mon–Fri 8am–6pm and Sat 8am–1pm. The daily rate (subject to change) is about 1,300 AS ($123.50) including tax, unlimited mileage, and insurance.

By Horse-Drawn Cab There are horse-drawn cabs (*fiakers*) at Residenzplatz. Four people usually pay 350 AS ($33.25) for 20 minutes, 680 AS ($64.60) for 50 minutes. But all fares are subject to negotiation, of course.

By Bicycle City officials have developed a network of bicycle paths, which are indicated on city maps. Between April and November, bicycles can be rented at the **Hauptbahnhof,** Desk 3 (☎ **0662/8887-5427**), on Südtirolerplatz. The cost is about 100 AS ($9.50) per day, unless you have a rail ticket; then the price is cut in half.

FAST FACTS: Salzburg

American Express The office is located at Mozartplatz 5 (☎ 0662/84-25-01), open Mon–Fri 9am–5:30pm and Sat 9am–noon.

Baby-sitters English-speaking students at the University of Salzburg often baby-sit; call 0662/8044-6001. Make arrangements as far in advance as possible.

Business Hours Most shops and stores are open Mon–Fri 9am–6pm and Sat, usually 9am–noon. Some of the smaller shops shut down at noon for a lunch break. Salzburg observes *langer Samstag,* which means that most stores stay open until 5pm on the first Saturday of every month.

Currency See "Fast Facts: Vienna" in section 1.

Currency Exchange Banks are open Mon–Fri 8am–noon and 2–4:30pm. Money can be exchanged at the Hauptbahnhof on Südtirolerplatz daily, 7am–10pm, and at the airport daily, 9am–4pm.

Dentists For an English-speaking dentist, call Dentistenkammer, Faberstrasse 2 (☎ 0662/87-34-66).

Doctors   Call Ärztekammer für Salzburg (☎ 0662/87-13-27). The Medical Emergency Center, Paris-London-Strasse 8A (☎ 141), is on duty from 7pm on Fri to 7am on Mon; it's also open on public holidays. See also **Hospitals** below.

Drugstores (Apotheke)   These are open Mon–Fri 8am–12:30pm and 2:30–6pm, and Sat 8am–noon. For night or Sunday service, shops display a sign giving the address of the nearest open pharmacy. You can also go to Elisabeth-Apotheke, Elisabethstrasse 1 (☎ 0662/87-14-84).

Embassies/Consulates   The Consular Agency of the **United States** is at Herbert-von-Karajan-Platz 1 (☎ 0662/84-87-76). The office is open Mon, Wed, and Fri 9am–noon to assist U.S. citizens with emergencies. The Consulate of **Great Britain** is at Alter Markt 4 (☎ 0662/84-81-33) and is open Mon–Fri 9am–noon.

Emergencies   Police (☎ 133), fire (☎ 122), and ambulance (☎ 144).

Eyeglasses   The best place to go is Preee Optik, Griesgasse 2 (☎ 0662/84-59-66), open Mon–Fri 9am–6pm and Sat 9am–12:30pm.

Hospitals   Accident Hospital is on Dr.-Franz-Rehrl-Platz (☎ 0662/65-80-0), and Krankenhaus und Konvent der Barmherzigen Brüder is at Kajetanerplatz 1 (☎ 0662/80-88-0).

Lost Property   Fundamt/Bundespolizeidirektion, the lost-and-found bureau, is supervised by the Salzburg Polizei at Alpenstrasse 90. Call 0662/6383-2330 for information, but only Mon–Fri 7:30am–3:30pm. You can show up in person at the office Mon–Fri 7:30am–12:30pm.

Luggage Storage/Lockers   Both are available at the Hauptbahnhof, Südtirolerplatz (☎ 0662/888-87), open 24 hours daily. For 2 days, you can rent a large locker for 30 AS ($2.85) or a small locker for 20 AS ($1.90). The luggage storage counter is open from 4am to midnight and costs 30 AS ($2.85) per day.

Photographic Needs   Herlango, Schwarzstrasse 10 (☎ 0662/87-36-41), on the right bank of the Salzach, lying between two bridges, Staatsbrücke and Makartsteg, is open Mon–Fri 8:30am–6pm and Sat 8:30am–noon.

Post Office   The main post office is at Residenzplatz 9 (☎ 0662/844-1210). The post office at the main railway station is open all year 24 hours a day.

ACCOMMODATIONS
ON THE LEFT BANK (ALTSTADT)
Very Expensive

✪ **Goldener Hirsch.** Getreidegasse 37, A-5020 Salzburg. ☎ **0662/8084.** Fax 0662/8485-178-45. 71 rms, 3 suites. A/C MINIBAR TV TEL. 3,300–7,300 AS ($313.50–$693.50) double; from 5,700 AS ($541.50) suite. Higher rates reflect prices at festival time (the first week of April and mid-July through Aug). AE, DC, MC, V. You can double-park in front of the Getreidegasse entrance or at the Karajanplatz entrance, and a staff member will take your vehicle to the hotel's garage for 250 AS ($23.75). Bus: 55.

The award for the finest hotel in Salzburg goes to this establishment, steeped in legend and with a history going back to 1407. Near Mozart's birthplace, the hotel is composed of four medieval town houses, three of which are joined together in a labyrinth of rustic hallways and staircases. A fourth, called "The Coppersmith's House," is across the street, containing 17 charming and elegant rooms, each with a marble bathroom and lots of space. All rooms are beautifully furnished and maintained. The hotel is host to two of the most important restaurants of Salzburg, the more formal being Goldener Hirsch. The hotel's charm and personal service are outstanding.

Inexpensive

⑤ Hotel Blaue Gans. Getreidegasse 43, A-5020 Salzburg. ☎ **0662/84-13-17.** Fax 0662/84-13-179. 45 rms (23 with bath). TEL. 650–750 AS ($61.75–$71.25) double without bath, 850–1,700 AS ($80.75–$161.50) double with bath. Rates include breakfast. AE, DC, MC, V. Parking 162 AS ($15.40). Bus: 1 or 2.

"The Blue Goose" has an ash-colored facade and a convenient location in the Old Town near the underground garages of the Mönchsberg. This building is probably 700 years old, although its bedrooms were renovated in the early 1990s. The rooms are cozy and comfortable, and all but two contain a minibar and TV. The Mexicano Keller in the same building is one of the nighttime diversions of Salzburg. There is also an informal beerhall and cafe-restaurant on the ground floor.

⑤ Hotel Elefant. Sigmund-Haffner-Gasse 4, A-5020 Salzburg. ☎ **0662/84-33-97.** Fax 0662/84-01-0928. 36 rms. MINIBAR TV TEL. 1,600 AS ($152) double. Rates include buffet breakfast. AE, DC, MC, V. Parking 100 AS ($9.50). Bus: 1, 2, 5, 6, or 51.

Near the Rathaus in the Old Town, in a quiet alley off Getreidegasse, is this well-established, family-run hotel, one of the most ancient buildings of Salzburg—it's more than 700 years old. In the lobby you'll see a pink-and-white marble checkerboard floor as well as a 400-year-old marquetry cabinet. One of our favorite rooms is the vaulted Bürgerstüberl, where high wooden banquettes separate the tables. The well-furnished and high-ceilinged bedrooms have radios, safes, and hair dryers.

Hotel Weisse Taube. Kaigasse 9, A-5020 Salzburg. ☎ **0662/84-24-04.** Fax 0662/84-17-83. 33 rms (31 with bath). MINIBAR TV TEL. 980–1,680 AS ($93.10–$159.60) double (all with bath). Rates include breakfast. AE, DC, MC, V. Parking garage 120 AS ($11.40). Bus: 5, 51, or 55.

The reception area here lies behind a stone-trimmed, wrought-iron and glass door a few steps from Mozartplatz. The hotel is in the pedestrian area of the Old Town, but you can drive up to it to unload baggage. Constructed in 1365, the Weisse Taube has been owned by the Haubner family since 1904. Some of the public rooms contain the massive ceiling beams of their original construction, but the bedrooms are for the most part renovated and comfortably streamlined. The hotel has an elevator, a TV room, and a bar.

ON THE RIGHT BANK

Expensive

✪ Österreichischer Hof. Schwarzstrasse 5–7, A-5020 Salzburg. ☎ **800/223-5652** in the U.S. and Canada, or 0662/889-77. Fax 0662/889-77-14. 120 rms, 17 suites. A/C MINIBAR TV TEL. 2,500–5,900 AS ($237.50–$560.50) double; from 6,900 AS ($655.50) suite. Rates include buffet breakfast. AE, DC, MC, V. Parking 300 AS ($28.50). Bus: 1, 5, 29, or 51.

Built originally as the Hotel d'Autriche in 1866 on the right bank of the River Salzach, this hotel over the years has survived the toils of war and has been renovated countless times to keep up to date. A new era began when the hotelier family Gürtler, owners of the Hotel Sacher in Vienna, took over in 1988. The tremendous renovation work, which took a year, has turned the "ÖH," as guests fondly call it, into a jewel amid the villas on the riverbank. The cheerful rooms are well furnished, all quite spacious, and each bedroom is decorated individually; most have high ceilings. Try to reserve one of the bedrooms overlooking the river. A host of drinking and dining facilities is available, including the Roter Salon, an elegant dining room facing the river, and the Zirbelzimmer, an award-winning wood-paneled restaurant.

Moderate

Hotel Auersperg. Auerspergstrasse 61, A-5027 Salzburg. ☎ **0662/889-44-0.** Fax 0662/88-944-55. 57 rms, 6 suites. MINIBAR TV TEL. 1,050–2,060 AS ($99.75–$195.70) double;

2,980 AS ($283.10) suite. Rates include breakfast. AE, DC, MC, V. Parking garage 80 AS ($7.60). Bus: 29.

Two buildings comprise this charming, family-run hotel. The less expensive villa lies adjacent to the main building. Both structures offer comfortable rooms and a relaxed atmosphere amid elegant surroundings. Centrally located near the train station and old town, it has a pleasant garden and a sauna, steam bath, and sun terrace on the top floor. The hotel also offers a comfortable bar and a good restaurant with a traditional Austrian ambience.

Hotel Mozart. Franz-Josef-Strasse 27, A-5020, Salzburg. ☎ **0662/87-22-74.** Fax 0662/87-00-79. 33 rms, 2 apartments. MINIBAR TV TEL. 1,360–1,860 AS ($129.20–$176.70) double; from 3,000 AS ($285) suite. Rates include breakfast. AE, DC, MC, V. Closed Jan–Feb. Free parking. Bus: 27 or 29.

Mozart is a comfortable family-run hotel located a 10-minute walk from the train station and only 5 minutes from the pedestrian area Linzergasse and the famous Mirabell Garden. It greets visitors with a buff-colored stucco six-story facade. Bedrooms are often sunny and have all the standard amenities. The hotel, with its careful service and courteously attentive staff, contains many thoughtful touches, such as drawings of the old city of Salzburg.

Inexpensive

Dr. Wührer's Haus Gastein. Ignaz-Rieder-Kai 25, A-5020 Salzburg. ☎ **0662/62-25-65.** Fax 0662/62-25-659. 13 rms, 3 suites. MINIBAR TV TEL. 1,400–2,000 AS ($133–$190) double; from 2,200 AS ($209) suite. Rates include breakfast. MC, V. Parking 180 AS ($17.10). Bus: 49.

This prosperous-looking Teutonic villa was built as a private home in 1953, lying amid calm scenery on the bank of the Salzach River. The house evokes an upper-class private home. Guests appreciate the spacious flowering garden, a setting for breakfast or afternoon tea. The interior is sparsely but pleasantly furnished, with conservative pieces and oriental carpets. Bedrooms contain cozy Salzburg furniture crafted by Salzburg artisans. Many accommodations have private balconies.

DINING

Two special desserts you'll want to sample while here include the famous *Salzburger nockerln*, a light mixture of stiff egg whites, as well as the elaborate confection known as the *Mozart-Kugeln*, with bittersweet chocolate, hazelnut nougat, and marzipan. You'll also want to taste the beer in one of the numerous Salzburg breweries.

ON THE LEFT BANK (ALTSTADT)

Very Expensive

✪ **Goldener Hirsch.** Getreidegasse 37. ☎ **0662/84-85-11.** Reservations required. Main courses 180–330 AS ($17.10–$31.35); five-course fixed-price menu 690 AS ($65.55). AE, DC, MC, V. Daily noon–2:30pm and 6:30–9:30pm. Bus: 55. AUSTRIAN/VIENNESE.

The best restaurant in the best hotel attracts the brightest luminaries of the international music and business community. It's staffed with a superb team of chefs and waiters in an atmosphere of elegant simplicity. Specialties include parfait of smoked trout in a mustard-dill sauce, grilled hare, veal in saffron sauce, roast filet of char with dill mustard and asparagus, tafelspitz (boiled beef), and, in season, venison served with red cabbage and Bohemian dumplings. Dishes are impeccably prepared and beautifully served.

Expensive

✪ **Alt-Salzburg.** Bürgerspitalgasse 2. ☎ **0662/84-14-76.** Reservations required. Main courses 98–248 AS ($9.30–$23.55); fixed-price menu 560 AS ($53.20). AE, DC, MC, V.

Mon–Sat 11:30am–2pm and 6–11:30pm (open Sun and until midnight in Aug). Closed Feb 3–16. Bus: 1, 15, or 49. AUSTRIAN/INTERNATIONAL.

A retreat into old-world elegance and one of the most venerated restaurants in the city, it's a bastion of formal service and refined cuisine. The building dates from 1648, and it's right in the town center in a wood-ceilinged room, crafted to reveal part of the chiseled rock of the Mönchsberg. The crystal shines, the waiters are formally dressed (often better than the clients), and the food choices include main dishes such as filet of river char sautéed with tomatoes, mushrooms, and capers, leaf spinach, and potatoes; and lamb chops sautéed in an herb crust and thyme sauce with zucchini and potato cakes.

Purzelbaum. Zugallistrasse 7. ☎ **0662/84-88-43.** Reservations required. Main courses 210–260 AS ($19.95–$24.70); two-course fixed-price lunch 160 AS ($15.20); five-course fixed-price dinner 530 AS ($50.35). AE, DC, MC, V. Mon–Sat noon–2pm and 6–11pm (open Sun in Aug). Closed July 1–14. Bus: 55. AUSTRIAN/VIENNESE.

In a residential neighborhood, this restaurant is near a duck pond at the bottom of a steep incline leading up to Salzburg Castle. Guests reserve tables in one of the trio of rooms containing marble buffets from a French buttery and an art nouveau ceiling. Menu items change according to the inspiration of the chef, and include turbot-and-olive casserole, sole meunière, beefsteak cooked in a savory casserole or grilled and served with pepper sauce, and the house specialty, scampi Grüstl, composed of fresh shrimp with sliced potatoes and baked with herbs in a casserole.

Moderate

Restaurant K & K. Waagplatz 2. ☎ **0662/84-21-56.** Reservations required. Main courses 110–260 AS ($10.45–$24.70); fixed-price menu 180–365 AS ($17.10–$34.65). AE, DC, MC, V. Daily 11:30am–2pm and 6–10:30pm; drinks and snacks daily 11:30am–midnight. Bus: 55. AUSTRIAN/INTERNATIONAL.

Separated into about half a dozen intimate dining rooms, the K & K contains oiled wood paneling, slabs of salmon-colored marble, stone accents crafted from the porous rocks of Salzburg, flickering candles, antique accessories, and a well-dressed clientele. The menus range from the traditional to the "creative," concocted from perch trout, roast filet of beef in a cognac-cream sauce with fresh mushrooms and green peppercorns, tafelspitz (boiled beef), breast of chicken in a curry-cream sauce, and several kinds of fresh shellfish.

Inexpensive

Festungsrestaurant. Hohensalzburg Schloss, Mönchsberg 34. ☎ **0662/84-17-80.** Reservations required July–Aug. Main courses 115–225 AS ($10.95–$21.40). No credit cards. Mar–May and Oct Wed–Sun 10am–6pm; June–Sept daily 10am–10pm. Closed Nov–Feb. Transportation: Funicular from the Old Town. SALZBURGIAN/AUSTRIAN.

Here you have a chance to dine in the former stronghold of the prince-archbishops of Salzburg. The restaurants and gardens are in the fortress, perched 400 feet above the Altstadt and the River Salzach, with a panoramic view of Salzburg, the surrounding countryside, and towering alpine peaks. The kitchen offers robust local specialties, along with many other flavorful dishes. In winter, although the restaurant is closed, the Burg Taverne remains open inside the castle, dispensing food and drink.

⊗ Herzl. Karajanplatz 7. ☎ **0662/8084.** Reservations recommended. Main courses 90–190 AS ($8.55–$18.05); fixed-price menu 100–120 AS ($9.50–$11.40). AE, DC, MC, V. Daily 11:30am–9pm. Bus: 55. AUSTRIAN/VIENNESE.

With an entrance on the landmark Karajanplatz, Herzl tavern is next door to, and part of, the glamorous Goldener Hirsch. Because it offers such good value, it attracts both visitors and locals. You'll see photos of musicians who have dined here while performing at the annual Salzburg Festival. Waitresses in dirndls serve an appetizing roast pork with dumplings, game stew (in season), and, for the trencherperson, a farmer's plate of boiled pork, roast pork, grilled sausages, dumplings, and sauerkraut.

🟢 **Krimpelstätter.** Müllner Hauptstrasse 31. ☎ **0662/43-22-74.** Reservations recommended. Main courses 79–165 AS ($7.50–$15.70), fish plates 265 AS ($25.20). No credit cards. Tues–Sat 11:45am–2pm and 6–10:15pm (and on Monday, May through Sept). Closed Dec 23–Jan 10. Bus: 49 or 95. SALZBURGIAN/AUSTRIAN.

An enduring Salzburg favorite, with a history going back to 1548, it was originally constructed as an inn, with chiseled stone columns supporting vaulted ceilings and heavy timbers. In summer the establishment's beer garden, full of roses and trellises, attracts up to 300 visitors at a time. If you want a snack, a beer, or a glass of wine, head for the paneled door marked GASTEZIMMER in the entry corridor. If you're looking for a more formal, less visited area, a trio of cozy antique dining rooms sits atop a flight of narrow stone steps. The menu offers the same dishes in each of the different areas, a hearty Land Salzburg regional cuisine featuring homemade sausages and wild game dishes.

Sternbräu. Griesgasse 23. ☎ **0662/84-21-40.** Main courses 80–140 AS ($7.60–$13.30); fixed-price menu 140–200 AS ($13.30–$19). No credit cards. Daily 9am–11pm. Bus: 2, 5, 12, 49, or 51. AUSTRIAN.

This place seems big enough to have fed half the Austro-Hungarian army, with a series of rooms that follow one after the other in varying degrees of formality. The Hofbräustübl is a rustic fantasy combining masonry columns with hand-hewn beams and wood paneling. You can also eat in the chestnut tree–shaded beer garden, usually packed on a summer's night, or under the weathered arcades of an inner courtyard. Daily specials, which are served by a battalion of aproned waiters, include typical Austrian dishes such as Wiener and chicken schnitzels, some trout recipes, cold marinated herring, Hungarian goulash, hearty regional soups, and lots of other *Gutbürgerlich* selections.

🟢 **Stiftskeller St. Peter (Peterskeller).** St.-Peter-Bezirk 1–4. ☎ **0662/84-12-680.** Reservations recommended. Main courses 80–225 AS ($7.60–$21.40). AE, MC, V. Mon–Sat 11am–midnight, Sun 10:30am–midnight. Bus: 29. AUSTRIAN/VIENNESE.

Legend has it that Mephistopheles met with Faust in this tavern, which isn't that far-fetched, considering that it was established by Benedictine monks in A.D. 803. In fact, it's the oldest restaurant in Europe, and is housed in the abbey of the church that supposedly brought Christianity to Austria. Aside from a collection of baroque banqueting rooms, there's an inner courtyard with vaults cut from living rock, a handful of dignified wood-paneled rooms, and a brick-vaulted cellar with a tile floor and rustic chandeliers. In addition to the wine fermented from the abbey's vineyards, the tavern serves good home-style Austrian cooking, including braised oxtail with mushrooms and fried polenta, and braised veal knuckle with anchovy sauce.

On the Right Bank
Moderate
Hotel Stadtkrug Restaurant. Linzer Gasse 20. ☎ **0662/87-35-45.** Reservations recommended. Fixed-price menu 195–230 AS ($18.50–$21.85) lunch, 295–450 AS ($28.05–$42.75) dinner. AE, DC, MC, V. Wed–Mon noon–3pm and 5pm–midnight. Bus: 27 or 29. AUSTRIAN/INTERNATIONAL.

Across the river from the Altstadt, on the site of what used to be a 14th-century farm, this restaurant occupies a structure rebuilt from an older core in 1458. In the 1960s, a modern hotel was added in back. The old-fashioned dining rooms in front now serve as one of the neighborhood's most popular restaurants. In an antique and artfully rustic setting, illuminated by gilded wooden chandeliers, you can enjoy hearty conservative and flavorful Austrian cuisine such as cream of potato soup "Old Vienna" style, braised beef with burgundy sauce, roast duckling with bacon dumplings and red cabbage/apple dressing, and glazed cutlet of pork with caraway seeds and deep-fried potatoes.

⑤ Zum Fidelen Affen. Priesterhausgasse 8. ☎ **0662/877361.** Main courses 85–110 AS ($8.05–$10.45). No credit cards. Mon–Sat 5–midnight. AUSTRIAN.

On the eastern edge of the river near the Staatsbrücke, this is the closest thing in Salzburg to a loud, animated, and jovial pub with food service. It's in one of the city's oldest buildings and contains an eclectically crowded bar. Management's policy is to allow only three reserved tables on any particular evening; the remainder are given to whoever happens to show up. Menu items are simple, inexpensive, and based on regional culinary traditions. A house specialty is a gratin of green (spinach-flavored) noodles in cream sauce with strips of ham. Also popular are casseroles of seasonal meats and mushrooms, and at least three different kinds of main-course dumplings flavored with meats, cheeses, herbs, and various sauces.

Cafes

❸ Café-Restaurant Glockenspiel. Mozartplatz 2. ☎ **0662/84-14-03-0.** Summer, daily 9am–midnight (food served until 11pm). Rest of the year, daily 9am–8pm (food served until 6pm). Closed second and third weeks of Nov and Jan. Bus: 55.

This cafe is the city's most popular, with about 100 tables with armchairs out front. You might want to spend an afternoon here, particularly when there's live chamber music. Upon entering, you can't miss a glass case filled with every caloric delight west of Vienna. Coffee starts at 33 AS ($3.15), and comes in many varieties, including Maria Theresa, which contains orange liqueur.

Café Tomaselli. Alter Markt 9. ☎ **0662/84-44-88.** Mon–Sat 7am–9pm, Sun and holidays 8am–9pm (closed 10 days in Feb). Bus: 5, 6, or 55.

Established in 1705, this cafe opens onto one of the most charming cobblest one squares of the Altstadt. Aside from the summer chairs placed outdoors, you'll find a high-ceilinged room with many tables, small crystal lighting fixtures, and lots of elegant conversation among the *haute bourgeoisie* crowd. A waiter brings a pastry tray filled with 40 different kinds of cakes. Other menu items include omelets, wursts, ice cream, and a wide range of drinks. Pastries begin at 25 AS ($2.40) and the most elaborate cakes cost 37 AS ($3.50). Coffee costs 36 AS ($3.40) for a mélange.

ATTRACTIONS

The Old Town lies between the left bank of the Salzach River and the ridge known as the **Mönchsberg,** which rises to a height of 1,650 feet and is the site of Salzburg's gambling casino. The main street of the Altstadt is **Getreidegasse,** a narrow little thoroughfare lined with five- and six-story burghers' buildings. Most of the houses along the street are from the 17th and 18th centuries. Mozart was born at no. 9 (see below). Many lacy-looking wrought-iron signs are displayed, and a lot of the houses have carved windows.

You might begin your tour at **Mozartplatz,** with its outdoor cafes. From here you can walk to the even more expansive **Residenzplatz,** where torchlight dancing is staged every year, along with outdoor performances.

SIGHTSEEING SUGGESTIONS

If You Have 1 Day   Start slowly with a cup of coffee at the Café-Restaurant Glock-enspiel on Mozartplatz. Then from the Altstadt take the funicular to the Hohensalzburg Fortress for a tour. After lunch in an old tavern, visit Mozart's birthplace on Getreidegasse, and stroll along the narrow street, most typical in the city. Later, visit the Residenz.

If You Have 2 Days   In the morning of your second day, visit the Dom and the cemetery of St. Peter's. Take a walking tour through the Altstadt. In the afternoon, explore Hellbrunn Palace, 3 miles south of the city.

If You Have 3 Days   On day 3, visit the many attractions of Salzburg you've missed so far: the Mönchsberg, the Mozart Wohnhaus, and the museum Carolino Augusteum in the morning. In the afternoon, see the Mirabell Gardens and Mirabell Palace and at least look at the famous Festspielhaus (Festival Hall), dating from 1607; tours are sometimes possible.

If You Have 5 Days or More   On day 4, head for some of the sights in the environs of Salzburg. Go to Gaisberg in the morning, which at 4,250 feet offers a panoramic view of the Salzburg Alps. After lunch, head for Hallein, the second-largest town in Land Salzburg, for a look at its salt mines. On day 5, take the "*Sound of Music* Tour*"* (see "Organized Tours," below) and visit the places where this world-famous musical with Julie Andrews was filmed. Return to Salzburg in time to hear a Mozart concert, if one is featured (as it often is).

THE TOP ATTRACTIONS

✪ **Residenz.** Residenzplatz 1. ☎ **0662/80-42-26-90.** Admission to Residenz state rooms, 50 AS ($4.75) adults, 40 AS ($3.80) students 16–18 and senior citizens, 15 AS ($1.45) children 6–15, free for children 5 and under. Combined ticket to state rooms and gallery, 80 AS ($7.60). Residenz Gallery, 50 AS ($4.75) adults, 40 AS ($3.80) students 16–18 and senior citizens, free for children under 16. Conducted tours of the Residenz state rooms, July–Aug daily 10am–4:40pm; Sept–June Mon–Fri 10am–3pm. Residenz Gallery, Mar–Sept daily 10am–5pm; Oct–Jan Thurs–Tues 10am–5pm. Closed Feb–Mar 25. Bus: 5 or 6.

This opulent palace, just north of Domplatz in the pedestrian zone, was the seat of the Salzburg prince-archbishops after they no longer needed the protection of the gloomy Hohensalzburg Fortress of Mönchsberg. The Residenz dates from 1120, but work on its series of palaces, which comprised the ecclesiastical complex of the ruling church princes, began in the late 1500s and continued until about 1796. The lavish rebuilding was originally ordered by Archbishop Wolfgang ("Wolf") Dietrich. The Residenz fountain, from the 17th century, is one of the largest and most impressive baroque fountains north of the Alps. The child prodigy Mozart often played in the Conference Room for guests. More than a dozen state rooms, each richly decorated, are open to the public via guided tour. On the second floor you can visit the **Residenzgalerie Salzburg** (☎ 0662/84-04-57-19), an art gallery founded in 1923, now containing European paintings from the 16th to the 19th century, displayed in 15 historic rooms.

Glockenspiel (Carillon). Mozartplatz 1. ☎ **0662/80-42-27-84.** Admission 20 AS ($1.90) adults, 10 AS (95¢) children 6–14, free for children 5 and under. Tours daily at 10:45am and 5:45pm (in winter, Mon–Fri only); no tours in bad weather.

The celebrated glockenspiel with its 35 bells stands across from the Residenz. You can hear this 18th-century carillon at 7am, 11am, and 6pm. There's a 20-minute tour (minimum of three people).

✪ **Salzburg Cathedral.** South side of Residenzplatz. ☎ **0662/84-11-62.** Cathedral, free; excavations, 20 AS ($1.90) adults, 15 AS ($1.45) children 6–15, free for children 5 and under;

museum, 40 AS ($3.80) adults, 10 AS (95¢) children. Cathedral, daily 8am–8pm (until 6pm in winter); excavations, Easter to mid-Oct daily 9am–5pm (closed mid-Oct to Easter); museum, May 10–Oct 18 daily 10am–5pm. Closed Oct 19–May 9. Bus: 1.

Located where Residenzplatz flows into Domplatz, this cathedral is world renowned for its 4,000-pipe organ. The original foundation dates from A.D. 774, superseded in the 12th century by a late-romanesque structure that was destroyed by fire in 1598. Prince-Archbishop Wolf Dietrich commissioned a new cathedral, but his overthrow prevented the completion of the project. The Italian architect Santino Solari built the present cathedral, which was consecrated in 1628 by Archbishop Paris Count Lodron.

Hailed by some critics as the "most perfect" northern Renaissance building, the cathedral has a marble facade and twin symmetrical towers. The mighty bronze doors were created in 1959. The interior has a rich baroque style with elaborate frescoes, the most important of which, along with the altarpieces, were designed by Mascagni of Florence. In the crypt, traces of the old romanesque cathedral have been unearthed.

The treasure of the cathedral and the "arts and wonders" the archbishops collected in the 17th century are displayed in the **Dom Museum** (☎ 0662/84-41-89), entered through the cathedral. The **cathedral excavations** (☎ 0662/84-52-95), entered around the corner (left of the Dom entrance), show the ruins of the original foundation.

Stiftskirche St. Peter. St.-Peter-Bezirk. ☎ **0662/844-578.** Free admission. Daily 9am–12:15pm and 2:30–6:30pm.

Founded in A.D. 696 by St. Rupert, whose tomb is here, this is the church of St. Peter's Abbey and Benedictine Monastery. Once a romanesque basilica with three aisles, the church was completely overhauled in the 17th and 18th centuries in elegant baroque style. The west door dates from 1240. The church is richly adorned with art treasures including some altar paintings by Kremser Schmidt.

Petersfriedhof (St. Peter's Cemetery). St.-Peter-Bezirk. ☎ **0662/84-45-78-0.** Twenty-minute tours, 12 AS ($1.15) adults, 8 AS (75¢) children 6–15, free for children 5 and under. Tours of catacombs, May–Sept daily 10am–5pm every 45 minutes; Oct–Apr daily 10:30am, 11:30am, 1:30, 2:30 and 3:30pm. Bus: 1.

This cemetery lies at the stone wall that merges into the rock called the Mönchsberg. Many of the aristocratic families of Salzburg lie buried here as well as many other noted persons, including Nannerl Mozart, sister of Wolfgang Amadeus. You can also see the romanesque Chapel of the Holy Cross and St. Margaret's Chapel, dating from the 15th century.

✪ Hohensalzburg Fortress. Mönchsberg 34. ☎ **0662/84-24-30-11.** Admission (excluding guided tour but including museum) 35 AS ($3.35) adults, 20 AS ($1.90) children 6–19, free for children 5 and under. Fortress and museums, Nov–Mar daily 9am–5pm; Apr–June and Oct daily 9am–6pm; July–Sept daily 8am–7pm. The funicular from Festungsgasse (☎ 0662/84-26-82) runs every 10 minutes during daylight hours and the round-trip costs 32 AS ($3.05) for adults and 16 AS ($1.50) for children 6–16, free for children 5 and under.

The stronghold of the ruling prince-archbishops before they moved "downtown" to the Residenz, this fortress towers 400 feet above the Salzach River on a rocky Dolomite ledge. The massive fortress crowns the Festungsberg and literally dominates Salzburg. Work on Hohensalzburg began in 1077 and was not finished until 1681. This is the largest completely preserved castle left in central Europe. The elegant state apartments, once the courts of the prince-archbishops, are on display.

The **Burgmuseum** contains a collection of medieval art. Plans and prints tracing the growth of Salzburg are on exhibit, as well as instruments of torture and many gothic artifacts. The **Rainermuseum** has displays of arms and armor. The beautiful late-gothic St. George's Chapel, dating from 1501, is adorned with marble reliefs of the apostles.

If you're athletic you can reach the fortress on foot from Kapitelplatz by way of Festungsgasse or from the Mönchsberg via the Schartentor. You can explore the fortress grounds on your own. Conducted 50-minute tours of the interior are offered daily, but hours and departure times depend on the season: Nov–March 10am–4:30pm; Apr–June 9:30am–5pm; July–Aug 9am–5:30pm; and Sept–Oct 9:30am–5:30pm. The cost of a conducted tour of the fortress and the Rainier Museum is 30 AS ($2.60) adults, 25 AS ($2.20) senior citizens, 20 AS ($1.70) students 16–19, 15 AS ($1.30) children 6–15, free for children under 6.

MORE ATTRACTIONS

✪ Mozart Gerburtshaus (Mozart's Birthplace). Getreidegasse 9. ☎ **0662/84-43-13.** Admission 65 AS ($6.20) adults, 47 AS ($4.45) students, 17 AS ($1.60) children. July–Aug daily 9am–7pm; Sept–June daily 9am–6pm.

The house where Wolfgang Amadeus Mozart was born on January 27, 1756, houses exhibition rooms and the apartment of the Mozart family. The main treasures are the valuable paintings (such as the well-known oil painting—left unfinished—by Joseph Lange, *Mozart and the Piano*) and the original instruments: the violin Mozart used as a child, his concert violin, his viola, fortepiano, and the clavichord.

Schloss Mirabell (Mirabell Palace). Off Makartplatz. ☎ **0662/8072-0.** Free admission. Staircase: Mon–Fri 8am–6pm. Marmosaal: Mon, Wed, and Thurs 8am–4pm; Tues and Fri 1–4pm. Bus: 1, 5, 6, or 51.

This palace and its gardens (see "Parks and Gardens" below) were originally created by Prince-Archbishop Wolf Dietrich in 1606 as a luxurious private residence for his mistress and the mother of his children, Salome Alt. Not much remains of the original grand structure, which has been rebuilt and modified. Now the official residence of the mayor of Salzburg, it is like a smaller edition of the Tuileries. The ceremonial marble Barockstiege-Englesstiege (Angel Staircase) with sculptured cherubs, carved by Raphael Donner in 1726, leads to the Marmorsaal, a marble-and-gold hall used for concerts and weddings.

Museum Carolino Augusteum. Museumsplatz 1. ☎ **0662/84-31-45.** Admission 40 AS ($3.80) adults, 15 AS ($1.45) children 6–19, free for children 5 and under. Tues 9am–8pm, Wed–Sun 9am–5pm. Bus: 1, 49, or 95.

A museum reflecting Salzburg's cultural history, several collections are brought together under one roof here. The archeological collection contains the well-known Dürnberg beaked pitcher, as well as Roman mosaics. Some 15th-century Salzburg art is on view, and there are many paintings from the Romantic period, as well as works by Hans Makart, who was born in Salzburg in 1840.

Mozart Wohnhaus (Mozart Residence). Makartplatz 8. ☎ **0662/88-94-0,** ext. 40. Admission 55 AS ($5.25) adults, 20 AS ($1.90) children. June–Sept daily 10am–5pm; Oct–May daily 10am–4pm. Bus: 1 or 5.

In 1773 the Mozart family vacated the cramped quarters of Mozart's birthplace, and the young Mozart lived here with his family until 1780. In the rooms of the former Mozart family apartments, a museum documents the history of the house and the life and work of Wolfgang Amadeus.

This is not the original house. Destroyed by bombing in 1944, it was rebuilt according to the specifics of an 1838 engraving and reopened on January 26, 1996—the eve of Mozart's birthday anniversary. A mechanized audio tour in six languages with relevant musical samples accompanies the visitor through the rooms of the museum.

Mönchsberg. ☎ **0662/05-51-180.** Express elevators leave from Gstättengasse 13, daily 9am–11pm; round-trip fare 27 AS ($2.55) adults, 14 AS ($1.35) children 6–15, free for children 5 and under.

West of the Hohensalzburg Fortress, this heavily forested ridge extends for some 1¹/₂ miles above the Altstadt and has fortifications dating from the 15th century. Several vistas can be seen, and a panoramic view of Salzburg is possible from Mönchsberg Terrace just in front of the Grand Café Winkler.

PARKS & GARDENS

Mirabell Gardens, off Makartplatz, are on the right bank of the river. Laid out by Fischer von Erlach and now a public park, these baroque gardens are studded with statuary and reflecting pools, making the gardens a virtual open-air museum. Some of the marble balustrades and urns were also designed by von Erlach. There's also a natural theater. Be sure to visit the bastion with fantastic marble baroque dwarfs and other figures, by the Pegasus Fountains in the lavish garden west of Schloss Mirabell. From the garden you have an excellent view of the Hohensalzburg Fortress. Admission is free, and the gardens are open daily 7am–8pm. Bus: 1, 5, 6, or 51.

ORGANIZED TOURS

The best tours are offered by **Salzburg Panorama Tours,** Mirabellplatz (☎ **0662/88-32-11-0**), which is the Gray Line company for Salzburg. The original "*Sound of Music* Tour" combines the Salzburg city tour with an excursion to the lake district and the places where the film was shot. The English-speaking guide also shows you the historical and architectural landmarks of Salzburg, as well as a part of the Salzkammergut countryside. The tour departs daily at 9:30am and 2pm, costing 330 AS ($31.35).

You must take your passport along for any of three trips into Bavaria in Germany. One of these, called the "Eagle's Nest Tour," takes visitors to Berchtesgaden and on to Obersalzberg, where Hitler and his elite followers had a vacation retreat. The 4¹/₂-hour tour departs daily at 9am, May 15–Oct 20, and costs 550 AS ($52.25). Among other tours offered, "The City & Country Highlights" takes in historic castles and the surrounding Land Salzburg landscape. Departure is daily at 1pm; the tour lasts 5 hours and costs 550 AS ($52.25).

Bookings are possible at the bus terminal at Mirabellplatz/St. Andrä Kirche (☎ **0662/87-40-29**). Tour prices are the same for all ages.

SHOPPING

Salzburg obviously doesn't have Vienna's wide range of merchandise. However, if you're not going on to the Austrian capital, you may want to patronize some of the establishments recommended below. Good buys in Salzburg include souvenirs of Land Salzburg, dirndls, lederhosen, petit point, and all types of sports gear. **Getreidegasse** is a main shopping thoroughfare, but you'll also find some intriguing little shops on **Residenzplatz.**

Alois Wenger & Co., Getreidegasse 29 (☎ **0662/84-16-77**), offers Salzburg's finest selections of Austrian loden and traditional costumes. The shop is a member of an Austrian chain, but this is one of the most stylish. It sells adaptations of traditional dresses such as an alpine-inspired dirndl, crafted in satin and velvet, that a woman might wear to a fashionable party. The staff is available to give advice. It's open Mon–Fri 9am–6pm and Sat 9am–noon.

Drechslerei Lackner, Badergasse 2 (☎ **0662/84-23-85**), is the place if you like items made of wood. It offers both antique and modern country furniture. Among the new items are chests, chessboards, angels, cupboards, crèches, candlesticks, and most definitely chairs. Open Mon–Fri 9am–6pm and Sat 9am–noon.

Salzburger Heimatwerk, Am Residenzplatz 9 (☎ **0662/84-41-19**), is one of the best places in town to buy local Austrian handcrafts and original Austrian *tracht.* Items for sale include Austrian silver and garnet jewelry, painted boxes, candles, woodcarvings, copper and brass ceramics, tablecloths, and patterns for cross-stitched samplers in alpine designs. Another section sells dirndl, pfoadl, and the rest of the regalia native to the land and still donned during commemorative ceremonies and festivals. Open Mon–Fri 9am–6pm and Sat 9am–noon.

Wiener Porzellanmanufaktur Augarten Gesellschaft, Alter Markt 11 (☎ **0662/ 84-07-14**), might tempt you to begin a collection. It's the premier shop for Austrian porcelain, and specializes in Augarten porcelain. Patterns like Viennese Rose and Maria Theresia are still very popular, but its most famous item, which it still turns out, is the black-and-white coffee set created by architect/designer Josef Hoffmann. Open Mon–Fri 9am–6pm and Sat 9am–noon.

SALZBURG AFTER DARK
THE PERFORMING ARTS

It's said that there's a musical event—often a Mozart concert—staged virtually every night in Salzburg. To find the venue, visit the Salzburg tourist office, Mozartplatz 5 (☎ **0662/847568**). Here you'll be given a free copy of **"Offizieller Wochenspiegel,"** a monthly pamphlet listing all major—and many minor—local cultural events.

If you don't want to pay a ticket agent's commission, you can go directly to the box office of a theater or concert hall. However, many of the best seats may have already been sold, especially those at the Salzburg Festival.

The major ticket agency affiliated with the city of Salzburg is located adjacent to Salzburg's main tourist office, at Mozartplatz 5. The **Salzburger Ticket Office** (☎ **0662/84-03-10**) is open Mon–Fri 9am–6pm (until 7pm in midsummer) and Sat 9am–noon.

❂ The Salzburg Festival

One of the premier music attractions of Europe, the Salzburg Festival reached its 76th season in 1996. Composer Richard Strauss founded the festival, aided by director Max Reinhardt and writer Hugo von Hofmmansthal. Details on the festival are available by writing to Salzburg Festival, P.O. Box 140, A-5010 Salzburg, Austria (☎ **0662/8045**).

Festival tickets are in great demand, and there never are enough of them. Don't arrive expecting to get into any of the major events unless you've booked your tickets far ahead. Travel agents can often get tickets for you, and you can also go to branches of the Austrian National Tourist Office at home or abroad.

An annual event is Hofmannsthal's adaptation of the morality play *Everyman,* which is staged (in German) outside the cathedral in Domplatz.

Subject to many exceptions and variations, and without agent commissions, drama tickets generally run 200–1,600 AS ($19–$152). Opera tickets can begin as low as 600 AS ($57), ranging upward to 4,200 AS ($399).

Concerts & Other Entertainment

Besides the venues listed below, you can attend a concert in dramatic surroundings in the Fürstenzimmer (Prince's Chamber) of the **Hohensalzburg Fortress.** Guest musicians of international renown perform on occasion. The box office, at Adlgasser Weg 22 (☎ **0662/42-58-88**), is open daily 9am–9pm. Performances are daily from mid-May to mid-Oct, at either 8 or 8:30pm, and tickets are 300 AS ($28.50). For more information, call **0662/84-24-30-11.**

Festspielhaus. Hofstallgasse 1. ☎ **0662/8045.** Tickets 100–4,000 AS ($9.50–$380) (the higher cost for the best seats at the Salzburg Festival); average but good seats run 550–950 AS ($52.25–$90.25). Bus: 1, 5, or 6.

All the premier ballet, opera, and musical presentations are offered at this world-famous theater complex. The Grosses Haus (Big House) is the larger venue, seating 2,170. The Kleines Haus (Small House) seats 1,323, which isn't that small. You can purchase tickets in advance at the box office at Waagplatz 1A (☎ **0662/8045-326**), close to the tourist office; it's open Mon–Fri 9:30am–4:30pm. Most performances begin at 7:30pm, although there are matinee shows from time to time at 11am and 3pm.

Mozarteum. Schwarzstrasse 26 and Mirabellplatz 1. ☎ **0662/87-31-54.** Tickets range 200–650 AS ($19–$61.75); the best seats run 1,200-2,000 AS ($114–$190). Bus 1, 5, 6, or 51.

On the right back of the Salzach River, near Mirabell Gardens, this is the major music and concert hall of Salzburg. All the big orchestra concerts, as well as organ recitals and chamber-music evenings, are offered by the Mozarteum. In the old building at Schwarzstrasse there are two concert halls, the Grosser Saal and the Wiener Saal. However, in the newer building on Mirabellplatz, concert halls include the Grosses Studio, the Leopold-Mozart Saal, and the Paumgartner Studio. The box office is open Mon–Thurs 9am–2pm and Fri 9am–4pm. Performances are at 11am or 7:30pm.

BEER GARDENS & THE CASINO

✪ **Augustiner Bräustübl.** Augustinergasse 46. ☎ **0662/43-12-46.** Bus: 27.

Our recommendation for one of the most enjoyable, authentic evenings in Salzburg is to pay a visit to this famous beer garden. The bierstube has served suds of one kind or another since 1622, although over the years it has expanded massively. In fair weather the beer-drinking fraternity of the beerhalls gathers in the leafy chestnut garden to "taste the brew." The brew is excellent and it's served Mon–Fri 3–11pm and Sat–Sun 2:30–11pm. The activity gets loud and raucous, especially when young men invade from neighboring Bavaria. To get here, you climb a steep, narrow cobblestone street and go through a stone entranceway, passing statues of saints and cherubs.

✪ **Stiegelbräu Keller.** Festungsgasse 10. ☎ **0662/84-26-81.**

To get here, you'll have to negotiate a steep cobblestone street that drops off on one side to reveal a panoramic view of Salzburg. Part of the establishment is carved into the rocks of Mönchsberg mountain. The cavernous interior is open only in summer when, along with hundreds of others, you can drink beer and eat traditional bierkeller food such as sausages and schnitzels. "Sound of Music" dinner shows are presented May–Sept daily 7:30–10pm. A three-course meal plus the show costs 520 AS ($49.40). You can also show up at 8:15pm and see the show, with dessert and coffee, for 360 AS ($34.20). On the first Sunday of the month, 10:30pm–midnight, there's a *fruhschoppen,* a traditional Salzburger music fest presented along with regional food specialties.

Casino Salzburg Schloss Klessheim. A-5071 Walzsezenheim. ☎ **0662/854-4550.** Cover 260 AS ($24.70) includes 300 AS ($28.50) worth of casino chips.

This is the only year-round casino in Land Salzburg, occupying the Schloss Klessheim, a baroque palace. On the premises is a stylish restaurant, plus bars. Monday night is poker night. You must show some form of identification—a driver's license or a passport—and except during the hottest months of summer, men are encouraged to wear jackets and ties. The complex is open daily 3pm–3am. To get there, drive west along highway A-1, exiting at the "Schloss Klessheim" exit, about a mile west of the center of Salzburg. Also, the casino maintains a flotilla of red-sided shuttle buses that depart, without charge, from the rocky base of the Mönchsberg every hour on the half-hour, daily, 2:30pm–midnight.

DAY TRIPS FROM SALZBURG

SCHLOSS HELLBRUNN   This early 17th-century palace was built as a hunting lodge and summer residence for Prince-Archbishop Markus Sittikus. The Hellbrunn Zoo, also here, was formerly the palace's deer park. The palace **gardens,** some of the oldest baroque formal gardens in Europe, are known for their trick fountains. As you walk through, take care—you may be showered from a surprise source when you least expect it. Some 265 figures in a mechanical theater are set in motion by a hydraulic movement to the music of an organ, also powered by water. The rooms of the schloss are furnished and decorated in 18th-century style. See, in particular, the banquet hall with its trompe-l'oeil painting. The gardens are at Fürstenweg 37, Hellbrunn (☎ **0662/820-372**). Admission is 60 AS ($5.70) for adults and 30 AS ($2.85) for children. Open Apr–Oct daily 9am–4:30pm; May, June, and Sept daily 9am–5pm; July–Aug daily 9am–10pm. Bus 15 from Salzburg runs here in 18 minutes.

✪ **DÜRNBERG SALT MINES (SALZBERGWERK HALLEIN)**   These salt mines (☎ **06245/83511-0**) are the big lure at Hallein, south of Salzburg. On guided tours, you'll walk downhill from the ticket office to the mine entrance, then board an electric mine train that takes you deep into the caverns. From here, you go on foot through galleries, changing levels by sliding down polished wooden slides, then exit on the train that brought you in. An underground museum traces the history of salt mining back to remote times.

Hallein is connected to Salzburg, 10 miles away, by both train and bus. From here there's a cable railway to Dürnberg. Tours lasting 1 1/2 hours are conducted Apr–Oct daily 9am–5pm and Nov–Mar daily 11am–3pm. Admission is 170 AS ($16.15) for adults and 85 AS ($8.05) for children between 6 and 15 and 55 AS ($5.25) for children between 4 and 6. There's a modern road from Hallein directly to a large parking lot near the ticket office to the mines.

✪ **EISRIESENWELT**   Eisriesenwelt lies in the Pongau basin, on the western cliffs of the Hochkogel, towering over the Salzach Valley. Some 30 miles south of Salzburg by train is this "World of the Ice Giants," the largest known **ice caves** in the world. The caves, opening at some 5,500 feet up, stretch for about 26 miles, although only a portion of that length is open to the public. You'll see fantastic ice formations at the entrance, extending for half a mile. The climax of this chilly underworld tour is the spectacular "Ice Palace." To reach the Eisriesenwelt, head for Werfen, a village that's the center for exploring the ice caves.

If you come by train from Salzburg, you can take a taxi bus from Werfen's Hauptplatz (main square), going 3 1/2 miles by mountain road to the same point you'll reach if you're traveling in your own car, rising from 1,600 to 3,000 feet. A cable car goes to the entrance of the caves. The round-trip cable-car ride costs 110 AS ($10.45) for adults and 55 AS ($5.25) for children.

Tours begin at a mountain outpost set 5,141 feet above sea level. From here, you walk to the nearby entrance to the caves. Supervised tours take about 2 hours and cost 80 AS ($7.60) for adults and 40 AS ($3.80) for children. Tours are conducted May–Oct, daily, at 9am, 11am, 2pm, and 5pm. For more information, call **06468/248.**

BERCHTESGADEN Although it lies in Germany, Berchtesgaden is one of the most popular day trips from Salzburg, about 14 miles to the south of the city. Berchtesgaden is situated below the many summits of Watzmann Mountain (8,900 feet at the highest point)—according to legend, these mountain peaks were once a king and his family who were so evil that God punished them by turning them into rocks.

Many visitors expect to see one of Hitler's favorite haunts, since the name Berchtesgaden is often linked with the führer and the Nazi hierarchy. This impression is erroneous. Hitler's playground was actually at Obersalzberg (see below), on a wooded plateau about half a mile up the mountain. Berchtesgaden itself is an old alpine village with ancient winding streets and a medieval marketplace and castle square.

The **Schlossplatz** is partially enclosed by the castle and the **Stiftskirche** (Abbey Church), dating from 1122, a romanesque foundation with gothic additions. The church interior contains many fine works of art; the high altar has a painting by Zott dating from 1669. The **Königliches Schloss Berchtesgaden** (☎ **08652/2085**) is now a museum, and the exhibition is mainly devoted to the royal collection of sacred art, including wood sculptures by the famed artists Veit Stoss and Tilman Riemenschneider. You can also explore a gallery of 19th-century art. Admission is 7 DM ($4.90) for adults and 3 DM ($2.10) for children 6–16 (free for 5 and under). From Easter to Sept, hours are Sun–Fri 10am–1pm. Off-season, hours are Mon–Fri, 10am–1pm and 2–5pm.

On the opposite side of the square from the church is a 16th-century arcade that leads to **Marktplatz,** with typical alpine houses and a wooden fountain from 1677 (restored in 1860). Some of Berchtesgaden's oldest inns and houses border this square.

Salzbergwerk Berchtesgaden, Bergwerkstrasse 83 (☎ **08652/60-02-0**), lies at the eastern edge of town. These salt mines have been worked since 1517; the deposits are more than 990 feet thick and are still processed today. Older children will especially enjoy the guided tours that begin with a ride into the mine on a small wagonlike train after donning protective miner's clothing. After nearly a half-mile ride, visitors explore the rest of the mine on foot, sliding down a miner's slide and riding on the salt lake in a ferry. The highlight of the tour is the "chapel," a grotto containing unusually shaped salt formations illuminated for an eerie effect. The 1½-hour tour can be taken any time of the year, in any weather. Admission is 18 DM ($12.60) for adults and 9 DM ($6.30) for children. The mines are open May–Oct 15 daily 8:30am–5pm. In the off-season, hours are Mon–Sat 12:30–3:30pm.

✪ OBERSALZBERG The drive from Berchtesgaden to Obersalzberg at 3,300 feet is along one of Bavaria's most scenic routes. Here Hitler settled down in a rented cottage while he completed *Mein Kampf.* After he came to power in 1933, he bought Haus Wachenfeld and had it remodeled into his residence, the Berghof. Obersalzberg became the center for holiday living for Nazis such as Martin Bormann and Hermann Göring.

A major point of interest to visitors is the **Kehlstein,** or Eagle's Nest, which can be reached only by a thrilling bus ride up a 4½-mile-long mountain road that was blasted out of solid rock, an outstanding feat of construction and engineering when begun in 1937. To reach the spot, you must enter a tunnel and take a 400-foot elevator ride through a shaft to the summit of the Kehlstein Mountain. There you can enjoy the panoramic view and explore the rooms of the original teahouse, which includes Eva Braun's living room.

For information about trips to Kehlstein, call **08652/54-73.** RVO buses (local buses based in Berchtesgaden) run from the Berchtesgaden Post Office to Obersalzberg–Hintereck; the round-trip journey costs 7 DM ($4.90). From Obersalzberg (Hintereck) the special mountain bus to the Kehlstein parking lot leaves every half-hour. The ticket price of 20 DM ($14) includes the elevator ride to the top.

3 Innsbruck & the Tyrol

Land of ice and mountains, dark forests and alpine meadows full of spring wildflowers, summer holidays and winter sports—that's Tyrol. Those intrepid tourists, the British, discovered its holiday delights and made it a fashionable destination in the last century. Munich is only a few hours away, and even the Bavarians head for Tyrol when they want a change of scenery. Tyrol is the most frequented winter playground in Austria, and in summer the extensive network of mountain paths lures visitors.

Skiers flock here in winter for a ski season that runs from mid-December to the end of March. Many prefer its ski slopes to those of Switzerland, and Tyrol has produced such great skiers as Toni Sailer. It's been a long time since the eyes of the world focused on Innsbruck at the Winter Olympics in 1964 and 1976, but the legacy lives on in the ski conditions and facilities on some of the world's choicest slopes.

ONLY IN THE TYROL

A Stroll Through Innsbruck's Altstadt (Old Town) All tours of the medieval center begin at the Goldenes Dachl, or "Golden Roof," a three-story balcony on a late-gothic mansion capped with 2,657 gold-plated tiles. Emperor Maximilian I used the balcony as a royal box to watch tournaments in the square below. From this central point you can wander around at leisure—each street holds interest, sighteeing highlights, shops, and cafes where you can take a break.

Standing on Top of the Hungerburg This mountain plateau at 2,860 feet overlooking Innsbruck is the most beautiful spot in the Tyrol, a province known for its panoramic beauty. To stand here on a summer night, watching the fountains and the floodlit buildings of Innsbruck below, is worth the trip to Austria. In the unlikely event you won't be satisfied with this view, you can take a cable railway even higher to the Seegrube and the Hafelekar at 7,655 feet for a sweeping view of alpine peaks and glaciers. Mountain scenery rarely gets more spectacular than this.

Skiing on the Arlberg The mecca of the serious skier, the Arlberg has peaks that top the 9,000-foot mark. Its vast network of lifts, cableways, runs stretching for miles, and a world-renowned ski school introduce you to skiing as you'll rarely encounter it. A good base for this adventure is St. Anton am Arlberg, on the eastern side of the Arlberg. Alpine skiing as it's known today was launched from here at a point 71 miles west of Innsbruck. St. Anton's is a virtual cradle of alpine skiing.

Hiking in the Alps From June through September, hikers and climbers flock to the area around Innsbruck for the walks and climbs of a lifetime. Hikers take cable-car lifts to trails across lofty plateaus. The Innsbruck tourist office distributes a free brochure filled with tips about the best trails. For those who'd like to learn to climb, the Alpine School Innsbruck, In der Stille 1, Natters (☎ **0512/546000-0**), offers lessons.

The Ski Circus at Kitzbühel At one of the most famous resorts in the Tyrol, you can ski downhill for more than 50 miles. Runs suit every stage of proficiency. Because the terrain is so ideal, numerous championship ski events are held here, including the World Cup event each January. The so-called "circus" is an intricately linked and carefully planned combination of runs, cable railways, and lifts, designed to give you one of the great ski experiences of a lifetime.

Alpine Après-Ski Life   Many visitors flock here not for the skiing but the après-ski life. It's an institution unto itself. Each resort from Innsbruck to Seefeld has its own peculiar flavor and *joie de vivre,* and you'll quickly find the spot suitable for you. Notices of the "big events" of the evening are posted around the resorts, and patrons quickly learn what's "hot" on any given night. Hockey games, holiday parties, sleigh trips into secluded valleys, and toboggan rides are also part of the never-ending après-ski life.

INNSBRUCK

Innsbruck is a city with a long imperial past, and even though it is littered with cultural artifacts of a bygone era, most visitors don't come for the history but for the mountains. Alpine peaks surround Innsbruck, protecting it from the cold winds of the north (we've seen vegetable gardens growing in January).

Innsbruck has a particularly lovely medieval town center, and this historic Altstadt has been protected by town planners. New structures in the inner city are in harmony with the gothic, Renaissance, and baroque buildings already standing, and modern urban development spreads along the Inn River east and west, away from the center. Visitors can take countless excursions in the environs. At the doorstep of Innsbruck lie some of the most beautiful drives in Europe. Just take your pick: Head in any direction, up any valley, and you'll be treated to mountains and alpine beauty almost unmatched anywhere else, including Switzerland.

Innsbruck is easily reached from Salzburg (118 miles to the northeast) and from Munich (99 miles to the north). But it's a long, 304-mile haul west of Vienna.

ORIENTATION

ARRIVING   By Plane   Innsbruck's airport, **Flughafen Innsbruck-Kranebitten,** Fürstenweg 180 (☎ **0512/22525**), is 2 miles west of the city. It offers regularly scheduled air service from all major Austrian airports and from most major European cities. Tyrolean Airlines (☎ **0512/222277**) services the airport exclusively, although some foreign carriers will charter flights.

From the airport, bus line F leads to the center of the city. Tickets cost 21 AS ($2). A taxi ride takes about 10 minutes, costing 80 AS ($7.60) or more.

By Train   Innsbruck is connected with all parts of Europe by international railway links. Arrivals are at the **Hauptbahnhof,** Südtiroler Platz (☎ **0512/17-17** for all rail information). Frequent trains pull in here from all major European and Austrian cities. There are at least five daily trains from Munich (trip time: 3 hours); from Salzburg, eight trains per day arrive (trip time: 1 hour).

By Bus   Bus service to all Austrian cities is provided by both Postal Buses and Federal Railway Buses. You can take a bus from Salzburg, although the train is more efficient. For central information about various bus routings through Tyrol, call **0512/58-51-55.**

By Car   If you're driving down from Salzburg in the northeast, take Autobahn A-8 west, which joins Autobahn A-93 (later it becomes the A-12), heading southwest to Innsbruck. This latter autobahn (A-93/A-12) is the main artery in from Munich. From the south you can take the Brenner toll motorway.

VISITOR INFORMATION   The **tourist office,** located at Burggraben 3 (☎ **0512/59850**), is open daily 8am–6pm. It will supply you with a wealth of information, as well as a list of inexpensive private rooms for rent in Innsbruck. On the first floor of the same building is **Innsbruck-Information** (☎ **0512/5356**), which arranges tours, sells concert tickets, and makes hotel reservations. It's open daily 8am–7pm.

CITY LAYOUT   This historic city is divided by the Inn River into left- and right-bank districts The Inn has two major crossings, the **Universitätssbrücke** and the **Alte Innsbrücke (Old Inn Bridge).** Many of the attractions, including the Hofkirche and the Goldenes Dachl, are on the right. If you arrive at the Hauptbahnhof, take Salurner Strasse and Brixener Strasse to Maria-Theresien-Strasse, which will put you into the very heart of Innsbruck.

The **Altstadt** is bounded on the north by the Inn River and on the south by Burggraben and Marktgrabben. The main street of this historic district is **Herzog-Friedrich-Strasse,** which becomes **Maria-Theresien-Strasse,** the axis of the postmedieval new part of town. The Altstadt becomes strictly pedestrian after 10:30am (wear good shoes on the cobblestone streets).

GETTING AROUND   A network of three **tram** and 25 **bus** lines covers all of Innsbruck and its environs. Single tickets in the central area cost 21 AS ($2), and a booklet of four tickets goes for 44 AS ($4.20). For information about various routes, call the Innsbrucker Verkehrsbetriebe (☎ **0512/53070**). Tickets can be purchased at the Innsbruck tourist office (see above), tobacco shops, and vending machines.

Postal buses leave from the Central Bus Station, adjacent to the Hauptbahnhof on Sterzinger Strasse. Here buses head for all parts of Tyrol. The station is open Mon–Fri 7am–5:30pm and Sat 7am–1pm. For information about bus schedules, call **0512/58-51-55.**

Taxi stands are in all parts of town, or you can call a radio car (☎ **0512/5311**). You can take a ride in a **fiacre** (horse-drawn carriage), starting in front of Tiroler Landestheater, Rennweg. The cost for a ride is about 500 AS ($47.50) for an hour-and-a-half trot around the city.

Bikes can be rented at the Hauptbahnhof, the main rail station. The cost is 90 AS ($8.55) per day, although if you carry a Eurail or Interrail pass, the charge drops to only 45 AS ($4.30) per day. You can return bikes to any rail station in Austria if you don't plan to come back to Innsbruck. Bicycle rentals are available only from April to early November.

For exploring Tyrol by car, try **Avis,** Salurner Strasse 15 (☎ **0512/57-17-54**), open Mon–Fri 7:30am–6pm, Sat 8am–1pm, and Sun 9am–noon. An Opal or Ford Fiesta rental with unlimited mileage and collision insurance begins at about 1,273 AS ($120.95) per day. There's also a branch of **Hertz** in Innsbruck at Südtirolerplatz 1 (☎ **0512/58-09-01**), across from the Hauptbahnhof, open Mon–Fri 7:30am–6pm and Sat 8am–1pm (closed Sun). They rent the same cars with unlimited mileage and basic liability insurance for 993 AS ($94.35).

FAST FACTS: Innsbruck

American Express   The office at Brixnerstrasse 3 (☎ 0512/58-24-91) is open Mon–Fri 9am–5:30pm and Sat 9am–noon.

Baby-sitters   For an English-speaking baby-sitter, call Baby-sitter Zentrale (☎ 0512/29-41-32), Tues 9–11am or Wed–Thurs 4:30–6pm. Most hotel concierges will make arrangements for you.

Dentist/Doctor   The tourist office (see above) will supply a list of private English-speaking dentists and doctors in the Innsbruck area. Or you can contact the University Clinic, Anichstrasse 35 (☎ 0512/504).

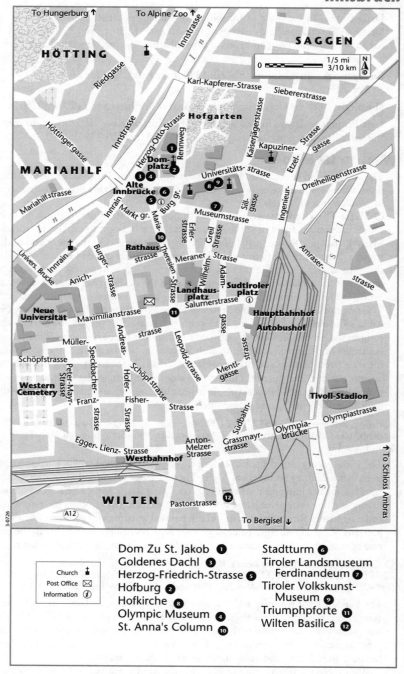

Innsbruck

To Hungerburg ↑ To Alpine Zoo ↑

HÖTTING

SAGGEN

0 1/5 mi
3/10 km

Karl-Kapferer-Strasse

Siebererstrasse

Innstrasse

Riedgasse

Höttinger gasse

Hofgarten

Herzog-Otto-Strasse

Rennweg

Kaiserjägerstrasse

Kapuziner- Strasse

MARIAHILF

①
Dom-
platz

②

Universitäts- strasse

Etzel- gasse

Dreiheiligenstrasse

③ ④

Alte
Innbrücke ⑥

⑤

Burg gr.

⑧ ⑨

Sill gasse

Ingenieur-

Mariahilfstrasse

Innrain

Markt gr.

Maria-

Museumstrasse

⑦

Amraser-

strasse

Univers. Brücke

Innrain

Burger-

strasse

Anich-

strasse

Theresien -Strasse

Erler- strasse

Meraner - Strasse

Wilhelm-

Greil Strasse

Adam-

⑩

Rathaus

Neue
Universität

Maximilianstrasse

Landhaus-
platz

Sudtiroler
platz

Salurnerstrasse

⑪

gasse

Hauptbahnhof

Autobushof

Müller-

Andreas-

strasse

Leopold-strasse

Mentl- gasse

Südbahn- strasse

Schöpfstrasse

Peter-Mayr-Strasse

Speckbacher-

strasse

Hofer-

Schöpf strasse

Fisher-

Strasse

Tivoli-Stadion

Western
Cemetery

Franz- strasse

Strasse

Olympiastrasse

Egger- Lienz- Strasse

Anton-
Melzer-
Strasse

Grassmayr- strasse

Olympia-
brücke

→ To Schloss Ambras

Westbahnhof

WILTEN Pastorstrasse **⑫**

(A12)

To Bergisel ↓

3-0726

Church ✝
Post Office ✉
Information ⓘ

Dom Zu St. Jakob **①**
Goldenes Dachl **③**
Herzog-Friedrich-Strasse **⑤**
Hofburg **②**
Hofkirche **⑧**
Olympic Museum **④**
St. Anna's Column **⑩**

Stadtturm **⑥**
Tiroler Landsmuseum
Ferdinandeum **⑦**
Tiroler Volkskunst-
Museum **⑨**
Triumphpforte **⑪**
Wilten Basilica **⑫**

Drugstores   In the heart of Innsbruck, St.-Anna Apotheke, Maria-Theresien-Strasse 4 (☎ 0512/58-58-47), is open Mon–Fri 8am–12:30pm and 2:30–6pm and Sat 8am–noon, and posts addresses of other pharmacies open on weekends or late at night.

Emergencies   In case of trouble, call 133 for the police, 122 for a fire, or 144 for an ambulance.

Hospitals   Try the University Clinic, located at Anichstrasse 35 (☎ 0512/504).

Lost Property   If you lose something (other than on a bus or train), go to the Bundespolizeidirektion, Kaiserjägerstrasse 8 (☎ 0512/5900-3395).

WHAT TO SEE & DO

The Altstadt and the surrounding Alpine countryside are Innsbruck's main attractions. Often it's fascinating just to watch the passersby, who are occasionally attired in Tyrolean regional dress.

✪ **Maria-Theresien-Strasse,** which cuts through the heart of the city from north to south, is the main street of Innsbruck, a good place to begin to explore Innsbruck. Many 17th- and 18th-century houses line this wide street. On the south end of the street, a Triumphpforte (Triumphal Arch), modeled after those in Rome, spans the shopping street. Maria Theresa ordered it built in 1765 with a twofold purpose: to honor her son's marriage and to commemorate the death of her beloved husband, Emperor Franz I. From this arch southward the street is called Leopoldstrasse.

Going north from the arch along Maria-Theresien-Strasse you'll see **Annasäule (St. Anna's Column)** in front of the 19th-century Rathaus (the present town hall). The column was erected in 1706 to celebrate the withdrawal in 1703 of invading Bavarian armies during the War of the Spanish Succession. Not far north of the Annasäule, the wide street narrows and becomes Herzog-Friedrich-Strasse, running through the heart of the medieval quarter. This street is arcaded and flanked by a number of well-maintained burghers' houses with their jumble of turrets and gables. Look for the multitude of dormer windows and oriels.

Hofburg. Rennweg 1. ☎ **0512/58-71-86.** Admission 50 AS ($4.30) adults, 20 AS ($1.90) students, 10 AS (95¢) children under 12. May–Oct daily 9am–5pm; Nov–Apr Mon–Sat 9am–5pm. Tram: 1 or 3.

The 15th-century imperial palace of Emperor Maximilian I was rebuilt in rococo style in the 18th century on orders of Maria Theresa. Later it held sad memories for the empress, for her husband died here in 1765. The palace, flanked by a set of domed towers, is a fine example of baroque secular architecture. The structure has four wings and a two-story Riesensaal (Giant's Hall), painted in white and gold and filled with portraits of the Habsburgs. You can visit the state rooms, the house chapel, the private apartment, and the Riesensaal on a guided tour, lasting about half an hour.

✪ **Goldenes Dachl (Golden Roof).** Herzog-Friedrich-Strasse 15. Admission to City Tower, 22 AS ($2.10) adults, 11 AS ($1.05) children. Museum, daily 9am–5pm. Tower, Mar–June and Sept–Oct daily 10am–5pm; July–Aug daily 10am–6pm. Closed Nov–Feb. Tram: 1 or 3.

The Golden Roof is Innsbruck's greatest tourist attraction, certainly its most characteristic landmark. It's a three-story balcony on a house in the Altstadt; the late-gothic oriels are capped with 2,657 gold-plated tiles. It was constructed for Emperor Maximilian I in the beginning of the 16th century to serve as a royal box where he could sit in luxury and enjoy tournaments in the square below.

With the same ticket, you can also visit the **Stadtturm (City Tower),** Herzog-Friedrich-Strasse 21 (☎ **0512/57-59-62**). Formerly a prison cell, the tower dates from the mid-1400s and stands adjacent to the Rathaus. Its top affords a panoramic view of the city rooftops and the mountains beyond. It's open daily 10am–5pm (July–Aug until 6pm).

Museums & Churches

The most important treasure in the **Hofkirche**, Universitätsstrasse 2 (☎ 0512/58-43-02), is the cenotaph of Maximilian I, although his remains, alas, are not in the elegant marble sarcophagus, a great feat of German Renaissance style. It has 28 bronze 16th-century statues of Maximilian's real and legendary ancestors surrounding the kneeling emperor on the cenotaph, with 24 marble reliefs on the sides depicting scenes from his life. Admission is 20 AS ($1.90) adults, 15 AS ($1.45) students, 10 AS (95¢) children under 15; open Mon–Sat 9am–5:30pm.

The **Dom zu St. Jakob (Cathedral of St. James),** Domplatz 6 (☎ 0512/58-39-02), was designed and rebuilt from 1717 to 1724 by Johann Jakob Herkommer. It has a lavishly embellished baroque interior, partly the work of the Asam brothers. A chief treasure is the *Maria Hilf (St. Mary of Succor),* painted by Lucas Cranach the Elder, on the main altar. It's open in winter daily 7:30am–6:30pm; summer daily 7:30am–7:30pm; closed Fri noon–3pm. Both churches can be reached on tram 1 or 3.

The **Tiroler Landesmuseum Ferdinandeum (Ferdinandeum Tyrol Museum),** Museumstrasse 15 (☎ 0512/59-489), has a gallery of Flemish and Dutch masters, and also traces the development of popular art in the Tyrolean country. You'll also see the original bas-reliefs used in designing the Goldenes Dachl. Admission is 50 AS ($4.75) adults, 20 AS ($1.90) children. Open May–Sept Fri–Wed 10am–5pm, Thurs 10am–5pm, and 7–9pm; Oct–Apr Tues–Sat 10am–noon and 2–5pm, Sun 10am–1pm. The **Tiroler Volkskunst-Museum (Tyrol Museum of Popular Art),** Universitätsstrasse 2 (☎ 0512/58-43-02), is in the Neues Stift, or New Abbey, and adjoins the Hofkirche on its eastern side. The museum contains one of the largest and most impressive collections extant of Tyrolean artifacts, ranging from handcrafts, furniture, Christmas cribs, and national costumes to religious and profane popular art. Admission is 40 AS ($3.80) adults, 15 AS ($1.45) children; open Mon–Sat 9am–5pm, Sun 9am–noon. Both museums can be reached by taking tram 1 or 3.

Zoos & Views

Alpenzoo. Weiherburggasse 37. ☎ **0512/29-23-23.** Admission 60 AS ($5.70) adults, 30 AS ($2.85) children 6–15, free for children 5 and under. Winter daily 9am–5pm; other seasons daily 9am–6pm. Bus: 2 (May 15–Sept only). Tram: 1 or 6 to the Hungerburgbahn (cog railway).

From this zoo, lying on the southern slope of the Hungerburg plateau, you'll get a panoramic view of Innsbruck and the surrounding mountains. The zoo contains only those animals indigenous to the Alps, plus alpine birds, reptiles, and fish. More than 800 animals belong to more than 140 different and sometimes rare species, including otters, eagles, elk, rabbits, vultures, wildcats, bison, and wolves.

✪ Hungerburg

The Hungerburg mountain plateau (2,860 feet) is the most beautiful spot in Tyrol, affording the best view of Innsbruck, especially on summer nights when much of the city, including fountains and historic buildings, is floodlit. You can drive to the plateau, or take the funicular, which departs about four times an hour 9am–8pm, then about every 30 minutes until 10:30pm; Fri–Sat nights until 11pm. The departure point for the funicular lies about half a mile east of the center of Innsbruck, at the corner of Rennweg and Kettenbrücke. (It's accessible from Innsbruck's center via tram no. 1 or bus C.) Round-trip fares are 50 AS ($4.75) for adults and 30 AS ($2.85) for children. For schedules and information, call **0512/29-22-50.**

Once you reach the plateau, you can progress even farther into the alpine wilds via the Nordkette cable railway, which will take you up to the Seegrube and the Hafelekar (7,655 feet) for a sweeping view of peaks and glaciers. This is the starting point of high mountain walks and climbing expeditions. In summer, the cable railway runs daily every hour 8am–6pm. A round-trip from Innsbruck to Hafelekar and back costs 284 AS ($27) for adults and 179 AS ($17) for children.

Outdoor Activities

Five sunny snow-covered, avalanche-free ski areas around the Tyrol are served by 5 cableways, 44 chairlifts, and ski hoists. The area is also known for bobsled and toboggan runs and ice-skating rinks.

In summer you can enjoy playing tennis at a number of courts, golfing on either a 9- or an 18-hole course, horseback riding, mountaineering, gliding, swimming, hiking, and shooting.

The **Hofgarten,** a public park containing lakes and many shade trees, lies north of Rennweg.

ORGANIZED TOURS

Short sightseeing tours of the town by bus are organized by an affiliate of Innsbruck's tourist office. Lasting about an hour, they depart from the Hofburg four times a day, at 10:15am, noon, 2pm, and 3:15pm. Tickets for the tour are available from the Innsbruck tourist information office at Burggraben 3 (☎ **0512/5356**). The cost is 150 AS ($14.25).

The tourist office also offers a 2-hour bus tour of the major monuments that departs from in front of the main railway station daily at 10am and 2pm (and July–Aug at noon) and costs 200 AS ($19); it ends with a 20-minute walking tour through parts of the Altstadt.

Daily bus excursions from Innsbruck to the most beautiful parts of Tyrol—including the Zillertal, Alpbach, and Kühtai—as well as visits across the border to northern Italy and southern Germany, can be arranged through the tourist office, your hotel, or any travel agency.

SHOPPING

You'll find a large selection of Tyrolean specialties and all sorts of skiing and mountain-climbing equipment. Stroll around Maria-Theresien-Strasse, Herzog-Friedrich-Strasse, and Museumstrasse, ducking in and making discoveries of your own. Here are some suggestions.

Lanz, Wilhelm-Greil-Strasse 15 (☎ **0512/58-31-05**), carries everything you'd need to look authentically Tyrolean—dirndls, lederhosen, hand-knit sweaters, sport coats, and accessories. The store sells children's clothing and apparel for men too. Open Mon–Fri 9am–6pm and Sat 9am–noon. **Lodenbaur,** Brixner Strasse 4 (☎ **0512/58-09-11**), is also devoted to regional Tyrolean dress, most of which is made in Austria. There's a full array for men, women, and children. Open Mon–Fri 9am–6pm and Sat 9am–noon.

Tiroler Heimatwerk, Meraner Strasse 2 (☎ **0512/58-23-20**), is one of the best stores in Innsbruck for handcrafted sculpture and pewter, carved chests, and furniture. The store carries textiles, lace, bolts of silk, and dress patterns for those who want to whip up their own dirndl (or whatever). The elegant decor includes ancient stone columns and vaulted ceilings. Open Mon–Fri 9am–6pm and Sat 9am–noon.

Zinnreproduktionen Rudolf Boschi, Kiebachgasse 8 (☎ **0512/58-92-24**), uses old molds discovered in abandoned Tyrolean factories to produce fine reproductions of century-old regional pewter at reasonable prices. Mr. Boschi also reproduces rare pewter objects acquired from auctions throughout Europe. Look for a copy of the 18th-century pewter barometer emblazoned with representations of the sun and the four winds. The work is done in a nearby foundry south of Innsbruck.

ACCOMMODATIONS
Very Expensive

✪ **Hotel Europa Tyrol.** Südtirolerplatz 2, A-6020 Innsbruck. ☎ **800/223-5652** in the U.S. and Canada, or 0512/5931. Fax 0512/58-78-00. 110 rms, 12 suites. MINIBAR TV TEL. 2,600–3,100 AS ($247–$294.50) double; from 5,000 AS ($475) suite. Rates include breakfast. AE, DC, MC, V. Parking 140 AS ($13.30).

Opposite Innsbruck's railway station, this elegant hotel has a formal paneled lobby with an English-style bar, accents of green marble, and oriental rugs. The rooms and suites are handsomely furnished, with all the modern conveniences and Tyrolean or Biedermeier-style decorations. Each tasteful unit offers a radio, a marble bathroom, and a hair dryer. The restaurant Europa Stüberl, the finest in Innsbruck, is recommended separately.

Expensive

✪ **Romantikhotel-Restaurant Schwarzer Adler.** Kaiserjägerstrasse 2, A-6020 Innsbruck. ☎ **0512/58-71-09.** Fax 0512/56-16-97. 26 rms, 2 suites. MINIBAR TV TEL. 1,680–1,840 AS ($159.60–$174.80) double; from 2,100 AS ($199.50) suite. Half board 310 AS ($29.45) per person extra. Rates include breakfast. AE, DC, MC, V. Parking 90 AS ($8.55). Tram: 1 or 3.

The hotel lies behind an antique facade of stucco, shutters, and a big-windowed tower. Its owners, the Ultsch family, have furnished the interior in an authentic Austrian style with lots of charm. Aged paneling, vaulted ceilings, hand-painted regional furniture, antiques, and lots of homey clutter make for a cozy and inviting ambience. The original Tiroler Stube has a history going back four centuries, and the K. u K. (Kaiser und König) Restaurant has won awards for its modern Austrian cuisine.

Moderate

✪ **Hotel Goldener Adler.** Herzog-Friedrich-Strasse 6, A-6020 Innsbruck. ☎ **0512/58-63-34.** Fax 0512/58-44-09. 35 rms, 2 suites. MINIBAR TV TEL. 1,460–2,100 AS ($138.70–$199.50) double; from 2,600 AS ($247) suite. Rates include breakfast. AE, DC, MC, V. Parking 132 AS ($12.55). Tram: 1 or 3.

Even the phone booth near the reception desk of this 600-year-old hotel is outfitted in antique style, concealed behind an old panel. Famous guests have included Goethe and the violinist Paganini, who cut his name into the windowpane of his room. The handsomely styled rooms in this family-run hotel sport leaded windows with stained-glass inserts, travertine floors, ornate carved Tyrolean furniture, and chandeliers with figures carved from rams' horns.

Hotel Maria Theresia. Maria-Theresien-Strasse 31, A-6020 Innsbruck. ☎ **800/528-1234** in the U.S. and Canada, or 0512/5933. Fax 0512/57-56-19. 105 rms, 2 suites. MINIBAR TV TEL. 1,500–2,200 AS ($142.50–$209) double; from 2,200 AS ($209) suite. Rates include American breakfast. AE, DC, MC, V. Parking 140 AS ($13.30). Tram: 1 or 3.

This Best Western hotel with its elegantly classic facade is on Innsbruck's famous shopping street a few blocks away from the winding alleys of the oldest parts of the city. A striking oil portrait of the empress herself hangs in the reception area. The helpful staff will do everything possible to make you feel comfortable. All rooms have been recently redecorated. The Restaurant Tyrol serves a local and international cuisine.

Inexpensive

City-Hotel Goldene Krone. Maria-Theresien-Strasse 46, A-6020. Innsbruck. ☎ **0512/ 58-61-60.** Fax 0512/580-18-96. 35 rms, 2 suites. TV. 880–1,320 AS ($83.60–$125.40) double; from 1,980 AS ($188.10) suite. Rates include breakfast. AE, MC, V. Bus: A, H, K, or N. Tram: 1.

Near the Triumphal Arch on Innsbruck's main street, this baroque house with its green-and-white facade offers three-star comfort: modern, well-maintained rooms, an elevator, soundproof windows, and a Viennese-inspired coffeehouse/restaurant, the Art Gallery-Café, where a salad buffet is set up daily 11:30am–2pm. The cafe/ restaurant is open Mon–Sat 7am–9pm.

☉ Gasthof-Hotel Weisses Kreuz. Herzog-Friedrich-Strasse 31, A-6020 Innsbruck. ☎ **0512/ 59479.** Fax 0512/59-47-990. 39 rms (28 with bath). TEL. 780–820 AS ($74.10–$77.90) double without bath, 1,020–1,120 AS ($96.90–$106.40) double with bath. Rates include breakfast. AE, MC, V. Parking 100 AS ($9.50). Tram: 1 or 3.

This atmospheric and historic inn located in the center of Innsbruck has not changed much during its lifetime, except for the addition of an elevator, which now carries newcomers up two flights to the reception area. In 1769, 13-year-old Wolfgang Mozart and his father, Leopold, stayed here. The hotel's facade is graced by an extended bay window, stretching from the second to the fourth floor.

DINING

Expensive

☉ Europastüberl. In the Hotel Europa Tyrol, Brixnerstrasse 6. ☎ **0512/5931.** Reservations required. Main courses 235–295 AS ($22.35–$28.05); fixed-price menu 500 AS ($47.50). AE, DC, MC, V. Daily 11:30am–3pm and 6pm–midnight. AUSTRIAN/INTERNATIONAL.

This distinguished restaurant with its delightful Tyrolean ambience serves both the hotel guests and the general public. Traditional regional and creative cookery is the chef's motto. Fresh Tyrolean trout almost always appears on the menu, and meat dishes range from red deer ragoût to saddle of venison to such exotica as fried jelly of calf's head Vienna style with a lamb's tongue salad. Many dishes are served for two people, including roast pike-perch with vegetables and buttery potatoes, and Bresse guinea hen roasted and served with an herb sauce.

☉ Restaurant Goldener Adler. Herzog-Friedrich-Strasse 6. ☎ **0512/58-63-34.** Reservations recommended. Main courses 100–275 AS ($9.50–$26.15); daily platters 85–160 AS ($8.05–$15.20). AE, DC, MC, V. Daily 11am–3pm and 6–11pm. Tram: 1 or 3. AUSTRIAN.

Richly Teutonic, this beautifully decorated restaurant has a firm reputation and a loyal following. All four dining rooms serve the same menu. This is good hearty fare; the chefs aren't into subtlety. Daily platter selections include braised beef, Tyrolean-style veal, and noodles with sauerkraut.

Moderate

Altstadtstüberl. Riesengasse 13. ☎ **0512/58-23-47.** Reservations recommended. Main courses 125–225 AS ($11.90–$21.40). AE, DC, MC, V. Mon–Sat 11am–3:30pm and 6–10pm. Tram: 1 or 3. AUSTRIAN.

This restaurant, located on the street level of a building whose walls date from 1360, has a cozy ambience and a flavorful cuisine. There's a salad buffet of fresh ingredients, along with several different kinds of wursts (sausages) and such specialties as rack of lamb and roulade of beef and pork.

Hirschen-Stuben. Kiebachgasse 5. ☎ **0512/58-29-79.** Reservations recommended. Main courses 150–235 AS ($14.25–$22.35); fixed-price lunch 90–140 AS ($8.55–$13.30). MC, V. Tues–Sat 11am–2pm; Mon–Sat 6–11pm. Tram: 1 or 3. AUSTRIAN/ITALIAN.

Beneath a vaulted ceiling in a house built in 1631, Hirshchen-Stuben is charming, well established, and well recommended. Down a short flight of stairs from the street, you'll find hand-chiseled stone columns, brocade chairs, and a warm ambience that is especially attractive in spring, autumn, and winter. The food is well prepared and the staff is charming. Menu items include steaming platters of pasta, fish soup, trout meunière, and sliced veal in cream sauce Zurich style.

Inexpensive

Ⓢ **Restaurant Ottoburg.** Herzog-Friedrich-Strasse 1. ☎ **0512/57-46-52.** Reservations recommended. Main courses 88–235 AS ($8.35–$22.35); two-course fixed-price lunch 98 AS ($9.30). AE, DC, MC, V. Daily 11am–3pm and 5–11pm. Tram: 1 or 3. AUSTRIAN/INTERNATIONAL.

This historic restaurant was originally established around 1745. It occupies two floors of a 13th-century building that some historians say is the oldest in Innsbruck. Inside, four intimate and atmospheric dining rooms with a 19th-century neogothic decor are scattered over two different floors. Dishes include venison stew, a special mixed grill, and fried trout.

Ⓢ **Stiegl-Bräu Innsbruck.** Wilhelm-Griel-Strasse 25. ☎ **0512/58-43-38.** Main courses 110–210 AS ($10.45–$19.95). No credit cards. Daily 10am–midnight (last orders at 11pm). Tram: 1 or 3. AUSTRIAN/INTERNATIONAL.

One of the most reliable and atmospheric of the cost-conscious restaurants of Innsbruck, this animated beerhall–restaurant is owned by a Salzburg-based brewery (Stiegl-Bräu). It contains three different dining rooms on two floors as well as an outdoor beer garden in summer. Well-prepared salads, roasts, schnitzels, sausages, and stews are the straightforward fare here.

INNSBRUCK AFTER DARK

The major venue for performing arts is the **Landestheater,** Rennweg 2 (☎ **0512/520744**). The theater offers a variety of programs. The box office is open Mon–Sat 8:30am–8:30pm, and performances usually begin at 7:30 or 8pm. Tickets cost 80–450 AS ($7.60–$42.75) for opera, 80–435 AS ($7.60–$41.35) for theater. Concerts are often presented at the Kunstpavillon in the **Hofgarten** in summer.

Bars, Clubs & Folk Music

In summer, the outdoor bar at **Club Filou,** Stiftsgasse 12 (☎ **0512/58-02-56**), blossoms with ivy-covered trellises and parasols. Inside you'll find an intimate hangout filled with Victorian settees and pop art. In a separate, very old room is the disco, with a ceiling is supported by medieval stone columns and ringed with a high-tech steel balcony. Long drinks in both the cafe and disco begin at around 68 AS ($6.45); a beer costs 38 AS ($3.60). The cafe is open daily 6pm–4am; the disco is open daily 9pm–4am. Food is available until 3am.

If you want to try an award-winning martini, go to **Sparkling Cocktails,** Innstrasse 45 (☎ **0512/28-78-80**). At this bar, virtually any kind of mixed drink or cocktail, including an almost lethal zombie, can be crafted by the highly experienced staff. Drinks range from 68 to 125 AS ($6.45 to $11.90), and are served Mon–Sat 7pm–2am.

Treibhaus, Angerzellgasse 8 (☎ **0512/58-68-74**), is the gathering place for young people. Within its battered walls, you can attend a changing roster of art exhibitions, cabaret shows, and protest rallies, daily from 10am to 1am, with live music presented at erratic intervals. Cover for live performances are 180–250 AS ($17.10–$23.75).

The **Goethe Stube,** Restaurant Goldener Adler, Herzog-Friedrich-Strasse 6 (☎ **0512/58-63-34**), offers authentic folk music programs that include the zither and "jodlers" throughout the Christmas–New Year's season, Easter, and the winter season. There's no cover, but a one-drink minimum; a large beer costs 40 AS ($3.80); meals start at 180 AS ($17.10). Open 7pm–midnight.

For adult entertainment, **Nightclub Lady-O,** Bruneckerstrasse 2 (☎ **0512/ 56-33-61**), has a collection of female artistes and an x-rated bar. Cover is 20 AS ($1.90); drinks begin at 150 AS ($14.25). It's open daily 9pm–5am, with shows beginning at 10pm and continuing nonstop until 5am.

ST. ANTON AM ARLBERG

A modern resort has grown out of this old village on the Arlberg Pass that was the scene of ski history in the making. At St. Anton (elev. 4,225 feet), Hannes Schneider developed modern skiing techniques and began teaching tourists how to ski in 1907. The Ski Club Arlberg was born here in 1901. In 1911 the first Arlberg–Kandahar Cup competition was held. Before his death in 1955, Schneider saw his ski school rated as the world's finest. Today the school is one of the world's largest and best, with about 300 instructors (most of whom speak English). St. Anton am Arlberg in winter is quite fashionable, popular with the wealthy and occasional royalty—a more conservative segment of the rich and famous than you'll see at other posh ski resorts.

There's so much emphasis on skiing here that few seem to talk of the summertime attractions. In warm weather St. Anton is tranquil and bucolic, surrounded by meadowland. A riot of wildflowers blooming in the fields announces the beginning of spring.

St. Anton is 372 miles west of Vienna and 62 miles west of Innsbruck.

ESSENTIALS

ARRIVING   By Train   St. Anton is an express stop on the main rail lines crossing over the Arlberg Pass between Innsbruck and Bregenz. Just to the west of St. Anton trains disappear into the Arlberg tunnel, emerging almost 7 miles later on the opposite side of the mountain range. About one train per hour arrives in St. Anton from both directions. Trip time from Innsbruck is 75–85 minutes, depending on the train; from Bregenz, around 85 minutes. Because of St. Anton's good rail connections to eastern and western Austria, most visitors arrive by train.

By Bus   The town is the point of origin for many bus travelers who travel from St. Anton on to such other resorts as Zürs and Lech.

By Car   Motorists should take Route 171 west from Innsbruck.

VISITOR INFORMATION   The **tourist office** is in the Arlberghaus in the center of town (☎ **05446/22690**).

SKIING IN ST. ANTON

The snow in this area is perfect for skiers, and the total lack of trees on the slopes makes the situation ideal. The ski fields of St. Anton stretch over a distance of some 6 square miles. Beginners stick to the slopes down below, and for the more experienced skiers there are the runs from the Galzig and Valluga peaks. A cableway will take you to **Galzig** (6,860 feet), where there's a self-service restaurant. You go from here to **Vallugagrat** (8,685 feet), the highest station reached. The peak of the **Valluga,** at 9,220 feet, commands a panoramic view. St. Christoph is the mountain annex of St. Anton.

In addition to these major ski areas, there are two other important sites attracting followers of the sport: the **Gampen/Kapall** and the **Rendl.**

OTHER ACTIVITIES & ATTRACTIONS

There are many other cold-weather pursuits than just skiing, including ski jumping, mountain tours, curling, skating, tobogganing, and sleigh rides, plus après-ski on the quiet side.

The **Ski und Heimat Museum** (Skiing and Local Museum), in the Arlberg-Kandahar House (☎ 05446/2475), traces the development of skiing in the Arlberg, as well as the history of the region from the days of tribal migrations in and around Roman times. The museum, in the imposing structure at the center of the Holiday Park in St. Anton, is open Thurs–Tues in summer 10am–6pm and Mon–Sat in winter 2:30pm–midnight. Admission is 20 AS ($1.90) for adults and 10 AS (95¢) for children in winter and 10 AS (95¢) for adults, free for children in summer.

ACCOMMODATION & DINING

✪ **Hotel Schwarzer Adler.** A-6580 St. Anton am Arlberg. ☎ **800/528–1234** in the U.S. and Canada, or 05446/22440. Fax 05446/224462. 56 rms. TV TEL. Winter, 2,400–4,300 AS ($228–$408.50) double. Summer, 650–980 AS ($61.75–$93.10) per person double. Rates includes half board. AE, DC, MC, V. Closed May and Oct–Nov. Free parking.

In the center of St. Anton, this hotel has been owned and operated by the Tschol family since 1885. The beautiful building was constructed as an inn in 1570, and became known for its hospitality to pilgrims crossing the treacherous Arlberg Passresa. The beautiful 400-year-old frescoes on the exterior were discovered during a restoration, and have been faithfully restored to their original grandeur.

The hotel's interior is rustic yet elegant, including blazing fireplaces, painted Tyrolean baroque armoires, and Oriental rugs. There are handsomely furnished and well-equipped bedrooms in the main hotel, plus 13 slightly less well-furnished (but less expensive) rooms in the annex, which is across the street above the Café Aquila. There's a sauna and a fitness center. The hotel's restaurant is well known for its excellent cuisine.

✪ **Raffl-Stube.** In the Hotel St. Antoner Hof, St. Anton am Arlberg. ☎ **05446/2910.** Reservations required. Main courses 140–320 AS ($13.30–$30.40); fixed-price menu 200–350 AS ($19–$33.25). AE, DC, MC, V. Daily 11am–2pm and 7–10pm. Closed May and Nov–Dec 1. AUSTRIAN.

In an enclosed corner of the hotel's lobby with only six tables, this place in the peak of the season can get very exclusive. Reservations are imperative, especially if you're a nonresident. Overflow diners are offered a seat in a spacious but less special dining room across the hall. The hotel has long enjoyed a reputation for its cuisine, but somehow the food in the stube tastes even better. Quality ingredients are always used, and the kitchen prepares such tempting specialties as roast goose liver with salad, cream of parsley soup with sautéed quail eggs, filet of salmon with wild rice and trout "prepared as you like it," along with the ever-popular fondue bourguignonne.

SEEFELD

Seefeld, 15 miles northwest of Innsbruck, is a member of Austria's "big three" international rendezvous points for winter-sports crowds. Seefeld hosted the 1964 and 1976 nordic events for the Olympic Winter Games and the 1985 Nordic Ski World Championships. The fashionable resort lies some 3,450 feet above sea level on a sunny plateau.

ESSENTIALS

ARRIVING   By Train   More than a dozen trains per day depart from Innsbruck; trip time is around 40 minutes. There is also train service from Munich and Garmisch-Partenkirchen.

By Bus   Buses depart daily from Innsbruck's Hauptbahnhof; trip time is around 45 minutes. For bus information, call **0512/58-51-55** in Innsbruck.

By Car   From Innsbruck, head west along Route 171 until you reach the junction with Route 313, at which point turn north.

VISITOR INFORMATION   The Seefeld tourist office is located at Klosterstrasse 43 (☎ **05212/2313**).

SKIING & OTHER ACTIVITIES

Skiers are served with one funicular railway, two cable cars, three chair lifts, and 14 drag lifts. The beginner slopes lie directly in the village center. The base stations of the lifts for the main skiing areas (known as Gschwandtkopt and Rosshutte/Seefelder Joch) are at most half a mile away from the center, and are serviced by free daily non-stop bus service. There are 124 miles of prepared cross-country tracks.

Other **winter activities** offered here include curling, horse-drawn sleigh rides, out-door skating (ice-skating school, with artificial and natural ice rink), horseback riding, indoor tennis (Swedish tennis school), tube sliding (you slide on rubber inner tubes—lying or sitting), indoor golf facilities, parasailing, bowling, squash, hiking (60 miles of cleared paths), fitness studio, swimming, and saunas.

Summer visitors can enjoy swimming in three lakes, in a heated open-air swimming pool on Seefeld Lake, or at the Olympia indoor and outdoor pools. Other **summer sports** include tennis on 18 open-air and 8 indoor courts (Swedish tennis school), riding (two stables with indoor schools), and golf on the 18-hole course, which has been rated by golf insiders as one of the 100 most beautiful courses in the world. Hiking on 124 miles of walks and mountain paths, cycling, minigolf, parasailing, and rafting can also be enjoyed.

While you're based in Seefeld, it's relatively easy to explore part of Bavaria in Germany. You may or may not get to see little **Wildmoos Lake.** It can, and sometimes does, vanish all in a day or so, and then there may be cows grazing on what has become meadowland. However, the lake will suddenly come back again, and if conditions are right, it will become deep enough for swimmers. Wildmoos Lake comes and goes more frequently than Brigadoon. The little German town of **Mittenwald,** one of the highlights of Bavaria, can also be easily explored on a day trip from Seefeld.

ACCOMMODATION

✪ **Hotel Klosterbräu.** Klosterstrasse 30, A-6100 Seefeld. ☎ **05212/26210.** Fax 05212/3885. 116 rms, 20 suites. MINIBAR TV TEL. Winter, 3,000–3,800 AS ($285–$361) double; from 4,000 AS ($380) suite. Summer, 2,400–2,800 AS ($228–$266) double; from 3,600 AS ($342) suite. Rates includes breakfast. AE, DC, MC, V. Closed Apr–May and Oct–Nov. Parking 150 AS ($14.25).

The town's most unusual and elegant hostelry is constructed around a 16th-century cloister. The dramatic entrance is under a thick stucco arch. The interior contains soaring vaults supported by massive columns of the same kind of porous stone that built Salzburg (you can still see prehistoric crustaceans embedded in the stone). Posh accessories here include thick carpeting, oriental rugs, antiques, and beautifully furnished paneling. The bedrooms are encased in a towering chalet behind the front entrance.

Restaurants on the premises include a country-style Bräukeller, a rustic Tyrolean room, and a more formal dining room where guests sit below ancient ceiling vaults. Dishes include international and Austrian specialties. The person at the next table might be a vacationing celebrity traveling incognito. À la carte dinners go for 350 to 600 AS ($33.25 to $57), and reservations are necessary.

In the evening Die Kanne is a nightclub, and a daily afternoon tea dance in winter allows the hotel guests to meet one another. There are indoor and outdoor swimming pools, a sauna, health club, solarium, golf, tennis, mountain climbing, and skiing within walking distance.

DINING

Birklstüberl. Geiggenbühelstrasse 79. ☎ **05212/2322.** Reservations recommended. Main courses 130–190 AS ($12.35–$18.05). No credit cards. Wed–Mon noon–2pm and 6–9pm. Closed Easter–June 14 and Sept 16–Christmas. AUSTRIAN/TYROLEAN.

Named after the original founders, the Birkl family, and capably run today by Robert Jenewein, this straightforward restaurant is housed in a 1900 chalet with thick walls and rustic interior paneling. Well-prepared specialties include fresh meats and vegetables, soups, cheeses, and homemade desserts, such as chocolate mousse. This is a likable *beisl,* an informal and pleasantly rustic stube without gastronomic pretensions.

✪ **Restaurant Wildsee-Schlössl.** In the Sporthotel Wildsee-Schlössl, Innsbruckerstrasse 195. ☎ **05212/2390.** Reservations required. Main courses 100–250 AS ($9.50–$23.75); fixed-price menu 390 AS ($37.05) for four courses, 550 AS ($52.25) for six courses. AE, DC, MC, V. Sept–Oct, Dec–Mar, and May–June daily 7–11pm; July–Aug daily 11am–2pm and 7–11pm. Closed Apr and Nov and on Wed to nonguests. AUSTRIAN/FRENCH.

This spot is one of the finest dining rooms in a region of fierce competition. In a re-creation of a Teutonic castle beside the lake, it consists of a trio of rooms. Everything in-house is made fresh, including trout strudel with potatoes and an herb-flavored mousse-like sauce, a ravioli of sole with wine-cream sauce, and rack of veal with baby carrots and a sauce made from local butter and the veal's natural juices.

THE KITZBÜHEL ALPS

Hard-core skiers and the rich and famous are attracted to this ski region. The Kitzbühel Alps are covered with such a dense network of lifts that they now form the largest skiing complex in the country, with a series of superlative runs. The action centers on the town of Kitzbühel, but there are many satellite resorts that are much less expensive, including St. Johann in Tyrol.

Kitzbühel is, in a sense, a neighbor of Munich, 81 miles to the northeast, whose municipal airport is the entry point for most wintertime visitors.

Edward, prince of Wales (you may remember him better as the duke of Windsor), may have put Kitzbühel on the international map with his 1928 "discovery" of what was then a town of modest guesthouses. Certainly his return a few years later with Mrs. Simpson caused the eyes of the world to focus on this town, and the "upper crust" of England and other countries began flocking here, placing a stamp of elegance on Kitzbühel. At the time of this 20th-century renaissance, however, Kitzbühel itself was already some eight centuries old, and a settlement has been here much, much longer than that.

ESSENTIALS

ARRIVING   By Train   Kitzbühel sits astride the main train lines between Innsbruck and Salzburg, receiving between two and three trains per hour (many of them express) from both these cities. Trip time from Innsbruck is about 70 minutes; from Salzburg, around 2¼ hours.

By Bus   About half a dozen buses travel daily from Salzburg's main railway station to Kitzbühel, with a trip time of around 2¼ hours. Nine local bus lines run into and up the surrounding valleys. A bus runs every 30 to 60 minutes between Kitzbühel and St. Johann in Tyrol; trip time is 25 minutes.

By Car   Kitzbühel is 62 miles east of Innsbruck. From Innsbruck, take Autobahn A-12 east to the junction with Route 312 heading to Ellmau. After bypassing Ellmau, continue east to the junction with Route 342, which you take south to Kitzbühel.

VISITOR INFORMATION   The **tourist office** is at Hinterstadt 18 (☎ 05356/ 2155-0), open Mon–Sat 8am–7pm and Sun 10am–noon and 4–8pm. In winter, call **182** for snow reports.

WHAT TO SEE

The town has two main streets, both pedestrian walkways, Vorderstadt and Hinterstadt. Kitzbühel has preserved its traditional style of structure, at least along these streets. You'll see three-story stone houses with oriels and scrollwork around the doors and windows, heavy overhanging eaves, and gothic gables.

The **pfarrkirche (parish church)** was built from 1435 to 1506 and renovated in the baroque style in the 18th century. The lower part of the **Liebfrauenkirche (Church of Our Lady)** dates from the 13th century, the upper part from 1570. Between these two churches stands the **Ölbergkapelle (Ölberg Chapel)** with a 1450 "lantern of the dead" and frescoes from the latter part of the 16th century.

In the **Heimatmuseum,** Hinterstadt 34 (☎ 05356/4588 or 2236), you'll see artifacts from prehistoric European mining eras and the north alpine Bronze Age, a winter-sports section with trophies of Kitzbüheler skiing greats, and exhibits detailing the town's history. The museum is open Mon–Sat 9am–noon, charging 30 AS ($2.85) for adults and 5 AS (45¢) for children and students.

SKIING & OTHER ACTIVITIES

In winter the emphasis in Kitzbühel, 2,300 feet above sea level, is on skiing, and facilities are offered for everyone from novices to experts. The ski season starts just before Christmas and goes until late March. With more than 62 lifts, gondolas, and mountain railroads on five different mountains, Kitzbühel has two main ski areas, the Hahnenkamm (renovated in 1995) and the Kitzbüheler Horn. Cable cars are within easy walking distance, even for those in ski boots.

The linking of the lift systems on the Hahnenkamm has created the celebrated ✪ **Kitzbühel Ski Circus,** which makes it possible to ski downhill for more than 50 miles, with runs that suit every stage of proficiency. Numerous championship ski events are held here; the World Cup event each January pits the skills of top-flight skiers against the toughest, fastest downhill course in the world, a stretch of the Hahnenkamm especially designed for maximum speed. Its name, *Die Strief,* is both feared and respected among skiers. A ski pass entitles the holder to use all the lifts that form the Ski Circus.

Skiing became a fact of life in Kitzbühel as long ago as 1892, when the first pair of skis was imported from Norway and intrepid daredevils began to slide down the snowy slopes at breakneck speeds. Many great names in skiing have since been associated with Kitzbühel, the most renowned being Toni Sailer, a native of the town, who was the triple Olympic champion in the 1956 Winter Games in Cortina.

There are many other **winter activities:** ski-bobbing, ski jumping, ice skating, tobogganing, hiking on cleared trails, curling, and hang gliding, as well as such indoor activities as tennis, bowling, and swimming. The children's ski school provides training for the very young. And don't forget the lively après-ski scene, with bars, nightclubs, and dance clubs rocking from teatime until the wee hours.

Kitzbühel has **summer pastimes** too, with activities including walking tours, visits to the Wild Life Park at Aurach (about 2 miles from Kitzbühel), tennis, horseback riding, golf, squash, brass band concerts in the town center, cycling, and swimming. There's an indoor swimming pool, but we recommend going to the Schwarzsee (Black Lake). About a 15-minute walk from the center of town, this is a peat lake and has bathing establishments, boats to rent, fishing, windsurfing, a waterski school, and restaurants.

One of the region's most exotic collections of alpine flora is clustered into the jagged and rocky confines of the **Alpine Flower Garden Kitzbühel,** where various species of entian, gorse, heather, and lichens are found on the sunny slopes of the Kitzbüheler Horn. Set at a height of around 6,000 feet above sea level, the garden— which is owned and maintained as an incentive to midsummer tourism by the municipality of Kitzbühel—is open late May–early Sept daily 8:30am–5:30pm, and is at its most impressive June–Aug. Admission to the garden is free, and many visitors opt to view it by taking the Kitzbüheler Horn gondola to its uppermost station and then descending on foot via the garden's labyrinth of footpaths to the gondola's middle station. The Kitzbüheler Horn cable car, priced at 150 AS ($14.25) for round-trip transit, departs from the Kitzbühel at half-hour intervals daily throughout the summer and winter months.

ACCOMMODATIONS

Hotel Bruggerhof. Reitherstrasse 24, A-6370 Kitzbühel. ☎ **05356/2806.** Fax 05356/447–930. 25 rms. TV TEL. Winter, 1,500–1,840 AS ($142.50–$174.80) double. Summer, 1,160–1,300 AS ($110.20–$123.50) double. Rates includes half board. AE, DC, V. Free parking. Closed Apr and Oct 15–Dec 15.

About a mile west of the town center, near the Schwarzsee, is this countryside chalet with a sun terrace. Originally a farmhouse, the interior has massive ceiling beams, some carved into Tyrolean patterns, and a corner fireplace. The dining room is graced with wooden ceilings and wrought-iron chandeliers. The owners, the Reiter family, run a well-maintained hotel. Rooms are comfortable and cozy, decorated in an alpine style. A whirlpool, steam bath, and solarium are just a hint of the amenities guests enjoy year round; tennis and miniature golf facilities are available in summer.

✪ **Hotel Zur Tenne.** Vorderstadt 8–10, A-6370 Kitzbühel. ☎ **05356/4444.** Fax 05356/480356. 34 rms, 16 suites. TEL. Winter, 2,400 AS ($228) double; 3,050 AS ($289.75) suite for three. Summer, 1,750 AS ($166.25) double; 1,950 AS ($185.25) suite for three. Rates include breakfast. Half board 480 AS ($45.60) per person extra in winter, 300 AS ($28.50) in summer. AE, DC, MC, V. Free parking outdoors, 100 AS ($9.50) in covered garage nearby.

This hotel combines Tyrolean *Gemütlichkeit* with urban style and panache. The staff show genuine concern for their clientele. The hotel was created in the 1950s when a trio of 700-year-old houses was joined into one unit. The hotel sports the most luxurious health complex in town, complete with a tropical fountain, two hot tubs, a sauna, and a hot and cold foot bath. The elegant Zur Tenne Restaurant serves an international cuisine, and accommodations are glamorous—suites have fireplaces.

DINING

Ⓢ Florianistube. In the Gasthof Eggerwirt, Goensbachgasse 12. ☎ **05356/2437.** Reservations recommended. Main courses 105–250 AS ($10–$23.75). AE, DC. Daily 11am–2pm and 6–10pm. INTERNATIONAL.

Named after St. Florian, patron saint of the hearth, this restaurant is in one of the resort's less ostentatious guesthouses, and it welcomes outsiders. The menu is comprehensive for such a stube-type place—it might include typical Austrian or Tyrolean dishes, or tournedos with mushroom sauce, spaghetti with clam sauce, or fondue bourguignonne. In summer a lunch or dinner buffet is served outside under the trees of the rear garden.

✪ **Wirtshaus Unterberger-Stuben.** Wehgasse 2. ☎ **05356/2101.** Reservations recommended. Main courses 150–320 AS ($14.25–$30.40); fixed-price menus 390–850 AS ($37.05–$80.75). No credit cards. Daily noon–1:30pm and 6–10:30pm. Closed June and Nov and Tues in summer. INTERNATIONAL.

Throughout the 1980s, this was the preferred hangout for the rich and famous names from industry, media, and show-biz. Although the stars of yesteryear might have faded a bit with the passage of time, the place still has a lot of prestige, and you're likely to be served one of your finest meals in Tyrol. If it's on the menu, try a poppyseed soufflé, or one of the specialties of the many countries that once belonged to the Austrian Empire. The establishment is open for snacks, coffee, and drinks 9am–midnight (see closings, above) but meals are only served during lunch and dinner hours.

Belgium 2

by George McDonald

As capital of the European Union (EU), Brussels is now taking its place among Europe's most important cities. Outside this busy place, the Flemish-speaking towns of Bruges and Ghent and the French-speaking towns of the Meuse Valley present two aspects of Belgium, each proud of its history, language, and traditions.

1 Brussels

In a way there are two Brussels. One is the brash new "capital of Europe," increasingly aware of its power and carrying a padded expense account in its elegant leather pocketbook. The other is the old Belgian city, more than a little provincial, but well aware of the fact that emperors once held court here, trying to hang on to its heritage against the wave of Eurobuilding that has rolled over it.

The two intersect, of course, usually in someone's favorite bar or restaurant. Yet they sit uneasily together. Most foreigners who live in the city long enough, or even stay on an extended vacation, find that they need to choose between the two. It's easy enough to live in the Eurocity as a privileged outsider. Getting below the surface to the real Brussels is harder, though finally well worth the effort. As a tourist you can try to experience both and decide for yourself which you prefer.

The experience is enhanced by the fact that the Bruxellois like things convivial—always ignoring the red-clawed agressiveness that consumes them when they enter their cars—and simple for the most part, still with a sense of style. If you like deploying assorted items of cutlery over a proud regional specialty, or feel at ease contemplating the consumption of a carefully crafted artisanal beer, or think that centuries-old traditions are not only worth keeping alive but still have meaning today—why, then, you should fit right in.

ONLY IN BRUSSELS

Your First Sighting of the Grand-Place   There is nothing in Brussels quite like strolling from one of the fairly ordinary sidestreets into the Grand-Place, the city's historic square. Your first look at the timeless perfection of the cobbled square, overlooked by gabled guildhouses and the gothic tracery of the Hôtel de Ville (Town Hall) and Maison du Roi (King's House), will be unforgettable.

Brussels Attractions & Accommodations

 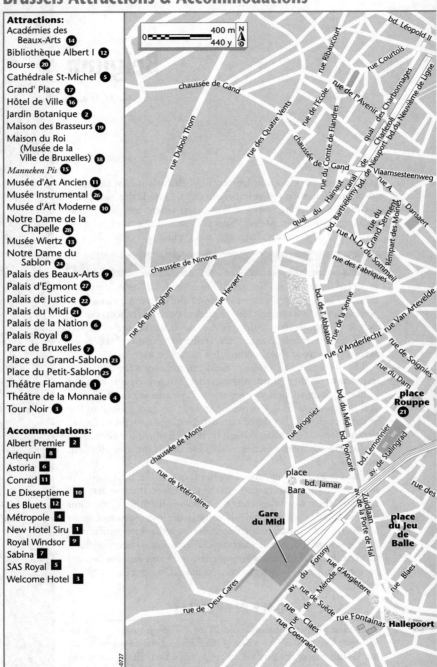

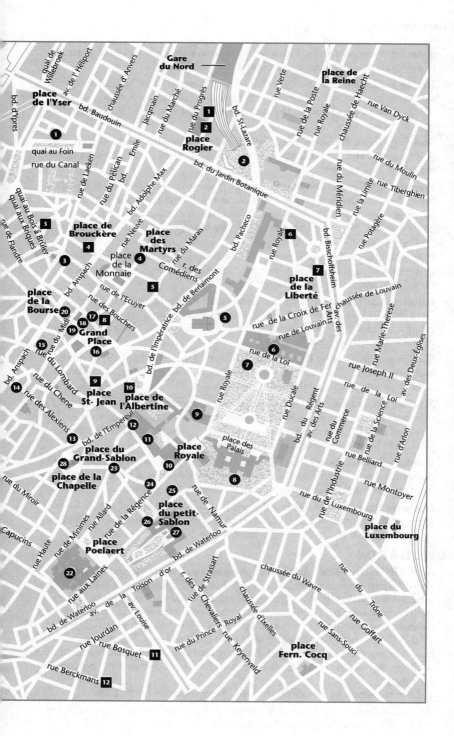

Gare du Nord

place de la Reine

place de l'Yser

quai de Willebroek
av. de l'Héliport
bd. Baudouin
chaussée d'Anvers
Jacqmain
rue du Marché
rue du Progrès
bd. St-Lazare
rue Verte
rue de la Poste
rue Royale
chaussée de Haecht
rue Van Dyck

bd. d'Ypres

1

quai au Foin
rue du Canal
rue de Laeken
rue du Pélican
bd. Emile
bd. Adolphe Max
rue Neuve
bd. du Jardin Botanique
rue du Moulin
rue du Méridien
rue de la Limite
rue Tiberghien

place Rogier

1
2

2

place de Brouckère

place des Martyrs

place de la Monnaie

rue du Marais
rue des Comédiens
bd. de Berlaimont
bd. Pacheco
rue Royale
bd. Bisschoffsheim
rue Potagère

place de la Liberté

3
4
3

4

5

6

7

quai au Bois à Brûler
quai aux Briques
rue de Flandre

place de la Bourse

bd. Anspach
rue de l'Ecuyer
rue des Bouchers
bd. de l'Impératrice

rue de la Croix de Fer
rue de Louvain
chaussée de Louvain
av. des Arts
rue Marie-Thérèse
rue Joseph II
av. des Deux-Églises

20
17
18
8
19
Grand Place
16
15
rue du Midi

rue de la Loi

6
7

rue du Lombard
rue du Chene
rue des Alexiens

14

place St-Jean

9
10
place de l'Albertine

place du Grand-Sablon

place de la Chapelle

rue du Miroir
bd. de l'Empereur

13
12
11
28
23

place Royale

10

place des Palais

9
rue Royale
rue Ducale
rue du Régent
av. des Arts
rue du Commerce
rue de la Science
rue d'Arlon
rue Belliard
rue Montoyer

8

place du Luxembourg

24
25
place du petit-Sablon

26
27

rue de Namur
rue de la Régence
rue Allard
rue de Minimes

place Poelaert

22

rue aux Laines
bd. de Waterloo
av. de la Toison d'or
av. Louise
rue de Strassart
rue des Chevaliers
Royal
chaussée du Wavre
chaussée d'Ixelles
rue du Trône
rue Goffart
rue Sans-Souci

Capucins
rue Haute

bd. de Waterloo
rue Jourdan
rue Bosquet
rue du Prince
rue Keyenveld

place Fern. Cocq

11

rue Berckmans

12

99

Shooting *Manneken-Pis*   With a camera, of course. Nobody can resist this statue of a gleefully piddling little boy. Should you be any different?

Dining at Comme Chez Soi   Three Michelin stars and just 45 places. It is probably easier to get into the kingdom of heaven than into the culinary holy-of-holies of master chef Pierre Wynant. If you do get a seat, though, you'll surely agree that heaven can wait.

Standing Under the Seven Giant Spheres of the Atomium   And hoping those seven giant spheres don't fall on your head. What on earth were its creators thinking about? Find out below.

Meeting with Bruegel and Magritte   The Historic section of the Royal Fine Arts Musea has Bruegels such as *The Fall of Icarus* and *Winter Landscape With Ice Skaters,* along with works by Rubens, Bosch, Van Dyck, Jordaens, and others. Go underground to the Modern section for works by Magritte, Delvaux, Ensor, Rops, Alechinsky, and others.

Pigging Out on Belgian Chocolates   Those devilish little critters—handmade Belgian pralines—should be sold with a government health warning, so addictive are they. Try Wittamer in place du Grand Sablon.

Enjoying Art Nouveau   Brussels considers itself the world capital of art nouveau. Local architect Victor Horta (1861–1947) was its foremost exponent and the master's colorful, sinuous style can be seen at his former home, now the Horta Museum, and in buildings dotted around the city.

Shopping at the Galeries Royales Saint-Hubert   Opened in 1847, the world's first shopping mall is a light and airy triple gallery enclosing boutiques, bookshops, cafes, restaurants, and a theater and cinema.

Strolling Around Europe   Mini-Europe, that is, a collection of emblematic buildings from the European Union's 15 member nations. These include the Leaning Tower of Pisa, Big Ben, the Acropolis, the Arc de Triomphe, and the Brandenburg Gate, all in beautifully rendered 1:25-scale detail.

Drinking Brussels Beer at Le Falstaff Cafe   A fanciful mix of art nouveau, art deco, and rococo, Falstaff boasts some of the most self-important waiters in the land. Ask them deferentially for a typical Brussels' brew, such as *gueuze.*

Hiking in the Forêt de Soignes   Brussels is a green city, and the Forêt de Soignes that stretches from the Bois de la Cambre to Waterloo is nature on the city's doorstep and a favorite place to escape maddening crowds and fuming traffic.

ORIENTATION

ARRIVING   By Plane   In addition to the national carrier Sabena, **Brussels National Airport** is served by virtually all major European airlines, as well as many other international carriers. Brussels National is at Zaventem, 9 miles from the city center. There is a direct train service to Brussels' three main stations (Gare du Nord, Gare Centrale, and Gare du Midi), operating 5:43am–11:14pm, with a one-way fare of BF 125 ($4.15) in first class and BF 85 ($2.80) in second class. Tickets are available at all railway stations—you pay more if you buy your ticket on the train. Journey time is 20 minutes to Gare du Nord, and the trains have wide corridors and extra space for baggage.

From the airport to the city center, taxis charge about BF 1,200 ($40).

By Train   Brussels is well served by high-speed trains, such as the Eurostar through the Channel Tunnel from London, the TGV from Paris, and the Thalys from Amsterdam, in addition to Eurocity (EC) and Intercity (IC) international services.

Schedule and fare information on travel in Belgium and abroad is available by calling **02/219-26-40.** Tickets are sold at all stations and through travel agents. Timetables are available at all stations, and main stations have information and reservation desks.

Travelers arriving from other European countries will probably want to get off at one of the three main stations: **Gare Centrale,** Carrefour de l'Europe 2; **Gare du Midi,** rue de France 2 (which is also the Eurostar and TGV terminal); and **Gare du Nord,** rue du Progrès 86.

By Bus   Most buses from continental destinations arrive in **rue Fonsny** beside Gare du Midi, although some stop at various city center locations around **place de Brouckère.** Many travel agents have schedules and fares. There are few really useful regional bus services within Belgium (trains do most of the work); many of those that do exist stop at **Gare du Nord.**

By Car   Anyone driving into Brussels would be well advised to park their car at the hotel car park (if it has one) and throw away the key—in a safe place, of course. For the reasons why, see "Getting Around," below.

VISITOR INFORMATION   The **Belgian Tourist Office** is located at rue du Marché-aux-Herbes 63 (☎ **02/504-03-90;** fax 02/504-02-70), and the **Tourist Information Brussels (T.I.B.)** is on the ground floor of the Hôtel de Ville (Town Hall) in the Grand-Place (☎ **02/513-89-40;** fax 02/514-40-91). T.I.B. provides very good tourist information, including the comprehensive visitors' booklet, "Brussels Guide & Map" (which has a fairly detailed street map of the inner city, with principal tourist attractions marked); makes hotel reservations; organizes paid-for guided walking tours in summer; and has well-trained, multilingual tourist guides who may be engaged by the hour or day. The Belgian Tourist Office is open Mon–Fri 9am–7pm; Sat–Sun 9am–1pm and 2–7pm. T.I.B. is open in summer daily 9am–6pm; winter Mon–Sat 9am–6pm, Sun 10am–2pm.

CITY LAYOUT   The heart-shaped inner city of Brussels—roughly 1 1/2 miles in diameter, lying within the inner ring-road that follows the line of the old city walls— is where most of the city's premier sightseeing attractions lie. **Brussels Capital Region** comprises some 62 1/2 square miles. Some 14% of the total area is occupied by parks, woods, and forest, making this one of the greenest urban centers in Europe.

The city center, once ringed by fortified ramparts, is now encircled by broad boulevards known collectively as the **Petite Ceinture.** Flat in its center and western reaches, where the now-vanished River Senne once flowed, to the east a range of low hills rises to the upper city, crowned by Royal Palace and some of the city's most affluent residential and prestigious business and shopping districts, reaching to place Stephanie and avenue Louise. The **Grand-Place** (Grote Markt in Dutch) stands at the very heart, and is both the starting point and reference point for most visitors.

GETTING AROUND   Maps of the integrated public transport network (métro, tram, and bus) are available free from the tourist office, from offices of the **S.T.I.B.** public transport company at Galerie de la Toison d'Or 20 (☎ **02/515-20-00**), and from the métro stations at Porte de Namur, place Rogier, and Gare du Midi. In addition, all stations and most bus and tram halts have maps. The full system operates 6am–midnight, after which a limited night-bus system operates.

By Métro (Subway)   While not extensive, the métro system is fast and efficient and covers many important city center locations on its 30-mile network, as well as reaching out to the suburbs. Stations are identified by signs with a white letter M on a blue background.

By Bus & Tram   Trams and urban buses are yellow, and stops are marked with red-and-white signs. Stop them by extending your arm as they approach. Tickets—which can also be used on the métro—cost BF 50 ($1.65) single (known as a "direct"); BF 230 ($7.65) for a 5-journey ticket bought from the driver; BF 320 ($10.65) for a 10-journey ticket available from métro stations; and BF 125 ($4.15) for a 1-day ticket valid on all urban services.

Insert your ticket into the orange electronic machines inside buses and trams and at the access to métro platforms. Your ticket must be inserted each time you enter a new vehicle, but it allows multiple transfers within a 1-hour period of the initial validation, so during that time period only one journey will be canceled by the electronic scanner.

By Taxi   The minimum rate is BF 100 ($3.35); charges per kilometer vary from BF 40 to BF 58, depending on location and time. You need not add an extra tip unless there has been extra service, such as helping with heavy luggage. All taxis are metered. They cannot be hailed in the street, but there are taxi stands on many principal streets. Call **ATR** (☎ 02/647-22-22); **Autolux** (☎ 02/411-12-21); **Taxis Bleus** (☎ 02/268-00-00); **Taxis Oranges** (☎ 02/511-22-33); **Taxis Verts** (☎ 02/349-49-49).

By Car   Don't do it: it's a jungle out there. Belgium has some of Europe's worst road accident statistics. Those normally polite citizens turn into red-eyed demons once they get behind the steering wheel. Do yourself a favor: Leave the car at the car park.

FAST FACTS: Brussels

American Express International, Inc., is located at pl. Louise 2, 1000 Brussels (☎ 02/512-17-40).

Area Code   Brussels' telephone area code is 02.

Baby-sitters   Many hotels can provide reliable baby-sitting service. A student baby-sitting roster is maintained by U. L. B. Service, "Jobs," CP 185, av. F. D. Roosevelt 50 (☎ 02/650-26-46).

Bookstores   At W. H. Smith & Sons, bd. Adolphe Max 71–75 (☎ 02/219-50-34 or 219-27-08), you'll find the best and most comprehensive selection of English-language books.

Business Hours   Banks are open Mon–Fri 9am–1pm and 2–4:30pm. Shopping hours are Mon–Sat 9 or 10am–6 or 7pm (some shops, such as bakers and news vendors, open earlier). Some shops also open the same hours on Sun. Many shops stay open on Fri until 8 or 9pm.

Currency   The exchange rate used in this chapter is 30 Belgian francs = $1 U.S.

Currency Exchange   Banks generally offer the best rates, but the station exchanges come close. Hotels and street *bureaux de change* offer poorer rates and may charge high commissions, but these are open in the evenings and on weekends. Thomas Cook, Grand-Place 4 (☎ 02/513-28-45) has reasonable rates.

Dentists/Doctors   For emergency dental service, call 02/426-10-26 or 02/428-58-58. For emergency medical service around the clock, call 02/479-18-18 or 02/648-80-00. Be sure to ask for an English-speaking doctor.

Embassies/Consulates   The **Australian** Embassy is in the Guimard Center, rue Guimard 6-8 (☎ 02/231-05-00); the **Canadian** Embassy is at av. de

Tervuren 2 (☎ 02/741-06-11); the **United Kingdom** Embassy is at rue Arlon 85 (☎ 02/287-62-11); the **United States** Embassy is at bd. du Regent 27 (☎ 02/508-21-11).

Emergencies   In case of an accident, call 100; for police assistance, 101; for fire, 100.

Lost Property   The bigger railway stations have lost property offices (☎ 02/203-36-40); for property lost on the métro, tram, or bus, go to S.T.I.B., av. de la Toison d'Or 15 (☎ 02/515-23-94).

Post Office   The post office at Gare du Midi, av. Fonsny 48A, is open 24 hours a day. Others are open Mon–Fri 9am–5pm; closed weekends and public holidays (the office in the Centre Monnaie shopping center is also open Sat 9am–1pm).

Safety   Brussels is generally a safe city, but there is a growing trend toward crime, much of it drug related, particularly pickpocketing, theft from cars, and muggings in places such as métro station foot tunnels.

ACCOMMODATIONS

Brussels has good accommodations in every price range. All the chains want to be represented in the "Capital of Europe," leading to a glut of hotel rooms—and therefore to the possibility of special rates—particularly on weekends and during July and August. All rates include VAT, a service charge, and often a complimentary continental or buffet breakfast.

Both the **T.I.B. office** in the Grand-Place (☎ **02/513-89-40**) and the **Belgian Tourist Office,** at rue du Marché-aux-Herbes 63 (☎ **02/504-03-90**), will make reservations, if made in person for the same day, for a small fee (which is then deducted by the hotel from its room rate). **Belgian Tourist Reservations,** bd. Anspach 111, 1000 Brussels (☎ **02/513-74-84;** fax 02/513-92-77), provides an identical service. The T.I.B. publishes an annual *Hotel Guide* with listings by price range. They can also provide complete information on **hostels** in Brussels.

An alternative to the hotels listed below is a stay in a B&B. Brussels has several excellent bed-and-breakfast organizations: **Bed & Breakfast Taxistop,** rue du Fossé-aux-Loups 28, 1000 Brussels (☎ **02/223-22-31;** fax 02/223-22-32); **Bed & Brussels,** rue V. Greyson 58, 1050 Brussels (☎ **02/646-07-37;** fax 02/644-01-14); and **Windrose,** av. Paul Dejaer 21a, 1060 Brussels (☎ **02/534-71-91;** fax 02/534-71-92). All will send you a list of host families (the Windrose includes a personal profile of the families) and the rates charged. There is a booking fee of BF 500 ($16.65) per reservation, and rates vary from BF 1,000–1,350 ($33–$45) single, and BF 1,600–2,200 ($53–$73) double. Phone or fax them for more details.

VERY EXPENSIVE

✪ **Conrad.** Av. Louise 71, 1000 Brussels. ☎ **02/542-42-42.** Fax 02/542-42-00. 254 rms, 15 suites. A/C MINIBAR TV TEL. BF 14,000 ($467) double; BF 27,000–73,000 ($900–$2,433) suite. Rates do not include breakfast. AE, DC, MC, V. Métro: Louise.

Big, bright and pretty fancy, the Conrad occupies a prime location on stylish avenue Louise, set back a little from the road. It offers all the services and facilities you would expect from a hotel in this price category, although at the time of writing a swimming pool was still only a gleam in the architect's eye. The French restaurant La Maison du Maître offers all the refinements of haute cuisine, while the Café Wiltshire maintains a less formal tone. There is 24-hour room service, a sports and fitness center, wheelchair access, and a parking garage.

Royal Windsor. Rue Duquesnoy 5, 1000 Brussels. ☎ **02/505-55-55.** Fax 02/505-55-00. 245 rms, 30 suites. A/C MINIBAR TV TEL. BF 10,900 ($363) double; BF 18,200–26,000 ($607–$867) suite. Rates include breakfast. AE, DC, MC, V. Métro: Gare Centrale.

Only 2¹/₂ short blocks from the Grand-Place, this sparkling modern hotel incorporates marble, polished wood, and gleaming brass and copper in a decor designed to suit its setting. Some rooms are wood paneled and all are luxuriously furnished, but it must be said that some of them are a tad on the small side, though none have a sense of cramped space. The bathrooms have such extras as hair dryers and scales. There's a fitness center, wheelchair access, and a parking garage.

Les Quatre Saisons restaurant is outstanding, where gourmet meals are served in a graceful setting. In the clubby, Edwardian-style Duke of Wellington pub, light lunches and snacks are available. You can dance into the wee hours at the hotel's nightclub, the Griffin's Club.

✪ **SAS Royal.** Rue du Fossé-aux-Loups 47. ☎ **02/219-28-28.** Fax 02/219-62-62. 263 rms, 18 suites. A/C MINIBAR TV TEL. BF 13,180 ($439) double; BF 15,000–48,000 ($500–$1,600) suite. Rates do not include breakfast. AE, DC, MC, V. Métro: Gare Centrale.

The SAS is a relatively new hotel which, when it opened, quickly captured the hearts and minds of many Bruxellois, who recommended it to those of their business and personal acquaintances who could afford to stay here. It's modern, but in a way that seems in keeping with its neighborhood a few streets away from the Grand-Place, and it incorporates a part of an ancient Roman wall. The hotel has a fitness center.

The very fine Sea Grill restaurant of course specializes in seafood; the Atrium serves Belgian and Scandinavian specialties; and the attached Henry J Bean's is an American-style bar and grill that has already become an institution with locals and expatriates alike.

EXPENSIVE

✪ **Astoria.** Rue Royale 103, 1000 Brussels. ☎ **02/217-62-90.** Fax 02/217-11-50. 107 rms, 13 suites. A/C MINIBAR TV TEL. BF 8,000 ($267) double; BF 14,000 ($467) suite. Rates do not include breakfast. AE, DC, MC, V. Métro: Botanique.

An absolute gem of a hotel, and one of Brussels' premier lodging experiences. From the minute you walk into the belle époque foyer, you are transported into a more elegant, less hurried age. The hotel dates from 1909, a few short years before Europe's age of innocence ended with World War I, and its plush ambience recalls the panache of that lost heyday—but now with the latest fixtures and fittings in the rooms. Corinthian columns, antique furnishings, and textured marble give an idea of the ambience. Le Palais Royal gastronomique is mostly French cuisine, and you can settle into the ornately decorated Pullman Bar, just off the lobby.

Bristol Stéphanie. Av. Louise 91–93, 1050 Brussels. ☎ **02/543-33-11.** Fax 02/538-03-07. 142 rms, 3 suites. A/C MINIBAR TV TEL. BF 8,950–9,950 ($298–$332) double; BF 15,000–35,800 ($500–$1,193) suite. Rates include breakfast. AE, DC, MC, V. Métro: Louise.

This sleekly modern hotel looks as if it was designed for the 21st century. Every feature, from lobby design and fittings to furnishings in the kitchenette suites, is streamlined, functional, and representative of the very best in avant-garde planning. It's located in a pretty section of avenue Louise, one of the city's most select shopping streets. The rooms include a lovely roof-garden suite, the luxurious Connoisseur Rooms as well as the spacious Classic Rooms, some of which have kitchenettes. The hotel has a swimming pool and parking gararge. The Gourmet Restaurant has a French and an international menu.

○ **Métropole.** Pl. de Brouckère 31, 1000 Brussels. ☎ **02/217-23-00.** Fax 02/218-02-20. 400 rms, 10 suites. A/C MINIBAR TV TEL. BF 8,400 ($280) double; BF 12,500 ($417) suite. Rates include buffet breakfast. AE, DC, MC, V. Métro: De Brouckère.

This classic old-world hotel dates from the late 1800s, and its splendidly ornate interior is a turn-of-the-century showcase of marble, gilt, and lavishly decorated public rooms. What's more, it is right in the middle of the city center, with popular shopping just out the back door and Grand-Place only a few blocks away. The spacious rooms have classic furnishings and also hark back to former days. Even if you don't stay at the hotel, it is well worth visiting, just for its own precious sense of itself.

Facilities include a relaxation center with sauna, Turkish bath, Jacuzzi, solarium, and flotation tank. The elegant L'Alban Chambon restaurant caters to the sophisticated gourmet, and the extravagantly Victorian Café Métropole, complete with gas lamps, is charming. There is also a heated sidewalk terrace, which creates its own sense of occasion, although the view of a busy street is uninspiring.

MODERATE

○ **Albert Premier.** Pl. Rogier 20, 1210 Brussels. ☎ **02/203-31-25.** Fax 02/203-43-31. 285 rms. MINIBAR TV TEL. BF 3,000–5,000 ($100–$167) double. Rates include breakfast. AE, DC, EU, V. Métro: Rogier.

A fine old hotel, now modernized, that has retained both popularity and cachet through the mixed fortunes of the square on which it stands. Finally, things in the neighborhood are looking up. The rooms are rather basic, but comfortable and attractive.

⊙ **Arlequin.** Rue de la Fourche 17–19, 1000 Brussels. ☎ **02/514-16-15.** Fax 02/514-22-02. 71 rms. TV TEL. BF 3,200–3,350 ($105–$110) double; BF 3,600–5,150 ($120–$185) suites. Rates include breakfast. AE, DC, MC, V. Métro: Bourse.

Among moderately priced hotels, the Arlequin rates high on several counts. First, it's in the very heart of the city, just steps away from Grand-Place, with the restaurant-lined Petite rue des Bouchers right outside its back entrance. Then there is the fine view of the Town Hall spire, overlooking rooftops and narrow, medieval streets. The guest rooms are rather plain, but the furnishings are modern and comfortable.

○ **Le Dixseptième.** Rue de la Madeleine 25, 1000 Brussels. ☎ **02/502-57-44.** Fax 02/502-64-24. 12 studios, 12 suites. MINIBAR TV TEL. BF 6,600 ($220) double; BF 9,800–13,600 ($327–$453) suite. Rates do not include breakfast. AE, DC, MC, V. Métro: Gare Centrale.

One of Brussels' delights, the Dixseptième is close to the Grand-Place in a neighborhood of restored houses. Its rooms are big enough to be more like suites than ordinary rooms and some have balconies. All are designed in 18th-century style, with wood paneling and marble chimneys, and named after famous Belgian painters from Brueghel to Magritte. Two beautiful lounges are decorated with carved wooden medallions and 18th-century paintings

○ **New Hotel Siru.** Pl. Rogier 1, 1210 Brussels. ☎ **02/203-35-80.** Fax 02/203-33-03. 100 rms. MINIBAR TV TEL. BF 5,900 ($197) double. Rates include buffet breakfast. AE, DC, MC, V. Métro: Rogier.

This is a fascinating mid-size hotel in what was formerly a rundown area—it used to be a red-light district and still has some peep-show joints and offbeat appliance shops—but that is going upmarket fast since a slew of fancy office blocks was built nearby. What sets the New Siru apart is that its owner has persuaded 100 contemporary Belgian artists, including some of the country's biggest names, to "decorate" each room with a work on the theme of travel. Given the unpredictable nature of reactions to modern art, some clients apparently reserve the same room time after time, while some ask for a room change in the middle of the night. In any case, it is not easily forgotten, and the rooms themselves are coolly modern.

INEXPENSIVE

⑤ Les Bluets. Rue Berckmans 124, 1060 Brussels. ☎ **02/534-39-83.** Fax 02/534-39-83. 17 rms (with shower only). TV TEL. BF 1,550–2,450 ($52–$82) double. Rates include breakfast. AE, MC, V. Métro: Hôtel des Monnaies.

Les Bluets is a sweet place, a fine old family hotel in a building that dates from 1864, and with a proprietress who looks on her guests almost as members of the family.

Sabina. Rue du Nord 78, 1000 Brussels. ☎ **02/218-26-37.** Fax 02/219-32-39. 24 rms. TV TEL. BF 2,200 ($73) double. Rates include buffet breakfast. V. Métro: Madou.

This small hostelry is like a private residence, presided over by its friendly and hospitable owners. The gracious living room has a warm, homey atmosphere, and although rooms vary in size, all are quite comfortable and nicely furnished.

✪ Welcome. Quai au Bois-à-Brûler 23, 1000 Brussels. ☎ **02/219-95-46.** Fax 02/217-18-87. 6 rms. A/C MINIBAR TV TEL. BF 2,200–3,000 ($75–$100) double. Rates do not include breakfast. AE, DC, MC, V. Métro: Sainte-Catherine.

It would be hard to imagine a smaller hotel (it is the smallest in Brussels), or one which will leave you with such fond memories. Regular guests' memories are so fond that the hotel is often fully booked—admittedly not a difficult feat—but you should reserve well in advance to be sure. The enthusiastic couple who own it, Michel and Sophie Smeesters, have created bright, cheerful guest rooms. A superb seafood restaurant, La Truite d'Argent (see "Dining," below), is attached—one of the best in the Fish Market area.

DINING

Food is a passion in Brussels, which boasts more Michelin star restaurants per head, or per stomach, than Paris. It's just about impossible to eat badly in this city, no matter what price range you are operating within. Belgian cuisine is based on the country's own regional traditions: roots that can be taken literally in the case of asparagus, chicory (endive), and even the humble Brussels sprout. A tradition in Brussels is cooking with local beers like gueuze and faro, while great steaming pots of Zeeland mussels have a fanatical following.

EXPENSIVE

✪ Comme Chez Soi. Pl. Rouppe 23. ☎ **02/512-29-21.** Reservations required, as far in advance as possible. À la carte meals BF 3,000–6,000 ($100–$200). AE, DC. Tues–Sat noon–2pm and 6:30–10pm. Closed July. Métro: Bourse. FRENCH.

An expedition inside the hallowed portals of Brussels' three-Michelin-star restaurant, whose name means "Just Like Home," is the undoubted culinary highlight of any trip to the city. The food is a long way from what one would really eat at home, but the welcome from Master Chef Pierre Wynants—one of Europe's most revered chefs— is warm and his standards are high enough for the most rigorous tastebuds on earth. This really is the stellar end of the spectrum, with unforgettable French cuisine presented in an art nouveau–style restaurant.

La Maison du Cygne. Rue Charles Buls 2. ☎ **02/511-82-44.** Reservations recommended. À la carte meals BF 2,000–4,000 ($65–$135). AE, DC, MC, V. Mon–Fri noon–3pm and Mon–Sat 7pm–midnight. Closed 3 weeks in Aug. Métro: Gare Centrale or La Bourse. FRENCH.

This *grande dame* of Brussels' internationally recognized restaurants has one Michelin star and overlooks the Grand-Place from the former Butchers' Guildhouse. The

House of the Swan features polished walnut walls, bronze wall sconces, and lots of green velvet. The service is as elegant as the decor, if possibly a tad stuffy. Because of its location, Cygne is usually crowded at lunchtime, but dinner reservations are likely to be available.

♦ Villa Lorraine. Chaussée de la Hulpe 28. ☎ **02/374-31-63.** Reservations recommended. À la carte meals BF 3,600 ($120). AE, DC, MC, V. Mon–Sat 6:30–10pm. Closed Aug. Train: Brésil. FRENCH.

Classic French creations are featured by one of the city's top kitchens in this renovated château on the fringes of the Bois de la Cambre park. The dining rooms are spacious, with wicker furnishings, flower arrangements everywhere, and a skylight. In good weather you may elect to have drinks outside under the trees. Among classic French offerings are saddle of lamb in a delicate red-wine-and-herb sauce, partridge cooked with apples, and baked lobster with butter rose.

MODERATE

♦ Brasserie de la Roue d'Or. Rue des Chapeliers 26. ☎ **02/514-25-54.** Reservations not necessary. À la carte meals BF 900–1,200 ($30–$40). AE, DC, MC, V. Daily noon–3pm and 6pm–12:30am. Métro: Gare Centrale or La Bourse. BELGIAN/GRILLS/SEAFOOD.

An excellent, high-ceilinged brasserie with art nouveau and Magritte-style decor, and fittings that include lots of dark wood and mirrors, and marble-topped tables. The extensive menu caters to just about any appetite, from grilled meat to a good selection of cooked salmon and other seafoods, as well as old Belgian favorites like stoemp—mixed mashed vegetables served with meat or sausage. It's a welcoming place, with an extensive wine, beer, and spirits list, and a loyal local following. Its characterful owner, Jef De Gelas (who also owns 't Kelderke, below), is known as the "King of Stoemp."

De l'Ogenblik. Galerie des Princes 1. ☎ **02/511-61-51.** Reservations recommended at peak times. À la carte meals BF 2,200 ($73). AE, DC, MC, V. Mon–Sat noon–2:30pm and 7pm–midnight (Fri–Sat until 12:30am). Métro: Gare Centrale or Bourse. FRENCH/BELGIAN.

In the elegant surroundings of the Galeries Royales Saint-Hubert, this restaurant offers good taste amid Parisian bistro-style ambience. It often gets busy and the ambience in its dining room, which is filled with wood and brass and is on two levels, is convivial, even if you might find yourself a little too close to other diners. Look for garlicky seafood and meat specialties.

♦ (Le) Falstaff Gourmand. Rue des Pierres 38. ☎ **02/512-17-61.** Reservations not necessary. À la carte meals BF 1,200 ($40); menu BF 900 ($30). AE, DC, MC, V. Tues–Sun 11:30am–3pm and 7–11pm (except Sunday evening). Métro: Bourse. BELGIAN/FRENCH.

Le Falstaff brasserie on rue Henri Maus across from the Bourse is widely renowned as a classic art nouveau bar and eatery. Just around the corner, however, is its sister establishment, a restaurant where the style is different but equally notable. Service in Le Falstaff Gourmand is superb, prompt, and friendly, and the surprising thing is that more people do not take advantage of its charms. First-class Belgian and French-oriented dishes include one of the best deals in Brussels: the three-course *menu gourmand,* with choice, for $30 per head, including an apéritif, a glass of wine with the entree, and a *pichet* of wine with the main course.

♦ Le Joueur de Flûte. Rue de l'Epée 26. ☎ **02/513-43-11.** Reservations essential. Fixed menu BF 1,100 ($40). AE, DC, MC, V. Mon–Fri 7–11pm. Bus: 20 or 48. FRENCH.

The choice in this tiny restaurant is nothing if not straightforward—take it or leave it. There is only one menu, with a couple of variations for the main course. Don't let that, or the fact that it only serves a dozen covers each evening, put you off. Owner and chef Philippe Van Cappelen has had more than a passing acquaintance with Michelin stars in his time and now he likes to keep it small, simple, and friendly. Van Cappelen cooks whatever he feels like; by the end of the evening it's just about guaranteed that the feeling will be mutual. Count on wine taking you up another $20 a head.

⊗ **Le Marmiton.** Rue des Bouchers 43. ☎ **02/511-79-10.** Reservations recommended at peak times. À la carte meals BF 1,200 ($40). AE, DC, MC, V. Daily noon–3pm and 6:30–11:30pm. Métro: Gare Centrale or La Bourse. BELGIAN/FRENCH.

The city center Ilot Sacré restaurant district is often dismissed as a tourist trap, and some restaurants, sadly, contribute to its image problems. Le Marmiton is emphatically not one of them—quite the reverse. A warm and welcoming environment, hearty servings, and a firm commitment to producing satisfied customers are the hallmarks of this restaurant.

La Quincaillerie. Rue du Page 45. ☎ **02/538-25-53.** Reservations recommended. À la carte meals BF 1,500 ($50). AE, DC, MC, V. Daily noon–2:30pm and 7pm–midnight. Tram: 23 or 90. FRENCH.

In the Ixelles district, a part of Brussels where good restaurants are about as common as streetlights, the Quincaillerie nevertheless stands out as a stylish devotee of good taste and fine ambience, although it may be a little too aware of its own modish good looks, and a shade pricey. Located in a former hardware store—which sounds terrible, but it is a traditional old hardware store, with wood paneling and masses of wooden drawers. It gets so busy that the waitstaff can be a little harrassed and absent-minded, yet always friendly and helpful.

✪ **La Sirène d'Or.** Pl. Sainte-Catherine 1a. ☎ **02/513-51-98.** Reservations recommended. À la carte meals BF 2,400–3,000 ($80–$100). AE, DC, MC, V. Wed–Sat noon–2pm and 6:30–10pm. Closed July. Métro: Sainte-Catherine. SEAFOOD/FRENCH.

In the colorful and atmospheric Fish Market, beside the now-vanished harbor in the heart of Brussels where fishing boats used to tie up, this restaurant's specialties are, not surprisingly, seafood. Chef Robert Van Düren was once chef to the then-prince of Liège, now King Albert II of Belgium, so the dishes have that royal touch. The setting is dark wood walls, overhead beams, velvet-seated chairs, and Belgian lace curtains. Specialties are grilled turbot with ginger and bouillabaisse Grand Marius (a garlicky mixed fish soup).

La Truite d'Argent. Quai aux Bois-à-Brûler 23. ☎ **02/218-39-26.** Reservations recommended. BF 2,800–3,400 ($95–$115). AE, DC, MC, V. Mon–Fri noon–2:30pm and 7–11:30pm. Métro: Sainte-Catherine. FRENCH/SEAFOOD.

The enthusiastic owners, Michel and Sophie Smeesters, positively insist on delivering taste with their seafood specialties. "Superb" is the best word to describe the food, which includes meat and fowl dishes. All are prepared from choice ingredients, and the presentation is exquisite, so pleasing to the eye you might well hesitate to destroy the image by eating it up—except that what's on the plate sort of demands it. The outdoor terrace looking onto the Fish Market is recommended in good weather.

INEXPENSIVE

L'Auberge des Chapeliers. Rue des Chapeliers 1–3. ☎ **02/513-73-38.** Reservations not necessary. À la carte meals BF 500–1,200 ($15–$40). AE, DC, MC, V. Daily noon–2:30pm and 6pm–midnight. Métro: Gare Centrale or La Bourse. BELGIAN.

Bistro food has been served up in this 150-year-old building, just off the Grand-Place, for more than a quarter of a century. Popular with locals who live and work in the area, as well as with tourists who are fortunate enough to find it, it can be chockablock at the height of lunch hour, so it's a good idea to come just after noon or just after 2pm. The menu features traditional Belgian dishes and servings are more than ample.

❸ Au Vieux Bruxelles. Rue Saint-Boniface 35. ☎ **02/513-01-81.** Reservations not necessary. À la carte meals BF 1,200 ($40). AE, DC, MC, V. Tues–Sat noon–2:30pm and 6–11pm. Métro: Porte de Namur. BELGIAN/SEAFOOD.

This is a convivial, brasserie-style, 1880s-era restaurant specializing in mussels and serving them in a wide variety of styles. One of those places beloved of the Bruxellois, tucked out of sight of foreign noses, it's no less welcoming to them if they follow the scent and find their way there. It somehow combines a buzz of friendly conversation with the appreciative silence of happy diners.

❸ In't Spinnekopke. Pl. du Jardin-aux-Fleurs 1. ☎ **02/511-86-95.** Reservations not necessary. À la carte meals BF 900 ($30); plat du jour BF 360 ($12). AE, DC, MC, V. Daily 6–11pm, Sun–Fri noon–3pm. Métro: Bourse. BELGIAN.

A Brussels institution since 1762, and where those hardy standbys of Belgian cuisine, such as stoemp and waterzooï, are given all the care and attention they deserve—from both the kitchen staff and the diners. You'll eat in a tilty, wood-floored building at simple tables, more likely than not pressed into a small space. But getting caught "In the Spider's Web" will be well worth it.

❸ La Mirabelle. Chaussée de Boondael 459. ☎ **02/649-51-73.** Reservations not necessary. À la carte meals BF 600–1,000 ($20–$35); plat du jour BF 360 ($12). MC, V. Daily noon–3pm and 6pm–2:45am. Train: Watermael. BELGIAN.

Popular with students from the nearby Free University of Brussels for its "democratic" prices, this brasserie-restaurant in Ixelles is equally popular with Bruxellois in general for its convivial atmosphere and consistently good food. There is a garden terrace, which is nice in summer.

❸ 't Kelderke. Grand-Place 15. ☎ **02/513-73-44.** Reservations not necessary. À la carte meals BF 900 ($30); plat du jour BF 360 ($12). AE, DC, MC, V. Daily noon–2am. Métro: Gare Centrale or La Bourse. BELGIAN.

Regular visitors to Brussels are rightly wary of some of the city-center restaurants. Too many look on their customers as "here today, gone tomorrow" and behave accordingly. 't Kelderke is not one of these, despite its classic tourist location on the Grand-Place. Excellent, if straightforward, traditional Belgian cuisine, well served in a superbly atmospheric downstairs cellar restaurant (its name means "The Little Cellar"), patronized by a great many Belgians as well as tourists. It serves up hearty dishes like lapin à la bière (rabbit cooked in beer), stoemp (mashed potatoes and vegetables served with a meat, such as steak or sausage), and great steaming pots of big Zeeland mussels.

ATTRACTIONS
SIGHTSEEING SUGGESTIONS

If You Have 1 Day Spend the day exploring the historic Center. Beginning with the magnificent Grand-Place, you can visit the 15th-century Town Hall, the Museum of the City of Brussels, and the guildhouses, before moving on to *Manneken-Pis,* the Cathedral of Saint-Michel, the Ilot Sacré restaurant zone, the Belgian Center of Comic Strip Art, the 19th-century Royal Saint Hubert Galleries shopping mall, La Monnaie Opera, and the Place des Martyrs.

If You Have 2 Days   The Royal Road begins at the Palace of Justice at the top end of rue de la Régence, and if you continue in a straight line onto rue Royale, you pass through a number of historic squares and sites that include the Synagogue, the Royal Conservatory of Music, the Musical Instruments Museum, the Royal Fine Arts Museums, the Royal Palace, the Palace of Fine Arts, Brussels Park, and the Botanique Cultural Center.

If You Have 3 Days   Take in the lower city on the third day, including the Fish Market, the course of the vanished River Senne, place Sainte-Catherine, the Convent of Notre-Dame des Riches Claires, the old Béguinage, and the baroque church of Saint Jean-Baptiste.

If You Have 5 Days or More   Spend the fourth day exploring green Brussels and its attraction park, Bruparck! on the city's northern edge. Bruparck! includes Mini-Europe, and the Océade water theme park. Have lunch at one of the restaurants in The Village area. Nearby are the Atomium, the Heysel soccer stadium, the Planetarium, and the Exhibitions Park. Take your pick from the many parks: Bois de la Cambre, Forêt de Soignes, the Ixelles Ponds, the Abbey of la Cambre, Josaphat Park, the Cinquantenaire Park, and many others. On the fifth day, take an excursion beyond the city, to the battlefield of Waterloo.

THE HISTORIC SQUARES & STREETS
Grand-Place
Ornamental gables, medieval banners, gilded facades, sunlight flashing off gold-filigreed rooftop sculptures, a general impression of harmony and timelessness—there's a lot to take in all at once when you first enter the Grand-Place (Grote Markt in Dutch). Once the pride of the Habsburg Empire, the Grand-Place has always been the very heart of Brussels. Characterized by Jean Cocteau as "a splendid stage," it is the city's theater of life.

Your tour should include a visit to the gothic Town Hall, the neogothic King's House (despite its name it has never been a royal palace), which houses the Museum of the City of Brussels, and the Brewers Museum, which is housed in the beautiful old brewers' guildhouse at Grand-Place 10.

Place du Grand Sablon
Considered a classier place by locals to see and be seen than the Grand-Place—although the busy traffic passing through it diminishes the cafe-terrace experience—the Grand Sablon is also lined with gabled mansions. This is antique territory and many of those mansions house antique shops, or private art galleries, with pricey merchandise on display. The dealerships have spread into neighboring sidestreets, and on Saturday and Sunday mornings an excellent antique market sets up its stalls in front of Notre-Dame au Sablon Church. This flamboyantly gothic church, with no fewer than five naves, was paid for by the city's Guild of Crossbowmen in the 15th century. The statue of Minerva in the square dates from 1751. Take bus 34, 95, or 96 from the Bourse.

Place du Petit Sablon
Just across rue de la Régence, the Grand Sablon's little cousin is an ornamental garden with a fountain and pool, and forms a magical little retreat from the city bustle. The 48 bronze statuettes adorning the surrounding wrought-iron fence symbolize Brussels' medieval guilds, while two statues in the center commemorate the counts of Egmont and Hornes, who were beheaded in 1568 for protesting the extravagant cruelties of the Council of Blood, the enforcement arm of Spain's Holy Inquisition in the Low Countries. Take bus 34, 95, or 96 from the Bourse.

Place Royale

Meeting point of rue de la Régence and rue Royale, streets where many of the city's premier attractions stand, the square is graced by a heroic equestrian statue of Duke Godefroi de Bouillon, leader of the First Crusade. Its inscription describes him as the "First King of Jerusalem," a title Godefroi himself refused, accepting instead that of Protector of the Holy Places (it amounted to the same thing anyway). Also in Place Royale is the neoclassical Church of St.-Jacques-sur-Coudenberg. Take bus 71 from Brouckère.

MUSEUMS, CHURCHES & MONUMENTS

Manneken-Pis. Corner of rue du Chêne and rue de l'Etuve. Métro: Gare Centrale or Bourse.

Brussels' favorite little boy, gleefully doing what a little boy's gotta do. More often than not he is watched by a throng of admirers snapping pictures. Children especially seem to enjoy his bravura performance. This is not the original statue, which was prone to theft and "maltreatment" and was removed for safekeeping. Louis XV of France began the tradition of presenting colorful costumes to "Little Julian" by way of making amends for Frenchmen having kidnapped the statue in 1747; the outfits are housed in the Museum of the City of Brussels in the Grand-Place.

Hôtel de Ville (Town Hall). Grand-Place. ☎ **02/279-43-55.** Admission BF 80 ($2.65). Métro: Gare Centrale or Bourse.

The spectacular gothic hall in the Grand-Place is open for visits when Brussels' council of aldermen is not in session. You should begin with the outside, however, particularly with the sculptures on the facade, many of which are 15th- and 16th-century jokes.

Inside are superb 16th- to 18th-century tapestries; one depicts the duke of Alba, whose cruel features bring instant insight into the brutal oppression he and his Council of Blood imposed on Belgium; others are scenes from the life of Clovis, first king of the Franks. The aldermen meet in a plush, mahogany-paneled room surrounded by mirrors—presumably so that each party can see what underhand maneuvers the others are up to.

Palais Royal (Royal Palace). Pl. des Palais. ☎ **02/551-20-20.** Free admission for guided tours only. July 21–Sept Tues–Sun 9:30am–3:30pm. Métro: Parc or Arts-Loi.

King Albert II has his offices in this palace that fronts onto the Parc de Bruxelles, but he and Queen Paola do not live there. It is also used for state receptions.

Cathédrale de Saints Michel et Gudule. Parvis Sainte-Gudule. ☎ **02/217-83-45.** Free admission to church; crypt BF 40 ($1.35). Métro: Gare Centrale.

Victor Hugo reckoned this magnificent church to be the "purest flowering of the gothic style." Begun in 1226, it was only officially dedicated as a cathedral in 1961, although the 16th-century Habsburg Emperor Charles V had taken a personal interest in its decoration, donating the superb stained-glass windows. In recent years its stonework has been undergoing a process of cleaning and restoration, and the dazzlingly bright exterior makes a superb sight. Inside, the cool and spare decoration focuses attention on its soaring columns and arches.

Musée d'Art Ancien (Museum of Historic Art). Rue de la Régence 3. ☎ **02/508-32-11.** Tues–Sun 10am–noon and 1–5pm. Free admission. Bus: 71 from De Brouckère.

Brueghel and Rubens are the stars of the show, but the history of Belgian painting is well represented. The collection also includes international masters, with works by Van Gogh and the French impressionists. Guided tours are available on request.

Musée d'Art Modern (Museum of Modern Art). Pl. Royale 1–2. ☎ **02/508-32-11.** Tues–Sun 11am–1pm and 2–5pm. Free admission. Bus: 71 from De Brouckère.

Next-door neighbor to the Museum of Historic Art and with an emphasis on underground works—if only because the museum's eight floors are all below ground level. Magritte is well represented; so are Delvaux, De Braekeleer, Dalí, Permeke, and many others. Guided tours are available on request.

Musée de la Ville de Bruxelles (Museum of the City of Brussels). Grand-Place. ☎ **02/279-43-50.** Mon–Thurs 10am–12:30pm and 1:30–5pm (Oct–Mar until 4pm); Sat–Sun 10am–1pm. Admission BF 80 ($2.65). Métro: Gare Centrale or Bourse.

Located in the neogothic King's House (which has never housed a king), the museum features Brussels through the ages, including its traditional arts and crafts of tapestry- and lace-making. Among its most fascinating exhibits are old paintings and scale reconstructions of the historic city center, particularly those showing the riverside ambience along the now-vanished River Senne. Pride of place, however, goes to the more than 500 costumes—including an Elvis costume—donated to Manneken-Pis.

Musée Horta (Horta Museum). Rue Américaine 25. ☎ **02/537-16-92.** Tues–Sun 2–5:30pm. Admission BF 120 ($4) on weekdays; BF 200 ($6.65) on weekends. Tram: 81 or 92.

Brussels owes much of its rich art nouveau heritage to the inspired creative vision of Victor Horta, a resident architect who led the development of the style. His home and an adjoining studio are now a museum. Restored to their original condition, they showcase his use of flowing, sinuous shapes and colors, in interior decoration as well as architecture.

Musée du Cinquantenaire (Cinquantenaire Museum). Parc du Cinquantenaire. ☎ **02/741-72-11.** Tues–Fri 9:30am–5pm, Sat–Sun 10am–5pm. Admission BF 150 ($5). Métro: Schuman or Mérode.

Formerly known as the Royal Museums of Art and History (Musées Royaux d'Art et d'Histoire), the monumental Cinquantenaire traces the story of civilization, particularly but not exclusively European civilization. Departments include archeology, antiquity (which features a giant model of Imperial Rome), and European decorative arts.

Musée du Costume et de la Dentelle (Museum of Costume and Lace). Rue de la Violette 6. ☎ **02/512-77-09.** Mon–Sat 10am–12:30pm and 1:30–5pm (Oct–Mar until 4pm); Sat–Sun 2–4:30pm. Admission BF 80 ($2.65). Métro: Gare Centrale or Bourse.

In a city famous for its lace, no visit would be complete without seeing the marvellous antique creations in this museum near the Grand-Place.

Belgian Center for Comic-Strip Art (Centre Belge de la Bande Dessinée). Rue des Sables 20. ☎ **02/219-19-80.** Tues–Sun 10am–6pm. Admission BF 180 ($6). Métro: Gare Centrale.

Often called the "CéBéBéDé" for short, the center features such popular cartoon characters as Lucky Luke, Thorgal, and, of course, Tintin, yet does not neglect the likes of Superman, Batman, and the Green Lantern. Grown-ups will love it as well. As icing on the cake it is housed in a Victor Horta–designed building, the Magasins Waucquez, which was slated for demolition when the center took it over.

PARKS & GARDENS

The **Parc de Bruxelles** borders rue Royale, standing between the Parliament building and the Royal Palace. Once the hunting preserve of the dukes of Brabant, it is now a landscaped garden. In 1830, Belgian patriots confronted Dutch troops here during the War of Independence. It is not so very big, yet manages to combine different aspects, from carefully trimmed verges to rough patches of trees and bushes, and has fine views along its main axes. The métro stop is Parc or Arts-Loi.

The big public park called the **Bois de la Cambre** begins at the top of avenue Louise in the southern section of Brussels. This is the city's lung and gets busy on sunny weekends. Its centerpiece is a small lake with an island in its center reached by an electrically operated pontoon. Some busy roads run through the park and traffic moves fast on them, so be careful with children at these points. Take tram 92 or 93 from Parc de Bruxelles.

Bruparck!, on the city's northern edge, includes Mini-Europe and the Océade water theme park. Kids especially enjoy the sights here. There's nothing else quite like the **Atomium,** a cluster of giant spheres representing the atomic model of an iron molecule enlarged 165 billion times—like something from *Close Encounters of the Third Kind.* You can wander around inside the spheres. The view from the viewing deck is marvellous. The whole thing was built for the 1958 World's Fair. Not just kids will get a kick out of strolling around the highlights of **Mini-Europe:** Big Ben, the Leaning Tower of Pisa, and the Bull Ring in Seville (complete with *Olé!*), as well as more modern emblems of continental achievement such as the Channel Tunnel and the Ariane rocket (which actually takes off, kind of). As the scale is 1:25, everyone will feel like giants. Beside Mini-Europe is the Océade water leisure center.

Bruparck! is at bd. du Centenaire, Laeken (☎ **02/477-09-77** or 02/478-05-50). The Atomium is open Apr–Aug 9am–8pm; Sep–Mar 10am–6pm. Admission BF 200 ($6.65); look out for reduced-rates combined tickets if you are also planning to visit Mini-Europe and the Océade. Mini-Europe is open July–Aug 9:30am–8pm; before and after this period Mini-Europe opens progressively later and closes progressively earlier; closed Jan–Feb. Métro: Heysel.

A STROLL THROUGH THE MAROLLES

The iconoclastic working-class Marolles district is a special place where the old Brussels dialect can still be heard and which remains resolutely unimpressed by the burgeoning "Capital of Europe." It is a generally poor community, and one that is under constant threat of encroachment and gentrification from neighboring, far wealthier areas—a process the Marolliens seem to want nothing to do with. Most people get their Marolles "initiation" by visiting the daily **flea market** in place du Jeu de Balle, which starts at 7am and finishes at 2pm, and where the weird and wonderful is commonplace.

The district lies beneath the long shadow of the **Palace of Justice (Palais de Justice),** whose domed magnificence must have seemed to its creators to loom as a salutary warning to the rebellious-minded, working-class Marolliens. Joseph Poelaert's 19th-century neoclassical temple, dedicated to the might and majesty of the law, at place Polaert, is worth seeing for its extravagant (some would say megalomaniac) architecture.

Somehow it makes a refreshing change to explore this other Brussels, a simple neighborhood of homes, welcoming cafes, and restaurants where the food is low-cost yet tasty. Simply wander around for an hour or two. Also here is the **Brueghel House,** at rue Haute 132. However, it is only open for groups on written request, and even then rarely. The métro stop for the area is Louise.

ORGANIZED TOURS

Coach tours, 3 hours in duration, are available from **Panorama Tours,** rue du Marché-aux-Herbes 105 (☎ **02/513-61-54**), and **De Boeck Sightseeing Tours,** rue de la Colline 8 (☎ **02/513-77-44**). Each tour costs BF 780 ($26). Bookings can be made through most hotels, and arrangements can be made for hotel pickup. Tours operate throughout the year, and private tours can also be arranged.

Chatterbus, rue des Thuyas 12 (☎ 02/673-18-35), operates a daily 3-hour tour, June–Sept, starting at 10am (also July, at 2pm) from the Galeries Royales Saint-Hubert, a 19th-century shopping mall next to rue du Marché-aux-Herbes 90, a few steps from the Grand-Place. It's a walking tour covering the historic center, followed by a bus ride through areas the average tourist will never see. You'll hear about life in Brussels and get a better feel for the city. The price is BF 350 ($11.65).

ARAU, the Workshop for Urban Research and Action, Adolphe Max 55 (☎ 02/219-33-45), is a committee of concerned Brussels residents who give 3-hour themed tours, including "Surprising Parks and Squares," "Brussels 1900 Art Nouveau," "Grand-Place and Its Surroundings," and "Alternative Brussels." Advanced reservations are advised. Prices are BF 350–BF 500 ($11.65–$16.65). Tours operate on a rotating basis, Sat, Mar–Nov. Private tours for groups can be arranged throughout the year.

SHOPPING

Brussels is not the place to come looking for bargains. As a general rule, the upper city around avenue Louise and the Porte de Namur is more expensive than the lower city around Rue Neuve and the shopping galleries on La Monnaie and place Brouckère. Shopping hours are generally Mon–Sat 9 or 10am–6pm, with late-night shopping Fri until 8 or 9pm. A useful source of information is the weekly English-language magazine *The Bulletin,* which keeps tabs on the latest shopping ideas and trends, reviews individual shops, and carries advertising.

Galeries Royales Saint-Hubert is Europe's oldest shopping mall, a light and airy arcade hosting boutiques, cafe terraces, and buskers playing classical music. Built in Italian neo-Renaissance style and opened in 1847, architect Pierre Cluysenaer's gallery has a touch of class, and is well worth a stroll through to admire even if you have no intention of so much as looking in a shop window. The elegant triple gallery—Galerie du Roi, Galerie de la Reine, and Galerie des Princes—was the forerunner of other city arcades such as the Burlington in London. You'll find it near the Grand-Place, between rue du Marché-aux-Herbes and rue de l'Ecuyer, and split by rue de Bouchers. There are accesses on each of these streets. Métro: Gare Centrale or Bourse.

At the **Flea Market** on place du Jeu-de-Balle, a large square in the Marolles district, you can find some exceptional decorative items, many recycled from the homes of the "recently deceased," as well as unusual postcards, clothing, and household goods. The market is held daily 7am–2pm.

Every weekend, the place du Grand Sablon hosts a fine **Antiques Market.** The salesmanship is low-key, the interest pure, and prices not unreasonable (don't expect bargains though), and the quality of the merchandise—including silverware, pottery, paintings, and jewelry—is high. The market is open Sat 9am–6pm and Sun 9am–2pm.

The Grand-Place boasts a **Flower Market,** daily 7am–2pm, and a weekly **Bird Market,** featuring many varieties of birds (many, sadly, with their wings clipped). Nearby at the top end of rue du Marché-aux-Herbes, in what is loosely called the Agora, there is a weekend **Crafts Market,** with lots of fine little specialized jewelry and other items, most of which are not expensive.

For books in English, **W. H. Smith,** bd. Adolphe Max 71 (☎ 02/219-27-08), is a branch of the major British bookshop chain. It also sells magazines and newspapers. Their books, however, may cost 30% to 50% more than in Britain. Métro: Rogier.

In case you want to see the world.

At American Express, we're here to make your journey a smooth one. So we have over 1,700 travel service locations in over 120 countries ready to help. What else would you expect from the world's largest travel agency?

do more

Travel

http://www.americanexpress.com/travel

In case you want to be welcomed there.

We're here to see that you're always welcomed at establishments everywhere. That's why millions of people carry the American Express® Card – for peace of mind, confidence, and security, around the world or just around the corner.

do more

In case you're running low.

We're here to help with more than 118,000 Express Cash locations around the world. In order to enroll, just call American Express before you start your vacation.

do more

Express Cash

And just in case.

We're here with American Express® Travelers Cheques
and Cheques *for Two*.® They're the safest way to carry
money on your vacation and the surest way to get a
refund, practically anywhere, anytime.

Another way we help you...

do more

**Travelers
Cheques**

Forget computer games and Disney stores—if you need to buy a gift for the kids, take home some Tintin mementos from **Boutique de Tintin,** rue de la Colline 13 (☎ **02/514-45-50**). ✪ **La Trotinette,** rue des Eperonniers 4 (☎ **02/511-00-41**), reaches back to a gentler and kinder era of children's toys, with tin cars, wooden soldiers, and Barbie dolls from the fifties. One of its more distinguished customers in recent times was President Bill Clinton. Métro: Gare Centrale.

Belgian chocolates are famous worldwide. Those handmade Belgian pralines should be sold with a government health warning, so addictively delicious are they. **Neuhaus,** Galerie de la Reine 25 (☎ **02/502-59-14**), sells some of the best handmade chocolates. **Wittamer,** pl. du Grand Sablon 12 (☎ **02/512-37-42;** tram 92 or 93), has the best in the world. Their rolls, breads, pastries, and cakes have also been winning fans here since 1910. To get there, take tram 92 or 93. ✪ **Dandoy,** rue au Beurre 31 (☎ **02/511-81-76;** métro: Bourse), is the place for sweet-toothed cookies-'n'-cakes fans. Try the traditional Belgian house specialties: spicy speculoos cookies and pain à grecque.

Don't miss **De Boe,** rue de Flandre 36 (☎ **02/511-13-73**), a small shop near the Fish Market. It's a place of heavenly smells from roasted and blended coffee, and has a superb selection of wines in all price categories, and an array of specialty crackers, nuts, spices, teas, and gourmet snacks, many of which come in tins that make them suitable to take home. Métro: Sainte-Catherine.

Among shops selling fashionable clothing and accessories, try **Delvaux,** Galerie de la Reine 31 (☎ **02/512-71-98**), a local company that makes and sells some of the best, if also the priciest, handbags and leather goods in Belgium. **Olivier Strelli,** av. Louise 72 (☎ **02/511-21-34**), is the top-rated Belgian fashion designer. His shop is strong on elegant, ready-to-wear items. Métro: Louise.

✪ **Les Fleurs Isabelle de Backer,** rue Royale 13 (☎ **02/217-26-69**), is a superb flower shop in a superb art nouveau location. Métro: Botanique.

Manufacture Belge de Dentelle, Galerie de la Reine 6–8 (☎ **02/511-44-77**), specializes in top-quality handmade Belgian lace. One of the best places for lace in Brussels is **Maison Antoine,** Grand-Place 26 (☎ **02/512-48-59;** métro: Gare Centrale or Bourse), with surely the best location, in a former guildhouse where Victor Hugo lived in 1852. The quality is superb, the service friendly, and the prices not unreasonable.

BRUSSELS AFTER DARK

The city offers a full range of evening activities, including dance, opera, classical music, jazz, film, theater, and discos. For an exhaustive listing of events, consult the "What's On" section of the English-language weekly *The Bulletin.*

PERFORMING ARTS

✪ **La Monnaie.** pl. de la Monnaie ☎ **02/229-12-11.** Métro: Brouckère.

The superb and historic Théâtre Royal de la Monnaie, founded in the 17th century, is home to the **Opéra National** and **l'Orchestre Symphonique de la Monnaie. Resident ballet companies** have included Maurice Béjart's Ballet du XXième Siècle and the Mark Morris Dance Group; at present it is local choreographer Anne Theresa de Keersmaeker's Group Rosas.

Music & Theater

The **Palais des Beaux-Arts,** rue Royale 10 (☎ **02/507-84-66;** métro: Parc), is the home of the Belgium National Orchestra. The **Cirque Royal,** rue de l'Enseignement 81 (☎ **02/218-20-15;** métro: Parc), was formerly a real circus, but having been transformed, is now more commonly used for music, opera, and ballet.

Brussels theater naturally concentrates on French- and Dutch-language plays, many of which are adapted from English, however. They also occasionally perform works in English. **Théâtre Royal du Parc,** rue de la Loi 3 (☎ **02/512-23-39;** métro: Parc), is a magnificent edifice occupying a corner of the Parc de Bruxelles opposite Parliament. Most performances of classic and contemporary drama and comedies here are in French.

In an atmospheric old Brussels cafe, the traditional art of Bruxellois marionette theater is maintained, at the **Théâtre Toone VII,** Impasse Schuddeveld, Petite rue des Bouchers 6 (☎ **02/217-27-53;** métro: Gare Centrale or Bourse). Often treating sophisticated subjects, puppet Master José Géal presents his adaptation of classic stories in the Brussels dialect, Brussels Vloms, but also in English, French, Dutch, and German.

THE CLUB & MUSIC SCENE

Brussels is not famous for its nightlife as are some of the neighboring capitals—dining out being the most popular local activity. However, nightlife is alive and well in Brussels, and if the range is inevitably thinner than in much bigger cities like London and Paris, the quality is not.

Cabarets & Discos
Black Bottom. Rue du Lombard 1. ☎ **02/511-06-08.** Métro: Bourse.

A Brussels institution, well loved by the "ordinary folks" of Brussels, if considered a bit passé by the smart Eurocrowd—which means, of course, that it's well worth visiting. The years have gone by for hosts Jerry and Martigny, but they still provide a warm welcome to their guests, they have some fine new performing talents, and the cabaret still retains much of the raffish air that first brought it fame.

Chez Flo. Rue au Beurre 25. ☎ **02/512-94-96.** Métro: Bourse.

It's a bit of a hoot, really, this transvestite cabaret and dinner. Kind of outrageous and kind of comfortable at the same time.

Le Garage. Rue Duquesnoy 16. ☎ **02/512-66-22.** Métro: Gare Centrale.

It always seems on the verge of going out of style, yet never quite gets there, even if it has lost the wild and wonderful cachet of its earlier days. A location just off the Grand-Place undoubtedly helps. So does a consistently up-to-date approach to the music.

(Le) Show Point. Pl. Stéphanie 14. ☎ **02/511-53-64.** Métro: Louise.

Brussels would not claim to be a competitor to Paris when it comes to Moulin Rouge–style shows, but in Show Point it has a place that adopts a similar approach. From 10pm until dawn, showgirls, scantily clad or wearing fanciful costumes, strut their stuff in a variety of fetching choreographies. Those who like this sort of thing will probably like this sort of thing.

Mirano Continental. Chaussée de Louvain 38. ☎ **02/218-57-72.** Métro: Madou.

More of a dance hall than a disco. A classy place for those whose wildest years belong to the history of disco yet who still like to enjoy themselves.

Jazz & Blues
Jazz has taken a hit in Brussels in recent years, with some of the best-loved spots closing down—worst missed of all may be the nightly shindig at L'Estaminet du Kelderke, which once set the foam flying in the beer glasses at this cellar bar in the Grand-Place. Still, some old places remain, and new ones have sprung up.

Blues Corner. Rue des Chapeliers 12. ☎ **02/511-97-94.** Métro: Gare Centrale.

Sometimes it seems that the thick clouds of cigarette smoke in this dark and lively dive have lingered there for decades. Like the blues themselves, this place just goes on and on. Which is how lovers of the heavy licks to be heard hereabouts like it.

Brussels Preservation Hall. Rue de Londres 3. ☎ **02/511-03-04.** Métro: Porte de Namur.

Lacks some (well, a lot really) of the New Orleans style to which it alludes. Don't let that put you off: It's just a name, after all, and the place itself is essential Brussels, the proprietor a genuine enthusiast, the clientele committed, and the music consistently outstanding. Visiting American musicians, some of whom might hail from that self-same New Orleans, are often to be found on the bill.

THE BAR SCENE

Now you're talking. Bars are where Brussels lives. It's hard to be disappointed, whether you just pop into a neighborhood watering hole where a *chope* or *pintje* (a glass of beer) will set you back a mere BF 30 ($1), or whether you prefer to fork out three or more times as much in one of the trendier places.

   La Morte Subite, rue Montagne-aux-Herbes Potagères 7 (☎ **02/513-13-18**) is also the name of one of the beers here. The name translates to "Sudden Death." Don't worry. You'll probably survive in this fine old Brussels cafe, which appeals to an eclectic cross-section of Brussels society, from little old ladies, to bank managers, to dancers and musicians from the top cultural venues, to students—oh yes, and to tourists as well. Stained-glass motifs, old photographs, paintings and prints on the walls; plain wooden chairs and tables on the floor. Specialties are traditional Brussels beers: gueuze, faro, and kriek, as well as abbey brews like Chimay, Maredsous, and Grimbergen. The staff's attitude can take a little getting used to, especially if you take more than 3 seconds flat to decide what you want. If you know straight away, you'll have a friend for life, or at any rate for the evening. Métro: Gare Centrale.

   Le Cirio, rue de la Bourse 18 (☎ **02/512-13-95**) is across the road from the Stock Exchange, many of the customers here seem like they've made their pile and retired to a state of genteel splendor. Which just about sums up Le Cirio, a quiet, refined sort of place to sip your beer, in surroundings that make the whole exercise seem worthwhile. Métro: Bourse.

   At **Le Falstaff,** rue Henri Maus 17 (☎ **02/511-87-89**), the waiters are widely considered to have an attitude problem; you can almost feel how privileged they consider you to be by the fact that you have them for waiting staff. Sometimes it can get a bit wearing, yet the big problem here is finding a seat, so popular is it. Opened in 1904, Falstaff's art nouveau enlivened with a dash of art deco helps to create the city's most stylish cafe. Métro: Bourse.

   The decor alone might give you the creeps at **Halloween,** rue des Grands-Carmes 10 (☎ **02/514-12-56**). Gargoyles, devils, and other assorted creatures from the darker recesses of the mind help create an unforgettable ambience. Fact is, though, that it is also a pretty good bar. Métro: Bourse.

A DAY TRIP TO WATERLOO

If you make a day trip to Waterloo, you'll be in good company. The French Emperor Napoléon started the tradition in 1815, but with any luck you'll have a better day out than he did. The first thing to note, however, is that you are not actually going to Waterloo, which although a pleasant enough suburb of Brussels is not really worth going out of your way for—the Battle of Waterloo was not actually fought there. A stretch of rolling farmland dotted with stoutly built manor-farmhouses several miles to the south got that "honor."

Waterloo was Europe's Gettysburg. The battlefield remains much as it was on June 18, 1815. Before exploring it you should take in the **Visitor Center,** route du Lion 252–254 (☎ **02/385-19-12**), where an audiovisual presentation of the tactical picture plus an extract from a fictional film version will give you an idea of the battle's impressive scale. It's open daily Apr–Sept 9am–6pm; Oct 9:30am–5:30pm; Nov–Feb 10:30am–4pm; Mar 10:30am–5pm. Admission to the Butte BF 40 ($1); to the audiovisual and Panorama BF 275 ($9); to all three, BF 300 ($10). Bus: W from avenue de Stalingrad to Centre Visiteur.

The view of the theater of war from the top of the great **Butte du Lion (Lion Mound)** beside the Visitor Center is worth the 226-step climb, although it takes an active imagination to fill the peaceful farmland spread out below you with slashing cavalry charges, thundering artillery, and 200,000 colorfully unifomed, struggling soldiers.

Also next to the center is the **Panorama,** featuring a painted diorama of the massed French cavalry charge led by Marshal Ney. It was a sensation in the pre-cinema era. Across the road is the **Musée des Cires (Waxworks Museum),** where Napoléon, Wellington, Blücher, and others appear as rather tatty wax figures. A pathway beside the Panorama leads to a memorial to Lieutenant Augustin Demulder, a Belgian trooper who fell in Napoléon's cause.

Farther on, a memorial records the position of British artillery that poured grapeshot into Napoléon's Old Guard during their doomed final assault. A stroll of 15 minutes more brings you to **Hougoumont Farm,** which played a key role in the fighting and which still bears the scars of battle. The owners let visitors wander around the grounds.

Returning to the Visitor Center, a little way down the Brussels–Charleroi road, is **La Haie-Sainte,** another farmhouse that played a crucial role in Napoléon's defeat by shielding Wellington's center from direct assault.

In Waterloo itself, the well-ordered **Musée Wellington (Wellington Museum),** chaussée de Bruxelles 147, Waterloo (☎ **02/354-78-06**), is in an old Brabant coaching inn that was the duke's headquarters. It was from here that he sent his historic victory dispatch. It's open daily Apr–Oct 9:30am–6:30pm; Nov–Mar 10:30am–5pm. Admission is BF 80 ($3). Take bus W from avenue de Stalingrad to Waterloo.

2 Bruges, Ghent & the Meuse Valley

The Flemish art cities of Bruges and Ghent bring back the Middle Ages, while Liège and the towns of the Meuse in French-speaking Wallonia present another side of Belgium. Both, however, hang on to their traditions and customs, and take considerable pride in their country's diversity.

ONLY IN THE ART CITIES & MEUSE VALLEY

Exploring Historic Bruges & Ghent   Walking around Bruges is like taking a step back in time. This perfectly preserved medieval city, with its squares, especially the Markt and the Burg, and its historic architecture, is a sight in itself. Ghent is grayer and more austere, but even more authentic with its forbidding castle and its three-towered cathedral.

Seeing the Treasures of the Art Cities   Some of the most outstanding paintings of the Northern Renaissance are found in the museums and churches of Bruges and Ghent, particularly the Church of Our Lady and the Groeninge Museum in Bruges, and St. Bavo's Cathedral in Ghent.

Sampling Classic Walloon Cuisine   Liège is the place to enjoy the classic Walloon cuisine. It lost ground in the past to more exotic tastes, but is making a strong comeback.

Touring the Meuse Valley   No less historic and interesting is a tour of the Meuse Valley, from Liège, the chief city, to the quaint resort town of Huy to Namur with its hilltop citadel to the fortress town of Dinant.

BRUGES (BRUGGE)

89km (55 miles) NW of Brussels, 46km (28 miles) NW of Ghent, 22km (14 miles) SE of Ostend

Bruges is a time capsule, drifting down the stream of time with all the graceful self-possession of the swans that cruise its canals. To step into the old city is to be transported instantly back to the Middle Ages, when Bruges was among the wealthiest cities of Europe. Unlike so many cities in Europe that have had their hearts torn out by war, Bruges has remained unravaged, its glorious monumental buildings intact.

ESSENTIALS

ARRIVING   By Train   Frequent trains arrive from Brussels and Antwerp (both via Ghent), and from the channel ferry ports of Ostend (Oostende) and Zeebrugge. Perhaps the most important first principle to be aware of is that although the city is called Bruges in English and French, to its own Flemish citizens it is Brugge, and that is what the station destination boards say. The station is on Stationsplein, about 1 mile south of town, a 20-minute walk to the town center or a short bus or taxi ride. For train information, call **050/38-23-82** from 6:30am–10:30pm.

By Bus   The bus station adjoins the train station. Schedule and fare information can be obtained by calling **059/56-53-53**.

By Car   Bruges is reached via the E40 from Brussels and Ghent; the E17 and E40 from Antwerp; and on the E40 from Ostend. You'll find it all but impossible to use a car in the confusing and narrow streets of the city center. Leave your car at your hotel car park (if it has one), at one of the big, prominently signposted underground car parks in the center (these get expensive for long stays), or at a free parking zone outside the center. It's a short walk into the heart of the old city from any of the car parks.

VISITOR INFORMATION   The **Tourist Office,** at Burg 11, 8000 Bruges (☎ **050/44-86-86;** fax 050/44-86-00), is open Apr–Sept Mon–Fri 9:30am–6:30pm, Sat–Sun 10am–noon and 2–6:30pm; Oct–Mar Mon–Fri 9:30am–5pm, Sat–Sun 9:30am–1pm and 2–5:30pm. Friendly and efficient, the tourist office has brochures that outline walking, coach, canal, and horse-drawn cab tours, as well as detailed information on many sightseeing attractions.

CITY LAYOUT   Bruges has two hearts in side-by-side monumental squares called the Markt and the Burg. Narrow streets fan out from these two squares, while a network of canals threads its way to every section of the small city. The center is almost encircled by a canal that opens at its southern end to become the Minnewater (Lake of Love), filled with swans and other birds and bordered by the Begijnhof and a fine park. On the outer side of the Minnewater is the railway station.

GETTING AROUND   By Bus   Most city buses depart from the Markt or one of the adjacent streets and from the bus station beside the train station, with schedules prominently posted.

By Bicycle   If you arrive in Bruges by train, you can rent a bicycle (you must present a valid rail ticket) at the Baggage Department of the railway station for BF 325

($10.85) per day (☎ **050/38-58-71**). Biking is a terrific way to get around or out of town to the nearby village of Damme (see below) by way of beautiful canalside roads.

By Taxi There are taxi ranks at the Markt (☎ **050/33-44-44**) and outside the train station on Stationsplein (☎ **050/38-46-60**).

By Boat Going around by tour boat is also the best way to see Bruges, especially on a fine day, and the view from those open-top boats is unforgettable.

EXPLORING HISTORIC BRUGES

Walking is the best way to see Bruges. Wear good walking shoes—those charming cobblestones can be hard going.

A leading contender for the title of Europe's most romantic town, Bruges is really one big attraction—a fairytale mixture of gabled houses, meandering canals, narrow cobblestone streets, a busy market square and civic square, and a populace that provides a warm welcome to its visitors. In some ways this last fact is the most astonishing. Those people actually *live* in Bruges and more often than not they are swamped by tourists. They don't let it get to them, however, and the reason is more than mere economics—they love their city and can well understand that visitors should want to see and experience it.

You should begin your tour at the **Markt square,** where you'll find the 13th–16th-century Belfry (Belfort) and Hallen, Markt 7 (☎ **050/38-69-01**). Much of the city's commerce was conducted in the Hallen in centuries past. The Belfry's octagonal tower soars 260 feet and holds a magnificent 47-bell carillon that peals out over the city every quarter hour and in longer concerts several times a day in summer. Climb the 366 steps to the Belfry's summit for a panoramic view of Bruges and the surrounding countryside all the way to the sea. The Belfry and Halls are open daily Apr–Sept 9:30am–5pm and Oct–Mar 9:30am–12:30pm and 1:30–5pm. Admission is BF 100 ($3.35) for adults, BF 50 ($1.65) for children.

The **sculpture group** in the center of the Markt depicts two Flemish heroes, butcher Jan Breydel and weaver Pieter de Coninck, who led an uprising in 1302 against the wealthy merchants and nobles who dominated the guilds, then went on to an against-all-odds victory over French knights later that same year in the Battle of the Golden Spurs. The large neogothic **Provinciaal Hof** dates from the 1800s and houses the government of West Flanders province.

An array of beautiful buildings, which adds up to a trip through the history of architecture, stands in the **Burg,** a public square just steps away from the Markt, where Baldwin "Iron Arm" once built a fortified castle around which a village (or "burg") developed.

The **Town Hall (Stadhuis),** Burg 11 (☎ **050/44-81-10**), is a beautiful gothic structure built in the late 1300s, making it the oldest town hall in Belgium. Don't miss the upstairs ✪ **Gothic Room (Gotische Zaal)** with its ornate decor and wall murals depicting highlights of Bruges's history. The Town Hall is open Apr–Sept daily 9:30am–5pm and Oct–Mar daily 9:30am–12:30pm and 1:30–5pm. Admission is BF 60 ($2) for adults, BF 20 (65¢) for children.

Next to the Town Hall is the richly decorated, romanesque **Basilica of the Holy Blood (Heilige-Bloedbasiliek),** Burg 10 (☎ **050/33-67-92**). Since 1149 this has been a repository of a fragment of cloth impregnated with what is said to be the blood of Christ, brought to Bruges during the Second Crusade by the Count of Flanders. Every Ascension Day, in the colorful Procession of the Holy Blood, the relic is carried by the bishop through Bruges's streets, accompanied by costumed residents

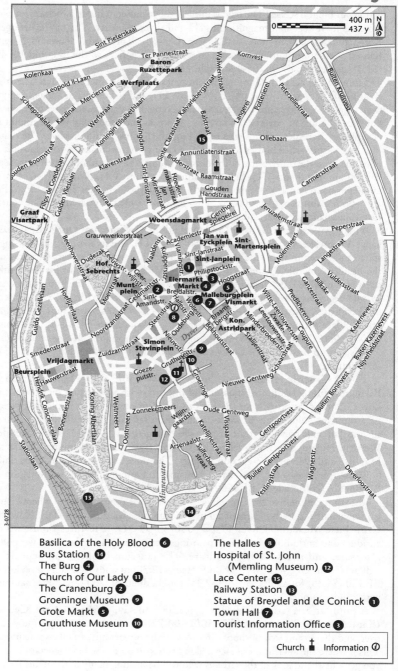

Bruges

Basilica of the Holy Blood ❻
Bus Station ⓮
The Burg ❹
Church of Our Lady ⑪
The Cranenburg ❷
Groeninge Museum ❾
Grote Markt ❺
Gruuthuse Museum ⑩

The Halles ❽
Hospital of St. John
(Memling Museum) ⑫
Lace Center ⑮
Railway Station ⑬
Statue of Breydel and de Coninck ❶
Town Hall ❼
Tourist Information Office ❸

Church ✝ Information ⓘ

acting out biblical scenes. The relic is in the basilica museum inside a rock-crystal vial which is itself kept in a magnificent gold-and-silver reliquary. The basilica is open Apr–Sept daily 9:30am–noon and 2–6pm, Oct–Mar daily 10am–noon and 2–4pm (closed Wed afternoon). Admission to the basilica is free; to the museum BF 40 ($1.35) for adults, BF 20 (65¢) for children.

Through the centuries, one of the most tranquil spots in Bruges has been the **Begijnhof,** Wijngaardstraat (☎ 050/33-00-11), and so it remains today. Begijns were religious women, similar to nuns, who accepted vows of chastity and obedience, but drew the line at poverty. Today, the begijns are no more, and the Begijnhof is occupied by Benedictine nuns who try to keep the begijns' traditions alive. The beautiful little whitewashed houses surrounding a lawn with trees makes a marvelous place of escape from the hurly-burly of the outside world. The Begijnhof is open Apr–Sept daily 10am–noon and 1:45–5:30pm (Sun until 6pm); Oct, Nov, and Mar, daily 10:30am–noon and 1:45–5pm; Dec–Feb, Wed, Thurs, Sat, Sun 2:45–4:15pm, Fri 1:45–6pm. Admission is BF 60 ($2) for adults, BF 30 ($1) for children. The courtyard is permanently open and admission is free.

It took two centuries (13th to 15th) to build the ✪ **Church of Our Lady (Onze-Lieve-Vrouwekerk),** Mariastraat (☎ 050/34-53-14), and its soaring 396-foot-high spire can be seen from a wide area around Bruges. Among its many art treasures are the beautiful marble *Madonna and Child* by Michelangelo (one of his few works to be seen outside Italy); a painting by Anthony Van Dyck; and the impressive side-by-side bronze tomb sculptures of Charles the Bold, who died in 1477, and Mary of Burgundy, who died in 1482. The church is open Apr–Sept Mon–Sat 10–11:30am and 2:30–5pm (Sat until 4pm); Oct–Mar Mon–Sat 10–11:30am and 2:30–4:30pm (Sat until 4pm). Admission to the church and the *Madonna and Child* altar is free; to the chapel of Charles and Mary, BF 60 ($2) for adults, BF 30 ($1) for children.

The ✪ **Groeninge Museum,** Dijver 12 (☎ 050/33-99-11), ranks among Belgium's leading traditional museums of fine arts, with a collection that covers the Low Countries' painting from the 15th to the 20th century. The Gallery of Flemish Primitives holds some 30 works, which seem far from "primitive," by painters such as Jan Van Eyck (Portrait of his wife, Margerita Van Eyck), Rogier van der Weyden, Hieronymus Bosch (*The Last Judgment*), and Hans Memling. Works by Magritte and Delvaux are also on display. The museum is open Apr–Sept daily 9:30am–5pm; Oct–Mar Wed–Mon 9:30am–12:30pm and 2–5pm. Admission is BF 200 ($6.65) for adults, BF 100 ($3.35) for children.

In a courtyard next to the Groeninge Museum is the ornate mansion where Flemish nobleman and herb merchant Louis de Gruuthuse lived in the 1400s. Now the **Gruuthuse Museum,** Dijver 17 (☎ 050/33-99-11), it features thousands of antiques and antiquities, including paintings, sculptures, tapestries, lace, weapons, glassware, and richly carved furniture. The museum is open Apr–Sept daily 9:30am–5pm; Oct–Mar Wed–Mon 9:30am–12:30pm and 2–5pm. Admission is BF 130 ($4.35) for adults, BF 70 ($2.35) for children, BF 260 ($8.65) for families with children under 18.

A popular attraction in Bruges, needless to say, is the ✪ **Lace Center (Kantcentrum),** Balstraat 14 (☎ 050/33-00-72). Bruges lace is famous the world over, and there is no lack of shops offering you the opportunity to take some home. This is where the ancient art of lace making is passed on to the next generation, and you get a firsthand look at the artisans who will be making many of the items for future sale in all those lace shops (ideally, you should specify handmade lace, although it is more expensive than the machine-made stuff). The center is open Mon–Sat

10am–noon and 2–6pm (Sat until 5pm). Lace-making demonstrations are in the afternoon. Admission is BF 40 ($1.35) for adults, BF 25 (85¢) for children.

ORGANIZED TOURS

If you'd like a trained, knowledgeable guide to accompany you, the tourist office can provide one for BF 1,200 ($40) for the first 2 hours, BF 600 ($20) for each additional hour. Or in July and August join a daily guided tour at 3pm from the tourist office for BF 120 ($4); children under 14, free.

A "must" for every visitor is a ✪ **boat trip** on the city canals, a fine way to see the city. The open-top boats operate year-round and there are several departure points, all marked with an anchor icon on maps available at the tourist office. The boats operate Mar–Nov daily 10am–6pm; Dec–Feb on weekends, school holidays, and public holidays 10am–6pm (except if the canals are frozen!). A half-hour cruise costs BF 170 ($5.65) for adults, BF 85 ($2.85) for children over 4. Wear something warm if the weather is cold or windy.

Another lovely way to tour Bruges is by ✪ **horse-drawn cab,** and Mar–Nov they are stationed in the Burg (Wed in the Markt). A 30-minute ride costs BF 900 ($30) per cab, and BF 450 ($15) for each additional 15 minutes.

Coach tours (50 minutes) depart hourly every day from the Markt, first bus at 10am and last bus at 7pm in July and August, and at 4, 5, or 6pm in other months. Fares are BF 330 ($11) for adults, BF 200 ($6.65) for children; ☎ **050/31-15-50.**

ACCOMMODATIONS

Bruges's hotels fill up easily, particularly at the obvious peak times. Don't arrive without a reservation, especially in summer. If you do, the tourist office has a reservation service, and can also book in advance for you, as can tourist offices throughout the country. Accommodations are less heavily booked during the week than on weekends.

Expensive

✪ **Duc de Bourgogne.** Huidenvettersplein 12, 8000 Bruges. ☎ **050/33-20-38.** Fax 050/34-40-37. 10 rms. A/C TV TEL. BF 5,250 ($175) double. Rates include breakfast. AE, DC, MC, V.

Perhaps the most elegant of the small hotels, the Duc de Bourgogne is located in a 17th-century building on a canal. The fairly large guest rooms here are luxuriously furnished and decorated, with antiques scattered all through the hotel. There's a very good restaurant on the ground floor, overlooking the canal (see "Dining," below).

✪ **De Snippe.** Nieuwe Gentweg 53, 8000 Bruges. ☎ **050/33-70-70.** Fax 050/33-76-62. 7 rms, 6 suites. MINIBAR TV TEL. BF 5,000–7,500 ($167–$250) double. Rates include breakfast. AE, DC, MC, V.

Set in an early 18th-century building in the town center and long known as one of Bruges's leading restaurants (see "Dining," below), De Snippe also offers truly luxurious and spacious rooms. Many of them have fireplaces, and all have furnishings of restrained elegance.

De Swaene. Steenhouwersdijk 1, 8000 Bruges. ☎ **050/34-27-98.** Fax 050/33-66-74. 21 rms, 3 suites. MINIBAR TV TEL. BF 5,500–6,800 ($183–$227) double; BF 8,500–10,400 ($283–$347) suite. Rates include breakfast. AE, DC, MC, V.

This small hotel overlooking a canal in the town center has rightly been called one of the most romantic hotels in Europe. All guest rooms are elegantly furnished and very comfortable, each with an individual decor. The lovely lounge is actually the Guild Hall of the Tailors that dates back to 1779. Its restaurant, whose specialty is fish, has also won honors from guests as well as critics, and there's a sauna and an indoor swimming pool.

Moderate

❍ **'t Bourgoensche Cruyce.** Wollestraat 41, 8000 Bruges. ☎ **050/33-79-26.** Fax 050/34-19-68. 8 rms. TV TEL. BF 3,200–3,800 ($91–$108) single or double. Rates include breakfast. AE, DC, MC, V.

Opening onto a lovely little inner courtyard right in the middle of things (the Belfry in the town center is just 100 yards away), this tiny family-run hotel provides the very epitome of a Bruges experience. The rooms are big enough and modernly furnished. Best of all, however, is the hospitality of the proprietors who also oversee their noted restaurant—one of the best in Bruges—which occupies the ground floor (see "Dining," below).

Egmond. Minnewater 15, 8000 Bruges. ☎ **050/34-14-45.** Fax 050/34-29-40. 8 rms. TV TEL. BF 3,200–3,600 ($107–$120) double. Rates include breakfast. No credit cards.

With only 8 rooms in a rambling mansion with its own grounds next to the Minnewater Park, the Egmond offers lots of space, plenty of family ambience, bags of local color, and heaps of peace and tranquility.

❍ **Hotel Erasmus.** Wollestraat 35, 8000 Bruges. ☎ **050/33-57-81.** Fax 050/33-47-97. 9 rms. MINIBAR TV TEL. BF 3,250 ($93) double. Rates include breakfast. AE, DC, MC, V.

Just steps away from the Belfry, this small, cozy hotel is set in a picturesque little square alongside a canal in the town center. All rooms have writing desks and attractive, modern furnishings.

De Markies. 't Zand 5, 8000 Bruges. ☎ **050/34-83-34.** Fax 050/34-87-87. 18 rms. TV TEL. BF 2,900–3,200 ($97–$107) double. Rates include breakfast. AE, DC, MC, V.

For anyone who wants to experience Bruges's old-world charm while hanging on to modern comforts, and without paying too steep a price, this relatively new hotel is a good bet. Its location on the corner of the big square called 't Zand makes it convenient for the old center. The rooms are stylishy furnished and equipped.

Inexpensive

❍ **Fevery.** Collaert Mansionstraat 3, 8000 Bruges. ☎ **050/33-12-69.** Fax 050/33-17-91. 11 rms. TV TEL. BF 2,000–2,300 ($67–$77) double. Rates include breakfast. AE, DC, MC, V.

Centrally located near Markt, the rooms in this small hotel are comfortable and nicely furnished, with a small table and adequate seating in bedrooms. There's a downstairs bar and dining room, and baby-sitting can be arranged.

Graaf van Vlaanderen. 't Zand 19, 8000 Bruges. ☎ **050/33-31-50.** Fax 050/34-59-79. 14 rms (5 with bath). BF 1,625–2,465 ($54–$82) double with bath. Rates include breakfast. AE, DC, MC, V.

Along the east side of 't Zand near the railway station, this small hotel provides basic but comfortable accommodations and has a budget-priced restaurant. There's no elevator in this three-story hotel.

❸ **Hotel 't Keizershof.** Oostmeers 126, 8000 Bruges. ☎ **050/33-87-28.** No fax. 7 rms (none with bath). BF 1,300 ($43) double. Rates include breakfast. No credit cards.

Despite being one of the least expensive hostelries in Bruges, the 't Keizershof gets high marks for clean, comfortable accommodations in a quiet, peaceful location. Several languages are spoken by the young couple who own and operate the hotel near the railway station, and they are most helpful to guests in planning their Bruges stay.

Rembrandt-Rubens. Walplein 38. ☎ **050/33-64-39.** 13 rms. TEL. BF 1,500–2,300 ($50–$77) double. Rates include breakfast. No credit cards.

This really is a marvelous place, of the kind that makes Bruges such a joy to be in. On a quiet square near the Begijnhof, this centuries-old mansion is packed with atmosphere and with the kind of antique decorations that seem to span every period of Bruges's history. The rooms are comfortable and clean, if not luxuriously equipped, and a stay here is sure to be a memorable one.

DINING

Expensive

○ **'t Bourgoensche Cruyce.** Wollestraat 41–43. ☎ **050/33-79-26.** Reservations required. Three-course fixed-price meal BF 1,400 ($47) at lunch, BF 2,200 ($73) at dinner. AE, DC, MC, V. Thurs–Mon noon–2:30pm and 7–9:30pm. Closed Nov. CONTINENTAL.

You'd be hard put to find a better location, finer food, or a friendlier welcome. The rustic charm of this small dining room overlooking a canal in the town center is just one intimation of the culinary delights in store. Its regional specialties are perfection itself and the menu reflects the best ingredients available in any season, including superb seafood dishes.

Duc de Bourgogne. Huidenvettersplein 12. ☎ **050/33-20-38.** Reservations required. Fixed-price meal BF 1,400 ($47) at lunch, BF 2,250 ($75) at dinner. AE, MC, DC, V. Daily 10am–11pm. Closed July. FRENCH.

This large dining room overlooking a canal illuminated at night joins 't Bourgoensche Cruyce as two of the classics of Bruges. The menu is a lengthy one; the fixed-price lunch menu changes daily, and the fixed-price dinner changes every 2 weeks.

○ **De Snippe.** Nieuwe Gentweg 53. ☎ **050/33-70-70.** Reservations required. À la carte meals BF 1,900–3,500 ($63–$117). AE, DC, MC, V. Tues–Sat noon–2:30pm; daily 7–10pm. FLEMISH/FRENCH.

Set in the hotel of the same name in an 18th-century mansion, De Snippe enjoys a reputation as one of Bruges's finest restaurants. It's a reputation well earned, especially for its regional dishes. Try the crayfish creations, scampi, or sliced wild duck.

Moderate

⑤ **Bistro de Stove.** Kleine Sint-Amandsstraat 4. ☎ **050/33-78-35.** Reservations not necessary. Menus from BF 850–1,350 ($28–$45). MC, V. Noon–2:30pm and 7–11pm. Closed all day Wed and Thurs; lunch in Apr–Oct; Wed–Thurs Nov–Mar. FLEMISH/SEAFOOD.

A fairly small restaurant, with just 30 places, that combines a rustic atmosphere that has a touch more modern style than is the norm in Bruges. The seafood specialties are well worth a try, particularly the hutsepot van vis (fish stew).

○ **Kasteel Minnewater.** Minnewater 4. ☎ **050/33-42-54.** Reservations not necessary. Menu du marché BF 890 ($30); menu gastronomique BF 1,600 ($53). No credit cards. Tues–Sun 11:30am–2:30pm and 6:30–9:30pm. FRENCH/SEAFOOD.

Occupying a superb location near the Begijnhof, with a terrace on the Minnewater (Lake of Love), this château-style restaurant exudes an easygoing charm along with its fine food. It's particularly rewarding to fetch up here at the end of a long sightseeing trail through Bruges.

Inexpensive

○ **Brasserie Erasmus.** Wollestraat 35. ☎ **050/33-57-81.** Reservations not required. Snacks and one-plate dishes BF 250–500 ($7–$14). AE, DC, MC, V. Wed–Mon 11am–midnight. FLEMISH.

This small, popular restaurant is one of the most conveniently located "drop-in" places in Bruges—a great stop after viewing the cathedral and museums. It serves a large variety of Flemish dishes, all prepared with beer. About 150 different brands of beer are available. If you need help making a selection, ask owner Tom for advice.

't Koffieboontje. Hallestraat 4. ☎ **050/33-80-27.** Reservations not necessary. À la carte meals BF 300–1,600 ($10–$53). MC, V. Daily noon–11pm. SEAFOOD.

A bright and cheerfully modern interior makes a noticeable contrast to the often gloomy Bruges restaurant interiors. Of course, not many people go to Bruges to find Scandinavian ambience, but the seafood specialties here, especially lobster, should more than make up for the bright lights.

GHENT (GENT)

48km (30 miles) NW of Brussels, 51km (31 miles) SW of Antwerp, 46km (28 miles) SE of Bruges

Standing at the confluence of the Rivers Leie and Scheldt, Ghent was the seat of the powerful counts of Flanders, whose great castle, built in 1180, still stands as a gloomy reminder of their former power.

Ghent is sometimes considered a poor relation of Bruges in tourism terms, with historical monuments and townscapes not quite so pretty as its sister city, and therefore only to be visited if there is time after seeing Bruges. From a tourist's point of view there is some truth in this—but not much. Ghent is more of a lived-in city, a real, vibrant place compared with Bruges's air of being a museum piece. Life moves faster in Ghent, which is an important port and industrial center, yet it compensates for its less precious appearance with a vigorous social and cultural scene.

ESSENTIALS

ARRIVING   By Train   Ghent is 32 minutes by train from Brussels. The main railway station, **Sint-Pieters** (☎ 09/222-44-44), is on Maria Hendrikaplein, a mile or so south of the city center, and there is good tram service into town.

By Bus   The bus station (☎ 09/210-94-91) adjoins Sint-Pieters railway station.

By Car   Ghent is reached via the E-40 from Brussels, the E-17 from Antwerp, and the E-40 from Bruges.

VISITOR INFORMATION   The **Tourist Office** is in the crypt of the Town Hall (Stadhuis), Botermarkt, 9000 Ghent (☎ 09/266-52-32; fax 09/224-15-55), open daily Apr–Oct 9:30am–6:30pm; Nov–Mar daily 9:30am–4:30pm.

CITY LAYOUT   The **Korenmarkt** lies at the heart of the city (the Centrum). If you arrive by rail at Sint-Pieters, take tram no. 1 to this square. Most of the city's important sights—including the Town Hall, Saint Bavo's Cathedral, and the Belfry— lie within half a mile of the Korenmarkt. The River Leie winds through the city center to connect with the River Scheldt and a network of canals that lead to the busy port area. The **Citadel Park,** location of the Museum of Fine Arts, is near Sint-Pieters railway station.

GETTING AROUND   Ghent has an excellent tram, bus, and trolleybus system, with many lines converging at the Korenmarkt. Walking is the best way to see Ghent, at least in the center, and to experience its effortless combination of history and modernity at a human pace. Beyond the center, however, it is best to use the excellent and easily understood public transport net.

SPECIAL EVENTS   The last week of July witnesses the **Ghent Festivities (Gentse Feesten),** a time of music, dancing, and generally riotous fun and games throughout the city.

EXPLORING HISTORIC GHENT

Ghent's historic monuments have not all been prettified. Some of them look down-right gray and forbidding. Oddly enough, this gives them a more authentic feel. In the case of the Castle of the Counts of Flanders it was *meant* to look gray and for-bidding, seeing as the citizens of Ghent were so often in revolt against its overlord. The "Three Towers of Ghent" you'll hear referred to often are those of St. Bavo's Cathedral, the Belfry, and St. Nicholas Church, which form a virtually straight line in the direction of St. Michael's Bridge.

Probably the best starting point is **Saint Bavo's Cathedral (Sint-Baafskathedraal)**, Sint-Baafsplein (☎ **09/223-10-46**). Its rather plain gothic lines, dating from the 14th and 15th centuries, have been impressively decorated in baroque style in the interior, where, in addition, the crypt contains traces of the earlier romanesque Church of St. John. The interior is filled with priceless paintings, sculp-tures, screens, memorials, and carved tombs, as well as a remarkable pulpit in white marble entwined with oak, reminiscent of Bernini.

St. Bavo's showpiece, however, is the 24-panel altarpiece *The Adoration of the Mys-tic Lamb,* completed by Jan Van Eyck in 1432. Van Eyck's luminous use of oils and the naturalistic portrayal of nature and people represented a giant step away from the rigid style of gothic religious art. Besides its art historic value, the *Mystic Lamb* is spell-binding in its own right. Other art treasures in the cathedral include Rubens's *The Conversion of St. Bavo,* painted in 1624. Recently restored, it's in the Rubens Chapel, in the semicircular ambulatory behind the high altar. St. Bavo's is open daily 8:30am–6pm.

The *Adoration of the Mystic Lamb* altar and the Crypt are open Apr–Oct Mon–Sat 9:30am–noon and 2–6pm, Sun 1–6pm; Nov–Mar Mon–Sat 10:30am–noon and 2:30–4pm, Sun 2–5pm. Admission is BF 60 ($2) for adults, BF 50 ($1.65) for children.

Just across the square from the cathedral is the 14th-century **Belfry and Lakenhalle (Cloth Hall)**, Sint-Baafsplein (☎ **09/223-99-22**), over which it tow-ers. Together they form a glorious medieval ensemble. From the Belfry, great bells have rung out Ghent's civic pride down through the centuries, and a 54-bell caril-lon still does so today. An iron chest kept in the Belfry held the charters that spelled out the rights wrested from the counts of Flanders by the guilds and citizens of me-dieval Ghent. The Cloth Hall dates from 1425 and was the gathering place of wool and cloth merchants during the Middle Ages. The Belfry tower and its carillon can be visited with a guide, and with the aid of an elevator. Tours leave daily at hourly intervals, 2:10–5:10pm. Tickets cost BF 100 ($3.35) for adults, BF 30 ($1) for chil-dren (under 7 free).

Crouching like a gray stone lion over the city, the grim-looking ✪ **Castle of the Counts (Het Gravensteen)**, Sint-Veereplein (☎ **09/225-93-06**), was clearly de-signed by the counts of Flanders to send a message to rebellion-inclined Gentenaars: Keep your thoughts to yourself, or better still, don't have any at all. When it came to a siege, the besieged could afford to poke fun at the besiegers, discounting the un-likely possibility of them getting inside, and having a good memory for faces.

Surrounded by the waters of the River Leie, the castle was begun by Philip of Alsace, count of Flanders, fresh from the Crusades in 1180. If its 6-foot-thick walls, battlements, and turrets failed to intimidate attackers, the counts could always turn to a well-equipped torture chamber, some of whose fixtures and fittings can be seen in a small museum in the castle. The view of Ghent from the ramparts of the central keep, the donjon, is worth the climb. The castle is open daily Apr–Sept

9am–6pm; Oct–Mar daily 9am–5pm. Admission is BF 100 ($3.35), children under 12 free.

The **Stadhuis (Town Hall)** stands at the corner of Botermarkt and Hoogpoort (☎ **09/223-99-22**). A bit of a split personality, the Town Hall looks fairly plain on the Renaissance face it shows on the Botermarkt side, and almost garishly ornamented on the gothic side facing Hoogpoort. Work began on the building in 1518, and continued in fits and starts until the 18th century. Those centuries of changing public tastes, and the availability (or otherwise) of money, are reflected in the building's style. In its Pacificatiezaal (Pacification Room), the Pacification of Ghent was signed in 1567, declaring the Low Countries' repudiation of Spanish Habsburg rule and their intention to permit religious freedom. Guided tours leave at variable times from the tourist office in the Town Hall crypt. Tickets cost BF 100 ($3.35) for adults, BF 30 ($1) for children.

Located in the Citadel Park, the **Fine Arts Museum (Museum voor Schone Kunsten),** Nicolaas de Liemaeckereplein 3 (☎ **09/222-17-03**), houses ancient and modern art masterpieces, including works by Rubens, Van Dyck, and Bosch, along with moderns such as James Ensor and Constant Permeke. The museum is open Tues–Sun 9:30am–5pm. Admission BF 100 ($3.35), children under 12 free.

Set in a group of former almshouses in the city center dating from the 1300s, the ✪ **Folklore Museum (Museum voor Volkskunde),** Kraanlei 65 (☎ **09/223-13-36**), bases its appeal on a series of authentic replicas of the rooms where the craft skills and trades of the period around 1900 were practiced. There is also an attached marionette theater that presents performances (check with the museum for the schedule). The museum is open Apr–Oct daily 9am–12:30pm and 1:30–5:30pm; Nov–Mar Tues–Sun 10am–noon and 1:30–5pm. Admission is BF 100 ($3.35) for adults, BF 50 ($1.65) for children over 12.

A row of gabled guildhouses was built along the ✪ **Graslei quay** between the 1200s and 1600s, when the waterway was the harbor of Ghent. They form a perfect ensemble of colored facades reflected in the waters of the River Leie. To fully appreciate them, walk across the bridge over the Leie to the Korenlei on the opposite bank and view them as a whole, then return to saunter past each, conjuring in your imagination the craftsmen, tradespeople, and merchants for whom these buildings were the very core of their commercial existence. This is an ideal spot for snapping a picture to capture the essence of Ghent.

The **Vrijdagmarkt (Friday Market Square)** is a popular meeting point for Gentenaars, as it was a popular rallying point for them in times past. A statue of Jacob Van Arteveld stands in the square, a tribute to the leader of a revolt in the 1300s, and its base is adorned by the shields of some 52 guilds. Today the square is a major shopping area and the scene of a lively street market every Friday. A short distance away, the smaller Kanonplein Square is guarded by a gigantic cannon known as Mad Meg (Dulle Griet), which thundered away in the 1400s in the service of Burgundian armies.

ORGANIZED TOURS

Qualified guides (☎ **09/233-07-72**) lead private walking tours Mon–Fri at a charge of BF 1,500 ($50) for the first 2 hours, BF 600 ($20) for each additional hour.

Horse-drawn carriages leave from Sint-Baafsplein and Korenlei daily 10am and 7pm, from Easter to about October, for half-hour rides at a cost of BF 700 ($23.35).

A ✪ **boat ride** along the canals is an ideal way to see the city's highlights. Apr–Oct, open and covered boats leave every 30 minutes, daily 10am–7pm from the

Graslei and Korenlei, with a narrative in several languages. The trip lasts about 35 minutes, with fares of BF 150 ($5) for adults, BF 70 ($2.35) for children under 12.

ACCOMMODATIONS

The tourist office provides an up-to-date "Hotels and Restaurants" booklet at no cost and will also make hotel reservations for a returnable deposit. Considering its popularity, Ghent has fewer hotels than might be expected and those in the city center are often full at peak times, so try to book in advance.

Expensive

Novotel Gent Centrum. Goudenleeuwplein 5, 9000 Ghent. ☎ **09/224-22-30.** Fax 09/224-32-95. 117 rms, 4 suites. A/C MINIBAR TV TEL. BF 3,050–4,650 ($102–$155) double; BF 5,500 ($183) suite. Rates do not include breakfast. AE, DC, MC, V.

The location of this modern hotel couldn't be more convenient for sightseeing—it's very near the Town Hall in the city center, within easy walking distance of all major sights. The modern edifice has been designed to fit, more or less, into its ancient surroundings. The guest rooms are nicely furnished and have individual heating controls. The facilities are all you'd expect from a top hotel, with light, airy public rooms and a garden terrace.

Sofitel Gent Belfort. Hoogpoort 63. ☎ **09/233-33-31.** Fax 09/233-11-02. 127 rms, 1 suite. A/C MINIBAR TV TEL. BF 4,500–6,750 ($150–$225) single or double; BF 12,900 ($430) suite. Rates do not include breakfast. AE, DC, MC, V.

Probably Ghent's top hotel, with an enviable location just across the road from the Town Hall and within easy distance of the city's premier tourist attractions. And then, the rooms have all the facilities and services expected by a demanding international business and tourist clientele. The hotel is bright and modern and has been designed to fit at least partway into its venerable surroundings.

Moderate

Carlton. Koningin Astridlaan 138, 9000 Ghent. ☎ **09/222-88-36.** Fax 09/220-49-92. 22 rms. MINIBAR TV TEL. BF 2,500–2,800 ($83–$93) double. Rates include breakfast. AE, DC, MC, V.

Close to the E-17/E-40 interchange near the railway station, this modern-style hotel features rooms with pretty standard decor and furnishings. It has no restaurant or bar, but there are several in the neighborhood, and there's convenient parking in a garage next door.

Europahotel. Gordunakaai 59, 9000 Ghent. ☎ **09/220-60-71.** Fax 09/220-06-09. 37 rms, 1 suite. MINIBAR TV TEL. BF 2,500–3,300 ($83–$110) double. Rates include breakfast. AE, DC, MC, V.

This is a modern hotel set in the greenery of the Blaarmeersen suburb on Ghent's outskirts, on the banks of the River Leie. The rooms are large, with bright, attractive furnishings. There's an attractive bar, a good restaurant, and easy parking.

✪ Gravensteen. Jan Breydelstraat 35, 9000 Ghent. ☎ **09/225-11-50.** Fax 09/225-18-50. 17 rms, 2 suites. MINIBAR TV TEL. BF 3,150–3,750 ($105–$125) double; BF 4,615–5,240 ($154–$175) suite. AE, DC, MC, V.

On Jan Breydelstraat, a short walk from Graslei and the Castle of the Counts, this lovely mansion was built in 1865 as the home of a Ghent textile baron. You enter through the old carriageway (made up of ornamented pillars and an impressive wall niche occupied by a marble statue), which sets the tone for the attractive rooms you'll find inside. Those in front look out on the moated castle, while those to the back have city views. There's a top-floor "Belvedere" with windows offering magnificent views of the city. There's no dining room, but plenty of good restaurants are within easy walking distance.

✪ **Sint-Jorishof (aka Cour St-Georges).** Botermarkt 2, 9000 Ghent. ☎ **09/224-24-24.** Fax 09/224-26-40. 28 rms. MINIBAR (on request) TV TEL. BF 3,500–3,900 ($117–$130) double. AE, DC, MC, V.

In the city center opposite the town hall, the Sint-Jorishof is a historical treasure dating back to 1228 that has been an inn of quality from the very beginning. If you stay here you'll be in good company, historically speaking: Mary of Burgundy, Charles V, and Napoléon Bonaparte have all stayed under its roof. Try to get a room in the old building rather than in the more modern annex across the street. The decor is traditional in the pleasant and comfortable rooms, and the rates are quite low for such a prime location (one of the most convenient in town for sightseeing) and all the inbuilt atmosphere. Reserve as far in advance as possible. Just sitting in the hotel's restaurant in the Gothic Hall is an experience; dining there is very heaven (see below under "Dining").

Inexpensive

Many of the cafes and restaurants along Korenmarkt have inexpensive upstairs rooms (perfectly respectable and comfortable, but without private baths or "extras"). The tourist office can supply a list of those with satisfactory standards, as well as hostels in the area. Also, inquire at the tourist office about availability of rooms in the **University of Ghent residence halls** from mid-July to mid-September at very low rates (☎ **09/233-70-50;** fax 09/264-72-96). The **Youth Hostel De Draecke** is at Sint-Widostraat 11 (☎ **09/233-70-50;** fax 09/233-80-01).

Eden. Zuidstationstraat 24. ☎ **09/223-51-51.** Fax 233-34-57. 28 rms. TV TEL. BF 2,200–3,000 ($73–$100) double. Rates include buffet breakfast. AE, DC, MC, V.

A nice hotel in its price category not far out of the center and with a small parking area in the courtyard. The facilities are straightforward, but each room has at least a toilet and shower, although some are on the cramped side.

DINING

In keeping with the city's tradition as a center of Flemish culture, many of Ghent's restaurants keep the culinary traditions alive and well, in dishes such as the thick, creamy waterzooï op Gentse wijze (a soup that borders on being a stew), and lapin à la flamande (rabbit with beer, vinegar, and currant juice); or if it's the right season, asparagus from the Mechelen area. Prices are generally well below those in the similar places in Brussels. The helpful, free "Hotels and Restaurants" booklet published by the tourist office lists the more prominent eateries in all price brackets.

Very Expensive

✪ **'t Buikske Vol.** Kraanlei 17. ☎ **09/225-18-80.** Reservations recommended. Lunch menu BF 1,300 ($43); business lunch BF 1,800–2,275 ($60–$76); dinner menu BF 1,900 ($63). AE, MC, V. Mon, Tues, Thurs, Fri noon–2pm and 7–9:30pm, Sat 7–9:30pm. SEAFOOD/FRENCH.

One of the gems of Ghent, thanks to chef Peter Vyncke's insistence on the best ingredients and the creation of a cosy, intimate atmosphere in which to dine. It isn't open much, all things considered, but when it is, it does the business.

Expensive

✪ **Jan Breydel.** Jan Breydelstraat 10. ☎ **09/225-62-87.** Reservations recommended. Average lunch BF 1,250 ($42); à la carte meals BF 1,500–2,500 ($50–$83). AE, DC, MC, V. Tues–Sat noon–2pm and 7–10pm; Mon 7–10pm. SEAFOOD/FLEMISH.

Top honors go to this exquisite restaurant on a quaint street near the Castle of the Counts. Its interior is a gardenlike delight of greenery, white napery, and light woods. Dishes issuing from the kitchen are as light and airy as their setting, with delicate sauces and seasonings making the most of fresh ingredients. Seafoods or regional specialties are all superb. Highly recommended.

✪ Sint-Jorishof. Botermarkt 2. ☎ **09/224-24-24.** Reservations required. Lunch BF 920–1,450 ($31–$48); à la carte BF 1,150–1,890 ($38–$63). AE, MC, DC, V. Mon–Sat noon–2:30pm and 7–10pm; Sun noon–2:30pm. FLEMISH.

The Gothic Hall in this ancient inn is a marvel of dark woodwork, a massive fireplace, and stained glass, surrounded by an upstairs balcony. One of the Flemish dishes in which it specializes is paling in 't groen (eel with green sauce), and chicken waterzooï. It's in the hotel of the same name in city center, opposite the Town Hall.

Moderate
Auberge de Fonteyne. Goudenleeuwplein 7. ☎ **09/225-48-71.** Reservations not necessary. À la carte meals BF 700–1,000 ($23–$33). MC, V. Mon–Fri noon–2:30pm and 6pm–midnight; Sat–Sun noon–2am. MUSSELS/FLEMISH.

It might seem difficult for the food quality to equal the extravagant good looks of this art deco restaurant, but it comes pretty close. Waterzooï is a particular favorite here, as are heaps of the big Zeeland mussels that Belgium loses its collective cool over.

✪ Graaf van Egmond. Sint-Michielsplein 21. ☎ **09/225-07-27.** Reservations required. À la carte BF 475–1,475 ($16–$49). AE, DC, MC, V. Daily noon–3pm and 6–11pm. FRENCH/ FLEMISH.

In a marvelous old Ghent town house of the 1200s on the River Leie in the city center, the Graaf van Egmond serves Flemish specialties like carbonnade flamande (beef stew) and asparagus à la flamande, along with French creations. If you can get a window seat, there's a spectacular view of the towers of Ghent.

Inexpensive
Ⓢ Buddhasbelly. Hoogpoort 30. ☎ **09/225-17-32.** Reservations not necessary. Lunch menu BF 250 ($8). Dinner menus BF 375–675 ($12–$22). No credit cards. Mon–Sat noon–2:30pm and 6–10pm. VEGETARIAN.

You might take one look at the name and think that this is a brown-rice-and-sandals sort of place—and you'd be absolutely right. Not only do they not accept credit cards here, they may not even know what one looks like. Okay, enough jokes. The food is good, healthy, inexpensive, and made and served by people who believe in it and treat their customers like fellow travelers on the road of life.

Guido Meerschaut. Kleine Vismarkt 3. ☎ **09/223-53-49.** Reservations not necessary. Fixed-price menu BF 880 ($29). AE, DC, MC, V. Tues–Sat noon–2:30pm and 6–10:30pm. SEAFOOD/ FLEMISH.

The Guido of the restaurant's name owns a fish shop in the Fish Market and this is the restaurant of the fish shop—so it is no surprise what Guido's specialties are. Fresh off the boat from the North Sea and served in a simple yet elegant room, with paintings on the walls of times gone by in the Fish Market.

GHENT AFTER DARK
PERFORMING ARTS   Opera is performed in the 19th-century **De Vlaamse Opera,** Schouwburgstraat 3 (☎ 09/225-24-25), Oct–mid-June. Ghent venues for **✪ puppet shows** are: the Museum of Folklore, Kraanlei 65 (☎ 09/223-13-36); the Taptoe Teater, Forelstraat 91c (☎ 09/223-67-58); and Magie, Haspelstraat 39

(☎ 09/226-42-18). Check with the tourist board for performance schedules during your visit.

BARS & TAVERNS In typical Flemish fashion, the favorite after-dark entertainment in Ghent is frequenting its atmospheric bars and taverns. You'll have a memorable evening in any one you choose, but **Oud Middelhuis,** Graslei 6, provides a 17th-century setting plus more than 300 varieties of beer—well worth searching out. The same recommendation applies to **Dulle Griet,** Vrijdagmarkt 50, where if you deposit one of your shoes you'll be given a glass of potent Kwak beer in the too-collectable wooden frame that a Kwak glass needs to stand up—you may also need artificial support to stand up if you drink too many Kwaks. The tiniest building on romantic Graslei is the former Toll House, now a nice little tavern called **Het Tolhuisje,** Graslei 10.

Groentenmarkt, near the Castle of the Counts, makes for a pretty good pub-crawl in an easily navigable area. Try **Het Waterhuis aan de Bierkant,** Groentenmarkt 9, which has more than 100 different Belgian beers (including the locally made *Stopken*). A couple of doors along is **'t Dreupelkot,** Groentenmarkt 12, a specialist in deadly little glasses of jenever. Ask owner Paul to recommend one of his 100 or so varieties, or walk straight in and boldly ask for a 32° Jonge Hertekamp or a 36° Pekèt de Houyeu; if they don't knock you down, you may be up for a 50° eight-year-old Filliers Oude Graanjenever or a 52° Hoogspanning. Across the tram lines is **Het Galgenhuisje,** Groentenmarkt 5, a tiny and perforce intimate place popular with students.

LIÈGE & THE RIVER MEUSE VALLEY

Covering approximately one-fifth of the country, the rugged Meuse Valley is a taste of a different kind of Belgium. Dotted with resort towns and villages where fine cuisine is a way of life, a visit here after being in Brussels and the Flemish art cities of Bruges and Ghent adds the third dimension to Belgium, in the heartland of French-speaking Wallonia.

It is best to do this as a driving tour, beginning at Liège, and heading upstream alongside the Meuse to Namur, Huy, and Dinant. It is also easy to do the tour by train and bus; the towns are connected by frequent service.

LIÈGE
112km (69 miles) SE of Brussels

Liège is the big city in these parts, a hot-blooded, lively kind of place ("la Cité Ardente"), and a mixture of aging industrial gloom, the gracefully down-at-heel monuments of its Victorian heyday, and the glorious remnants from the time of the powerful prince-bishops of Liège.

Essentials
ARRIVING   By Train   There are frequent train services to Liège from Brussels, as well as Paris, Maastricht (Holland), Cologne, and Luxembourg. The main railway station is Gare de Guillemins, rue des Guillemins (☎ 04/229-26-10), 1¹/₂ miles south of the city center, with the bus station in front.

By Car   From Brussels by car, take the E-40 highway east.

VISITOR INFORMATION   The **Tourist Office** is at en Féronstrée 92 (☎ 04/221-92-21; fax 04/221-92-22). The Tourist Office of Liège Province is at bd de la Sauvenière 77, 4000 Liège (☎ 04/222-42-10; fax 04/222-10-92).

Liège

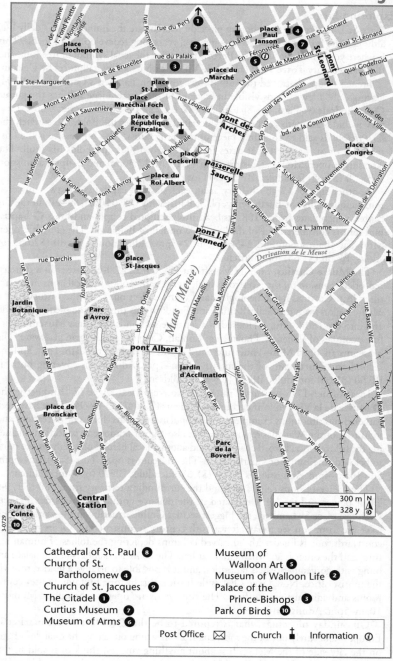

Cathedral of St. Paul **8**
Church of St.
   Bartholomew **4**
Church of St. Jacques **9**
The Citadel **1**
Curtius Museum **7**
Museum of Arms **6**

Museum of
   Walloon Art **5**
Museum of Walloon Life **2**
Palace of the
   Prince-Bishops **3**
Park of Birds **10**

Post Office ⊠   Church ✝   Information ⓘ

Exploring Liège

Place St-Lambert and neighboring place du Marché are the hub of Liège's daily life, although the former is undergoing a massive, years-long redevelopment process. This is where you'll find the 1698 **Le Perron fountain,** the local symbol of freedom, and the 18th-century **Town Hall (Hôtel de Ville),** with its lobby sculptures by Delcour. French troops destroyed the sumptuous gothic St. Lambert's Cathedral in 1794, leaving only a few stumps visible in place of St.-Lambert. Liège still has the gothic ✪ **Cathédrale St-Paul,** rue St-Paul 2A (☎ **04/222-04-26**), however, whose Treasury includes a superb gold reliquary donated by Charles the Bold. A bas-relief, the *Crucifixion,* is said to contain a piece of the True Cross. Also impressive is the bust reliquary of St. Lambert that dates from the early 1500s and holds his skull. The Treasury is open Mon–Sat 2–4pm, Sun 11:15am–12:30pm and 2–4pm; admission is BF 50 ($1.65) for adults, BF 30 ($1) for children.

Another sign of Liège's history as an ecclesiastical capital is the twin-towered romanesque **Eglise St-Barthélemy,** pl. St-Barthélemy (☎ **04/221-89-44**), in the city center, which dates from 1108. Its beautifully sculpted copper-and-brass ✪ **baptismal font** is considered one of the "Seven Wonders of Belgium." The church is open Mon–Sat 10am–noon and 2–5pm, Sun 2–5pm. Admission is BF 80 ($2.65) for adults, BF 50 ($1.65) for children.

The **Musée Curtius,** quai de Maestricht (☎ **04/223-20-68**), is set in a turreted red-brick mansion on the riverfront, built in the early 1600s by local arms manufacturer Jean Curtius. Its archeological and crafts collections trace the history of the Meuse region from the Gallo-Roman and Frankish eras through the medieval period and into the 18th century. Housed in a separate section is the **Glass Museum,** with fine examples of Venetian, Phoenician, Roman, Chinese, and Belgian glassware. The museums are open Mon–Thurs and Sat 2–5pm, Wed and Fri 10am–1pm, and the second and fourth Sun of the month 10am–1pm. Admission, covering both, is BF 50 ($1.65) for adults, BF 20 (65¢) for children.

In a former 17th-century Franciscan convent near place St-Lambert is the ✪ **Musée de la Vie Wallonne,** cour des Mineurs (☎ **04/223-60-94**). Here have been gathered multitudinous examples of the popular arts, crafts, forms of recreation, and industries of the Wallonia region. There is also a great marionette collection, including the beloved local hero, Tchantchès, and another local hero, if one perhaps not quite so beloved, the Emperor Charlemagne. The museum is open Tues–Sat 10am–5pm, Sun 10am–4pm. Admission is BF 50 ($1.65) for adults, BF 20 (65¢) for children.

The prince-bishops ruled Liège and the surrounding territory from 980 to 1794. Their power and wealth is reflected in the massive gothic ✪ **Palais des Prince-Evêques,** place St-Lambert, the biggest secular Gothic structure in the world, which took the form you see today after a 16th-century reconstruction. Of its two inner courtyards, one is lined with 60 carved columns depicting the follies of human nature, and the other is an ornamental garden. The council chambers of the palace are hung with gorgeous Brussels tapestries, and it is possible to arrange a guided tour via the tourist office. Now Liège's Palais de Justice, this historic building houses courtrooms and administrative offices. The courtyards are open to the public Mon–Fri 10am–5pm. Admission is free.

On Sunday morning, what is reputed to be the ✪ **oldest street market** in Europe—and surely one of the most colorful—is strung out along the quai de la Batte on the city side of the Meuse. Just about anything you can think of is sold in this mile-long bazaar of stalls: brass, clothes, flowers, foodstuffs, jewelry, toys, birds, animals, books, radios . . . the list is endless.

Accommodations

Bedford. Quai St-Léonard 36, 4000 Liège. ☎ **04/228-81-11.** Fax 04/227-45-75. 125 rms. A/C MINIBAR TV TEL. BF 6,950 ($232) double; weekend rates BF 2950 ($98) single and double. Rates include buffet breakfast. AE, DC, MC, V.

This a fairly new hotel with a good position beside the Meuse and whose front-room windows overlook the river. The old center is only a 10-minute walk away. It is fully and comfortably equipped to modern business standards, and has a restaurant and bar.

✪ **Cygne d'Argent.** Rue Beeckman 49, 4000 Liège. ☎ **04/223-70-01.** Fax 04/222-49-66. 23 rms. MINIBAR TV TEL. BF 2,500 ($98) double. AE, DC, MC, V.

There's a nice homey atmosphere at this small hotel near the railway station in the commercial and administrative center. The guest rooms vary in size, and furnishings are in traditional style. They can provide photocopying for guests, as well as limousine service and car rental. The hotel is located near the train station and the commercial and administrative district.

Ⓢ **Hôtel du Midi.** Place des Guillemins 1, 4000 Liège. ☎ **04/252-20-04.** Fax 04/252-16-13. 24 rms. TEL. BF 1,400 ($47) double (with shower). Rates include breakfast. MC, V.

A small but friendly, clean, and comfortable place close to the main railway station, which makes up for its relative lack of facilities with its location and reasonable prices.

Dining

Liège is the center of Walloon cuisine, being big enough to support a network of restaurants specializing in this tradition, whose popularity had waned in recent decades in favor of more "exotic" tastes but is now making a strong comeback.

✪ **Au Vieux Liège.** Quai de la Goffe 41. ☎ **04/223-77-48.** Reservations required. Fixed-price meal BF 1,100 ($37) at lunch, BF 2,000 ($67) at dinner. AE, DC, MC, V. Mon–Sat noon–2:45pm and 6:30–9:45pm. Closed mid-July to mid-Aug. SEAFOOD/CONTINENTAL.

This marvelous restaurant is located in the city center in a four-story 16th-century town house furnished in antiques of that era. Dinner is by candlelight, the waiters are in formal attire, and the food outshines even the setting. Almost any fish dish is a good choice.

Ⓢ **Brasserie as Ouhès.** Place du Marché 21. ☎ **04/223-32-25.** Reservations not required. Average three-course meal BF 750–2,000 ($25–$67). AE, MC, V. Mon–Fri noon–2:30pm; Mon–Sat 6pm–midnight. WALLOON.

Liège specialties are served with a flair in this tastefully decorated, rather large restaurant across from Town Hall and set on a narrow oblong public plaza that also holds a number of quite adequate, moderately priced eateries. Ouhès, however, is the best in its price range, and its menu is large enough to suit everyone's taste. Duck appears in more than one guise. It's extremely popular with local businesspeople at lunch, so go early or late.

✪ **Mamé V" Cou.** Rue de la Wache 9. ☎ **04/223-71-81.** Reservations not necessary. À la carte meals average BF 1,200 ($40). MC, V. Daily noon–2:30pm and 6:30–11:30pm. WALLOON.

The name is Walloon dialect for "A Nice Old Lady," and while it would be churlish to even consider owner Mme Dupagne's years, her welcome is certainly nice enough. Her oak-beamed restaurant serves traditional Walloon specialties such as pigs' kidneys flamed in Pekèt (geneva), chicken in beer, and hot black pudding with acid cherries.

HUY

A small and enchantingly quaint River Meuse resort town, 21 miles southwest of Liège, Huy was a center for tin- and copper-working in the Middle Ages, and has a long tradition of metalwork. Nowadays, pewter is the alloy of choice and in Huy there are shops filled with pewter objects crafted in and around the town.

Huy can be reached by car by taking the N-90 southwest. There are frequent train services from Liège to Huy's Gare du Nord, at place Zenobe Gramme (☎ 085/21-36-55), in front of which is the bus station (☎ 081/72-08-40). The **Tourist Office** is at quai de Namur 1 (☎ 085/21-29-15; fax 085/23-29-44).

What to See

Like many Mosan towns, Huy is dominated by its hilltop citadel, the **Fort de Namur,** chaussée Napoléon (☎ 085/21-53-34), built in 1818 on the site of earlier castles and forts going back to the Gallo-Roman period at least. In World War II it was used as a concentration camp by the Nazis and a museum on the site tells the tale as well as that of Belgium Resistance fighters. It can be reached on foot or by cable car from quai Batta, costing BF 100 ($3.35) single and BF 150 ($5) return for adults, BF 70 ($2.35) and BF 90 ($3) for children. The fort is open July–Aug daily 10am–8pm; Apr–June and Sept Mon–Fri 10am–6pm and Sat–Sun 10am–7pm. Admission is BF 120 ($4) for adults, BF 100 ($3.35) for children.

The 14th-century gothic ✪ **Notre-Dame Collegiate Church,** parvis Theoduin de Bavière (☎ 085/21-20-05), is famed for its magnificent stained-glass windows, including the beautiful rose window called *Li Rondia.* Its treasury contains the romanesque shrine of St. Mengold and many items in chiseled copper. The Treasury is open Sat–Thurs 9am–noon and 2–5pm (except during services). Admission is BF 50 (1.65).

NAMUR

A handsome riverside town, 18 miles from Huy, of some 40,000 inhabitants at the confluence of the Meuse and Sambre Rivers, Namur is the capital of Wallonia, and a pleasant yet bustling place considered to be the gateway to the Ardennes. Dominated by its vast hilltop Citadel, it also boasts fine museums and churches, a casino, and an elegant sufficiency of good cafes and restaurants, particularly along the narrow and atmospheric sidestreets of its old quarter.

From Huy by car, take the N-90 southwest to reach Namur. There are on average two trains an hour from Huy and Liège. The railway station is at square Léopold (☎ 081/25-22-23), with the bus station just in front (☎ 081/72-08-40). The **tourist information kiosk** is adjacent, at square de l'Europe Unie (☎ 081/22-28-59; fax 081/23-02-57). The **Tourist Office of Namur Province** is in the nearby village of Naninne, at rue Pieds d'Alouette 18, 5100 Naninne (☎ 081/40-80-10; fax 081/40-80-20).

What to See

The **Cathédrale St-Aubain,** place St-Aubain, is a domed structure dating from 1751, built on the site of a 1047 collegiate church of the same name that became the cathedral of the diocese of Namur in 1559, and whose belfry survives in the existing structure. Its Italian architect designed it in the light, ethereal Renaissance style of his native land, with columns, pilasters, cornices, vessels, and balustrades. In the adjacent **Musée Diocésain,** place du Chapitre 1 (☎ 081/22-21-64), is the cathedral's Treasury, a small but impressive collection of ecclesiastical relics, gold plate, and sculptures. The museum is open Easter Tues–Oct Tues–Sat 10am–noon and

2:30–6pm, Sun 2:30–6pm; Nov–Easter Sun, Tues–Sun 2:30–4:30pm. Admission is BF 50 ($1.65) for adults, BF 25 (85¢) for children.

Two scenic drives wind up the steep cliffside to Namur's hilltop ✪ **Citadel,** route Merveilleuse 8 (☎ **081/22-68-29**). An alternative is to take the cable car from rue Notre-Dame, which runs 10am–6pm daily Apr–Sept, weekends only Oct–Mar, and costs BF 160 ($5.35) for a single journey. There have been fortifications on the site for at least 2,000 years, with the present one dating mostly from the 18th and 19th centuries. The Citadel is now part of a 16-acre wooded estate that includes museums, children's play parks, restaurants, cafes, and craft shops. Visitors are shown a film on the history of the Citadel and given a tour of the fortifications. The Citadel is open June–Sept daily 11am–5pm; Easter–May Sat–Sun and public holidays 11am–5pm. Admission is BF 195 ($6.50) for adults, BF 100 ($3.35) each for the first two children, thereafter BF 80 ($2.65) per child from the same family.

Located in the former meat market on the banks of the River Sambre, and dating from the 15th century in the Renaissance style, the **Musée Archéologique,** rue du Pont (☎ **081/23-16-31**), displays important remains of the life and times of the Meuse Valley, from prehistoric through the Celtic, Roman, and Frankish periods into the Middle Ages. The museum is open Tues–Fri 10am–5pm; Sat–Sun 10:30am–5pm. Admission is BF 80 ($2.65) for adults, BF 40 ($1.35) for children over 6.

Namur sometimes seems unsure what to make of one of its best-known sons, the 19th-century painter and engraver Félicien Rops, who explored bizarre and erotic territory that the 19th century preferred to keep under wraps. The **Musée Rops,** rue Fumal 12 (☎ **081/22-01-10**), seems also to be kept under wraps, tucked away in a narrow sidestreet, but inside exposure is the name of the game. The museum is open July–Aug daily 10am–6pm; Sept–June Tues–Sun 10am–5pm. Admission is BF 100 ($3.35) for adults, BF 50 ($1.65) for children.

Accommodations

✪ **L' Excelsior.** Av de la Gare 4, 5000 Namur. ☎ **081/23-18-13.** Fax 081/23-09-29. 14 rms. TV TEL. BF 2,000 ($67) double; BF 2,700 ($90) triple. AE, DC, MC, V.

This comfortable small hotel with wheelchair access is conveniently located in the town center; the per-room rate may vary a little depending on whether you have a shower or full bath. There's a bar and restaurant on the premises.

✪ **Queen Victoria.** Av. de la Gare 21, 5000 Namur. ☎ **081/22-29-71.** Fax 081/24-11-00. 12 rooms. TV TEL. BF 1,250 ($42) single; BF 1,750 ($58) double. Rates include breakfast. AE, DC, MC, V.

Although small, it has comfortable, nicely furnished guest rooms and a convenient location across from the railway station. There's a bar and a good, moderately priced restaurant attached.

Les Tanneurs. Rue des Tanneries 13, 5000 Namur. ☎ **081/23-19-99.** Fax 081/22-97-03. 16 rms. MINIBAR TV TEL. BF 1,750–8,500 ($58–$283) double. Breakfast BF 300 ($10) extra. AE, DC, MC, V.

A luxuriously appointed hotel occupying a refurbished old building close to the confluence of the rivers Meuse and Sambre. There is a good restaurant and grill with the hotel, but these tend to specialize in seminars and groups, and can get a bit too busy as a result.

Dining

The best meals in and near Namur are in the hotel restaurants listed below and the small bistros (many with sidewalk cafe service in good weather) around place

Marché-aux-Legumes, rue des Frippiers, and rue de la Croix, with prices in the moderate range. For inexpensive meals, look to the cluster of restaurants near the Citadel.

✪ **Brasserie Henry.** Pl. St-Aubin 3. ☎ **081/22-02-04.** Reservations not required. Fixed-price lunch BF 260 ($9); à la carte meals BF 750–1,200 ($25–$40). AE, DC, MC, V. Daily 8am–1am. FRENCH.

Long, elegant brasserie with a plant-bedecked terrace at the back for dining in good weather. It's a pretty informal place, yet things are still done with a touch of class and the food is very good. Located just outside the Cathedral of St. Aubin in one of Namur's nicest squares, this is a good place to get a feel for the new Namurois style.

◎ **La Petite Fugue.** Pl. Chanoine Descamps 5. ☎ **081/23-13-20.** Reservations required. Fixed-price lunch BF 600 ($20); à la carte meals BF 700–1,300 ($23–$43). Tues–Fri noon–1:30pm and 7–9:30pm; Sat 7–9:30pm; Sun noon–2:30pm. FRENCH.

An intimately atmospheric little place in the heart of old Namur, where the emphasis is on quality rather than the quantity of customers. Prices are reasonable considering the good food and attentive service, and its 20 or so places fill up fast enough during its short opening hours. There is a good choice of wines and some good advice to go along with them.

✪ **Le Queen.** In the Queen Victoria Hotel, av. de la Gare 12. ☎ **081/22-29-71.** Reservations not required. Menu of the day BF 600 ($17); fixed-price meal BF 1,200 ($40); average à la carte meal BF 800 ($23). AE, DC, MC, V. Daily noon–2:30pm and 6–11:30pm. SEAFOOD/FRENCH.

This pleasant hotel restaurant in the town center offers an extensive menu, with such specialties as sole meunière and an excellent bouillabaisse of the North Sea.

En Route to Dinant

On the N-92 out of Namur, you'll pass Wépion, a sleepy riverside village that is an important strawberry-growing center. Further along, at Annevoie-Rouillon, then a short way along the N-932, you reach the ✪ **Jardins d'Annevoie,** route des Jardins (☎ **082/61-15-55**), in the grounds of a château whose 18th-century ornamental gardens and fountains make a splendid display. The many ways that water is used to create visual delight—fountains, waterfalls, lagoons, streams, canals—is reminiscent of Tivoli's Villa d'Este, although not on quite so dramatic a scale.

The 18th-century Château d'Annevoie and its outbuildings are laid out in a harmonious design reflected in the lagoon alongside, and inside there are fine architectural details in the woodwork, stuccos, fireplaces, and the family chapel. The gardens are open Apr–Oct daily 9:30am–6:30pm; the château, July–Aug daily 9:30am–1pm and 1:30–6:30pm; Apr–June and Sept Sat–Sun and public holidays only. Admission to both gardens and château are BF 200 ($6.65) adult, BF 140 ($4.65) child; for gardens only, BF 170 ($5.65) adult, BF 120 ($4) child; for château only, BF 100 ($3.35) adult, BF 70 ($2.35) child.

DINANT

Like Liège, Huy, and Namur, Dinant is a fortress town, and like them has suffered over the centuries for its Citadel, perched on its highest hilltop overlooking the Meuse. Now, the Citadel is a museum piece, and Dinant is perhaps the handsomest resort town on the river. When not trying to fend off invaders, its people developed such skill in working beaten copper that their engravings were sought after as early as the 13th century, and Dinanderie-ware still makes prized souvenirs from the area.

On average there are two trains an hour from Namur, as well as regular bus services. The **Tourist Office** is at rue Grande 37 (☎ **082/22-28-70;** fax 082/22-77-88).

What to See

The ✪ **Citadel,** Le Prieuré (☎ **082/22-36-70**), built in 1530 and perched on a cliff high above the town and river, can be reached by car or cable car. If you're feeling particularly energetic or can't turn down the challenge, there are 400 steep steps leading to the bluff top and its spectacular view. The Citadel is open Apr–Sept daily 10am–6pm; Oct–Dec and Feb–Mar Sat–Thurs 10am–4pm; Jan Sat–Sun 10am–4pm. Admission is BF 180 ($6) for adults and BF 140 ($4.65) for children; includes the cable-car fare.

Accommodations

✪ **L'Auberge de Bouvignes.** Rue Fétis 112, route de Namur, 5500 Dinant. ☎ **082/61-16-00.** 6 rms. TV TEL. BF 3,000 ($100) double. Rates include breakfast. AE, DC, MC, V.

Two miles from Dinant, this lovely soft-rose brick inn on the banks of the Meuse has one of the best kitchens around, and its six charming guest rooms, beautifully decorated and furnished, are perfect retreats after a day of busy sightseeing. Try to book well in advance.

Ⓢ **Hôtel de la Citadelle.** Pl. Reine-Astrid 5, 5500 Dinant. ☎ **082/22-35-43.** 20 rms (7 with bath). TV TEL. BF 1,700 ($57) double without bath, BF 2,300 ($77) double with bath. Rates include breakfast. No credit cards.

This well-kept hotel, centrally located in Dinant, has comfortable rooms, a nice bar, and a reasonably priced restaurant.

Hôtel de la Couronne. Rue Adolphe-Sax 1, 5500 Dinant. ☎ **082/22-24-41.** 22 rms (some with bath), 2 suites. TV TEL. BF 2,200 ($73) double with bath; BF 3,000 ($100) suite. AE, MC.

In the center of town, this pleasant hotel has a good, moderately priced restaurant and tavern. There's a homey feeling about the place, which features traditional decor and furnishings in its comfortable and attractive rooms.

Dining

Le Thermidor. Rue de la Station 3. ☎ **082/22-31-35.** Reservations recommended. Average meal BF 2,000–2,500 ($67–$83). AE, MC, V. Wed–Mon noon–2:30pm; Wed–Sun 6–10pm. SEAFOOD.

Widely considered the best Dinant restaurant, the Thermidor specializes in such delicacies as crayfish dinantaise, and the country-style pâté is terrific. It's located in the town center.

3

The Czech Republic

by John Mastrini & Alan Crosby

If you have time to visit only one Eastern European city, the place to
go is Prague. The quirky and compact Czech capital, often called
"baroque Disneyland" because of its fairy-tale architecture, is a
perfect end-of-millennium European destination—here you'll
encounter the triumphs and tragedies of the past 10 centuries spiked
with the peculiarity of the postcommunist reconstruction.

And in west Bohemia, home to the country's spas, a lively tourist scene is already in place.

1 Prague & Environs

by John Mastrini

Prague today is much too busy to spend a lot of time looking
back before 1989's bloodless citizens' revolt known as the "Velvet
Revolution," but the mixture of its turbulent past, its pristine architecture, and its promising future gives it an eclectic energy. The
six-centuries-old Charles Bridge is now jammed with an army of
friendly invaders—tourists and entrepreneurs looking to take home
memories, or profit, from a once-captive city, now fully employing
its born-again freedoms.

ONLY IN PRAGUE

Strolling Across Charles Bridge at Dawn or Dusk The silhou-
ettes of the statues lining the crown jewel of Czech heritage hover
like ghosts in the still of the sunrise skyline. Early in the morning you
can stroll across the bridge without encountering the crowds that will
be there by midday. At dusk, the statues are the same, but the odd
light play makes the bridge and the city completely different than in
the morning.

Romping Late at Night on Charles Bridge "Peace, Love, and
Spare Change" describes the scene, as musicians, street performers,
and flower people come out late at night to become one with the
bridge.

Proceeding Down the Royal Route The downhill jaunt from
Prague castle, through Malá Strana (Lesser Town), across Charles
Bridge to Old Town Square, is a day in itself. The trip recalls the

route taken by the carriages of the Bohemian Kings; today it's lined with quirky galleries, shops, and cafes.

Spending a Moment with the Children of Terezín   On display at the Ceremonial Hall of the Old Jewish Cemetery are sketches drawn by children held at the Terezín concentration camp. These drawings are a moving lesson in the Nazi occupation of Czechoslovakia.

Getting Lost in Staré Město   Every week a new cafe nook or gallery cranny seems to pop up along the narrow winding streets of Staré Město (Old Town). Prague is best discovered by those who easily get lost on foot, and Old Town's impossible-to-navigate streets are made for it.

Wandering Around the Practice Halls   During hotter weather, many windows of rehearsal rooms scattered throughout Staré Město (Old Town) and Malá Strana (Lesser Town) are open. Lucky wanderers may stumble upon a free concert amid the ancient alleys.

Enjoying an Afternoon in the Letná Beer Garden   Nice weather sends Czechs in search of open air and affordable beer. The tree-covered Letná Chateau (Letenský Zámeček) garden on the Letná plain is a hidden treasure that serves up a local favorite brew from Velké Popovice called "Kozel" (Goat), as well as a great city view.

Experiencing Beer and Oompah-Pah at U Fleků   A more raucous and touristy beer experience can be found at the U Fleků beerhall in New Town. You can wash down traditional Czech dishes with U Fleků's own dark home brew, accompanied by traditional drinking music.

Picnicking on Vyšehrad   Of all the parks where you could picnic in Prague, the citadel above the Vltava that guards the south end of the old city is the most calm and interesting spot. Its more remote location means less tourist traffic, and the gardens, city panoramas, and national cemetery provide pleasant walks and poignant history.

Making a Trip to Karlštejn Castle   A 30-minute train ride south puts you in the most visited Czech landmark outside of Prague, built by King Charles IV (Karel IV in Czech, who is the namesake of Charles Bridge) in the 14th century to protect the crown jewels of the Holy Roman Empire. This romanesque hilltop bastion fills the image of the castles of medieval lore.

ORIENTATION

ARRIVING   By Plane   Prague's **Ruzyně Airport** (☎ **02/36-77-60** or 36-78-14) lies 12 miles west of the city center. There's a bank for changing money (usually open daily 7am–11pm), telephones, and several car-rental offices.

Taxis are plentiful and line up in front of the airport. The fancy cars parked directly in front of the terminal will cost about twice the price of the rickety Škoda and Lada taxis waiting off to the right. ČSA, the Czech national airline, operates an airport shuttle to and from nám Republiky in downtown Prague, which runs every 30 minutes or so from 7:30am–7:30pm. The ČSA main office, at Na celnici 5 (☎ **02/2431 4270**) is centrally located, about five blocks from the náměstí Republiky metro station. The shuttle costs 30 Kč ($1) per person. You can also take city bus no. 119, which goes to the Dejvická metro station (Line A).

By Train   Passengers traveling to Prague by train typically pull into one of two centrally located stations: Hlavní Nádraží (Main Station) or Nádraží Holešovice (Holešovice Station). Both are on Line C of the metro system and offer a number

Prague Attractions & Accommodations

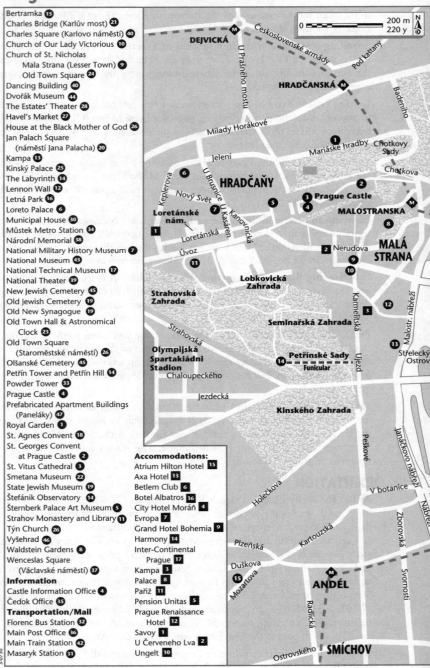

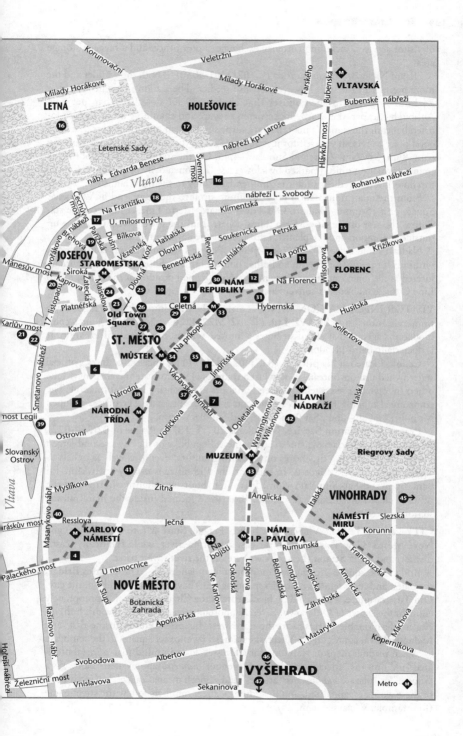

of visitor services, including currency exchange, a post office, and a luggage-storage area.

Hlavní Nádraží, Wilsonova třída (☎ **02/2461-4030**), is both the grander and the more popular of the two; however, it's also seedier. The station's basement holds a 24-hour luggage-storage counter that charges 20 Kč (74¢) per bag per day. Although cheaper, the nearby lockers aren't secure and should be avoided. Also located beneath the station's main hall are surprisingly clean public showers that are a good place to refresh yourself for just 30 Kč ($1.11); the showers are open Mon–Fri 6am–8pm, Sat 7am–7pm, and Sun 8am–4pm. On the station's second floor is the train information office (marked by a lowercase "i"), open daily 6am–10pm. On the top floor is a tattered restaurant recommendable only to the most famished.

From the main train station it's a 5-minute stroll to the "top" end of Wenceslas Square or a 15-minute walk to Old Town Square. Metro Line C connects the station to the rest of the city. Metro trains depart from the lower level. Taxis line up outside the station and are plentiful throughout the day and night.

Nádraží Holešovice (☎ **02/2461-5865**), Prague's second station, is usually the terminus for trains from Berlin and other points north. Although it's not as centrally located as the main station, its more manageable size and position at the end of metro Line C make it almost as convenient.

VISITOR INFORMATION   If you're arriving by train into either of Prague's two primary stations, stop by **AVE Ltd.** (☎ **02/2422-3226** or 2422-3521), an accommodations agency that also distributes a limited amount of printed information. It is open daily 6am–11:30pm.

Čedok, located at Na příkopě 18 (☎ **02/2419-7111**), once the country's official state-owned visitors bureau, is now just a traditional semiprivate travel agency. Like others in town, it prefers selling tickets and tours to dispensing free information. The company also books rail tickets and accepts major credit cards. The offices are open Mon–Fri 8:30am–6pm, Sat 9am–1pm, and Sun 9am–2pm.

Prague Information Service, Na příkopě 20 (☎ **187** in Prague or **02/264-022**), located between Václavské náměstí and náměstí Republiky, is the city's second-largest tourist office, offering brochures on upcoming cultural events as well as tickets to sightseeing tours and concerts. In summer, the PIS office is usually open Mon–Fri 9am–6pm and Sat–Sun 9am–5pm. In winter, hours are slightly shorter and the office is closed on Sunday. A second PIS office is located inside the main railway station.

CITY LAYOUT   The Vltava River bisects Prague. **Staré Město** (Old Town) and **Nové Město** (New Town) are on the east side of the river, while **Hradčany** (castle district) and **Malá Strana** (Lesser Town) are on the river's west bank.

Bridges and squares are Prague's most prominent landmarks. The **Charles Bridge,** the oldest and most famous of the 15 spanning the Vltava, is in the middle of the city. **Old Town Square,** a few winding blocks east of the Charles Bridge, is, appropriately enough, the center of Old Town. Several important streets radiate from this hub, including fashionable **Pařížská** to the northwest, historic **Celetná** to the east, and **Melantrichova,** connecting to **Václavské náměstí** (Wenceslas Square) to the southeast.

When reading maps or searching for addresses, keep in mind that *ulice* (abbreviated "ul.") means "street," *třída* means "avenue," *náměstí* (abbreviated "nám.") is a "square" or "plaza," *most* means "bridge," and *nábřeží* means "quay." In Czech none of these words is capitalized, and in addresses, street numbers follow the street name (for example, Václavské nám. 25).

GETTING AROUND   Prague's public transportation network is both vast and efficient—one of the few sound communist-era legacies.

Fares for Public Transportation   The city's metros, trams, and buses all share the same price structure and ticket system. A new system of fares took effect in summer 1996.

You have two choices for single-use tickets. Tickets that cost 6 Kč (22¢) allow up to 15 minutes of travel on a bus or tram, without transfers, or for a trip of no more than four stations within the metro. We recommend this option if you want to go between two sights within the old districts of the city. This ticket is not valid on trams, buses after midnight, and on the funicular on Petřín hill. Tickets that cost 10 Kč (37¢) allow unlimited travel, including transfers, on all forms of municipal transport for 60 minutes during work days from 5am to 8pm, or you can use it for 90 minutes between 8pm and 5am and on Saturday and Sunday.

It may be more convenient to buy a tourist pass. The fares are 50 Kč ($1.85) for a 1-day pass; 130 Kč ($4.81) for a 3-day pass; 190 Kč ($7.30) for a 7-day pass; and 220 Kč ($8.14) for a 15-day pass. No picture is necessary.

You can buy tickets from yellow coin-operated machines in metro stations or at most newsstands marked "Tabák" or "Trafika." Hold on to your validated ticket throughout your ride—you'll need to show it if a plain-clothes ticket collector (be sure to check for his badge) asks you. If you're caught without a valid ticket, you'll be asked (not so kindly) to pay a 200 Kč ($7.40) fine on the spot.

By Metro   Metro trains operate daily from 5am to midnight and run every 2 to 6 minutes or so. On the three lettered lines (A, B, and C) the most convenient central Prague stations are Můstek, at the foot of Václavské náměstí (Wenceslas Square); Staroměstská, for Old Town Square and Charles Bridge; and Malostranská, serving Malá Strana and the Castle District.

By Tram   The city's two dozen electric tram (streetcar) lines run practically everywhere. There's always another tram with the same number traveling back. You never have to hail trams; like trains, they automatically make every stop. The most popular tram, no. 22 (dubbed the "tourist tram" or the "pickpocket express"), runs past top sights like the National Theater and Prague Castle.

By Bus   As with other means of public transportation, bus riders must purchase the same tickets in advance, and validate them on boarding. Regular bus and tram service stops at midnight, after which selected routes run reduced schedules, usually only once per hour. If you miss a night connection, expect a long wait for the next.

By Funicular   The funicular, a cog railway, dashes up and down Petřín Hill every 15 minutes or so from 9:15am–8:45pm. It requires the 10 Kč (37¢) ticket, and departs from a small house in the park just above the middle of Újezd in Malá Strana. The incline tram makes two stops—one at the Nebozízek Restaurant in the middle of the hill and the other at the top.

By Taxi   Taxis can be hailed in the streets or found in front of train stations, large hotels, and popular tourist attractions. *Be warned:* The great majority of cab drivers routinely rip off unsuspecting tourists. The meter should start no higher than 10 Kč (37¢). When riding within the city center, the meter should then climb at a rate of 12 Kč (44¢) per kilometer (although city hall was in the process of changing regulated rates at this writing). If you phone for a taxi, chances are pretty good that you'll be charged the official rate, as your trip is logged in an office and is a matter of public record. Reputable taxi companies with English-speaking dispatchers include **AAA**

Taxi (☎ 312-2112 or 3399); **RONY Taxi** (☎ 692-1958 or 43-04-03); and the unfortunately named **ProfiTaxi** (☎ 6104-5555 or 6104-5550 or 1035).

By Car   Driving in Prague is not worth the money or effort. The roads are frustrating and slow, parking minimal and expensive. But if you must drive, you can rent a car from **Europcar/InterRent,** Pařížská 28 (☎ 02/2481-0515 or 2481-1290), open daily 8am–8pm; **Hertz,** Karlovo nám. 28 (☎ 02/292-147); **Budget,** at Ruzyně Airport (☎ 02/316-5214) and in the Hotel Inter-Continental, náměstí Curieových (☎ 02/231-9595); and **Avis,** E. Krásnohorské 9 (☎ 02/231-5515). For possible lower rates, check with the following local car-rental companies: **Prague Car Rent,** Opletalova 33 (☎ 02/2422-9848); and **SeccoCar,** Přístavní 39 (☎ 02/684-3403).

FAST FACTS: Prague

American Express   The sole office is located at Václavské nám. (Wenceslas Square) 56 (☎ 02/2421-9992; fax 02/2422 7708), open Mon–Fri 9am–6pm and Sat 9am–2pm, sometimes closing for lunch from 1:30–2pm. To report lost or stolen Amex cards, call 2/2421-9978.

Business Hours   Most banks are open Mon–Fri 9:30am–3:30pm, and some on Sat 9:30am–noon. Stores are open Mon–Fri 10am–6pm, Sat 10am–1pm, with those in the tourist center keeping longer hours and open Sunday as well. Some small food shops that keep long hours charge up to 20% more for all their goods after 8pm or so.

Currency   **The Czech crown (koruna),** abbreviated Kč, is divided into 100 hellers. There are seven banknotes and nine coins. Notes, each of which bears a forgery-resistant metal strip and a prominent watermark, are issued in 20, 50, 100, 200, 500, 1,000, and 5,000 crown denominations. Coins are valued at 10, 20, and 50 hellers and 1, 2, 5, 10, 20, and 50 crowns. At this writing $1 = approximately 27 Kč, or 1 Kč= 3.5¢.

Currency Exchange   When changing money in Prague, you'll get a better rate for cash than for traveler's checks. Banks generally offer the best exchange rates, but American Express is competitive and doesn't charge commission. Beware of CheckPoint and other private money-changing places that charge obscenely high commissions. Automated-teller machines (ATMs) are located throughout the city center, and many accept cards linked to the CIRRUS network. Some convenient locations include Na příkopě 5; Václavské nám. (Wenceslas Square) 42; and by the Kotva department store at nám. Republiky 8.

Doctors & Dentists   For emergency medical aid call the Foreigners' Medical Clinic, Na Homolce Hospital (☎ 02/5292-2146 or 5292-2191). For other medical needs, visit the First Medical Clinic of Prague Ltd., Vyšehradská 35 (☎ 02/292-286). The clinic provides 24-hour emergency health care as well as house calls, and referrals to specialists. Normal walk-in hours are Mon–Sat 7am–8pm.

Drugstores   The most centrally located pharmacy (*lékárna*) is at Václavské nám. 8 (☎ 02/2422-7532), open only Mon–Fri 8am–6pm. The nearest 24-hour pharmacy "U Anděla" is at Štefánikova 6 (☎ 02/2451-1112), on metro line B at the Anděl station.

Embassies   The **U.S.** Embassy, at Tržiště 15 (☎ 02/2451-0847), is open Mon–Fri 8–11:30am and 2:30–4pm. The **Canadian** Embassy, Mickiewiczova 6 (☎ 02/2431-1108), is open Mon–Fri 10am–noon and 2–4pm. The **British** Embassy, Thunovská 14 (☎ 02/2451 0439), is open Mon–Fri 9am–noon. Call for an

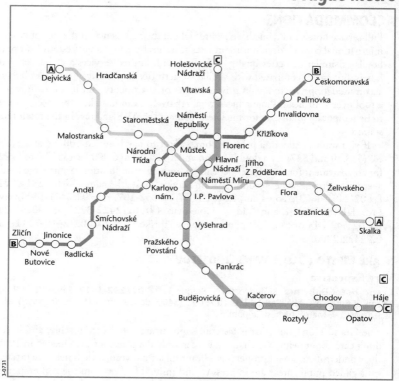

appointment at the **Australian** Honorary Consul, Na Ořechovce 38 (☎ 02/2431-0743).

Emergencies   Police (☎ 158), fire (☎ 158), ambulance (☎ 155).

Eyeglasses   There are spectacle shops on Na příkopě and Václavské náměstí. The best place for repairs is Lumina Optic, Skořepka 1 (☎ 02/2421-9915).

Hospitals   Particularly welcoming to visitors is University Hospital Motol, V úvalu 84 (Motol) (☎ 02/2443-1111). Their English-speaking doctors also make house calls.

Lost Property   Stop by the city's Lost Property Office, Karolíny Světlé 5 (☎ 02/2423-5085).

Luggage Storage/Lockers   The train stations Hlavní Nádraží and Nádraží Holešovice both charge 20 Kč (74¢) per bag per day, and storage is technically open 24 hours, but if your train is departing late at night, make sure someone will be around. All city train stations have luggage lockers, but they are not secure and should be avoided. The Ruzyně Airport Luggage Storage Office never closes, and charges 60 Kč ($2.22) per item per day. You can also often leave luggage at some hotels, even if you're not a guest; the Hotel Paříž charges approximately 50 Kč ($1.85) per item.

Tax   A 22% value-added tax (VAT) applies to most restaurant, hotel, and shop items and is included in the menu, rate card, or ticket price, rather than tacked on at the register.

ACCOMMODATIONS

Full-service hotels in Prague have had to tighten their efficiency in the face of heavier international competition, but room rates still top those in many Western European hotels of similar or better quality. Pensions with limited services are cheaper than hotels, but again, compared with similar western B&Bs, are pricey. The best budget accommodations are rooms in private homes or apartments. But if you require just a roof over your head, Prague has several relatively clean hostels. Most hostels seem to be temporary affairs, so for the latest, contact the **AVE agency,** in the main train station.

If you want to stay in a private room, expect to pay between 500 Kč and 1,000 Kč ($18.50 and $37) for a double room, and 1,500 Kč to 6,000 Kč ($55.50 to $222) for an apartment for two. Rates depend on both size and location. Some large rental agencies include Prague Accommodation Service, Haštalské nám. (☎ **02/231-0202;** fax 02/2481-0603); Top Tour, Rybná 3 (☎ **02/232-1077;** fax 02/2481-1400); Ave Ltd., Hlavní Nádraží and Nádraží Holešovice (☎ **02/2422-3226** or 2422-3521; fax 02/549-743 or 542-239); and Čedok, Napříkopě 18 (☎ **02/2419-7111;** fax 02/2422-2300).

STARÉ MĚSTO (OLD TOWN) & JOSEFOV

Very Expensive

Grand Hotel Bohemia. Královdvorská 4, Prague 1. ☎ **02/232-3417.** Fax 02/232-9545. 78 rms, 8 suites. A/C MINIBAR TV TEL. 10,790 Kč ($400) double; from 15,000 Kč ($555) suite. AE, DC, MC, V. Metro: náměstí Republiky.

The Grand Hotel Bohemia is tasteful, sophisticated, and comfortable, and if you don't care about being overcharged, it's certainly the place to stay. Opened in 1994, the wonderfully restored property is a beautiful art nouveau–style hotel. The extravagant gilded public areas are impressive and quite different from the contemporary guest rooms. The bright and cheerful accommodations are not large, but are fitted with business-oriented extras such as trouser presses, faxes, and answering machines. The unspectacular hotel restaurant should only be used as a matter of convenience. There's also a small cafe.

Hotel Inter-Continental Prague. Curieových 5, Prague 1. ☎ **02/2488-1111.** Fax 02/2481-1216. 365 rms, 27 suites. A/C MINIBAR TV TEL. 8,200–9,000 Kč ($303–$333) double; from 14,000 Kč ($518) suite. Rates include buffet breakfast and entrance to pool with sauna. Children under 10 stay free in parents' room. AE, DC, MC, V. Metro: Staroměstská.

It's hard to blame the building's ugly exterior on the communist regime; 1970s architecture was unsightly the world over. None of the standard guest rooms are particularly large, though they are well dressed in top business style, with good closets, computer ports, and marble baths. Zlatá Praha, the top-floor continental restaurant with wraparound windows, offers terrific views of Prague's spires and rooftops.

Expensive

✪ **Hotel Paříž.** U Obecního domu 1, Prague 1. ☎ **02/2422-2151.** Fax 02/2422-5475. 96 rms, 4 suites. TV TEL. 5,900–6,200 Kč ($218–$229) double; from 9,600 Kč ($355) suite. Rates include breakfast. AE, CB, DC, MC, V. Metro: náměstí Republiky.

Although the Paříž is one of Prague's best hotels, it still doesn't compare to deluxe hotels in most western cities. The building is a neogothic historical landmark, packed with plenty of eye-catching art nouveau elements. Every guest room is different and, although amenities can vary slightly, all are handsomely decorated, with firm beds and soft couches. The restaurant Sarah Bernhardt features a beautiful dining room, but style outweighs substance.

Ungelt. Štupartská 1, Prague 1. ☎ **02/2481-1330.** Fax 02/231-9505. 10 suites. TV TEL. 4,900 Kč ($181) one-bedroom suite; 5,740 Kč ($212) two-bedroom suite. AE, V. Metro: Staroměstská or line B to náměstí Republiky.

You can't find a more centrally located hotel in all of Prague. Nestled on a small backstreet, just east of Staroměstské náměstí, the three-story Ungelt is a hidden gem. Each unit contains a living room, full kitchen, and hand-held shower in the bath. Bedrooms, which are meagerly dressed with communist-era beds and couches, are enlivened with antique dressers, Bohemian glass chandeliers, and other nice objects.

Moderate

Betlem Club. Betlémské nám 9, Prague 1. ☎ **02/2421-6872.** Fax 02/2421-8054. 22 rms. MINIBAR TV TEL. 3,500 Kč ($120) double. Rates include breakfast. No credit cards. Metro: Národní třída.

The location is fantastic—just opposite Old Town's Bethlehem Chapel. About half the rooms are decorated in typical Czech 1970s style, while others are more contemporary with black lacquer furnishings. Breakfast is served each morning in a vaulted medieval cellar.

Inexpensive

Pension Unitas. Bartolomějská 9, Prague 1. ☎ **02/232-7700.** Fax 02/232-7709. 34 rooms (none with bath). 1,100 Kč ($40) double. No credit cards. Metro: Staroměstská.

This hotel, located smack in the middle of Old Town, is just about as plain a place as you can find. The building was occupied by the Czech Secret Police in the 1950s, when it was turned into a prison. Cells in the basement once held political prisoners, including Václav Havel. You too can stay in the President's Cell P6 though conditions don't seem to have improved much since Havel's day. It's cheerier upstairs, where rooms are bright but basic. Smoking and drinking are banned, and there's a 1am curfew.

NOVÉ MĚSTO (NEW TOWN)

Very Expensive

✪ **Palace.** Panská 12, Prague 1. ☎ **02/2409 3111.** Fax 02/2422-1240. 125 rms, 17 suites. A/C MINIBAR TV TEL. 9,100 Kč ($337) double; from 11,383 Kč ($421) suite. AE, DC, MC, V. Metro: Můstek.

One of Prague's finest and most expensive hotels, the Palace is a stylish luxury hotel set in a beautifully restored art nouveau palace. Guests enter through an impressive front door flanked by imposing sconce-wielding statues. Although rooms are still considered small by American standards, these are some of the largest luxury accommodations in Prague. Only rivaled by the Savoy for comfort, the Palace beats the competition in terms of location, situated only a block from Wenceslas Square and Old Town.

Expensive

Atrium Hilton Hotel. Pobřežní 1, Prague 8. ☎ **02/2484-1111.** Fax 02/2481-1973. 788 rms. 20 suites. A/C MINIBAR TV TEL. 8,250 Kč ($305) double; from 9,015 Kč ($333) suite. AE, CB, DISC, MC, V. Metro: Florenc.

The glass-and-steel cube-shaped Atrium Hilton is as imposing as it is huge, built around an enormous glass-topped atrium. Thankfully, guest rooms are quite a bit more intimate than the chilly common areas. Most are identical to each other, making this hotel perfect for large tour groups and conventioneers. While guest rooms are not large, they are of a relatively high standard. The location, just outside of center city, is not ideal, but hearty travelers can walk to náměstí Republiky in about 15 minutes.

City Hotel Morán. Na Moráni 15, Prague 2. ☎ **02/2491-5208.** Fax 02/29 75 33. 57 rms. MINIBAR TV TEL. 4,000–6,000 Kč ($148–$222) double. AE, DC, MC, V. Metro: Karlovo náměstí.

Built in the 19th century, this recently restored lime-green hotel is far from fancy, but for style and comfort it ranks as one of the best in its price range. Top-floor rooms are your best bet, and those facing north enjoy a good view of Prague Castle. The hotel is located about a 20-minute walk from Old Town Square, just outside of the main tourist center. There's a small restaurant and bar on the premises.

✪ **Hotel Harmony.** Na Poříčí 31, Prague 1. ☎ **02/232-0016** or 232-0720. Fax 02/231-0009. 54 rms, 6 suites. TEL. 3,341 Kč ($123) double; from 3,541 Kč ($131) suite. Rates include breakfast. AE, MC, V. Metro: náměstí Republiky or Florenc.

Completely overhauled in 1992, the Harmony is easily the nicest hotel in its price range. The sparkling white hotel has a contemporary design and postcommunist furnishings. Double rooms, with two single beds pushed together as one, make up the bulk of the hotel's seven floors. There are two restaurants on the ground floor, and the reception desk becomes the concierge when you need concert tickets or tour reservations.

Prague Renaissance Hotel. V Celnici 7, Prague 1. ☎ **02/2481-0396.** Fax 02/2182 -2200. 309 rms, 14 suites. A/C MINIBAR TV TEL. 6,800 Kč ($251) double; from 11,600 Kč ($429) suite. Children under 18 stay free in parents' room. Rates include breakfast. AE, CB, DC, MC, V. Metro: náměstí Republiky.

The Prague Renaissance, a marble monolith completed in 1993, is a top European-style business hotel with well-designed standardized rooms and unusually responsive management. Guest rooms are almost all identically dressed, and feature good closets and lighting.

Inexpensive

Axa Hotel. Na Poříčí 40, Prague 1. ☎ **02/2481-2580.** Fax 02/232-2172. 127 rms, 5 suites. TEL. 3,100 Kč ($114) double; 4,300 Kč ($159) suite. Children under 6 stay free in parents' room. Rates include continental breakfast. MC, V. Metro: náměstí Republiky or Florenc.

Built in 1932, and completely overhauled in 1992, Axa has all the hallmarks of a typical Prague hotel. It's rather drab on the outside, and sterile within. Frills are few, and so are towels. Beds are "Eastern European Specials"—thin mattresses on pull-out sofalike beds. The hotel has one of the best health clubs in town, containing a six-lane indoor lap pool, sauna, and solarium.

Botel Albatros. Nábřeží Ludvíka Svobody, Prague 1. ☎ **02/2481-0541.** Fax 02/2481-1214. 80 rms, 4 suites. TEL. 2,100 Kč ($77) double; from 4,000 Kč ($148) suite. Rates include continental breakfast. AE, MC, V. Tram: 5, 14, 26, or 53.

Located at the end of Revoluční on the River Vltava, the permanently moored blue-and-white Albatros is a converted hotel boat, or "botel." Rooms are predictably cramped; each is just large enough for two single beds and the tiny table that separates them. Suites, located toward the back of the boat, are bright exceptions to these otherwise restricted accommodations. Although there is a small restaurant on the boat, guests will have more fun on the lively bar barge docked just behind the Albatros.

Hotel Evropa. Václavské náměstí 25, Prague 1. ☎ **02/2422-8117.** Fax 02/2422-4544. 104 rms (50 with bath), 3 suites. 2,120 Kč ($78) double without bath, 3,360 Kč ($124) double with bath; from 4,660 Kč ($172) suite. Rates include continental breakfast. AE, MC, V. Metro: Můstek.

Erected in 1889 and rebuilt in the art nouveau style during 1903–1905, the Evropa remains one of Prague's most magnificent turn-of-the-century structures. The fantastic, statue-topped facade is a festival for the eyes, beautifully painted and wrapped with hand-sculpted wrought-iron railings. The outdoor terrace of the ground-floor cafe is coveted—for style and people-watching, not food or service. The best rooms are the front-facing doubles; a half-dozen have balconies overlooking Václavské náměstí. These are relatively large and have high ceilings. There's no trick to getting a good room here; luck is the only mitigate. Reservations are accepted by fax.

MALÁ STRANA

Expensive

U Červeného Lva. Nerudova 41, Prague 1. ☎ **02/537-239** or 538-192. Fax 02/538-193. 9 rms, 2 suites. MINIBAR TV TEL. 4,800 Kč ($177) double; from 5,900 Kč ($218) suite. Rates include breakfast. Metro: Malostranská.

The publisher of Frommer's stayed in three places when he recently visited Prague, and "The House at the Red Lion" was his favorite. This pension is expensive, but costs less than the big hotels, and it has a very sophisticated and friendly atmosphere. Suites have a double bed in the bedroom and two twin beds in the living room. This historical burgher house, which dates back to the 15th century, is located on the Royal Route, near the entrance to Prague Castle.

Moderate

Hotel Kampa. Všehrdova 16, (Malá Strana) Prague 1. ☎ **02/2451-0409.** Fax 02/2451-0377. 85 rms. TEL. 3,100 Kč ($114) double. AE, MC, V. Metro: Malostranská.

Located on one of the city's cutest, quietest, and best-located streets, Hotel Kampa occupies what was once an armory, built in the early 17th century. The incredibly simple rooms probably will not be acceptable to first-class travelers. Try to reserve a double furnished with an extra bed, as these are the largest rooms. You can request a room with a view of the river or the park. A restaurant on the premises serves lunch and dinner, but smart guests dine elsewhere.

HRADČANY

Very Expensive

✪ Savoy. Keplerova 6, Prague 1. ☎ **02/2430-2122.** Fax 02/2430-2128. 61 rms, 6 suites. A/C MINIBAR TV TEL. 7,670 Kč ($284) double; from 10,900 Kč ($403) suite. AE, DC, MC, V. Tram: 22.

Opened in 1994, the Savoy is widely considered to be Prague's best hotel. Located on a moderately busy street three blocks from Prague Castle, the hotel's location is not ideal. But once inside, the hotel is hard to top. Opulent even by western standards, the hotel's dressy public areas lead into equally well-decorated guest rooms, outfitted with every convenience one would expect from a top hotel. Rooms have all the requisite fittings, including firm oversize beds, marble baths, safes, and fax machines.

DINING

The true Czech dining experience can be summed up in three native words: *vepřo-knedlo-zelo*—pork-dumplings-cabbage. If that's what you want, try most any *hostinec* (Czech pub). Most have a hearty gulás or pork dish with dumplings and cabbage, usually for about 60–100 Kč ($2.22–$3.70), and after you wash it down with Czech beer, you won't care about the taste.

At most restaurants, menu prices include VAT. Tipping has become more commonplace in restaurants where the staff is obviously trying harder; rounding up the bill to about 10% or more is usually adequate. *Beware:* Some restaurants gouge customers by charging exorbitant amounts for nuts or other seemingly free premeal snacks. Ask before you eat.

STARÉ MĚSTO (OLD TOWN) & JOSEFOV

Expensive

Opera Grill. Karolíny Světlé 35, Prague 1. ☎ **02/265-508.** Reservations recommended. Main courses 250–350 Kč ($10–$14). AE, MC, V. Daily 7pm–2am. Metro: Staroměstská. CONTINENTAL.

This intimate 25-seat restaurant caters to those in search of a quiet meal in beautiful surroundings. A firm knock on the door summons the maitre d', who then whisks you away to a small, attractive dining room furnished with flowing drapery, overstuffed armchairs, and elegantly laid tables. A short list of continental dishes, presented on a hand-lettered menu, includes steaks, game, and seafood, as well as fish and pasta.

✪ **Parnas.** Smetanovo nábřeží 2, Prague 1. ☎ **02/2422-7614** or 2422-9248. Reservations recommended. Main courses 350–550 Kč ($14–$22); Sunday brunch 450 Kč ($18). AE, DC, MC, V. Mon–Sat noon–3pm and 5:30–11pm, Sun 11am–3pm and 7–11pm. Metro: Národní třída. INTERNATIONAL.

One of the few Czech restaurants that would still be considered superior outside Eastern Europe, Parnas can always be counted on for very good food served with studied precision by highly trained career waiters. Located on the embankment facing the Vltava, the lofty dining room is quite elegant. The luckiest diners have window seats with great views of distant Prague Castle.

Little on the menu is either traditional or plain. Appetizers may include cold North Sea shrimp with fresh kiwi, venison pátě with blue cheese, and a piping hot onion, leek, and mushroom tart. Spinach tagliatelle—a house specialty—is tossed with salmon and cream, garlic and herbs, or tomato and olives. Salmon with dill (poached to order and served either hot or cold) and prawns in a hot garlic sauce are the best of almost a dozen seafood main dishes.

Vinárna V Zátiší. Liliová 1, Prague 1. ☎ **02/2422-8977.** Reservations recommended. Main courses 300–500 Kč ($12–$20); Sun brunch 350 Kč ($14). AE, DC, MC, V. Mon–Sat noon–3pm and 5:30–11pm, Sun 11am–3pm and 5:30–11pm. Metro: Národní třída. CONTINENTAL.

Owned by the same group that runs the restaurant Parnas, Vinárna V Zátiší's self-consciously elegant dining room is designed to appeal to Prague's business crowd at both lunch and dinner. The chefs cook what is essentially the same food as Parnas at distinctly lower prices. The menu changes often, but almost always contains homemade pasta, fresh fish, rabbit, and roast duck.

Moderate

La Provance. Štupartská 9, Prague 1. ☎ **02/232-4801.** Reservations recommended. Main courses 150–300 Kč ($6–$12). AE, MC, V. Daily noon–11:30pm. Metro: Náměstí Republiky. FRENCH.

Opened in 1995, La Provance is the first of a new breed of Prague restaurants—a colorful, ultra-stylish international eatery. Located below Banana Cafe, a popular bar that has become a mainstay of the city's trendies, it serves some adventurous dishes, albeit with mixed results. Escargots are more novel than tasty, as are any of their pâtés. Sliced grilled duck breast served over a garden salad is a much better appetizer. Main courses run the gamut from mediocre grilled scampi and bouillabaisse to very good coq au vin and a roasted half-duck.

Reykjavik. Karlova 20, Prague 1. ☎ **02/2422-9251.** Reservations not necessary. Main courses 150–250 Kč ($6–$10). AE, MC, V. Daily 11am–midnight. AE, MC, V. Metro: Staroměstská. SEAFOOD/CONTINENTAL.

Everyone who visits Prague passes Reykjavik restaurant, located on the main pedestrian street between Old Town Square and Charles Bridge. Despite the tourists, Reykjavik is surprisingly recommendable. The kitchen stresses fish in general, and salmon in particular—both frozen Icelandic filets and fresh Norwegian steaks are competently prepared.

Inexpensive

It's well worth finding ❸ **U Bakálaře,** a small sandwich bar at Celetná 12, hidden inside a reconstructed building on the main street connecting Old Town Square and náměstí Republiky. The restaurant (☎ **02/2481-1870,** ext. 257) serves little toasties—inexpensive ready-to-eat open-face sandwiches (*chlebíčky*)—with toppings that include sardines, cheese, salami spread, and tuna. It's open Mon–Fri 9:30am–7pm, Sat–Sun 12:30–7pm.

Hogo Fogo. Salvátorská 4, Prague 1. ☎ **02/231-7023.** Reservations not accepted. Main courses 40–75 Kč ($1.60–$3). AE, MC, V. Mon–Fri 11:30pm–midnight, Fri–Sat noon–2am. Metro: Staroměstská. CZECH.

It's not hard to determine exactly what attracts Hogo Fogo's loyal following of Americans and Czechs in their 20s. The bare basement dining room is unremarkable, service is sluggish, and most of the food is just tolerable. But, located just two blocks from Old Town Square, Hogo Fogo is one of the cheapest full-service restaurants in Old Town. There are some menu standouts, such as the lentil soup and fried cheese, and the rock music is good. Half liters of beer are just 30 Kč ($1.20), and diners are encouraged to sit all day if they wish.

Klub Architektů. Betlémské nám. 5a, Prague 1. ☎ **02/2440-1214.** Reservations recommended. Main courses 60–100 Kč ($2.40–$4). No credit cards. Daily 11:30am–midnight. Metro: Národní třída. CZECH.

This hard-to-find restaurant, located in a dimly lit, labyrinthine, 12th-century cellar, combines medieval tranquility with big-city chic. The architect owners have designed an excellent space. Soft rock music bounces off centuries-old whitewashed vaulted ceilings. The funky environment appeals to in-the-know young Czechs. Less distinctive is the food, which, for the most part, is strictly functional. Few dishes are great—the cheese-stuffed chicken is a standout. The restaurant is located under Bethlehem Church; go through the church's front gates and turn right. Make a reservation, then be prepared to wait.

Red Hot & Blues. Jakubská 12, Prague 1. ☎ **02/231-4639.** Reservations not necessary. Main courses 90–250 Kč ($3.60–$10). AE, MC, V. Daily 9am–11pm. Metro: Náměstí Republiky. REGIONAL AMERICAN.

A popular American ex-pat hangout at its inception, Red Hot & Blues has evolved into a Czech-oriented regional American theme restaurant serving decent shrimp creole, etouffee, burgers, and nachos. The front dining room is smaller and holds the bar, while the rear room accommodates a dozen wood-topped iron tables and the live jazz combo that regularly performs. An adjacent atrium opens during warmer months. Red Hot & Blues is at its blistering best on Sunday, when they serve a good à la carte brunch that includes French toast and creole omelets.

✪ **Zlatá Ulička.** Masná 9, Prague 1. ☎ **02/232-0884.** Reservations not necessary. Main courses 110–200 Kč ($4.40–$8). No credit cards. Daily 10am–midnight. Metro: Náměstí Republiky. YUGOSLAV.

Hidden in the backstreets of Staré Město near Kostel sv. Jakuba (St. James Church), and named after the Hradčany street of colorful 16th-century cottages, pint-sized Zlatá Ulička is one of central Prague's unique finds. The restaurant's low-kitsch interior suggests a surreal Renaissance-era courtyard surrounded by faux yellow-and-blue cottage facades complete with shingle roofs. Diners discover the food's Yugoslavian qualities—savory spices that are almost completely absent in Bohemia. Whole trout is pan fried in olive oil with garlic and parsley, while a medley of piquant spices enliven giant homemade hamburgers. The very traditional Yugoslavian shish kebab alternates marinated veal and vegetables.

NOVÉ MĚSTO (NEW TOWN)

Expensive

✪ Fakhreldine. Klimentská 48, Prague 1. ☎ **02/232-7970.** Main courses 250–350 Kč ($10–$14) AE, DC, MC, V. Daily noon–midnight. Metro: Florenc. LEBANESE.

Fakhreldine is exceptional because it is one of Prague's only top-of-the-line non-European restaurants. This very upscale eatery is the only other branch of London's most famous Lebanese restaurant, and the quality here rivals its English parent in both flavor and atmosphere. The chandeliered dining room is uncluttered and elegant. A long list of entrees includes char-grilled lamb, marinated veal, and steaks. The beautifully presented starters are the tastiest treats, and include raw lamb, grilled spicy Armenian sausages, babaganush, Lebanese cream cheese, hummus, and plenty of homemade Arabic bread. Three kinds of baklava and cardamom-scented coffee round out the meal.

Moderate

Bella Napoli. V jámě 8, Prague 1. ☎ **02/2422-7315.** Reservations recommended on weekends. Main courses 130–220 Kč ($5.20–$8.80). No credit cards. Mon–Sat 11:30am–11:30pm, Sun 6–11:30pm. Metro: Můstek. SOUTHERN ITALIAN.

The best thing about Bella Napoli is the antipasti bar, a table of cold appetizers that on any given night might include roasted peppers, calamari rings, marinated mushrooms, or grilled eggplant. First courses include a wide range of pasta dishes, including a particularly good tortellini gorgonzola. The best main courses are made with local beef, cheese, and red sauces. The restaurant's single small dining room feels warm and comfortable, and is a nice place to relax with friends. This remains one of Prague's best southern Italian restaurants.

✪ Na Rybárně. Gorazdova 17, Prague 2. ☎ **02/299-795.** Reservations recommended. Main courses 130–220 Kč ($5.20–$8.80). AE, DC, MC, V. Daily noon–midnight, Sun 5pm–midnight. Metro: Karlovo náměstí. SEAFOOD.

One of Prague's oldest fish restaurants, Na Rybárně specializes in local freshwater offerings like trout, carp, and eel. Meals here are almost always great. The fish is prepared simply, usually grilled with lemon and butter. Typical Czech meat dishes are also available. The atmosphere is informal; the best tables are located in the back room, where famous visitors, including rocker Paul Simon and members of the Rolling Stones, have autographed the white walls. President Václav Havel was a familiar face here a few years ago, when he lived around the corner.

Inexpensive

Gany's. Národní třída 20, Prague 1. ☎ **02/297-472.** Reservations not accepted. Main courses 90–180 Kč ($3.60–$7.20). AE, DC, MC, V. Daily 8am–11pm. Metro: Můstek. CZECH/INTERNATIONAL.

You will almost certainly walk past Gany's on your wanderings around Prague; it's situated on a major thoroughfare, equidistant from Václavské náměstí and the

National Theater. But unless you're looking for it hovering above the street, you could easily pass by. Its fabulous, understated art nouveau interior has been perfectly restored and enlivened with trendy, period-style oil paintings. The curious combination of cuisine includes smoked salmon, battered and fried asparagus, and ham au gratin with vegetables, and main dishes that encompass everything from trout with horseradish to beans with garlic sauce. In between is a long list of chicken, beef, veal, and pork dishes, each drowned in a complementary, if not extraordinary, sauce. They serve postcurtain. There's also a well-appointed billiards parlor in the back.

MALÁ STRANA

Expensive

Circle Line Brasserie. Malostranské nám. 12, Prague 1. ☎ **02/530-276.** Reservations recommended. Main courses 180–300 Kč ($7.20–$12). AE, MC, V. Mon–Sat 6–11pm. Metro: Malostranská. SEAFOOD.

This cellar restaurant, located below the American-style eatery Avalon, primarily serves fresh fish in an upbeat basement dining room. Oysters, shrimp, crab, and lobster are served either on their own or as a shellfish medley that arrives on a giant platter of crushed ice. Large parties of locals are common here, and the food has gotten fresher since their supplier started delivering from Belgium almost daily. A whimsical nautical theme, evoked by murals of cruise-ship lounges, almost makes up for the fact that this restaurant is situated in a basement.

Kampa Park. Na Kampě 8b, Prague 1. ☎ **02/534-800.** Reservations recommended. Main courses 200–400 Kč ($8–$16). AE, DC, MC, V. Daily 11:30am–1am. Metro: Malostranská. CONTINENTAL.

In summer, there is no prettier place for a meal than on the outdoor waterside patio at Kampa Park. The water of the Vltava practically laps at your feet, and you'll enjoy the most magnificent view of Charles Bridge and the Old Town skyline. Owned by an intelligent team of Scandinavian businessmen, the restaurant looks like a top European eatery. Vested waiters and well-composed plates make diners feel special. Sometimes meals here are superlative; fillet of venison in red-wine sauce or fresh grilled salmon steak topped with a light creamy caper sauce can be sublime. Other times, however, mediocrity reigns.

U Malířů. Maltézské náměstí 11. ☎ **02/2451-0269.** Reservations recommended. Main courses 1,200–1,700 Kč ($48–$68); Menu Gourmand 3,500 Kč ($140). AE, DC, MC, V. Daily 11:30am–2:30pm and 7–10pm. Metro: Malostranská. FRENCH.

When U Malířů opened in 1991 with a French chef in the kitchen and hand-painted murals in three small, elegant dining rooms, no other restaurant could even come close to the quality and beauty that was offered here. And nothing wowed Prague's restaurant-going public more than this restaurant's famously high prices—dinner here still costs two or three times more than a meal at Parnas, its closest competitor. Czech-born chef Jaromír Froulik is an excellent student, and he has mastered the traditional French menus that rotate here on a seasonal basis. Summer starters include herb-marinated salmon and goose-liver pâté. Entrees include braised sole fillets with mushrooms and fillet of beef rolled in bacon with truffle sauce. While the food is good and the service excellent, only the high prices make the meal particularly memorable.

✪ U Modré Kachničky (The Blue Duckling). Nebovidská 6, Prague 1. ☎ **02/2451-0217.** Reservations recommended. Main courses 150–320 Kč ($6–$12.80). AE, MC, V. Daily noon–3:30pm and 6:30–11:30pm. Metro: Malostranská. CZECH.

It's hard to complain about a restaurant that has everything: charm, intimacy, style, good service, and fine food. Each of the three small dining rooms has vaulted ceilings covered with contemporary frescoes, antique furnishings, and oriental carpets. Cold starters include Russian malossol caviar, smoked salmon, goose liver with apples and red wine, and asparagus baked with ham and cheese. Boar goulash is an interesting twist on the original, duck is smoked before being served with the traditional cabbage, and rabbit is cooked with a cream sauce and cranberries. Carp, a popular Czech fish, is baked with anchovies, and the single vegetarian main dish, risotto, is made to order with mushrooms and cheese.

Moderate

Avalon Bar & Grill. Malostranské nám. 12, Prague 1. ☎ **02/530-276.** Reservations not necessary. Main courses 120–250 Kč ($4.80–$10). AE, MC, V. Daily 11am–1am. Metro: Malostranská. AMERICAN.

This California theme restaurant is a fun eatery, where good American food is served in ultra-contemporary surroundings. The dining room, which feels something like Los Angeles, is both authentic and unique—not just someone's idea of California kitsch. Locals can always count on this restaurant's overstuffed sandwiches, grilled chicken, burgers, potato skins, and buffalo wings.

۞ Vinárna U Maltézských Rytířů (Knights of Malta). Prokopská 10, Prague 1. ☎ **02/536-357.** Reservations recommended. Main courses 150–300 Kč ($6–$12). AE, MC. Daily 11:30am–11pm. Metro: Malostranská. CZECH.

The Wine Tavern of the Knights of Malta, opened in 1993, is one of the city's best buys. The restaurant occupies the ground floor and cellar of a charming house that once functioned as a knights-operated hospice. Nadia Černíková, the restaurant's eternally cheerful co-owner and hostess, keeps a watchful eye on the front of the house, personally greeting and seating the majority of the restaurant's patrons. Many are loyal regulars. Asparagus-filled turkey breast, salmon steak with herb butter, lamb cutlet with spinach, and chateaubriand are among the consistent main courses.

Inexpensive

Jo's Bar. Malostranské náměstí 7, Prague 1. No phone. Reservations not accepted. Main courses 100–150 Kč ($4–$6). No credit cards. Daily 11am–1am. Metro: Malostranská. MEXICAN/ AMERICAN.

One of the first North American–owned restaurants in postcommunist Eastern Europe, Jo's was once Prague's chief hangout for expatriates. The restaurant/bar is still packed with foreigners in their 20s, but the majority are now tourists who have heard about this legendary place. Jo's great attraction has never been the tacos, guacamole, and salsa; rather the beer and camaraderie with other English speakers draw the crowds.

HRADČANY

Expensive

Peklo. Strahovské nádvoří 1, Prague 1. ☎ **02/2451-0032.** Reservations recommended. Main courses 300–400 Kč ($12–$16). AE, DC, MC, V. Daily 6pm–2am. Tram: 22. CONTINENTAL.

Located in the ancient wine cellars of Strahov Monastery, Peklo (which means "hell") is a stunningly beautiful subterranean restaurant serving good food. Although sauces can sometimes be mild to the point of being a whisper, most meals are generally as flavorful as the presentations thoughtful. Sturgeon and vegetables baked in puff pastry and perfectly broiled steak are typical entrees. Peklo is expensive, but the prices are justified if you are staying in the neighborhood and don't want to descend into Old Town or Malá Strana. However, those coming from down below might question whether it's worth the trip.

Moderate

Nebozízek. Petřínské sady 411, Prague 1. ☎ **02/537-905.** Reservations recommended. Main courses 80–200 Kč ($3.20–$8). AE, MC, V. Daily 11am–6pm and 7–11pm. Tram: 12 or 22 to Újezd, then funicular up Petřín Hill. CZECH/CONTINENTAL.

Getting to Nebozízek is half the fun. No, make that three-quarters. Located in the middle of Petřín Hill, the restaurant is accessible by funicular, a kind of cable car on a track. Unlike the food, which is mediocre at best, the view overlooking Prague is truly unmatched. In fact, dining above the storybook rooftops is so enchanting that dinner reservations are sometimes required days in advance. Main dishes, which are heavy on steak and pork, should be chosen with an eye toward simple preparations like pepper steak and roast pork. The garlic soup is exceptional.

Inexpensive

⑤ Saté Grill. Pohořelec 3, Prague 1. No phone. Main courses 50–100 Kč ($2–$4). No credit cards. Daily 12:30–10pm. Tram: 22. INDONESIAN.

Begun as a take-out shop, Saté Grill has proved so popular that it has become a restaurant. Pork saté with peanut sauce is the centerpiece of a short Indonesian menu that also features Migoreng, a spicy noodle dish that some pundits think tastes a bit too close to the ramen that got you through college. Prices are extremely low for a restaurant so close to the castle.

ELSEWHERE IN PRAGUE

Moderate

Le Bistro de Marlene. Plavecká 4, Prague 2. ☎ **02/291-077.** Reservations recommended. Main courses 150–350 Kč ($6–$14). No credit cards. Mon–Fri noon–2:30pm and 7:30–10:30pm, Sat 7:30–10pm. Metro: Vyšehrad. FRENCH.

It doesn't matter that Le Bistro de Marlene is hidden on a small residential street near Vyšehrad Castle. The restaurant is packed anyway, with locals and visitors. The bistro atmosphere is made upbeat with mirrored walls, good music, plenty of plants, and a very friendly, very French staff. Many appetizers are recommendable, including flan aux champignons, a wonderful mushroom loaf served on a parsley sauce, and terrine de lapin, a subtle rabbit terrine. Of entrees, roast leg of lamb is herb infused and arrives perfectly pink. A petit steak is topped with a sweet curry sauce, and a fresh fish dish is usually available nightly. Most everything comes with a side of vegetables, simply steamed, or baked in a gratin with layers of cheese.

❍ Quido. Kubelíkova 22, Prague 3. ☎ **02/270-950.** Reservations recommended. Main courses 130–250 Kč ($5.20–$10). AE, MC, V. Daily 11:30am–11pm. Metro: Jiřího z Poděbrad. CZECH.

Quido is a veritable survey of Bohemian cooking. One of the best traditional appetizers is pork tongue—home smoked, sliced thin, and pleasantly arranged. The garlic soup is full of meat and potatoes, and the sautéed chicken livers are simply out of this world. The most successful main courses come from the restaurant's gas-fired lava grill. These include a cheese-filled hunter's steak, and chicken breast with pineapple, both of which are served with white cabbage and carrots.

Inexpensive

✪ Radost F/X Café. Bělehradská 120, Prague 2. ☎ **02/251-210.** Reservations not accepted. Main courses 55–120 Kč ($2.20–$4.40). MC, V. Daily 11am–5am. Metro: I. P. Pavlova. VEGETARIAN.

One of Prague's few completely vegetarian restaurants, Radost is recommendable for good soup, like garlicky spinach and oniony lentil, and hearty sandwiches, like tofu with stir-fried vegetables. There are some disappointments, including an anchovy-less

Greek salad and lackluster pizzas. But for the most part, Radost gets a rave. The funky and stylish restaurant looks more like a cafe than a serious dining establishment above a popular American-style dance club of the same name. It's also one of the few restaurants in the city that's open all night. Their fine Bloody Marys compliment 4am breakfasts. On weekends, the restaurant serves the best down-scale brunch in town.

CAFES

Prague's reputation as a "Left Bank of the '90s" leads many to believe that there is a thriving cafe culture in the capital. Truth is, the city's coffeehouses and tearooms are only now catching up to the cliche. Most cafes listed below have espresso machines and some employees actually know how to operate one.

Cafe Evropa. Václavské náměstí 25, Prague 1. ☎ **02/2422-8117.** Cappuccino 30 Kč ($1.20); pastries 30–100 Kč ($1.20–$4). AE, MC, V. Daily 7am–midnight. Metro: Můstek.

Spin through the etched-glass revolving door into the otherworldliness of Prague's finest art nouveau cafe. Built in 1906, the cafe is bedecked with period chandeliers and hand-carved woods, all made even more elegant by musicians, who entertain every afternoon. Drinks are relatively expensive and service is terrible. But compared to Western European standards, it's cheap, and few diners are in a mood to hurry. There's a 40 Kč ($1.20) cover charge after 3pm.

Café Milena. Staroměstské nám. 22, Prague 1. ☎ **02/260-843.** Light snacks and desserts 60–150 Kč ($2.40–$6). No credit cards. Daily 10am–10pm. Metro: Staroměstská.

Located on the second floor of a beautiful building directly across from Old Town Square's astronomical clock, this Viennese-style cafe operated by the Franz Kafka Society is named for Milena Jesenská, one of the famous writer's lovers. Decent light snacks and ice cream are served in comfortable surroundings. The luckiest patrons snare window seats, from which the clock's 12 apostles appear at almost eye level.

The Globe. Janovského 14, Prague 7. ☎ **02/6671-2610.** Sandwiches and desserts 60–100 Kč ($2.40–$4). No credit cards. Daily 10am–midnight. Metro: Vltavská.

Prague's only bookstore/coffeehouse is not only the best place in the city for used paperback literature and nonfiction, it's one of the best places for young American expats to meet. The smart-looking barroom serves espresso-based drinks, sandwiches, salads, and desserts, and stocks a full bar.

ATTRACTIONS

The concept of an itinerary should be a loose one when visiting Prague. The most intrigue comes from its outdoor sights—the architecture, the atmosphere. The most enjoyment comes from a slow, aimless wander through the city's heart. If you have the time and the energy, try taking a broad view of the grand architecture of Prague Castle and the Old Town skyline (best from Charles Bridge) at sunrise, and then at sunset. You will see two completely different cities.

Except for the busy main streets, where you may have to dodge traffic, Prague is an ideal city for walking. Actually, walking is really the only way to explore Prague. Most of the town's oldest areas are walking zones, with motor traffic restricted.

SIGHTSEEING SUGGESTIONS

If You Have 1 Day Do what visiting kings and potentates do on a 1-day visit: walk the Royal Route from the top of the Hradčany hill (tram 22 or a taxi is suggested for the ride up unless you're very fit). Tour Prague Castle in the morning, and then after lunch, stroll across Charles Bridge, on the way to the winding alleys of Old Town (Staré Město).

If You Have 2 Days During your second day, explore the varied sights of Old Town, Lesser Town, and the Jewish Quarter (Josefov)—what you didn't have time for the day before. Just wander and browse through numerous shops and galleries offering the finest Bohemian crystal, porcelain, and modern artwork, as well as top fashion boutiques, cafes, and restaurants.

If You Have 3 Days On your first day, go lighter on touring Prague Castle, as your ticket is good for 3 days. On your third day, after seeing what you held over from the first day at the Castle, visit the National Art Gallery at Šternberk Palace, the Strahov Monastery with its ornate libraries, and the Loreto Palace with its peculiar artwork.

If You Have 5 Days or More On days 4 and 5, head for one of the many other museums or galleries or venture out of the city center. Visit the old southern citadel over the Vltava, Vyšehrad, where you get a completely different view of the city you've explored the past 3 days.

THE TOP ATTRACTIONS
Charles Bridge

Dating from the 14th century, Prague's most celebrated structure links the castle to Staré Město. For most of its 600 years, the 1700-foot-long span has been a pedestrian promenade, just as it is today. From dawn to dusk, Charles Bridge is filled with folks crossing the Vltava. The best times to stroll across are in early morning or around sunset, when the crowds have thinned and the shadows are more mysterious.

Prague Castle (Pražský Hrad). Hradčany. Combined entrance to the three main attractions 80 Kč ($2.96) for adults, 40 Kč ($1.48) for students without a tour guide; 120 Kč ($4.44) for adults, 80 Kč ($2.96) for students with an English-speaking guide. Tues–Sun 9am–5pm (until 4pm Nov–March). Buy entrance tickets at the Information Center in the second courtyard after passing through the main gate from Hradčanské náměstí. The center also arranges tours in various languages and sells tickets for concerts and exhibitions held on castle grounds.

The huge hilltop complex that's known collectively as Prague Castle (Pražský Hrad), on Hradčanské náměstí, encompasses dozens of houses, towers, churches, courtyards, and monuments. A visit to the castle could easily take an entire day or more. Still, the top sights—St. Vitus Cathedral, Royal Palace, and St. George's Basilica, plus Golden Lane—can be seen in the space of a morning or afternoon. While you can wander the castle grounds for free, you need to buy an entrance ticket for St. Vitus Cathedral, the Royal Palace, and St. George's Basilica.

St. Vitus Cathedral, originally constructed in A.D. 926 as the court church of the Přemyslid princes, has long been the center of Prague's religious and political life. The key part of its gothic construction took place in the 14th century under the direction of Mathias of Arras and Peter Parler of Gmuend. In the 18th and 19th centuries, subsequent baroque and neogothic additions were made.

The Royal Palace, located in the third courtyard of the castle grounds, served as the residence of kings between the 10th and 17th centuries. Vaulted Vladislav Hall, the interior's centerpiece, was used for coronations and special occasions. Here Václav Havel was inaugurated president. The adjacent Diet was where the king met with his advisors and where the supreme court was held.

St. George's Basilica, adjacent to the Royal Palace, is the oldest romanesque structure in Prague, dating from the 10th century. It was also the first convent in Bohemia. No longer serving a religious function, the building now houses a museum of historic Czech art.

(Golden Lane) **Zlatá ulička** is a picturesque street of tiny 16th-century servants' houses built into the castle fortifications. The houses now contain small shops, galleries, and refreshment bars. In 1917, Franz Kafka lived briefly at house #22. You'll find a good selection of guidebooks, maps, and other related information in the entrance to the Royal Palace.

Jewish Museum in Prague. Maisel Synagogue, Maiselova St., between Široká St. and Jáchymová St., Prague 1. ☎ **02/2481-0099.** Admission 340 Kč ($12.60) for adults, 260 Kč ($9.60) for children 8–15 years old includes: The Ceremonial Hall, Old Jewish Cemetery, Old-New Synagogue, Pinkas Synagogue, Klaus Synagogue, and Maisel Synagogue (Admission to individual sites also available). Sun–Fri 9am–6:30pm. Metro: Line A to Staroměstská.

Most of Prague's ancient Judaica was destroyed by the Nazis during World War II. Ironically, it was the same Germans who constructed an "exotic museum of an extinct race" which allowed thousands of the objects to be salvaged—including valued Torah covers, books, and silver now on display at the Maisel Synagogue.

Down the road at Červená 2, the **Old New Synagogue (Staronová Synogoga),** built around 1270, is the oldest Jewish house of worship in Europe. Worshipers have prayed continuously for over 700 years, interrupted only between 1941 and 1945 because of the Nazi occupation.

The **Old Jewish Cemetery (Starý židovský hřbitov),** one of Europe's oldest Jewish burial grounds, located just one block from the Old New Synagogue, dates from the mid-15th century. Because the local government of the time didn't allow Jews to bury their dead elsewhere, graves were dug deep enough to hold 12 bodies vertically, with each tombstone placed in front of the last. The result is one of the world's most crowded cemeteries: a one-block area filled with more than 20,000 graves.

Strahov Monastery and Library (Strahovský klášter). Strahovské nádvoří. ☎ **02/2451-1137.** Admission 40 Kč ($1.48) adults, 20 Kč (74¢) students. Daily 9am–noon and 1–5pm. Tram: 22 from Malostranská metro station.

The second-oldest monastery in Prague, Strahov was founded high above Malá Strana in 1143 by Vladislav II. It is still home to Premonstratensian monks, a scholarly order closely related to the Jesuits. What draws visitors here are the monastery's ornate libraries, which hold over 125,000 volumes. The Philosophical Library's 46-foot-high ceiling is decorated with a 1794 fresco entitled *The Struggle of Mankind to Know Real Wisdom.* Paths leading through the monastery grounds take you to a breathtaking overlook of the city.

Famous Squares

The most celebrated square in the city, **Old Town Square (Staroměstské náměstí),** is surrounded by baroque buildings and packed with colorful craftsmen, cafes, and entertainers. In ancient days, the site was a major crossroad on central European merchant routes. In its center stands a memorial to Jan Hus, the 15th-century martyr who crusaded against Prague's German-dominated religious and political establishment. Unveiled in 1915, on the 500th anniversary of Hus's execution, the monument's most compelling features are the asymmetry of the composition and the fluidity of the figures.

The **Astronomical Clock (orloj)** at **Old Town Hall (Staroměstská radnice)** performs a glockenspiel spectacle daily on the hour from 8am–8pm. Originally constructed in 1410, the clock has long been an important symbol of Prague.

Wenceslas Square (Václavské náměstí), one of the city's most historic squares, has thrice been the site of riots and revolutions—in 1848, 1968, and 1989.

MORE ATTRACTIONS

Bertramka (W. A. Mozart Museum). Mozartova 169, Praha 5. ☎ **02/543-893.** Admission 50 Kč ($1.85) adults, 30 Kč ($1.11) students. Daily 9:30am–6pm. Tram: 2, 6, 7, 9, 14, or 16 from Anděl metro station.

Mozart loved Prague, and when he visited, the composer often stayed here, with the family who owned this villa, the Dušeks. Now a museum, the villa contains displays that include his written work and his harpsichord. There's also a lock of Mozart's hair, encased in a cube of glass. Much of the Bertramka villa was destroyed by fire in the 1870s, but Mozart's rooms, where he finished composing the opera *Don Giovanni,* have miraculously remained untouched.

Estates' Theater (Stavovské divadlo). Ovocný trh 1. ☎ **02/2421-5001.** Metro: A or B to Můstek.

Completed in 1783 by the wealthy Count F. A. Nostitz, Wolfgang Amadeus Mozart staged the premier of *Don Giovanni* here in 1787 because he said the conservative patrons in Vienna did not appreciate him or his passionate and sometimes shocking work. "Praguers understand me," Mozart was quoted as saying. Czech director Miloš Forman returned to his native country to film his Oscar-winning *Amadeus,* shooting the scenes of Mozart in Prague with perfect authenticity at the Estates' Theater.

The theater does not have daily tours, but tickets for performances and the chance to sit in one of the many elegant private boxes are usually available. Tour events are occasionally scheduled, and individual tours can be arranged through the city heritage group **Pražská vlastivěda** (☎ 02/2481-6184).

Church of St. Nicholas (Kostel Sv. Mikuláše). Malostranské náměstí 1. Free admission. Metro: A to Malostranská.

This church is critically regarded as one of the best examples of high baroque north of the Alps. K. I. Dienzenhofer's original 1711 design was augmented by his son Kryštof's 260-foot-high dome that dominates the Malá Strana skyline and was completed in 1752.

Veletržní Palace (National Gallery). Veletržní at Dukelských hrdinů, Prague 7. ☎ **02/2430-1015.** Admission 80 Kč ($2.96); family pass 120 Kč ($4.80). Tues–Sun 10am–6pm, Thurs until 9pm. Metro: C to Vltavská or tram 17.

This newly remodeled 1925 constructionist palace, originally built for trade fairs (and reopened in December 1995), now holds the bulk of the National Gallery's collection of 20th-century works by Czech and other European artists. Three atrium-lit concourses provide a comfortable setting for some catchy and kitschy Czech sculpture and multimedia works. Unfortunately the best cubist works from Braque and Picasso, Rodin bronzes, and many other French pieces have been relegated to a chalky, poorly lit section on the second floor.

PARKS & GARDENS

From **Vyšehrad,** Soběslavova 1 (☎ 02/2491-1353), legend has it, Princess Libuše looked out over the Vltava valley toward the present-day Prague Castle and predicted the founding of a great state and capital city. Vyšehrad was the first seat of the first Czech kings in the Přemyslid dynasty before the dawn of this millennium.

Today, the fortifications remain on the rocky cliffs, blocking out the increasing noise and confusion below. Within the confines of the citadel, lush lawns and gardens are crisscrossed by dozens of paths, leading to historic buildings and cemeteries. Vyšehrad is still somewhat of a hidden treasure for picnics and romantic walks, and from here you'll see one of the most panoramic views of the city. Admission is 10 Kč (37¢). Take tram 17, 3 from Karlovo náměstí to Výtoň south of New Town.

The **Royal Garden (Královská zahrada)** at Prague Castle, once the site of the sovereigns' vineyards, was founded in 1534. Dotted with lemon trees and surrounded by 16th-, 17th-, and 18th-century buildings, the park is consciously and conservatively laid out with abundant shrubbery and fountains. Enter from u Prašného mostu street north of the castle complex.

In Hradčany, the castle's **Garden on the Ramparts (Zahrada na Valech),** on the city-side ramparts below the castle, was reopened in spring 1995 after being thoroughly refurbished. Beyond the beautifully groomed lawns and sparse shrubbery there is a tranquil low-angle view of the Castle above and the city below. Enter the garden from the south side of Castle complex below Hradčanské náměstí. The park is open Tues–Sat 9am–5pm.

Located near the foot of Charles Bridge in Malá Strana, **Kampa (Na Kampě)** was named by Spanish soldiers who set up camp here after the Roman Catholics won the Battle of White Mountain in 1620.

Part of the excitement of **Waldstein (Wallenstein) Gardens (Valdštejnská zahrada)** is its location, behind a 30-foot wall on the back streets of Malá Strana. Inside, elegant, leafy gravel paths, dotted by classical bronze statues and gurgling fountains, fan out in every direction.

ORGANIZED TOURS

If you're traveling in a larger group and you really want a unique sightseeing experience, why not rent your own classic trolley? With enough people in your party it really can be affordable thanks to the ✪ **Historic Tram Tour (Elektrické dráhy DP),** Patočkova 4 (☎ and fax **02/312-3349**). If you send a fax with details 1 day ahead, the city transport department will arrange a private tour using one of the turn-of-the-century wooden tram cars that actually traveled on regular lines through Prague. Up to 24 people can fit in one car, which sports wooden-planked floors, cast-iron conductor's levers, and the "ching-ching" of a proper tram bell. It costs 1,995 Kč ($73) per hour. Up to 60 people can fit into a double car for 2,310 Kč ($85) per hour.

SHOPPING

Czech porcelain, glass, and cheap but well constructed clothing draw hoards of day-trippers from nearby Germany. Private retailers have only been allowed to operate here since late 1989, but many top international retailers have already arrived. Shops that line the main route from Old Town Square to Charles Bridge are also great for browsing. For clothing, porcelain, jewelery, garnets, and glass, stroll around Wenceslas Square and Na příkopě, the street connecting Wenceslas Square with náměstí Republiky.

For glass and crystal, try **Moser,** Na příkopě 12 (☎ **02/2421-1293**), Prague's most prestigious crystal shop that opened in 1857. Even if you're not buying, the inimitable old-world shop is definitely worth a browse. A second shop is located at Malé nám. 11.

At **Cristallino,** Celetná 12 (☎ **02/261-265**), you'll find a good selection of stemware and vases in traditional designs. The shop's central location belies its excellent prices.

At **Pavilon,** Vinohradská 50 (☎ **02/257-633**), fashion junkies can browse in stores from Lacoste to Diesel, have their hair done, buy some Timberlands, and bring home a hunk of bacon from the Belgian Butcher. The only thing this brand new four-tiered galleria lacks is 14-year-old mall rats.

Located inside the lobby of Charles University's philosophy building, **Bohemian Ventures,** nám. Jana Palacha 2 (☎ **02/231-95-16**), sells English-language books with an Eastern European slant. There's a good guide selection and translations of the most famous Czech bards.

PRAGUE AFTER DARK

Check the *Prague Post* for listings of cultural events and nightlife. Large, centrally located ticket agencies include **Prague Tourist Center,** Rytířská 12 (☎ **02/ 2421-2209**); **Bohemia Ticket International,** Na příkopě 16 (☎ **02/2421-5031**); and **Čedok,** Na příkopě 18 (☎ **02/2481-1870**).

THE PERFORMING ARTS

Although there is plenty of music year-round, the city's symphonies and orchestras all come to life during the **Prague Spring Festival,** a 3-week-long series of classical music and dance performances. The country's top performers usually participate in the festival, which runs from May 12 to June 2. Concert tickets range from 250 Kč to 2,000 Kč ($10 to $80), and are available in advance from Hellichova 18 (☎ **02/ 2451-0422**).

The **Czech Philharmonic Orchestra** and **Prague Symphony Orchestra** usually perform at the Rudolfinum, náměstí Jana Palacha (☎ **02/2489-3352**). Tickets are 100–600 Kč ($3.70–$22).

In a city full of spectacularly beautiful theaters, the masive, pale green **Estates' Theater (Stavovské divadlo),** Ovocný trh 1 (☎ **02/2421-5001**), ranks as one of the most awesome. Built in 1783, it once saw the premiere of Mozart's *Don Giovanni*, conducted by the composer himself. It's worth coming to Prague just to see a performance of the opera here. The theater now also hosts many productions of opera and classic drama from all over Europe. Simultaneous English translation, transmitted via headphone, is available for most performances.

Lavishly constructed in the late-Renaissance style of northern Italy, the gold-crowned **National Theater (Národní divadlo),** Národní třída 2 (☎ **02/ 2491-2673**), which overlooks the Vltava River, is one of Prague's most recognizable landmarks. The productions of the National Opera are staged in a larger setting than at the Estates' Theater, but with about the same ticket prices.

THE CLUB & MUSIC SCENE

Bunkr. Lodecká 2, Prague 1. ☎ **02/2481-0665.** Cover 20–70 Kč (70¢–$2.35). Metro: náměstí Republiky.

A long, deep basement that once was a 1950s Civil Guard bunker and nuclear shelter, club Bunkr opened in November 1991, followed a few months later by a like-named street-level cafe. Despised by its neighbors, the club features loud deejay nights and a plethora of live bands. Owner Richard Nemčok has honest credentials; he was jailed by the socialists and signed Charter 77. Packed with lots of young twentysomething European tourists, Bunkr is sometimes laughed at by knowledgeable locals.

Radost F/X. Bělehradská 120, Prague 2. ☎ **02/251-210.** Cover 40–50 Kč ($1.60–$2). Metro: I. P. Pavlova.

Popular with a very mixed gay and model crowd, Radost is built in the American mold. A subterranean labyrinth of nooks and crannies has a pulsating techno-heavy dance floor with good sight lines for wallflowers. Radost is extremely stylish and self-consciously urban. It's a great place, but a boring shame that it's the only game in town. There's a vegetarian cafe upstairs (reviewed above). Open daily 9pm–5am.

Roxy. Dlouhá 33, Prague 1. ☎ **02/231-6331.** Cover 30 Kč ($1.20), more for concerts. Metro: Náměstí Republiky.

One of the city's most unusual venues, Roxy is a great subterranean theater with a wraparound balcony overlooking a concrete dance floor. The club is ultra-downscale, and extremely popular on Friday and Saturday nights. Persian rugs and lanterns soften the atmosphere but don't improve the lousy acoustics. Acid jazz, funk, techno, ambient, and other danceable tunes attract an artsy crowd. Arrive after midnight. Open Tues–Sat 8pm–6am.

Jazz Clubs

AghaRTA Jazz Centrum. Krakovská 5, Prague 1. ☎ **02/2421-2914**. Cover 60–100 Kč ($2.40–$4). Metro: Muzeum.

Relatively high prices guarantee this small jazz room a predominantly foreign clientele. Upscale by Czech standards, the AghaRTA jazzery regularly features some of the best music in town, running the gamut from standard acoustic trios to Dixieland, funk, and fusion. Bands usually begin at 9pm. Open Mon–Fri 4pm–1am, Sat–Sun 7pm–1am.

Reduta Jazz Club. Národní 20, Prague 1. ☎ **02/2491-2246**. Cover 80–100 Kč ($3.20–$4). Metro: Národní třída.

Reduta is a smoky subterranean jazz room that looks exactly like a jazz cellar is supposed to look. An adventurous booking policy means different bands play almost every night of the week. Music usually starts around 9:30pm. Open Mon–Sat 9pm–midnight.

PUBS & THE BAR SCENE

You'll experience true nightly Czech entertainment in only one kind of place—a smoky local pub serving some of the world's best beer. Remember to put a cardboard coaster in front of you to show you want a mug, and never wave for service, as the typically surly waiter will just ignore you.

An excellent traditional 14th-century pub on a charming Old Town back street, **U Vejvodů,** Jilská 4 (☎ **02/2421-0591**), attracts a good mix of locals and visitors who come here for good Staropramen beer and decent Czech pub food. Open daily 11am–11pm.

One of the most famous Czech pubs, **U Zlatého tygra,** Husova 17 (☎ **02/ 2422-9020**), translated as At the Golden Tiger, is one of the favorite watering holes of both President Havel and writer Bohumil Hrabal. Particularly smoky, and not especially tourist friendly, this place is a one-stop education in Czech culture. Havel and President Bill Clinton joined Hrabal for a traditional Czech pub evening here during Clinton's 1994 visit to Prague. Open daily 3pm–11pm.

Originally a brewery dating back to 1459, **U Fleků,** Křemencova 11 (☎ **02/ 2491-5118**), is Prague's most famous beer hall, and one of the only pubs that still brews its own beer. This huge place has a myriad of timber-lined rooms and a large, loud courtyard where an oompah band performs. Tourists come here by the busload, so U Fleků is avoided by disparaging locals who don't like its German atmosphere anyway. The pub's special dark beer is excellent, however, and not available anywhere else. Open daily 9am–11pm.

Hidden on a small Old Town back street, the loud and lively **Chapeau Rouge/ Banana Cafe,** Jakubská 2 (no phone), has twin bars, plank floors, and a good sound system playing contemporary rock music. They sell four types of beer on tap and feature regular drink specials. It's busy and fun—if you avoid the headache-inducing concoctions from the frozen drink machine. Open daily noon–5am.

CASINOS

Prague has many casinos, most offering blackjack, roulette, and slot machines. House rules are usually similar to Las Vegas. **Casino Palais Savarin,** Na příkopě 10

(☎ 02/2422-1636), occupying a former rococo palace, is the city's most beautiful game room, open daily 1pm–4am (metro: Můstek). Other recommended casinos include **Casino de France,** in the Hotel Hilton Atrium, Pobřežní 1 (☎ 02/ 2484-1111), open daily 2pm–6am; and **Casino Admirál,** Vodičkova 30 (☎ 02/ 2416-2427), open daily 1pm–5am.

DAY TRIPS FROM PRAGUE

KARLŠTEJN CASTLE   By far the most popular destination in the Czech Republic after Prague, this medieval castle, located 18 miles southwest of Prague, was built by Charles IV in the 14th century to safeguard the crown jewels of the Holy Roman Empire. As you approach the castle, which has been renovated to its original state, little can prepare you for your first view: a spectacular, Disney-like castle perched high on a hill, surrounded by lush forests and vineyards. If you decide to take the tour, be prepared: The **Holy Rood Chapel,** famous for the more than 2,000 precious and semiprecious inlaid gems that adorn its walls, is closed. So is the **Chapel of St. Catherine,** King Karel IV's own private oratory. What is open are several rooms, most in the south palace. But the tour isn't a total waste of time. Both the **Audience Hall** and the **Imperial Bedroom** are impressive, despite being stripped of their original furnishings.

The best way to get to Karlštejn is by train (there is no bus service). Most trains leave from Prague's Smíchov Station (at the Smíchovské nádraží metro stop) hourly throughout the day and take about 45 minutes to reach Karlštejn. The one-way second-class fare is 14 Kč (52¢). You can also take a scenic half-hour drive, leaving Prague from the southwest along Highway 4 in the direction of Strakonice, and taking the Karlštejn cutoff and following the signs (and traffic). Castle admission is 90 Kč ($3.33) for adults, 45 Kč ($1.67) for children. Open May, June, and Sept 9am–noon and 12:30–6pm; July–Aug 9am–noon and 12:30–7pm; Nov–Dec 9am–noon and 1–4pm.

KUTNÁ HORA   A medieval town that grew fantastically rich from the silver deposits beneath it, Kutná Hora, 45 miles east of Prague, is probably the second most popular day trip from Prague. The town's ancient heart is quite decayed, making it hard to believe that this was once the second most important city in Bohemia.

The town's main attraction is the enormous **St. Barbara's Cathedral** (Chrám Sv. Barbory) at the southwestern edge of the town. The cathedral's soaring arches, dozens of spires, and intricate designs raise expectations that the interior will be just as impressive—you won't be disappointed. Upon entering the cathedral (you have to enter from the side, not the front), you'll see several richly decorated frescoes full of symbols denoting the town's two main industries of mining and minting. Admission is 20 Kč (74¢) for adults, 10 Kč (37¢) for children. Open Tues–Sun 9am–noon and 1–5pm.

When you leave the cathedral, head down the statue-lined **Barborská street,** where you will pass the early **Baroque Jesuit College** built in the late 17th century.

A visit to Kutná Hora isn't complete without a trip to **Kostnice,** the "bone church." It's located a mile down the road in Sedlec; those who don't want to walk can board a local bus on Masarykova street—the fare is 6 Kč (22¢).

From the outside, Kostnice looks like most other gothic churches. But once you go inside, you know this is no ordinary church. All of the decorations in the church were made from human bones by František Rint. The bones came from victims of the 14th-century plague and the 15th-century Hussite wars; both events left thousands of dead, who were buried in mass graves. As the area developed, the bones were uncovered, and the local mons came up with this idea. Admission is 20 Kč (74¢) for adults, 10 Kč (37¢) for children. Open July–Aug daily 9am–noon and 1–5pm; Sept–June Tues–Sun 9am–noon and 1–4pm.

TEREZÍN (THERESIENSTADT) The name Terezín (*Theresienstadt* in German) occupies a unique place in the atrocious history of Nazism. This former Austro-Hungarian imperial fortress-turned-concentration camp, 30 miles northwest of Prague, has no gas chambers, mass machine-gun executions, or medical testing rooms; it was used instead as a transit camp. About 140,000 people passed though Terezín's gates; many died here, and more than half ended up at the death camps of Auschwitz and Treblinka.

Terezín will live in infamy for the cruel trick played by the SS chief Heinrich Himmler. On June 23, 1944, three foreign observers came to Terezín to find out if the rumors of Nazi atrocities were true. They left under the impression that all was well, duped by a carefully planned "beautification" of the camp. So the observers wouldn't think the camp was overcrowded, the Nazis transported some 7,500 of the camp's sick and elderly prisoners to Auschwitz. The trick worked so well that the Nazis made a film of the camp while it was still "self-governing" called *A Town Presented to the Jews from the Fuehrer*. Terezín was liberated by Russian forces on May 10, 1945, eight days after Berlin had fallen to the Allies.

Today, the Terezín Camp exists as a memorial to the dead, and a monument to human depravity. Once inside the **Major Fortress,** you'll immediately be struck by its drab, plain streets. Just off the main square lies the **Museum of the Ghetto,** which chronicles the rise of Nazism and life in the camp. Admission is 50 Kč ($1.85) for adults, 25 Kč (93¢) for children. A ticket to enter both the Major and Minor Fortresses is 80 Kč ($2.96) for adults, 40 Kč ($1.48) for children. The Major Fortress is open daily 9am–6pm.

The **Minor Fortress** is about a 10-minute walk from the Major Fortress over the Ohře River. Just in front of the fortress's main entrance is the **National Cemetery** (Národní Hřbitov), where the bodies exhumed from the mass graves were buried. As you enter the main gate, the sign above *Arbeit Macht Frei* ("Work Sets One Free") sets a gloomy tone. You can walk through the prison barracks, execution grounds, workshops, and isolation cells.

Terezín is a 45-minute drive from Prague, on the main highway that leads north out of Prague and goes to Berlin via Dresden. Six buses leave daily from Florenc Bus Station (metro line C) for the 1-hour trip. Prague-based **Wittman Tours** (☎ 02/25-12-35) offers a bus tour that costs 950 Kč ($35.15) for adults; call for tour times.

2 West Bohemia & the Spas

by Alan Crosby

The Czech Republic is comprised of two regions: Bohemia and Moravia. The bigger of the two, Bohemia, which occupies the central and western areas of the country, has for centuries been caught between a rock (Germany) and a hard place (the Austrian Empire). Bohemia was almost always in the center of regional conflicts, both secular and religious. But the area also flourished, as witnessed by the wealth of castles that dot the countryside and spa towns that were once the playgrounds of the rich and famous.

Though Bohemia is historically undivided, there are clear-cut distinctions in the region's geography that make going from town to town easier if you "cut" Bohemia into sections. This section focuses on west Bohemia, home to the country's spa towns.

It's also one of the few regions within the Czech Republic where a full-blown tourist infrastructure is already in place. Its main towns—Karlovy Vary (Carlsbad), Mariánské Lázně (Marienbad), and to a lesser extent Plzeň and Cheb—offer a wide array of accommodations, restaurants, and services.

A relatively inexpensive network of trains and buses covers the region, allowing travel between towns and to and from Prague with a minimum of fuss and confusion. West Bohemia is generally rougher terrain, so only serious cyclists should consider touring the area on two wheels. For those with a car, the region's highways can range from top-notch, such as the newly built Prague-Plzeň motorway, to an asphalt horror ride such as the Prague-Karlovy Vary route. Roads generally are much slower than in Western Europe, so leave yourself plenty of time. Gas stations are constantly springing up, so stops for food and fuel are rarely hard to come by. Please note that if you drive the D5 (Prague-Plzeň) and D1 (Prague-Brno) highways, your car must display the country's highway sticker; these stickers, which can be bought at most every gas station and border crossing, cost 400 Kč ($15) and save you from being hassled by the police and fined 500 Kč ($18.50).

Most towns are distant enough that you should drive from one to another. However, if you'd rather stay in one place and make day trips, I'd recommend staying in Karlovy Vary and then taking excursions from there. The **Kur-Info Vřídelní Kolonáda,** 360 01 Karlovy Vary (☎ **017/203-569** or **240-97;** fax 017/246-67) can provide information on bus trips to Mariánské Lázně and other regional sights.

ONLY IN WEST BOHEMIA

Relaxing at Karlovy Vary and Mariánské Lázné These two spas are excellent examples of what was once central Europe's resort area. You can enjoy the hot springs that provide everything from drinking samples to body treatments.

Drinking the Original Pilsner Pilsner Urquell and Budvar, two of the world's best and most famous beers, come from Bohemia, from the city of Plzeň in the west and České Budějovice in the south, respectively.

Touring Český Krumlov Bohemia's second largest castle is one of the most celebrated in Europe.

KARLOVY VARY (CARLSBAD)

The discovery of Karlovy Vary (Carlsbad), 75 miles west of Prague, by King Charles IV reads something like a 14th-century episode of the television show *The Beverly Hillbillies.* According to local lore, the king was out hunting for some food when up from the ground came some bubbling water (though discovered by his dogs and not an errant gun shot). Knowing a good thing when he saw it, Charles immediately set to work on building a small castle in the area, naming the town that evolved around it Karlovy Vary, which translates to Charles's Boiling Place. The first spa buildings were built in 1522, and before long, notables such as Albrecht of Wallenstein, Russian Czar Peter the Great, and later Bach, Beethoven, Freud, and Marx all came to Karlovy Vary as a holiday retreat.

After World War II, East Bloc travelers (following in the footsteps of Marx no doubt) discovered the town, and Karlovy Vary became a destination for the proletariat. On doctor's orders, most workers would enjoy regular stays of 2 or 3 weeks, letting the mineral waters ranging from 43.5° to 72° Celsius from the town's 12 spas heal their tired and broken bodies. Even now, most spa guests are there by doctor's prescription.

But most of the 40-plus years of communist neglect—they even took out most of the social aspect of spa-going and turned it into a science—have been erased as a barrage of renovators are restoring almost all of the spa's former glory. Gone is the statue of Yuri Gregarin, the Russian cosmonaut. Gone are almost all of the fading, crumbling building facades that used to line both sides of the river. In their place now stand restored buildings, cherubs, charatids, and more in the center.

Today, nearly 100,000 people travel annually to the spa resort to sip, bathe, and frolic, though most enjoy the 13th spring, a hearty herb-and-mineral liqueur called Becherovka, more than the 12 nonalcoholic versions. Czechs will tell you that all have medical benefits.

ESSENTIALS

ARRIVING   By Train   At all costs, avoid the train from Prague, which takes over 4 hours on a circuitous route. If you're arriving from another direction, Karlovy Vary's main train station is connected to the town center by bus no. 13.

By Bus   Frequent express buses make the trip from Prague's Florenc station to Karlovy Vary's náměstí Dr. M. Horákové in about 2¹/₂ hours. Buses leave from platforms 21 or 22 daily at 7am, 9am, 9:40am, noon, and 4pm. Take a 10-minute walk or local bus no. 4 into Karlovy Vary's town center. Note that unlike Prague, you must have a ticket (4 Kč/15¢) to board local transportation. Tickets can be purchased at the main station stop, or, if you have no change, the kiosk across the street sells tickets during regular business hours.

By Car   The nearly 2-hour drive from Prague to Karlovy Vary is not difficult, but can be at times a little hair-raising. From Prague, take highway E-48 from the western end of the city and follow it straight through to Karlovy Vary. This two-lane highway widens in a few spots to let cars pass slow-moving vehicles on hills. However, be warned that this highway is a popular route for reckless drivers heading to and from the capital. Please take extra care when driving.

VISITOR INFORMATION   Kuri-Info, located inside the Vřídelní Kolonáda, is open Mon–Fri 7am–5pm, Sat–Sun 9am–3pm. It provides accommodation services, arranges guided tours and spa treatments, and sells tickets for some events. Be sure to pick up the *Cultural Calendar,* a comprehensive collection of events with a small map of the town center.

There are also two privately run **Info-Centrum** booths in Karlovy Vary: one in the train station and the other in a parking lot at the base of Jana Palácha ulice. Both give away free maps and a brochure of current cultural listings and events called *Promenáda.* Info-Centrum also books accommodations in private rooms and sells tours.

SPECIAL EVENTS   The **Karlovy Vary International Film Festival** is one of the few places to see and be seen. Each summer (usually at the beginning of July), the film stars and celebrities take part in one of Europe's biggest film festivals. Six venues screen more than 200 films during the 8- to 10-day festival.

Karlovy Vary plays host to several events including a **jazz festival** and **beer Olympiad** in May, the **Dvořák singing contest** in June, the **Summer Music Festival** in August, and the **Dvořák Autumn Music Festival** in September and October.

For more information on any of the festivals, contact **Kur-Info Vřídelní Kolonáda,** 360-01 Karlovy Vary (☎ **017/203-569** or **240-97;** fax 017/246-67).

CITY LAYOUT   Karlovy Vary is shaped like a T, with the Teplá River running up the stem and the Ohře River at the top of the T. Most of the major streets are pedestrian promenades lining both sides of the Teplá River.

Bohemia

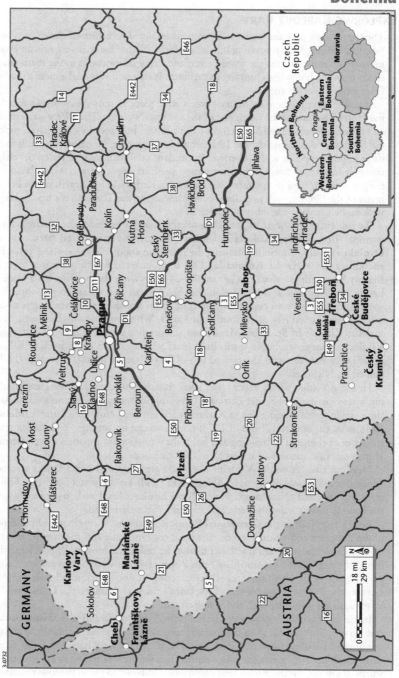

EXPLORING KARLOVY VARY

The town's slow pace and pedestrian promenades, lined with turn-of-the-century art nouveau buildings, turn strolling into an art form. Nighttime walks take on an even more mystical presence as the sewers, river, and many major cracks in the roads emit steam from the hot springs running underneath. It feels as if you might meet Vincent Price around every corner.

If you're traveling here by train or bus, a good place to start your walking tour is the **Hotel Thermal** at the north end of the old town's center. The 1960s glass, steel, and concrete hotel, nestled between the town's eastern hills and the Ohře River, sticks out like a sore thumb amidst the 19th-century architecture. Nonetheless, you'll find three important places at the Thermal: its outdoor pool with mineral water, the only centrally located, outdoor public swimming pool; its upper terrace, which boasts a truly spectacular view of the town; and its theater, Karlovy Vary's largest, which holds many of the film festival's premier events. After seeing the Thermal, it's best to keep walking before you remember too much of it.

As you enter the heart of the town on the river's west side, the ornate white wrought-iron **Sadová Kolonáda** adorns a beautifully manicured park named **Dvořákový Sady.** Continue following the river, and about 100 meters later you will encounter the **Mlýnská Kolonáda.** This long, covered walkway houses several Karlovy Vary springs, which can be sampled 24 hours a day. Each spring has a plaque beside it telling which mineral elements are present and what temperature the water is. Bring your own cup, or buy one just about anywhere to sip the waters since most are too hot to just drink from your hands. When you hit the river bend, the majestic **Church of St. Mary Magdalene** sits perched atop a hill, overlooking the **Vřídlo,** the hottest spring in town. Built in 1736, the church is the work of Kilian Ignac Dientzenhofer, who also created two of Prague's more notable churches—both named St. Nicholas.

Housing Vřídlo, which blasts water some 50 feet into the air, is the glass building where the statue of Soviet astronaut Gregarin once stood. (Gregarin's statue has since made a safe landing at the Karlovy Vary airport.) Now called the **Vřídelní Kolonáda,** the structure, built in 1974, houses several hot springs. You can sample these free of charge. The building also holds the Kuri-Info information center, where visitors can find answers to almost all of their questions.

Heading away from the Vřídelní Kolonáda are Stará and Nova Louka streets, which line either side of the river. Along **Stará (Old) Louka** you'll find several fine cafes and glass and crystal shops. **Nova (New) Louka** is lined with many hotels and the historic town's main theater, currently under reconstruction.

Both streets lead to the **Grandhotel Pupp.** Both the main entrance and building of the Pupp are under heavy reconstruction as the hotel attempts to erase the effects of 40 years of communism (the hotel used to be called the Moskva-Pupp). Regardless of capitalism or communism, the Pupp remains what it always was: the grand-dame of hotels in the area. Once catering to nobility from all over central Europe, the Pupp still houses one of the town's finest restaurants, the Grand, while its grounds are a favorite with the hiking crowd.

If you still have the energy, atop the hill behind the Pupp stands the **Diana Lookout Tower.** Footpaths lead to the tower through the forests and eventually spit you out at the base of the tower, as if to say, "Ha, the trip is only half over." The five-story climb up the tower tests your stamina, but the view of the town is more than worth it. Oh yes, for those who aren't up to the climb just to get to the tower, a cable car runs to the tower every 15 minutes or so.

Spa Cures & Treatments

Most visitors to Karlovy Vary come for the specific reason of getting a spa treatment, a therapy that lasts 1 to 3 weeks. After consulting with a spa physician, guests are given a regimen of activities that may include mineral baths, massages, waxings, mud packs, electrotherapy, and pure oxygen inhalation. After spending the morning at a spa, or sanatorium, guests are usually directed to walk the paths of the town's surrounding forest.

The common denominator of all the cures is an ample daily dose of hot mineral water, which bubbles up from 12 different springs. This water definitely has a distinct odor and taste. You'll see people chugging down the water, but it doesn't necessarily taste very good. Some thermal springs actually taste and smell like rotten eggs. You may want to take a small sip at first.

You'll also notice that almost everyone in town seems to be carrying "the cup." This funny-looking cup is basically a mug with a built-in straw that runs through the handle. Young and old alike parade through town with their mugs, filling and refilling them at each new thermal water tap. You can buy these mugs everywhere for as little as 50 Kč ($1.85) or as much as 500 Kč ($18.50); they make a quirky souvenir. But be warned: None of the mugs can make the hot springs taste any better!

The minimum spa treatment lasts 1 week and must be arranged in advance. A spa treatment package traditionally includes room, full board, and complete therapy regimen; the cost varies from about $40 to $100 per person per day, depending on season and facilities. Rates are highest from May through September, and lowest from November through February.

For information and reservations in the United States, contact **Čedok,** 10 E. 40th St., New York, NY 10016 (☎ **212/689-9720**). For information and reservations in Prague, contact Čedok, Na příkopě 18. Many hotels also provide spa and health treatments, so ask when you book your room. Most hotels will happily arrange a treatment if they don't provide them directly.

Visitors to Karlovy Vary for just a day or two can experience the waters on an "outpatient" basis. The **State Baths III** (☎ **017/256-41**) welcomes day-trippers with mineral baths, massages, saunas, and a cold pool. They're open for men on Tues, Thurs, and Sat, and for women on Mon, Wed, and Fri 7:45am–3pm. **Vojensky lázeňsky ústav,** Mlynské nábřeží 7 (☎ **017/22206**), offers similar services and costs about 750 Kč ($27.75) per day.

Shopping

Crystal and porcelain are Karlovy Vary's other claims to fame. Dozens of shops throughout town sell everything from plates to chandeliers.

Ludvík Moser founded his first glassware shop in 1857, and became one of this country's foremost names in glass. You can visit the **Moser Factory,** kapitána Jaroše 19 (☎ **017/41-61-11**), just west of the town center; take bus nos. 1, 10, or 16. It's open Mon–Fri 7:30am–3:30pm. The **Moser Store,** Stará Louka 40, is right in the heart of town, open Mon–Fri 9am–5pm.

Accommodations

Private rooms are the best places to stay in Karlovy Vary with regard to quality and price. Arrange your room through **Info-Centrum** (see "Visitor Information" above) or **Čedok,** Karla IV č. 1 (☎ **017/26110** or 267-05; fax 017/278-35), open Mon–Fri 9am–5pm, Sat 9am–noon. Expect to pay about 500–800 Kč ($18.50–$29.62) for a single and 750–1,200 Kč ($27.75–$44.44) for a double.

The town's major spa hotels only accommodate those who are paying for complete treatment, unless, for some reason, their occupancy rates are particularly low. The hotels listed below accept guests for stays of any length.

Expensive

Grandhotel Pupp. Mírově náměstí 2, 360-91, Karlovy Vary. ☎ **017/209-631.** Fax 017/ 32-240-32. 270 rms and suites. MINIBAR TV TEL. From April 14–Nov 5 and Dec 28–Jan 4, 3,600–4200 Kč ($133–155) double, 5,350–16,900 Kč ($198–$626) suite; Jan 5–April 13 and Nov 6–Dec 27, 2,550–2,990 Kč ($94–$110) double, 3,750–16,900 Kč ($138–$626) suite. AE, DC, MC, V.

Well known as one of Karlovy Vary's best hotels, Grandhotel Pupp, built in 1701, is also one of Europe's oldest. While the hotel's public areas are oozing with splendor and charm, the guest rooms are not as consistently enchanting. The best rooms tend to be those that face toward the town center and are located on the upper floors; these rooms have good views and sturdy wooden furniture.

Hotel Dvořák. Nova Louka 11, 360-21, Karlovy Vary. ☎ **017/310-2111.** Fax 017/322-2814. 79 rms and suites. MINIBAR TV TEL. May–Oct, 4,750 Kč ($176) double, 6,480 Kč ($240) suite; Jan–April and Nov–Dec, 3,240 ($117) double. AE, DC, MC, V.

This hotel is within sight of the Grandhotel Pupp, but people who have stayed here say it's far beyond Karlovy Vary's vaunted hotel. If the Pupp has the history and elegance, they say, the Dvořák has the facilities, including a well-equipped fitness center. The rooms are spacious and well appointed, and the staff is very attentive.

Moderate

Hotel Puškin. Tržiště 37, 360-90 Karlovy Vary. ☎ **017/322-2646.** Fax 017/322-4134. 20 rms. TV TEL. May–Oct, 1,980–2,200 Kč ($73–$81) double, 3,093 Kč ($115) 4-person junior suite; Jan 3–April and Nov–Dec, 1,620–1,800 Kč ($60–$67) double, 2,500 Kč ($93) 4-person junior suite. No credit cards.

Named for the great Russian poet we know as Pushkin, this hotel occupies an intricately ornamented 19th-century building that has just been renovated. The hotel has a terrific location, close to the springs. The rooms are rather basic, but they are comfortable enough; ask for one that has a balcony facing St. Mary Magdalene church.

DINING

Expensive

Grand Restaurant. In the Grand Hotel Pupp, Mírově náměstí 2. ☎ **017/22121.** Reservations recommended. Main courses 290–590 Kč ($10.74–$21.85). AE, V. Daily noon–3pm and 6–10pm. CONTINENTAL.

It's no surprise that the Grandhotel Pupp has the nicest dining room in town, an elegant eatery with tall ceilings, huge mirrors, and glistening chandeliers. A large menu gives way to larger portions of salmon, chicken, veal, pork, turkey, and beef in a variety of heavy and heavier sauces. Even the trout with mushrooms is smothered in a butter sauce.

✪ **Promenáda.** Tržiště 31. ☎ **017/322-5648.** Reservations highly recommended. Main courses 180–350 Kč ($6.66–$12.96). AE, V. Daily noon–11pm. CZECH/CONTINENTAL.

This cozy, intimate spot may not be as elegant as the Grand Restaurant in the Pupp, but for Karlovy Vary residents, it remains one of *the* places to dine. Located directly across from the Vřídelní Kolonáda, the Promenáda offers a wide selection of meals that come in generous portions. The daily menu usually includes well-prepared wild game, but most will tell you that the mixed grill for two or the chateaubriand, both flambéed at the table, are the chef's best dishes. The wine list features a large selection from around Europe, but don't sell short the Czech wines on the menu, especially the white Ryslink and the red Frankovka. An order of crépes Suzette big enough to satisfy the sweet tooth of two diners rounds out a wonderful meal.

Moderate

Abbazia. Vřdelní 51. ☎ **017/322-5648.** Reservations recommended. Main courses 99–300 Kč ($3.67–$11.11). AE, V. Daily noon–11pm. CZECH/CONTINENTAL.

From the outside, the Abbazia is easy to miss, but it's well worth finding. Located near the Vřídelní Kolonáda on the second floor, Abazzia has a wooden interior dominated by huge tables, making it one of the few places where large groups are always welcome. The rather large menu offers a wide assortment of Czech and international meals at reasonable prices. This is one of the few places in the Czech Republic where I would recommend the scampi; I usually order it as an appetizer to share with my dining partner.

As an added bonus, Ondřej Havelka and his Prague Syncopated Orchestra regularly stop by to play music from the 1920s and 1930s, complete with flappers dancing away. It's some of the best music you'll hear on either side of the Atlantic. Always check to see if he is in town, and if he is, reserve a place as quickly as possible so you don't miss him.

Inexpensive

Cafe Elefant. Stará Louka 32. ☎ **017/23406.** Cakes and desserts 20–75 Kč (74¢–$2.77). Daily 9am–10pm. DESSERTS.

Save yourself a trip to Vienna. A cafe in the true sense of the word, all you will find is coffee, tea, alcoholic and nonalcoholic drinks, desserts, and enough ambience to satisfy the hordes of Germans and Austrians who flock to this landmark. The Elefant, widely known for its belle époque style that includes pink walls and mirrors, is famous for its freshly baked cakes. A large number of outdoor tables overlook the pedestrian promenade.

MARIÁNSKÉ LÁZNĚ (MARIENBAD)

When Thomas Alva Edison visited Mariánské Lázně in the late 1800s, he proclaimed: "There is no more beautiful spa in all the world." The town is 29 miles southwest of Karlovy Vary, and 100 miles west of Prague.

While the spa town of Mariánské Lázně now stands in the shadow of the Czech Republic's most famous spa town, Karlovy Vary, it was not always that way. First mentioned in 1528, the town's mineral waters gained prominence at the end of the 18th and beginning of the 19th centuries. Nestled among forested hills and packed with romantic and elegant pastel hotels and spa houses, the town, commonly known by its German name, Marienbad, has played host to such luminaries as Goethe (where his love for Ulrika von Levetzow took root), Mark Twain, composers Chopin, Strauss, and Wagner, as well as Freud and Kafka. England's King Edward VII found the spa resort so enchanting he visited nine times, and even commissioned the building of the country's first golf club.

ESSENTIALS

ARRIVING   By Train   The express train from Prague takes just over 3 hours. Mariánské Lázně train station, Nádražní náměstí 292 (☎ **0165/625-321**), is located south of the town center; take bus no. 5 into town. The one-way fare costs 136 Kč ($5) first class, 96 Kč ($3.55) second class.

By Bus   The 3-hour bus trip from Prague costs about 65 Kč ($2.40). The Mariánské Lázně bus station is situated adjacent to the train station on Nádražní náměstí; take bus no. 5 into town.

By Car   Driving from Prague, take the E-50 highway through Plzeň to Stříbo—about 22km (13.64 miles) past Plzeň—and head northwest on highway 21. The clearly marked route can take up to 2 hours. From Karlovy Vary the trip is about 80km (49.60 miles). Take highway 20 south and then turn right onto highway 24 in the town of Bečov.

VISITOR INFORMATION   Just across from the Hotel Bohemia, **City Service,** at Hlavní třída 1 (☎ and fax **0165/624-218** or 623-816), on the town's main street, is the best place for information. In addition to dispensing advice, the staff sells maps and arranges accommodations in hotels and private homes. Open Mon–Fri 7am–7pm, Sat–Sun 9am–6pm.

SPECIAL EVENTS   One of the few places in central Europe not to claim Mozart as one of its sons, Mariánské Lázně has instead chosen to honor one of its frequent visitors, Chopin, with a yearly festival devoted entirely to the Polish composer and his works. The **Chopin Festival** usually runs for 8–10 days near the end of August. Ticket prices range from 70 to 300 Kč ($2.60 to $11).

Each June, the town also plays host to a **classical music festival** with many of the Czech Republic's finest musicians, as well as those from around the world. For more information or ticket reservations for either event, contact **Infocentrum KaSS,** Dům Chopin, Hlavní 47, 353-01, Mariánské Lázně (☎ **0165/622-427;** fax 0165/625892).

Patriotic Americans can show up on **July 4** for a little down-home fun, including a parade and other flag-waving special events commemorating the town's liberation by U.S. soldiers in World War II.

In mid-August, the sports-minded traveler can see some of Europe's top golfers at the **Czech Open,** one of the newest events on the European PGA golf tour.

CITY LAYOUT   Mariánské Lázně is laid out around **Hlavní třída,** the main street. A plethora of hotels, restaurants, travel agencies, and stores front this street. **Lázeňské Colonnade,** a long, covered block beginning at the northern end of Hlavní třída, contains six of the resort's eight major springs.

TAKING THE WATERS AT MARIÁNSKÉ LÁZNĚ

When walking through the town, it's almost impossible to miss the **Lázeňské Colonnade,** located just off Skalníkovy sady. From Hlavní třída, walk east on Vrchlického ulice. Recently restored to its former glory, the eye-catching cast-iron and glass colonnade is adorned with ceiling frescoes and Corinthian columns. Built in 1889, the colonnade connects a half-dozen major springs in the town center; this is the focal point of those partaking in the ritual. Bring a cup to fill, or, if you want to fit in with the thousands of guests who are serious about their spa water, buy one of the porcelain mugs with a built-in straw that are offered just about everywhere. Do keep in mind that the waters are used to treat internal disorders, so the minerals may act to cleanse the body thoroughly. You can wander the colonnade any time; water is distributed daily 6am–noon and 4–6pm.

For a relaxing mineral bubble bath or massage, make reservations through the **State Spa Office,** Masarykova 22 (☎ **0165/622-170**). Also ask at your hotel since most provide spa treatments and massages or can arrange them. Treatments cost from 300 Kč ($11) and up.

MORE TO SEE & DO

There's not much town history, since Mariánské Lázně only officially came into existence in 1808. But engaging brevity is what makes the two-story **Muzeum**

Hlavního Města (City Museum), Goetheovo náměstí 11 (☎ **0165/622-740**), recommendable. Chronologically arranged displays include photos and documents of famous visitors. Goethe slept here, in the upstairs rooms in 1823, when he was 74 years old. If you ask nicely, the museum guards will play an English-language tape that describes the contents of each of the museum's rooms. You can also request to see the museum's English-language film about the town. Admission is 20 Kč (74¢). Open Tues–Sun 9am–4pm.

You can also take a walk in the woods. The surrounding **Slavkovský les (Slavkov Forest)** has about 70 kilometers of marked footpaths and trails through the gentle hills that abound in the area.

If you're a diehard golfer, or just looking for a little exercise, the **Mariánské Lázně Golf Club,** a 6,195-meter yard par-72 championship course, lies on the edge of town. The club takes pay-as-you-play golfers, with a fully equipped pro shop that rents clubs. Greens fees are 900 Kč ($33), club rental 300 Kč ($11).

ACCOMMODATIONS

The main strip along Hlavní třída is lined with hotels, many with rooms facing the Colonnade. I suggest walking the street and shopping around for a room; most hotels charge 2,000–3,500 Kč ($55–$110) for a double in high season (May–Sept). Off-season prices can fall by as much as half.

For private accommodations, try Paláckého ulice, which runs south of the main spa area.

Expensive

Hotel Golf. Zádub 55, 353-01 Mariánské Lázně. ☎ **0165/622651.** Fax 2655. 96 rms. MINIBAR TV TEL. 3,200 Kč ($119) double; 5,400 Kč ($200) suite. Rates include breakfast. AE, DC, MC, V.

One of the more luxurious hotels in town, the Hotel Golf is not actually in town, but across the street from the golf course about 2 miles away on the road leading to Karlovy Vary. This hotel is busy, so reservations are recommended. An English-speaking staff delivers on their pledge to cater to every wish. The rooms are bright and spacious, plus there's an excellent restaurant and terrace on the first floor. Not surprisingly, given the hotel's name, staff can help arrange a quick 18 holes across the street. The hotel plans to open its own spa center in 1996 to pamper guests a little more.

Hotel Villa Butterfly. Hlavní třída 72, 353-01 Mariánské Lázně. ☎ **0165/626201.** Fax 0165/626210. 26 rms. MINIBAR TV TEL. 4,000 Kč ($148) double; 5,550–7,400 Kč ($206–$274) suite. Rates include breakfast. AE, DC, MC, V.

One of the newest hotels on the main street, the Villa Butterfly has rather ordinary rooms that are comfortable and spotlessly clean. An English-speaking staff and a good selection of foreign-language newspapers at the reception are an added bonus that few hotels here provide.

Moderate

Hotel Palace. Hlavní třída 67, 353-01 Mariánské Lázně. ☎ **0165/622223.** Fax 0165/624262. 40 rms, 5 suites. MINIBAR TV TEL. May–Sept, 3,400 Kč ($126) double, 5,100 Kč ($189) suite; Apr and Oct, 2,720 Kč ($101) double, 3,400 Kč ($126) suite; Nov–March, 1,870 Kč ($69) double, 2,550 Kč ($94) suite. AE, DC, MC, V.

One of the top hotels in town, the 1920s-era Palace is a beautiful art nouveau–style hotel located just 300 feet from the spa colonnade. The rooms are extremely comfortable. In addition to a good Bohemian restaurant, the hotel contains a cafe, wine room, and snack bar.

Hotel Zvon. Hlavní třída 68, 353-01 Mariánské Lázně. ☎ **0165/622015.** Fax 0165/623245. 79 rms. MINIBAR TV TEL. 2,800 Kč ($104) double; 4,000 Kč ($148) 3-room suite. AE, DC, MC, V.

Next door to the Palace, the newly renovated Zvon lacks a bit of the panache that its smaller neighbor has, but still ranks as one of the town's nicer hotels.

Inexpensive

🟢 **Hotel Koliba.** Dusíkova 592, 35301 Mariánské Lázně. ☎ **0165/625169.** Fax 0165/76310. 10 rms. MINIBAR TV TEL. 1,600 Kč ($59) double.

Away from the main strip, but still only a 7-minute walk from the Colonnade, the Koliba is a rustic hunting lodge set in the hills on Dusíkova, the road that leads to the golf course and Karlovy Vary. Rooms are very comfortable. The hotel provides a wide array of spa and health treatments, which cost extra.

DINING

Moderate

✪ **Hotel Koliba Restaurant.** Dusíkova 592. ☎ **0165/5169.** Reservations recommended. Main courses 120–400 Kč ($4.44–$14.81). No credit cards. Daily 11am–11pm. CZECH.

Like the hotel built into it, the Koliba restaurant is a shrine to the outdoors. The dining room is well appointed with a hearty rustic atmosphere, which goes perfectly with the restaurant's strength: wild game. Check the daily menu to see what's new, or choose from the wide assortment of *specialty na roštu* (specialties from the grill), including wild boar and venison. The Koliba also has an excellent selection of Moravian wines that can be ordered with your meal, or at its wine bar, which also has dancing from 7pm to midnight (except Mon).

Hotel Palace Restaurant. Hlavní třída 67. ☎ **0165/622222.** Reservations not needed. Main courses 140–320 Kč ($5.19–$11.85). AE, DC, MC, V. Daily 7am–11pm. CZECH/ INTERNATIONAL.

The restaurant's mirror- and glass-packed neoclassical dining room is one of the prettiest in town, with a good view of the Colonnade. Bow-tied waiters serve traditional Bohemian specialties like succulent roast duck, broiled trout, and chateaubriand. Most everything comes with dumplings and sauerkraut. During good weather, the best tables are outside on a small street-front porch or on the second-floor terrace.

Inexpensive

Churchill Club Restaurant. Hlavní třída 121. No phone. Reservations not needed. Main courses 110–180 Kč ($4.07–$6.66). No credit cards. Daily 11am–11pm. CZECH.

A lively bar atmosphere makes the Churchill one of the few fun places to be after dark in this quiet town. Don't let the name fool you—the food here is traditional Czech, not British, with few surprises, which is both good and bad. A large selection of beers also sets the Churchill apart from other restaurants along the main strip.

Classic Cafe/Restaurant. Hlavní třída. No phone. Reservations not needed. Salads 51–110 Kč ($1.89–$4.07); main courses 50–130 Kč ($1.85–$4.81). AE, MC, V. Daily 10am–11pm. CZECH.

A nice place to stop for a light bite to eat, the Classic offers a large assortment of good fresh salads. The open and airy cafe/restaurant has one of the friendliest staffs in town. It also brews a mean espresso.

PLZEŇ (PILSEN)

Some 400 years ago, a group of men formed Plzeň's first beer-drinking guild, and today, beer is probably the only reason you will want to stop at this otherwise industrial town. Unfortunately for the town, its prosperity and architecture were ravaged during World War II, leaving few buildings untouched. The main square, náměstí Republiky, is worth a look, but after that, there's not much to see.

ESSENTIALS

ARRIVING   Plzeň is 55 miles southwest of Prague.

By Train   It's more comfortable taking the train to Plzeň than the bus. A fast train from Prague whisks travelers to Plzeň in just under 2 hours, about the same time the bus takes. Trains between the two cities are just as plentiful and fit most every schedule. The one-way train fare costs 88 Kč ($3.25) first class, 64 Kč ($2.37) second class. To get from the train station to town, walk out the main entrance and take Americká street across the river and turn right onto Jungmannova street, which leads to the main square.

By Bus   The bus from Prague also takes about 2 hours, but tends to be cramped. If you do take the bus, head back into town along Husova to get to the square.

By Car   A newly finished highway makes the drive between Prague and Plzeň one of the few worry-free trips a motorist can make in the country. Leave Prague to the west on the D-5 highway and 45 minutes later you'll be there.

VISITOR INFORMATION   The **City Information Center Plzeň,** náměstí Republiky 41, 301 16 Plzeň (☎ **019/7236-535;** fax 019/7224-473), is packed with literature to answer travelers' questions.

SPECIAL EVENTS   If you're an American, or speak English, being in Plzeň in May is quite an experience. May 8 marks when General George S. Patton was forced to halt his advance after liberating the area, thanks to an Allied agreement to stop. The Russians were allowed to free Prague, becoming its successor superpower as agreed. Forty years of communist oppression, however, means that the town now celebrates May 8 or **Liberation Day** with a vengeance. You will be féted and praised into the wee hours of the night, as the city's people give thanks to the forces that ended Nazi occupation.

Anxious to capitalize on its beer heritage, and always happy to celebrate, Plzeň has started its own Octoberfest, called **Pivní slavností.**

For more information on festivities for the two events, contact the City Information Center Plzeň, náměstí Republiky 41, 301-16 Plzeň (☎ **019/7236-535;** fax 019/ 7224-473).

CITY LAYOUT   Plzeň's old core is centered around náměstí Republiky. All of the sites, including the brewery, are no more than a 10-minute walk from here.

TOURING THE BEER SHRINES

Founded in 1295 by Přemysl King Václav II, Plzeň was, and remains, western Bohemia's administrative center. King Václav's real gift to the town, however, was not making it an administrative nerve center, but granting it brewing rights. As a result, more than 200 microbreweries popped up in almost every street-corner basement. Realizing the brews they were drinking had become mostly plonk by the late 1830s, rebellious beer drinkers demanded quality, forcing the brewers to try harder. "Give us what we want in Plzeň, good and cheap beer!" became the battle cry. Before long, in 1842, the brewers combined their expertise to produce a superior brew through what became known as the Pilsner brewing method. If you don't believe it's the best method, look in your refrigerator at home. Most likely, the best beer in there has written somewhere on its label "Pilsner brewed."

Widely regarded as one of the best beers the world over, **Plzeňské Pivovary** (Pilsner Breweries), at U Prazdroje 7, will interest anyone who wants to learn more about the brewing process. The brewery actually is comprised of several different breweries, pumping out brands like Pilsner Urquell and Gambrinus, the most widely consumed beer in the Czech Republic. The 1-hour tour of the factory (which has barely changed since its creation) includes a 15-minute film and visits to the fermentation cellars and brewing rooms. There's only one tour a day at 12:30pm Mon–Sat. It costs 30 Kč ($1.11) weekdays, 50 Kč ($1.85) Saturday; the price includes a dozen beer-oriented postcards and some freshly brewed beer.

If you didn't get your fill of beer facts at the brewery, the **Pivovarské Muzeum** (Beer Museum) is one block away on Veleslavínova street. Inside this former 15th-century house you'll learn everything there is to know about beer, but were afraid to ask. In the first room, once a 19th-century pub, the guard winds up an old German polyphone music box from 1887 that plays the sweet, though somewhat scratchy, strains of Strauss's *Blue Danube*. Subsequent rooms display a wide collection of pub artifacts, brewing equipment, and mugs. Most displays have English captions, but ask for a more detailed museum description in English when you enter. Admission is 20 Kč (74¢). It's open Tues–Sun 10am–6pm.

EXPLORING PLZEŇ

Safely full of more knowledge than you may want about the brewing process, proceed to the main square to see what's hopping (sorry, I couldn't resist). Dominating the center of the square is the **Gothic Cathedral of St. Bartholomew,** with the tallest steeple in the Czech Republic at 333 feet. Inside the church, a beautiful marble Madonna graces the main altar.

You'll see an Italian flair in the first four floors of the 16th-century **Town Hall** and in the *sgrafitto* adorning its facade. Later on, more floors were added, as well as a tower, gables, and brass flags, making the building appear as though another had fallen on top of it. In front of the town hall, a **memorial** built in 1681 commemorates victims of the plague.

Just west of the square on Sady pětatřicátníku lies the shattered dreams of the 2,000 or so Jews who once called Plzeň home. The **Great Synagogue,** the third largest in the world, was built in the late 19th century. But sadly, its doors remain locked, with the building in need of urgent repairs.

ACCOMMODATIONS

For private rooms that are usually outside of the town center but a little cheaper, try **Čedok** at Sedláčkova 12 (☎ 019/723-6648), open Mon–Fri 9am–noon and 1–5pm (until 6pm in summer), Sat 9am–noon. Expect to pay about 300–600 Kč ($11–$22) for a double room with a shower and toilet.

Hotel Continental. Zbrojnická 8, 305-34 Plzeň. ☎ **019/723-5291.** Fax 019/723-6479. 42 rms. TV TEL. 802 Kč ($30) double without shower or bath, 2,150 Kč ($80) double with shower but without toilet, 2,400 Kč ($89) double with bath and WC. AE, MC, V.

Located about one block from the old town square, the modern Continental is considered by locals to be one of the best in town. Velvet-covered furniture and blue-tiled bathrooms greet guests in spacious, comfortable rooms. If you're not looking for the creature comforts, ask for a room without a bathroom or WC. The staff is usually loathe to admit it, but these rooms do exist and are a cheap alternative. Downstairs the casino stays open late if you're feeling lucky, or just thirsty.

I love 0-800-99-0011
in the springtime.

All you need for the fastest, clearest connections home.

Every country has its own AT&T Access Number which makes calling from France and other countries really easy. Just dial the AT&T Access Number for the country you're calling from and we'll take it from there. And be sure to charge your calls on your AT&T Calling Card. It'll help you avoid outrageous phone charges on your hotel bill and save you up to 60%.* 0-800-99-0011 is a great place to visit any time of year, especially if you've got these two cards. So please take the attached wallet card of worldwide AT&T Access Numbers.

Hotel Slovan. Smetanovy sadý 1, 305-28 Plzeň. ☎ **019/722-7256.** Fax 019/722-7012. 110 rms. TV. 1,800 Kč ($67) double. AE, MC, V.

An elegant turn-of-the-century staircase graces the entrance foyer to this venerable hotel. But after that, the rooms fall into the same 1970s-modern decor that, hard as it is to believe, was once in fashion. Nonetheless, the rooms are clean and comfortable, and the square is only about two blocks north.

DINING

Pivnice Prazdroj. 1, U Prazdroje (just outside the brewery gates). No phone. Reservations not needed. Main courses 40–120 Kč ($1.48–$4.44). No credit cards. Mon–Fri 10am–10pm, Sat–Sun 11am–9pm. CZECH.

Unlike the Na Spilce, this is not a tourist-oriented pub; mostly brewery workers frequent this eatery, just outside the brewery gates. Literally in the same building that houses the brewery's management, the pub has remained true to those who supply it with beverages by cooking hearty basic Czech meals.

Restaurace Na Spilce. U Prazdroje (just inside the brewery gates). No phone. Reservations not needed. Main courses 70–150 Kč ($2.59–$5.56). No credit cards. Daily 11am–10pm. CZECH.

Just inside the brewery gates, Restaurace Na Spilce looks like a 600-seat tourist trap, but the food is quite good and reasonably priced. Standard *Řízký* (schnitzels), goulash, and *svičková na smetaně* (pork tenderloin in a cream sauce) are hearty, and complement the beer that flows in a never-ending stream from the brewery.

CHEB (EGER) & FRANTIŠKOVY LÁZNĚ

Like Plzeň, few people who travel through Cheb actually stop and take a look around. From the outside, that's understandable, but it's too bad, since the center of Cheb is one of the more architecturally interesting places in west Bohemia. Its history is fascinating as well.

A former stronghold for the Holy Roman Empire on its eastern flank, Eger, as it was then known, became part of Bohemia in 1322. Cheb stayed under Bohemian rule until it was handed to Germany as part of the 1938 Munich Pact. Soon after the end of World War II, it returned to Czech hands, whereupon most of the area's native Germans, known as Sudeten Germans, were expelled for their open encouragement of the invading Nazi army. This bilingual, bicultural heritage can be seen in the town's main square, which could be mistaken for being on either side of the border, if it weren't for the Czech writing on windows. These days, the Germans have returned, but only for a few hours at a time, many for the town's thriving sex trade and cheap alcohol. Don't be surprised to see women around almost every corner looking to ply their trade. Still, Cheb is worth exploring for its melange of styles in the buildings, the eerie Jewish quarter Špalíček, and the enormous, romanesque Chebsky Hrad (Cheb Castle).

Only about 20 minutes up the road from Cheb is the smallest of the three major west Bohemian spa towns, **Františkovy Lázně.** Though it pales in comparison to Karlovy Vary and Marianské Lázně, Františkovy Lázně has taken great strides in the past few years to try and erase the decline it experienced under communism. There's not much to see save for the **Spa Museum,** which holds an interesting display of bathing artifacts, but it's a much quieter and cleaner place to spend the night than Cheb. I've listed places to stay and dine in both Cheb and Františkovy Lázně.

To get to Františkovy Lázně from Cheb by car, take highway E-49. The trip takes about 20 minutes. You can also take a taxi; just agree with the driver before you get in that the fare won't be more than 150 Kč ($5.55).

ESSENTIALS

ARRIVING   Cheb is 105 miles west of Prague and 25 miles southwest of Karlovy Vary.

By Train   Express trains from Prague usually stop in Cheb, as do several trains daily from Karlovy Vary. Cheb is on a main train route of the Czech Republic, so it's easy to catch many international connections here. The train takes $3^1/_2$ hours and costs 151 Kč ($5.60) one way in first class, 106 Kč ($3.92) in second class.

By Bus   Cheb is a long bus ride from Prague, and I suggest avoiding taking the bus if possible. It's more manageable to take the bus from Karlovy Vary to Cheb.

By Car   Cheb is located on the E-48, one of the main highways leading to Germany. If you're driving from Prague, take the same route as you would to Karlovy Vary, which eventually brings you to Cheb. The drive takes about $2^1/_2$ hours.

CITY LAYOUT   At the center of the old town lies the triangular náměstí Krále Jiřího z Poděbrad. Most of the main sights lie either directly on the square or on one of the many streets leading off of it.

VISITOR INFORMATION   You'll find maps, guidebooks, lodging, and even a currency exchange (at a fairly steep price, so only use it if desperate) at the **Informacní Centrum Goetz & Hanzlík,** náměstí Přemysla Otakara II 2 (☎ **0166/594-80;** fax 0166/592-91).

EXPLORING CHEB

The main square, **náměstí Krále Jiřího z Poděbrad,** attracts most of the attention, and is a good place to begin a tour of the old town. Though it has been overrun with touristy shops and cafes that serve uniformly mediocre German fare, the square still shines with gothic burgher houses and the baroque **old town hall (stará radnice).** At its south end, the **statue Kašna Roland,** built in 1591 and a former symbol of capital punishment, reminds people of the strength justice can wield. At the other end of the square stands the **Kašna Herkules,** a monument to the town's former strength and power. Next to it stands a cluster of 11 timber houses, called **Špalíček.** These houses used to be owned by Jews in the early 14th century, but a fervently anti-Semitic clergy in the area incited such hatred against the Jews that they were forced up Židská ulice (Jews Street) and into an alleyway called ulička Zavražděnych (Murderer's Lane), where they were unceremoniously slaughtered in 1350.

Across from Špalíček is the **Cheb Museum,** where another murder took place almost 300 years later—that of Albrecht von Wallenstein in 1634. On the upper level a display vividly depicts the assassination. The museum's first floor displays many 20th-century paintings from which one can trace the town's slow demise. Admission is 20 Kč (74¢). Open Tues–Sun 9am–noon and 1–5pm.

The old town of Cheb is also packed with several churches. The most interesting church is **St. Nicholas,** just around the corner from the museum. It's a hodgepodge of architecural styles: Its romanesque heritage is reflected in the tower windows, while a gothic portal added later and baroque interior round out the renovations over the years.

TOURING CHEB CASTLE

A better example of romanesque architecture can be found in the northeast part of the old town, where the **Cheb Castle** stands. Overlooking the Elbe River, the castle, built in the late 12th century, is one of central Europe's largest romanesque structures.

The castle's main draws are its **chapel of Sts. Erhard and Ursala** and the **Černá věž** (Black Tower). The two-tiered, early gothic chapel has a dark, somber first floor where the proletariat would congregate, while the emperor and his family went to the much cheerier and brighter second floor with its gothic windows. Unfortunately, there are no tours of the castle, and the English text provided at the entrance does little to inform visitors. Admission is 20 Kč (74¢). Open June–Aug Tues–Sun 9am–noon and 1–6pm; May and Sept Tues–Sun 9am–noon and 1–5pm; April and Oct Tues–Sun 9am–noon and 1–4pm.

Across the courtyard from the chapel stands the **Černá věž** (Black Tower). From its 60-foot-high lookout, you'll see the best views of the town. The tower seems dusty and smeared with pollution, but its color is not from the emissions of the Trabats and Škodas that drive through the streets. Rather the tower is black because the blocks it is made from are actually lava rocks taken from the nearby Komorni Hurka volcano (which is now dormant).

ACCOMMODATIONS

In Cheb

Hotel Hvězda (Hotel Star). náměstí Krále Jiřího z Poděbrad 3, 350-01 Cheb. ☎ **0166/ 225-49.** Fax 0166/225-46. 44 rms. TV TEL. 1,000 Kč ($37) double. AE, MC, V.

Overlooking the rather noisy main square, the Hvězda is a lone star in the Cheb hotel universe. Small but clean rooms make it bearable, and the staff does try to make your stay comfortable. If you can't stay in Františkovy Lázně, and you don't want to drive further, this is really the only hotel I would recommend staying at in town.

In Františkovy Lázně

Hotel Tří Lilie (Three Lillies Hotel). Jiráskova 17, 351-01 Františkovy Lázně. ☎ **0166/ 942-350.** Fax 0166/942-970. 32 rms. TV TEL. 2,970 Kč ($110) double; 4,140 Kč ($153) suite. AE, MC, V.

In 1808, Goethe stayed here and he knew what he was doing. The Three Lillies is worth the extra money since it's the only luxury hotel in the area. Cheb needs a nice hotel like this. You can relax here; at night, you can block out noise in the spotless, spacious, well-appointed rooms. The staff is very attentive and can arrange spa treatments, massages, and other health services. On the main floor there is a nice, if not pricey, bar and restaurant.

Interhotel Slovan. Národní Třída 5, 351-01 Františkovy Lázně. ☎ **0166/942-841.** Fax 0166/ 942-843. 25 rms. TV TEL. 1,400–1,600 Kč ($52–$59) double. AE, MC, V.

This hotel is not as elegant as the Three Lillies just down the main street, but it's a nice place nonetheless. Rooms are a little plain and small, but for the money, they're one of the best bets in town. The only drawback is a staff that at times forgets that the customer is also paying for service.

DINING

In Cheb

Staročeská Restaurace. Kamenná 1, Cheb. No phone. Reservations not necessary. Main courses 65–140 Kč ($2.41–$5.19). No credit cards. Daily 10am–10pm. CZECH/CHINESE.

This restaurant serves much the same fare as all of the other restaurants on or around the square, but what caught my eye were the few Chinese meals offered. The *Kuře Kung-Pao* (Kung pao chicken) was a good spicy alternative to the sausages and meat and dumplings most of the other diners were having.

In Františkovy Lázně

Restaurace Interhotel Slovan. Národní Třída 5, Františkovy Lázně. No phone. Main courses 85–220 Kč ($3.15–$8.15). No credit cards. Daily 8am–10pm. CZECH.

As the prices show, this restaurant tries to appeal to every budget. Be prepared for more heavy central European cuisine, with all four Czech food groups—meat, potatoes, dumplings, and cabbage—well represented. The fish tends to be a lighter meal than the pork cutlet smothered in cheese and ham, but both proved to be excellent choices. Oddly, the service at the restaurant is markedly better than the hotel.

ČESKÝ KRUMLOV

If you only have time on your visit to the Czech Republic for one excursion, seriously consider making it Český Krumlov, which is 96 miles south of Prague. One of Bohemia's prettiest towns, Krumlov is a living gallery of elegant Renaissance-era buildings housing charming cafes, pubs, restaurants, shops, and galleries. In 1992 UNESCO named Český Krumlov a World Heritage Site for its historical importance and physical beauty.

Bustling since medieval times, the town, after centuries of embellishment, is exquisitely beautiful. In 1302 the Rožmberk family inherited the castle and moved in, using it as their main residence for nearly 300 years. You'll feel that time has stopped as you look from the Lazebnický bridge, with the waters of the Vltava below, snaking past the castle's gray stone. At night, with the castle light, the view becomes even more dramatic.

Few deigned to change the appearance of Český Krumlov over the years, not even the Schwarzenbergs, who had a flair for opulence. At the turn of the 19th century, several facades of houses in the town's outer section were built, as were inner court-yards. Thankfully, economic stagnation in the area during communism meant little money for "development," so no glass-and-steel edifice like the Hotel Thermal in Karlovy Vary juts out to spoil the town's architectural beauty. Instead, a medieval sense reigns supreme in Český Krumlov, now augmented by the many festivals and renovations that keep the town's spirit alive.

Consider yourself warned, however, that word has spread about this town. Summer season can be unbearable as thousands of tourists blanket its medieval streets. If possible, try to visit in the off-season when the crowds recede, prices decrease, and the town's charm can really shine. Who knows, you may even hear some Czech!

ESSENTIALS

ARRIVING **By Train** The only way to reach Český Krumlov by train from Prague is via České Budějovice, a slow ride that will deposit you at a station relatively far from the town center. It takes $3^{1}/_{2}$ hours; the one-way fare is 136 Kč ($5.03) first class, 96 Kč ($3.56) second class.

By Bus The nearly 3-hour bus ride from Prague usually involves a transfer in České Budějovice. The bus station in Český Krumlov is a 15-minute walk from the town's main square.

By Car From Prague, it's a 2-hour drive along the E-55 highway.

CITY LAYOUT Surrounded by a circular sweep of the Vltava River, Český Krumlov is very easy to negotiate. The main square, náměstí Svornosti, is located at the very center of the Inner town. The bridge that spans the Vltava a few blocks away leads to a rocky hill and Latrán, above which is a castle known as the Český Krumlov Château.

VISITOR INFORMATION   Located right on the main square, the **Information Centrum,** náměstí Svornosti 1, 381-00 Český Krumlov (☎ and fax **0337/5670**) provides a complete array of tourist services from booking accommodations to ticket reservations for events, as well as a phone and fax service. Open daily 9am–6pm.

Be warned that the municipal hall is located in the same building—it's crowded with weddings on weekends. If someone holds out a hat, throw some change into it, take a traditional shot of liquor from them, and *blahopřát* (congratulate) just about everyone in the room.

SPECIAL EVENTS   After being banned during communism (a little too feudalistic for Gottwald), the **Slavnost pětilisté růže** (Festival of the Five-Petaled Rose) has made a triumphant comeback. It's held each year at the summer solstice. Residents of Český Krumlov dress up in Renaissance costume and parade through the streets. Afterward, the streets become a stage with plays, chess games with people dressed as pieces, music, and even duels "to the death."

Český Krumlov also plays host to a 2-week **International Music Festival** every August, attracting performers from all over the world. Performances are held in nine spectacular venues. For information or ticket reservations, contact the festival organizer, **Auviex,** Obrovskéo 10, 141-00, Prague 4 (☎ **02/767-275** or 769-443; fax 02/ 2-768-881; in Český Krumlov 0337/4275-3350).

Exploring Český Krumlov

Bring a good pair of walking shoes, and be prepared to wear them out. Český Krumlov not only lends itself to hours of strolling, but its hills and alleyways demand it. No cars, thank goodness, are allowed in the historic town, and the cobblestones keep most other vehicles at bay. The town is split into two parts—the **Inner town** and **Latrán,** which houses the castle. Each is better tackled separately, rather than crisscrossing the bridges several times.

Begin your tour at the **Okresní Muzeum** (Regional Museum) at the top of Horní ulice. Once a Jesuit seminary, the three-story museum now contains artifacts and displays relating to Český Krumlov's 1,000-year history. The highlight of this mass of folk art, clothing, furniture, and statues is a giant model of the town that offers a bird's-eye view of the buildings. Admission is 20 Kč (74¢). Open Tues–Sun 10am–12:30pm and 1–6pm.

Across the street from the museum is the **Hotel Růže** (Rose), which was once a Jesuit student house. Built in the late 16th century, the hotel and the prelature next to it show the development of architecture: gothic, Renaissance, and rococo influences are all present. If you're not staying at the hotel, don't be afraid to walk around and even ask questions at the reception desk.

Continue down the street to the impressive late gothic **St. Vitus Cathedral.** Be sure to climb the church tower, which offers one of the most spectacular views of both the Inner town and the castle across the river.

Farther down the street you will come to **náměstí Svornosti.** Few buildings show any character, making the main square of such an impressive town a little disappointing. The **Radnice** (Town Hall) located at náměstí Svornosti 1 is one of the few exceptions. Its gothic arcades and renaissance vault inside are exceptionally beautiful in this otherwise rundown area. From the square, streets fan out in all directions. Take some time just to wander through the streets. You might want to grab a light snack before crossing the bridge and heading for the castle.

One of Český Krumlov's most famous residents was the Austrian-born artist Egon Schiele. A bit of an eccentric who on more than one occasion raised the ire of the town's residents (many were distraught with his use of their young women as his nude models), Schiele's stay was cut short as residents' patience ran out. But the town readopted the artist in 1993, setting up the **Egon Schiele Foundation and the Egon Schiele Centrum** in Inner town Široká 70-72, 381-01, Český Krumlov (☎ **0337/4232;** fax 0337/2820). The center documents his life and work, housing a permanent selection of his paintings as well as other exhibitions. Admission depends on the exhibition. Open daily 10am–6pm.

For a different perspective on what the town looks like, take the stairs from the **Městské divadlo** (Town Theater) on Horní ulice down to the riverfront and rent a boat from **Maláček boat rentals.** Always willing to lend his advice, the affable Pepa Maláček will tell you what to watch out for, and where the best fishing is (even if you don't want him to!).

Český Krumlov Château

From here you will begin the long climb up to the castle, perched high atop a rocky hill. Reputedly the second largest castle in Bohemia (after Prague Castle), **Český Krumlov Château** was constructed in the 13th century as part of a private estate. Throughout the ages, the castle has passed on to a variety of private owners.

Greeting visitors is a round 12th-century **tower,** with its Renaissance balcony. You'll pass over the moat, now occupied by two brown bears. Next is the **Dolní Hrad** (Lower Castle) and then the **Horní Hrad** (Upper Castle).

The château is open to tourists from April to October only, exclusively by guided tour. Visits begin in the palace's rococo **Chapel of St. George,** continue through portrait-packed **Renaissance Hall,** and end with the **Royal Family Apartments,** outfitted with ornate furnishings that include Flemish wall tapestries and European paintings. Tours last 1 hour and depart frequently; tours cost 90 Kč ($3.33) for adults, 45 Kč ($1.67) for students. Most are in Czech or German—if you want an English-language tour, arrange it ahead of time (☎ **0337/2075**).

The castle is open May–Aug Tues–Sun 7:45am–noon and 12:45–4pm; Sept Tues–Sun 8:45am–noon and 12:45–4pm; Apr and Oct Tues–Sun 8:45am–noon and 12:45–3pm. The last entrance is 1 hour before closing.

Once past the main castle building, one of the more stunning views of Český Krumlov can be seen from **Most Na Plášti,** a walkway that doubles as a belvedere to the Inner town.

Most visitors don't realize that beyond this part of the castle they can have one of the Czech Republic's finest dining experiences at **Krčma Markéta,** Latrán 67 (☎ **0337/3829**).

To get there, walk all the way up the hill through the castle, past the Horní Hrad (Upper Castle) and past the Zámecké Divadlo (Castle Theater). Walk through the raised walkway and into the Zámecká Zahrada (Castle Garden) where you will eventually find this Renaissance pub. When you go inside, you'll feel like you've left this century. There's no need for plates here, as meals are served on wooden blocks. Drinks come in pewter mugs.

The restaurant recently underwent a change of ownership, but the atmosphere and good times are still the same. There's no menu—just go up to the spit and see what's roasting; usually there's a wide variety of meats, including succulent pork cutlets, rabbit, chickens, and pork knees, a Czech delicacy. The waiter/cook will bring bread and a slab of spiced pork fat (considered a good base for drinking), but do not worry—refusing to eat it won't raise his ire. Instead, wait until the plate comes—but don't wait for the vegetables—only a smattering of cabbage for decoration is on offer. Vegetarians need not apply. Krčma Markéta is open daily 6–11pm. Reservations are recommended. Main courses are 60–130 Kč ($2.22–$4.81); no credit cards are accepted.

ACCOMMODATIONS

Hotels are sprouting up, or are getting a "new" old look; PENSION and ZIMMER FREI signs line Horní and Rooseveltova streets, and offer some of the best values in town. For a comprehensive list of area hotels and help with bookings, call or write to the Infocentrum listed above in "Visitor Information."

Moderate

Hotel Růže (Rose Hotel). Horní 153, 381-01 Český Krumlov. ☎ **0337/2245** or 5481. Fax 3381. 50 rms. MINIBAR TV TEL. May–Sept 1,980–2,070 Kč ($73–$77) double; 3,420–4,140 Kč ($127–$153) suite. Oct–April 1,570–1,660 Kč ($58–$61) double; 2,750–3,320 Kč ($102–$123) suite. AE, MC, V.

Once a Jesuit seminary, this stunning Italian Renaissance structure has been turned into a well-appointed hotel. Comfortable in a big-city kind of way, the hotel is packed with amenities, and is one of the top places to stay in Český Krumlov. But for all of the splendor the building holds, you may find the Růže a bit of a disappointment. Rooms are not period furnished, but look as though they were furnished from the floor of a Sears warehouse in the U.S. Midwest. While rooms are clean and spacious, the promise of a Renaissance stay dissipates quickly. For families or large groups, the larger suites, which have eight beds, provide good value.

Inexpensive

Hotel Krumlov. Náměstí Svorností 14, 381-01 Český Krumlov. ☎ **0337/2040.** 33 rms (5 with full bath and WC, 4 with shower and WC). TV TEL. 770 Kč ($29) double without shower, 1,100–1,250 Kč ($41–$46) double with bath and toilet; 2,400 Kč ($89) suite with bath and WC. AE, DC, V.

Located on the town's main square, a few minutes' walk from Český Krumlov Château, Hotel Krumlov is an aging belle dating from 1309. Like so many others in the republic, there's nothing fancy here, just satisfactory rooms right in the heart of the city. The hotel's restaurant serves typical Bohemian fare daily 7am–11pm.

Hotel U Zlatého Anděla. Náměstí Svorností 10, 381-01 Český Krumlov. ☎ **0337/2473.** 4 rms. 1,000 Kč ($37). Rates include breakfast. No credit cards.

The publisher of Frommer's stayed here and preferred it to the Hotel Růže. He thought this hotel had a more comfortable and friendly atmosphere. The attractive rooms are also much less expensive, but those over the bar are noisy.

✪ Pension Anna. Rooseveltova 41, 381-01 Český Krumlov. ☎ **0337/4418.** 8 rms. 1,000 Kč ($37) double; 1,200 Kč ($44) suite (with four beds). Rates include breakfast. No credit cards.

Along "pension alley," Anna is a very comfortable and rustic place to stay. What makes this pension a favorite among the others is the friendly management and homey feeling you get as you walk up to your room. Forget hotels—this is the kind of place where you can relax. The owners even let you buy drinks and snacks at the bar downstairs and take them to your room. The suites with four beds and a living room are great for families and group travelers.

Pension Na louži. Kájovská 66, 381-01 Český Krumlov. ☎ and fax **0337/5495.** 5 rms. 900 Kč ($33) single/double; 1,200 Kč triple ($44); 1,400 Kč ($52) suite. No credit cards.

Smack-dab in the heart of the Inner town, the small Na louži, decorated with early 20th-century wooden furniture, is oozing with charm. The only drawback is beds with foot boards that can be a little short for those over 6 feet tall.

⚫ **Pension Ve Věži (In the Tower).** Latrán 28, 381-01 Český Krumlov. ☎ **0337/5287** or 4972. 4 rms (none with bath, common shower and toilet for 2 rooms). May–Sept, 990 Kč ($37) double; 1,540 Kč ($57) quad. Oct–Apr, 770 Kč ($29) double, 1,320 Kč ($49) quad. Rates include breakfast. No credit cards.

A private pension located in a renovated medieval tower just a 5-minute walk from the castle, Ve Věži is one of the most magnificent places to stay in town. It's not the accommodations themselves that are so grand; none have a private bath and all are sparsely decorated. Instead, what's wonderful is the ancient ambience that fills this place. Advance reservations are always recommended.

DINING

Kavárna. At the Hotel Konvice, Horní ul. 144. ☎ **0337/4180.** Reservations not necessary. Main courses 84–200 Kč ($3.11–$7.40). AE, MC, V. Daily 8am–10pm. CZECH.

If weather permits, eat outside overlooking the river at the Kavárna at the Hotel Konvice. Try the boned chicken breast smothered in cheese or any of the steaks and salads.

Rybařská Bašta Jakuba Krčína. Kájovská 54. ☎ **0337/67183.** Reservations recommended. Main courses 120–300 Kč ($4.44–$11.11). AE, MC, V. Daily 7am–11pm. CZECH.

One of the town's most celebrated restaurants, this place specializes in freshwater fish from surrounding lakes. Trout, perch, pike, and eel are sautéed, grilled, baked, and fried in a variety of herbs and spices. Venison, rabbit, and other game are also available, along with the requisite roast beef and pork cutlet dinners.

U Města Vídně. Latrán 78. No phone. Reservations not necessary. Main courses 50–95 Kč ($1.85–$3.52). No credit cards. Daily 10am–10pm. CZECH.

This locals' kind of pub is not only a good restaurant but one of the best hangouts in town. Traditional meat-and-dumplings–style food is augmented by a few egg-based vegetarian dishes. Natives swear by the pub's locally brewed Českokrumlovské beer.

Denmark 4

by Darwin Porter & Danforth Prince

The name for Copenhagen, Denmark's capital, came from the word *københavn,* meaning "merchants' harbor." This city grew in size and importance because of its position on the Øresund (the Sound) between Denmark and Sweden, guarding the entrance to the Baltic. From its humble beginnings, Copenhagen has become the largest city in Scandinavia, home to 1.5 million people. It's the seat of the oldest kingdom in the world.

Copenhagen

Copenhagen is a city with much charm, as reflected in its canals, narrow streets, and old houses. Its most famous resident was Hans Christian Andersen, whose memory still lives on. Another of Copenhagen's world-renowned inhabitants was Søren Kierkegaard, who used to take long morning strolls in the city, planning his next essay; his completed essays eventually earned him the title "father of existentialism."

But few modern Copenhageners are reading Kierkegaard today; they're also not as melancholy as Hamlet either. Most of them are out having too much fun. Copenhagen epitomizes a Nordic *joie de vivre,* and the city is filled with a lively atmosphere, good times (none better than at the Tivoli Gardens), sex shows, countless outdoor cafes, and all-night dance clubs. Of course, if you come in winter, the fierce realities of living above the 55th parallel set in. That's when Copenhageners retreat inside their smoky jazz clubs and beer taverns. The fun goes on: It's just not outdoors.

Modern Copenhagen still retains some of the characteristics of a village. If you forget the suburbs, you can cover most of the central belt on foot, which makes it a great tourist spot. It's almost as if the city were designed for pedestrians, as reflected by its Strøget (strolling street), Europe's longest and oldest walking street.

ONLY IN COPENHAGEN

Reliving the Past at Dragør   At the doorstep of Copenhagen, this seafaring town once flourished as a bustling herring port on the Baltic. Life, however, passed it by, and for that we can be grateful, because it looks much as it used to, with half-timbered ocher-and-pink 18th-century cottages—all with thatch or red-tile roofs. The entire village is under the protection of the National Trust of Denmark. In a 35-minute ride from the Danish capital, you can be delivered back in a time capsule.

Biking in Copenhagen & Zealand   Vying with Amsterdam, Copenhagen is the virtual biking capital of Europe. It's a flat city and ideal for touring by bike. You can pedal along canals, past palaces, and even beyond the capital to the highlights of the island of Zealand itself, on which Copenhagen lies. Cyclists are given high priority in traffic. Pick up a copy of *Bike Denmark,* available at Aboulevard 1, DK-1637 Copenhagen (☎ 35-36-41-00), and set out—of course, singing "Wonderful, Wonderful Copenhagen" as you do.

Spending a Day & a Night at the Tivoli   These pleasure gardens are worth the air ticket to Copenhagen. They're not Disneyland, but these 150-year-old gardens are unique. They're a little bit of everything: open-air dancing, restaurants, theaters, concert halls, an amusement park . . . and, oh yes, gardens as well. From the first bloom of spring until the autumn leaves start to fall, they're devoted to harmless fun, often of the type enjoyed back in the belle époque. The gardens are worth a visit any time, but best at twilight when the lights begin to glint among the trees.

Shopping for Danish Design   The simple but elegant line that became fashionable in the 1950s has made a comeback—nowhere more so than in Denmark. Danish modern in chairs, glassware, and even buildings has returned. "Old Masters" such as Arne Jacobsen, Hans Wegner, and Poul Kjærhom are celebrated, their designs from the 1940s and 1950s sold today in antique stores. Wegner is now viewed as the grand old man of Danish design, noted for his sculptural teak chairs. Younger designers have followed, creating everything from chairs, desks, and furnishings to table settings and silverware. For the best display of Danish design, walk along the pedestrian-only Strøget, Copenhagen's major shopping street. The best single showcase is Illums Bolighus at Amagertorv 10.

Visiting the Palaces   At Copenhagen's Christianborg Palace, the queen officially receives guests in the Royal Reception Chamber, where you must don slippers to protect the floors. The complex also contains the Parliament House and the Supreme Court. From 1441 until the fire of 1795, this was the official residence of Denmark. You can tour the richly decorated rooms, including the Throne Room and banqueting hall. Below you can see the well-preserved ruins of the 1167 castles of Bishop Absalon, founder of Copenhagen. The other monument of note is Rosenborg Castle, founded by Christian IV in the 17th century. This red-brick Renaissance castle remained a royal residence until the early 19th century, when it was converted into a museum. It still houses the crown jewels, and its collection of costumes and royal memorabilia is unequaled in Denmark.

Viewing the Beer People's Art   Cultural capital of Europe in 1996, Copenhagen has a rich treasure trove of art. The Glyptotek, behind the Tivoli Gardens, was founded by Mr. Carlsberg Beer himself, Carl Jacobsen, in the 19th century. It contains everything from the Egyptians to Rodin and van Gogh, Manet to Monet to Renoir—especially Gauguin.

ORIENTATION

ARRIVING   By Plane   When you arrive—perhaps on an SAS plane from New York—at **Kastrup Airport** (☎ 31-54-17-01) outside Copenhagen, you can reduce costs by taking an SAS coach to the city terminal; the fare is 35Kr ($5.95). A taxi to the city center costs around 130Kr ($22.10). Even cheaper is a local bus, no. 2505, leaving from the international arrivals terminal every 15–20 minutes for the Town Hall Square in central Copenhagen and costing 15Kr ($2.55).

By Train   Trains from the continent arrive at the **Hoved Banegård (Central Railroad Station),** in the very center of Copenhagen, near the Tivoli and the Rådhuspladsen. For rail information, call **33-14-17-01.** The station operates a luggage-checking service but room bookings are available only at the tourist office (see "Visitor Information" below). You can also exchange money at Den Danske Bank (☎ **33-12-04-11**), open Sept–August 8 daily 7am–9pm.

From the Central Railroad Station, you can connect with **S-tog,** the local subway, with trains departing from platforms in the terminus itself. Ask at the information desk near Tracks 5 and 6 about which train you should board to reach your destination.

By Bus   Buses from Zealand or elsewhere in Denmark also pull into the Central Railroad Station (see above). For bus information, call **36-45-45-45.**

By Car   If you're driving from Germany, a car-ferry will take you from Travemünde to Gedser in southern Denmark. From Gedser, get on E-55 north, an express highway that will deliver you to the southern outskirts of Copenhagen. If you're coming from Sweden and crossing at Helsingborg, you'll land on the Danish side at Helsingør. From here, take express highway E-55 south to the northern outskirts of Copenhagen.

By Ferry   Most ferryboats land at Havnegade at the end of the south side of Nyhavn, a short walk to the center of Copenhagen. Taxis also wait here for ferry arrivals. Most arrivals are from Malmö, Sweden; ferries from continental Europe usually land in South Zealand.

VISITOR INFORMATION   The **Copenhagen Tourist Information Center,** Bernstorffsgade 1 (☎ **33-11-13-25**), is across from Tivoli's main entrance. It's open Sept 16–Apr Mon–Fri 9am–5pm, Sat 9am–2pm; May–June and Sept 1–15 daily 9am–9pm; July–Aug Mon–Sat 8am–11pm and Sun 9am–11pm.

CITY LAYOUT   The heart of Old Copenhagen is a maze of pedestrian streets, formed by Nørreport Station to the north, Town Hall Square (Rådhuspladsen) to the west, and Kongens Nytorv to the east. One continuous pedestrian route, **Strøget,** the world's longest pedestrian street, goes east from Town Hall Square to Kongens Nytorv and is made up of five streets: Frederiksberggade, Nygade, Vimmelskaftet, Amagertorv, and Østergade. Strøget is lined with shops, bars, restaurants, and sidewalk cafes (in summer). **Pistolstraede** is a maze of galleries, restaurants, and boutiques, all housed in restored 18th-century buildings.

Fiolstraede (Violet Street), a dignified street with antique shops and bookshops, cuts through the university (Latin Quarter). If you turn into Rosengaarden at the top of Fiolstraede, you'll come to **Kultorvet** (Coal Square) just before you reach Nørreport Station. Here you join the third main pedestrian street, **Købmagergade** (Butcher Street), which winds around and finally meets Strøget on Amagertorv.

At the end of Strøget you approach **Kongens Nytorv** (King's Square), the site of the Royal Theater and Magasin, the latter the largest department store in Copenhagen. This will put you at the beginning of **Nyhavn,** the former seamen's quarter that has been gentrified into an upmarket area of expensive restaurants, apartments, cafes, and boutiques. The government of Denmark is centered on the small island of **Slotsholmen,** connected to the center by eight bridges. Several museums, notably Christiansborg Castle, are found here.

The center of Copenhagen is **Rådhuspladsen** (Town Hall Square). From here it's a short walk to the Tivoli Gardens, the major attraction, and the Central Railroad Station, the main railroad and subway terminus. The wide boulevard, **Vesterbrogade,** passes by Tivoli until it reaches the Central Railroad Station. Another major street

Copenhagen Attractions & Accommodations

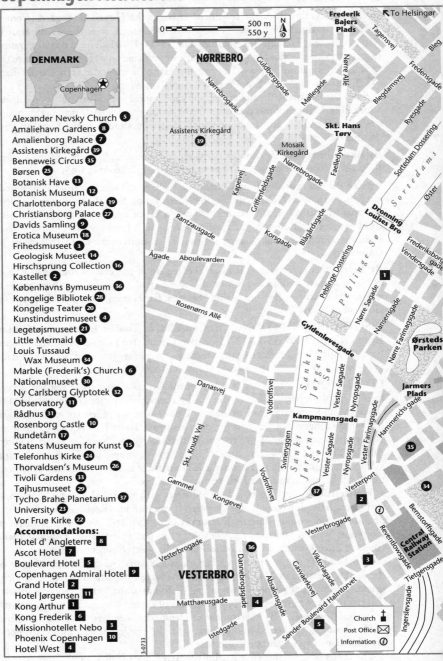

DENMARK

Copenhagen

Alexander Nevsky Church **5**
Amaliehavn Gardens **8**
Amalienborg Palace **7**
Assistens Kirkegård **39**
Benneweis Circus **35**
Børsen **25**
Botanisk Have **13**
Botanisk Museum **12**
Charlottenborg Palace **19**
Christiansborg Palace **27**
Davids Samling **9**
Erotica Museum **18**
Frihedsmuseet **3**
Geologisk Museet **14**
Hirschsprung Collection **16**
Kastellet **2**
Københavns Bymuseum **36**
Kongelige Bibliotek **28**
Kongelige Teater **20**
Kunstindustrimuseet **4**
Legetøjsmuseet **21**
Little Mermaid **1**
Louis Tussaud
   Wax Museum **34**
Marble (Frederik's) Church **6**
Nationalmuseet **30**
Ny Carlsberg Glyptotek **32**
Observatory **11**
Rådhus **31**
Rosenborg Castle **10**
Rundetårn **17**
Statens Museum for Kunst **15**
Telefonhus Kirke **24**
Thorvaldsen's Museum **26**
Tivoli Gardens **33**
Tøjhusmuseet **29**
Tycho Brahe Planetarium **37**
University **23**
Vor Frue Kirke **22**
Accommodations:
Hotel d' Angleterre **8**
Ascot Hotel **7**
Boulevard Hotel **5**
Copenhagen Admiral Hotel **9**
Grand Hotel **2**
Hotel Jørgensen **11**
Kong Arthur **1**
Kong Frederik **6**
Missionhotellet Nebo **3**
Phoenix Copenhagen **10**
Hotel West **4**

NØRREBRO

Frederik Bajers Plads

↖To Helsingør

Assistens Kirkegård **39**

Skt. Hans Tørv

Mosaik Kirkegård

Nørrebrogade

Dronning Louises Bro

Peblinge Sø

Sortedams

Øster

Frederiksborggade

Vendersgade

Ørsteds Parken

Jarmers Plads

Kampmannsgade

Sankt Jørgens Sø

Gyldenløvesgade

Central Railway Station

VESTERBRO

Church ✝
Post Office ✉
Information ⓘ

3-0733

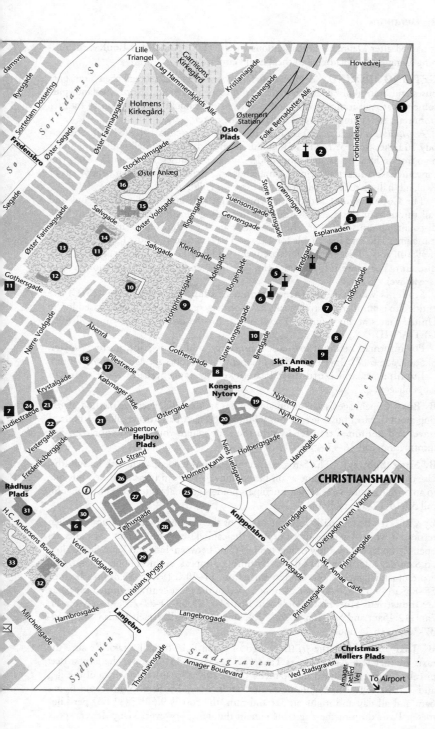

Lille
Triangel

Garnisons
Kirkegård

Hovedvej

Ryesgade

damsvej

Dag Hammerskjölds Allé

Kristianiagade

Østbanegade

Folke Bernadottes Allé

Forbindelsesvej

①

Sorterdam Dossering

Holmens
Kirkegård

Østerport
Station

Østergade

Oslo
Plads

② †■

Fredensbro

Øster Søgade

Stockholmsgade

Søgade

Øster Anlæg

Øster Farimagsgade

Grønningen

†

③

Esplanaden

④

Suensonsgade

Store Kongensgade

Øster Farimagsgade

⑯

Sølvgade

⑮

Gernersgade

Bredgade

†■

⑭

Øster Voldgade

Rigensgade

Klerkegade

Borgergade

⑤ † ■

⑬

⑪

Sølvgade

Adelgade

⑥ † ■

Toldbodgade

⑫

Gothersgade

Kronprinsessegade

⑩

⑨

Store Kongensgade

⑦

⑪

Gothersgade

⑧

Abenrå

⑩

Bredgade

⑨

Nørre Voldgade

⑱

Pilestræde

⑰

Bredgade

⑧

Skt. Annae
Plads

Krystalgade

⑦ ⑳ ⑳

Studiestræde

Købmager gade

Østergade

Kongens
Nytorv

⑲ Nyhavn

⑫ ⑳

Amagertorv

Nyhavn

Vestergade

Frederiksberggade

Højbro
Plads

Holbergsgade

Havnegade

Inderhavnen

Gl. Strand

Niels Juelsgade

CHRISTIANSHAVN

Rådhus
Plads

ⓘ

⑳

Holmens Kanal

②⑤

H.C. Andersens Boulevard

③①

③⓪

⑥

Tøjhusgade

②⑧

Knippelsbro

Strandgade

Overgaden oven Vandet

Vester Voldgade

③③

②⑨

Christians Brygge

Torvegade

Skt. Annae Gade

Prinsessegade

Skt. Prinsessegade

③②

Mitchellgade

Hambrosgade

Langebrogade

Langebro

Sydhavnen

Stadsgraven

Christmas
Møllers Plads

Thorshavnsgade

Amager Boulevard

Ved Stadsgraven

Amager
Fælled
Vej

To Airport

is named after Denmark's most famous writer, **H. C. Andersens Boulevard,** running along Rådhuspladsen and the Tivoli Gardens.

GETTING AROUND   A joint zone fare system includes Copenhagen Transport buses and State Railway and S-tog trains in Copenhagen and North Zealand, plus some private rail routes in a 25-mile radius of the capital, enabling you to transfer from train to bus and vice versa with the same ticket.

A *grundbillet* (basic ticket) for both buses and trains costs 10Kr ($1.70). You can buy 10 tickets for 75Kr ($12.75). Children under 12 ride for half fare; those under 5 go free on local trains, and those under 7 go free on buses. For 65Kr ($11.05) you can purchase a ticket allowing 24-hour bus and train travel through nearly half of Zealand; half price for children 7 to 11; free for children under 7.

The **Copenhagen Card** entitles you to free and unlimited travel by bus and rail throughout the metropolitan area (including North Zealand), 25% to 50% discounts on crossings to and from Sweden, and free admission to many sights and museums. The card is available for 1, 2, or 3 days and costs 140Kr ($23.80), 230Kr ($39.10), and 295Kr ($50.15), respectively. Children 11 and under are given a 50% discount. For more info, contact the Copenhagen Tourist Information Center (see above).

Students who have an **International Student Identity Card (ISIC)** are entitled to a number of travel breaks in Copenhagen. A card can be purchased in the United States at any Council Travel office; for the office nearest you, call **800/ GET-AN-ID.**

For information about low-cost train, ferry, and plane trips, go to **Waastel,** Skoubogade 6 (☎ **33-14-46-33**), in Copenhagen. Hours are Mon–Fri 9am–6pm.

Eurailpasses and Nordturist Pass tickets are accepted on local trains in Copenhagen.

By Bus   Copenhagen's well-maintained buses are the least expensive method of getting around. Most buses leave from Rådhuspladsen. A basic ticket allows 1 hour of travel and unlimited transfers within the zone where you started your trip. For information, call **36-45-45-45.**

By S-tog (Subway)   The S-tog connects heartland Copenhagen with its suburbs. Use of the tickets is the same as on buses (above). You can transfer from a bus line to an S-train on the same ticket. Eurailpass holders generally ride free. For more info, call **33-14-17-01** at any time.

By Car   It's best to park your car in any of the dozens of city parking lots, then retrieve it when you're ready to explore the capital's environs. Many car parks are open 24 hours a day; a few others tend to close between 1am and 7am. Some close on Saturday afternoon and on Sunday during nonpeak business hours when traffic is presumably lighter. Costs tend to range from 11–20Kr ($1.85–$3.40) per hour or 55–85Kr ($9.35–$14.45) per 24 hours. Two of the most centrally located car parks are **Industriens Hus,** H. C. Andersens Blvd. 18 (☎ **33-91-21-75**), open Mon–Fri 7am–12:45am and Sat–Sun 10am–12:45am; and **Statoil,** Israels Plads (☎ **33-14-37-76**), open 24 hours.

By Taxi   Watch for the *fri* (free) sign or green light to hail a taxi. Be sure the taxis are metered. **Københavns Taxa** (☎ **31-35-35-35**) operates the largest fleet of cabs. Tips are included in the meter price: 20Kr ($3.40) at the drop of the flag and 7.70Kr ($1.30) per kilometer thereafter, Mon–Fri 6am–6pm. From 6pm–6am and all day and night on Sat and Sun, the cost is 9.60Kr ($1.65) per kilometer. Basic drop-of-the-flag costs remain the same, however. Many drivers speak English.

By Bicycle   To reduce pollution from cars, Copenhageners ride bicycles. For 40Kr ($6.80) per day, you can rent a bike at **Københavns Cyklebors,** Gothersgade 157 (☎ **33-14-07-17**).

FAST FACTS: Copenhagen

American Express   The office in Copenhagen, at Amagertorv 18 (☎ 33-12-23-01), is open Mon–Fri 9am–5pm and Sat 9am–noon (until 2pm on Sat in May–Aug).

Business Hours   Most **banks** are open Mon–Fri 9:30am–4pm (Thurs until 6pm). **Stores** are generally open Mon–Thurs 9am–5:30pm, Fri 9am–7 or 8pm, and Sat 9am–2pm; most are closed Sun.

Currency   The Danish currency is the **krone** (crown), or **Kr** in its plural form, made up of 100 **øre**. Banknotes are issued in 20, 50, 100, 500, and 1,000Kr. Coins come in 25 and 50 øre, and 1, 2, 5, 10, and 20Kr; the 1-, 2-, and 5-krone coins have a hole in the center. The rate of exchange used in this chapter was $1 = 5.88Kr, or 1Kr = 17¢.

Currency Exchange   Banks are generally your best bet to exchange currency. When banks are closed, you can exchange money at Forex (☎ 33-11-29-05) in the Central Railroad Station, daily 8am–9pm, or The Change Group (☎ 33-93-04-55), Østergade 61, Mon–Sat 9am–10pm and Sun 10am–8pm.

Dentists/Doctors   For emergency dental treatment, go to Tandlaegevagten, Oslo Plads 14 (☎ 31-38-02-51), near Østerport Station and the U.S. Embassy. Open Mon–Fri 8am–9:30pm and Sat, Sun, and holidays 10am–noon. Be prepared to pay in cash. To reach a doctor, dial 33-93-63-00, 9am–4pm, or 38-88-60-41 after hours. The doctor's fee is payable in cash. Virtually every doctor speaks English.

Embassies   The embassy of the **United States** is at Dag Hammarsjölds Allé 24, DK-2100 København (☎ 31-42-31-44); the embassy of the **United Kingdom,** at Kastelsvej 36–40, DK-2100 København (☎ 35-26-46-00); of **Canada,** on Kristen Berniskowsgadei, DK-1105 København K (☎ 33-12-22-99); and of **Australia,** at Kristianiagade 21, DK-2100 København (☎ 35-26-22-44).

Emergencies   Dial **112** for the fire department, the police, an ambulance, or to report a sea or air accident. Emergency calls from public phone kiosks are free (no coins needed).

Post Office   For information about the Copenhagen post office, call 33-33-89-00. The main post office, where you can pick up your general delivery (*poste restante*) letters, is Tietgensgade 35–39, DK-1704 København (☎ 33-33-89-00), open Mon–Fri 10am–6pm, Sat 9am–1pm. The post office at the Central Railroad Station is open Mon–Fri 8am–10pm, Sat 9am–4pm, and Sun 10am–5pm.

Telephone   Danish phones are fully automatic. Dial just the eight-digit number, for there are no city area codes. At public phone booths, use two 50-øre coins or a 1-krone or 5-krone coin only. Don't insert coins until your party answers. You can make more than one call on the same payment if your time hasn't run out. Remember that it can be expensive to phone from your hotel room. Emergency calls are free. The country code for Denmark is 45. This two-digit number will precede any call that's intended for Denmark dialed from another country. To make phone calls or send faxes or telexes, go to the Telecommunications Center at the Central Railroad Station (☎ 33-14-20-00), open Mon–Fri 8am–10pm and Sat–Sun 9am–9pm.

ACCOMMODATIONS
NEAR KONGENS NYTROV & NYHAVN
Very Expensive
- **Hotel d'Angleterre.** Kongens Nytorv 34, DK-1050 København. ☎ **800/44-UTELL** in the U.S., or 33-12-00-95. Fax 33-12-11-18. 118 rms, 12 suites. AC MINIBAR TV TEL. 2,050–2,900Kr ($348.50–$493) double; from 3,440Kr ($584.80) suite. AE, DC, MC, V. Parking 150Kr ($25.50). Bus: 1, 6, or 9.

At the top of Nyhavn, this hotel is the premier choice for Denmark, though it's a bit staid and stodgy. Still, there's no better address in Copenhagen. The seven-story hotel was built in 1755 and extensively renovated in the 1980s. It's a medley of styles, and rooms are beautifully furnished with art objects and occasional antiques. Light color schemes, subdued lighting, and modern amenities continue to make this a desirable address. Facilities include a health club, pool, sauna, Turkish bath, and solarium.

- **Phoenix Copenhagen.** Bredgade 37, DK-1260 København. ☎ **33-95-95-00.** Fax 33-33-98-33. 209 rms, 3 suites. MINIBAR TV TEL. Mon–Thurs, 990–2,250Kr ($168.30–$382.50) double; 1,850–6,000Kr ($314.50–$1,020) suite. Fri–Sun, 990–1,850Kr ($168.30–$314.50) double; 1,850–4,500Kr ($314.50–$765) suite. AE, DC, MC, V. Parking 90Kr ($15.30). Bus: 1, 5, 9, or 10.

More than any other hotel in Copenhagen, this top-of-the-line newcomer poses a serious challenge to the discreet grandeur of the nearby d'Angleterre. Opened in 1991, the Phoenix rose from the ruined neoclassicism of a royal house built in the 1700s to house aristocratic courtiers of Amalienborg Palace. Beginning in 1988, tons of white and colored marble were imported to create the Louis XVI decor that has so impressed newcomers ever since. The rooms are tastefully elegant and discreet interpretations of Louis XVI. On the premises is a Danish/French restaurant, the Von Plessen, as well as an English-inspired pub, Murdoch's.

Moderate
Copenhagen Admiral Hotel. Toldbodgade 24–28, DK-1253 København. ☎ **31-11-82-82.** Fax 33-32-36-07. 313 rms, 52 suites. TV TEL. 890–1,120Kr ($151.30–$190.40) double; from 1,670Kr ($283.90) suite. AE, MC, V. Free parking. Bus: 1, 9, 10, 28, or 41.

Two blocks from Nyhavn Canal, this hotel was built as a granary in 1787 but was turned into a hotel in 1988. Even though the rooms are showing wear, readers' reaction is more favorable here than it is at the highly touted 71 Nyhavn nearby. You navigate between the thick timbers and stone arches of the infrastructure, where modern partitions have created a series of well-furnished first-class rooms, which lack a certain coziness and charm but are well maintained. Some rooms have harbor views. A popular lunch buffet is served in the restaurant; at dinner, formal service and an international cuisine greet you.

NEAR RÅDHUSPLADSEN & TIVOLI
Expensive
- **Kong Frederik.** Vester Voldgade 25, DK-1552 København. ☎ **800/44-UTELL** in the U.S., or 33-12-59-02. Fax 33-93-59-01. 107 rms, 3 suites. MINIBAR TV TEL. 1,240–1,650Kr ($210.80–$280.50) double; from 1,600Kr ($272) suite. AE, DC, MC, V. Parking 85Kr ($14.45). Bus: 1, 6, or 28.

The smallest of Copenhagen's ultra-chic hotels, Kong Frederik still has the feeling of an unpretentious but elegant private club because of its discreet service, dark paneling, and labyrinth of antique-filled lounges. Many discriminating guests prefer it as a cozier choice than the Angleterre. Renovated in 1996, the rooms have conservatively traditional furniture in a wide array of styles and contain hair dryers, separate shower cabinets, and radios. The Restaurant Queen's Garden is recognized for its fine cuisine and excellent service.

Moderate

Ascot Hotel. Studiestraede 61, DK-1554 København. ☎ **33-12-60-00.** Fax 33-14-60-40. 123 rms, 20 suites. TV TEL. 1,090–1,390Kr ($185.30–$236.30) double; from 1,390Kr ($236.30) suite. Rates include buffet breakfast. Winter discounts available. AE, DC, MC, V. Free parking. Bus: 14 or 16.

On a side street, about a 2-minute walk from Town Hall Square, the Ascot was built in 1902 on 492 wooden pilings rescued from a section of a medieval fortification that had previously stood on the site. In 1994 the hotel annexed the premises of an adjacent building that had been a 19th-century bathhouse. The rooms were renovated and modernized, and the resulting structure is one of Copenhagen's best small hotels. The atmosphere is inviting.

Grand Hotel. Vesterbrogade 9A, DK-1620 København. ☎ **31-31-36-00.** Fax 31-31-33-50. 149 rms, 2 suites. MINIBAR TV TEL. 1,025–1,395Kr ($174.25–$237.15) double; from 2,400Kr ($408) suite. Rates include buffet breakfast. AE, DC, MC, V. Bus: 1, 6, 16, 27, 28, or 29.

Built in 1880, this surprisingly elegant landmark hotel near the Central Railroad Station received in 1988 a renovation that brought it new life. The charm of the old building was preserved, but the rooms and baths were updated—each tastefully furnished and well maintained, with in-room movies. The Grand Bar overflows in summer onto a sidewalk cafe and Oliver's Restaurant serves freshly prepared Danish specialties.

⑤ Kong Arthur. Nørre Søgade 11, DK-1370 København. ☎ **33-11-12-12.** Fax 33-32-61-30. 100 rms, 7 suites. MINIBAR TV TEL. 750–1,145Kr ($127.50–$194.65) double; from 2,700Kr ($459) suite. Rates include buffet breakfast. AE, DC, MC, V. Free parking. Bus: 5, 7, or 16.

An orphanage when it was built in 1882, this good-value hotel sits behind a private courtyard next to the tree-lined Peblinge Lake in a residential part of town. It has been completely renovated into a contemporary hostelry; a new wing with more spacious rooms, including 17 no-smoking rooms, was added in 1993. Each of the comfortably furnished and carpeted rooms is freshly painted and has a safe and hair dryer. The hotel's Restaurant Brøchner is recommended for its reasonably priced Danish and French cuisine. A Japanese restaurant is also on site.

Inexpensive

Boulevard Hotel. Sønder Blvd. 53, DK-1720 København. ☎ **33-25-25-19.** Fax 33-25-25-83. 20 rms (none with bath). TV TEL. 500Kr ($85) double. No credit cards. Bus: 10.

Simple and plain but well kept, this five-story hotel is about a 10-minute walk from the main rail station. Renovated in the late 1980s from an older core, it's unpretentious and unassuming, with bright and acceptably decorated rooms. Each has a sink with hot and cold running water; the toilets and showers are in rooms off the central corridors. Breakfast is the only meal served.

⑤ Hotel West. Dannebrogsgade 8, DK-1661 København. ☎ **31-24-27-61.** 24 rms (10 with bath). 300Kr ($51) double without bath; 500Kr ($85) double with bath. Extra bed 125Kr ($21.25). No credit cards. Bus: 6, 27, or 28.

This hotel occupies the fourth floor of a 1900 corner building a 10-minute walk from the rail station. There's no elevator, so reaching your somewhat Spartan accommodation requires a climb. The rooms are small but clean and well maintained. Only a few singles are available; most are twin-bedded but can be used as three-, four-, or five-bedded units. No breakfast is served, but many restaurants are nearby. Ten rooms have a small refrigerator (not a minibar).

Missionshotellet Nebo. Istedgade 6, DK-1650 København. ☎ **31-21-12-17.** Fax 31-23-47-74. 150 rms (72 with bath). TV TEL. 540Kr ($91.80) double without bath, 840Kr ($142.80) double with bath. Extra bed 160Kr ($27.20). AE, DC, MC, V. Parking 25Kr ($4.25). Bus: 1, 6, 16, 28, or 41.

This hotel near the rail station is a quiet retreat, with a tiny lobby and a lounge that opens onto a side courtyard. The small rooms are clean and up-to-date, though Spartan; they're furnished in a Nordic functional style. There are bathrooms on all floors.

ON HELGOLANDSGADE & COLBJØRNSENSGADE

Copenhagen's main accommodations street is near the Central Railroad Station, where Helgolandsgade runs parallel to Colbjørnsensgade. The many moderately priced hostelries here can be booked through a central office at Helgolandsgade 4 (☎ **31-31-43-44**). Adjacent to the **Triton Hotel,** it's operated jointly by the Triton and the well-recommended **Absalon Hotel.** Admittedly, most callers phoning this service are siphoned off to either of those hotels, but if space in those hotels is full, lodgings are found in other decent and acceptable hotels in the neighborhood.

A GAY HOTEL

Hotel Jørgensen. Rømersgade 11, DK-1362 København. ☎ **33-13-81-86.** Fax 33-15-51-05. 12 doubles, 12 dorm rms. 580Kr ($98.60) double with bath; 100Kr ($17) per person dorm room. Rates include breakfast. MC, V. Bus: 14 or 16.

In 1984 the Jørgensen was transformed into Denmark's first gay hotel. A white stucco establishment, it's on a busy boulevard in the central city, with a patronage mainly of gays and lesbians, though straights are welcome. The rooms are conventional and well organized, and 12 dormitory rooms accommodate 6–14 each.

DINING

The national institution, the ubiquitous *smørrebrød* open-face sandwiches, is introduced at lunch. Literally, this means "bread and butter," but the Danes stack this sandwich as if it were the Leaning Tower of Pisa—then they throw in a slice of curled cucumber and bits of parsley or perhaps sliced peaches or a mushroom for added color.

NEAR KONGENS NYTORV & NYHAVN

Expensive

✪ **Kommandanten.** Ny Adelgade 7. ☎ **33-12-09-90.** Reservations required. Main courses 205–250Kr ($34.85–$42.50); fixed-price menu 520Kr ($88.40). AE, DC, MC, V. Mon–Fri noon–2:30pm; Mon–Sat 5:30–10pm. Bus: 1 or 6. INTERNATIONAL.

Built in 1698 and the former residence of the military commander of Copenhagen, Kommandanten is the epitome of Danish chic and charm. The menu offers a mouthwatering array of classical dishes mixed with innovative selections. Each dish is given a pleasing personal touch. The finest seasonal ingredients are used, and the menu changes every 2 weeks. You might be offered the grilled catch of the day, breast of duck with port-wine sauce, grilled turbot with spinach sauce, or gratinée of shellfish.

✪ **Kong Hans Kaelder.** Vingårdsstraede 6. ☎ **33-11-68-68.** Reservations required. Main courses 165–325Kr ($28.05–$55.25); fixed-price menus 375–850Kr ($63.75–$144.50). AE, DC, MC, V. Mon–Sat 6pm–midnight. Closed July 15–Aug 15 and Dec 24–26. Bus: 1, 6, or 9. INTERNATIONAL.

This vaulted gothic cellar, once owned by King Hans, may be the best restaurant in Denmark. Its most serious competition comes from Kommandanten, which many discriminating palates hail as the best. Located on "the oldest corner of Copenhagen," it has been carefully restored and is now a Relais Gourmand. H. C. Andersen lived above it and even wrote some of his finest stories here. The chef creates dishes that one critic claimed "to have been prepared by Matisse or Picasso." You might prefer to order one of the fixed-price menus; one is offered at lunch and five are offered at dinner. A typical three-course dinner would be smoked salmon from the restaurant's own smokery, breast of duck with bigarade sauce, then plum ice cream with Armagnac for dessert.

Moderate

Café Lumskebugten. Esplanaden 21. ☎ **33-15-60-29.** Reservations recommended. Main courses 168–250Kr ($28.55–$42.50); three-course fixed-price lunch 265Kr ($45.05); four-course fixed-price dinner 435Kr ($73.95). AE, DC, MC, V. Mon–Fri 11am–4:30pm; Mon–Sat 4:30–10:30pm. Bus: 1, 6, or 9. DANISH.

This restaurant is a clean, well-managed bastion of Danish charm, with an unpretentious elegance. It was established in 1854 as a rowdy tavern for sailors by a now-legendary matriarch named Karen Marguerita Krog. Today, a tastefully gentrified version of the original beef hash is still served. Two glistening-white dining rooms are decorated with antique ships' models, oil paintings, and pinewood floors. The food and service are excellent. Menu specialties include Danish fish cakes with mustard sauce and minced beetroot, fried platters of herring, sugar-marinated salmon with mustard-cream sauce, and a symphony of fish with saffron sauce and new potatoes.

Inexpensive

⑤ Nyhavns Faergekro. Nyhavn 5. ☎ **33-15-15-88.** Reservations required. Fixed-price dinner 140Kr ($23.80); herring buffet 68Kr ($11.55); Danish open-face sandwiches 39–60Kr ($6.65–$10.20). DC, MC, V. Daily 11:30am–4pm and 5–11pm. Closed Jan 1 and Dec 24–25. Bus: 1, 6, or 9. DANISH/FRENCH.

The Nyhavn Ferry Inn has a long tradition and many devotees. The house dates from the final years of the 18th century. At the harbor area, it offers a popular summer terrace, where diners can enjoy not only their food but a view of the 18th-century houses and boats in the canal. Inside, the decor is unusual, with a spiral stairway from an antique tram and a black-and-white checkerboard marble floor. The kitchen prepares a daily homemade buffet of 10 types of herring in many styles and sauces. You can also order *smørrebrød*, everything from smoked eel with scrambled eggs to chicken salad with bacon. For dinner you can have one of Copenhagen's tenderest and most succulent entrecôtes.

NEAR RÅDHUSPLADSEN & TIVOLI

Moderate

Copenhagen Corner. H. C. Andersens Blvd. 1A. ☎ **33-91-45-45.** Reservations recommended. Main courses 75–185Kr ($12.75–$31.45); three-course fixed-price menu 275Kr ($46.75). AE, DC, MC, V. Daily 11:30am–11pm. Bus: 1, 6, or, 8. SCANDINAVIAN.

This restaurant opens onto Rådhuspladsen, around the corner from the Tivoli Gardens. Outfitted with some of the accessories of a greenhouse-style conservatory for plants, it offers well-prepared and unpretentious meals. Menu choices include marinated slices of Parma ham with salad greens, several preparations of marinated or smoked salmon, thin-sliced duck with potatoes and orange sauce, fried fillet of veal with lobster sauce, and a dessert specialty of hazelnut parfait.

Inexpensive

City Rock Café. In Scala, Axeltorv 2. ☎ **33-15-45-40.** Burgers, sandwiches, and platters 60–120Kr ($10.20–$20.40). DC, MC, V. Daily 11am–11pm (Bar, daily 11am–1 or 2am). Bus: 1, 6, or 8. AMERICAN.

Inspired by the successful international appeal of the Hard Rock Cafe chain, this is one of the busiest cafe-bars in the Scala shopping/restaurant complex. Rock from the 1960s to the 1990s is played against a backdrop of banquettes made from the rear end of a 1959 Cadillac and an old-fashioned Würlitzer jukebox. Live concerts are presented about twice a month in winter, after the nearby Tivoli Gardens are closed. Menu choices, which are copious and inexpensive, consist of several kinds of burgers, T-bone steaks, and an array of salads bearing such distinctly non-Danish names as Malibu, Tijuana, and Pacific.

NEAR ROSENBORG SLOT

Very Expensive

✪ St. Gertruds Kloster. Hauser Plads 32. ☎ **33-14-66-30.** Reservations required. Fixed-price menus 340–750Kr ($57.80–$127.50); children's menu 90Kr ($15.30). Main courses 215–268Kr ($36.55–$45.55). AE, DC, MC, V. Daily 5–11:15pm. Closed Dec 25–Jan 1. Bus: 4E, 7E, 14, or 16. INTERNATIONAL.

Near Nørreport Station and south of Rosenborg Castle, this is the most romantic restaurant in Copenhagen. There's no electricity in the labyrinth of 14th-century underground vaults, and the 1,500 flickering candles, open grill, iron sconces, and rough-hewn furniture create an elegant medieval ambience. The chefs display talent and integrity, their cuisine reflecting a precision and sensitivity. Every flavor is fully focused, each dish balanced to perfection. Try the fresh homemade foie gras with black truffles, lobster served in turbot bouillon, scallops sautéed with herbs in sauterne, or venison (year-round) with asparagus and truffle sauce.

AT GRÅBRØDRETORV

Moderate

Bøf & Ost. Gråbrødretorv 13. ☎ **33-11-99-11.** Reservations required. Main courses 100–165Kr ($17–$28.05); fixed-price meals 95Kr ($16.15) at lunch, 235Kr ($39.95) at dinner. DC, MC, V. Mon–Sat 11:30am–10:30pm. Closed Jan 1 and Dec 24–25. Bus: 5. DANISH/FRENCH.

Beef & Cheese is housed in a 1728 building, and its cellars come from a medieval monastery. In summer a pleasant outdoor terrace overlooks Gray Friars Square. Specialties include lobster soup, fresh Danish bay strips, a cheese plate with six selections, and some of the best grilled tenderloin in town.

Peder Oxe's Restaurant/Vinkaelder Wine Bar. Gråbrødretorv 11. ☎ **33-11-00-77.** Reservations recommended. Main courses 69–159Kr ($11.75–$27.05); fixed-price lunch 69–89Kr ($11.75–$15.15). DC, MC, V. Daily 11:30am–midnight. Bus: 5. DANISH.

In the Middle Ages this was the site of a monastery, but the present building dates from the 1700s. The restaurant/wine bar was established in the 1970s and is still popular among young people. A salad bar is included in the price of the main course, but it's so tempting that many prefer to enjoy it alone for 59Kr ($10.05) per person. Dishes include lobster soup, Danish bay shrimp, open-face sandwiches, hamburgers, and fresh fish. The bill of fare, though standard, is well prepared.

Inexpensive

⊗ Pasta Basta. Valkendorfsgade 22. ☎ **33-11-21-31.** Reservations recommended. Main courses 65–115Kr ($11.05–$19.55). DC, MC, V. Sun–Wed 11:35am–3:30am, Thurs–Sat 11:30am–5:30am. Bus: 5. ITALIAN.

Its main attraction is a loaded table of cold antipasti and salads, which many diners believe is one of the best values in town. The restaurant is divided into half a dozen cozy dining rooms, each with a decor inspired by ancient Pompeii. Menu choices include at least 15 kinds of pasta (all made fresh on the premises), raw marinated fillet of beef (carpaccio) served with olive oil and basil, a platter with three kinds of Danish caviar (whitefish, speckled trout, and vendace, all served with chopped onions, lemon, toast, and butter), and fresh mussels cooked in a dry white wine with pasta and creamy saffron sauce.

NEAR CHRISTIANSBORG

Expensive

Krogs Fiskerestaurant. Gammel Strand 38. ☎ **33-15-89-15.** Reservations required. Main courses 185–365Kr ($31.45–$62.05); fixed-price menu 225Kr ($38.25) for three courses, 425Kr ($72.25) for five courses. AE, DC, MC, V. Mon–Sat 11:30am–4pm and 5:30–10:30pm. Bus: 2, 10, or 16. SEAFOOD.

This restaurant's premises were built in 1789 as a fish shop. The canalside plaza where fishers moored their boats is now the site of the outdoor dining terrace. Converted into a restaurant in 1910, the establishment serves very fresh seafood in a single large room decorated in an antique style with old oil paintings and rustic colors. The well-chosen menu includes lobster soup, bouillabaisse, natural oysters, mussels steamed in white wine, and poached salmon-trout with saffron sauce. Each dish is impeccably prepared and filled with flavor. A limited selection of meat dishes is also available.

Moderate

Fiskekaelderen. Ved Stranden 18. ☎ **33-12-20-11.** Reservations recommended. Main courses 175–270Kr ($29.75–$45.90); three-course fixed-price menu 260Kr ($44.20). AE, DC, MC, V. Mon–Fri noon–3pm; daily 5–10pm. Bus: 1, 6, or 10. SEAFOOD.

Though the building dates from 1750, Fiskekaelderen was opened in 1975 and is today the best seafood restaurant in Copenhagen. The restaurant prides itself on very fresh fish either imported from the Mediterranean or caught in the waters of the North Atlantic. Warmly nautical in decor, it has a bubbling lobster tank and an ice table displaying the fish of the day. Try the lobster bisque with fish and lobster roe, Danish fish soup, stuffed sole poached in white wine and glazed with hollandaise sauce, or fricassée of three types of fish in saffron-flavored bouillon with noodles. Some beef dishes, such as Charolais sirloin, are also served.

IN TIVOLI

Food prices inside Tivoli are about 30% higher than elsewhere. Try skipping dessert at a restaurant and picking up a less expensive treat at one of the many stands. Take bus no. 1, 6, 8, 16, 29, 30, 32, or 33 to reach the park and either of the following restaurants. *Note:* These restaurants are open only from May to mid-September.

✪ **Belle Terrasse.** Vesterbrogade 3. ☎ **33-12-11-36.** Reservations required. Main courses 225–295Kr ($38.25–$50.15); fixed-price menu 465Kr ($79.05) for three courses, 545Kr ($92.65) for four courses. AE, DC, MC, V. Daily noon–11pm. DANISH/FRENCH.

A seductive menu and a glamorous flower-filled terrace lure diners to Tivoli's best restaurant. Since its opening in 1946 in a position overlooking Tivoli Lake, it has been owned by the same family. Guests such as Marlene Dietrich, who performed at the Tivoli, have enjoyed the belle époque atmosphere in the octagonal greenhouse-like dining room. The cuisine is refined and dignified, the service formal. The menu presents an array of tempting appetizers, from medaillons of fresh pan-fried duck liver with blackberry sauce to freshly peeled Danish fjord shrimp. The fish courses, often from the Baltic, range from fillet of Danish turbot baked with fennel to sole meunière. Roasted pigeon served with potato purée with black olives and truffle sauce is a worthy selection, as is the rack and leg of Danish spring lamb roasted with thyme and garlic pesto. Many dishes are from the charcoal grill, including tenderloin of Charolais beef.

✪ **Divan II.** Vesterbrogade 3. ☎ **33-12-51-51.** Reservations recommended. Main courses 245–345Kr ($41.65–$58.65); fixed-price meal 295Kr ($50.15) at lunch, 385–585Kr ($65.45–$99.45) at dinner. AE, DC, MC, V. Daily 11:30am–11pm. DANISH/FRENCH.

This is the second finest restaurant in Tivoli, and certainly one of the most expensive. It was established in 1843, the same year as Tivoli itself, and despite its designation as Divan II, it's nonetheless older than its nearby competitor, the less formal Divan I. Service is almost unrelentingly impeccable in a garden setting where the cuisine is among the most urbane in the Danish capital. Examples include fried fillet of salmon served with a turbot bisque and tomato-and-basil concassé, a paupiette of fillet of sole with lobster mousseline with fried oyster mushrooms and a turbot bisque, and monkfish medaillons fried with veal bacon and served with fricassée of morels. Dinners here are elaborate, memorable, and highly ritualized.

ATTRACTIONS
SIGHTSEEING SUGGESTIONS

If You Have 1 Day   Take a walking tour through the heart of the old city, which will give you time to recover from jet lag. Spend the late afternoon at Christiansborg Palace on Slotsholmen island where the queen of Denmark receives guests. Early in the evening head to the Tivoli.

If You Have 2 Days   On day 2, visit Amalienborg Palace, the queen's residence. Try to time your visit to witness the changing of the guard. Continue beyond the palace to *The Little Mermaid* statue. In the afternoon, see the art treasures of Ny Carlsberg Glyptotek. At night, visit Scala, the restaurant/shopping complex.

If You Have 3 Days   In the morning of the third day, visit Rosenborg Castle, summer palace of King Christian IV, then wander through the park and gardens. Have lunch at one of the restaurants lining the canal at Nyhavn, the traditional seamen's quarter of Copenhagen. In the afternoon, go to Rundetårn (Round Tower) for a panoramic view of the city, and if time remains, stop in at the National Museum and Denmark's Fight for Freedom Museum.

If You Have 5 Days   On day 4, head north to Louisiana, the modern-art museum, and continue on to Helsingør to visit Kronborg Castle, famously associated with Shakespeare's Hamlet. Return by train to Copenhagen in time for a stroll along the Strøget, Europe's longest walking street. For dinner, head to Dragør. On the fifth day, visit Frilandsmuseet, at Lyngby, a half-hour train ride from Copenhagen. Have lunch at the park. Return to Copenhagen and take a walking tour along its canals. If time remains, tour the Carlsberg brewery. Pay a final visit to the Tivoli to cap your adventure in the Danish capital.

THE TIVOLI & *THE LITTLE MERMAID*

✪ **Tivoli Gardens.** Vesterbrogade 3. ☎ **33-15-10-01.** Admission 11am–1pm, 30Kr ($5.10) adults, 20Kr ($3.40) children under 12; 1–9:30pm, 44Kr ($7.50) adults, 20Kr ($3.40) children; 9:30pm–midnight, 20Kr ($3.40) for everyone. Rides 15Kr ($2.55) each. Daily 11am–midnight. Closed mid-Sept to May. Bus: 1, 16, or 29.

Since it opened in 1843, this 20-acre garden and amusement park in the center of Copenhagen has been a resounding success, with its thousands of flowers, merry-go-round of tiny Viking ships, games of chance and skill (pinball arcades, slot machines, shooting galleries), and Ferris wheel of hot-air balloons and cabin seats. There's even a playground for children.

An Arabian-style fantasy palace, with towers and arches, houses more than two dozen restaurants in all price ranges, from a lakeside inn to a beer garden. Take a walk around the edge of the tiny lake with its ducks, swans, and boats.

A parade of the red-uniformed Tivoli Boys Guard takes place on weekends at 6:30 and 8:30pm, and their regimental band gives concerts Saturday at 3:30pm on the open-air stage. The oldest building at Tivoli, the Chinese-style Pantomime Theater, with its peacock curtain, stages pantomimes in the evening.

Den Lille Havfrue. Langelinie. Bus: 1, 6, or 9.

The one statue *everybody* wants to see in Copenhagen is the life-size bronze of *Den Lille Havfrue,* inspired by H. C. Andersen's *The Little Mermaid,* one of the world's most famous fairy tales. The statue, unveiled in 1913, was sculpted by Edvard Eriksen. It rests on rocks right off the shore. The mermaid has been attacked more than once, losing an arm in one misadventure, decapitated in another.

In summer, a special "Mermaid Bus" leaves from Rådhuspladsen (Vester Voldgade) at 10:30am and then at half-hour intervals until 5:30pm. On the "Langelinie" bus there's a 20-minute stop at *The Little Mermaid.* If you want more time, take bus no. 1, 6, or 9.

THE TOP MUSEUMS

✪ **Ny Carlsberg Glyptotek.** Dantes Plads 7. ☎ **33-41-81-41.** Admission 15Kr ($2.55) adults, free for children. Free admission Wed and Sun. Tues–Sun 10am–4pm. Bus: 1, 2, 5, 6, 8, or 10.

The Glyptotek, behind the Tivoli, is one of Scandinavia's most important art museums. Founded by 19th-century art collector Carl Jacobsen, the museum comprises two distinct departments: modern works and antiquities. The modern section has both French and Danish art, mainly from the 19th century. Sculpture, including works by Rodin, is on the ground floor, and works of the Impressionists and related artists, including van Gogh's *Landscape from St. Rémy,* are on the upper floors. Egyptian, Greek, and Roman art are on the main floor; and Etruscan and Greek art are on the lower floor. The Egyptian collection is outstanding; the prize is a prehistoric rendering of a hippopotamus. A favorite of ours is the Etruscan art display. In 1996, the Ny Glyptotek added a French Masters' wing, where you'll find an extensive collection of masterpieces.

Statens Museum for Kunst (Royal Museum of Fine Arts). Sølvgade 48–50. ☎ **33-91-21-26.** Admission 20–40Kr ($3.40–$6.80) adults, free for children under 16. Tues and Thurs–Sun 10am–4:30pm, Wed 10am–9pm. Bus: 10, 14, 43, or 184.

This well-stocked museum houses painting and sculpture from the 13th century to the present. There are Dutch golden-age landscapes and marine paintings by Rubens and his school, plus portraits by Frans Hals and Rembrandt. The Danish golden age is represented by Eckersberg, Købke, and Hansen. French 20th-century art includes 20 works by Matisse. In the Royal Print Room are 300,000 drawings, prints, lithographs, and other works by such artists as Dürer, Rembrandt, Matisse, and Picasso.

Den Hirschsprungske Samling (The Hirschsprung Collection). Stockholmsgade 20. ☎ **31-42-03-36.** Admission 20Kr ($3.40) adults; free for children under 16; 35Kr ($5.95) for special exhibitions. Wed 11am–9pm, Thurs–Mon 11am–4pm. Bus: 10, 14, 42, or 43.

This collection of Danish art from the 19th and early 20th centuries is in Ostre Anlaeg, a park in the city center. Heinrich Hirschsprung (1836–1908), a tobacco merchant, created the collection and it has been growing ever since. The emphasis is on the Danish golden age, with such artists as Eckersberg, Købke, and Lundbye, and on the Skagen painters, P. S. Krøyer, and Anna and Michael Ancher. Some furnishings from the artists' homes are exhibited.

Nationalmuseet (National Museum). Ny Vestergade 10. ☎ **33-13-44-11.** Admission 30Kr ($5.10) adults, free for children. Tues–Sun 10am–5pm. Closed Dec 24–25 and 31. Bus: 1, 2, 5, 6, 8, 10, 28, 29, 30, 32, 33, 34, or 35.

A gigantic repository of anthropological artifacts, this museum is divided primarily into five departments. The first section focuses on Prehistory, the Middle Ages, and the Renaissance in Denmark. These collections date from the Stone Age and include Viking stones, helmets, and fragments of battle gear. Especially interesting are the "lur" horn, a Bronze Age musical instrument, among the oldest instruments in Europe, and the world-famous "Sun Chariot," an elegant Bronze Age piece of pagan art. The Royal Collection of Coins and Medals contains various coins from antiquity. The Collection of Egyptian and Classical Antiquities offers outstanding examples of art and artifacts from ancient civilizations.

Frihedsmuseet (Museum of Danish Resistance, 1940–45). Churchillparken. ☎ **33-13-77-14.** Free admission. May–Sept 15 Tues–Sat 10am–4pm, Sun 10am–5pm; Sept 16–Apr Tues–Sat 11am–3pm, Sun 11am–4pm. Bus: 1, 6, or 9.

On display here are relics of torture and concentration camps, the equipment used for the wireless and illegal films, British propaganda leaflets, satirical caricatures of Hitler, information about Danish Jews and conversely about Danish Nazis, and the paralyzing nationwide strikes. An armed car, used for drive-by shootings of Danish Nazi informers and collaborators, is on the grounds. All exhibition texts are in English.

Frilandsmuseet (Open-Air Museum). Kongevejen 100. ☎ **42-85-02-92.** Admission 30Kr ($5.10) adults, free for children. Easter–Sept Tues–Sun 10am–5pm; Oct 1–15 Tues–Sun 10am–4pm. Closed Oct 16–Easter. S-tog: From Copenhagen Central Station to Sorgenfri (leaving every 20 minutes). Bus: 184 or 194.

This reconstructed village in Lyngby, on the fringe of Copenhagen, captures Denmark's one-time rural character. The "museum" is nearly 90 acres, a 2-mile walk around the compound, and includes a dozen authentic buildings—farmsteads, windmills, fishers' cottages. Exhibits include a half-timbered 18th-century farmstead from one of the tiny windswept Danish islands, a primitive longhouse from the remote Faroe Islands, thatched fishers' huts from Jutland, tower windmills, and a potter's workshop from the mid-19th century.

Erotica Museum. Købmagergade 24. ☎ **33-12-03-11.** Admission 49Kr ($8.35). May–Sept daily 10am–11pm; Oct–Apr Mon–Fri 11am–8pm, Sat 10am–9pm, Sun 10am–8pm. Bus: 1, 16, or 29.

The only museum in the world where you learn about the sex lives of such famous people as Freud, Nietzsche, and Duke Ellington, this museum of erotica opened in the summer of 1992. Founded by Ole Ege, a well-known Danish photographer of nudes, it's within walking distance of the Tivoli and the Central Railroad Station. In addition to revealing a glimpse into the sex lives of the famous, it presents a survey of erotica around the world as well as through the ages. The exhibitions range from "the tame to the tempestuous"—from Etruscan drawings and Chinese paintings to Greek vases depicting a lot of sexual activity.

Tøjhusmuseet (Royal Arsenal Museum). Tøjhusgade 3. ☎ **33-11-60-37.** Admission 20Kr ($3.40) adults, 5Kr (85¢) children 6–17, free for children under 6. Tues–Sun 10am–4pm. Closed Jan 1 and Dec 24–25 and 31.

This museum features a fantastic display of weapons used for hunting and warfare. On the ground floor—the longest vaulted Renaissance hall in Europe—is the Canon Hall, stocked with artillery equipment from 1500 up to the present day. Above the Canon Hall is the impressive Armory Hall with one of the world's finest collections of small arms, colors, and armor. The building was erected during the years 1598–1604.

THE ROYAL PALACES

✪ **Amalienborg Palace.** Slotsplads. ☎ **33-12-21-86.** Admission 35Kr ($5.95) adults, 5Kr (85¢) children 5–15, free for children under 5. Mar–Oct daily 11am–4pm; Nov–Feb Tues–Sun 11am–4pm. Bus: 1, 6, 9, or 10.

These four 18th-century French-style rococo mansions have been the home of the Danish royal family since 1794, when Christiansborg burned. Visitors flock to witness the changing of the guard at noon when the royal family is in residence. A swallowtail flag at mast signifies that the queen is in Copenhagen and not at her North Zealand summer home, Fredensborg Palace.

The Royal Life Guard in black bearskin busbies (like the hussars) leaves Rosenborg Castle at 11:30am and marches along Gothersgade, Nørrevold, Frederiksborggade, Købmagergade, Østergade, Kongens Nytorv, Bredgade, Sankt Annae Plads, and Amaliegade to Amalienborg. After the event, the guard, still accompanied by the band, returns to Rosenborg Castle via Frederiksgade, Store Kongensgade, and Gothersgade.

In 1994 some of the official and private rooms in Amalienborg were opened to the public for the first time. The rooms, reconstructed to reflect the period 1863–1947, belonged to members of the reigning royal family, the Glücksborgs, who ascended the throne in 1863. The highlight is the period devoted to the long reign (1863–1906) of King Christian IX and Queen Louise.

✪ **Christiansborg Palace.** Christiansborg Slotsplads. ☎ **33-92-64-92.** Admission to Royal Reception Rooms, 33Kr ($5.60) adults, 10Kr ($1.70) children; parliament, free; castle ruins, 20Kr ($3.40) adults, 5Kr (85¢) children. Reception Rooms, May and Sept, guided tours Tues–Sun at 11am and 3pm; June–Aug, guided tours daily at 11am, 1pm, and 3pm; Oct–Apr, guided tours Tues, Thurs, and Sun at 11am and 3pm. Closed Jan. Parliament, English-language tours given only mid-June to late Sept Sun–Fri 10am–4pm. Ruins, May–Sept Tues–Fri and Sun 9:30am–3:30pm. Bus: 1, 2, 5, 8, or 9.

This granite-and-copper palace on the Slotsholmen—a small island that has been the center of political power in Denmark for more than 800 years—houses the Danish parliament, the Supreme Court, the prime minister's offices, and the Royal Reception Rooms. A guide will lead you through richly decorated rooms, including the Throne Room, banqueting hall, and Queen's Library. Before entering, you'll be asked to put on soft overshoes to protect the floors. Under the palace, visit the well-preserved ruins of the 1167 castle of Bishop Absalon, founder of Copenhagen.

✪ **Rosenborg Castle.** Øster Voldgade 4A. ☎ **33-15-32-86.** Admission 40Kr ($6.80) adults, 10Kr ($1.70) children under 15. Palace and treasury (imperial jewels), June–Aug daily 10am–4pm; mid-Apr to May and Sept to mid-Oct daily 11am–3pm; off-season Tues, Fri, and Sun 11am–3pm. S-tog: Nørreport. Bus: 5, 7, 10, 14, 16, 17, 43, or 84.

This red-brick Renaissance-style castle houses everything from narwhal-tusked and ivory coronation chairs to Frederik VII's baby shoes—all from the Danish royal family. Its biggest draws are the dazzling crown jewels and regalia in the basement Treasury, where a lavishly decorated coronation saddle from 1596 is also shown. Try to see the Knights Hall (Room 21), with its coronation seat, three silver lions, and relics from the 1700s. Room 3 was used by founding father Christian IV, who died in this bedroom decorated with Asian lacquer art and a stucco ceiling.

CHURCHES & OTHER ATTRACTIONS

Marble Church (Frederik's Church). Frederiksgade 4. ☎ **33-15-01-44.** Admission 20Kr ($3.40) adults, 10Kr ($1.70) children. Church, Mon, Tues, Thurs, and Fri 11am–2pm; Wed 11am–6pm; Sat 11am–4pm; Sun noon–4pm. Dome, Apr–May Sat–Sun 12:45pm; June–Sept daily 11am–12:45pm. Bus: 1, 6, or 9.

This two-centuries-old church, with its green copper dome—one of the largest in the world—is a short walk from Amalienborg Palace. After an unsuccessful start during the neoclassical revival of the 1750s in Denmark, the church was finally completed in Roman baroque style in 1894. In many ways it's more impressive than Copenhagen's cathedral.

Vor Frue Kirke (Copenhagen Cathedral). Nørregade. ☎ **33-14-41-28.** Free admission. Mon–Fri 9am–5pm. Bus: 5.

This Greek Renaissance–style church, built in the early 19th century near Copenhagen University, features Bertel Thorvaldsen's white marble neoclassical works, including *Christ and the Apostles.* The funeral of H. C. Andersen took place here in 1875, and that of Søren Kierkegaard in 1855.

Rådhus (Town Hall). Rådhuspladsen. ☎ **33-66-25-82.** Admission to Rådhus, 30Kr ($5.10); clock, 10Kr ($1.70) adults, 5Kr (85¢) children. Guided tour, Rådhus, Mon–Fri 3pm, Sat 10am; tower, Mon–Sat at noon. Bus: 1, 6, or 8.

Built in 1905, the Town Hall has impressive statues of H. C. Andersen and Niels Bohr, the Nobel Prize–winning physicist. Jens Olsen's famous **World Clock** is open for viewing Mon–Fri 10am–4pm and Sat at noon. The clockwork is so exact that the aberration over 300 years is 0.4 seconds. Climb the tower for an impressive view.

Rundetårn (Round Tower). Købmagergade 52A. ☎ **33-93-66-60.** Admission 15Kr ($2.55) adults, 5Kr (85¢) children. Tower, Sept–May Mon–Sat 10am–5pm, Sun noon–5pm; June–Aug Mon–Sat 10am–8pm, Sun noon–8pm. Observatory, Sept 26–Mar 20 Tues–Wed 7–10pm. Bus: 5, 7E, 14, 16, or 42.

This 17th-century public observatory, attached to a church, is visited by thousands who climb the spiral ramp (no steps) for a panoramic view of Copenhagen. The tower is one of the crowning architectural achievements of the Christian IV era. Peter the Great, in Denmark for a state visit, galloped up the ramp on horseback.

Botanisk Have (Botanical Gardens). Gothersgade 128. ☎ **35-32-22-22.** Free admission. Apr–Sept daily 8:30am–6pm; Oct–Mar daily 8:30am–4pm. S-tog: Nørreport. Bus: 5, 7, 14, 16, 24, 40, or 43.

Planted from 1871–74, the Botanical Gardens, across from Rosenborg Castle, are at a lake that was once part of the city's defensive moat. Special features include a cactus house and a palm house, all of which appear even more exotic in the far northern country of Denmark. An alpine garden contains mountain plants from all over the world.

ORGANIZED TOURS

BUS & BOAT TOURS   For orientation, try the 1½-hour **City Tour** (2½ hours with a visit to a brewery) that covers major scenic highlights like *The Little Mermaid,* Rosenborg Castle, and Amalienborg Palace. On workdays, tours also visit the Carlsberg brewery. Tours depart May 12–June 15 daily at 9:30am and 4pm; June 16–Sept 15 daily at 9:30am, 1pm, 3pm, and 4pm; Sept 16–Oct 15 daily at 4pm. Tours cost 120Kr ($20.40) per person.

The **City and Harbor Tour,** a 2½-hour trip by launch and bus, departs from Town Hall Square. The boat tours the city's main canals, passing *The Little Mermaid* and the Old Fish Market. It operates May 12–June 15 daily at 9:30am and June 16–Sept 15 daily at 9:30am, 1pm, and 3pm. Tours cost 160Kr ($27.20) per person.

Shakespeare buffs will be interested in an afternoon excursion to the castles of North Zealand. The 4½-hour tour explores the area north of Copenhagen, including visits to Kronborg (Hamlet's Castle), a brief visit to Fredensborg, the Queen's residence, and a stopover at Frederiksborg Castle and the National Historical Museum. Tours depart from the Town Hall Square, June–Sept 15, daily at 1:30pm; Sept 16–May, Tues and Fri at 1:30pm. Tours cost 270Kr ($45.90).

Another popular trip is the Hans Christian Andersen Tour, an 11-hour journey to Roskilde, Egeskov Castle, and the house and museum of the storyteller in Odense. Tours cost 480Kr ($81.60) per person and depart May 12–June 15 and Aug 16–Sept 30 on Sun at 8:30am; June 16–Aug 15 on Wed and Sun at 8:30am. Reserve in advance. For more info about these tours and the most convenient place for you to purchase tickets in advance, call **Vikingbus** at 31-57-26-00 or **Copenhagen Excursions** at 31-54-06-06.

GUIDED WALKS English-language guided walking tours of Copenhagen are offered during the summer at 40Kr ($6.80) for adults and 20Kr ($3.40) for children. Contact the Copenhagen Tourist Information Center, Bernstorffsgade 1 (☎ **33-11-13-25**).

SHOPPING

Boghallen, Rådhuspladsen 37 (☎ **33-11-85-11;** Bus: 2, 8, or 30), is a big store carrying many books in English (including translations of Danish works) as well as a wide selection of travel-related literature, including maps. The shop is at Town Hall Square. Open Mon–Fri 9:30am–6pm and Sat 9:30am–1pm.

One of Denmark's top department stores, **Illum's,** Østergade 52 (☎ **33-14-40-02;** Bus: 1, 6, 9, or 10), is on the Strøget. Take time to browse through its vast world of Scandinavian design. There's a restaurant and a special export cash desk at street level. Open Mon 10am–7pm, Tues–Wed 10am–6pm, Thurs–Fri 10am–8pm, and Sat 10am–5pm. The elegant ✪ **Magasin,** Kongens Nytorv 13 (☎ **33-11-44-33;** Bus: 1, 6, 9, or 10), is the biggest department store in Scandinavia. It offers an assortment of Danish designer fashion, glass and porcelain, and souvenirs. Goods are shipped abroad tax-free. Open Mon 10am–7pm, Tues–Wed 10am–6pm, Thurs–Fri 10am–8pm, and Sat 10am–5pm.

In the Royal Copenhagen retail center, legendary ✪ **Georg Jensen,** Amagertorv 6 (☎ **33-11-40-80;** Bus: 1, 6, 8, 9, or 10), is known for its fine silver. For the connoisseur, there's no better address—this is the largest and best collection of Jensen hollowware in Europe. Jewelry in traditional and modern design is also featured. One department specializes in seconds. Open Mon–Thurs 10am–6pm, Fri 10am–7pm, Sat 10am–5pm, and Sun noon–5pm. In the Royal Copenhagen retail center, **Holmegaards Glasvaerker,** Amagertorve 6 (☎ **33-12-44-77;** Bus: 1, 6, 8, 9, or 10), is the only major producer of glasswork in Denmark. Its Wellington pattern, created in 1859, is available once again. The Holmegaard glasses and Regiment Bar set reflect solid craftsmanship. Open Mon–Thurs 10am–6pm, Fri 10am–7pm, Sat 10am–5pm, and Sun noon–5pm.

A center for modern Scandinavian and Danish design, ✪ **Illums Bolighus,** Amagertorv 10, on Strøget (☎ **33-14-19-41;** Bus: 28, 29, or 41), is one of Europe's finest showcases for household furnishings and accessories of every kind. The store also sells fashions and accessories for women and men. There's even a gift shop. Open Mon–Thurs 10am–6pm, Fri 10am–7pm, and Sat 10am–5pm. ✪ **Royal Copenhagen** and **Bing & Grøndahl Porcelain,** Amagertorv 6 (☎ **33-13-71-81;**

Bus: 1, 2, 6, 8, 28, 29, or 41 for the retail outlet or 1 or 14 for the factory), was founded in 1775. Royal Copenhagen's trademark, three wavy blue lines, has come to symbolize quality in porcelain throughout the world. The factory was a royal possession for a century before passing into private hands in 1868 and has turned out a new plate each year since 1908, most of the motifs depicting the Danish countryside in winter. On the top floor is a huge selection of seconds, and unless you're an expert, you can't tell.

Established in 1926, **Kunsthallens Kunstauktioner,** Gothersgade 9 (☎ **33-32-52-00;** Bus: 1, 6, 9, or 10), is Europe's leading dealer in the pan-European school of painting known as COBRA (*Co*penhagen, *Br*ussels, and *A*msterdam). These works, produced from 1948 to 1951, were an important precursor of abstract expressionism. The gallery holds 12 auctions yearly, 8 with modern art; the others concentrate on the 19th century. Aug–June, the shop is open Mon–Fri 9:30am–6pm and Sat 9:30am–4pm. July is slow, though the premises are open for inspection and appraisals Mon–Fri 10am–4pm. At **Sweater Market,** Frederiksberggade 15 (☎ **33-15-27-73;** Bus: 2, 8, or 30), take your pick from Scandinavian and Icelandic top-grade sweaters, hats and scarves, handknit in 100% wool. There's also a large selection of Icelandic wool jackets and coats. Open Mon–Fri 9:30am–6pm, Sat 9:30am–4 or 5pm.

COPENHAGEN AFTER DARK

In Copenhagen, a good night means a late night. On warm weekends hundreds of rowdy revelers crowd Strøget until sunrise, and jazz clubs, traditional beer houses, and wine cellars are routinely packed. The city has a more serious cultural side as well, exemplified by excellent theaters, operas, and ballets. There's also a circus that shouldn't be missed. **Half-price tickets** for some concerts and theater productions are available the day of the performance from the ticket kiosk opposite the Nørreport rail station, at Nørrevoldgade and Fiolstræde; it's open Mon–Fri noon–7pm and Sat noon–3pm. On summer evenings there are outdoor concerts in Fælled Park near the entrance, near Frederik V's Vej; inquire about dates and times at the Copenhagen Tourist Office.

THE PERFORMING ARTS

❂ **Det Kongelige Teater (Royal Theater).** Kongens Nytorv. ☎ **33-69-69-69.** Tickets, 60–325Kr ($10.20–$55.25), half price for seniors 67 and over and those under 26. Bus: 1, 6, 9, or 10.

The Royal Theater, which dates from 1748, is home to the renowned **Royal Danish Ballet,** one of the world's premier ballet companies, which performs all over the globe, and the **Royal Danish Opera.** Because the arts are state subsidized in Denmark, ticket prices are comparatively low, and some seats may be available at the box office the day before a performance. The season runs Aug–May.

NIGHTCLUBS

Crazy Dayzi. Nørregade 41. ☎ **33-13-67-88.** Cover Fri–Sat 45Kr ($7.65). Tram: Nørreport Station.

In the early 1990s, a popular provincial nightclub in Jutland broadened its horizons and expanded into 16 locations in Denmark. The Copenhagen branch is the largest and busiest of the chain. No one under 21 is admitted, but those who make it past the doorman will find a whimsical collection of five bars, each outfitted in a distinctly different theme—like the cowboys of Montana, the monuments of ancient Rome, the sultry nights of old Havana, the volcanic jungles of Hawaii, and the Creole earthiness of New Orleans. Open Thurs 6pm–4am and Fri–Sat 6pm–5am.

Den Røde Pimpernel. H. C. Andersens Blvd. 7. ☎ **33-12-20-32.** No cover Tues–Thurs, 40Kr ($6.80) Fri–Sat. Bus: 2, 8, or 30.

The lively clublike atmosphere of the Scarlet Pimpernel, near Rådhuspladsen, makes it a good place for dancing. There's a bit of an attitude; people are admitted only after being inspected through a peephole. A live band plays a variety of dance music. It's open Tues–Sat 9pm–8am.

Fellini. Hammeritchsgade 1. ☎ **33-93-32-39.** Cover charge 50Kr ($8.50). Bus: 2, 6, 9, or 43.

This is Copenhagen's most luxurious and upscale nightclub, with a distinctly international theme. Set in, but independent from, the Radisson SAS Royal Hotel, it has a decor that's sheathed in mauve and scarlet. You'll find two bars, a dance floor, and a series of entertainment themes that are continued on the three nights per week that the place is open. These have included African music night, Latin salsa night, and American night, a venue that usually coincides with the arrival of whatever U.S. sports team happens to be in residence that week. It's open Thurs–Sat 10pm–5am. Men aren't expected to wear jackets and ties.

Jazz & Blues Clubs

Jazzhaus/Laurits Betjent. Ved Stranden 16. ☎ **33-12-03-01.** Cover 20Kr ($3.40). Bus: 1, 10, 27, 28, or 29.

A popular nightspot has stood here since 1850. There's more than just the ground floor. The upstairs, which offers a menu to satisfy the fast-food crowd with offerings of pizza, hamburgers, and french fries, attracts all ages, who flock to this barnlike place for the beer. It's open Mon–Sat noon–6am.

Mojo Blues Bar. Løngangsstraede 21C. ☎ **33-11-64-53.** No cover Sun–Thurs, 40Kr ($6.20) Fri–Sat. Bus: 2, 8, or 30.

Mojo is a candlelit drinking spot that offers blues music, 90% of which is performed by Scandinavian groups. It's open daily 8pm–5am.

A Dance Club

X-Ray Underground, Gothersgade 11, Bolthensgaard (☎ **33-93-74-15**), is one of the hotter venues for a late-night crowd about ages 19–28, most of whom are avid fans of whatever musical innovation is happening at the moment in London or New York. The decorative themes in this two-story place are derived from a surprisingly stylish adaptation of the themes of the 1960s cult classic *A Clockwork Orange.* The club is open Thurs–Sat midnight–6am. Cover is 50Kr ($8.50). Bus: 1, 6, or 9.

Bars

Det Lille Apotek, Stor Kannikestraede 15 (☎ **33-12-56-06;** Bus: 2, 5, 8, or 30), is a good spot for English-speaking foreign students to meet their Danish contemporaries. Though the menu varies, keep an eye out for the prawn cocktail and tenderloin. The main courses run from about 88–128Kr ($14.95–$21.75). It's open daily 11am–midnight (closed Dec 24–26). Frequented by celebrities and royalty, the **Library Bar,** in the Hotel Plaza, Bernstorffsgade 4 (☎ **33-14-92-62;** Bus: 6), was rated by the late Malcolm Forbes as one of the top five bars in the world. In a setting of antique books and works of art, you can order everything from a cappuccino to a cocktail. The setting is the lobby level of the landmark Plaza, commissioned in 1913 by King Frederik VIII. The bar was designed and built as the hotel's ballroom and Oregon pine was used for the paneling. The oversize mural of George Washington and his men dates from 1910. It's open Mon–Sat 11:30am–1am and Sun 11:30am–midnight.

Nyhavn 17, Nyhavn 17 (☎ **33-12-54-19;** Bus: 1, 6, 27, or 29), is the last of the honky-tonks that used to make up the former sailors' quarter. This cafe is a short walk from the patrician Kongens Nytorv and the d'Angleterre luxury hotel. In summer you can sit outside. It's open Sun–Thurs 10am–2am and Fri–Sat until 4am. A dancing, drinking, singing, and snack complex, **Vin & Olgod,** Skindergade 45 (☎ **33-13-26-25;** Bus: 5, 7, or 14), is complete with a tavern, a pub, a bodega, and a main beer hall. It's a Teutonic import of Bavarian oompah into Danish territory; definitely not for trendies or punkers, but perfect for fans of old-time evergreen music. When the band plays on stage, everybody sings along. It's open Mon–Sat 8pm–2am, except in July and part of Aug. The cover is 25Kr ($4.25) Mon–Thurs and 50Kr ($8.50) Fri–Sat.

GAY & LESBIAN CLUBS

Geo 2, Studiestraede 31 (Bus 14 or 16), is a disco that caters mostly to gay men who appreciate the fact that dialogue isn't drowned out by music. It occupies the street level under a straight bar, Blue Note, whose clients sometimes pop in for curiosity's sake. The cover is 20Kr ($3.40); it's open Thurs–Sat 10pm–6am. Beer costs from 25Kr ($4.25).

Café Babooshka, Turensensgade 6 (☎ **33-15-05-36;** Bus: 5, 7, or 16), is Copenhagen's premier lesbian bar, owned and managed by women. Near the Ørsteds Parken and Gyldenløvesgade, it welcomes men, gay and straight, but primarily identifies itself as a spot where lesbians can be themselves. After 8pm the cafe-style format is transformed into a disco. There's no cover, and Fri and Sat nights are reserved for women only. The place is open Mon–Wed noon–1am, Thurs–Fri noon–2am, Sat 4pm–2am, and Sun 4pm–1am.

GAMBLING

Danish authorities allowed the country's first fully licensed casino, **Casino Copenhagen,** in the SAS Scandinavia Hotel, Amager Blvd. 70 (☎ **33-11-51-15;** Bus: 5, 11, 30, or 34), to open just after Christmas 1990. Today gamblers play such popular games as roulette, baccarat, punto banco, blackjack, and slot machines. The operation is overseen by Casinos of Austria, Europe's largest casino operator. It's open daily 2pm–4am. The cover is 60Kr ($10.20); guests of any of Copenhagen's Radisson SAS hotels enter free.

DAY TRIPS FROM COPENHAGEN

DRAGØR   Visit the past in this old seafaring town on the island of Amager, 3 miles south of Copenhagen's Kastrup Airport. It's filled with well-preserved half-timbered, ocher-and-pink 18th-century cottages with steep red-tile or thatch roofs, many of which are under the protection of the National Trust. Dragør is a 35-minute trip on bus no. 30, 33, or 73E from Rådhuspladsen (Town Hall Square) in Copenhagen.

Dragør (pronounced *Drah-wer*) was a busy port on the herring-rich Baltic Sea in the early Middle Ages, and when fishing fell off it became just another sleepy waterfront village. After 1520, Amager Island and its villages—Dragør and Store Magleby—were inhabited by the Dutch, who brought their own customs, Low-German language, and agricultural expertise to Amager, especially their love of bulb flowers. In Copenhagen, you still see wooden-shoed Amager selling their hyacinths, tulips, daffodils, and lilies in the streets.

A rich trove of historic treasures is found in the **Amager Museum,** Hovedgaden 4–12, Store Magleby (☎ **32-53-93-07;** Bus: 30, 33, or 350S), outside Dragør. The exhibits reveal the affluence achieved by the Amager Dutch, with rich textiles, fine embroidery, and amenities like carved silver buckles and buttons. The interiors of a

Dutch house are especially interesting, showing how these people decorated their homes and lived in comfort. Admission is 20Kr ($3.40) for adults, 10Kr ($1.70) for children. It's open Apr–Sept Wed–Sun noon–4pm; Oct–Apr Wed and Sun noon–4pm.

The exhibits at the harborfront **Dragør Museum,** Havnepladsen 2–4 (☎ **32-53-41-06;** Bus: 30, 33, or 350S), show how the Amager Dutch lived from prehistoric times to the 20th century. Farming, goose breeding, seafaring, fishing, ship piloting, and ship salvage are delineated through pictures and artifacts. Admission is 20Kr ($3.40) for adults, 10Kr ($1.70) for children. It's open May–Sept Tues–Fri 2–5pm, Sat–Sun and holidays noon–6pm; closed Oct–Apr.

LOUISIANA Established in 1958, the ✪ **Louisiana Museum of Modern Art,** Gl. Strandvej 13 (☎ **49-19-07-19**), is idyllically situated in a 19th-century mansion on the Danish Riviera surrounded by elegant gardens, opening directly onto the Øresund. It's 20 miles north of Copenhagen. The art displayed is paintings and sculptures by modern masters (Giacometti and Henry Moore, to name two) as well as the best and most controversial works of modern art. In particular, look for paintings by Carl-Henning Pedersen. Occasionally, there are Chinese or Egyptian art exhibits as well as concerts. The museum name came from the first owner of the estate, Alexander Brun, who had three wives, each named Louise. Admission is 48Kr ($8.15) for adults, 15Kr ($2.55) for children 4–16; free for children under 4. It's open Thurs–Tues 10am–5pm and Wed 10am–10pm; closed Dec 24–25 and 31.

Humlebaek, the nearest town to Louisiana, may be reached by train from Copenhagen (København–Helsingør). Two trains per hour leave from the main station in Copenhagen (trip time 40 min.). Once you're at Humlebaek, the museum is a 10-minute walk.

HELSINGØR (ELSINORE) Once you reach Helsingør, 25 miles north of Copenhagen, you'll be deposited in the center of town and can cover all the major attractions on foot. Helsingør (Elsinore in English) is visited chiefly for "Hamlet's Castle." Aside from its literary associations, the town has a certain charm: a quiet market square, medieval lanes, and old half-timbered and brick buildings, remains of its once-prosperous shipping industry. There are frequent trains from Copenhagen, taking 50 minutes. Some 30 buses daily leave Copenhagen for the 1-hour trip to Helsingør. The **Tourist Office,** at Havnepladsen 3 (☎ **49-21-13-33**), is open Mon–Fri 9:30am–5pm and Sat 10am–1pm.

There's no evidence that Shakespeare ever saw this sandstone-and-copper Dutch Renaissance–style castle, full of intriguing secret passages and casements, but he made **Kronborg Slot,** Kronborg (☎ **49-21-30-78**), famous in *Hamlet.* According to 12th-century historian Saxo Grammaticus, though, if Hamlet had really existed, he would've lived centuries before Kronborg was erected (1574–85). Over the years some famous productions of the Shakespearean play have been staged here.

During its history, the castle has been looted, bombarded, gutted by fire, and used as a barracks (1785–1922). The starkly furnished Great Hall is the largest in northern Europe. The church with its original oak furnishings and the royal chambers are also worth exploring. Its bleak and austere atmosphere adds to its drama. Also on the premises is the **Danish Maritime Museum** (☎ **49-21-06-85**), which explores the history of Danish shipping.

Admission is 30Kr ($5.10) for adults, 10Kr ($1.70) for children 6–14, free for children under 6. It's open May–Sept daily 10:30am–5pm; Oct and Apr Tues–Sun 11am–4pm; Nov–Mar Tues–Sun 11am–3pm; closed Christmas Day. Guided tours are given every half hour Oct–Apr. In summer you can walk around on your own. The castle is half a mile from the rail station.

5 England

by Darwin Porter & Danforth Prince

England is filled with wonderful places to visit, and here we offer a sampling: No one would want to miss London or the legendary Stonehenge. The university at Oxford offers one side of England, and the unspoiled villages of the Cotswolds another. The classic city of Bath is a museum of the past, from the Romans to the 18th-century Jane Austen.

1 London

Dr. Samuel Johnson said, "When a man is tired of London, he is tired of life, for there is in London all that life can afford." In this section, we'll survey only a fraction of that life: ancient monuments, literary shrines, museums, walking tours, Parliament debates, royal castles, waxworks, palaces, cathedrals, and parks.

ONLY IN LONDON

Enjoying a Traditional English Tea   In London, it has a special ambience. Try the Hotel Goring, 15 Beeston Place, SW1 (☎ **0171/ 396-9000**), dating from 1910. From the lounge, you'll have a view of a small garden as you enjoy finger sandwiches, the hotel's special Ceylon blend tea, scones, and the chef's famous "light fruit cake," offered from a trolley.

Going to the West End Theater   London is the theatrical capital of the world. The live stage offers a unique combination of variety, accessibility, and economy—and perhaps a look at next year's Broadway hit.

Studying the Turners at the Tate   Upon his death in 1851, J. M. W. Turner bequeathed his personal collection of 19,000 watercolors and some 300 paintings to the people of Britain. He wanted his finished works, some 100 paintings, displayed under one roof. For 125 years, Turner's wish was unfulfilled. The expansion of the Clore Gallery changed this. The artist lived and died on the Thames' banks in Chelsea and painted the river in its many changing moods.

Shopping at Harrods   This vast emporium at Knightsbridge, spread over 15 acres, proclaims as its motto *Omnia Omnibus Ubique* or "everything for everyone, everywhere." They mean it, too. Want an elephant? Go to Harrods—in 1975 someone called Harrods at midnight and ordered a baby elephant to be delivered to the home of the then governor of California, Ronald Reagan. The animal arrived safely, albeit a bit bewildered. You can even arrange your funeral at the store.

Dining at Rules   Rules, at 35 Maiden Lane (☎ **0171/836-5314**), dates from 1798, when it was first established as an oyster bar. It may, in fact, be London's oldest restaurant. Long a venue for the theatrical elite and literary *beau monde,* it still serves the same dishes that delighted Edward VII and his mistress, Lillie Langtry. Charles Dickens liked the place so much he had a regular table. If it's feathered or furred, it's likely to be served here.

Doing a Pub Crawl   Americans bar hop, Londoners do a pub crawl. With thousands of pubs within the city limits, you would be crawling indeed if you tried to have a drink in each of them. Many pubs today are only for "lager louts," with Formica, loud jukeboxes, and an obsessive concern with football (soccer) scores. But traditional pubs remain, especially in central London, with their long mahogany bars, dark wood paneling, and Victorian curlicue mirrors to make it worthwhile to go on a crawl and partake of pub grub.

Spending a Rainy Day at the British Museum   It shelters one of the most comprehensive collections of art and artifacts in the world. Everything is here, from the finest assembly of Islamic pottery outside the Muslim world to the Elgin Marbles. Just when you think you've seen everything, you stumble into the room displaying sculptures from the Mausoleum at Halicarnassus, one of the Seven Wonders of the Ancient World. Even if it's not raining, you'll savor a visit here.

ORIENTATION

ARRIVING   By Plane   Heathrow Airport, west of London, in Hounslow (☎ **0181/759-4321**), one of the world's busiest airports, is divided into four terminals, each of which is relatively self-contained. Terminal 4, the most modern, handles the long-haul and transatlantic operations of British Airways, where most U.S airline flights arrive. Terminals 1 and 2 receive the intra-European flights of several European airlines. There is an Underground (subway) connection from Heathrow Central to the center of London; the 50-minute trip costs £3.10 ($4.95). Airbuses will also take you to central London in about an hour; they cost £6 ($9.60) for adults and £4 ($6.40) for children. A taxi costs at least £30 ($48).

Gatwick (☎ **01293/535353** for flight information), a smaller and more remote airport, lies 25 miles south of London, in West Sussex. Charter flights as well as many scheduled flights arrive here. Trains leave for London every 15 minutes during the day and every hour at night; they cost £9 ($14.25) for adults and half price for children aged 5 to 15 (under 5 free). There is also an express Flightline bus (no. 777) from Gatwick to Victoria Station that departs every half hour from 6:30am to 8pm and every hour from 8 to 11pm; it costs £7.50 ($12) per person. A taxi from Gatwick to central London usually costs £50 to £60 ($80 to $96).

By Train   Most trains originating in Paris and traveling through the Chunnel arrive at **Waterloo Station.** Visitors from Amsterdam arrive at the **Liverpool Street Station,** and those journeying south by rail from Edinburgh pull in at **King's Cross Station.** All are connected to London's vast bus and Underground network, and have phones, restaurants, pubs, luggage-storage areas, and London Regional Transport Information Centres.

By Car   If you're taking a car across the channel, you can quickly connect with a motorway into London. *Remember to drive on the left.* London is encircled by a ring road. Determine which part of the city you wish to enter and follow the signs there.

You should confine your driving in London to the *bare minimum,* so after you arrive, find a place to park.

VISITOR INFORMATION   The **British Travel Centre,** Rex House, 4–12 Lower Regent St., London SW1 4PQ (tube: Piccadilly Circus), caters to walk-in visitors (note that telephone information has been suspended). It's often a long wait. On the premises you'll find a British Rail ticket office, a travel agency, theater-ticket agency, hotel-booking service, bookshop, and souvenir shop—all in one well-equipped and very modern facility, open Mon–Fri 9am–6:30pm, Sat–Sun 10am–4pm, with extended Sat hours June–Sept.

The tourist board has a 24-hour recorded information service, **"Visitorcall"** (☎ **01839/123456**), which, for fees of 39p (60¢) or 49p (80¢) per minute (depending on when you call), will play a recorded message about tourist attractions that change every day. For a full information pack on London, write to the London Tourist Board, P.O. Box 151, London E15 2HF.

CITY LAYOUT   Our London begins at **Chelsea,** on the north bank of the river, and stretches for roughly 5 miles north to **Hampstead.** Its western boundary runs through Kensington, whereas the eastern boundary lies 5 miles away, at Tower Bridge. Inside this 5-by-5-mile square, you'll find all the hotels and restaurants and nearly all the sights that are usually of interest to visitors.

The logical (although not geographical) center of this area is **Trafalgar Square,** which we'll take as our orientation point. Stand here facing the steps of the imposing National Gallery—you're looking northwest. That is the direction of **Piccadilly Circus**—the real core of tourist London—and the maze of streets that makes up **Soho.** Farther north runs **Oxford Street,** London's gift to moderately priced shopping, and still farther northwest lies Regent's Park and the zoo.

At your back—that is, south—runs **Whitehall,** which houses or skirts nearly every British government building, from the Ministry of Defence to the official residence of the prime minister, at **10 Downing Street.** In the same direction, a bit farther south, stand the Houses of Parliament and Westminster Abbey.

Flowing southwest from Trafalgar Square is the table-smooth **Mall,** flanked by parks and mansions and leading to Buckingham Palace, the queen's residence. Farther along in the same direction lie **Belgravia** and **Knightsbridge,** the city's plushest residential areas, and south of them is **Chelsea,** with its chic flavor, plus **King's Road,** principally a boulevard for shopping.

Due west stretches the superb and high-priced shopping area bordered by **Regent Street** and **Piccadilly Street** (as distinct from the Circus). Farther west lie the equally elegant shops and even more elegant homes of **Mayfair.** Then comes **Park Lane.** On the other side of Park Lane is **Hyde Park,** the biggest park in central London and one of the largest in the world.

Charing Cross Road runs north from Trafalgar Square, past **Leicester Square,** and intersects with **Shaftesbury Avenue.** This is London's theater land. A bit farther along, Charing Cross Road turns into a browser's paradise, lined with shops selling new and secondhand books. At last it funnels into **St. Giles Circus.** This is where you enter **Bloomsbury,** site of the University of London, the British Museum, and erstwhile stamping ground of the famed "Bloomsbury group," led by Virginia Woolf.

Northeast of your position lies **Covent Garden,** known for its Royal Opera House and today a major shopping, restaurant, and cafe district.

Follow **The Strand** eastward from Trafalgar Square and you'll come to **Fleet Street.** Beginning in the 19th century, this corner of London became the most concentrated newspaper district in the world. **Temple Bar** stands where The Strand becomes Fleet Street, and only here do you enter the actual City of London, or "the City." Its focal point and shrine is the Bank of England on **Threadneedle Street,** with the Stock Exchange next door and the Royal Exchange across the street. In the midst of all the hustle and bustle rises **St. Paul's Cathedral,** Sir Christopher Wren's monument to beauty and tranquility.

At the far eastern fringe of the City looms the **Tower of London,** shrouded in legend, blood, and history and permanently besieged by battalions of visitors.

GETTING AROUND   By Public Transportation   Both the Underground (subway) and bus systems are operated by London Transport—with Travel Information Centres in the Underground stations at King's Cross, Hammersmith, Oxford Circus, St. James's Park, Liverpool Street Station, and Piccadilly Circus, as well as in the British Rail stations at Euston and Victoria and in each of the terminals at Heathrow Airport. They take reservations for London Transport's guided tours and have free Underground and bus maps and other information. A **24-hour telephone information** service is available by calling **0171/222-1234.**

London Transport, Travel Information Service, 55 Broadway, London SW1H 0BD, also offers **Travelcards** for use on the bus, Underground, and British Rail service inside Greater London. Available in a number of combinations for adjacent zones, Travelcards can be purchased for periods of from 7 days to a year. A Travelcard allowing travel in two zones for 1 week costs £14.80 ($23.65) for adults and £4.90 ($7.85) for children.

For shorter stays in London, a **1-Day Off-Peak Travelcard** can be used on most bus, Underground, and British Rail services throughout Greater London Mon–Fri after 9:30am and at any time on weekends and bank holidays. The Travelcard is available at Underground ticket offices, Travel Information Centres, and some newsstands. A two-zone card costs £2.80 ($4.50) for adults, £1.50 ($2.40) for children aged 5 to 15; children 4 and under ride free.

By Underground (Subway)   Known locally as "the tube," all Underground stations are clearly marked with a red circle and blue crossbar. You pick your station on the large diagram displayed on the wall, which has an alphabetical index. You note the color of the line it happens to be on (Bakerloo is brown, Central is red, and so on). By following the colored band, you can see at a glance where—or whether—you'll have to change and how many stops there are to your destination.

You can transfer as many times as you like as long as you stay in the Underground. The flat fare for one trip within the central zone is £1 ($1.60). Trips from the central zone to destinations in the suburbs range from £1 to £4 ($1.60 to $6.40) in most cases.

By Bus   The comparably priced bus system is almost as good as the Underground, and you'll have a better view. To find out about current routes, pick up a free bus map at one of London Regional Transport's Travel Information Centres listed above. The map is not available by mail.

Fares vary according to the distance traveled. Generally, the cost is 50p to £1.70 (80¢ to $2.70)—less than tube fares. If you travel for two or three stops, the cost is 60p (95¢); longer runs within zone 1 cost 80p ($1.30). If you want to be warned when to get off, simply ask the conductor. Call a 24-hour hotline (☎ **0171/ 222-1234**) for schedules and fares.

By Taxi   For a radio cab, phone **0171/272-0272** or 0171/253-5000. The minimum fare is £1.20 ($1.90) for the first third of a mile or 1 minute and 51 seconds, with increments of 20p (30¢) thereafter, based on distance or time. Each additional passenger is charged 30p (50¢). Passengers pay 10p (16¢) for each piece of luggage in the driver's compartment and any other item more than 2 feet long. Surcharges are imposed after 8pm and on weekends and public holidays. All these tariffs include VAT. Fares usually increase annually. It's recommended that you tip 10% to 15% of the fare.

By Car   Rent a car in London only if you plan to take excursions into the environs. Because of impossible traffic and parking difficulties, it's virtually impossible to see London by car.

By Bicycle   One of the most popular bike rental shops is **On Your Bike,** 52–54 Tooley St., London Bridge, SE1 (☎ **0171/378-6669;** tube: London Bridge), open Mon–Fri 9am–6pm, Sat 9:30am–5:30pm, Sun 11am–4pm. The 10-speed sports bikes, with high seats and low-slung handlebars, cost £8 ($12.80) per day or £25 ($40) per week and require a £50 ($80) deposit.

FAST FACTS: London

American Express   The main office is at 6 Haymarket, SW1 (☎ 0171/930-4411; tube: Piccadilly Circus). Full services are available Mon–Fri 9am–5:30pm, Sat 9am–4pm. At other times—Sat 9am–6pm and Sun 10am–6pm—only the foreign-exchange bureau is open.

Baby-sitters   The best is Childminders, 9 Paddington St., London W1M 3LA (☎ 0171/935-3000; tube: Baker Street). You pay £4.40 ($7.05) per hour in the daytime and £3.15 to £4.05 ($5.05 to $6.50) per hour at night. There is a 4-hour minimum, and hotel guests are charged a £5 ($8) booking fee each time they use a sitter.

Business Hours   Banks are usually open Mon–Fri 9:30am–3:30pm. Pubs and bars are open Mon–Sat 11am–11pm, Sun noon–10:30pm. Many pubs observe these extended Sunday hours; others prefer to close during the late afternoon (3–7pm). Stores are generally open 9am–5:30pm, until 7pm on Wed or Thurs. Most central shops close on Sat around 1pm.

Currency   The basic unit of currency is the **pound sterling** (£), which is divided into 100 pence (p). There are 1p, 2p, 10p, 20p, 50p, and £1 coins; banknotes are issued in £1, £5, £10, £20, and £50 denominations. The rate of exchange used in this chapter was $1 = 62.5p or £1 = $1.60.

Dentists/Doctors   For dental emergencies, call Emergency Dental Service (☎ 0181/302-8106), available 24 hours a day. Some hotels have doctors on call. In an emergency, contact Doctor's Call (☎ 0181/900-1000). Medical Express, 117A Harley St., W1 (☎ 0171/499-1991; tube: Regent's Park), is a private British clinic that's not part of the free British medical establishment.

Drugstores   In Britain they're called "chemist shops." Bliss The Chemist, 5 Marble Arch, W1 (☎ 0171/723-6116; tube: Marble Arch), is open daily 9am–midnight. Every London neighborhood has a branch of Boots, Britian's leading chain.

Embassies/High Commissions   The **U.S.** Embassy is at 24 Grosvenor Sq., W1 (☎ 0171/499-9000; tube: Bond Street). However, for passport and visa information, go to the U.S. Passport and Citizenship Unit, 55–56 Upper Brook St., London, W1 (☎ 0171/499-9000, ext. 2563; tube: Marble Arch), open Mon–Fri 8:30am–noon and 2–4pm (on Tues the office closes at noon). The **Canadian** High Commission, MacDonald House, 38 Grosvenor Sq., W1 (☎ 0171/258-6600; tube: Bond Street), handles visas for Canada; it's open Mon–Fri 10am–noon and 2–3pm.

London Underground

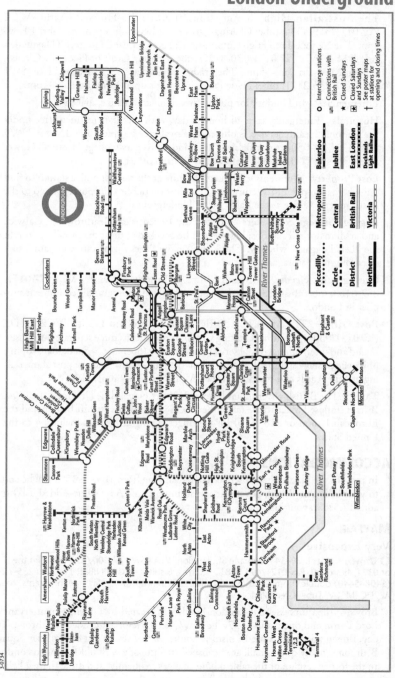

The **Australian** High Commission, at Australia House, Strand, WC2 (☎ 0171/379-4334; tube: Charing Cross or Aldwych), is open Mon–Fri 10am–4pm. The **New Zealand** High Commission, at New Zealand House, 80 Haymarket at Pall Mall SW1 (☎ 0171/930-8422; tube: Charing Cross or Piccadilly Circus), is open Mon–Fri 9am– 5pm. The **Irish** Embassy, at 17 Grosvenor Place, SW1 (☎ 0171/235-2171; tube: Hyde Park Corner), is open Mon–Fri 9am–4pm.

Emergencies   In London, for police, fire, or an ambulance, dial **999.**

Hospitals   Emergency care 24 hours a day, with the first treatment free under the National Health Service, is offered by Royal Free Hospital, Pond Street, NW3 (☎ 0171/794-0500; tube: Belsize Park), and University College Hospital, Gower Street, WC1 (☎ 0171/387-9300; tube: Warren Street).

Lost Property   For items left in taxis, inquire at the nearest police station to find out where to apply for its return; for items lost on public transportation, go to the Lost Property Office at the Baker Street Underground.

Luggage Storage & Lockers   Lockers can be rented at Heathrow and Gatwick and at all major rail stations; luggage can be checked at most major rail stations at the "Left Luggage" window. Check the Yellow Pages for private companies that offer long-term storage.

Photographic Needs   The Flash Centre, 54 Brunswick Centre, WC1 (☎ 0171/837-6163; tube: Russell Sq.), is the best professional photographic equipment supplier in London.

Post Office   The Main Post Office is at 24 William IV St., WC2N 4DL (☎ 0171/930-9580; tube: Charing Cross). It operates as three separate businesses: inland and international postal service and banking (open Mon–Sat 8:30am–8pm); philatelic postage stamp sales (open Mon–Sat 8am–8pm); and the post shop, selling greeting cards and stationery (open Mon–Sat 8am–8pm).

Taxes   The British government levies a 25% tax on gasoline ("petrol"). In 1994, Britain imposed a departure tax: either £5 ($8) for flights within Britain and the European Union or £10 ($16) for passengers flying elsewhere, including to the United States.

ACCOMMODATIONS

In most of the places listed, a service charge ranging from 10% to 15% will be added to your bill. The British government also imposes a VAT (Value-Added Tax) that adds 17.5% to your bill.

MAYFAIR

Very Expensive

✪ **Brown's Hotel.** 29–34 Albemarle St., London W1A 4SW. ☎ **800/225-5843** in the U.S., or 0171/493-6020. Fax 0171/493-9381. 110 rms, 6 suites. A/C MINIBAR TV TEL. £255–£275 ($408–$440) double; from £335 ($536) suite. Children up to 12 stay free in parents' room. AE, DC, MC, V. Tube: Green Park.

Brown's, the quintessential London hotel, was created by a former manservant of Lord Byron and opened in 1837, the year Queen Victoria ascended the throne. Today, Brown's occupies some 14 historic houses on two streets just off Berkeley Square. Bedrooms, many quite small, are furnished traditionally with old-fashioned comfort. In the formal restaurant the table d'hôte changes frequently, and dishes have a lighter, more contemporary touch than before, although the "trolley roast" is still here for longtime devotees.

○ **Claridge's.** Brook St., London W1A 2JQ. ☎ **800/223-6800** in the U.S., or 0171/629-8860. Fax 0171/499-2210. 132 rms, 58 suites. A/C TV TEL. £255–£295 ($408–$472) double; from £390 ($624) suite. AE, DC, MC, V. Tube: Bond St.

Claridge's has cocooned royal visitors in an ambience of discreet elegance since the time of the Battle of Waterloo. This is the hotel for British Empire nostalgists—even Queen Victoria dined here. Many of the spacious guest rooms have generous-sized baths complete with dressing rooms and numerous amenities. The rooms have old-fashioned layouts instead of modern comforts. Excellent food is stylishly served in the intimacy of the Causerie, renowned for its lunchtime smorgasbord and pretheater suppers, and in the more formal Restaurant, with its English and French specialties. Guests can use nearby health clubs.

Expensive

○ **Park Lane Hotel.** Piccadilly, London W1Y 8BX. ☎ **800/223-5652** in the U.S., or 0171/499-6321. Fax 0171/499-1965. 308 rms, 42 suites. MINIBAR TV TEL. £195–£210 ($312–$336) double; from £230 ($368) suite. AE, DC, MC, V. Parking £25 ($40). Tube: Hyde Park Corner or Green Park.

The most traditional and longstanding of the Park Lane deluxe hotels, it has far more style and personal warmth than so many of its competitors. The Park Lane offers luxurious and comfortable accommodations. Many suites have marble fireplaces and the original marble-sheathed bathrooms. The hotel's award-winning restaurant, Bracewells, competes favorably with any of the other London grand hotel dining rooms. There are fitness facilities and a business center on the premises.

PICCADILLY

Inexpensive

Regent Palace Hotel. 12 Sherwood St., near Piccadilly Circus, London W1A 4BZ. ☎ **0171/734-7000.** Fax 0171/734-6435. 950 rms (none with bath). TV TEL. £79 ($126.40) double without breakfast. For stays of 2 or more nights, £39 ($62.40) per person, including English breakfast. AE, DC, MC, V. Tube: Piccadilly Circus.

A major focal point since it was built in 1915 at the edge of Piccadilly Circus, this is one of the largest hotels in Europe. Today, it's known for its staunch loyalty to its original design, whereby none of the simply furnished rooms has a private bathroom. The hotel's Original Carvery makes for good, inexpensive dining and The Dome bistro is open for pretheater meals.

ST. JAMES'S

Expensive

Dukes Hotel. 35 St. James's Place, London SW1A 1NY. ☎ **0171/491-4840.** Fax 0171/493-1264. 64 rms, 12 suites. A/C TV TEL. £160–£185 ($256–$296) double; from £210 ($336) suite. AE, DC, MC, V. Parking £37 ($59.20). Tube: Green Park.

Dukes provides elegance without ostentation and, along with its nearest competitors, The Stafford and 22 Jermyn Street, attracts the urbane guest who's looking for charm, style, and tradition in a hotel. Since 1908 it has stood in a quiet courtyard off St. James's Street. Dukes Restaurant is small, tasteful, and elegant, combining both classic British and continental cuisine.

BLOOMSBURY

Expensive

Hotel Russell. Russell Sq., London WC1 B5BE. ☎ **800/435-4542** in the U.S., or 0171/837-6470. Fax 0171/837-2857. 329 rms, 16 suites. TV TEL. £145 ($232) double; from £170 ($272) suite. AE, DC, MC, V. Tube: Russell Sq.

London Accommodations

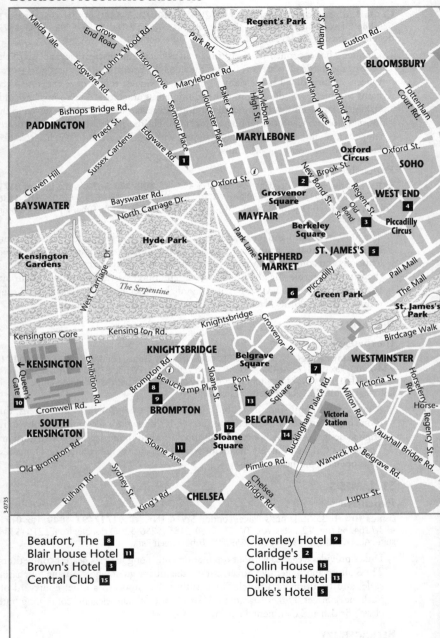

Beaufort, The **8**
Blair House Hotel **11**
Brown's Hotel **3**
Central Club **15**

Claverley Hotel **9**
Claridge's **2**
Collin House **13**
Diplomat Hotel **13**
Duke's Hotel **5**

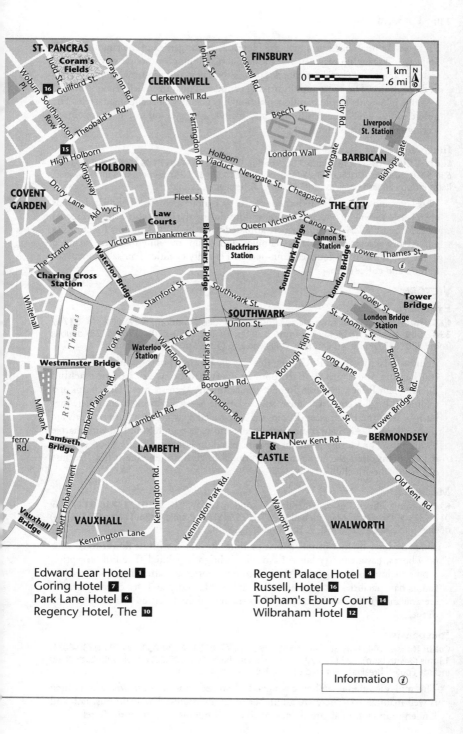

Edward Lear Hotel **1**
Goring Hotel **7**
Park Lane Hotel **6**
Regency Hotel, The **10**

Regent Palace Hotel **4**
Russell, Hotel **16**
Topham's Ebury Court **14**
Wilbraham Hotel **12**

Information *i*

This late Victorian hotel, run by Forte Hotels, faces the garden of the famous Russell Square, and is within easy reach of theaters and shopping. Although way down the scale as London or even Forte hotels go, it is the finest and most traditional address in Bloomsbury. The bedrooms, in striking contrast to the ornate belle époque facade, are done in a rather sterile traditional, although generally well-maintained, style. The public rooms have been refurbished and include Fitzroy Doll's, a main restaurant serving modern British food.

Inexpensive

Central Club. 16–22 Great Russell St., London WC1B 3LR. ☎ **0171/636-7512.** Fax 0171/636-5278. 109 rms. TV TEL. £61.25 ($98) double; £14.50 ($23.20) per person in triple or quad. Rates include English breakfast. MC, V. Tube: Tottenham Court Rd.

This large and attractive building, designed by famous architect Sir Edwin Lutyens (1869–1944), will be undergoing renovations during the life of this edition. Erected in 1932 as a YWCA and still vaguely affiliated with the YWCA, it now functions as a hotel and accepts men, women, families, and groups traveling together. Included in the rate is use of the lounges, coin-operated laundry facilities, hair salon, gym, solarium, and coffee shop.

VICTORIA

Expensive

✪ **Goring Hotel.** 15 Beeston Place, Grosvenor Gardens, London SW1W 0JW. ☎ **0171/396-9000.** Fax 0171/834-4393. 74 rms, 3 suites. TV TEL. £180–£205 ($288–$328) double; from £270 ($432) suite. AE, DC, MC, V. Parking £15 ($24). Tube: Victoria Station.

Built in 1910 by Mr. O. R. Goring, this was the first hotel in the world to have central heating and a private bathroom in every bedroom. Located just behind Buckingham Palace, it is our premier choice for the Victoria area. The charm of a traditional English country home is reflected in the paneled drawing room, where fires burn in the ornate fireplaces. Rooms here are called apartments and some units are air-conditioned. All the well-furnished bedrooms have been refurbished with marble bathrooms. The Goring is one of the best places in London for afternoon tea, and its restaurant offers the area's finest traditional English dishes. Guests have free use of a nearby health club.

Moderate

🅢 **Topham's Ebury Court.** 28 Ebury St., London SW1W 0LU. ☎ **0171/730-8147.** Fax 0171/823-5966. 42 rms (23 with bath). TV TEL. £95 ($152) double without bath; £115 ($184) double with bath. AE, DC, MC, V. Tube: Victoria Station.

Three minutes by foot from Victoria Station, this hotel, with its flower-filled window boxes, has a country-house flavor and is brightly painted. The little reception rooms are informal and decorated with flowery chintzes and attractive antiques. Most rooms have facilities for making coffee and tea. Laundry and dry-cleaning service are available. Topham's Restaurant offers traditional English food at both lunch and dinner.

Inexpensive

Collin House. 104 Ebury St., London SW1W 9QD. ☎ **0171/730-8031.** Fax 0171/730-8031. 13 rms (8 with bath). £52 ($83.20) double without bath; £62 ($99.20) double with bath. Rates include English breakfast. No credit cards. Tube: Victoria Station.

This mid-Victorian town house is a good, clean bed-and-breakfast, where everything is well maintained. There are a number of family rooms. The main bus, rail, and Underground terminals are all located about a 5-minute walk from the hotel.

KNIGHTSBRIDGE

Expensive

⭘ **The Beaufort.** 33 Beaufort Gardens, London SW3 1PP. ☎ **800/888-1199** in the U.S or Canada, or 0171/584-5252. Fax 0171/589-2834. 21 rms, 7 suites. TV TEL. £150–£215 ($240–$344) double; £240 ($384) junior suite for two. AE, DC, MC, V. Free overnight parking on street. Tube: Knightsbridge.

One of London's finest boutique hotels has an elegant town-house atmosphere with personal service and the ultimate in tranquility. Only 200 yards from Harrods, it sits behind two Victorian porticoes and an iron fence. The owner combined a pair of adjacent houses, ripped out the old decor, and created an updated ambience of merit and charm. Each bedroom features at least one painting by a London artist, a modern color scheme, plush carpeting, and a kind of grace throughout. Light meals are available from room service.

Moderate

⭘ **Claverley Hotel.** 13–14 Beaufort Gardens, London SW3 1PS. ☎ **800/747-0398** in the U.S, or 0171/589-8541. Fax 0171/584-3410. 32 rms (29 with bath). TV TEL. £100–£180 ($160–$288) double with bath. Rates include English breakfast. AE, DC, MC, V. Free parking available on street 6:30pm–8:30am. Tube: Knightsbridge.

Located on a quiet cul-de-sac, this tasteful hotel is just a few blocks from Harrods and is one of the neighborhood's very best hotels. It's a small, cozy place accented with Georgian-era accessories. The lounge evokes a country house. Most rooms have Victorian-inspired wallpaper, wall-to-wall carpeting, and comfortably upholstered armchairs. A few singles are without bath.

BELGRAVIA

Moderate

Ⓢ **Diplomat Hotel.** 2 Chesham St., London SW1X 8DT. ☎ **0171/235-1544.** Fax 0171/259-6153. 27 rms. TV TEL. £115–£145 ($184–$232) double. Rates include English breakfast buffet. AE, DC, MC, V. Tube: Sloane Sq. or Knightsbridge.

This is a small, reasonably priced hotel in an otherwise expensive neighborhood filled with privately owned Victorian homes and highrise first-class hotels. It was built in 1882 by one of the neighborhood's most famous architects (Thomas Cubitt) on a wedge-shaped street corner near the site of today's Belgravia Sheraton. Each of the comfortable high-ceilinged bedrooms—many of which were renovated in 1996—boasts well-chosen wallpaper in Victorian-inspired colors, as well as a modern bath equipped with a hair dryer, among other accessories. The staff is very helpful.

CHELSEA

Moderate

Ⓢ **Blair House Hotel.** 34 Draycott Place, London SW3 2SA. ☎ **0171/581-2323.** Fax 0171/823-7752. 16 rms. TV TEL. £90–£98 ($144–$156.80) double. Rates include continental breakfast. AE, DC, MC, V. Tube: Sloane Sq.

This comfortable hotel is a good, reasonably priced choice in the heart of Chelsea if you're seeking a B&B-type establishment and can't afford the prices of some of Chelsea's luxurious hotels. This old-fashioned building of architectural interest has been modified and completely refurbished, with every comfortable room sporting radios and tea- or coffee-making equipment. The quieter rooms are in the back.

Inexpensive

Wilbraham Hotel. 1–5 Wilbraham Place (off Sloane St.), London SW1X 9AE. ☎ **0171/730-8296.** Fax 0171/730-6815. 53 rms (42 with bath), 4 suites. TV TEL. £66–£75

($105.60–$120) double with bath; from £80 ($128) suite. Rates include English breakfast. No credit cards. Nearby parking £20 ($32). Tube: Sloane Sq.

This is a dyed-in-the-wool British hotel set on a quiet residential street just a few hundred yards from Sloane Square. It occupies three Victorian town houses that have been joined together. The well-maintained bedrooms are furnished in a traditional style. Some singles are rented without bath. On the premises is an attractive and old-fashioned lounge, The Bar and Buttery.

KENSINGTON
Inexpensive
🄢 **Abbey House.** 11 Vicarage Gate, London W8 4AG. ☎ **0171/727-2594.** 16 rms (none with bath). TV. £58 ($92.80) double; £68 ($108.80) triple; £78 ($124.80) quad. Rates include English breakfast. No credit cards. Tube: Kensington High St.

Some hotel critics have rated this the best bed-and-breakfast in London. Thanks to renovations, this hotel, which was built in about 1860 on a typical Victorian square, is modern, although many of the original features have been retained. The spacious bedrooms have central heating, electrical outlets for shavers, vanity lights, and hot-and cold-water basins. The hotel offers shared baths, one to each two lodging units. The rooms are each refurbished annually.

SOUTH KENSINGTON
Moderate
🄢 **Regency Hotel.** 100 Queen's Gate, London SW7 5AG. ☎ **800/328-9898** or 0171/370-4595. Fax 0171/370-5555. 198 rms, 11 suites. A/C MINIBAR TV TEL. £115–£120 ($184–$192) double; from £179 ($286.40) luxury suite for two; £199 ($318.40) double suite with Jacuzzi. AE, DC, MC, V. Tube: South Kensington.

The Regency—close to museums, Kensington, and Knightsbridge—takes its name from the historical period of the Prince Regent, later George IV. Located on a street lined with Doric porticoes, six Victorian terrace houses were converted into one stylish, seamless whole. The hotel's restaurant, the Pavillion, serves moderately priced international dishes. At your disposal are the Regency Health Club (with steam rooms, minigym, saunas, and a sensory-deprivation tank), plus a business center.

ST. MARYLEBONE
Moderate
Durrants Hotel. George St., London W1H 6BJ. ☎ **0171/935-8131.** Fax 0171/487-3510. 96 rms, 3 suites. TV TEL. £105 ($168) double; from £210 ($336) suite. AE, MC, V. Tube: Bond St.

Established in 1789 off Manchester Square, this historic hotel with its brown-brick facade ornamented with Georgian details is a snug, cozy, and traditional retreat—almost like a poor man's Browns. The establishment's oldest bedrooms face the front and have slightly higher ceilings than the newer ones. Even the most recent accommodations, however, have elaborate cove moldings and very comfortable furnishings.

Inexpensive
Edward Lear Hotel. 28–30 Seymour St., London W1H 5WD. ☎ **0171/402-5401.** Fax 0171/706-3766. 31 rms (8 with bath), 4 suites. TV TEL. £55 ($88) double without bath, £74 ($119.20) double with bath; £85 ($136) suite. Rates include English breakfast. MC, V. Tube: Marble Arch.

Edward Lear is a popular budget hotel, made all the more desirable by the bouquets of fresh flowers in the public rooms. It's one block from Marble Arch in a pair of brick town houses dating from 1780. Steep stairs lead up to the bedrooms. The cozy units are fairly small but have all the usual facilities. The only major drawback is that this is an extremely noisy part of London.

DINING

All restaurants and cafes in Britain are required to display the prices of their food and drink in a place that the customer can see before entering the eating area. Charges for service and any minimum charge or cover charge must also be made clear. The prices shown must include 17.5% VAT. Most restaurants add a 10% to 15% service charge to your bill, but if nothing has been added, leave a 12% to 15% tip.

MAYFAIR

Very Expensive

✪ **Chez Nico at Ninety Park Lane.** 90 Park Lane, W1. ☎ **0171/409-1290.** Reservations required (2 days in advance for lunch, 10 days for dinner). Fixed-price three-course lunch £29 ($46.40); dinner £59 ($94.40) for two courses, £60 ($96) for three courses. AE, DC, MC, V. Mon–Fri noon–2pm; Mon–Sat 7–11pm. Closed 10 days around Christmas/New Year's. Tube: Marble Arch. FRENCH.

Nico Ladenis is one of the most talked-about chefs of Great Britain—the only one who is a former oil company executive, economist, and self-taught cook. As befits any three-star Michelin restaurant, dinners are memorable in the very best gastronomic tradition of postnouvelle cuisine, in which the tenets of classical cuisine are creatively adapted to local fresh ingredients. The menu changes frequently, according to Nico's inspiration. Specialties include a warm salad of foie gras on toasted brioche with caramelized orange, or a Bresse pigeon rivaled only by Gavroche. Desserts are sumptuous.

✪ **Le Gavroche.** 43 Upper Brook St., W1. ☎ **0171/408-0881.** Reservations required, as far in advance as possible. Main courses £27–£36 ($43.20–$57.60); fixed-price lunch £38 ($60.80); fixed-price dinner £58–£80 ($92.80–$128). AE, DC, MC, V. Mon–Fri noon–2pm and 7–11pm. Tube: Marble Arch. FRENCH.

Le Gavroche has long stood for quality French cuisine, perhaps the finest in Great Britain, although Michelin gives it only two stars as opposed to Chez Nico (see above), which rates three. It's the creation of a Burgundy-born father-and-son team, Albert and Michel Roux. Service is faultless, the ambience chic and formal without being stuffy. The menu changes constantly, depending on what fresh produce is available, and, more important, the chefs' inclinations. Their wine cellar is among London's most interesting, with many quality Burgundies and Bordeaux. Try, if featured, soufflé Suissesse, *papillote* of smoked salmon, or *tournedos gratinés*.

Inexpensive

Hard Rock Cafe. 150 Old Park Lane, W1. ☎ **0171/629-0382.** Reservations not accepted. Main dishes £7–£15 ($11.20–$24). AE, MC, V. Sun–Thurs 11:30am–12:30am, Fri–Sat 11:30am–1am. Closed Dec 25–26. Tube: Green Park or Hyde Park Corner. AMERICAN.

This down-home cum-American roadside diner serves good food at reasonable prices with taped music and smiling servers in an atmosphere of relaxed hospitality. It's popular with the young, visiting rock and film stars, and American tennis players, and almost every night there's a line waiting to get in. Portions are generous, and main dishes come with a salad and fries. Specialties include a smokehouse steak, filet mignon, and a T-bone, plus charbroiled burgers and hot chili.

ST. JAMES'S

Inexpensive

Bubbles. 41 N. Audley St., W1. ☎ **0171/491-3237.** Reservations recommended. Main courses £4.80–£12.50 ($7.70–$20); fixed-price dinner £14.50 ($23.20); fixed-price vegetarian menu £7 ($11.20); glass of wine £2 ($3.20). AE, DC, MC, V. Daily 11am–11pm. Tube: Marble Arch or Bond St. ENGLISH/CONTINENTAL/VEGETARIAN.

At this wine bar between Upper Brook Street and Oxford Street (near Selfridges), the owners attach equal importance to their food and their impressive wine list. Some wines are available by the glass. On the ground floor guests enjoy fine wines but also draft beer and liquor, along with a limited but well-chosen selection of bar food. Downstairs an à la carte restaurant serves both English and continental dishes, including a selection appealing to vegetarians.

Red Lion. 2 Duke of York St., off Jermyn St., SW1. ☎ **0171/930-2030.** Sandwiches £2.20 ($3.50); fish and chips £8 ($12.80). No credit cards. Mon–Sat noon–11pm. Tube: Piccadilly Circus. BRITISH.

Ian Nairn (1930–83), a noted British writer on architecture, compared the Red Lion's spirit to that of Edouard Manet's painting *A Bar at the Folies-Bergère* (see the collection at the Courtauld Institute Galleries). The menu is composed of a set number of premade sandwiches, so once they are gone you're out of luck. On Friday and Saturday homemade fish and chips are also served. The food is prepared in upstairs kitchens and sent down in a century-old dumbwaiter; orders are placed at the bar.

PICCADILLY

Moderate

Greens Restaurant and Oyster Bar. 36 Duke St., SW1. ☎ **0171/930-4566.** Reservations recommended for dinner. Main courses £9.50–£33 ($15.20–$52.80). AE, DC, MC, V. Restaurant daily 12:30–3pm; Mon–Sat 6–11pm. Oyster bar Mon–Sat 11:30am–3pm and 5:30–11pm, Sun noon–3pm. Tube: Piccadilly Circus or Green Park. SEAFOOD.

The excellence of its menu, the charm of its staff, and its central location make Greens a great choice. This busy place has a cluttered entrance leading to a crowded bar where you can stand at what the English call "rat-catcher counters," if the tables are full, to sip fine wines and, from September through April, enjoy oysters. Other foods complementing wines are quails' eggs, king prawns, smoked Scottish salmon, "dressed" crab, and baby lobsters. If you go into the dining room, you can order from a long menu with a number of seafood dishes, from fish cakes with parsley sauce to poached Scottish lobster.

LEICESTER SQUARE

Moderate

Cork & Bottle Wine Bar. 44–46 Cranbourn St., WC2. ☎ **0171/734-7807.** Reservations recommended. Main courses £5.95–£8.95 ($9.50–$14.30); glass of wine from £2.20 ($3.50). AE, DC, MC, V. Mon–Sat 11am–midnight, Sun noon–10:30pm. Tube: Leicester Sq. INTERNATIONAL.

New Zealander Don Hewitson, a connoisseur of fine wines for more than 30 years, presides over this trove of blissful fermentation. He maintains a particular fondness for labels from "Down Under." The most successful dish is a raised cheese-and-ham pie. It has a cream-cheesy filling, and the well-buttered pastry is crisp—not your typical quiche. (In one week the bar sold 500 portions of this alone.) The kitchen also offers a chicken-and-apple salad, Lancashire sausage hot pot, and lamb in ale.

Sheekeys. 28–32 St. Martin's Court, off Charing Cross Rd., WC2. ☎ **0171/240-2565.** Reservations required. Main courses £13.95–£25.95 ($22.30–$41.50); fixed-price lunch £15.95 ($25.50). AE, DC, MC, V. Mon–Sat noon–3pm and 5:30–11:30pm (pretheater 5:30–7:30pm). Tube: Leicester Sq. SEAFOOD.

Established in 1896 by an Irish-born vaudevillian, Sheekeys is a series of small but intimate dining rooms, its walls covered with the photographs of stage-and-screen stars. Seafood is the specialty here, one of the few places in London that almost never (and only when specifically requested) fries its food. Instead, the delicate and fresh ingredients are steamed, grilled, or stewed, and then laden with such ingredients as sherry, cream, garlic, lemon, and herbs. The result is usually rich and delicious. Specialties include lobster Thermidor, Dover sole, jellied eels (a British delicacy), and grilled sea bass with endive.

SOHO

Moderate

Alastair Little. 49 Frith St., W1. ☎ **0171/734-5183.** Reservations recommended. Fixed-price dinner £25 ($40). AE, DC, MC, V. Mon–Fri noon–3pm; Mon–Sat 6–11:30pm. Tube: Leicester Sq. or Tottenham Court Rd. BRITISH.

In a circa-1830 brick-fronted town house—which for a brief period is said to have housed John Constable's art studio—this monochromatic restaurant provides an informal and cozy place for a well-prepared lunch or dinner. Owned by the British–Danish–Spanish trio of Alastair Little, Kirsten Pedersen (who directs the dining room), and André-Vega, it features a well-chosen menu with dishes that reflect whatever is available that day from the market. Examples include a fully flavored roasted sea bass with parsley salad, a tender rack of lamb with rosemary, or Tuscan squab.

The Ivy. 1–5 West St., WC2. ☎ **0171/836-4751.** Reservations required. Main courses £7–£15 ($11.20–$24); Sat–Sun lunch £14.50 ($23.20). AE, DC, MC, V. Daily noon–3pm and 5:30pm–midnight (last order). Tube: Leicester Sq. ENGLISH.

Effervescent and sophisticated, The Ivy has been intimately associated with the West End theater district since it was established in 1911. Meals are served until very late, ideal for after the theater. With its ersatz 1930s look, The Ivy is fun, humming, and throbbing. The menu choices appear deceptively simple, but they use fresh ingredients and are skillfully prepared. Dishes include white asparagus with sea kale and truffle butter; seared scallops with spinach, sorrel, and bacon; and salmon fish cakes.

Inexpensive

Chuen Cheng Ku. 17 Wardour St., W1. ☎ **0171/437-1398.** Reservations recommended on weekend afternoons. Main courses £6.40–£16.80 ($10.25–$26.90); fixed-price menus £9.50–£30 ($15.20–$48). AE, DC, MC, V. Daily 11am–11:45pm. Closed Dec 24–25. Tube: Piccadilly Circus or Leicester Sq. CHINESE.

This is one of the finest eateries in Soho's "New China." This large restaurant on several floors, which seats 400 diners, is noted for its Cantonese food and has the longest and most interesting such menu in London. Specialties are paper-wrapped prawns, rice in lotus leaves, steamed spareribs in black-bean sauce, and shredded pork with cashew nuts, all served in generous portions.

BLOOMSBURY

Moderate

Ⓢ **Museum Street Café.** 47 Museum St., W1. ☎ **0171/405-3211.** Reservations required. Lunch, £12.50 ($20) for two courses, £15.50 ($24.80) for three courses; dinner, £17.50 ($28) for two courses, £21.50 ($34.40) for three courses. MC, V. Mon–Fri 12:30–2:15pm (last order) and 6:30–9:30pm (last order). Tube: Tottenham Court Rd. MODERN BRITISH.

In an undistinguished building that's a 2-minute walk from the British Museum, this small-scale and charming dining room was the neighborhood's least appealing "greasy spoon" until it was transformed by Boston-born Gail Koerber and her English partner, Mark Nathan. Today—in a deliberately underfurnished setting filled with simple tables and chairs and lined with primitive paintings—you can sample up-to-date dishes, including smoked halibut fish cakes with a sherry-cayenne mayonnaise sauce or char-grilled swordfish with coriander, soy, and ginger. The kitchen is best when it's char-grilling.

THE STRAND
Moderate

Joe Allen's. 13 Exeter St., WC2. ☎ **0171/836-0651.** Reservations required. Main courses £6.50–£13.50 ($10.40–$21.60). No credit cards. Mon–Sat noon–1am, Sun noon–midnight. Tube: Covent Garden or Embankment. AMERICAN.

This fashionable American restaurant, lying north of The Strand near the Savoy Hotel, attracts primarily theater crowds. The decor is inspired by its New York branch, with theater posters and red-and-white gingham tablecloths. The menu lists such specialties as salmon, herb, and cheese quesadilla; broccoli with olive oil and lemon; and pecan pie. The menu has grown increasingly sophisticated in the past few years and might include such modern dishes as grilled corn-fed chicken with sunflower-seed pesto.

Simpson's-in-the-Strand. 100 The Strand, WC2. ☎ **0171/836-9112.** Reservations required. Jacket and tie for men. Main courses £14.50–£17.50 ($23.20–$28); fixed-price breakfast £10.50 ($16.80); fixed-price two-course lunch £10.50 ($16.80). AE, DC, MC, V. Mon–Fri 7am–noon; daily noon–2:30pm and 6–11pm. Tube: Charing Cross or Embankment. BRITISH.

Simpson's is more of an institution than a restaurant. Located next to the Savoy Hotel, it has been in business since 1828. All this very Victorian place needs is an empire. It has everything else: Adam paneling, crystal, and an army of grandly formal waiters hovering about. Nouvelle cuisine here means anything after Henry VIII. However, there is one point on which most diners agree: Simpson's serves the best roasts in London. Huge roasts are trolleyed to your table and you can have slabs of meat carved off and served with traditional Yorkshire pudding.

COVENT GARDEN
Moderate

Rules. 35 Maiden Lane, WC2. ☎ **0171/836-5314.** Reservations recommended. Main courses £11.95–£15.95 ($19.10–$25.50). AE, DC, MC, V. Daily noon–11:30pm. Tube: Covent Garden. ENGLISH.

London's most quintessentially British restaurant was established in 1798 as an oyster bar, and is lined with the framed memorabilia of the British Empire at its height. Around the turn of the century, Edward VII, portly future king of England, used to arrive here with his infamous mistress, Lillie Langtry. Their signed portraits still embellish the yellowing walls, along with that of Charles Dickens, who crafted several of his novels here. You can order such classic dishes as jugged hare, Aylesbury duckling in orange sauce, and game dishes year-round.

Inexpensive

Nag's Head. 10 James St., WC2. ☎ **0171/836-4678.** Reservations not accepted. Sandwich platters with salad £2.50–£4.95 ($4–$7.90); full-meal salads £4.25 ($6.80); main courses £4.95 ($7.90); pint of lager £1.80 ($2.90). AE, DC, MC, V. Mon–Sat 11:30am–11pm, Sun noon–10:30pm. Tube: Covent Garden. ENGLISH.

Nag's Head is one of the most famous Edwardian pubs of London. With the moving of the market, 300 years of British tradition faded away. Today, the pub is patronized mainly by young people who fill up all the tables every evening, including drinking space around the bar counter. Try a draft Guinness. Lunch is typical pub grub: sandwiches, salads, pork cooked in cider, and garlic prawns.

⑤ Porter's English Restaurant. 17 Henrietta St., WC2. ☎ **0171/836-6466.** Reservations recommended. Main courses £7–£8 ($11.20–$12.80); fixed-price menu £16.50 ($26.40). AE, DC, MC, V. Mon–Sat noon–11:30pm, Sun noon–10:30pm. Tube: Covent Garden or Charing Cross. ENGLISH.

Porter's specializes in classic English meat pies. Main courses are so generous that the menu eliminates appetizers. The traditional bangers and mash plate is featured daily. With whipped cream or custard, the "puddings" come hot or cold, including bread-and-butter pudding or steamed syrup sponge. The English call all desserts puddings, but at Porter's they are the real puddings, as the word is known in the American sense.

FLEET STREET
Inexpensive

🟢 Ye Olde Cheshire Cheese. Wine Office Court, 145 Fleet St., EC4. ☎ **0171/353-6170.** Main courses £11.95–£14.95 ($19.10–$23.90). AE, DC, MC, V. Daily noon–2:30pm and 6–9:30pm. Drinks and bar snacks available daily 11:30am–11pm. Tube: St. Paul's or Blackfriars. ENGLISH.

Dating from the 13th century, this is the most famous of the old City chophouses and pubs. It claims to be the spot where Dr. Samuel Johnson entertained admirers with his acerbic wit. Later, many of the ink-stained journalists and scandalmongers of 19th- and early 20th-century Fleet Street made its four-story premises their "local." Within, you'll find six bars and two dining rooms. The house specialties include "ye famous pudding"—steak, kidney, mushrooms, and game—and Scottish roast beef, with Yorkshire pudding and horseradish sauce.

WESTMINSTER
Moderate

Tate Gallery Restaurant. Millbank, SW1. ☎ **0171/887-8877.** Reservations required 2 days in advance. Main courses £10–£16 ($16–$25.60); two-course fixed-price lunch £12.50 ($20); three-course fixed-price lunch £15.50 ($24.80). MC, V. Mon–Sat noon–3pm. Tube: Pimlico. Bus: 77 or 88. ENGLISH.

The restaurant is particularly attractive to wine fanciers, offering what may be the best bargains for superior wines to be found anywhere in the country. It is especially strong on Bordeaux and Burgundies. Wine connoisseurs frequently come for lunch, regardless of whatever exhibits may be on view at the museum. If you're looking for food instead of (or in addition to) wine, the restaurant specializes in an English menu that changes about every month. Menu choices might include seafood crêpes; roast duck with spiced apricots; and steak, kidney, and mushroom pie.

CHELSEA
Very Expensive

🔵 La Tante Claire. 68–69 Royal Hospital Rd., SW3. ☎ **0171/352-6045.** Reservations required at least 2 weeks in advance. Main courses £24.50–£32 ($39.20–$51.20); three-course fixed-price lunch £26 ($41.60); minimum charge £60 ($96) per person. AE, DC, MC, V. Mon–Fri 12:30–2pm and 7–11pm. Closed Dec 24 and Jan 3. Tube: Sloane Sq. FRENCH.

This "Aunt Claire" has become, in the eyes of many critics, the leading choice among the capital's gaggle of French restaurants. A discreet doorbell, set into the Aegean blue-and-white facade, prompts an employee to usher you inside. Pierre Koffman is the celebrated chef, creating such specialties as ravioli langostino. Every gastronome in London talks about the pigs' trotters stuffed with morels and the exquisite sauces that complement many of the dishes. These include grilled scallops served on a bed of squid-ink sauce, baked filet of turbot with mustard-seed sauce on a bed of roasted leeks, and duck in red-wine sauce and confit.

Moderate

English Garden. 10 Lincoln St., SW3. ☎ **0171/584-7272.** Reservations required. Main courses £8.50–£17.25 ($13.60–$27.60); fixed-price lunch £15.75 ($25.20). AE, DC, MC, V.

Mon–Sat 12:30–2:30pm and 7:30–11:30pm, Sun 12:30–2pm and 7–10:30pm. Closed Dec 25–26. Tube: Sloane Sq. ENGLISH.

In this historic Chelsea town house, the Garden Room on the ground floor is white-washed brick with panels of large, stylish flowers. Rattan chairs in a Gothic theme and candy-pink napery complete the scene. With the domed conservatory roofs and banks of plants, this is a metropolitan restaurant par excellence. Every component of our last meal here was chopped or cooked to the right degree and well proportioned. Interesting dishes are a checkerboard of freshwater fish, including a steamed fish of the day, or roast rack of Welsh lamb with roasted garlic.

KENSINGTON

Moderate

Launceston Place Restaurant. 1A Launceston Place, W8. ☎ **0171/937-6912.** Reservations required. Main courses £14–£17 ($22.40–$27.20); fixed-price menu £14.50 ($23.20) for two courses, £17.50 ($28) for three courses. AE, MC, V. Mon–Sat 12:30–2:30pm and 7–11:30pm, Sun 12:30–3pm. Tube: Gloucester Rd. BRITISH.

In an almost village-like neighborhood, the architecturally stylish restaurant comprises a series of uncluttered Victorian parlors illuminated by a rear skylight and decorated with Victorian oils and watercolors, plus contemporary paintings. Known for its new British cuisine, the menu changes every 6 weeks, but might include such dishes as poached smoked haddock with parsley sauce, medaillons of pork with mustard sauce, or breast of duck with cider brandy.

SOUTH KENSINGTON

Expensive

♦ **Bibendum/Oyster Bar.** 81 Fulham Rd., SW3. ☎ **0171/581-5817.** Reservations required in Bibendum; not accepted in Oyster Bar. Main courses £15–£20 ($24–$32); three-course fixed-price lunch £27 ($43.20); cold seafood platter in Oyster Bar £22 ($35.20) per person. AE, MC, V. Bibendum, Mon–Fri 12:30–2:30pm and 7–11:15pm, Sat 12:30–3pm and 7–11:15pm, Sun 12:30–3pm and 7–10:15pm. Oyster Bar, Mon–Sat noon–11:30pm, Sun noon–3pm and 7–10:30pm. Tube: South Kensington. MODERN FRENCH/MEDITERRANEAN.

This fashionable eatery occupies two floors of a building that is one of the art-deco masterpieces of London. Built in 1911, it housed the British headquarters of the Michelin tire company. Bibendum, the more visible eatery, is located one floor above street level in a white-tiled room whose stained-glass windows, streaming sunlight, and chic clientele make meals extremely pleasant. Menu choices are carefully planned interpretations of seasonal ingredients, known for their freshness and simplicity, including red pepper and basil risotto, sautéed squid with aïoli and salsa, deep-fried cod with chips and tartar sauce, or breast of duck with garlic and sherry cream sauce. Simpler meals and cocktails are available on the building's street level, in the Oyster Bar.

Moderate

Hilaire. 68 Old Brompton Rd., SW7. ☎ **0171/584-8993.** Reservations recommended. Two-course fixed-price lunch £16.50 ($26.40); three-course fixed price lunch £20.50 ($32.80); three-course fixed-price dinner £29.50 ($47.20); four-course fixed-price dinner £34 ($54.40); dinner main courses £14.50–£19.50 ($23.20–$31.20). AE, DC, MC, V. Mon–Fri 12:15–2:30pm; Mon–Sat 6:30–11:30pm. Closed bank holidays. Tube: South Kensington. CONTINENTAL.

Hilaire is a jovially cramped restaurant, housed in what was originally a Victorian storefront. Chef Bryan Webb prepares a mixture of classical French and *cuisine moderne;* thus, this has become one of London's most stylish restaurants. The menu always reflects the best of the season's offerings, and main courses at dinner might include rack of lamb with tapenade and wild garlic, saddle of rabbit, or grilled tuna with Provençal vegetables.

AFTERNOON TEA

۞ Brown's Hotel. 29–34 Albemarle St., W1. ☎ **0171/493-6020.** Reservations not accepted. Afternoon tea £14.95 ($23.90). AE, DC, MC, V. Daily 3–5:45pm. Tube: Green Park.

The lounge is decorated with English antiques, wall panels, oil paintings, and floral chintz, much like a private English country estate. Give your name to the concierge upon arrival; arrangements will be made for you to be seated on clusters of sofas and settees or at low tables. The regular afternoon tea includes a choice of 10 different teas.

Claridge's. Brook St., W1. ☎ **0171/629-8860.** Reservations recommended. Jacket and tie for men. High tea £16.50 ($26.40). AE, DC, MC, V. Daily 3–5pm. Tube: Bond St.

Claridge's teatime rituals manage to persevere through the years with as much pomp and circumstance as the British Empire itself. A portrait of Lady Claridge gazes beneficently from the paneled walls as a choice of 17 kinds of tea is served ever-so-politely.

۞ Georgian Restaurant. On the fourth Floor of Harrods Department Store, 87–135 Brompton Rd., SW1. ☎ **0171/581-1656.** Teatime Mon–Sat 3:45–5:15pm (last order). High tea £12.75 ($20.40) per person. AE, DC, MC, V. Tube: Knightsbridge.

A flood of visitors is somehow gracefully herded into a high-volume but nevertheless elegant teatime venue, which is in a fourth-floor room that's so long its staff refers to its shape and size as "the Mississippi River." The list of teas available—at least 50—is sometimes so esoteric that the experience might remind you of the vintages within a sophisticated wine cellar.

۞ The Orangery. In the gardens of Kensington Palace, W8. ☎ **0171/376-0239.** Reservations not accepted. Pot of tea £1.60 ($2.55), summer cakes and puddings £1.90–£3.50 ($3.05–$5.60), sandwiches £5.95 ($9.50). MC, V. Apr–Sept 10am–6pm; Oct–Mar 10am–4pm. Tube: Kensington High St. or Queensway.

Set about 50 yards north of Kensington Palace, this tearoom occupies a long and narrow garden pavilion (The Orangery) built in 1704 by Queen Anne as a site for her tea parties. Rows of potted orange trees bask in sunlight from soaring windows, and tea is still served amid Corinthian columns, ruddy-colored bricks, and a pair of Grinling Gibbons woodcarvings.

ATTRACTIONS

SIGHTSEEING SUGGESTIONS

If You Have 1 Day   No first-time visitor should leave London without visiting Westminster Abbey. Then walk over to see Big Ben and the Houses of Parliament. You can walk up to 10 Downing St., home of the prime minister, or walk over to watch the Changing of the Guard at Buckingham Palace if it's being held. Have dinner at a restaurant in Covent Garden, perhaps Porter's English Restaurant. For your nightcap, head over to the Red Lion, 2 Duke of York St., in Mayfair, quite a Victorian pub.

If You Have 2 Days   Devote a good part of your second day to exploring the British Museum, one of the world's biggest and best museums. Spend the afternoon visiting the Tower of London and seeing the collection of crown jewels (expect slow-moving lines). Cap your day by boarding one of the London Launches to experience the city from the river. Go to one of London's landmark restaurants such as Simpson's-in-The-Strand, 100 The Strand.

If You Have 3 Days   In the morning of your third day, go to the National Gallery, facing Trafalgar Square. Then enjoy an afternoon at Madame Tussaud's Waxworks. Take some time to stroll through St. James's and try to catch a cultural performance at the South Bank Centre, site of the Royal Festival Hall.

If You Have 5 Days   In the morning of your fourth day, head for the City, the financial district in the East End. Here you'll tour Sir Christopher Wren's St. Paul's Cathedral. Spend a few hours strolling the City and visit a few of its many metropolitan attractions. In the late afternoon, head down King's Road in Chelsea to shop the many and varied boutiques. On your fifth day, explore the Victoria and Albert Museum in the morning, then head to the Tate Gallery for lunch at its restaurant. Finally, see where history was made during the dark days of World War II; visit the Cabinet War Rooms at Clive Steps (see below), where Churchill directed the British operations against the Nazis. In the evening, attend the theater.

THE TOP ATTRACTIONS

✪ **Tower of London.** Tower Hill, on the north bank of the Thames, EC3. ☎ **0171/709-0765.** Admission £8.30 ($13.30) adults, £6.25 ($10) students and senior citizens, £5.50 ($8.80) children. Free for children under 5. Family ticket for five (but no more than two adults), £20 ($32). Mar–Oct Mon–Sat 9am–6pm, Sun 10am–6pm; Nov–Feb Mon–Sat 9am–5pm, Sun 10am–5pm. Closed Dec 24–26, Jan 1. Tube: Tower Hill. Boats: From Westminster Pier.

This ancient fortress continues to pack in visitors because of its macabre associations with all the legendary figures who were imprisoned and/or executed here. The fortress is actually a compound, in which the oldest and finest structure is the White Tower, begun by William the Conqueror. Here you can view the Armouries, which dates from the reign of Henry VIII. A display of instruments of torture and execution will recall some of the most ghastly moments in the history of the Tower. To see the **Jewel House,** where the crown jewels are kept, go early in the day during summer because long lines often form. A palace once inhabited by King Edward I in the late 1200s was opened to visitors for the first time in 1993. Above Traitor's Gate, it is the only surviving medieval palace in Britain. One-hour tours are given by the Yeoman Warders at frequent intervals, starting at 9:30am from the Middle Tower near the main entrance. The tour includes the Chapel Royal of St. Peter ad Vincula (St. Peter in Chains). The last guided walk starts about 3:30pm in summer, 2:30pm in winter.

✪ **Westminster Abbey.** Broad Sanctuary, SW1. ☎ **0171/222-7110.** Free admission to abbey; £1.35 ($2.15) donation suggested. Royal Chapels, Royal Tombs, Coronation Chair, Lady Chapel, £4 ($6.40) adults, £1 ($1.60) children; free Wed evenings. Mon–Fri 9am–3:45pm, Sat 9:15am–1:45pm and 4–4:45pm. Tube: Westminster or St. James's Park.

In 1065 the Saxon king, Edward the Confessor, founded the Benedictine abbey and rebuilt the old minster church on this spot, overlooking Parliament Square. The first English king crowned in the abbey was Harold in 1066, before he was killed at the Battle of Hastings later that same year. The man who defeated him, Edward's cousin, William the Conqueror, was also crowned at the abbey; the coronation tradition has continued to the present day, broken only twice (Edward V and Edward VIII). The essentially early English Gothic structure existing today owes more to Henry III's plans than to those of any other sovereign, although many architects, including Wren, have contributed to the abbey. Built on the site of the ancient lady chapel in the early 16th century, Henry VII Chapel is one of the loveliest in Europe, with its fan vaulting, Knights of Bath banners, and Torrigiani-designed tomb of the king. You can also visit the most hallowed spot in the abbey, the shrine of Edward the Confessor (canonized in the 12th century). In the saint's chapel is the Coronation Chair, made at the command of Edward I in 1300 to display the Stone of Scone. Another noted spot is the Poets' Corner, to the right of the entrance to the Royal Chapel, with monuments to Chaucer, Shakespeare, "O Rare Ben Johnson" (his name misspelled), Samuel Johnson, the Brontë sisters, Thackeray, Dickens, Tennyson, Kipling, even the American Longfellow.

Houses of Parliament. Westminster Palace, Old Palace Yard, SW1. ☎ **0171/219-4272** for the House of Commons, or **0171/219-3107** for the House of Lords. Free admission. House of Lords, open to the public Mon–Thurs 9:30am–2:30pm; also some Fri (check by phone). House of Commons, open to the public Mon, Tues, and Thurs from 2:30pm, Wed and Fri from 9:30am. Join line at St. Stephen's entrance. Tube: Westminster.

These Houses are the stronghold of Britain's democracy, the assemblies that effectively trimmed the sails of royal power. Both Houses (Commons and Lords) are situated in the former royal Palace of Westminster, the king's residence until Henry VIII moved to Whitehall. The present Houses of Parliament were built in 1840, but the Commons chamber was bombed and destroyed by the Luftwaffe in 1941. The 320-foot tower that houses Big Ben, however, remained standing and the "symbol of London" continues to strike its chimes. Except for the Strangers' Galleries, the two Houses of Parliament are closed to tourists. To be admitted to the Strangers' Galleries, join the public line outside the St. Stephen's entrance; often there is a delay before the line is admitted.

✪ **British Museum.** Great Russell St., WC1. ☎ **0171/636-1555.** Free admission. Mon–Sat 10am–5pm, Sun 2:30–6pm (the galleries start to close 10 minutes earlier). Closed Jan 1, Good Friday, early May, Dec 24–26. Tube: Holborn, Tottenham Court Rd., or Russell Sq.

The British Museum shelters one of the world's most comprehensive collections of art and artifacts, including countless treasures of ancient and modern civilizations. Even on a cursory first visit, be sure to see the Asian collections (the finest assembly of Islamic pottery outside the Islamic world), the Chinese porcelain, the Indian sculpture, and the Prehistoric and Romano–British collections. The overall storehouse splits basically into the national collections of antiquities; prints and drawings; coins and medals; and ethnography. The Assyrian Transept on the ground floor displays the winged and human-headed bulls and lions that once guarded the gateways to the palaces of Assyrian kings. From here you can continue into the angular hall of Egyptian sculpture to see the Rosetta stone, whose discovery led to the deciphering of hieroglyphs. Also on the ground floor is the Duveen Gallery, housing the Elgin marbles, now subject of much controversy. The Sutton Hoo Anglo-Saxon burial ship, discovered in Suffolk, is, in the words of an expert, "the richest treasure ever dug from English soil." The Portland Vase, one of the most celebrated possessions of the British Museum, was found in 1582 outside Rome. In the Manuscript "Saloon" (yes, that's right) are two of the four surviving copies of the Magna Carta (1215).

✪ **Buckingham Palace.** At the end of The Mall (the street running from Trafalgar Sq.). ☎ **0171/839-1377.** Palace tours £8 ($12.80) adults to age 60, £6 ($9.60) adults over 60, £4.50 ($7.20) children under 17. (*Warning:* These ticket prices, or even the possibility of public admission to Buckingham Palace, depend entirely on the whim of the queen, since it is her home.) Changing of the guard free. Palace tours: Check tourist information offices, local publications. Changing of the guard: Call Visitorcall at **01839/123-411** for the most up-to-date information about the ceremony. Toll charges 39p–49p (60¢–80¢) per minute. Tube: St. James's Park, Green Park, or Victoria.

This massively graceful building is the official residence of the queen, and you can tell whether Her Majesty is at home by the Royal Standard flying at the masthead. In spring 1993, Queen Elizabeth II agreed to allow visitors for the first time to tour her state apartments and picture galleries. The palace will be open to the public for

Central London Attractions

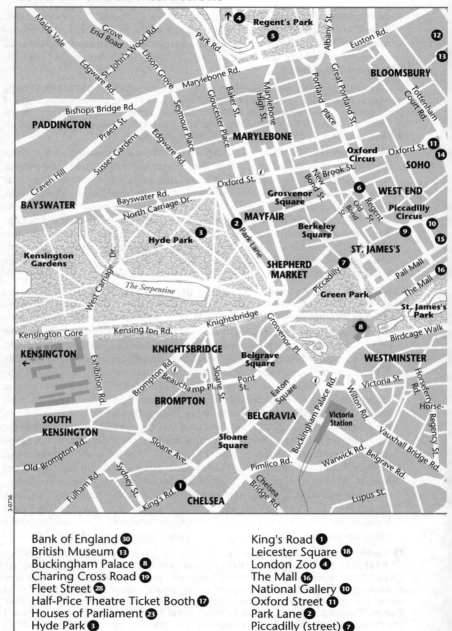

Bank of England ⓾
British Museum ⓭
Buckingham Palace ➑
Charing Cross Road ⓳
Fleet Street ⓰
Half-Price Theatre Ticket Booth ⓱
Houses of Parliament ㉓
Hyde Park ➌

King's Road ➊
Leicester Square ⓲
London Zoo ➍
The Mall ⓰
National Gallery ➓
Oxford Street ⓫
Park Lane ➋
Piccadilly (street) ➐

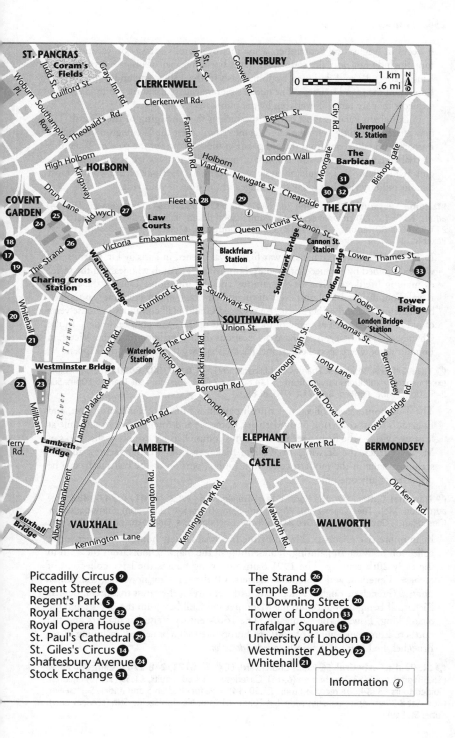

Piccadilly Circus ⑨
Regent Street ⑥
Regent's Park ⑤
Royal Exchange ㉜
Royal Opera House ㉕
St. Paul's Cathedral ㉙
St. Giles's Circus ⑭
Shaftesbury Avenue ㉔
Stock Exchange ㉛

The Strand ㉖
Temple Bar ㉗
10 Downing Street ⑳
Tower of London ㉝
Trafalgar Square ⑮
University of London ⑫
Westminster Abbey ㉒
Whitehall ㉑

Information ⓘ

8 weeks in August and September, when the royal family is away on vacation. The tours include not only the state apartments but a number of other rooms used by King George IV and designed by John Nash in the 1800s, including the Throne Room and the grand staircase. The queen's picture gallery has some world-class masterpieces that are rarely if ever seen by the public.

Buckingham Palace's most famous spectacle is the **Changing of the Guard.** The new guard, marching behind a band, comes from either the Wellington or Chelsea Barracks and takes over from the old guard in the forecourt of the palace. When this martial ceremony occurs is the subject of mass confusion—when it happens, it begins at 11:30am. You should always check locally to see if one of the world's most famous military rituals is likely to be staged at the time of your visit.

Madame Tussaud's. Marylebone Rd., NW1. ☎ **0171/935-6861.** Admission £8.75 ($14) adults, £5.75 ($9.20) children under 16. Combination tickets, including the new planetarium, £11.75 ($18.80) adults, £7.50 ($12) children under 16. Mon–Sat 10am–5:30pm. Tube: Baker St.

In 1770, an exhibition of life-size wax figures was opened in Paris by Dr. Curtius. He was soon joined by his niece, Strasbourg-born Marie Tussaud, who learned the secret of making lifelike replicas of the famous and the infamous. During the French Revolution, the head of almost every distinguished victim of the guillotine was molded by Madame Tussaud or her uncle. An enlarged Grand Hall continues to house years of old favorites, as well as many of today's heads of state and political leaders. In the Chamber of Horrors, you can have the vicarious thrill of walking through a Victorian London street where special effects include the shadowy terror of Jack the Ripper.

✪ **Tate Gallery.** Beside the Thames on Millbank, SW1. ☎ **0171/887-8000.** Free admission, except special exhibitions varying from £3 ($4.80) to £7 ($11.20). Mon–Sat 10am–5:50pm, Sun 2–5:50pm. Tube: Pimlico. Bus: 77A, C10, or 88.

The Tate houses two collections: British paintings from the 16th century on, and England's finest collection of modern art, domestic and foreign. Try to schedule at least two visits—the first to see the museum's comprehensive exhibit of the works of M. W. Turner, the drawings of William Blake, and the pre-Raphaelites, and the second to take in the modern collection. Only a portion of the collections can be displayed at any one time.

✪ **National Gallery.** On the north side of Trafalgar Sq., WC2. ☎ **0171/747-2885.** Free admission. Mon–Tues 10am–6pm, Wed 10am–8pm, Thurs–Sat 10am–6pm, Sun noon–6pm. Closed Jan 1, Good Friday, and Dec 24–26. Tube: Charing Cross, Embankment, or Leicester Sq.

In an impressive neoclassical building the National Gallery houses a comprehensive collection of Western painting, representing all the major schools from the 13th to the early 20th century. The 1991 Sainsbury wing houses the large collection of Sienese, Venetian, and Florentine masters. Of the early gothic works, the *Wilton Diptych* (French or English school, late 14th century) is the rarest treasure; it depicts Richard II being introduced to the Madonna and Child by John the Baptist and the Saxon king, Edward the Confessor. The 16th-century Venetian masters and the northern European painters of northern Europe are well represented, including Pieter Brueghel the Elder's Bosch-influenced *Adoration*.

✪ **St. Paul's Cathedral.** St. Paul's Churchyard, EC4. ☎ **0171/248-2705.** Cathedral £3.50 ($5.60) adults, £2 ($3.20) children (6–16). Galleries £3 ($4.80) adults, £1.50 ($2.40) children. Guided tours £3 ($4.80), recorded tours £2.50 ($4). Free for children 5 and under. Sightseeing Mon–Sat 8:30am–4pm; galleries Mon–Sat 10am–4:15pm. No sightseeing Sun (services only). Tube: St. Paul's.

It was during the Great Fire of 1666 that the old St. Paul's was razed, making way for a new Renaissance structure designed by Sir Christopher Wren and built between 1675 and 1710. The classical dome of St. Paul's dominates the City's square mile. Inside, the cathedral is laid out like a Greek cross; it houses few art treasures but has many monuments, including a memorial chapel to American service personnel who lost their lives in World War II. Encircling the dome is the Whispering Gallery, where discretion in speech is advised. Wren lies in the crypt, along with the Duke of Wellington and Lord Nelson.

✪ **Victoria and Albert Museum.** Cromwell Rd., SW7. ☎ **0171/938-8500.** Free admission, but donations of £4.50 ($7.20) suggested for adults, £1 ($1.60) for students and senior citizens. Children under 12 are not asked for a donation. Mon noon–5:50pm, Tues–Sun 10am–5:50pm. Jazz Brunch Sun 11am–3pm. Tube: South Kensington.

The general theme here is the fine and decorative arts. Medieval holdings include many treasures, such as the Eltenberg Reliquary (Rhenish, second half of the 12th century); the Early English Gloucester Candlestick; the Byzantine Veroli Casket, with its ivory panels based on Greek plays; and the Syon Cope, a highly valued embroidery made in England in the early 14th century. An area devoted to Islamic art houses the Ardabil carpet from 16th-century Persia (320 knots per square inch). The Victoria and Albert has the largest collection of Renaissance sculpture outside Italy, including a Donatello marble relief. Raphael's cartoons for tapestries for the Sistine Chapel, owned by the queen, can also be seen here.

MORE ATTRACTIONS

Official London

Whitehall, SW1, the seat of the British government, grew up on the grounds of Whitehall Palace and was turned into a royal residence by Henry VIII, who snatched it from its former occupant, Cardinal Wolsey. Whitehall extends south from Trafalgar Square to Parliament Square. Along it you'll find the Home Office, the Old Admiralty Building, and the Ministry of Defence.

Visitors today can see the **Cabinet War Rooms,** the bombproof bunker suite of rooms, just as they were left by Winston Churchill at the end of World War II. You can see the Map Room with its huge wall maps; the Atlantic map is a mass of pinholes (each hole represents at least one convoy). Next door is Churchill's bedroom-cum-office, which has two BBC microphones on the desk for his broadcasts of those famous speeches that stirred the nation. The entrance to the War Rooms is by Clive Steps at the end of King Charles Street, SW1 (☎ **0171/930-6961;** tube: Westminster or St. James's), off Whitehall near Big Ben. Admission is £4.20 ($6.70) for adults and £2.10 ($3.35) for children. The rooms are open Apr–Sept daily 9:30am–6pm (last admission 5:15pm); Oct–March daily 10am–5:30pm; closed on Christmas holidays.

Museums

Imperial War Museum. Lambeth Rd., SE1. ☎ **0171/416-5000.** Admission £4.50 ($7.20) adults, £2.25 ($3.60) children; free daily 4:30–6pm. Daily 10am–6pm. Closed Dec 24–26. Tube: Lambeth North or Elephant & Castle.

Built around 1815, this large domed building, the former Bethlehem Royal Hospital for the Insane (or Bedlam), houses collections relating to the two world wars and other military operations. There are four floors of exhibitions, including a vast area showing historical displays, two floors of art galleries, and a dramatic re-creation of London at war during the blitz.

Apsley House. The Wellington Museum, 149 Piccadilly, Hyde Park Corner, W1. ☎ **0171/499-5676.** Admission £3 ($4.80) adults, £1.50 ($2.40) seniors and children (12–17), free for children under 12, £7 ($11.20) family ticket. Tues–Sun 11am–5pm. Closed Jan 1, May Day, Dec 24–26. Tube: Hyde Park Corner.

This former town house of the Iron Duke, the British general (1769–1852) who defeated Napoléon at the Battle of Waterloo and later became prime minister, was opened as a public museum in 1952. The building was designed by Robert Adam and was constructed in the late 18th century.

Museum of London. 150 London Wall, EC2. ☎ **0171/600-3699.** Admission £3.50 ($5.60) adults, £1.75 ($2.80) children. Tues–Sat 10am–5:50pm, Sun noon–5:50pm. Tube: St. Paul's, Barbican, or Moorgate.

In London's Barbican district near St. Paul's Cathedral, the Museum of London traces the history of London from prehistoric times to the postmodern era through relics, costumes, household effects, maps, and models. Anglo-Saxons, Vikings, Normans—they're all here, displayed on two floors around a central courtyard.

Galleries

National Portrait Gallery. St. Martin's Place, WC2. ☎ **0171/306-0055.** Free admission, except for special exhibitions. Mon–Sat 10am–6pm; Sun noon–6pm. Tube: Charing Cross or Leicester Sq.

The National Portrait Gallery was founded in 1856 to collect the likenesses of famous British men and women. Today the collection is the most comprehensive of its kind in the world and constitutes a unique record of those who created the history and culture of the nation. A few paintings will catch your eye, including Sir Joshua Reynold's portrait of Samuel Johnson ("a man of most dreadful appearance"). You'll also see a portrait of William Shakespeare, which is claimed to be the most "authentic contemporary likeness" of its subject of any work yet known, and the portrait of the Brontë sisters, painted by their brother Branwell.

London's Parks

London's parklands easily rate as the greatest "green lung" system of any large city. One of the biggest is **Hyde Park.** With the adjoining Kensington Gardens, it covers 636 acres of central London with velvety lawn interspersed with ponds, flower beds, and trees. **Kensington Gardens** are home to the celebrated statue of Peter Pan with the bronze rabbits that toddlers are always trying to kidnap. East of Hyde Park, across Piccadilly, stretch **Green Park** and **St. James's Park,** forming an almost-unbroken chain of landscaped beauty. This is an ideal area for picnics. You'll find it hard to believe this was once a festering piece of swamp near the leper hospital. **Regent's Park,** north of Baker Street and Marylebone Road, was designed by the 18th-century genius John Nash to surround a palace that never materialized. The **open-air theater** and the **London Zoo** are in this most classically beautiful of London's parks.

ORGANIZED TOURS

One of the most popular bus tours is called **"The Original London Sightseeing Tour,"** where London unfolds from a traditional double-decker bus, with live commentary by a guide. The 1½-hour sightseeing tour costs £10 ($16) for adults, £5 ($8) for children under 16. The tour plus Madame Tussaud's is £17 ($27.20) for adults and £9 ($14.40) for children. You can buy tickets on the bus or from any London Transport or London Tourist Board Information Centre, where you can receive a discount. Departures are from various convenient points within the city. For information or ticket purchases on the phone, call **0181/877-1722.** It's also possible to write for tickets: **London Coaches,** Jews Row, London SW18 1TB.

Touring boats operate on the Thames all year and can take you to various places within Greater London. Main embarkation points are Westminster Pier, Charing Cross Pier, and Tower Pier—a system that enables you, for instance, to take a "water taxi" from the Tower of London to Westminster Abbey. Several companies operate motor launches, offering panoramic views of one of Europe's most historic waterways en route. For information and reservations, call **Westminster Passenger Service Association** (Upstream Division), Westminster Pier, Victoria Embankment, SW1 (☎ **0171/930-2062**).

John Wittich, of **J. W. Promotions,** 66 St. Michael's St., W2 (☎ **0171/262-9572**), started walking tours of London in 1960. He is a Freeman of the City of London and a member of two of the ancient guilds of London. There's no better way to search out the unusual, the beautiful, and the historic than to take his walking tour. A 1¹/₂- to 2-hour walking tour costs £15 ($24) for one or two adults, with £10 ($16) per hour assessed for extended walks. A whole-day guided tour costs £60 ($96). **Discovery Tours** (☎ **0171/256-8973**) offers a number of interesting walks, including a ghost walk and a Jack the Ripper walk.

SHOPPING

Together with Kensington and Brompton roads, **Knightsbridge** (tube: Knightsbridge) forms an extremely busy shopping district south of Hyde Park. It's patronized for furniture, antiques, jewelry, and Harrods department store. **Harrods,** 87–135 Brompton Rd., Knightsbridge (☎ **0171/730-1234**), is London's—indeed Europe's—top department store. It's an institution, and visitors have come to view it as a sightseeing attraction. The sheer range, variety, and quality of merchandise is dazzling—be sure not to miss the delicatessen and food halls. The store has been refurbished to restore it to the elegance and luxury of the 1920s and 1930s.

Beauchamp Place (tube: Knightsbridge), pronounced like "Beecham," is a block off Brompton Road, near Harrods department store. Whatever you're looking for— from a pâté de marcassin to a carved pine mantelpiece—you are likely to find it here.

Kensington High Street (tube: Kensington High St.) has been called "the Oxford Street of West London." Stretching for about 1¹/₂ miles, it includes numerous shops. Many establishments are on adjacent side streets, including Earl's Court and Abington roads. From Kensington High Street, you can walk up Kensington Church Street, which, like Portobello Road, is one of the city's main shopping avenues.

King's Road (tube: Sloane Sq.), the main street of Chelsea, which starts at Sloane Square, will forever remain a symbol of London in the "swinging sixties." In the 1990s, King's Road is a lineup of markets and "multistores," large or small conglomerations of in- and outdoor stands, stalls, and booths within one building or enclosure.

Oxford Street (tube: Tottenham Court Rd.), the main shopping artery of London, runs from St. Giles Circus to Marble Arch. It's an endless, faceless, totally uninspiring but utility-crammed strip of stores, stores, and yet more stores. Here you'll find six of London's major department stores. One of Europe's largest, **Selfridges,** 400 Oxford St. (☎ **0171/629-1234**), has more than 500 divisions selling everything from artificial flowers to groceries. The specialty shops are particularly enticing, with good buys in Irish linens, Wedgwood china, leather goods, silver-plated goblets, cashmere items, and woolen scarves. There's also the Miss Selfridge Boutique.

Curving down elegantly from Oxford Circus to Piccadilly Circus, **Regent Street** (tube: Piccadilly Circus) is crammed with fashionable stores selling everything from silks to silverware. This stylish thoroughfare has both department stores and boutiques, but the accent is on the medium-size establishment in the upper-medium price range.

Divided into New and Old, **Bond Street** (tube: Bond St.) connects Piccadilly with Oxford Street and is synonymous with the luxury trade. Here are found the very finest—and most expensive—antique shops, hatters, jewelers, milliners, tailors, shoe stores, and sporting goods establishments.

Burlington Arcade (tube: Piccadilly Circus), the famous glass-roofed, Regency-style passage leading off Piccadilly, looks like a period exhibition and is lined with intriguing shops and boutiques.

After four centuries, **Covent Garden Market** (☎ 0171/836-9136), the most famous market in all England—possibly all Europe—has gone suburban. The actual fruit-and-vegetable market followed the lead of Les Halles in Paris and shifted to more contemporary but less colorful quarters south of the River Thames. Today's Covent Garden (tube: Covent Garden) has developed into an impressive array of shops, pubs, and other attractions in the old market buildings.

A magnet for collectors of virtually anything, **Portobello Market** (tube: Ladbroke Grove or Notting Hill Gate) is mainly a Saturday happening from 6am (it's best to go early) to 5pm. Portobello in the past four decades has become synonymous with antiques. But don't take the stallholder's word for it that the fiddle he's holding is a genuine Stradivarius left to him in the will of his Italian great-uncle. It might just as well have been "nicked" from an East End pawnshop.

LONDON AFTER DARK

Weekly publications such as *Time Out* and *Where,* available at newsstands, give full entertainment listings and contain information on restaurants, nightclubs, and theaters. You'll also find listings in daily newspapers, notably *The Times* and *The Telegraph.*

THE PERFORMING ARTS

If you want to see specific shows—especially hit ones—purchase your tickets in advance. The best way to do this is to buy your ticket from the theater's box office. Often you can call in advance—many theaters will accept bookings by telephone if you give your name and credit-card number when you call. You can also make theater reservations through ticket agents, such as **Keith Prowse/First Call,** Suite 1000, 234 W. 44th St., New York, NY 10036 (☎ 800/669-8687 or 212/398-1430, or 0171/836-9001 in London). The fee for booking a ticket in the United States is 35%; in London, it's 25%.

Theater

A recent addition to London's theater scene is the replica of Shakespeare's **Globe Theater,** on its original site at New Globe walk, Bankside, SE1 (☎ 0171/928-6406). Performances are staged as they were in Elizabethan times, without lighting or scenery or such luxuries as cushioned seats or a roof over the audience. Tours are given daily 10am–5pm and cost £5 ($8) adults, £3 children. Performance tickets and schedules vary; call for details. Tube: Mansion House.

✪ **Royal Shakespeare Company (RSC).** Barbican Centre, Silk St., Barbican, EC2. ☎ 0171/ 638-8891 (box office). Barbican Theatre, £7.50–£22 ($12–$35.20); The Pit, £15 ($24) matinees and evening performances. Tube: Barbican or Moorgate.

One of the world's finest theater companies is based in Stratford-upon-Avon and here at the Barbican Centre. The central core of the company's work remains the plays of William Shakespeare, but it also presents a wide-ranging program. There are three different productions each week in the Barbican Theatre—the 1,200-seat main auditorium, which has excellent sight lines throughout, thanks to a raked orchestra—and the Pit, the small studio space where much of the company's new writing is presented.

✪ **Royal National Theatre.** South Bank, SE1. ☎ **0171/928-2252.** Tickets £9.50–£22.50 ($15.20–$36); midweek matinees, Sat matinees, and previews cost less. Mon–Sat 10am–11pm. Tube: Waterloo, Embankment, or Charing Cross.

Occupying a prime site on the South Bank of the River Thames is the flagship of British theater, the Royal National Theatre. Home to one of the world's greatest stage companies, the National houses three theaters. The largest is named after Lord Olivier, with 1,200 seats and a style reminiscent of the Greek amphitheater with its fan-shaped open stage.

Classical Music & Opera

The fabled **Royal Opera House** in Covent Garden will be closed for renovation in June of 1997, and will not reopen until fall 1999. In the meantime, the **Royal Opera** and the **Royal Ballet** will be performing in venues to be announced. For information and tickets, call 0171/304-4000.

London Coliseum. London Coliseum, St. Martin's Lane, WC2. ☎ **0171/632-8300** for reservations. Tickets, £6–£12 ($9.60–$19.20) balcony, £10–£50 ($16–$80) upper dress circle or stalls. Tube: Charing Cross or Leicester Sq.

The London Coliseum, built in 1904 as a variety theater and converted into an opera house in 1968, is London's largest and most splendid theater. The **English National Opera,** one of the two national opera companies, performs a wide range of works, from great classics to Gilbert and Sullivan to new and experimental works, staged with flair and imagination.

Royal Albert Hall. Kensington Gore, SW7. ☎ **0171/589-8212.** Tickets £8–£120 ($12.80–$192). Tube: South Kensington, Kensington High St., or Knightsbridge.

Since 1941, the hall has been the setting for the BBC Henry Wood Promenade Concerts ("The Proms"), 8 weeks mid-July–mid-Sept. A British tradition since 1895, the programs are outstanding and often present newly commissioned works for the first time. For tickets, call Ticketmaster at **0171/379-4444** instead of Royal Albert Hall directly.

✪ **South Bank Centre, Royal Festival Hall.** On the South Bank, SE1. ☎ **0171/928-8800.** Tickets £5–£35 ($8–$56); credit cards accepted. Box office 10am–9pm. Tube: Waterloo or Embankment.

Across Waterloo Bridge rise three of the most comfortable and acoustically perfect concert halls in the world: Royal Festival Hall, Queen Elizabeth Hall, and the Purcell Room. Within their precincts, more than 1,200 performances a year are presented.

THE CLUB & MUSIC SCENE

Nightclubs & Cabarets

Camden Palace. 1A Camden High St., NW1. ☎ **0171/387-0428.** Cover £2–£4 ($3.20–$6.40) Tues–Wed, £8–£15 ($12.80–$24) Fri–Sat. Tube: Camden Town or Mornington Crescent.

Camden Palace is housed inside what was originally a theater built around 1910. It draws an over-18 crowd that flocks there in various costumes and energy levels according to the night of the week. Since it offers a rotating style of music, it's best to phone in advance to see if that evening's musical genre appeals to your taste. Open Tues–Wed 9pm–2:30am, Fri 9pm–4am, Sat 9pm–6am.

The Green Room at the Café Royal. 68 Regent St., W1. ☎ **0171/437-9090.** Reservations recommended. Tues–Sat dinner at 7:15pm followed by 60- to 90-minute show. Tube: Piccadilly Circus.

Set one floor above street level, in a sober and modern function room poised amid the gilded and frescoed premises of the Café Royal, the establishment offers a changing cast of well-known singers and comics. Many visitors opt for dinner before the show begins; others arrive just for the entertainment. A three-course dinner, without wine, followed by the show, costs £48 ($76.80) per person Tues–Thurs and £55 ($88) Fri–Sat; the cover charge for the show without dinner is £20 ($32) Tues–Thurs and £25 ($40) Fri–Sat. Drinks cost from £4 ($6.40) each.

Tiddy Dols. 55 Shepherd Market, Mayfair, W1. ☎ **0171/499-2357.** Main courses £8.95–£13.95 ($14.30–$22.30). Tube: Green Park.

Housed in nine small atmospheric Georgian houses that were built around 1741, Tiddy Dols is named after the famous gingerbread baker and eccentric. Guests come to Tiddy Dols to enjoy such dishes as jugged hare, cock-a-leekie, plum pudding, and the original gingerbread of Tiddy Dol. While dining, they are entertained with madrigals, Noël Coward tunes, Gilbert and Sullivan music, and vaudeville and music-hall songs. Open Mon–Sat noon–midnight, Sun noon–11pm.

Comedy

The Comedy Store, Coventry Street and Oxendon, off Piccadilly Circus (☎ **01426/914433**), is London's most visible showcase for both established and emerging comic talent. Even if the performers are unfamiliar to you, you will still enjoy the spontaneity of live British comedy. Visitors must be over 18 years of age. Reservations are accepted through Ticketmaster at 0171/344-4444, and the club opens 1½ hours before each show. Cover is £8 ($12.80) Mon–Thurs, £10 ($16) Sat, £9 ($14.40) Fri and Sun. Open daily 8pm–midnight.

Rock

A long-established venue for electronic and rock-and-roll bands, **The Rock Garden,** 6–7 The Piazza, Covent Garden (☎ **0171/836-4052**), maintains a bar and a stage in the cellar and a restaurant on the street level. The cellar area, known as The Venue, has hosted such names as Dire Straits, The Police, and U2 before they became more famous (and more expensive). Cover is £2–£12 ($3.20–$19.20); diners enter free. Open Mon–Thurs 5pm–3am, Fri 5pm–6am, Sat 4pm–4am, Sun 7:30–11pm.

Jazz & Blues

Blue Note. 1 Hoxton Sq., N1. ☎ **0171/729-2476.** Cover £4–£10 ($6.40–$16). Drinks from £3 ($4.80). Tube: Old St.

This club presents performances that range from traditional jazz, such as the music of Jessica Williams, all the way to contemporary hip-hop and funk. Friday and Saturday are club nights with deejays. Open Mon–Sat 10pm–3am, Sun 1pm–midnight.

Ronnie Scott's. 47 Frith St., W1. ☎ **0171/439-0747.** Cover Mon–Thurs £12 ($19.20), Fri–Sat £14 ($22.40). Tube: Tottenham Court Rd., Leicester Sq., or Piccadilly Circus.

Mention the word *jazz* in London and people immediately think of Ronnie Scott's, long the citadel of modern jazz in Europe, where the best English and American groups are booked. Featured on almost every bill is an American band, often with a top-notch singer. In the Main Room you can either stand at the bar to watch the show or sit at a table, where you can order dinner. The Downstairs Bar is more intimate. On weekends the Upstairs Room is separate and it has a disco called Club Latino. Drinks begin at £2.30 ($3.70); a half pint of beer, £1.20 ($1.90). Open Mon–Sat 8:30pm–3am.

Dance Clubs & Discos

Equinox. Leicester Sq., WC2. ☎ **0171/437-1446.** Cover £5–£10 ($8–$16). Tube: Leicester Sq.

The Equinox has nine bars, the largest dance floor in London, and a restaurant modeled along the lines of an American diner from the 1950s. With the exception of "rave" music, virtually every kind of dance music is featured here. Open Mon–Thurs 9pm–3am, Fri–Sat 9pm–4am.

Hippodrome. Leicester Sq., WC2. ☎ **0171/437-4311.** Cover £4–£10 ($6.40–$16). Tube: Leicester Sq.

This is one of London's greatest discos, an enormous place where light and sound beam in on you from all directions. Revolving speakers even descend from the roof to deafen you in patches, and you can watch yourself on closed-circuit video. Drinks run £3 ($4.80) and up. Open Mon–Sat 9pm–3am.

Gay & Lesbian Clubs & Bars

The most reliable source of information on gay clubs and activities is the **Gay Switchboard** (☎ **0171/837-7324**). The staff runs a 24-hour service for information on places and activities catering to homosexual men and women.

Heaven, The Arches, Craven St. (☎ **0171/930-2020**), is set within the vaulted cellars of Charing Cross Railway Station. Painted black inside, and reminiscent of a very large air-raid shelter, Heaven is the biggest and best-established gay venue in Great Britain. Call before you go to learn the latest format. Cover is £4–£8 ($6.40–$12.80). Open Tues–Sat 10:30pm–3:30am, Sun 9pm–1am.

Brief Encounter, 41 St. Martin's Lane (☎ **0171/240-2221**), is the most frequented West End gay pub. Bars are on two levels, but even so it's hard to find room to stand up, much less drink. Some men are in jeans, leather, or whatever, whereas others are dressed in business suits from their stockbroker jobs in the City. Lager starts at £1.88 ($3). Open Mon–Sun noon–11pm; in winter, closed Sun.

The Duke of Wellington, 110 Balls Pond Rd. (☎ **0171/249-3729**), is now one of the most popular gay bars in North London, with a good percentage of gay women. Divided into two rooms, each with its own bar and its own devoted corps of aficionados, it hosts Saturday night disco parties (free entrance) and live music at least one night a week. Open Mon–Sat noon–midnight, Sun noon–11pm. Pints of lager start at £1.95 ($3.10).

THE BAR SCENE

At the **American Bar,** in The Savoy, The Strand (☎ **0171/836-4343**), still one of the most sophisticated gathering places in London, the bartender is known for such special concoctions as the "Savoy Affair" and the "Prince of Wales," as well as for making the best martini in town. Jazz piano music is featured Mon–Sat 7–11pm. Drinks cost £6.15 ($9.85). Open Mon–Sat 11am–3pm and 5:30–11pm, Sun noon–3pm and 7–10:30pm.

Rumours, 33 Wellington St. (☎ **0171/836-0038**), is the kind of place where you might expect Tom Cruise to turn up as bartender. Set within what functioned a century ago as a wholesale flower market, Rumours combines 1990s sophistication with a flamboyant marine theme. Cocktails cost from £3 to £5 ($4.80 to $8). Open Mon–Sat 5–11pm.

Smollensky's Balloon, in the basement of 1 Dover St. (☎ **0171/491-1199**), is an American eatery and drinking bar that's packed with Mayfair office workers during happy hour. The place has a 1930s piano bar atmosphere and serves standard

American-style fare. House cocktails (good measures) cost £3.95 ($6.30); beer, £2.25 ($3.60). Open Mon–Sat noon–midnight, Sun noon–10:30pm.

CASINOS

There are at least 25 casinos in the West End alone, with many more scattered throughout the suburbs. But we cannot make specific recommendations. Under a new law, casinos aren't allowed to advertise, which in this context would mean appearing in a guidebook. It isn't illegal to gamble, only to advertise a gambling establishment. Most hall porters can tell you where you can gamble in London. You will be required to become a member of your chosen club, and then you must wait 24 hours before you can play at the tables . . . and then it must be strictly for cash. The most common games are roulette, blackjack, punto banco, and baccarat.

DAY TRIPS FROM LONDON

✪ **HAMPTON COURT PALACE**   On the north side of the Thames, 13 miles west of London in East Molesey, Surrey, this 16th-century palace of Cardinal Wolsey (☎ **0181/781-9500**) can teach us a lesson: Don't try to outdo your boss— particularly if he happens to be Henry VIII. The rich cardinal did just that, and he eventually lost his fortune, power, and prestige and ended up giving his lavish palace to the Tudor monarch. Henry took over, even outdoing the Wolsey embellishments. Although the palace enjoyed prestige and pomp in Elizabethan days, it owes much of its present look to William and Mary—or rather to Sir Christopher Wren, who designed and had built the Northern or Lion Gates. You can parade through the apartments today, filled as they are with porcelain, furniture, paintings, and tapestries. The King's Dressing Room is graced with some of the best art, mainly paintings by old masters on loan from Queen Elizabeth II.

The gardens—including the Great Vine, King's Privy Garden, Great Fountain Gardens, Tudor and Elizabethan Knot Gardens, Board Walk, Tiltyard, and Wilderness—are open daily year-round 7am–dusk (but not later than 9pm) and can be visited free except for the Privy Garden for which admission is £1.70 ($2.70), unless you pay for a palace ticket. The cloisters, courtyards, state apartments, great kitchen, cellars, and Hampton Court exhibition are open mid-March to mid-Oct daily 9:30am–6pm, and mid-Oct to mid-March Mon 10:15am–6pm and Tues–Sun 9:30am–6pm. The Tudor tennis court and banqueting house are open the same hours as above, but only from mid-March to mid-Oct. Admission to all these attractions is £7.50 ($12) for adults, £5.60 ($8.95) for students and senior citizens, and £4.90 ($7.85) for children 5 to 15 (free for children under 5).

You can get to Hampton Court by bus, train, boat, or car. London Transport buses no. 111, 131, 216, 267, and 461 make the trip, as do Green Line Coaches (ask at the nearest London Country Bus office for routes 715, 716, 718, and 726). Frequent trains from Waterloo Station (Network Southeast) go to Hampton Court Station. If you have the time (about 4 hours), boat service is offered to and from Kingston, Richmond, and Westminster.

✪ **WINDSOR CASTLE**   When William the Conqueror ordered a castle built on this spot, he began a legend and a link with English sovereignty that has known many vicissitudes, the most recent being a 1992 fire. The state apartments display many works of art, porcelain, armor, furniture, three Verrio ceilings, and several 17th-century Gibbons carvings. Several works by Rubens adorn the King's Drawing Rooms. Of the apartments, the grand reception room, with its Gobelin tapestries, is the most spectacular.

Queen Mary's Doll's House is a palace in perfect miniature. The Doll's House was given to Queen Mary in 1923 as a symbol of national goodwill. The house, designed by Sir Edwain Lutyens, was created on a scale of 1 to 12. It took 3 years to complete and involved the work of 1,500 tradesmen and artists.

St. George's Chapel is a gem of the Perpendicular style, sharing the distinction with Westminster Abbey of being a pantheon of English monarchs (Victoria is a notable exception). The present St. George's was founded in the late 15th century by Edward IV on the site of the original Chapel of the Order of the Garter (Edward III, 1348).

Admission is £9.50 ($15.20) for adults, £7 ($11.20) for students and senior citizens, and £5.50 ($8.80) for children 16 and under. The castle at Castle Hill is open March–Oct daily 10am–5pm; Nov–Feb daily 10am–4pm. Lying 21 miles west of London, Windsor Castle (☎ **01753/868286**) is reached in 50 minutes on a train from Paddington Station.

2 Oxford, the Cotswolds & Stratford-upon-Avon

One of England's most picturesque areas is the Cotswolds, with its sleepy old wool towns, and the country around Shakespeare's birthplace, Stratford-upon-Avon. After visiting London, many move on to visit the ancient university city of Oxford and the still untouched Cotswold villages that, despite tourism, retain their authentic character. Both time and tradition beckon you on to these places.

ONLY IN THE HEART OF ENGLAND

Visiting the Colleges   Every Oxford student has his or her favorite college—usually the one they attend. But all 36 of them are worth seeing, although some are more impressive than others. Our favorite is University College or "Univ," as it is popularly known. It is the oldest building foundation in Oxford, dating from 1249, and legend has it that it was founded by Alfred the Great, although few scholars seriously believe that. There's even a memorial here to the poet Shelley, although the college expelled him.

Experiencing the Romance of Oxford   It's all here waiting for you: Walk down the long sweep of The High, one of the most striking streets in England; have a mug of cider in one of the old student pubs; listen to the sound of May Day when the choristers sing in Latin from Magdalen Tower; hear the Great Tom bell from Tom Tower, whose 101 peals traditionally signal the closing of the college gates; see towers and spires rising majestically; swim nude at Parson's Pleasure; find a tiny, dusty bookstall where you can pick up a valuable first edition—all this in Oxford, home of one of the world's greatest universities.

Town Hopping in the Cotswolds   Less than 100 miles west of London are the rolling limestone uplands of the Cotswold Hills. This is picture-postcard England, as you visit villages built from honey-colored stone, bearing names like Upper and Lower Slaughter, Bourton-on-the-Water, and Moreton-in-Marsh. The Cotswolds stretch northeast in a curving 60-mile arc, all the way from the elegant city of Bath to the Bard's Stratford-upon-Avon. The most glamorous Cotswold towns are Broadway and Chipping Campden.

Entering the World of Shakespeare   Five of the most important buildings connected with the Bard are, miraculously, still standing. Shakespeare's Birthplace, a modest half-timbered and gabled Tudor house, is virtually the spiritual center of

Stratford. Other Tudor buildings include Anne Hathaway's Cottage and Mary Arden's House. You can even visit Shakespeare's grave at Holy Trinity Church.

Where the Play's the Thing   Regardless of where you see a Shakespearean production, no theater seems to equal the Royal Shakespeare Theatre. Over the years, the greatest Shakespearean actors in the world, from Laurence Olivier or John Gielgud on down, have performed here. At its riverside location, and under the patronage of the queen, this theater opened on April 23, 1932, on the Bard's birthday. Shakespeare is the only fare on these boards; the season runs from April 17 to October 5.

Downing a Pint with the Actors at the Dirty Duck   This pub, the most famous in Stratford, is called the Black Swan. But over the years actors appearing in local Shakespearean productions have nicknamed it the Dirty Duck. In the old days you might have shared a pint with Olivier, Gielgud, Glenda Jackson, or Peter O'Toole. Today it's likely to be Emma Thompson, Kenneth Branagh, or Derek Jacobi. Stratford players have been enjoying a pint here—many quite a few—since the 18th century. As for the food, it's not at all as bad as legend has it.

OXFORD

Oxford is a city of business and commerce, home to several industries, and, as such, is more of a real city than Cambridge. Oxford isn't entirely dominated by its university, although the colleges at its core are the reason the hordes, including tour buses, flock here. The fast-flowing pedestrian traffic may cause you to think you've been transported back to London instead of delivered to not-so-sleepy Oxford.

At any time of the year you can tour the colleges, many of which represent a peak in England's architectural kingdom, as well as a valley of Victorian contributions. The Oxford Information Centre (see below) offers guided walking tours daily throughout the year. Just don't mention the other place (Cambridge) and you shouldn't have any trouble. Comparisons between the two universities are inevitable of course, Oxford being better known for the arts and Cambridge more for the sciences.

The city predates the university—in fact, it was a Saxon town in the early part of the 10th century. By the 12th century, Oxford was growing in reputation as a seat of learning, at the expense of Paris, and the first colleges were founded in the 13th century. The story of Oxford is filled with local conflicts—the relationship between town and gown wasn't as peaceful as it is today, and riots often flared over the rights of the university versus the town. Nowadays, the young people of Oxford take out their aggressiveness in sporting competitions.

Ultimately, the test of a great university lies in the caliber of the people it turns out. Oxford can name-drop a mouthful: Roger Bacon, Sir Walter Raleigh, John Donne, Sir Christopher Wren, Samuel Johnson, William Penn, Lewis Carroll, Harold Macmillan, Graham Greene, T. E. Lawrence, and many, many others.

ARRIVING   Oxford is 54 miles northwest from London.

By Train   Trains from Paddington Station (☎ **01865/722330**) reach Oxford in 1¼ hours. Service is every hour. A cheap, same-day round-trip ticket costs £12.40 ($19.85).

By Bus   The X90 London Express departs from Victoria Station (☎ **01990/808080**) for the Oxford Bus Station daily. Coaches usually leave about every 20 minutes during the day, taking 1¾ hours. A same-day round-trip ticket costs £7 ($11.20). Or take the Oxford Tube (☎ **01865/772250** for schedules), an express coach that makes the trip in 1½ hours. Coaches operate every 20 minutes, 24 hours a day. Fares are £5.70 ($9.10) single and £6 ($9.60) for a 24-hour round-trip return.

By Car   Take M-40 west from London and follow the signs.

Oxford

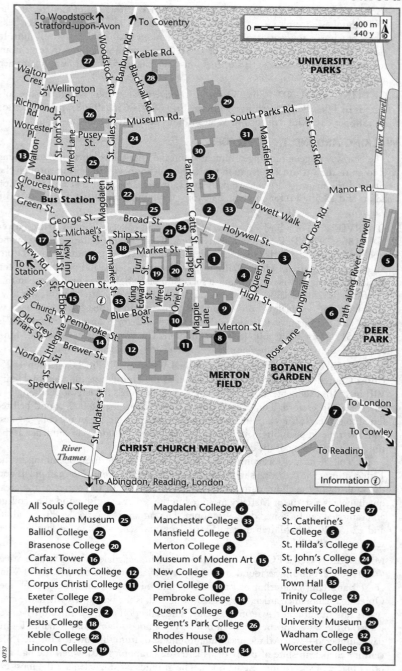

To Woodstock ↑
Stratford-upon-Avon   → To Coventry

0 _____ 400 m
             440 y
N↑

Woodstock Rd.
Banbury Rd.
Blackhall Rd.
Keble Rd.

UNIVERSITY PARKS

River Cherwell

Walton
Cres.
St. Wellington
Sq.

Richmond
Rd.
Worcester
Pl.
Walton
St.
St. John's St.
Alfred Lane
Pusey
St.
St. Giles St.

Museum Rd.

South Parks Rd.

St. Cross Rd.

Manor Rd.

Beaumont St.
Gloucester
St.
Green St.
Bus Station
Magdalen St.

Broad St.
Catte St.
Holywell St.
Jowett Walk

Parks Rd.

Mansfield Rd.

St. Cross Rd.

Longwall St.

Path along River Charwell

DEER PARK

George St.
St. Michael's
St.
New Rd.
To →
Station
New Inn
Hall St.
Cornmarket St.
Ship St.
Market St.
Turl St.
Queen St.
St. Ebbes St.
Castle St.
Church
St.
Old Grey
Friars St.
Littlegate St.
Pembroke St.
Brewer St.
Norfolk
St.
Speedwell St.
St. Aldates St.

Radcliffe Sq.
Alfred
St.
King
Edward
St.
Oriel St.
Blue Boar
St.

Magpie Lane
High St.
Queen's
Lane
Merton St.
Rose Lane

MERTON FIELD

BOTANIC GARDEN

River Thames

CHRIST CHURCH MEADOW

↓ To Abingdon, Reading, London

To London →
To Cowley →
To Reading

Information ⓘ

All Souls College ❶	Magdalen College ❻	Somerville College ㉗
Ashmolean Museum ㉕	Manchester College ㉝	St. Catherine's
Balliol College ㉒	Mansfield College ㉛	College ❺
Brasenose College ⓴	Merton College ❽	St. Hilda's College ❼
Carfax Tower ⑯	Museum of Modern Art ⑮	St. John's College ㉔
Christ Church College ⑫	New College ❸	St. Peter's College ⑰
Corpus Christi College ⑪	Oriel College ⑩	Town Hall ㉟
Exeter College ㉑	Pembroke College ⑭	Trinity College ㉓
Hertford College ❷	Queen's College ❹	University College ❾
Jesus College ⑱	Regent's Park College ㉖	University Museum ㉙
Keble College ㉘	Rhodes House ㉚	Wadham College ㉜
Lincoln College ⑲	Sheldonian Theatre ㉞	Worcester College ⑬

3-0737

245

VISITOR INFORMATION   The **Oxford Tourist Information Centre,** at The Old School Gloucester Green, opposite the bus station (☎ **01865/726871**), sells maps, brochures, souvenir items, as well as the famous Oxford University T-shirt. It also provides hotel booking services for £2.50 ($4). Guided walking tours leave from the center daily (see below). It's open Mon–Sat 9:30am–5pm and Sun in summer and bank holidays 10am–3pm.

GETTING AROUND   Since Oxford is relatively flat, a good way to see the colleges is by bike. **Pennyfarthing,** 5 George St. (☎ **01865/249368**), rents bikes for £5 ($8) per day, with a deposit of £25 ($40); it's open Mon–Sat 8am–5:30pm.

WALKING AROUND THE COLLEGES

The best way to get a running commentary on the important sightseeing attractions is to go to the Oxford Information Centre. **Two-hour walking tours** through the city and the major colleges leave daily at 11am and 2pm, and cost £4 ($6.40) for adults and £2.50 ($4) for children. The tours do not include New College or Christ Church.

OVERVIEW   For a bird's-eye view of the city and colleges, climb **Carfax Tower** (☎ **01865/792653**), located in the city center. This structure is distinguished by the clock and figures that strike the quarter hours. Carfax Tower is all that remains from St. Martin's Church, where William Shakespeare once stood as godfather for William Davenant, who also became a successful playwright. A church stood on this site from 1032 until 1896. The tower used to be higher, but after 1340 it was lowered, following complaints from the university to Edward III that townspeople threw stones and fired arrows at students during town-and-gown disputes. Admission is £1.20 ($1.90) for adults, 60p (95¢) for children. The tower is open Apr–Oct Mon–Sat 10am–6pm, Sun 10am–7pm; Nov–March Mon–Sat 10am–3:30pm.

✪ CHRIST CHURCH   Begun by Cardinal Wolsey as Cardinal College in 1525, Christ Church (☎ **01865/276499**), known as the House, was founded by Henry VIII in 1546. Facing St. Aldate's Street, Christ Church has the largest quadrangle of any college in Oxford. Tom Tower houses Great Tom, the 18,000-pound bell referred to earlier. It rings at 9:05pm nightly, signaling the closing of the college gates. The 101 times it peals originally signified the number of students in residence at the time of the founding of the college.

The college chapel was constructed over a period of centuries, beginning in the 12th century. The cathedral's most distinguishing features are its Norman pillars and the vaulting of the choir, dating from the 15th century. In the center of the great quadrangle is a statue of Mercury mounted in the center of a fish pond. The college and cathedral can be visited daily 9am–6pm. The entrance fee is £3 ($4.80) for adults and £2 ($3.20) for children under 18, students, and senior citizens. A family ticket sells for £6 ($9.60).

MAGDALEN COLLEGE   Pronounced *Maud*-lin, Magdalen College, High Street (☎ **01865/276000**), was founded in 1458 by William of Waynflete, bishop of Winchester and later chancellor of England. Its alumni range from Wolsey to Wilde. Opposite the botanic garden, the oldest in England, is the bell tower, where the choristers sing in Latin at dawn on May Day. The reflection of the 15th-century tower is cast in the waters of the Cherwell below. On a not-so-happy day, Charles I—his days numbered—watched the oncoming Roundheads from this tower. Visit the 15th-century chapel, in spite of many of its latter-day trappings. Ask when the hall and other places of special interest are open. The grounds of Magdalen are the most extensive of any Oxford college; there's even a deer park. You can visit Easter–June daily 2–6pm; July–Sept daily noon–6pm. Admission costs £2.20 ($3.50).

MERTON COLLEGE   Founded in 1264, Merton College, Merton Street (☎ **01865/276310**), is among the three oldest colleges at the university. It stands near Corpus Christi College on Merton Street, the sole survivor of Oxford's medieval cobbled streets. Merton College is noted for its library, built between 1371 and 1379 and said to be the oldest college library in England. There was once a tradition of keeping some of its most valuable books chained. Now only one book is so secured, to illustrate that historical custom. One treasure of the library is an astrolabe (an astronomical instrument used for measuring the altitude of the sun and stars) thought to have belonged to Chaucer. You pay £1 ($1.60) to visit the ancient library, as well as the Max Beerbohm Room (the satirical English caricaturist who died in 1956). The library and college are open Mon–Fri 2–4pm, Sat–Sun 10am–4pm (closed for 1 week at Easter and Christmas).

A favorite pastime is to take **Addison's Walk** through the water meadows. The stroll is so named after a former alumnus, Joseph Addison, the 18th-century essayist and playwright noted for his contributions to the *The Spectator* and *The Tatler*.

UNIVERSITY COLLEGE   University College, High Street (☎ **01865/276602**), is the oldest one at Oxford and dates back to 1249, when money was donated by an ecclesiastic, William of Durham (the old claim that the real founder was Alfred the Great is more fanciful). The original structures have all disappeared, and what remains today represents essentially the architecture of the 17th century, with subsequent additions in Victoria's day as well as in more recent times. For example, the Goodhart Quadrangle was added as late as 1962. The college's most famous alumnus, Shelley, was "sent down" for his part in collaborating on a pamphlet on atheism. However, all is forgiven today, as the romantic poet is honored by a memorial erected in 1894. The hall and chapel of University College can be visited daily during vacations from 2 to 4pm for a charge of £1.50 ($2.40) for adults, 60p (95¢) for children.

NEW COLLEGE   New College, New College Lane, off Queen's Lane (☎ **01865/ 279555**), was founded in 1379 by William of Wykeham, bishop of Winchester and later lord chancellor of England. His college at Winchester supplied a constant stream of students. The first quadrangle, dating from before the end of the 14th century, was the initial quadrangle to be built in Oxford and formed the architectural design for the other colleges. In the antechapel is Sir Jacob Epstein's remarkable modern sculpture of *Lazarus* and a fine El Greco painting of St. James. One of the treasures of the college is a crosier (pastoral staff of a bishop) belonging to the founding father. In the garden, you can stroll among the remains of the old city wall and the mound. The college (entered at New College Lane) can be visited Easter–Sept daily 11:30am–5pm; off-season daily 2–5pm. Admission is £1 ($1.60).

PUNTING—A LOCAL SPORT

At **Punt Station,** Cherwell Boathouse, Bardwell Road (☎ **01865/515978**), you can rent a punt (flat-bottom boat maneuvered by a long pole and a small oar) for £6– £8 ($9.60–$12.80) per hour, plus a £30–£40 ($48–$64) deposit. Similar charges are made for punt rentals at Magdalen Bridge Boathouse. Punts are rented from March to mid-June and late Aug to Oct daily 10am–dusk; from mid-June to late Aug, when a larger inventory of punts is available, daily 10am–10pm.

SHOPPING

In its way, **Alice's Shop,** 83 St. Aldate's (☎ **01865/723793**), might have played a more important role in English literature than any other shop in Britain. Set within a 15th-century building that has housed some kind of shop since 1820, it functioned as a general store (selling brooms, hardware, etc.) during the period that Lewis

Carroll, at the time a professor of mathematics at Christ Church College, was composing *Alice in Wonderland.* As such, it is believed to have been the model for important settings within the book. Today, the place is a favorite stop of Lewis Carroll fans, who gobble up commemorative pencils, chess sets, party favors, bookmarks, and in rare cases, original editions of some of Carroll's works.

Bodleian Library Shop, Old School's Quadrangle, Radcliffe Square, Broad Street (☎ **01865/277175**), specializes in Oxford-derived souvenirs that might be appropriate for anyone with academic pretensions. There are more than 2,000 objects inventoried here, including books describing the history of the university and its various colleges, paperweights made of pewter and crystal, and Oxford banners and coffee mugs.

Castell & Son (The Varsity Shop), 13 Broad St. (☎ **01865/244000**), is the best outlet for clothing emblazoned with the Oxford logo or heraldic symbol. Objects include both whimsical and dead-on-serious neckties, hats, T-shirts, sweatshirts, pens, bookmarks, beer and coffee mugs, and cuff links. You'll find more Oxford souvenirs at **The Oxford Collection,** 1 Golden Cross Courtyard, off Cornmarket (☎ **01865/247414**), such as glass beer steins etched with the university's logo, and a wool cardigan–like sweater with brass buttons bearing the university crest.

Magna Gallery, 41 High St. (☎ **01865/245805**), is one of the best-respected antiquarian galleries in Oxford, with engravings, maps, and prints made between 1550 and 1896. Although the botanical prints and maps are among the most intriguing in the store, connoisseurs usually ask for the prints and engravings of 19th-century caricaturist Robert Cruikshank.

Few other shops in England glorify trees and wood products as artfully as **Once a Tree,** 99 Gloucester Green (☎ **01865/793558**). A member of a rapidly blossoming chain, it stocks wood-carved objects that range from the functional and utilitarian (kitchen spoons and breadboards) to the whimsical and exotic (carved wooden flowers, chunky jewelry, boxes, bowls, mirror frames, furniture, mantelpieces).

ACCOMMODATIONS

The **Oxford Tourist Information Centre,** Gloucester Green, opposite the bus station (☎ **01865/726871**), operates a year-round room-booking service for a fee of £2.50 ($4), plus a refundable deposit. The center has a list of accommodations, maps, and guidebooks.

Expensive

✪ **Old Parsonage Hotel.** 1 Banbury Rd., Oxford OX2 6NN. ☎ **01865/310210.** Fax 01865/311262. 26 rms, 4 suites. MINIBAR TV TEL. £155 ($248) double; £195 ($312) suite. Rates include English breakfast. AE, DC, MC, V. Free parking. Bus: 7.

This extensively renovated hotel near St. Giles Church and Keble College is so old (1660) it looks like an extension of one of the ancient colleges. Originally a 13th-century hospital named Bethleen, it was restored in the early 17th century. Oscar Wilde once lived here for a time and is famed for the remark, "Either this wallpaper goes, or I do." In the 20th century a modern wing was added, and in 1991 it was completely renovated and made into a first-rate hotel. The bedrooms are individually designed but not large, with such amenities as a remote-control radio and hair dryer. The marble bathrooms are air-conditioned, with their own phone extensions. All suites and some bedrooms have sofa beds. The bedrooms open onto the private gardens, and 10 are on the ground floor.

The Randolph. Beaumont St., Oxford, Oxfordshire OX1 2LN. ☎ **800/225-5843** in the U.S. and Canada, or 01865/247481. Fax 01865/791678. 102 rms, 7 suites. TV TEL. £139–£179

($217.60–$286.40) double; £225–£380 ($360–$608) suite. AE, DC, MC, V. Free parking. Bus: 7.

Since 1864, the Randolph has overlooked St. Giles, the Ashmolean Museum, and the Cornmarket. Its arched stone entrance is striking. The hotel illustrates how historic surroundings can be combined with modern conveniences to make for elegant accommodations. The furnishings are traditional, and all rooms have a private bath, hair dryer, and hot beverage-making facilities. Some rooms are quite large, although others are a bit cramped. The double glazing on the windows seems inadequate to keep out the midtown traffic noise. In this price range, we'd opt first for the Old Parsonage before checking in here. The hotel's Spires Restaurant presents both a time-tested English and a modern cuisine in a high-ceilinged Victorian dining room. There's also a wine bar.

Moderate

Eastgate Hotel. 23 Merton St., The High, Oxford, Oxfordshire, OX1 4BE. ☎ **800/225-5843** in the U.S. and Canada, or 01865/248244. Fax 01865/791681. 42 rms, 1 suite. TV TEL. £110 ($176) double; £130 ($208) suite. AE, DC, MC, V. Free parking. Bus: 7.

The Eastgate, built on the site of a 1600s structure, stands opposite the ancient Examination Halls, next to Magdalen Bridge, within walking distance of Oxford colleges and the city center. Recently refurbished, it offers modern facilities while retaining in the public rooms the atmosphere of an English country house. The comfortably furnished rooms have radios as well as hot beverage-making equipment. The Shires Restaurant offers roasts and traditional English fare, complemented by a choice of wines.

Oxford Moat House. Godstow Rd., Wolvercote Roundabout, Oxford, Oxfordshire OX2 8AL. ☎ **01865/489988.** Fax 01865/310259. 155 rms. TV TEL. £115 ($184) double. AE, DC, MC, V. Closed Dec 24–Jan 2. Free parking. Bus: 60.

This hostelry is one of the Queens Moat Houses group, incorporating the principles of motel design, with an emphasis on spacious, glassed-in areas and streamlined bedrooms. Patronized mainly by motorists, it's at the northern edge of Oxford 2 miles from the center, hidden from the traffic at the junction of A-40 and A-34. Each refurbished room features a radio, video, and trouser press. The Moat House has a swimming pool, squash courts, sauna, solarium, and snooker (billiards) room. Its Oxford Blue Restaurant serves an English menu.

Inexpensive

☉ **Adams Guest House.** 302 Banbury Rd., Oxford, Oxfordshire OX2 7ED. ☎ **01865/56118.** 6 rms. TV. £42 ($67.20) double. Rates include English breakfast. No credit cards. Bus: 2 or 7 from Cornmarket.

In Summertown, 1¹⁄₄ miles from Oxford, opposite Radio Oxford, is the Adams Guest House, operated by John Strange; it's one of the best B&Bs in the northern Oxford area. The comfortable and cozy rooms have private showers and tea or coffeemakers. Breakfast is served in a dining room decorated in old-world style.

Tilbury Lodge Private Hotel. 5 Tilbury Lane, Eynsham Rd., Botley, Oxford, Oxfordshire OX2 9NB. ☎ **01865/862138.** Fax 01865/863700. 10 rms. TV TEL. £64 ($102.40) double, £80 ($128) double with four-poster. Rates include English breakfast. MC, V. Free parking. Bus: From Cornmarket St. to Botley.

On a quiet country lane about 2 miles west of the center of Oxford, this small hotel is less than a mile from the railway station. Eddie and Eileen Trafford accommodate guests in their well-furnished and comfortable bedrooms. The most expensive room has a four-poster bed. The guest house also has a Jacuzzi and welcomes children. If you don't arrive by car, Eddie can pick you up at the train station.

DINING

Very Expensive

✪ **Le Manoir aux Quat' Saisons.** Great Milton, Oxfordshire OX44 7PD. ☎ **01844/278881.** Fax 01844/278847. Reservations required. Main courses £30–£33 ($48–$52.80); lunch *menu du jour* £29.50–£36.50 ($47.20–$58.40); lunch or dinner *menu gourmand* £69 ($110.40). AE, DC, MC, V. Daily noon–2:15pm and 7:15–10:15pm. Take Exit 7 off M-40 and head along A-329 toward Wallingford; look for signs for Great American Milton Manor around a mile later. FRENCH.

Some 12 miles southeast of Oxford, Le Manoir aux Quat' Saisons offers the finest cuisine in the Midlands. The gray- and honey-colored stone manor house was originally built by a Norman nobleman in the early 1300s. The connection with France has been masterfully revived by the Gallic owner and chef, Raymond Blanc. You can enjoy such highly creative specialties as quail eggs, spinach, parmesan, and black truffle ravioli in a poultry *jus* and *meunière* butter and swiss chard; grilled fillet of turbot with red-wine butter and *beurre blanc* (white butter) garnished with deep-fried vegetables; or braised boned oxtail filled with shallots and wild mushrooms in a Hermitage red-wine sauce with purée of parsnips. Each dish is an exercise in studied perfection.

The gabled house was built in the 1500s and improved and enlarged in 1908. An outdoor swimming pool, still in use, was added much later. Inside, there are 19 luxurious bedrooms, each decorated boudoir style with lots of flowery draperies, ruffled canopies, radio, color TV, phone, private bath, springtime colors, and high-quality antique reproductions; the cost is £125–£375 ($200–$600) for a double.

Moderate

Cherwell Boathouse Restaurant. Bardwell Rd. ☎ **01865/52746.** Reservations recommended. Main courses £10–£12 ($16–$19.20); fixed-price lunch £10–£16.50 ($16–$26.40); fixed-price dinner from £17.50 ($28). AE, DC, MC, V. Tues–Sat noon–2pm and 6–11:30pm, Sun noon–2pm. Closed Dec 24–30. Bus: Banbury Rd. ENGLISH/FRENCH.

This Oxford landmark on the River Cherwell is owned by Anthony Verdin, who is assisted by a young crew. The cooks change the menu every 2 weeks to take advantage of the availability of fresh vegetables, fish, and meat. There is a very reasonable, even exciting, wine list. In summer, the restaurant also serves on the terrace. The chefs turn out the best roast pheasant in Oxford, and other dishes are delicately handled as well, including a loin of free-range pork in a creamy tarragon and green peppercorn sauce.

Elizabeth. 82 St. Aldate's St. ☎ **01865/242230.** Reservations recommended. Main courses £13.25–£17.75 ($21.20–$28.40); lunch £15 ($24). AE, DC, MC, V. Tues–Sun 12:30–2:30pm and 6:30–11pm. Closed Easter weekend and Christmas week. Bus: 7. FRENCH/CONTINENTAL.

Despite the portraits of Elizabeth II that hang near the entrance, this restaurant is named after its original owner, a matriarch who founded the place in this stone-sided house in the 1930s opposite Christ Church College. Today, you're likely to find a well-trained staff from Spain, who serve beautifully presented dishes in the French style. The larger of the two dining rooms displays reproductions of paintings by Goya and Velázquez and exudes a restrained kind of dignity; the smaller room is devoted to *Alice in Wonderland* designs inspired by Lewis Carroll. The dishes that show the kitchen at its best include chicken royale; the Scottish steaks; grilled salmon, Dover sole, and sea bass, served in white-wine or lemon-butter sauce; and Basque pipérade.

Inexpensive

⑤ Munchy Munchy. 6 Park End St. ☎ **01865/245710.** Reservations recommended. Main courses £4.50–£8.75 ($7.20–$14). MC, V. Tues–Sun noon–2pm; Tues–Sat 5:30–10pm. Closed 2 weeks in Sept and 2 weeks in Dec. Bus: 52. SOUTHEAST ASIAN/INDONESIAN.

Some Oxford students, who frequent this restaurant near the station, claim that it offers the best food value in the city. Main dishes depend on what's available in the marketplace, and there are no appetizers. Ethel Ow is adept at herbs and seasoning, and often uses fresh fruit creatively, as reflected in such dishes as king prawns sautéed with tumeric, coriander, and a purée of apricots or a spicy lamb with eggplant, Szechuan red pepper, star anise, and crushed yellow bean sauce. Indonesian and Malaysian dishes are popular. Sometimes, especially on Friday and Saturday, long lines form at the door. Children 5 and under are not permitted on Friday and Saturday evenings.

PUBS

Bear Inn. Alfred St. ☎ **01865/721783.** Reservations not accepted. Snacks and bar meals £1.85–£4.75 ($2.95–$7.60). No credit cards. Mon–Sat noon–11pm, Sun noon–3pm and 7–10:30pm. Bus: 2A or 2B. ENGLISH.

A short block from The High, overlooking the north side of Christ Church College, this is the village pub and an Oxford tradition since the 13th century. Its swinging inn sign depicts the bear and ragged staff, old insignia of the earls of Warwick, who were among the early patrons. Some former owners developed an astonishing habit: clipping neckties. Around the lounge bar you'll see the remains of thousands of ties, which have been labeled with their owners' names. For those of you who want to leave something behind, a thin strip from the bottom of your tie will be cut off (with your permission, of course).

Turf Tavern. 4 Bath Place (off Holywell St.). ☎ **01865/243235.** Reservations not accepted. Main dishes £4.85 ($7.75). MC, V. Mon–Sat 11am–11pm, Sun noon–3pm and 7–10:30pm. Bus: 52. ENGLISH.

This 13th-century tavern lies on a very narrow passageway near the Bodleian Library. Thomas Hardy used the place as the setting for *Jude the Obscure.* During his student days at Oxford, Bill Clinton frequently came here. At night, the nearby old tower of New College and part of the old city wall are floodlit, and during warm weather you can sit in any of the three gardens that radiate outward from the pub's central core. For wintertime warmth, braziers are lighted in the courtyard and in the gardens. A separate food counter, set behind a glass case, displays the day's fare.

A DAY TRIP FROM OXFORD

✪ **BLENHEIM PALACE**   Just 8 miles northwest of Oxford stands the extravagant baroque Blenheim Palace (☎ **01993/811091**), England's answer to Versailles. Blenheim is the home of the 11th duke of Marlborough, a descendant of John Churchill, the first duke, who was an on-again, off-again favorite of Queen Anne's. In his day (1650–1722), the first duke became the supreme military figure in Europe. Fighting on the Danube near a village named Blenheim, Churchill defeated the forces of Louis XIV, and the lavish palace of Blenheim was built for the duke as a gift from the queen. It was designed by Sir John Vanbrugh, who was also the architect of Castle Howard; the landscaping was created by the famous 18th-century landscape gardener, Capability Brown.

The palace is loaded with riches: antiques, porcelain, oil paintings, tapestries, and chinoiserie. North Americans know Blenheim as the birthplace of Sir Winston Churchill. His birth room is included in the palace tour, as is the Churchill exhibition, four rooms of letters, books, photographs, and other relics. Today the former prime minister lies buried in Bladon Churchyard, near the palace.

Blenheim Palace is open mid-March to Oct daily 10:30am–4:45pm. Admission costs £7.30 ($11.70) for adults, £3.70 ($5.90) for children 5 to 15 (free for children 4 and under).

If you're driving, take the A-44 from Oxford; otherwise, the no. 20 Gloucester Green bus (☎ **01865/711312**) leaves Oxford about every 30 minutes during the day for the half-hour trip.

BURFORD: GATEWAY TO THE COTSWOLDS

This unspoiled medieval town, built of Cotswold stone, is 20 miles west of Oxford. The town is largely famous for its **Norman church** (ca. 1116) and its **High Street** lined with coaching inns. Oliver Cromwell passed this way, as (in a happier day) did Charles II and his mistress, Nell Gwynne. Burford was one of the last of the great wool centers. You may want to photograph the bridge across the Windrush River where Queen Elizabeth I once stood. Burford today is definitely equipped for tourists, as the antiques shops along the High will testify.

ESSENTIALS

ARRIVING   By Train   The nearest station is at Oxford, so take a train from London (a 45-minute trip), and then at Oxford, walk a very short distance to the entrance of the Taylor Institute, from which about three or four buses per day make the 30-minute run to Burford.

By Bus   A National Express coach runs from London's Victoria Coach Station to Burford several times a day; the trip, with many stops, takes 2 hours.

By Car   From Oxford, take the A-40 west for 20 miles.

VISITOR INFORMATION   The **Tourist Information Centre,** at the Old Brewery, Sheep Street (☎ **01993/823558**), is open Nov–March Mon–Fri 10am–4:30pm, Sat 9:30am–1pm, and April–Oct Mon–Sat 9:30am–1pm and 2–5:30pm.

ACCOMMODATIONS & DINING

✪ **Bay Tree Hotel.** 12–14 Sheep St., Burford, Oxfordshire OX18 6LW. ☎ **01993/822791.** Fax 01993/823008. 23 rms, 7 suites. TV TEL. £110 ($176) double; £155–£195 ($248–$312) suite. Rates include English breakfast. AE, DC, MC, V. Free parking.

The house was built for Sir Lawrence Tanfield, the unpopular lord chief baron of the Exchequer to Elizabeth I, definitely not noted for his hospitality. But time has erased his unfortunate memory, and the splendor of this Cotswold manor house remains, even more so after a major overhaul. The house has oak-paneled rooms with stone fireplaces. In the tastefully decorated rooms, 20th-century comforts have been discreetly installed, and the beds are a far cry from the old rope-bottom contraptions of the days of Queen Elizabeth I. Try to get a room overlooking the terraced gardens at the rear of the house. The 65-seat oak-beamed restaurant, which overlooks the gardens, retains all of its original charm. The chef is well known for his tempting menus, with dishes based on local and seasonal produce.

Golden Pheasant Hotel. 91 High St., Burford, Oxfordshire OX18 4QA. ☎ **01993/823223.** Fax 01993/822621. 12 rms. TV TEL. £65–£85 ($104–$136) double. Rates include English breakfast. AE, MC, V. Free parking.

On the main street, the Golden Pheasant has the oldest set of property deeds surviving in Burford. It's the second best place to stay in town. In the 1400s it was the home of a prosperous wool merchant, but it began serving food and drink in the 1730s. Inside, within view of dozens of old beams and a blazing fireplace, a candlelit restaurant serves both French and English specialties; the new bar also merits a visit. The rooms are comfortable and cozy; one has a four-poster bed.

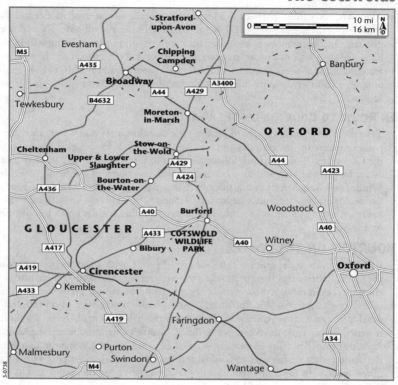

A SIDE TRIP TO BIBURY

Most visitors in a rush head north from Burford to Stow-on-the-Wold and Broadway (see below). But if you have the time you can dip south and in less than an hour you'll be in Bibury. From Burford, go southwest along the A-433 to reach one of the loveliest spots in the Cotswolds.

The utopian romancer of Victoria's day, poet William Morris, called it England's most beautiful village. It is matched only by Painswick for its scenic village beauty and purity. Both villages are still unspoiled by modern invasions. On the banks of the tiny Coln River, Bibury is noted for Arlington Row, a group of 15th-century gabled cottages, its most-photographed attraction, which is protected by the National Trust. You can admire the cottages from the outside; you're not, however, supposed to peer into the windows, as they are still people's homes.

The main thing to do here is enjoy the village scene. Attractions in the area include the **Cotswold Country Museum** (☎ **01451/860715**), located in a former mill, with an impressive collection of old carts and industrial machines. Rooms show how locals lived and worked in the 19th century. Admission is £1.50 ($2.40) for adults, £1.25 ($2) for senior citizens, and 75p ($1.20) for children. Open mid-March to mid-Nov Mon–Sat 10:30am–5pm, Sun 2–5pm; off-season Sat–Sun 10:30am–dusk.

If you'd like to stay in Bibury, the finest hotel and restaurant in the village is **The Swan,** Bibury, Gloucestershire GL7 5NW (☎ **01285/740695;** fax 01285/740473).

The owners outfitted parts of the interior in a cozily overstuffed mode, and the charming and tasteful bedrooms have antique furniture, and all have TV and telephones. On the premises is an informal brasserie, with outdoor seating within the hotel's courtyard. A more formal restaurant, with crystal chandeliers and heavy damask curtains, specializes in modern British food. Rates are £115–£210 ($184–$336) double; £280 ($448) suite, and include English breakfast. AE, MC, and V are accepted.

EN ROUTE TO BOURTON-ON-THE-WATER

Take the A-433 northeast toward Burford, the direction from which you came. Here you can escape the main routes and take some back roads for better scenic views of the Cotswolds. From Burford, follow the signs to Great Barrington, about 4 miles away, by turning left onto an unclassified road just north of the bridge over the Windrush River. After passing through Great Barrington with its double row of Cotswold cottages, continue west toward Windrush. From here, take an unnumbered road northwest to Sherborne, and, once here, go another 6 miles north to Bourton-on-the-Water.

BOURTON-ON-THE-WATER

Its fans define it as the quintessential Cotswold village, with a history going back to the Celts. Its residents fiercely protect their heritage of 15th- and 16th-century architecture, even though their town is singled out for practically every bus tour that rolls through the Cotswolds. Populated in Anglo-Saxon times, Bourton-on-the-Water developed into a strategic outpost along the ancient Roman road, Fosse Way, that traversed Britain from the North Sea to the St. George's Channel. During the Middle Ages, its prosperity came from wool, shipped all over Europe. During the Industrial Revolution when profits were in finished textiles, it became a backwater as a producer of raw wool, with the happy result for us that it was never "modernized," and its traditional appearance was preserved.

ESSENTIALS

ARRIVING   By Train   Trains go from Paddington Station in London to nearby Moreton-in-Marsh; the trip takes 2 hours. From Moreton-in-Marsh, Pulhams Bus Company runs buses for the 15-minute (6-mile) journey to Bourton-on-the-Water. Other cities with train service into London include Cheltenham or Kingham, and both of those, while somewhat more distant, also have bus connections into Bourton-on-the-Water.

By Bus   National Express coaches, from Victoria Coach Station in London, travel to both Cheltenham and Stow-in-the-Wold. From either of those towns, Pulhams Bus Company operates about four buses per day into Bourton-on-the-Water.

EXPLORING THE TOWN

A handful of minor museums can be visited within the town, each of which grew up from idiosyncratic collections amassed over the years by local residents. They include the **Cotswold Motor Museum** (☎ 01451/821255), the **Bourton Model Railway Exhibition and Toy Shop** (☎ 01451/820686), and **Birdland** (described below). But these museums don't compare with the evocative history of Bourton-on-the-Water itself.

The **Model Village at the Old New Inn,** High St. (☎ 01451/820467), was constructed by a local hotelier, Mr. Morris, to while away some of the doldrums of the Great Depression. His scale model (1:9) is big enough to allow viewers to walk through a re-creation of the town. If you opt to visit this place, you won't be alone:

The Queen of England has marveled at the site's workmanship and detailing, and Ford Motor Company used it as the centerpiece of an ad campaign for its compact Fiesta (i.e., a small-scale car photographed within a small-scale village). Admission £1.30 ($2.10) adults, £1.10 ($1.75) senior citizens, 90p ($1.45) children; it's open daily 9:30am–6pm or until dusk.

About a mile east of Bourton-on-the-Water, on the banks of Windrush River, is **Birdland,** Rissington Rd. (☎ **01451/820480**). Established in 1958 on 8¹/₂ acres of field and forests, this handsomely designed homage to ornithological splendors houses about 1,200 birds representing 361 species. Included is the largest and most varied collection of penguins in any zoo, with glass-walled tanks that allow observers to appreciate their agile underwater movements. Birdland provides a picnic area and a children's playground in a wooded copse. Admission is £3 ($4.80) for adults, £2.50 ($4) for senior citizens, £1.50 ($2.40) for children 4–14; open Apr–Oct daily 10am–6pm; Nov–Mar daily 10am–4pm.

ACCOMMODATIONS & DINING

Old Manse Hotel. Victoria St., Bourton-on-the-Water, Cheltenham, Gloucestershire GL54 2BX. ☎ **01451/820082.** Fax 01451/810381. 14 rms. TV TEL. Sun–Thurs £59–£79 ($94.40–$126.40) double; £99 ($158.40) suite. Fri–Sat £71–£95 ($113.60–$152) double; £119 ($190.40) suite. Rates include English breakfast. AE, DC, MC, V. Free parking.

An architectural gem reminiscent of the setting of Nathaniel Hawthorne's *Mosses from an Old Manse,* this hotel in the town center sits by the slow-moving river that wanders through the village green. Built of Cotswold stone in 1748, with chimneys, dormers, and small-paned windows, it has been modernized inside. The bedrooms have recently been refurbished to a high standard. Dining is a treat in the Secret Garden, which serves dinner Mon–Sat 6–9pm and Sun 7–9pm. Typical dishes include such appetizers as homemade venison sausage or sautéed breast of pigeon, followed by Dover sole, stuffed Bibury trout, and roast English lamb. Sometimes roast pheasant is featured.

⑤ Old New Inn. High St., Bourton-on-the-Water, Cheltenham, Gloucestershire GL54 2AF. ☎ **01451/820467.** Fax 01451/810236. 17 rms (6 with bath). TV. £55 ($88) double without bath; £68 ($108.80) double with bath. Rates include English breakfast. MC, V. Free parking.

Old New Inn can lay claim to being the landmark hostelry in the village. On the main street, overlooking the river, it's a good example of Queen Anne design (the miniature model village in its garden was referred to earlier). Hungry or tired travelers are drawn to the old-fashioned comforts and cuisine of this most English inn. The comfortable rooms have homelike furnishings and soft beds. Nonresidents are also welcome here for meals, with lunches at £10 ($16) and dinner from £15 ($24). You may want to spend an evening in the redecorated pub lounge either playing darts or chatting with the villagers.

A COTSWOLD RAMBLE: WALKING BETWEEN THE SLAUGHTERS

Midway between Bourton-on-the-Water and Stow-on-the-Wold are the twin villages of Upper and Lower Slaughter, two of the prettiest villages in the Cotswolds. (The name "Slaughter" is a corruption of *de Scoltre,* the name of the original Norman landowner.) The houses are constructed of honey-colored Cotswold stone, and a stream meanders right through, providing a home for the ducks that wander freely about, begging scraps from kindly visitors.

Of course, you can drive to these delightful villages, lying on backroads, but it's more fun to walk. The walk between the two villages, with an optional extension to Bourton-on-the-Water, is 1 mile each way between the Slaughters, or 2¹/₂ miles from

Upper Slaughter to Bourton-on-the-Water. Your walk could take between 2 and 4 hours. A well-worn footpath, **Warden's Way,** meanders beside the edge of the swift-moving River Eye. Originating in Upper Slaughter (where its start is marked at the town's central car park), the path beckons all kinds of nature enthusiasts. En route, you will pass sheep grazing in meadows, antique houses crafted from honey-colored local stone, stately trees arching over ancient millponds, and footbridges that have endured centuries of foot traffic and rain.

Don't think for a moment that the rivers of this region (including the Eye, Colne, Diklar, and Windrush) are sluggish, slow-moving streams: Between Upper and Lower Slaughter, the water literally rushes down the incline, powering a historic mill that you'll find on the northwestern edge of Lower Slaughter. In quiet eddies, you'll see ample numbers of waterfowl and birds, including wild ducks, gray wagtails, mute swans, coots, and Canadian geese. You could follow this route in reverse, although since parking is more plentiful in Upper Slaughter than in Lower Slaughter, it's more convenient to begin in the former town.

Most visitors prefer to end their outdoor ramble here, retracing their steps upstream to the car park at Upper Slaughter. But you could continue your walk for another 1 1/2 miles to Bourton-on-the-Water. To extend your trip, follow Warden's Way across the A-429 highway, which is identified by locals as Fosse Way. Your path will leave the river's edge and strike out across cattle pastures in a southerly direction. Most of the distance from Lower Slaughter to Bourton-on-the-Water is tarmac covered; it's closed to motor traffic, but ideal for trekkers or cyclists. Watch for bird life, and remember that you're legally required to close each of the several gates that stretch across the footpath.

Warden's Way will introduce you to Bourton-on-the-Water through the hamlet's northern edges. The first landmark you'll see will be the tower of St. Lawrence's Anglican Church. From the base of the church, walk south along The Avenue (one of the hamlet's main streets) and end your Cotswold ramble on the Village Green, directly in front of the War Memorial.

EN ROUTE TO STOW-ON-THE-WOLD

If you've ended the walk in Upper Slaughter, you can take the B-4068 directly northeast to Stow-on-the-Wold, our next stop. However, if you're back in Bourton-on-the-Water, you can head northeast on A-429, which will in just a short time deliver you to Stow.

STOW-ON-THE-WOLD

This Cotswold market town remains unspoiled, despite the busloads of tourists who stop off en route to Broadway and Chipping Campden. Stow-on-the-Wold lies 9 miles southeast of Broadway, 10 miles south of Chipping Campden, 4 miles south of Moreton-in-Marsh, and 21 miles south of Stratford-upon-Avon. The town is the loftiest in the Cotswolds, built on a wold (rolling hill) about 800 feet above sea level. In its open market square you can still see the stocks where offenders in the past were jeered at and punished by the townspeople, who threw rotten eggs at them. The final battle between the Roundheads and the Royalists took place in Stow-on-the-Wold. This is a good base for exploring the Cotswold wool towns, as well as Stratford-upon-Avon.

ESSENTIALS

ARRIVING   By Train   From London, take a train to Moreton-in-Marsh (see below) from London's Paddington Station, a service that runs several times a day. From

Moreton-in-Marsh, continue by a Pulhams bus for the 10-minute ride to Stow-on-the-Wold.

By Bus National Express coaches also run daily from London's Victoria Coach Station to Moreton-in-Marsh, where a Pulhams Bus Company coach goes the rest of the way to Stow-on-the-Wold. Several Pulhams coaches also run daily to Stow-on-the-Wold from Cheltenham.

VISITOR INFORMATION The **Tourist Information Centre,** at Hollis House, The Square (☎ **01451/831082**), is open April–Oct Mon–Sat 10am–5:30pm and Sun 10:30am–4pm; Nov–March Mon–Sat 9:30am–4:30pm.

ANTIQUES GALORE

Don't be fooled by the hamlet's sleepy, country-bucolic setting: Stow-on-the-Wold has developed over the last 20 years into the antique buyer's centerpiece of Britain, and as such has at least 60 merchandisers scattered throughout the village and its environs. Some visitors thrill to rummaging at random through the town's various venues, dusty and otherwise, looking for whatever appeals to them. Here is a selection of the town's most interesting and unusual emporiums.

Set within four showrooms inside an 18th-century building on the town's main square, **Anthony Preston Antiques, Ltd.,** The Square (☎ **01451/831586**), specializes in English and French furniture, including some very large pieces such as bookcases, and decorative objects that include paperweights, lamps, paintings on silk, and more.

Baggott Church Street, Ltd., Church Street (☎ **01451/830370**), is the smaller, and perhaps more intricately decorated, of two shops founded and maintained by a well-regarded local antiques merchant, Duncan ("Jack") Baggott. The shop contains four showrooms loaded with furniture and paintings from the 17th to the 19th century. More eclectic and wide-ranging in its inventory is **Woolcomber House,** Sheep Street (☎ **01451/830662**), the second of Baggott's two shops. This contains about 17 rooms that today are decorated according to a particular era of English history. Serious buyers and wholesalers of antiques usually ask for access to the bulging inventories of antique furniture stocked within a warehouse that's about 50 feet from this shop. There, it's understood that purchases will usually be made in bulk, and shipped as part of containers to other antique stores around the world.

Covering about half a block of terrain in the town center, **Huntington's Antiques, Ltd.,** Church Street (☎ **01451/830842**), contains one of the largest stocks of quality antiques dating from the Middle Ages through the 17th century, and for informal (country "vernacular") pieces includes the Middle Ages to the end of the 18th century. Wander at will through 10 ground-floor rooms, then climb to the second floor, where a long gallery and a quartet of additional showrooms bulge with refectory tables, unusual cupboards, and much more.

ACCOMMODATIONS & DINING

Fosse Manor Hotel. Fosse Way, Stow-on-the-Wold, Cheltenham, Gloucestershire GL54 1JX. ☎ **01451/830354.** Fax 01451/832486. 20 rms, 2 suites. TV TEL. £106 ($169.60) double; £150 ($240) suite. Rates include English breakfast. "Bargain Breaks" (2-night minimum required): £53–£75 ($84.80–$120) per person, including half board. AE, DC, MC, V. Free parking. Take A-429 1¼ miles south of Stow-on-the-Wold.

Although lacking the charm of the Grapevine, Fosse Manor is at least "second best" in town. Its stone walls and neogothic gables almost concealed by strands of ivy, the hotel lies near the site of an ancient Roman road that used to bisect England. From some of the high stone-sided windows you can enjoy a view of a landscaped garden with a sunken lily pond, flagstone walks, and an old-fashioned sundial. Inside, the interior is conservatively modernized with such touches as a padded and upholstered bar and a dining room where dinners cost £18.50 ($29.60). The bedrooms are home-like, with matching fabrics and wallpaper, and two rooms are favorites of honey-mooners.

Grapevine Hotel. Sheep St., Stow-on-the-Wold, Cheltenham, Gloucestershire GL54 1AU. ☎ **800/528-1234** in the U.S. and Canada, or 01451/830344. Fax 01451/832278. 23 rms. TV TEL. £60–£77 ($96–$123.20) per person. Rates include breakfast. "Bargain Breaks" (2-night minimum): £55–£80 ($88–$128) per person, including half board. AE, DC, MC, V. Free parking.

The Grapevine, facing the village green, mixes urban sophistication with reasonable prices, rural charm, and intimacy. Although it's the best inn within the town, it doesn't have the charm and grace of Wyck Hill House on the outskirts. The Grape-vine was named after the ancient vine whose tendrils shade and shelter the beauti-ful conservatory restaurant. Each bedroom has tasteful furnishings, radio, hair dryer, and a tea and coffeemaker. Six rooms offer a minibar. Full meals feature English, French, and Italian cuisine.

✪ Wyck Hill House. Burford Rd., Stow-on-the-Wold, Cheltenham, Gloucestershire GL54 1HY. ☎ **01451/831936.** Fax 01451/832243. 30 rms, 2 suites. TV TEL. £105 ($168) double; £180 ($288) suite. Rates include English breakfast. AE, DC, MC, V. Free parking. Drive 2¹/₂ miles south of Stow-on-the-Wold on A-424.

This Victorian country house contains parts that date back even earlier—to 1720 when its stone walls were first erected. Today, it is the area's showcase country inn. One wing of the manor house, it was discovered in the course of recent restoration, rested on the foundations of a Roman villa. Wyck Hill House is located on 100 acres of grounds and gardens. The well-furnished bedrooms are in the main hotel, in the coach-house annex, or in the orangery. Excellent food is also served, with a two-course lunch costing £11.95 ($19.10) and a three-course lunch going for £13.50 ($21.60). Dinners are à la carte, averaging £30–£50 ($48–$80) per meal.

EN ROUTE TO MORETON-IN-MARSH

From Stow-on-the-Wold you can continue directly north along A-429 into Moreton-in-Marsh in 15 minutes. Or else you can take a detour and visit the two "Swells"—Lower Swell, a mile west of Stow on B-4068, and Upper Swell, a mile from Lower Swell on an unnumbered but signposted road. Like the Slaughters, these are very charming and unspoiled 18th-century villages lying on back roads. From these two villages, you can take side roads north to Bourton-on-the-Hill en route to Moreton-in-Marsh 7 miles away.

MORETON-IN-MARSH

Moreton-in-Marsh is an important center for rail passengers headed for the Cotswolds because it's near many villages of interest. The town is 4 miles north of Stow-on-the-Wold, 7 miles south of Chipping Campden, and 17 miles south of Stratford-upon-Avon. Don't take the name "Moreton-in-Marsh" too literally, as "marsh" derives from an old word meaning "border."

It's the town as a whole that is the attraction—not specific sights or museums. The town once lay on the ancient Fosse Way. Look for the 17th-century market hall and the old curfew tower, and then walk down the shop-flanked High (the main street), where Roman legions trudged centuries ago. Look for the Market Hall on High Street, a Victorian Tudor structure from 1887. The Curfew Tower on Oxford Street is from the 1600s (in the 19th century its bell rang daily). However, far more alluring are the antique shops along the wide Fosse Way. Moreton-in-Marsh doesn't rival Stow-on-the-Wold in shopping, but everybody seems to be a shopkeeper here.

ESSENTIALS

ARRIVING   By Train   You can take a train from London Paddington Station, arriving in about 2 hours.

By Bus   National Express coaches run from London's Victoria Coach Station to Moreton-in-Marsh daily.

VISITOR INFORMATION   The nearest tourist office is at Stow-on-the-Wold (see above).

ACCOMMODATIONS

Manor House Hotel. High St., Moreton-in-Marsh, Gloucestershire GL56 0LJ. ☎ **800/ 876-9480** in the U.S., or 01608/650501. Fax 01608/651481. 39 rms, 1 family suite. TV TEL. £85–£125 ($136–$200) double; £135 ($216) suite. Rates include English breakfast. AE, DC, MC, V. Free parking.

The town's best address, the Manor House comes complete with its own ghost, a priest's hiding hole, a secret passage, and a moot room used centuries ago by local merchants to settle arguments over wool exchanges. On the main street, it's a formal yet gracious house, and its rear portions reveal varying architectural periods of design. Here, the vine-covered walls protect the garden. The hotel has a heated indoor pool, a spa bath, and a sauna. The bedrooms are tastefully furnished, often with antiques or fine reproductions. Many have fine old desks set in front of window ledges, with a view of the garden and ornamental pond.

ⓢ White Hart Royal Hotel. High St., Moreton-in-Marsh, Gloucestershire GL56 0BA. ☎ **01608/650731.** Fax 01608/650880. 19 rms. TV TEL. £65–£70 ($104–$112) double. Rates include English breakfast. AE, DC, MC, V. Free parking.

A mellow old Cotswold inn once graced by Charles I (in 1644), the White Hart provides modern amenities without compromising the personality of yesteryear. It long ago ceased being the premier inn of town, and Michelin has dropped it altogether, but it's still a good, comfortable place to spend the night. The well-furnished bedrooms all have hot and cold running water, innerspring mattresses, and a few antiques intermixed with basic 20th-century pieces.

DINING

ⓞ Marsh Goose. High St. ☎ **01608/652111.** Reservations recommended. Lunch main courses £10–£13 ($16–$20.80); three-course fixed-price lunch £13.50 ($21.60), on Sun £18.50 ($29.60); four-course fixed-price dinner £24 ($38.40). AE, MC, V. Tues–Sun 12:30–2:30pm; Tues–Sat 7:30–9:45pm. MODERN BRITISH.

In a highly competitive area of England, the food here ranks at the top, a creative seasonal cuisine that showcases the talents of chef Sonya Kidney. Despite its unique allure and country-house elegance, this is very much an outpost of young and sophisticated Londoners. The unusual cuisine is modern British, with good doses of Caribbean style thrown in. Examples include calves' liver with mangoes and Dubonnet sauce; breast of roasted guinea fowl with a creamy mustard sauce and prunes wrapped in bacon; and a suprême of salmon with mussels and a saffron-flavored cream sauce.

CHIPPING CAMPDEN

The English, regardless of how often they visit the Cotswolds, are attracted in great numbers to this town, once an important wool center. Off the main road, it's easily accessible to major points of interest, and double-decker buses frequently run through here on their way to Oxford or Stratford-upon-Avon. It lies 36 miles northwest of Oxford, 12 miles south of Stratford-upon-Avon, and 93 miles northwest of London.

On the northern edge of the Cotswolds above the Vale of Evesham, Campden, a Saxon settlement, was recorded in the *Domesday Book*. In medieval times, rich merchants built homes of Cotswold stone along its model High Street, described by historian G. M. Trevelyan as "the most beautiful village street now left in the island." Today the houses have been so well preserved that Chipping Campden remains a gem of the Middle Ages. Its church dates from the 15th century, and its old market hall is the loveliest in the Cotswolds. Look, also, for its almshouses, which, along with the market hall, were built by a great wool merchant, Sir Baptist Hicks, whose tomb is in the church.

ESSENTIALS

ARRIVING   By Train   Trains depart from London's Paddington Station for Moreton-in-Marsh; the trip takes 1¹/₂ to 2 hours. At Moreton-in-Marsh, a bus operated by Castleway's travels the 7 miles to Chipping Campden five times a day. Many visitors opt for a taxi at Moreton-in-Marsh to go to Chipping Campden.

By Bus   The largest and most important nearby bus depot is Cheltenham, which receives service several times a day from London's Victoria Coach Station. From Cheltenham, however, bus service (by Barry's Coaches) is infrequent and uncertain, departing at the most only three times per week.

VISITOR INFORMATION   The summer-only **Tourist Information Centre** is at Woolstaplers Hall Museum, High Street (☎ **01386/840101**), open Mon–Fri 9:30am–5pm.

ACCOMMODATIONS & DINING

✪ **Cotswold House Hotel.** The Square, Chipping Campden, Gloucestershire GL55 6AN. ☎ **01386/840330.** Fax 01386/840310. 15 rms. TV TEL. £100–£140 ($160–$224) double; £160 ($256) four-poster room. Rates include English breakfast. AE, DC, MC, V. Free parking.

A stately, formal Regency house dating from 1800, right in the heart of the village, opposite the old wool market, Cotswold House sits amid 1¹/₂ acres of tended, walled garden with shaded seating. It's the best place to stay within the town. Note the fine winding Regency staircase in the reception hall. The bedrooms are furnished with themes ranging from Gothic to French to military, with many others included along the way. You can dine in the restaurant, which serves first-class English and French food in a formal, elegant room, or in Greenstocks Brasserie.

Noel Arms Hotel. High St., Chipping Campden, Gloucestershire GL55 6AT. ☎ **800/528-1234** in the U.S. and Canada, or 01386/840317. Fax 01386/841136. 26 rms. TV TEL. £80–£110 ($128–$176) double. Children up to 10 stay free in parents' room. Rates include English breakfast. AE, DC, MC, V. Free parking.

This old coaching inn has been famous in the Cotswolds since the 14th century, although it long ago lost its number one position to the Cotswold House. In 1651 Charles II rested here after his defeat at the Battle of Worcester. Tradition is kept alive in the decor, with fine antiques, muskets, swords, and shields. There's a private sitting room for residents, but you may prefer the lounge with its 12-foot-wide fireplace. Twelve bedrooms date back to the 14th century; the others, comfortably furnished and well appointed, are in a more sterile modern wing built of Cotswold stone. The oak-paneled Gainsborough Restaurant offers an extensive menu, with an international wine list. Typical English dishes such as venison and mushroom pie or roast prime sirloin of beef with Yorkshire pudding are featured.

BROADWAY

The most overrun and tourist-trodden town of the Cotswolds is also one of the most beautiful—hence, its enduring popularity. Many of the Cotswolds' prime attractions, as well as Shakespeare country, lie within easy reach of Broadway, which is near Evesham at the southern tip of Hereford and Worcester. Broadway lies 15 miles southwest of Stratford-upon-Avon, 5 miles west of Chipping Campden, and 93 miles northwest of London.

The best-known of the Cotswold villages, Broadway has a wide and beautiful High Street flanked with honey-colored stone buildings, remarkable for their harmony of style and design. Overlooking the Vale of Evesham, it's a major stop for bus tours and is mobbed in summer; however, it manages to retain its charm in spite of the invasion.

ESSENTIALS

ARRIVING   By Train   Connections are possible from London's Paddington Station via Oxford. The nearest railway stations are at Moreton-in-Marsh (7 miles away) or at Evesham (5 miles away). Frequent buses arrive from Evesham, but one has to take a taxi from Moreton.

By Bus   From London's Victoria Coach Station, one coach daily runs to Broadway, taking 2$^1/_2$ hours.

By Car   From Chipping Campden take the B-4081 southwest to the junction with A-44, at which point you cut northwest to Broadway.

VISITOR INFORMATION   The **Tourist Information Centre,** 1 Cotswold Court (☎ **01386/852937**), is open Mar–Dec Mon–Sat 10am–1pm and 2–5pm.

ACCOMMODATIONS & DINING

Broadway Hotel. The Green, Broadway, Hereford and Worcester WR12 7AA. ☎ **01386/852401.** Fax 01386/853879. 18 rms. TV TEL. £70–£85 ($112–$136) double. Rates include English breakfast. AE, DC, MC, V. Free parking.

Right on the village green, one of the most colorful places in Broadway, is this converted 15th-century house, formerly used by the abbots of Pershore, combining the half-timbered look of the Vale of Evesham with the stone of the Cotswolds. While keeping its old-world charm, the hotel has been modernized and converted to provide comforts. All the pleasantly furnished rooms have hot-beverage facilities and central heating. One room with full private bath has a four-poster bed. The cooking is fine, the service personal, and the dining room attractive.

Dormy House. Willersey Hill, Broadway, Hereford and Worcester WR12 7LF. ☎ **01386/852711.** Fax 01386/858636. 46 rms, 3 suites. TV TEL. £120–£145 ($192–$232) double; £155 ($248) suite. Rates include English breakfast. AE, DC, MC, V. Closed Dec 24–28. Free parking. Take A-44 2 miles southeast of Broadway.

This manor house high on a hill above the village boasts views in all directions. Its panoramic position has made it a favorite place for those who desire a meal, afternoon tea, or lodgings. The owners transformed it from a sheep farm, furnishing the 17th-century house with a few antiques, good soft beds, and full central heating; they also extended these amenities to an old adjoining timbered barn, which they converted into studio rooms, with open-beamed ceilings. The establishment serves an excellent cuisine, and the cellar houses a superb selection of wines.

✪ **Lygon Arms.** High St., Broadway, Hereford and Worcester WR12 7DU. ☎ **01386/852255.** Fax 01386/858611. 60 rms, 5 suites. TV TEL. £150–£160 ($240–$256) double; from £235 ($376) suite. VAT extra. Rates include continental breakfast. AE, DC, MC, V. Free parking.

This many-gabled structure basks in its reputation as one of the greatest Old English inns. In the rear the inn opens onto a private garden, with 3 acres of lawns, trees, and borders of flowers, stone walls with roses, and nooks for tea or sherry. The oldest portions date from 1532 or earlier, but builders many times since then have made their additions. Today an earlier century is evoked by the almost overwhelmingly charming cluster of antique-laden public rooms. Many but not all the rooms are in the antique style; a new wing offers a more 20th-century environment. Each room is furnished with a radio, hair dryer, and trouser press. You dine in the oak-paneled Great Hall, with a Tudor fireplace, a vaulted ceiling, and a minstrels' gallery.

DINING

Tapestry Restaurant. In Dormy House, off the A-44, Willersey Hill, Broadway. ☎ **01386/852711.** Reservations recommended. Set price Sun lunch £17 ($27.20); dinner main courses £14.80–£20.95 ($23.70–$33.50). Table d'hôte menus (dinner only) £26.50–£34 ($42.40–$54.40). AE, DC, MC, V. Daily noon–2pm; Mon–Sat 7–9:30pm; Sun 7–9pm. MODERN BRITISH.

Set 2 miles from the center of Broadway, beside the highway leading to Moreton-in-Marsh and Oxford, this is one of the most charming and well-managed restaurants in the district, with an elegant but less stringent formality than the Lygon Arms. The setting is as pastoral as a painting by Constable. You'll dine within a room ringed with Cotswold stone or in an adjacent glass-sided conservatory (no-smoking). The cuisine prepared by Alan Cutler and Simon Boyle has been praised for its intelligence and its logic. Menu items change every 3 months, but might include a roasted suprême of pigeon served on a bed of risotto scented with sage; grilled fillet of turbot accompanied with a pink grapefruit and butter sauce; and a suprême of locally reared Barbary duckling with a fig and ginger confit.

STRATFORD-UPON-AVON

Stratford is virtually overrun by visitors in the summer months, the crowds dwindling in winter when you can at least walk on the streets and seek out the places of genuine historic interest. It's located 91 miles northwest of London and 40 miles northwest of Oxford.

David Garrick, the actor, really launched the shrine in 1769 when he organized the first of the Bard's commemorative birthday celebrations. William Shakespeare, of course, was born here. Little is known about his early life, and many of the stories connected with Shakespeare's days in Stratford are largely fanciful, invented to amuse the vast number of literary fans who make the pilgrimage.

A magnet for tourists is the Royal Shakespeare Theatre, and the Swan Theatre, where the Royal Shakespeare Company performs during a long season (early Apr to late Jan). Visitors often rush back to London after a performance, but despite the crowds, the literary pilgrimage sights deserve your interest. Stratford today aggressively hustles the Shakespeare connection, a bit suffocatingly so, as everybody seems in business to make a buck off the Bard.

ESSENTIALS

ARRIVING   By Train   Those using public transport can take frequent trains from Paddington Station; the trip takes 2¼ hours. Call **0171/262-6767** for schedules. Same-day round-trip tickets cost £18 ($28.80) or £21 ($33.60) to return the next day.

By Bus   Eight National Express (☎ **0990/808080**) coaches a day leave from Victoria Station; the trip takes 3¼ hours. A single-day round-trip ticket costs £13 ($20.80) except Friday when the price is £15.50 ($24.80).

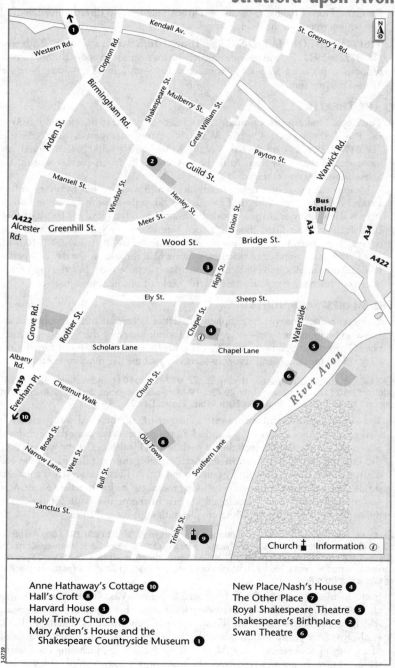

Stratford-upon-Avon

Anne Hathaway's Cottage ❿
Hall's Croft ❽
Harvard House ❸
Holy Trinity Church ❾
Mary Arden's House and the
 Shakespeare Countryside Museum ❶

New Place/Nash's House ❹
The Other Place ❼
Royal Shakespeare Theatre ❺
Shakespeare's Birthplace ❷
Swan Theatre ❻

Church ✝ Information ⓘ

3-0739

By Car   From Broadway, continue northeast along A-46 directly into Stratford-upon-Avon to call on the Bard.

VISITOR INFORMATION   The **Tourist Information Centre,** Bridgefoot (☎ **01789/293127**), will provide any details you might wish about the Shakespeare properties. It's open Mar–Oct Mon–Sat 9am–6pm, Sun 11am–5pm; Nov–Feb Mon–Sat 9am–5pm.

✪ THE THEATER

The **Royal Shakespeare Company** has a major showcase in Stratford-upon-Avon, the Royal Shakespeare Theatre, Waterside, Stratford-upon-Avon CV37 6BB (☎ **01789/295623**), on the banks of the Avon. Seating 1,500 patrons, the theater has a season that runs from April 17 to October 5. In an average season, five Shakespearean plays are staged.

It's important to reserve tickets in advance, which you can book by phone or from a travel agent. In New York try Edwards and Edwards or Keith Prowse in London (they will add a service charge), or call the theater box office (payment by major credit card) at the number listed above; it's open Mon–Sat 9am–8pm, closing at 6pm on days with no performances. Seat prices range from £6.50 to £45.50 ($10.40 to $72.80). A small number of tickets are always held for sale on the day of a performance. You can pick up your ticket on the day it is to be used, but you can't cancel once your reservation is made unless 2 full weeks of advance notice is given.

THE SHAKESPEARE SIGHTS

Besides the attractions on the periphery of Stratford, there are many Elizabethan and Jacobean buildings in town—many of them administered by the Shakespeare Birthplace Trust. One ticket—costing £9 ($14.40) for adults, £4 ($6.40) for children, £7.50 ($12) for seniors and students—lets you visit the five most important sights.

✪ **Shakespeare's Birthplace.** Henley St. ☎ **01789/204016.** Admission £3.30 ($5.30) adults, £1.50 ($2.40) children. Mar 20–Oct 19 Mon–Sat 9am–5pm, Sun 9:30am–5pm; off-season Mon–Sat 9:30am–4pm, Sun 10am–4pm. Closed Dec 23–26.

The son of a glover and whittawer (leather worker), the Bard was born on St. George's day (April 23) in 1564 and died 52 years later on the same day. Filled with Shakespeare memorabilia, including a portrait and furnishings of the writer's time, the Trust property is a half-timbered structure, dating from the first part of the 16th century. The house was bought by public donors in 1847 and preserved as a national shrine. You can visit the oak-beamed living room, the bedroom where Shakespeare was probably born, a fully equipped kitchen of the period (look for the "baby-minder"), and a Shakespeare Museum, illustrating his life and times.

✪ **Anne Hathaway's Cottage.** Cottage Lane, Shottery. ☎ **01789/292100.** Admission £2.40 ($3.85) adults, £1.20 ($1.90) children. Mar 20–Oct 19 Mon–Sat 9:30am–5:30pm, Sun 10am–5:30pm; off-season Mon–Sat 9:30am–4:30pm, Sun 10am–4pm. Closed Dec 23–26. You can walk across the meadow to Shottery from Evesham Place in Stratford (pathway marked), or take a bus from Bridge St.

In the hamlet of Shottery 1 mile from Stratford-upon-Avon is the thatched, wattle-and-daub cottage where Anne Hathaway lived before her marriage to Shakespeare. It's the most interesting of the Trust properties, and the most unchanged. The Hathaways were yeoman farmers, and the cottage provides a rare insight into the life of a family of Shakespeare's day. Many original furnishings, including the courting settle and utensils, are preserved inside the house, which was occupied by descendants of Shakespeare's wife's family until 1892.

New Place/Nash's House. Chapel St. ☎ **01789/292325.** Admission £2 ($3.20) adults, £1 ($1.60) children. Mar 20–Oct 19 Mon–Sat 9:30am–5pm, Sun 10am–5pm; Oct 20–Mar 19 Mon–Sat 10am–4pm, Sun 10:30am–4pm. Closed Dec 23–26. Walk west down High St. Chapel St. is a continuation of High St.

This is the site where Shakespeare retired in 1610, a prosperous man as judged by the standards of his day. He died 6 years later, at the age of 52. Regrettably, his former home was torn down, and only the site remains. You enter the gardens through Nash's House (Thomas Nash married a granddaughter of the poet). Nash's House has 16th-century period rooms and an exhibition illustrating the history of Stratford. The delightful Knott Garden adjoins the site and represents the style of a fashionable Elizabethan garden. New Place has its own great garden, which once belonged to Shakespeare.

Mary Arden's House and the Shakespeare Countryside Museum. Wilmcote. ☎ **01789/293455.** Admission £3.30 ($5.30) adults, £1.50 ($2.40) children. Mar 20–Oct 19 Mon–Sat 9:30am–5pm, Sun 10am–5pm; off-season Mon–Sat 10am–4pm, Sun 10:30am–4pm. Closed Dec 23–26. Take the A-3400 (Birmingham) road for 3¹/₂ miles.

This Tudor farmstead, with its old stone dovecote and various outbuildings, was the girlhood home of Shakespeare's mother, or so it was determined by some entrepreneur in the 18th century. There is no definite evidence, however, that this was the actual home where Mary Arden dwelled. It's situated at Wilmcote, 3¹/₂ miles from Stratford. The house contains country furniture and domestic utensils. In the barns, stable, cowshed, and farmyard you'll find an extensive collection of farming implements illustrating life and work in the local countryside from Shakespeare's time to the present.

TOURS

Guided tours of Stratford-upon-Avon leave daily from the Guide Friday Tourism Center, Civic Hall, Rother Street (☎ **01789/294466**). In summer, open-top double-decker buses depart every 15 minutes from 9:30am to 5:30pm. You can take a 1-hour ride without stops, or you can get off at any or all of the town's five Shakespeare's Properties. Anne Hathaway's Cottage and Mary Arden's House are the two likely stops to make outside the town center. Although the bus stops are clearly marked along the historic route, the most logical starting point is on the sidewalk in front of the Pen & Parchment Pub, at Bridgefoot, at the bottom of Bridge Street. Tour tickets are valid all day, so you can hop on and off the buses wherever you want. The tour price is £7 ($11.20) for adults or £2.50 ($4) for children under 12, £5 ($8) for senior citizens or students.

SHOPPING

The largest shop of its kind in the Midlands, **Arbour Antiques, Ltd,** Poet Arbour, off Sheep Street (☎ **01789/293493**), sells antique weapons, used for both warfare and sport, from Britain, Europe, and in some cases, India and Turkey. If you've always hankered after a full suit of armor, this place will be able to sell you one.

More than any other pottery studio in Stratford, **Dianthus,** 1 Centre Craft Yard, off Henley St. (☎ **01789/292252**), benefits from an intimate knowledge of California pottery as practiced in San Francisco, with emphasis on unique creative statements cast in stoneware. It's within spacious quarters where a trio of potters display their technique on their potter's wheels.

At the **National Trust Shop,** 45 Wood St. (☎ **01789/262197**), you'll find textbooks and guidebooks describing esoteric places in the environs of Stratford, descriptions of National Trust properties throughout England, stationery, books, china, pewterware, and toiletries, each inscribed, embossed, or painted with logos that evoke some aspect of English tastes and traditions.

Everything in the **Pickwick Gallery,** 32 Henley St. (☎ **01789/294861**), is a well-crafted work of art produced by copper or steel engraving plates, or printed by means of a carved wooden block. Look for the engravings by William Hogarth showing satirical scenes that lampooned Parliamentary corruption during the late 18th century.

Set within an antique house with ceiling beams that lies across from the Shakespeare Birthplace Center, the **Shakespeare Bookshop,** 39 Henley St. (☎ **01789/292176**), is the region's premier source for textbooks and academic treatises on the Bard and his works. It specializes in books conceived for every level of expertise, from picture books for junior high school students to weighty tomes geared to anyone pursuing a Ph.D. in literature.

Scattered over three floors of an Elizabethan House said to have been occupied by one of Shakespeare's daughters as an adult, **Trading Post,** 1 High St. (☎ **01789/ 267228**), offers a jammed and slightly claustrophobic assortment of gift items that might appeal to your taste for the kitschy and nostalgic. Included in the roster of items are doll's houses and the furnishings to go inside, a scattering of small, easy-to-transport antiques, and memorabilia of your visit to the Midlands.

ACCOMMODATIONS

Very Expensive

Welcombe Hotel. Warwick Rd., Stratford-upon-Avon, Warwickshire CV37 ONR. ☎ **01789/ 295252.** Fax 01789/414666. 67 rms, 9 suites. TV TEL. £150 ($240) double; £175–£275 ($280–$440) suite. Rates include English breakfast. AE, DC, MC, V. Free parking. Take A-439 1¹/₂ miles northeast of the town center.

For a formal, historic hotel, there is none better in Stratford. One of England's great Jacobean country houses, this hotel is a 10-minute ride from the heart of Stratford-upon-Avon. Its keynote feature is an 18-hole golf course. The home once belonged to Sir Archibald Flower, the philanthropic brewer who helped create the Shakespeare Memorial Theatre. Converted into a hotel, it is surrounded by 157 acres of grounds and has a formal entrance on Warwick Road, a winding driveway leading to the main hall. The public rooms are heroic in size, with high mullioned windows providing views of the park. Regular bedrooms—some big enough for tennis matches—are luxuriously furnished; however, those in the garden wing, although comfortable, are small.

Expensive

Alveston Manor Hotel. Clopton Bridge, Stratford-upon-Avon, Warwickshire CV37 7HP. ☎ **800/225-5843** in the U.S. and Canada, or 01789/204581. Fax 01789/414095. 103 rms, 3 suites. TV TEL. £110–£145 ($176–$232) double; £185 ($296) suite. AE, DC, MC, V. Free parking.

This black-and-white timbered manor is perfect for theatergoers—it's just a two-minute walk from the Avon off B-4066. Whereas the Welcombe is on the outskirts and has cornered the deluxe trade, the Alveston along with the Shakespeare (see below) are tied for the most atmospheric choices within the town itself. The hotel has a wealth of chimneys and gables, and everything from an Elizabethan gazebo to Queen Anne windows. Mentioned in the *Domesday Book,* the building predates the arrival of William the Conqueror. The rooms in the manor house will appeal to those who appreciate old slanted floors, overhead beams, and antique furnishings. Some triples or quads are available in the modern section, which is connected by a covered walk through the rear garden. The rooms here have built-in pieces and a color-coordinated decor, and 20 are set aside for nonsmokers.

Shakespeare. Chapel St., Stratford-upon-Avon, Warwickshire CV37 6ER. ☎ **800/225-5843** in the U.S. and Canada, or 01789/294771. Fax 01789/415411. 63 rms, 4 suites. TV TEL. £120 ($192) double; £145–£170 ($232–$272) suite. Children up to 16 stay free in parents' room. AE, DC, MC, V. Free parking.

Filled with historical associations, the original core of this hotel, which dates from the 1400s, has seen many additions in its long life. It's been called both the Four Gables Hotel and the Five Gables Hotel. In the 1700s a demure facade of Regency brick was added to conceal the intricate timber framing, but in the 1880s, with a rash of Shakespearean revivals, the hotel was restored to its original Tudor look. It is equaled within the central core of Stratford only by Alveston Manor. Residents relax in the post-and-timber-studded public rooms, within sight of fireplaces and play-bills from 19th-century productions of Shakespeare's plays. The bedrooms are named in honor of noteworthy actors, Shakespeare's plays, or Shakespearean characters. The oldest are capped with hewn timbers, and all have modern comforts. Even the newer accommodations are at least 40 to 50 years old and have rose-and-thistle patterns carved into many of their exposed timbers.

Moderate

Arden Thistle Hotel. 44 Waterside, Stratford-upon-Avon, Warwickshire CV37 6BA. ☎ **01789/294949.** Fax 01789/415874. 63 rms. TV TEL. £98 ($156.80) double. AE, DC, MC, V. Free parking.

Across the street from the main entrance of the Royal Shakespeare and Swan theaters, this hotel's interior was completely refurbished in 1993 after it was purchased by the Thistle chain. Theatergoers flock here. Its redbrick main section dates from the Regency period, although over the years a handful of adjacent buildings were included and an uninspired modern extension was added. Today, the interior has a well-upholstered lounge and bar; a dining room (Bards) with bay windows; a covered garden terrace; and comfortable but narrow bedrooms with trouser presses, hair dryers, and hot-beverage facilities.

Falcon. Chapel St., Stratford-upon-Avon, Warwickshire CV37 6HA. ☎ **01789/279953.** Fax 01789/414260. 72 rms, 1 suite. TV TEL. £105 ($168) double; £125 ($200) suite. AE, DC, MC, V. Free parking.

The Falcon blends the very old and the very new. At the rear of a black-and-white timbered inn, licensed a quarter of a century after Shakespeare's death, is a more sterile 1970 bedroom extension, joined by a glass-covered passageway. In the heart of Stratford, the inn faces the Guild Chapel and the New Place Gardens. The recently upgraded bedrooms in the mellowed part have oak beams, diamond leaded-glass windows, some antique furnishings, and good reproductions. Each room includes a radio, electric trouser press, and hot-beverage facilities, but not enough soundproofing to prevent you from hearing what BBC show your neighbor is watching next door.

Inexpensive

ⓢ Stratford House. 18 Sheep St., Stratford-upon-Avon, Warwickshire CV37 6EF. ☎ **01789/268288.** Fax 01789/295580. 11 rms, 1 suite. TV TEL. £82–£88 ($131.20–$140.80) double; £120 ($192) suite. Rates include English breakfast. AE, DC, MC, V. Parking £3 ($4.80).

This Georgian house stands 100 yards from the River Avon and the Royal Shakespeare Theatre. The staff of this small hotel extends a warm welcome to North American guests. The house is furnished tastefully and with style, somewhat like a private home, with books and pictures along with a scattering of antiques. Everything is spotlessly maintained. There is a walled courtyard on the side with flowering plants. All bedrooms have tea- and coffeemakers.

⑤ Stratheden Hotel. 5 Chapel St., Stratford-upon-Avon, Warwickshire CV37 6EP. ☎ **01789/ 297119.** Fax 01789/297119. 9 rms. TV TEL. £56–£62 ($89.60–$99.20) double. Rates include English breakfast. MC, V.

First mentioned in a property deed in 1333, this hotel lies a short walk north of the Royal Shakespeare Theatre. The Stratheden, built in 1673 (and today the oldest remaining brick building in the town center), has a tiny rear garden and top-floor rooms with slanted, beamed ceilings. It has improved in both decor and comfort with the addition of fresh paint, new curtains, and good beds. The dining room, with a bay window, has an overscale sideboard that once belonged to the "insanely vain" Marie Corelli, an eccentric novelist, poet, and mystic, and a favorite author of Queen Victoria.

DINING

Box Tree Restaurant. In the Royal Shakespeare Theatre, Waterside. ☎ **01789/293226.** Reservations required. Matinee lunch £16.50 ($26.60); dinner £25 ($40). AE, MC, V. Thurs–Sat noon–2:30pm; Mon–Sat 5:45pm–midnight. FRENCH/ITALIAN/ENGLISH.

This restaurant is right in the theater itself, with glass walls providing an unobstructed view of the Avon and its swans. During intermission there is a snack feast of smoked salmon and champagne. You dine by flickering candlelight. There's a special phone for reservations in the theater lobby. Many dishes are definitely Old English (apple and parsnip soup); others reflect a continental touch. For your main course, you might select Dover sole, salmi of wild boar, pheasant suprême, or roast loin of pork. Homemade desserts are likely to include crème brûlée, an old-time favorite at the Box Tree. Better food can be had at Hussain's or Liaison, but none is as convenient for theatergoers as this choice.

⑤ Hussain's. 6A Chapel St. ☎ **01789/267506.** Reservations recommended. Main courses £5.75–£10.95 ($9.20–$17.50). AE, DC, MC, V. Daily noon–2pm and 5:15–11:45pm. INDIAN.

Dining here has been compared to a visit to a private Indian home. The restaurant has many admirers—some consider it one of the brighter spots on the bleak culinary landscape. The well-trained, alert staff welcome guests, advising them about special dishes. Against a setting of pink crushed-velvet paneling, you can select from an array of northern Indian dishes. Herbs and spices are blended imaginatively in the kitchen to impart a distinctive flavor. Many tandoori dishes are offered, along with various curries with lamb or prawn. Hussain's is across from the Shakespeare Hotel and historic New Place.

Liaison. 1 Shakespeare St. ☎ **01789/293400.** Reservations recommended. Main courses £13.95–£15.95 ($22.30–$25.50); fixed-price lunch £11.50–£13.95 ($18.40–$22.30); fixed-price dinner £21.95 ($35.10). AE, DC, MC, V. Mon–Fri noon–2:30pm; Mon–Sat 6–10:30pm. MODERN BRITISH.

Conveniently close to Shakespeare's birthplace (within a 3-minute walk), this restaurant occupies the high-ceilinged premises of what was formerly a Methodist chapel. Menu choices are modern and elegant, loosely based on traditional British cuisine, with creative input from contemporary sources. You get a better and more imaginative fare here than you do at any other restaurant in Stratford. Patricia Plunkett is the culinary star behind this place, and she has an appealing way of cooking, using carefully selected ingredients chosen fresh daily, each dish transformed by her talent. Tempting main courses include a delectable boned guinea fowl with wild rice coated with an orange mustard glaze or a paupiette of sole with a crabmeat soufflé on a mild curry sauce.

PUBS

Black Swan (also known as the Dirty Duck). Waterside. ☎ **01789/297312.** Reservations required for dining. Main courses £6–£14 ($9.60–$22.40); pint of ale £1.80 ($2.90). MC, V (restaurant only). Pub, Mon–Sat 11am–11pm, Sun noon–3pm and 7–10:30pm. Restaurant, Tues–Sun noon–2pm; Mon–Sat 6–11:30pm. ENGLISH.

Affectionately known as the Dirty Duck, this has been a popular hangout for Stratford players since the 18th century. The wall is lined with autographed photos of its patrons, some of long ago, such as Laurence Olivier. The front lounge and bar crackles with intense conversation. In the spring and fall an open fire blazes. In the Dirty Duck Grill Room, typical English grills, among other dishes, are featured, although no one ever accused the Dirty Duck of serving the best food in Stratford. Main dishes include braised kidneys or oxtails, roast chicken, or honey-roasted duck.

Garrick Inn. 25 High St. ☎ **01789/292186.** Main courses £5–£9 ($8–$14.40). MC, V. Meals daily noon–8:30pm. Pub, Mon–Sat 11am–11pm, Sun noon–3pm and 7–10:30pm. ENGLISH.

This black-and-white timbered Elizabethan pub from 1595 near Harvard House has an unpretentious charm. It's named after David Garrick, one of England's greatest actors. The front bar is decorated with tapestry-covered settles, an old oak refectory table, and an open fireplace that attracts the locals. The black bar has a circular fireplace with a copper hood and mementos of the triumphs of the English stage. The specialty is homemade pies such as steak and ale, steak and kidney, or chicken and mushroom.

A DAY TRIP FROM STRATFORD

✪ **WARWICK CASTLE**   Perched on a rocky cliff above the Avon in the town center, this stately late-17th-century–style mansion is surrounded by a magnificent 14th-century fortress. The first significant fortifications at Warwick were built by Ethelfleda, daughter of Alfred the Great, in 915. Two years after the Norman Conquest in 1068, William the Conqueror ordered the construction of a motte and bailey castle. The castle mound is all that remains today of the Norman castle.

The Beauchamp family, earls of Warwick, is responsible for the appearance of the castle today, and much of the external structure remains unchanged from the mid-14th century. The staterooms and Great Hall house fine collections of paintings, furniture, arms, and armor. The armory, dungeon, torture chamber, ghost tower, clock tower, and Guy's tower create a vivid picture of the castle's turbulent past and its important role in the history of England.

Warwick Castle was described by Sir Walter Scott in 1828 as "that fairest monument of ancient and chivalrous splendor which yet remains uninjured by time." Visitors can also see the Victorian rose garden, a re-creation of an original design from 1868 by Robert Marnock. On Castle Hill, Warwick Castle (☎ **01926/408000**) is open daily 10am–5pm. Admission is £8.75 ($14) for adults, £5.25 ($8.40) for children 4–16, and £6.25 ($10) for senior citizens and students (free for children 3 and under).

Trains run frequently between Stratford and Warwick, and a Midland Red Bus leaves every hour (no. 18 or X16) during the day; the trip takes 15 to 20 minutes. Motorists should take A-46 north from Stratford.

3 Stonehenge & Bath

Many visitors with very limited time head for the "West Countree" of England, where they explore its two major attractions: Stonehenge—the most important prehistoric monument in Britain—and Bath, England's most elegant city, famed for its architecture and its hot springs. If you have the time, you should not miss having a look at Salisbury Cathedral and the other prehistoric sites in the area, at Avebury and Old Sarum.

ONLY IN STONEHENGE & BATH

Visiting Stoneghenge at Twilight   We like to go at twilight when the bus hordes have departed and you can watch the last rays of sunshine reflected off these ancient stones, which seem to heighten their mystery. You can speculate as to their origin some 3,500 to 5,000 years ago. Only the silent Salisbury Plain knows for sure. But whatever their purpose, these stones have captured the imagination of the world.

Taking Afternoon Tea at the Pump Room   The best way to return to the glory of Beau Nash's elegant 18th-century Bath is to come here for afternoon tea. Tradition dictates that first you sip the foul-tasting waters of the hot springs. After that, you can cleanse and sweeten your palate with afternoon tea and freshly baked cakes as you listen to the sounds of violin music.

Tasting Gingerbread at the American Museum   If you ever wondered what made George Washington grow up to be the founder of his country, it was probably the spice in his mother's gingerbread. You can still taste that gingerbread—baked fresh every day—based on her old recipe at the American Museum at Claverton Manor on Bathwick Hill 2¹/₂ miles outside Bath. This was the first American museum established outside the United States, and it remains the best. There's everything here from a copy of Washington's flower garden at Mount Vernon to a Conestoga wagon.

Enjoying a Leisurely Cruise on a Summer Afternoon   The Kennet and Avon Canal, just outside of Bath, is lined with leafy banks. The canal links the Thames River at Reading in the east with the docks of the city of Bristol in the west. Long neglected, this 1810 canal has been redredged and its more than 100 locks restored to their former glory—in all some 90 miles of navigable canal open to the public once again. Instead of industrial craft, they are now filled with pleasure craft, or else a waterbus plying the waters between Bath and Folly Swing Bridge, which is the most romantic part of the canal. Hop aboard *Scenic I* running on the hour daily from 11am to 7pm, upstream from Pulteney Weir opposite Parade Gardens. Check with tourist information for more details about other boat trips.

Spending a Morning at Bath Abbey   Before this 1499 church was begun, both a Saxon abbey and a Norman cathedral had stood on the site. A sunny morning is the best time to view it when the light pours through the sparkling panes of glass in the towering clerestory windows, providing a natural illumination for the fan vaulting, one of the purest forms of English Perpendicular architecture.

Downing a Pint at the Saracen's Head   This is the oldest pub in Bath, dating from 1713. Back when it was an inn, Charles Dickens boarded in 1835. Saracen's Head, 42 Broad St. (☎ 01225/426518), no longer puts up overnight guests, but still welcomes visitors for a pint under its beamed ceilings, which still possess their original plasterwork. You'd be assured of a warm welcome at this unpretentious place. It's cozy and filled with chatty, friendly locals. In summer you might refresh yourself with a good Pimms.

✪ STONEHENGE

Two miles west of Amesbury at the junction of A-303 and A-344/A-360, about 9 miles north of Salisbury, stands the renowned monument of Stonehenge, a stone

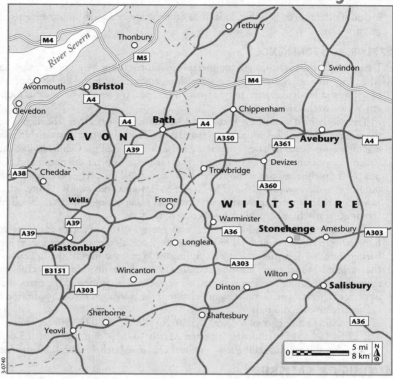

circle believed to be anywhere from 3,500 to 5,000 years old. This huge circle of lintels and megalithic pillars is the most important prehistoric monument in Britain.

ESSENTIALS

ARRIVING **By Car** To reach Stonehenge from London, head in the direction of Salisbury, 90 miles to the southwest. Take the M-3 to the end of the run, continuing the rest of the way on A-30. Once at Salisbury, after stopping to view its cathedral (see below), head north on Castle Road from the center of town. At the first roundabout or traffic circle, take the exit toward Amesbury (A-345) and Old Sarum. Continue along this route for 8 miles and then turn left onto A-303 in the direction of Exeter. Stonehenge is signposted, leading you up the A-344 to the right. In all, it's about 12 miles total from Salisbury.

By Train or Bus You can also reach Stonehenge by train and bus from London. A Network Express train departs hourly from Waterloo Station in London bound for Salisbury; the trip takes 2 hours. Buses also depart four or five times per day from London's Victoria Station, heading for Salisbury; the trip takes 2¹/₂ hours. Once at Stonehenge, you can take a Wilts & Dorset bus (☎ **01722/336-855** for schedules), which runs several vehicles daily—depending on demand—from Salisbury to Stonehenge. This company's buses depart from the train station at Salisbury, heading directly to Stonehenge; the trip takes 30 minutes and a round-trip passage costs £4.10 ($6.55). Use Salisbury (see below) as a refueling stop, as the visitors center, including the toilets, is rather squalid at Stonehenge, although improvements are promised.

EXPLORING STONEHENGE

Despite its familiarity through photographs, visitors cannot help but be impressed when they first see Stonehenge, an astonishing engineering feat—the boulders, the bluestones in particular, were moved many miles, possibly from as far away as southern Wales, to this site.

The widely held view of the 18th- and 19-century romantics that Stonehenge was the work of the Druids is without real foundation. The boulders, many weighing several tons, are believed to have predated the arrival in Britain of the Celtic Druidic cult. Recent excavations continue to bring new evidence to bear on the origin and purpose of the prehistoric circle; controversy has surrounded the site, especially since the publication of *Stonehenge Decoded* by Gerald S. Hawkins and John B. White, which maintains that Stonehenge was an astronomical observatory—that is, a Neolithic "computing machine" capable of predicting eclipses.

The site is now surrounded by a fence to protect it from vandals and souvenir hunters. Your ticket permits you to go inside the fence, all the way up to a short rope barrier about 50 feet from the stones. Spring 1996 saw the start of the full circular tour around Stonehenge; a modular walkway has been introduced to cross the archeologically important area that runs between the Heel Stone and the main circle of stones. This lets you complete a full circuit of the stones, an excellent addition to the well-received audio tour.

Admission to Stonehenge is £3.50 ($5.60) for adults, £1.80 ($2.90) for children, and £2.60 ($4.15) for students. It's open March 16–May and Sept–Oct 15 daily 9:30am–6pm; June–Aug daily 9am–7pm; and Oct 16–March 15 daily 9:30am–4pm.

AVEBURY & SALISBURY

After visiting Stonehenge, you can move on to Bath. But if you have an extra day or so, you should not miss the other attractions nearby.

AVEBURY

Lying 20 miles north of Stonehenge, Avebury, one of Europe's largest prehistoric sites, is on the Kennet River 7 miles west of Marlborough. Unlike Stonehenge, you can walk around the 28-acre site at Avebury, winding in and out of the circle of more than 100 stones, some weighing up to 50 tons. The stones are made of sarsen, a sandstone found in Wiltshire. Inside this large circle are two smaller ones, each with about 30 stones standing upright. Native Neolithic tribes are believed to have built these circles.

Avebury is on A-361 between Swindon and Devizes and a mile from the A-4 London–Bath road. The closest rail station is at Swindon, some 12 miles away, which is served by the main rail line from London to Bath. A limited bus service (no. 49) runs from Swindon to Devizes through Avebury.

You can also reach Avebury by bus from Salisbury by taking one of two buses (nos. 5 and 6) run by Wilts & Dorset (☎ **01722/336855**). The buses leave three times a day Mon–Sat (twice on Sun). The one-way trip takes 1¹⁄₂ hours.

What to See & Do

Founded by Alexander Keiller, the **Avebury Museum** (☎ **01672/539250**) houses one of Britain's most important archeological collections. It began with Keiller's material from excavations at Windmill Hill and Avebury, and now includes artifacts from other prehistoric digs at West Kennet, Long Barrow, Silbury Hill, West Kennet

Avenue, and the Sanctuary. Admission is £1.50 ($2.40) for adults, 80p ($1.30) for children. Open Apr–Oct daily 10am–6pm; Nov–Mar daily 10am–4pm.

Housed in a 17th-century thatched barn is the **Great Barn Museum of Wiltshire Rural Life** (☎ **01672/539555**), a center for the display and interpretation of Wiltshire life during the last three centuries. There are displays on cheese making, blacksmithing, thatching, sheep and shepherds, the wheelwright, and other rural crafts, as well as local geology and domestic life. Admission is 95p ($1.50) for adults, 50p (80¢) for children. Open mid-Mar to Oct daily 10am–5:30pm; Nov to mid-Mar Sat–Sun 11am–4:30pm.

SALISBURY

Long before you enter Salisbury, the spire of the Cathedral will come into view, just as John Constable painted it many times. Salisbury lies in the Avon River Valley, and is a fine place to stop for lunch and a look at the cathedral on your way to Stonehenge.

For driving directions, see above. Salisbury can be reached by bus from the Victoria Coach Station in London. There is also direct rail service from London from Waterloo Station.

✪ Salisbury Cathedral

You can search all of England, but you'll find no better example of the Early English, or pointed, style than Salisbury Cathedral. Construction was begun as early as 1220 and took 38 years to complete; this was rather fast in those days since it was customary for a cathedral building to require at least three centuries. The soaring spire was completed at the end of the 13th century. Despite an ill-conceived attempt at renovation in the 18th century, the architectural integrity of the cathedral has been retained.

The cathedral's 13th-century octagonal chapter house (note the fine sculpture), which is especially attractive, possesses one of the four surviving original texts of the Magna Carta, along with treasures from the diocese of Salisbury and manuscripts and artifacts belonging to the cathedral. The cloisters enhance the beauty of the cathedral, and the exceptionally large close, with at least 75 buildings in its compound (some from the early 18th century and others predating that), sets off the cathedral most effectively.

The cathedral at The Close in Salisbury (☎ **01722/328726**) is open May–Aug daily 8:30am–8:30pm; Sept–Apr daily 8am–6:30pm. To visit the cathedral costs £2.50 ($4), plus another 30p (50¢) to see the Chapter House.

Attractions Nearby

Old Sarum. Castle Road, 2 miles north of Salisbury off A-345.

Old Sarum is believed to have been an Iron Age fortification. The earthworks were known to the Romans as *Sorbiodunum*. Much later, Saxons also used the fortification. The Normans built a cathedral and a castle here in what was then a Middle Ages walled town. Parts of the old cathedral were taken down to build the city of New Sarum (Salisbury).

For information, call **01722/335398**. Admission is £1.70 ($2.70) for adults, 90p ($1.45) for children. Open Apr–Sept daily 10am–6pm; off-season daily 10am–4pm. Bus nos. 3, 5, 6, 7, 8, and 9 out of Salisbury run every 20 minutes to the site.

✪ Wilton House. About 2¹⁄₂ miles west of Salisbury in the town of Wilton on A-30.

Wilton House, one of England's great country estates, is the home of the earls of Pembroke. Wilton House dates from the 16th century, but has undergone numerous alterations, most recently in Victoria's day. It is noted for its 17th-century staterooms by the celebrated architect Inigo Jones. It is believed that Shakespeare's troupe may have entertained here. Preparations for the D-day landings at Normandy were laid out here by Eisenhower and his advisors, with only the silent Van Dyck paintings in the Double Cube room as witnesses.

The house displays paintings by Sir Anthony Van Dyck, Rubens, Brueghel, and Reynolds. A dynamic film introduced and narrated by Anna Massey brings to life the history of the family since 1544, the year it was granted the land by Henry VIII. You then visit a reconstructed Tudor kitchen and Victorian laundry plus "The Wareham Bears," a unique collection of some 200 miniature dressed teddy bears.

Growing on the 21-acre estate are giant Cedars of Lebanon, the oldest of which were planted in 1630. The Palladian Bridge was built in 1737 by the ninth earl of Pembroke and Roger Morris. There are rose and water gardens, riverside and woodland walks, and a huge adventure playground for children.

For information, call **01722/74315.** Admission is £6.50 ($10.40) for adults, £4 ($6.40) for children 5–15 (under 5 free). To enter the grounds costs £4 ($6.40) for adults, £2.50 ($4) for children. Open Apr–Oct daily 11am–6pm (last admission at 5pm).

Where to Dine

Harper's Restaurant. 7–9 Ox Row, Market Sq. ☎ **01722/333118.** Reservations recommended. Main courses £8.50–£11.90 ($13.60–$19.05); fixed-price three-course lunch £7.90 ($12.65); fixed-price three-course dinner £12.90 ($20.65). AE, DC, MC, V. Mon–Sat noon–2pm and 6–9:30pm, Sun 6–9:30pm. ENGLISH.

The chef-owner of this place prides himself on specializing in "real food" that's homemade and wholesome. The pleasantly decorated restaurant is on the second floor of a redbrick building at the back side of Salisbury's largest parking lot, in the town center. Within the same all-purpose dining room, you can order from two different menus, one featuring cost-conscious bistro-style platters, including beefsteak casserole with "herbey dumplings." A longer menu includes all-vegetarian pasta diavolo or spareribs with french fries and rice.

Salisbury Haunch of Venison. 1 Minster St. ☎ **01722/322024.** Main courses £8.50–£11.95 ($13.60–$19.10); bar platters for lunches, light suppers, and snacks £4.50–£8 ($7.20–$12.80). AE, DC, MC, V. Daily noon–3pm; Mon–Sat 7–9:30pm. Pub, Mon–Sat 11am–11pm, Sun noon–3pm and 7–11pm. Closed on Christmas, Easter. ENGLISH.

Right in the heart of Salisbury, this creaky-timbered 1320 chophouse serves excellent dishes, especially English roasts and grills. Stick to its specialties and you'll rarely go wrong. Begin perhaps with tasty grilled venison sausages in a Dijon mustard sauce, then follow with the time-honored house specialty: roast haunch of venison with gin and juniper berries. Many other classic English dishes are served, such as a medley of fish and shellfish or else grilled Barnsley lamb chops with "bubble and squeak" (cabbage and potatoes).

Silver Plough. White Hill, Pitton, near Salisbury. ☎ **01722/712266.** Reservations recommended. Main courses £7–£13 ($11.20–$20.80); bar platters £4.50–£6 ($7.20–$9.60). AE, DC, MC, V. Restaurant, daily noon–2:30pm; Mon–Sat 7–10pm, Sun 7–9pm. Pub, Mon–Sat 11am–3pm and 6–11pm, Sun noon–3pm and 7–10:30pm. Closed Dec 25–26 and Jan 1. Take A-30 for 5 miles east of Salisbury; it's at the southern end of the hamlet of Pitton. ENGLISH.

Built as a stone-sided farmhouse 150 years ago, the Silver Plough is now a charming country pub with an attached restaurant. Snacks available in the bar include ratatouille au gratin and grilled sardines with garlic butter and freshly baked bread. In the somewhat more formal dining room, the chef prepares such dishes as fresh

Dorset mussels in a white wine, garlic, and cream sauce; sliced breast of duck in cracked pepper or orange sauce; and roast guinea fowl in a sharp strawberry sauce. The Silver Plough has known many famous visitors, but the management prefers to stick to its quiet, country atmosphere and to concentrate on making its guests feel at home.

EN ROUTE TO BATH

From Stonehenge follow the sign south to the A-303 heading west. Continue past Chicklade until you come to the junction of A-350 heading directly north. Follow this route toward Warminster, where you can connect with the A-36 into Bath. You'll enter at the southern tier of the city.

BATH

In 1702 Queen Anne made the trek from London 115 miles west to the mineral springs of Bath, thereby launching a fad that was to make the city England's most celebrated spa.

The most famous personage connected with Bath's popularity was the 18th-century dandy Beau Nash. Master of ceremonies of Bath, Nash cut a striking figure. In all the plumage of a bird of paradise, he was carted around in a sedan chair, dispensing (at a price) trinkets to courtiers and aspirant gentlemen. This polished arbiter of taste and manners succeeded in making dueling déclassé.

The 18th-century architects John Wood the Elder and his son provided a proper backdrop for Nash's activities. These architects designed a city of honey-colored stone from the nearby hills, a feat so substantial and lasting that Bath today is the most harmoniously laid-out city in England. The city attracted a following among leading political and literary figures, such as Dickens, Thackeray, Nelson, and Pitt, and most important, of course, Jane Austen. Canadians may already know that General Wolfe lived on Trim Street, and Australians may want to visit the house at 19 Bennett St. where their founding father, Admiral Phillip, lived.

Bath has had two lives. Long before its Georgian and Victorian popularity, it was known to the Romans as *Aquae Sulis*. The foreign legions founded their baths here (which may be visited today) to ease their rheumatism in the curative mineral springs.

Remarkable restoration and careful planning have ensured that Bath retains its handsome look today. It has somewhat of a museum appearance, with the attendant gift shops. Prices—because of massive tourist invasion—tend to be high. But Bath remains one of the high points of the West Country.

ESSENTIALS

ARRIVING   By Train   At least one train per hour leaves London's Paddington Station bound for Bath during the day; the trip takes 70 to 90 minutes.

By Bus   One National Express coach leaves London's Victoria Coach Station every 2 hours during the day for the 2¹/₂-hour trip.

By Car   Coming from London, drive west on M-4 to the junction with A-4, on which you continue west to Bath.

VISITOR INFORMATION   The **Bath Tourist Information Centre,** at Abbey Chambers, Abbey Church Yard (☎ **01225/462831**), opposite the Roman Baths, is open June–Sept Mon–Sat 9:30am–7pm, Sun 10am–6pm; off-season Mon–Sat 9:30am–5pm, Sun 10am–4pm.

SPECIAL EVENTS   For 17 days in late May and early June each year the city is filled with more than 1,000 performers. The **Bath International Music Festival**

focuses on classical music, jazz, new music, and the contemporary visual arts, with orchestras, soloists, and artists from all over the world. There is also all the best in walks, tours, and talks, plus free street entertainment and a free Festival Club in Bath's famous Pump Room. For more information, contact the Bath Festivals Booking Office, Linley House, 1 Pierrepont Place, Bath BA1 1JY (☎ **01225/463362**).

GETTING AROUND One of the best ways to explore Bath is by bike. You can rent one from Avon Valley Bike Hire (☎ **01225/4651880**), behind the train station, open daily 9am–6pm. Rentals are £10.50–£22.50 ($16.80–$36) per day, with a deposit ranging from £20 to £75 ($32 to $120).

EXPLORING BATH

In addition to the attractions listed below, you'll want to visit some of the buildings, crescents, and squares in town. The **North Parade** (where Oliver Goldsmith lived) and the **South Parade** (where English novelist and diarist Frances Burney once resided) represent harmony and are the work of John Wood the Elder. The younger Wood designed the elegant half-moon row of town houses, the **Royal Crescent.** One of the most beautiful squares is **Queen Square**—both Jane Austen and Wordsworth once lived here—showing off the work of Wood the Elder. Also of interest is **The Circus,** built in 1754, as well as the shop-lined **Pulteney Bridge,** designed by Robert Adam and often compared to the Ponte Vecchio of Florence.

✪ **Bath Abbey.** Orange Grove. ☎ **01225/422462.** Free admission; donation requested £1.50 ($2.40). Heritage Vaults £2 ($3.20) adults, £1 ($1.60) students, children, and senior citizens. Abbey, Apr–Oct Mon–Sat 9am–6pm; Nov–Mar Mon–Sat 9am–4:30pm; year-round, Sun 1–2:30pm and 4:30–5:30pm. Heritage Vaults, Mon–Sat 10am–4pm.

Built on the site of a much larger Norman cathedral, the present-day abbey is a fine example of the late Perpendicular style. When Queen Elizabeth I came to Bath in 1574, she ordered a national fund to be set up to restore the abbey. When you go inside and see its many windows, you'll understand why the abbey is called the "Lantern of the West." Note the superb fan vaulting, with its scalloped effect. Beau Nash was buried in the nave and is honored by a simple monument totally out of keeping with his flamboyant character. In 1994 the Bath Abbey Heritage Vaults opened on the south side of the abbey. This subterranean exhibition traces the history of Christianity at the abbey site since Saxon times.

Pump Room and Roman Baths. Abbey Church Yard. ☎ **01225/477000,** ext. 2785. Admission £5.60 ($8.95) adults, £3.30 ($5.30) children. Apr–Sept daily 9am–6pm; Oct–Mar Mon–Sat 9:30am–5pm, Sun 10:30am–5pm. Evenings in Aug 8–10pm.

Founded in A.D. 75 by the Romans, the baths were dedicated to the goddess Sulis Minerva; in their day they were an engineering feat. Even today they're among the finest Roman remains in the country, and are still fed by Britain's most famous hot-spring water. After centuries of decay, the original baths were rediscovered during Queen Victoria's reign. The site of the Temple of Sulis Minerva has been excavated and is now open to view. The museum displays many interesting objects from Victorian and recent digs (look for the head of Minerva). Coffee, lunch, and tea, usually with music from the Pump Room Trio, can be enjoyed in the 18th-century pump room, overlooking the hot springs. There's also a drinking fountain with hot mineral water that tastes horrible, but is supposedly beneficial.

No. 1 Royal Crescent. 1 Royal Crescent. ☎ **01225/428126.** £3.50 ($5.60) adults, £2.50 ($4) children; £8 ($12.80) family ticket. Mar–Oct Tues–Sun 10:30am–5pm, Nov–Dec 1 Tues–Sun 10:30am–4pm (last admission 30 minutes before closing). Closed Good Friday.

The interior of this Bath town house has been redecorated and furnished by the Bath Preservation Trust to look as it might have toward the end of the 18th century. The house is located at one end of Bath's most magnificent crescent, west of the Circus.

American Museum. Claverton Manor, Bathwick Hill. ☎ **01225/460503.** Admission £5 ($8) adults, £2.50 ($4) children. Late Mar–late Oct Tues–Sun 2–5pm. Bus: 18.

Some 2½ miles outside Bath is the first American museum established outside the United States. In a Greek Revival house (Claverton Manor), the museum sits on extensive grounds high above the Avon valley. Authentic exhibits of pioneer days have been shipped over from the States. On the grounds is a copy of Washington's flower garden at Mount Vernon and an American arboretum. A permanent exhibition in the New Gallery displays the Dallas Pratt Collection of Historical Maps.

ORGANIZED TOURS

The **Heart of England Tourist Board** (☎ 019051/763436) and the **West Country Tourist Board** (☎ 01392/76351) have details of numerous guided tours within their regions, and the staff can book you with registered guides for outings ranging from short walks to luxury tours that include accommodations in stately homes.

Free, 1¾-hour walking tours are conducted throughout the year by the Mayor's Honorary Society (☎ **01225/477786**). Tours depart from outside the Roman Baths Mon–Fri at 10:30am and 2pm, Sun at 2:30pm, and Tues, Fri, and Sat at 7pm. A slightly different tour by Bath Parade Tours, costing £3 ($4.80) per person, leaves Saturday at 2:30pm from outside the Roman Baths. Reservations aren't needed for either tour.

Jane Austen Tours take you in the footsteps of the author and her characters. These tours leave Saturday from the Abbey Lace Shop, York Street (☎ **01225/436030**), and cost £3 ($4.80) per person. You'll be told the time to meet when you make a reservation.

To tour Bath by bus, you can choose among several tour companies—some with open-top buses leaving from the Tourist Information Centre, which can be called for changing schedules and prices. Among the best are **Patrick Driscoll/Beau Nash Guides,** Elmsleigh, Bathampton, BA2 6SW (☎ **01225/46210**), as these tours are more personalized than most. Another good outfitter is **Sulis Guides,** 2 Lansdown Terrace, Weston, Bath BA1 4BR (☎ **01225/429681**).

SHOPPING

Bath has the finest shopping possibilities outside of London. Here is a sampling to get you started.

The **Bath Stamp & Coin Shop,** 12–13 Pulteney Bridge (☎ **01225/463073**), is the largest purveyor of antique coins and stamps in Bath, with hundreds of odd or unusual numismatics from throughout England and its former empire. Also look for antique Venetian glass and a scattering of English antiques.

The **Beaux Arts Gallery,** 13 York St. (☎ **01225/464850**), is the most important gallery of contemporary art in Bath, specializing in well-known British artists. The gallery occupies a pair of interconnected, stone-fronted Georgian houses, set close to Bath Abbey.

The four floors of merchandise at **Rossiter's,** 38–41 Broad St. (☎ **01225/462227**), might remind you of a very English version of a department store. They'll ship any of the Royal Doulton, Wedgwood, or Spode to anywhere in the world. Look especially for the displays of ginger jars, vases, and clocks manufactured by Moorcroft, and perfumes by London-based Floris.

   Walcot Reclamation, 108 Walcot St. (☎ **01225/444404**), is a sprawling and dusty storeroom that sells 19th-century architectural remnants. The 20,000-square-foot warehouse is located a quarter-mile northeast of Bath. Anything can be shipped or altered on site.

   Whittard of Chelsea, 10 Union Passage (☎ **01225/447787**), is the most charming and unusual emporium in Bath for whatever you'll need to duplicate the tea-drinking ritual. If you want a quite exotic tea to wow your friends with back home, ask for Monkey-Picked Oolong, a Chinese tea from plants so inaccessible that leaves can be gathered only by trained monkeys.

ACCOMMODATIONS

Expensive

✪ **Bath Spa Hotel.** Sydney Rd., Bath, Avon BA2 6JF. ☎ **01225/444424.** Fax 01225/444006. 90 rms, 8 suites. MINIBAR TV TEL. £149–£229 ($238.40–$366.40) double; £219–£329 ($350.40–$526.40) suite for two. AE, DC, MC, V. Free parking. East of the city off A-36.

   This restored 19th-century mansion—an even more stunning addition to the Bath hotel scene than the Royal Crescent—is a 10-minute walk from the center of Bath. It lies at the end of a tree-lined drive on 7 acres of landscaped grounds. The drawing room of what was once an English general's house has been restored, and log-burning fireplaces, elaborate moldings, oak paneling, and staircases are used to create country-house charm. The rooms are handsomely furnished with the best of English furniture and well-chosen and coordinated fabrics. Most rooms are spacious.

   Dining/Entertainment: The former owner called his home Vellore House, which is now the name of the restaurant where continental cuisine is served. You're given immaculate service and superb food and wine for a fixed-price dinner served 7–10pm daily. A second restaurant, the Alfresco Restaurant, offers a Mediterranean-style menu. In summer, guests can dine outside in an informal garden with a fountain.

   Services: 24-hour room service, valet and laundry service, beauty treatments, hairdressing salon.

   Facilities: Indoor swimming pool, gymnasium, tennis court, sauna and whirlpool bath, croquet lawn, children's nursery, beauty treatment rooms, healthy snack cafe, health and leisure spa.

Fountain House. 9–11 Fountain Buildings, Lansdown Rd., Bath, Avon BA1 5DV. ☎ **01225/ 338622.** Fax 01225/445855. 14 suites. MINIBAR TV TEL. £120–£168 ($192–$268.80) one-bedroom suite for two; £168–£202 ($268.80–$323.20) two-bedroom suite for four. Rates include continental breakfast. AE, DC, MC, V. Parking £11.75 ($18.80).

   On the northern edge of the city center, the three buildings that comprise this hotel are a trio of Georgian neoclassic, natural stone-fronted structures dating from 1735. British entrepreneur Robin Bryan created an all-suite hotel that has been favorably compared to the most prestigious in England. There are no public rooms. Each suite has original or reproduction antiques, at least one bedroom, a sitting room, private bath, and all the electronic equipment you'd expect in such an elegant hotel. The hotel stands within 100 yards of Milsom Street, the city's main shopping and historic thoroughfare. It doesn't serve a formal breakfast—breakfast is delivered in a basket to your door.

Priory Hotel. Weston Rd., Bath, Avon BA1 2XT. ☎ **01225/331922.** Fax 01225/448276. 29 rms. TV TEL. £160 ($256) standard double; £190 ($304) deluxe room for two. Rates include English breakfast. AE, DC, MC, V. Free parking.

   Converted from one of Bath's Georgian houses in 1969, the Priory is situated on 2 acres of formal and award-winning gardens with manicured lawns and flower beds, a swimming pool, and a croquet lawn. It is currently being upgraded as its public and private rooms have grown a little tired. It's not as overly commercial as the Francis, but is less expensive than the Bath Spa or Royal Crescent, yet offering somewhat the same town-house aura. The bedrooms are individually decorated and furnished with antiques; our personal favorite is Clivia (all rooms are named after flowers or shrubs), a nicely appointed duplex in a circular turret.

The restaurant consists of three separate dining rooms, one in a small salon in the original building; the others have views over the garden. The menu is varied and reflects seasonal availability. Grouse, partridge, hare, and venison are served in season, as is the succulent best end of lamb roasted with herb-flavored bread crumbs. A three-course dinner is offered, and on Sunday traditional roasted meats are featured.

Queensberry Hotel. Russel St., Bath, Avon BA1 2QF. ☎ **800/323-5463** in the U.S., or 01225/447928. Fax 01225/446065. 22 rms. TV TEL. £110–£175 ($176–$280) double. Rates include continental breakfast. MC, V. Parking 50p (80¢) per hour.

Although hardly as grand as the addresses previously considered, this place derives much of its beauty from the many original fireplaces, ornate ceilings, and antiques, which the creators of the property, Stephen and Penny Ross, have preserved. The Marquis of Queensberry commissioned John Wood to build this house in 1772. Each of three interconnected town houses that form this hotel was constructed in the early Georgian era. Today each bedroom has antique furniture and carefully chosen upholstery, in keeping with the character of the house. Open since 1988, the Queensberry has become one of Bath's most important hotels. You can dine at the exceptional Olive Tree, offering a contemporary English cuisine (reviewed below).

✪ Royal Crescent Hotel. 16 Royal Crescent, Bath, Avon BA1 2LS. ☎ **800/457-6000** in the U.S., or 01225/319090. Fax 01225/339401. 31 rms, 15 suites. TV TEL. £165–£225 ($264–$360) double; £285–£385 ($456–$616) suite. AE, DC, MC, V. Free parking.

Standing proudly in the center of the famed Royal Crescent, this Georgian colonnade of town houses was designed by John Wood the Younger in 1767. It's long been regarded as Bath's premier hotel, before the arrival of the even better Bath Spa. Crystal chandeliers, period furniture, and paintings add to the rich adornment. The bedrooms, including the Jane Austen Suite, are often lavishly furnished with four-poster beds and Jacuzzi baths. Each bedroom also offers such comforts as a trouser press, hair dryer, bathrobes, fruit plates, and other special touches. Excellent English cuisine is served in the Dower House Restaurant. Reservations are essential for rooms or meals. The continental cuisine is imaginative, with ever-so-polite and formal service.

Moderate

Francis Hotel. Queen Sq., Bath, Avon BA1 2HH. ☎ **800/225-5843** in the U.S. and Canada, or 01225/424257. Fax 01225/319715. 94 rms, 1 suite, 2 minisuites. TV TEL. £100 ($160) double; £130 ($208) triple; £120–£180 ($192–$288) suite. AE, DC, MC, V. Free parking.

An integral part of Queen Square, the first major development of John Wood the Elder, architect and creator of Bath's most prestigious buildings, the Francis is an example of 18th-century building taste, but suffers today from a too commercial aura. Although the building has style, the hotel is very tourist oriented. Originally consisting of six private residences dating from 1729, the Francis was opened as a private hotel by Emily Francis in 1884 and has offered guests first-class service for more than 100 years. Many of the well-furnished and traditionally styled bedrooms overlook Queen Square—named in honor of George II's consort, Caroline. The public rooms feature some 18th-century antiques, a cocktail bar, and the Edgar Restaurant, which offers both British and international food.

Inexpensive

Apsley House Hotel. 141 Newbridge Hill, Bath, Avon BA1 3PT. ☎ **01225/336966.** Fax 01225/425462. 5 rms, 2 suites. TV TEL. £65 ($104) double; £75–£85 ($120–$136) suite. Rates include English breakfast. DC, MC, V. Free parking. Take A-4 to Upper Bristol Rd. and fork right at the traffic signals into Newbridge Hill.

This charming and stately building, just a mile west of the center of Bath, dates back to 1830—the reign of William IV. It's set in its own gardens, with a square tower, arched windows, and a walled garden with south views. In 1994 new owners refurbished the hotel, filling it with country-house chintzes and antiques borrowed from the showrooms of an antique store they own. (Some hotel furniture is for sale.) The bedrooms are comfortably furnished and filled with fine fabrics and attractive accessories.

Dukes' Hotel. 53–54 Great Pulteney St., Bath, Avon BA2 4DN. ☎ **01225/463512.** Fax 01225/483733. 22 rms. TV TEL. £65–£90 ($104–$144) double; £75–£100 ($120–$160) family room. Rates include English breakfast. AE, MC, V. Free parking. Bus: 18.

A short walk from the heart of Bath, this building dates from 1780 but has been completely restored and rather elegantly furnished and modernized, both in its public rooms and its bedrooms. Many of the original Georgian features, including cornices and moldings, have been retained. Amenities include electric trouser presses and hair dryers. Guests can relax in a refined drawing room or patronize the cozy bar. A traditional English menu is also offered.

✪ **Laura Place Hotel.** 3 Laura Place, Great Pulteney St., Bath, Avon BA2 4BH. ☎ **01225/463815.** Fax 01225/310222. 8 rms, 1 suite. TEL. £65–£85 ($104–$136) double; £100 ($160) family suite. Rates include English breakfast. AE, MC, V. Free parking. Bus: 18 or 19.

Built the year of the French Revolution (1789), this hotel has won a civic award for the restoration of its stone facade. Set on a corner of a residential street overlooking a public fountain, it lies within a 2-minute walk of the Roman Baths and Bath Abbey. The hotel has been skillfully decorated with antique furniture and fabrics evocative of the 18th century.

Number Ninety Three. 93 Wells Rd., Bath, Avon BA2 3AN. ☎ **01225/317977.** 4 rms. TV. £38–£47 ($60.80–$75.20) double. Rates include English breakfast. AE, MC, V. Bus: 3, 13, 14, 17, 23, or 33.

This well-run guest house is a traditional B&B British style: small but immaculately kept and well maintained. Its owner is a mine of local information. The elegant Victorian house serves a traditional English breakfast, and it is within easy walking distance from the city center, rail and National Bus stations. Evening meals are available by prior arrangement. Parking can be difficult in Bath, but the hotel will advise.

Pratt's Hotel. South Parade, Bath, Avon BA2 4AB. ☎ **01225/460441.** Fax 01225/448807. 46 rms. TV TEL. £85 ($136) double. Rates include English breakfast. Children under 15 stay free in a room shared with two adults. AE, DC, MC, V. Parking £7.50 ($12).

Once the home of Sir Walter Scott, Pratt's is conveniently located for sightseeing and has functioned as a hotel since 1791. Several elegant terraced Georgian town houses were joined together to make a comfortable hotel with warm, cheerful lounges, a bar, and a high-ceilinged dining room. A well-thought-out cuisine is served in the dining room.

✪ **Sydney Gardens Hotel.** Sydney Rd., Bath, Avon BA2 6NT. ☎ and fax **01225/464818.** 6 rms. TV TEL. £69 ($110.40) double. Rates include English breakfast. MC, V. Free parking.

This spot is reminiscent of the letters of Jane Austen, who wrote to friends about the long walks she enjoyed in Sydney Gardens, a public park just outside the city center. In 1852 an Italianate Victorian villa was constructed here of gray stone on a lot immediately adjacent to the gardens. Three rooms have twin beds and the other three have 5-foot-wide double beds. Each accommodation is individually decorated with an English country-house charm. Amenities include hair dryers and beverage-making facilities. Only breakfast is served. No smoking is allowed. There's also a foot-path running beside a canal.

Nearby Places to Stay

Homewood Park. Hinton Charterhouse, Bath, Avon BA3 6BB. ☎ **01225/723731.** Fax 01225/723820. 19 rms, 2 suites. £95–£170 ($152–$272) double; £210 ($336) suite. Rates include English breakfast. AE, DC, MC, V. Free parking. Take A-36 (Bath–Warminster Rd.) 6 miles south of Bath.

This small, family-run hotel, set on 10 acres, was built in the 18th century and enlarged in the 19th. Overlooking the Limpley Stoke Valley, it's a large Victorian house with grounds adjoining the 13th-century ruin of Hinton Priory. You can play tennis and croquet in the garden. Riding and golfing are available nearby, and beautiful walks in the Limpley Stoke Valley lure guests. Each bedroom is luxuriously decorated and furnished with taste and charm. Most rooms overlook the gardens and grounds or offer views of the valley.

Most visitors come here for the cuisine, served in a dining room facing south, overlooking the gardens. The French and English cooking is prepared with skill and flair.

Hunstrete House. Hunstrete, Chelwood, near Bristol, Avon BS18 4NS. ☎ **01761/490490.** Fax 01761/490732. 21 rms, 2 suites. TV TEL. £150–£180 ($240–$288) double; £230–£250 ($368–$400) suite. Half board £205–£230 ($328–$368) double; £280 ($448) suite for two. Rates include English breakfast. AE, DC, MC, V. Free parking. Take A-4 about 4 miles west of Bath, then A-368 another 4¹⁄₂ miles toward Weston-super-Mare.

This fine Georgian house, a Relais & Châteaux, is situated on 92 acres of private parkland. Six units are in the Courtyard House, attached to the main structure and overlooking a paved courtyard with its Italian fountain and flower-filled tubs. Swallow Cottage, which adjoins the main house, has its own private sitting room, double bedroom, and bath. Units in the main house are individually decorated. There is a heated swimming pool in a sheltered corner of the walled garden. Part of the pleasure of staying at Hunstrete is the contemporary and classic cuisine served in the dining room.

✪ Ston Easton Park. Ston Easton, Somerset BA3 4DF. ☎ **01761/241631.** Fax 01761/241377. 21 rms, 1 cottage, 1 stateroom. TV. £145–£195 ($232–$312) double; £245–£265 ($392–$424) cottage; £245–£320 ($392–$512) stateroom. Children under 7 not accepted. AE, DC, MC, V. Free parking.

From the moment you pass a group of stone outbuildings and the century-old beeches of the 30-acre park, you know you've come to a very special place. The mansion was created in the mid-1700s from the shell of an existing Elizabethan house. In 1977, after many years of neglect, Peter and Christine Smedley acquired the property and poured money, love, and labor into its restoration. Now it's one of the great country hotels of England. A pair of carved mahogany staircases are ringed with ornate plaster detailing, and the place is full of antiques. Tasteful bedrooms are filled with flowers. A gardener's cottage comprises two separate suites, and the stateroom is regal with a large bedroom with a four-poster bed and a private seating area.

A sunflower-colored formal dining room displays museum-quality oil portraits, grandeur, and exquisite attention to detail. The chef prepares superb food, offering imaginative menus.

DINING

Moderate

Hole in the Wall. 16 George St. ☎ **01225/425242.** Reservations recommended. Main courses £12 ($19.20); fixed-price two-course lunch £9 ($14.40), fixed-price three-course lunch £11.50 ($18.40); fixed-price three-course dinner £19.50 ($31.20). AE, MC, V. Mon–Sat noon–2pm and 6–11pm. MODERN ENGLISH/FRENCH.

After an unsuccessful interlude as an Italian restaurant, this much-renovated Georgian town house reopened in 1994 as the rebirth of an establishment that was among the most famous restaurants in Britain during the 1970s. Its owners are Gunna and Christopher Chown, whose successful restaurant in Wales has already received critical acclaim. The pair of interconnected dining rooms are accented with polished copper pots, darkened ceiling beams, whitewashed walls, and a large fireplace. The menu choices change frequently, according to the chef's inspiration and ingredient availability, but dishes might include a warm salad of monkfish with Parma ham and exotic mushrooms; summer mushroom cutlet; braised lamb shank with roasted potatoes, garlic, and tomatoes; braised pork tenderloin wrapped in bacon with a brandy cider, and applesauce; and chocolate sorbet along with various warm and cold puddings. The house that accommodates the restaurant was built of honey-colored Bath stone around 1790.

Ⓢ **Moon and Sixpence.** 6A Broad St. ☎ **01225/460962.** Reservations recommended. Main courses £8.50–£11.95 ($13.60–$19.10); fixed-price lunch £13.50 ($21.60); two-course lunch buffet in the wine bar £5.95 ($9.50); fixed-price dinner £14.95–£18.95 ($23.90–$30.30). AE, MC, V. Daily noon–2:30pm and 5:30–10:30pm (until 11pm Fri–Sat). INTERNATIONAL.

One of Bath's leading restaurants and wine bars, the Moon and Sixpence occupies a stone structure east of Queen Square, with an extended conservatory and sheltered patio. Situated just off Broad Street, it has a cobbled passageway that leads you past a fountain into its courtyard.

The food may not be as good as that served at more acclaimed choices, including the Hole in the Wall, but the value is unbeatable. At lunch a large cold buffet with a selection of hot dishes is featured in the wine bar section. In the upstairs restaurant overlooking the bar, full service is offered. Main courses might include such dishes as fillet of lamb with caramelized garlic or medaillons of beef fillet with a bacon, red wine, and shallot sauce. Look for the daily specials on the continental menu.

Olive Tree. In the Queensberry Hotel, Russel St. ☎ **01225/447928.** Reservations recommended. Main courses £12.75–£15 ($20.40–$24); fixed-price three-course lunch £12.50 ($20); fixed-price three-course dinner £19 ($30.40). MC, V. Mon–Sat noon–2pm and 7–10pm, Sun 7–9:30pm. MODERN ENGLISH/MEDITERRANEAN.

In the basement of this previously reviewed hotel, Stephen and Penny Ross operate one of the most sophisticated little restaurants in Bath. Stephen uses the best of local produce, with an emphasis on freshness. The menu is changed to reflect the season, with game and fish being the specialties. You might begin with a Provençal fish soup with *rouille* and croutons or eggplant and mozzarella fritters with a sweet red pepper sauce, unless the grilled scallops with noodles and pine nuts tempts you instead. Then you could go on to Gressingham duck breast lightly grilled with shallots and kumquats or else loin of venison with wild rice and morels delicately flavored with a tarragon sauce. Stephen is also known for his desserts, which might include a hot chocolate soufflé or an apricot and almond tart.

Popjoy's Restaurant. Sawclose. ☎ **01225/460494.** Reservations recommended. Main courses £7.95–£10.95 ($12.70–$17.50); fixed-price three-course lunch £7 ($11.20); fixed-price three-course dinner £15 ($24). AE, DC, MC, V. Tues–Sat noon–2pm; Tues–Wed 6–9:30pm, Thurs–Sat 6–10pm. FRENCH/INTERNATIONAL.

Owned by Malcom Burr, this restaurant is named after Bath's most famous English Regency couple, Beau Nash and his mistress, Julianna Popjoy. Two dining rooms are located on separate floors of the circa 1720 Georgian home where the couple entertained their friends and established the fashions of the day. Inventiveness and a solid technique go into the dishes. Menu choices include a terrine of duck and chicken liver wrapped in bacon with a tomato coulis, watercress and potato soup, sautéed lamb kidneys with crispy smoked bacon, braised lamb shoulder with a sage and garlic stuffing, and tagliatelle with leeks and cream sauce.

Inexpensive

Beaujolais. 5 Chapel Row, Queen Sq. ☎ **01225/423417.** Reservations recommended. Fixed-price two-course lunch £5.80 ($9.30), fixed-price three-course lunch £8.50 ($13.60); dinner main courses £10.50–£14 ($16.80–$22.40). AE, MC, V. Daily noon–2pm and 7–11pm. FRENCH.

This is the best-known bistro in Bath, maintaining its old habitués but also attracting new admirers every year. Established in 1973, it is the oldest restaurant in Bath under its original ownership. Diners are drawn to the good, honest cookery and the decent value. One area of the restaurant is reserved for nonsmokers. Persons with disabilities (wheelchair access), children (special helpings), and vegetarians will all find comfort here. The house wines are modestly priced. Begin perhaps with a salad of warm scallops or else rabbit terrine served with chutney, then follow with an excellent grilled loin of lamb topped with a crispy julienne of ginger and leeks.

Woods. 9–13 Alfred St. ☎ **01225/314812.** Reservations recommended. Main courses £11.45 ($18.30); fixed-price lunches £5–£12 ($8–$19.20); fixed-price dinners £10–£13.50 ($16–$21.60). AE, MC, V. Mon–Sat noon–2:30pm and 6–10:30pm, Sun noon–4pm. Closed Dec 25–26. ENGLISH/FRENCH/ORIENTAL.

Named after John Wood the Younger, architect of Bath's famous Assembly Room, which lies across the street, this restaurant, within a Georgian building, is run by horse-racing enthusiast David Price and his French-born wife, Claude. A fixed-price menu is printed, while the seasonally changing array of à la carte items is noted on a chalkboard. Good bets might include pear and parsnip soup; smoked chicken salad with Stilton and avocado; pan-fried cod roe; and a perfectly prepared breast of chicken with tomatoes, mushrooms, red wine, and tarragon.

BATH AFTER DARK

Theatre Royal, located next to the new Seven Dials development at Sawclose (☎ 01225/448844; for credit-card bookings, call 01225/448861), was restored in 1982 and refurbished with plush seats, red carpets, and a painted proscenium arch and ceiling; it is now the most beautiful theater in Britain. It has 940 seats, with a small pit and grand tiers rising to the upper circle. A **studio theater** at the rear of the main building opened in 1996. The theater publishes a list of forthcoming events; its repertoire includes, among other offerings, West End shows.

Beneath the theater, reached from the back of the stalls or by a side door, are the theater vaults, where you will find a bar and a restaurant, serving an array of dishes from soup to light à la carte meals.

DAY TRIPS FROM BATH

✪ **LONGLEAT HOUSE**　Between Bath and Salisbury, Longleat House, Warminster, in Wiltshire (☎ **01985/844400**), owned by the seventh marquess of Bath, lies 4 miles southwest of Warminster and 4¹/₂ miles southeast of Frome on A-362. The first view of this magnificent Elizabethan house, built in the early Renaissance style, is romantic enough, but the wealth of paintings and furnishings in its lofty rooms is dazzling. From the Elizabethan Great Hall to the library, the state rooms, and the grand staircase, the house is filled with fine tapestries and paintings. The library represents the finest private collection in the country. The Victorian kitchens are open, and various exhibitions are mounted in the stable yard.

Events are staged frequently on the grounds, and the Safari Park has a vast array of animals in open parklands, including Britain's only white tiger. The Maze, the longest in the world, was added to the attractions by the current marquess. It has more than 1 1/2 miles of paths. The first part is comparatively easy, but the second part is more complicated.

Admission is £4.80 ($7.70) for adults, £3.50 ($5.60) for children; admission to Safari Park, £5.50 ($8.80) for adults, £4 ($6.40) for children. Special exhibitions and rides require separate admission tickets. Passport tickets for all Longleat's attractions cost £11 ($17.60) for adults and £9 ($14.40) for children, including admission to the Butterfly Garden, Simulator Dr. Who Exhibition, Postman Pat's Village, Adventure Castle, and more. It's open mid-March to Sept daily 10am–6pm; Oct–Easter daily 10am–4pm. The park is open mid-March to Nov 3 daily 10am–6pm (last cars are admitted at 5:30pm or sunset).

STOURHEAD   After Longleat, you can drive 6 miles down B-3092 to Stourton, a village just off the highway, 3 miles northwest of Mere (A-303). A Palladian house, Stourhead (☎ 01747/841152) was built in the 18th century by the banking family of Hoare. The magnificent gardens, which blended art and nature, became known as *le jardin anglais*. Set around an artificial lake, the grounds are decorated with temples, bridges, islands, and grottoes, as well as statuary. The gardens are open daily 9am–7pm (or until dusk), and cost £4.20 ($6.70) for adults and £2.20 ($3.50) for children from March to Oct. Off-season tickets cost £3.20 ($5.10) for adults and £1.60 ($2.55) for children. The house is open Mar 30–Oct 30 Sat–Wed noon–5:30pm, costing £4.20 ($6.70) for adults and £2.20 ($3.50) for children.

France 6

by Darwin Porter & Danforth Prince

France presents visitors with an embarrassment of riches—no other country concentrates such a diversity of sights and scenery into so compact an area. This chapter explores that diversity: Paris and the Ile de France; the Loire Valley in the northwest with its châteaux and vineyards; Provence, in the southwest, with its ancient culture; and the lush semitropical coast of the Mediterranean.

1 Paris

Paris today is, in many ways, less French and more international. Those Parisians who were born and bred in the city and who have French ancestry have accepted the fact that they may one day become a minority in their own hometown, as waves of immigrants from the far stretches of the former empire, including Vietnam and North Africa, flood their gates. And with the millions of visitors pouring in annually from all over the world, you can no longer separate Paris from its visitors—they have virtually become one and the same.

Legendary Paris style and chic are changing, too. Unless you frequent upscale watering holes, you'll see very few Parisians dressed quite as alluringly and formally as they did a few years ago. Many young Parisians have adopted the casual attire of their American counterparts. And while the old haute couture houses have experienced rough times, prêt-à-porter designers are flourishing.

The late president François Mitterrand, though a Socialist, wanted to leave an architectural legacy to rival or surpass that of the autocratic "Sun King," Louis XIV. His dream was to make Paris the undisputed capital of the European Union. To do that, he virtually painted Paris in gold (well, gilt at least), cleaned the Louvre's facade, spruced up the Champs-Elysées, and ran up a $6-billion tab as he built, restored, or recast. The most famous and most controversial of the *grand projects* was I. M. Pei's metal-and-glass pyramid entrance for the Louvre, a design selected by Mitterrand himself.

Thanks to Mitterrand, Paris looks more glamorous than ever. And lovers still walk arm in arm along the Seine and children still scamper about in the Tuileries and cafes still fill with animated conversation and women still dance the cancan at the Moulin Rouge.

ONLY IN PARIS

Strolling Along the Seine   Painters like Sisley, Turner, and Monet have fallen under the Seine's spell. Lovers still walk hand in hand alongside it and anglers still cast their lines here. The *clochards* still seek a home for the night under its bridges and on its banks the *bouquinistes* still peddle postcards, perhaps some 100-year-old pornography, or a tattered edition of an old history of Indochina. Some athletic visitors walk the full 7-mile stretch of the river, but you may want to confine your stroll to central Paris, passing the Louvre, Notre-Dame, and the pont Neuf.

Window-Shopping Along the Faubourg St-Honoré   In the 1700s this was home to the wealthiest of Parisians; today it's home to the stores that cater to them. Even if you don't purchase anything, you'll enjoy some great window-shopping with all the big names, like Hermès, Larouche, Courrèges, Cardin, Saint Laurent, and Lagerfeld.

Spending a Languid Afternoon in a Cafe   The Parisian cafe is an integral part of life. Even if it means skipping a museum, spend some time at a cafe. Whether you have one small coffee or the most expensive cognac in the house, nobody will hurry you and you can see how the French really live.

Attending an Opera or a Ballet   In 1989, the acoustically perfect Opéra Bastille was inaugurated to compete with the *grande dame* of Paris's musical scene, the Opéra Garnier. Now the Garnier has reopened, its recent renovation having returned it to its rococo splendor. A night here will take you back to the Second Empire, beneath a ceiling by Chagall. Whether it be for a performance of Bizet or Tharp, check out these two major Paris landmarks. Dress with pomp and circumstance.

Discovering Hidden Montmartre   This district is the most touristy part of Paris. However, far removed from the area's top draw, Sacré-Coeur, another neighborhood unfolds—that of the true Montmartrois. Wander on any of the back streets away from the souvenir shops. Arm yourself with a good map and seek out such streets as rue Lepic (refresh yourself at the Lux Bar, no. 12), rue Constance, rue Tholozé (with a view over the rooftops), lively rue des Abbesses, and rue Germain-Pilon—none of these is famous, none receives hordes of visitors, but each is flanked with buildings whose detailing shows the pride and care that permeates Paris's architecture. You'll discover dozens of other streets on your own.

Checking Out the Marchés   A daily Parisian ritual is ambling through one of the open-air markets to purchase fresh food to be consumed that day—some ripe and properly creamy Camembert or a pumpkin-gold cantaloupe at its peak when consumed before sundown. Even if you're staying in a hotel with no kitchen facilities, you can partake of this tradition and gather supplies for a picnic in one of the city's parks. The vendors arrange their wares into a mosaic of vibrant colors. *Sanguine,* an Italian citrus whose juice is the color of an orange sunset; ruby-red peppers; golden yellow bananas from Martinique—all dazzle the eye. Our favorite market is on rue Montorgueil, beginning at rue Rambuteau, 1er (Métro: Les-Halles).

ORIENTATION

ARRIVING   By Plane   Paris has two major international airports: Aéroport d'Orly, 8¹/₂ miles south, and Aéroport Roissy–Charles de Gaulle, 14 miles northeast of the city. A shuttle operates between the two about every 30 minutes, taking 50 to 75 minutes to make the journey.

At **Charles de Gaulle (Roissy) Airport** (☎ **01-48-62-22-80**), foreign carriers use Aérogare 1 and Air France uses Aérogare 2. From Aérogare 1, you take a moving walkway to the passport checkpoint and the Customs area. The two terminals are linked by a shuttle bus (*navette*). The free shuttle bus connecting Aérogare 1 with Aérogare 2 also transports passengers to the Roissy rail station, from which fast RER trains leave every 15 minutes heading to such Métro stations as Gare-du-Nord, Châtelet, Luxembourg, Port-Royal, and Denfert-Rochereau. A typical fare from Roissy to any point in central Paris is 40F ($8).

You can also take an Air France shuttle bus to central Paris for 48F ($9.60). It stops at the Palais des Congrès (Port Maillot), then continues on to place de l'Etoile, where subway lines can carry you farther along to any other point in Paris. That ride, depending on traffic, takes between 45 and 55 minutes. The shuttle departs about every 12 minutes between 5:40am and 11pm. Another option is the Roissybus, departing from the airport daily from 5:45am to 11pm and costing 35F ($7) for the 45- to 50-minute ride. Departures are about every 15 minutes, and the bus will take you near the corner of rue Scribe and place de l'Opéra in the heart of Paris.

A taxi from Roissy into the city will cost about 200F ($40). From 8pm to 7am, fares are 35% higher. Long queues of both taxis and passengers form outside each of the airport's terminals and are surprisingly orderly.

Orly Airport (☎ 01-49-75-15-15) also has two terminals—Orly Sud (south) for international flights and Orly Ouest (west) for domestic flights. They're linked by a free shuttle bus. Air France buses leave from Exit E of Orly Sud and from Exit F of Orly Ouest every 12 minutes between 5:45pm and 11pm, heading for Gare des Invalides. At Exit D you can board bus no. 215 for place Denfert-Rochereau in central Paris. Passage on any of these buses costs 32F ($6.40).

An alternative method for reaching central Paris involves taking a free shuttle bus that leaves both of Orly's terminals at intervals of approximately every 15 minutes for the nearby Métro and RER train station (Pont-de-Rungis/Aéroport-d'Orly), from which RER trains take 30 minutes for rides into the city center. A trip to Les Invalides, for example, costs 34F ($6.80). (When you're returning to the airport, buses leave the Invalides terminal heading either to Orly Sud or Orly Ouest every 15 minutes, taking about 30 minutes.)

A taxi from Orly to the center of Paris costs about 170F ($34) and is higher at night. Don't take a meterless taxi from Orly Sud or Orly Ouest—it's much safer (and usually cheaper) to hire a metered cab from the lines, which are under the scrutiny of a police officer.

By Train There are six major train stations in Paris: **Gare d'Austerlitz,** 55 quai d'Austerlitz, 13e (servicing the southwest with trains to the Loire Valley, the Bordeaux country, and the Pyrénées); **Gare de l'Est,** place du 11-Novembre-1918, 10e (servicing the east, with trains to Strasbourg, Nancy, Reims, and beyond to Zurich, Basel, Luxembourg, and Austria); **Gare de Lyon,** 20 bd. Diderot, 12e (servicing the southeast with trains to the Côte d'Azur, Provence, and beyond to Geneva, Lausanne, and Italy); **Gare Montparnasse,** 17 bd. Vaugirard, 15e (servicing the west with trains to Brittany); **Gare du Nord,** 18 rue de Dunkerque, 15e (servicing the north with trains to Holland, Denmark, Belgium, and the north of Germany); and **Gare St-Lazare,** 13 rue d'Amsterdam, 8e (servicing the northwest with trains to Normandy).

For general train information and to make reservations, call **01-45-82-50-50** daily 7am–8pm. Buses operate between the stations.

By Bus Most buses arrive at **Gare Routière Internationale du Paris-Gallieni,** avenue du Général-de-Gaulle, Bagnolet (☎ 01-49-72-51-51; Métro: Gallieni).

By Car Driving a car in Paris is definitely *not* recommended. Parking is difficult and traffic dense. If you do drive, remember that Paris is encircled by a ring road called the *périphérique*. The major highways into Paris are A1 from the north (Great Britain and Benelux); A13 from Rouen, Normandy, and other points of northwest France; A109 from Spain, the Pyrénées, and the southwest; A7 from the French Alps, the Riviera, and Italy; and A4 from eastern France.

VISITOR INFORMATION   The main **tourist information office** is at 127 av. des Champs-Elysées, 8e (☎ **01-49-52-53-54**), where you can secure information about both Paris and the provinces. The office is open daily (except May 1) 9am–8pm. **Welcome Offices** in the city's rail stations (except Gare St-Lazare) will give you free maps, brochures, and *Paris Selection,* a monthly French-language listing of all current events and performances.

CITY LAYOUT

Paris is surprisingly compact. Occupying 432 square miles (6 more than San Francisco), it's home to more than 10 million people. The River Seine divides Paris into the **Right Bank (Rive Droite)** to the north and the **Left Bank (Rive Gauche)** to the south. These designations make sense when you stand on a bridge and face downstream, watching the waters flow out toward the sea—to your right is the north bank; to your left the south. Thirty-two bridges link the Right Bank and the Left Bank, some providing access to the two small islands at the heart of the city, **Ile de la Cité**—the city's birthplace and site of Notre-Dame—and **Ile St-Louis,** a moat-guarded oasis of sober 17th-century mansions.

Between 1860 and 1870 Baron Georges-Eugène Haussmann, at the orders of Napoléon III, forever changed the look of Paris by creating the legendary *grands boulevards:* St-Michel, St-Germain, Haussmann, Sébastopol, Magenta, Voltaire, and Strasbourg.

The "main street" on the Right Bank is the **avenue des Champs-Elysées,** beginning at the Arc de Triomphe and running to **place de la Concorde.** Haussmann also created avenue de l'Opéra and the 12 avenues that radiate starlike from the Arc de Triomphe, giving it its original name, place de l'Etoile (*étoile* means "star"). It was renamed place Charles-de-Gaulle following the general's death; today it's often referred to as **place Charles-de-Gaulle–Etoile.**

ARRONDISSEMENTS IN BRIEF   The heart of medieval Paris was the Ile de la Cité and the areas immediately surrounding it; as Paris grew it absorbed many of the once-distant villages, and today these are *arrondissements* (districts) of the city—each of the 20 arrondissements has a character of its own. They're numbered from 1 to 20 starting at the center around the Louvre and progressing in a clockwise spiral. The key to finding any address in Paris is looking for the arrondissement number, rendered either as a number followed by "e" or "er" (1er, 2e, and so on) or, more formally, as part of the postal code (the last digit or last and penultimate digits indicate the arrondissement—75007 indicates that the address is in the 7th arrondissement; 75017 means the 17th arrondissement).

On the Right Bank, the **1er** is home to the Musée du Louvre, place Vendôme, rues de Rivoli and St-Honoré, Palais Royal, and Comédie-Française—an area filled with grand institutions and grand stores; at the center of the **2e** is the Bourse (stock exchange), making it the city's financial center; most of the **3e** and the **4e** is referred to as the Marais, the old Jewish quarter that in the 17th century was home to the aristocracy—today it's a trendy area of boutiques and restored mansions as well as the center of Paris's gay and lesbian community. On the Left Bank, the **5e** is known as the Latin Quarter, home to the Sorbonne and Panthéon and associated with the intellectual life that thrived in the 1920s and 1930s; the **6e,** known as St-Germain-des-Prés, stretches from the Seine to boulevard du Montparnasse, and is associated

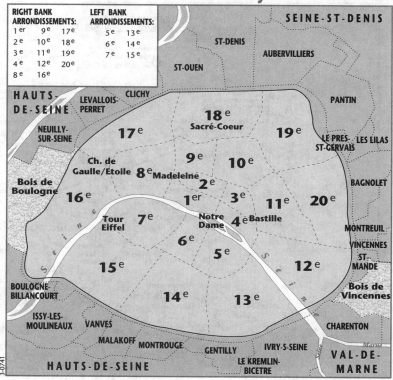

RIGHT BANK
ARRONDISSEMENTS:
1er	9e	17e
2e	10e	18e
3e	11e	19e
4e	12e	20e
8e	16e	

LEFT BANK
ARRONDISSEMENTS:
5e	13e
6e	14e
7e	15e

SEINE-ST-DENIS

ST-DENIS

AUBERVILLIERS

ST-OUEN

HAUTS-
DE-SEINE

LEVALLOIS-
PERRET

CLICHY

PANTIN

NEUILLY-
SUR-SEINE

17e

18e
Sacré-Coeur

19e

LE-PRÉS-
ST-GERVAIS

LES LILAS

Ch. de
Gaulle/Étoile

9e

10e

BAGNOLET

8e
Madeleine

Bois de
Boulogne

16e

2e

1er

3e

11e

20e

Tour
Eiffel

7e

Notre
Dame

4e

Bastille

MONTREUIL

6e

5e

VINCENNES
ST-
MANDE

12e

Bois de
Vincennes

15e

BOULOGNE-
BILLANCOURT

14e

13e

ISSY-LES-
MOULINEAUX

VANVES

CHARENTON

MALAKOFF

MONTROUGE

GENTILLY

IVRY-S-SEINE

VAL-DE-
MARNE

HAUTS-DE-SEINE

LE KREMLIN-
BICETRE

with the 1920s and 1930s—as well as being a center for art and antiques, it boasts the Palais and Jardin du Luxembourg within its boundaries. The **7e,** containing both the Tour Eiffel and Hôtel des Invalides, is a residential district for the well-heeled.

On the Right Bank, the **8e** epitomizes monumental Paris: with the triumphal avenue des Champs-Elysées, the Elysées Palace, and the fashion houses along avenue Montaigne and the Faubourg St-Honoré. The **18e** is home to Sacré-Coeur and Montmartre and all that the name conjures of the bohemian life painted most notably by Toulouse-Lautrec. The **14e** incorporates most of Montparnasse, including its cemetery, whereas the **20e** is where the the city's famous lie buried in Père-Lachaise and where today the recent immigrants from North Africa live. Beyond the arrondissements stretch the vast *banlieue* (suburbs) of Greater Paris, where the majority of Parisians live.

GETTING AROUND

Paris is a city for strollers whose greatest joy is rambling through unexpected alleys and squares. Given a choice of conveyance, try to make it on your own two feet whenever possible.

You can purchase a **Paris-Visite,** a tourist pass valid for 3 or 5 days on the public transportation system, including the Métro, buses, and RER (Réseau Express Régional) trains. (The RER has both first- and second-class compartments, and the pass lets you travel in first class.) The cost is 95F ($19) for 3 days or 150F ($30) for

Paris Métro

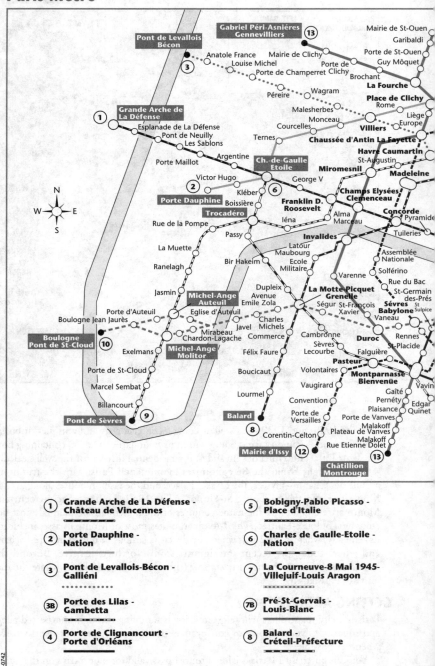

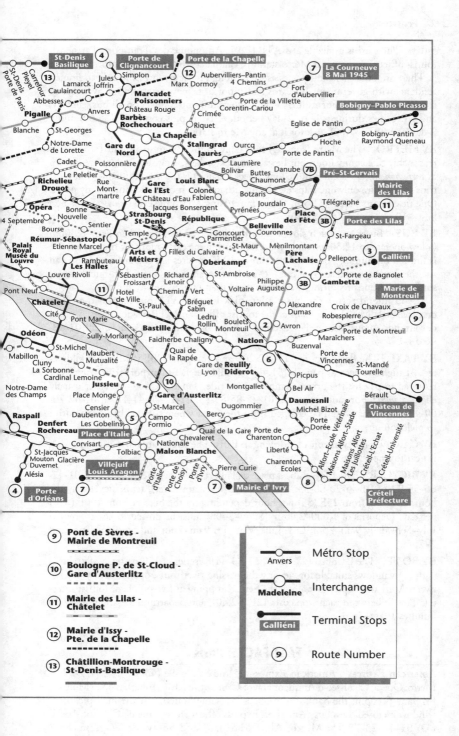

5 days. The card is available at RATP (Régie Autonome des Transports Parisiens), tourist offices, or the main Métro stations; call **01-44-68-20-20** for information.

There are other discount passes as well, though most are available only to French residents with government ID cards and proof of taxpayer status. One available to temporary visitors is **Formule 1,** which allows unlimited travel on all bus, subway, and RER lines during a 1- or 2-day period. A 1-day pass costs 28F ($5.60) and a 2-day pass 38F ($7.60). Ask for it at any Métro station.

BY METRO   The Métro (subway) runs daily from 5:30am to around 1:15am. It's reasonably safe at any hour, but beware of pickpockets. Transfer stations are known as *correspondances*—some require long walks; Châtelet is the most difficult—but most trips will require only one transfer. On the urban lines, it costs the same to any point. One ticket costs 7.50F ($1.50). When purchasing Métro tickets, a *carnet* is the best buy—10 tickets for 44F ($8.80).

BY BUS   Buses are much slower than the subway. Most buses run 7am–8:30pm (a few operate to 12:30am, and 10 operate during the early-morning hours). Service is limited on Sunday and holidays. Bus and Métro fares are the same and you can use the same *carnet* tickets on both. Most bus rides require one ticket, but there are some destinations requiring two (never more than two in the city limits).

If you intend to use the buses a lot, pick up an RATP bus map at the office on place de la Madeleine, 8e, or at the tourist offices at RATP headquarters, 55 quai des Grands-Augustins, 6e. For detailed info on bus and Métro routes, call **01-43-46-14-14.**

BY TAXI   The flag drops at 11F ($2.20), and you pay 5.20F ($1.05) per kilometer. At night, expect to pay 7F ($1.40) per kilometer. On airport trips you're not required to pay for the driver's empty return ride. Tip 12–15%—the latter usually elicits a *merci*. For radio cabs, call 01-45-85-85-85, 01-42-70-41-41, or 01-42-70-00-42—note that you'll be charged from the point where the taxi begins the drive to pick you up.

BY CAR   Don't even consider driving in Paris. The streets are narrow and parking is next to impossible.

BY BICYCLE   The **Bicy-club,** 8 place de la Porte-de-Champerret, 17e (☎ **01-47-66-55-92** or 01-45-20-60-33; Métro: Porte-de-Champerret), rents bicycles by the hour, charging from 25F ($5) per hour depending on the bike or from 100F ($20) per day. Deposits of 1,000–2,000F ($200–$400) must be posted. Bikes are rented July–Sept daily 9am–7pm; Oct–June Mon–Fri 9am–7pm and Sat 9am–1pm and 2–7pm.

BY BOAT   The **Batobus** (☎ **01-44-11-33-44**), a series of 150-passenger ferryboats with big windows suitable for viewing the passing riverfronts, operates every day between April and September along the Seine, stopping at five points of tourist interest. Transit between each stop costs 12F ($2.40), and departures are about every 30 minutes 10am–7pm.

FAST FACTS: Paris

American Express   American Express, 11 rue Scribe, 9e (☎ 01-47-77-77-07; Métro: Opéra, Chaussée-d'Antin, or Havre-Caumartin; RER: Auber), is open Mon–Fri 9am–6:30pm; the bank is also open Sat (same hours), but the mail pickup window is closed. Less busy American Express offices are at 5 rue de Chaillot, 16e (☎ 01-47-23-72-15; Métro: Alma-Marceau) and 38 av. de Wagram, 8e

(☎ 01-42-27-58-80; Métro: Ternes). Both offices operate Mon–Fri 9am–1pm and 2–5:30pm.

Baby-sitters   The Institut Catholique, 21 rue d'Assas, 6e (☎ 01-45-48-31-70), runs a service staffed by students. The price is 32F ($6.40) per hour plus 10F ($2) for insurance. The main office is open Mon–Sat 9am–noon and 2–6pm.

Business Hours   Normally, **banks** are open Mon–Fri 9am–noon and 1 or 1:30–4:30pm. Some banks have long hours on Sat morning. The *grands magasins* **(department stores)** are generally open Mon–Sat 9:30am–6:30pm; **smaller shops** close for lunch and reopen around 2pm, but this has become rarer than it used to be. Many stores stay open to 7pm in summer; others are closed Mon, especially in the morning. Large **offices** remain open all day, but some also close for lunch.

Currency   The French **franc** (**F**) is divided into 100 **centimes.** There are coins of 5, 10, and 20 centimes, and ¹/₂, 1, 2, 5, and 10 francs. Sometimes there are two types of coins for one denomination, especially after the 1989 bicentennial of the French Revolution, when new commemorative coins were minted. Bills come in denominations of 20, 50, 100, 500, and 1,000 francs. At this writing, $1 = approximately 5F (or 1F = 20¢), and this is the rate of exchange we've used to calculate the dollar values in this chapter.

Dentists/Doctors   For emergency dental service, call 01-43-37-51-00 daily 8am–11:40pm. The American Hospital, 63 bd. Victor-Hugo, Neuilly (☎ 01-46-41-25-41; Métro: Pont-de-Levallois or Pont-de-Neuilly; Bus: 82), operates a bilingual (English–French) dental clinic on the premises, open 24 hours. Some large hotels have a doctor on staff, or try the American Hospital (see above), which operates a 24-hour emergency service.

Drugstores   After regular hours, have your concierge contact the Commissariat de Police for the nearest 24-hour *pharmacie.* You'll find the address posted on the doors or windows of all other drugstores. One of the most central all-night pharmacies is Pharmacy "les Champs," 84 av. des Champs-Elysées, 8e (☎ 01-45-62-02-41; Métro: George-V).

Embassies/Consulates   The Embassy of the **United States** is at 2 av. Gabriel, 75008 Paris (☎ 01-43-12-22-22; Métro: Concorde), open Mon–Fri 9am–6pm. Passports are issued at its consulate at 2 rue St-Florentin (☎ 01-42-96-12-02, ext. 2531; Métro: Concorde).

   The Embassy of **Australia** is at 4 rue Jean-Rey, 75015 Paris (☎ 01-45-59-33-00; Métro: Bir-Hakeim), open Mon–Fri 9am–1pm and 2:30–5pm. The Embassy of **Canada** is at 35 av. Montaigne, 75008 Paris (☎ 01-47-23-01-01; Métro: Franklin-D.-Roosevelt or Alma-Marceau), open Mon–Fri 9–noon and 2–5pm; the Canadian Consulate is at the same address. The Embassy of the **United Kingdom** is at 35 rue du Faubourg St-Honoré, 75383 Paris CEDEX (☎ 01-42-66-91-42; Métro: Concorde or Madeleine), open Mon–Fri 9:30am–1pm and 2:30–6pm; the U.K. consulate is at the same address (☎ 01-44-51-31-00). Hours are Mon–Fri 9:30am–12:30pm and 2:30–5pm. The Embassy of **New Zealand** is at 7 ter rue Léonard-de-Vinci, 75116 Paris (☎ 01-45-00-24-11; Métro: Victor-Hugo), open Mon–Fri 9am–1pm and 2–5:30pm.

Emergencies   For the police, call **17;** to report a fire, call 18. For an ambulance, call the fire department at 01-45-78-74-52; a fire vehicle rushes cases to the nearest emergency room. S.A.M.U., call 15, is an independently operated, privately owned ambulance company. You can reach the police at 9 bd. du Palais, 4e (☎ 01-53-71-53-71 or 01-53-73-53-73; Métro: Cité).

Holidays   On national holidays, shops, businesses, government offices, and most restaurants close. They include New Year's Day (Jan 1); Easter Monday (late Mar or early Apr); Labor Day (May 1); Ascension Thursday (in May or June, 40 days after Easter); Whit Monday, also called Pentecost Monday (51st day after Easter in June or July); Bastille Day (July 14); Assumption Day (Aug 15); All Saints Day (Nov 1); Armistice Day (Nov 11); and Christmas Day (Dec 25). In addition, schedules may be disrupted on Shrove Tuesday (the Tuesday before Ash Wednesday, in Jan or Feb) and Good Friday (late Mar or early Apr).

Hospitals   See "Dentists/Doctors" above.

Lost & Found   The central office is Objets Trouvés, Prefecture de Police, 36 rue des Morillons 15e (☎ 01-45-31-14-80; Métro: Convention), at the corner of rue de Dantzig; for objects left in a taxi, ask for extension 4208. It's open Mon and Wed 8:30am–5pm, Tues and Thurs 8:30am–8pm, and Fri 8:30am–5:30pm. For Lost and Found on the Métro, call 01-40-06-75-27.

Mail   Airmail letters within Europe cost 2.80F (55¢); to the United States, 4.30F (85¢). See "Post Office" below.

Police   In an emergency call **17**. The principal Prefecture is at Place Baudoyer 4e (☎ 01-53-71-53-71; Métro: Hôtel-de-Ville).

Post Office   The main post office (P.T.T.) for Paris is Bureau de Poste, 52 rue du Louvre, 75001 Paris (☎ 01-40-28-20-00; Métro: Louvre). Your mail can be sent here *poste restante* (general delivery) for a small fee. Take an ID, such as a passport, if you plan to pick up mail. It's open daily 8am–7pm for most services, 24 hours for telegrams and phone calls.

Safety   Especially beware of child pickpockets. They roam the capital, preying on tourists around such sites as the Louvre, Eiffel Tower, Notre-Dame, and Montmartre, and they especially like to pick pockets in the Métro, often blocking the entrance and exit to the escalator.

Transit Information   For information on public transport, stop in at the office of the Services Touristiques de la RATP, 55 quai des Grands-Augustins, 6e (Métro: St-Michel), or call 01-43-46-14-14 for recorded information, in French, about stoppages, subway or bus breakdowns, or exceptionally heavy traffic on any particular bus or Métro line.

ACCOMMODATIONS
RIGHT BANK: 1ST ARRONDISSEMENT
Very Expensive

✪ **Le Ritz.** 15 place Vendôme, 75001 Paris. ☎ **01-43-16-30-30.** Fax 01-43-16-36-68. 142 rms, 45 suites. A/C MINIBAR TV TEL. 3,350–4,250F ($670–$850) double; from 5,500F ($1,100) suite. AE, DC, MC, V. Parking 180F ($36). Métro: Opéra.

Le Ritz is Europe's greatest hotel, an enduring symbol of elegance on one of Paris's most beautiful and historic squares. César Ritz, the "little shepherd boy from Niederwald," opened the hotel in 1898, and with the help of culinary master Escoffier, made the Ritz a miracle of opulence. The salons are furnished with museum-caliber antiques, ornate mirrors, and handwoven tapestries. The Espadon grill room is one of the finest in Paris. The Ritz Club includes a bar, a salon with a fireplace, a restaurant, and a dance floor. You can order drinks in either the Bar Vendôme or the Bar Hemingway. At ground level is a luxury health club with a pool and massage parlor.

Expensive

Hôtel Cambon. 3 rue Cambon, 75001 Paris. ☎ **01-42-60-38-09.** Fax 01-42-60-30-59. 42 rms, 6 suites. A/C MINIBAR TV TEL. 1,480F ($296) double; 1,980F ($396) suite. AE, MC, V. Parking in nearby lot 170F ($34) per 24 hours. Métro: Concorde.

This stone-fronted 19th-century building recently was renovated in a contemporary decor—too contemporary for some, who find the new Cambon a bit antiseptic. Nevertheless, the Cambon's address is impeccable, right in the chic heart of Paris. The public rooms are richly furnished with 19th- and 20th-century sculptures and paintings, including the cozy street-level bar. The guest rooms are individually decorated, with fabric wall coverings, marble-sheathed baths, and much exposed wood.

Moderate

Hôtel Regina. 2 place des Pyramides, 75001 Paris. ☎ **01-42-60-31-10.** Fax 01-40-15-95-16. 121 rms, 14 suites. A/C MINIBAR TV TEL. 1,820F ($364) double; from 2,620F ($524) suite. AE, DC, MC, V. Métro: Pyramides or Tuileries.

Until a radical renovation upgraded its old-fashioned grandeur in 1995, this hotel slumbered peacefully in a prime location. All that changed when the management poured funds into the site's recent renovation, retaining the patina and beeswax of the art nouveau interior and adding hundreds of thousands of francs' worth of historically appropriate improvements, especially to the guest rooms. Pluvinel serves a conservative French cuisine in an art deco ambience of deliberate nostalgia.

Inexpensive

⑤ Britannique. 20 av. Victoria, 75001 Paris. ☎ **01-42-33-74-59.** Fax 01-42-33-82-65. 40 rms. MINIBAR TV TEL. 720–830F ($144–$166) double. AE, DC, MC, V. Parking 90F ($18). Métro: Châtelet.

After a complete renovation, the Britannique has been rated three stars. It's in the heart of Paris, near Les Halles, the Centre Pompidou, and Notre-Dame. The rooms may be small but they're clean, comfortable, and adequately equipped. The building was a Quaker mission during World War I. Though the 1st arrondissement has far superior hotels, the Britannique is a superior value.

RIGHT BANK: 3RD & 4TH ARRONDISSEMENTS

Expensive

✪ Pavillon de la Reine. 28 place des Vosges, 75003 Paris. ☎ **01-42-77-96-40.** Fax 01-42-77-63-06. 30 rms, 17 duplexes, 15 suites. A/C MINIBAR TV TEL. 1,700F ($340) double; 2,100F ($420) duplex for one or two; 2,700–3,200F ($540–$640) suite. AE, DC, MC, V. Free parking. Métro: Bastille.

Built in 1986, this neoclassical villa blends into an area that was once home to Victor Hugo. You enter through a tunnel that opens onto a small formal garden. The Louis XIII decor evokes the heyday of place des Vosges. Wing chairs with flame-stitched upholstery combined with iron-banded Spanish antiques create a rustic feel. Each room is different; some are duplexes with sleeping lofts set above cozy salons. All have a warm decor of weathered beams, reproductions of famous oil paintings, and marble baths.

Moderate

Hôtel de Lutèce. 65 rue St-Louis-en-l'Ile, 75004 Paris. ☎ **01-43-26-23-52.** Fax 01-43-29-60-25. 23 rms. A/C TV TEL. 840F ($168) double; 990F ($198) triple. V. Métro: Pont-Marie.

Walking into this hotel is much like walking into a country house in Brittany. The lounge is graciously furnished with antiques, original tile floors, a fireplace, and contemporary paintings. Each of the individualized rooms comes furnished with antiques, creating a refined atmosphere. The hotel is comparable in style and

Paris Accommodations

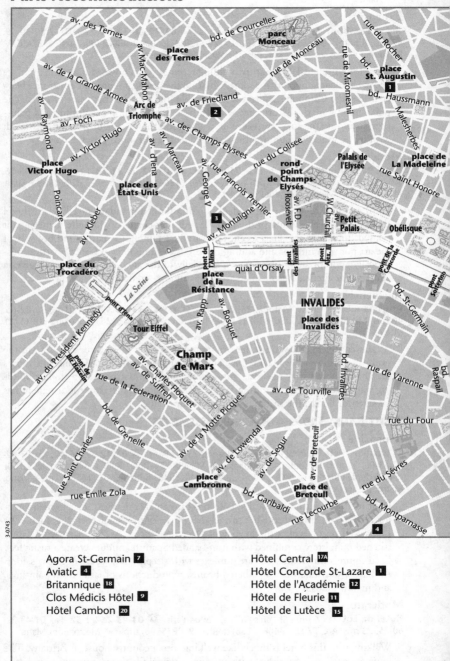

Agora St-Germain **7**
Aviatic **4**
Britannique **18**
Clos Médicis Hôtel **9**
Hôtel Cambon **20**

Hôtel Central **17A**
Hôtel Concorde St-Lazare **1**
Hôtel de l'Académie **12**
Hôtel de Fleurie **11**
Hôtel de Lutèce **15**

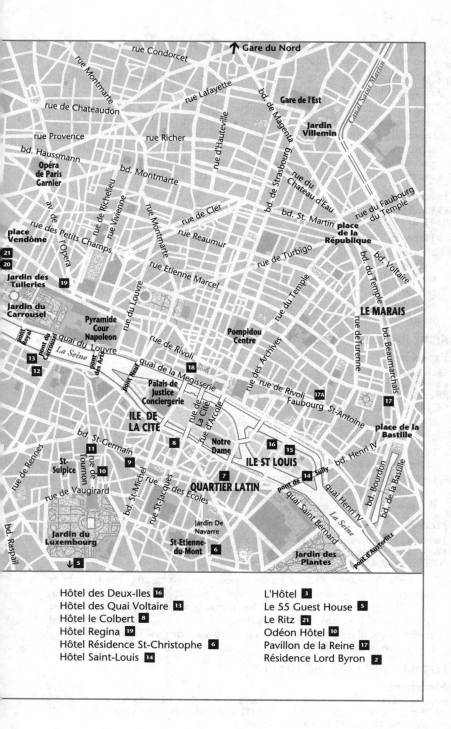

Hôtel des Deux-Iles 16
Hôtel des Quai Voltaire 13
Hôtel le Colbert 8
Hôtel Regina 19
Hôtel Résidence St-Christophe 6
Hôtel Saint-Louis 14

L'Hôtel 3
Le 55 Guest House 5
Le Ritz 21
Odéon Hôtel 10
Pavillon de la Reine 17
Résidence Lord Byron 2

amenities with Deux-Iles (same ownership). Together they outpace their nearby competition on the island, Hôtel St-Louis.

Hôtel des Deux-Iles. 59 rue St-Louis-en-l'Ile, 75004 Paris. ☎ **01-43-26-13-35.** Fax 01-43-29-60-25. 17 rms. TV TEL. 840F ($168) double. V. Métro: Pont-Marie.

This 17th-century hotel is the largest and most glamorous on the island. The collection of furnishings is eclectic, mostly bamboo and reed, blended with period pieces. Downstairs is a rustic tavern with an open fireplace; the lounge has a central garden of plants and flowers. The Deux-Iles has nowhere near the style, charm, comfort, and grace of the Pavillon de la Reine, but then it's a lot cheaper. In its category, its rooms and amenities are superior to those of the nearby Hôtel St-Louis.

Inexpensive

☉ Hôtel St-Louis. 75 rue St-Louis-en-l'Ile, 75004 Paris. ☎ **01-46-34-04-80.** Fax 01-46-34-02-13. 21 rms. TEL. 695F ($139) double. MC, V. Métro: Pont-Marie.

This small hotel occupies a 17th-century town house romantically positioned on Ile St-Louis. Guy Record discovered this hotel and did a good job refurbishing it. Along with his wife, Andrée, he maintains a charming family atmosphere that's becoming harder to find in Paris. It may not be in the same league as its major rivals, Lutéce and Deux-Iles, but it's an even better value. Many of the upper-level rooms offer views over the rooftops. We prefer those on the fifth floor, which have the most atmosphere and are decorated with old wood and attractive furniture.

RIGHT BANK: 8TH ARRONDISSEMENT

Expensive

✪ Hôtel Concorde St-Lazare. 108 rue St-Lazare, 75008 Paris. ☎ **800/888-4747** in the U.S. and Canada, 0171/630-1704 in London, or 01-40-08-44-44. Fax 01-42-93-01-20. 277 rms, 23 suites. A/C MINIBAR TV TEL. 1,260–1,960F ($252–$392) double; from 3,500F ($700) suite. AE, DC, MC, V. Parking 100F ($20). Métro: St-Lazare.

This is the best hotel in the Gare St-Lazare area, across from the rail station. In the 1990s the St-Lazare's main lobby (a historic monument) was restored under the supervision of the Concorde chain. The guest rooms were elevated to modern standards of comfort, redecorated, and soundproofed. An American bar, Le Golden Black, bears fashion designer Sonia Rykiel's signature decor of black lacquer with touches of gold and amber. Bistrot 108 offers provincial dishes with great vintages you can order by the glass.

Moderate

Résidence Lord Byron. 5 rue de Chateaubriand, 75008 Paris. ☎ **01-43-59-89-98.** Fax 01-42-89-46-04. 31 rms, 6 suites. MINIBAR TV TEL. 800–900F ($160–$180) double; from 1,250F ($250) suite. AE, MC, V. Métro: George-V. RER: Etoile.

The Lord Byron, just off the Champs-Elysées on a curving street, may not be as monumentally grand as other hotels of the 8th, but its prices are a lot more democratic. No style setter, it's solid and reliable and maybe a little stuffy. Owner Françoise Coisne has added many personal touches, and throughout are framed prints of butterflies and historic French scenes. The furnishings are good reproductions of antiques or restrained modern pieces.

LEFT BANK: 5TH ARRONDISSEMENT

Moderate

Hôtel le Colbert. 7 rue de l'Hôtel-Colbert, 75005 Paris. ☎ **01-43-25-85-65.** Fax 01-43-25-80-19. 36 rms, 2 suites. MINIBAR TV TEL. 1,010F ($202) double; from 1,630F ($326) suite. AE, DC, MC, V. Métro: Maubert-Mutualité or St-Michel.

Not only is this centuries-old inn a minute from the Seine but it provides a fine view of Notre-Dame from many rooms. There's even a small courtyard to set it apart from the Left Bank bustle. Built during the 18th century, the building was converted into a hotel in 1966. You enter a tasteful lobby with marble floors and antique furniture. The rooms are well designed and tailored, most providing comfortable chairs and a breakfast area. Those on the uppermost floor seem like garrets, and the suites feature old exposed beams. Some rooms are suitable for persons with disabilities.

Inexpensive

⑤ Agora St-Germain. 42 rue des Bernardins, 75005 Paris. ☎ **01-46-34-13-00.** Fax 01-46-34-75-05. 39 rms. MINIBAR TV TEL. 720F ($144) double; 820F ($164) triple. AE, DC, MC, V. Parking 110F ($22). Métro: Maubert-Mutualité.

One of the best of the district's reasonably priced hotels, the building Agora St-Germain was constructed in the early 1600s, probably to house a group of guardsmen protecting the brother of the king at his lodgings on nearby rue Monsieur-le-Prince. The hotel offers compact soundproof rooms, comfortably furnished and equipped with an alarm clock, a hair dryer, and a safety-deposit box.

Hôtel Résidence St-Christophe. 17 rue Lacépède, 75005 Paris. ☎ **01-43-31-81-54.** Fax 01-43-31-12-54. 31 rms. MINIBAR TV TEL. 550–750F ($110–$150) double. AE, DC, MC, V. Métro: Place-Monge.

This hotel has a gracious English-speaking staff and a location in one of the undiscovered but charming districts of the Latin Quarter. It was created in 1987 when a derelict hotel was connected to a butcher shop. Millions of francs later, the result is clean and comfortable, with traditional furniture and wall-to-wall carpeting. Breakfast is the only meal served.

LEFT BANK: 6TH ARRONDISSEMENT

Expensive

✪ L'Hôtel. 13 rue des Beaux-Arts, 75006 Paris. ☎ **01-44-41-99-00.** Fax 01-43-25-64-81. 24 rms, 3 suites. A/C MINIBAR TV TEL. 1,000–1,700F ($200–$340) small double; 2,300–2,800F ($460–$560) large double; from 3,600F ($720) suite. AE, DC, MC, V. Métro: St-Germain-des-Prés.

L'Hôtel was once a 19th-century "fleabag" called the Hôtel d'Alsace, and its major distinction was that Oscar Wilde, broke and in despair, died here. However, today's guests aren't exactly on poverty row: Through the lobby march many show-business and fashion personalities. You'll feel like a movie star when you bathe in your tub of rosy-pink Italian marble. Throughout the building is an eclectic collection of antiques that includes Louis XV and Louis XVI, Empire, and Directoire pieces.

Moderate

Clos Médicis Hôtel. 56 rue Monsieur-le-Prince, 75006 Paris. ☎ **01-43-29-10-80.** Fax 01-43-54-26-90. 37 rms, 1 duplex. A/C MINIBAR TV TEL. 786–892F ($157.20–$178.40) double; 1,212F ($242.40) duplex. AE, DC, MC, V. RER: Luxembourg.

In 1994, the neighborhood's newest hotel opened on the premises of what had been a private home in 1860. You'll find a verdant garden with lattices and exposed stone walls, a lobby with modern spotlights and simple furniture, and a multilingual staff. Its location, adjacent to the Luxembourg Gardens in the heart of the Latin Quarter, is one of the establishment's major advantages. The warmly colored rooms are uncomplicated and comfortable. Breakfast is the only meal served.

Odéon-Hôtel. 3 rue de l'Odéon, 75006 Paris. ☎ **01-43-25-90-67.** Fax 01-43-25-55-98. 34 rms. TV TEL. 850–1,000F ($170–$200) double. AE, DC, MC, V. Métro: Odéon.

Near both the Théâtre de l'Odéon and boulevard St-Germain, this hotel stands on what in 1779 was the first Paris street to have pavements and gutters. With its exposed beams, rough stone walls, high crooked ceilings, and tapestries mixed with contemporary fabrics, mirrored ceilings, and black leather furnishings, the Odéon is reminiscent of a modernized Norman country inn. After modern plumbing was added, each room was individually designed.

Inexpensive

Aviatic. 105 rue de Vaugirard, 75006 Paris. ☎ **01-45-44-38-21.** Fax 01-45-49-35-83. 43 rms. MINIBAR TV TEL. 750–780F ($150–$156) double. AE, DC, MC, V. Parking 100F ($20). Métro: Montparnasse–Bienvenue.

This is a bit of old Paris, with a modest inner courtyard and a vine-covered lattice on the walls. It has been a family-run hotel of character and elegance for a century. The reception lounge, with its marble columns, brass chandeliers, antiques, and petit salon, provides an attractive traditional setting. It doesn't have the decorative style and flair of some hotels in the 6th but offers good comfort and a warm ambience.

Hôtel de Fleurie. 32–34 rue Grégoire-de-Tours, 75006 Paris. ☎ **01-53-73-70-00.** Fax 01-53-73-70-20. 29 rms. A/C MINIBAR TV TEL. 850–1,200F ($170–$240) double. Children stay free in parents' room. AE, DC, MC, V. Métro: Odéon.

Just off boulevard St-Germain on a colorful little street, the Fleurie is one of the best of the "new" old hotels. Restored to its former glory in 1988, the facade is studded with statuary spotlit by night, recapturing its 17th-century elegance. The stone walls have been exposed in the reception salon, with a refectory desk where you check in. An elevator takes you to the well-furnished modern rooms, each with a safe; a spiral staircase leads down to the breakfast room.

LEFT BANK: 7TH ARRONDISSEMENT

Moderate

Hôtel de l'Académie. 32 rue des Sts-Peres, 75007 Paris. ☎ **01-45-48-36-22.** Fax 01-45-44-75-24. 34 rms. A/C MINIBAR TV TEL. 490–1,290F ($98–$258) double. AE, DC, MC, V. Métro: St-Germain-des-Prés.

The exterior walls and old ceiling beams are all that remain of this 17th-century residence of the private guards of the duc de Rohan. In 1983 the hotel was completely renovated to include an elegant reception area. The comfortably up-to-date guest rooms have Directoire beds, an Ile-de-France decor upholstered in soft colors, and views over the 18th- and 19th-century buildings of the neighborhood.

Inexpensive

⑤ Hôtel du Quai-Voltaire. 19 quai Voltaire, 75007 Paris. ☎ **01-42-61-50-91.** Fax 01-42-61-62-26. 32 rms. TV TEL. 600–690F ($120–$138) double; 800F ($160) triple. AE, DC, MC, V. Parking 120F ($24) nearby. Métro: Palais-Royal.

Built in the 1600s as an abbey, then transformed into a hotel in 1856, the Quai-Voltaire is best known for its illustrious guests, who have included Wilde, Baudelaire, and Wagner, who occupied rooms 47, 56, and 55, respectively. Many rooms in this modest inn have been renovated and most overlook the bookstalls and boats of the Seine. You can have drinks in the bar or the small salon, and simple meals can be prepared for those who prefer to eat in.

GAY HOTELS

Hôtel Central. 33 rue Vieille-du-Temple, 75004 Paris. ☎ **01-48-87-99-33.** Fax 01-42-77-06-27. 7 rms (1 with bath). TEL. 485F ($97) double with or without bath. MC, V. Métro: Hôtel-de-Ville.

This is the most visible gay hotel in Paris. The rooms are on the third, fourth, and fifth floors of this 18th-century building, which contains the Marais's major gay bar, Le Central (see later). If you arrive between 8:30am and 3pm, you'll find a registration staff one floor above street level; if you arrive at any other time, you'll have to retrieve your key and register at the street-level bar. The rooms are simple and serviceable. Women are welcome but rare.

✪ **Le 55 Guest House.** 55 av. Reille, 75014 Paris. ☎ **01-45-89-91-82.** Fax 01-45-89-91-83. 2 suites. MINIBAR TV TEL. 900–1,200F ($180–$240) suite. Rates include breakfast. No credit cards. Métro: Porte-d'Orléans. RER: Cité-Universitaire.

This upscale B&B offers two monochromatic suites accented with oak paneling and art deco furnishings. It's on the periphery of Paris, between the trees of the Parc Montsouris and an expansive lawn. The owner since 1993 is Jean-Marc Perry. Breakfast is served in your suite or on a flowering terrace.

DINING
RIGHT BANK: 1ST ARRONDISSEMENT
Very Expensive

✪ **Le Grand Véfour.** 17 rue de Beaujolais, 1er. ☎ **01-42-96-56-27.** Reservations required. Main courses 230–380F ($46–$76); fixed-price lunch 325–750F ($65–$150); fixed-price dinner 750F ($150). AE, DC, MC, V. Mon–Fri 12:30–2:15pm and 7:30–10:15pm. Métro: Louvre. FRENCH.

Since the reign of Louis XV this has been a restaurant, though the exact date of its opening as the Café de Chartres isn't known. In 1812 it was named after owner Jean Véfour, a former chef to a member of the royal family. Jean Taittinger of the champagne family purchased the restaurant, and the meticulous restoration has improved its former glories. Dining here is a great gastronomic experience. Specialties, served on Limoges china, include terrine of half-cooked roe salmon with "smoked milk" (you heard right) and deboned poached fillet of sole Grand Véfour (stuffed with mushrooms and served with mustard-flavored mousseline sauce). Try the grand *gourmandises au chocolate*, a richness of chocolate served with chocolate sorbet.

Moderate

Pharamond. 24 rue de la Grande-Truanderie, 1er. ☎ **01-42-33-06-72.** Reservations required. Main courses 90–150F ($18–$30); fixed-price lunch 180F ($36); fixed-price dinner 250F ($50). AE, DC, MC, V. Tues–Sat 12:30–2:30pm; Mon–Sat 7:30–10:45pm. Métro: Les-Halles or Châtelet. FRENCH.

The restaurant, part of an 1832 neo-Norman structure, sits on a Les Halles street once frequented by the vagabonds of Paris. For an appetizer, work your way through half a dozen Breton oysters (available Oct–Apr). But the dish to order is *tripes à la mode de Caen,* served over a charcoal burner. Tripe is a delicacy, and if you're at all experimental you'll find no better introduction to it. Try the *coquilles St-Jacques au cidre* (scallops in cider) if you're not up to tripe.

⑤ **Restaurant Paul.** 15 place Dauphine, 1er. ☎ **01-43-54-21-48.** Reservations required. Main courses 98–155F ($19.60–$31). AE, MC, V. Tues–Sun noon–2:30pm and 7:30–10:15pm. Métro: Pont-Neuf. FRENCH.

When this century was young this address was given with strictest confidence to first-time Paris visitors. Since then it has become a cliche for the hidden little bistro, serving the same good food it always did. Why not sample the chicken liver grandmother style, then try the filet mignon *en papillote* (cooked in parchment)? The dessert specialty is *baba à la confiture flambé au rhum* (cake made of leavened dough, mixed with raisins, and steeped in rum after cooking).

Inexpensive

❸ **Lescure.** 7 rue de Mondovi, 1er. ☎ **01-42-60-18-91.** Reservations not accepted. Main courses 38–90F ($7.60–$18); fixed-price four-course menu 100F ($20). MC, V. Mon–Fri noon–2:15pm and 7–10:15pm. Closed 2 weeks in Aug. Métro: Concorde. FRENCH.

This minibistro is a major discovery because reasonably priced restaurants near place de la Concorde are difficult to find. The tables on the sidewalk are tiny and there isn't much room inside, but what this place does have is rustic charm. The kitchen is wide open, and the aroma of drying bay leaves, salami, and garlic pigtails hanging from the ceiling fills the room. Expect *cuisine bourgeoise* here—nothing overly thrilling, just hearty fare. Perhaps begin with *pâté en croûte* (pâté encased in pastry). House specialties include *confit de canard* (duckling) and salmon in green sauce. A favorite dessert is one of the chef's fruit tarts.

RIGHT BANK: 3RD ARRONDISSEMENT

Inexpensive

L'Ambassade d'Auvergne. 22 rue de Grenier St-Lazare, 3e. ☎ **01-42-72-31-22.** Reservations recommended. Main courses 86–120F ($17.20–$24). MC, V. Daily noon–2pm and 7:30–11pm. Métro: Rambuteau. FRENCH.

In an obscure district, this rustic tavern serves the hearty *cuisine bourgeoise* of Auvergne. You enter through a busy bar, with heavy oak beams and hanging hams; rough wheat bread is stacked in baskets, and rush-seated ladderback chairs are placed at tables covered with bright cloths, mills to grind your own salt and pepper, and a jug of mustard. Specialties include cassoulet with lentils, *pot-au-feu* (beef simmered with vegetables), *confit de canard* (duckling), and codfish casserole. For a side dish, try aligot, a medley of fresh potatoes, garlic, and Cantal cheese.

RIGHT BANK: 4TH ARRONDISSEMENT

Very Expensive

❸ **L'Ambroisie.** 9 place des Vosges, 4e. ☎ **01-42-78-51-45.** Reservations required. Main courses 300–500F ($60–$100). AE, MC, V. Tues–Sat noon–1:30pm and 8–9:30pm. Métro: St-Paul. FRENCH.

Bernard Pacaud is one of the most talented chefs in Paris, and his restaurant occupies an early 17th-century town house built for the duc de Luynes. In summer there's outdoor seating. The dishes change seasonally but may include crayfish tails with sesame seeds and curry sauce; fillet of turbot braised with celery and celeriac, served with a julienne of black truffles; and one of our favorites, Bresse chicken roasted with black truffles and truffled vegetables.

Moderate

Bofinger. 5–7 rue de la Bastille, 4e. ☎ **01-42-72-87-82.** Reservations recommended. Main courses 100–150F ($20–$30). AE, DC, MC, V. Mon–Fri noon–3pm and 6:30pm–1am, Sat–Sun noon–1am. Métro: Bastille. FRENCH/ALSATIAN.

This is Paris's oldest Alsatian brasserie, tracing its origins back to 1864. The brasserie offers not only excellent Alsatian fare but also hearty portions served by waiters in floor-length white aprons. The chef prepares a different main dish every day, like savory stew in casserole (*cassolette toulousain*). Most diners order the *choucroute formidable* (sauerkraut), complete with sausages, smoked bacon, and pork chops.

Inexpensive

Chez Jo Goldenberg. 7 rue des Rosiers, 4e. ☎ **01-48-87-20-16.** Reservations recommended. Main courses 70–90F ($14–$18). AE, DC, MC, V. Daily noon–1am. Métro: St-Paul. JEWISH/CENTRAL EUROPEAN.

This is the best-known restaurant on the "Street of the Rose Bushes." Albert Goldenberg, the doyen of Jewish restaurateurs in Paris, long ago moved to a restaurant in choicer surroundings (at 69 av. de Wagram, 17e), but his brother Joseph has remained here. Dining here is on two levels, one reserved for nonsmokers. Look for the collection of samovars and the white fantail pigeon in a wicker cage. Strolling musicians add to the ambience. The *carpe farcie* (stuffed carp) is a preferred selection, but the beef goulash and eggplant moussaka are also good. The menu also offers Israeli wines, but M. Goldenberg admits that they're not as good as French wine.

RIGHT BANK: 8TH ARRONDISSEMENT

Very Expensive

✪ **Lucas-Carton (Alain Senderens).** 9 place de la Madeleine, 8e. ☎ **01-42-65-22-90.** Reservations required several days ahead for lunch, several weeks ahead for dinner. Main courses 300–700F ($60–$140); fixed-price lunch 395F ($79); *menu dégustation* 1,500–1,900F ($300–$380). AE, DC, MC, V. Mon–Fri noon–2:30pm; Mon–Sat 8–10:15pm. Closed 3 weeks in Aug. Métro: Madeleine. FRENCH.

This landmark restaurant was designed by an Englishman named Lucas and a talented French chef named François Carton. Since Senderens has taken over as restaurateur, he's added some welcome modern touches. French food critics are divided into two camps: those claiming Lucas-Carton is Paris's best restaurant and those claiming Taillevent. The battle may never be settled as the race is too close. The two dining rooms downstairs and the private rooms upstairs are decorated with mirrors, fragrant bouquets, and wood paneling that's been polished weekly since 1900. Every dish is influenced by Senderens's creative flair. Menu items change seasonally and include *ravioli aux truffes* (truffles), foie gras with cabbage, vanilla-flavored lobster, duckling Apicius (roasted with honey and spices), and a wonderful *millefeuille* with vanilla sauce.

Moderate

Androuët. 41 rue d'Amsterdam, 8e. ☎ **01-48-74-26-93.** Reservations required. Main courses 100–130F ($20–$26); fixed-price lunch 175F ($35) or 195F ($39); *dégustation de fromages* 250F ($50). AE, DC, MC, V. Mon–Sat noon–3pm and 7:30–10pm. Métro: St-Lazare or Liège. FRENCH.

Brightly lit and decorated in pastels, this is an unusual restaurant, because cheese is the basic ingredient in most dishes. It all began in World War I, when founder M. Androuët started inviting favored guests down to his cellar to sample cheese and good wine. The idea caught on. Today Androuët isn't merely chic—it's an institution. For a first course, the *ravioles de chèvre frais* (ravioli stuffed with fresh goat cheese) is wonderful. A good main dish is *filet de boeuf cotentin* (beef filet with Roquefort sauce, flambéed with Calvados).

RIGHT BANK: 9TH & 10TH ARRONDISSEMENTS

Expensive

Restaurant Opéra. In the Hôtel Inter-Continental, place de l'Opéra, 9e. ☎ **01-40-07-30-10.** Reservations recommended. Main courses 140–225F ($46–$48); fixed-price menu 230–335F ($46–$67). AE, DC, MC, V. Mon–Fri noon–2:30pm and 7–11pm. Métro: Opéra. FRENCH.

If you opt for a meal here, your predecessors will have included Dalí, Josephine Baker, Dietrich, Chevalier, Callas, and also Chagall, who often came here while working on the famous ceiling of the nearby Opéra Garnier. On August 25, 1944, de Gaulle placed this restaurant's first food order in a newly free Paris—a cold plate to go. Today you can enjoy a before-dinner drink in a lavishly ornate bar before heading for a table in what some diners compare to a gilded jewel box. Among the fish selections are lightly salted cod with green-olive cream and fillet of sea bass with herb-flavored crust. Main dishes may be breast of Challans duckling and roast rack of veal for two. The desserts are sumptuous, like chestnut cake with a hazelnut milk sauce.

Moderate

Brasserie Flo. 7 cour des Petites-Ecuries, 10e. ☎ **01-47-70-13-59.** Reservations recommended. Main courses 70–100F ($14–$20); fixed-price lunch 112F ($22.40); fixed-price dinner 185F ($37); fixed-price late-night supper (after 10pm) 112F ($22.40). AE, DC, MC, V. Daily noon–3pm and 7pm–1:30am. Métro: Château-d'Eau or Strasbourg–St-Denis. ALSATIAN.

This restaurant in a remote area is a bit hard to find, but once you arrive (after walking through passageway after passageway), you'll see that fin-de-siècle Paris lives on. The restaurant was established in 1860 and has changed its decor very little since. The house specialty is *la formidable choucroute* (a heaping mound of sauerkraut surrounded by boiled ham, bacon, and sausage) for two. It's bountiful in the best tradition of Alsace. The onion soup is always good, as is the guinea hen with lentils. Look for the *plats du jour* (plates of the day), ranging from roast pigeon to fricassée of veal with sorrel.

LEFT BANK: 5TH ARRONDISSEMENT

Very Expensive

✪ **La Tour d'Argent.** 15–17 quai de la Tournelle, 5e. ☎ **01-43-54-23-31.** Reservations required. Main courses 255–500F ($51–$100); fixed-price lunch 395F ($79). AE, DC, MC, V. Tues–Sun noon–2:30pm and 8–10:30pm. Métro: Maubert-Mutualité or Pont-Marie. FRENCH.

From La Tour d'Argent, a national institution, the view over the Seine and the apse of Notre-Dame is panoramic. Although this penthouse restaurant's long-established position as "the best" in Paris has long been taken over by Taillevent and others, dining at this temple of gastronomy remains unsurpassed as a theatrical event. Since the 16th century there's always been a restaurant on this spot. The restaurant became famous when it was owned by Frédéric Delair, who began issuing certificates to diners who ordered the house specialty, pressed duck (*caneton*)—it's sensational. Other selections include fillets de sole cardinal and fillet Tour d'Argent. Begin with the potage (soup) Claudius Burdel made with sorrel, egg yolks, fresh cream, chicken broth, and butter whipped together.

Moderate

Au Pactole. 44 bd. St-Germain, 5e. ☎ **01-46-33-31-31.** Reservations recommended. Main courses 130–190F ($26–$38); fixed-price menu 149–285F ($29.80–$57). AE, MC, V. Sun–Fri noon–2:45pm; daily 7:15–10:45pm. Métro: Maubert-Mutualité. FRENCH.

Pactole consistently remains one of the 5th arrondissement's best restaurants and continues to offer good value. Roland Magne is not as celebrated as some Paris chefs, but his is an award-winning cuisine. He's assisted by his gracious wife, Noëlle, who is your host. His *ravioli d'escargots* (snails) is surely better than that made by good ol' maman. He also prepares the best ribs of beef you're likely to be served in the 5th, roasted in a crust of salt. He also does an excellent cabillaud (large cod found in the Northern Atlantic)—the flesh is white and flaky, and he seasons it perfectly with green olive oil and herbs.

Inexpensive

Brasserie Balzar. 49 rue des Ecoles, 5e. ☎ **01-43-54-13-67.** Reservations recommended. Main courses 90–115F ($18–$23). AE, MC, V. Daily noon–midnight. Métro: Cluny/La Sorbonne. FRENCH.

Opened in 1898, this brasserie is a bit battered yet cheerful, with some of the friendliest waiters in Paris (all male). The menu makes almost no concessions to nouvelle cuisine and includes *steak au poivre* (pepper steak), sole meunière, sauerkraut garnished with ham and sausage, pigs' feet, and calves' liver. The food is decently prepared, and who wants to come up with anything new when what has been served for 40 years is just fine?

🇸 **La Petite Hostellerie.** 35 rue de la Harpe (just east of boulevard St-Michel), 5e. ☎ **01-43-54-47-12.** Fixed-price lunch 59F ($11.80); fixed-price dinner 89F ($17.80). AE, DC, MC, V. Métro: St-Michel or Cluny/La Sorbonne. FRENCH.

This place has two dining rooms: a usually crowded ground-floor one and a larger (seating 100) upstairs one with attractive 18th-century woodwork. People come for the cozy ambience and decor, decent French country cooking, polite service, and excellent prices. The 89F ($17.80) menu might feature favorites like *coq au vin* (chicken cooked in wine), *canard* (duckling) *à l'orange,* or *entrecôte à la moutarde* (steak with mustard sauce). Start with onion soup or stuffed mussels and finish with cheese or salad and *pêches Melba* (peach Melba) or *tarte aux pommes* (apple tart).

LEFT BANK: 6TH ARRONDISSEMENT

Expensive

Closerie des Lilas (Pleasure Garden of the Lilacs). 171 bd. du Montparnasse, 6e. ☎ **01-43-26-70-50.** Reservations required. Main courses 190–250F ($38–$50) in restaurant, 90–130F ($18–$26) in brasserie. AE, DC, MC, V. Restaurant, daily 12:30–2:30pm and 7:30pm–12:30am; brasserie, daily noon–1am. Métro: Port-Royal or Vavin. FRENCH.

The number of famous people who've dined at the Closerie watching the fallen leaves blow along the Montparnasse streets is almost countless: Stein and Toklas, Ingres, Henry James, Whistler, Proust, Sartre and de Beauvoir. In the *bateau,* you can select such rustic dishes as poached haddock, beef with a salad, and steak tartare. In the chic restaurant inside the Closerie, the cooking is classic. Try the *escargots* (snails) *façon Closerie* for openers. Of the main-course selections, the *rognons de veau à la moutarde* (veal kidneys with mustard) and ribs of veal in cider sauce are highly recommended.

Inexpensive

🇸 **Aux Charpentiers.** 10 rue Mabillon, 6e. ☎ **01-43-26-30-05.** Reservations required. Main courses 90–180F ($18–$36); fixed-price lunch 122F ($24.40); fixed-price dinner 153F ($30.60). AE, DC, MC, V. Mon–Sat noon–3pm and 7:30–11:30pm. Métro: Mabillon. FRENCH.

Aux Charpentiers used to be the rendezvous of master carpenters, whose guild was next door. Now it's where St-Germain-des-Prés youth go for inexpensive meals at a bistro opened more than 130 years ago. Though not imaginative, the food is well prepared in the best tradition of *cuisine bourgeoise.* Especially recommended as a main course is the roast duck with olives. Each day a different *plat du jour* (plate of the day) is offered, with time-tested French home cooking: *pot-au-feu* (beef simmered with vegetables) and *petit salé* of pork (derived from boiling salted pork, then reheating it with richly seasoned lentils) are among the main dishes.

🇸 **Crémerie-Restaurant Polidor.** 41 rue Monsieur-le-Prince, 6e. ☎ **01-43-26-95-34.** Reservations not accepted. Main courses 40–69F ($8–$13.80); fixed-price lunch (Mon–Fri) 50F ($10); fixed-price menu 100F ($20). No credit cards. Daily noon–2:30pm; Mon–Sat 7pm–12:30am, Sun 7–11pm. Métro: Odéon. FRENCH.

This bistro serving *cuisine familiale,* frequented by students and artists, opened in 1930 and has changed little since. Its name still contains the word *crémerie,* referring to its specialty: frosted crème desserts. This has become one of the Left Bank's most established literary bistros; it was André Gide's favorite. Lace curtains and brass hat racks, drawers in the back where repeat customers lock up their cloth napkins, and clay water pitchers on the tables create an old-fashioned atmosphere. The overworked but smiling waitresses serve grandmother's favorites, like pumpkin soup, snails from Burgundy, and veal in white sauce.

LEFT BANK: 7TH ARRONDISSEMENT
Moderate

La Petite Chaise. 36–38 rue de Grenelle, 7e. ☎ **01-42-22-13-35.** Reservations required. Fixed-price menu 180F ($36). MC, V. Daily noon–2:15pm and 7–11pm. Métro: Sèvres-Babylone. FRENCH.

This is Paris's oldest restaurant, established by the baron de la Chaise in 1680 as an inn at the edge of what was then a large hunting preserve. (The baron, according to the restaurant's lore, maintained a series of upstairs rooms for afternoon dalliances.) Very Parisian, the "Little Chair" invites you into a world of cramped but attractive tables, old wood paneling, and ornate wall sconces. The only option is a cost-conscious four-course set menu with a large choice of dishes. The menu may include thin slices of salmon cooked simply with salt and olive oil, Bourgogne snails with garlic butter, or tender beef in wine sauce.

Inexpensive

L'Auberge Basque. 51 rue de Verneuil, 7e. ☎ **01-45-48-51-98.** Reservations recommended. Main courses 80–120F ($16–$24); fixed-price lunch 120F ($24); fixed-price dinner 180F ($36). MC, V. Mon–Sat noon–2:30pm and 7:30–10:30pm. Métro: Rue-du-Bac. FRENCH.

The fixed-price meal of the day offered here depends on the *cuisine du marché* (whatever is fresh at the market). Owners M. and Mme Rourre come from the Basque country near the Spanish border, and their meals reflect the rich cuisine of that region. You might begin with Basque pâté, then follow with a pipérade, a regionally famous omelet. They also prepare *magrêt* and *confit de canard* (duck). Various fresh fish dishes also are served, along with a selection of cheese and fresh-fruit tarts.

GAY RESTAURANTS

Au Rendezvous des Camionneurs. 72 quai des Orfèvres, 1er. ☎ **01-43-54-88-74.** Reservations recommended on weekends. Main courses 78–98F ($15.60–$19.60); fixed-price dinner 120F ($24). AE, MC, V. Daily noon–2:30pm and 7–11:30pm (last order). Métro: Pont-Neuf. FRENCH.

On the Ile de la Cité, this restaurant has the look, feel, cuisine, and service of a traditional bistro; the distinct difference is that 80% of the clientele is gay. The food is reasonably priced and well prepared. Offered are terrine of rabbit, *crottin de chavignol* (a traditional appetizer layered with goat cheese), snails with garlic cream sauce, and blanquette of veal (veal in white sauce). The staff is intelligent and charming.

L'Amazonial. 3 rue Ste-Opportune, 1er. ☎ **01-42-33-53-13.** Reservations recommended. Main courses 75–120F ($15–$24); fixed-price menus 75–120F ($15–$24). AE, MC, V. Daily noon–3pm and 7pm–1am (last order). Métro: Châtelet. SOUTH AMERICAN/FRENCH.

In the heart of the Marais, this is one of Paris's busiest and most popular gay restaurants. Housed in a 19th-century building, its flowered terrace extends onto the pavement, and it features an eclectic decor. Menu items include codfish cooked in coconut milk, prawns grilled in the style of Barbados, Bahia (Brazil)-style lamb curry, tacos, guacamole, and Brazilian-style feijoida.

CAFES

Brasserie Lipp, 151 bd. St-Germain, 6e (☎ **01-45-48-53-91;** Métro: St-Germain-des-Prés), is known as the "rendezvous for *le tout Paris.*" There's an upstairs dining room, but it's more fashionable to sit in the back room. Open daily 9am–1am, though restaurant service is only noon–12:30am. Across from the Centre Pompidou, the avant-garde **Café Beaubourg,** 100 rue St-Martin, 4e (☎ **01-48-87-63-96;** Métro: Rambuteau or Hôtel-de-Ville), boasts a minimalist decor by architect Christian de Portzamparc. In summer tables are set on the terrace, providing a panoramic view of the neighborhood. Open Sun–Thurs 8am–1am and Sat–Sun 8am–2am.

Café Marly, 93 rue de Rivoli, 1er (☎ **01-49-26-06-60;** Métro: Palais-Royal–Musée-du-Louvre), occupies the Louvre's historic cour Napoléon. It's accessible only from a point close to the pyramid and has become a favorite refuge for Parisians escaping the roar of traffic. Anyone is welcome to sit for just a *café au lait* whenever meals aren't being served (noon–3pm and 8–11pm). In summer, outdoor tables overlook the majestic courtyard. Open daily 8am–2am.

At **La Coupole,** 102 bd. Montparnasse, 14e (☎ **01-43-20-14-20;** Métro: Vavin), the clientele ranges from artists' models to young men dressed like Rasputin. The dining room looks like a rail station but serves surprisingly good food. Open daily 7:30am–2am. The legendary **Deux Magots,** 6 place St-Germain-des-Prés, 6e (☎ **01-45-48-55-25;** Métro: St-Germain-des-Prés), is still the hangout for sophisticated neighborhood residents and is a tourist favorite in summer. Inside are two large oriental statues that give the cafe its name. Open daily 7:30am–1:30am.

Fouquet's, 99 av. des Champs-Elysées, 8e (☎ **01-47-23-70-60;** Métro: George-V), is the premier cafe on the Champs-Elysées. The outside tables are separated from the sidewalk by a barricade of potted flowers. Inside is an elegant grill room with leather banquettes and rattan furniture, private banquet rooms, and a restaurant. The cafe and grill room are open daily 9am–2am; the restaurant is open daily noon–3pm.

ATTRACTIONS

The best way to discover the City of Light is on foot. Walk along the grand avenue des Champs-Elysées, tour the quays of the Seine, wander around Ile de la Cité and Ile St-Louis, browse through the countless shops and stalls, wander through the famous squares and parks. Each turn will open a new vista.

Le Pass-Musée (Museum and Monuments Pass) is available at any of the museums that honor it or at any branch of the Paris Tourist Office (above). It offers free entrance to the permanent collections of 65 monuments and museums in Paris and the Ile de France. A 1-day pass is 70F ($14), a 3-day pass 140F ($28), and a 5-day pass 200F ($40).

SIGHTSEEING SUGGESTIONS

If You Have 1 Day The most practical way to see Paris in a day is to take a guided tour. Start the day by ordering a *café au lait* or *café crème* and croissants at a sidewalk cafe. At 9:30am the Cityrama tour's double-decker bus leaves for its 2-hour ride around the city, past such sights as Notre-Dame and the Eiffel Tower (see "Organized Tours"). After the tour, have lunch and go to the Louvre for a guided tour of its most important works. With what's left of the afternoon, stroll along the Seine, ending up at Notre-Dame as the sun sets. If you have an early dinner at a nearby bistro, you may still have the time and energy to attend the Lido or Folies-Bergère.

If You Have 2 Days Start your second day by taking a Bateaux-Mouche cruise on the Seine (see "Organized Tours"). Next head for the Arc de Triomphe, a perfect place to begin a stroll down the Champs-Elysées, the main boulevard, until you reach the Egyptian obelisk at place de la Concorde. This grand promenade is one of the world's most famous long walks. That night, visit a Left Bank boîte or jazz club.

If You Have 3 Days On your third morning, explore the Sainte-Chapelle and the Conciergerie. Have lunch on Ile St-Louis, then take a walking tour of that island in

Paris Attractions

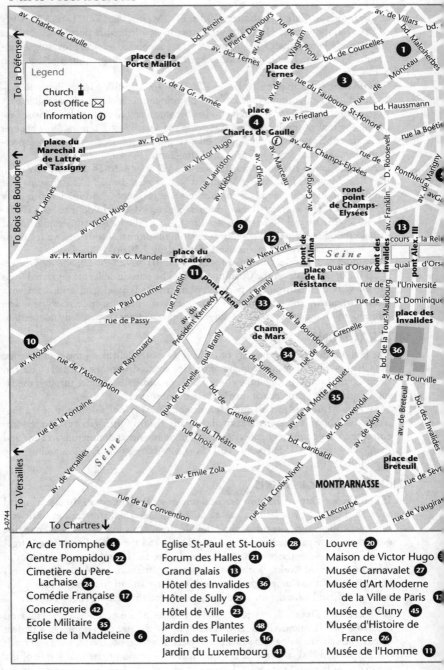

Legend

Church ✝
Post Office ✉
Information ⓘ

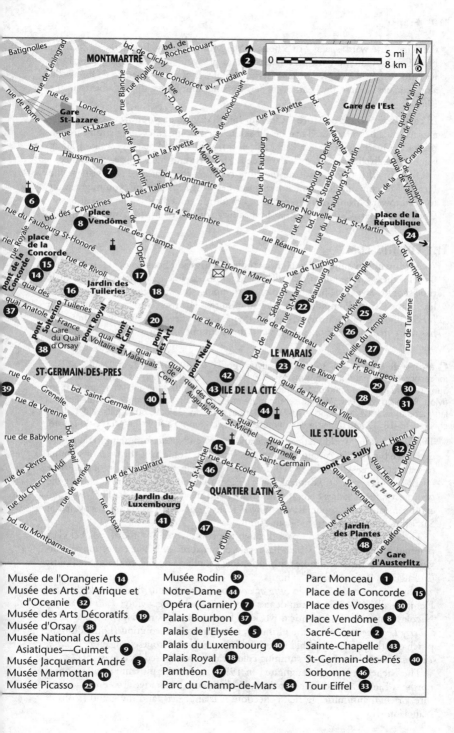

Musée de l'Orangerie (14)
Musée des Arts d' Afrique et d'Oceanie (32)
Musée des Arts Décoratifs (19)
Musée d'Orsay (38)
Musée National des Arts Asiatiques—Guimet (9)
Musée Jacquemart André (3)
Musée Marmottan (10)
Musée Picasso (25)

Musée Rodin (39)
Notre-Dame (44)
Opéra (Garnier) (7)
Palais Bourbon (37)
Palais de l'Elysée (5)
Palais du Luxembourg (40)
Palais Royal (18)
Panthéon (47)
Parc du Champ-de-Mars (34)

Parc Monceau (1)
Place de la Concorde (15)
Place des Vosges (30)
Place Vendôme (8)
Sacré-Cœur (2)
Sainte-Chapelle (43)
St-Germain-des-Prés (40)
Sorbonne (46)
Tour Eiffel (33)

the Seine. Afterward, spend 2 or 3 hours at the Musée d'Orsay. Before the day is over, head for the Cimetière du Père-Lachaise and pay your respects to Jim Morrison, Richard Wright, Oscar Wilde, and Gertrude Stein. In the early evening go for a walk along rue des Rosiers, the heart of the Jewish community, then dine at a bistro in the Marais.

If You Have 5 Days or More   On your fourth day, go on your own or take an organized tour to Versailles. Then head back to the city for an evening stroll through the Latin Quarter, dining in a Left Bank bistro. With a good map, try walking along some of the livelier streets, such as rue de la Hachette and rue Monsieur-le-Prince.

On your fifth day, spend the morning roaming the Marais. Pay a visit to the Picasso Museum and have lunch near place des Vosges. Afterward, you might want to head toward Montmartre to explore. Try to time your visit so you'll be at Sacré-Coeur at sunset. Cap the evening by heading for one of Montparnasse's famous cafes.

THE TOP MUSEUMS

Note: Museums require that you check shopping bags and book bags, and sometimes lines for these can be longer than ticket and admission lines. Visitors who value their time should leave these bags behind or do shopping afterward. For instance, the coat line at the Centre Pompidou can take 30 minutes. The trick is to go to the coat line for the photo exhibit downstairs, where there's almost never a wait. Ask if a museum has more than one coat line; if so, avoid the main one and go to the less frequented ones.

✪ **Musée du Louvre.** 34–36 quai du Louvre, 1er. ☎ **01-40-20-53-17,** or 01-40-20-51-51 for recorded information. Admission 45F ($9) before 3pm, 26F ($5.20) after 3pm and all day Sun; free for children 17 and under. Free first Sun of every month. Mon and Wed 9am–9:45pm (Mon, Richelieu wing only; Wed the entire museum), Thurs–Sun 9am–6pm. 90-minute English-language tours leave Mon and Wed–Sat at various times for 33F ($6.60) adults, 22F ($4.40) children 13–18; 12 and under free with museum ticket. Métro: Palais-Royal–Musée-du-Louvre.

The Louvre is the world's largest palace and largest and greatest museum. You'll have no choice but to miss certain masterpieces since you won't have the time or stamina to see everything—the Louvre's collection is truly staggering. People on one of those "Paris-in-a-day" tours try to break track records to stand with the crowds and see the two most famous ladies here: the *Mona Lisa* and the *Venus de Milo.* Those with an extra 5 minutes go in pursuit of *Winged Victory,* the headless statue discovered at Samothrace and dating from about 200 B.C.

To enter the Louvre, you pass through the controversial 71-foot I. M. Pei glass pyramid in the courtyard, which has received mixed reviews. The collections are divided into departments; those with little time should go on one of the guided tours (in English), lasting about 1½ hours.

Our favorite works include *Ship of Fools* by Hieronymous Bosch (tucked in the Flemish galleries)—no one can depict folly and greed more vividly; *Four Seasons* by Nicolas Poussin, the canonical work of French classicism; Eugène Delacroix's *Liberty Leading the People,* the ultimate endorsement of revolution (Louis-Philippe purchased the painting and hid it during his reign); and Veronese's gigantic *Wedding Feast at Cana,* showing how stunning colors can be when used by a master.

The Richelieu Wing, inaugurated in 1993, houses the museum's collection of northern European and French paintings, along with decorative arts, French sculpture, oriental antiquities (a rich collection of Islamic art), and the grand salons of Napoléon III.

○ **Musée d'Orsay.** 1 rue de Bellechasse or 62 rue de Lille, 7e. ☎ **01-40-49-48-14.** Admission 35F ($7) adults, 24F ($4.80) ages 18–24 and seniors, free for children 17 and under. Tues–Wed and Fri–Sat 10am–6pm, Thurs 10am–9:45pm, Sun 9am–6pm. June 20–Sept 20, museum opens 9am. Métro: Solférino. RER: Musée-d'Orsay.

The defunct but handsome neoclassical Gare d'Orsay rail station, across the Seine from the Louvre and the Tuileries, has been transformed into a repository of 19th-century art and civilization. The museum houses sculptures and paintings spread across 80 galleries, plus belle époque furniture, photographs, objets d'art, architectural models, and even a cinema.

One of Renoir's most joyous paintings is here—*Moulin de la Galette* (1876). Another celebrated work is by American James McNeill Whistler—*Arrangement in Gray and Black: Portrait of the Painter's Mother.* The most famous piece in the museum is Manet's 1863 *Déjeuner sur l'herbe (Picnic on the Grass)*, which created a scandal when it was first exhibited.

Centre Pompidou. Place Georges-Pompidou, 4e. ☎ **01-44-78-12-33.** All-day pass, 70F ($14) adults, 45F ($9) ages 16–25 and over 60, free for age 17 and under. Musée National d'Art Moderne, 35F ($7) adults, 24F ($4.80) ages 16–24 and over 60, free for age 15 and under. Mon and Wed–Fri noon–10pm, Sat–Sun 10am–10pm. Métro: Rambuteau, Hôtel-de-Ville, Châtelet, or Les Halles.

In 1969 Georges Pompidou, then president of France, decided to create a large cultural center to spotlight every form of 20th-century art. The structure has been the subject of much controversy because of its radical exoskeletal design. The Tinker Toy–like array of colorful pipes and tubes surrounding the transparent shell are functional, serving as casings for the center's heating, air-conditioning, electrical, and phone systems.

The Centre Pompidou encompasses four separate attractions. The **Musée National d'Art Moderne** offers a large collection of 20th-century art; with some 40,000 works, only some 850 can be displayed at one time. If you want to view a real charmer, see Alexander Calder's *1926 Josephine Baker,* one of his earliest versions of the mobile, an art form he invented. In the **Public Information Library** the public (for the first time in Paris's history) has free access to 1 million French and foreign books, periodicals, films, records, slides, and microfilms in nearly every area of knowledge. The **Center for Industrial Design** emphasizes the contributions made in the fields of architecture, visual communications, and community planning. The **Institute for Research and Coordination of Acoustics/Music** brings together musicians and composers interested in furthering the cause of music, both contemporary and traditional.

○ **Musée Picasso.** 5 rue de Thorigny, 3e. ☎ **01-42-71-25-21.** Admission 28F ($5.60) adults, 18F ($3.60) ages 19–25, free for age 18 and under. Apr–Sept Wed–Mon 9:30am–5:30pm; Oct–Mar Wed–Mon 9:30am–5:30pm. Métro: St-Paul, Filles-du-Calvaire, or Chemin-Vert.

When it opened in the beautifully restored Hôtel Salé (salt mansion, built in 1656 for Aubert de Fontenay, collector of the dreaded salt tax), a state-owned property in Le Marais, the press hailed it as a "museum for Picasso's Picassos," meaning those he chose not to sell. The greatest Picasso collection in the world, acquired by the state in lieu of $50 million in inheritance taxes, consists of 203 paintings, 158 sculptures, 16 collages, 19 bas-reliefs, 88 ceramics, and more than 1,500 sketches and 1,600 engravings, along with 30 notebooks. These works span 75 years of Picasso's life and changing styles. The range of paintings includes a remarkable 1901 self-portrait and embraces such masterpieces as *Le Baiser (The Kiss),* painted at Mougins in 1969, and *Reclining Nude* and *The Man with a Guitar.*

On the Champs-Elysées

In late 1995, Paris's most prominent triumphal promenade was reinaugurated with several important improvements. The *contre-allées* (side lanes that had always been clogged with parked cars) had been removed, new lighting added, the pedestrian sidewalks widened, new trees planted, and underground parking garages added. Now the Grand Promenade truly is grand again.

Arc de Triomphe. Place Charles-de-Gaulle–Etoile, 16e. ☎ **01-43-80-31-31.** Admission 32F ($6.40) adults, 21F ($4.20) ages 18–24 and over 60, 15F ($3) children 12–17, free for children 11 and under. Apr–Sept daily 9:30am–11pm; Oct–Mar daily 10am–10:30pm, Sun and Mon 10am–6:30pm. Métro: Charles-de-Gaulle–Etoile.

At the western end of the Champs-Elysées, the Arc de Triomphe is the world's largest triumphal arch, about 163 feet high and 147 feet wide. This arch has witnessed some of France's proudest moments—and some of its more humiliating defeats, notably those of 1871 and 1940. Commissioned by Napoléon in 1806 to commemorate his Grande Armée's victories, it wasn't completed until 1836, under Louis-Philippe. Four years later Napoléon's remains—brought from his grave on St. Helena—passed under the arch on their journey to his tomb at the Invalides. Since then it has become the focal point for state funerals. It's also the site of the tomb of the unknown soldier, where an eternal flame is kept burning.

On the Ile de la Cité & Ile St-Louis

Ile de la Cité

Medieval Paris, that architectural blending of grotesquerie and gothic beauty, began on this island in the Seine. Explore as much of it as you can, but if you're in a hurry, try to visit at least Notre-Dame, the Sainte-Chapelle, and the Conciergerie.

✪ **Cathédrale Notre-Dame.** 6 place du Parvis Notre-Dame, 4e. ☎ **01-42-34-56-10.** Cathedral, free; towers, 27F ($5.40) adults, 18F ($3.60) ages 18–24 and over 60, 10F ($2) children 7–17, free for children under 7. Treasury or crypt, 15F ($3) adults, 10F ($2) ages 18–24 and over 60, 5F ($1) children 10–17, free for children under 10. Cathedral, daily 8am–6:45pm (closed Sat 12:30–2pm); towers, daily 9:30am–5pm; museum, Wed and Sat–Sun 2:30–6pm; treasury and crypt, Mon–Sat 9:30am–5:30pm. Six masses are celebrated on Sun, four on weekdays, and one on Sat. Métro: Cité or St-Michel. RER: St-Michel.

This is surely the world's most famous gothic cathedral. From square Parvis, you can view the trio of 13th-century sculptured portals: On the left, the Portal of the Virgin depicts the signs of the Zodiac and the Virgin's coronation. The restored central Portal of the Last Judgment is divided into three levels: The first shows Vices and Virtues; the second, Christ and his Apostles; the third, Christ in triumph after the Resurrection. On the right is the Portal of St. Anne, depicting such scenes as the Virgin enthroned with Child, the most perfect piece of sculpture in Notre-Dame. Equally interesting (though often missed) is the Portal of the Cloisters (around on the left).

The interior is typical gothic, with slender, graceful columns. Over the central portal is the remarkable rose window, 31 feet in diameter. The carved-stone choir screen from the early 14th century depicts such biblical scenes as the Last Supper. Near the altar stands the highly venerated 14th-century Virgin and Child.

To visit those grimy gargoyles, immortalized by Victor Hugo, where Quasimodo hung out, you have to scale steps leading to the twin square towers, rising to a height of 225 feet. It may be visited 10am–noon and 2–7pm. Admission is free.

Sainte-Chapelle. Palais de Justice, 4 bd. du Palais, 1er. ☎ **01-43-54-30-09.** Admission 32F ($6.40) adults, 21F ($4.20) ages 18–25, 15F ($3) ages 12–17, free for children under 12.

Apr–Sept daily 9:30am–6:30pm; Oct–Mar daily 10am–5pm. Métro: Cité, St-Michel, or Châtelet. RER: St-Michel.

The Sainte-Chapelle is Paris's second most important medieval monument after Notre-Dame. It was erected in the flamboyant Gothic style to enshrine relics (no longer there) including the Crown of Thorns, and two pieces from the True Cross. The walls of the upper chapel consist almost entirely of 15 superb stained-glass windows, and viewed on a bright day with the sun streaming in, they glow with marvelous ruby reds and Chartres blues, a sight not to be missed. The lower level of the chapel is supported by flying buttresses and ornamented with fleurs-de-lis—it was used by the palace servants, the upper chapel by the king and his courtiers.

Conciergerie. 1 quai de l'Horloge, 1er. ☎ **01-43-54-30-06.** Admission 28F ($5.60) adults, 18F ($3.60) ages 12–17, 15F ($3) children under 12. Apr–Sept daily 9:30am–6:30pm; Oct–Mar daily 10am–5pm. Métro: Cité, Châtelet, or St-Michel. RER: St-Michel.

The Conciergerie has been called the most sinister building in France. Though it had a long regal history before the revolution, it's visited today chiefly by those wishing to bask in the Reign of Terror's horrors. You approach the Conciergerie through its landmark twin towers, the Tour d'Argent and Tour de César, but the 14th-century vaulted Guard Room is the actual entrance. Also from the 14th century—and even more interesting—is the vast, dark, foreboding Salle des Gens d'Armes (People at Arms), chillingly changed from the days when the king used it as a banqueting hall.

Ile St-Louis

As you walk across the iron footbridge from the rear of Notre-Dame, you descend into a world of tree-shaded quays, aristocratic town houses and courtyards, restaurants, and antique shops.

The sibling island of the Ile de la Cité is primarily residential; its denizens fiercely guard their heritage, privileges, and special position. It was originally two "islets," one named Island of the Heifers. Plaques on the facades make it easier to identify former residents. Madame Curie, for example, lived at 36 quai de Bethune, near ponte de la Tournelle, from 1912 until her death in 1934.

The most exciting mansion is the **Hôtel de Lauzun,** built in 1657, at 17 quai d'Anjou; it's named after a 17th-century rogue, the duc de Lauzun, famous lover and on-again/off-again favorite of Louis XIV. French poet Charles Baudelaire lived here in the 19th century with his "Black Venus," Jeanne Duval. Voltaire lived in the **Hôtel Lambert,** 2 quai d'Anjou, with his mistress, Emilie de Breteuil, the marquise du Châteley, who had an "understanding" husband.

THE EIFFEL TOWER & ENVIRONS

From place du Trocadéro, you can step between the two curved wings of the Palais de Chaillot and gaze out on a breathtaking view. At your feet lie the Jardins du Trocadéro, centered by fountains. Directly in front, pont d'Iéna spans the Seine, leading to the the iron immensity of the Tour Eiffel. And beyond, stretching as far as your eye can see, is the Champ-de-Mars, once a military parade ground but now a garden with arches, grottoes, lakes, and cascades.

✪ Tour Eiffel. Champ-de-Mars, 7e. ☎ **01-44-11-23-23.** First landing, 20F ($4); second landing, 40F ($8); third landing, 56F ($11.20); stairs to second landing, 12F ($2.40). Sept–June daily 9:30am–11pm; July–Aug daily 9am–midnight (in fall and winter the stairs close at 6:30pm). Métro: Trocadéro, Ecole-Militaire, or Bir-Hakeim. RER: Champ-de-Mars/Tour-Eiffel.

Except for perhaps the Leaning Tower of Pisa, this is the single most recognizable structure in the world—the symbol of Paris. Weighing 7,000 tons but exerting about the same pressure on the ground as an average-size person sitting in a chair, the tower was never meant to be permanent. It was built for the Universal Exhibition of 1889 by Gustave-Alexandre Eiffel, the engineer whose fame rested mainly on his iron bridges. The tower, including its 55-foot TV antenna, is 1,056 feet tall. On a clear day you can see it from some 40 miles away. An open-framework construction, the tower ushered in the almost-unlimited possibilities of steel construction, paving the way for the 20th century's skyscrapers. You can visit the tower in three stages: Taking the elevator to the first landing, you have a view over the rooftops of Paris; the second landing provides a panoramic look at the city; the third gives the most spectacular view, allowing you to identify monuments and buildings.

Hôtel des Invalides (Napoléon's Tomb). Place des Invalides, 7e. ☎ **01-44-42-37-72.** Admission (good for 2 consecutive days for the Musée de l'Armée, Napoléon's Tomb, and the Musée des Plans-Reliefs) 35F ($7) adults, 25F ($5) children 7–18 and people over 60, free for children 6 and under. Apr–Sept daily 10am–6pm (Napoléon's Tomb until 7pm June–Aug); Oct–Mar daily 10am–5pm. Closed Jan 1, May 1, Nov 1, and Dec 25. Métro: Latour-Maubourg, Varenne, or Invalides.

The glory of the French military lives on here in the Musée de l'Armée, the world's greatest army museum. It was the Sun King who decided to build the "hotel" to house soldiers who'd been disabled. Among the collections are Viking swords, Burgundian bacinets, 14th-century blunderbusses, Balkan khandjars, salamander-engraved Renaissance serpentines, and American Browning machine guns. As a sardonic touch, there's even General Daumesnil's wooden leg.

To accommodate the Tomb of Napoléon—of red porphyry, with a green granite base—the architect Visconti had to redesign the high altar in 1842. First buried at St. Helena, Napoléon's remains were returned to Paris in 1840. Surounding the tomb are a dozen amazon-like figures representing his victories. Almost lampooning the smallness of the man, everything is made awesome: You'd think a real giant were buried here, not a symbolic one.

IN MONTMARTRE

From the 1880s to just before World War I, Montmartre enjoyed its golden age as the world's best-known art colony. *La Vie de bohème* reigned supreme. Following World War I the pseudoartists flocked here in droves, with camera-snapping tourists hot on their heels. The real artists had long gone to such places as Montparnasse.

Before its discovery and subsequent chic, Montmartre was a sleepy farming community, with windmills dotting the landscape. Since it's at the highest point in the city, if you find it too much of a climb you may want to take the miniature train along the steep streets: **Le Petit Train de Montmartre,** which passes all the major landmarks, seats 55 passengers who can listen to the English commentary. Board at place du Tertre (at the Eglise St-Pierre) or place Blanche (near the Moulin Rouge). Trains run daily 10am–7pm. For information, contact Promotrain, 131 rue de Clignancourt, 18e (☎ **01-42-62-24-00**).

The simplest way to reach Montmartre is to take the Métro to Anvers, then walk up rue du Steinkerque to the funicular, which runs to the precincts of Sacré-Coeur every day 6am–11pm.

✪ Basilique du Sacré-Coeur. Place St-Pierre, 18e. ☎ **01-42-51-17-02.** Basilica, free; dome, 15F ($3) adults, 8F ($1.60) students 6–25; crypt, 15F ($3) adults, 5F ($1) students. Basilica, daily 7am–10:30pm. Dome and crypt, Apr–Sept daily 9:15am–7pm; Oct–Mar daily 9:15am–6pm. Métro: Abbesses; then take the elevator to the surface and follow the signs to the funiculaire, which goes up to the church for the price of one Métro ticket.

Montmartre's crowning achievement is Sacré-Coeur, though the view of Paris from its precincts takes precedence over the basilica itself. One Parisian called it "a lunatic's confectionery dream." Zola declared it "the basilica of the ridiculous." But Utrillo never tired of drawing and painting it, and he and Max Jacob came here regularly to pray.

In gleaming white, it towers over Paris—its five bulbous domes suggesting some 12th-century Byzantine church and its campanile inspired by Roman–Byzantine art. After France's defeat by the Prussians in 1870, the basilica was planned as an offering to cure the country's misfortunes. Both rich and poor contributed money to build it. Construction began in 1873, but the church was not consecrated until 1919. On a clear day the vista from the dome can extend for 35 miles.

IN THE LATIN QUARTER

This is the Left Bank precinct of the **University of Paris** (often called the **Sorbonne**), where students meet and fall in love over coffee and croissants. Rabelais called it the Quartier Latin, because of the students and professors who spoke Latin in the classrooms and on the streets. The sector teems with belly dancers, exotic restaurants (from Vietnamese to Balkan), sidewalk cafes, bookstalls, and *caveaux*.

A good starting point might be **place St-Michel** (Métro: Pont-St-Michel), where Balzac used to get water from the fountain when he was a youth. This center was the scene of much Resistance fighting in the summer of 1944. The quarter centers around **boulevard St-Michel,** to the south (the students call it "Boul Mich").

Musée National du Moyen Age/Thermes de Cluny (Musée de Cluny). 6 place Paul-Painlevé, 5e. ☎ **01-43-25-62-00.** Admission 28F ($5.60) adults, 18F ($3.60) ages 18–25, free for age 17 and under. Wed–Mon 9:15am–5:45pm. Métro: Cluny/La Sorbonne.

There are two reasons to go here: The museum houses the world's finest collection of art from the Middle Ages, including jewelry and tapestries, and it's all displayed in a well-preserved manor house built on top of Roman baths. In the cobblestone Court of Honor you can admire the flamboyant Gothic building with its clinging vines, turreted walls, gargoyles, and dormers with seashell motifs. Along with the Hôtel de Sens in Le Marais, this is all that remains in Paris of domestic medieval architecture. Most people come primarily to see the Unicorn Tapestries—all the romance of the age of chivalry lives on in these remarkable yet mysterious tapestries, showing a beautiful princess and her handmaiden, beasts of prey, and just plain pets. They were discovered only a century ago in the Château de Boussac in the Auvergne. Downstairs are the ruins of the Roman baths, dating from around A.D. 200. You wander through a display of Gallic and Roman sculptures and an interesting marble bathtub engraved with lions.

HISTORIC GARDENS & SQUARES

GARDENS   Bordering place de la Concorde, the statue-studded ✪ **Jardin des Tuileries** (☎ **01-44-50-75-01;** Métro: Tuileries) are as much a part of Paris as the Seine. They were designed by Le Nôtre, Louis XIV's gardener and planner of the Versailles grounds. About 100 years before that, Catherine de Médici ordered a palace built here, connected to the Louvre. Twice attacked by enraged Parisians, it was finally burnt to the ground in 1871 and never rebuilt.

Hemingway told a friend that the ✪ **Jardin du Luxembourg,** 6e (Métro: Odéon; RER: Luxembourg), "kept us from starvation." He related that in his poverty-stricken days in Paris, he wheeled a baby carriage through the gardens because it was known "for the classiness of its pigeons." When the gendarme left to get a glass of wine, the writer would eye his victim, then lure it with corn and snatch it. "We got a little tired of pigeon that year," he confessed, "but they filled many a void." Before it became a feeding ground for struggling artists in the 1920s, the Luxembourg Gardens knew greater days. But they've always been associated with artists, though students from the Sorbonne and children predominate nowadays. The gardens are the best on the Left Bank (if not in all of Paris). Marie de Médici, the much-neglected wife and later widow of the roving Henri IV, ordered the Palais du Luxembourg built on this site in 1612.

SQUARES   In **place de la Bastille** on July 14, 1789, a mob of Parisians attacked the Bastille and thus sparked the French Revolution. Nothing remains of the historic Bastille, built in 1369, for it was torn down. Many prisoners—some sentenced by Louis XIV for "witchcraft"—were kept within its walls, the best known being the "Man in the Iron Mask." When the fortress was stormed, only seven prisoners were discovered (the marquis de Sade had been transferred to the madhouse 10 days earlier). Bastille Day is celebrated with great festivity on July 14. In the center of the square is the Colonne de Juillet (July Column), but it doesn't commemorate the revolution. It honors the victims of the 1830 July revolution, which put Louis-Philippe on the throne.

✪ Place des Vosges, 4e (Métro: St-Paul or Chemin-Vert), is Paris's oldest square and was once the most fashionable. In the heart of the Marais, it was called the Palais Royal in the days of Henri IV, who planned to live here—but his assassin, Ravaillac, had other intentions for him. Henry II was killed while jousting on the square in 1559. Place des Vosges was one of the first planned squares in Europe. Its *grand siècle* red-brick houses are ornamented with white stone. Its covered arcades allowed people to shop at all times, even in the rain—quite an innovation at the time.

In the east, avenue des Champs-Elysées begins at **place de la Concorde,** an octagonal traffic hub ordered built in 1757 to honor Louis XV and one of the world's grandest squares. The statue of the king was torn down in 1792 and the name of the square changed to place de la Révolution. Floodlit at night, it's dominated now by an Egyptian obelisk from Luxor, the oldest man-made object in Paris; it was carved circa 1200 B.C. and presented to France in 1829 by the viceroy of Egypt. During the Reign of Terror, Dr. Guillotin's little invention was erected on this spot and claimed thousands of lives—everybody from Louis XVI, who died bravely, to Mme du Barry, who went kicking and screaming all the way.

For a spectacular sight, look down the Champs-Elysées—the view is framed by Coustou's Marly horses, which once graced the gardens at Louis XIV's Château de Marly (these are copies—the originals are in the Louvre).

HISTORIC PARKS & A CEMETERY

PARKS   One of the most spectacular parks in Europe is the **✪ Bois de Boulogne,** Porte Dauphine, 16e (☎ **01-40-67-90-80;** Métro: Les-Sablons, Porte-Maillot, or Porte-Dauphine). Horse-drawn carriages traverse it, but you can also drive through. Many of its hidden pathways, however, must be discovered by walking. West of Paris, the park was once a forest kept for royal hunts. When Napoléon III gave the grounds to the city in 1852, they were developed by Baron Haussmann. Separating Lac Inférieur from Lac Supérieur is the Carrefour des Cascades (you can stroll under its waterfall). The Lower Lake contains two islands connected by a footbridge.

The **Parc Monceau,** 8e (☎ **01-42-27-39-56;** Métro: Monceau or Villiers), is ringed with 18th- and 19th-century mansions, some of them evoking Proust's *Remembrance of Things Past.* It was built in 1778 by the duc d'Orléans, or Philippe Egalité, as he became known. Parc Monceau was laid out with an Egyptian-style obelisk, a medieval dungeon, a thatched alpine farmhouse, a Chinese pagoda, a Roman temple, an enchanted grotto, various chinoiseries, and a waterfall. The park was opened to the public during Napoléon III's Second Empire.

A CEMETERY   The ✪ **Cemetière du Père-Lachaise,** 16 rue de Repos, 20e
(☎ **01-43-70-70-33;** Métro: Père-Lachaise), is Paris's largest and contains more illustrious dead than any other. When it comes to name-dropping, this cemetery knows
no peer—it's been called the "grandest address in Paris." Everybody from Sarah
Bernhardt to Oscar Wilde (his tomb by Epstein) was buried here. So were Balzac,
Delacroix, and Bizet. Colette's body was taken here in 1954, and her black granite
slab always sports flowers (legend has it that cats replenish the red roses). In time, the
"little sparrow," Edith Piaf, followed. Marcel Proust's black tombstone rarely lacks
a tiny bunch of violets. Some tombs are sentimental favorites—that of Jim Morrison,
the American rock star who died in 1971, reportedly draws the most visitors. Another
stone is marked GERTRUDE STEIN on one side and ALICE B. TOKLAS on the other.
Open Mon–Fri 8am–6pm, Sat 8:30am–6pm, and Sun 9am–6pm (closes at 5:30pm
Nov 6–Mar 14).

ORGANIZED TOURS

BY BUS   You can take the most popular get-acquainted tour in Paris: **Cityrama,**
4 place de Pyramides, 1er (☎ **01-44-55-60-00;** Métro: Palais-Royal or Musée-du-
Louvre). On a double-decker bus with enough windows for the Palace of Versailles,
you're taken on a leisurely 2-hour ride through the city. Since you don't go inside
any attractions, you must settle for a look at the outside of such places as Notre-Dame
and the Eiffel Tower. Tours depart daily at 9:30, 10:30, and 11:30am and 1:30, 2:30,
and 3:30pm. A 2-hour orientation tour of Paris costs 150F ($30). A morning tour
with interior visits to Notre-Dame and the Louvre goes for 260F ($52). Tours to
Versailles and Chartres are also offered. Another Cityrama offering, a tour of the
nighttime illuminations, leaves daily at 10pm in summer, at 9pm in winter. The cost
is 150F ($30).

BY BOAT   A boat tour on the Seine provides sweeping views of the riverbanks and
some of the best views of Notre-Dame. Many of the boats have open sundecks, bars,
and restaurants. **Bateaux-Mouche** cruises (☎ **01-42-25-96-10** for info and reservations; Métro: Alma-Marceau) depart from the Right Bank of the Seine, adjacent
to pont de l'Alma, and last about 75 minutes each. Tours leave every day, at 30-
minute intervals between 10am and 11:30pm, and at 15-minute intervals in good
weather. Dinner cruises depart at 8:30pm; on these, ties and jackets are required for
men. Fares are 40F ($8) for adults and 20F ($4) for children.

SHOPPING

Perfumes and **cosmetics,** including such famous brands as Guerlain, Chanel,
Schiaparelli, and Jean Patou, are almost always cheaper in Paris than in the United
States. Paris is also a good place to buy Lalique and Baccarat **crystal.** They're expen-
sive but still priced below international market value.

Of course, many people come to Paris just to shop for **fashions.** From Chanel to
Yves Saint Laurent, from Nina Ricci to Sonia Rykiel, the city overflows with
fashion boutiques, ranging from haute couture to the truly outlandish. Fashion accessories, such as those designed by Louis Vuitton and Céline, are among the finest
in the world. **Lingerie** is another great French export. All the top lingerie designers
are represented in boutiques as well as in the major department stores, Galeries
Lafayette and Le Printemps.

✪ **Le Louvre des Antiquaires,** 2 place du Palais-Royal, 1er (☎ **01-42-97-
27-00;** Métro: Palais-Royal–Musée-du-Louvre), is Europe's largest antique center,
stocking everything from Russian icons to art deco pieces. On three floors, it houses
250 dealers in its 2¹/₂ acres of well-lit modern salons. Open Tues–Sun 11am–7pm.

Maeght Editeur & Adrien Maeght Gallery, 42 rue du Bac, 7e (☎ 01-45-48-31-01; Métro: Rue-du-Bac), boasts an interesting collection of posters and pictorial books by important artists, like Matisse. Exhibits include modern sculpture and engravings by established and unknown artists. Open Tues–Sat 10am–1pm and 2–7pm.

Purveyor to kings and presidents since it was established in 1764, ✪ **Baccarat,** 30 bis rue de Paradis, 10e (☎ 01-47-70-64-30; Métro: Château-d'Eau, Poissonière, or Gare-de-l'Est), produces some of the world's most famous full-lead crystal. Their glittering showroom is open Mon–Fri 9am–6:30pm and Sat 10am–6pm. A museum one floor above street level displays some of the company's historic models. The museum is open Mon–Sat 10am–6pm. **Limoges-Unic,** 12 and 58 rue de Paradis, 10e (☎ 01-47-70-54-49; Métro: Gare-de-l'Est or Poissonnière), sells an extensive stock of Limoges china—such as Ceralane, Haviland, and Bernardaud—as well as Baccarat, Villeroy & Boch, Hermès, Lalique, and Sèvres crystal. Open Mon–Sat 10am–6:30pm.

A landmark in the Parisian fashion world, **Galeries Lafayette,** 40 bd. Haussmann, 9e (☎ 01-42-82-34-56; Métro: Chausée-d'Antin or Opéra; RER: Auber), is one of the world's leading department stores. An entrance marked WELCOME directs you to English-speaking hostesses available to assist you. Finish your shopping day with an exceptional view of Paris on the rooftop terrace. Open Mon–Wed and Fri–Sat 9:30am–6:45pm, Thursday 9:30am–9pm. The city's largest department store, ✪ **Le Printemps,** 64 bd. Haussmann, 9e (☎ 01-42-82-50-00; Métro: Havre-Caumartin; RER: Auber), has three stores connected by bridges on the second and third floors. Brummell offers men's clothing, whereas Printemps de la Mode sells clothes for women, juniors, and children. Printemps de la Maison is mainly for records, books, furniture, and housewares. The ground floor has a large perfumerie, as well as cosmetics, gifts, and handcrafts. Interpreters at the ground-floor Welcome Service will help you claim your discounts and guide you. Open Mon–Wed and Fri–Sat 9:35am–7pm, Thurs 9:35am–10pm.

Anna Loew, 104 rue du Faubourg St-Honoré, 8e (☎ 01-40-06-02-42; Métro: Franklin-D.-Roosevelt), was conceived and is managed by former fashion model Anna Loew. It's Paris's premier boutique for high-quality clothing, usually by famous designers, that's sold at discounted prices. All items come with the original designer's label still attached, as well as with the label of Anna Loew, and include garments by Chanel, Valentino, Givenchy, Ungaro, and Lacroix. Some of the merchandise comes from last season's (usually discontinued) collection. Open Mon–Sat 10:30am–7pm.

Michel Swiss, 16 rue de la Paix, 2e (☎ 01-42-61-61-11; Métro: Opera), looks like the other chic boutiques near place Vendôme. But once you're inside (there's no storefront window), you'll see major brands of luxury perfumes, makeup, leather bags, pens, neckties, accessories, and giftware—all discounted. Open Mon–Sat 9am–6:30pm.

Vast ✪ **Fauchon,** 26 Place de la Madeleine, 8e (☎ 01-47-42-60-11; Métro: Madeleine), is one of the most popular city sights. The window display, often including plump chickens or lamb filled with fresh vegetables, entices passersby. English-speaking clerks help you choose from the incredible selection. The fruit-and-vegetable department offers such items as rare mushrooms and wild strawberries. The confectionery features pastries and especially good candies. Also on the premises are a self-service stand-up bar, a cocktail department, a gifts department, a selection of porcelain and table settings, and an impressive collection of wines. Open Mon–Sat 9:40am–7pm. A "mini-Fauchon" selling mainly foods is open Mon–Sat 7–9pm.

The **Marché aux Puces** (flea market), av. de la Porte de Clignancourt (Métro: Vanves), has an enormous mixture of vintage bargains and old junk. It's estimated that the complex has 2,500 to 3,000 open stalls spread over half a mile. Monday is traditionally the day for bargain hunters, and negotiating is a must. Once you arrive at Porte de Clignancourt, turn left and cross boulevard Ney, then walk north on avenue de la Porte de Clignancourt. You'll pass stalls offering cheap clothing, but continue walking until you see the entrances to the first maze of flea-market stalls on the left. Open Sat–Sun 6:30am–4:30pm.

PARIS AFTER DARK

Parisians tend to do everything later than their Anglo-American counterparts. Once the workday is over, people head straight to the cafe to meet up with friends, and from there they go to the restaurant or bar, and finally to the nightclub.

THE PERFORMING ARTS

Listings of what's playing can be found in *Pariscope,* a weekly entertainment guide, or the English-language *Paris Passion.* Performances start later in Paris than in London or New York City—anywhere from 8 to 9pm—and Parisians tend to dine after the theater. There are many ticket agencies in Paris, but most are found near the Right Bank hotels. *Avoid them if possible.* The cheapest tickets can be purchased at the theater box office.

Several agencies sell tickets for cultural events and plays at discounts of up to 50%. One outlet for discount tickets is the **Kiosque Théâtre,** 15 place de la Madeleine, 8e (no phone; Métro: Madeleine), offering leftover tickets for about half price on the day of a performance. Tickets for evening performances are sold Tues–Fri 12:30–8pm and Sat 2–8pm. If you'd like to attend a matinee, buy your ticket Sat 12:30–2pm or Sun 12:30–4pm.

For discounts of 20% to 40% on tickets for festivals, concerts, and theater performances, try one of two locations of the **FNAC** department store chain: 136 rue de Rennes, 6e (☎ **01-44-09-18-00;** Métro: Montparnasse-Bienvenue), or in the Forum des Halles, 1–7 rue Pierre-Lescot, 1er (☎ **01-40-41-40-00;** Métro: Châtelet–Les Halles). To obtain discounts on tickets, you must purchase a *carte FNAC,* which is valid for 3 years and costs 150F ($30).

For light-opera productions, try the **Opéra-Comique,** place Boïeldieu, 2e (☎ **01-42-66-45-45;** Métro: Richelieu-Drouot). If possible, make arrangements 2 weeks before the performance. The box office is open Mon–Sat 11am–6pm (closed July–Aug). At the **Salle Pleyel,** 252 rue du Faubourg St-Honoré, 8e (☎ **01-45-61-53-00;** Métro: Ternes), you can enjoy the Orchestre de Paris, whose season runs from September to Easter. Tickets are sold daily 11am–6pm on the day of concerts.

For the best orchestra in France, try the **Radio France Salle Olivier Messian,** 116 av. Président-Kennedy, 16e (☎ **01-42-30-15-16;** Métro: Passy-Ranelagh), which offers topnotch concerts with guest conductors. The box office is open Mon–Sat 11am–6pm. Tickets are 50–190F ($10–$38) for the Orchestre National de France and 120F ($24) for the Orchestre Philharmonique. Of the half-dozen *grands travaux* conceived by the Mitterrand administration, the **Cité de la Musique,** 221 av. Jean Jaurès, 19e (☎ **01-44-84-45-00,** or 01-44-84-44-84 for tickets and info; Métro: Porte de Pantin), has been the most widely applauded, the least criticized, and the most innovative. It incorporates a network of concert halls, a library and research center for the study of all kinds of music from around the world, and a museum. Concerts at 4:30pm cost 60–100F ($12–$20); those at 8pm 100–160F ($20–$32).

Comédie-Française. 2 rue de Richelieu, 1er. ☎ **01-40-15-00-15.** Tickets 50–175F ($10–$35). Métro: Palais-Royal–Musée-du-Louvre.

Those with a modest understanding of French can still delight in a sparkling production of Molière at this national theater, established to keep the classics alive and promote the most important contemporary authors. Nowhere else will you see the works of Molière and Racine so beautifully staged. In 1993, a much-neglected wing of the building was renovated and launched as Le Théâtre du Vieux Colombier. The box office is open daily 11am–6pm (closed Aug 1–Sept 15).

✪ Opéra Bastille. Place de la Bastille, 120 rue de Lyon. ☎ **01-44-73-13-00.** Tickets 100–370F ($20–$74). Métro: Bastille.

Now the home of the **Paris Opera,** the controversial building was designed by Canadian architect Carlos Ott, with curtains created by Japanese fashion designer Issey Miyake. The showplace was inaugurated in July 1989 (for the Revolution's bicentennial), and on March 17, 1990, the curtain rose on Hector Berlioz's *Les Troyens.* The main hall is the largest of any French opera house, with 2,700 seats. The building contains two additional concert halls, including an intimate room, usually used for chamber music, with only 250 seats. Both traditional operas and symphony concerts are presented. Several concerts are presented free, in honor of certain French holidays. Write ahead for tickets to the Opéra Bastille, 120 rue de Lyon, 75012 Paris.

✪ Opéra Garnier (Palais Garnier). Place de l'Opéra, 9e. ☎ **01-40-01-17-89.** Tickets 60–160F ($12–$32) opera, 30–380F ($6–$76) dance. Métro: Opéra.

The Opéra Garnier is the home of the **Paris Ballet,** one of the world's great companies, always a leading innovator in the world of dance. This rococo wonder was designed as a contest entry by architect Charles Garnier in the heyday of the empire. Now months of painstaking restorations have returned the Garnier to its former glory. Its boxes and walls are lined with flowing red damask, its gilt gleaming, its ceiling (painted by Marc Chagall) cleaned, and a new air-conditioning system added. Opera is once again presented here: In mid-1995 the Garnier reopened grandly with Mozart's *Così fan tutte.*

NIGHTCLUBS & CABARETS

✪ Crazy Horse Saloon. 12 av. George-V, 8e. ☎ **01-47-23-32-32.** Cover 220–620F ($44–$124), including two drinks; third drink from 100F ($20). Métro: George-V or Alma-Marceau.

Alain Bernardin's stripteasery is no ordinary cabaret. It's a French parody of a western saloon, and became the first emporium in France where the strippers tossed their G-strings to the winds, throwing up their hands for the big "revelation." Shows are Sun–Fri at 8:30 and 11pm and Sat at 8 and 10:35pm and 12:50am.

✪ Folies-Bergère. 32 rue Richer, 9e. ☎ **01-44-79-98-98.** Cover 150–265F ($30–$53); dinner and show 670F ($134). Performances are Tues–Sat at 9pm, Sun at 5pm. Restaurant opens at 7pm. Reservations at box office window Tues–Sun 11am–6pm. Métro: Rue-Montmartre or Cadet.

The Folies-Bergère is a Paris institution. Since 1886 foreigners have been flocking here for the performances, the excitement, and the scantily clad dancers. Josephine Baker, the African-American singer who used to throw bananas into the audience, became "the toast of Paris" at the Folies-Bergère. The Folies has radically changed its context into a less titillating, more conventional format. It often presents bemused, lighthearted French-language comedies and musical comedies.

✪ Moulin Rouge. Place Blanche, 18e. ☎ **01-46-06-00-19.** Dinner and revue 720F ($144); revue only, 495F ($99), including champagne. No minimum if you sit at the bar (where the view isn't as good). Drinks around 90F ($18). Nightly dinner at 8pm, revue at 10pm. Métro: Blanche.

The Moulin Rouge was immortalized in the paintings of Toulouse-Lautrec. Colette created a scandal here by offering an on-stage kiss to Mme de Morny. Today the shows still have shock value. The revue itself is stunning, with elaborate feather costuming and the best cancan in France. Once a nude couple jumped into a tank for some underwater recreation. Try to get a table, as the view is much better on the main floor than from the bar. Reservations are essential. The bar opens 15 minutes before each show.

JAZZ CLUBS

Le Bilboquet. 13 rue St-Benoît, 6e. ☎ **01-45-48-81-84.** No cover. Drinks 120F ($24) in Biblioquet and 100F ($20) in Club St-Germain. Dinner in Le Biblioquet 200–50F ($40–$10) 8am–1am. Métro: St-Germain-des-Prés.

This restaurant/jazz club/piano bar offers some of the best music in Paris. The film *Paris Blues* was shot here. Jazz is played on the upper level in Le Biblioquet restaurant, a wood-paneled room with a copper ceiling, brass-trimmed sunken bar, and Victorian candelabra. The menu is limited but classic French. Open nightly 8pm–2:45am. Jazz music is presented 10:45pm–2:45am. Under separate management is the downstairs Club St-Germain disco, open Tues–Sun 11pm–5am. Entrance is free, but drinks cost 90F ($18). You can walk from one club to the other but have to buy a new drink each time you change venue.

Jazz Club La Villa. In the Hotel La Villa, 29 rue Jacob, 6e. ☎ **01-43-26-60-00.** Cover 120–150F ($24–$30), including first drink. Drinks 60F ($12). Mon–Sat 10:30pm–2am. Closed Aug. Métro: St-Germain-des-Prés.

This club is unusual in the fact that it lies in the red-velour cellar of a small but chic four-star hotel in the Latin Quarter. It has a reputation for bringing in famous artists as well as hard-core aficionados of jazz. Much of the musical venue derives from New Orleans, mainly Dixieland or any of the schools that followed. Artists rotate once a week; no food is served.

DANCE CLUBS

Chic **Les Bains,** 7 rue du Bourg-l'Abbé, 3e (☎ **01-48-87-01-80;** Métro: Réaumur), has been pronounced "in" and "out" of fashion, but lately it's very "in." The name Les Bains comes from the place's old function as a Turkish bath attracting gay clients, none more notable than Marcel Proust. Sometimes it may be hard to get in if the bouncer doesn't like your looks. Open nightly midnight–6am. The cover is 140F ($28), including the first drink. Drinks cost 100F ($20).

One of the leading Paris nightclubs, **Le Palace,** 8 rue du Faubourg-Montmartre, 9e (☎ **01-42-46-10-87;** Métro: Rue Montmartre), re-creates 1940s Hollywood glamor. There's plenty of room to dance. In 1992 it was acquired by Régine, empress of the Paris night, who plans to retain its youthful ambience. The management doesn't allow sneakers or jeans with holes pierced in indiscreet places. Open Tues–Sun 11:30pm–6am, with the gay men's tea dance Sun 5–11pm. The cover at night is 100F ($20) and the cover for the gay men's tea dance is 60F ($12). Cover after 6am on Fri–Sun is 50F ($10). Drinks are 50F ($10).

WINE BARS

The tiny **Au Sauvignon,** 80 rue des Sts-Pères, 7e (☎ **01-45-48-49-02;** Métro: Sèvres-Babylone), has tables overflowing onto a covered terrace. Wines served here range from the cheapest Beaujolais to the most expensive Puligny-Montrachet. To go with your wine, choose an Auvergne specialty, including goat cheese and terrines. Open Mon–Sat 8:30am–10:30pm. Closed major religious holidays, 2 weeks in Feb, and 3 weeks in Aug.

Journalists and stockbrokers patronize the increasingly popular **Willi's Wine Bar,** 13 rue des Petits-Champs, 1er (☎ **01-42-61-05-09;** Métro: Bourse, Louvre, or

Palais-Royal), in the center of the financial district. About 250 kinds of wine are offered, including a dozen "wine specials" you can taste by the glass. Lunch is the busiest time—on quiet evenings, you can better enjoy the warm ambience and 16th-century beams. Open Mon–Sat noon–2:30pm and 7–11pm.

GAY & LESBIAN CLUBS

Le Bar Central, 33 rue Vielle-du-Temple, 4e (☎ 01-48-87-99-33; Métro: Hôtel-de-Ville), is one of the leading bars for men in the Hôtel-de-Ville area. Open daily 2pm–1am, Fri–Sat 2pm–2am. The club has opened a small hotel upstairs. Both the bar and its hotel are in a 300-year-old building in the heart of the Marais. The hotel caters mostly to gay men, less frequently to lesbians. No cover.

In the center of Montparnasse, **Le New Monocle,** 60 bd. Edgar-Quinet, 14e (☎ 01-43-20-81-12; Métro: Edgar-Quinet), has been a traditional lesbian hangout since the days of Gertrude and Alice. It's a *disco féminin* but does admit gay male couples. Inside is a bar, plus a dance floor ringed with seats and banquettes and 1950s-look accessories. Live entertainment is interspersed with dance music. Open Mon–Sat 3pm–4am and Sun 5pm–4am. The cover is 150F ($30), including the first drink.

DAY TRIPS FROM PARIS: THE ILE DE FRANCE

✪ **VERSAILLES**   Within 50 years the **Château de Versailles** (☎ 01-30-84-74-00) was transformed from Louis XIII's simple hunting lodge into an extravagant palace, a monument to the age of absolutism. What you see today is the greatest living museum of a vanished way of life. Begun in 1661, the construction of the château involved 32,000 to 45,000 workmen, some of whom had to drain marshes—often at the cost of their lives—and move forests. Louis XIV set out to create a palace that would awe all Europe. He created a symbol of pomp and opulence that was to be copied, yet never quite duplicated, all over Europe and even in America.

The six magnificent **Grands Appartements** are in the Louis XIV style, each taking its name from the allegorical painting on its ceiling. The most famous room at Versailles is the 236-foot-long **Hall of Mirrors.** Begun by Mansart in 1678 in the Louis XIV style, it was decorated by Le Brun with 17 large arched windows matched by corresponding beveled mirrors in simulated arcades.

Spread across 250 acres, the **Gardens of Versailles** were laid out by the great landscape artist André Le Nôtre. A long walk across the park will take you to the **Grand Trianon,** in pink-and-white marble, designed by Hardouin-Mansart for Louis XIV in 1687. Traditionally it's been a place where France has lodged important guests. Gabriel, the designer of place de la Concorde in Paris, built the **Petit Trianon** in 1768 for Louis XV. Actually, its construction was inspired by Mme de Pompadour, who died before it was completed. In time, Marie Antoinette adopted it as her favorite residence.

The palace is open Tues–Sun 9am–6:30pm May 2–Sept 30; until 5:30pm the rest of the year. The grounds are open daily from dawn to dusk. Admission to the palace is 42F ($8.40) for adults, 28F ($5.60) for those under 25, and free for those under 18 and over 60. Admission on Sunday for adults is reduced to 35F ($7). Admission to the Grand Trianon is 23F ($4.60) for adults, 15F ($3) for those 18–25, and free for those under 18. Admission to the Petit Trianon is 13F ($2.60) for adults, 9F ($1.80) for those 18–25, and free for those under 18. Admission to both Trianons is 29F ($5.80) for adults, 19F ($3.80) for those 18–25, and free for those under 18.

To get to Versailles, 13 miles southwest of Paris, catch the RER line C5 at the Gare d'Austerlitz, St-Michel, Musée d'Orsay, Invalides, Pont-de-l'Alma, Champ-de-Mars, or Javel station and take it to the Versailles Rive Gauche station, from which there's a shuttle bus to the château. The 35F ($7) trip takes about 35 to 40 minutes; Eurailpass holders travel free. A regular train also leaves from the Gare St-Lazare to the Versailles Rive Gauche RER station. If you go by Métro, get off at the Pont-de-Sèvres stop and transfer to bus no. 171. The trip takes 15 minutes. To get there from Paris, it's cheaper to pay with three Métro tickets from a *carnet*. You'll be let off near the gates of the palace. If you're driving, take Route N-10 and park on place d'Armes in front of the château.

FONTAINEBLEAU   Napoléon joined in the grand parade of French rulers who used the **Palais de Fontainebleau** (☎ **01-60-71-50-70**) as a resort, hunting in its magnificent forest. Under François I the hunting lodge was enlarged into a royal palace, in the Italian Renaissance style that the king admired. Artists from the School of Fontainebleau adorned the 210-foot-long **Gallery of François I.** If it's true that François I built Fontainebleau for his mistress, then Henri II, his successor, left a fitting memorial to the woman he loved, Diane de Poitiers: Sometimes called the Gallery of Henri II, the splendid **Ballroom** is in the mannerist style, with the monograms H & D interlaced in the decoration.

Fontainebleau found renewed glory under Napoléon. You can wander around much of the palace on your own, but the **Napoleonic Rooms** are accessible by guided tour only. Most impressive are his throne room and his bedroom (look for his symbol, a bee). The furnishings in the grand apartments of Napoléon and Joséphine evoke the imperial heyday.

The interior is open Wed–Mon 9:30am–12:30pm and 2–5pm. In July–Aug, it's open Wed–Mon 9:30am–6pm. A combination ticket allowing visits to the *grands appartements,* the Napoleonic Rooms, and the Chinese Museum is 31F ($6.20) for adults and 20F ($4) for students 18–20; under 18 free. A ticket allowing access to the *petits appartements* goes for 15F ($3) for adults and 10F ($2) for students 18–20; under 18 free.

Trains to Fontainebleau, 37 miles south of Paris, depart from the Gare de Lyon in Paris, and the trip takes 35 minutes to an hour. The Fontainebleau station is just outside the town in Avon, a suburb of Paris; a local bus makes the 2-mile trip to the château every 10–15 minutes Mon–Sat (every 30 minutes Sun).

✪ CHARTRES   The architectural aspirations of the Middle Ages reached their highest expression in the **Cathédrale Notre-Dame de Chartres,** 16 Cloutre Notre-Dame (☎ **01-37-21-58-65**). One of the greatest of the world's high Gothic cathedrals, it contains some of the oldest and most beautiful medieval stained glass that gave the world a new color, Chartres blue. A mystical light seems to stream through the stained glass, some of it created as early as the 12th century. It was spared in both world wars; the glass was removed painstakingly piece by piece for storage and safekeeping.

The cathedral you see today dates principally from the 13th century. It was the first to use flying buttresses, giving it a higher and lighter construction. French sculpture in the 12th century broke into full bloom when the Royal Portal was added; the sculptured bodies are elongated and formalized in their long flowing robes, but the faces are amazingly lifelike.

The cathedral is open daily 7:30am–7:30pm. Chartres is 60 miles southwest of Paris. From the Gare Montparnasse, trains run directly to Chartres, taking less than an hour and passing through the sea of wheat fields that characterize Beauce, the granary of France.

2 The Loire Valley

Bordered by vineyards, the winding Loire Valley cuts through the land of castles deep in France's heart. When royalty and nobility built châteaux throughout this valley during the French Renaissance, sumptuousness was uppermost in their minds. An era of excessive pomp reigned here until Henri IV moved his court to Paris, marking the Loire's decline.

The Loire is blessed with abundant attractions—there's even the castle that inspired the fairy tale *Sleeping Beauty.* Tours is the traditional gateway; once there you can explore either east or west, depending on your interests. From Paris, you can reach Tours by autoroute (take A-10 southwest).

ONLY IN THE LOIRE VALLEY

Wandering Through the Gardens of Villandry   These are the most splendid gardens in the Loire, containing 10½ miles of boxwood sculpture alone. Borders represent the many facets of love: Pink tulips and dahlias suggest sweet love; red, tragic; and yellow, unfaithful. Crazy love is symbolized by all colors. The vine arbors, citrus hedges, and shady walks keep six men busy full-time. One Renaissance garden contains all the common French vegetables except the potato, which wasn't known in France in the 16th century.

Seeing Where French History Was Made   If you don't like to read books on French history, you can learn about it on the spot. Every château has a juicy story. For example, at the Château de Blois you learn about the events of December 23, 1588, when the duc de Guise, a ladies' man in spite of his being called Balafré (Scarface), met his end. Summoned to meet his archrival, Henri III, the duc reluctantly left the bed of one of his loves and was met by the daggers of the guards. Stabbed repeatedly, he fell to the floor in a pool of blood. Only then did Henri emerge from behind the curtains. *"Mon Dieu,"* the king exclaimed, "he's taller dead than alive."

Calling on Les Dames de Chenonceau   The Château de Chenonceau is called the most feminine in the Loire because it's associated with six "lionesses." The most famous was Diane de Poitiers, mistress of Henri II and 20 years his senior. The virtual queen of France, she was presented with the château in 1547. Henri's wife, Catherine de Médici, took over upon her husband's death, sending Diane to Chaumont. The wife of Henri III, Louise de Lorraine, also lived here; she became known as Le Reine Blanche (white queen) after her husband was assassinated. She mourned his death for the rest of her life, even though Henri, who often went about in drag, had preferred his curly haired minions to her. A famous 18th-century occupant was Mme Dupin, grandmother of George Sand.

Following in the Footsteps of Leonardo   The town of Amboise with its château evokes memories of Leonardo da Vinci, the greatest Renaissance artist. He spent his last years here, where his remains were entombed. You can still visit Clos-Lucé, the charming 15th-century manor house that François I, a great patron of the arts, gave to Leonardo after summoning him from Italy in 1514. Obviously Leonardo was happy in these idyllic surroundings, as he left this message: "A well-filled day gives a good sleep. A well-filled life gives a peaceful death."

Calling at the Gates of Chambord   In the middle of a royal game forest, this château is the largest in the Loire—hailed as the most outstanding experience in the valley. There are 440 rooms, plus 365 chimneys. Admittedly, it doesn't have the extravagant beauty of Chenonceau, but it's mammothly impressive. Of course, you'll arrive at the gates less encumbered than François I used to. He required 12,000 horses to haul his luggage, servants, and court hangers-on.

Sampling the Cuisine of the Loire   The châteaux district is one of the world's great gastronomic centers. Patricia Wells, author of *The Food Lover's Guide to France,* said that the Loire's cuisine reminds her "of the daffodil days of spring and blue skies of summer." Particularly superb are salmon caught in the Loire River, often served with sorrel. The region's rivers are stocked with other fish as well, like pike, carp, shad, and mullet. Gourmets highly prize pâté d'alouettes (lark pâté) and matelote d'anguille (stewed eel). From the mushroom-rich Sologne comes wild boar, deer, miniature quail, hare, pheasant, and mallard duck. The valley's Atlantic side produces an astonishing variety of grapes used to make wines ranging from dry to lusciously sweet and from still to sparkling and fruity.

TOURS

Tours, 144 miles southwest of Paris and 70 miles southwest of Orléans, is at the junction of the Loire and Cher rivers. The devout en route to Santiago de Compostela in northwest Spain once stopped off here to pay homage at the tomb of St. Martin, the Apostle of Gaul, bishop of Tours in the 4th century. It is the traditional place to begin your exploration of the Loire Valley.

ESSENTIALS

ARRIVING   If you're not driving, Tours can be reached in 2¹/₂ hours from Gare d'Austerlitz in Paris. Some 22 trains per day make this run. Once at Tours, you can rely on public transport to see much of the Loire; you can also rent a bike and tour—the region is relatively flat. Try **Montaubin,** 2 rue Nationale (☎ **02-47-05-62-27**). Ten-speeds rent for 85F ($17) per day, with a deposit of 1,000F ($200).

VISITOR INFORMATION   The **Office de Tourisme** is at 78 rue Bernard-Palissy (☎ **02-47-70-37-37**).

DEPARTING BY CAR   To reach your first major château in the Loire, follow D-7 for 11 miles west to Villandry.

EXPLORING TOURS

The heart of town is place Jean-Jaurès. Rue Nationale is the principal street (the valley's Champs-Elysées), running north to the Loire River. Head along rue du Commerce and rue du Grand-Marché to reach *la vieille ville* (the old town).

The **Cathédrale St-Gatien,** 5 place de la Cathédrale (☎ **02-47-05-05-54**), has a facade in the flamboyant Gothic style, flanked by towers with bases from the 12th century, though the lanterns are Renaissance. The choir is from the 13th century, and each century through the 16th saw new additions. Some of the glorious stained-glass windows are from the 13th century. The cathedral is open daily 8:30am–5:45pm; admission is free.

In the Château Royal, quai d'Orléans, is the **Musée de l'Historial de la Touraine** (☎ **02-47-61-02-95**). A perfect (although a bit kitschy) introduction to the region, this museum features 30 scenes and 165 wax figures tracing 1,000 years of Touraine history. The museum is open daily: Apr–Sept 9am–noon and 2–5:30pm and Oct–Mar 2–5:30pm. Admission is 35F ($7) for adults and 20F ($4) for age 15 and under.

The **Musée des Beaux-Arts,** 18 place François-Sicard (☎ **02-47-05-68-73**), is a fine provincial museum housed in the Palais des Archevêques, worth visiting for its lovely rooms and gardens. There are also works by Degas, Delacroix, Rembrandt, and Boucher, and sculpture by Houdon and Bourdelle. The museum is open Wed–Mon 9am–12:45pm and 2–6pm. Admission is 30F ($6) for adults and 15F ($3) for children. You can tour the gardens for free daily 7am–8:30pm.

ACCOMMODATIONS

Moderate

Hôtel Alliance. 292 av. de Grammont, 37000 Tours. ☎ **02-47-28-00-80.** Fax 02-47-27-77-61. 110 rms, 6 suites. A/C MINIBAR TV TEL. 450F ($90) double; from 600F ($120) suite. AE, DC, MC, V. Free parking. Bus: 1, 2, 5, or 9.

This is the largest and most modern hotel in Tours, about a mile south of the town center. It's decorated in *grand siècle* style and boasts a reception area with chandeliers and marble columns. The bright-colored soundproof rooms contain a blend of modern pieces and antique reproductions. There's plenty of open space, a French garden, and a pool. Breakfast and drinks are served in a sitting area, and the hotel has a distinguished restaurant with a terrace.

Hôtel de l'Univers. 5 bd. Heurteloup, 37000 Tours. ☎ **02-47-05-37-12.** Fax 02-47-61-51-80. 85 rms. TV TEL. 780F ($156) double. AE, DC, MC, V. Parking 50F ($10).

This highly regarded hotel on the main artery of Tours is the oldest in town and has hosted Edison, Hemingway, and the former kings of Spain, Portugal, and Romania. The rooms are decorated partly with modern pieces and partly with art deco pieces. La Touraine, the main dining room (open daily), serves excellent meals from a fixed-price menu.

Inexpensive

ⓢ Le Central. 21 rue Berthelot, 37000 Tours. ☎ **02-47-05-46-44.** Fax 02-47-66-10-26. 40 rms (38 with bath, 2 with wash basin and bidet only). TEL. 180F ($36) double without bath, 360F ($72) double with bath. AE, DC, MC, V. Parking 35F ($7). Bus: 1, 4, or 5.

Off the main boulevard, this old-fashioned hotel is within walking distance of the river and cathedral, surrounded by gardens, lawns, and trees. It's much more modest but also more economical than the previous choices. The Tremouilles family offers comfortable rooms (38 with TVs and minibars) at reasonable rates, as well as two salons with reproductions of 18th- and 19th-century pieces. A parking garage is available.

DINING

Expensive

❉ La Roche le Roy. 55 route St-Avertin. ☎ **02-47-27-22-00.** Reservations recommended. Main courses 110–160F ($22–$32); fixed-price lunch 160–350F ($32–$70); fixed-price dinner 200–350F ($40–$70). AE, DC, MC, V. Tues–Fri 12:15–1:45pm and 7:15–10pm, Sat 7:15–10pm. Closed first 3 weeks in Aug. FRENCH.

One of Tours's hottest chefs, Alain Couturier, blends new and old culinary techniques at this restaurant, housed in a 15th-century manor 2 miles south of the town center. Couturier's repertoire includes scalloped foie gras with lentils, crayfish sautéed with vanilla and mint, and *fraicheur* of lobster with roe-enhanced vinaigrette. His masterpiece is suprême of pigeon with a "roughly textured" sauce. For dessert, try his mélange of seasonal fruit with sabayon made from Vouvray Valley wine.

Moderate

La Rôtisserie Tourangelle. 23 rue du Commerce Tours. ☎ **02-47-05-71-21.** Reservations required. Main courses 90–135F ($18–$27); fixed-price menus 90–170F ($18–$34). AE, DC, MC, V. Tues–Sat 12:15–1:45pm and 7:30–9:45pm, Sun 12:15–1:45pm. Bus: 1, 4, or 5. FRENCH.

The Loire Valley

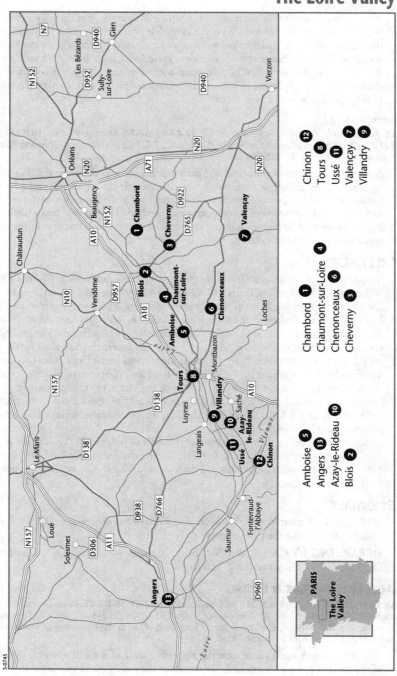

Chinon ⑫
Tours ⑧
Ussé ⑪
Valençay ⑦
Villandry ⑨

Chambord ①
Chaumont-sur-Loire ④
Chenonceaux ⑥
Cheverny ③

Amboise ⑤
Angers ⑬
Azay-le-Rideau ⑩
Blois ②

PARIS
The Loire Valley

This is a local favorite. You can dine on a terrace in summer, but there's not much to see. It's better to concentrate on the ever-changing menu, which may include homemade foie gras, snails in red-wine sauce, and white fish caught in the Loire served with *beurre blanc* (white butter sauce). Regional ingredients mix well with the local wines, as exemplified by pike-perch with sabayon and *aiguillettes de fillet de canard* (duckling), followed in summer by strawberry parfait with raspberry coulis. If only the service were a little better.

Inexpensive

Le Relais Buré. 1 place de la Résistance. ☎ **02-47-05-67-74.** Main courses 65–105F ($13–$21); fixed-price menu (Mon–Fri only) 98F ($19.60). AE, DC, MC, V. Daily noon–3pm and 7pm–midnight. Bus: 1, 4, or 5. FRENCH.

A 5-minute walk east of the center of Tours, this brasserie specializes in shellfish and regional recipes, though it's somewhat unimaginative. It has a busy bar and a front terrace, with tables scattered inside on the street level and mezzanine. Menu items include six well-flavored versions of sauerkraut, a wide choice of grilled meats (including a peppery steak au poivre), foie gras and smoked salmon (both prepared in-house), and a tempting array of desserts.

VILLANDRY

The extravagant 16th-century–style gardens of the Renaissance **Château de Villandry,** 37510 Joué-les-Tours (☎ 02-47-50-02-09), are celebrated throughout the Touraine. Forming a trio of superimposed cloisters, with a water garden on the highest level, the gardens were purchased in a decaying state and restored by Spanish doctor/scientist Joachim Carvallo, the present owner's grandfather. The grounds contain $10^1/_2$ miles of boxwood sculpture, which the gardeners must cut to style in only 2 weeks in September. Every square of the gardens seems like a geometric mosaic. The borders represent the many faces of love: for example, tender, tragic (with daggers), or crazy, the last evoked by a labyrinth that doesn't get you anywhere.

Originally a feudal castle stood at Villandry, but in 1536 Jean Lebreton, the chancellor of François I, built the present château, whose buildings form a U and are surrounded by a two-sided moat.

Admission to the gardens with a tour of the château is 40F ($8). Visiting the gardens separately without a guide costs 30F ($6). The château is open mid-Feb–mid-Nov, and guided tours are conducted daily 9am–6:30pm. The gardens are open 9am–sunset.

ESSENTIALS

ARRIVING   Unfortunately, Villandry doesn't have bus service from Tours. Rent a bike and ride along the Cher or go by car.

DEPARTING BY CAR   From Villandry, continue west along D-7, then take D-39 south for 7 miles to Azay-le-Rideau.

ACCOMMODATIONS & DINING

Le Cheval Rouge. Villandry, 37510 Joué-les-Tours. ☎ **02-47-50-02-07.** Reservations recommended. Fax 02-47-50-08-77. Fixed-price menus 95–200F ($19–$40). MC, V. Tues–Sat noon–2pm and 7:30–9pm; Sun noon–2pm. Closed end of Jan to the beginning of Mar. Open Sun night and Mon if it's a holiday. FRENCH.

This is the major lunch venue near the château in spite of the stiff welcome. Many of the château's famous gardens are visible from the dining room windows, and the Cher flows 100 yards from the hotel. Specialties include fresh grilled salmon, farm-bred pigeon with garlic, and fillet of pork with plums. The food is competent enough, but chances are this won't be one of your most memorable meals in the Loire. This inn also rents 20 comfortable rooms, 18 with bath. A double rents for 295F ($59) and a triple for 400F ($80).

AZAY-LE-RIDEAU

Its machicolated towers and blue-slate roof pierced with dormers shimmer in the moat, creating a reflection like one in a Monet painting. But the defensive medieval look is all for show. The **Château d'Azay-le-Rideau,** 37190 Azay-le-Rideau (☎ **02-47-45-42-04**), was created as a private residence during the Renaissance at an idyllic spot on the Indre River. Gilles Berthelot, François I's finance minister, commissioned the castle, and his spendthrift wife, Philippa, supervised its construction. So elegant was the creation that the chevalier king grew immensely jealous. In time, Berthelot was forced to flee and the château reverted to the king.

Before entering, circle the château, enjoying the perfect proportions of the crowning achievement of the Renaissance in Touraine. Its most fancifully ornate feature is a bay enclosing a grand stairway with a straight flight of steps. The Renaissance interior is a virtual museum. From the second-floor Royal Chamber, look out at the gardens. This bedroom, also known as the Green Room, is believed to have sheltered Louis XIII.

The château is open daily July–Aug 9am–7pm, Apr–June and Oct 9:30am–6pm, and Nov–Mar 9:30am–12:30pm and 2–5:30pm. Admission is 32F ($6.40) for adults and 21F ($4.20) for children. May–July, *son-et-lumière* performances are staged at 10:30pm; Aug–Sept, at 10pm. Tickets cost 60F ($12) for adults and 35F ($7) for children.

ESSENTIALS

ARRIVING   Seven trains or buses a day arrive from Tours (trip time: 30 min.).

VISITOR INFORMATION   The **Syndicat d'Initiative** (tourist office) is at place de l'Europe (☎ **02-47-45-44-40**).

DEPARTING BY CAR   After seeing Villandry and Azay-le-Rideau, return to Tours. From there, head east for 22 miles to Amboise. To reach it, you can take good roads on either side of the Loire, D-751 on the south bank or N-152 on the north bank. If you take the northern route, you can follow the signs to Vouvray, which turns out the most famous white wine of the Touraine. Vintners post signs if they allow visits and tastings.

DINING

L'Aigle d'Or. 10 av. Adélaïde-Riché. ☎ **02-47-45-24-58.** Reservations recommended. Main courses 72–110F ($14.40–$22); fixed-price lunch Mon–Fri 92F ($18.40); fixed-price dinner Mon–Fri 143–270F ($28.60–$54). V. Thurs–Tues 12:30–2pm and 7:30–9:30pm. Closed Sun and Tues night in low season, Feb and Dec 10–25. FRENCH.

This restaurant is the most enduring favorite of everyone visiting the château. The service is professional, the welcome is often charming, but the food isn't what it used to be. But dining choices at Azay are very limited. The choices always include lobster with foie gras or fillet of Chinon beef and may feature stingray with artichokes or minced lamb with zucchini flan. The chef needs to perk up the flavors a bit. In spite of these drawbacks, it's nevertheless the finest dining choice in town.

AMBOISE

On the banks of the Loire, Amboise is in the center of vineyards known as Touraine-Amboise. Leonardo da Vinci, the quintessential Renaissance man, spent his last years in this city.

ESSENTIALS

ARRIVING   Amboise lies on the main Paris–Blois–Tours rail line, with 14 trains per day arriving from both Tours and Blois. Trip time from Tours is only 20 minutes. Touraine Voyages, 1 rue Voltaire (☎ **02-47-37-81-81**), runs buses connecting Tours and Amboise at the rate of five per day (trip time: 25 min.).

VISITOR INFORMATION   The **Office de Tourisme** is on quai du Général-de-Gaulle (☎ **02-47-57-09-28**).

DEPARTING BY CAR   To reach Blois from Amboise, continue along either the south bank (D-751) or the north bank (N-152), at a distance of 37 miles northeast of Tours.

EXPLORING AMBOISE

Dominating the town is the **Château d'Amboise** (☎ **02-47-57-14-47**), the first in France to reflect the Italian Renaissance. A combination of both Gothic and Renaissance, this 15th-century château is mainly associated with Charles VIII, who built it on a rocky spur separating the valleys of the Loire and the Amasse.

You enter via a ramp, opening onto a panoramic terrace fronting the river. At one time this terrace was surrounded by buildings, and *fêtes* were staged in the enclosed courtyard. At the time of the revolution, the castle declined and only a quarter or even less remains of this once-sprawling edifice. First you come to the flamboyant Gothic Chapelle St-Hubert, distinguished by its lacelike tracery. It allegedly contains Leonardo's remains; actually the great artist was buried in the castle's Collegiate Church, which was destroyed between 1806 and 1810. During the Second Empire, excavations were done here and discovered bones were "identified" as Leonardo's.

Today the walls of the château are hung with tapestries and the rooms furnished grandly. The Logis du Roi (king's apartment) escaped destruction and can be visited. The château is open daily July–Aug 9am–7pm, Apr–June 9am–6:30pm, Sept–Oct 9am–6pm, and Nov–Mar 9am–noon and 2–5pm. Admission is 34F ($6.80) for adults, 24F ($4.80) for students, and 15F ($3) for children.

You might also wish to visit **Clos-Lucé,** 2 rue de Clos-Lucé (☎ **02-47-57-62-88**), a 15th-century brick-and-stone manor. In what had been an oratory for Anne de Bretagne, François I installed "the great master in all forms of art and science," Leonardo da Vinci. Venerated by the chevalier king, Leonardo lived here for 3 years, dying at the manor in 1519. (Those paintings of Leonardo dying in François's arms are symbolic; the king was supposedly out of town at the time.) The manor's rooms are well furnished, some with reproductions from Leonardo's time. Clos-Lucé is open daily Mar–Oct 9am–7pm and Nov–Feb 9am–6pm. Admission is 37F ($7.40) for adults and 18F ($3.60) for children.

ACCOMMODATIONS

Expensive

✪ **Le Choiseul.** 36 quai Charles-Guinot, 37400 Amboise. ☎ **02-47-30-45-45.** Fax 02-47-30-46-10. 32 rms, 4 suites. MINIBAR TV TEL. 560–1,100F ($112–$220) double; 1,250–1,650F ($250–$330) suite. AE, DC, MC, V. Free parking. Closed Nov 26–Jan 15.

This 18th-century hotel's rooms, 16 of which are air-conditioned, are luxurious; though recently modernized, they've retained their old-world charm. There's no better address in Amboise or any better place for cuisine. The food is better than that found in Tours or the surrounding area. On the grounds is a garden with flowering terraces. This hotel is set in the valley between a hillside and the Loire River, close to the château. The formal dining room has a view of the Loire and welcomes nonguests who phone ahead. It's open daily noon–2pm and 7–9:30pm, with fixed-price menus. The dishes are ingenious and only the freshest and highest-quality products are used. The wine list is also the freshest in the area. Facilities include an outdoor pool, a tennis court, and a Ping-Pong table.

Hostellerie du Château-de-Pray. Route de Chargé (D751), 37400 Amboise. ☎ **02-47-57-23-67.** Fax 02-47-57-32-50. 19 rms, 1 suite. TEL. 470–750F ($94–$150) double; 650–894F ($130–$178.80) suite. Half board 195F ($39) extra. AE, DC, MC, V. Closed Jan 2–27. Free parking.

From its position above parterres surveying the Loire in a park about a mile east of the town center, this château resembles a tower-flanked castle on the Rhine. Inside, you'll find antlers, hunting trophies, venerable antiques, and a paneled drawing room with a fireplace and a collection of antique oils. The guest rooms are stylishly conservative and comfortable—if they're in the main building. Try to avoid the four rooms in the annex. Open to nonguests, the hotel restaurant offers fixed-price menus of excellent quality. In summer, tables are placed on a terrace overlooking formal gardens. The menu might include grilled salmon with beurre blanc, lobster cannelloni, or roast rabbit with wine sauce.

Moderate

Belle-Vue. 12 quai Charles-Guinot, 37400 Amboise. ☎ **02-47-57-02-26.** Fax 02-47-30-51-23. 32 rms. TV TEL. 280–330F ($56–$66) double. MC, V. Closed Dec–Mar 15. Free parking.

This modest inn lies at the bridge crossing the Loire at the foot of the château. It has rows of French doors and outside tables on two levels shaded by umbrellas in summer. The interior lounges are well maintained and the modernized guest rooms are comfortable, with traditional French pieces. Try to stay here and not in the annex across the river. Breakfast is the only meal served.

Dining

Le Manoir St-Thomas. Place Richelieu. ☎ **02-47-57-22-52.** Reservations required. Fixed-price menu 175–300F ($34–$60). AE, DC, MC, V. Tues–Sat 12:15–2:30pm and 7:15–9:30pm, Sun 12:15–2:30pm. Closed Jan 15–Mar 15. FRENCH.

The best food in town outside of Le Choiseul is served at this Renaissance house, in the shadow of the château. The restaurant is in a pleasant garden, and the elegant dining room is richly decorated with a polychrome ceiling and a massive stone fireplace. Owner/chef François Le Coz's specialties include truffles with foie gras, lamb fillet with pork, duck liver confit with Vouvray sauce, and red mullet fillet with cream of sweet pepper sauce. The tender saddle of hare is perfectly flavored.

BLOIS

Blois is the most attractive of the major Loire towns. It rises on the right bank of the Loire, its skyline dominated by its château, where the duc de Guise was assassinated on December 23, 1588 on orders of his archrival, Henri III; it's one of the most famous murders in French history. Several French kings lived here and the town has a rich architectural history.

ESSENTIALS

ARRIVING   The Paris–Austerlitz line via Orléans delivers eight trains per day from Paris (trip time: 1 hr.). From Tours, 10 trains arrive per day (trip time: 1 hr.), and from Amboise, 10 trains per day arrive (trip time: 20 min.). If you'd like to explore the area by bike, go to **Atelier Cycles,** 44 levée des Tuileries (☎ **02-54-74-30-13**), where 10-speeds range in price from 25F to 50F ($5 to $10) per day. Mountain bikes are also available, costing 35F to 100F ($7 to $20) per day. You have to leave your passport as a deposit.

VISITOR INFORMATION   The **Office de Tourisme** is at Pavillon Anne-de-Bretagne, 3 av. Jean-Laigret (☎ **02-54-74-06-49**).

DEPARTING BY CAR   To reach Chaumont, take D-751 for 12 miles south of Blois.

EXPLORING THE CHÂTEAU

The murder of the duc de Guise is only one of the memories evoked by the **Château de Blois** (☎ **02-54-74-16-06**), begun in the 13th century by the comtes de Blois. Charles d'Orléans (son of Louis d'Orléans, assassinated by the Burgundians in 1407) lived at Blois after his release from 25 years of English captivity. He'd married Mary of Cleves and brought a "court of letters" to Blois. In his 70s, Charles became the father of the future Louis XII, who was to marry Anne de Bretagne. Blois was then launched in its new role as a royal château. In time it was to be called the second capital of France, with Blois the city of kings.

However, Blois soon became a palace of banishment. Louis XIII got rid of his interfering mother, Marie de Médici, by sending her here; but this plump matron escaped by sliding into the moat down a mound of dirt left by the builders. Then in 1626 the king sent his conspiring brother, Gaston d'Orléans, here; he stayed.

If you stand in the courtyard, you'll find the château is like an illustrated storybook of French architecture. The Hall of the Estates-General is a beautiful 13th-century work; the Charles d'Orléans gallery was actually built by Louis XII from 1498 to 1501, as was the Louis XII wing. The Gaston d'Orléans wing was constructed by Mansart between 1635 and 1637. The most remarkable is the François I wing, a masterpiece of the French Renaissance, containing a spiral staircase with elaborately ornamented balustrades and the king's symbol, the salamander.

The château is open daily Apr–Oct 9am–6pm; Nov–Mar 9am–noon and 2–5pm. Admission is 30F ($6) for adults and 25F ($5) for children. A *son-et-lumière* presentation (in French) is sponsored daily at 8:15 or 10pm June–Sept, costing 60F ($12) for adults and 30F ($6) for children 7–15 (free for 6 and under).

ACCOMMODATIONS

L'Horset Blois. 26 av. Maunoury, 41000 Blois. ☎ **02-54-74-19-00.** Fax 02-54-74-57-97. 78 rms. MINIBAR TV TEL. 505F ($101) double. AE, DC, MC, V. Children 11 and under stay free in parents' room. Free parking. Bus: 1.

This leading hotel has all the modern amenities as well as a respect for traditional charm. A three-star hotel, it's a member of a small but widely respected French-based chain. The rooms are furnished with contemporary flair. There's a good restaurant, where meals are moderately priced and children's meals are available. The hotel is more reliable than exciting.

Mercure Centre. 28 quai St-Jean, 41000 Blois. ☎ **02-54-56-66-66.** Fax 02-54-56-67-00. 96 rms. MINIBAR TV TEL. 495–600F ($94.10–$114.05) double. AE, DC, MC, V. Parking 35F ($7). Bus: Quayside marked PISCINE.

This is the newest and best-located hotel in Blois, beside the quays of the Loire, a 5-minute walk from the château. It's on a par with L'Horset, though both are rather impersonal. Three stories of reinforced concrete, with big windows, it contains larger-than-expected rooms filled with contemporary furniture and soothing colors. The greenhouse-style lobby leads into a pleasant restaurant where meals are served daily.

DINING

Le Médicis. 2 allée François-1er, 41000 Blois. ☎ **02-54-43-94-04.** Fax 02-54-42-04-05. Reservations required. Main courses 90–145F ($18–$29); fixed-price menus 98F ($19.60), 148F

($29.60), and 198F ($39.60). AE, DC, MC, V. Daily 12:30–2pm and 7–10pm. Closed Jan 1–15. Bus: 149. FRENCH.

Christian and Annick Garanger maintain the most sophisticated inn in Blois—ideal for a gourmet meal or an overnight stop. Fresh fish is the chef's specialty. Typical main courses are asparagus in mousseline sauce, scampi ravioli with saffron sauce, suprême of perch with morels, and thinly sliced duck breast with Cassis sauce. Chocolate in many manifestations is the dessert specialty. In addition, the Garangers rent 12 elegant rooms with bath. The rates are 420–550F ($84–$110) double.

✪ **Rendezvous des Pêcheurs.** 27 rue du Foix. ☎ **02-54-74-67-48.** Reservations recommended. Main courses 95–140F ($19–$28); fixed-price menu 145F ($29). MC, V. Mon 7:30–9:30pm, Tues–Sat 12:30–2pm and 7:30–9:30pm. Closed 3 weeks in Aug and 1 week in Feb. FRENCH.

This restaurant is in an old building beside the quays of the Loire. The chef makes sure that the fish—his specialty—is always fresh and well prepared. As a result, some dishes may seem overly simple, but the result is usually a taste sensation. Only fish, not shellfish of any kind, is served. The menu changes daily according to the availability of fish in the markets; sea urchins raw from the shell are a favorite. Other specialties are a fillet of Loire valley sandre (zander) in wine-and-butter sauce and crayfish-stuffed cabbage. You can order dishes other than fish—for example, sautéed foie gras with warm potatoes.

CHAUMONT-SUR-LOIRE

On the morning when Diane de Poitiers crossed the drawbridge, the ✪ **Château de Chaumont** (☎ **02-54-20-97-76**) looked fiercely grim with its battlements and pepper-pot turrets crowning the towers. Henri II, her lover, had recently died. The king had given her Chenonceau, but his widow, Catherine de Médici, banished her from her favorite château and sent her into exile at Chaumont. Inside, portraits reveal that Diane truly deserved her reputation as forever beautiful. Another portrait—of Catherine looking like a devout nun—invites unfavorable comparisons.

Chaumont (Burning Mount) was built during the reign of Louis XII by Charles d'Amboise. It was privately owned and inhabited until it was acquired by the state in 1938. The castle spans the period between the Middle Ages and the Renaissance. Its prize exhibit is a rare collection of medallions by Nini, an Italian artist. A guest of the château for a while, he made medallion portraits of kings, queens, and nobles—even Benjamin Franklin, who once visited. In the bedroom once occupied by Catherine de Médici is a rare portrait, painted when she was young.

The château is open daily Apr–Sept 9:30am–6:30pm; Oct–Mar 10am–4:30pm. Admission is 28F ($5.60) for adults and 15F ($3) for children. For 30F ($6) per adult and 20F ($4) per child, you can ride around Chaumont in horse-drawn carriages; ☎ **02-54-20-90-60.**

ESSENTIALS

ARRIVING   From Blois, Chaumont is reached by 17 trains per day (trip time: 15 min.). Seventeen trains also arrive from Tours (trip time: 25 min.). The train station is in Onzain, 1½ miles north of the château, a pleasant walk.

VISITOR INFORMATION   The **Office de Tourisme** is on rue du Maréchal-Leclerc (☎ **02-54-20-91-73**).

DEPARTING BY CAR   Blois (above) also makes a perfect launching pad for visiting another important château in the area, that of Chambord, which lies 11 miles east of Blois along D-33 near Bracieux.

ACCOMMODATIONS & DINING

Hostellerie du Château. 2 rue du Maréchal-de-Lattre-Tassigny, 41150 Chaumont-sur-Loire. ☎ **02-54-20-98-04.** Fax 02-54-20-97-98. 13 rms, 2 suites. TEL. 350–400F ($70–$80) double; 480F ($96) suite. V. Free parking.

This early 20th-century house has the kind of exposed timbers and black-and-white facade you'd expect to find in Normandy. A 10-minute walk downhill from the château, in a village of no more than 900, it has a small garden and a pool. The hotel has a kind staff, comfortable but rather dull rooms, and the best and most reasonably priced restaurant in the village. Regional specialties are served, with fixed-price meals priced at 80F ($16), 150F ($30), and 180F ($36).

CHAMBORD

When François I used to say, "Come on up to my place," he meant the ✪ **Château de Chambord,** 41250 Bracieux (☎ **02-54-50-50-08**), not Fontainebleau or Blois. Some 2,000 workers began to piece together "the pile" in 1519. What emerged after 20 years was the pinnacle of the French Renaissance, the largest château in the Loire Valley. It was ready for the visit of Charles V of Germany, who was welcomed by nymphets in transparent veils gently tossing wildflowers in his path. French monarchs like Henri II and Catherine de Médici, Louis XIII, and Henri III came and went from Chambord, but none developed an affection for it to match François I's. The state acquired Chambord in 1932.

The château is in a park of more than 13,000 acres, enclosed within a wall stretching some 20 miles. Looking out a window in one of the 440 rooms, François is said to have carved these words on a pane with a diamond ring: "A woman is a creature of change; to trust her is to play the fool." Chambord's facade is dominated by four monumental towers. The keep has a spectacular terrace the ladies of the court used to stand on to watch the return of their men from the hunt.

The three-story keep also encloses a corkscrew staircase, superimposed so one person may descend at one end and a second ascend at the other without ever meeting. The apartments of Louis XIV, including his redecorated bedchamber, are also in the keep.

The château is open daily mid-June to mid-Sept 9:30am–6:30pm (until 7:30 in July–Aug); mid-Sept to mid-June 9:30am–5:30pm. Admission is 35F ($7) for adults and 15F ($3) for children. At the tourist office you can pick up tickets for the *son-et-lumière* presentation in summer, called *Jours et Siècles* (Days and Centuries), but check the times.

ESSENTIALS

ARRIVING   It's best to travel to Chambord by car. Otherwise, you could rent a bicycle in Blois and cycle to Chambord or take one of the organized tours to Chambord leaving from Blois in summer.

VISITOR INFORMATION   The **Office de Tourisme** is on place St-Michel (☎ **02-54-20-34-86**).

DEPARTING BY CAR   Back at the launching pad of Blois, you can strike out in another direction for yet another major château. Cheverny lies 12 miles south of Blois, reached by taking D-765.

ACCOMMODATIONS & DINING

Hôtel du Grand-St-Michel. 103 place St-Michel, 41250 Chambord, near Bracieux. ☎ **02-54-20-31-31.** Fax 02-54-20-36-40. 39 rms. TV TEL. 320–450F ($64–$90) double. MC, V. Closed Nov 14–Dec 20. Free parking.

Across from the château, this inn is about the only one of any substance in town. Try for a front room overlooking the château, which is dramatic when floodlit at night. The rooms are plain but comfortable, with provincial decor. The staff is rather blasé and inarticulate even in French. Most visitors arrive for lunch, which in summer is served on an awning-shaded terrace; the regional dishes rarely match the Loire wines.

CHEVERNY

The *haut monde* still come to the Sologne area for the hunt as if the 17th century had never ended. However, 20th-century realities like taxes are *formidable* here—hence the **Château de Cheverny** (☎ **02-54-79-96-29**) must open some of its rooms for inspection by paying guests. At least that keeps the tax collector at bay and the hounds fed in winter.

Unlike most of the Loire châteaux, Cheverny is actually lived in by the descendants of the original owner, the vicomte de Sigalas. The family's lineage can be traced back to Henri Hurault, the son of the chancellor of Henri III and Henri IV, who built the château here in 1634. Designed in classic Louis XIII style, it boasts square pavilions flanking the central pile.

Inside, the antique furnishings, tapestries, decorations, and objets d'art are quite impressive. A 17th-century French artist, Jean Mosnier, decorated the fireplace with motifs from the legend of Adonis. In the Guards' Room is a collection of medieval armor.

The château is open daily June–Sept 15 9:15am–6:45pm; Sept 16–May 9:15am–noon and 2:15–5:30pm. Admission is 32F ($6.40) for adults and 21F ($4.20) for children. In July–Aug, a daily *son-et-lumière* show called *Rêves en Sologne (Dreams in Sologne)* is presented at 10pm for 85F ($17) per ticket.

ESSENTIALS

DEPARTING BY CAR   If after exploring Cheverny you have enthusiasm for one more château, strike out for Valençay. From Cheverny head south on D-102 for 6 miles, crossing the border of the forest of Cheverny. At the town of Contres, connect with the junction of D-956, which traverses the Cher River 12 miles farther south at Selles-sur-Cher. From here, continue the final 9 miles (well signposted) to Valençay.

DINING

Saint-Hubert

Rue Nationale. 41700 Cour-Cheverny. ☎ **02-54-79-96-60.** Fax 02-54-79-21-17. Main courses 90–160F ($18–$32); fixed-price menus 98–250F ($19.60–$50). MC, V. Thurs–Tues 12:15–1:15pm and 7:30–8:45pm (closed Sun night in low season). Closed Jan 10–Feb 17. FRENCH.

About 800 yards from the château, this roadside inn was built in the old provincial style. Chef Jean-Claude Pillaut is the secret of the Saint-Hubert's success. The least expensive menu might include terrine of quail, pike-perch with beurre blanc (white butter), a selection of cheese, and a homemade fruit tart. The most expensive menu may offer lobster or fresh spring asparagus. Game is featured here in season. Most visitors pass through Cour-Cheverny on a day trip, but it's also possible to spend the night. The Saint-Hubert offers 20 rooms with bath, charging 190–300F ($38–60) double.

Les Trois Marchands. Place de l'Eglise, 41700 Cour-Cheverny. ☎ **02-54-79-96-44.** Fax 02-54-79-25-60. Fixed-price menus 115F ($23), 200F ($40), and 320F ($64). AE, DC, MC, V. Daily noon–2pm and 7:30–9pm. Closed Feb 5–Mar 15 and Mon in Oct–June. FRENCH.

This much-renovated coaching inn, more comfortable than Saint-Hubert, has been handed down for many generations from father to son. Today Jean-Jacques Bricault owns the three-story building that sports awnings, a mansard roof, a glassed-in courtyard, and sidewalk tables with bright umbrellas. In the large tavern-style dining room, the menu might include frogs' legs, fresh asparagus in mousseline sauce, or cassoulet of lobster. The inn also rents 38 well-furnished and comfortable rooms, costing 250–340F ($50–$68) double.

VALENÇAY

One of the Loire's handsomest Renaissance châteaux, 35 miles south of Blois, the **Château de Valençay** (☎ **02-54-00-10-66**) was acquired in 1803 by Talleyrand on the orders of Napoléon, who wanted his minister of foreign affairs to receive dignitaries in great style. In 1838 Talleyrand was buried at Valençay, the château passing to his nephew, Louis de Talleyrand-Périgord. Before the Talleyrand ownership, Valençay was built in 1550 by the d'Estampes family. The dungeon and great west tower are of this period, as is the building's main body; other wings were added in the 17th and 18th centuries. The effect is grandiose, almost too much so, with domes, chimneys, and turrets. The private apartments are open to the public; they're sumptuously furnished, mostly in the Empire style but with Louis XV and Louis XVI trappings as well.

Admission to the castle, an antique car museum, and the park is 40F ($8) for adults, 32F ($6.40) for seniors and students, and 20F ($4) for children 17 and under. It's open mid-Mar–mid-Nov daily 9am–noon and 2–6:30pm; mid-Nov–mid-Mar Sat–Sun 9am–noon and 2–5:30pm.

ESSENTIALS

ARRIVING   There are frequent SNCF rail connections from Blois.

VISITOR INFORMATION   The **Office de Tourisme** is on route de Blois (☎ **02-54-00-04-42**).

DEPARTING BY CAR   To continue château-hopping, drive north from Valençay until you come to Selles-sur-Cher at the river. This time head west in the direction of Amboise, taking N-76 along the south bank. Chenonceaux lies 10 miles south of Amboise.

ACCOMMODATIONS & DINING

✪ **Hôtel d'Espagne.** 9 rue du Château, 36600 Valençay. ☎ **02-54-00-00-02.** Fax 02-54-00-12-63. 8 rms, 6 suites. TV TEL. 450–650F ($90–$130) double; from 900F ($180) suite. AE, DC, MC, V. Parking 25F ($5). Closed Jan–Feb.

M. and Mme Fourré and their family provide an old-world ambience with a first-class kitchen. The rooms have names—yours might have an authentic Empire, Louis XV, or Louis XVI decor. Lunch (Tues–Sun) is served in the dining room or gardens. The specialties include noisettes of lamb in tarragon and sweetbreads with morels. Fixed-price menus begin at 200F ($40), with a spectacular à la carte meal, including wine, costing 350F ($70) and up. The restaurant is open daily June–Sept; off-season, closed Mon. They've also opened the less formal Bistro des Gourmets, with fixed-price meals for 70–120F ($14–$24).

CHENONCEAUX

A Renaissance masterpiece, the **Château de Chenonceau** (☎ **02-47-23-90-07**) is best known for the *dames de Chenonceau* who've occupied it. (Note that the town is spelled with a final *x* but the château is not.) Originally it was owned by the Marqués family, but its members were far too extravagant. Deviously, Thomas Bohier, the comptroller-general of finances in Normandy, began buying up land around the château. The Marqués family was forced to sell to Bohier, who tore down Chenonceau, preserving only the keep and building the rest in the emerging Renaissance style.

Many of the château's walls are covered with Gobelin tapestries, including one depicting a woman pouring water over the back of an angry dragon, another of a three-headed dog and a seven-headed monster. The chapel contains a delicate marble *Virgin and Child*, plus portraits of Catherine de Médici in her traditional black and white. There's even a portrait of the stern Catherine in the former bedroom of her rival, Diane de Poitiers. In François I's Renaissance bedchamber the most interesting portrait is that of Diane de Poitiers as the huntress Diana.

The history of Chenonceau is related in 15 tableaux in the wax museum, which charges 10F ($2). Diane de Poitiers, who, among other accomplishments, introduced the artichoke to France, is depicted in three tableaux. One portrays Catherine de Médici tossing out her husband's mistress.

The château is open daily mid-Mar–mid-Sept 9am–7pm, mid-Sept–mid-Mar 9am–6:30pm. Admission is 40F ($8) for adults and 25F ($5) for children 7–15; 6 and under free. A *son-et-lumière* spectacle, *In the Old Days of the Dames of Chenonceau*, is staged daily in summer at 10:15pm; admission is 40F ($8).

ESSENTIALS

ARRIVING There are three daily trains from Tours to Chenonceaux (trip time: 45 min.). The train deposits you half a mile from the château.

VISITOR INFORMATION The **Syndicat d'Initiative** (tourist office) is at 13 bis rue du Château (☎ **02-47-23-94-45**), open Easter to September.

DEPARTING BY CAR Continue back to Tours, branching out this time for the best of the châteaux in the west. The first stop is Ussé, of *Sleeping Beauty* fame. Follow the directions to the previously visited Azay-le-Rideau. From there, it's but a short ride down the Indre Valley on D-17 and then D-7 to Ussé.

ACCOMMODATIONS

Hôtel du Bon-Laboureur et du Château. 6 rue du Dr.-Bretonneau, Chenonceaux, 37150 Bléré. ☎ **02-47-23-90-02.** Fax 02-47-23-82-01. 31 rms, 3 suites. TV TEL. 350–700F ($70–$140) double; 800–1,000F ($160–$200) suite. AE, DC, MC, V. Free parking.

This country inn, with an ivy-covered facade and tall chimneys, is within walking distance of the château and is your best bet for a comfortable night's sleep and good food. The rear garden has a little guest house, plus formally planted roses. The owner/chef is Antoine Jeudi. Founded in 1880, the hotel maintains the flavor of that era, but modern baths have been added to the rooms, plus satellite TV. In fair weather, request a table in the courtyard, under a maple tree. The fixed-price menus in Le Bon Laboureur are a family tradition. You can order grill specialties in a second restaurant, Les Gourmandises de Touraine, in summer only. There's also an outdoor heated pool.

La Roseraie. Chenonceaux, 37150 Bléré. ☎ **02-47-23-90-09.** Fax 02-47-23-91-59. 16 rms. TV TEL. 265–485F ($53–$97) double. AE, DC. Closed Nov 15–Feb 15. Free parking.

This is a traditional French inn, in a leafy setting with a rear garden, a short walk from the château. A bit down the scale from Bon Laboureur, it nevertheless also offers a comfortable night's lodging and good food. The rooms are furnished in classic boudoir style and offer much comfort at reasonable rates. Some of the finest meals in town are served in the restaurant with its steak house. Good regional specialties are featured, and meals can be served on a terrace in the garden.

DINING

🕲 **Au Gateau Breton.** 16 rue Bretonneau. ☎ **02-47-23-90-14.** Reservations required July–Aug. Fixed-price menus 66–110F ($13.20–$22). MC, V. Tues 7–9:30pm, Wed 11:30am–2pm, Thurs–Mon 11:30am–2pm and 7–9:30pm. Closed mid-Nov to mid-Dec. FRENCH.

The sun terrace in back of this Breton-type inn, a short walk from the château, is a refreshing place for dinner or tea. Gravel paths run among beds of pink geraniums and lilacs, and the red tables have bright canopies and umbrellas. The chef provides home cooking and cherry liqueur—a specialty of the region. In cool months meals are served in rustic dining rooms. Specialties are small chitterling sausages of Tours, chicken with Armagnac sauce, and coq au vin (chicken cooked in wine). The medallions of veal with mushroom-cream sauce are excellent, though you may want to skip the blood sausage with apples, highly touted locally. Tasty pastries are sold in the front room.

USSÉ

At the edge of the hauntingly dark forest of Chinon, the **Château d'Ussé** (☎ **02-47-95-54-05**) was the inspiration behind Perrault's legend of *Sleeping Beauty (La Belle au Bois Dormant)*. On a hill overlooking the Indre River, it's a complex of steeples, turrets, towers, chimneys, and dormers. Conceived as a medieval fortress, Ussé was erected at the dawn of the Renaissance. Two powerful families—the Bueil and d'Espinay—lived here in the 15th and 16th centuries. The terraces, laden with orange trees, were laid out in the 18th century.

The guided tour begins in the Renaissance chapel, with its sculptured portal and handsome stalls. Then you proceed to the royal apartments, furnished with tapestries and antiques, like a four-poster bed draped in red damask. One gallery displays an extensive collection of swords and rifles. A spiral stairway leads to a tower with a panoramic view of the river and a waxwork Sleeping Beauty waiting for her prince to come.

The château is open daily Mar–Oct 9am–6:30pm and Nov–Feb 10am–noon and 2–5:30pm. Admission is 59F ($11.80) for adults and 19F ($3.80) for children.

ESSENTIALS

DEPARTING BY CAR   Chinon is easily reached from Ussé via D-7 and D-17. You approach this ancient town with its rock-of-ages castle looming on the horizon.

CHINON

Remember in the film *Joan of Arc* when Ingrid Bergman sought out the dauphin as he tried to conceal himself among his courtiers? The action in real life took place at the Château de Chinon, one of the oldest fortress-châteaux in France. Charles VII, mockingly known as the King of Bourges, centered his government at Chinon from 1429 to 1450. In 1429, with the English besieging Orléans, the Maid of Orléans, that "messenger from God," prevailed on the weak dauphin to give her an army. The rest is history. The seat of French power stayed at Chinon until the Hundred Years' War ended.

ESSENTIALS

ARRIVING   There are three trains daily from Tours (trip time: 1 hr.).

VISITOR INFORMATION   The **Office de Tourisme** is at 12 rue Voltaire (☎ **02-47-93-17-85**).

DEPARTING BY CAR   Angers is generally considered the western end of the Loire Valley, though the Loire River continues for another 80 miles before reaching Nantes. To reach Angers, continue north from Chinon toward the river. The D-7 connects to the N-152 heading west all the way to Saumur. Once at Saumur, the D-952 continues west into Angers, a distance of 32 miles.

EXPLORING CHINON

On the banks of the Vienne, the town of Chinon retains a medieval atmosphere. It consists of winding streets and turreted houses, many built in the 15th and 16th centuries in the heyday of the court. For the best view, drive across the river, turning right onto quai Danton. From that vantage point you'll have the best perspective, seeing the castle in relation to the village and the river. The gables and towers make Chinon look like a toy village. The most typical street is **rue Voltaire,** lined with 15th- and 16th-century town houses. At no. 44, Richard the Lion-Hearted died on April 6, 1199, after being mortally wounded while besieging Chalus in Limousin. In the heart of Chinon, the **Grand Carroi** was the crossroads of the Middle Ages.

The most famous son of Chinon, Rabelais, the Renaissance writer, walked these streets. He was born at La Devinière, on D-17 near N-751, now the **Musée Rabelais.** Of Chinon's equally famous wine he once remarked, "Drink it always, and you will never die."

The **Château de Chinon** (☎ 02-47-93-13-45) is three separate strongholds, once badly ruined, but today at least two of the buildings, the Château du Milieu and Château du Coudray, have been entirely restored, with the exception of their still nonexistent roofs. Some of the grim walls from other dilapidated edifices remain, though many of the buildings—including the Great Hall where Joan of Arc sought out the dauphin—have been torn down. Some of the most destructive owners were the heirs of Cardinal Richelieu. Now gone, the Château de St Georges was built by Henry II of England, who died here in 1189. The Château du Milieu dates from the 11th to the 15th century, containing the keep and the clock tower, where the Musée Jeanne d'Arc has been installed. Separated from the latter by a moat, the Château du Coudray contains the Tour du Coudray, where Joan of Arc stayed during her time at Chinon. In the 14th century the Knights Templar were imprisoned here before meeting their violent deaths.

The château is open Feb–Nov daily 9am–6pm, charging 25F ($5) for adults and 18F ($3.60) for children.

ACCOMMODATIONS

Chris' Hôtel. 12 place Jeanne-d'Arc, 37500 Chinon. ☎ **02-47-93-36-92.** Fax 02-47-98-48-92. 40 rms. TV TEL. 350–400F ($70–$80) double. AE, DC, MC, V. Free parking.

This well-run hotel is housed in a 19th-century building near the town's historic district. Many of the rooms offer views of the castle and river; most are furnished in a Louis XV style and all have modern amenities. Breakfast is the only meal served.

DINING

✪ **Au Plaisir Gourmand.** 2 rue Parmentier. ☎ **02-47-93-20-48.** Reservations required. Main courses 95–130F ($19–$26); fixed-price menus 175–245F ($35–$49). AE, MC, V. Tues–Sat noon–2pm and 7:30–9:30pm, Sun noon–2pm. Closed Jan–Feb. FRENCH.

This is the premier restaurant in the area, owned by Jean-Claude Rigollet, who used to direct the chefs at the fabled Les Templiers in Les Bézards. His restaurant offers an intimate dining room with a limited number of tables in a charming 18th-century building. Menu items are likely to include roast rabbit in aspic with foie-gras sauce, sandre in beurre blanc (white butter), and sautéed crayfish with a spicy salad. For dessert, try the prunes stuffed in puff pastry.

ANGERS

Once the capital of Anjou, Angers straddles the Maine River. Although it suffered extensive damage in World War II, it has been considerably restored, somehow blending provincial charm with the suggestion of sophistication. The town is often used as a base for exploring the château district to the west.

ESSENTIALS

ARRIVING   From Saumur it's a 30-minute train trip to Angers; from Tours, it's 1 hour. Trains also leave Paris–Austerlitz for the 2³/₄-hour trip. The train station at place de la Gare in Angers is a convenient walk from the château.

VISITOR INFORMATION   The **Office de Tourisme** is on place du Kennedy (☎ 02-41-23-51-11).

EXPLORING ANGERS

The moated **Château d'Angers** (☎ 02-41-87-43-47), from the 9th century, was once the home of the comtes d'Anjou. After the castle was destroyed, it was reconstructed by St. Louis. From 1230 to 1238 the outer walls and 17 massive towers were built, creating a formidable fortress well prepared to withstand invaders. The château was favored by Good King René, during whose reign a brilliant court life flourished here until he was forced to surrender Anjou to Louis XI. Louis XIV turned the château into a prison, dispatching his finance minister, Fouquet, to a cell here. In the 19th century the castle again became a prison, and during World War II it was used by the Nazis as a munitions depot. Allied planes bombed it in 1944.

The castle displays the **Apocalypse Tapestries,** one of the masterpieces of art from the Middle Ages. This series of tapestries wasn't always so highly regarded—they once served as a canopy for orange trees to protect the fruit from unfavorable weather and at another time to cover the damaged walls of a church. They were made by Poisson beginning in 1375 for Louis I of Anjou and in the 19th century were purchased for a nominal sum. Seventy-seven pieces of them stretch a distance of 335 feet, the series illustrating the book of St. John. One scene is called *La Grande Prostituée,* and another shows Babylon invaded by demons; yet another is a peace scene with two multiheaded monsters holding up a fleur-de-lis.

You can tour the fortress, including the courtyard of the nobles, prison cells, ramparts, windmill tower, 15th-century chapel, and royal apartments. The château is open daily June–Sept 15 9am–7pm and Sept 16–May 9:30am–12:30pm and 2–6pm. Admission is 32F ($6.40) for adults, 21F ($4.20) for seniors, and 6F ($1.20) for children 7–17; 6 and under free.

The **Cathédrale St-Maurice,** place Freppel (☎ 02-41-87-58-45), is mostly from the 12th and 13th centuries; the main tower, however, is from the 16th century. The statues on the portal represent everybody from the Queen of Sheba to David at the harp. On the tympanum is depicted Christ Enthroned; the symbols, such as the lion for St. Mark, represent the Evangelists. The stained-glass windows from the 12th through the 16th century have made the cathedral famous. The oldest one illustrates the martyrdom of St. Vincent (the most unusual is of former St. Christopher with the head of a dog). Once all the Apocalypse Tapestries were shown here; now only a few remain. The 12th-century nave is a landmark in cathedral architecture, a clear, coherent plan that's a work of harmonious beauty, the start of the Plantagenet architecture. It's open daily 8am–5pm.

ACCOMMODATIONS

Hôtel d'Anjou. 1 bd. Foch, 49100 Angers. ☎ **02-41-88-24-82.** Fax 02-41-87-22-21. 53 rms (46 with bath). MINIBAR TV TEL. 370F ($74) double without bath, 630F ($126) double with bath. AE, DC, MC, V. Parking 45F ($9).

The prices are reasonable at this four-story hotel on the main boulevard, next to a large park, even though it's clearly the best choice for overnighting, even better than the Hôtel de France because of its superior appointments and amenities. The clean rooms are comfortably furnished with traditional pieces, and you're politely welcomed and cared for. The hotel restaurant, La Salamandre, is one of the better ones in town, offering regional specialties and fresh fish.

Hôtel de France. 8 place de la Gare, 49100 Angers. ☎ **02-41-88-49-42.** Fax 02-41-86-76-70. 57 rms. MINIBAR TV TEL. 480F ($96) double. AE, DC, MC, V. Parking 40F ($8).

One of the most respected in town, this 19th-century hotel has been run by the Bouyers since 1893. It's the preferred choice near the rail station. The rooms are soundproof, but only four are air-conditioned (it can get hot on a summer night). The restaurant, Les Plantagenets, serves reliable fixed-price meals.

DINING

Provence Caffè. 9 place du Ralliement. ☎ **02-41-87-44-15.** Reservations recommended. Main courses 68F ($13.60); fixed-price menus 89F ($17.80). AE, MC, V. Mon 7–10pm, Tues–Sat noon–2pm and 7–10pm, Sun noon–2pm (open for lunch on Mon and closed all day Sun from Easter to Sept). PROVENÇAL.

This restaurant opened in 1994 celebrating the herbs, spices, and seafood of Provence. The decor includes bundles of herbs, bright colors, and souvenirs of the Mediterranean, and the ambience is unstuffy and sunny. Menu items include a risotto with asparagus and basil, grilled salmon with Provençal herbs, and a ballotine of chicken with ratatouille.

Le Toussaint. 7 place du Président-Kennedy. ☎ **02-41-87-46-20.** Reservations recommended. Main courses 80–150F ($16–$30); fixed-price menus 98–250F ($19.60–$50). AE, MC, V. Tues–Sat noon–2pm and 7:45–9:30pm, Sun noon–2pm. FRENCH.

This leading restaurant, on the same street as the cathedral, serves the imaginative cuisine of well-known chef Michel Bignon. The second-floor dining room boasts a sweeping château view. The recipes include only the freshest ingredients, and specialties are foie gras with Layon wine, farm-bred pigeon stuffed with foie gras, and an array of fresh fish and shellfish. The dessert specialty is an ice-cream soufflé with Cointreau.

3 Provence & the Côte d'Azur

Provence has been called a bridge between the past and present, where yesterday blends with today in a quiet, often melancholy way. Peter Mayle's best-selling *A Year in Provence* (as well as his other books about the area) has played no small part in the burgeoning popularity that this sunny corner of southern France has enjoyed during recent years.

The Greeks and Romans first filled the landscape with cities boasting Hellenic theaters, Roman baths, amphitheaters, and triumphal arches. These were followed in medieval times by romanesque fortresses and gothic cathedrals. In the 19th century Provence's light and landscapes attracted illustrious painters like Cézanne and van Gogh to Aix and Arles and other towns. Despite the changes over the years, the mistral will forever howl through the broad-leaved plane trees.

Provence has its own language and customs. The region is bounded on the north by the Dauphine, the west by the Rhône, the east by the Alps, and the south by the Mediterranean. We cover the northern area of this region, what's traditionally thought of as Provence, and then head down to the southern part, what's known as the glittering Côte d'Azur or French Riviera.

The Riviera has been called the world's most exciting stretch of beach and "a sunny place for shady people." Each resort on the Riviera—be it Beaulieu by the sea or eagle's-nest Eze—offers its unique flavor and special merits. Glitterati and eccentrics have always been drawn to this narrow strip of fabled real estate. A trail of modern artists, attracted to the brilliant light, have left a rich heritage: Matisse in his chapel at Vence, Cocteau at Menton and Villefranche, Picasso at Antibes and seemingly everywhere else, Léger at Biot, Renoir at Cagnes, and Bonnard at Le Cannet. The best collection of all is at the Maeght Foundation in St-Paul-de-Vence.

The Riviera's high season used to be winter and spring only. However, with changing tastes, July and August have become the most crowded months, and reservations are imperative. The average summer temperature is 75°F; the average winter temperature, 49°F.

The Corniches of the Riviera, depicted in countless films, stretch from Nice to Menton. The Alps drop into the Mediterranean and roads were carved along the way. The lower road, about 20 miles long, is the **Corniche Inférieure.** Along this road are the ports of Villefranche, Cap-Ferrat, Beaulieu, and Cap-Martin. Built between World War I and the beginning of World War II, the **Moyenne Corniche** (Middle Road), 19 miles long, also runs from Nice to Menton, winding spectacularly in and out of tunnels and through mountains. The highlight is at mountaintop Eze. The **Grande Corniche**—the most panoramic—was ordered built by Napoléon in 1806. La Turbie and Le Vistaero are the principal towns along the 20-mile stretch, which reaches more than 1,600 feet high at Col d'Eze.

Our tour begins in Avignon, 425 miles south of Paris, 50 miles northwest of Aix-en-Provence, and 66 miles northwest of Marseille. Most motorists approach the city from Lyon in the north, taking the autoroute (A-7) south.

ONLY IN PROVENCE & THE CÔTE D'AZUR

Dining in the South of France Some of the greatest French chefs are sons and daughters of Provence, and to sample the regional produce and to drink the classic local wine is reason enough to visit, even without the beach. No chef elsewhere can successfully duplicate the bouillabaisse you get on home turf—perhaps it's the scorpion fish and conger eel that's added in. But don't confine your tasting to bouillabaisse. Such goodies as salade Niçoise, "fruits of the sea," grilled sea bass with fennel, and ratatouille are also waiting to win your heart.

Seeing the Riviera by Boat What could be more alluring than the glittering Côte d'Azur as seen from the Mediterranean? Every port along the coast has boats for rent. Whether you join a local fisher on a day's outing, or travel on an expensive yacht, the sight of the southern Provençal coast is the same. Villefranche, Monaco, St-Tropez—each name seems more glamorous than the last. Our favorite? A day sail to the Iles d'Hyéres.

Wandering the Hill Towns The old fortified villages built on hilltops or terraced along the mountainsides are the big bait when you tire of beaches and bikinis. Some, like Eze, perched above the Riviera, are so giddily situated they seem ready to spill

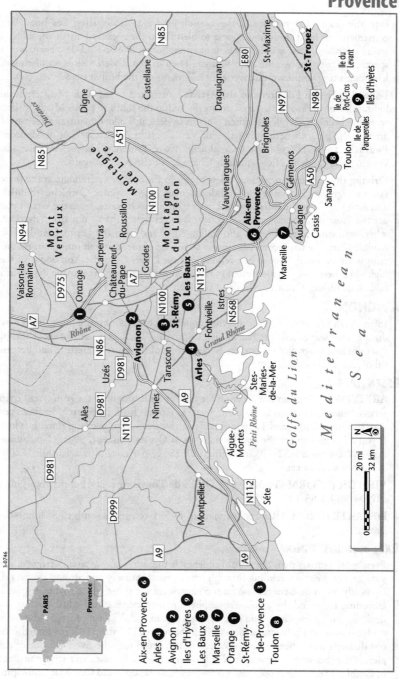

into the sea at any minute. Others, such as dramatically sited Les Baux, are constructed of local stone and appear to blend into the rocks. Many of the villages are so steep and narrow that cars cannot enter. Some, like St-Paul-de-Vence, are so spectacular they are overrun with tourists. The fun of a Riviera visit is wandering at leisure, making your own discoveries of hill towns off the beaten track.

Following in the Footsteps of the Artists   Attracted to the clear Mediterranean light, some of the world's greatest artists flocked to the south to paint. Much of their work has been carted off, but much remains to delight. Follow their trail to see great art and the places where they painted: Van Gogh in Arles, Cocteau in Menton, Picasso in Antibes, Léger in Biot, Cézanne in Aix-en-Provence, Matisse in Vence, and virtually everybody in Nice—notably Chagall, but also Matisse again.

Driving the Riviera Corniches   Few routes in Europe are as dramatic as the three famous highways known as the Grande Corniche, the Moyenne Corniche (middle), and even the Corniche Inférieure or Lower Corniche. Of course from the Grand you get the most panoramic vistas—the view is never better than from Eze Belvedere, where you can see the French and Italian Alps, and even the Lerins Islands. The Middle Corniche has coastal panoramas as you zip along, through tunnels in mountains when necessary. Not to be overlooked is the Lower Corniche. You don't get the high vistas here, but you are treated to the sea and all the resorts that made the Riviera fabled, including Monaco, Nice, and Beaulieu.

AVIGNON

In the 14th century, Avignon was the capital of Christendom; the popes lived here during what was called "the Babylonian Captivity." The legacy left by that "court of splendor and magnificence" makes Avignon one of the most interesting and beautiful of Europe's medieval cities.

ESSENTIALS

ARRIVING   Avignon is a junction for bus routes throughout the region and train service from other towns is frequent. The TGV trains from Paris arrive 13 times per day (trip time: 4 hr.), and 17 trains per day arrive from Marseille (trip time: 1¹/₂ hr.). If you'd like to explore the area by bike, go to **Cycles Peugeot,** 80 rue Guillaume-Puy (☎ **04-90-86-32-49**), charging 60F ($12) per day, plus a 1,000F ($200) deposit or a credit card.

VISITOR INFORMATION   The **Office de Tourisme** is at 41 cours Jean-Jaurès (☎ **04-90-82-65-11**).

DEPARTING BY CAR   From Avignon, D-571 continues south to St-Rémy-de-Provence.

EXPLORING AVIGNON

Even more famous than the papal residency is the ditty *"Sur le pont d'Avignon, l'on y danse, l'on y danse,"* echoing through every French nursery and around the world. Ironically, **pont St-Bénézet** was far too narrow for the danse of the rhyme, inspired, according to legend, by a vision a shepherd named Bénézet had while tending his flock. Spanning the Rhône and connecting Avignon with Villeneuve-lèz-Avignon, the bridge is now only a fragmented ruin. Built between 1117 and 1185, it suffered various disasters from then on; in 1669 half of it toppled into the river. On one of the piers is the two-story Chapelle St-Nicolas—one story in Romanesque style, the other in Gothic. The bridge is open daily Apr–Sept 9am–6:30pm and Oct–Mar 9am–5pm. Admission is 15F ($3) for adults, 7F ($1.40) for students and seniors.

Dominating Avignon from a hill is the **Palais des Papes,** place du Palais-des-Papes (☎ **04-90-27-50-74**). You're shown through on a guided tour, usually lasting 50 minutes. Most of the rooms have been stripped of their finery; the exception is the Chapelle St-Jean, known for its beautiful frescoes of scenes from the life of John the Baptist and John the Evangelist, attributed to the school of Matteo Giovanetti and painted between 1345 and 1348. The Grand Tinel (banquet hall) is about 135 feet long and 30 feet wide, and the pope's table stood on the southern side. The pope's bedroom is on the first floor of the Tour des Anges.

The palace is open daily Apr–Aug 5 from 9am to 6pm, Aug 6–Sept from 9am to 8pm, and Oct–Mar from 9am to noon and 2 to 6pm. Admission is 35F ($7) for adults and 26F ($5.20) for students and those over 65. A 12F ($2.40) supplement is charged when an exhibition is displayed. Guided tours in English depart daily, costing 43F ($8.60) for adults and 35F ($7) for children.

Near the palace is the 12th-century **Cathédrale Notre-Dame,** place du Palais-des-Papes, containing the flamboyant Gothic tomb of Pope John XXII, who died at age 90. Benedict XII is also buried here. The cathedral's hours vary, but generally it's open daily 11am–6pm and admission is free. From the cathedral, enter the promenade du Rocher-des-Doms to stroll through its garden and enjoy the view across the Rhône to Villeneuve-lèz-Avignon.

SHOPPING

Since the 1960s, **Antiquités Bourret,** 5 rue Linas (☎ **04-90-86-65-02**), has earned a reputation as far away as Paris as a repository for 18th- and 19th-century Provençal antiques, inspired by Louis XV French models and painted in 18th-century pigments of ocher, pale green, or blue. Other pieces are crafted from Provençal walnut and waxed to a luster. Open Tues–Sat 9:30am–12:30pm and 2:30–7pm. **Véronique Pichon,** place Crillon (☎ **04-90-85-89-00**), is the newest branch of a porcelain manufacturer whose colorful products have been a regional fixture since the 1700s. Manufactured in the nearby town of Uzès, the tableware, decorative urns, statues, and lamps are cost-effective enough to be shipped virtually anywhere. Open Mon–Sat 9am–7:30pm.

The Avignon branch of **Les Olivades,** 28 rue des Marchands (☎ **04-90-86-13-42**), is one of the most visible of a chain of outlets associated in the States with Pierre Deux. Look for fabrics by the yard, bedcovers, slipcovers, draperies, and tablecloths. Fabrics, printed in a factory only 6 miles from Avignon, tend to feature intricate designs in colors inspired by 19th-century models or, to a somewhat lesser extent, Créole designs with butterflies, pineapples, bananas, and flowers. Open Mon–Sat 9:30am–1pm and 2–7pm.

The vision that launched **Les Indiens de Nîmes,** 4 rue College de Roure (☎ **04-90-86-32-05**), in the early 1980s involved the duplication of 18th- and 19th-century Provençal fabric patterns. They're sold as fabric by the meter as well as clothing for men, women, and children. Kitchenware and a selection of furniture inspired by originals from Provence and the steamy wetlands west of Marseille are also sold. Open Tues–Sat 9:30am–noon and 2–7pm. All the clothing at **Souleiado,** 5 rue Joseph-Vernet (☎ **04-90-86-47-67**), derives from a Provençal model, and even the Provençal name (which translates as "first ray of sunshine after a storm") evokes a spirit on which the owners want to capitalize. Most, but not all, of the clothing is designed for women and comes in a wider choice than the garments (mostly shirts) available for men. Fabrics are also sold by the meter. Open Mon–Sat 9am–noon and 2–7pm.

ACCOMMODATIONS

Mercure Palais-des-Papes. Quartier de la Balance, rue Ferruce, 84000 Avignon. ☎ **04-90-85-91-23.** Fax 04-90-85-32-40. 86 rms. A/C TV TEL. 525–565F ($105–$113) double. AE, DC, MC, V. Parking 50F ($10). Bus: 11.

This chain hotel is one of the best in Avignon, though nothing to equal La Mirande. It lies within the city walls, at the foot of the Palace of the Popes. The rooms are well furnished yet functional and without any particular style. There's a small bar but no restaurant, as breakfast is the only meal served. Avoid the skimpy room service tray and head for the buffet breakfast.

✪ **La Mirande.** 4 place Amirande, 84000 Avignon. ☎ **04-90-85-93-93.** Fax 04-90-86-26-85. 20 rms, 1 suite. A/C MINIBAR TV TEL. 1,700–2,100F ($340–$420) double; 2,800F ($560) suite. AE, DC, V.

In the heart of Avignon, this restored 700-year-old town house is one of the grand little luxuries of France, far better than anything else in town. Behind the Palais des Papes, the hotel treats you to two centuries of decorative art in France. All the rooms are stunning, with huge tubs. The restaurant earns its one star in Michelin and is among the finest in Avignon. Chef Eric Coisel has a light, sophisticated touch.

DINING

✪ **Christian Etienne.** 10 rue Mons. ☎ **04-90-86-16-50.** Reservations recommended. Main courses 80–250F ($16–$50); fixed-price lunch (Mon–Fri) 160F ($32); fixed-price dinners 300F ($60), 420F ($84), 480F ($96). AE, DC, MC, V. July daily noon–2:30pm and 8–10:30pm; the rest of the year, Mon–Sat noon–2:30pm and 8–10:30pm. FRENCH.

This restaurant serves the best food in Avignon. The dining room contains very old ceiling and wall frescoes honoring the marriage of Anne de Bretagne to the French king in 1491. Several of the fixed-price menus present specific themes, from vegetarian to lobster. À la carte specialties include fennel soup with sea barnacles, terrine of foie gras cooked with sauterne, and roast pigeon with escalope of foie gras.

⑤ **La Fourchette II.** 7 rue Racine. ☎ **04-90-85-20-93.** Fixed-price lunch 115F ($23); fixed-price dinner 148F ($29.60). MC, V. Mon–Fri noon–2pm and 7:30–9:30pm. Closed Aug 5–29. Bus: 11. FRENCH.

This bistro offers creative cooking at a moderate price. There are two dining rooms, one like a summer house with walls of glass, the other more like a tavern with oak beams. You might begin with parfait of chicken liver with spinach flan or mousseline of fish in saffron sauce. Two specialties are daube of beef avignonnaise style with macaroni and grilled lambs' liver with raisins.

ST-RÉMY-DE-PROVENCE

Nostradamus, the French physician/astrologer, author of more than 600 obscure verses whose reputation is enjoying great vogue today, was born here in 1503. In 1922 Gertrude Stein and Alice B. Toklas found St-Rémy after "wandering around everywhere a bit," as Ms. Stein once wrote to Cocteau. But mainly St-Rémy is associated with van Gogh. He committed himself to an asylum here in 1889 after cutting off his left ear. Between moods of despair, here he painted such works as *Olive Trees* and *Cypresses*. The town lies 16 miles northeast of Arles and 8 miles north of Les Baux.

ESSENTIALS

ARRIVING   There are local buses from Avignon, taking 45 minutes and costing 27F ($5.40) one way.

VISITOR INFORMATION   The **Office de Tourisme** is at place Jean-Jaurès (☎ **04-90-92-05-22**).

DEPARTING BY CAR   From St-Rémy-de-Provence, head south for 8 miles along the winding D-5 until you reach Les Baux.

EXPLORING ST-RÉMY & ENVIRONS

You can visit the cloisters of the asylum van Gogh made famous in his paintings at the 12th-century **Monastère de St-Paul-de-Mausolée.** Now a psychiatric hospital, the former monastery is east of D-5, a short drive north of Glanum (see below). You can't visit the cell in which this genius was confined from 1889 to 1890, but it's still worth coming here to explore the Romanesque chapel and cloisters with their circular arches and columns, which have beautifully carved capitals. The cloisters are open daily 9am–noon and 2–6pm in summer and 9am–noon and 1–5pm in winter. On your way to the church you'll see a bust of van Gogh. Admission is currently free but may not remain gratis for long. There's no number to call for information.

In the center of St-Rémy, the **Musée Archéologique,** in the Hôtel de Sade, rue du Parage (☎ **04-90-92-64-04**), displays both sculptures and bronzes excavated at Glanum. It's open June–Oct daily 9am–noon and 2–6pm; Apr–May Mon–Fri 3–6pm and Sat–Sun 10am–noon. Admission is 12F ($2.40) for adults and 6F ($1.20) for children.

A mile south of St-Rémy on D-5 is **Ruines de Glanum,** avenue Vincent-van-Gogh (☎ **04-90-92-23-79**), a Gallo-Roman city (follow the signs to Les Antiques). Its historical monuments include an Arc Municipal, a triumphal arch dating from the time of Julius Caesar, and a cenotaph called the Mausolée des Jules. Garlanded with sculptured fruits and flowers, the arch dates from 20 B.C. and is the oldest in Provence. The mausoleum was raised to honor the grandsons of Augustus and is the only extant monument of its type. In the area are entire streets and foundations of private residences from the 1st-century town. Some remains are from an even earlier Gallo-Greek town dating from the 2nd century B.C. Admission is 32F ($6.40) for adults and 10F ($2) for children under 10. The excavations are open daily Apr–Sept 9am–7pm and Oct–Mar 9am–noon and 2–5pm.

ACCOMMODATIONS & DINING

Ⓢ **Bar/Hôtel/Restaurant des Arts.** 32 bd. Victor-Hugo, 13210 St-Rémy-de-Provence. ☎ **04-90-92-08-50.** Reservations recommended. Main courses 60–150F ($12–$30); fixed-price menus 90–160F ($18–$32). AE, DC, MC, V. Wed–Mon noon–2pm and 7:30–9:30pm. Closed Feb and Nov 1–12. FRENCH.

This old-style cafe/restaurant and hotel is on the east side. The wait for dinner can be as long as 45 minutes, so you may want to spend some time in the bar, with its wooden tables and slightly faded decor. The restaurant is time-tested, with pine paneling, copper pots, and original paintings. The menu lists old-fashioned specialties like rabbit terrine, pepper steak with champagne, tournedos with madeira and mushrooms, duckling in orange sauce, and trout served three ways.

If you want to spend the night, the 17 rooms upstairs are basic, some in Provençal style, with rustic ceiling beams and exposed timbers; 8 have baths. A double is 278–350F ($55.60–$70).

LES BAUX

Cardinal Richelieu called Les Baux a nesting place for eagles. It lies 12 miles north of Arles and 50 miles north of Marseille and the Mediterranean. In its lonely position high on a windswept plateau overlooking the southern Alpilles, Les Baux is a mere ghost of its former self. Once it was the citadel of the powerful *seigneurs* of Les Baux, who ruled with an iron fist and sent their conquering armies as far as Albania. The town is nestled in a valley surrounded by mysterious, shadowy rock formations. In medieval times troubadours from all over Europe came to this "court of love," where they recited Western Europe's earliest-known vernacular poetry. Eventually, the notorious "Scourge of Provence" ruled Les Baux, sending his men throughout the land to kidnap people. If no one would pay ransom for a victim, the poor wretch was forced to walk a gangplank over the cliff's edge.

Fed up with the rebellions against Louis XIII in 1632, Richelieu commanded his armies to destroy Les Baux. Today the castle and ramparts are a mere shell, though you can see remains of great Renaissance mansions.

ESSENTIALS

ARRIVING   From Arles you can take one of six daily buses (trip time: 30 min.), costing 27F ($5.40) one way.

VISITOR INFORMATION   The **Office de Tourisme** is on Ilôt Post Tenebras Lux (☎ **04-90-54-34-39**).

DEPARTING BY CAR   From Les Baux continue southwest on D-17 for 12 miles to Arles.

ACCOMMODATIONS & DINING

✪ **La Riboto de Taven.** Le Val d'Enfer, 13520 Les Baux. ☎ **04-90-54-34-23.** Fax 04-90-54-38-88. Reservations required. Main courses 140–180F ($28–$36); fixed-price menus 198F ($39.60) (lunch only) and 280–420F ($56–$84). AE, DC, MC, V. Tues noon–2pm, Thurs–Mon noon–2pm and 7:30–10pm. Closed Jan 5–Mar 15. FRENCH.

This 1835 farmhouse outside the medieval section of town has been owned by two generations of the Novi family, of which Christine and Philippe Theme are the English-speaking daughter and son-in-law. In summer, you can sit out at the beautifully laid tables, one of which is a millstone. Menu items may include sea bass in olive oil, fricassée of mussels flavored with basil, and lamb en croûte with olives—plus homemade desserts. The cuisine is a personal statement of Jean-Pierre Novi, whose cookery is filled with brawny flavors and the heady perfumes of Provençal herbs.

It's also possible to rent two double rooms so large they're like suites, each at 990F ($198), breakfast included.

ARLES

Arles, 22 miles southwest of Avignon and 55 miles northwest of Marseille, has been called "the soul of Provence," and art lovers, archeologists, and historians are attracted to this town on the Rhône. Many of its scenes, painted so luminously by van Gogh in his declining years, remain to delight. The great Dutch painter left Paris for Arles in 1888. He was to paint some of his most celebrated works in this Provençal town, including *Starry Night, The Bridge at Arles, Sunflowers,* and *L'Arlésienne.*

Although Arles doesn't possess quite as much charm as Aix-en-Provence, it has first-rate museums, excellent restaurants, and summer festivals such as an international photography festival in early June. The city today isn't quite as lovely as it was when Picasso came here, but it has enough antique Provençal flavor to keep the appeal alive.

ESSENTIALS

ARRIVING   Arles lies on the Paris–Marseille and the Bordeaux–St-Raphaël rail lines, so has frequent connections from most French cities. Ten trains arrive daily from Avignon (trip time: 20 min.) and 10 per day from Marseille (trip time: 1 hr.).

From Aix-en-Provence, 10 trains arrive per day (trip time: 1³/₄ hr.). There are about five buses per day from Aix-en-Provence (trip time: 1³/₄ hr.).

VISITOR INFORMATION The **Office de Tourisme,** where you can buy a *Billet Globale,* is on the esplanade des Lices (☎ **04-90-18-41-20**). If you'd like to get around by bicycle, go to **L'Arène du Cycle,** 10 rue Portugal (☎ **04-90-96-46-83**), which charges 60F ($12) per day, plus a deposit of 500F ($100). Mountain bikes are rented for 100F ($20) per day, with a 1,000F ($200) deposit.

DEPARTING BY CAR From Arles, head east toward Aix-en-Provence on N-113. Once at Salon-de-Provence, take the autoroute southeast for 23 miles to Aix-en-Provence, the conclusion of your driving tour of Provence. After that, it's south to the French Riviera.

Exploring Arles

At the tourist office you can purchase a *Billets Global,* the all-inclusive pass that admits you to the town's museums, Roman monuments, and all the major attractions, at a cost of 55F ($11) for adults and 35F ($7) for children.

The town is full of monuments from Roman times. The general vicinity of the old Roman forum is occupied by **place du Forum,** shaded by plane trees. Once the Café de Nuit, immortalized by van Gogh, stood on this square. Two columns in the Corinthian style and pediment fragments from a temple can be viewed at the corner of the Hôtel Nord-Pinus. South of here is **place de la République,** the principal plaza, dominated by a 50-foot-tall blue porphyry obelisk. On the north is the impressive Hôtel-de-Ville (town hall) from 1673, built to Mansart's plans and surmounted by a Renaissance belfry.

On the east side of the square is the **Eglise St-Trophime** (☎ **04-90-49-36-36**), noted for its 12th-century portal, one of the finest achievements of southern Romanesque style. In the pediment Christ is surrounded by the symbols of the Evangelists. The cloister, in both the Gothic and Romanesque styles, is noted for its medieval carvings. The church is open daily 8am–7pm and admission is free. The cloister's hours are daily Oct–Mar 9–11:30am and 2–4:30pm and Apr–Sept 9am–7pm. An admission of 15F ($3) is collected from adults and 9F ($1.80) from students.

The **Museon Arlaten** (☎ **04-90-96-08-23**) is entered at 29 rue de la République—its name is written in old Provençal style. It was founded by Frédéric Mistral, the Provençal poet and leader of a movement to establish Modern Provençal as a literary language, using the money from his Nobel Prize for literature in 1904. This is really a folklore museum, with regional costumes, portraits, furniture, dolls, a music salon, and one room devoted to mementos of Mistral. Admission is 15F ($3) for adults and 10F ($2) for children. The museum is open Apr–Oct daily 9am–noon and 2–6:30pm; Nov–Mar Tues–Sun 9am–noon and 2–5pm.

The two great classical monuments are the **Théâtre Antique,** rue du Cloître (☎ **04-90-96-93-30**), and the Amphitheater. The Roman theater, begun by Augustus in the 1st century, was mostly destroyed and only two Corinthian columns remain. Now rebuilt, the theater is the setting for an annual drama festival in July. The theater was where the *Venus of Arles* was discovered in 1651. Take rue de la Calade from the town hall. The theater is open daily June–Sept 8:30am–7pm, Mar–Oct 9am–12:30pm and 2–6pm, Apr 9am–12:30pm and 2–6:30pm, May 9am–12:30pm and 2–7pm, and Nov–Feb 9am–noon and 2–4:30pm. Admission is 15F ($3) for adults and 9F ($1.80) for children.

Nearby, the **Amphitheater,** Rond-Point des Arènes (☎ **04-90-96-03-70**), also built in the 1st century, seats almost 25,000 and still hosts bullfights in summer. The government warns you to visit the old monument at your own risk. For a good view, you can climb the three towers that remain from medieval times, when the amphitheater was turned into a fortress. Open daily June–Sept 8:30am–7pm, Oct and March–May 9am–12:30pm and 2–7pm, and Nov–Feb 9am–noon and 2–4:30pm. Admission is 15F ($3) for adults and 9F ($1.80) for children.

The most memorable sight in Arles is **Les Alyscamps,** rue Pierre-Renaudel, once a necropolis established by the Romans, converted into a Christian burial ground in the 4th century. As the latter, it became a setting for legends in epic medieval poetry and was even mentioned in Dante's *Inferno.* Today it's lined with poplars as well as any remaining sarcophagi. Arlesiens escape here to enjoy a respite from the heat. Open daily June–Sept 8:30am–7pm, Oct and Mar–May 9am–12:30pm and 2–7pm, and Nov–Feb 9am–noon and 2–4:30pm. Admission is 15F ($3) for adults and 9F ($1.80) for children. Another ancient monument is the **Thermes de Constantín,** rue Dominique-Maisto, near the banks of the Rhône. Today only the baths (*thermae*) remain of a once-grand imperial palace. Visiting hours are the same as at Les Alyscamps, and admission is 15F ($3) for adults and 9F ($1.80) for children.

ACCOMMODATIONS

Hôtel d'Arlatan. 26 rue du Sauvage, 13631 Arles. ☎ **04-90-93-56-66.** Fax 04-90-49-68-45. 33 rms, 7 suites. MINIBAR TV TEL. 605–750F ($121–$150) double; 858F ($171.60) suite. AE, DC, MC, V. Parking 58F ($11.60).

In the former residence of the comtes d'Arlatan de Beaumont, near place du Forum, this hotel has been managed by the same family since 1920. It was built in the 15th century on the ruins of an old palace—in fact, there's still a 4th-century wall. The rooms are furnished with authentic Provençal antiques, the walls covered with tapestries in the Louis XV and Louis XVI styles. Try to get a room overlooking the garden; 25 rooms are air-conditioned.

Ⓢ **Hôtel le Cloître.** 16 rue du Cloître, 13200 Arles. ☎ **04-90-96-29-50.** Fax 04-90-96-02-88. 33 rms. TEL. 210–295F ($42–$59) double; 365–395F ($73–$79) triple. AE, MC, V. Parking 30F ($6). Bus: 4.

Between the ancient theater and the cloister, this hotel is one of the best-value stops in Arles. Originally part of a 12th-century cloister, it still retains the original Romanesque vaultings. The restored old house has a Provençal atmosphere, pleasant rooms, and a TV lounge, though 17 rooms have their own TVs. Parking is available nearby.

DINING

Ⓢ **Hostellerie des Arènes.** 62 rue du Refuge. ☎ **04-90-96-13-05.** Reservations required. Main courses 45–100F ($9–$20); fixed-price menus 75F ($15), 99F ($19.80), and 129F ($25.80). MC, V. Wed–Mon noon–2pm and 7–9pm. Closed Jan 10–Feb 20. Bus: Free minibus. PROVENÇAL.

Close to the arena, this hostelry offers Provençal meals whose well-prepared specialties include seafood in puff pastry, braised duckling laced with green peppercorns, brochette of mussels with tartar sauce, and veal Marengo. In warm weather, meals are served on the terrace. Chef Didier Pirouault prepares a wonderful bouillabaisse. Inexpensive wines, by the carafe or bottle, provide an added element to any meal.

AIX-EN-PROVENCE

Founded in 122 B.C. by a Roman general, Caius Sextius Calvinus, who named it Aquae Sextiae after himself, Aix was first a Roman military outpost and then a civilian colony, the administrative capital of a province of the later Roman Empire, the seat of an archbishop, and the official residence of the medieval comtes de Provence. After the union of Provence with France, Aix remained until the revolution a judicial and administrative headquarters.

The celebrated son of this old capital city of Provence is Paul Cézanne, who immortalized the countryside nearby. Just as he saw it, Montagne Ste-Victoire looms over the town today, though a string of highrises has now cropped up on the landscape. The most charming center in all Provence, this faded university town was once a seat of aristocracy, its streets walked by counts and kings. The location is 50 miles southeast of Avignon and 20 miles north of Marseille.

ESSENTIALS

ARRIVING   As a rail and highway junction, the city is easily accessible, with trains arriving hourly from Marseille, taking 40 minutes. Independent bus companies service Aix-en-Provence. SATAP (☎ **04-42-26-23-78**) operates four buses a day to and from Avignon, taking 1¹/₂ hours. If you'd like to explore the area by bike, call on **Troc Vélo,** 62 rue Boulegon (☎ **04-42-21-37-40**), which rents 10-speeds for 80F ($16) per day or mountain bikes for 100F ($20) per day. A passport deposit is required.

VISITOR INFORMATION   The **Office de Tourisme** is at 2 place du Général-de-Gaulle (☎ **04-42-16-11-61**).

DEPARTING BY CAR   From Aix-en-Provence, the best way to reach St-Tropez is to take the autoroute (A-8) southeast to the junction with Route 25, then cut south to Ste-Maxime. Once at Ste-Maxime, follow N-98 west to Port Grimaud, at which point you connect with D-98a going east for the final lap to St-Tropez.

EXPLORING AIX

✪ **Cours Mirabeau,** the main street, is one of the most beautiful in Europe. Plane trees stretch their branches across the top to shade it from the hot Provençal sun like an umbrella, filtering the light into shadows that play on the rococo fountains. On one side are shops and sidewalk cafes, on the other richly embellished sandstone *hôtels particuliers* (mansions) from the 17th and 18th centuries. Honoring Mirabeau, the revolutionary and statesman, the street begins at the 1860 landmark fountain on place de la Libération.

The **Cathédrale St-Sauveur,** place des Martyrs de la Résistance (☎ **04-42-21-10-51**), is dedicated to Christ under the title St-Sauveur (Holy Savior or Redeemer). Its baptistery dates from the 4th and 5th centuries, but the architectural complex as a whole has seen many additions. It contains a brilliant Nicolas Froment triptych, *The Burning Bush,* from the 15th century. One side depicts the Virgin and Child, the other Good King René and his second wife, Jeanne de Laval. It's open daily 7:30am–noon and 2–6pm.

Nearby in a former archbishop's palace is the **Musée des Tapisseries,** 28 place des Martyrs de la Résistance (☎ **04-42-23-09-91**). Lining its gilded walls are three series of tapestries from the 17th and 18th centuries collected by the archbishops to decorate the palace: *The History of Don Quixote* by Notoire, *The Russian Games* by Leprince, and *The Grotesques* by Monnoyer. In addition, the museum exhibits rare furnishings from the 17th and 18th centuries. Charging 15F ($35) for admission, it's open daily 10am–noon and 2–5:45pm.

Up rue Cardinale is the **Musée Granet,** place St-Jean-de-Malte (☎ **04-42-38-14-70**), which owns several Cézannes but not a very typical collection of the great artist's work. Matisse donated a nude in 1941. Housed in the former center of the Knights of Malta, the fine-arts gallery contains work by van Dyck, van Loo, and Rigaud; portraits by Pierre and François Puget; and (the most interesting) a *Jupiter* *and Thetis* by Ingres. Ingres also did an 1807 portrait of the museum's namesake, François Marius Granet. Granet's own works abound. The museum is open Wed–Mon 10am–noon and 2:30–6pm; closed January. Admission is 18F ($3.60) for adults and 10F ($2) for children.

Outside town, at 9 av. Paul-Cézanne, is the **Atelier de Cézanne** (☎ **04-42-21-06-53**), the studio of the painter who was the major forerunner of cubism. Surrounded by a wall, the house was restored by American admirers. Repaired again in 1970, it remains much as Cézanne left it in 1906, "his coat hanging on the wall, his easel with an unfinished picture waiting for a touch of the master's brush," as Thomas R. Parker wrote. It may be visited Oct–May Wed–Mon 10am–noon and 2–5pm, and June–Sept 10am–noon and 2:30–6pm. Admission is 16F ($3.20) for adults and 10F ($2) for children.

SHOPPING

Established a century ago and a standard fixture on the shopping list of anyone planning a dinner party in and around Aix, **Bechard,** 12 cours Mirabeau (☎ **04-26-06-78**), is the most famous bakery/*patissier* in town. On the ground floor of a building on the town's main street, it takes its work so seriously that it refers to its underground kitchens as a *laboratoire* (laboratory). The pastries are truly delectable, in most cases made fresh every day. Open daily 7am–8pm.

Few boutiques other than **La Boutique du Pays d'Aix,** in the Aix-en-Provence Tourist Information Office, 2 place du Général-de-Gaulle (☎ **04-42-16-11-61**), carry so many *santos* (carved figurines inspired by the Nativity of Jesus), locally woven textiles and carvings, and an assortment of *calissons* (sugared confections made with almonds and a *confit* of melon) that some local residents define as the national confection. The shop is open Sept and Apr–June Mon–Sat 8:30am–8pm; Oct–Mar Mon–Sat 8:30am–9pm; and July–Aug Mon–Sat 8:30am–10pm, Sun 9am–1pm and 2–10pm.

Founded in 1934 and set on a busy boulevard about half a mile from the center of Aix, the showroom and factory of **Santons Fouque,** 65 cours Gambetta (Route de Nice, RN7) (☎ **04-42-26-33-38**), stocks the largest assortment of *santos* in Aix. More than 1,800 figurines are cast in terra-cotta, finished by hand, then decorated with oil-based paint according to 18th-century models. Each of the trades practiced in medieval Provence is represented in the inventories, which include representations of grizzled but awestruck shoemakers, barrelmakers, copper and iron smiths, and ropemakers, each poised to welcome the newborn Jesus. Depending on their size and complexity, figurines range from 40F ($8) to 5,300F ($1,060). Open Mon–Fri 9am–5pm and Sat 9am–1pm.

ACCOMMODATIONS

Hôtel la Caravelle. 29 bd. du Roi-René, 13100 Aix-en-Provence. ☎ **04-42-21-53-05.** Fax 04-42-96-55-46. 32 rms. TV TEL. 260–390F ($52–$78) double. AE, DC, MC, V. Bus: 1, 2, 3, 6, or 9.

A 3-minute walk from the center at cours Mirabeau is this conservatively furnished three-star hotel, run by M. and Mme Henri Denis, who offer breakfast in the stone-floored lobby, part of their continuing tradition of hospitality toward travelers from across the world. The majority of the rooms were restored in 1995; they have double-glazed windows to help muffle the noise.

✪ **Villa Gallici.** Av. de la Violette (impasse des Grands Pins), 13100 Aix-en-Provence. ☎ **04-42-23-29-23.** Fax 04-42-96-30-45. 19 rms, 4 suites. A/C MINIBAR TV TEL. 900–1,950F ($180–$390) double; from 1,950F ($390) suite. AE, DC, MC, V. Free parking.

This elegant inn is the most stylishly decorated hotel in Aix, created by a trio of architects and interior designers (Mssrs. Dez, Montemarco, and Jouve). Each room contains a private safe and an individualized decor of subtlety and charm, richly infused with the decorative traditions of Aix. Some rooms boast a private terrace or garden. The villa sits in a large enclosed garden in the heart of town, close to one of the best restaurants, Le Clos de la Violette. Simple meals can be ordered from this restaurant and served at lunchtime beside the pool. They also have their own restaurant, Gourmande d'Yvonne, but they still work with La Violette. On the premises are limited spa facilities.

DINING

🟢 **Le Bistro Latin.** 18 rue de la Couronne. ☎ **04-42-38-22-88.** Reservations recommended. Fixed-price lunch 75F ($15); fixed-price dinners 99–160F ($19.80–$32). AE, DC, MC, V. Tues–Sat noon–2pm and 7–10:30pm. Bus: 27, 42, or 51. FRENCH.

The best little bistro in Aix-en-Provence—for the price, that is—is run by Bruno Ungaro, who prides himself on his fixed-price menus. He offers two intimate dining rooms, decorated with antiques. The staff is young and enthusiastic, and Provençal music plays in the background. Try the chartreuse of mussels, one of the meat dishes with spinach-and-saffron cream sauce, or crêpe of hare with basil sauce. We've enjoyed the classic cuisine on all our visits, particularly the scampi risotto.

✪ **Le Clos de la Violette.** 10 av. de la Violette. ☎ **04-42-23-30-71.** Reservations required. Main courses 170–195F ($34–$39); fixed-price menus 370–490F ($74–$98). AE, V. Mon noon–1:30pm, Tues–Sat noon–1:30pm and 7:30–9:30pm. Bus: 27, 42, or 51. FRENCH.

In an elegant residential neighborhood, which most visitors reach by taxi, this is the most innovative restaurant in town. This imposing Provençal villa has an octagonal reception area and several modern dining rooms. The food produced by Jean-Marc and Brigitte Banzo has been called a "song of Provence." Typical dishes—though they change every 2 months—are an upside-down tart of snails with parsley juice, fricassée of sole with lobster, and a sumptuous array of desserts. The service is extremely professional and even gracious.

ST-TROPEZ

Sun-kissed lasciviousness is rampant in this carnival town, 47 miles southwest of Cannes, but the true Tropezian resents the fact that the port has such a bad reputation. "We can be classy, too," one native has insisted. Creative people in the lively arts along with ordinary folk create a volatile mixture. One observer has said that St-Tropez "has replaced Naples for those who accept the principle of dying after seeing it. It is a unique fate for a place to have made its reputation on the certainty of happiness."

Colette lived here for many years. Even the late diarist Anaïs Nin, confidante of Henry Miller, posed for a little cheesecake on the beach in 1939 in a Dorothy Lamour bathing suit. Earlier, St-Tropez was known to Guy de Maupassant, Matisse, and Bonnard.

Artists, composers, novelists, and the film colony are attracted to St-Tropez in summer. Trailing them is a line of humanity unmatched anywhere else on the Riviera for sheer flamboyance.

ESSENTIALS

ARRIVING The nearest rail station is in St-Raphaël, a neighboring resort; at the *vieux port,* four or five boats per day leave the Gare Maritime de St-Raphaël, rue Pierre Auble (☎ **04-94-95-17-46**), for St-Tropez (trip time: 50 min.), costing 100F

($20) round-trip. Some 15 Sodetrav buses per day, leaving from the *gare routière* in St-Raphaël (☎ 04-94-95-24-82), go to St-Tropez, taking 1¹/₂–2¹/₄ hours, depending on the bus. A one-way ticket costs 45F ($9). Buses run directly to St-Tropez from Toulon and Hyères.

VISITOR INFORMATION   The **Office de Tourisme** is on quai Jean-Jaurès (☎ 04-94-97-45-21).

DERPARTING BY CAR   After leaving St-Tropez, take the D-98a northwest again (the same route you traveled to get here), and link up with D-559 at the junction, heading east to Ste-Maxime. This route, which becomes N-98, will take you all the way to Cannes, a distance of 101 miles east of Marseille.

EXPLORING ST-TROPEZ & ENVIRONS

Near the harbor is the **Musée l'Annonciade (Musée de St-Tropez)** at place Georges-Grammont (☎ 04-94-97-04-01), installed in the former chapel of the Annonciade. As a legacy from the artists who loved St-Tropez, the museum shelters one of the finest modern-art collections on the Riviera. Many of the artists, including Paul Signac, depicted the port of St-Tropez. Opened in 1955, the collection includes such works as Van Dongen's yellow-faced *Women of the Balustrade* and paintings and sculpture by Bonnard, Matisse, Braque, Utrillo, Seurat, Derain, and Maillol. The museum is open June–Sept Wed–Mon 10am–noon and 3–7pm and Oct and Dec–May 10am–noon and 2–6pm. Admission is 30F ($6) for adults and 15F ($3) for children.

Two miles from St-Tropez, **Port Grimaud** makes an interesting outing. If you approach the village at dusk, when it's softly bathed in Riviera pastels, it'll look like some old hamlet, perhaps from the 16th century. But this is a mirage. Port Grimaud is the dream fulfillment of its promoter, François Spoerry, who carved it out of marshland and dug canals. Flanking these canals, fingers of land extend from the main square to the sea. The homes are Provençal style, many with Italianate window arches. Boat owners can anchor right at their doorsteps. One newspaper called the port "the most magnificent fake since Disneyland."

SHOPPING

Although better stocked than the norm, **Choses,** quai Jean-Jaurès (☎ 04-94-97-03-44), is a women's clothing store typical of the hundreds of middle-bracket, whimsically nonchalant emporiums that thrive throughout the Riviera. Its specialty includes clingy and often provocative T-shirt dresses. It's open only mid-Mar to mid-Nov July–Aug daily 10am–11pm; the rest of the season, daily 10am to between 6 and 9pm, depending on the whim of the owner. **Galeries Tropéziennes,** 56 rue Gambetta (☎ 04-94-97-02-21), crowds hundreds of unusual gift items, some worthwhile, some rather silly, and textiles into its rambling showrooms near place des Lices. The inspiration is Mediterranean, breezy and sophisticated. It's open Mon–Sat 9:30am–12:30pm and 3:30–7:30pm and Sun 10:30am–12:30pm and 3:30–7:30pm.

In a resort that's increasingly loaded with purveyors of suntan lotion, touristy souvenirs, and T-shirts, **Jacqueline Thienot,** 12 rue Georges-Clemenceau (☎ 04-94-97-05-70), maintains an inventory of Provençal antiques that is prized by dealers from as far away as Paris. The three-room shop is housed in a late 18th-century building that shows the 18th- and 19th-century antiques to their best advantage. Also inventoried are antique examples of Provençal wrought iron and rustic farm and homemaker's implements. Open May–Sept daily 10:30am–1pm and 4–8pm; Oct–Apr daily 10am–noon and 3–7pm.

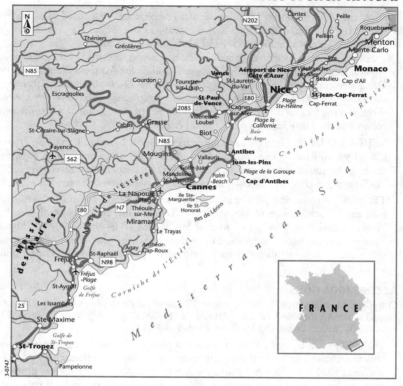

ENJOYING THE OUTDOORS

BEACHES   The best Riviera beaches are at St-Tropez. The best for families are those closest to the center, including the amusingly named **Bouillabaisse** and **Plage des Greniers.** The more daring beaches are the 6-mile sandy crescents at **Les Salins** and **Pampellone,** begining some 2 miles from the town center and best reached by bike (below) if you're not driving. If you ever wanted to go topless or wear a daring bikini, this is the place.

BICYCLING   The largest and most solidly established outfitter for bikes and motorscooters is **Louis Mas,** 5 rue Josef-Quaranta (☎ **04-94-97-00-60**). Open Oct–Apr Mon–Sat 9am–7pm and Sun 9am–1pm and 5:30–7pm, it requires a deposit of 1,000F ($200; payable with AE, MC, or V), plus 48F ($9.60) per hour for a bike and 190–275F ($38–$55) per hour for a motorscooter, depending on its size.

BOATING   The well-recommended **Suncap Company,** 15 Quai de Suffren (☎ **04-94-97-11-23**), rents boats that range from 18 feet to 40 feet. The smallest can be rented to qualified sailors without a captain, whereas the larger ones come with a captain at the helm. Prices, per day, range from 3,000F ($600) to 13,800F ($2,760). From Apr–Oct, it's open daily 9am–10pm; the rest of the year, daily 9am–7pm.

GOLF   The nearest golf course, at the edge of Ste-Maxime, across the bay from St-Tropez, is the **Golf Club de Beauvallon,** bd. des Collines, Grimaud, 83120

Ste-Maxime (☎ **04-94-96-16-98**), a popular 12-hole course that added an additional 6 holes late in 1996. Known for a terrain that allows you to walk, rather than rent a cart, it charges between 280F ($56) and 320F ($64) for 18 holes.

Sprawling over a rocky, vertiginous landscape that requires a golf cart and a lot of physical labor is the Don Harradine–designed **Golf de Ste-Maxime-Plaza,** Route de Débarquement, B.P. 1, 83120 Ste-Maxime (☎ **04-94-49-26-60**). Built in 1991 with the four-star Plaza de Ste-Maxime, it welcomes nonguests; phone to reserve tee-off times. Greens fees for 18 holes are 280F ($56) per person; rental of a cart for two golfers and their equipment is 125F ($25) per 18 holes.

SCUBA DIVING　Head for **Les Plongeurs du Golfe,** Nouveau Port de St-Tropez (☎ **04-94-56-81-27**). Their boat, *L'Idéal,* offers first-timers a one-on-one *Baptême,* teaching the rudiments of scuba; it costs 200F ($40). Experienced divers pay 235F ($47) for a one-tank dive, all equipment included. Reservations are needed.

TENNIS　Anyone who phones in advance can use the eight courts (both artificial grass and "Quick," a form of concrete) at the **Tennis-Club de St-Tropez,** Route des Plages, in St-Tropez's industrial zone of St-Claude (☎ **04-94-97-80-76**). About ¹/₂ mile from the resort's center and open throughout the year, daily 10am–10pm, the courts rent for 100F ($20) per hour until 5pm and 120F ($24) per hour after 5pm.

ACCOMMODATIONS

✪ **Byblos.** Av. Paul-Signac, 83990 St-Tropez. ☎ **04-94-56-68-00.** Fax 04-94-56-68-01. 47 rms, 55 suites. A/C MINIBAR TV TEL. 1,740–2870F ($348–$574) double; from 2,960F ($592) suite. AE, DC, MC, V. Closed Oct 15–Easter. Parking 140F ($28).

The builder said he created "an anti-hotel, a place like home." That's true if your home resembles a palace in Beirut with salons decorated with Phoenician gold statues from 3000 B.C. On a hill above the harbor, this deluxe complex has intimate patios and courtyards. Every room is different. For example, one has a fireplace on a raised hearth, paneled blue-and-gold doors, and a bed recessed on a dais. Le Hameau contains 10 duplex apartments built around a small courtyard with an outdoor spa. Some rooms have balconies overlooking an inner courtyard; others open onto a terrace of flowers. You can dine by the pool at Les Arcades, enjoying Provençal food, or try an Italian restaurant offering an antipasti buffet, many pasta courses, and other typical fare.

Hôtel Ermitage. Av. Paul-Signac, 83990 St-Tropez. ☎ **04-94-97-52-33.** Fax 04-94-97-10-43. 26 rms. TEL. 590–990F ($118–$198) double. AE, DC, MC, V. Free parking.

Attractively isolated amid the rocky heights of St-Tropez, this hotel was built in the 19th century as a private villa. Today its red-tile roof and green shutters shelter a plush hideaway. A walled garden is illuminated at night, and a cozy corner bar near a woodburning fireplace takes the chill off blustery evenings. The rooms are pleasantly but simply furnished, and the staff can be charming. Breakfast is the only meal served.

La Ponche. 3 rue des Remparts, 83990 St-Tropez. ☎ **04-94-97-02-53.** Fax 04-94-97-78-61. 18 rms. A/C MINIBAR TV TEL. 700–2,200F ($140–$440) double. AE, MC, V. Closed Nov–Mar 15.

Overlooking the old fishing port, this has long been a cherished address, run by the same family for more than half a century. The hotel is filled with the original paintings of Jacques Cordier, which adds to the elegant atmosphere. Each room has been newly redecorated and is well equipped, opening onto views of the sea. The hotel restaurant is big on Provençal charm and cuisine and a sophisticated crowd can be found on its terrace almost any night in fair weather.

DINING

✪ **Bistrot des Lices.** 3 place des Lices. ☎ **04-94-97-29-00.** Reservations required in summer. Main courses 100–200F ($20–$40); fixed-price lunch 175F ($35); fixed-price dinner 280–430F ($56–$86). AE, MC, V. Daily noon–2pm and 7:30pm–midnight. Closed 1 day midweek in winter and Jan–Feb. FRENCH.

This first-class restaurant boasts St-Tropez's most celebrated cuisine and a glamorous clientele. There's a glass-enclosed outdoor cafe, with a piano bar/cafe in the outer room. In summer, tables are placed in the rear garden. Chef Laurent Tarridec features a menu filled with Provençal flavor. He's known for his creative use of local produce in its prime. Aïoli, the garlicky mayonnaise of Provence, is delectable with certain fresh fish, like John Dory. The classic ratatouille appears with oven-roasted turbot. Even young rabbit is sometimes offered with fresh herbs.

L'Echalotte. 35 rue Allard. ☎ **04-94-54-83-26.** Reservations recommended in summer. Main courses 60–110F ($12–$22); fixed-price menus 98–150F ($19.60–$30). AE, MC, V. Fri–Wed 12:30–2pm and 8–11:30pm. Closed Nov 15–Dec 15. FRENCH.

This charming restaurant, with a tiny garden and clean dining room, serves consistently good food for moderate prices. You can enjoy lunch on the veranda or dinner indoors. The tables may be difficult to get, especially in peak summer weeks. The cuisine is solidly bourgeois, including grilled veal kidneys, crayfish with drawn-butter sauce, and fillet of turbot with truffles. The major specialty is several kinds of fish, like sea bass and daurade royale cooked in a salt crust.

ST-TROPEZ AFTER DARK

On the lobby level of the hyperexpensive, hyperelegant Hôtel Byblos, **Les Caves du Roi**, av. Paul-Signac (☎ **04-94-58-68-00**), is the most prestigious and most self-consciously chic nightclub in St-Tropez. It's the kind of place where, if Aristotle Onassis were still alive and roving, he'd camp out with a cellular phone for late-night trysts. Entrance is free, but the price of drinks begins at 140F ($28). Open May–Oct daily 11:30pm–5 or 6am, depending on the crowd.

Le Papagayo, in the Residence du Nouveau Port, rue Gambetta (☎ **04-94-97-07-56**), is one of the largest nightclubs in St-Tropez, with two floors, three bars, and lots of attractive women and men from throughout the Mediterranean eager to pursue their bait. The decor was inspired by the psychedelic 1960s in an urban setting like New York. Entrance costs 90F ($18) and includes the first drink. Between April and October, it's open nightly 11:30pm to around 6am; the rest of the year, it's open Fri–Sun 11:30pm–6am.

Le Pigeonnier, 13 rue de la Ponche (☎ **04-94-97-36-85**), rocks, rolls, and welcomes a clientele that's 80% to 85% gay, male, and aged 20 to 50. Most of the socializing revolves around the long and narrow bar, where drinks cost 70F ($14) and where menfolk from all over Europe seem to enjoy chitchatting. There's also a dance floor. Entrance costs 70F ($14) and includes your first drink. Other than a reopening for a brief sojourn at Christmas and New Year's, the place is open only Apr–Oct, every night from 11:45pm to sometime between 6 and 8am, depending on the energy of the crowd.

CANNES

When Coco Chanel went here and got a suntan, returning to Paris bronzed, she startled the ladies of society. But they quickly began copying her. Today the bronzed bodies—in nearly nonexistent swimsuits—still line the sandy beaches of this chic resort.

Popular with celebrities, Cannes is at its most frenzied during the **International Film Festival** at the Palais des Festivals on promenade de la Croisette, held in either April or May. On the seafront boulevards flashbulbs pop as the stars emerge. International regattas, galas, *concours d'élégance,* even a Mimosa Festival in February—something is always happening at Cannes, except in November, traditionally a dead month.

Sixteen miles southwest of Nice, Cannes is sheltered by hills. For many it consists of only one street, **promenade de la Croisette** (or just La Croisette), curving along the coast and split by islands of palms and flowers.

A port of call for cruise liners, the seafront of Cannes is lined with hotels, apartment houses, and chic boutiques. Many of the bigger hotels, some dating from the 19th century, claim part of the beaches for the private use of their guests. But there are also public areas.

ESSENTIALS

ARRIVING   Cannes lies on the major coastal rail line along the Riviera, with trains arriving frequently throughout the day. From Antibes to Cannes by rail takes only 15 minutes, or 35 minutes from Nice. The TGV from Paris going via Marseille also services Cannes. Buses pick up passengers at the Nice airport every 40 minutes during the day, delivering them to Cannes, and service is also available from Antibes with one bus every half-hour. The international airport at Nice is only 20 minutes northeast.

VISITOR INFORMATION   The **Office de Tourisme** is on esplanade du Président-Georges-Pompidou (☎ **04-93-39-24-53**).

DEPARTING BY CAR   From Cannes, N-7 heads directly east to the resort of Juan-les-Pins, a distance of 6 miles.

EXPLORING CANNES

Above the harbor, the old town of Cannes sits on Suquet Hill, where you'll see a 14th-century tower, which the English dubbed the **Lord's Tower.**

Nearby is the **Musée de la Castre,** in the Château de la Castre, Le Suquet (☎ **04-93-38-55-26**), containing fine arts, with a section on ethnography. The latter includes relics and objects from everywhere from the Pacific islands to Southeast Asia, including both Peruvian and Mayan pottery. There's also a gallery devoted to relics of ancient Mediterranean civilizations. Five rooms are devoted to 19th-century paintings. The museum is open Apr–June Wed–Mon 10am–noon and 2–6pm, July–Sept Wed–Mon 10am–noon and 3–7pm, and Oct–Mar Wed–Mon 10am–noon and 2–5pm. Admission is 10F ($2), free for children.

Another museum of note, the **Musée de la Mer,** Fort Royal (☎ **04-93-38-55-26**), displays artifacts from Ligurian, Roman, and Arab civilizations, including paintings, mosaics, and ceramics. You can also see the jail where the "Man in the Iron Mask" was incarcerated. Temporary exhibitions of photography are also shown. Open June–Sept daily 10am–noon and 2–6pm. Admission is 10F ($2).

SHOPPING

By the standards of virtually every well-dressed woman in Cannes, **Alexandra,** Rond Point Duboys-d'Angers (☎ **04-93-38-41-29**), behind the Noga Hilton, is loaded with upscale designs, in the words of the owners, *"pour la ville, le soir, et les cérémonies."* Prices begin at 4,000F ($800) and include garments by Mori, Givenchy,

Rochas, Lacroix, and Montana. Open Mon–Sat 9:30am–12:30pm and 2:30–7pm. In July–Aug, it's also open Sun 10am–1pm and 3–7:30pm.

Richly stocked with books and periodicals from virtually every English-speaking country in the world, **Cannes English Bookshop,** 11 rue Bivouac Napoléon (☎ **04-93-99-40-08**), near the main post office, has attracted readers since 1984. The shop is open Mon–Sat 9:30am–7pm; in midwinter or whenever business is slow, the well-mannered and congenial staff might close the shop between 1 and 2pm.

Cannolive, 16–20 rue Vénizelos (☎ **04-93-39-08-19**), a distinctive and charmingly old-fashioned shop, is owned by the Raynaud family, who founded the place in 1880. It sells Provençal olives and all of their by-products—purées (*tapenades*) that connoisseurs refer to as "Provençal caviar," black "olives de Nice," and green "olives de Provence," as well as three grades of olive oil from several regional producers. Oils and food products are dispensed from no. 16, but gift items (fabrics, porcelain, and Provençal souvenirs) are sold next door. Open Tues–Sat 9am–noon and 2:30–7pm; closed the last 2 weeks of Aug.

Maiffret, 31 rue d'Antibes (☎ **04-93-39-08-29**), specializes in chocolates and candied fruit, made by culinary processes that must be seen to be fully appreciated. Pâtés and confits of fruit, some of which decorate cakes and tarts, are also sold as desirable confections in their own right. Look for the Provençal national confection, *calissons,* crafted from almonds, a confit of melon, and sugar. It's open Mon–Sat 9:15am–7:30pm and Sun 9:15am–12:30pm and 3:30–7:30pm. During July–Aug, hours are daily 9:15am–10pm. Tours of the kitchens are available Tues–Sat 2–4pm.

ENJOYING THE OUTDOORS

BEACHES The best beach is **Plage du Midi,** west of the old harborfront, with the best sun in the afternoon. **Plage Gazagnaire,** another good beach, is east of the new port, ideal in the morning. Between these two public beaches are many private ones where you can gain entrance by paying a fee that includes a mattress and sun umbrella. Waiters at these private beach clubs come by to take your orders for lunch.

BICYCLING & MOTORSCOOTERING Despite the roaring traffic, the flat landscapes between Cannes and such satellite resorts as La Napoule are well suited for riding a bike or motorscooter. **Cannes Location Deux Roues,** 11 rue Hélène-Vagliano (☎ **04-93-39-46-15**), across from the Gray d'Albion, rents pedal bikes for 62F ($12.40) per day and requires a 1,000F ($200) deposit (payable with AE, MC, or V). Motorscooters rent for 165–200F ($33–$40) per day and require a deposit of 4,000–10,000F ($800–$2,000) per day, depending on their value. None of the motor-scooters rented here requires a driver's license or special permit. It's open May–Sept daily 9:30am–9:30pm.

BOATING **New Boat,** in an annex of the Hôtel Latitude, rue de la Laiterie (☎ **04-93-93-12-34**), is in Mandelieu, 4 miles west of Cannes. With a good reputation and a hardworking staff, it maintains a flotilla of powerboats and small yachts, ranging from 12 to 45 feet long. They rent, usually with a staff included for navigation and safety, for 3,500–15,000F ($700–$3,000) per day. It's open daily 9am–9:30pm.

GOLF The dry and rolling landscapes of Provence contribute to memorable golfing. One of the region's most challenging and interesting courses, **Country-Club de Cannes-Mougins,** 175 rte. d'Antibes, Mougins (☎ **04-93-75-79-13**), 4 miles north of Cannes, was a 1976 reconfiguration by Dye & Ellis of an outmoded, under-accessorized course laid out in the 1920s. Noted for olive trees and cypresses that adorn a relatively flat terrain, it has many water traps and a deceptively tricky layout loaded with technical challenges. It has a par of 72 and a much-envied role, since 1981, as host to the Cannes–Mougins Open, an important stop on the PGA European Tour. The course is open to anyone with proof of his or her handicap willing to pay greens fees of 340–380F ($68–$76), depending on the day of the week. An electric golf cart rents for 280F ($56), and golf clubs can be rented for 150F ($30) per set. Reservations are recommended.

SWIMMING   Most of the larger hotels in Cannes have their own pools. In addition to the tennis courts described below, the **Complexe Sportif Montfleury,** 23 av. Beauséjour (☎ 04-93-38-75-78), boasts a large modern pool that's about 100 feet long. Anyone who pays the entrance fee of 22F ($4.40) can spend the entire day lounging beside its borders. From April to mid-November, it's open Mon–Fri 10am–7pm and Sat–Sun 10am–7pm. The rest of the year, it's open daily 12:30–2pm and 4:30–6:45pm.

TENNIS   Its 10 tennis courts are one of the highlights of the **Complexe Sportif Montfleury,** 23 av. Beauséjour (☎ 04-93-38-75-78). You'll find eight hard-surfaced courts, at 70F ($14) per hour, and two clay-surfaced courts, at 90F ($18) per hour. The courts, as well as the complex, are open daily 8am–8pm.

ACCOMMODATIONS

Very Expensive

✪ **Hôtel Carlton Intercontinental.** 58 bd. de la Croisette, 06400 Cannes. ☎ **800/ 327-0200** in the U.S., or 04-93-06-40-06. Fax 04-93-06-40-25. 326 rms, 28 suites. A/C MINIBAR TV TEL. 1,400–3,690F ($280–$738) double; from 5,800F ($1,160) suite. AE, DC, MC, V. Parking 150F ($30). Bus: 11.

Shortly after it was built in 1912, the Carlton attracted the most prominent members of the *haut monde* of Europe, including members of royalty. They were followed decades later by the most important screen personalities. The guest rooms were renovated in 1990. Double-glazing, big combination baths with hair dryers, and luxurious appointments are part of the features. The most spacious rooms are in the west wing, and many of the upper-floor rooms open onto balconies fronting the sea. The Carlton Casino Club opened in 1989, and La Côte restaurant is one of the most distinguished along the Riviera. There's a private beach, health club with spa facilities, and a glass-roofed indoor pool.

Expensive

Hôtel Gray-d'Albion. 38 rue des Serbes, 06400 Cannes. ☎ **04-92-99-79-79.** Fax 04-93-99-26-10. 172 rms, 14 suites. A/C MINIBAR TV TEL. 960–1,650F ($192–$330) double; 3,700–6,200F ($740–$1,240) suite. AE, DC, MC, V. Bus: 1.

The smallest of the major hotels isn't on La Croisette, but this one contains pastel-colored rooms, each outfitted with all the luxury a modern hotel can offer—some critics consider the Gray-d'Albion among France's most luxurious hotels. Groups form a large part of its clientele, but it also caters to individuals. Rooms on the 8th and 9th floors have views of the Mediterranean. Dining selections include Le Royal Gray, one of Cannes' best, a beach-club restaurant, and a brasserie featuring special dishes from Lebanon.

Moderate

Hôtel le Fouquet's. 2 rond-point Duboys-d'Angers, 06400 Cannes. ☎ **04-93-38-75-81.** Fax 04-92-98-03-39. 10 rms. A/C MINIBAR TV TEL. 480–780F ($96–$156) double. AE, DC, MC, V. Closed Oct 30–Mar 20. Parking 50F ($10).

This is an intimate hotel drawing a discreet clientele, often from Paris, who'd never think of patronizing the grand palace hotels, even if they could afford them. Very

"Riviera French" in design and decor, it's several blocks from the beach. Each of the attractive, airy rooms is decorated in bold colors, containing a loggia, dressing room, and hair dryer. Most rooms are spacious. There's no restaurant.

Inexpensive

Hôtel de Provence. 9 rue Molière, 06400 Cannes. ☎ **04-93-38-44-35.** Fax 04-93-39-63-14. 30 rms. A/C MINIBAR TV TEL. 450–500F ($90–$100) double. AE, MC, V. Parking 35F ($7). Bus: 1.

In 1992 the rooms at this family-owned hotel were renovated into a comfortably uncluttered format. Most have private balconies and many overlook the garden. The hotel stands in its own walled garden of palms and flowering shrubs on a quiet inner street. In warm weather, breakfast is served under the vines and flowers of an arbor.

A Gay Hotel

Hôtel Les Charmettes. 47 rue de Grasse, 06400 Cannes. ☎ **04-93-39-17-13.** Fax 04-93-68-08-41. 260–350F ($52–$70) double. AE, DC, MC, V.

This is a modern, somewhat boxy three-story hotel near the center of Cannes, with a laissez-faire attitude. It welcomes a goodly number of gays. Each room is sound-proofed and individually decorated into a tasteful and pleasing style. Breakfast is the only meal served, though you can get drinks in the lobby.

DINING

Expensive

✪ **La Palme d'Or.** In the Hôtel Martinez, 73 bd. de la Croisette. ☎ **04-92-98-74-14.** Reservations required. Main courses 180–480F ($36–$96); fixed-price menus 295F ($59), 350F ($70), and 580F ($116). AE, DC, MC, V. Tues 7:30–10:30pm, Wed–Sun 12:30–2pm and 7:30–10:30pm. Closed Nov 20–Dec 20. Bus: 1. FRENCH.

When this hotel was renovated by the Taittinger family (of champagne fame), one of their primary concerns was to establish a restaurant that could rival the tough competition in Cannes. And they've succeeded. The result was a light wood–paneled, art deco marvel overlooking the pool and La Croisette. Alsatian-born chef Christian Willer has worked at some of France's greatest restaurants. Here his sublime special-ties include warm foie gras with fondue of rhubarb, nage of sole with Bellet wine, and salmon with caviar-cream sauce.

Moderate

Gaston-Gastounette. 7 quai St-Pierre. ☎ **04-93-39-49-44.** Reservations required. Main courses 130–200F ($26–$40); fixed-price lunches 125–168F ($25–$33.60); fixed-price dinner 199F ($39.80). AE, DC, MC, V. Daily noon–2pm and 7–11pm. Closed Dec 1–22 and Jan. Bus: 1. FRENCH.

This is the best restaurant to offer views of the marina. Located in the old port, it has a stucco exterior with oak moldings and big windows and a sidewalk terrace surrounded by flowers. Inside you'll be served bouillabaisse, breast of duckling in garlic-cream sauce, pot-au-feu de la mer (a stew of seafood), and such fish platters as turbot and sole.

La Mère Besson. 13 rue des Frères-Pradignac. ☎ **04-93-39-59-24.** Reservations required. Main courses 75–120F ($15–$24); fixed-price lunch 90F ($18); fixed-price dinners 140–170F ($28–$34). AE, DC, MC, V. Mon–Fri 12:15–2pm and 7:30–10:30pm, Sat 7:30–10:30pm (open Sun in summer). Bus: 1. FRENCH.

The culinary traditions of Mère Besson are carried on in one of Cannes' favorite res-taurants. All the specialties are prepared with consummate skill, especially the Provençal dishes featured daily. Most delectable is estouffade Provençal—beef braised with red wine and rich stock flavored with garlic, onions, herbs, and mushrooms. Every Wednesday you can order *lou piech,* a Niçoise name for veal brisket stuffed with white-stemmed vegetables, peas, ham, eggs, rice, grated cheese, and herbs. The meat is cooked in salted water with vinegar, carrots, and onions, then served with thick tomato coulis.

CANNES AFTER DARK

In the Carlton International, 50 bd. de la Croisette, is **Le Casino du Carlton** (☎ **04-93-68-00-33**). Considerably smaller than its major competitor (below), its modern decor nonetheless draws its share of devotees. Jackets are required for men, and a passport or government-issued identity card is required for admission. It's open daily 7:30pm–4am. Admission is 70F ($14).

The largest and most legendary casino in Cannes is the **Casino Croisette,** in the Palais des Festivals, 1 jetée Albert-Edouard, near promenade de la Croisette (☎ **04-93-38-12-11**). Within its glittering confines you'll find all the gaming tables you'd expect—open daily 5pm–4 or 5am—and one of the best nightclubs in town, **Le Jimmy's** (☎ **04-93-68-00-07**), outfitted in shades of red. Jimmy's is open Wed–Sun 11pm–dawn. You must present your passport to enter the gambling room. Admission is 100F ($20) and includes a drink.

Jane's is in the cellar of the Gray d'Albion, 38 rue des Serbes (☎ **04-92-99-79-79**). This is a stylish and appealing nightclub with an undercurrent of coy permissiveness. The crowd is well dressed (often with the men wearing jackets and ties) and from a wide gamut of age groups. The cover ranges from 50F ($10) to 100F ($20), depending on business, and on some slow nights women enter for free. Open Wed–Sun 11pm–5am.

Check out the action in the gay bar, **Le Vogue,** open Tues–Sun 7:30pm–2:30am.

JUAN-LES-PINS

This suburb of Antibes is a resort that was developed in the 1920s by Frank Jay Gould. At that time, people flocked to "John of the Pines" to escape the "crassness" of nearby Cannes. In the 1930s Juan-les-Pins drew a chic crowd during winter. Today Juan-les-Pins is often called a honky-tonk town or the "Coney Island of the Riviera," but anyone who calls it that hasn't seen Coney Island in a long time. One newspaper writer labeled it "a pop-art Monte Carlo, with burlesque shows and nude beaches"—a description much too provocative for such a middle-class resort.

The town offers some of the best nightlife on the Riviera, and the action reaches its frenzied height during the July jazz festival. Many revelers stay up all night in the smoky jazz joints, then sleep the next day on the beach. The **casino,** in the town center, offers cabaret entertainment, often until daybreak. During the day, skin-diving and waterskiing predominate. The pines sweep down to a good beach, crowded with summer sunbathers, most often in skimpy swimwear.

ESSENTIALS

ARRIVING   Juan-les-Pins is connected by rail and bus to most other coastal resorts. Frequent trains arrive from Nice throughout the day (trip time: 30 min.).

VISITOR INFORMATION   The **Office de Tourisme** is at 51 bd. Charles-Guillaumont (☎ **04-92-90-53-05**).

DEPARTING BY CAR   After Juan-les-Pins, ignore the "Direct to Antibes" signs and follow D-2559 around the cape. You'll come first to Cap d'Antibes before approaching the old city of Antibes itself.

ACCOMMODATIONS

Belles-Rives. Bd. Baudoin, 06160 Juan-les-Pins. ☎ **04-93-61-02-79.** Fax 04-93-67-43-51. 41 rms, 4 suites. A/C MINIBAR TV TEL. 980–2,350F ($196–$470) double; from 3,500F ($700) suite. Half board 380F ($76) per person extra. AE, MC, V. Closed Oct 8–Mar.

This is one of the fabled addresses on the Riviera. Once it was a holiday villa occupied by Zelda and F. Scott Fitzgerald and the scene of many a drunken brawl. In the following years it hosted the illustrious, like the duke and duchess of Windsor, Josephine Baker, and even Edith Piaf. A certain 1930s aura still lingers in the decor. The view of the sea that those celebrities enjoyed is still there to enchant. A major restoration began in 1988 but has slowed because of the economic downturn. The best accommodations are half a dozen sea-view rooms sparked up in 1990; some, however, remain a tad behind the times and are on the small scale. Double glazing and a new air-conditioning system help a lot. Also on the premises are a private beach and a landing dock.

✪ **Hôtel Juana.** La Pinède, av. Gallice, 06160 Juan-les-Pins. ☎ **04-93-61-08-70.** Fax 04-93-61-76-60. 45 rms, 5 suites. A/C TV TEL. 850–2,050F ($170–$410) double; from 1,800F ($360) suite. MC, V. Closed Nov–Mar.

This balconied art deco building, owned by the Barache family since 1931, is separated from the sea by the park of pines that gave Juan-les-Pins its name. The hotel has a private swimming club where guests can rent a "parasol and pad" on the sandy beach. It's constantly being refurbished, as reflected by the rooms, which are very attractive, with mahogany pieces, well-chosen fabrics, tasteful carpets, and large baths in marble or tile. The rooms also have such extras as safes and (in some) balconies. There's a bar in the poolhouse. Also on the premises are a private beach and a heated outdoor pool.

DINING

✪ **La Terrasse.** In the Hôtel Juana, La Pinède, av. Gallice. ☎ **04-93-61-20-37.** Reservations required. Main courses 250–400F ($50–$80); fixed-price lunch 260F ($52); fixed-price dinners 450–620F ($90–$124). AE, MC, V. July–Aug daily 12:30–2pm and 7:30–10:30pm; Apr–June and Sept–Oct Thurs–Tues 12:30–2pm and 7:30–10:30pm. Closed Nov–Mar. FRENCH.

Bill Cosby loves this gourmet restaurant so much that he's been known to fly chef Christian Morisset and his Dalí mustache to New York to prepare dinner for him. Morisset, who trained with Vergé and Lenôtre, cooks with a light, precise, and creative hand. His cuisine is the best in Juan-les-Pins. The ideal place to dine in summer is the terrace, among a lively, sophisticated crowd. The chef interprets traditional dishes and creates his own. Milk-fed veal, John Dory, and scampi-stuffed ravioli—all we've sampled has been delectable.

ANTIBES & CAP D'ANTIBES

On the other side of the Bay of Angels, 13 miles southwest of Nice, is the port of Antibes. This old Mediterranean town has a quiet charm, unusual for the Côte d'Azur. Its little harbor is filled with fishing boats, the marketplaces with flowers, mostly roses and carnations. If you're in Antibes in the evening, you can watch fishers playing the popular Riviera game of *boule*.

Spiritually, Antibes is totally divorced from Cap d'Antibes, a peninsula studded with the villas and pools of the *haut monde*. In *Tender Is the Night*, F. Scott Fitzgerald described it as a place where "old villas rotted like water lilies among the massed pines."

ESSENTIALS

ARRIVING Trains from Cannes arrive every 30 minutes (trip time: 16 min.), costing 16F ($3.20) one way, and trains from Nice arrive every 30 minutes (trip time: 18 min.), costing 22F ($4.40) one way.

VISITOR INFORMATION The **Office de Tourisme** is on place du Général-de-Gaulle (☎ **04-92-90-53-00**).

DEPARTING BY CAR After leaving Antibes, you can take an excursion to the most famous hill towns on the French Riviera: St-Paul-de-Vence and Vence. Follow N-7 to Cagnes-sur-Mer, where you can connect with D-36 heading first to St-Paul-de-Vence, then continuing north to Vence.

EXPLORING ANTIBES & CAP D'ANTIBES

On the ramparts above the port is the Château Grimaldi, place du Château, which contains the **Musée Picasso** (☎ **04-92-90-54-20**). Once the home of the princes of Antibes of the Grimaldi family, who ruled the city from 1385 to 1608, today it houses one of the greatest Picasso collections in the world. Picasso came to the small town after his bitter war years in Paris and stayed in a small hotel at Golfe-Juan until the museum director at Antibes invited him to work and live at the museum. Picasso then spent 1946 painting at the museum. When he departed he gave the museum all the work he'd done that year—two dozen paintings, nearly 80 pieces of ceramics, 44 drawings, 32 lithographs, 11 oils on paper, 2 sculptures, and 5 tapestries. In addition, a gallery of contemporary art exhibits Léger, Miró, Ernst, and Calder, among others. The museum is open July–Sept Tues–Sun 10am–noon and 2–6pm; Oct–June Tues–Sun 10am–noon and 2–5pm. Admission is 20F ($4) for adults and 10F ($2) for those 15–24 and over 60; 14 and under free.

Cap d'Antibes has the **Musée Naval et Napoléonien,** Batterie du Grillon, boulevard J-F-Kennedy (☎ **04-93-61-45-32**). This ancient military tower contains an interesting collection of Napoleonic memorabilia, naval models, paintings, and mementos. Open Mon–Fri 9:30am–noon and 2:15–6pm and Sat 9:30am–noon. Admission is 15F ($3) for adults and 7F ($1.40) for children 9 and under.

ACCOMMODATIONS

⑤ Auberge de la Gardiole. Chemin de la Garoupe, 06600 Cap d'Antibes. ☎ **04-93-61-35-03.** Fax 04-93-67-61-87. 21 rms. MINIBAR TV TEL. 420–640F ($84–$128) per person. Rates include half board. AE, DC, MC, V. Closed Nov–Feb. Bus: A2.

M. and Mme Courtot run this country inn with a delightful personal touch. The large villa, surrounded by gardens and pergola, is in an area of private estates. The charming rooms, on the upper floors of the inn and in the little buildings in the garden, contain personal safes; 15 are air-conditioned. The cuisine is French/Provençal. The cheerful dining room has a fireplace and hanging pots and pans, and in good weather you can dine under a wisteria-covered trellis.

✪ Hôtel du Cap–Eden Roc. Bd. J-F-Kennedy, 06601 Cap d'Antibes. ☎ **04-93-61-39-01.** Fax 04-93-67-76-04. 130 rms, 10 suites. A/C TEL. 2,050–3,000F ($410–$600) double; from 4,000F ($800) suite. No credit cards. Closed mid-Oct to mid-Apr. Free parking. Bus: A2.

This Second Empire hotel, opened in 1870, is surrounded by 22 splendid acres of gardens. It's like a great country estate, with spacious public rooms, marble fireplaces, scenic paneling, chandeliers, and clusters of richly upholstered armchairs. Some rooms and suites have regal period furnishings. The staff is famed for its snobbery. The world-famous Pavillon Eden Roc, near a rock garden apart from the hotel, has a panoramic Mediterranean view.

DINING

La Bonne Auberge. Quartier de Brague, route N7. ☎ **04-93-33-36-65.** Reservations required. Fixed-price menu 188F ($37.60). MC, V. May–Sept daily noon–2pm and 7–10:30pm; Oct–Nov 14 and Dec 16–Apr Tues–Sun noon–2pm and 7–10:30pm. Closed end of Oct–Dec 5. Take the coastal highway (N-7) 2^1/$_2$ miles from Antibes. FRENCH.

For many years following its 1975 opening, this was one of the most famous restaurants on the French Riviera. In 1992, following the death of its famous founder, Jo Rostang, his culinary heir Philippe Rostang wisely limited its scope and transformed it into a worthwhile but less ambitious restaurant. The fixed-price menu offers a wide selection. Choices vary but may include Basque-inspired pipérade with poached eggs, savory swordfish tart, chicken with vinegar and garlic, and perch-pike dumplings Jo Rostang. Dessert might be an enchanting peach soufflé.

✪ **Restaurant de Bacon.** Bd. de Bacon. ☎ **04-93-61-50-02.** Reservations required. Fixed-price menus 250–400F ($50–$80). AE, DC, MC, V. Tues–Sun 12:30–2pm and 8–10pm (open Mon lunch in July–Aug). Closed Nov–Feb 1. SEAFOOD.

Bouillabaisse aficionados claim that Bacon's offers France's best version. This fish stew, conceived as a simple fisher's supper, is now one of the world's great dishes. In its deluxe version, saltwater crayfish float atop the savory brew; we prefer the simple version—a waiter adds the finishing touches at your table. You can also try a fish soup with the traditional garlic-laden rouille sauce, fish terrine, sea bass, John Dory, or something from an exotic collection of fish unknown in North America. These include sar, pageot, and denti, prepared in several ways.

ST-PAUL-DE-VENCE & VENCE

Of all the perched villages of the Riviera, St-Paul-de-Vence is the best known, 17 miles east of Cannes and 19 miles north of Nice. It was popularized in the 1920s when many noted artists lived here, occupying the 16th-century houses flanking the narrow cobblestone streets. The feudal hamlet grew up on a bastion of rock, almost blending into it. Its ramparts (allow about 30 minutes to encircle them) overlook a peaceful setting of flowers and olive and orange trees. As you make your way through the warren of streets, you'll pass endless souvenir shops, a charming old fountain carved in the form of an urn, and a 13th-century Gothic church.

ESSENTIALS

ARRIVING Some 20 buses per day leave from Nice's *gare routière*, taking 55 minutes.

VISITOR INFORMATION The **Office de Tourisme** is at Maison Tour, rue Grande (☎ **04-93-32-86-95**).

DEPARTING BY CAR To Nice, take the N202 south to the junction with the N7; follow the N7 east to Nice.

EXPLORING ST-PAUL-DE VENCE & VENCE

The ✪ **Fondation Maeght** (☎ **04-93-32-81-63**) is one of the most modern art museums in Europe. On a hill in pine-studded woods, the Maeght Foundation is like a Shangri-la. Not only is the architecture avant-garde but the building houses one of the finest collections of contemporary art on the Riviera. Nature and human creations blend harmoniously in this unique achievement of architect José Luís Sert. Its white concrete arcs give the impression of a giant pagoda.

A stark Calder rises like some futuristic monster on the grassy lawns. In a courtyard, the elongated bronze works of Giacometti form a surrealistic garden, creating a hallucinatory mood. Sculpture is also displayed inside, but it's at its best in a natural setting of surrounding terraces and gardens.

There is a library, a cinema, and a cafeteria here. In one showroom original lithographs by artists like Chagall and Giacometti and limited-edition prints are for sale. Admission is 40F ($8) for adults and 30F ($6) for children. It's open daily July–Sept 10am–7pm and Oct–June 10am–12:30pm and 2:30–6pm.

North of St-Paul, you can visit the sleepy old town of Vence, with its **Vieille Ville** (Old Town). If you're wearing the right kind of shoes, the narrow, steep streets are worth exploring. The cathedral on place Godeau is unremarkable except for some 15th-century choir stalls. But if it's the right day of the week, most visitors quickly pass through the narrow gates of this once-fortified walled town to where the sun shines more brightly.

It was a beautiful golden autumn along the Côte d'Azur. The great Henri Matisse was 77, and after a turbulent time of introspection, he set out to create his masterpiece, the ✪ **Chapelle du Rosaire**—in his own words, "the culmination of a whole life dedicated to the search for truth." Just outside Vence, on avenue Henri-Matisse (☎ 04-93-58-03-26), you might pass by the chapel of the Dominican nuns of Monteils, finding it unremarkable—until you spot a 40-foot crescent-adorned cross rising from a blue-tile roof.

The light inside picks up the subtle coloring in the simply rendered leaf forms and abstract patterns—sapphire blue, aquamarine, and lemon yellow. In black-and-white ceramics, St. Dominic is depicted in a few lines. The Stations of the Cross are also black-and-white tile, with Matisse's self-styled "tormented and passionate" figures. The bishop of Nice himself came to bless the chapel in the late spring of 1951 when the artist's work was completed. Matisse died 3 years later. The chapel is open Dec 13–Oct Tues and Thurs 10–11:30am and 2:30–5:30pm. Admission is 5F ($1); donations are welcomed.

NICE

The Victorian upper class and tsarist aristocrats loved Nice in the 19th century, but it's solidly middle class today. Of all the major resorts, from Deauville to Biarritz to Cannes, Nice is the least expensive. It's also the best excursion center on the Riviera, especially if you're dependent on public transportation. For example, you can go to San Remo, "the queen of the Italian Riviera," returning to Nice by nightfall. From the Nice airport, the second largest in France, you can travel by bus along the entire coast to resorts like Juan-les-Pins and Cannes, the latter only 20 miles to the west.

Nice is the capital of the Riviera, the largest city between Genoa and Marseille (also one of the most ancient, having been founded by the Greeks, who called it Nike, or Victory). Because of its brilliant sunshine and relaxed living, Nice has attracted artists and writers, among them Matisse, Dumas, Nietzsche, Apollinaire, Flaubert, Hugo, Stendhal, and Mistral.

ESSENTIALS

ARRIVING   Visitors who arrive at **Aéroport Nice–Côte d'Azur** (☎ 04-93-21-30-30) can take an airport bus departing every 20 minutes to the Station Centrale in the city center. Buses run 6am–10:30pm and cost 8F ($1.60). For 25F ($5) you can take a *navette* (airport shuttle) that goes several times a day from the train station or airport. A taxi ride into the city center will cost at least 180F ($36). Trains arrive at **Gare Nice-Ville,** avenue Thiers (☎ 04-93-87-50-50). From here you can take frequent trains to Cannes, Monaco, and Antibes, among other destinations.

VISITOR INFORMATION   The **Office de Tourisme** is on avenue Thiers, at the Station Centrale (☎ **04-93-87-07-07**), near place Masséna. This office will make you a hotel reservation; the fee depends on the classification of the hotel. You can rent bicycles and mopeds at **Nicea Rent,** 9 av. Thiers (☎ **04-93-82-42-71**), near the Station Centrale. Mar–Oct, it's open daily; Nov–April, Mon–Sat 9am–noon and 2–6pm. The cost begins at 120F ($24) per day, plus a 1,500F ($300) deposit.

DEPARTING BY CAR   Leaving Nice, drive east along the Corniche Inférieure (the ancient via Aurelia) until reaching Villefranche; turn right onto D-25, which takes you in a very short distance to the wooded peninsula of St-Jean-Cap-Ferrat, 6 miles east of Nice.

EXPLORING NICE

The wide **boulevard des Anglais** fronts the bay. Split by "islands" of palms and flowers, it stretches for about 4 miles. Fronting the beach are rows of grand cafes, the Musée Masséna, villas, and hotels—some good, others decaying.

Crossing this boulevard in the briefest of bikinis or thongs are some of the world's most attractive people. They're heading for the beach—"on the rocks," as it's called here. Tough on tender feet, the beach is shingled, one of the least attractive (and least publicized) aspects of the cosmopolitan resort. Many bathhouses provide mattresses for a charge.

In the east, the promenade becomes **quai des Etats-Unis,** the original boulevard, lined with some of the best restaurants in Nice, each specializing in bouillabaisse. Rising sharply on a rock is the **château,** the spot where the ducs de Savoie built their castle, which was torn down in 1706. The steep hill has been turned into a garden of pines and exotic flowers. To reach the château, you can take an elevator; actually, many prefer to take the elevator up, then walk down. The park is open daily 8am–7:30pm.

The center of Nice is **place Masséna,** with pink buildings in the 17th-century Genoese style and the **Fontaine du Soleil (Fountain of the Sun)** by Janoit. Stretching from the main square to the promenade is the **Jardin Albert-Ier,** with an open-air terrace and a Triton Fountain. With palms and exotic flowers, it's the most relaxing oasis at the resort.

The ✪ **Musée des Beaux-Arts,** 33 av. des Baumettes (☎ **04-93-44-50-72**), is housed in the former residence of Ukrainian Princess Kotchubey. It has an important gallery devoted to the masters of the Second Empire and belle époque, with an extensive collection of the 19th-century French experts. The gallery of sculptures includes works by J. B. Carpeaux, Rude, and Rodin. Note the important collection by a dynasty of painters, the Dutch Vanloo family. A fine collection of 19th- and 20th-century art is displayed, including works by Ziem, Raffaelli, Boudin, Renoir, Monet, Guillaumin, and Sisley. The museum is open Tues–Sun May–Sept 10am–noon and 3–6pm and Oct–Apr 10am–noon and 2–5pm. Admission is 25F ($5) for adults and 15F ($3) for children. Take bus no. 9, 12, 22, 23, or 38.

The fabulous villa housing the **Musée Masséna,** 65 rue de France (☎ **04-93-88-11-34**), was built in 1900 in the style of the First Empire as a residence for Victor Masséna, the prince of Essling and grandson of Napoléon's marshal. The city of Nice has converted the villa, next door to the Négresco, into a museum of local history and decorative art. A remarkably opulent drawing room, with mahogany-veneer pieces and ormolu mounts, is on the ground floor. The museum is open Tues–Sun in May–Sept 10am–noon and 3–6pm and in Oct–Apr 10am–noon and 2–5pm; closed holidays. Admission is 25F ($5) for adults, 15F ($3) for children, or free one Sunday per month. Take bus no. 3, 7, 8, 9, 10, 12, 14, or 22.

EXPLORING NEARBY CIMIEZ   Founded by the Romans, who called it Cemenelum, Cimiez, a hilltop suburb, was the capital of the Maritime Alps province. To reach this suburb, take bus no. 15 or 17 from place Masséna.

The **Monastère de Cimiez** (Cimiez Convent), place du Monastère (☎ 04-93-81-55-41), embraces a church that owns three of the most important works from the primitive painting school of Nice by the Brea brothers. See the carved and gilded wooden main altarpiece. In a restored part of the convent where some Franciscan friars still live, the **Musée Franciscain** is decorated with 17th-century frescoes. Some 350 documents and works of art from the 15th to the 18th century are displayed, and a monk's cell has been re-created. See also the 17th-century chapel. In the gardens you can get a panoramic view of Nice and the Bay of Angels. Matisse and Dufy are buried in the cemetery. The museum is open Mon–Sat 10am–noon and 3–6pm; the church is open daily 8am–12:30pm and 2–7pm.

The **Musée Matisse,** in the Villa des Arènes-de-Cimiez, 164 av. des Arènes-de-Cimiez (☎ 04-93-81-08-08), honors the great artist who spent the last years of his life in Nice; he died here in 1954. The museum has several permanent collections, many donated by Matisse and his heirs. These include *Nude in an Armchair with a Green Plant* (1937), *Nymph in the Forest* (1935/1942), and a chronologically arranged series of paintings from 1890 to 1919. The most famous of these is *Portrait of Madame Matisse* (1905), usually displayed near another portrait of the artist's wife, by Marquet, painted in 1900. The museum is open Wed–Mon Apr–Sept 11am–7pm and Oct–Mar 10am–5pm. Admission is 25F ($5) for adults and 15F ($3) for children.

SHOPPING

Since 1925, **Allées de la Côte d'Azur,** 1 rue St-François-de-Paul (☎ 04-93-85-87-30), has sold food products inspired by the bounty of Provence. Near La Mairie (Town Hall) in the old town, it specializes in anything concocted from a fig, including fig sausages, fig loafs, fresh figs, and fig liqueur. Equally tempting are tinned or glass-encased *tapenades* concocted from pulverized black olives, various types of basil and herbs from the foothills of the Alps, perfumes, dried lavender, and gift items carved from olivewood. Open Mon–Sat 8am–7pm and Sun 8am–1pm.

Established in 1949 by the grandfather (Joseph Fuchs) of the present English-speaking owners, the **Confiserie du Vieux-Nice,** 14 quai Papacino (☎ 04-93-45-43-50), is near the historic center's Old Port. The specialty is glazed fruits crystallized in sugar or artfully arranged into chocolates. Look for exotic jams (rose-petal preserves or mandarin marmalade) and the free recipe leaflet as well as candied violets, verbena leaves, and rosebuds. Prices run from 15F ($3) to 600F ($120) for a large gift basket. Open daily 9am–noon and 2–6:30pm.

Façonnable, 7–9 rue Paradis (☎ 04-93-87-88-80), is the site that sparked the creation of what is today several hundred Façonnable menswear stores around the world. This is one of the largest Façonnable stores, with a wide range of men's suits, raincoats, overcoats, sportswear, and jeans. The look is youthful and conservatively stylish, for relatively slim (French) bodies. From May–Sept, it's open Mon–Sat 10am–8pm; from Oct–Apr, it's open 10am–7pm.

If you're thinking of indulging in a Provençal *pique-nique,* **Nicola Alziari,** 14 rue St-François de Paule (☎ 04-93-85-77-98), will provide everything you'll need: from olives, anchovies, and pistous to aïolis and tapenades. It's one of the oldest stores of its kind in Nice. The house brand comes in two strengths, a light version that aficionados claim is vaguely perfumed with Provence and a stronger version well suited to the earthy flavors and robust ingredients of a Provençal winter. Also look for a range of objects crafted from olive wood. Open Tues–Sat 8:15am–12:30pm and 2:15–7:15pm.

ENJOYING THE OUTDOORS

GOLF   The oldest golf course on the Riviera is about 10 miles from Nice: **Golf Bastide du Roi** (also known as the Golf de Biot), avenue Jules-Grec, Biot (☎ **04-93-65-08-48**). This is a flat, not particularly challenging, and much-used sea-fronting course. (Regrettably, it's necessary to cross over a highway midway through the course to complete the full 18 holes.) Open daily throughout the year, tee-off times begin at 8am, continue until 6pm, with the understanding that players then continue their rounds as long as the daylight allows. Reservations aren't necessary, though on weekends you should expect a delay. Greens fees are 200F ($40) for 18 holes, and clubs can be rented for 50F ($10). No carts are available.

HORSEBACK RIDING   The only equestrian venue in the area, **Club Hippique de Nice,** 368 rte. de Grenoble (☎ **04-93-13-13-16**), contains about 40 horses, 13 of which are available for rentals. About 3 miles from Nice, near the airport, it's hemmed in on virtually every side by busy roads and highways and conducts all its activities in a series of riding rinks. Riding sessions should be reserved in advance, last about an hour, and cost 65F ($13).

SCUBA DIVING   The best-respected underwater outfit is the **Centre International de Plongée de Nice,** 2 Ruelle des Moulins (☎ **04-93-55-59-50**). Adjacent to the city's old port, midway between quai des Docks and boulevard Stalingrad, it's maintained by Champagne-born Raymond Lefevre, whose dive boat, *René-Madeleine,* is an amalgam of the names of his parents. A *Baptême* (initiatory dive for first-timers) costs 180F ($36) and a one-tank dive for experienced divers, with all equipment included, is 200F ($40).

TENNIS   The oldest tennis club in Nice is the **Nice Lawn Tennis Club,** Parc Impérial, 5 av. Suzanne-Lenglen (☎ **04-93-96-17-70**). Near the rail station, it's open daily 8:30am–9pm, and charges 120F ($24) per person for two noncontiguous hours of court time, or a reduced rate of 250F ($50) per person for unlimited access to the courts for a 1-week period. The club contains a cooperative staff, a loyal clientele, 13 clay courts, and 6 hard-surfaced courts. Reservations should be made the evening before.

ACCOMMODATIONS

Very Expensive

✪ **Hôtel Négresco.** 37 promenade des Anglais, 06007 Nice CEDEX. ☎ **04-93-16-64-00.** Fax 04-93-88-35-68. 132 rms, 18 suites. A/C MINIBAR TV TEL. 1,300–2,350F ($260–$470) double; from 3,950F ($790) suite. AE, DC, MC, V. Parking 160F ($32). Bus: 8.

The Négresco is one of the many superglamorous hotels along the French Riviera. This Victorian wedding-cake hotel is named after founder Henry Négresco, a Romanian, who died franc-less in Paris in 1920. It was built on the seafront, in the French château style, with a mansard roof and domed tower, and its interior design was inspired by the country's châteaux and museums. The guest rooms contain antiques, tapestries, paintings, and art. Some rooms have personality themes, like the Louis XIV chamber, which has a green-velvet bed under a brocaded rose canopy. The most expensive rooms have balconies and face the Mediterranean. The staff wears 18th-century costumes. Less expensive meals are served in La Rotonde, though the featured restaurant—one of the greatest on the Riviera—is Chantecler (See "Dining," below).

Expensive

Abela Regency Hôtel. 223 promenade des Anglais, 06200 Nice. ☎ **04-93-37-17-17.** Fax 04-93-71-21-71. 321 rms, 12 suites. A/C MINIBAR TV TEL. 820–1,200F ($164–$240) double; from 1,450F ($290) suite. AE, DC, MC, V. Parking 100F ($20). Bus: 8.

Alongside the major beachside thoroughfare, this streamlined contemporary hotel is one of the most alluring palaces in town, though nowhere near as grand as the Négresco. A discreet portico leads into the sun-flooded lobby. Most of the attractive guest rooms open onto the promenade des Anglais, with balconies fronting the sea; they're filled with amenities. Les Mosaïques offers Mediterranean cuisine and Lebanese specialties.

Moderate

Busby. 36–38 rue du Maréchal-Joffre, 06000 Nice. ☎ **04-93-88-19-41.** Fax 04-93-87-73-53. 80 rms. A/C TV TEL. 500–700F ($100–$140) double. AE, DC, MC, V. Closed Nov 15–Dec 20. Bus: 9, 10, 12, or 22.

This place should please you if you want an elegant central hotel that has all the modern amenities. Totally renovated and air-conditioned, the hotel has kept its old Niçois facade, with balconies and shutters at the tall windows. The guest rooms are dignified yet colorful, and some contain pairs of mahogany twin beds and two white-and-gold wardrobes. The bar is cozy, and the long dining room has marble columns, mirrors, and ladderback chairs. The restaurant is open from Dec 20 to May.

Grand Hôtel Aston. 12 av. Félix-Faure, 06000 Nice. ☎ **04-93-80-62-52.** Fax 04-93-80-00-30. 156 rms. 600–1,100F ($120–$220) double. AE, DC, MC, V. Parking 90F ($18).

One of the most alluring in its price bracket, this elegantly detailed 19th-century hotel has been radically renovated. Most rooms overlook the splashing fountains of the city's showcase, the Espace Masséna, a few blocks from the water. The rooftop garden offers dance music and a bar on summer evenings and has a panoramic coastline view.

Inexpensive

⑤ Hôtel Villa Eden. 99 bis promenade des Anglais, 06000 Nice. ☎ **04-93-86-53-70.** Fax 04-93-97-67-97. 15 rms. A/C TV TEL. 170–360F ($34–$72) double. AE, DC, MC, V. Free parking. Bus: 9, 10, 12, 23, or 24.

In 1925, an exiled Russian countess built this art deco villa on the seafront, surrounded it with a wall, and planted a tiny garden. The villa still remains, despite the construction of much taller modern buildings on both sides. You can enjoy the ivy and roses in the garden and stay in old-fashioned partly modernized rooms whose sizes vary greatly. The owner maintains a wry sense of humor and greets guests at breakfast, the only meal served.

DINING

Expensive

✪ Chantecler. In the Hôtel Négresco, 37 promenade des Anglais. ☎ **04-93-16-64-00.** Reservations required. Main courses 190–250F ($38–$50); fixed-price menus 395–560F ($79–$112). AE, DC, MC, V. Daily 12:30–2:30pm and 7:30–10:30pm. Closed mid-Nov to mid-Dec. Bus: 8. FRENCH.

Of all France's great palace hotels, none has a chef to equal Dominique Le Stanc— this culinary genius merits high praise. Beautifully restored and redecorated, Chantecler is a delight. Monsieur Le Stanc's cuisine is excellent and attractively presented. To begin, try one of his specialties: ravioli stuffed with a small lobster, asparagus, and artichokes. He also does a "symphony" of truffles, scallops, potatoes, and leeks in a feathery-thin "potato hamburger," as one food critic called it.

Moderate

Chez Michel (Le Grand Pavois). 11 rue Meyerbeer. ☎ **04-93-88-77-42.** Reservations required. Main courses 120–190F ($24–$38); bouillabaisse 300–450F ($60–$90); fixed-price menus 195–250F ($39–$50). AE, DC, MC, V. Daily noon–2:30pm and 7–11pm. Bus: 8. SEAFOOD.

Chez Michel is nestled under an art deco apartment building near the water. One of the partners, Jacques Marquise, is from Golfe-Juan, where for 25 years he managed the famous fish restaurant Chez Tétou. His bouillabaisse has been widely celebrated. Other delectable specialties are baked sea bass in white wine, herbs, and lemon sauce and grilled flambé lobster.

Inexpensive

Ⓢ **La Nissarda.** 17 rue Gubernatis. ☎ **04-93-85-26-29.** Reservations recommended. Main courses 40–75F ($8–$15); fixed-price menus 78–138F ($15.60–$27.60). MC, V. Mon–Sat noon–2pm and 7–10pm. Closed Aug. NIÇOISE/NORMAN.

About a 10-minute walk from place Masséna, this restaurant is maintained by the Normandy-born Prunier family, who work hard to maintain the aura and some of the culinary traditions of Nice. In an intimate setting lined with old engravings and photographs of the city, the place serves local versions of ravioli, lasagne, spaghetti carbonara, and grilled salmon with herbs. A handful of Norman-based specialties also manage to creep onto the menu, like escalopes of veal with cream sauce and apples.

Ⓢ **Restaurant l'Estocaficada.** 2 rue de l'Hôtel-de-Ville. ☎ **04-93-80-21-64.** Reservations recommended. Main courses 50–95F ($10–$19); fixed-price menus 58–95F ($11.60–$19); pizzas 30–45F ($6–$9). AE, MC, V. Mon–Fri noon–2pm and 7–10pm, Sun 7–10pm. Bus: 1, 2, or 5. NIÇOISE.

Estocaficada is the Provençal word for stockfish, the ugliest fish in Europe. You can see one for yourself—there might be a dried-out, balloon-shaped version on display in the cozy dining room. Brigitte Autier is owner/chef, devoted to the preservation of recipes prepared by her Niçois grandmother. Examples include gnocchi, beignets, several types of farcies (tomatoes, peppers, or onions stuffed with herbed fillings), grilled sardines, or bouillabaisse served as a main course or in a miniversion. As a concession to popular demand, the place also serves pizzas and pastas.

NICE AFTER DARK

A quarterly booklet, *L'Infor,* available free at the tourist office, lists the city's cultural attractions. You can also pick up a copy of *La Semaine des Spectacles,* outlining the week's nighttime diversions.

The major cultural center along the Riviera is the **Opéra de Nice,** 4 rue St-François-de-Paule (☎ **04-92-17-40-44**), with a busy season in winter. A full repertoire is presented, including both operas and the popular French Opéra Comique. In one season you might see *La Bohème, Tristan und Isolde,* and *Carmen,* as well as a *saison symphonique,* dominated by the Orchestre Philharmonique de Nice. The opera hall is also the major venue for concerts and recitals. The box office is open Mon–Sat 10am–5:55pm. Tickets cost 80–300F ($16–$60).

Charming and cosmopolitan, the double-tiered **Piano Bar Louis XV/Disco Inferno,** 10 rue Cité du Parc (☎ **04-93-80-49-84**), contains a piano bar in its 200-year-old vaulted cellar and a modern disco on its street level. Most visitors begin in the piano bar, dancing on a small floor to rhythms produced by a Brazilian pianist who's sometimes accompanied by a small dance band. Audiences call out their favorite melody and musical style (bossa novas, merengues, or whatever) and the staff do their best to comply. Cover is 80F ($16), including the first drink. Open year-round Tues–Sun 11pm–5 or 6am.

Near the Hôtel Ambassador, **L'Ambassade,** 18 rue de Congrés (☎ 04-93-88-88-87), was deliberately designed in a mock-Gothic style that includes the wrought-iron accents you'd expect to find in a château, two bars, and a dance floor. At least 90% of its clients are straight, or at least profess to be, and come in all physical types and age ranges. Cover is 80F ($16), including the first drink. It's open Wed–Sat midnight–7am, with an additional opening on Sun night May–Sept.

Near the Négresco and the promenade des Anglais, **Le Blue Boy,** 9 rue Spinetta (☎ 04-93-44-68-24), is the oldest and most deeply entrenched gay disco on the Riviera. With two bars and two floors, it's a vital nocturnal stopover for passengers aboard the dozens of all-gay cruises (most of which are administered from Holland) that make regular stops at Nice and such nearby ports as Villefranche. Cover is 50F ($10) on Sat or 30F ($6) otherwise. It's open every night 11pm–6 or 7am.

ST-JEAN-CAP-FERRAT

This has been called Paradise Found. Of all the oases along the Côte d'Azur, no place has the snob appeal of Cap-Ferrat. It's a 9-mile promontory sprinkled with luxurious villas, outlined by sheltered bays, beaches, and coves. The vegetation is lush. In the port of St-Jean, the harbor accommodates yachts and fishing boats.

The Italianate **Musée Ile-de-France,** avenue Denis-Séméria (☎ 04-93-01-33-09), affords you a chance to visit one of the most legendary villas along the Côte d'Azur, built by the Baronne Ephrussi Rothschild. She died in 1934, leaving the building and its magnificent gardens to the Institut de France on behalf of the Académie des Beaux-Arts. The wealth of her collection is preserved: 18th-century furniture; Tiepolo ceilings; Savonnerie carpets; screens and panels from the Far East; tapestries from Gobelins, Aubusson, and Beauvais; original drawings by Fragonard; canvases by Renoir, Sisley, and Boucher; rare Sèvres porcelain; and more. Covering 12 acres, the gardens contain fragments of statuary from churches, monasteries, and torn-down palaces.

The museum and its gardens are open daily July–Aug 10am–7pm, Feb 15–June and Sept–Oct 10am–6pm, and Nov–Feb 14 from 2–6pm. Admission to the museum and gardens is 45F ($9) for adults and 30F ($6) for children.

ESSENTIALS

DEPARTING   From St-Jean-Cap-Ferrat, you can head east toward Monaco by taking D-25 along the coast to the resort of Beaulieu, which is almost as chic as Cap-Ferrat. Continue along N-98 for about 7 miles into Monaco.

ACCOMMODATIONS

✪ **Grand Hôtel du Cap-Ferrat.** Bd. du Général-de-Gaulle, 06290 St-Jean-Cap-Ferrat. ☎ 04-93-76-50-50. Fax 04-93-76-04-52. 59 rms, 11 suites. A/C MINIBAR TV TEL. 1,800–2,950F ($360–$590) double; from 6,000F ($1,200) suite. Rates include continental breakfast. AE, DC, MC, V. Free parking.

This turn-of-the-century palace is at the tip of the peninsula in the midst of a 14-acre garden of semitropical trees and manicured lawns. Parts of the exterior have open loggias and big arched windows, and guests enjoy the views from the elaborate flowering terrace over the sea. The guest rooms are conservatively modern with dressing rooms, and rates include admission to the pool, Club Dauphin. The hotel's indoor/outdoor restaurant serves *cuisine du marché,* based on market-fresh ingredients.

◎ **Hôtel Clair Logis.** 12 av. Centrale, 06230 St-Jean-Cap-Ferrat. ☎ 04-93-76-04-57. Fax 04-93-76-11-85. 18 rms. TEL. 370–680F ($74–$136) double. AE, DC, MC, V. Free parking. Closed Jan–Feb and Nov–Dec 15.

A rare find here, this hotel occupies what was a 19th-century villa surrounded by 2 acres of semitropical gardens. The pleasant rooms are scattered over three buildings in the confines of the garden. The hotel's most famous guest was General de Gaulle, who lived in a room called Strelitzias (Bird of Paradise) during many of his retreats from Paris. Each room is named after a flower. The most romantic and spacious accommodations are in the main building; the rooms in the annex are the most modern but have the least character.

DINING

✪ **Le Provençal.** 2 av. Denis-Séméria. ☎ **04-93-76-03-97.** Reservations required. Main courses 150–200F ($30–$40); fixed-price menu 560F ($112). MC, V. Apr–Sept Tues–Wed 7:30–9:30pm, Thurs–Mon noon–2:30pm and 7:30–9:30pm; Oct Tues–Sat noon–2:30pm and 7:30–9:30pm, Sun noon–2:30pm. Closed Nov–Mar. FRENCH.

In this Provence-inspired dining room high above the village, with a sweeping panorama, you can enjoy marinated artichoke hearts with half a lobster, John Dory roasted in fig leaves and served with fresh figs, roast pigeon with cinnamon, classic bourride Provençal, and a choice of five "petits desserts" that might be macaroons with chocolate or crème brûlée. The cooking seems more inspired than ever. The food is solemnly served, as if part of a grand ritual.

MONACO

Monaco—or rather its capital of Monte Carlo—has for a century been a symbol of glamor. Its legend was further enhanced by the 1956 marriage of the man who was at that time the world's most eligible bachelor, Prince Rainier III, to American actress Grace Kelly. Although not always happy in her role, Princess Grace soon won the respect and adoration of her people. The Monégasques still mourn her death in a 1982 car accident.

Monaco became a property of the Grimaldi clan, a Genoese family, as early as 1297. With shifting loyalties, it has maintained something resembling independence ever since. In a fit of impatience, the French annexed it in 1793, but the ruling family recovered it in 1814, though the prince at the time couldn't bear to tear himself away from the pleasures of Paris for "dreary old Monaco."

ESSENTIALS

ARRIVING Monaco has rail, bus, and highway connections from other coastal cities, especially Nice. Trains arrive every 30 minutes from Cannes, Nice, Menton, and Antibes. There are no border formalities for anyone entering Monaco from mainland France.

VISITOR INFORMATION The **Direction du Tourisme** is at 2A bd. des Moulins (☎ **92-16-61-16**).

EXPLORING MONACO

The second-smallest state in Europe (Vatican City is the tiniest), Monaco consists of four parts: The old town, **Monaco-Ville,** on a promontory, The Rock, 200 feet high, is the seat of the royal palace and the government building, as well as the Oceanographic Museum. To the west of the bay, **La Condamine,** the home of the Monégasques, is at the foot of the old town, forming its harbor and port sector. Up from the port (walking is steep in Monaco) is **Monte Carlo,** once the playground of European royalty and still the center for wintering wealthy, the setting for the casino and its gardens and the deluxe hotels. The fourth part, **Fontvieille,** is a neat industrial suburb.

Ironically, **Monte-Carlo Beach,** at the far frontier, is on French soil. It attracts a chic crowd, including movie stars in bikinis and thongs. The resort has a freshwater pool, an artificial beach, and a sea-bathing establishment.

The Italianate home of Monaco's royal family, the **Palais du Prince,** dominates the principality from "The Rock." When touring Les Grands Appartements du Palais, place du Palais (☎ **93-25-18-31**), you're shown the Throne Room and allowed to see some of the art collection, including works by Brueghel and Holbein, as well as Princess Grace's stunning state portrait. The palace was built in the 13th century and part of it is from the Renaissance. The ideal time to arrive is 11:55am to watch the 10-minute changing of the guard. The palace is open daily in June–Sept 9:30am–6:30pm and in Oct 10am–5pm. Admission is 30F ($6) for adults and 15F ($3) for children.

The **Jardin Exotique,** boulevard du Jardin-Exotique (☎ **93-30-33-65**), was built on the side of a rock and is known for its cactus collection. The gardens were begun by Prince Albert I, who was both a naturalist and a scientist. He spotted some succulents growing in the palace gardens, and knowing that these plants were normally found only in Central America or Africa, he created the garden from them. You can also explore the grottoes here, as well as the **Musée d'Anthropologie Préhistorique** (☎ **93-15-80-06**). The view of the principality is splendid. The site is open daily June–Sept 9am–7pm and Oct–May 9am–6pm. Admission is 36F ($7.20) for adults and 18F ($3.60) for children 6–18; 5 and under free.

The **Musée de l'Océanographie,** avenue St-Martin (☎ **93-15-36-00**), was founded by Albert I, great-grandfather of the present prince. In the main rotunda is a statue of Albert in his favorite costume—that of a sea captain. Displayed are specimens he collected during 30 years of expeditions aboard his oceanographic boats. The aquarium, one of the finest in Europe, contains more than 90 tanks. The Oceanography Museum is open daily July–Aug 9am–8pm; Apr–May and Sept 9am–7pm; Mar and Oct 9:30am–7pm; and Nov–Feb 10am–6pm. Admission is 60F ($12) for adults and 30F ($6) for children 6–18; 5 and under free.

SHOPPING

Rising costs and an increase in crime have changed women's tastes in jewelry, perhaps forever. **Bijoux Cascio,** Les Galeries du Metropole, 207 av. des Spélugues (☎ **93-50-17-57**), sells only imitation gemstones. They're rather shamelessly copied from the real McCoys sold by Cartier and Van Cleef & Arpels. Made in Italy of gold-plated silver, cubic zirconia, and glittering chunks of Austrian-made Swarovski crystal, the fake jewelry costs between 200F ($40) and 2,000F ($400) per piece, many thousands of francs less than what you might have paid for the authentic gems. Open Mon–Sat 10am–7:30pm.

The **Boutique du Rocher,** 1 av. de la Madone (☎ **93-30-91-17**), is the larger of two roughly equivalent boutiques opened in 1966 by Princess Grace as the official retail outlets of the charitable foundation that was established by the Grimaldis in her name. In a discreet way, the organization merchandizes Monégasque (and Provençal) handcrafts, with an emphasis on keeping the artisanal traditions of Monaco alive and thriving. A short walk from place du Casino, the shop sells carved frames for pictures or mirrors; housewares; gift items crafted from porcelain, textiles, and wood; children's toys; and dolls. On the premises are workshops where local artisans produce the goods you'll find for sale. Hours are Mon–Sat 9am–noon and 2:30–7pm.

Old River, 17 bd. des Moulins (☎ **93-50-33-85**), is a menswear store aiming at a solid middle-bracket market who simply want to dress appropriately and look good.

You can pick up a swimsuit, shorts, slacks, a blazer, and a pair of socks to replace the ones you ruined by too many walking tours, at prices that won't require that you remortgage your house. It's open Mon–Sat 9:30am–12:30pm and 2:30–7:30pm.

ENJOYING THE OUTDOORS

GOLF   The **Monte Carlo Golf Club,** Rte. N7, La Turbie (☎ **04-93-41-09-11**), is a par-72 golf course with ample amounts of prestige, scenic panoramas, and local history. Certain perks (including use of electric golf buggies) are reserved exclusively for members. Before they're allowed to play, nonmembers will be asked to show proof of membership in another golf club and provide evidence of their handicap ratings. Greens fees for 18 holes are 350F ($70) Mon–Fri and 450F ($90) Sat–Sun. Clubs can be rented for 120F ($24). The course is open daily 8am–sunset.

SWIMMING/BEACHES   Monaco, in its role as the quintessential kingdom by the sea, offers sea bathing at its most popular beach, **La Plage de Larvetto,** off avenue du Princesse-Grace (☎ **93-15-28-76**). There's no charge for bathing on this strip of beach, whose sands are frequently replenished with sand hauled in by barge. The beach is open to public access at all hours.

If a pool is more to your tastes, most of the large hotels in town boast pools, but the dowager empress, across the border in neighboring France, is **Le Monte Carlo Beach Club,** av. Princesse-Grace, Roquebrune–St-Roman (☎ **93-28-66-66**). Founded in 1929, it's one of the most evocative and envied beach, pool, and social clubs on the Riviera. Some privileges and perks are reserved for members, but nonmembers who pay 150F ($30) can use the facilities on a day pass. An additional 800F ($160) will get you a striped private cabana. Most of the socializing occurs around the edges of the Olympic-size pool. On the premises are bars and three restaurants. From April to October, windsurfing and waterskiing are popular diversions that are conducted from the stony beach of this club.

TENNIS & SQUASH   The **Monte Carlo Country Club,** av. Princesse-Grace, Roquebrune–St-Roman (☎ **93-41-30-15**), includes 23 tennis courts (21 clay and 2 concrete), but if that isn't enough, they lie within a cornucopia of other warm-weather distractions that could amuse virtually anyone for at least a week. Payment of the 215F ($43) entrance fee will provide access to a restaurant, a health club with Jacuzzi and sauna, a putting green, a beach, squash courts, and the above-mentioned roster of well-maintained tennis courts. Plan to spend at least a half-day, ending a round of tennis with use of any of the other facilities. It's open daily 8am–8 or 9pm, depending on the season.

ACCOMMODATIONS

Very Expensive

✪ **Hôtel de Paris.** Place du Casino, 98000 Monaco. ☎ **92-16-30-00.** Fax 93-16-38-50. 206 rms, 41 suites. A/C MINIBAR TV TEL. 1,900–3,000F ($380–$600) double; from 5,500F ($1,100) suite. AE, DC, MC, V. Parking 120F ($24). Bus: 1 or 2.

On the main plaza, this is one of the most famous hotels in the world and the choice address in the principality. The hotel is furnished with a dazzling decor of marble pillars, statues, crystal chandeliers, sumptuous carpets, Louis XVI chairs, and a wall-size fin-de-siècle mural. The guest rooms are fashionable and, in many cases, sumptuous. On top of the Hôtel de Paris, the Louis XIV royal galley-style Le Grill has an impressive sliding roof. The elegant Le Louis XV is recommended under "Dining." Thermes Marins spa, connected to the hotel, offers complete cures of thalassotherapy under medical supervision.

Expensive

Hôtel Mirabeau. 1 av. Princesse-Grace, MC 98000 Monaco. ☎ **92-16-65-65.** Fax 93-50-84-85. 93 rms, 10 suites. MINIBAR TV TEL. 1,200–2,300F ($240–$460) double; from 3,000F ($600) suite. AE, DC, MC, V. Bus: 1 or 2.

In the heart of Monte Carlo, next to the casino, the contemporary Mirabeau combines modern design with refined atmosphere. Each guest room is appointed elegantly, many featuring terraces with a romantic view overlooking the pool and Mediterranean. La Coupole restaurant is highly praised among restaurants of the Riviera for its inventive yet classical cooking (closed Aug).

Moderate

Hôtel Alexandra. 33 bd. Princesse-Charlotte, 98000 Monaco. ☎ **93-50-63-13.** Fax 92-16-06-48. 56 rms. A/C TV TEL. 600–850F ($120–$170) double. AE, DC, MC, V. Parking 40F ($8). Bus: 1 or 2.

This hotel is in the center of the business district, on a busy and often noisy street corner. Its comfortably furnished guest rooms don't generate much excitement, but they're reliable and respectable. The Alexandra knows it can't compete with the giants of Monaco and doesn't even try. But it attracts those who'd like to visit the principality without spending a fortune.

Inexpensive

⊙ **Hôtel Cosmopolite.** 4 rue de la Turbie, 98000 Monaco. ☎ **93-30-16-95.** Fax 93-30-23-05. 24 rms (none with bath). 222–310F ($44.40–$62) double. No credit cards. Free parking on street. Bus: 1, 2, or 4.

This century-old hotel is down a set of steps from the train station. Madame Gay Angèle, the English-speaking owner, is proud of her "Old Monaco" establishment. Her more expensive rooms have showers, but the cheapest way to stay here is to request a room without shower—there are adequate facilities in the hall.

DINING

Very Expensive

✪ **Le Louis XV.** In the Hôtel de Paris, place du Casino. ☎ **92-16-30-01.** Reservations recommended. Jacket/tie for men. Main courses 300–400F ($60–$80); fixed-price menus 790–890F ($158–$178). AE, DC, MC, V. July–Aug Wed 8–10pm, Thurs–Mon noon–2pm and 8–10pm; Sept–June Thurs–Mon noon–2pm and 8–10pm. Bus: 1 or 2. FRENCH/ITALIAN.

On the lobby level of the five-star Hôtel de Paris, Le Louis XV offers what one critic called "down-home Riviera cooking within a Fabergé egg." Despite the place's regal trappings (or as a reaction against them?), the chef creates a simple cuisine, which is served by the finest waitstaff in Monaco. Everything is light, attuned to the seasons, with an intelligent modern interpretation of both Provençal and northern Italian courses. The service is superb.

Expensive

Café de Paris. Place du Casino. ☎ **92-16-20-20.** Main courses 100–170F ($20–$34); fixed-price menus from 210F ($42). AE, DC, MC, V. Daily 8am–4am. Bus: 1 or 2. INTERNATIONAL.

Opposite the casino and the Hôtel de Paris, this cafe provides a front-row seat for the never-ending spectacle of Monte Carlo. It's owned by the Société des Bains de Mer and was completely rebuilt in the late 1980s. The Grand Café with its terrace and adjacent bar are still here, as are several boutiques and a Parisian-style "drugstore." One room is devoted to "one-armed bandits." Around six *plats du jour* are offered, and the cuisine is international with a varied menu—so varied in fact that guest chefs are invited in for "theme weeks" that highlight various world cuisines. The chefs are best with fresh seafood.

Monaco After Dark

The **Loews Casino**, 12 av. des Spélugues (☎ **93-50-65-00**), is a huge room filled with the one-armed bandits, adjoining the lobby in the Loews Monte-Carlo. It also features blackjack, craps, and American roulette. Additional slot machines are available on the roof starting at 11am—for those who want to gamble with a wider view of the sea. It's open daily 4pm–4am (until 5am for slot machines). Admission is free.

A speculator, François Blanc, made the ✪ **Monte Carlo Casino**, place du Casino (☎ **92-16-21-21**), the most famous in the world, attracting Sarah Bernhardt, Mata Hari, King Farouk, and Aly Khan (Onassis used to own a part-interest). The architect of Paris's Opéra Garnier, Charles Garnier, built the oldest part of the casino, and it remains an extravagant example of period architecture. The Salle Américaine, containing only Las Vegas–style slot machines, opens at noon, as do doors for roulette and trente-quarente. A section for roulette and chemin-de-fer opens at 3pm. The hottest action begins at 4pm when the full casino swings into action, with more roulette, craps, and blackjack. The gambling continues until very late, the closing depending on the crowd. To enter the casino, you must carry a passport, be at least 21, and pay an admission of 50–100F ($10–$20) if you want to enter the private rooms. In lieu of a passport, an identity card or driver's license will suffice.

The foremost winter establishment, under the same ownership, is the **Cabaret** in the Casino Gardens, where you can dance to the music of a smooth orchestra. A good cabaret is featured, often with ballet numbers. It's open from mid-September until the end of June, but closed Tuesday. From 9pm you can enjoy dinner for 420F ($84). Drinks ordered separately begin at 150F ($30). For reservations, call **92-16-36-36**.

In the **Salle Garnier** of the casino, concerts are held periodically; for information, contact the tourist office (above). The music is usually classical, featuring the Orchestre Philharmonique de Monte Carlo.

The casino also contains the **Opéra de Monte-Carlo,** whose patron is Prince Rainier. This world-famous house, opened in 1879 by Sarah Bernhardt, presents a winter and spring repertoire that traditionally includes Puccini, Mozart, and Verdi. The famed Ballets Russes de Monte-Carlo, starring Nijinsky and Karsavina, was created in 1918 by Sergei Diaghilev. The national orchestra and ballet company of Monaco appear here. Tickets may be hard to come by; your best bet is to ask your hotel concierge. You can make inquiries about tickets on your own at the Atrium du Casino (☎ **92-16-22-99**), open Tues–Sun 10am–12:30pm and 2–5pm. Standard tickets generally cost 100F ($20) to 580F ($116).

7

Germany

by Darwin Porter & Danforth Prince

Berlin is almost, but not quite yet, the capital of unified Germany; here you can see history in the making. What was once the city's biggest tourist attraction, the Berlin Wall, is now a bicycle path where Berliners push baby strollers. Restored baroque Munich, in the south, known as Germany's "secret capital," is the gateway to the Bavarian Alps and the picturesque Alpine villages. For a taste of medieval Germany, explore the untouched towns of the Romantic Road and Ludwig II's fairy-tale castle of Neuschwanstein.

1 Berlin

When Heinrich Heine arrived in Berlin in 1819, he exclaimed, "Isn't the present splendid!" Were he to arrive today, he might make the same remark. Visitors who come by plane to Berlin see a splendid panorama. Few metropolitan areas are blessed with as many lakes, woodlands, and parks—these cover one-third of the city's area, and small farms with fields and meadows still exist within the city limits.

Berlin today is an almost completely modern city. As it fortifies its position as the capital of a unified Germany, dizzying changes are going on, one of the compelling reasons to visit. Regrettably, Berlin is hardly the architectural gem that old-time visitors remember from the pre-Nazi era; it wasn't rebuilt with the same kind of care lavished on Munich and Cologne. But in spite of its decades-long "quadripartite status," it's a vibrant city, always receptive to new ideas, a major economic and cultural center, and a leader in development and research. Because of its excellent facilities, it is a favored site for trade fairs, congresses, and conventions, attracting 6 million visitors a year.

Today, the metamorphosis making the two Berlins into one is still going on. Phone systems, transportation, and air arrivals are just some of the thousands of elements that must be blended to make the city whole again.

ONLY IN BERLIN

Strolling the Kurfürstendamm Launched by Bismarck in 1870 to surpass the Champs-Elysées in Paris, this bustling neon-lit boulevard celebrates the victory of capitalism even though deep in the heart of Eastern Europe. Two miles of pure consumerism, the Ku'damm is glitzy, showy, and great for a shopping stroll. Stop in at one of the grand cafes (Kranzler or Möhring) for a milchkaffee and a slice of apfel strudel.

Walking Unter den Linden   By all means stroll along Berlin's second great street. This is that architectural showpiece of the old East Berlin, where you follow in the footsteps of Prussian emperors, under linden trees that were replanted to replace the ones Hitler had removed. Be awed by the imposing Deutsches Historisches Museum (designed by Germany's most famous baroque architect, Andreas Schlüter) and relax in the Lustgarten before walking across Schlossbrücke, Berlin's most beautiful bridge.

Spending a Day at the Dahlem Museums   Investigating these museums, in a southwestern suburb, is reason enough to visit Berlin. Here is the capital's largest and densest concentration of museums, a treasure trove guaranteed to please almost everyone. Save special time for the Gemäldegalerie, Germany's top art museum, a virtual encyclopedia of the great periods of European art, even if the most famous painting, *Man with the Golden Helmet,* is no longer attributed to Rembrandt. (Avoid the hordes and visit the Brücke Museum, devoted to the works of the *Die Brücke* artists who introduced Expressionism to Germany.)

Looking at the Past at the Pergamon   Dedicated to ancient times, this museum shelters the altars, gates, and gathering places of antiquity—none more enthralling than the Hellenistic Pergamon Altar from 180 to 160 B.C. Built of white marble, it's carved with figures of the gods. And that's only one of the attractions here at one of the major architectural museums of the world. The two-story Market Gate of Miletus was erected in A.D. 120, and a dazzling Babylonian Processional Street leads to the Gate of Ishtar.

Taking a Kneipen Crawl Through the Heart of Town   Forget London's pub crawl. Berliners have their own brand of this nighttime tradition. Every neighborhood is filled with *kneipen* (bars and taverns) waiting to lure you. These are cozy rendezvous where patrons meet their friends, and you can easily get caught up in the oldtime atmosphere and conviviality. Favorites include Gaststätte Hoeck, Wilmersdorferstrasse 149 (☎ **030/341-31-10**), the oldest kneipe in Charlottenburg (1892), and Ax-Bar, Leibnizstrasse 34 (☎ **030/313-85-94**), the hot spot near the Savignyplatz.

Calling on Marlene   Gone but hardly forgotten, Marlene Dietrich was the seductive femme fatale of the 20th century, a legend ever since she appeared as prostitute Lola-Lola in *The Blue Angel.* Born in Berlin on Christmas 1904, she stood for ambiguously erotic glamor, and her sultry voice singing her signature tune, "Lili Marlene," added to her mystique. This great personality and the most famous German woman of the 20th century died in 1992. Loyal fans can purchase some of her favorite red roses and lay them on her grave in Berlin-Friedenau cemetery, along Stubenrauchstrasse.

Picnicking in the Tiergarten   What better place for a picnic than the former hunting grounds of the Prussian electors since the 1500s? No longer the bare and denuded forest it was in 1946, the Tiergarten today blossoms with trees from all over the world, including some contributed by Queen Elizabeth II and many towns from throughout Germany. The Tiergarten is ideal for strolling, including crossing the Löwenbrücke or Lion Bridge. Wander at leisure through the 412-acre park until you find a suitable oasis. But first stop at the sixth-floor food emporium of KaDeWe at Wittenbergplatz, the major department store, to secure the makings of one of life's memorable picnics—everything from fresh bread to grilled chicken, sausages, salads, and wine.

Western Berlin Attractions & Accommodations

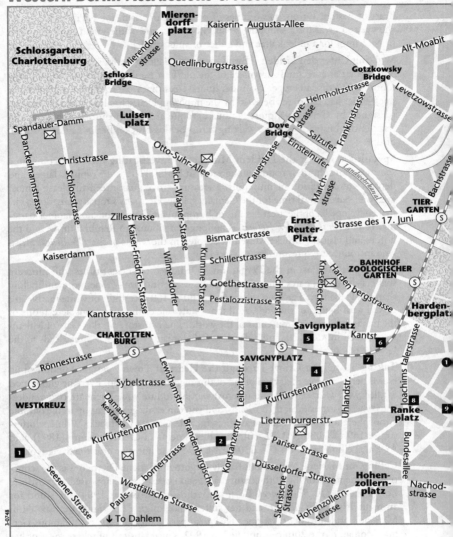

BERLIN

Western Berlin

Attractions:

Brandenburger Tor ❹

Europa-Center ❷

Kaiser-Wilhelm-
Gedächtniskirche ❶

Kungstgewerbe Museum ❺

Musikinstrumenten
Museum ❼

Neue Nationalgalerie ❽

Philharmonie ❻

Schloss Bellevue ❸

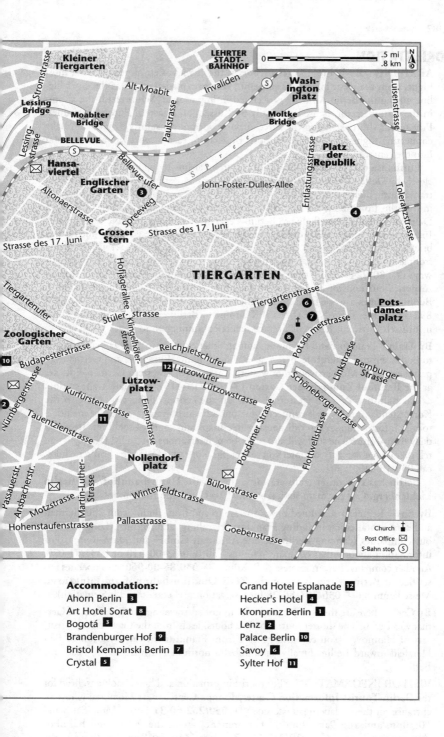

Accommodations:

Ahorn Berlin **3**
Art Hotel Sorat **8**
Bogotá **3**
Brandenburger Hof **9**
Bristol Kempinski Berlin **7**
Crystal **5**

Grand Hotel Esplanade **12**
Hecker's Hotel **4**
Kronprinz Berlin **1**
Lenz **2**
Palace Berlin **10**
Savoy **6**
Sylter Hof **11**

ORIENTATION

ARRIVING   By Plane   Tegel Airport is the city's busiest airport, serving most flights from the west. Historic **Tempelhof Airport** (made famous as the city's lifeline during the Berlin Airlift) has declined in importance. **Schönefeld,** the airport in the eastern sector, is used primarily by Russian and Eastern European airlines. Private bus shuttles among the three airports operate constantly so you can make connecting flights at a different airport. Buses from each airport will also take you into the center of Berlin.

Lufthansa (☎ 800/645-3880) is the premier airline flying into Berlin, followed closely by **Delta** (☎ 800/241-4141). Lufthansa routes Berlin-bound passengers from transatlantic flights onto one of the 100 or more domestic flights it offers every day into Berlin from about a dozen cities in western Germany and the rest of Europe. Delta offers daily direct flights to Berlin–Tegel every evening from New York's JFK International Airport and from its home base in Atlanta. These planes touch down briefly in Hamburg, with no change of equipment en route. Delta's service to Atlanta from around the United States is without equal in the airline industry. **British Airways** (☎ 800/247-9297) offers direct flights into Berlin from London's Heathrow Airport. Four nonstop flights depart every day for Tegel. BA also flies nonstop to Berlin six times a week from both Manchester and Birmingham. **TWA** (☎ 800/892-4141) flies from New York's JFK airport to Berlin every day, touching down in Brussels (with no change of aircraft) before continuing on to Tegel.

By Train   Frankfurt and Hamburg, among other cities, have good rail connections to Berlin. From Frankfurt to Berlin takes about 7 hours. Eurailpass and GermanRail passes are valid. Most arrivals from western European and western German cities are at the **Bahnhof Zoologischer Garten** (☎ 030/19-419), the main train station, called Bahnhof Zoo, in western Berlin. In the center of the city, close to the Kurfürstendamm, it's well connected for public transportation. Facilities include a tourist information counter dispensing free maps and tourist brochures. It's open daily 8am–11pm. The staff will also make hotel reservations for 5 DM ($3.50) if you tell them what category of hotel you're seeking. For rail information and schedules, call 030/19-419.

Berlin has two other train stations, the **Berlin Hauptbahnhof** and **Berlin Lichtenberg.** Call the main station at 030/19-419 for information.

By Bus   Regularly scheduled buses operate to and from Berlin from 250 German and continental cities, including Frankfurt, Hamburg, and Munich. Long-distance bus companies servicing Berlin include Autokraft GmbH and Haru-Reisen. For information about either company's routes, call **030/33-00-010** or 0431/71-070. Another company, Bayern Express & P. Kühn (☎ **030/86-00-960**) also operates bus service to Berlin. Arrivals are at the **ZOB Omnibusbahnhof am Funkturm,** Messedamm 8 (☎ **030/301-80-28** for reservations, schedules, and information).

By Car   There are three major routes for motorists traveling from the west of Germany to Berlin. The shorter route (about 2 hours) leads from the town of Helmstedt, east of Hannover. You can also go east from Frankfurt in the direction of Bad Herzfeld toward Berlin. Finally, an autobahn north of Nürnberg (A-9) heads for Berlin.

VISITOR INFORMATION   For tourist information and hotel bookings, head for the **Berlin Tourist Information Center,** Europa-Center (near Memorial Church), entrance on the Budapesterstrasse side (☎ 030/262-60-31), open Mon–Sat 8am–10:30pm and Sun 9am–9pm. Other branches are at the rail station Bahnhof Zoologischer Garten (☎ **030/313-90-63**), open Mon–Sat 8am–10:30pm; in the main lobby of the Tegel Airport (☎ **030/4101-31-45**), open daily 8am–11pm; and in the Hauptbahnhof, in the eastern part of Berlin (☎ **030/279-52-09**), open daily 8am–8pm.

CITY LAYOUT

The center of activity in the western part of Berlin is the 2-mile-long **Kurfürstendamm,** called the Ku'damm by Berliners. Along this wide boulevard you'll find the best hotels, restaurants, theaters, cafes, nightclubs, shops, and department stores. The huge **Tiergarten** is the city's largest park. The Tiergarten is crossed by Strasse des 17 Juni, which leads to the famed **Brandenburg Gate** (just north of here is the Reichstag). On the southwestern fringe of the Tiergarten is the **Berlin Zoo.** From the Ku'damm you can take Hardenbergstrasse, crossing Bismarckstrasse and traversing Otto-Suhr-Allee, which leads to Schloss Charlottenburg and museums, one of your major sightseeing goals. The Dahlem Museums are on the southwestern fringe, often reached by going along Hohenzollerndamm.

The **Brandenburger Tor,** which once separated the two Berlins, is the start of eastern Berlin's most celebrated street, **Unter den Linden,** the cultural heart of Berlin before World War II. The famous street runs from west to east, cutting a path through the city. It leads to **Museumsinsel** (Museum Island), where the most outstanding museums of eastern Berlin, including the Pergamon, are situated. As it courses along, Unter den Linden crosses another major eastern Berlin artery, **Friedrichstrasse.** If you continue south along Friedrichstrasse, you'll reach the former location of Checkpoint Charlie, a famous site of the cold war days.

Unter den Linden continues east until it reaches **Alexanderplatz,** the center of eastern Berlin, with its TV tower (Fernsehturm). A short walk away is the restored **Nikolai Quarter** (Nikolaiviertel), a neighborhood of bars, restaurants, and shops that evoke life in the prewar days.

GETTING AROUND

The Berlin transport system consists of buses, trams, and U-Bahn and S-Bahn trains. For information about public transport, call **030/752-70-20.**

The **BVG standard ticket** (Einzelfahrschein) costs 3.70 DM ($2.60) and is valid for 2 hours of transportation in all directions, transfers included. Also available at counters and vending machines is the four-ride **multiple ticket** (Sammelkarte) for 12.50 DM ($8.75). On buses only standard tickets can be purchased, and for a ride by tram you have to buy your ticket in advance. Tickets should be kept until the end of the journey; otherwise you'll be liable for a fine of 60 DM ($42).

A special **30-Studen-Karte** is valid for 30 hours of transportation. For two adults, accompanied by three children under 14, the charge for this card is 20 DM ($14). The card is good for unlimited travel on the U-Bahn, S-Bahn, and buses, and it can be purchased at the BVG information booth in front of the Bahnhof Zoo as well as staffed counters of the rapid rail system and at some special vending machines.

If you're going to be in Berlin for 3 days, you can purchase a WelcomeCard for 29 DM ($20.30), entitling holders to 72 free hours on public transportation in Berlin and Brandenburg. It is valid for one adult and three children.

By U-Bahn & S-Bahn U-Bahn trains are run by Berliner Verkehrsbetriebe (BVG). S-Bahn trains are run by Deutsche Bundesbahn (DB). Trains throughout the city operate from about 4:30am–12:30am daily (except for some 62 night buses and trams, and two U-Bahn lines).

By Taxi Taxis are available throughout Berlin. The meter starts at 4–6 DM ($2.80–$4.20), with additional kilometers ranging from 1.70–2.30 DM ($1.20–$1.60). The

Berlin U-Bahn & the S-Bahn

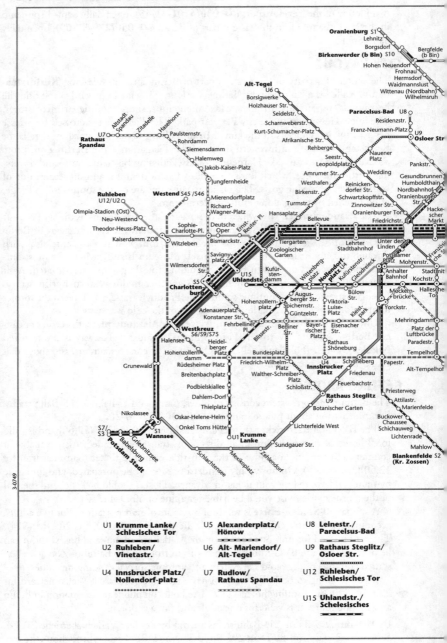

U1 **Krumme Lanke/ Schlesisches Tor**

U2 **Ruhleben/ Vinetastr.**

U4 **Innsbrucker Platz/ Nollendorf-platz**

U5 **Alexanderplatz/ Hönow**

U6 **Alt- Mariendorf/ Alt-Tegel**

U7 **Rudlow/ Rathaus Spandau**

U8 **Leinestr./ Paracelsus-Bad**

U9 **Rathaus Steglitz/ Osloer Str.**

U12 **Ruhleben/ Schlesisches Tor**

U15 **Uhlandstr./ Schelesisches**

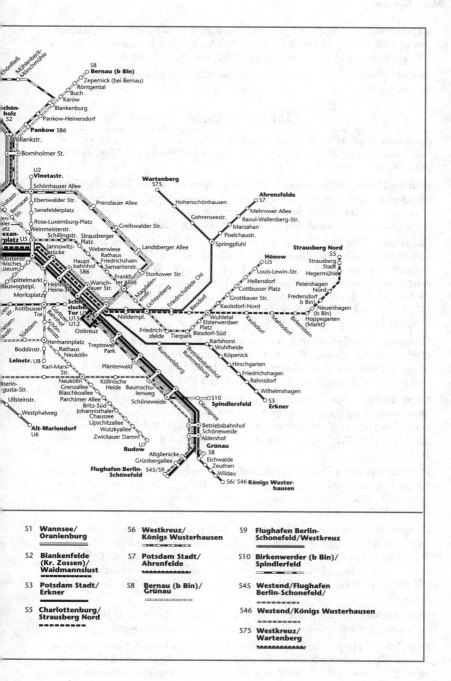

S1 **Wannsee/ Oranienburg**

S2 **Blankenfelde (Kr. Zossen)/ Waidmannslust**

S3 **Potsdam Stadt/ Erkner**

S5 **Charlottenburg/ Strausberg Nord**

S6 **Westkreuz/ Königs Wusterhausen**

S7 **Potsdam Stadt/ Ahrenfelde**

S8 **Bernau (b Bin)/ Grünau**

S9 **Flughafen Berlin-Schonefeld/Westkreuz**

S10 **Birkenwerder (b Bin)/ Spindlerfeld**

S45 **Westend/Flughafen Berlin-Schonefeld/**

S46 **Westend/Königs Wusterhausen**

S75 **Westkreuz/ Wartenberg**

longer the ride, the cheaper the price per kilometer. For short distances (either 5 minutes or 2 kilometers) the fare is 5 DM ($3.50). Visitors can flag down taxis that have a T-sign illuminated. For a taxi, call **21-02-02,** 69022, or 26-10-26.

By Car   Touring Berlin by car isn't recommended. Free parking places are difficult to come by.

FAST FACTS: Berlin

American Express   Amex offices are at Uhlandstrasse 173–174 (☎ 030/884588-0), just off Kurfürstendamm; it's open Mon–Fri 9am–5:30pm and Sat 9am–noon.

Business Hours   Most **banks** are open Mon–Fri 9am–1 or 3pm. Most other **businesses** and **stores** are open Mon–Fri 9 or 10am–6 or 6:30pm and Sat 9am–2pm. On langer Samstag, the first Saturday of the month, shops stay open until 4 or 6pm. Some stores observe late closing on Thursday (usually 8:30pm).

Consulates   The **U.S.** Consulate is at Clayallee 170, D-14169 Berlin (☎ 030/832-9233). The consular information hotline is 0130/82-63-64. The **British** Embassy is at Unter den Linden 32–34, D-10117 Berlin (☎ 030/20-18-40). The **Australian** Consulate is at Uhlandstrasse 181–183, D-10623 Berlin (☎ 030/880-08-80). The **Canadian** Consulate is at Friedrichstrasse 95, D-10117 Berlin (☎ 030/261-11-61). The **New Zealand** Consulate is at Heimhuderstrasse 56, D-20148 Hamburg (☎ 040/442-555-0).

Currency   The German unit of currency is the Deutsche Mark (DM), which is divided into 100 pfennig. Bills are in denominations of 5, 10, 20, 50, 100, 200, 500, and 1,000 marks; coins come in 1, 2, 5, 10, and 50 pfennig. The rate of exchange used in this book was $1 = 1.43 DM, or 1 DM = 70¢.

Currency Exchange   You can exchange money at all airports, at major department stores, at any bank, and at the American Express office (above). The **deutsche mark** (DM) is divided into 100 **pfennig.** Coins come in 1, 2, 5, 10, or 50 pfennig, and 1, 2, and 5 DM. Notes are issued in 5, 10, 20, 50, 100, 200, 500, and 1,000 DM.

Dentists/Doctors   The Berlin tourist office in the Europa-Center (above) keeps a list of English-speaking dentists and doctors in Berlin. In case of a medical emergency, dial 31-00-31 for information. For a dental emergency, call 11-41 on weekends, on holidays, and at night.

Drugstores   If you need a pharmacy (*apotheke*) at night, go to one on any corner. There you'll find a sign in the window giving the address of the nearest drugstore open at night (such posting is required by law). Otherwise, call 011-41 to find out what's open. A central pharmacy is Europa-Apotheke, Tauentzienstrasse 9–12 (☎ 030/261-41-42), by the Europa-Center. It's open Mon–Fri 9am–7pm and Sat 9am–2pm.

Emergencies   Call the police at 110; dial 112 to report a fire or to summon an ambulance. For a dental or medical emergency, see "Dentists/Doctors," above.

Post Office   The post office at the Bahnhof Zoo is open Mon–Sat 6am–midnight and Sun 8am–midnight. If you have mail sent there, have it marked Hauptpostlagernd, Postamt 120, Bahnhof Zoo, D-10612, Berlin. There's also a post office at Hauptbahnhof, open Mon–Fri 7am–7pm and Sat 8am–1pm. For postal info, call 030/311-00-235. You can make long-distance calls at post offices at far cheaper rates than at hotels.

Taxes   A 15% government value-added tax (VAT) is included in the price of restaurants, hotels, and material goods in Germany. On many objects, however, temporary visitors to Germany can obtain a refund of the VAT.

Telephone   Local and long-distance calls may be placed from all post offices and coin-operated public phone booths. The unit charge is 0.30 DM or three 10-pfennig coins. More than half the phones in Germany require an advance-payment phone card from Telekom, the German telephone company. Phone cards are sold at post offices and newsstands, costing 12 DM ($8.40) and 50 DM ($35). The 12 DM card offers about 40 minutes and the 50 DM card is useful for long-distance calls. Rates are measured in units rather than minutes. USA direct can be used with all phone cards and for collect calls. The number in Germany is 01-30-00-10. Canada Direct can be used with Bell Telephone cards and for collect calls. This number from Germany is 01-30-00-14. Telephone calls to Germany from the United States and Canada can be made by dialing 0-11-49.

ACCOMMODATIONS
ON OR NEAR THE KURFÜRSTENDAMM
Very Expensive

✪ **Bristol Kempinski Berlin.** Kurfürstendamm 27, D-10719 Berlin. ☎ **800/426-3135** in the U.S., or 030/88-43-40. Fax 030/833-60-75. 315 rms, 33 suites. A/C MINIBAR TV TEL. 390–530 DM ($273–$371) double; 600–1,800 DM ($420–$1,260) suite. AE, DC, MC, V. Parking 30 DM ($21). U-Bahn: Kurfürstendamm.

The legendary Kempinski enjoys a position in Berlin similar to that of the Waldorf-Astoria in New York. The only hotels that match it in style are the Grand Hotel Esplanade and the Maritim Grand. The glass-enclosed winter garden of the recently expanded lobby along with comfortable groupings of fine furniture set the relaxed mood. The guest rooms, with marble baths and soundproof windows, match the public rooms in elegance. The hotel contains three dining areas, the most expensive and elegant of which is the Restaurant Kempinski. Facilities include a recreation center with an indoor pool, a sauna, massage facilities, a solarium, and a fitness center.

Grand Hotel Esplanade. Lützowufer 15, D-10785 Berlin. ☎ **030/26-10-11.** Fax 030/262-91-21. 369 rms, 33 suites. A/C MINIBAR TV TEL. 430–520 DM ($301–$364) double; from 680 DM ($476) suite. AE, DC, MC, V. Free parking. U-Bahn: Kurfürstenstrasse, Nollendorfplatz, or Wittenbergplatz.

One of "The Leading Hotels of the World," the Esplanade rivals the Kempinski for supremacy in Berlin. The hotel's public and guest rooms are filled with contemporary art, some of museum caliber. Opened in 1988, it's uncompromisingly modern. Each of the well-furnished, bright, and cheerful accommodations contains a cable TV, video, and sound insulation. Thirty-three rooms are reserved for nonsmokers. The gourmet restaurant, Harlekin, is devoted to *cuisine moderne* and serves some of the town's best food. Facilities include an indoor pool, whirlpool, solarium, and sauna.

Expensive

✪ **Brandenburger Hof.** Eislebener Strasse 14, D-10789 Berlin. ☎ **030/214-050.** Fax 030/214-05-100. 87 rms. A/C MINIBAR TV TEL. 330–445 DM ($231–$311.50) double. Rates include breakfast. AE, DC, MC, V. Parking 18 DM ($12.60). U-Bahn: Kurfürstendamm or Augsburger Strasse. S-Bahn: Zoologischer Garten.

This white-fronted property is a redesigned classic in the Bauhaus style. Many of the rooms, however, are too severe and minimalist for some tastes. Its lofty status as a Relais & Château means better food, service, and amenities than most hotels of its rank. The restrained architecture reflects a harmony of contrasting elements. The

Wintergarten just past the lobby is a unique combination of an Italian monastery and a Japanese garden. The hotel features two restaurants. The best, Die Quadriga, a Frank Lloyd Wright design whose cherrywood walls and chairs emit reddish brown hues, boasts French cuisine with an Asian influence.

Kronprinz Berlin. Kronprinzendamm 1, D-10711 Berlin. ☎ **030/89-60-30.** Fax 030/89-31-215. 66 rms, 1 suite. MINIBAR TV TEL. 250–295 DM ($175–$206.50) double; 380 DM ($266) suite. Children 12 and under stay free in parents' room. Rates include buffet breakfast. AE, DC, MC, V. Parking 12 DM ($8.40). Bus: 119 or 129.

The Kronprinz may lack the style of the Bradenburger Hof, but it remains a worthy runner-up. It was built in 1894 and restored in 1995, and its location is away from Berlin's center at the far western edge of the Ku'damm, about half an hour walk from the Gedchtniskirche (though linked by bus). The hotel creates the feel of a boutique hotel. The rooms accommodate one or two and include a balcony. For extra comfort, inquire about a Bel-Etage room—spacious and elegant, these rooms additionally offer two private phones and a private safe. Many guests congregate in the cozy in-house bar, or in summer they gather in the garden under the chestnut trees for draft beer and wine.

✪ Savoy. Fasanenstrasse 9–10, D-10623 Berlin. ☎ **800/223-5652** in the U.S. and Canada, or 030/311-03-0. Fax 030/311-03-333. 125 rms, 15 suites. MINIBAR TV TEL. 314–394 DM ($219.80–$275.80) double; 520–900 DM ($364–$630) suite. Children under 12 stay free in parents' room. AE, DC, MC, V. U-Bahn: Kurfürstendamm.

If you don't demand the full-service facilities of the grander choices, this might be the hotel for you. The quiet, unassuming Savoy continues as a reliable and durable favorite year after year. Better than many in its category, it attracts some of the most illustrious people of Berlin and discriminating foreigners. Although modernization has cost it some of its old-world Berlin flavor, it remains the choice for the diehard traditionalist. Rated first-class and not deluxe because of the absence of a pool, the Savoy exhibits muted colors in beautifully furnished rooms and luxurious suites. Try the restaurant Belle Époque and its cozy Times Bar. There's also a sauna and a fitness club.

Moderate

Ahorn Berlin. Schlüterstrasse 40, D-10707 Berlin. ☎ **030/881-43-44.** Fax 030/881-65-00. 27 rms. MINIBAR TV TEL. 160 DM–210 DM ($112–$147) double; 195 DM–240 DM ($136.50–$168) triple or quad; 5 DM ($3.80) supplement for kitchenette. Discounts sometimes granted in Dec and Aug. Rates include continental breakfast. AE, DC, MC, V. Parking 5 DM ($3.50). U-Bahn: Adenauerplatz.

This simple, clean, cost-conscious hotel is located near a corner of the Kurfürstendamm in a neighborhood liberally sprinkled with *kneipen* and restaurants. Its wall-to-wall carpeted rooms and optional kitchenettes are very functional. Families often book in here, not only for the kitchenettes, but because so many rooms are suitable for three or four guests.

✪ Lenz. Xantenerstrasse 8, D-10707 Berlin. ☎ **030/881-51-58.** Fax 030/881-55-17. 28 rms. TV TEL. 160–180 DM ($112–$126) double. Rates include continental breakfast. AE, DC, MC, V. U-Bahn: Adenauerplatz.

Although it may be a bit creaky for some, many appreciate the old-fashioned ambience of the Lenz since much of Berlin is just *too* modern. Built as a private home just before World War I, the Lenz retains a cozy, homelike atmosphere. Accommodations vary in size and decor, so your reaction to the Lenz may depend entirely on your room assignment. There's also a small but convivial bar and breakfast room.

Inexpensive

Bogotà. Schlüterstrasse 45, D-10707 Berlin. ☎ **030/881-50-01.** Fax 030/88-35-887. 130 rms (12 with shower only, 65 with bath). TEL. 125 DM ($87.50) double without bath, 145 DM ($101.50) double with shower only, 190 DM ($133) double with bath. Rates include continental breakfast. AE, DC, MC, V. Parking 7–12 DM ($4.90–$8.40). U-Bahn: Adenauerplatz or Uhlandstrasse.

One of the town's most patronized budget hotels, the Bogotà's maintenance facilities are less than state-of-the-art. The elevator and floor lobbies are old-fashioned if not outdated. You might forget you're in Berlin because of the Bogotà's Spanish flair. The 1890s structure displays an Iberian lobby with lofty ceiling beams, an open wooden staircase, a wooden balcony, and a heavy bronze chandelier.

✪ Crystal. Kantstrasse 144, D-10623 Berlin. ☎ **030/312-90-47.** Fax 030/312-64-65. 33 rms (28 with bath). TEL. 90 DM ($63) double without bath, 130 DM ($91) double with bath. Rates include continental breakfast. MC, V. Free parking. S-Bahn: Savignyplatz.

Essentially a "back-to-basics" hotel, the Crystal offers clean and comfortable surroundings. The plumbing seems hodgepodge at best, but it's one of the cheapest rates for those who want to be in the heart of town and don't mind weathering an inconvenience or two.

NEAR THE MEMORIAL CHURCH & ZOO

Expensive

✪ Art Hotel Sorat. Joachimstalerstrasse 28–29, D-10719 Berlin. ☎ **030/88-44-7-0.** Fax 030/88-44-77-00. 133 rms. A/C MINIBAR TV TEL. 280 DM ($196) double. AE, DC, MC, V. U-Bahn: Kurfürstendamm.

Those partial to the more famous and highly regarded Bradenburger Hof (below) also like this hotel of discretion and taste. Though not in the league of some full-service hotels, the Sorat stands out because top designers added decorative nuances to enliven interiors. Philippe Starck designed the barstools, for example, and Arne Jacobsen the chairs. Artwork by Wolf Vostel, a well-known artist in Berlin, grace the guest-room walls. Both chic and avant-garde, the Sorat is unlike any other in Berlin.

Palace Berlin. In the Europa-Center, Budapesterstrasse 41, D-10789 Berlin. ☎ **800/528-1234** in the U.S., or 030/2502-0. Fax 030/262-65-77. 321 rms, 11 suites. A/C MINIBAR TV TEL. 330–530 DM ($231–$371) double; from 650 DM ($455) suite. AE, DC, MC, V. U-Bahn: Wittenbergplatz.

The Palace outranks such landmarks as the Berlin Hilton against whom it competes. The best rooms are in the more recently built Casino Wing, with marble baths and separate showers and tubs. Opposite the Memorial Church, the stylish and comfortable Palace is much improved over recent years. It offers many styles of accommodations and state-of-the-art maintenance. However, in some rooms the double glazing on the windows is unable to deafen the noise from the adjacent Europa-Center. All of the 7th floor and some of the 6th is set aside for nonsmokers. The hotel maintains its own elegant dining room serving continental food. The Thermen am Europa-Center, a large health club, offers indoor and outdoor pools, exercise equipment, and a sauna.

Moderate

Hecker's Hotel. Grolmanstrasse 35, D-10623 Berlin. ☎ **030/88-900.** Fax 030/889-0260. 72 rms. A/C MINIBAR TV TEL. 280–350 DM ($196–$245) double; 280–350 DM ($196–$245) junior suite or studio. AE, DC, MC, V. Parking 10 DM ($7). U-Bahn: Uhlandstrasse. Bus: 109 from Tegel Airport to Uhlandstrasse or 119, 129, or 219.

Opened in the late 1960s, this hotel was greatly extended in 1994. For years it had enjoyed a reputation as a "small, private hotel," but now it's not that small. The location is convenient, near the Ku'damm and the many bars, cafes, and restaurants around the Savignyplatz. The original 42 rooms are smaller than the newer units (that was the cold war hotel room style in the 1960s). A somber blue dominates most of the rooms, some of which are rented exclusively for nonsmokers. There's also a bar and a little cafe in the lobby. In summer, guests sit on the rooftop terrace, enjoying the lights of Berlin at night.

Sylter Hof. Kurfürstenstrasse 116, D-10787 Berlin. ☎ **030/2-12-00.** Fax 030/214-28-28. 154 rms, 16 suites. MINIBAR TV TEL. 220–272 DM ($154–$190.40) double; 296–402 DM ($207.20–$281.40) suite. Rates include buffet breakfast. AE, DC, MC, V. Free parking. U-Bahn: Wittenbergplatz.

The Sylter Hof offers rich trappings at good prices. It trails comparable hotels but outclasses many rivals. The main lounges are warmly decorated in an old-world style, with chandeliers, Louis XV–style and provincial chairs, and such antiques as an armoire and a grandfather clock. The well-maintained rooms—the majority of which are singles—may be too small for most tastes but might be a good choice for business travelers visiting Berlin alone. The Friesenstube is a conservative dining room serving Prussian and continental cuisine.

BERLIN-MITTE

Very Expensive

✪ Maritim Grand Hotel. Friedrichstrasse 158–164, D-10117 Berlin. ☎ **800/843-3311** in the U.S., or 030/23-270. Fax 030/23-27-33-62. 327 rms, 22 suites. A/C MINIBAR TV TEL. 480–660 DM ($336–$462) double; 700–800 DM ($490–$560) junior suite; 900–1,200 DM ($630–$840) deluxe suite. AE, DC, MC, V. Parking 25 DM ($17.50). U-Bahn: Französische Strasse. S-Bahn: Friedrichstrasse.

Many hotels call themselves grand—this one truly is. In Berlin the Maritim is rivaled only by the Kempinski. Amazingly, this monument to capitalistic decadence was first built on socialist soil by a Japanese company at a reported cost of $120 million. Blending belle époque features with contemporary styling, its rooms rise, atrium style, and come in a wide range of styles, from beautifully appointed standard singles and doubles all the way up to the Schinkel Suite, named to honor the famed early 19th-century architect. There's a wide choice for dining; your best bet is the posh Le Grand Silhouette, though the Goldene Gans is more traditional. Facilities include a fitness club, whirlpool, marble pool, saunas, and solarium.

Expensive

Hotel Luisenhof. Köpenicker Strasse 92, 10179 Berlin. ☎ **030/270-0543.** Fax 030/279-2983. 27 rms, 1 suite. MINIBAR TV TEL. 230 DM ($161) double; 350 DM ($245) suite. Rates include breakfast. AE, DC, MC, V. Free parking. U-Bahn: Märkisches Museum.

One of the most desirable small hotels of Berlin's eastern district, this hotel occupies a dignified house built in 1822 as the home of an iron-and-coal magnate. Its five floors of high-ceilinged rooms have been comfortably outfitted in a conservative and traditional style and upgraded with small but attractive baths. Beneath vaulted ceilings in the cellar, you'll find a very appealing restaurant, the Alexanderkeller.

Radisson Plaza. Karl-Liebknecht-Strasse 5, D-10178 Berlin. ☎ **800/333-3333** in the U.S. or 030/23828. Fax 030/2382-7590. 530 rms, 37 suites. A/C MINIBAR TV TEL. 370 DM ($259) double; 600 DM ($420) suite. AE, DC, MC, V. Parking 22 DM ($15.40). S-Bahn: Alexanderplatz.

In 1992, the Inter-Hotel Group poured $43 million into the Radisson's renovation, ripped out much of the cold war sterility, and radically changed its interior configuration of bars and restaurants. The Radisson Plaza now ranks near the top of the four-star choices, trailing the Steigenberger Berlin, the Berlin Hilton, the Palace, and Schweizerhof, but at least it's up and running in the big league. The Orangerie is an intimate restaurant on the second floor, amid a network of cubbyhole-style bars and potted plants. The cuisine is elegant and international. The hotel has a gymnasium with the biggest hotel pool in Berlin.

GRÜNEWALD

Very Expensive

✪ **Schlosshotel Vier Jahreszeiten Berlin.** Brahmsstrasse 10, D-14193 Berlin-Grunewald. ☎ **030/89-58-40.** Fax 030/89-58-48-00. 42 rms, 12 suites. MINIBAR TV TEL. 595–695 DM ($416.50–$486.50) double; from 950 DM ($665) suite. AE, DC, MC, V. Parking 29 DM ($20.30). Bus: 219.

This Italian Renaissance–style palace was built in 1912 by the personal attorney to Kaiser Wilhelm II and is a good choice for those who gravitate to German castle hotels. Its remote location in the leafy suburb of Grünewald saved it from destruction by bombing in World War II. For years the hotel functioned as a sleepily bourgeois hideaway; in 1994 it reopened after a three-year renovation with a lavish new decor by German-born fashion superstar Karl Lagerfeld. The rooms are elegantly furnished and beautifully maintained. The hotel contains a pair of restaurants, the more unusual and best of which is Vivaldi's.

GAY HOTELS

Arco Hotel. Gaisbergstrasse 30, D-10777 Berlin. ☎ **030/882-63-88.** 23 rms (14 with bath). 120 DM ($84) double without bath, 170 DM ($119) double with bath. AE, DC, MC, V. U-Bahn: Wittenbergplatz.

The Arco is a gay-friendly hotel occupying an older, rather old-fashioned building with four floors—access to which is possible only by stairs. The rooms are simple and a bit Spartan, but well scrubbed and decent. The clientele is about half gay, including women traveling as couples.

Pension Niebuhr. Niebuhrstrasse 74, D-10629 Berlin. ☎ **030/324-9595.** Fax 030/324-8021. 12 rms (7 with bath). 120 DM ($84) double without bath, 170 DM ($119) double with bath. Rates include breakfast. AE, MC, V. S-Bahn: Savignyplatz.

The Neibuhr is a clean, safe haven—and quite gay friendly—occupying one and a half floors of a turn-of-the-century apartment building. Your amiable host, Willi Heidasch, maintains simple but clean accommodations, decorating the public areas with paintings for sale by aspirant Berlin artists. About half the guests are gay, and that percentage is growing.

DINING

ON OR NEAR THE KURFÜRSTENDAMM

Very Expensive

✪ **Bamberger Reiter.** Regensburgerstrasse 7. ☎ **030/218-42-82.** Reservations required. Main courses 52–58 DM ($36.40–$40.60); six- or seven-course fixed-price menu 145–185 DM ($101.50–$129.50). AE, DC, MC, V. Tues–Sat 6pm–1am (last order 10pm). U-Bahn: Spichernstrasse. CONTINENTAL.

Bamberger Reiter is the city's best restaurant, serving French, German, and Austrian dishes. The quality of the food is beyond question. Only Rockendorf's or Alt Luxemburg can pretend to have better fare. Don't judge it by its location in an undistinguished 19th-century apartment house. Excellent in its forthright approach to fresh ingredients and meticulous in its preparation and service, the restaurant enjoys a loyal following among Berlin's business elite. The decor evokes old Germany, with lots of mirrors and fresh flowers. The menu changes daily according to the availability of fresh ingredients and the chef's inspiration.

Expensive

✪ **Harlekin.** In the Grand Hotel Esplanade, Lützowufer. ☎ **030/254-78-858.** Reservations recommended. Main courses 44–46 DM ($30.80–$32.20); four- to six-course fixed-price menu 95–130 DM ($66.50–$91). AE, DC, MC, V. Tues–Fri noon–3pm; Tues–Sat 6–11pm. Closed 3 weeks late July–Aug (dates vary). U-Bahn: Nollendorfplatz or Wittenbergplatz. FRENCH/INTERNATIONAL.

This restaurant's rise to prominence chagrined jealous chefs at traditional favorites like the Kempinski. The *carte* is perfectly balanced between tradition and innovation. Appetizers are likely to include such dishes as calves' consommé with crayfish or the more traditional medaillons of lobster. For your main course, you might be won over by the piccata of veal with truffle sauce (of course what doesn't taste good with truffle sauce?) or veer to the traditional medaillon of venison with port-wine sauce and fresh mushrooms. Both are perfectly prepared here.

Paris Bar. Kantstrasse 152. ☎ **030/313-80-52.** Reservations recommended. Main courses 35–50 DM ($24.50–$35). AE. Daily noon–1am. U-Bahn: Uhlandstrasse. FRENCH.

This French bistro has been a local favorite since the postwar years, when two expatriate Frenchmen established the restaurant to bring a little Parisian cheer to the dismal gray of bombed-out Berlin. The place is just as crowded with elbow-to-elbow tables as a Montmartre tourist trap. In Berlin, however, you'll find it a genuinely pleasing little eatery. It's a true restaurant on the see-and-be-seen circuit between Savinngyplatz and Gedchtniskiche. The food is invariably fresh and well prepared but not particularly innovative. That's left to such swank addresses as the Harlekin or Bamberger Reiter.

Moderate

Estiatorio (also called **Fofi**). Fasanenstrasse 70. ☎ **030/881-87-85.** Reservations required. Main courses 28–52 DM ($19.60–$36.40). AE. Daily 6pm–midnight (bar and cafe, daily 6pm–3am). U-Bahn: Uhlandstrasse. GREEK/GERMAN.

Estiatorio is decidedly chic. In summer, the doors open and the action spills onto the sidewalk. Otherwise, on a winter's night, you're likely to see some of the dazzling Berlin personalities around the metal bar. You might begin with a selection of Greek hors d'oeuvres, such as stuffed grape leaves, and then go on to grilled scampi or moussaka. Lamb is also imaginatively prepared. Sea bass cooked with olive oil and herbs in the Mediterranean style evokes languid days on the Riviera. The German dishes, however, including sauerbraten, rouladen of beef, and tafelspitz (boiled beef), are served in better versions in dozens of other places. There's more glitz and glitter the later you go.

✪ **Hardtke's.** Meinekestrasse 27A. ☎ **030/881-98-27.** Reservations required. Main courses 22–32 DM ($15.40–$22.40); three-course fixed-price menu 35 DM ($24.50). No credit cards. Daily 10am–1am. U-Bahn: Kurfürstendamm. BERLINER.

These Teutonic recipes haven't changed during the 40 years of Hardtke's operation. German retirees like dining here; they're fond of the cuisine they enjoyed in the 1940s and 1950s before the "new German cookery" became all the rage. Hardtke's serves the most authentic German cooking in town. You can eagerly OD on all the potatoes and sauerkraut, the blood-and-liver sausage (from the in-house butcher shop), and the monstrous bockwurst. The true Berliner asks for grosse schlachteplatte—fresh black pudding and liver sausage, small pickled knuckle of pork, liver dumpling, shredded pickled white cabbage, mashed peas, and boiled potatoes.

Heinz Holl. Damaschkestrasse 26. ☎ **030/323-14-04.** Reservations required. Main courses 21–50 DM ($14.70–$35). AE, MC. Mon–Sat 7pm–1am. Closed holidays and certain weeks in summer (dates vary). U-Bahn: Adenauerplatz. GERMAN.

West of the center, Heinz Holl has gained a reputation as a select dining spot and social center. Your host is Heinz Holl, who has a devoted local following among theater and media personalities. Savor the recipes that much of Berlin craves, including kohlroulade, a stuffed cabbage roll, the best in town. Few other chefs would want to compete with it. The tafelspitz, boiled beef with vegetables, would've pleased Emperor Josef of Austria (it was his favorite dish). Look also for the market-fresh daily specials, especially if fresh fish is featured. The chef believes in strong flavors and good hearty cookery.

Ⓢ Marjellchen. Mommsenstrasse 9. ☎ **030/883-26-76.** Reservations required. Main courses 20–40 DM ($14–$28). AE, DC, MC, V. Daily 5pm–midnight. Closed Dec 23, 24, 31. U-Bahn: Adenauerplatz or Uhlandstrasse. Bus: 109, 119, or 129. EAST PRUSSIAN.

This is the only restaurant in Berlin specializing in the cuisine of Germany's long-lost province of East Prussia, along with the cuisines of Pomerania and Silesia. Deriving its unusual name from an East Prussian word meaning "young girl," the establishment divides its space among three rooms, the first dominated by a Kneipe-style bar. Amid a Bismarckian ambience of still-lifes, vested waiters, and oil lamps, you can enjoy a savory version of red-beet soup with strips of beef, East Prussian potato soup with crabmeat and bacon, falscher gänsebraten (pork spare ribs stuffed with prunes and breadcrumbs), and Mecklenburger kümmelfleisch (lamb with chives and onions).

Zlata Praha. Meinekestrasse 4. ☎ **030/881-97-50.** Reservations recommended. Main courses 24–46 DM ($16.80–$32.20). AE, MC, V. Daily 5pm–midnight. U-Bahn: Joachimstaler Strasse. BOHEMIAN/HUNGARIAN.

Zlata Praha serves the best Bohemian cuisine of any restaurant in Berlin. German, French, and Austrian wines are featured. However, the pièce de résistance is the special tap beer, Pilsner Urquell das Echte. Many of the food items spark an instant recognition (paprika lovers take note) and evoke childhood memories from the restaurant's many regular clients. The Szegendiner goulash is as fine as any we've had during our tours of Hungary. Specialties are "Bohemian forest" goulash, Eszterhazy rostbraten, filet Stroganoff Paprikaschnitzel, an original Wiener schnitzel, and honey-glazed roast duck with red cabbage and dumplings. The portions are gargantuan.

NEAR THE MEMORIAL CHURCH & ZOO

Inexpensive

Ⓢ Schwejk-Prager Gasthaus. Ansbacherstrasse 4. ☎ **030/213-78-92.** Reservations recommended. Main courses 22–28 DM ($15.40–$19.60). No credit cards. Daily 6pm–1am. U-Bahn: Wittenbergplatz. CZECH.

The taste of Eastern Europe is alive and flourishing at this bistro where Bohemian specialties are served in generous portions. It's almost as if, at any moment, you expect to see the Hapsburg emperor, Ferdinand the gracious, arriving to proclaim, "I am the emperor and I want dumplings." There's a small bar for drinking. Try Pilsner Urquell or the original Tschech Budweiser with your food. Most of the dishes are quite decent, including specialties like crackling broiled pork shanks (*schweinehaxen*).

CHARLOTTENBURG

Expensive

✪ **Alt-Luxemburg.** Windscheidstrasse 31. ☎ **030/323-87-30.** Reservations required. Fixed-price three-course menu 95 DM ($66.50); fixed-price four-course menu 108 DM ($75.60); fixed-price five-course menu 118 DM ($82.60); fixed-price six-course menu 135 DM ($94.50). AE, DC, V. Mon–Sat 7–11pm. U-Bahn: Sophie-Charlotteplatz. CONTINENTAL.

The Bamberger Reiter is the leader among Berlin restaurants, but the Alt-Luxemburg is nipping at its heels. Chef Karl Wannemacher is one of the most outstanding in eastern Germany. Known for his quality and market-fresh ingredients, he prepares a seductively sensual plate. Everything shows his flawless technique, especially the stuffed and stewed oxtail or the saddle of venison with elderberry sauce. Taste his excellent lacquered duck breast with honey sauce or saddle of lamb with stewed peppers. The Alt-Luxemburg offers a finely balanced wine list. The service is both unpretentious and gracious.

Ponte Vecchio. Spielhagenstrasse 3. ☎ **030/342-19-99.** Reservations required. Main courses 32–46 DM ($22.40–$32.20). DC. Wed–Mon 6:30–11pm. Closed 4 weeks in summer. U-Bahn: Bismarckstrasse. TUSCAN.

Although we've dined here many times and were moderately pleased, that impression has improved. We now view this as Berlin's finest Italian restaurant. It's not the most elaborately decorated restaurant, but it caters to patrons primarily concerned with what's on the plate. Market-fresh ingredients produce a winning cuisine with a Tuscan focus. If you don't wisely opt for fresh fish of the day, you'll find any number of other dishes to tempt the palate, especially several variations of veal. Assorted shellfish is always deftly handled according to Tuscan style, with fresh basil and olive oil.

Moderate

Ernst-August. Sybelstrasse 16. ☎ **030/324-55-76.** Reservations required. Main courses 22–32 DM ($15.40–$22.40). No credit cards. Wed–Sun 6:30pm–1am (kitchen stops serving hot food at midnight). Closed July 15–Aug 15. U-Bahn: Adenauerplatz. FRENCH/INTERNATIONAL.

This unprepossessing restaurant is the type of place a local might take a friend from out of town. The setting is as quiet and unobtrusive as the antique bric-a-brac that adorns its walls. If you don't opt for the filet steak, the chef might prepare one of two variations of hare. Even the simple rumpsteak gets the care and attention of a fresh herb and green pepper sauce. This restaurant, though outclassed by dozens of establishments, still maintains a special niche.

Inexpensive

Bierhaus Luisen-Bräu. Luisenplatz 1, Charlottenburg. ☎ **030/341-93-88.** Reservations recommended on Sat and Sun. Salads, snacks, and platters 8–15 DM ($5.60–$10.50). No credit cards. Sun–Thurs 11am–1am, Sat–Sun 11am–2am. U-Bahn: Richard-Wagner-Platz. GERMAN.

One of the city's largest breweries, Luisen-Bräu opened this restaurant, close to Charlottenburg Castle, in 1987. The decor includes enormous stainless-steel vats of the fermenting brew, from which the waiters happily refill your mug. There's no subtlety of cuisine here: It's robust and hearty fare, the kind Germans enjoyed "between the wars." Victuals are offered from a long buffet table, where you serve yourself from a display of traditional German foods. The seating is indoor or outdoor, depending on the season, at long picnic tables that encourage a sense of beerhall camaraderie.

BERLIN-MITTE

Expensive

✪ Le Grand Restaurant Silhouette. In the Maritim Grand Hotel, Friedrich-strasse 158. ☎ **030/2327-4500.** Reservations required. Main courses 50–55 DM ($35–$38.50); fixed-price four-course menu 125 DM ($87.50); fixed-price seven-course menu 169 DM ($118.30). AE, DC, MC, V. Tues–Sat 6pm–1am (restaurant open until 3am). Closed July–Aug 4. S-Bahn: Friedrichstrasse. INTERNATIONAL.

This posh restaurant, offering both classic cuisine and cuisine moderne, is the finest in eastern Berlin. Although its setting is grand, it's not in the same league as the Bamberger Reiter, the Alt-Luxemburg, or Rockendorf's. Michelin, for reasons known only to its inspectors, has removed Silhouette's star, but we'll keep ours. Nowhere else in Berlin will you dine in such a sumptuous setting. An attentive staff will propose tempting hors d'oeuvres, including freshly smoked fish straight from the ovens. Main dishes include stewed venison in juniper-cream sauce and medaillons of veal with lobster slices and oysters (one of the most succulent dishes we've sampled in Berlin).

Moderate

Französischer Hof. Jagerstrasse 56. ☎ **030/229-39-69.** Reservations recommended. Main courses 28–40 DM ($19.60–$28). AE, DC, MC, V. Daily noon–1am. Closed Dec 24. U-Bahn: Hausvogteiplatz. GERMAN.

Französischer Hof opened its art nouveau doors in 1989. It fills two floors connected by a belle époque staircase, evoking a turn-of-the-century Paris bistro. One recent memorable dinner included roast duck breast with Calvados along with zucchini and potato pancakes. Admittedly, the cookery is hardly the finest in Eastern Berlin, but the ingredients are fresh and deftly handled. You'll experience far greater and more innovative meals than those served here, but sometimes you want a reasonable, unthreatening meal in a relaxed atmosphere. Many guests begin with the delectable selection of fish canapés, then proceed to the main courses. Saddle of lamb is always admirably done, though you may be more distracted by the theatrical flambéed filet Stroganoff with almond-studded dumplings.

✪ Goldene Gans. In the Maritim Grand Hotel, Friedrichstrasse 158. ☎ **030/2327-3246.** Reservations recommended. Main courses 20–46 DM ($14–$32.20). AE, DC, MC, V. Daily noon–midnight. S-Bahn: Friedrichstrasse. GERMAN.

The "Golden Goose" is a deliberate contrast to the beaux arts glamor of the hotel containing it. This rustic stube is one flight above the lobby. It has a wooden ceiling, colorfully embroidered napery, and an open-to-view kitchen. The cuisine is based on Thuringian recipes vividly evocative of old Germany. Although cholesterol counters shun it, the special appetizer of the kitchen (it doesn't appear on the menu) is goose fat with mixed pickles and freshly baked rolls. The restaurant's namesake goose appears in three preparations that are very Thuringian and very much a delicacy. A host of other regional dishes is also offered, but since this place prepares the premier goose dishes in all Berlin, why order anything else?

Inexpensive

⑤ Keller Restaurant im Brecht-Haus-Berlin. Chausseestrasse 125. ☎ **030/28-23-843.** Main courses 14–25 DM ($10.85–$19.60). AE, MC, V. Daily 5pm–midnight. U-Bahn: Oranienblurger Tor. SOUTH GERMAN/AUSTRIAN.

An unusual restaurant, it occupies the cellar of a building where Bertolt Brecht and his wife Helene Weigel once lived. The restaurant is trimmed with white plaster and exposed stone, and has scores of photographs of the playwright's theatrical productions. It serves copious portions of traditional South German and Austrian food, including fleisch laberln, tasty meatballs made with minced pork, beef, green beans, and bacon, served with dumplings. No one will mind if you just stop for a glass of its many wine offerings.

Zur Letzten Instanz. Waisenstrasse 14–16. ☎ **030/242-55-28.** Soup, 6 DM ($4.20); main courses 14–22 DM ($9.80–$15.40); fixed-price menu from 25 DM ($17.50). AE, DC, V. Daily noon–1am. S-Bahn: Kloster Strasse. GERMAN.

Reputedly Berlin's oldest restaurant, dating from 1525, Zur Letzten Instanz in its day was frequented by everybody from Napoléon to Beethoven. Prisoners used to stop off here for one last beer before going to jail. It occupies two floors of a baroque building whose facade is ornamented with a row of stone bas-reliefs of medieval faces. Double doors open on a series of small woodsy rooms, one with a bar and ceramic stove. At the back a circular staircase leads to another series of rooms, where every evening at 6, only food and wine (no beer) are served. On both floors you can select from a limited and old-fashioned menu of Berlin staples.

WAIDMANSLUST

Very Expensive

✪ **Rockendorf's Restaurant.** Düsterhauptstrasse 1. ☎ **030/402-30-99.** Reservations required. Fixed-price lunch 110–175 DM ($77–$122.50); fixed-price dinner 175–225 DM ($122.50–$157.50). AE, DC, MC, V. Tues–Sat noon–2pm and 7–9:30pm. Closed Dec 22–Jan 6 and July. S-Bahn: Waidmannslust. CONTINENTAL.

Rockendorf's occupies a 19th-century art nouveau villa near the Englischer Garten in north Berlin, a 20-minute taxi ride from the center. Chef Siegfried Rockendorf achieves a happy wedding between modern cuisine and classic specialties. The restaurant mounts a serious challenge to the Bamberger Reiter or the Alt-Luxemburg, the only one in Berlin to do so. Try such dishes as fillet of turbot in Ricard sauce, which succeeds despite being neither new nor exciting. The same could be said of the goosemeat pâté in sauterne with cranberries. The service is exquisitely refined—attentive without being cloying.

ATTRACTIONS

On the Kurfürstendamm in the western part of the city, Berliners often glance at a sobering reminder of less happy days. At the end of the street stands the **Kaiser Wilhelm Memorial Church,** with only the shell of its neo-romanesque bell tower (1895) remaining. (You can wander through the ruins Mon–Sat 10am–4:30pm.) In striking contrast is the new church, constructed west of the old tower in 1961, and nicknamed "lipstick and powder box" by the Berliners. Its octagonal hall is lit solely by thousands of colored-glass windows set into the honeycomb framework and can hold 1,200 people. Ten-minute services are held in the church daily at 5:30 and 6pm for those going home from work. There's a Saturday concert at 6pm, and an English-language service is held daily at 9am June–Aug. This remarkable combination of old and new is what Berlin is all about. Although there's more new than old in this city, which was almost flattened in World War II, Berlin offers a multitude of sights for the visitor.

SIGHTSEEING SUGGESTIONS

If You Have 1 Day   Get up early and visit the Brandenburg Gate, symbol of Berlin, then walk down Unter den Linden and have coffee and pastry at the Operncafe. Then head for Dahlem to visit the Gemäldegalerie, to see some of the world's greatest masterpieces. Afterward, go to Charlottenburg Palace and its museums to see the celebrated bust of Queen Nefertiti in the Egyptian Museum. In the evening, walk along the Kurfürstendamm, visit the Kaiser Wilhelm Memorial Church, and dine in a local restaurant.

If You Have 2 Days On day 2, return to eastern Berlin and visit the Pergamon Museum on Museum Island, seeing the Pergamon Altar. Explore the National Gallery and the Bode Museum, then head for Alexanderplatz. Take the elevator up for a view from its TV tower, before exploring the Nikolai Quarter on foot.

If You Have 3 Days On the third day, go to Potsdam (see "Day Trips from Berlin").

If You Have 5 or More Days On day 4, return to the museums of Dahlem, this time to visit the Sculpture Gallery and Ethnographical Museum. In the afternoon return to Charlottenburg Palace and explore the Historical Apartments, and in the evening visit the modern Europa-Center for drinks and dinner. On day 5, see some of the sights you might've missed. Take some walks through Berlin and stop at the cold war's Checkpoint Charlie, with its Museum Haus am Checkpoint Charlie. If time remains, visit the Berlin Zoo, stroll through the Tiergarten, and attend a cabaret in the evening.

DAHLEM MUSEUMS

Gemäldegalerie and Other Dahlem Museums. Arnimallee 23–27. ☎ **030/83-01-1.** Admission 4 DM ($2.80) adults, 2 DM ($1.40) children. All collections, Tues–Fri 9am–5pm, Sat–Sun 10am–5pm. U-Bahn: Dahlem-Dorf.

The ✪ **Gemäldegalerie (Picture Gallery)** is one of Germany's finest galleries. Of the nearly 3,000 paintings it owns, more than 600 are on display in Dahlem, another 300 in the picture gallery in the Bodesmuseum on Museum Island in eastern Berlin. The ground floor has several rooms devoted to early German masters, with panels from altarpieces dating from the 13th, 14th, and 15th centuries. Note the panel of *The Virgin Enthroned with Child* (1350), surrounded by angels that resemble the demons so popular in the later works of Hieronymus Bosch. Eight paintings make up the Dürer collection in the adjacent rooms, including several portraits.

Another ground-floor gallery is given over to Italian painting. Here are five Raphael madonnas, works by Titian (*The Girl with a Bowl of Fruit*), Fra Filippo Lippi, Botticelli, and Correggio (*Leda with the Swan*). There are early Netherlands paintings from the 15th and 16th centuries (Van Eyck, Van der Weyden, Bosch, and Brueghel) as well.

The floor above is devoted to Flemish and Dutch masters of the 17th century, with no fewer than 15 works by Rembrandt. Among the most famous of the great painter's works here is the *Head of Christ*. One painting, famous for years as a priceless Rembrandt, *The Man with the Golden Helmet,* was proven by radioactive testing in 1986 to be painted in Rembrandt's era by an imitator of his style. This remarkable painting is now accepted as an independent original.

The building also houses the **Skulpterengalerie (Sculpture Gallery),** with 1,200 works, including a bas-relief in Carrara marble by Donatello. The **Museum für Völkerkunde (Ethnographical Museum)** contains arts and artifacts from Africa, the Far East, the South Seas, and South America. Many of the figures and ritualistic masks are grotesquely beautiful, presenting a striking contrast in art, especially after a visit to the gallery of paintings. In addition, the Dahlem houses the **Museums of Far Eastern Art, Islamic Art,** and **Indian Art.**

Note: The Gemäldegalerie will begin moving part of its collection to new quarters by the end of 1997, followed by the Sulpturengalerie after the turn of the century.

Tiergarten will become the center for European art, while Dahlem will house the non-European collections.

SCHLOSS CHARLOTTENBURG & MUSEUMS

Charlottenburg is in the quarter of Berlin of the same name, just west of the Tiergarten. In addition to viewing the exhaustive collections in the palace buildings, you can enjoy a relaxing ramble through Schlossgarten Charlottenburg. The gardens have been restored and landscaped much as they were in the days of Friedrich Wilhelm II.

✪ **Schloss Charlottenburg (Charlottenburg Palace).** Luisenplatz. ☎ **030/3-20-91.** Combined ticket for all buildings and historical rooms 8 DM ($5.60) adults, 4 DM ($2.80) children under 14. Guided tours of the Historical Rooms (in German), Tues–Fri 9am–5pm, Sat–Sun 10am–5pm (last tour at 4pm) U-Bahn: Sophie-Charlotte-Platz or Richard-Wagner-Platz. Bus: 109, 121, 145, or 204.

Perhaps Napoléon exaggerated a bit in comparing Schloss Charlottenburg to the great Versailles when he invaded Berlin in 1806, but in its heyday this palace was the most elegant residence for the Prussian rulers outside the castle in Potsdam. Begun in 1695 as a summer palace for the Electress Sophie Charlotte, patron of philosophy and the arts and wife of King Frederick I (Elector Frederick III), the little residence got out of hand until it grew into the massive structure you see today. Parts of the palace were badly damaged during the war, but most of it has now been completely restored. Many furnishings were saved, especially the works of art, and are again on display. The main wing contains the apartments of Frederick I and his "philosopher queen." The **new wing,** known as the Knobelsdorff-Flügel and built from 1740 to 1746, contains the apartments of Frederick the Great, which have in essence been converted into a museum of paintings, many of which were either collected or commissioned by the king.

✪ **Ägyptisches Museum.** Schloss-strasse 70. ☎ **030/32-09-11.** Admission 4 DM ($2.80) adults, 2 DM ($1.40) children; Sun free. Mon–Thurs 9am–5pm, Sat–Sun 10am–5pm. U-Bahn: Sophie-Charlotte-Platz or Richard-Wagner-Platz. Bus: 109, 145, or 204.

The western Berlin branch of the Egyptian Museum is housed in the east guardhouse, built for the king's bodyguard. It's worth the trip just to see the famous colored bust of Queen Nefertiti, dating from the Egyptian Amarna period (about 1340 B.C.) and discovered in 1912. The bust, stunning in every way, is all by itself in a dark first-floor room, illuminated by a spotlight. It is believed that the bust never left the studio in which it was created but served as a model for other portraits of the queen. The left eye of Nefertiti was never drawn in. In addition, look for the head of Queen Tiy and the world-famous head of a priest in green stone.

MUSEUMSINSEL MUSEUMS

✪ **Pergamon Museum.** Kupfergraben, Museumsinsel. ☎ **030/203-55-0.** Admission 4 DM ($2.80) adults, 2 DM ($1.40) children; Sun free. Tues–Sun 9am–5pm. U-Bahn/S-Bahn: Friedrichstrasse. Tram: 1, 2, 3, 4, 5, 13, 15, or 53.

The Pergamon Museum complex houses several departments, but if you have time for only one exhibit, go to the central hall of the U-shaped building to see the **Pergamon Altar.** This Greek altar (180–160 B.C.) is so large it has a huge room all to itself. Some 27 steps lead from the museum floor up to the colonnade. Most fascinating is the frieze around the base, tediously pieced together over a 20-year period. Depicting the struggle of the Olympian gods against the Titans as told in Hesiod's *Theogony,* the relief is strikingly alive, with its figures projected as much as a foot from the background. This, however, is only part of the attraction of the **Department of**

Attractions in Charlottenburg

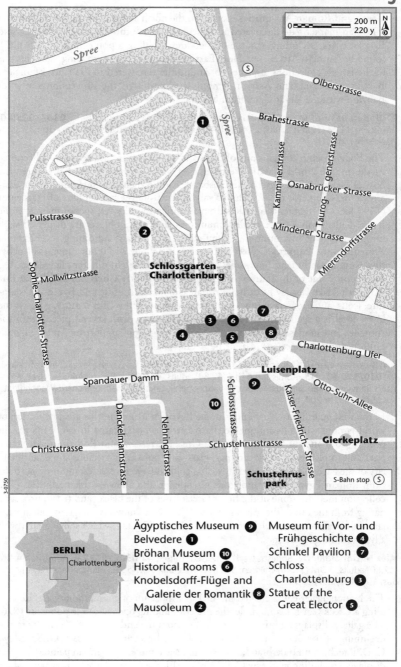

0 ————— 200 m
————— 220 y

Spree

Olberstrasse

Brahestrasse

Kamminerstrasse

generstrasse

Osnabrücker Strasse

Taurog-

Mindener Strasse

Mierendorffstrasse

Pulsstrasse

Sophie-Charlotten-Strasse

Mollwitzstrasse

Schlossgarten Charlottenburg

Charlottenburg Ufer

Luisenplatz

Spandauer Damm

Schlossstrasse

Otto-Suhr-Allee

Danckelmannstrasse

Nehringstrasse

Kaiser-Friedrich-Strasse

Gierkeplatz

Christstrasse

Schustehrusstrasse

Schustehrus-park

S-Bahn stop Ⓢ

BERLIN
Charlottenburg

Ägyptisches Museum **9**
Belvedere **1**
Bröhan Museum **10**
Historical Rooms **6**
Knobelsdorff-Flügel and
   Galerie der Romantik **8**
Mausoleum **2**

Museum für Vor- und
   Frühgeschichte **4**
Schinkel Pavilion **7**
Schloss
   Charlottenburg **3**
Statue of the
   Great Elector **5**

Greek and Roman Antiquities, housed in the north and east wings. You'll also find a Roman market gate discovered in Miletus and sculptures from many Greek and Roman cities, including a statue of a goddess holding a pomegranate (575 B.C.), found in southern Attica. The **Near East Museum,** in the south wing, contains one of the largest collections anywhere of antiquities discovered in the lands of ancient Babylonia, Persia, and Assyria. Among the exhibits is the Processional Way of Babylon with the Ishtar Gate, from 580 B.C.

✪ **Bodemuseum.** Monbijoubrücke, Bodestrasse 1–3, Museumsinsel. ☎ **030/20355-0.** Admission 4 DM ($2.80) adults, 2 DM ($1.40) children; Sun free. Tues–Sun 9am–5pm. S-Bahn: Hackescher Markt.

The Bodemuseum contains one of the world's most significant Egyptian collections. At the end of World War II, West Berliners broke up a set when they secured the bust of Nefertiti. The head of her husband, King Akhenaton, remained in the eastern sector, where it is today. Exhibits vary in size from the huge sphinx of Hatshepur (1490 B.C.) to fragments of reliefs from Egyptian temples. Of special interest is the Burial Cult Room, where coffins, mummies, and grave objects are displayed with lifesize X-rays of the mummies of humans and animals. Adjoining the Egyptian Museum is the **Papyrus Collection,** containing about 25,000 documents of papyrus, ostraca, parchment, limestone, wax, and wood in eight different languages. On the opposite side of the staircase is the **Museum of Early Christian and Byzantine Art,** with a rich display of early Christian sarcophagi, Coptic and Byzantine sculpture, icons, and even gravestones from the 3rd through the 18th century. Also on the lower level is a section of the **Sculpture Collection,** with several pieces from the churches and monasteries, including a sandstone pulpit support by Anton Pilgram (1490) carved in the shape of a medieval craftsman.

Antikensammlung (Museum of Greek and Roman Antiquities). Schloss-strasse 1. ☎ **030/320-91-215.** Admission 4 DM ($2.80) adults, 2 DM ($1.40) children; Sun free. Mon–Thurs 9am–5pm, Sat–Sun 10am–5pm. U-Bahn: Sophie-Charlotte-Platz or Richard-Wagner-Platz. Bus: 145, 109, or 204.

In the west guardhouse, just opposite the Egyptian Museum, this great collection of world-famous works of antique decorative art was inaugurated in 1960. It's rich in pottery from ancient Greece and Italy; Greek, Etruscan, and Roman bronze statuettes and implements; ivory carvings, glassware, objects in precious stone, and jewelry of the Mediterranean region, as well as gold and silver treasures; mummy portraits from Roman Egypt; wood and stone sarcophagi; and a few marble sculptures. The collection includes some of the finest Greek vases of the black- and red-figures style dating from the 6th to the 4th century B.C. The best known is a large Athenian wine jar (amphora) found in Vulci, Etruria, dating from 490 B.C., which shows a satyr with a lyre and the god Hermes.

Alte Nationalgalerie. Bodestrasse 1–3, Museumsinsel. ☎ **030/20355-0.** Admission 4 DM ($2.80) adults, 2 DM ($1.40) children; Sun free. Tues–Sun 9am–5pm. S-Bahn: Hackescher Markt. Bus: 100, 157, 257, or 348.

The Nationalgalerie was created in 1861 as a museum of contemporary art. Resembling a Greek Corinthian temple, the present building opened to the public in 1876. The gallery displays paintings and sculpture from the end of the 18th century to the beginning of the 20th. These include sculpture by such masters as J. G. Schadow, C. D. Rauch, von Hilderbrand, and Rodin. Masterpieces by German painters are also displayed, including works by Graff, Krüger, Blecken, and Slevogt. International art is represented by works of Constable, van Gogh, Rodin, Manet, Monet, Renoir, and Cézanne.

Attractions & Accommodations in Berlin-Mitte

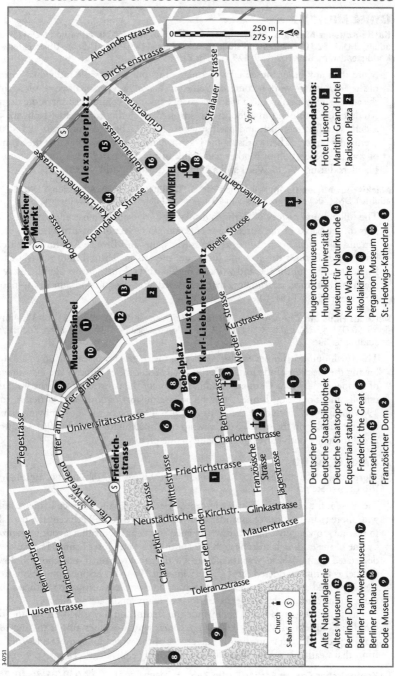

Accommodations:
Hotel Luisenhof **3**
Maritim Grand Hotel **1**
Radisson Plaza **2**

Attractions:

Alte Nationalgalerie **11**
Altes Museum **12**
Berliner Dom **13**
Berliner Handwerksmuseum **17**
Berliner Rathaus **16**
Bode Museum **9**

Deutscher Dom **1**
Deutsche Staatsbibliothek **6**
Deutsche Staatsoper **4**
Equestrian statue of
Frederick the Great **5**
Fernsehturm **15**
Französicher Dom **2**

Hugenottenmuseum **2**
Humboldt-Universität **7**
Museum für Naturkunde **14**
Neue Wache **7**
Nikolaikirche **8**
Pergamon Museum **10**
St.-Hedwigs-Kathedrale **3**

Church ✠■
S-Bahn stop Ⓢ

3-0751

OTHER MUSEUMS

Käthe-Kollwitz-Museum. Fasanenstrasse 24. ☎ **030/882-52-10.** Admission 6 DM ($4.20) adults, 3 DM ($2.10) children and students. Wed–Mon 11am–6pm. U-Bahn: Uhlandstrasse or Kurfürstendamm. Bus: 109, 119, 129, 219, or 249.

More than any other museum in Germany, this one reflects the individual sorrow of the artist whose work it contains. Some visitors call it a personalized revolt against the agonies of war, as well as a welcome change from the commercialism of the nearby Ku'damm. Established in 1986, it was inspired by Berlin-born Käthe Kollwitz, an ardent socialist, feminist, and pacifist whose stormy social commentary led to the eventual banning of her works by the Nazis. Many Kollwitz works show the agonies of wartime separation of mother and child, inspired in part by her loss of a son in Flanders during World War I and a grandson during World War II.

Märkisches Museum. Am Källnischen Park 5. ☎ **030/30-86-60.** Admission 3 DM ($2.10) adults, 1 DM (70¢) children. Tues–Sun 10am–6pm. U-Bahn: Märkisches Museum.

The full cultural history of Berlin is displayed in one of the most prominent buildings on the banks of the Spree; 42 rooms contain collections of artifacts from excavations, plus such art treasures as Slav silver items and Bronze Age finds. You can learn about Berlin's theaters and literature, the arts in Berlin and in the March of Brandenburg, and the life and work of Berlin artists. Most visitors like the array of mechanical musical instruments that are played Wed 3–4pm and Sun 11am–noon, for an extra 2 DM ($1.40).

Museum Haus am Checkpoint Charlie. Friedrichstrasse 44. ☎ **030/251-10-31.** Admission 7.50 DM ($5.25) adults, 4.50 DM ($3.15) children. Daily 9am–10pm. U-Bahn: Kochstrasse or Stadtmitte. Bus: 129.

This small building houses exhibits depicting the tragic events leading up to and following the erection of the former Berlin Wall. You can see some of the instruments of escape used by East Germans. Photos document the construction of the wall, the establishment of escape tunnels, and the postwar history of both parts of Berlin from 1945 until today, including the airlift of 1948–49. One of the most moving exhibits is the display on the staircase of drawings by schoolchildren who, in 1961–62, were asked to depict both halves of Germany in one picture.

A PARK & A ZOO

✪ **Tiergarten.** From the Bahnhof Zoo to the Brandenburger Tor. Take bus no. 100, 141, or 341 to Grosser Stern.

Tiergarten, the largest green space in central Berlin, covers just under 1 square mile, with more than 14 miles of meandering walkways. Late in the 19th century, partially to placate growing civic unrest, it was opened to the public, with a layout formalized by one of the leading landscape architects of the era, Peter Josef Lenné. The park was devastated during World War II, and the few trees that remained were chopped down for fuel as Berlin shuddered through the winter of 1945–46. Beginning in 1955, trees were replanted and alleyways, canals, ponds, and flower beds rearranged in their original patterns through the cooperative efforts of many landscape architects.

The park's largest monuments include the Berlin Zoo, described below, and the **Golden Goddess of Victory** (*Die Siegessäule*), which perches atop a soaring red-granite pedestal from a position in the center of the wide boulevard (Strasse des 17 Juni) that neatly bisects the Tiergarten into roughly equivalent sections.

✪ **Zoologischer Garten Berlin (Berlin Zoo).** Hardenbergplatz 8. ☎ **030/25-40-10.** Zoo, 10 DM ($7) adults, 5.50 DM ($3.85) children. Aquarium, 10 DM ($7) adults, 5 DM ($3.50) children. Combined ticket 16 DM ($11.20) adults, 8 DM ($5.60) children. Zoo, Apr–Oct daily

9am–6:30pm; Nov–Mar daily 9am–5pm. Aquarium, year-round, daily 9am–6pm, last Sat in the month, 9am–9pm.

In Berlin, with its surprisingly vast green expanse, you can see Germany's oldest and finest zoo. Founded in 1844, it's a short walk north from the Ku'damm, occupying almost the entire southwest corner of the Tiergarten. Until World War II, the zoo boasted thousands of animals of every imaginable species and description—many familiar to Berliners by nicknames. The tragedy of the war struck here as well, and by the end of 1945, only 91 animals had survived. Since the war the city has been rebuilding its large and unique collection; today more than 13,000 animals are housed here, some to prevent their extinction. The zoo has Europe's most modern birdhouse, with more than 550 species. The zoo's most valuable inhabitants are giant pandas.

ORGANIZED TOURS

BY BUS   Some of the best tours are operated by **Severin + Kühn,** Kurfürstendamm 216 (☎ **030/883-10-15**), which offers half a dozen tours of Berlin and its environs. Their 2-hour "Berlin City Tour" departs daily in winter at 11am and 2:30pm and daily in summer at 11am, 1:30pm, and 4pm. Priced at 30 DM ($21) per person, the tour passes most of the important attractions using buses equipped with taped commentaries of the sights en route. Among the attractions visited are the Europa-Center, the Brandenburg Gate, and Unter den Linden.

More appealing and personalized is the 3-hour "Big Berlin Tour," which departs at 10am daily, costs around 39 DM ($27.30) per visit, and—depending on the itinerary—usually incorporates sights not included on the shorter tour. Among the attractions is a section of the Grünewald Forest.

One interesting tour Tues–Sun lasts 4 hours and visits Potsdam, especially Sans Souci Palace, former residence of Frederick the Great. The price is 54 DM ($37.80) per person. Departures in winter are at 9:30am and in summer at 10am.

BY BOAT   The city's best-known boat operator is **Stern- und Kreisschiffahrt,** Pushkinallee 60–70 (☎ **030/61-73-900**). Since Germany's unification, the company has absorbed piers and ferryboats of its former East German counterparts and now offers boat rides through areas of the city that weren't accessible before the crumbling of the wall. One of these is the Historische Stadtfahrt, a ride along the banks of the river that helped build Berlin, the Spree. Departing from a quay near Berlin's cathedral, Am Palast Ufer, about six tours (in German only) a day embark on boat rides that offer good views of the Reichstag, the Pergamon Museums, the Royal Library, and the monumental heart of the former Soviet zone.

SHOPPING

The central shopping destinations are Kurfürstendamm, Tauentzienstrasse, Am Zoo, and Kantstrasse. You might also want to walk up streets that intersect with Tauentzienstrasse: Marburger, Ranke, and Nürnberger.

Despite its abbreviated name, ✪ **KPM,** Kurfürstendamm 26A (☎ **030/ 881-18-02**), is one of Europe's most prestigious emporiums of luxury dinnerware. It was founded in 1763 when Frederick the Great invested his personal funds in a lackluster porcelain factory, elevated it to royal status, and superimposed a new name (Känigliche Porzellan-Manufaktur). Each item is hand-painted, hand-decorated, and hand-packed in almost-unbreakable formats that can be shipped virtually anywhere. Open Mon–Fri 9am–6pm and Sat 9am–2pm.

Known popularly as KaDeWe (pronounced "kah-day-vay"), the luxury department store **Kaufhaus des Westens,** Wittenbergplatz (☎ **030/21-21-0**), is about two blocks from the Kurfürstendamm. The huge store, whose name means "department store of the west," was established some 75 years ago. Displaying extravagant items, it's known mainly for its sixth-floor food department, open Mon–Fri 9:30am–6:30pm (Thurs until 8:30pm) and Sat 9am–2pm. It's been called the greatest food emporium in the world. More than 1,000 varieties of German sausages are displayed, and delicacies from all over the world are shipped in. You can also explore the six floors of merchandise.

Berlin-Grafik, Schloss-strasse 60 (☎ 030/342-85-44), is one of the richest treasure troves of memorabilia related to Berlin anywhere in Germany. Its inventory includes artwork (mostly prints and drawings) of the city's past and present architecture, some steeped with respect for the imperial age's 19th-century grandeur; others more concerned with the rapid developments engulfing the city since 1945. Unframed engravings of the city start at 10 DM ($7). The establishment also sells both new and antique books on Berlin, its art, and its history. Open Mon–Fri 11am–6pm and Sat 11am–2pm.

The **Flohmarkt,** Strasse des 17 Juni (☎ 030/332-81-99), is a favorite weekend venue of countless Berliners, who wander amid its stalls looking for an appropriate piece of nostalgia, kitsch, a battered semiantique, or new or used clothing. The market is held every Sat, Sun, and Easter Mon 10am–6pm. It sprawls near the corner of the Bachstrasse and the Strasse des 17 Juni, at the western edge of the Tiergarten, adjacent to the Tiergarten U-bahn station. The **Turkish Bazaar** is held on the bank of the Maybachufer in Kreuzberg (☎ 030/781-58-44). This area adjacent to the Maybachufer Canal has been converted by Germany's "guest workers." Although much of the merchandise involves food (especially grilled kebabs), there's also a good selection of jewelry, glassware, onyx, and copper items. Open Tues and Fri noon–6pm; Friday is livelier. To reach the bazaar, take the U-Bahn to Kottbusser Tor.

Berlin's largest indoor shopping center, topped by the Mercedes-Benz star, is the **Europa-Center,** Tauentzienstrasse, in the heart of the western city. Take the U-Bahn to Kurfürstendamm. You'll also find the Berlin casino and a number of restaurants and cafes. An array of 100 shops offers wide-ranging merchandise that runs up and down the price-scale ladder.

BERLIN AFTER DARK

For information about cultural events, there are at least three magazines devoted exclusively to publicizing various happenings within the city limits. These include the English-language *Checkpoint Berlin,* a monthly magazine, which, if not available free at hotel reception desks or at tourist offices, is sold at news kiosks. Also useful is the German-language *Berlin Programm,* available at newsstands. A final German-language publication, issued at biweekly intervals, is *zitty.*

THE PERFORMING ARTS

✪ **Berliner Philharmonisches Orchester (Berlin Philharmonic).** Matthäikirchstrasse 1. ☎ **030/254-88-189.** Tickets 11–140 DM ($7.70–$98). Bus: 129.

The Berlin Philharmonic is one of the world's premier orchestras. Claudio Abbado is music director. It's home, **the Philharmonie,** is a significant piece of modern architecture; you may want to visit even if you do not attend a performance. None of the 2,218 seats is more than 100 feet from the rostrum. The box office is open in the main lobby Mon–Fri 3:30–6pm and Sat–Sun 11am–2pm. You can't place orders by phone. If you're staying in a first-class or deluxe hotel, you can usually get the concierge to obtain seats for you. Located in the Tiergarten sector, the hall can be reached from the center of the Ku'damm by taking bus no. 129.

☸ **Deutsche Oper Berlin.** Bismarckstrasse 35. ☎ **030/34-384-01.** Tickets 15–135 DM ($10.50–$94.50). U-Bahn: Deutsche Oper and Bismarckstrasse. Bus: 101 or 109.

The famed Berlin Opera performs in one of the world's great opera houses, built on the site of the prewar opera house in Charlottenburg. The present structure is a notable example of modern theater architecture that seats 1,885. A ballet company performs once a week. Concerts, including Lieder evenings, are also presented on the opera stage.

Deutsche Staatsoper (German State Opera). Unter den Linden 7. ☎ **030/20-35-45-55.** Tickets, concerts 8–57 DM ($5.60–$39.90); opera 6–190 DM ($4.20–$133). U-Bahn: Französische Strasse.

Because of the east-west split, Berlin has two famous opera companies. The Deutsche Staatsoper presents some of the finest opera in the world, along with a regular repertoire of ballet and concerts. Its home is a reproduction of the original 1740s Staatsoper, destroyed in World War II. The box office generally sells tickets Mon–Fri 10am–6pm and Sat–Sun noon–6pm. However, if you visit near the end of summer, the opera will be closed.

Komische Oper Berlin. Behrensstrasse 55–57. ☎ **030/229-25-55.** Tickets 10–82.50 DM ($7–$57.75). S-Bahn: Friedrichstrasse or Unter den Linden. U-Bahn: Französische Strasse.

The Komische Oper lies in the middle of the city near Brandenburger Tor. Over the years, the opera has become one of the most innovative theater ensembles in Europe, presenting many avant-garde productions. Opening hours for the box office are Mon–Sat 11am–7pm and Sun 1pm until 1 1/2 hours before the performance.

CABARETS

Die Stachelschweine. Tauentzienstrasse and Budapester Strasse (in the basement of Europa-Center). ☎ **030/261-47-95.** Cover 25–50 DM ($17.50–$35). U-Bahn: Kurfürstendamm.

If you know how to sing "Life is a cabaret, old chum," in German no less, you may enjoy an evening in this postwar "Porcupine." Like its namesake, it pokes prickly fun at both German and often American politicians. Get a ticket early, because the Berliners love this one. Tickets at the box office are sold Mon–Fri 10:30am–12:30pm, with performances Mon–Fri at 7:30pm and Sat at 6 and 9:15pm.

Wintergarten. Postsdamer Strasse 96. ☎ **030/262-70-70.** Cover Fri–Sat 68–92 DM ($47.60–$64.40), Sun–Thurs 50–73 DM ($35–$51.10), depending on the seat. U-Bahn: Kurfürstenstrasse.

Opened in 1893 as one of the most popular purveyors of vaudeville in Europe, it operated in fits and starts throughout the war years, until it was demolished in 1944 by Allied bombers. In 1992 it reopened in a modernized design. Today, it's the largest and most nostalgic Berlin cabaret, laden with schmaltzy reminders of yesteryear and staffed with performers who include chorus girls; magicians from America, Britain, and countries of the former Soviet bloc; circus acrobats; political satirists; and musician/dancer combos. Shows begin Mon–Fri at 8pm, Sun at 6pm, with an occasional Sat matinee at 3:30pm; they last around 2 1/4 hours each.

MUSIC CLUBS

A-Trane. Bleibtreustrasse 1. ☎ **030/313-25-50.** Cover 10–20 DM ($7–$14), depending on whomever happens to be playing at the time of your arrival. Music begins around 10pm. S-Bahn: Savignyplatz.

The name is a hybrid of the old Big Band standard, "Take the A-Train," with the suffix derived from the name of the legendary John Coltrane. This small and smoky jazz house is where virtually everyone seems to have a working familiarity with great names from the jazz world's past and present. It's open Wed–Sat at 9pm, with musicians from all over the world.

Eierschale. Rankestrasse 1. ☎ **030/882-53-05.** Cover of 4 DM ($2.80) applied to first drink. Sun–Thurs 8am–2am, Fri–Sat 8am–4am. U-Bahn: Kurfürstendamm.

Eierschale, which means "eggshell" in German, presents live music of one kind or another nightly beginning at 8:30pm. In days gone by, the club attracted such famous musicians as Louis Armstrong and Duke Ellington. Possibilities include country and western, rock, and, on Fri and Sat, jazz. When music is presented there's an admission charge. It's a Berlin tradition to visit the Eierschale for its fixed-price Sunday brunch, served 8am–2pm for 11.90 DM ($8.35).

CAFES

At the turn of the century, the imposing neoclassical decor, overstuffed sofas, and formal waiters made the **Cafe Adlon,** Kurfürstendamm 69 (☎ **030/883-76-82;** U-Bahn: Kurfürstendamm), one of the most prestigious cafes in its neighborhood. It still offers charming summer vistas from its sidewalk tables and a view of Berlin kitsch from its interior. You'll find a huge selection of cakes. Open Sun–Mon 8am–midnight and Fri–Sat 8am–1am.

The family-owned **Cafe/Bistro Leysieffer,** Kurfürstendamm 218 (☎ **030/885-74-80;** U-Bahn: Kurfürstendamm), was opened in the early 1980s within what had been the Chinese embassy. The street level contains a pastry and candy shop, but most clients climb the flight of stairs to a marble- and wood-sheathed cafe with a balcony overlooking the busy Ku'damm. The breakfast menu is one of the most elegant in town: Parma ham, smoked salmon, a fresh baguette, French butter, and—to round it off—champagne. Open Mon–Sat 9:30am–8pm and Sun 10am–7pm.

✪ **Cafe Kranzler,** Kurfürstendamm 18–19 (☎ **030/882-69-11;** U-Bahn: Kurfürstendamm), one of Berlin's most famous and visible cafes, opened in 1825 on the eastern side of Berlin, near Unter den Linden. About a century later, it moved to the then less imposing district around the Kurfürstendamm. Today owned by Swiss investors, the cafe/restaurant offers a variety of Swiss specialties, among them shredded veal Zurich style. Also available are ice creams, pastries, coffee, and drinks. Open daily 8am–midnight.

DANCE CLUBS

Big Eden, Kurfürstendamm 202 (☎ **030/882-61-20;** U-Bahn: Uhlandstrasse; Bus: 109, 119, or 129), one of Germany's most famous dance clubs, attracts disco lovers like a magnet—some 10 million and counting. In the center of Berlin, the club accommodates some 1,000 gyrating dancers nightly on a mega dance floor. Top deejays play the latest international hits. Happy hour is featured nightly. Cover is 5 DM ($3.50) Sun–Thurs and 8 DM ($5.60) Fri–Sat (includes one drink). Open Sun–Thurs 8pm–4am and Fri–Sat 8pm–7am.

The **Metropole,** Nollendorfplatz 5, Schöneberg (☎ **030/216-41-22;** U-Bahn: Nollendorfplatz), one of the leading dance clubs in Berlin, opens only on weekends for patrons in the 18- to -38 age group. Built as a theater around the turn of the century, the Metropole also contains a smaller area on its street level, La Cumbia, for dancing to the waltz, polka, tango, fox-trot, and jitterbug. Both are open Fri–Sat 9pm–dawn. Cover is 10 DM ($7) to Metropole and 15 DM ($10.50) to La Cumbia.

GAY & LESBIAN CLUBS

Motzstrasse is the center of many gay and lesbian bars. The **Knast Bar,** Fuggerstrasse 34 (☎ **030/218-10-26;** U-Bahn: Wittenbergplatz), is Berlin's leading leather bar.

No entrance fee is charged, and beer costs 4 DM ($2.80) and up. Open daily 9pm–dawn. The **Begine Cafe-und-Kulturzentrum für Frauen,** Potsdamerstrasse 139 (☎ **030/215-14-14;** Bus: 19 or 48), is Berlin's most visible headquarters for feminists and the most obvious launching pad for women seeking to meet other women. Open daily 6pm–1am.

DAY TRIPS FROM BERLIN

POTSDAM   Of all the tours possible from Berlin, the three-star attraction is the baroque town of Potsdam, 15 miles southwest of Berlin on the Havel River, often called Germany's Versailles. From the beginning of the 18th century it was the residence and garrison town of the Prussian kings. Soviet propagandists once called it a "former cradle of Prussian militarism and reactionary forces." World attention focused on Potsdam from July 17 to August 2, 1945, when the Potsdam Conference shaped postwar Europe.

The center of town is Sans Souci Park, with palaces and gardens, which lies to the west of the historic core. In the northern part of the town is the New Garden, on the Heiliger See, a mile northwest of Sans Souci. This garden contains the Cecilienhof Palace.

There are 29 daily connections with the rail stations of Berlin, taking 23 minutes to/from the Bahnhof Zoo in Berlin and 54 minutes to/from the Berliner Hauptbahnhof. For rail info in Potsdam, call **0331/322-386.** Potsdam can also be reached by S-Bahn lines S3, S4, and S7 of the Berlin rapid-transit system, connecting at Wannsee station with lines R1, R3, and R4 (trip time: 30 min.). For more information, call BVG Berlin at **0331/291-65-088.** Car access is via the E-30 autobahn east and west or the E-53 north and south.

For tourist information, contact **Potsdam-Information,** FriedrichStrasse 5 (☎ **0331/291-100**). Its hours are Apr–Oct Mon–Fri 9am–8pm, Sat 10am–6pm, and Sun 10am–4pm; Nov–Mar Mon–Fri 10am–6pm and Sat–Sun 10am–2pm.

Exploring Potsdam   With its palaces and gardens, ✪ **Sans Souci** (or **Sanssouci) Park,** Zur historischen Mühle (☎ **0331/96-94-190**), was the work of many architects and sculptors. The park covers an area of about a square mile. Once at Potsdam, you might consider an organized tour of the park and various palaces. Take tram no. 94 or 96 or bus no. 612, 614, 631, 632, 692, or 695.

Frederick II ("the Great") chose Potsdam rather than Berlin as his permanent residence. The style of the buildings he ordered erected is called Potsdam rococo, an achievement primarily of Georg Wenzeslaus von Knobelsdorff. Knobelsdorff built **Sans Souci (or Sanssouci) Palace,** with its terraces and gardens, as a summer residence for Frederick II. The palace, inaugurated in 1747, is a long one-story building crowned by a dome and flanked by round pavilions. The music salon is the supreme example of the rococo style, and the elliptical Marble Hall is the largest in the palace. As a guest of the king, Voltaire visited in 1750. Sans Souci is open daily Apr–Sept 9am–5pm; Nov–Jan 9am–3pm; and Feb, Mar, and Oct 9am–4pm; closed the first and third Mon of every month. Admission is 8 DM ($5.60) for adults and 4 DM ($2.80) for children to both Sans Souci Palace and the Bildergalerie.

Schloss Charlottenhof, south of Okonomieweg (☎ **0331/969-42-28;** Tram: 1 or 4), was built between 1826 and 1829 to the designs of Karl Friedrich Schinkel, the greatest master of neoclassical architecture in Germany. He erected the palace in the style of a villa and designed most of the furniture inside. Open daily Apr–Sept 9am–5pm; Nov–Jan 9am–3pm; Feb–Mar and Oct 9am–4pm; closed fourth

Thurs of every month. Admission is 8 DM ($5.60) adults and 4 DM ($2.80) children.

North of the 200-acre park, the ✪ **Cecilienhof Palace,** Im Neuer Garten (☎ **0331/969-42-44;** bus: 695), was ordered built by Kaiser Wilhelm II between 1913 and 1917 and was completed in the style of an English country house. The 176-room mansion became the new residence of Crown Prince Wilhelm of Hohenzollern. It was occupied as a royal residence until March 1945, when the crown prince and his family fled to the West, taking many of their possessions. Cecilienhof was the headquarters of the 1945 Potsdam Conference. Open daily 9am–5pm. Admission is 5 DM ($3.50) for adults and 3 DM ($2.10) for children.

Dining In 1878, one of the courtiers in the service of the Prussian monarchs built an elegant villa on the shore of the Heileger See. During the 1920s it was used by author Bernhardt Kellerman as the place where he wrote some of his best work. After a cold war stint as a base for Russian officers, it now functions as the most talked-about restaurant in Potsdam: **Villa Kellerman,** Mangerstrasse 34–36 (☎ **0331/29-15-72;** Bus: 695). The classically Italian cuisine might include marinated carpaccio of seawolf; a mixed platter of antipasti; spaghetti with scampi, herbs, and garlic; or John Dory in butter-and-caper sauce. Reservations are recommended. American Express and Visa accepted. Open Tues–Sun noon–midnight.

THE SPREEWALD This landmass southeast of Berlin is flat and water-soaked—but celebrated for its eerie beauty. For at least a thousand years, residents of the region have channeled the marshlands there into a network of canals, streams, lakes, and irrigation channels and built unusual clusters of houses, barns, and chapels on the high points of otherwise marshy ground. Ethnologists consider it one of central Europe's most distinctive adaptations of humans to an unlikely landscape, and botanists appreciate the wide diversity of bird and animal life that flourishes, according to the seasons, on its lush and fertile terrain. And legends abound, with tales of the spirits that inhabit the thick forests of the Spreewald.

Many of the people you'll meet here belong to a linguistic subdivision of the German-speaking people, the Sorbs, descendants of Slavic tribes who settled in the region around 600 B.C. Most modern-day Sorbs remain fiercely proud of their dialect and traditions and continue to till the soil of the Spreewald using labor-intensive methods, producing crops of mostly cucumbers and radishes.

The Spreewald is at its most appealing in early spring and autumn, when the crowds of sightseers depart and a spooky chill descends with the fog over these primeval forests and shallow medieval canals. The Spreewald lies 60 miles southeast of Berlin, and the best gateway is Lübben, reached in 60 minutes by train from the Berlin–Lichtenberg station. Once at the Lübben train station, head straight out the front exit and walk in the same direction on a tree-lined street leading into the center of town. Once here, follow the signs directing you to Kahfahrten (boat rides) or Paddlebooten (paddleboats) and you're off to discover Spreewald.

Fahrmannsverein Lübben/Spreewald, Ernst-von-Houwald Damm 16 (☎ **03546/71-22**), offers three boat trips daily exploring the Spreewald, costing 4–5 DM ($2.80–$3.50) per hour. Tours are daily 9am–4pm, departing from the Standcafé-Kahnanlegestelle. **Kahnfahrhafen Flottes Rudel,** Eisenbahnstrasse 3 (☎ **03546/35-45**), offers both boat and barge trips for the same price. You can also rent your own boats (a canoe, paddleboat, or rowboat) at **Bootsverleih Gebauer** on Lindenstrasse (☎ **03546/71-94**).

2 Munich & the Bavarian Alps

Sprawling Munich, home of some 1.3 million people and such industrial giants as Siemens and BMW, is the pulsating capital and cultural center of Bavaria. One of Germany's most festive cities, Munich exudes a hearty Bavarian *gemütlichkeit*.

Longtime resident of Munich, Thomas Mann, wrote: "Munich sparkles." Although the city he described was swept away by two world wars and some of the most severe bombing in the history of Europe, Munich continues to sparkle, as it introduces itself to thousands of new visitors annually.

The cliche notion of Munich as a beer-drinking town of folkloric charm is marketed by the city itself. Despite a roaring GNP, Munich likes to present itself as a large, agrarian village peopled by jolly beer drinkers who cling to rustic origins despite the presence on all sides of symbols of the computer age, high-tech industries, a sophisticated business scene, a good deal of Hollywood-style glamor, and fairly hip night action. Bavarians themselves are in danger of becoming a minority in Munich—more than two-thirds of the population comes from outside Germany or from other parts of the country—but everybody buys into the folkloric charm and schmaltz.

ONLY IN MUNICH

Nude Sunbathing in the Englischer Garten   On any summery sunny day, it seems that half of Munich can be seen letting it all hang out in the Volksgarten (People's Park), much to the delight of camera-toting tourists. The sentimental founding fathers of this park with their Romantic-era ideas surely had no idea they were creating a public nudist colony. If you're not much of a voyeur, and feel that most people look better with their clothes on, you can still come here to enjoy the park's natural beauty.

Snacking on Weisswürst   This sausage is the classic "street food" of Munich. Traditionally the freshly made "white sausage" of calf's head, veal, and seasoning, about the size of a hot dog, must be consumed before you hear the chimes of midday. Even in this day of refrigeration, that tradition is maintained. Smooth and light in flavor, it is eaten with pretzels and beer—nothing else. Weisswürst etiquette calls for you to remove the sausage from a bowl of hot water, cut it crosswise in half, dip the cut end in sweet mustard, then suck the sausage out of the casing in a single gesture. When you learn to do this properly, you will have become a true Münchener.

Attending Oktoberfest   It's called the "biggest keg party" in the world. Müncheners had so much fun in 1810 celebrating the wedding of Prince Ludwig to Princess Therese von Sachsen-Hildburghausen that they've been rowdying it up ever since—16 full days from September 21 to October 6. The festival becomes a tent city at the Theresienwiese. The Middle Ages live on as oxen are roasted on open spits, brass bands oompah-pah you into oblivion, and some 750,000 kegs of the brew are tapped.

Spending a Day at Nymphenburg   Just northwest of the city center lies Nymphenburg Palace, begun in 1664, an exquisite baroque extravaganza that was the summer home of the Bavarian kings. Nowhere in Munich will you experience such grandeur—a 495-acre park with lakes and hunting lodges and a spectacular palace. We prefer to visit when the summer outdoor concerts are presented, or else May–June when the rhododendrons are in bloom. Have a look at the painted ceiling in the Great Hall; here Bavarian rococo reached its apogee.

Munich Attractions & Accommodations

 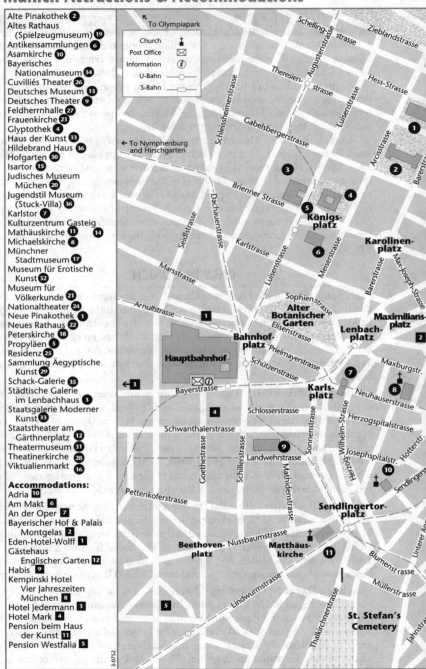

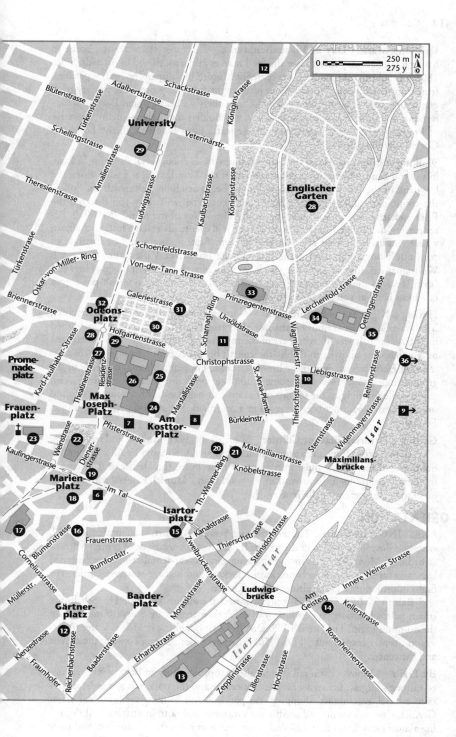

Enjoying Market Day at Viktualienmarkt The most characteristic scene in Munich is a Saturday morning at the food market at the south end of Altstadt. Since 1807 Viktualienmarkt has been the center of Munich life, dispensing fresh vegetables, fruit from the Bavarian countryside, just-caught fish, dairy produce, poultry, rich grainy breads, and farm-fresh eggs. Naturally, there's a beer garden. Even more interesting than the market produce are the stall holders themselves—many evocative of Professor Higgins's "squashed cabbage leaf," Eliza Doolittle in the London's Covent Garden of yore.

Walking and Rafting Along the Isar Admittedly, it doesn't rival the Seine in Paris, but if you can't make it for a country walk in the Bavarian Alps, a walk along the left bank of the Isar is an alternative option. Begin at Höllriegelskreuth and follow the scenic path along the Isar's high bank. Your trail will carry you through the Römerschanze into what Müncheners call "The Valley of the Mills" (Mühltal). After passing the Bridge Inn (Brückenwirt) you will eventually reach Kloster Schäftlarn where you'll find—what else?—a beer garden. After a mug you'll be fortified to continue along signposted paths through the Isar River Valley until you reach Wolfrathausen. Instead of walking back, you can often board a raft made of logs and "drift" back to the city, enjoying beer (what else?) and often the oompah-pah sound of a brass band as you head toward Munich.

Having a Night at the Hofbräuhaus Not just the city's major tourist attraction, it's the world's most famous beerhall, seating more than 4,000 drinkers. Established in 1589, at first it was for members of the royal court only, but in 1828 the citizens of Munich were allowed to drink "the court's brew." A popular song, *In München steht ein Hofbräuhaus,* spread the brewery's fame. For real authenticity, drink in the ground-floor *Schwemme* where some 1,000 beer buffs down their brew at wooden tables while listening to the sounds of an oompah-pah band. More rooms are found upstairs, and in summer beer is served in a colonnaded courtyard patio with a Lion Fountain.

Getting a Bavarian Blast of Culture With all this beer drinking and having fun, it's easy to forget Munich is a great cultural capital of Germany. Its Alte Pinakothek holds one of Germany's most important art collections; the Deutsches Museum is the largest technological museum in the world, and Munich's opera and its three orchestras are internationally renowned.

ORIENTATION

ARRIVING   By Plane The **Franz Josef Strauss Airport,** inaugurated in 1992, is among the most modern in the world. It lies 18 miles northeast of central Munich at Erdinger Moos. Facilities include parking garages; car-rental centers; restaurants, bars, and cafes; currency-exchange kiosks; lockers; and luggage-storage facilities. For flight information, call the airline of your choice.

   S-Bahn (☎ 089/55-75-75) trains connect the airport with the Hauptbahnhof (main railroad station) in downtown Munich. Departures are every 30 minutes for the 40-minute trip. The fare is 13.20 DM ($9.25); Eurailpass holders ride free. A taxi into the center costs about 90 DM ($63). Airport buses also run between the airport and the center.

   By Train Munich's main rail station, the **Hauptbahnhof,** on Bahnhofplatz, is one of Europe's largest. Located near the city center and the trade-fair grounds, it contains a hotel, restaurants, shopping, car parking, and banking facilities. All major German cities are connected to this station, most with a train arriving and departing almost every hour. Some 20 daily trains connect Munich to Frankfurt, and there

Munich U-Bahn & the S-Bahn

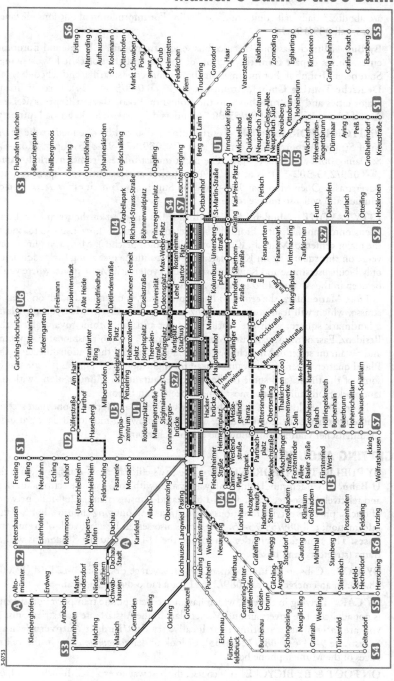

are about 23 daily rail connections to Berlin. For information about long-distance trains, call **089/194-19.**

By Bus   Munich has long-distance bus service from many German and European cities. Buses depart from the section of the Hauptbahnhof called West-wing-Starnberger Bahnhof. For information about connections, tariffs, and schedules, call **Deutsche Touring GmbH,** Arnulf Strasse 3 (☎ **089/59-18-24).** It covers many major cities and also runs buses to the Romantic Road. **Bayern Express Reisen,** Arnulf Strasse 16–18 (☎ **089/55-30-74),** offers daily service to Berlin via Nürnberg.

VISITOR INFORMATION   Tourist information can be obtained at the Franz Josef Strauss Airport in the central area (☎ **089/975-92-815),** open Mon–Sat 8:30am–10pm and Sun 1–9pm. The main tourist office, **Fremdenverkehrsamt,** (☎ **089/233-302-56),** is at the Hauptbahnhof at the south exit opening onto Bayerstrasse. Open Mon–Sat 9am–9pm and Sun 11am–7pm, it offers a free map of Munich and will also reserve rooms.

CITY LAYOUT   Munich's **Hauptbahnhof** lies just west of the town center and opens onto Bahnhofplatz. From the square you can take Schützenstrasse to one of the major centers of Munich, **Karlsplatz** (nicknamed Stachus). Many tram lines converge on this square. From Karlsplatz, you can continue east along the pedestrians-only Neuhauserstrasse and Kaufingerstrasse until you reach Marienplatz, where you'll be deep in the **Altstadt** (old town) of Munich.

From **Marienplatz,** the center and heart of the city, you can head north on Diener-strasse, which will lead you to Residenzstrasse and finally to **Max-Joseph-Platz,** a landmark square, with the Nationaltheater and the former royal palace, the Residenz. East of this square runs **Maximilianstrasse,** the most fashionable shopping and restaurant street of Munich. Between Marienplatz and the Nationaltheater is the **Platzl** quarter, where you'll want to head for nighttime diversions, as it's the seat of some of the finest (and some of the worst) restaurants in Munich, along with the landmark Hofbräuhaus, the most famous beerhall in Europe.

North of the old town is **Schwabing,** the university and former Bohemian section whose main street is Leopoldstrasse. The large, sprawling municipal park grounds, the Englischer Garten, are found due east of Schwabing.

GETTING AROUND

BY PUBLIC TRANSPORTATION   The city's efficient rapid-transit system is the **U-Bahn,** or Undergrundbahn, a subway system with convenient electronic devices and relatively noise-free rides. The **S-Bahn** rapid-transit system, a 260-mile network of tracks, provides service to various city districts and outlying suburbs. For S-Bahn information, call **089/55-75-75.** The city is also served by a network of **trams** and **buses.** The same ticket entitles you to ride the U-Bahn and the S-Bahn, as well as trams (streetcars) and buses.

BY TAXI   Cabs are relatively expensive—the average ride costs 8–12 DM ($5.60–$8.40). In an emergency, call **089/21611** for a radio-dispatched taxi.

BY CAR   Driving in the city, which has an excellent public transportation system, is not advised. The streets around Marienplatz in the Altstadt are pedestrian only. If you are interested in renting a car locally, try **Sixt/Budget Autovermietung,** Seitzstrasse 9–11 (☎ **089/22-33-33),** or look under *Autovermietung* in the yellow pages of the Munich phone book.

ON FOOT & BY BICYCLE   Of course, the best way to explore Munich is on foot, since it has a vast pedestrian zone in the center. Many of its attractions can, in fact, be reached only on foot. Pick up a good map and set out.

The tourist office also sells a pamphlet called *Radl-Touren für unsere Gäste,* costing only 0.50 DM (35¢). It outlines itineraries for touring Munich by bicycle. One of the most convenient places to rent a bike is **Lenbach + Pöge,** Hans-Sachs-Strasse 7 (☎ **089/26-65-06**), near the U-Bahn station at Frauen-hoferstrasse. It's open Mon–Fri 9am–1pm and 2–6:30pm, Sat 9am–1pm. Charges are 18 DM ($12.60) for a full day.

FAST FACTS: Munich

American Express   American Express, Promenadeplatz 6 (☎ 089/290-900), is open for mail pickup and check cashing Mon–Fri 9am–5:30pm and Sat 9:30am–noon. Unless you have an American Express card or traveler's checks, you'll be charged 2 DM ($1.40) for picking up your mail.

Business Hours   Most **banks** are open Mon–Fri 8:30am–12:30pm and 1:30–3:30pm (many stay open until 5:30pm on Thurs). Most **businesses** and **stores** are open Mon–Fri 9am–6pm and Sat 9am–2pm. On *langer Samstag* (first Sat of the month) stores remain open until 6pm. Many observe a late closing on Thurs, usually 8 or 9pm.

Currency   See "Fast Facts: Berlin."

Currency Exchange   You can get a better rate at a bank rather than at your hotel. American Express traveler's checks are best cashed at the local American Express office (see above). On Sat–Sun or at night, you can exchange money at the Hauptbahnhof exchange, open daily 6am–11:30pm.

Dentists/Doctors   For an English-speaking dentist, go to Universitäts-Kieferklinik, Lindwurmstrasse 2A (☎ 089/5160-2911); it deals with emergency cases and is always open. The American, British, and Canadian consulates keep a list of recommended English-speaking physicians.

Drugstores   For an international drugstore where English is spoken, go to International Ludwig's Apotheke, Neuhauserstrasse 11 (☎ 089/260-30-21), in the pedestrian shopping zone; open Mon–Fri 9am–6:30pm and Sat 9am–2pm.

Emergencies   For emergency medical aid, phone 089/55-77-55. Call the police at **089/110.**

Post Office   The Postamt München (main post office) is across from the Hauptbahnhof, at Bahnhofplatz 1 (☎ 089/5454-2732). You can make long-distance calls here (far cheaper than at your hotel). Mark mail "Poste Restante" (for general delivery), D-80074 München. Take along your passport to reclaim it at counter 8, 9, or 10. The office is open Mon–Fri 6am–10pm, Sat, Sun, and holidays 7am–10pm.

ACCOMMODATIONS
VERY EXPENSIVE

✪ **Bayerischer Hof & Palais Montgelas.** Promenadeplatz 2–6, D-80333 München. ☎ **800/223-6800** in the U.S., or 089/2-12-00. Fax 089/21-20-906. 440 rms, 45 suites. MINIBAR TV TEL. 430–510 DM ($301–$357) double; from 730–1,950 DM ($511–$1,365) suite. Rates include buffet breakfast. AE, DC, MC, V. Parking 28 DM ($19.60). Tram: 19.

A Bavarian version of New York's Waldorf-Astoria, in a swank location, opening onto a little tree-filled square, it is now better than ever, after zillions of marks spent on integrating the sumptuously decorated Palais Montgelas into the Bayerischer Hof. The renovation added deluxe suites and double rooms. Eighty of the guest rooms are air-conditioned. The major dining room, the Garden-Restaurant, evokes the grandeur of a small palace. Generous drinks and charcoal specialties from the rôtisserie are served in the clublike bar. There's also Trader Vic's for Polynesian nights. Facilities include a rooftop pool and garden with bricked sun terrace, sauna, and massage rooms.

✪ **Kempinski Hotel Vier Jahreszeiten München.** D-80539 München. ☎ **800/426-3135** in the U.S., or 089/221-50. Fax 089/212-52-000. 316 rms, 48 suites. A/C MINIBAR TV TEL. 480–780 DM ($336–$546) double; from 950 DM ($665) suite. AE, DC, MC, V. Parking 30 DM ($21). Tram: 19.

The most elegant place to stay in Munich is this grand hotel with a tradition stretching back to 1858. Rebuilt after a 1944 air raid destroyed it, it is still in its number-one position. The guest rooms and suites, which have hosted royalty, heads of state, and famed personalities, combine the charm of days gone by with modern amenities. Vier Jahreszeiten Restaurant, its finest dining spot, is open daily. The completely refurnished Bistro Eck surprises guests with its modern yet classical atmosphere. There's an indoor pool and sauna, solarium, and sun terrace.

EXPENSIVE

Eden-Hotel-Wolff. Arnulfstrasse 4–8, D-80335. ☎ **089/55-11-50.** Fax 089/551-15-555. 214 rms, 4 suites. MINIBAR TV TEL. 260–450 DM ($182–$315) double; from 370–500 DM ($259–$350) suite. One child up to age 6 stays free in parents' room. Rates include buffet breakfast. AE, DC, MC, V. Parking 19 DM ($13.30). U-Bahn or S-Bahn: Hauptbahnhof.

Opposite the Hauptbahnhof, the Eden-Hotel-Wolff misleads with its sedate exterior—the interior is decorated in a richly traditional style with chandeliers and dark-wood paneling. If you must stay in the station area, this stone-clad house is your best bet. The guest bedrooms have a rather fashionable decor, often with marble-clad baths. In the main dining room the theme is Bavarian—a natural-pine ceiling, gleaming brass lantern sconces, and thick stone arches. Excellent Bavarian dishes and a savory international cuisine are served.

Moderate

Adria. Liebigstrasse 8a, D-80538 München. ☎ **089/29-30-81.** Fax 089/22-70-15. 47 rms. MINIBAR TV TEL. 180–250 DM ($126–$175) double. Rates include buffet breakfast. AE, MC, V. Closed Dec 23–Jan 6. U-Bahn: 4 or 5. Tram: 20.

The Adria offers many special touches and has an inviting, friendly atmosphere. The lobby sets the stylish contemporary look. The guest rooms are furnished with armchairs or sofas, small desks, and hair dryers. Breakfast, a buffet with waffles, cakes, homemade rolls, health-food selections, and even sparkling wine, is served in the garden room. Services include money exchange, laundry, theater tickets, and arrangements for sightseeing tours. For 50 DM ($35) the hotel will give you a "license" allowing you to park free in the neighborhood; when you return the license at checkout time, the fee is returned.

An der Oper. Falkenturmstrasse 11, D-80331 München. ☎ **089/290-02-70.** Fax 089/290-02-729. 55 rms. TEL. 195–220 DM ($136.50–$154) double. Rates include buffet breakfast. AE, MC, V. Tram: 19.

Located just off Maximilianstrasse, near Marienplatz, this is a superb choice for sightseeing or shopping in the traffic-free malls, just steps from the Bavarian National Theater. It's one of the best-run hotels in this price category. Guest rooms offer first-class amenities; each has a small sitting area with armchairs and a table for breakfast. The rooms have been renovated in a light contemporary style with soft and subdued colors. A restaurant with French-style cuisine, Bosuirth, occupies space in the same building.

✪ Gästehaus Englischer Garten. Liebergesellstrasse 8, D80802 München-Schwabing. ☎ **089/39-20-34.** Fax 089/39-12-33. 12 rms (6 with bath), 15 apts. MINIBAR TV TEL. 130 DM ($91) double without bath, 138–168 DM ($96.60–$117.60) double with bath. No credit cards. Parking 10 DM ($7). U-Bahn: U3 or U6 to Münchner Freiheit.

This oasis of charm and tranquility, close to the Englischer Garten, is one of our preferred stopovers in the Bavarian capital. The ivy-covered villa was once the site of a mill. It later became a private villa, but for some two decades now Frau Irene Schlüter-Hubscher has operated it as a hotel. All the rooms are attractively furnished. In an annex across the street are 15 units that are small apartments, each with bath and a tiny kitchenette. Try for Room 16, 23, 26, or especially 20. In fair weather, breakfast is served in a rear garden.

Habis. Maria-Theresia-Strasse 2A, D-81675 München-Haidhausen. ☎**089/470-50-71.** Fax 089/47-05-101. 25 rms. TV TEL. 190 DM ($133) double. Rates include buffet breakfast. AE, DC, MC, V. U-Bahn: U4 or U5 to Max-Weber-Platz.

This small hotel of special character is across from Isarpark, overlooking the river. Over the bridge are some of Munich's leading museums. The renovated hotel, on a corner, has five floors of individualized guest rooms and a wine restaurant. The general decor, especially the entrance with its curving staircase, is modified art nouveau. The bedrooms have strong earth colors, with built-in pieces, trim beds, and casual wicker armchairs.

Hotel Mark. Senfelderstrasse 12, D-80336 München. ☎ **089/55-98-20.** Fax 089/ 559-82-333. 90 rms. MINIBAR TV TEL. 190–220 DM ($133–$154) double. Rates include buffet breakfast. AE, DC, MC, V. Parking 15 DM ($10.50). S-Bahn or U-Bahn: Hauptbahnhof.

This hotel near the Hauptbahnhof's south exit should be considered for its comfort and moderate prices. Rebuilt in 1956, it offers serviceable amenities and up-to-date plumbing. The guest rooms are modern and functionally furnished, although a bit cramped. Breakfast is the only meal served.

INEXPENSIVE

⑤ Am Markt. Heiliggeistrasse 6, D-80331 München. ☎ **089/22-50-14.** Fax 089/22-40-17. 32 rms (13 with bath). TEL. 110 DM ($77) double without bath, 160 DM ($112) double with bath. Rates include continental breakfast. No credit cards. Parking 12 DM ($8.40). S-Bahn: From the Hauptbahnhof, take any S-Bahn train headed for Marienplatz, a two-stop ride from the station.

This popular Bavarian hotel stands in the heart of the older section. The hotel is not luxurious, and owner Harald Herrler has wisely maintained a nostalgic decor in the lobby and dining room. As Mr. Herrler points out, when you have breakfast here, you're likely to find yourself surrounded by opera and concert artists who stay here to be close to where they perform. The guest rooms are basic modern—small but trim and neat. All units have hot and cold running water, with free use of the corridor baths and toilets.

Hotel Jedermann. Bayerstrasse 95, D-80335 München. ☎ **089/53-32-67.** Fax 089/ 53-65-06. 55 rms (34 with shower or toilet). TEL TV. 95–140 DM ($66.50–$98) double without shower and toilet; 130–220 DM ($91–$154) double with shower and toilet; 120–185 DM ($84–$129.50) triple without shower and toilet; 155–265 DM ($108.50–$185.50) triple with shower and toilet. Rates include buffet breakfast. Parking 8 DM ($5.60). Ten-minute walk from Hauptbahnhof (turn right on Bayerstrasse from south exit).

This pleasant, cozy spot has been deftly run by the Jenke family since 1961. Renovated and enlarged in 1990, its central location and value make it a desirable choice, with a wood-paneled interior and Bavarian furnishing. An apt choice for families, cribs or cots are available. A generous breakfast buffet is served in a charming room;

Bavarian fare can be arranged for lunch or dinner from one of the restaurants in the vicinity.

☉ Pension beim Haus der Kunst. Bruderstrasse 4, D-80802 München. ☎ **089/22-21-27.** Fax 089/834-8248. 9 rms (none with bath), 1 apt (with bath). 90 DM ($63) double; 200 DM ($140) apt for four. Rates include breakfast. AE. U-Bahn: Lehel.

Noted for its ideal location near the Englischer Garten, its copious breakfasts, and warm hospitality, this inexpensive and well-run small pension is one of Munich's best. Early reservations are important. The establishment's apartment contains the only private bath; guests in the other rooms (no singles) must share the facilities in the hallways. Built in 1956, the hotel is low-key and decent. Parking, when available, is free on the street.

☉ Pension Westfalia. Mozartstrasse 23, D80336 München. ☎ **089/53-03-77.** Fax 089/ 54-39-120. 19 rms (11 with bath). TEL. 85 DM ($59.50) double without bath, 130 DM ($91) double with bath. Rates include buffet breakfast. AE, V. U-Bahn: 3 or 6 to Goetheplatz. Bus: 58 from the Hauptbahnhof.

Facing the meadow where the annual Oktoberfest takes place, this four-story town house near Goetheplatz is one of Munich's best pensions, offering immaculately maintained guest rooms, many with TVs. Owner Peter Deiritz speaks English, and parking is free on the street, when available.

DINING
VERY EXPENSIVE

✪ A. Boettner. Theatinerstrasse 8, off Marienplatz. ☎ **089/22-12-10.** Reservations required. Main courses 50–66 DM ($35–$46.20); fixed-price lunch 87 DM ($60.90). AE, DC, MC, V. Mon–Fri 11:30am–11pm, Sat 11:30am–2:30pm. Tram: 19. INTERNATIONAL.

Boettner is a citadel of fine taste, good food, and impeccable service—all wrapped in a discreet and distinguished ambience. It's tiny and totally intimate, and has been run by the same family since 1901. Lobster is a specialty, sometimes appearing in a soufflé of pike or in an exquisite lobster stew Boettner. In season fresh venison attracts the aficionado of game. For dessert, the chocolate mousse is a particularly velvety choice.

✪ Restaurant Königshof. In the Hotel Königshof, Karlsplatz 25 (Am Stachus). ☎ **089/ 55-13-60.** Reservations required. Main courses 44–64 DM ($30.80–$44.80); fixed-price menus 128–148 DM ($89.60–$103.60). AE, DC, MC, V. Daily noon–2:30pm and 7–11pm. S-Bahn: S3, S7, or S8 to Karlsplatz. Tram: 19. INTERNATIONAL.

The owners of this deluxe hotel want the Königshof to surface near the top in culinary delights. This is no longer the finest hotel dining room in Munich, that honor having passed to others, but it still surfaces near the top. The Geisel family has made major renovations to the dining room, with its oyster-white panels of oak, polished bronze chandeliers, silver candelabra, and porcelain. Chef Martin Bräuer is both inventive and creative. His "culinary masterpieces" depend on his whim, and, almost as important, on what's available in season. He likes extremely fresh ingredients, and the food here reflects his passion. Perhaps you'll get to try his foie gras with sauternes, loin of lamb with *fines herbes*, lobster with vanilla butter, or sea bass suprême.

✪ Tantris. Johann-Fichte-Strasse 7, Schwabing. ☎ **089/36-20-61.** Reservations required. Fixed-price five-course lunch 148 DM ($103.60); fixed-price dinner 192 DM ($134.40) for five courses, 218 DM ($152.60) for eight courses; special five-course dinner Tues–Thurs (including red and white wine) 215 DM ($150.50). AE, DC, MC, V. Tues–Fri noon–3pm; Tues–Sat 6:30pm– 1am. Closed public holidays; annual holidays in Jan and May. U-Bahn: U6 to Dietlindenstrasse. FRENCH/INTERNATIONAL.

Tantris serves Munich's finest cuisine. Chef Hans Haas was voted the top in Germany in 1994, and, if anything, he has refined and sharpened his culinary technique since winning that honor. His penchant for exotic cookery carries him into greater achievements. There is no restaurant in Munich that comes close to equaling this place. The setting is unlikely—but once you're inside, you're transported into an ultramodern atmosphere with fine service.

The food is a treat to the eye as well as to the palate and the choice of dishes is wisely limited, the cooking both subtle and original. You might begin with a terrine of smoked fish served with green cucumber sauce, then follow with classic roast duck on mustard-seed sauce, or perhaps a delightful concoction of lobster medaillons on black noodles. These dishes show a refinement and attention to detail, plus a quest for technical perfection, that is found nowhere else in Munich.

EXPENSIVE

○ **Gastehaus Glockenbach.** Kapuzinerstrasse 29, corner of Maistrasse. ☎ **089/53-40-43.** Reservations recommended. Main courses 35–50 DM ($24.50–$35); fixed-price menus 60–125 DM ($42–$87.50). DC, MC, V. Tues–Fri noon–1:30pm (last order); Tues–Sat 7–9:30pm (last order). Closed for 3 weeks in August, 1 week at Christmas. U-Bahn: U3 or U6 to Goetheplatz. MODERN CONTINENTAL.

The setting is a 200-year-old building, close to a tributary (the Glockenbach) of the nearby Isar. The dignified country-baroque interior is accented with vivid modern paintings, and the most elegant table settings in town, including a lavish array of porcelain by a company not well known in the New World, Hutchenreuther. Cuisine changes with the season and according to the inspiration of the chef, Karl Ederer. Examples include imaginative preparations of venison and pheasant in autumn, lamb and veal dishes in springtime, preparations of whatever shellfish is seasonal at the time, and a medley of ultra-fresh vegetables and exotica imported from local farms and from sophisticated purveyors throughout Europe and the world.

Spatenhaus. Residenzstrasse 12. ☎ **089/290-70-60.** Reservations recommended. Main courses 24.50–42.50 DM ($17.15–$29.75). AE, DC, MC, V. Daily 10:30am–12:30pm. U-Bahn: U3, U4, or U6 to Odeonsplatz or Marienplatz. BAVARIAN/INTERNATIONAL.

One of Munich's best-known beer restaurants has wide windows overlooking the opera house on Max-Joseph-Platz. Of course, to be loyal, you should accompany your meal with the restaurant's own beer, Spaten-Franziskaner-Bier. You can sit in an intimate, semiprivate dining nook or at a big table. The Spatenhaus has old traditions, offers typical Bavarian food, and is known for generous portions and reasonable prices. If you want to know what all this fabled Bavarian gluttony is all about, order the "Bavarian plate," which is loaded down with various meats, including lots of pork and sausages.

MODERATE

○ **Alois Dallmayr.** Dienerstrasse 14–15. ☎ **089/213-51-00.** Reservations required. Main courses 28–46 DM ($19.60–$32.20). AE, DC, MC, V. Mon–Wed and Fri 9am–6:30pm, Thurs 9am–8:30pm, Sat 9am–3pm. Tram: 19. CONTINENTAL.

Alois Dallmayr's history can be traced back to 1700. Near the Rathaus, it is Germany's most famous delicatessen. After looking at its tempting array of delicacies from around the globe, you'll think you're lost in a millionaire's supermarket. Dallmayr has been a purveyor to many royal courts.

The upstairs dining room serves a subtle German version of continental cuisine, owing a heavy debt to France. The food array is dazzling, ranging from the best herring and sausages we've ever tasted to such rare treats as perfectly vine-ripened tomatoes flown in from Morocco and papayas from Brazil. The famous French poulet de Bresse, believed by many gourmets to be the world's finest, is also shipped in.

Austernkeller. Stollbergstrasse 11. ☎ **089/29-87-87.** Reservations required. Main courses 22–46 DM ($15.40–$32.20). AE, DC, MC, V. Tues–Sun 6pm–1am. Closed Dec 23–26. U-Bahn: Isartorplatz. SEAFOOD.

You get the largest selection of the finest oysters in town; many gourmets make an entire meal of raw oysters here. Others prefer them elaborately prepared. A delectable dish to start is the shellfish platter with fresh oysters, mussels, clams, scampi, and sea snails, or you might begin with a richly stocked fish soup and go on to lobster thermidor to shrimp grilled in the shell. French meat specialties are also offered. The decor, under a vaulted ceiling, is a kitsch collection of everything from plastic lobsters to old porcelain.

Ratskeller München. Im Rathaus, Marienplatz 8. ☎ **089/22-03-13.** Reservations required. Main courses 15–33 DM ($10.50–$23.10). AE, MC, V. Daily 10am–midnight. U-Bahn: U2 or U3 to Marienplatz. BAVARIAN.

Munich is proud to possess one of the best ratskellers in Germany. The decor is typical: lots of dark wood and carved chairs. The most interesting tables, the ones staked out by in-the-know locals, are the semiprivate dining nooks in the rear, under the vaulted painted ceilings. Bavarian music adds to the ambience. The menu, a showcase of regional fare, includes many vegetarian choices, which is unusual for a ratskeller. Some of the dishes are a little heavy and too porky—best left for your overweight Bavarian uncle—but you can find lighter fare if you search the menu.

INEXPENSIVE

Ⓢ **Donisl.** Weinstrasse 1. ☎ **089/22-01-84.** Reservations recommended. Main courses all 11.95 DM ($8.35). AE, DC, MC, V. Daily 9am–midnight. U-Bahn: U2 or U3 to Marienplatz. S-Bahn: All trains. BAVARIAN/INTERNATIONAL.

Donisl is Munich's oldest beerhall, dating from 1715. Some readers praise this Munich-style restaurant with its relaxed and comfortable atmosphere. The seating capacity is about 550, and in summer you can enjoy the hum and bustle of Marienplatz while dining in the garden area out front. The standard menu offers traditional Bavarian food as well as a weekly changing specials menu. The little white sausages, Weisswürst, have been a decades-long tradition here.

Hundskugel. Hotterstrasse 18. ☎ **089/26-42-72.** Reservations required. Main courses 14–37 DM ($9.80–$25.90). No credit cards. Daily 10am–midnight. U-Bahn: U2 or U3 to Marienplatz. BAVARIAN.

The city's oldest tavern, Hundskugel dates back to 1440, and apparently serves the same food as it did back then. If it was good a long time ago, why mess with the menu? Built in an alpine style, it's within easy walking distance of Marienplatz. Perhaps half the residents of Munich at one time or another have made their way here to be wined and dined in style. The cookery is honest Bavarian with no pretensions. Although the chef makes a specialty of *spanferkel* (roast suckling pig with potato noodles), you might prefer *tafelspitz* (boiled beef) in dill sauce, or roast veal stuffed with goose liver.

Ⓢ **Nürnberger Bratwurst Glöckl Am Dom.** Frauenplatz 9. ☎ **089/29-52-64.** Reservations recommended. Main courses 15–29 DM ($10.50–$20.30). No credit cards. Daily 9am–midnight. U-Bahn: U2 or U3 to Marienplatz. S-Bahn: All trains. BAVARIAN.

In the coziest and warmest of Munich's local restaurants, the chairs look as if they were made by some Black Forest woodcarver, and the place is full of memorabilia—

pictures, prints, pewter, and beer steins. Upstairs, reached through a hidden stairway, is a dining room decorated with reproductions of Dürer prints. The restaurant has a strict policy of shared tables, and service is on tin plates. The homesick Nürnberger comes here just for one dish: *Nürnberger Schweinwurstl mit Kraut*. Last food orders go in at midnight.

Wirtshaus im Weinstadl. Burgstrasse 5. ☎ **089/290-40-44.** Reservations required. Main courses 12–30 DM ($8.40–$21). AE, MC. Mon–Sat 10:30am–1am. U-Bahn: U2 or U3 to Marienplatz. GERMAN.

A weinhaus since 1850 and reputedly the oldest in Munich, Weinstadl was built in 1551 for use as a municipal wine cellar. Real old-world charm is found here: vaulted ceilings, a *trompe l'oeil* facade, and wrought-iron sconces. Dining is on three levels. Hearty Bavarian food and Palatinate wines are served; especially invigorating is the bean soup with ham. A typical main dish is roast pork with potato dumplings and mixed salad. Watch for the daily specials. In summer the activities spill over into an outdoor beer garden with a view of the neighborhood's medieval buildings.

BEER GARDENS

Bamberger Haus. Brunnerstrasse 2. ☎ **089/308-89-66.** Main courses 15.50–32 DM ($10.85–$22.40). Restaurant, daily noon–midnight; beer hall, daily 5pm–1am. AE, MC, V. U-Bahn: U3 or U6 to Scheidplatz.

In a century-old house northwest of Schwabing at the edge of Luitpold Park, Bamberger Haus is named after the city most noted for the quantity of its beer drinking. Bavarian and international specialties in the street-level restaurant include well-seasoned soups, grilled steak, veal, pork, and sausages. If you want only to drink, you might visit the rowdier and less expensive beerhall in the cellar. A large beer costs 4.50 DM ($3.15).

✪ Biergärten Chinesischer Turm. Englischer Garten 3. ☎ **089/38-38-730.** Daily 10am–midnight; Nov–Apr, closing may vary. MC, V. U-Bahn: U3 or U6 to Giselastrasse.

Our favorite is in the Englischer Garten, the park lying between the Isar River and Schwabing. The biggest city-owned park in Europe, it has several beer gardens, of which the Biergärten Chinesischer Turm is preferred. It takes its name from its location at the foot of a pagoda-like tower. Beer and Bavarian food, and plenty of it, are what you get here. A large glass or mug of beer (ask for *ein mass Bier*), enough to bathe in, costs 9.50 DM ($6.65). The food is very cheap—a simple meal begins at 15 DM ($10.50). Homemade dumplings are a specialty, as are all kinds of tasty sausage. Oompah bands often play, and it's most festive.

ATTRACTIONS
SIGHTSEEING SUGGESTIONS

If You Have 1 Day Local tourist tradition calls for a morning breakfast of Weisswürst; head for Donisl (see "Dining," earlier in this chapter), which opens at 9am. A true Münchener downs them with a mug of beer. Then walk to Marienplatz, with its glockenspiel and altes rathaus (town hall). Later stroll along Maximilianstrasse, one of Europe's great shopping streets. In the afternoon, visit the Neue Pinakothek and see at least some exhibits at the Deutsches Museum. Cap the evening with a night of Bavarian food, beer, and music at the Hofbräuhaus am Platzl.

If You Have 2 Days In the morning of day 2, visit the Staatsgalerie Moderner Kunst and, if the weather's right, plan a lunch in one of the beer gardens of the Englischer Garten. In the afternoon, visit the Nymphenburg Palace, summer residence of the Wittelsbach dynasty, longtime rulers of Bavaria.

If You Have 3 Days Occupy your third day exploring the sights you've missed so far: the Residenz, the Städtische Galerie im Lenbachhaus, and the Bavarian National Museum. If you have any more time, return to the Deutsches Museum. Enjoy dinner or at least a drink at Olympiapark, enjoying a panoramic view of the Alps.

If You Have 5 or More Days As fascinating as Munich is, tear yourself away for a day's excursion to the Royal Castles once occupied by the "mad king" Ludwig II (see "Organized Tours" and section 3, "The Romantic Road"). On Day 5, take an excursion to Dachau, the notorious World War II concentration camp, and in the afternoon visit Mittenwald for a taste of the Bavarian Alps.

THE ALTSTADT

Marienplatz, dedicated to the patron of the city whose statue stands on a huge column in the center of the square, is the heart of the Altstadt. On its north side is the **Neues Rathaus** (New City Hall) built in 19th-century gothic style. Each day at 11am, and also at noon and 5pm in the summer, the glockenspiel on the facade performs a miniature tournament, with enameled copper figures moving in and out of the archways. Since you're already at the rathaus, you may wish to climb the 55 steps to the top of its tower (an elevator is available if you're conserving energy) for a good overall view of the city center. The **Altes Rathaus** (Old City Hall), with its plain gothic tower, is to the right. It was reconstructed in the 15th century, after being destroyed by fire.

MUSEUMS & PALACES

Alte Pinakothek. Barer Strasse 27. ☎ **089/238-05215.** Scheduled to reopen in 1997. Check with tourist board for hours and admission prices. U-Bahn: U2 to Königsplatz. Tram: 18. Bus: 53.

This is not only Munich's most important art museum but one of the most significant collections in Europe. The nearly 900 paintings on display (many thousands more are in storage) in this huge neoclassical building represent the greatest European artists of the 14th through the 18th century. Begun as a small court collection by the royal Wittelsbach family in the early 1500s, the collection grew and grew. There are only two floors with exhibits, but the museum is immense.

The landscape painter *par excellence* of the Danube school, Albrecht Altdorfer, is represented by no fewer than six monumental works. The works of Albrecht Dürer include his greatest—and final—*Self-Portrait* (1500). Here the artist has portrayed himself with almost Christ-like solemnity. Also displayed is the last great painting by the artist, his two-paneled work called *The Four Apostles* (1526).

✪ **Residenz.** Max-Joseph-Platz 3. ☎ **089/29-06-71.** Museum and Treasure House, 5 DM ($3.50) adults, 3 DM ($2.10) students and seniors; Theater, 3 DM ($2.10) adults, 2.50 DM ($1.75) students and seniors; free for children under 15. Museum and Treasure House, Tues–Sun 10am–4:30pm (last tickets sold at 4pm); Theater, Mon–Sat 2–5pm, Sun 10am–5pm. U-Bahn: U3, U5, or U6 to Odeonsplatz.

This palace was the official residence of the rulers of Bavaria from 1385 to 1918. Added to and rebuilt over the centuries, the complex is a conglomerate of various styles of art and architecture. Depending on how you approach the Residenz, you might first see a German Renaissance hall (the western facade), a Palladian palace (on the north), or a Florentine Renaissance palace (on the south facing Max-Joseph-Platz). The Residenz has been completely restored since its almost total destruction in World War II and now houses the Residenz Museum, a concert hall, the Cuvilliés Theater, and the Residenz Treasure House.

The **Residenz Museum,** Max-Joseph-Platz 3 (☎ **089/29-06-71**), comprises the southwestern section of the palace, some 120 rooms of art and furnishings collected by centuries of Wittelsbachs. To see the entire collection, you'll have to take two tours, one in the morning and the other in the afternoon. You may also visit the rooms on your own.

If you have time to view only one item in the **Schatzkammer** (Treasure House), make it the 16th-century Renaissance statue of *St. George Slaying the Dragon*. The equestrian statue is made of gold, but you can barely see the precious metal for the thousands of diamonds, rubies, emeralds, sapphires, and semiprecious stones embedded in it.

From the Brunnenhof, you can visit the **Cuvilliés Theater,** whose rococo tiers of boxes are supported by seven bacchants. The huge box, where the family sat, is in the center. In summer this theater is the scene of frequent concert and opera performances. Mozart's *Idomeneo* was first performed here in 1781.

✪ Bayerisches Nationalmuseum (Bavarian National Museum). Prinzregentenstrasse 3. ☎ **089/21-124-1.** Admission 3 DM ($2.10) adults, 2 DM ($1.40) students and seniors, free for children under 15. Tues–Sun 9:30am–5pm. U-Bahn: U4 or U5 to Lehel. Tram: 20. Bus: 53.

Three vast floors of sculpture, painting, folk art, ceramics, furniture, textiles, and scientific instruments exhibit Bavaria's artistic and historical riches. Entering the museum, turn to the right and go into the first large gallery (called the Wessobrunn Room). Devoted to early church art from the 5th through the 13th century, this room holds some of the oldest and most valuable works. The desk case contains ancient and medieval ivories, including the so-called Munich ivory, from about A.D. 400.

The Riemenschnneider Room is devoted to the works of the great sculptor Tilman Riemenschneider (ca. 1460–1531) and his contemporaries. The second floor contains a fine collection of stained and painted glass—an art in which medieval Germany excelled—baroque ivory carvings, Meissen porcelain, and ceramics.

✪ Schloss Nymphenburg. Schloss Nymphenburg 1. ☎ **089/17-908-668.** If you have the better part of a day, buy the 8 DM ($5.60) ticket to the palace, Marstallmuseum (carriages), museum of porcelain, and the pavilions in the park; 5 DM ($3.50) for children 6–14. For Nymphenburg palace, Amalienburg, Marstallmuseum, and museum of porcelain only, 6 DM ($4.20) for adults, 4 DM ($2.80) for children. Apr–Sept Tues–Sun 9am–5pm; Oct–Mar Tues–Sun 10am–4pm. Parking beside the Marstallmuseum. U-Bahn: U1 to Rotkreuzplatz, then tram no. 12 toward Amalienburgstrasse. Bus: 41.

In summer, the Wittelsbachs would pack up their bags and head for their country house, Schloss Nymphenburg. A more complete, more sophisticated palace than the Residenz in Munich, it was begun in 1664 in Italian villa style and took more than 150 years and several architectural changes to complete.

Entering the main building, you're in the great hall, decorated in rococo colors and stuccos, with frescoes by Zimmermann (1756). This hall was used for both banquets and concerts in the 18th century. Concerts are still presented here in summer. From the main building, turn left and head for the arcaded gallery connecting the northern pavilions. The first room in the arcade is the Great Gallery of Beauties. More provocative, however, is Ludwig I's Gallery of Beauties in the south pavilion (the apartments of Queen Caroline). Ludwig commissioned no fewer than 36 portraits of the most beautiful women of his day. The paintings by J. Stieler (painted from 1827 to 1850) include the *Schöne Münchnerin (Lovely Munich Girl)* and a portrait of Lola Montez, the dancer whose "friendship" with Ludwig I caused a scandal that factored into the Revolution of 1848.

Neue Pinakothek. Barer Strasse 29. ☎ **089/23-80-51-95.** Admission 6 DM ($4.20) adults, 3.50 DM ($2.45) students and seniors, free for children 15 and under; free Sun. Tues and Thurs 10am–8pm, Wed and Fri–Sun 10am–5pm. U-Bahn: U2 to Königsplatz. Tram: 27. Bus: 53.

The Neue Pinakothek offers a survey of 18th- and 19th-century art. Across Theresienstrasse from the Alte Pinakothek, the museum has paintings by Gainsborough, Goya, David, Manet, van Gogh, and Monet. Among the more popular German artists represented are Wilhelm Leibl and Gustav Klimt; you'll encounter a host of others whose art is less well known. Note particularly the genre paintings by Carl Spitzweg.

◆ Deutsches Museum (German Museum of Masterpieces of Science and Technology). Museumsinsel 1. ☎ **089/2-17-91.** Admission 9 DM ($6.30) adults, 6 DM ($4.20) seniors, 3 DM ($2.10) students, 2.50 DM ($1.75) children 6–12, free for children 5 and under. Daily 9am–5pm (closes at 2pm the second Wed in Dec). Closed major holidays. S-Bahn: Isartor. Tram: 18.

On an island in the Isar River is the largest technological museum of its kind in the world. Its huge collection of priceless artifacts and historic originals includes the first electric dynamo (Siemens, 1866), the first automobile (Benz, 1886), the first diesel engine (1897), and the laboratory bench at which the atom was first split (Hahn, Strassmann, 1938). There are hundreds of buttons to push, levers to crank, and gears to turn, as well as a knowledgeable staff to answer questions and demonstrate how steam engines, pumps, or historical musical instruments work. Among the most popular displays are those on mining, with a series of model coal, salt, and iron mines, as well as the electrical power hall, with high-voltage displays that actually produce lightning. There are many other exhibits, covering the whole range of science and technology.

Antikensammlungen (Museum of Antiquities). Königsplatz 1. ☎ **089/59-83-59.** Admission 5 DM ($3.50) adults. Joint ticket to the Museum of Antiquities and the Glyptothek, 8 DM ($5.60) adults, free for children under 14. Free Sun. Tues and Thurs–Sun 10am–4:30pm, Wed noon–8:30pm. U-Bahn: U2 to Königsplatz.

On the south side of Königsplatz, the five main-floor halls house more than 650 Greek vases. The oldest piece is "the goddess from Aegina" from 3000 B.C. Technically not pottery, this pre-Mycenaean figure, carved from a mussel shell, is on display with the Mycenaean pottery exhibits in Room I. Take the stairs down to the lower level to see the collection of Greek, Roman, and Etruscan jewelry.

Glyptothek. Königsplatz 3. ☎ **089/28-61-00.** Admission 5 DM ($3.50) adults. Joint ticket to the Museum of Antiquities and the Glyptothek, 6 DM ($4.20) adults, free for children under 14. Free Sun. Tues–Sun 10am–4:30pm. U-Bahn: U2 to Königsplatz.

The Glyptothek supplements the pottery and smaller pieces of the main museum with an excellent collection of ancient Greek and Roman sculpture. Included are the famous pediments from the temple of Aegina, two marvelous statues of *kouroi* (youths) from the 6th century B.C., the colossal figure of a *Sleeping Satyr* from the Hellenistic period, and a splendid collection of Roman portraits. The collection is the country's largest assemblage of classical art.

CHURCHES

Peterskirche (St. Peter's Church), Rindermarkt 1, is Munich's oldest church (1180). Its tall steeple is worth the climb in clear weather for a view as far as the Alps. In its gilded baroque interior are murals by Johann Baptist Zimmerman. The **Asamkirche,** Sendlinger Strasse, is a remarkable example of rococo, designed by the Asam brothers, Cosmas Damian and Edgar Quirin, in 1733–46. The **Michaelskirche,** Neuhauser Strasse 52, has the distinction of being the largest Renaissance church north of the Alps. The lovely **Theatinerkirche,** Theatinerstrasse 22, with its graceful fluted columns and arched ceilings, is the work of the court architect, François Cuvilliés and his son.

❂ **Frauenkirche (Cathedral of Our Lady).** Frauenplatz 12. Free admission. Daily 7am–7pm. U-Bahn and S-Bahn: Marienplatz.

When the smoke cleared from the 1945 bombings, only a fragile shell remained of Munich's largest church. Workmen and architects who restored the 15th-century gothic cathedral used whatever remains they could find in the rubble, along with modern innovations. The overall effect of the rebuilt Frauenkirche is strikingly simple yet dignified. The twin towers, which remained intact, have been the city's landmark since 1525. Instead of the typical flying buttresses, huge props on the inside that separate the side chapels support the edifice. The gothic vaulting over the nave and chancel is borne by 22 simple octagonal pillars.

Entering the main doors at the cathedral's west end, you first notice no windows (actually, except for the tall chancel window, they're hidden by the enormous pillars). According to legend, the devil laughed at the notion of hidden windows and stamped in glee at the stupidity of the architect—you can still see the strange footlike mark called "the devil's step" in the entrance hall.

ORGANIZED TOURS

Blue buses, with sightseeing tours conducted in both German and English, leave from the square in front of the Hauptbahnhof, at Hertie's, all year round. Tickets are sold on the bus and no advance booking is necessary.

A number of city tours are offered daily, costing 15–27 DM ($10.50–$18.90) for adults and 8–14 DM ($5.60–$9.80) for children 6 to 12. Nymphenburg Palace can be visited on a 2¹/₂-hour tour, costing 27 DM ($18.90) for adults and 14 DM ($9.80) for children, Tues–Sun at 2:30pm.

For bookings and information, contact **Panorama Tours,** an affiliate of Gray Line. The office is at Arnulfstrasse 8 (☎ **089/59-15-04,** after hours 0177-20-33-037), to the north of the Hauptbahnhof. Hours are Mon–Fri 7:30am–6pm, Sat 7:30am–noon, and Sun and holidays 7:30–10am. Panorama Tours as well as several local bus companies offer excursions to Berchtesgaden, Garmisch–Partenkirchen, and to Ludwig II's fairy-tale castles.

Pedal pushers will want to try Mike Lasher's **Mike's Bike Tour,** St. Bonifatiusstrasse 2 (☎ **089/651-8275**). His bike rental services for 25 DM ($17.50) include maps and locks, child and infant seats, and helmets at no extra charge. English and bilingual tours of central Munich run Mar–Nov, leaving daily at 11:30am and 4pm (call to confirm) for 28 DM ($19.60).

SHOPPING

The most interesting shops are concentrated on Munich's pedestrians-only streets between Karlsplatz and Marienplatz.

Germany's cameras are world renowned, and **Photo-Kohlroser,** Maffeistrasse 14 (☎ 089/29-52-50), carries a good assortment of cameras and equipment. Look for the Minox cameras (sometimes referred to humorously as "spy cameras"). Open Mon–Fri 9am–6pm and Sat 9am–1pm.

Handmade crafts can be found on the fourth floor of Munich's major department store, **Ludwig Beck am Rathauseck,** Am Marienplatz 11 (☎ 089/236-91-00), open Mon–Fri 9:30am–6:30pm and Sat 9am–2pm. ❂ **Wallach,** Residenzstrasse 1 (☎ 089/22-08-71), is a fine place to obtain handcrafts and folk art, both new and antique. Shop here for a memorable object to remind you of your trip. You'll find antique churns, old hand-painted wooden boxes and trays, painted porcelain clocks, and many other items. It's open Mon–Fri 9:30am–6pm and Sat 9:30am–2pm.

❂ **Dirndl-Ecke,** Am Platzl 1/Sparkassenstrasse 10 (☎ **089/22-01-63**), one block up from the famed Hofbräuhaus, gets our unreserved recommendation as a stylish place specializing in dirndls, feathered alpine hats, and all the clothing associated with the alpine regions. Everything is of the best quality—there's no tourist junk. Bavarian clothing for children is also available. Open Mon–Fri 9am–6pm and Sat 9am–1pm.

The founders of **Gebruder Hemmerle,** Maximilianstrasse 14 (☎ **089/22-01-89**), made their fortune designing bejeweled fantasies for the Royal Bavarian Court of the fairy-tale king, Ludwig II. Today, all pieces are limited editions, designed and made in-house by Bavarian craftspeople. Open Mon–Fri 9:30am–6pm and Sat 9:30am–1pm.

On the grounds of Schloss Nymphenburg you'll find **Nymphenburger Porzellan-manufaktur** (☎ **089/17-91-970**), one of Germany's most famous porcelain makers. You can visit the exhibition and sales rooms Mon–Fri 8:30am–noon and 12:30–5pm. Shipments can be arranged if you make purchases. There's also a branch in Munich's center, at Odeonsplatz 1 (☎ **089/28-24-28**).

MUNICH AFTER DARK

To find out what's happening in the Bavarian capital, go to the tourist office and request a copy of "Monats-programm" (costing 2.50 DM/$1.75). This pamphlet contains complete information about what's going on in Munich, and how to purchase tickets.

THE PERFORMING ARTS

Nowhere else in Europe, other than London and Paris, will you find so many musical and theatrical performances. And the good news is the low cost of the seats—you'll get good tickets if you're willing to pay anywhere from 15–75 DM ($10.50–$52.50).

○ Altes Residenztheater (Cuvilliés Theater). Residenzstrasse 1. ☎ **089/2185-19-20.** Opera tickets, 30–250 DM ($21–$175); play tickets, 10–71 DM ($7–$49.70).

A part of the Residenz (see "Museums & Palaces," above) this theater is a sightseeing attraction in its own right, Germany's most outstanding example of a rococo tier-boxed theater. During World War II the interior was dismantled and stored. The **Bavarian State Opera** and the **Bayerisches Staatsschauspiel (State Theater Company)** perform smaller works here in keeping with the tiny theater's intimate character. Box-office hours are the same as those for the Nationaltheater. U-Bahn to Odeonsplatz.

Deutsches Theater. Schwanthalerstrasse 13. ☎ **089/552-34-360.** Tickets, 35–100 DM ($24.50–$70), higher for special events.

The regular season of the Deutsches Theater lasts throughout the year. Musicals, operettas, ballets, and international shows are performed here. During carnival season (Jan–Feb) the theater becomes a ballroom for more than 2,000 guests. Take the U-Bahn to Karlsplatz/Stachus.

○ Gasteig Kulturzentrum. Rosenheimer Strasse 5. ☎ **089/48-09-80.** Tickets, 23–120 DM ($16.10–$84).

The Gasteig Cultural Center is the home of the **Münchner Philharmoniker (Munich Philharmonic Orchestra),** which was founded in 1893. Its present home, which opened in 1985, also shelters the Richard Strauss Conservatory and the Munich Municipal Library. The orchestra performs in Philharmonic Hall, which has the largest seating capacity of the center's five performance halls. In the Haidhausen district, Gasteig stands on the bluffs of the Isar River. Take the S-Bahn to Rosenheimer Platz, tram no. 18 to Gasteig, or bus no. 51. You can purchase tickets at the ground-level Glashalle Mon–Fri 10am–6pm and Sat 10am–2pm. The Philharmonic season begins in mid-September and runs to July.

✪ **Nationaltheater.** Max-Joseph-Platz 2. ☎ **089/21-85-01.** Tickets, 10–250 DM ($7–$175), including standing room.

Practically any night of the year, except August to mid-September, you'll find a performance at the opera house, home of the **Bavarian State Opera,** one of the world's great opera companies. The productions are beautifully mounted and presented, and sung by famous singers. Hard-to-get tickets may be purchased Mon–Fri 10am–6pm, plus 1 hour before each performance (during the weekend, only on Sat 10am–1pm). For ticket information, call **089/2185-1919.** Take the U-Bahn or S-Bahn to Marienplatz.

BEERHALLS

Augustinerbrau. Neuhäuserstrasse 27. ☎ **089/55-199-257.**

On the principal pedestrians-only street of Munich, this beerhall offers generous helpings of food, good beer, and mellow atmosphere. It's only been around for less than a century, but beer was first brewed on this spot in 1328, as the literature about the establishment claims. The cuisine is not for dieters: It's hearty, heavy, and starchy, but that's what customers want. Half a liter of beer begins at 5.20 DM ($3.65); meals cost 20–39 DM ($14–$27.30). It's open Mon–Sat 11am–midnight. Take the U-Bahn or S-Bahn to Stachus or tram no. 19.

✪ **Hofbräuhaus am Platzl.** Am Platzl 9. ☎ **089/22-16-76.**

The world's most famous beerhall, the Hofbräuhaus is a legend. Visitors with only one night in Munich usually target the Hofbräuhaus as their number-one nighttime destination. Owned by the state, the present Hofbräuhaus was built at the end of the 19th century, but the tradition of a beer house on this spot dates from 1589. In the 19th century it attracted artists, students, and civil servants. It was called the Blue Hall because of its dim lights and smoky atmosphere. When it grew too small to contain everybody, architects designed another in 1897. This one was the 1920 setting for the notorious meeting of Hitler's newly launched German Workers Party.

Today 4,500 beer drinkers can crowd in here on a given night. Several rooms are spread over three floors, including a top-floor room for dancing. The ground floor, with its brass band (which starts playing at 11am), is exactly what you expect of a beerhall—here it's eternal Oktoberfest. A liter of beer costs 9.90 DM ($6.95); meals run 9–25 DM ($6.30–$17.50). It's open daily 9am–midnight. Take the U-Bahn or S-Bahn to Marienplatz.

Mathäser Bierstadt. Bayerstrasse 5. ☎ **089/59-28-96.**

Mathäser Bierstadt is a rowdy "beer city," filled both afternoons and evenings with happy imbibers. To reach the bierhalle, walk through to the back, then go upstairs. In addition to the main hall, there is a rooftop garden and a downstairs tavern. Daily the Mathäser holds a special program featuring a big brass band and yodeling. A liter of beer begins at 9.90 DM ($6.95); meals are 9–25 DM ($6.30–$17.50). Open daily from 8am to 11:30pm. Take the U-Bahn or S-Bahn to Stachus.

THE CLUB & MUSIC SCENE

Bayerischer Hof Night Club. In the Hotel Bayerischer Hof, Promenadeplatz 2–6. ☎ **089/ 212-09-94.** Cover 18 DM ($12.60) Fri–Sat.

This is one of the city's most sophisticated venues. A piano bar from 7–10pm, at 10pm an orchestra mounts the bandstand and plays for dancing until 3 or 4am, depending upon business. The piano bar has no cover, but the nightclub has a cover charge Fri–Sat. Drinks begin at 15.50 DM ($10.85); meals run 35–40 DM ($24.50–$28). Take tram no. 19.

Jazzclub Unterfahrt. Kirchenstrasse 96. ☎ **089/448-27-94.** Cover Tues–Sat 15–28 DM ($10.50–$19.60), Sun jam session 5 DM ($3.50).

This is Munich's leading jazz club, lying near the Ostbahnhof in the Haidhausen district. The club presents live music Tues–Sun 9pm–1am (it opens at 8pm). Wine, small snacks, beer, and drinks are sold as well. Sunday night there's a special jam session for improvisation. Beer begins at 4.80 DM ($3.35); snacks run 6.50–10 DM ($4.55–$7). Take the S-Bahn or U-Bahn to Ostbahnhof.

Schwabinger Podium. Wagnerstrasse 1. ☎ **089/39-94-82.** No cover.

This club offers varying nightly entertainment. Some evenings are dominated by oldies and rock 'n' roll. Beer begins at 5.80 DM ($4.05). It's open Sun–Thurs 8pm–1am and Fri–Sat 8pm–2am. Take U-Bahn U3, U4, U5, or U6 to Münchner Freiheit.

THE BAR & CAFE SCENE

Once a literary cafe, **Alter Simpl,** Türkenstrasse 57 (☎ **089/272-30-83**), takes its name from a satirical review of 1903. There's no one around anymore who remembers that revue, but Alter Simpl is still on the scene, made famous by its legendary owner, Kathi Kobus. It attracts a wide segment of locals, including young people. The real fun of the place occurs after 11pm, when the iconoclastic artistic ferment becomes more reminiscent of Berlin than Bavaria. Drinks begin at 7 DM ($4.90), with a beer costing 4.70 DM ($3.30) and up, and light meals costing 10–20 DM ($7–$14). It's open Mon–Sat 7pm–3 or 4am. Take tram no. 18 or bus no. 53.

Nachtcafé, Maximilianplatz 5 (☎ **089/59-59-00**), hums, thrives, and captures the nocturnal imagination of everyone—no other nightspot in Munich attracts such an array of soccer stars, film celebrities, literary figures, and, as one employee put it, "ordinary people, but only the most sympathetically crazy ones." Waves of patrons appear at different times of the evening: at 11pm, when live concerts begin; at 2am, when the restaurants close; and at 4am, when die hard revelers seek a final drink in the predawn hours. The music is jazz, blues, and soul. Beer costs 7 DM ($4.90), drinks run 12 DM ($8.40), and meals go for 18–40 DM ($12.60–$28). It's open daily 9pm–6am. Take tram no. 19.

Schumann's, Maximilianstrasse 36 (☎ **089/22-90-60**), doesn't waste any money on decor—it depends on the local *beau monde* to keep it fashionable. In warm weather the terrace spills out onto the street. Schumann's is known as a "thinking man's bar." Charles Schumann, author of three bar books, wanted a bar that would be an artistic, literary, and communicative social focus of the metropolis. Popular with the film, advertising, and publishing worlds, his place is said to have contributed to a remarkable renaissance of bar culture in the city. Drinks run 9 DM to 30 DM ($6.30 to $21). Beer is 5.50 DM ($3.85). It's open Sun–Fri 5pm–3am and closed Sat. Take tram no. 19.

GAY & LESBIAN CLUBS

Much of Munich's gay and lesbian scene takes place in the blocks between the Viktualienmarkt and Gärtnerplatz, particularly on Hans-Sachs-Strasse.

The strident rhythms and electronic sounds of **New York,** Sonnenstrasse 25 (☎ **089/59-10-56**), might just have been imported from New York, Los Angeles, or Paris. The sound system is accompanied by laser-light shows. This is Munich's premier gay (male) disco. Most clients, ranging in age from 20 to 35, wear jeans. There's no cover Mon–Thurs; Fri–Sun cover is 10 DM ($6.60) including the first drink. Beer begins at 6.50 DM ($4.55), and drinks are 16.50 DM ($11.55) and up. It's open daily 11pm–4am. Take U-Bahn U1, U2, U3, or U6 to Sendlingertorplatz.

Teddy Bar, Hans-Sachsstrasse 1 (☎ **089/260-33-59**), is a small, cozy gay bar decorated with teddy bears. It draws a congenial crowd, both foreign and domestic. There's no cover. Oct–Apr, Sun brunch is 11am–3pm. Beer costs 4.50 DM ($3.15); drinks run 11 DM ($7.70). The bar is open Sun–Thurs 6pm–1am and stays open Fri–Sat until 3am. Take the U-Bahn to Sendlingertor, or tram no. 18 or 25.

DAY TRIPS FROM MUNICH

DACHAU   In 1933 what had once been a quiet little artists' community just 10 miles from Munich became a tragic symbol of the Nazi era. In March, shortly after Hitler became chancellor, Himmler and the SS set up the first German concentration camp on the grounds of a former ammunition factory. Countless prisoners arrived at Dachau between 1933 and 1945. Although the files show a registry of more than 206,000, the exact number of people imprisoned here is unknown.

Entering the camp, **KZ-Gedenkstätte Dachau,** Alte-Roemar-Strasse 75 (☎ **08131/84566**), you are faced by three memorial chapels—Catholic, Protestant, and Jewish. Immediately behind the Catholic chapel is the Lagerstrasse, the main camp road lined with poplar trees, once flanked by 32 barracks, each housing 208 prisoners. Two barracks have been rebuilt to give visitors insight into the conditions endured by the prisoners.

The **museum** is housed in the large building that once contained the kitchen, laundry, and shower baths where the SS often brought prisoners for torture. Photographs, documents, and exhibits depict the rise of the Nazi regime and the history of the camp.

You can get to the camp by taking the frequent S-Bahn trains (train no. S2) from the Hauptbahnhof to the Dachau station (direction: Petershausen), and then bus no. 722 from the station to the camp. Admission is free, and the camp is open Tues–Sun 9am–5pm. The English version of a documentary film, *KZ-Dachau,* is shown at 11:30am and 3:30pm.

HERRENCHIEMSEE & THE NEUES SCHLOSS   Known as the "Bavarian Sea," Chiemsee is one of the Bavarian Alps most beautiful lakes in a serene landscape. Its main attraction lies on the island of Herrenchiemsee where "Mad" King Ludwig II built one of his fantastic castles.

✪ **Neues Schloss,** begun by Ludwig II in 1878, was never completed because of the king's death in 1886. The castle was to have been a replica of the grand palace of Versailles that Ludwig so admired. One of the architects of Herrenchiemsee was Julius Hofmann, who the king had also employed for the construction of his alpine castle, Neuschwanstein. When work was halted in 1886, only the center of the enormous palace had been completed. The palace and its formal gardens remain one of the most fascinating of Ludwig's adventures, in spite of their unfinished state.

The splendid Great Hall of Mirrors most authentically replicates Versailles. The 17 door panels contain enormous mirrors reflecting the 33 crystal chandeliers and the 44 gilded candelabra. The vaulted ceiling is covered with 25 paintings depicting the life of Louis XIV. The dining room is a popular attraction for visitors because of the table nicknamed "the little table that lays itself." A mechanism in the floor permitted the table to go down to the room below to be cleared and relaid between courses.

You can visit Herrenchiemsee at any time of the year. Apr–Sept 30, tours are given daily 9am–5:30pm; off-season, daily 10am–4:30pm. Admission (in addition to the round-trip boat fare) is 7 DM ($4.90) for adults, 4 DM ($2.80) for students, and free admission for children under 15.

You can reach Herrenchiemsee taking the train to Prien am Chiemsee, about an hour's trip. For train information, call **08051/1-94-19**. There is also regional bus service, offered by **RVO Regionalver-kehr Oberbayern,** Betrieb Rosenheim (☎ **08031/62-006** for schedules and information). Access by car is via the A-8 autobahn from Munich.

From Prien, lake steamers make the trip to Herrenchiemsee. They are operated by **Chiemsee-Schiffahrt Ludwig Fessler** (☎ **08051/60-90** for information). The round-trip fare is 9.50 DM ($6.65). For visitor information, contact the **Kur und Verkehrsamt,** Alte Rathausstrasse 11, in Prien am Chiemsee (☎ **0851/6-90-50**), open Mon–Fri 8:30am–6pm, Sat 9am–noon.

OUTDOORS IN THE BAVARIAN ALPS

The Bavarian Alps are both a winter wonderland and a summer playground. **Winter skiing** is the best in Germany. A regular winter snowfall in January and February measures from 12 to 20 inches. This leaves about 6 feet of snow in the areas served by ski lifts. Of course, the great Zugspitzplatt snowfield can be reached in spring or autumn by a rack railway. The Zugspitze at 9,720 feet above sea level is the tallest mountain peak in Germany. Ski slopes begin at a height of 8,700 feet.

The second great ski district in the Alps is Berchtesgadener Land, with alpine skiing centered on Jenner, Rossfeld, Götschen, and Hochschwarzeck, with consistently good snow conditions until March. There are a cross-country skiing center and many miles of tracks kept in first-class condition, natural toboggan runs, one artificial ice run for toboggan and skibob runs, artificial ice skating, and ice-curling rinks.

In summer, **alpine hiking** is a major attraction—climbing mountains, enjoying nature, watching animals in the forest. Hikers are able at times to observe endangered species firsthand. One of the best areas for hiking is the 4,060-foot Eckbauer, lying on the southern fringe of Partenkirchen (the tourist office at Garmisch–Partenkirchen will supply maps and details). Many visitors come to the Alps in summer just to hike through the Berchtesgaden National Park, bordering the Austrian province of Salzburg. The 8,091-foot Watzmann Mountain, the Königssee (Germany's cleanest, clearest lake), and parts of the Jenner (the pride of Berchtesgaden's four ski areas) are within the boundaries of the national park, which has well-mapped trails cut through protected areas, leading the hiker along spectacular flora and fauna. Information about hiking in the park is provided by the **National Park Information Post Königssee** in the former railway station at Königssee (☎ **08652/62222**).

From Garmisch–Partenkirchen, serious hikers can take overnight trips, staying in mountain huts belonging to the German Alpine Association (Deutscher Alpenverein). Some huts are staffed and serve meals. At unsupervised huts, you'll need to get a key. For information, inquire at the local tourist office or write to the German Alpine Association, Am Perlacher Forst 186, D-80997 München (☎ **089/651-0720**).

If you are a true outdoorsperson, you will use Garmisch–Partenkirchen as a base and will branch out to take advantage of all the attractions of the Berchtesgaden National Park, which is within an easy commute of Garmisch. You can also stay at one of the inns in Mittenwald or Oberammergau and take advantage of the suggested activities. Any of the outfitters below will provide directions and link-ups with their sports programs from your inn.

Other summertime activities include **ballooning,** through Outdoor Club Berchtesgaden, Ludwig-Ganghofer-Strasse 20¹/₂, (☎ 08652/50-01). Summer **curling** can be played every Tuesday evening at 7pm on the asphalt surface of the ice rink Eisstadion, Berchtesgaden. **Cycling and mountain biking** give outdoor enthusiasts an opportunity to enjoy the outdoors and exercise simultaneously. Maps are available from the **Kurdirektion** (the local tourist office) at Berchtesgaden (☎ 08652/967-0) and bikes can be rented at the train station (☎ 08652/50-74). Licensed anglers will find plenty of **fishing** opportunities at Lake Hintersee and the rivers Ramsauer Ache and Königsseer Ache with passes available from the Ramsau tourist office (☎ 08657/98 89-20). **Hang gliding** (with permission) is available from Mount Jenner through Sport Roberto (☎ 08652/32-18). **Horseback riding** lessons are available to beginners through advanced riders (☎ 08651/45-20). Practice your **kayaking** technique on one of the many rivers (water level permitting) in the area such as the Ramsauer, Königisser, Bischofswiesener, and the Berchtesgadener Aches. Beautiful valleys provide scenic **paragliding** opportunities. Contact Berchtesgadener Gleitschirmflieger e.V., Königsseestrasse 15 (☎ 08652/23-63). Go **whitewater rafting** with the Outdoor-Club Berchtesgaden (☎ 08652/50-01).

Of course there's plenty to do outdoors during the winter as well. In addition to some of the greatest **alpine and cross-country skiing** in all of Europe (☎ 08652/967-297 for current snow conditions), visitors can go **ice skating** at the rink in Berchtesgaden (☎ 08652/61405) from October through February or on the Hintersee Lake once it's sufficiently frozen. A nice way to spend a winter's night is huddled with a companion in the back of a **horse-drawn sled** (☎ 08652/34-53).

If you'd like to go **swimming** in an alpine lake—not to everyone's body temperature—there are many "lidos" found in the Bavarian Forest.

GARMISCH-PARTENKIRCHEN

In spite of its urban flair, Garmisch-Partenkirchen, Germany's top alpine resort, has maintained the charm of an ancient village. Even today you occasionally see country folk in traditional costumes, and you may be held up in traffic while the cattle are led from their mountain grazing grounds down through the streets of town. Garmisch is about 55 miles southwest of Munich.

ESSENTIALS

ARRIVING   By Train   The Garmisch-Partenkirchen Bahnhof lies on the major Munich–Weilheim–Garmisch–Mittenwald–Innsbruck rail line with frequent connections in all directions. Twenty trains per day arrive from Munich (trip time: 1 hr. 22 min.). For rail information and schedules, call **08821/19-419.** Mountain rail service to several mountain plateaus and the Zugspitze is offered by the Bayerische Zugspitzenbahn at Garmisch (☎ **08821/7970**).

By Bus   Both long-distance and regional buses through the Bavarian Alps are provided by **RVO Regionalverkehr Oberbayern** in Garmisch–Partenkirchen (☎ **08821/51-822** for information).

By Car   Access is via the A-95 autobahn from Munich; exit at Eschenlohe.

VISITOR INFORMATION   For tourist information, contact the **Kurverwaltung und Verkehrsamt,** Richard-Strauss-Platz (☎ **08821/18-06**), open Mon–Sat 8am–6pm; Sun 10am–noon.

GETTING AROUND   An unnumbered municipal bus services the town, depositing passengers at Marienplatz or the Bahnhof, from where you can walk to all centrally located hotels. This free bus runs every 15 minutes.

WHAT TO SEE & DO

The symbol of the city's growth and modernity is the **Olympic Ice Stadium,** built for the 1936 Winter Olympics and capable of holding nearly 12,000 people. On the slopes at the edge of town is the much larger **Ski Stadium,** with two ski jumps and a slalom course. In 1936 more than 100,000 people watched the events in this stadium. Today it's still an integral part of winter life in Garmisch—the World Cup Ski Jump is held here every New Year.

Garmisch–Partenkirchen is a center for winter sports, summer hiking, and mountain climbing. In addition, the town environs offer some of the most panoramic views and colorful buildings in Bavaria. The 18th-century pilgrimage **Chapel of St. Anton,** on a pinewood path at the edge of Partenkirchen, is all pink and silver, inside and out. Its graceful lines are characteristic of the time it was built. The **Philosopher's Walk** in the park surrounding the chapel is a delightful spot to enjoy the views of the mountains around the low-lying town.

EXPLORING THE ENVIRONS

From Garmisch–Partenkirchen, you can see the tallest mountain peak in Germany, the ✪ **Zugspitze,** at the frontier of Austria and Germany. Its summit towers 9,720 feet above sea level. Ski slopes begin at a height of 8,700 feet. For a panoramic view of both the Bavarian and the Tyrolean (Austrian) Alps, go all the way to the peak. The Zugspitze summit can be reached from Garmisch by taking the cogwheel train to Zugspitzeplatz. The train leaves Zugspitzeplatz daily every hour between 8:35am and 2:35pm. Travel time from Garmisch is 75 minutes. The Eibsee cable car (Eibsee–Seilbahn) may be taken from Eibsee, a small lake at the foot of the mountain. It makes the 10-minute run at least every half hour 8:30am–4:30pm (July–Aug until 5:30pm).

The cable car to the Zugspitze summit (Gletscherbahn), a 4-minute ride, departs from Sonn Alpin to the summit at least every half hour during the operating hours of the cogwheel train and the Eibsee cable car. The Zugspitze round-trip is 72 DM ($50.40) for adults and 42 DM ($29.40) for children 4 to 16; children under 4 ride free. More information is available from the Bayerische Zugspitzbahn, Olympiastrasse 27 in Garmisch–Partenkirchen (☎ **08821/79-70**).

The ✪ **Alpspitz** region can also be explored. It's a paradise for hikers and nature lovers in general. From early spring until late fall, its meadows and flowers are a delight and its rocks evoke a prehistoric world. At altitudes of 4,600 to 6,300 feet, the Alps present themselves in a storybook fantasy. Those who want to explore the northern foot of the Alpspitz can take the Alpspitz round-trip by going up on the Alpspitz cable car, over the Hochalm, and back down on the Kreuzeck or Hausberg cable car, allowing time in between for hikes lasting from half an hour to an hour and a half. Snacks are served at the Alpspitz cable car's top station or at the more rustic Hochalm Chalet.

The Alpspitz cable car to Osterfelderkopf, at a height of 6,300 feet, makes its 9-minute run at least every hour 8am–5pm. The round-trip cost is 35 DM ($24.50) for adults and 21 DM ($14.70) for children 4–14.

The Hochalm cable car from the Hochalm to Osterfelderkopf makes its 4-minute run at least every hour during the operating hours of the Alpspitz cable car. A single ride costs 6 DM ($4.20) for adults and 4 DM ($2.80) for children. The Alpspitz round-trip with the Osterfelder cable car, the Hochalm cable car, and Kreuzeck or the Kreuzwankl/Hausberg cable car is 40 DM ($28) for adults and 24 DM ($16.80) for children.

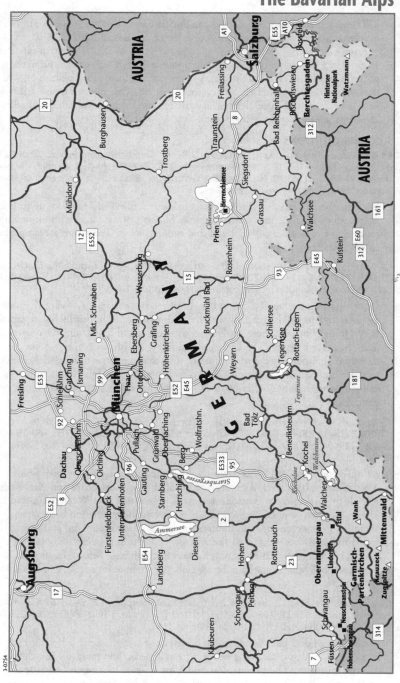

These fares and times of departure can fluctuate from season to season. Therefore, for the latest details, check with the tourist office, or else call **08821/7970.**

From Garmisch–Partenkirchen, many other peaks of the Witterstein range are accessible via the 10 funiculars ascending from the borders of the town. From the top of the **Wank** (5,850 feet) to the east, you get the best view of the plateau on which the twin villages of Garmisch and Partenkirchen sit. This summit is also a favorite with the patrons of Garmisch's spa facilities because the plentiful sunshine makes it ideal for the *Liegekur* (deck-chair cure).

ACCOMMODATIONS

☉ Gästehaus Trenkler. Kreuzstrasse 20, D-82467 Garmisch–Partenkirchen. ☎ **08821/ 34-39.** Fax 08821/1562. 10 rms (5 with shower). 77–85 DM ($53.90–$59.50) double without shower, 91–95 DM ($63.70–$66.50) double with shower. Rates include continental breakfast. No credit cards. Free parking. Bus: Eibsee no. 1.

For a number of years Frau Trenkler has made travelers feel well cared for in her guest house, which enjoys a quiet central location. She rents five doubles with showers and toilets and five doubles with hot and cold running water. The rooms are simple but comfortably furnished.

○ Posthotel Partenkirchen. Ludwigstrasse 49, D-82467 Garmisch–Partenkirchen. ☎ **08821/5-10-67.** Fax 08821/78-568. 56 rms, 3 suites. MINIBAR TV TEL. 300–350 DM ($210–$245) double. Rates include continental breakfast. AE, DC, MC, V.

Once a posting inn, the Posthotel Partenkirchen has emerged as one of the town's most prestigious hotels especially with the added asset of its unusually fine restaurant (see "Dining," below). Here you'll experience old-world living, and the owners of-fer personalized service. The U-shaped rooms are stylish, with antiques and hand-decorated or elaborately carved furnishings. The balconies are sun traps; they overlook a garden and parking for your car, and offer a view of the Alps. Golf, tennis, swim-ming, hiking, mountain climbing, skiing, cycling, hiking, horseback riding, and paragliding can be arranged.

○ Reindl's Partenkirchner Hof. Bahnhofstrasse 15, D-82467 Garmisch–Partenkirchen. ☎ **08821/5-80-25.** Fax 08821/73-401. 65 rms, 23 suites. MINIBAR TV TEL. 160–190 DM ($112–$133) double; 320–550 DM ($224–$385) suite. AE, DC, MC, V. Closed Nov 11–Dec 12. Parking 12 DM ($8.40).

Reindl's opened in 1911, and from the beginning it attracted a devoted following. Maintaining a high level of luxury and hospitality, owners Bruni and Karl Reindl have kept this a special Bavarian retreat. The annexes, the Wetterstein and the House Alpspitz, have balconies, and the main four-story building has wraparound verandas, giving each room an unobstructed view of the mountains and town. The well-furnished rooms have all the amenities, including safes. The place is also known for Reindl's much-honored restaurant (see "Dining," below). Facilities include a covered pool, sauna, sun room, health club, open terrace for snacks, and two attrac-tive gardens.

○ Romantik-Hotel Clausing's Posthotel. Marienplatz 12, D-82467 Garmisch–Partenkirchen. ☎ **08821/7090.** Fax 08821/70-92-05. 42 rms, 1 suite. TV TEL. 160–200 DM ($112–$140) double; 450 DM ($315) suite. AE, DC, MC, V.

Set behind a florid pink facade in the heart of town, it was originally built in 1512 as a tavern—it began accepting refugees from besieged and ravaged Munich within its walls during the Thirty Years War, and it has retained its *gemütlich* antique charm. In the early 1990s it was radically upgraded. What had been unused space beneath the eaves was transformed into the finest accommodations at the inn. The rooms successfully mingle a traditional ambience with all the modern, well-insulated comforts you'd expect. The most glamorous restaurant here is the Stüberl, a paneled enclave of warmth and carefully presented cuisine.

DINING

⑤ Flösserstuben. Schmiedstrasse 2. ☎ **08821/28-88.** Reservations recommended. Main courses 12–32.50 DM ($8.40–$22.75). AE, MC. Daily 11am–2:30pm and daily 4:30–11pm (or as late as 1:30am, depending on business). Town bus. GREEK/BAVARIAN/INTERNATIONAL.

Regardless of the season, a bit of the Bavarian Alps always seems to flower amid the wood-trimmed nostalgia of this intimate restaurant that lies close to the town center. On certain evenings, the weathered beams above the dining tables are likely to reverberate with laughter and good times. You can select a seat at a colorful wooden table or on an ox yoke–inspired stool in front of the spliced saplings that decorate the bar. Moussaka and souvlaki, as well as sauerbraten and all kinds of Bavarian dishes, are abundantly available.

Posthotel Partenkirchen. Ludwigstrasse 49, Partenkirchen. ☎ **08821/5-10-67.** Reservations required. Main courses 22–50 DM ($15.40–$35); fixed-price menus 32–76 DM ($22.40–$53.20). AE, DC, MC, V. Daily noon–2pm and 6–9:30pm. CONTINENTAL.

The Posthotel Partenkirchen is renowned for its distinguished cuisine. The interior dining rooms are rustic, with lots of mellow, old-fashioned atmosphere. You could imagine meeting Dürer here. Everything seems comfortably subdued, including the guests. The best way to dine here is to order one of the fixed-price menus, which change daily, depending on the availability of seasonal produce. The à la carte menu is extensive, featuring game in the autumn. You can order main dishes such as schnitzel cordon bleu or mixed grill St. James. The Wiener schnitzel served with a large salad is the best we've had in the resort.

○ Reindl's Restaurant. In the Partenkirchner Hof, Bahnhofstrasse 15. ☎ **08821/5-80-25.** Reservations required. Main courses 27–41 DM ($18.90–$28.70); fixed-price lunch 50 DM ($35); fixed-price dinner 120 DM ($84). AE, DC, MC, V. Daily noon–2:30pm and 6:30–11pm. Closed Nov 11–Dec 12. CONTINENTAL.

Reindl's is first class in every sense of the word. The seasonal menu comprises cuisine moderne as well as regional Bavarian dishes. The chef de cuisine is Marianne Holzinger, daughter of founding father Karl Reindl. The restaurant is known for honoring each "food season": For example, if you're here in asparagus season in spring, a special menu samples the dish in all the best-known recipes.

Among main dishes, we recommend coq au Riesling (chicken in Riesling wine) with noodles, or veal roasted with *steinpilzen,* a special mushroom from the Bavarian mountains. Among the fish dishes, try wild salmon with white and red wine and butter sauce.

MITTENWALD

Seeming straight out of *The Sound of Music,* the year-round resort of Mittenwald lies in a pass in the Karwendel Range, 11 miles southeast of Garmisch–Partenkirchen. Especially noteworthy and photogenic are the painted Bavarian houses with overhanging eaves. Even the baroque church tower is covered with frescoes. On the square stands a monument to Mathias Klotz, who introduced violin making to Mittenwald in 1684. The town is a major international center for this highly specialized craft.

ESSENTIALS

ARRIVING   By Train   Mittenwald can be reached by almost hourly train service, since it lies on the express rail line between Munich and Innsbruck (Austria). From Munich, trip time is 1½ to 2 hours, depending on the train. Call **908102/19-419** for information.

BY BUS   Regional bus service from Garmisch–Partenkirchen and nearby towns is frequently provided by RVO Regionalverkehr Oberbayern at Garmisch (☎ **08821/ 51-822** for schedules and information).

BY CAR   Access by car is via the A-95 autobahn from Munich.

Visitor Information   Contact the **Kurverwaltung und Verkehrsamt,** Dammkarstrasse 3 (☎ **08823/3-39-81**), open Mon–Fri 8am–noon and 1–5pm; Sat 10am–noon.

WHAT TO SEE & DO

The town's museum, with a workshop, has exhibits devoted to violins and other string instruments, from their invention through various stages of their evolution. The **Geigenbau- und Heimatmuseum,** Ballenhausgasse 3 (☎ **08823/25-11**), is open Mon–Fri 10–11:45am and 2–4:45pm and Sat–Sun 10–11:45am, charging an admission of 2.50 DM ($1.75) for adults and 1 DM (70¢) for children. The museum is closed Nov 1–Dec 20.

In the countryside, you are constantly exposed to the changing scenery of the Wetterstein and Karwendel ranges. Horse and carriage trips are available as well as coach tours from Mittenwald to nearby villages. In the evening there is typical Bavarian entertainment, often consisting of folk dancing and singing, zither playing, and yodeling, but you also have your choice of concerts, dance bands, discos, and bars. Mittenwald has good spa facilities, in large gardens landscaped with tree-lined streams and trout pools. Concerts during the summer are held in the music pavilion.

OUTDOOR ACTIVITIES

In winter the town is a skiing center and remains equally active throughout the summer with an array of outdoor activities beckoning visitors. Some 80 miles of paths wind up and down the mountains around the village. Chairlifts make the hiking trails readily accessible. Of course where there are trails there is mountain hiking. A biking map is available from the tourist office (see above). Mountain climbing expeditions are also available. You can always go swimming to cool off on a hot summer's day—the Lautersee and Ferchensee are brisk waters that, even in summer, might be forfeited by the faint-hearted for the heated adventure pool in Mittenwald.

ACCOMMODATIONS

Alpenrose. Obermarkt 1, D-82481 Mittenwald. ☎ **08823/50-55.** Fax 08823/37-20. 20 rms, 2 suites. MINIBAR TV TEL. 124–185 DM ($86.80–$129.50) double; 185 DM ($129.50) suite. Rates include buffet breakfast. AE, DC, MC, V. Free parking.

In the village center at the foot of a rugged mountain, the facade of this inn is covered with decorative designs; window boxes hold flowering vines. In the 14th century, the inn was part of a monastery. The present inn is comfortable, with suitable plumbing facilities. The hotel has a less desirable annex, the Bichlerhof. The tavern room, overlooking the street, has many ingratiating features, including coved ceilings.

ⓢ Berghotel Latscheneck. Kaffeefeld 1, D-82481 Mittenwald. ☎ **08823/14-19.** Fax 08823/ 10-58. 12 rms. TV TEL. 200–230 DM ($140–$161) double. Rates include continental breakfast. No credit cards. Closed Apr 18–May and Nov 25–Dec. Free parking.

Set against a craggy backdrop of rock and forest a short walk above the center of town, this chalet is ringed with green shutters, wraparound balconies, and a flagstone-covered sun terrace. The guest rooms are modern and attractively furnished. During chilly weather an open fireplace illuminates the knickknack-covered walls of the eating areas (open only to guests). The Kranzberg ski lift is nearby, and a covered pool and sauna can provide a relaxing prelude to a quiet evening.

Ⓢ **Gästehaus Franziska.** Innsbruckerstrasse 24, D-82481 Mittenwald. ☎**08823/92030.** Fax 08823/38-93. 14 rms, 4 suites. MINIBAR TEL. 98–138 DM ($68.60–$96.60) double; 158–178 DM ($110.60–$124.60) suite. Rates include buffet breakfast. AE, V. Closed Nov 11–Dec 13. Free parking.

When Olaf Grothe built this guest house, he named it after the most important person in his life—his wife, Franziska. Both have labored to make it the most personalized guesthouse in town by furnishing it tastefully and giving their guests sympathetic attention. Each room and suite is furnished with traditional Bavarian styling. All have balconies opening onto mountain views; the suites also have safes and tea or coffee facilities. Breakfast is the only meal served, but there are plenty of restaurants nearby. It's extremely difficult to obtain bookings June 20–Oct 2.

DINING

Ⓢ **Restaurant Arnspitze.** Innsbruckerstrasse 68. ☎ **08823/24-25.** Reservations not required. Main courses 25–38 DM ($17.50–$26.60); fixed-price lunch 36.50 DM ($25.55); fixed-price dinner 76.50 DM ($53.55). AE. Thurs–Mon noon–2pm; daily 6–9pm. Closed Oct 25–Dec 19. Bus: RVO. BAVARIAN.

Housed in a modern chalet hotel on the outskirts of town, the Restaurant Arnspitze is the finest dining room in Mittenwald. The restaurant is decorated in the old style; the cuisine is solid, satisfying, and wholesome. You might order sole with homemade noodles or veal steak in creamy smooth sauce, then finish with one of the freshly made desserts. There's an excellent fixed-price lunch.

OBERAMMERGAU

In this alpine village, 12 miles north of Garmisch–Partenkirchen, the world-famous passion play is presented, usually every 10 years; the next one is scheduled for the year 2000. Surely the world's longest-running show (in more ways than one), it began in 1634 when the town's citizens took a vow after they were spared from the devastating plague of 1633. Lasting about 8 hours, the play is divided into episodes, each introduced by an Old Testament tableau connecting predictions of the great prophets to incidents of Jesus's suffering.

A visit to Oberammergau is ideal in summer or winter. It stands in a wide valley surrounded by forests and mountains, with sunny slopes and meadows. It has long been known for the skill of its woodcarvers. Here in this village right under the Kofel, farms are still intact, and tradition still prevails.

ESSENTIALS

ARRIVING   By Train   The Oberammergau Bahnhof is on the Murnau–Bad Kohlgrum–Oberammergau rail line, with frequent connections in all directions. Through Murnau, all major German cities can be reached. Daily trains from Munich take 2 hours; from Frankfurt, 7 hours. For rail information and schedules, call **08821/19-419.**

By Bus   Regional bus service to nearby towns is offered by RVO Regionalverkehr Oberbayern in Garmisch–Partenkirchen (☎ **08821/51-822**). An unnumbered bus goes back and forth between Oberammergau and Garmisch–Partenkirchen.

By Car   The trip from Munich takes about 1¹/₂ hours, and 5¹/₂ hours from Frankfurt. Take the A-95 Munich–Garmisch–Partenkirchen autobahn and exit at Eschenlohe.

VISITOR INFORMATION   Contact the **Verkehrsbüro,** Eugen-Papst-Strasse 9A (☎ **08822/10-21**), open Mon–Fri 8:30am–6pm and Sat 8:30am–noon.

WHAT TO SEE & DO

The **Passionspielhaus,** Passionwiese, where the passion play is performed, is at the edge of town. The roofed auditorium holds 4,700 spectators, and the open-air stage is a wonder of engineering, with a curtained center stage flanked by gates opening onto the so-called streets of Jerusalem. The auditorium is open to the public daily 10am–noon and 1:30–4pm. Admission is 4 DM ($2.80) for adults and 2.50 DM ($1.75) for children and students.

Aside from the actors, Oberammergau's most respected citizens include another unusual group, the woodcarvers, many of whom have been trained in the village's woodcarver's school. In the **Pilatushaus,** Ludwigthomstrasse (☎ **08822/1682**), you can watch local artists at work, including woodcarvers, painters, sculptors, and potters. Hours are Mon–Fri 10:30am–5:30pm. You'll see many examples of these art forms throughout the town, on the painted cottages and inns and in the churchyard. Also worth seeing when strolling through the village are the houses with frescoes by Franz Zwink (18th century) that are named after fairy-tale characters, such as "Hansel and Gretel House" and the "Little Red Riding Hood House."

The **Heimatmuseum,** Dorfstrasse (☎ **08822/94136**), has a notable collection of Christmas crèches, all hand-carved and -painted, and dating from the 18th through the 20th century. It's open May 15–Oct 15 Tues–Sat 2–6pm; off-season, Sat 2–6pm. Admission is 3 DM ($2.10) for adults and 1.50 DM ($1.05) for children.

NEARBY ATTRACTIONS   The Ammer Valley, with Oberammergau in the (almost) center, offers easy access to many nearby attractions. **Schloss Linderhof,** designed as a French rococo palace, the smallest and perhaps the most successful of Ludwig II's constructions, is open throughout the year. The 18th-century **Kloster Ettal,** one of the finest examples of Bavarian rococo architecture, lies 2 miles from Oberammergau. Both can be reached by frequent bus service; inquire at the tourist office for details.

OUTDOOR ACTIVITIES

Numerous hiking trails lead through the mountains around Oberammergau to hikers' inns such as the **Kolbenalm** and the **Romanshohe.** You can, however, simply go up to the mountaintops on the Laber cable railway or the Kolben chairlift. Oberammergau also offers opportunities to tennis buffs, minigolf players, cyclists, swimmers, hang-gliding enthusiasts, and canoeists. The recreation center **Wellenberg,** with its large alpine swimming complex with open-air pools, hot water and fountains, sauna, solarium, and restaurant, is one of the Alps' most beautiful recreation centers.

ACCOMMODATIONS & DINING

Ⓢ **Alte Post.** Dorfstrasse 19, D-82487 Oberammergau. ☎ **08822/91-00.** Fax 08822/910-100. 32 rms (28 with bath). TV TEL. 120 DM ($84) double without bath, 140 DM ($98) double with bath. Rates include continental breakfast. AE, MC, V. Closed Oct 25–Dec 19. Parking 6 DM ($4.20). Bus: 30.

A provincial inn in the village center, the Alte Post is built in chalet style—wide overhanging roof, green-shuttered windows painted with decorative trim, and tables set on a sidewalk under a long awning. It's the village social hub. The interior has storybook charm, with a ceiling-high green ceramic stove, alpine chairs, and shelves of pewter plates. The rustic guest rooms have wood-beamed ceilings and wide beds with giant posts; most have views. The main dining room is equally rustic, and there's an intimate drinking bar. The restaurant serves excellent Bavarian dishes.

Ⓢ **Hotel Café-Restaurant Friedenshöhe.** König-Ludwig-Strasse 31, D-82487 Oberammergau. ☎ **08822/35-98.** Fax 08822/43-45. 14 rms. TEL. 100–160 DM ($70–$112) double. Rates include buffet breakfast. AE, DC, MC, V. Closed Oct 27–Dec 14. Free parking. Bus: 30.

Built in 1906, the villa enjoys a beautiful location, and is one of the better inns in town. The villa once hosted Thomas Mann, who wrote here. The guest rooms, furnished in tasteful modern style, are well maintained; TVs are available on request. The hotel offers a choice of four dining rooms, including an indoor terrace with a panoramic view and an outdoor terrace. The Bavarian and international cuisine is known for its taste and the quality of its ingredients.

Hotel Restaurant Böld. König-Ludwig-Strasse 10, D-82487 Oberammergau ☎ **08822/ 30-21.** Fax 08822/71-02. 57 rms (all with bath). TV TEL. 180–200 DM ($126–$140) double. Rates include continental breakfast. AE, DC, MC, V. Free outside parking, 10–15 DM ($7–$10.50) in the garage. Bus: 30.

This inn has steadily improved in quality and now is among the town's premier choices. Only a stone's throw from the river, this well-designed chalet hotel offers comfortable public rooms in its central core and well-furnished guest rooms in its contemporary annex; most units also open onto balconies. A sauna is offered for guests' relaxation, as are a solarium and whirlpool. The restaurant features both international and regional cuisine. In the bar, you'll find a tranquil atmosphere, plus attentive service. Raimund Hans and family are the hosts.

3 The Romantic Road

No area of Germany is more aptly named than the Romantische Strasse. Stretching for 180 miles from Würzburg in the north to Füssen in the foothills of the Bavarian Alps in the south, it passes through untouched medieval villages and 2,000-year-old towns.

The best way to see the Romantic Road is by car, stopping whenever the mood suggests and then driving on through vineyards and over streams until you arrive at the alpine passes in the south. Frankfurt and Munich are convenient gateways. Access is by the A7 autobahn from the north and south, or the A3 autobahn from the east and west. The A81 autobahn has links from the southwest.

Although this section has been structured as a driving tour, you can also explore the Romantic Road by train or bus, or by organized tour.

ONLY ALONG THE ROMANTIC ROAD

Visiting the Fairy-tale Castles   Nothing along the Romantic Road equals the appeal of the two royal castles, Hohenschwangau and the fairy-tale castle of Neuschwanstein, forever associated with the enduring legend of "Mad King" Ludwig. The most enthralling is the multiturreted Disney-like Neuschwanstein. From a distance the castles appear more dreamlike than real. Neuschwanstein is the most photographed and most visited castle in Germany, even though it was never finished after the king's mysterious death.

Walking in "Outer Space"   Before the American Apollo 14 and 17 astronauts headed into outer space, they toured the Ries crater at Nördlingen to give them a preview of the terrain of other planets. This 25km-wide circular Ries crater resulted from a kilometer-wide meteorite smashing into the earth some 15 million years ago. It had the power of 250,000 atomic bombs and caused massive worldwide environmental havoc. The pressure created a new mineral, *suevite,* similar to rocks found on the moon. Tours of this ancient crater plain are possible.

Wandering the Ancient Streets of Rothenburg   Rothenburg is Europe's most perfectly preserved medieval city, and the architectural gem of the Romantic Road. Miraculously Rothenburg emerged after World War II with its 14th-century fortified walls and towers intact.

Attending a Medieval Banquet At the Welser Küche, Maximilianstrasse 83 (☎ 0821/96-11-0), in Augsburg, the Middle Ages live on—at least at the banquet staged here. You eat with a dagger and fingers, enjoying recipes from a 16th-century cookbook discovered in 1970.

Escaping the Crowds at Donauwörth If you want to avoid the hordes who descend on the Romantic Road in summer, head to the old walled town of Donauwörth. Here the Wörnitz River meets the Danube, and time stands still—prosperity and progress left Donauwörth long ago, leaving the town to enchant today's visitor. Explore the Altstadt on an island in the river and stroll down the Reichsstrasse, lined with shops and houses that are centuries old—the finest street along the Romantic Road.

ROTHENBURG OB DER TAUBER

Sometimes abbreviated as Rothenburg o.d.T. (ob der Tauber), or just Rothenburg, this city was first mentioned in written records in 804 as Rotinbure, a settlement above (*ob* in German) the Tauber River that grew to be a free imperial city, reaching its apex of prosperity under a famous Burgermeister, Heinrich Toppler, in the 14th century.

The place is such a gem and so well known that its very popularity is its chief disadvantage—tourist hordes march through here, especially in summer, and the concomitant souvenir peddlers hawk kitsch. If your time is limited and you can visit only one town on the Romantic Road, make it Rothenburg.

Contemporary life and industry have made an impact, and if you arrive at the railroad station, the first thing you'll see are factories and office buildings. But don't be discouraged. Inside those undamaged 13th-century city walls is a completely preserved medieval town, relatively untouched by the passage of time.

ESSENTIALS

ARRIVING By Train Daily trains arrive from Frankfurt (trip time: 3 hours), from Hamburg (trip time: 5¹/₂ hours), or from Berlin (trip time: 7 hours). Rothenburg lies on the Steinach–Rothenburg rail line, with frequent connections to all major German cities, including Nürnberg and Stuttgart. For information, call **0821/19-419.**

By Bus The Romantic Road bus **(Deutsche Touring Frankfurt)** includes Rothenburg on its itinerary Mar–Oct. Any travel agent in Germany or abroad can book you a seat. Regular long-distance buses (lines EH190 and 190A) service the Romantic Road from Frankfurt, Würzburg, Augsburg, and Munich, as well as Füssen. For information and reservations, phone **069/79-03-256** in Frankfurt. Regional bus service is provided by **OVF Omnibusverkehr Franken GmbH,** Kopernikusplatz 14, 90459 Nürnberg (☎ **0911/43-91-06-66**) for information.

Visitor Information Contact **Stadt Verkehrsamt,** Rathaus (☎ **09861/40-492**); open Mon–Fri 9–12:30pm and 2–6pm and Sat 9am–noon.

EXPLORING ROTHENBURG

✪ The **Rathaus (Town Hall)** on the Marktplatz (☎ **09861/40-492**) and the Jacobskirche are the outstanding attractions, along with the medieval walls. The town hall consists of two sections: The older, gothic section dates from 1240. From the 165-foot tower of the gothic hall you get an overview of the town. The belfry has quite a history—in 1501, fire destroyed part of the building, and after that the belfry became a fire watchtower. Guards had to ring the bell every quarter hour to prove

The Romantic Road

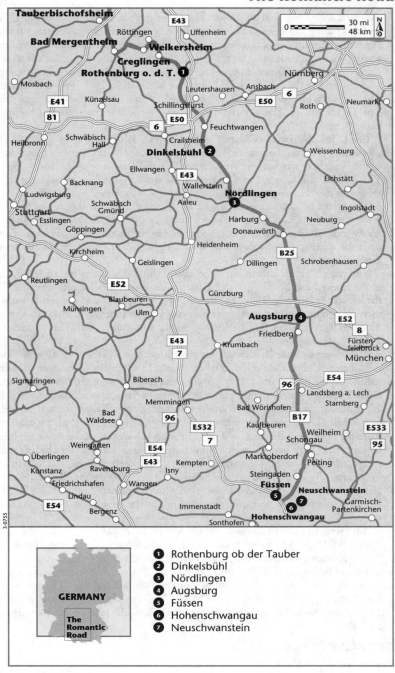

GERMANY

The Romantic Road

1. Rothenburg ob der Tauber
2. Dinkelsbühl
3. Nördlingen
4. Augsburg
5. Füssen
6. Hohenschwangau
7. Neuschwanstein

they were wide awake and on the job. The newer Renaissance section, built in 1572, replaced the portion destroyed in the fire. It's decorated with intricate friezes, an oriel extending the building's full height, and a large stone portico opening onto the square. The octagonal tower at the center of the side facing the square contains a grand staircase leading to the upper hall. On the main floor is the large courtroom.

Admission to the tower is 1 DM (70¢) for adults, 0.50 DM (35¢) for children. The Rathaus is open Mon–Fri 8am–6pm, Sat–Sun 7am–4pm; the tower is open daily Apr–Oct 9:30am–12:30pm and 1–5pm, and Nov–Mar Sat–Sun and holidays noon–3pm.

✪ **St. Jakobskirche (Church of St. James),** Klostergasse 15 (☎ 09861/ 70-06-20), contains the famous *Altar of the Holy Blood* (west gallery), a masterpiece of the Würzburg sculptor and woodcarver Tilman Riemenschneider (1460–1531). The Rothenburg Council commissioned the work in 1499 to provide a worthy setting for the *Reliquary of the Holy Blood.* The relic is contained in a rock-crystal capsule set in the reliquary cross (about 1270) in the center of the shrine, and beneath it the scene of the *Last Supper* makes an immediate impact on the viewer—Jesus is giving Judas the morsel of bread, marking him as the traitor. The altar wings show (left) the *Entry of Christ into Jerusalem* and (right) *Christ Praying in the Garden of Gethsemane.*

The vertical gothic church has three naves. The choir, dating from 1336, is the oldest section, and has fine painted-glass windows from the late gothic period. To the left is the tabernacle (1390–1400), which was recognized as a "free place," a sanctuary for condemned criminals where they could not be touched. The church is open Mon–Fri 9am–5:30pm, Sun 10:30am–5:30pm. Admission 2.5 DM ($1.75) adults, 1 DM (70¢) children.

Also of interest is the **Reichsstadtmuseum,** Klosterhof 5 (☎ 09861/40-458). This is Rothenburg's historical collection, housed in a 13th-century Dominican nunnery with well-preserved cloisters. You'll find on display here an enormous tankard that holds 3½ liters—more than 6 pints—whose story has echoes all over the city. In 1631, during the Thirty Years' War, the Protestant city of Rothenburg was captured by General Tilly, commander of the armies of the Catholic League. He promised to spare the town from destruction if one of the town burghers would drink the huge tankard full of wine in one draught. Burgermeister Nusch accepted the challenge and succeeded, and so saved Rothenburg. There's a festival every spring at Whitsuntide to celebrate this event. Among the exhibits is the 1494 *Rothenburg Passion* series, 12 pictures by Martinus Schwartz, and works by English painter Arthur Wasse (1854– 1930), whose pictures managed to capture in a romantic way the many moods of the city.

Admission to the museum is 4 DM ($2.80) adults, 2 DM ($1.40) children; family card 9 DM ($6.30). It's open Apr–Oct daily 10am–5pm; Nov–Mar daily 1–4pm.

The **Kriminal Museum,** Burggasse 3 (☎ 09861/53-59), is the only museum of its kind in Europe. Housed in a structure built in 1395 with later renovations, it provides insight into the life, laws, and punishments of medieval days. The museum's four floors display 10 centuries of legal history. You'll see chastity belts, shame masks, a shame flute for bad musicians, and a cage for bakers who baked bread too small or too light.

ACCOMMODATIONS

Expensive

✪ **Burg Hotel.** Klostergasse 1–3, D-91541 Rothenburg o.d.T. ☎ 09861/50-37. Fax 09861/ 14-87. 14 rms, 5 suites. MINIBAR TV TEL. 210–300 DM ($147–$210) double; from 250– 290 DM ($175–$203) suite. Rates include buffet breakfast. AE, DC, MC, V. Parking 10 DM ($7).

This fine inn is at the end of a cul-de-sac in an old-fashioned timbered house—just the kind of place Red Riding Hood might have gone to visit Grandma. Its Tauber Valley view, picket fences, and window boxes make it a cliche of German charm. Parking is a delight in the barn of a former Dominican monastery—the most historic garage in Rothenburg. Rooms are spread across three floors, sans elevator, and decorated with antiques, carpets, and tastefully selected fabrics.

✪ **Eisenhut (Iron Helmet).** Herrengasse 3–5, D-91541 Rothenburg o.d.T. ☎ **09861/ 70-50.** Fax 09861/70-545. 80 rms, 4 suites. MINIBAR TV TEL. 285–380 DM ($199.50–$266) double; from 580 DM ($406) suite. AE, DC, MC, V. Parking 15 DM ($10.50).

The most celebrated inn on the Romantic Road, the Eisenhut is the finest small hotel in Germany. Four medieval patrician houses, dating from the 12th century, were joined to make this distinctive inn, just across the street from the Rathaus. Demand for rooms is great, and the staff appears forever overworked. No two guest rooms are alike—yours may contain hand-carved, monumental pieces or have a 1940s Hollywood touch with a tufted satin headboard. Most impressive is the three-story galleried dining hall, with ornate classic wood paneling and balconies. Other places to dine are richly decorated and furnished, although in sunny weather they're all deserted in favor of the multitiered flagstone terrace on the Tauber.

✪ **Hotel Bären.** Hofbronnengasse 9, D-91541 Rothenburg o.d.T. ☎ **09861/94-410.** Fax 09861/94-41-60. 35 rms. MINIBAR TV TEL. 250–320 DM ($175–$224) double. Rates include buffet breakfast. AE, MC, V. Closed Jan 4–Mar 15. Parking 8 DM ($5.60).

One of the leading old inns of town, directly south of the Rathaus, dates back to 1577. Although modernized by the Müller family, it still has 15-inch oak beams and ornate wainscoting. Each of the traditional guest rooms is styled differently, with coordinated colors. A major improvement was to reduce the number of rooms and increase the spaciousness of those remaining. The owner is a gifted chef who offers some of the best food of any inn in town. Three dining rooms with varied cuisine provide both Bavarian and international dishes. The Bären continues as one of the best equipped hotels in town replete with a solarium, sauna, and gym. Rooms include fine carpets, both antique and contemporary furniture, and minibars.

Goldener Hirsch. Untere Schmiedgasse 16–25, D-91541 Rothenburg o.d.T. ☎ **09861/ 70-80.** Fax 09861/70-81-00. 72 rms. MINIBAR TEL. 190–320 DM ($133–$224) double. Rates include breakfast. AE, DC, MC, V. Parking 6 DM ($4.20).

This first-class hotel is a remake of an inn that dates from 1600. In the heart of town off Wenggasse, it lies just three blocks from the main square. It looks more austere and institutional and lacks the coziness of some of the other leading inns. Nevertheless, it is extremely comfortable and well maintained, and so popular that the hostelry annexed another patrician house across the street. Room service and laundry are available. The Blue Terrace, for dining, offers a panoramic view of the Tauber Valley, or you may prefer to take your dinner in the wood-paneled, cozy Ratsherrenstube.

Hotel Tilman Riemenschneider. Georgengasse 11–13, D-91541, Rothenburg o.d.T. ☎ **09861/20-86.** Fax 09861/29-79. 65 rms. TV TEL. 200–340 DM ($140–$238) double. Rates include buffet breakfast. AE, DC, MC, V. Parking 10 DM ($7).

Named for the famous sculptor, this hotel's half-timbered facade rises directly above one of Rothenburg's busy historic streets. Its rear courtyard, adorned with geraniums, offers a cool and calm oasis from the heavy pedestrian traffic in front. It's traditionally styled and well furnished with alpine-inspired furniture, stone floors, and an occasional porcelain stove set into a wall niche. Room service, laundry, and dry cleaning are available, and facilities include a fitness center with a sauna, a turbo-skylab solarium, and two whirlpool baths. For its restaurant, see "Dining," below.

Romantik Hotel Markusturm. Rödergasse 1, D-91541 Rothenburg o.d.T. ☎ **09861/ 20-98.** Fax 09861/26-92. 24 rms, 2 suites. TV TEL. 180–350 DM ($126–$245) double; from 350 DM ($245) suite. Rates include buffet breakfast. AE, DC, MC, V. Parking 12 DM ($8.40).

When this hotel was built in 1264, one of Rothenburg's defensive walls was incorporated into the building. Today that wall has been torn down except for the section that is part of the hotel. Its bold masculine style favorably contrasts the many cute and cozily cluttered inns; much of the hotel, despite its ancient pedigree, dates from 1988. Guest rooms have been modernized but furnished in a traditional style with quality antique and rustic furniture. Five spacious rooms are set aside for non-smokers. The hotel employs one of the most helpful staffs in town. The hotel is open all year, but its well-regarded restaurant closes from mid-January to mid-February.

Moderate

Hotel Gasthof Glocke. Am Plönlein 1, D-91541 Rothenburg o.d.T. ☎ **09861/30-25.** Fax 09861/86-711. 25 rms. TV TEL. 148–178 DM ($103.60–$124.60) double. Rates include continental breakfast. AE, DC, MC, V. Closed Dec 24–Jan 6. Parking 8 DM ($5.60).

The designer of this comfortable hotel, which lies south of the town center off Wenggasse, took pains to re-create a country-rustic decor. Nearly at the bottom of the pecking order, this hotel does not have the charm and style of the premier inns, but it's a good choice for those who want plain, simple, affordable rooms and good food. The owners are justifiably proud of their restaurant (see "Dining," below). Guests enjoy the family atmosphere at this gemütlich hotel.

Ⓢ **Hotel Reichs-Küchenmeister.** Kirchplatz 8, D-91541 Rothenburg o.d.T. ☎ **09861/9700.** Fax 09861/86-965. 50 rms, 3 suites. TV TEL. 130–220 DM ($91.00–$154.00) double; 220 DM ($154) suite for two, 330 DM ($231) suite for five. Rates include buffet breakfast. AE, DC, MC, V. Parking 6 DM ($4.20) lot, 10 DM ($7) garage.

This hotel, one of Rothenburg's oldest structures, near St. Jacobskirche, is built on different levels. We like this hotel a lot and rank it alongside the Tilman Riemenschneider and the Goldener Hirsch. It successfully blends a taste of the past with modern amenities and a sense of style, and is one of the best equipped hotels in Rothenburg, with Finnish sauna, whirlpool, solarium, and Turkish bath. You wander down the corridors to nicely furnished rooms with painted, regional, wooden furniture. Use of the sauna costs 20 DM ($14) extra. An extra 17 rooms are available in the duller annex across the street. For its restaurant, see "Dining," below.

Inexpensive

Ⓢ **Bayerischer Hof.** Ansbacherstrasse 21, D-91541 Rothenburg o.d.T. ☎ **09861/34-57.** Fax 09861/86-56-1. 9 rms. TV TEL. 100–130 DM ($70–$91) double. Rates include breakfast. AE, MC, V. Closed Jan. Free parking.

Petra and Harald Schellhaas welcome guests to their recently renovated, clean, and well-furnished accommodations, midway between the Bahnhof and the medieval walled city. This little place doesn't even try to compete with the grand inns of the town. And why should it? It has found its niche as a B&B, and although the outside looks rather sterile, many cozy warm Bavarian touches, such as painted furniture, grace the interior. The food is very good, with international and Bavarian specialties.

Gasthof Goldener Greifen. Obere Schmiedgasse 5, D-91541 Rothenburg o.d.T. ☎ **09861/ 22-81.** Fax 09861/86-374. 21 rms (16 with shower or bath). 74 DM ($51.80) double without bath, 135 DM ($94.50) double with shower or bath. Rates include buffet breakfast. AE, MC, V. Closed Aug 22–Sept 2 and Dec 22–Feb.

One of the better little inns, the Gasthof Goldener Greifen offers well-cooked meals at modest prices as well as pleasant rooms. It's one of the very best B&Bs in town if you want homestyle warmth and comfort. Off Marktplatz in a patrician 1374 house, it stands next door to the prestigious Baumeisterhaus restaurant (see "Dining," below). You can order your morning coffee in the garden amid roses and geraniums. The simple rooms offer good comfort, eiderdowns, and hot and cold running water. The dining room is closed Monday.

DINING

Expensive

✪ **Restaurant Bärenwirt.** In the Hotel Bären, Hofbronnengasse 9. ☎ **09861/94410.** Reservations recommended. Main courses 39–55 DM ($27.30–$38.50); fixed-price menus 118–162 DM ($82.60–$113.40). MC, V. Daily 6–10pm. FRANCONIAN/INTERNATIONAL.

Many food critics, including the magazine *VIF Gourmet Journal*, cite the "Bear," owned by Fritz and Elisabeth Müller, as one of the finest restaurants in all Germany. The decor is elegantly subdued and the service impeccable. In-the-know patrons like to visit just to sample its "Gourmet Menu of the Month," a fixed-price dinner. The menu changes are based on the chef's inspiration and use the best seasonal produce.

Moderate

Baumeisterhaus. Obere Schmiedgasse 3. ☎ **09861/94-700.** Reservations required for courtyard tables. Main courses 10.50–35 DM ($7.35–$24.50). AE, DC, MC, V. Daily 11am–2:30pm and 6–9:30pm. FRANCONIAN.

Right off Marktplatz, the Baumeisterhaus is housed in an ancient patrician residence, built in 1596. It has Rothenburg's most beautiful courtyard (which only guests can visit), with colorful murals, serenely draped by vines. Frankly, although the menu is good, the setting is even more romantic. The food, for the most part, is rib-sticking fare beloved of Bavarians, including roast suckling pig with potato dumplings, and one of the chef's best dishes, sauerbraten (braised beef marinated in vinegar), served with spätzle (small flour dumplings).

⑤ **Ratsstube.** Marktplatz 6. ☎ **09861/55-11.** Reservations recommended. Main courses 19–34 DM ($13.30–$23.80). MC, V. Mon–Sat 9am–11pm, Sun noon–6pm. Closed Jan 7–Feb. FRANCONIAN.

The Ratsstube enjoys a position right on the market square, one of the most photographed spots in Germany. It's a bustling center of activity throughout the day—a day that begins when practically every Rothenburger stops by for a cup of morning coffee. Inside, a true tavern atmosphere prevails with hardwood chairs and tables, vaulted ceilings, and pierced copper lanterns. The à la carte menu of Franconian wines and dishes includes sauerbraten and venison, both served with fresh vegetables and potatoes. For dessert, you can order homemade Italian ice cream and espresso. This is a longtime favorite of those who prefer typical Franconian cookery without a lot of fuss and bother. If you arrive at 9am, the staff will serve you an American breakfast.

Inexpensive

⑤ **Hotel Gasthof Glocke.** Am Plönlein 1. ☎ **09861/30-25.** Reservations recommended. Main courses 14–66 DM ($9.80–$46.20). AE, DC, MC, V. Daily 11am–2pm; Mon–Sat 6–9pm. Closed Dec 24–Jan 6. FRANCONIAN.

This traditional hotel and guest house (previously recommended) serves regional specialties along with a vast selection of local wine. Meals emphasize seasonal dishes. Service is polite and attentive.

Reichs-Küchenmeister. Kiirchplatz 8. ☎ **09861/20-46.** Reservations required. Main courses 17.80–39.80 DM ($12.45–$27.85). AE, DC, MC, V. Daily 11:30am–2pm and 6–9:30 pm. FRANCONIAN.

The main dishes served here are the type Bavarians have loved for years, including sauerbraten or pork tenderloin; white herring and broiled salmon are also available. The Lebensknodel (liver dumpling) or goulash soup is perfect for cold days. We recently discovered that the chef makes one of the best Wiener schnitzels in town. The restaurant is near St. Jacobskirche and has a typical weinstube decor, along with a garden terrace and a konditorei. Service is warm and efficient.

☺ Tilman Riemenschneider. Georgengasse 11. ☎ **09861/20-86.** Main courses 17.50–34 DM ($12.25–$23.80); fixed-price menu 26–35 DM ($18.20–$24.50). AE, DC, MC, V. Daily 11:30am–2pm and 6–9pm. FRANCONIAN.

A traditional old weinstube is housed in one of Rothenburg's finest hotels (see above). The chef shows elevated respect for old-fashioned cookery served in generous portions. You might begin with air-dried beef or smoked fillet of trout, then follow with poached eel, halibut steak, or loin of pork.

DINKELSBÜHL

Still surrounded by medieval walls and towers, Dinkelsbühl is straight out of a Brothers Grimm story, even down to the gingerbread, which is one of its main products. Behind the ancient 10th-century walls is a town that retains its quiet, provincial ambience in spite of the many tourists who come here. The cobblestone streets are lined with fine 16th-century houses, many with carvings and paintings depicting biblical and mythological themes. In the center of town, on Marktplatz, is the late gothic **Georgenkirche,** built between 1448 and 1499. It contains a carved Holy Cross Altar from the same period and pillar sculptures, many from the 15th century.

ESSENTIALS

GETTING THERE   By Train The nearest train station is in Ansbach, which has several trains arriving daily from Munich and Frankfurt (trip time 2¹/₂ to 3 hours), Nürnberg, and Stuttgart. From Ansbach, Dinkelsbühl can be reached by bus. For rail information, call **0821/19-419.**

By Bus For long-distance bus service along the Romantic Road, see Rothenburg. Regional buses link Dinkelsbühl with local towns. There are three to five buses a day to Rothenburg and five or six to Nördlingen.

By Car Take B-25 south from Rothenburg.

VISITOR INFORMATION Contact **Stadt Verkehrsamt,** Marktplatz (☎ **09851/9-02-40**). Hours are Mon–Fri 9am–6pm and Sat 10am–1pm.

SPECIAL EVENTS The **Kinderzeche (Children's Festival),** held for 10 days in July, commemorates the saving of the village by its children in 1632. According to the story, the children pleaded with conquering Swedish troops to leave their town without pillaging and destroying it—and got their wish. The pageant includes concerts given by the local boys' band dressed in historic military costumes.

ACCOMMODATIONS & DINING

Blauer Hecht. Schweinemarkt 1, D-91150 Dinkelsbühl. ☎ **09851/8-11.** Fax 09851/8-14. 44 rms. TV TEL. 150–165 DM ($105–$115.50) double. Rates include continental breakfast. AE, DC, MC, V. Closed Jan 2–31.

The inn is the second best in town. The elegant ocher building, dating from the 17th century, has three hand-built stories of stucco, stone, and tiles. The hotel was once a brewery tavern, and the owners still brew in the backyard. Although it's centrally located, rooms are tranquil. The hotel has been renovated and kept up to date and rooms are large and sunny. A good regional cuisine is served in the hotel restaurant.

Deutsches Haus. Weinmarkt 3, D-91550 Dinkelsbühl. ☎ **09851/60-58.** Fax 09851/79-11. 6 rms, 1 suite. TV TEL. 165–210 DM ($115.50–$147) double; 210 DM ($147) suite. Rates include continental breakfast. AE, DC, MC, V. Closed Dec 23–Jan 6. Parking 15 DM ($10.50).

The facade of Deutsches Haus dates from 1440; rich in painted designs and festive wood carvings, in a niche on the second floor of the arched entrance is a 17th-century madonna. The rooms are unique—you may find yourself in one with a ceramic stove or in another with a Biedermeier desk. Casually run, the Deutsches Haus features a dining room with an elaborately decorated ceiling, inset niches with provincial scenic pictures, and parquet floors.

Its **Altdeutsches Restaurant** is one of the finest in Dinkelsbühl. It's intimate and convivial, an attractive rendezvous. The restaurant serves Franconian and regional specialties daily 11:30am–2pm and 6–10pm. In the afternoon many visitors drop in for coffee and freshly baked pastries.

✪ **Eisenkrug.** Dr.-Martin-Luther-Strasse 1, D-91550 Dinkelsbühl. ☎ **09851/57-00.** Fax 09851/57-070. 12 rms, 1 suite. MINIBAR TV TEL. 135–160 DM ($94.50–$112) double; 250 DM ($175) suite. Rates include continental breakfast. AE, DC, MC, V.

The sienna walls of this centrally located hotel were originally built in 1620. Today the Eisenkrug's forest-green shutters are familiar to everyone in town; many celebrate family occasions at the hotel restaurant. There's even a cafe with al fresco tables in warm weather. The stylish rooms are wallpapered with flowery prints and filled with engaging old furniture. An additional nine rooms are in an equally fine guest house nearby where doubles cost 125–135 DM ($87.50–$94.50).

Zum kleinen Obristen serves a gourmet international cuisine—the finest dining along the entire road. Chef Martin Scharff invents his own recipes and carefully selects ingredients that go into his market-fresh cuisine. His is an indigenous Franconian–Swabian approach, with many innovative touches. The superior wine cellar has some really unusual vintages. À la carte meals cost 35–62 DM ($24.50–$43.40). It's also possible to order fixed-price menus for 72 DM ($50.40) and 115 DM ($80.50). It's open noon–2pm and 6–10pm; closed Mon and Tues evenings.

✪ **Goldene Rose.** Marktplatz 4, D-91550, Dinkelsbühl. ☎ **09851/57-750.** Fax 09851/57-75-75. 34 rms. MINIBAR TV TEL. 120–200 DM ($84–$140) double. Rates include continental breakfast. AE, DC, MC, V. Parking 6 DM ($4.20) lot, 15 DM ($10.50) garage.

A landmark in the heart of this village since 1450, the intricately timbered Goldene Rose rises three stories, with a steeply pitched roof and overflowing window boxes. It offers the best value in Dinkelsbühl. Guest rooms are modernized, with comfortable beds.

The dining rooms are country-inn style, with an international cuisine (the menu is in English). The à la carte menu offers such tempting items as lobster and crab with dill, and rumpsteak Goldene Rose. Meals cost 26–60 DM ($18.20–$42), and service is daily 11am–midnight.

NÖRDLINGEN

One of the most irresistible and perfectly preserved medieval towns along the Romantic Road, Nördlingen is still completely encircled by the well-preserved 14th–15th-century **city fortifications.** You can walk around the town on the covered parapet, which passes 11 towers and 5 fortified gates set into the walls.

Things are rather peaceful around Nördlingen today, and the city still employs sentries to sound the message, *"So G'sell so"* ("All is well"), as they did in the Middle Ages. However, events around here weren't always so peaceful. The valley sits in a gigantic crater, the Ries. Once thought to be the crater of an extinct volcano, it is now known that a meteorite at least half a mile in diameter is responsible for the Ries. It hit the ground at more than 100,000 miles per hour, the impact having the destructive force of 250,000 atomic bombs of that type that wiped out Hiroshima in 1945. Debris was hurled as far as Slovakia, and all plant and animal life within a radius of 100 miles was destroyed. This momentous event took place some 15 million years ago. Today it is the best preserved and scientifically researched meteorite crater on earth. The American Apollo 14 and 17 astronauts had their field training in the Ries from August 10 to 14 in 1970.

ESSENTIALS

ARRIVING   By Train   Nördlingen lies on the main Nördlingen–Aalen–Stuttgart line, with frequent connections in all directions. Telephone **0821/19-419** for schedules and more information. Nördlingen can be reached from Stuttgart in 2 hours, from Nürnberg in 2 hours, and from Augsburg in an hour.

By Bus   The long-distance bus that operates along the Romantic Road includes Nördlingen; see Rothenburg above.

By Car   Take B-25 south from Dinkelsbühl.

VISITOR INFORMATION   Contact the **Verkehrsamt,** Marktplatz 2 (☎ **09081/ 43-80**), open Mon–Thurs 9am–6pm and Fri 9am–4:30pm, Sat and holidays 9:30am–12:30pm.

WHAT TO SEE & DO

At the center of the circular Altstadt within the walls is **Rübenmarkt.** If you stand in this square on market day, you'll be swept into a world of the past—the country people have preserved many traditional customs and costumes here, which, along with the ancient houses, create a living medieval city. Around the square stand a number of buildings, including the gothic **Rathaus.** An antiquities collection is displayed in the **Stadtmuseum,** Vordere Gerbergasse 1 (☎ **09081/84-120**), open Tues–Sun 10am–noon and 1:30–4:30pm; closed Nov–Feb. Admission is 5 DM ($3.50) for adults and 2.50 DM ($1.75) for children. Guided tours available only. Hours are Mon–Thurs 9am–5pm and Fri 9am–3pm.

The gothic Hallenkirche, the **Church of St. George,** on the square's northern side, is the town's most interesting sight and one of its oldest buildings, from the 15th century. Plaques and epitaphs commemorating the town's more illustrious 16th- and 17th-century residents decorate the fan-vaulted interior. Although the original gothic altarpiece by Friedrich Herlin (1470) is now in the Reichsstadt Museum, a portion of it, depicting the crucifixion, remains in the church. Above the high altar today stands a more elaborate baroque altarpiece. The church's most prominent feature, however, is the 295-foot French gothic tower, called the "Daniel." At night, the town watchman calls out from the steeple, his voice ringing through the streets. The tower is accessible Mon–Fri 9am–noon and 2–5pm and Sat and Sun 9am–5pm. Admission is 2.50 DM ($1.75) for adults and 1.50 DM ($1.05) for children.

The **Rieskrater-Museum,** Hintere Gerbergasse (☎ **0981/84-11-16**), documents the impact of the stone meteorite that created the Ries. Examine fossils from Ries Lake deposits and learn about the fascinating evolution of this geological wonder. Hours are Tues–Sun 10am–noon and 1:30–4:30pm. Entrance fees for adults are 5 DM ($3.50) and 2.5 DM ($1.75) for students, seniors, and large groups. Tours of the crater are possible through the museum.

ACCOMMODATIONS

Flamberg Hotel Klösterle. Am Klösterle 1, D-86720 Nördlingen. ☎ **09081/88-054.** Fax 09081/22-740. 80 rms, 10 suites. MINIBAR TV TEL. 216 DM ($151.20) double; 246 DM ($172.20) suite. Rates include breakfast. AE, DC, MC, V. Parking 15 DM ($10.50).

These accommodations are the town's best. White-sided and red-roofed, this historic building was a monastery in the 1200s. Since then, its ziggurat-shaped gables and steep roof have been an essential part of Nördlingen's medieval center. In 1991 the monastery was renovated, a new wing added, and the entire complex transformed into the town's most luxurious hotel. Rated four stars, it offers elevator access, a cozy bar (the Tarantelstube), and a hardworking, polite staff. Under the sloping eaves of its top floor are a sauna, a fitness center, and a series of conference rooms. The bedrooms have dark-wood fixtures, modern upholstery, lots of electronic extras, and large bathrooms. The restaurant serves lunch and dinner every day noon–2pm and 6–10pm.

Ⓢ **Kaiser Hotel Sonne.** Marktplatz 3, D-86720 Nördlingen. ☎ **09081/50-67.** Fax 09081/23-999. 40 rms (32 with bath), 3 suites. MINIBAR TV TEL. 125 DM ($87.50) double without bath, 175 DM ($122.50) double with bath; 230 DM ($161) suite. Rates include breakfast. AE, DC, MC, V. Free parking.

In a bull's-eye position, next to the cathedral and the Rathaus, is the Sonne, with a heady atmosphere from having entertained so many illustrious personalities since it opened as an inn in 1405. Among its guests have been Frederick III, Maximilian I, and Charles V, the great poet Goethe, and, in more recent times, the American Apollo astronauts. The hotel's interior, completely modernized in 1995, provides tasteful accommodations. In a choice of dining rooms, you can order the soup of the day, main courses such as rumpsteak Mirabeau, and fattening German desserts. It's all quite casual; the waitresses even urge you to finish the food on your plate.

DINING

Meyer's Keller. Marienhöhe 8. ☎ **09081/44-93.** Reservations required. Main courses 38–52 DM ($26.60–$36.40); fixed-price meals 39–119 DM ($27.30–$83.30). AE, MC, V. Wed–Sun noon–2pm; Tues–Sun 6–10pm. Local bus to Marktplatz. CONTINENTAL.

The conservative, modern decor here seems a suitable setting for the restrained *neue Küche* of the talented chef and owner of this place, Joachim Kaiser, who is adroit with both rustic and refined cuisine. The menu changes according to availability of ingredients and the chef's inspiration; typical selections are likely to include roulade of seawolf and salmon with baby spinach and wild rice, or John Dory with champagne-flavored tomato sauce. The wine list is impressive, and many are quite reasonable in price.

EN ROUTE TO AUGSBURG

After Nördlingen, B-25 heads south to Augsburg. After a 12-mile ride you can stop to visit **Schloss Harburg** (it's signposted), one of the best-preserved medieval castles in Germany. It once belonged to the Hohenstaufen emperors and contains treasures collected by the family over the centuries. It is open mid-Mar to Sept Tues–Sun 9am–5pm; Oct Tues–Sun 9:30am–4:30pm. Admission is 5 DM ($3.50) for adults, 3 DM ($2.10) for children, including a guided tour.

After exploring the castle, drive 7 miles south to the walled town of **Donauwörth**, where you can stop to walk through the oldest part of the town, on an island in the river, connected by a wooden bridge. Here the Danube is only a narrow, placid stream. The town's original walls overlook its second river, the Woernitz.

After a brief stopover, continue your southward trek for 30 miles to Augsburg, the largest city on the Romantic Road.

AUGSBURG

Augsburg is near the center of the Romantic Road and the gateway to the Alps and the south. Founded 2,000 years ago by the Roman emperor Augustus, for whom it was named, it once was the richest city in Europe. Little remains from the early Roman period. However, the wealth of Renaissance art and architecture is staggering. Over the years, Augsburg boasts an array of famous native sons, including painters Hans Holbein the Elder and Hans Holbein the Younger, and playwright Bertolt Brecht. In 1518 it was here that Martin Luther was summoned to recant his 95 theses before a papal emissary. Only 15% of the city was left standing after World War II, but there is still much here to intrigue. Today Augsburg is an important industrial center on the Frankfurt–Salzburg autobahn. It is Bavaria's third largest city after Munich and Nürnberg.

ESSENTIALS

GETTING THERE   By Train   Around 90 Euro and InterCity trains arrive here daily from all major German cities. For railway information, call **0821/1-94-19.** There are 60 trains per day from Munich (trip time: 30–50 minutes), and 35 from Frankfurt (trip time: 3–4¹/₂ hours).

By Bus   Long-distance buses (lines EB190 and 190A, plus line 189) service the Romantic Road. The buses are operated by **Deutsche Touring GmbH** in Frankfurt (☎ **069/790-32-56** for reservations and information).

VISITOR INFORMATION   Contact **Tourist-Information,** Bahnhofstrasse 7 (☎ **0821/50-20-70**), Mon–Fri 9am–6pm and Sat 10am–1pm.

GETTING AROUND   The public transportation system in Augsburg consists of three tram lines and 31 bus lines covering the inner city and reaching into the suburbs. Public transportation operates daily 5am–midnight, and service is provided by **Augsburger Verkehrsverband AVV** (☎ **0821/15-70-07**).

✪ THE FUGGEREI

Throughout its history, Augsburg has been an important city, but during the 15th and 16th centuries it was one of Europe's wealthiest communities, mainly because of its textile industry and the political and financial clout of its two banking families, the Welsers and the Fuggers. The Welsers, who once owned nearly all of Venezuela, have long since faded from the minds of Augsburgers. But the founders of the powerful Fugger family have established themselves forever in the hearts of townsfolk by an unusual legacy, the Fuggerei, created in 1519 to house poorer Augsburgers. A master mason fallen on hard times, Franz Mozart, once lived at Mittlere Gasse 14—he was the great-grandfather of Wolfgang Amadeus Mozart. The quarter consists of several streets lined with well-maintained Renaissance houses, as well as a church and administrative offices, all enclosed within walls. The Fugger Foundation still owns the Fuggerei.

A house at Mittlere Gasse 13, next to the one once occupied by Mozart's ancestor, is now the Fuggerei's museum (☎ **0821/30-868**). The rough 16th- and 17th-century furniture, wood-paneled ceilings and walls, and cast-iron stove, as well as other objects of everyday life, show what it was like to live there in earlier times. Admission to the museum is 1 DM (70¢), open Mar–Oct daily 9am–6pm. Tram: 1.

OTHER SIGHTS

The **Rathaus** (☎ **0821/32-41**) was built by Elias Holl in 1620. In 1805 and 1809, Napoléon visited; regrettably, it was also visited by an air raid in 1944, leaving a mere shell from a building that had once been known as a palatial eight-story monument to the glory of the Renaissance. The destruction left its celebrated "golden chamber" in shambles. Now, after costly restoration, the Rathaus can be visited by the public. Admission is 2 DM ($1.40) adults, 1 DM (70¢) children 7–14; open daily 10am–6pm. Tram: 1.

Dom St. Maria, Hoher Weg (☎ **0821/31-66-353**), has the distinction of containing the oldest stained-glass windows in the world. The romanesque windows, from the 12th century, are younger than the cathedral itself, which was begun in 944. You'll find the ruins of the original basilica in the crypt beneath the west chancel. Partially gothicized in the 14th century, the church stands on the edge of the park, which also fronts the **Episcopal Palace,** where the basic Lutheran creed was presented at the Diet of Augsburg in 1530. The cathedral remains the episcopal see of the Catholic bishop to this day. The 11th-century bronze doors, leading into the three-aisle nave, are adorned with bas-reliefs of a mixture of biblical and mythological characters. The cathedral's interior, restored in 1934, contains side altars with altarpieces by Hans Holbein the Elder and Christoph Amberger. The windows in the south transept are the oldest, depicting Old Testament prophets in a severe but colorful romanesque style. The church is open Mon–Sat 7am–6pm, Sun noon–6pm. Tram: 1.

The **Church of St. Ulrich and St. Afra,** Ulrichplatz 19 (☎ **0821/15-60-49**), is the most attractive church in Augsburg. It was constructed between 1476 and 1500 on the site of a Roman temple. The church and the dom, one Protestant, one Catholic, stand side by side, a tribute to the 1555 Peace of Augsburg, which recognized the two denominations, Roman Catholic and Lutheran. Many of the church's furnishings, including the three altars representing the birth and resurrection of Christ and the baptism of the church by the Holy Spirit, are baroque. In the crypt are the tombs of the Swabian saints, Ulrich and Afra. It's open daily 9am–6pm.

Facing the Hercules Fountain, the **Schaezlerpalais,** Maximilianstrasse 46 (☎ **0821/324-21-71**), contains the city's art galleries. Constructed as a 60-room mansion between 1765 and 1770, it was willed to Augsburg after World War II. Most of the paintings are from the Renaissance and baroque periods. One of the most famous is Dürer's portrait of Jakob Fugger the Rich, founder of the dynasty that was once powerful enough to influence the elections of the Holy Roman emperors. Other works are by local artists Hans Burgkmair and Hans Holbein the Elder, and Rubens, Veronese, and Tiepolo are also represented. Admission is 4 DM ($2.80) adults, 2 DM ($1.40) children; open Wed–Sun 10am–4pm. Tram: 1.

ACCOMMODATIONS

Very Expensive

✪ **Steigenberger Drei Mohren.** Maximilianstrasse 40, D-86150 Augsburg. ☎ **800/223-5652** in the U.S. and Canada, or **0821/5-03-60.** Fax 0821/15-78-64. 107 rms, 5 suites. MINIBAR TV TEL. 279–350 DM ($195.30–$245)double; 490–550 DM ($343–$385) suite. Rates include buffet breakfast. AE, DC, MC, V. Parking 19 DM ($13.30). Tram: 1.

The original hotel, dating from 1723, was renowned in Germany before its destruction in an air raid. In 1956 it was rebuilt in a modern style, and it remains the premier hotel in town. The interior treatment of the "Three Moors" incorporates stylish contemporary pieces with traditional furnishings. Guest rooms are restrained and restful, handsomely proportioned, and some are reserved for nonsmokers. The formal dining room offers an international cuisine. Staff can arrange golf nearby.

Moderate

Dom Hotel. Frauentorstrasse 8, D-86152 Augsburg. ☎ **0821/15-30-31.** Fax 0821/51-0126. 43 rms. TV TEL. 150–195 DM ($105–$136.50) double. Rates include buffet breakfast. AE, DC, MC, V. Free parking or 8 DM ($5.60) garage. Tram: 2.

Although it may not have the decorative flair of the more expensive hotels, it does have an indoor pool. That, combined with the low rates, makes this one of the most appealing choices in town. The hotel is a half-timbered structure, next to Augsburg's famous cathedral, built in the 15th century to house the town's provost. It offers clean, comfortable rooms, and the attic-style rooms, with sloping ceilings, on the top floor have good views of Augsburg. In warm weather, breakfast—the only meal served—can be enjoyed in a garden beside the town's medieval fortifications.

Hotel Am Rathaus. Am Hinteren Perlachberg 1, D-86150 Augsburg. ☎ **0821/50-90-00.** Fax 0821/51-77-46. 32 rms. MINIBAR TV TEL. 205 ($143.50) double. Rates include buffet breakfast. AE, DC, MC, V. Parking 12 DM ($8.40). Tram: 1.

Many repeat guests consider its location to be its best asset, just behind Augsburg's famous town hall. Built in a three-story contemporary format in 1986, the hotel offers comfortable, monochromatic bedrooms accented with darkly stained wood, and a well-stocked breakfast buffet. It may be short on style but it's long on value. There's no restaurant or bar on the premises.

Romantik Hotel Augsburger Hof. Auf dem Kreuz 2, D-86152 Augsburg. ☎ **0821/31-40-83.** Fax 0821/3-83-22. 36 rms. TV TEL. 145–240 DM ($101.50–$168) double. Rates include buffet breakfast. AE, DC, MC, V. Parking 10 DM ($7). Tram: 1.

Originally built in 1767 in a solid, thick-walled design with exposed beams and timbers, this hotel was carefully restored in 1988. In the town center, it's a favorite for its romantic and traditional atmosphere, its good location, and its excellent food. Its bedrooms are clean, modernized, and cozy. Those overlooking the calm inner courtyard are more expensive than ones facing the street. On the premises a restaurant serves German and international food.

Inexpensive

🛇 **Hotel Garni Weinberger.** Bismarckstrasse 55, D-86391 Stadtbergen. ☎ **0821/2439-1-0.** Fax 0821/43-88-31. 31 rms (26 with bath). 110 DM ($77) double without shower or bath; 140 DM ($98) double with shower or bath. Rates include buffet breakfast. No credit cards. Closed Aug 15–30. Free parking. Tram: 2.

One of the best budget accommodations in the area lies about 2 miles from the heart of Augsburg, along Augsburgerstrasse in the western sector. The owner rents light and airy rooms. The place is well patronized by Germans, who know a good bargain, and its cafe is one of the most popular in the area for snacks.

DINING

Expensive

✪ **Cheval Blanc.** In the Hotel Gregor, Landsberger Strasse 62, D-86171 Augsburg. ☎ **0821/8-00-50.** Fax 0821/80-05-69. Reservations recommended. Main courses 40–50 DM ($28–$35); fixed-price menu 78 DM ($54.60) for four courses, 115 DM ($80.50) for five courses. AE, DC, MC, V. Tues–Sat 7–10pm. Bus: 730, 731, 732, or 733. SWABIAN/BAVARIAN/FRENCH.

The restaurant is 5 miles south of Augsburg, and the cuisine is outstanding, ranking with the Eisenkrug in Dinkelsbühl (see above). The menu is seasonally adjusted to market-fresh ingredients, and dishes are marked by intense, refined flavors. The chef presents a classic cuisine, impeccably prepared, with some innovation and experimentation. Much attention is paid to game and fish. Begin, perhaps, with a delectable carpaccio of venison with virgin olive oil, and follow with fillet of redfish with eggplant and pesto. An even more enticing suprême dish is pheasant with marinated wild mushrooms.

You can stay here in one of the 40 well-appointed guest rooms with private baths, TVs, and phones. Doubles range from 140–180 DM ($98–$126), including a continental breakfast.

✪ Oblinger. Pfäarrle 14. ☎ **0821/345-83-92.** Reservations required. Main courses 19.50–39.50 DM ($13.65–$27.65); fixed-price five-course menu 78 DM ($54.60). AE, DC, MC, V. Tues–Sun 11:30am–2pm; Tues–Sat 6–11pm. Closed Aug 1–19. Tram: 12. CONTINENTAL.

Near the cathedral, in the heart of the historic section, Oblinger is the best restaurant within the city. It's a charming, intimate 20-seat restaurant offering a changing array of seasonal specialties. The surroundings are unpretentious, the waiters attentive, and there's a superb collection of wine, more than 200 varieties. Recently we savored the goose-liver terrine with mushrooms and cabbage, going on to an equally well-prepared sole roulade with crepes. The turbot with chanterelles or the stuffed Bresse pigeon were also successes. The cuisine here has personality.

Moderate

Die Ecke. Elias-Holl-Platz 2. ☎ **0821/51-06-00.** Reservations required. Main courses 22–45 DM ($15.40–$31.50); fixed-price lunches 35–45 DM ($24.50–$31.50); fixed-price dinner 57 DM ($39.90) for four courses, 98 DM ($68.60) for six courses. AE, DC, MC, V. Daily 11:30am–2pm and 6pm–1am. Tram: 2. FRENCH/SWABIAN.

Since the restaurant was founded in the year Columbus sighted the New World, its guests have included Hans Holbein the Elder, Wolfgang Amadeus Mozart, and, in more contemporary times, Bertolt Brecht, whose sharp-tongued irreverence tended to irritate diners of more conservative political leanings. The weinstube ambience belies the skilled cuisine of the chef, which continues to win us over year after year. Breast of duckling might be preceded by a pâté or pheasant, and the fillet of sole in Riesling is deservedly a classic. Venison dishes in season are a specialty—the best in town.

Inexpensive

Ⓢ Sieben-Schwaben-Stuben. Bürgermeister-Fischer-Strasse 12. ☎ **0821/31-45-63.** Reservations recommended. Main courses 19–36 DM ($13.30–$25.20). AE, DC, MC, V. Daily 11am–11pm. Tram: 1. SWABIAN.

This unusual place has a high barrel-vaulted ceiling, with half-moon windows. Each day a different menu reigns. A hearty Swabian cuisine is featured, including such well-prepared regional dishes as bacon dumplings bedded on cider sauerkraut, a 7-Swabians Pot (tenderloin of pork with spätzle), and boiled breast of beef with horseradish. For dessert, try the apfelstrudel with vanilla sauce.

NEUSCHWANSTEIN & HOHENSCHWANGAU

The 19th century saw a great classical revival in Germany, especially in Bavaria, mainly because of the enthusiasm of Bavarian kings for ancient art forms. Beginning with Ludwig I (1786–1868), who was responsible for many Greek revival buildings in Munich, this royal house ran the gamut of ancient architecture in just three short decades. It culminated in the remarkable flights of fancy of Ludwig II, often called "Mad King Ludwig," who died under mysterious circumstances in 1886. In spite of his rather lonely life and controversial alliances, both personal and political, he was a great patron of the arts.

Although the name "Royal Castles" is limited to the castles of Hohenschwangau (built by Ludwig's father, Maximilian II) and Neuschwanstein, the extravagant king was responsible for the creation of two other magnificent castles, Linderhof (near Oberammergau) and Herrenchiemsee (Chiemsee).

In 1868, after a visit to the great castle of Wartburg, Ludwig wrote to his good friend, composer Richard Wagner: "I have the intention to rebuild the ancient castle ruins of Hohenschwangau in the true style of the ancient German knight's castle." The following year, construction began on the first of a series of fantastic edifices, a series that stopped only with Ludwig's untimely death in 1886, only 5 days after he was deposed because of alleged insanity.

The nearest towns to the castles are **Füssen,** 2 miles away at the very end of the Romantic Road, and **Schwangau,** where accommodations can be found.

ESSENTIALS

ARRIVING   By Train   There are frequent trains from Munich and Augsburg to Füssen. For information, call **0821/1-94-19.** A train from Munich takes $2^1/_2$ hours; frequent buses travel to the castles.

By Bus   Long-distance bus service from Augsburg to Füssen is provided by line EB190. Regional service is provided by **RVA Regionalverkehr Schwäben Allgau GmbH** in Füssen (☎ **08362/3-77-71**), which runs at least 10 buses a day to the royal castles.

By Car   Take B-17 south to Füssen, then head east from Füssen on B-17.

VISITOR INFORMATION   For information about the castles and the region in general, contact the **Kurverwaltung,** Kaiser-Maximilian-Platz 1, Füssen (☎ **08362/ 70-77** and 70-78), open Mon–Fri 8am–noon and 2–5pm, Sat 10am–noon. Information is also available at the **Kurverwaltung,** Rathaus, Münchenerstrasse 2, in Schwangau (☎ **08362/8-19-80**), open Mon–Fri 8am–5pm.

VISITING THE ROYAL CASTLES

There are often very long lines in summer, especially August. With 25,000 people a day visiting, the wait in peak summer months can range from a startling 4–5 hours for a 20-minute tour. The telephone number for Neuschwanstein is **08362/8-10-35;** for Hohenschwangau, **08362/8-11-27.**

✪ Neuschwanstein

This is the fairy-tale castle of Ludwig II. Construction went on for 17 years, until the king's death, when all work stopped, leaving a part of the interior uncompleted. From 1884 to 1886 Ludwig lived on and off in the rooms that were completed for a total of only about 6 months.

The doorway off the left side of the vestibule leads to the king's apartments. The study, like most of the rooms, is decorated with wall paintings showing scenes from the Nordic legends (which also inspired Wagner's operas). The theme of the study is the Tannhäuser saga, painted by J. Aigner. The curtains and chair coverings are in hand-embroidered silk, designed with the gold-and-silver Bavarian coat-of-arms.

From the vestibule, you enter the throne room through the doorway at the opposite end. This hall, designed in Byzantine style by J. Hofmann, was never completed. The floor, a mosaic design, depicts the animals of the world. The columns in the main hall are the deep copper red of porphyry.

The king's bedroom is the most richly carved and decorated in the entire castle—it took $4^1/_2$ years to complete this room alone. Aside from the mural showing the legend of Tristan and Isolde, the walls are decorated with panels carved to look like gothic windows. In the center is a large wooden pillar completely encircled by gilded brass sconces. The ornate bed is on a raised platform with an elaborately carved canopy.

The fourth floor of the castle is almost entirely given over to the Singer's Hall, the pride of Ludwig II and all of Bavaria. Modeled after the hall at Wartburg, where the legendary song contest of Tannhäuser supposedly took place, this hall is decorated with marble columns and elaborately painted designs interspersed with frescoes depicting the life of Parsifal.

The castle can be visited year round, and in September visitors have the additional treat of hearing Wagnerian concerts along with other music in the Singer's Hall. For information and reservations, contact the tourist office, Verkehrsamt, Schwangau, at the Rathaus (☎ **08362/8-19-80**). The castle is open (guided tours only) Apr–Sept daily 9am–5:30pm; off-season daily 10am–4pm. Admission is 10 DM ($7) for adults, 7 DM ($4.90) for students and seniors over 65; children 15 and under enter free.

Reaching Neuschwanstein involves a steep half-mile climb from the parking lot of Hohenschwangau Castle, about a 25-minute walk for the energetic, an eternity for anybody else. To cut down on the climb, you can take a bus to Marienbrücke, a bridge that crosses over the Pollat Gorge at a height of 305 feet. From that vantage point you, like Ludwig, can stand and meditate on the glories of the castle and its panoramic surroundings. If you want to photograph the castle, don't wait until you reach the top, where you'll be too close to the edifice. It costs 3 DM ($2.10) for the bus ride up to the bridge or 2.50 DM ($1.75) if you'd like to take the bus back down the hill. From the Marienbrücke bridge it's a 10-minute walk to Neuschwanstein over a very steep footpath that is not easy to negotiate for anyone who has trouble walking up or down precipitous hills.

The most picturesque way to reach Neuschwanstein is by horse-drawn carriage, costing 7 DM ($4.90) for the ascent, 3.50 DM ($2.45) for the descent. However, some readers have objected to the rides, complaining that too many people are crowded in.

✪ Hohenschwangau

Not as glamorous or spectacular as Neuschwanstein, the neo-gothic Hohenschwangau Castle nevertheless has a much richer history. The original structure dates back to the 12th-century knights of Schwangau. When the knights faded away, the castle began to do so too, helped along by the Napoleonic Wars. When Ludwig II's father, Crown Prince Maximilian (later Maximilian II), saw the castle in 1832, he purchased it and 4 years later he had completely restored it. Ludwig II spent the first 17 years of his life here and later received Richard Wagner in its chambers, although Wagner never visited Neuschwanstein on the hill above.

The rooms of Hohenschwangau are styled and furnished in a much heavier gothic mode than those in Ludwig's castle, and are typical of the halls of medieval knights' castles. But also unlike Neuschwanstein, this castle has a comfortable look about it, as if it actually were a home at one time, not just a museum. The small chapel, once a reception hall, still hosts Sunday mass. The suits of armor and the gothic arches here set the stage. Among the most attractive chambers is the Hall of the Swan Knight, named for the wall paintings that tell the saga of Lohengrin.

Hohenschwangau is open Apr–Sept daily 8:30am–5:30pm; Oct–Mar daily 10am–4pm. Admission is 10 DM ($7) for adults and 7 DM ($4.90) for children 6–15 and seniors over 65; children 5 and under enter free. Several parking lots nearby enable you to leave your car there while visiting both castles.

NEARBY ACCOMMODATIONS

In Hohenschwangau

Hotel Lisl and Jägerhaus. Neuschwansteinstrasse 1–3, D-87643 Hohenschwangau. ☎ **08362/88-70.** Fax 08362/81-107. 51 rms. MINIBAR TV TEL. 280 DM ($196) double. AE, DC, MC, V. Closed Jan to mid-Mar. Free parking. Bus: Füssen.

This graciously styled villa with an annex across the street was seemingly made to provide views as well as comfort. Both houses sit in a narrow valley, surrounded by their own gardens. Most rooms have a view of at least one of the two royal castles and some units open onto views of both schlosses. In the main house, two well-styled dining rooms serve good-tasting meals. The restaurant features an international as well as a local cuisine.

Hotel Müller Hohenschwangau. Alpseestrasse 16, D-87645 Hohenschwangau. ☎ **08362/ 8-19-90.** Fax 08362/81-99-13. 43 rms, 2 suites. TV TEL. 200–260 DM ($140–$182) double; 300–400 DM ($210–$280) suite. Rates include continental breakfast. AE, DC, MC, V. Closed Nov–Dec 20. Free parking. Bus: Füssen.

The yellow walls, green shutters, and gabled alpine detailing of this hospitable inn are enough incentive for you to stay here. However, its location near the foundation of Neuschwanstein Castle makes it even more alluring. An enlargement and upgrading in 1984 added extra modern conveniences. On the premises are two pleasant restaurants. Nature lovers usually enjoy hiking the short distance to nearby Hohenschwangau Castle.

In or Near Füssen

Hotel Christine. Weidachstrasse 31, D-87629 Füssen. ☎ **08362/72-29.** 15 rms. TV TEL. 150– 180 DM ($105–$126) double. Rates include continental breakfast. No credit cards. Closed Jan 15–Feb 15. Free parking.

The Christine is one of the best local choices for accommodation, 5 minutes by taxi from the train station in Füssen. The staff spends the long winter months refurbishing the rooms so they'll be fresh and sparkling for spring visitors. Breakfast, the only meal, is served on beautiful regional china as classical music plays in the background. The rooms are quite spacious, with balconies.

Hotel-Schlossgasthof Zum Hechten. Ritterstrasse 6, D-87629 Füssen. ☎ **08362/91-600.** Fax 08362/91-6099. 34 rms (25 with shower or bath), 4 suites. 85–95 DM ($59.50–$66.50) double without shower or bath; 100–130 DM ($70–$91) double with shower or bath. Rates include buffet breakfast. MC, V. Free outside parking, 5 DM ($3.50) garage.

The family owners have maintained this impeccable guest house for generations. Directly below the 15th-century castle of Füssen, it's one of the oldest in town. On a central street with a white-walled facade, it has been unpretentiously and tastefully modernized into a functional format with the added charm of the family's personal atmosphere and hospitality. The guest house offers two restaurants. A typical Swabian and Bavarian cuisine is served, with plenty of dishes to please the vegetarian as well.

Ⓢ **Seegasthof Weissensee.** An der B-310, D-87629 Füssen–Weisssensee. ☎ **08362/70-95.** Fax 08362/23-76. 24 rms. MINIBAR TEL. 100–130 DM ($70–$91) double. Rates include breakfast. No credit cards. Free parking.

The paneled rooms at this hotel have sliding glass doors opening onto a balcony overlooking the lake, 4 miles from central Füssen on B-310. Each accommodation contains a minibar stocked with beer, wine, and champagne. Breakfast is an appetizing and generous meal of cheese, cold cuts, bread, pastry, eggs, and beverages. The fish that your obliging hosts serve you during dinner might have been caught in the ice-blue waters of the nearby lake, whose far shore you can see from the dining room.

Ⓢ **Steig Mühle.** Alte Steige 3, D-87629 Füssen–Weisssensee. ☎ **08362/73-73.** Fax 08362/ 31-48. 10 rms. 100–110 DM ($70–$77) double. Rates include buffet breakfast. No credit cards. Closed Nov 23–Dec 24. Free outside parking, 4.50 DM ($3.15) garage. From Füssen, take Route 310 toward Kempten, a 5-minute drive.

Owners and obliging hosts Josef and Guste Buhmann like things to be cozy—their chalet-like guesthouse is almost a cliche of Bavarian charm. It's a pension garni (serving breakfast). The rooms open onto a view of the lake or mountains, and many have their own balconies. Six contain TVs. They're furnished in a neat, functional style and are kept immaculately clean. The public rooms are paneled in wood and decorated with local artifacts.

DINING

Fischerhütte. Uferstrasse 16, Hopfen am See. ☎ **08362/71-03.** Reservations recommended. Main courses 16–39.50 DM ($11.20–$27.65). AE, DC, MC, V. Daily 11:30am–2pm and 6–9:30 pm. Closed Mon–Tues Jan–Mar. SEAFOOD.

Three miles northwest of Füssen in the hamlet of Hopfen am See, at the edge of the lake within sight of dramatic mountain scenery, lie four gracefully paneled old-fashioned dining rooms, plus a terrace in summer. As its name (Fisherman's Cottage) suggests, the establishment specializes in an array of fish whose origins read like an international atlas: half an entire Alaskan salmon (for two); a garlicky version of French bouillabaisse; fresh alpine trout, pan-fried or with aromatic herbs in the style of Provence; North Atlantic lobster; and grilled halibut. A limited array of meat dishes is also offered, as well as succulent desserts.

Zum Schwanen. Brotmarkt 4. Füssen. ☎ **08362/61-74.** Reservations required. Main courses 11–32 DM ($7.70–$22.40). AE. Tues–Sun 11:30am–2pm; Tues–Sat 5:30–9pm. SWABIAN/ BAVARIAN.

A conservative yet flavorful blend of Swabian and Bavarian specialties is served to the loyal clients of Zum Schwanen, a small, attractively old-fashioned restaurant. Good-tasting and hearty specialties include homemade sausage, roast pork, lamb, and venison.

DAY TRIPS & OUTDOOR ACTIVITIES IN THE AREA

The lakes around Füssen are excellent for windsurfing and sailing. Dinghies and windsurfing boards can be rented at **Selbach Bootsvermietung** at either their Hopfensee or Weissensee boathouse. Call **08362/71-64** for more information.

There are many hiking trails in the mountains around Füssen and Schwangau. Maps, guide services, and other information are available from the tourist office. For information about skiing, contact the tourist offices. Instruction can be provided by **Skischule Tegelberg-Füssen** at Schwangau (☎ **08362/8-10-18**).

A fascinating excursion is to the ✪ **Wieskirche,** one of the most extravagant and flamboyant rococo buildings in the world, a masterpiece of Dominikus Zimmermann. On the slopes of the Ammergau Alps, between Ammer and Lech, the Wieskirche is a noted pilgrimage church, drawing visitors from all over the globe. It's located in an alpine meadow just off the Romantic Road near Steingaden. Inquire at the tourist office for a map and the exact location before setting out. Also, confirm that the church will be open at the time of your visit. The church, which in German means "in the meadows," was built to honor the memory of Jesus Scourged. With the help of his brother, Johann Baptist, Zimmermann worked on the building from 1746 to 1754. Around the choir the church has "upside-down" arches, and its ceiling is richly frescoed. A bus heading for the church leaves Füssen Mon–Sat at 11:15am; Sun at 1:05pm. You can return on the 3:50pm bus from the church. The trip takes an hour and costs 12 DM ($8.40) round-trip.

8

Greece

by John Bozman & Sherry Marker

Greece is, of course, the land of ancient sites and treasures: the Acropolis in Athens, the amphitheater of Epidauros, the museum at Delphi, Olympia where the games began, and many others. It is also a place of sun, beaches, and spectacular islands like Santorini and Mykonos.

1 Athens

by John Bozman

When you arrive in central Athens, your first impressions probably will be of bright sunlight, drab concrete buildings, and congested streets—not the romantic wonderland you've dreamed about. But when you catch your first glimpse of the Acropolis, floating high against the sky, you'll remember why you came. You'll soon encounter sights you've heard and read about all your life, recognizing them from a thousand pictures, and you'll be impressed and delighted.

While Athens's modern center may not be beautiful, the attractions in its ancient heart are awe-inspiring. Athina is older than Rome, a democratic Greek city heavily influenced by the Orient and given to free growth rather than Roman order, inhabited by some of the world's most open, friendly, and boisterous people.

ONLY IN ATHENS

Seeing the Ancient Monuments The Acropolis, with the Parthenon, the world's most beautiful public building, is an incredible sight. And below it is the Ancient Greek Agora, the political, civil, commercial, and religious center of ancient Athens.

Exploring Athens's Neighborhoods Climb Lykavitos Hill for a bird's-eye view over much of Athens and down to the Saronic Gulf. Wander through Plaka, which has streets that were laid out in antiquity. Stroll in Anafiotika, a neighborhood that still feels like a Cycladic village.

Spending an Afternoon at the National Archeological Museum You can view the best Greek relics anywhere in this vast warehouse of history, art, and archeological treasures.

Having a Night on the Town Enjoy Athens's lively nightlife at a traditional music tavern into the wee hours.

Exploring Eleusis   Take a side trip for the imagination to one of the oldest and most mysterious sanctuaries in the world.

Shopping the Flea Market   The flea market, filled with small stores and tourist stalls selling trinkets—fun and cheap—to reproductions of ancient works, many convincing and relatively inexpensive.

ORIENTATION

ARRIVING   By Plane   Athens's **Hellenikon International Airport** is 7 miles south of Syntagma (Constitution) Square. Most visitors arrive at the East Air Terminal, on the eastern side of the airport runways. It offers a few convenient facilities: branches of the major Greek banks (open 24 hours) giving you the official exchange rate, luggage carts available for 200 Dr (85¢), a managed taxi rank outside to the right, and buses to the left. The information desk, slightly to the left as you come out of Customs, is helpful and for a small fee will book you into a hotel in your price range. For information about flights, call 01/969-4466. A cab into the center (*kentro*) of town will cost you about 2,500 Dr ($10.50), twice that between midnight and 5am. A far better deal is to take bus no. 091 to Syntagma Square or Omonia Square for less than $1, though the wait can sometimes be nearly an hour. (The bus stops first near Omonia, which most Greeks consider the center of town because it's the commercial heart.)

All domestic and international flights of the national airline, Olympic, arrive at the newer West Air Terminal, on the west side of the runways. For information about incoming Olympic flights, call 01/926-9111. Bank offices are in the arrivals area, open 7am–11pm, with ATMs for after hours. Olympic has an information booth, and the Tourist Police have a corner office in the building across from the terminal entrance. A rather expensive—700 Dr ($3) for 24 hours—unofficial luggage storage is across the parking lot from the entrance.

You can take bus no. 019 directly to Piraeus from either the East or the West Terminal.

By Train   Trains from the west, including Eurail connections via Patras, arrive at the **Peloponnese Station** (Stathmos Peloponnissou), about a mile northwest of Omonia Square. A taxi into the center of town should cost about 500 Dr ($2.15). Trains from the north arrive at **Larissa Station** (Stathmos Larissis), northeast across the tracks, where you'll find a currency-exchange office, open daily 8am–9:15pm, and a luggage-storage office charging 250 Dr ($1.05) per bag per day, open 6:30am–9:30pm.

By Boat   Athens's main seaport, Piraeus, 7 miles southwest, is a 15-minute subway ride from Monasteraki and Omonia Squares. The subway runs from about 5am to midnight and costs 75 Dr (35¢), with a surcharge of another 75 Dr after Omonia. See "Day Trips from Athens," at the end of this section, for further information.

VISITOR INFORMATION   The **Greek National Tourist Organization** has a walkup window outside the National Bank of Greece at the northwest corner of Syntagma Square, 2 Karayiori Servias St. (☎ **01/322-3111**), open Mon–Thurs 8:30am–2pm, Fri 8:30am–1:30pm, and Sat 9am–12:30pm (closed holidays). Information about Athens, free city maps, hotel lists, and other general booklets are available in English, though the line can get rather long.

CITY LAYOUT   Central Athens is based on an almost equilateral triangle, with its points at **Syntagma (Constitution) Square, Omonia (Harmony) Square,** and **Monasteraki (Little Monastery) Square,** near the Acropolis—all now construction sites for a future Athens subway. This is sanctioned as the Commercial Center, from

Athens Attractions & Accommodations

Attractions:
Academy of Arts
& Letters **18**
Acropolis Museum **11**
Athens Cathedral **20**
Ayios Yióryios **19**
Benaki Museum **21**
Byzantine Museum **23**
Hadrian's Arch **27**
Hadrian's Library **6**
Ilias Lalaounis
Jewelry Museum **13**
Keramikós Cemetery **1**
Monasteráki Church **5**
Museum of Cycladic Art **22**
Museum of Greek
Folk Art **24**
National Archaeological
Museum **14**
National Historical
Museum **15**
National Library **16**
National Picture Gallery **26**
Odeum of Heródes
Atticus **9**
Parthenon **10**
Presidential Palace **25**
Roman Agora **7**
Stoa of Attalos **4**
Stoa of Zeus **3**
Temple of Olympian
Zeus **28**
Theater of Dionysus **12**
Theseum (Hephaestium) **2**
Tower of Winds (Aerides) **8**
University **17**

Accommodations:
Achilleas Hotel **11**
Acropolis View **2**
Adonis Hotel **7**
Amalia Hotel **9**
Athenian Inn **14**
Athens Hilton **13**
Attalos Hotel **1**
Austria **3**
Carolina Hotel **12**
Dioskouros Guest House **5**
Dryades Hotel **16**
Elektra Palace **8**
Exarchion Hotel **15**
Hotel Hera **4**
Hotel Plaka **10**
Nefeli Hotel **6**

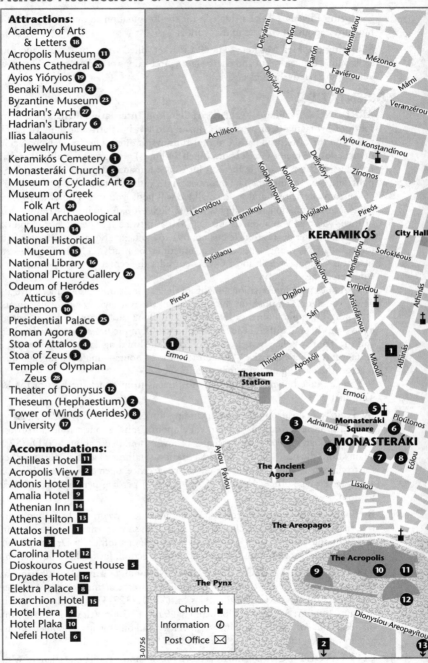

3-0756

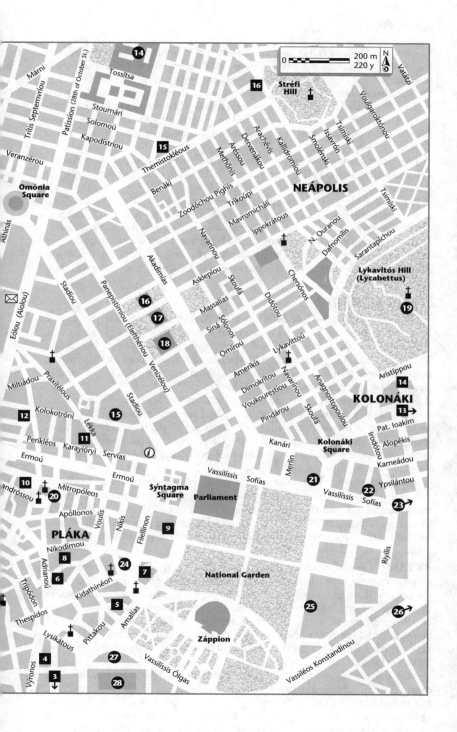

Márni
Trítis Septemvríou
Patissíon (28th of October St.)
Tossítsa
Stournári
Solomoú
Kapodístriou
Veranzérou

14

16
Stréfi
Hill

Tsímiski
Issavrón
Smolénski
Voulgaroktónou
Vatátzi

0 —————— 200 m
220 y
N

Themistokléous
15

Arachóvis
Dervenákou
Arésou
Methónis
Kallidromíou

Benáki
Zoodóchou Pighís
Trikoúpi
Mavromicháli
Ippokrátous

NEÁPOLIS

N. Ouranoú
Dafnomílis
Sarantapíchou

Tsímiski

Omónia
Square

Athinás

Navarínou
Asklepíou
Skoufá
Massalías
Sólonos
S1ná
Omirou
Amerikís
Dimokrítou
Voukourestíou
Pindárou

Didótou
Chersónos

Lykavittoú
Navarínou
Anagnostopoúlou
Skoufá

Lykavitós Hill
(Lycabettus)

19

Aristíppou

Eólou (Aiólou)
Stadíou
Panepistimíou (Eleftheríou Venizélou)

Akadimías
16
17
18

Stadíou

Miltiádou
Praxitélous
Kolokotróni
Lékka
12
11
Perikléos
Karayióryi
Servías
Ermoú
15

14

KOLONÁKI
13 →
Pat. Ioakím
Iródotou
Alopékis
Karneádou

Kanári
Kolonáki
Square

Merlin
21

10
androssou
20
Mitropóleos
Ermoú
Apóllonos
Voulís
Nikis
Filellínon

PLÁKA
Nikodímou
8
Adrianoú
6
Tripódon
Thespídos
Lysikátous
Výronos
4
3
↓

Kidathinéon
24
7
5
Amalías
Pittakou

28
27

Vassilíssis Ólgas

Záppion

**Syntagma
Square**
Parliament

Vassilíssis
Sofías

Vassilíssis
Sofías

22
Ypsilántou
23 →

Ríyílis

National Garden

25

26 →

Vassiléos Konstandínou

9

(i)

461

which cars are banned except for three cross streets. Omonia and Syntagma Squares are connected by the parallel **Stadiou Street** and **Panepistimiou Street,** which is also called Eleftheriou Venizelou. West from Syntagma Square, ancient Ermou Street and broader **Mitropoleos Street** lead slightly downhill to Monasteraki Square. Here you'll find the flea market, the **Ancient Agora (Market)** below the Acropolis, and Plaka, the oldest neighborhood, with names and monuments from ancient times. From Monasteraki Square, **Athinas Street** leads north past the modern market to Omonia Square.

Two helpful landmarks for orientation are the Acropolis and, to its northeast, **Lykavitos (Lycabettus) Hill,** higher, with a small white church on top—both visible from most parts of the city.

In general, finding your way around Athens is relatively easy. An exception is Plaka, with its small winding streets at the foot of the Acropolis, a labyrinth that'll challenge even the best navigators, but the neighborhood is small enough that you can't go far astray and so charming that you won't mind being lost. One excellent map, the *Historical Map of Athens,* produced by the Greek Archeological Service, has the sites of Athens clearly identified and an enlarged map of Plaka as well; it costs about 500 Dr ($2.15).

GETTING AROUND

BY BUS, TROLLEY BUS & METRO (SUBWAY)   In general, the regular blue buses and the orange trolley buses (powered by electric lines above) serve areas in the city center. The blue A line buses head out of town to transfer points. Tickets cost 75 Dr (35¢) and must be purchased in advance, usually in groups of 10, from any news kiosk or special bus-ticket kiosks at main stations. When you board, validate your ticket in the automatic machine and keep it.

Sometimes inspectors board and check all tickets to see if everybody has paid the fare. You don't want the hassle of explaining why you didn't cancel, or don't have, a ticket—not to mention paying the fine. Buses run all the time but with limited night service. The Athens map distributed by the Greek National Tourist Office indicates the major stops and routes, but you probably won't use the bus often, as many sights of interest can be reached on foot.

The metro presently links Piraeus, the seaport of Athens, and Kifissia, an upscale northern suburb. (A second line is under construction.) In the city center the trains run underground, and the main stops are Monasteraki, Omonia, and Viktorias (Victoria). Tickets cost 75 Dr (35¢), with a 75-Dr surcharge after Omonia. (Metro and bus tickets aren't interchangeable.) Trains run about every 15 minutes 5am–midnight.

BY TAXI   Taxis are inexpensive in Athens and the vast majority of drivers are honest men trying to wrest a living by driving on crowded streets. However, some drivers, notably those in Piraeus and a few working the airport, have been known to overcharge severely. Insist that the meter be used and set on "1" rather than "2," except between midnight and 5am or outside the city (when and where the fare doubles), and don't let the driver move the decimal point. Only if the cab is caught in heavy traffic should your trip to the center of town from the airport cost more than 3,000 Dr ($12.80).

As of this writing, the minimum fare is 200 Dr (85¢), typical for a short hop in central Athens. Additional charges include a luggage fee of 55 Dr (25¢) per 22-lb. bag and an extra 300 Dr ($1.25) for stops at transportation centers like the airport or train station. If you have a problem with your driver, enlist your hotel or place of business in negotiations and protests or call the helpful Tourist Police at 171.

You may see locals shouting at the windows or running alongside taxis trying to get in a word with the driver. Taxis can pick up several passengers along their route, and people are trying to see if the taxi is going their way. If you're picked up half-way through another passenger's ride, note the amount on the meter as you board and subtract it from the final fare, but be prepared to simply accept the charge the driver asks. It'll probably be reasonable. If a taxi flashes its lights, it's available.

There are about 15 radio-taxi companies, including **Express** (☎ **01/993-4812**), **Kosmos** (☎ **01/801-9000**), and **Parthenon** (☎ **01/581-4711**). If you're trying to make travel connections, your hotel will have more clout and can usually save you some hassle.

ON FOOT   Like so many other European cities, Athens is creating pedestrian zones, mostly in major shopping areas, making window-shopping and strolling a pleasure. Most of Plaka and the Commercial Triangle are closed to traffic.

You can do most sightseeing in Athens on foot. When crossing a street, keep in mind that a red traffic light or a stop sign doesn't necessarily mean that all cars will stop.

BY CAR & MOPED   Parking is so difficult and traffic so heavy in Athens that you should use a car only for trips outside the city.

You can rent mopeds from **Meintanis,** 4 Dionysiou Areopayitou in Plaka, at the foot of the Acropolis near the intersection with Amalias Street (☎ **01/323-2346**), for about 4,200 Dr ($17.50) per day, tax included (less 20% if rented for a week).

FAST FACTS: Athens

Banks   Banks are generally open Mon–Thurs 8am–2pm and Fri 8am–1:30pm. All banks have currency-exchange counters working at the rates set daily by the government, and give better rates than the exchange bureaus. The American Express Bank, 31 Panepistimiou St. (☎ 01/323-4781), offers currency-exchange and other services Mon–Fri 8:30am–4pm and Sat 8:30am–1:30pm. The National Bank of Greece operates a 24-hour ATM next to the Tourist Information Office on Syntagma Square.

Business Hours   In winter, shops and businesses are generally open Mon and Wed 9am–5pm, Tues and Thurs–Fri 10am–7pm, and Sat 8:30am–3:30pm. In summer, hours are Mon, Wed, and Sat 8am–3pm, and Tues and Thurs–Fri 8am–1:30pm and 5:30–10pm. Note that shops geared to tourists keep especially long hours, and some close for "siesta" from about 2 to 5pm.

Currency   The **drachma (Dr)** is the Greek national currency. Coins are issued in 1, 2, 5, 10, 20, 50, and 100 Dr; bills are denominated in 50, 100, 500, 1,000, 5,000, and 10,000 Dr. At this writing, $1 = approximately 235 Dr (or 1 Dr = 4¢), and this was the rate of exchange used to calculate the dollar values given in this chapter.

Drugstores   *Pharmakia,* identified by green crosses, are scattered all over. The usual working hours are 8am–2pm weekdays. In the evening and on weekends most are closed, but there will be a sign on the door listing the names and addresses of pharmacies that are open. Newspapers, including the *Athens News,* list the pharmacies open outside regular hours.

Embassies/Consulates   The Embassy of **Australia** is at 37 D. Soutsou Ave. (☎ 01/644-7303); the Embassy of **Canada,** at 4 Ioannou Yenadiou St. (☎ 01/723-9511 or 01/725-4011); the Consulate of **New Zealand,** at 15 Tsocha St.

(☎ 01/721-0112); the Embassy of the **United Kingdom,** at 1 Ploutarchou St. (☎ 01/723-6211); and the Embassy of the **United States,** at 91 Vasilissis Sofias Ave. (☎ 01/721-2951).

Emergencies   In an emergency, dial 100 for fast **police** assistance and 171 for the effective Tourist Police. Dial 199 to **report a fire** and 166 for an **ambulance** and hospital. If you need an English-speaking doctor or dentist, call your embassy for advice or try SOS Doctor (☎ 01/331-0310 or 01/331-0311).

Holidays   Public holidays in Athens include New Year's Day (Jan 1), Epiphany (Jan 6), Ash Wednesday, Independence Day (Mar 25), Good Friday, Greek Orthodox Easter Sunday and Monday (can coincide with or vary by 2 weeks from Catholic/Protestant Easter), Labor Day (May 1), Assumption Day (Aug 15), National Day (Oct 28), and Christmas (Dec 25–26).

Laundry   The laundry at 10 Angelou Yeronda St., off Kydathineon Street, in Plaka, is open daily 8:30am–7pm. It charges 1,500 Dr ($6.40) for wash, dry, and soap. There's the Self Service Maytag Launderette, at the corner of Didotou and Zoodochou Piyis in Exarchia (☎ 01/381-0661), open Mon–Sat 8am–9pm; it charges 2,500 Dr. ($10.65) for you to wash and dry 5 kilos (11 lb.) or 3,000 Dr ($12.75) if they do the work.

Lost & Found   If you lose something on the street or on public transport, contact the Police Lost and Found Office, 173 Alexandras Ave. (☎ 01/642-1616), open Mon–Sat 9am–3pm. Lost passports and other documents may be returned by the police to the appropriate embassy, so check there as well.

Mail   The main post offices in central Athens are at 100 Eolou, just off Omonia Square, and in Syntagma Square on the corner of Mitropoleos Street. These are open Mon–Fri 7:30am–8pm, Sat 7:30am–2pm, and Sun 9am–1pm. The two post offices at the East and West Air Terminals also keep these extensive hours.

You can receive correspondence in Athens ℅ American Express, 31 Panepistimiou St., 102 25 Athens (☎ 01/323-4781). If you have an American Express card or traveler's checks, the service is free; otherwise, each article you collect costs a steep 600 Dr ($2.55). It's open Mon–Fri 8:30am–4pm and Sat 8:30am–1:30pm.

All the post offices can accept parcels, but the parcel post office at 4 Stadiou St., inside the arcade (☎ 01/322-8940), is specifically geared to do so. It sells cardboard shipping boxes in four sizes and is open Mon–Fri 7:30am–8pm.

Newspapers/Magazines   There's no shortage of local English-language news. Most central-Athens newsstands carry the local daily *Athens News;* weeklies include the *Greek Times* and *Greece's Weekly,* good for in-depth local news and entertainment listings. *Athenscope,* a weekly magazine costing 400 Dr ($1.70), is a fairly comprehensive guide to the arts and entertainment.

Police   In an emergency, dial 100. For help dealing with a troublesome taxi driver, hotel, restaurant, or shop owner, call the Tourist Police at 171—they're powerful advocates for visitors.

Radio/TV   There are nine major Greek TV stations in Athens and at least two local stations. In addition, foreign-language channels from Italy, Spain, and Germany can be seen, as well as CNN around the clock. The foreign-language films shown on Greek TV, like the foreign-language movies shown in Greek cinemas, have the original soundtracks with Greek subtitles, so you'll have no trouble understanding any English-language film.

Tax   VAT is included in the ticket price of all goods and services in Athens, ranging from 4% on books to 36% on certain luxury items.

Telephone   Many of the city's public phones now accept only phone cards, available at newsstands and OTE offices for 1,300 Dr ($5.50) and good for 100 short local calls. Some kiosks still have metered phones; you pay what the meter records. A local call costs 20 Dr (10¢).

You can place international calls without a hotel surcharge at the Telephone Office (OTE), 15 Stadiou St., 3 blocks from Syntagma Square, open Mon–Fri 7am–midnight and Sat–Sun and holidays 8am–midnight.

Tipping   Restaurants already include a service charge in the bill, but many locals add a 10% tip. The same applies to taxi fares.

ACCOMMODATIONS

Don't expect high style and ornamentation in most Greek hotels. They're usually plain and unadorned, but should be clean and comfortable. The area south and west of Syntagma Square, and the neighborhoods of Plaka, Koukaki, Makriyanni, and Monasteraki, offer the most convenient and comfortable choices. We especially recommend Koukaki for its quiet residential backstreets and the feeling it offers of a real Greek neighborhood; although it's not as conveniently situated as Plaka or Syntagma Square, it's only a short walk or bus ride from those areas. For pure convenience, the Syntagma hotels, as well as those in the lively Plaka area, can't be beaten.

Note: We strongly advise that you write or fax ahead of time for reservations, because the best-value hotels sell out in the summer. If you arrive without a reservation, you can book a room at the **tourist information booth** at the West Air Terminal, run by a private tourist agency, open 7am–1am. The staff's English is excellent, and they're very helpful, but the service costs a small fee. You can also book rooms through the **Hellenic Chamber of Hotels** in the National Bank of Greece on Syntagma Square, 2 Karayioryis Servias St. (☎ **01/323-7193**), open Mon–Thurs 8:30am–2pm, Fri 8:30am–1:30pm, and Sat 9am–12:30pm. Both offices can make reservations for hotels elsewhere in Greece.

IN PLAKA

Expensive

Elektra Palace. 18 Nikodimou St., Plaka, 105 57 Athens. ☎ **01/324-1401** or 01/324-1407. Fax 01/324-1875. 106 rms. A/C MINIBAR TV TEL. 26,500 Dr ($112.75) double. Rates include breakfast. AE, DC, MC, V.

A good choice for comfort and a convenient location, the Elektra is just a few blocks southwest of Syntagma Square at the edge of Plaka. The rooms are decorated in warm muted tones; those on the upper levels are smaller, but their larger balconies have a view that merits their use. There's a nice rooftop pool for soaking up the rays and the view and for a refreshing splash after a hot day of sightseeing.

Moderate

Hotel Plaka. 7 Kapnikereas St. (at Mitropoleos), Plaka, 105 56 Athens. ☎ **01/322-2096** or 01/322-2098. Fax 01/322-2414. 67 rms (52 with shower, 15 with tub). A/C TV TEL. 21,000 Dr ($89) double. Air-conditioning 2,000 Dr ($8.50) extra. AE, MC, V.

The bright new white lobby is impressive, as is the roof garden's wonderful view of the Acropolis, particularly in the evening. Request one of the more attractive rooms facing the Acropolis, though the street-facing rooms have double-paned windows. Mini-fridges are available by request.

Inexpensive

Adams Hotel. Thalou and Herefondos Sts., 105 58 Athens. ☎ **01/322-5381** or 01/324-6582. 15 rms, 11 with bath. 11,000 Dr ($46.80) double with bath. Breakfast 1,000 Dr ($4.25) extra.

No credit cards. From Syntagma Square, walk south on Amalias Avenue; as you approach Hadrian's Arch you'll find Thalou Street on your right, and the hotel is 2 blocks along it.

Many of the rooms here boast good views of the Acropolis. All have balconies and some (notably no. 303) have large terraces. In the lobby lounge is a big cafe/bar where English is spoken fluently. Each of the rooms without an en suite bath (all singles) has its own bathroom across the hall.

Adonis Hotel. 3 Kodrou, Plaka, 105 58 Athens. ☎ **01/324-9737.** Fax 01/324-9737. 25 rms, 1 suite. TEL. 12,600 Dr ($54) double; 16,000 Dr ($70) suite. No credit cards. Rates include breakfast.

This clean, quiet hotel, near Voulis Street has central heating, an elevator, and a pleasant rooftop garden with a great Acropolis view. The rooms are quite plain but comfortable enough, some with balconies large enough for sunbathing. If you stay more than two nights, request the 20% discount. Breakfast is served on the roof terrace, which doubles as a cafe in the evening.

Dioskouros Guest House. 6 Pittakou St., Plaka, 105 58 Athens. ☎ **01/324-8165.** 12 rms, none with bath. 8,000 Dr ($34) double. Breakfast 700 Dr ($3) extra. No credit cards.

This small guest house occupies an old home that has seen better days. The staff, however, keeps the place clean, and it's fairly quiet, as it's shielded from busy Amalias by a much larger building.

Nefeli Hotel. 16 Iperidou St., Plaka, 105 58 Athens. ☎ **01/322-8044.** Fax 01/323-1114. 18 rms. TEL. 13,800 Dr ($59) double. Rates include breakfast. No credit cards.

This charming, well-run little hotel is at the end of Voulis Street, in a quiet corner in the heart of Plaka. The rooms are small but spotless, some with old-fashioned ceiling fans and six with air-conditioning.

NEAR MONASTERAKI SQUARE
Inexpensive

✪ **Attalos Hotel.** 29 Athinas St., 105 54 Athens. ☎ **01/321-2801.** Fax 01/324-3124. 80 rms. A/C TEL. 9,500 Dr ($40) double. Buffet breakfast 1,100 Dr ($4.50) per person extra. Air-conditioning 1,500 Dr ($6.40) extra. V.

The Attalos has a good location: 2 blocks north of the Monasteraki metro station and a short walk to the Acropolis, Plaka, and Syntagma Square. Excellent management, a friendly and attentive staff, and comfortable lodgings make this an exceptional value. Bustling Athinas Street is nearly deserted and quiet at night, and there's a handsome roof garden with fine views of the city and the Acropolis. The rooms are plain, but very well maintained and especially clean. The Attalos provides free luggage storage.

Carolina Hotel. 55 Kolokotroni St., 105 60 Athens. ☎ **01/331-1784** or 01/331-1785. Fax 01/324-0944. 31 rms, 15 with bath. 8,000 Dr ($34) double without bath, 9,000 Dr ($39) double with bath. Breakfast 1,000 Dr ($4.25) per person extra. AE, EU, MC, V.

The three-story Carolina (with elevator) is a good affordable standby, offering clean, quiet rooms with balconies. Solar-heating units were installed in 1996 for a regular supply of hot water. Rooms without an en suite bath have a separate private bathroom down the hall. Co-owner George Papagiannoulas (who runs the place with his brother) lived in Australia for 10 years and speaks English well.

ON & AROUND SYNTAGMA SQUARE
Very Expensive

Hotel Grande Bretagne. Syntagma Sq., 105 63 Athens. ☎ **01/323-0251.** Fax 01/322-8034. 365 rms, 33 suites. A/C MINIBAR TV TEL. 63,000–125,650 Dr ($268–$535) double; from 86,000 Dr ($366) suite. AE, CB, DC, MC, V.

This grande dame is still a favorite for old-world elegance. Built in 1864, it remains a venerable institution; its beaux-arts design is without equal in all of Greece. The polished marble floors and classical pillars of the lobby, with its ornately carved wood paneling and soaring ceilings, lend a true continental air, a feeling that the clientele only enhances. Yet the Greek flavor prevails, as the movers and shakers of Greek society pass through for power lunches at the popular GB Corner.

Softly lit hallways with marble wainscoting lead to old-fashioned rooms with 12-foot ceilings and wall-to-wall coziness. The hotel was renovated in 1992, but we occasionally hear of a room that was apparently overlooked. The front rooms, with views of Syntagma Square and the Acropolis, are usually preferred, but the inner courtyard rooms are quieter.

Expensive

Amalia Hotel. 10 Amalias Ave., 105 57 Athens. ☎ **01/323-7301** or 01/323-7309. Fax 01/ 323-8792. 98 rms. A/C MINIBAR TV TEL. 25,800 Dr ($110) double. Rates include breakfast. AE, DC, MC, V.

This is one of the best values in Athens, especially considering its convenient Syntagma Square location. The rooms are large, comfortable, and quiet, and the busy staff is helpful, if sometimes a bit curt.

Esperia Palace Hotel. 22 Stadiou St., 105 61 Athens. ☎ **01/323-8001.** 185 rms. A/C MINIBAR TV TEL. 30,000 Dr ($127) double. Rates include breakfast. AE, DC, MC, V.

This is another good-value hotel with a convenient location. The rooms are rather plain but large and comfortable, with direct-dial telephones. The buffet breakfast is especially good. Many tour groups stay here and the staff is used to handling a high turnover well. (You can make reservations through Best Western.)

Inexpensive

Ⓢ **Achilleas Hotel.** 21 Lekka St., 105 62 Athens. ☎ **01/323-3197.** Fax 01/324-1092. 34 rms (27 with shower, 7 with tub). A/C TEL. 15,700 Dr ($67) double. Rates include continental buffet breakfast. AE, V.

The Achilleas is on a quiet street just off Syntagma Square. Don't be put off by the entrance off the street; this hotel was completely renovated in 1995, and all the rooms are spacious and bright. It's a very good value, especially for families, who will enjoy the twin bedrooms that share a sitting room and bath.

IN KOLONAKI

Moderate

Athenian Inn. 22 Haritos St., Kolonaki, 106 75 Athens. ☎ **01/723-8097.** Fax 01/724-2268. 28 rms. A/C TV TEL. 23,500 Dr ($100) double; 29,500 Dr ($125) triple. AE, DC, V.

This is a favorite hotel for many return visitors. The quiet location 3 blocks east of Kolonaki Square is a blessing, as are the clean accommodations and friendly staff. (A quote from the guest book: "At last the ideal Athens hotel, good and modest in scale but perfect in service and goodwill. Hurrah. Lawrence Durrell.") Many of the balconies look out upon Lykavitos Hill. You can have breakfast in the cozy lounge with a fireplace and piano.

IN THE EMBASSY DISTRICT

Very Expensive

Athens Hilton. 46 Vassilissis Sofias Ave., 115 28 Athens. ☎ **01/722-0301.** Fax 01/721-3110. 427 rms, 19 suites. A/C MINIBAR TV TEL. 66,000–140,000 Dr ($280–$595) double; 117,000 Dr ($498) Plaza Executive double; from 155,000 Dr ($660) suite. AE, DC, EC, MC, V.

The Athens Hilton, near the U.S. Embassy, is something of an institution in the capital—it's the place where the international business community and diplomats meet for a drink or a meal in one of its many restaurants. Made of polished marble and quietly elegant, the lobby and other public spaces are a bit too cool and impersonal for some. The guest rooms have marble bathrooms and a pleasantly neutral style.

The Hilton often runs promotional sales, so check about special weekend rates before booking. The hotel has a Plaza Executive floor of rooms and suites with a separate business center and higher level of service. Sports options include a pool and a health club. The lobby Polo Club and top-floor Galaxy Roof Terrace, with superb city views, are fine venues for a drink.

NEAR THE ACROPOLIS

Very Expensive

✪ **Divani-Palace Acropolis.** 19–25 Parthenonos St., Makriyanni, 117 42 Athens. ☎ **01/92-22-2945.** Fax 01/92-14-993. 242 rms, 11 suites. A/C MINIBAR TV TEL. 52,000–72,000 Dr ($221–$306) double; from 72,500 Dr ($308) suite. AE, DC, MC, V.

For luxury, comfort, and location, you'd have a hard time beating this recently renovated beauty, just 3 blocks south of the Acropolis. The rooms are quietly elegant and service is friendly and professional. The spacious modern lobby has copies of classical sculpture, but sections of the actual walls built by Themistocles during the Persian Wars are exhibited in the basement. The hotel has a small, handsome pool and a bar, a good restaurant, and a lovely roof garden with the view you'd expect.

Expensive

Herodion Hotel. 4 Rovertou Gali St., Makriyanni, 117 42 Athens. ☎ **01/923-6832** or 01/923-6836. Fax 01/923-5851. 90 rms (12 with shower, 78 with tub). A/C TV TEL. 32,000 Dr ($135) double. Rates include breakfast. AE, DC, MC, V.

This attractive hotel is just a block south of the Acropolis, near the Herodes Atticus theater. The lobby leads to a lounge and patio garden where you can have drinks and snacks under the trees. The dining room has a set three-course menu for about 4,500 Dr ($20). The large rooms are tastefully decorated, many with a balcony, some with good views. The roof terrace has a fine view of the Acropolis, and you can have room service bring up snacks and meals.

Moderate

Acropolis View Hotel. 10 Webster St., Acropolis, 117 42 Athens. ☎ **01/921-7303** or 01/921-7305. Fax 01/923-0705. 32 rms (12 with shower, 20 with tub). A/C TEL. 20,000 Dr ($85) double. AE, MC, V.

This is a fine little hotel on a small winding side street with no traffic near the Herodes Atticus theater, between Roverto Galli and Propileon. The rooms are small but have most modern amenities; some have the view from which it takes its name. The view from the rooftop bar is sensational, especially at sunset and at night.

Hera Hotel. 9 Falirou St., Makriyani, 117 42 Athens. ☎ **01/923-6682.** Fax 01/924-7334. 45 rms (35 with shower, 4 with tub). A/C TEL. 19,500 Dr ($83) double. No credit cards. Free parking.

This is an attractive, modern hotel with a rooftop bar looking out on the Acropolis. The spacious lobby includes a coffee shop and breakfast lounge and bar with a view of the back garden. The compact rooms are simply furnished and carpeted. Some rooms have TVs. Garage parking is provided at no extra cost.

Hotel Philippos. 3 Mitseon, Makriyani, 117 42 Athens. ☎ **01/922-3611.** Fax 01/922-3615. 50 rms (all with shower). A/C TV TEL. 22,500 Dr ($96) double. AE, DC, MC, V.

Completely renovated in 1993 in keeping with its sleek art deco design, this hotel is amazingly quiet for its busy location 3 blocks south of the Acropolis. The rooms are small but pretty and quite comfortable, and there's a laundry service.

IN KOUKAKI
Moderate
Austria Hotel. 7 Mousson St., Filopappou, 117 42 Athens. ☎ **01/923-5151.** Fax 01/902-5800. 37 rms. A/C TEL. 22,000 Dr ($94) double. Rates include breakfast. AE, DC, EU, MC, V.

This quiet, well-maintained little hotel at the base of Philopappou Hill is operated by a nice Greek-Austrian family. The rooms are rather spartan but especially neat and clean. The view from the rooftop is especially fine, and it's a good base for taking in the sights.

Inexpensive
Art Gallery Pension. 5 Erechthiou St., Koukaki, 117 42 Athens. ☎ **01/923-8376.** Fax 01/923-3025. 22 rms. TEL. 12,000 Dr ($51) double; 13,900 Dr ($59) triple; 15,700 Dr ($67) quad. V.

The Art Gallery Pension takes its name from the many paintings displayed here by artists who have lived in this 40-year-old family house. Polished hardwood floors, ceiling fans, and a tiny cage elevator provide a warm, homey atmosphere.

Ⓢ Marble House Pension. 35A Zinni St., Koukaki, 117 41 Athens. ☎ **01/923-4058** or 01/922-6461. 17 rms (9 with bath). 8,900 Dr ($38) double without bath, 9,990 Dr ($43) double with bath. Oct–May, doubles available for $277 per month. No credit cards.

This place is a favorite of repeat visitors for its good value and friendly atmosphere. It's 2 blocks from Syngrou Avenue and the Olympic Airlines Office, on a cul-de-sac just after the church on Zinni Street, and decked in fuchsia-colored bougainvillea. The rooms facing the cul-de-sac have balconies; all are small, simple, functional, and clean, with solid ceiling fans. The affable Thanos and his staff are informative, caring, and helpful.

DINING
You'll find every sort of ethnic food in the capital, but Greek cooking is still the best and least expensive. Seafood is almost always very expensive, and we often have doubts about its freshness. The traditional difference between Greek restaurants and tavernas used to be that a restaurant (*estiatorion*) served food cooked in or on a stove in advance and a *taverna* prepared grilled food to order. Athens provides a full array of restaurants offering good Greek food and going all the way up to fine French or "international" cooking served in luxurious surroundings.

Most places have menus printed in both Greek and English, but many don't keep their printed (or handwritten) menus up-to-date. When in doubt, go to the display case often outside the kitchen and point. A frequent dish, sometimes quite good, is *moussaka*—baked eggplant casserole, usually with ground meat. *Souvlaki* is chunks of meat, usually beef, grilled on a skewer—what we call shish kebab, its Turkish name. *Pastitsio* (baked pasta with tomato sauce, usually with ground meat) looks rather like lasagne, though it's usually much blander. Another staple is *dolmodakia* (meat wrapped in grape leaves). For a snack, ask for a *tyropitta* (cheese pie), a *spanokopita* (spinach-and-cheese pie), or a *gyro* (*yiro* or *souvlaki me pita*), which you probably already know.

Mezedes (appetizers served with bread) are another Greek specialty you should try. Common ones are *tzatziki* (garlic, cucumber, and yogurt), *melitzanosalata* (eggplant dip), *skordalia* (garlic dip), *taramasalata* (fish roe dip), *keftedes* (meatballs), *kalamaria* (squid), *yigantes* (giant white beans in tomato sauce), and *loukanika* (little sausages).

The most popular Greek table wine is *retsina,* usually white, flavored with pine resin. Some retsina is rotgut, but some can be very good indeed. If you don't like the taste, order *krassi* or *aretsinato* (wine without resin). The most common Greek hard drink is *ouzo,* an anise-flavored liqueur, about 200–300 Dr (90¢–$1.35) per shot, taken either straight or with water, which turns it cloudy white.

Coffeehouses are abundant. The largest concentrations of them are on Syntagma and Kolonaki Squares. They're expensive but are places to be seen, and in summer they're busy throughout the day and well into the evening. In addition to coffee, you can usually get soft drinks, sandwiches, ice cream, and beer. Expect to pay about 800 Dr ($3.55) for a coffee; if you stand up you'll pay considerably less.

Try the **Firenze Gelateria Pasticceria,** 42 Dimitrakopoulou St. (☎ **01/ 922-7156**), for delicious ice cream, pastries, and the best cappuccino in town.

IN PLAKA
Moderate

Eden Vegetarian Restaurant. 12 Lissiou St. ☎ **01/324-8858.** Main courses 1,200–2,100 Dr ($5.10–$8.95). No credit cards. Daily noon–midnight. From Adrianou, take Mnissikleos up 2 blocks toward the Acropolis. VEGETARIAN.

One of the few vegetarian restaurants in Greece, this place serves up good low-cost food in an attractive contemporary setting. The decor includes 1920s-style prints, mirrors, and wrought-iron lamps, and there are views of a pretty Plaka street. Greeks and tourists alike come here to enjoy such dishes as soya mousaka, mushroom, wheat germ, and onion pie, and the delicious brown bread. They also have separate sections for smokers and nonsmokers, a blessing in this country.

Piccolino Restaurant. 26 Sotiros St. (at corner of Kidatheneon, near the Metamorfossi Church). ☎ **01/324-6692.** Main courses 1,500–2,800 Dr ($6.40–$11.90). No credit cards. Daily 6pm–3am. GREEK/ITALIAN.

Piccolino is popular with both Greeks and tourists. Dishes include generous portions of spaghetti carbonara, macaroni and cheese, pastitsio, octopus with french fries, mussels stewed in white wine, fish and chips, and 10 varieties of pizza baked in a traditional wood-fired oven.

Platanos Taverna. 4 Dioyenous St. ☎ **01/322-0666.** Main courses 1,500–2,500 Dr ($6.40–$10.65). No credit cards. Mon–Sat noon–4:30pm and 8pm–midnight. From Adrianou, take Mnissikleos up a block toward the Acropolis. GREEK.

This traditional taverna is on a quiet pedestrian square near the Tower of the Winds. Inside is a pleasant ambience of paintings, photos, and certificates on the walls beneath the modern wooden ceiling. If it's warm, sit at a table beneath the eponymous plane (sycamore) tree in front. Platanos is famous for its Greek specialties and its large list of white, red, and rose wines.

Ta Bakaliarakia Taverna (Damigos). 41 Kidatheneon St. (just before Adrianou). ☎ **01/ 322-5084.** Main courses 1,500–2,600 Dr ($6.40–$11.05). No credit cards. Daily 7pm–midnight. Closed July–Sept. GREEK.

Down a short flight of steps, this long-time budget favorite is where you'll find solid Greek food at low prices. Bakaliarakia are deep-fried patties made from salted cod, soaked for hours to reduce the salt and served with garlic sauce. There are many other dishes as well.

☼ Taverna Xinos. Angelou Yeronda 4 (a narrow lane near Iperidou St.). ☎ **01/322-1065.** Reservations recommended. Main courses 2,000–2,800 Dr ($8.50–$12). No credit cards. Mon–Fri 8pm–12:30am. Closed July. GREEK.

This classic taverna with live music as well as superb food is worth making reservations for, but make them for after 9pm. Its informal atmosphere draws guests in aloha shirts as well as the suit-and-tie crowd. It's highly recommended by Greeks, who consider it one of the finest restaurants in Athens. Try the excellent lemony stuffed grape leaves, the tasty moussaka with fresh ground spices, the lamb fricassee in an egg-lemon and dill sauce, or the veal stew with tomatoes and potatoes in rich olive oil.

☼ To Tristato. 34 Dedalou St. (near Ayiou Yeronda Sq.). ☎ **01/324-4472.** Light meals 1,000–2,000 Dr ($4.25–$8.50); desserts 800–1,500 Dr ($3.40–$6.40). No credit cards. Mon–Fri 2pm–midnight, Sat 10am–midnight, Sun 11am–midnight. Closed Aug 10–Sept 10. SNACKS/DESSERTS.

This small 1920s-style tearoom, adjoining a triangular rose garden, is one of our favorite light-meal and dessert places in Athens. This New Age cafe run by a group of lovely women has it all: fresh fruits and yogurt, omelets, fresh-squeezed juices, scrumptious cakes—everything healthful and homemade. It's the perfect spot for a late breakfast, afternoon tea, light supper, or late-night dessert.

Inexpensive

Grill House Plaka. 28 Kidathineon St. (between the Metamorfossi Church and the Acropolis). ☎ **01/324-6229.** Light meals 900–1,800 Dr ($3.85–$7.65). No credit cards. Daily 11am–1am. GREEK.

At this simple, clean, family-run gyro joint in the heart of Plaka, 1,800 Dr ($7.65) will get you a full plate of souvlaki (beef, pork, or chicken), fresh greens, fries, pita bread, and tzatziki.

Kouklis Ouzeri (To Yerani). 14 Tripodon St. ☎ **01/324-7605.** Mezedes 400–800 Dr ($1.70–$3.40). No credit cards. Daily 11am–2am. GREEK.

In summer, small wrought-iron tables are moved to the rooftop terrace and the sidewalk. Diners are presented with a dozen plates of mezedes: appetizers of fried fish, beans, grilled eggplant, taramosalata, cucumber-and-tomato salad, olives, fried cheese, and other seasonal specialties. With a liter of the house krassi (wine) for 800 Dr ($3.40), you can dine on a budget at Kouklis.

NEAR MONASTERAKI SQUARE

Moderate

Taverna Sigalas. 2 Monasteraki Sq. ☎ **01/321-3036.** Main courses 1,000–1,800 Dr ($4.25–$7.65). No credit cards. Daily 7am–2am. Walk east across the square from the metro station. GREEK.

This worthy taverna is housed in a vintage 1879 commercial building with a newer outdoor pavilion. Its lively interior has huge, old retsina kegs in the back and dozens of black-and-white photos of Greek movie stars on the walls. After 8pm nightly, there's Greek Muzak. At all hours, Greeks and tourists are wolfing down large portions of stews, moussaka, grilled meatballs, baked tomatoes, gyros, and other tasty dishes.

Inexpensive

☺ Epirus. 15 Ayiou Filippou Sq. ☎ **01/324-5572.** Main courses 1,200–2,000 Dr ($5.10–$8.50). No credit cards. Daily noon–midnight. Walk 2 blocks west of the Monasteraki metro station. GREEK.

This marvelous restaurant a few yards from the entrance to the Ancient Greek Agora, past the awnings in the square, is worth finding. It has no pretensions, good food, generous portions, and fair prices.

🟢 **Thanasis.** 69 Metropoleos St. (just off the northeast corner of Monasteraki Sq.). ☎ **01/324-4705.** Main courses 350–1,700 Dr ($1.50–$7.25). No credit cards. Daily 8:30am–1 or 2am. GREEK.

This specialized *souvlakatzidiko* (souvlaki stand) is truly an institution. It serves souvlaki wrapped "to go" or on a plate with pita bread at one of two dozen wooden tables. The french fries are superb and cooked in olive oil—no cholesterol. It's almost always packed with locals who don't seem to notice the brusque service or blaring TVs.

NEAR SYNTAGMA SQUARE

Expensive

Far East. 7 Stadiou St. ☎ **01/323-4996.** Reservations recommended. Main courses 1,400–7,000 Dr ($6–$30). AE, EU, DC, MC, V. Daily 11:30am–2am. CHINESE/JAPANESE/KOREAN.

Several Asian restaurants have opened in central Athens in recent years, but this is the only one we can fully recommend. Though expensive, it turns out the town's best chicken and beef dishes, some tofu and mixed-vegetable dishes, and light, steamed dumplings. The decor is 1960s Chinatown, with teak paneling and floral patterns, and with waitresses (some even Chinese) in classic cheongsam.

Moderate

Apotsos. 10 Panepistimiou St. (at end of the arcade by the Zalotas jewelry store, 2 blocks from Syntagma Sq.). ☎ **01/363-7046.** Mezedes 400–2,000 Dr ($1.70–$8.50). AE, DC, MC, V. Mon–Sat 11am–5pm. GREEK.

This quintessentially Greek establishment specializes in mezedes, small plates of delicacies that fill your table. Regional cheeses and various salads are also served. It has been an Athenian haven for decades and maintains a 1920s atmosphere.

Diros Restaurant. 10 Xenofondos St. ☎ **01/323-2392.** Main courses 1,400–2,500 Dr ($5.95–$10.65). AE, DC, V. Daily noon–midnight. Walk 1 block south from Syntagma Square. GREEK.

You can count on good home-cooked food here. Menu items include avgolemono (rice, egg, and lemon soup), bean soup, a large selection of spaghetti dishes, and roast chicken with french fries. There's seating for 50 both inside and out, and the waiter and manager speak some English.

Inexpensive

Apollonion Bakery. 10 Nikis St. (off the southwest corner of Syntagma Sq.). ☎ **01/331-2590.** Snacks 300–1,000 Dr ($1.25–$4.25). No credit cards. SANDWICHES/PASTRIES.

This new arrival is a branch of a well-known chain. Their sandwiches and croissants are good and fresh.

IN KOLONAKI

Expensive

L'Abreuvoir. 51 Xenokratous. ☎ **01/722-9106.** Reservations recommended. Main courses 4,600–8,700 Dr ($19.60–$37). AE, DC, MC, V. Daily 12:30–4:30pm and 8:30pm–midnight. FRENCH.

This fine French restaurant has tables set under mulberry trees, a wonderful place to have lunch or dinner. From the fluffy spinach tart or smoked trout to the steak au poivre, entrecôtes provençals (a filet cooked in marvelous garlic, mushroom, and parsley sauce) to the soufflé au Grand Marnier or chocolate mousse, it's all a delight. L'Abreuvoir has all the attributes of a perfect splurge evening: a quiet, elegant setting, wonderful food, and good service. For what you get, the prices are reasonable.

Moderate

Dimokritos. 23 Dimokritou St. ☎ **01/361-3588.** Meals 2,500–4,000 Dr ($10.65–$17). No credit cards. Mon–Sat 1–5pm and 8pm–1am. Walk 4 blocks northwest of Kolonaki Square on Skoufa Street and turn right onto Dimokritou; it's 1 block up, up one floor, marked only by the word *taverna* on the doors. GREEK.

Overlooking the Church of Ayios Dionysios, this two-room taverna serves good food to a dedicated clientele. The large menu, in both Greek and English, features grilled veal, rabbit, fish, and lamb, though many knowledgeable locals swear by the sword-fish souvlaki. A variety of Greek salads are displayed in a case by the entrance. It's a spotless, pretty interior.

Rodia Taverna. 44 Aristipou St. ☎ **01/722-9883.** Main courses 600–2,500 Dr ($2.55–$10.65). No credit cards. Mon–Sat 8pm–2am. GREEK.

This is a romantic, old-fashioned taverna below street level in one of Kolonaki's oldest homes, at the foot of Lykavitos Hill. In the winter, dining is in Rodia's dark interior, with its patterned tiled floors and lace curtains; kegs of the house *krassi* (wine) are on display. During the other seasons, the small tables are put in the vine-shaded back garden. Specials include octopus in mustard sauce, oregano or lemon beef, fluffy *bourekis* (vegetable pastries), and for dessert, fresh halva.

Inexpensive

Kioupi. 4 Kolonaki Sq. ☎ **01/361-4033.** Meals 1,200–2,100 Dr ($5.10–$8.95). No credit cards. Daily 11am–11pm. Closed evenings in summer. GREEK.

This friendly basement restaurant is a favorite with people who want good food without frills, and it's an especially good value for this expensive neighborhood. Once you've gone down the steps, turn left toward the kitchen and point out what you want.

AROUND OMONIA SQUARE

Expensive

Restaurant Costoyanis. 37 Zaimi St. (2 blocks behind the Archeological Museum). ☎ **01/822-0624.** Meals 2,400–6,000 Dr ($10.20–$25.55). No credit cards. Mon–Sat 8am–2am. GREEK/SEAFOOD.

As you enter the Costoyanis, you'll see an impressive display of fish and other foods, and you can choose the items you'd like to sample. You can also order from the menu. The attractive dining room has wooden ceiling beams and a long array of windows covered by curtains.

Moderate

Cafe Neon. 1 Dorou St. (on the northeast side of the square). ☎ **01/523-6409.** Main courses 1,000–2,600 Dr ($4.25–$11); bowl of salad 1,000 Dr ($4.25). No credit cards. Daily 8am–2am. INTERNATIONAL.

The Kafenion was built in 1924 and was one of Omonia Square's grandest old edifices; it was recently completely restored as an air-conditioned "free-flow" restaurant. The staff, clad in sailor suits, assist customers at several self-service stations. You can choose from the salad bar, the omelet kitchen, the hot-entree counter, or the pastry counter. Everything is freshly made, tasty, and a good value. Vegetarians will appreciate the cold and hot vegetable dishes, and all will enjoy the breakfast choices.

Restaurant Nea-Olympia. 3 Emanuil Benaki St. ☎ **01/321-7972.** Meals 1,300–3,200 Dr ($5.75–$14.25). No credit cards. Mon–Fri 11am–midnight, Sat 11am–4pm. Walk 2 blocks southeast of Omonia Square and turn left (north) off Stadiou Street. GREEK/INTERNATIONAL.

This is one of the largest restaurants in town, with a slightly more attractive decor than some of the area's other budget picks. Windows overlook the street and Greek prints adorn the blond-wood walls. Daily specials are posted at each table in Greek, so make sure to ask the waiter for a translation; the regular menu is in English.

NEAR THE OLYMPIC STADIUM
Very Expensive

Myrtia. 32–34 Trivonianou St. ☎ **01/924-7175.** Reservations recommended. Fixed-price menu 10,000–17,000 Dr ($42.55–$72.35). AE, DC, EC, MC, V. Mon–Sat 8:30pm–2am. Closed Aug. GREEK.

You'll want to dress your best and take a cab up to the serious feast at this most famous of the fixed-price-menu tavernas in Athens, up the hill behind the Olympic Stadium in Mets. The atmosphere is charmingly bucolic, like a Greek village, with strolling musicians, outdoors in the summer. You'll be served a full array of mezedes, tender roast chicken, delicious lamb, fruit, sweets, various wines, and much more—all you can eat, prepared to perfection.

NEAR THE ACROPOLIS
Moderate

Socrates' Prison. 20 Mitseon St. (half a block down from the southeast corner of the Acropolis). ☎ **01/922-3434.** Reservations recommended. Main courses 1,400–2,700 Dr ($6–$11.50). Mon–Sat 7pm–1am. Closed Aug. GREEK/CONTINENTAL.

Situated near the Acropolis, this is a local favorite for travelers and hip young locals. You dine at long, family-style tables or outdoors in summer. The meat dishes are well prepared and come in large portions, the salads are fresh, and the retsina is flavorful. New additions on the menu include such continental dishes as pork roll stuffed with vegetables and salade niçoise.

✪ **Strofi Tavern.** 25 Rovertou Galli St. (2 blocks south of the Acropolis). ☎ **01/921-4130.** Reservations recommended. Main courses 2,400–3,500 Dr ($10–$15). Mon–Sat 7pm–2am. GREEK.

The view of the Acropolis from the rooftop garden of this long-time favorite restaurant is wonderful. The Strofi Tavern offers a varied cuisine marked by interesting cheeses, fine olive oil, and fresh ingredients. Every dish is well presented and served. We especially like the fine mezedes and the excellent lamb and veal courses. In the winter there's a Saturday brunch with 20 mezedes and ouzo.

Inexpensive

Panathinea Pizzeria/Cafeteria. 27–29 Makriyanni St. (across from the Center for Acropolis Studies). ☎ **01/923-2721.** Main courses 900–2,600 Dr ($3.85–$11.05). V. Daily 8:30am–1am. GREEK/ITALIAN.

This is an unpretentious place that serves really good food at very reasonable prices. If the streetside is too noisy for you, go inside for air-conditioned comfort. The pizza is especially good, the country salad is fresh and ample, the chicken souvlaki is tender and juicy, and the moussaka is delicious.

ATTRACTIONS
SIGHTSEEING SUGGESTIONS

If You Have 1 Day   The Acropolis with its Parthenon is a wonder you shouldn't miss. Afterward, walk down the slope to the Ancient Greek Agora and then on into

Monasteraki and Plaka, where you can find remarkable places for both lunch and dinner and lots of shopping.

If You Have 2 Days   It's worth spending 3 or 4 hours of Day 2 at the National Archeological Museum. The top of Lykavitos Hill, accessible either by taking the funicular from the top of Ploutarchou Street for 500 Dr ($2.15), which operates every 20 minutes 8am–10pm in summer, or by walking up from Dexameni Square, is a good change of pace. The air is clear and you'll have a wonderful view of Athens, Piraeus, Aegina, and even Hydra. Also consider taking in another museum or two.

If You Have 3 Days or More   For the rest of your time, visit more of the museums below or consider a day trip to one of the great sights of antiquity (see section 2) or take a day-long excursion by boat from Piraeus to the three islands of Aegina (Eyina), Poros, and Hydra (Idra) in the nearby Saronic Gulf.

✪ THE ACROPOLIS

Standing high above Plaka, the **Acropolis** (☎ **01/321-0219**) is the most famous site in Greek history, for more than 3,000 years the center of life in Athens. In antiquity it was the center primarily for the goddess Athena but also for all Athenian religious cults. The structures on this site were built during the Classical Period, when Athens was at the peak of its political, economic, artistic, and intellectual strength.

Crowning the Acropolis is the **Parthenon,** named after the statue of Athena Parthenos (Virgin) that once stood inside the temple. Nothing of this huge gold-and-ivory statue by Phidias remains, but a small Roman copy is in the Archeological Museum (below). The building was erected between 447 and 438 B.C., though the sculptural decorations weren't completed until 432 B.C. Work on what's called the Older Parthenon began on this site a few years after the Athenian defeat of the Persians at Marathon in 490 B.C. When the Persians occupied and burned Athens in 480 B.C., they destroyed the Older Parthenon, still under construction. The Athenians vowed not to rebuild the desecrated shrines and temples, but 33 years later, under Pericles, Athens had amassed enough political and economic strength to begin major temple construction.

To support the Older Parthenon the Athenians had created an artificial terrace by building retaining walls and laying many courses of stone foundation. There are as many as 22 courses of this foundation, approximately five times a man's height, under the southeast corner where the Acropolis falls off steeply to the south. Pericles added to the rampart wall and raised the terrace to today's level just before work began on the present Parthenon.

The Athenians spared no expense on their new temple. The only material used throughout the building was marble from Mt. Penteli, and the sculptural decoration filled all available space. It had 17 Doric columns along each side and 8 (instead of the usual 6) at each end. The columns are narrower and set more closely together than usual, giving an impression of solidity in contrast to the large central room, or *cella,* designed to accommodate Phidias's 36-foot-high statue of Athena. The architect ("master builder") Iktinus produced a design unsurpassed for balance and harmony. Any possible appearance of disproportion was corrected: Lines were slightly curved to appear straight—an optical illusion called *entasis* (intensification).

When the Ottoman Turks settled on the Acropolis, they used the Parthenon to store munitions, among other things. In 1687 the Venetians besieged the Turks, and one shell fell directly into the powder room. The resulting explosion was devastating. The Parthenon, for the first time since it had been built, suffered major damage.

The pediment sculptures left after this explosion were carted off to London by Lord Elgin in the first decade of the 19th century. Known as the Elgin Marbles, they are on display in the British Museum. On the west pediment the only remnants in their original position are the badly damaged remains of statues of Kekrops and his daughter and, in the southern corner, of a nymph. On the east pediment the only original sculptures are the heads of two horses from the sun god's chariot in the southern corner and the head of one horse from the moon goddess's chariot in the northern corner. (The reclining figure on the east pediment, probably Dionysos, is a modern copy.) The western pediment showed the contest for the city between Athena and Poseidon. The eastern pediment, over the entrance to the temple, showed the birth of Athena.

Beneath the pediments a frieze, consisting of triglyphs and metopes, continued around all four sides of the temple. The triglyphs are three vertical bands separated by grooves, and the metopes are the panels between them. All 92 of these metopes, for the first time in a Greek temple (doing so was expensive), had sculptural decoration. The triglyphs and traces of the badly damaged metopes can be seen easily. The western side showed the battle between Theseus and the Athenians against the Amazons; the eastern side, the battle between the gods and the giants; the southern side, the battle with the centaurs; and the northern side, scenes from the Trojan War. Most of the surviving metopes are from the southern side and are now in the British Museum. The most recent danger to the Parthenon is from air pollution and tourism, which is why buses may no longer drive up toward the entrance nor visitors walk inside.

The **Propylaia,** the monumental entrance gate, was built right after the Parthenon in 437–432 B.C. The other buildings on the Acropolis you should note are the small **Temple of Athena Nike,** high up on the right as you come up to the Acropolis. This beautiful Ionic temple was built in 424 B.C. and reconstructed in the 1930s. The **Erechtheion,** with its famous Caryatid Porch, is the most complex of all the temples here and housed the most ancient Athenian cult objects.

The **Acropolis Archeological Museum** is in the southeastern corner, set low in the ground to be as inconspicuous as possible. Several objects inside are well worth seeing, particularly the four Caryatids from the Erechtheion that remain in Athens (one disappeared during the Ottoman occupation and one is in the British Museum).

The main approach to the Acropolis is the path from near the intersection Dioskouron and Theorias Streets in the southwest corner of Plaka. You can also enter through the Ancient Agora from Adrianou Street or from the south side to the left of the Odeum of Herodes Atticus. Admission is 2,000 Dr ($8.50) for adults and 1,000 Dr ($4.25) for students; it's free for everyone on Sunday and holidays. It's open in summer, Mon–Fri 8am–7pm and Sat–Sun and holidays 8:30am–7pm; check with Greek Tourist Organization (EOT) (☎ 01/323-4130) for winter hours. Photographing with a simple camera without flash and amateur videotaping is free.

Those interested in learning more should visit the **Center for Acropolis Studies,** on Makriyani Street just southeast of the Acropolis (☎ **01/923-9381**), which contains plaster casts of the most significant sculpture from the Acropolis, artifacts, reconstructions, photographs, drawings, and other exhibits. It's open Mon–Fri 9am–2pm, with evening hours Mon, Wed, and Fri 6–10pm and Sat–Sun 10am–2pm. Admission is free.

THE ANCIENT AGORA

The Ancient Greek Agora (pronounced ah-gor-*ah*) is below the Acropolis on the edge of Monasteraki Square. If you plan to vsit after seeing the Acropolis, take the

The Acropolis & Ancient Agora

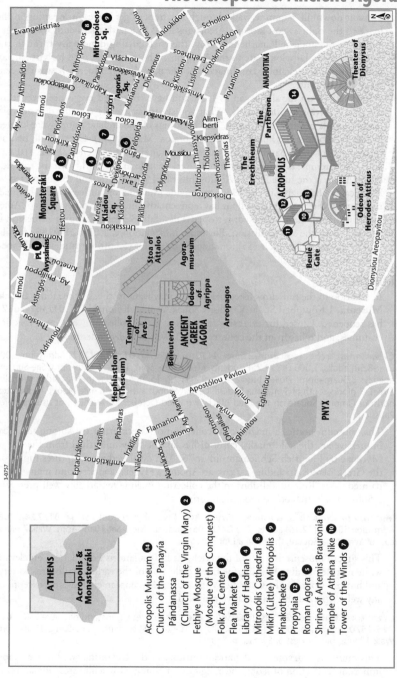

ATHENS

Acropolis & Monasteráki

Acropolis Museum **14**
Church of the Panayía
Pándanassa
(Church of the Virgin Mary) **2**
Fethiye Mosque
(Mosque of the Conquest) **6**
Folk Art Center **3**
Flea Market **1**
Library of Hadrian **4**
Mitropólis Cathedral **8**
Mikrí (Little) Mitropólis **9**
Pinakotheke **11**
Propylaia **12**
Roman Agora **5**
Shrine of Artemis Brauronia **13**
Temple of Athena Nike **10**
Tower of the Winds **7**

3-0757

pleasant downhill 5-minute walk through the trees to get there. An opening in the fence to the right as you face the Areopagos leads to a path that bends to the right and joins the ancient Panathenaic Way, the road cutting diagonally through the Agora from the Dipylon Gate to the Acropolis. The Agora was used for virtually all public pursuits—religious, commercial, political, and even athletic. It was the center of Athenian life.

Excavations on the site began in 1931 and have continued ever since, except for the period during World War II. What you see today are the remains of many different periods of life in the Agora. The buildings of the archaic Agora were located in the west, before the hill of Kolonos Agoraios (Market Hill). On the hill, behind the remains of the Stoa of Zeus, is the Haphaition, built between 460 and 410 B.C. This Doric temple is the best-preserved Greek temple in the world. On the east side of the Agora is the huge Stoa of Attalos, built in 159–38 B.C., and reconstructed by American archeologists in the 1950s to provide museum and office space. The small museum on the Stoa's ground floor has representative finds from 5,000 years of Athenian history, all clearly marked; it's open Tues–Sun 8:30am–2:45pm; admission is included with the site admission. For more information call **01/321-0185.** Admission to the site is 1,200 Dr ($5) for adults and 600 Dr ($2.50) for students; it's open daily 8:30am–3:45pm.

MUSEUMS

In addition to the museums listed below, you may want to check to see if the **Benaki Museum,** 1 Koumbari St., at Vassilissis Sofias Avenue, Kolonaki (☎ **01/361-1617**), has reopened. Closed for extensive renovation, it has collections of Greek folk art, costumes, and relics from the country's 1821 War of Independence.

✪ **National Archeological Museum.** 44 Patission St. ☎ **01/821-7717.** Admission 2,000 Dr ($8.50) adults, 1,000 Dr ($4.25) students. Mon 11am–5pm, Tues–Fri 8am–5pm, Sat–Sun and holidays 8:30am–3pm. Trolley bus: 2, 4, 5, 9, 11, 12, 15, or 18 from the east side of Amalias Street, 3 blocks south of Syntagma Square. Or walk about a third of a mile (about 10 minutes) north of Omonia Square on the road officially named October 28 Avenue but usually called Patission.

This museum houses a magnificent collection of Greek artifacts. Among the most impressive are the gold masks, cups, dishes, and jewelry unearthed from the site of Mycenae by Heinrich Schliemann in 1876. Also displayed are sculptures found on the Greek islands, including a Zeus, an Apollo, a Hygeia, a jockey, and many hand-painted vases. Recent additions to the collection include remarkably well-preserved 3,500-year-old frescoes found on Santorini.

Museum of Cycladic and Ancient Greek Art. 4 Neophytou Douka St. ☎ **01/724-9706.** Admission 500 Dr ($2.15) adults, 250 Dr ($1.05) students. Mon–Sat 10am–4pm. Walk 7 blocks east of Syntagma Square, then half a block north.

This superb museum is a gift of the Nicholas P. Goulandris Foundation, an elegant white marble building housing the finest collection of the earliest sculpture, pottery, and bronzes from the the the Cycladic, Minoan, and Mycenaean civilizations, exceptionally well displayed and informatively labeled.

Byzantine Museum. 22 Vassilissis Sofias Ave. (at Vassileos Konstantinou Ave.). ☎ **01/ 723-1570.** Admission 500 Dr ($2.15) adults, 250 Dr ($1.05) students. Tues–Sun 8:30am–3pm. Walk 12 long blocks west of Syntagma Square.

This museum is devoted to the art and history of the Byzantine era. Greece's most important collection of icons and religious art, along with sculptures, altars, mosaics, bishops' garments, bibles, and a small-scale reconstruction of an early Christian basilica, are exhibited on three floors around a courtyard.

MORE ATTRACTIONS

Athens Cathedral. Mitropoleos St. (between Syntagma and Monasteraki squares). Free admission. Daily 6am–1pm and 4–7pm. Walk 5 minutes west from Syntagma Square.

A big but architecturally disappointing Byzantine-style cathedral, Athens's Greek Orthodox headquarters features a modern stone facade and is decorated with silver votive offerings. The smaller cathedral in its shadow, built in the 13th century, is a gem from the Byzantine era, built with all sorts of pieces from antique structures. Its facade of white marble and red brick and its cupolas are an eye-catching sight amid the modern apartment buildings.

Cemetery of Keramikos. 148 Ermou St. (west of Monasteraki Sq.). ☎ **01/346-3552.** Admission 500 Dr ($2.15) adults, 250 Dr ($1.05) students. Tues–Sun 8:30am–3pm.

This ancient cemetery by what was once the Eridanos River has some very interesting funerary monuments and the remains of the colossal Dipylon Gate, the main entrance to the ancient city of Athens. It's a refreshing retreat, too often missed by tourists.

Greek Folk Art Museum. 17 Kidatheneon St., Plaka. ☎ **01/322-9031.** Admission 500 Dr ($2.15) adults, 250 Dr ($1.05) students. Tues–Sun 10am–4pm.

Embroideries and costumes from all over the country are displayed here, but the most interesting collection is the series of folk paintings done by the eccentric artist Theofilos Hadjimichael in the early years of this century.

National Historical Museum. 13 Stadiou St. ☎ **01/323-7617.** Admission 500 Dr ($2.15) adults, 250 Dr ($1.05) students. Tues–Sun 9am–1:30pm. Walk 2 blocks northeast of Syntagma Square.

The country's primary ethnological museum contains traditional costumes and the personal effects of famous Greeks. There are objects relating to local life from the Byzantine period, the Turkish occupation, the Balkan Wars, and the War of Independence.

A GARDEN & A VIEW

The **National Garden,** between Amalias Avenue and Irodou Attikou, south of Vasilissis Sofias, was planted as the king's private palace garden. Now public, the area combines a park, garden, and zoo with shady trees, benches, a cafe, and small lakes and ponds with ducks, swans, and a few peacocks. A favorite meeting place on hot summer days, it's a good picnic spot. The palacelike building in the southern section is an exhibition/reception hall built by the brothers Zappas and so is known as the Zappion. The garden is open daily 7am–10pm.

Lykavitos (Lycabettus) Hill, which dominates the northeastern section of the city, is a favorite retreat for Athenians and a great place to get a bird's-eye view of Athens and its environs, especially spectacular at sunrise and sunset. The summit is topped by the lovely little chapel of Ayios Yioryios (St. George), whose name day is celebrated there on April 23. There's also the Lykavitos Theater, an important venue for music performances in summer, as well as a couple of overpriced cafes. You can take the funicular from the top of Ploutarchou Street for 500 Dr ($2.15), which operates in summer every 20 minutes 8am–10pm, or walk up from Dexameni, which is the route preferred by young lovers.

ORGANIZED TOURS

You won't need to take a bus tour to get acquainted with Athens, but you can book a tour through your hotel or any travel agency. A half-day tour of the city highlights should cost about 8,000 Dr ($34). Night tours can include a sound-and-light show,

Greek folk dancing at the Dora Stratou Dance Theater, or dinner and Greek dancing, and cost about 7,000–10,000 Dr ($30–$43). **Educational Tours & Cruises,** 1 Artemidos St., Glyfada (☎ **01/898-1741**), can arrange tours in Athens and throughout Greece, including individual tours with emphasis on historical and educational aspects. **C.H.A.T. Tours,** 4 Stadiou St. (☎ **01/322-3137**), is another reliable agency.

SHOPPING

Athens is a great place to buy unusual and inexpensive **gifts** and has a good variety of offbeat clothes and craft shops. The greatest variety of items, some of them at the best prices, are sold in and around the **flea market,** a daily spectacle between Plaka and Monasteraki Square. It's most colorful on Sunday, when it's packed to the gills. Other days are good too, offering the usual tourist-oriented trinkets, copies of ancient artifacts, jewelry, sandals, and various handmade goods. Poke around some of the nearby side streets for antiques and other finds.

Inexpensive to mid-price **fashions** can be found on the many streets in the Omonia/Syntagma/Monasteraki Squares triangle. The city's three major **department stores** are all near Omonia Square: Athenee, at 33 Stadiou St.; Lambropouli Bros., at Eolou and Lykourgos Streets; and the largest, Minion, at Patission (a continuation of Eolou) and Veranzerou Streets. BHS (British Home Stores), 2 blocks south of Omonia, at Athinas and Elfpolidos Streets, has an excellent self-service restaurant (open 9am–8:30pm) on the eighth floor, with indoor and outdoor seatings and a great view.

For **top-of-the-line goods,** including designer wear—not at bargain prices—wander around the smaller streets near Kolonaki Square, between Syntagma Square and Lykavitos Hill.

Compendium, 28 Nikis St., on the edge of Plaka near Syntagma Square (☎ **01/ 322-1248**), is a good English-language bookstore, selling both new and used fiction and nonfiction, plus magazines and maps. Winter hours usually are Mon–Wed 9am–5pm, Tues and Thurs–Fri 10am–7pm, and Sat 9am–3:30pm. Summer hours are Mon–Wed 9am–3pm, Tues and Thurs–Fri 9am–1:30pm and 5:30–8:30pm, and Sat 9am–3:30pm. The biggest foreign-language bookstore in Athens is **Eleftheroudakis,** up the street at 4 Nikis St., which has similar hours.

ATHENS AFTER DARK

When it comes to nightlife, Greeks are all for it. An evening's activities usually start with dinner around 9:30pm, an extremely leisurely event that often seems to be more about socializing than eating. When midnight rolls around and the last glass of wine is emptied, revelers seek out a bouzouki place for some traditional entertainment or head to a dance club, bar, or cafe. The cafes on Syntagma and Kolonaki Squares front busy street scenes and are good places to idle an evening away.

Check the daily *Athens News,* sold at most major newsstands, for current cultural and entertainment events, including films, lectures, theater, music, and dance. The weekly *Athenscope* is even better, filled with a good list of nightspots, restaurants, movies, theater, and much else.

THE PERFORMING ARTS

The **Athens Festival,** at the Odeum of Herodes Atticus, has famous Greek and foreign artists performing music, plays, opera, and ballet from the beginning of June to the beginning of October in this beautiful open-air setting. Find out what's being presented through the English-language press or at the Athens Festival office, at 4 Stadiou (☎ **01/322-1459** or 01/322-3111 to 01/322-3119, ext. 137). The office is open Mon–Sat 8:30am–2pm and 5–7pm and Sun 10am–1pm. If available, tickets can also be purchased at the Odeum of Herodes Atticus (☎ 01/323-2771) on the day of performance. Performances begin at 9pm.

The acoustically marvelous new **Megaron Mousikis Concert Hall,** 89 Vasilissis Sofias Ave. (☎ **01/729-0391**), hosts a wide range of classical music programs that include quartets, operas in concert, symphonies, and recitals. Check the listings magazines to see what's on. The box office is open Mon–Fri 10am–6pm and Sat 10am–2pm. Tickets run 5,000–20,000 Dr ($21.25–$85.10), depending on the performance. Most major jazz and rock concerts, as well as some classical performances, are held at the **Pallas Theater,** 1 Voukourestiou St. (☎ **01/322-8275**).

The Greek National Opera performs at the **Olympia Theater,** 59 Akadimias St., at Mavromihali (☎ **01/361-2461**).

The **Dora Stratou Folk Dance Theater,** performing at 8 Scholio St., on Philopappou Hill in Plaka (☎ **01/924-4395,** or 01/921-4650 after 5:30pm), is the best known of the traditional dance troupes. Various regional dances are performed in costume and with appropriate musical accompaniment nightly at 10:15, with additional matinees at 8:15pm on Wednesday and Sunday. You can buy tickets at the theater's box office 8am–2pm; prices run 1,800–2,500 Dr ($7.65–$10.65).

Sound and Light Shows, seen from the Pnyx, glorify history on the Acropolis. The shows are held Apr–Oct. English performances begin at 9pm and last for 45 minutes. Get tickets from the Athens Festival office, at 4 Stadiou St. (☎ 01/322-7944), or at the entrance to the Sound and Light (☎ **01/922-6210**). Tickets are 1,200 Dr ($5) for adults and 600 Dr ($2.50) for students. Grab seats farthest away from the public address system.

There's English-language theater and American-oriented music at the **Hellenic American Union Auditorium,** 22 Massalias St., between Kolonaki and Omonia squares (☎ **01/362-9886**); tickets are around 3,000 Dr ($12.75) or lower. Arrive early and check out the art show or photo exhibition at the adjacent gallery.

THE CLUB, MUSIC & BAR SCENE

TRADITIONAL MUSIC CLUBS Walk the streets of Plaka on any night and you'll hear many tavernas offering traditional live music. The most reliable are **Nefeli,** 24 Panos St. (☎ 01/321-2475); **Dioyenis,** 3 Sellei (Shelley) St. (☎ 01/324-7933); and **Stamatopoulou,** 26 Lissiou St. (☎ 01/322-8722).

If you want to check out the local rock and blues scene along with small doses of metal, Athenian popsters play at **Memphis,** 5 Ventiri St., near the Hilton Hotel (☎ 01/722-4104), open Tues–Fri 10:30pm–2:30am. The downscale smoke-filled **Rebetiki Istoria,** housed in a neoclassical building at 181 Ippokratous St. (☎ 01/642-4937), features old-style *rebetika* music, played to a mixed crowd of older regulars and younger students and intellectuals. The music usually starts at 11pm, but arrive earlier to get a seat.

The **Taverna Mostrou,** 22 Mnissikleos St., Plaka (☎ 01/324-2441), is one of the largest, oldest, and best-known clubs for traditional Greek music and dancing. Shows here begin about 11pm and usually last until 2am. The entrance cost of 3,500 Dr ($14.90) includes a fixed-menu supper; à la carte is available but expensive. In the heart of Plaka, **Zoom,** 37 Kidathineon St. (☎ 01/322-5920), is the place to go to hear the best of Greek pop music. The performers, who are likely to have current hit albums, are showered with carnations by adoring audience members. The minimum order is 4,500 Dr ($19.15).

BOUZOUKIA Bouzouki clubs—with abundant but expensive wine, amplified bands, and guests dancing up a storm—are enjoyed by many in spite of the loud music, high prices, and late hours. Plate-smashing, the accepted method of showing appreciation, has been outlawed, but the tradition persists in some clubs; check with the management before you join in, because you'll be charged by the plate.

The boundaries between *dimotika* (country folk music) and *rebetika* (music of the urban poor), which is what many people consider bouzouki (after the most important instrument used to play it), have blurred, and purists seeking authentic rebetika will have to look harder and pay a lot more.

Plaka has always been the center of the tourist-oriented bouzouki clubs. It's an area where a few key streets are just wall-to-wall sound, and the clubs have only pink or blue neon signs to differentiate them. Many of the tavernas with musicians or elaborate floor shows serve a high-priced meal beforehand to get you in the mood; count on spending at least 6,000 Dr ($25) a head.

Those who are serious about bouzoukiing should consult their hotel receptionist or the current issue of *Athenscope* magazine (in English and available at newsstands) to find out which clubs are featuring the best performers. The really Greek clubs are a distance from the Syntagma/Plaka area, so budget another 2,500–4,000 Dr ($10–$17) for round-trip taxi fare. Two of the better-known nightspots are **Dias,** 25 Ionias and Ayiou Meletiou (Patissia) (☎ 01/832-6888); and **Fantastiko,** 140 Syngrou Ave. (Kallithea) (☎ 01/922-8902). The downscale smoke-filled **Rebetiki Istoria,** housed in a neoclassical building at 181 Ippokratous St. (☎ 01/642-4937), near the university, features old-style rebetika music, played to a mixed crowd of older regulars and younger students and intellectuals. The music usually starts at 11pm, but arrive earlier to get a seat.

GAY & LESBIAN BARS   Despite the prestige of homosexuality among the aristocracy in ancient times, the current gay scene is fairly discrete, mostly centered along Syngrou Street in Makriyani, where there's a transvestite cruising area. **Granazi,** 20 Lebesi St. (☎ 01/325-3979), is popular, and the best-known alternative is **E . . . Kai?** ("So What?"), across Syngrou at 12 Iossif ton Rogon (☎ 01/922-1742). In more upscale Kolonaki, **Alexander's,** 44 Anagnostopoulou, is more sedate.

DANCE CLUBS   Hidden on the outskirts of Plaka, the second-floor **Booze,** 57 Kolokotroni St. (☎ 01/324-0944), blasts danceable rock to a hip student crowd. There's art on every wall, jelled stage lights, and two bars. Admission is 1,500 Dr ($6.40), plus 700 Dr ($3) per drink. If it's disco you're craving, head east to **Absolut,** 23 Fillelinon St. If you feel a bit too old there, head north to the **Wild Rose,** in the arcade at 10 Panepistimiou St. Up the street, **Mercedes Rex,** 48 Panepistimiou St. (☎ 01/361-4591), has even more diversity.

DAY TRIPS FROM ATHENS
PIRAEUS

Piraeus has been the port of Athens since antiquity. It's essentially an extension of Athens and of interest mostly because it's where you catch boats to the islands. It's one of the most seen—but least appealing—places on the Greek itinerary. It has the seamier side of a sailors' port of call, yet the color and bustle of an active harbor. The fish restaurants are the other reason people go down to Piraeus.

Essentials
GETTING THERE   By Metro   The fastest and easiest way to Piraeus is to take the metro from Omonia Square or Monastiraki to the last stop, for 75 Dr (35¢), which will leave you 1 block from the domestic port.

By Bus   From Syntagma Square, take the Green Depot bus no. 40 from the corner of Filellinon Street; it will leave you 1 block from the international port, about a 10-minute walk along the water from the domestic port. From the airport, bus no. 19 goes to Piraeus; the fare is 300 Dr ($1.25).

By Taxi   A taxi from Syntagma Square will cost up to 1,800 Dr ($7.50). A taxi from the airport to the port costs about 1,500 Dr ($6.40). From the port to Athens, taxi drivers have a conspiracy to overcharge tourists disembarking from the boats—they often charge two or three times the legal fare. If you stand on the dock you'll get no mercy. The only option is to walk to a nearby street and hail a cab.

VISITOR INFORMATION   For boat schedules, transit information, and other tourist information 24 hours a day, dial **171.**

If you need a travel agency to make reservations or to recommend a particular service, try **Explorations Unlimited,** at 2 Kapodistriou St. (☎ **01/411-6395** or 01/411-1243), just off Akti Posidonos near the metro station, open Mon–Fri 8am–7pm and Sat 9am–2pm.

FERRIES TO THE ISLANDS   Ferry tickets can be purchased at a ticket office up to 1 hour before departure; after that they can be purchased on the boat. To book first-class cabins or for advance-sale tickets, see one of the harborside travel agents around Karaïskaki Square by the domestic ferries and along Akti Miaouli, opposite the Crete ferries. Most open at 6am and will hold your baggage for the day (but there's no security). The EOT publishes a list of weekly sailings, and the Tourist Police (☎ 171) or the Port Authority (☎ 01/451-1311) can provide you with schedule information.

The boats to the islands are opposite the metro station. Both boats to the Saronic Gulf and hydrofoils (Flying Dolphins) to Aegina are found opposite and to the left of the metro station; the hydrofoils leave from the foot of Gounari Street. Boats to the other islands are around to the right and away from the station. Boats to Italy and Turkey are found a mile or so to the left. Hydrofoils to other destinations leave from Zea Marina, a separate harbor some distance from the metro station.

Where to Dine

While there are some good restaurants in Piraeus, the places to eat along the harbor are generally mediocre. If you decide to try one of the seafood restaurants in Mikrolimani and Piraeus, make sure you know the price before ordering, insist on a receipt, and take any complaints immediately to the Tourist Police. Some recommendable restaurants are below.

Dourambeis. 29A Dilaveri St., Piraeus. ☎ **01/412-2092.** Reservations suggested. Fish dishes 9,000–14,000 Dr ($38–$60) per kilo. No credit cards. Mon–Sat 8:30pm–1am. SEAFOOD.

This fish taverna near the Delphinario theater in Piraeus is where Greeks go when they want to splurge on a good fish dinner. The decor is simple, the food excellent. The crayfish soup alone is worth the trip and the lettuce salad still remains in our memory, but the whole point of going here is for the excellent grilled fish.

Stou Delivoria. 8 Milonos St., Paleo Faliro. ☎ **01/985-0257.** Meals 2,000–3,500 Dr ($8.50–$14.90). No credit cards. Mon–Sat 8:30pm–midnight. GREEK.

If you want very good, very unusual Greek food, take a cab to this restaurant run by Nikolaos Delivorias just off Filiki Etairias Square in Paleo Faliro, south of town. The decor is reconstructed Byzantine and the food is prepared from very old Greek recipes: Lamb with plums and almonds, chicken with almonds, stuffed peppers with cheese, eggplant salad with walnuts, and Greek broad beans with spinach—all are dishes we'd never heard of and found surprisingly good.

☉ Vasilainas. 72 Etolikou, Ayia Sofia. ☎ **01/461-2457.** Reservations recommended Fri–Sat. Meals 4,000 Dr ($17). No credit cards. Mon–Sat 8pm–midnight. SEAFOOD/GREEK.

There's no menu at this interesting restaurant in a suburb just north of Piraeus; for a flat fee of 4,000 Dr ($17) per person you're presented with a steady flow of more than 15 dishes. Come here hungry, and even then you probably won't be able to eat everything set before you. There's plenty of seafood, plus good Greek dishes. In the winter you eat downstairs in what used to be a grocery store; in the summer tables are set on the roof. This is a deservedly popular spot, well worth the trip.

ANCIENT ELEUSIS

Eleusis was the site of the most famous and revered of all the ancient Mysteries. The names of the illustrious people initiated into the sacred rites here would fill pages, yet we know almost nothing for certain about those ceremonies.

The **Sanctuary of Eleusis** (☎ 01/554-6019) was used from Mycenaean times through the Roman period and was famous throughout the Greek and Roman worlds. The site and its history are complex. The path from the entrance leads south past a **Temple of Artemis,** on the right. To the left of the huge sculpted marble medallion of Antonius Pius, its builder, is the **Greater Propylaea,** which was built in the 2nd century A.D. and modeled after the Propylaea in Athens. To the left of the Greater Propylaea, you can see one of two triumphal arches dedicated to the Great Goddesses and to the emperor Hadrian. (This arch inspired the Arc de Triomphe, on the Champs-Elysées in Paris.) Nearby is the Kallichoron Well, where Demeter wept, and where women later danced and chanted in her honor.

A little farther south, the **Lesser Propylaia,** the entrance into the main part of the sanctuary, is distinguished by two curved grooves for the doors. (You can see one of the two colossal caryatids that supported the Lesser Propylaia in the museum; the other was carted off to Cambridge, England, in 1801.)

Beyond the Lesser Propylaia on the right is the **Ploutonion,** a cave said to be sacred to Pluto and that, according to the Hymn to Demeter, was an entrance to Hades. The path continues to the **Telesterion,** the Temple of Demeter, where initiates were presented with the cult's mysteries.

The **museum** is above the Telesterion to the south. The collection isn't large or well labeled, but it does contain the greater part of a famous Demeter by Agoracritis, a caryatid from the Lesser Propylaia, a cast of Demeter and Persephone sending Triptolemos off to teach mankind agriculture, and several Roman statues.

The site of Eleusis is in the modern industrial city of Elefsina, 14 miles west from central Athens on the highway to Corinth. Take bus no. 853 or no. 862 from Eleftheri, a square off Pireos Avenue (northwest of Monasteraki), or bus no. A 15, marked ELEFSINA, from Sachtouri Street, southeast of Eleftheria Square. (This trip can be combined with a visit to Daphni Monastery. Ask the driver to let you off at the sanctuary, or *heron,* which is off to the left of the main road, before the center of town.) It's open Tues–Sun and holidays 8:30am–3pm; admission is 500 Dr ($2.15), free on Sunday.

THE MONASTERY OF DAFNI

The mosaics in the Monastery of Dafni (☎ 01/581-1558) are masterpieces of Byzantine art, dating from approximately 1100. The second monastery on this site, the present building dates from the late 11th century. Two Corinthian capitals from the earlier period are to the right and left of the church entrance. After the Crusaders captured Constantinople in 1204, Daphni was used as a Catholic monastery by the Cistercian monks who installed the twin gothic arches in front of the west entrance to the church. After the Ottomans captured Athens, the monastery was returned to the Greek Orthodox church.

Excellent restoration work has been going on for the last several years, and most of the mosaics are brilliantly clear. The central dome has the commanding mosaic of Christ Pantocrator (the Almighty), whose powerful gaze looks left. The image is of an awesome judge rather than the Western conception of a suffering mortal. Sixteen prophets are displayed between the windows of the dome. The Annunciation, Nativity, Baptism, and Transfiguration are in the squinches supporting the dome. The Adoration of the Magi and the Resurrection are in the barrel vault inside the main (southern) entrance of the church, and the Entry into Jerusalem and the Crucifixion are in the northern barrel vault.

Mosaics showing scenes from the life of the Virgin are in the south bay of the narthex (passage between the entrance and nave).

Dafni is 5¹/₂ miles west of Athens on the highway to Corinth. Take bus no. 860 from Panepistimiou Street north of Sina (behind the university); bus no. 853, 862, 873, or 880 from Eleftheria Square off Pireos Avenue (northwest of Monasteraki); or bus no. A 15, marked ELEFSINA, from Sachtouri Street, southeast of Eleftheria Square. The trip should take about half an hour, and the bus stop at Dafni is about 150 yards from the monastery. The monastery is open daily, except major holidays, 8:30am–3pm. Admission is 800 Dr ($3.40).

THE MONASTERY OF KESSARIANI & MT. IMITTOS (HYMETTUS)

Some 10 miles east of central Athens, the beautiful **Kessariani Monastery** (☎ 01/ 723-6619) is in a cool, bird-inhabited forest at the foot of Mt. Imittos. The spring waters pouring forth from the marble goat's head at the monastery's entrance have distinguished this as a holy site for centuries.

The monastery was built in the 11th century over the ruins of a 5th-century Christian church, which in turn probably covered an ancient Greek temple. The small church is constructed in the form of a Greek cross, with four marble columns supporting the dome. Most of the lovely frescoes date from the 16th century. On the west side of the paved, flower-filled courtyard are the old kitchen and the refectory, which now house some sculptural fragments. To the south, the old monks' cells and a bathhouse are being restored (exploration at your own risk is permitted).

On a clear day, **Mt. Imittos** offers prospects over Athens, Attica, and the Saronic Gulf. At every scenic parking spot, you'll find men playing backgammon, couples holding hands, and old people strolling. After sunset, Imittos becomes Athens's favorite lovers' lane. The road winds around these forested slopes for nearly 11 miles, and the choice of sun, shade, cool breezes, and picnic spots is unlimited.

Bus no. 224 leaves from Panepistimiou and Vassilissi Sofias, northeast of Syntagma Square, every 20 minutes heading for the suburb of Kessariani. It's a pleasant 1¹/₄-mile walk up the road to the wooded site. The monastery is open Tues–Sun, and admission is 800 Dr ($3.40).

2 Delphi & the Northern Peloponnese

by Sherry Marker

With the exception of the Acropolis in Athens, the most famous and beautiful ancient sites in Greece bracket the Gulf of Corinth—Apollo's sanctuary at Delphi is on the mainland north of the Gulf of Corinth, while Agamemnon's palace at Mycenae, the Mycenaean fortress of Tiryns, the spectacular 4th-century B.C. theater of Epidauros, and the birthplace of the Olympic games at Olympia are just across the gulf in the northern Peloponnese.

EXPLORING THE REGION BY CAR   Thanks to the excellent road linking Athens and the Peloponnese at Corinth and the frequent ferry service across the Gulf of Corinth between Rio and Anti-Rio, it's easy to combine a visit to Delphi with a tour of the most important ancient sites in the Peloponnese. Try to allow at least 4 days (spending 2 nights at Nafplion and 1 night each at Olympia and Delphi) and keep in mind that although most Greek roads are quite good, much of your journey will be on the beautiful, but sometimes vertiginous winding mountain and coastal roads that make distances deceptive. Therefore, we're suggesting how long you should expect each part of the trip to take, rather than giving you a false sense of how quickly you can travel by just telling you how many miles you'll cover.

If traffic is light (and it almost never is), you can drive the 55 miles from Athens to Corinth on the National Road in just over an hour. After taking a look at the Corinth canal and the sprawling site of ancient Corinth, an hour's drive (less if you take the new National Road to Argos and double back to Mycenae) through the farmland of Corinthia and Argolis will take you to Mycenae (71 miles southwest of Athens). From Mycenae, it's less than an hour to Nafplion (90 miles southwest of Athens), generally conceded to be the prettiest town in the Peloponnese and the perfect spot to spend the night before visiting Epidauros. Although it's only 20 miles from Nafplion to Epidauros, this road is usually clogged with tour buses, especially when there are performances at the ancient theater; allow at least an hour for the drive. From Nafplion, you can continue across the Peloponnese to Olympia, with a choice of routes: you can return to Corinth and join the National Road which runs as far as Patras, where you take the good coast road on to Olympia, or you can join the new National Road at Argos and drive through the Arcadian mountains via Tripolis to Olympia (199 miles west of Athens). Either way, expect to spend at least 4 hours en route and try to spend more, so that you can enjoy the coastal scenery or the mountain villages of Arcadia. Then, to reach Delphi from Olympia, simply head to Rio, just north of Patras, and catch one of the frequent ferries across the gulf to Anti-Rio, where a new road runs all the way to Delphi (110 miles west of Athens). Again, allow at least 5 hours for the trip from Olympia to Delphi and 3 hours to get from Delphi to Athens.

ONLY AT THE CLASSICAL SITES

Imagining the Ancient Past   Sitting in the shade of the pine trees above the stadium where Greek athletes once raced to win a crown of laurel leaves, you can almost see the famous charioteer of Delphi urging his team of horses around the track. And you can run a lap in the stadium at Olympia and imagine the cheers of spectators.

Attending a Play at Epidauros   After the sun sinks over the horizon, you can watch a classic Greek tragedy in the acoustically perfect theater of Epidaurus, where a whisper from the stage can be heard in the back row.

Exploring Mount Parnassus   You can trek up the slopes of Mount Parnassus to the upland plain of Livadi, which the ancient Greeks thought was the home of Pan and the Nymphs—or you can take the easy way up and drive to the summit.

Enjoying the Life in the Towns   Walk under balconies dripping with bouganvillia on the narrow side streets of Nafplion or have an ouzo in the village square of Arachova, where the waiter will get you a glass of water from one of the springs that gush from marble fountains.

Central Greece & the Northern Peloponnese

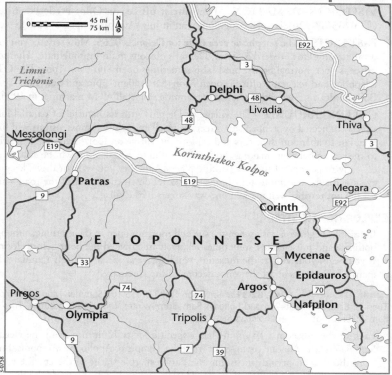

DELPHI

Delphi, which the ancient Greeks believed was the center of the world, is the big enchilada of Greek sites. Even more than Olympia, this place has everything: a long and glorious history as the scene of Apollo's famous oracle and the Pythian games; spectacular ancient remains, including the Temple of Apollo and the well-preserved stadium where the ancient games took place; a superb museum; and a heart-achingly beautiful location on the slopes of Mount Parnassus. Look up and you see the cliffs and crags of Parnassus; look down and you see Greece's most beautiful plain of olive trees stretching as far as the eye can see toward the town of Itea on the Gulf of Corinth.

ESSENTIALS

ARRIVING   By Bus   There are five daily buses to Delphi from the Athens station at 260 Odos Liossion (☎ **01/831-7096**).

By Car   Take the Athens–Corinth National Highway 46 miles west of Athens to the Thebes turnoff and continue 25 miles west to Levadia. If you wish to stop at the monastery of Osios Loukas, take the Distomo turnoff for 5¹/₂ miles. Return to Distomo and continue via Arachova for 16 miles or via the seaside town of Itea for 40 miles to Delphi. The approach from Itea is well worth the time if you aren't in a hurry.

VISITOR INFORMATION The **tourist office,** on Odos Frederikis Street (☎ **0265/89-920**), is open 8am–3pm, and in July–Aug often open 6–8pm as well.

FAST FACTS The **telephone area code** for Delphi is **0265.** Most services you may want are on Odos Frederikis Street, Delphi's obvious main thoroughfare. The **post office** is open normal hours, but is also sometimes open Sun 9am–1pm. The **OTE** telephone and telegraph office is open Mon–Sat 7:30am–3pm and Sun 9am–1pm. Both **banks** on Frederikis Street were planning to install ATM machines in 1996.

GETTING AROUND The village of Delphi, with its handful of parallel long streets connected by stepped side streets, is small enough that most visitors will find it easiest to abandon their cars and explore the village on foot. If you have to drive to the site rather than making the 5- to 10-minute walk from town, be sure to set off early to get one of the few parking places. Whether you walk or drive, keep an eye out for the enormous tour buses that barrel down the center of the road—and for the not terribly well marked one-way streets in the village.

EXPLORING THE SITE

If possible, begin your visit when the site and museum open in the morning, although both site and museum are sometimes relatively uncrowded the hour before closing. If you begin your visit at the museum, you'll arrive at the site already familiar with many of the works of art that once decorated the sanctuary.

Delphi Museum. ☎ **0265/82-313.** Admission 1,200 Dr ($5.10). Summer, Mon 11am–7pm, Tues–Fri 8am–7pm, Sat–Sun and holidays 8am–3pm; winter, Mon 11am–5:30pm, Tues–Fri 8am–5:30pm, Sat–Sun and holidays 8am–3pm.

Each of the museum's 13 rooms has a specific focus: sculpture from the elegant Siphnian treasury in one room, finds from the Temple of Apollo in two rooms, finds from the Roman period (including the Parian marble statue of the epicine youth Antinous, the beloved of the emperor Hadrian) in another. Just outside the first display room stands a 4th-century B.C. marble egg, a symbol of Delphi's position as the center of the world. According to legend, when Zeus wanted to determine the earth's center, he released two eagles from Mount Olympus. When the eagles met over Delphi, Zeus had his answer. (You may still see eagles in the sky above Delphi, but as often as not, the large birds circling overhead are the less distinguished Egyptian vultures.) The star of the museum, with a room to himself, is the famous 5th-century B.C. *Charioteer of Delphi,* a larger-than-life bronze figure that was part of a group that originally included a four-horse chariot. The *Charioteer* is an irresistible statue—don't miss the handsome youth's delicate eyelashes shading wide enamel and stone eyes, or the realistic veins that stand out in his hands and feet.

Although the *Charioteer* is the star of the collection, he's in good company here. Delphi was chockablock with superb works of art given by wealthy patrons, such as King Croesus of Lydia, who gave the massive silver bull that's on display. Many of the finest exhibits, however, are quite small, such as the elegant bronzes in the museum's last room, including one that shows Odysseus clinging to the belly of a ram. According to Homer, this is how the wily hero escaped from the cave of the ferocious (but nearsighted) monster Cyclops.

Sanctuary of Apollo, Castalian Spring & Sanctuary of Athena Pronaia. ☎ **0265/82-313.** Admission 1,200 Dr ($5.10). Summer, Mon 11am–7pm, Tues–Fri 8am–7pm, Sat–Sun and holidays 8am–3pm; winter, Mon 11am–5:30pm, Tues–Fri 8am–5:30pm, Sat–Sun and holidays 8am–3pm.

As you enter the **Sanctuary of Apollo,** just past the museum, you'll be on the marble Sacred Way, following the route that visitors to Delphi have taken for thousands of years. The **Sacred Way** twists uphill past the remains of Roman stoas and a number of Greek **treasuries** (including the Siphnian and Athenian treasuries, whose sculpture is in the museum). Just as modern cities vie in building the tallest skyscraper, ancient cities tried to build the most elegant of these elaborate small temples, which were storehouses for works of art dedicated to Apollo. Take a close look at the treasury walls: You'll see not only beautiful dry-wall masonry but countless inscriptions. The ancient Greeks were never shy about using the walls of their buildings as bulletin boards. Alas, so many contemporary visitors have added their own names to the ancient inscriptions that the Greek archeological service no longer allows visitors inside the massive 4th-century B.C. **Temple of Apollo,** which was built here after several earlier temples were destroyed. In antiquity, one of the three priestesses on duty gave voice to Apollo's oracles from a room deep within the temple. That much is known, although the details of precisely what happened here are obscure: Did the priestess sit on a tripod balanced over a chasm, breathing in hallucinatory fumes? Did she chew various herbs, including the laurel leaf sacred to Apollo, until she spoke in tongues, while priests interpreted her sayings? Perhaps wisely, the oracle has kept its secrets. From the temple, it's a fairly steep uphill climb to the remarkably well-preserved 4th-century B.C. **theater** and the **stadium,** which was extensively remodeled by the Romans. In antiquity, contests in the Pythian festivals took place in both the stadium and the theater. Today the theater and stadium are used most summers for the Festival of Delphi, which, on occasion, has featured exceptionally unclassical pop music.

Keep your ticket as you leave the Sanctuary of Apollo and begin the 10-minute walk along the Arakova–Delphi road to the Sanctuary of Athena (also called the Marmaria, which simply refers to all the marble found here). En route, you'll pass the famous **Castalian Spring,** where Apollo planted a laurel. Above are the rose-colored cliffs known as the Phaedriades (the Bright Ones), famous for the way they reflect the sun's rays. Drinking from the Castalian Spring has inspired legions of poets; however, poets now have to find their inspiration elsewhere, as the spring is off-limits to allow repairs to the Roman fountain facade. Poets be warned: Once an antiquity is closed in Greece, it often stays closed quite a while.

A path descends from the main road to the **Sanctuary of Athena,** goddess of wisdom, who shared the honors at Delphi with Apollo. As the remains here are quite fragmentary, except for the large 4th-century B.C. gymnasium, you may choose simply to wander about and enjoy the site without trying too hard to figure out what's what. The round 4th-century tholos with its three graceful standing Doric columns is easy to spot, although, no one knows why this building was built, why it was so lavishly decorated, or what went on inside. Again, the oracle keeps its secrets.

ACCOMMODATIONS

There's no shortage of hotels in Delphi and you can usually get a room here even in July or August. Still, if you want a room in a specific price category (or with a view), it's best to make a reservation. Finally, consider staying in nearby Arachova, where hotels are usually less crowded and the restaurants better (see below).

Amalia Hotel. Signposted on the Delphi–Itea road. ☎ **0265/82-101.** Fax 0265/82-290. 184 rms. TEL. 40,000 Dr ($170) double. Rates include breakfast. AE, MC, V.

The Amalia has all the creature comforts—swimming pool, garden, several shops, restaurants, and a vast lobby—but is outside the village, so you probably won't want to stay here unless you have a car.

Castalia Hotel. 13 Frederikis (at Vasileos Pavlou), Delphi. ☎ **0265/82-205.** 26 rms. TEL. 21,000 Dr ($90) double. Rates include breakfast. AE, DC, V. Closed weekdays Jan–Feb.

The Castalia, a white stucco building with projecting balconies on Delphi's main street, has been here since 1938, but was completely remodeled in 1986. Most of the good-sized bedrooms have hand-loomed rugs, and the rear bedrooms have fine views over the olive plain.

Hotel Varonos. 27 Frederikis (at Vasileos Pavlou), Delphi. ☎ **0265/82-345.** 9 rms. 12,000 Dr ($51) double. AE, MC, V.

This small, family-owned hotel has very clean, spare bedrooms, many overlooking the olive plain. This is a very welcoming hotel—we once arrived here with an ailing gardenia plant and the entire family pitched in to make sure that it was well taken care of.

Hotel Vouzas. 1 Frederikis (at Vasileos Pavlou), Delphi. ☎ **0265/82-232.** Fax 0232/82-033. 59 rms. TV TEL. 32,500 Dr ($138) double. AE, DC, MC, V.

If you don't mind missing the swimming pool at the Amalia, this is the place to stay—a cozy fireplace in the lobby, spectacular views, and a short walk to everything you've come to see. The bedrooms and bathrooms here are very comfortable, and the balconies not only have a table and chairs, but a welcoming pot of basil.

DINING

You won't starve in Delphi, but there's no really outstanding restaurant here so you may prefer to head to the village of Arachova, 6 miles to the north (see below).

Topiki Gefsi. 19 Frederikis (at Odos Pavlou). ☎ **0265/82-480.** Main courses 3,000–4,200 Dr ($12.75–$19.15). AE, DC, MC, V. GREEK.

This large restaurant on Delphi's main street has a good view and reasonably good food. Unfortunately, as with most restaurants here, the staff is pretty sure that they'll never see you again and the service is haphazard. That said, the stuffed vine leaves are good and there are sometimes interesting stews on the menu. A guitar and piano duo sometimes appears in the evening.

DAY TRIPS FROM DELPHI

ARACHOVA   The mountain village of Arachova, 6 miles north of Delphi, clings to Mount Parnassus some 3,100 feet above sea level. Arachova is famous for its hand-loomed *tagari* shoulder bags, heavy blankets, and fluffy *flokakia* rugs. When several tour buses stop here during the daytime, this tiny village can be seriously crowded. Don't despair—come in the evening, when the shops are still open and the cafes and restaurants give you a chance to escape from the tourist world of Delphi to the village world of Greece. There's usually an energetic evening *volta* (stroll) on main street, and if you climb the steep stairs to the upper town, you'll find yourself on quiet neighborhood streets where children play and families sit in front of their homes.

On main street, have a look at the weavings in Georgia Charitou's shop, **Anemi** (☎ **0267/31-701**), which also has some nice reproductions of antiques. **Katina Panagakou's shop,** on the main street (☎ **0267/31-743**), also has examples of local crafts.

For lunch or dinner here, try the **Taverna Karathanassi,** by the coffee shops in the main street square that has the lovely freshwater springs. You'll have simple family fare, served by the Karathanassi family; expect to pay about $10 for dinner. Just off the square, the **Taverna Dasargyri** (also known as Barba Iannis) specializes in delicious loukanika (sausages), chops, and the koukoretsi (stuffed entrails) that are much tastier than they sound. This is a popular local hangout; the meat here is usually priced by the kilo, and you can eat well from about $12.

If you want to stay in Arachova, the **Xenia Hotel** (☎ **0267/31-230;** fax 0267/ 32-175), with 43 rooms, each with a balcony, has doubles at 15,000 Dr ($63.85). The very pleasant **Best Western Anemolia** (☎ **0276/31-640**), with 52 rooms, on a hill just outside Arachova above the Delphi road, charges 18,000 Dr ($77) for a double Sun–Thurs, 27,000 Dr ($115) double per night for a Fri–Sat stay, and 30,000 Dr ($128) for Sat alone. Both these hotels are usually full winter weekends when Greeks flock here to ski on Mt. Parnassus.

MOUNT PARNASSUS   Parnassus is an odd mountain: it's difficult to see its peaks from either Delphi or Arachova, although if you approach from the north, you'll have fine views of the twin summits. You can drive up to the ski resort at **Fterolaki** in about an hour. It's a lively place in winter during the ski season, but nothing is open during the summer.

If you want to go **hiking on Mount Parnassus,** there are two possibilities: You can head uphill in Delphi on the paved road that runs above the cemetery and stadium and keep going. Four hours will bring you to the upland meadows known as the Plateau of Livadi, where shepherds traditionally pasture their flocks. As always in the mountains, it's not a good idea to make such an excursion alone. If you plan to continue on past the meadows to the Corcyrian Cave (known locally as Sarantavli, or "Forth Rooms"), where Pan and the Nymphs once were thought to live, or to the summits, you should check on conditions locally or with the **Hellenic Mountaineering Club in Athens** (☎ **01/323-4555**).

THE MONASTERY OF OSIOS LOUKAS   You can visit Osios Loukas en route to or from Delphi, or do the 60-mile round-trip from Delphi as a day trip. If you go to Osios Loukas via Levadia, pause at **Schiste (Triodos),** where three roads cross. This is the spot where the ancients believed that Oedipus unknowingly slew his father. Things got worse—still unknowing, he married his mother and brought down tragedy on himself and his descendants.

The 10th-century Monastery of Saint Luke (Osios Loukas) is a lavishly decorated complex: A wide variety of different jewel-like polychrome marbles were used in the monastery's construction. The two churches have superb mosaics; along with the mosaics at Dafni, outside Athens (see section 1), and the splendid churches of Thessaloniki, these are the finest mosaics in Greece.

Osios Loukas is not a tourist destination, but a holy spot for Greek Orthodox visitors—something to keep in mind during your visit. This is not the place for sleeveless shirts, shorts, or a casual attitude toward the icons or still less toward the tomb of Saint Luke.

THE NORTHERN PELOPONNESE & THE CLASSICAL SITES

One of the delights of visiting the northern Peloponnese is that when many of the Aegean islands are sagging under the weight of tourists each summer, the Peloponnese is still relatively uncrowded. That doesn't mean that you're going to have famous spots like Mycenae, Epidauros, and Olympia to yourself if you arrive at high noon in August, but it does mean that if you arrive at these sites just as they open, or just before they close, you may have an hour under the pine trees at Olympia or Epidauros virtually alone, and be able to stand in Mycenae's Treasury of Atreus with swallows as your only companions.

Since even the most avid tourists do not live by culture alone, it's good to know that one of the great delights of spending time in the northern Peloponnese comes from quiet hours in shady *plateias* (squares), watching fishers mend their nets while Greek families settle down for a leisurely meal. An hour in a seaside cafe watching the locals watching you watch them is the ideal way to unwind after a day's sightseeing.

CORINTH

In antiquity, Corinth exported its pottery around the Mediterranean and dominated trade in Greece for much of the 8th and 7th centuries B.C. before having a second golden age under the Romans in the 2nd century A.D. Today, as in antiquity, Corinth, along with Patras, is still one of the two major "gateways" to the Peloponnese, and as you pause here, you'll want to take a look at the Corinth canal and visit ancient Corinth before heading deeper into the northern Peloponnese.

Essentials

ARRIVING   By Train   There are several trains a day from Athens's Stathmos Peloponnisou (Train Station for the Peloponnese) to the **Corinth station** off Odos Demokratias (☎ **0741/22-522**). These trains are almost invariably late, often taking 3 hours or more. Refreshments sometimes are—and sometimes are not—available on board. For information on schedules and fares call **01/512-4913** in Athens.

By Bus   There are at least 15 buses a day from the Stathmos Leoforia Peloponnisou (Bus Station for the Peloponnese) at 100 Odos Kifissou in Athens to the **Corinth bus station** at Ermou and Koliatsou streets (☎ **0741/25-645**), where you can catch a bus (15–20 minutes) to Archaia Korinthos. For information on Athens–Corinth–Athens schedules and fares call 01/512-8233 in Athens. Buses from Corinth for the Peloponnese leave from the station at the corner of Konstantinou and Aratou streets (☎ **0741/24-403**).

By Car   Corinth is 55 miles west of Athens, connected to it by the National Highway; the toll is 400 Dr ($1.70). The highway is in the process of being widened to seven lanes, but still contains some three-lane stretches which are particularly dangerous. The highway ends just before the Corinth canal; just after the canal, you'll see signs for Ancient Corinth (the archeological site) and Corinth (the uninteresting modern town).

VISITOR INFORMATION   The **telephone area code** for Corinth is **0741**. The **police station** is on Ermou Street (☎ **0741/22-143**).

The Corinth Canal

Almost everyone stops here for a coffee, a souvlaki, and a look at the canal that separates the Peloponnese from the mainland. There's a small post office at the canal, and a kiosk with postcards and English-language newspapers, and most of the large souvlaki places have surprisingly clean toilet facilities (and very tough souvlaki). One word of warning that's necessary here and almost nowhere else in Greece: Be sure to lock your car door. This is a popular spot for thieves to prey on unwary tourists.

The French engineers who built the Corinth canal between 1881 and 1893 used lots of dynamite, blasting through 285 feet of sheer rock to make this 4-mile-long, 30-yard-wide passageway. The canal utterly revolutionized shipping in the Mediterranean. Boats that previously had spent days making their way around Cape Matapan at the southern tip of the Peloponnese could dart through the canal in hours.

Exploring Ancient Corinth

Archeological Museum. Old Corinth, on the site of Ancient Corinth. ☎ **0741/31-207.** Admission (including admission to the archeological site) 1,000 Dr ($4.25). Summer, Mon–Fri 8am–7pm, Sat–Sun 8am–3pm; winter, Mon–Fri 8:45am–3pm, Sat–Sun 8:30am–3pm.

As you'd expect, the museum has a particularly fine collection of the famous Corinthian pottery that's often decorated with charming red and black figures of birds and animals. There are also a number of statues of Roman worthies and several mosaics, including one in which Pan is shown piping away to a clutch of cows. The museum courtyard is a shady spot to sit and read up on the ancient site, which has virtually no shade.

Ancient Corinth. Old Corinth. ☎ **0741/31-207.** Admission (including admission to the museum; see above) 1,000 Dr ($4.25). Summer, Mon–Fri 8am–7pm, Sat–Sun 8am–3pm; winter, Mon–Fri 8:45am–3pm, Sat–Sun 8:30am–3pm.

The most conspicuous—and the most handsome—surviving building at Ancient Corinth is clearly the 6th-century B.C. Temple of Apollo, which stands on a low hill overlooking the extensive remains of the Roman Agora (marketplace). Only 7 of the temple's 38 monolithic Doric columns are standing, the others having been long-since toppled by earthquakes.

Ancient Corinth's main drag, the 40-foot-wide marble-paved road that ran from the port of Lechaion into the heart of the marketplace, is clearly visible from the temple. Along the road, and throughout the agora, are the foundations of hundreds of the stores that once stocked everything from spices imported from Asia Minor to jugs of wine made from Corinth's still-excellent grapes. Two spots in the agora are especially famous—the Bema and the Fountain of Peirene. In the 2nd century A.D., the famous Roman traveler, philhellene, and benefactor, Herodes Atticus encased the modest Greek fountain in the elaborate two-storied building with arches, arcades, and the 50-square-foot courtyard whose remains you see today. Peirene, by the way, was a woman who wept so hard when her son died that she dissolved into the spring that still flows here. The Bema was the public platform where St. Paul had to plead his case when the Corinthians, irritated by his constant criticisms, hauled him up in front of the Roman governor Gallo in 52 A.D.

Acrocorinth. Old Corinth. Free admission during the current restoration. Summer, daily 8am–7pm; winter, daily 8am–5pm.

A signposted road twists from the ancient site to the summit of Acrocorinth, the rugged limestone sugarloaf mountain 1,885 feet above the plain. A superb natural acropolis, Acrocorinth was fortified first by the Greeks and later by the Byzantines, Franks, Venetians, and Turks, whose elaborate walls still crown this citadel.

NAFPLION

With two hilltop Venetian fortresses, shady parks, an interesting assortment of small museums, and better-than-average hotels, restaurants, and shops—and even a miniature castle (the Bourtzi) in the harbor—this port town on the northeast coast of the Gulf of Argos is almost everyone's first choice as the most charming town in the Peloponnese. A good deal of Nafplion's charm comes from the fact that for several years after the Greek War of Independence (1821–28) this was Greece's first capital. Although the palace of Greece's young King Otto—a mail-order monarch from Bavaria—burnt down in the 19th century, an impressive number of handsome neoclassical civic buildings and private houses have survived, as well as a scattering of Turkish fountains and several mosques.

Essentials

ARRIVING   By Bus   There are at least a dozen buses a day to Nafplion from the Stathmos Leoforia Peloponnisou (Bus Station for the Peloponnese) in Athens at 100 Odos Kifissou (☎ **01/513-4110** and 01/513-4588). The trip takes about 4 hours because the bus goes into both Corinth and Argos before reaching Nafplion.

By Boat There is Flying Dolphin hydrofoil service from Marina Zea, Piraeus, to Nafplion, Mon–Sat, weather permitting. The hydrofoil makes a number of stops and takes almost as long as the bus to reach Nafplion. For information on fares and schedules call **01/324-2281** or 01/453-6107 in Athens.

By Car From Athens, head south to the Corinth canal. Take the new Corinth–Tripolis road as far as the Argos exit. Follow the signs first into Argos itself and thence to Nafplion (about 12 miles in all). You'll almost certainly get lost at least once in Argos, which has an abysmal system of directional signs. Allow at least 3 hours for the drive from Athens to Nafplion. When you reach Nafplion, park in the large municipal lot (no charge) by the harbor. If you want to stop at Mycenae and/or Nemea en route, take the winding old road to Nafplion. If you want to stop at Epidauros en route, turn left just after the canal at the sign for Epidauros.

VISITOR INFORMATION The office of the **Greek National Tourist Organization (EOT)** is at 16 Photomara St. (☎ **0752/28-131**), catercorner from the bus station in Plateia Nikitara. It's usually open Mon–Fri 9am–2pm.

FAST FACTS The **telephone area code** for Nafplion is **0752.** The **post office** is open Mon–Fri 8am–2pm, and the **OTE** telephone and telegraph offices, Mon–Fri 8am–7pm. Both are signposted from the bus station. There's a branch of the **National Bank of Greece** on the main square, Plateia Syntagma (Constitution Square). There are a number of travel agencies in Nafplion, such as **Staikos Travel,** by the harbor (☎ **0757/27-950**). The best place to swim is at the **beach** beneath the Palamidi, a 15-minute walk (with the sea on your right) from the harborside cafes.

What to See & Do

Nafplion is a stroller's delight and one of the great pleasures here is simply walking through the parks, up and down the stepped side streets, and along the harbor. Don't make the mistake of stopping your harborside stroll when you come to the last of the large seaside cafes by the Hotel Agamemnon: if you continue on, you can watch fishing boats putting in at the pier and explore several cliffside chapels. Nafplion is so small that you can't get seriously lost, so have fun exploring. Here are some suggestions on how to take in the official sights after you've had your initial stroll.

ACRONAFPLIA & PALAMIDI There's no charge to visit the cliffs above Nafplion known as Acronafplia, where there are considerable remains of Greek, Frankish, and Venetian fortresses, as well as two modern hotels, the Xenia and Xenia Palace. Nafplion's two massive fortresses, Acronafplia and the Palamidi, dominate the skyline. The easiest way to get up **Acronafplia** is to drive, or hitch a ride on the elevator (signposted) that conveys guests from the lower town to the Xenia Palace Hotel. If you want to walk up, follow signs in the lower town to the Church of Saint Spyridon, one of whose walls has the mark left by one of the bullets that killed Ianni Kapodistria, the first governor of modern Greece. From Saint Spyridon, follow the signs farther uphill to the Catholic Church of the Metamorphosis.

This church is as good a symbol as any for Nafplion's vexed history: Built by the Venetians, it was converted into a mosque by the Turks, and then reconsecrated as a church after the War of Independence. Inside, an ornamental doorway has an inscription listing philhellenes who died for Greece, including nephews of Lord Byron and George Washington. As you continue to climb to Acronafplia, keep an eye out for several carvings of the winged lion that was the symbol of Saint Mark, the patron saint of Venice.

If you're not in the mood to climb the 800-plus steps to the summit of **Palamidi,** you can take a taxi up and then walk down. The Venetians spent 3 years building the Palamidi, only to have it conquered the next year (1715) by the Turks. You'll enter the fortress the way the Turkish attackers did, through the main gate to the east. Once inside, you can trace the course of the massive wall that encircled the entire summit and wander through the considerable remains of the five defense fortresses that failed to stop the Turkish attack. The Palamidi is open Mon–Fri 8am–7pm in summer, 8:30am–5pm in winter. Admission 500 Dr ($2.15).

NAFPLION'S MUSEUMS   All four of Nafplion's museums are within easy walking distance of each other, and one—the Folk Art Museum—is one of the most delightful museums in Greece.

Everything about the **Folk Art Museum,** 1 Odos V. Alexandros (☎ **0752/ 28-379**), is charming: It's housed in an elegant 18th-century house with a shady courtyard and welcome snack bar, and it has a superb shop—and one of the finest collections of costumes in Greece. Labels are in English as well as Greek, which means that you can learn just how cotton was harvested and silk was spun and what kind of loom was used to make which kind of costume. It's open May–Sept, Wed–Mon 9am–2pm and 5–7pm; Oct–Apr, Wed–Mon 9am–2pm; closed Feb. Admission is 400 Dr ($1.70).

The **Museum of Childhood,** Stathmos, Kolokotronis Park, an offshoot of the Folk Art Museum, has an ecclectic collection of dolls, baby clothes, and toys. It's open year-round Mon–Fri 4–8pm and Sat 9am–1pm (with frequent unscheduled closings); admission is 400 Dr ($1.70).

The **Archeological Museum,** Syntagma Square (☎ **0752/27-502**), is housed in the handsome 18th-century Venetian arsenal that dominates Syntagma Square. The thick walls make this a deliciously cool place to visit on even the hottest day. Displays are from sites in the area and include pottery, jewelry, and some quite horrific Mycenaean terra-cotta idols as well as a handsome bronze Mycenaean suit of armor. Open Tues–Sun 8:30am–1pm; admission is 500 Dr ($2.15).

If you like old prints and old photographs, not to mention muskets, you'll enjoy strolling through the exhibits at the **Military Museum,** on Leoforos Amalias (☎ **0752/25-591**), which cover Greek wars from the War of Independence to World War II. Open Tues–Sun 9am–2pm; admission is free.

Accommodations

Nafplion has enough hotels that you can usually find a room here, although you may end up on the outskirts of town in high season. Be sure to make a reservation if you want a view of the harbor or if you're going to be here when there's a performance at Epidauros, when tour groups reserve entire hotels.

Byron Hotel. Plateia Agiou Spiridona, 211 00 Nafplion. ☎ **0752/22-351.** Fax 0752/26-338. 13 rms. TEL. 13,000–16,000 Dr ($55–468) double. AE, EC, MC, V.

This very pleasant small hotel, painted a distinctive pink with blue shutters, is in a quiet, breezy location overlooking the Church of Agiou Spiridona. There are a number of nice bits of Victoriana in the bedrooms and sitting rooms. Word has got out about the Byron's charm, so it's almost never possible to stay here in July or August without a reservation.

Hotel Agamemnon. 3 Akti Miaouli, 211 00 Nafplion. ☎ **0752/28-021.** 40 rms. TEL. TV. 27,000 Dr ($115) double. Rates include breakfast and either lunch or dinner. AE, EC, MC, V.

The Agamemnon is on the harbor just past the string of cafes, which means that you're bound to hear voices if you have a front room with a balcony. Still, friends who have stayed here claim that they weren't bothered by the noise and loved the view.

Hotel Amphitriton. Plateia Speliadon, 211 00 Nafplion. ☎ **0752/27-366.** 42 rms. TEL. 24,000 Dr ($102) double. Rates include breakfast. AE, MC, V.

Many of the rooms in this pleasant, usually quiet, in-town hotel have views of the harbor and Bourtzi castle. Like many Nafplion hotels, the Amphitriton does a brisk tour business and you can feel a bit odd-man-out here if everyone else is with "the group." Still, the rooms are large, clean, and comfortable and the hotel itself is just steps from the shops that line Spiliadou Street.

King Otto. 4 Farmakopoulou, 211 00 Nafplion. ☎ **0752/27-585.** 12 rms (4 with shower). 10,000 Dr ($42) double. AE, MC, V.

The small, venerable, King Otto Hotel, in a pleasant neoclassical building with a handsome suspension staircase, is the best bargain in town. Don't expect frills here, but the rooms have high ceilings and some overlook a pleasant small garden.

Xenia Palace Hotel. Acronaufplia, 210 00 Nafplion. ☎ **0752/28-981.** Fax 0752/28-987. 48 rms, 3 suites, 50 bungalows. A/C MINIBAR TV TEL. 51,000–65,000 Dr ($217–$276) double. Rates include breakfast and either lunch or dinner. Off-season reductions possible. AE, DC, EC, MC, V.

The Xenia Palace has the best view in town; whether you think it has the best location depends on whether you want to be in town or up here on the slopes of Acronafplia looking across the harbor to the Bourtzi and the mountains of the Peloponnese. Unfortunately, the rugs and chairs in many of the bedrooms are showing signs of wear and the dining room has indifferent "international" and Greek cuisine. One big plus is the swimming pool, the perfect place to cool off after a day's sightseeing. You can sometimes make arrangements to use the pool here if you're staying at the nearby Xenia Hotel, the Xenia Palace's less expensive sibling hotel, where rooms are usually at least $20 cheaper (same phone and fax).

Dining

Oddly enough, the restaurants in and just off Syntagma Square are not the tourist traps you'd expect. Furthermore, you'll see a good number of Greeks at the big harborside cafes on Akti Miaoulis. In short, Nafplion has lots of good restaurants as well as one superb pastry shop and any number of ice cream parlors selling elaborate gooey confections.

Hellas Restaurant. Syntagma Sq. ☎ **0752/27-278.** Main courses 1,500–2,500 Dr ($6.40–10.65). AE, MC, V. Daily 9am–midnight. GREEK.

Kostas, the patron of the Hellas, says that there's been a restaurant here for more than 100 years. Shady trees and awnings make this a cool spot to eat outdoors; there's also an inside dining room, where locals tend to congregate year-round. Excellent dolmades with egg-lemon sauce are usually on the menu, as well as stuffed tomatoes and peppers in season. Just about everyone in town passes through Syntagma Square, so this is a great spot to people-watch.

Karamanlis. 1 Leoforos Bouboulinas. ☎ **0752/27-668.** Main courses 1,500–2,000 Dr ($6.40–$8.50); fresh fish priced by the kilo. AE, EC, MC, V. 11am–midnight. GREEK

This simple harborfront taverna several blocks east of the cluster of harborfront cafes tends to get fewer tourists than most of the places in town and has good grills and several kinds of meatballs (keftedes, sousoutakia, and yiouvarlakia). If you like the food here, you'll probably also enjoy the Kanares Taverna and the Hundalos Taverna, both also on Bouboulinas.

Noufara. Syntagma Sq. ☎ **0752/23-648.** Main courses from 2,500 ($10.65). AE, EC, MC, V. Open all day. GREEK/INTERNATIONAL.

With its shady awnings, the elegant Noufara is one of "the" places in Nafplion to see and be seen. Appetizers range from Greek favorites such as octopus to prociutto and melon. The pasta is excellent here, especially since the chef doesn't indulge in the Greek passion for overcooking. You can get breakfast, lunch, and dinner here—and some fans do just that.

The Pharos. Akti Miaoulis (by the childrens' playground). ☎ **0752/26-043.** Ouzo and standard mezedes from 600 Dr ($2.55); ouzo and a meal of mezedes from 2,000 Dr ($8.50). Daily 10am–midnight. SNACKS.

It's easy to stop at the Pharos for a drink and a snack and end up eating enough octopus, fried cheese, keftedes (meatballs), and saganaki (fried cheese) to make a meal. This is a great spot for enjoying the waterfront away from the main tourist bustle.

Savouras Psarotaverna. 79 Leoforos Bouboulinas. ☎ **0752/27-704.** Fish priced by the kilo, according to availability. AE, EC, MC, V. Daily noon–11pm. FISH.

This restaurant has been here more than 20 years and its fresh fish attracts Greek daytrippers from Tripolis and even Athens. What you eat depends on what was caught that day—it's always a good idea to check the price before ordering. Expect to pay at least $30 for two fish dinners, a salad, and some house wine. On summer weekends this restaurant can be terribly crowded.

Cafes & Pastry
The Aladdin, Plateia Saint George (☎ **0752/21-221**), has honey-drenched Anatolian pastries that are the next best thing to the pastries sold at the superb Karavan pastry shops in Athens. If you arrive in Nafplion by bus, you could do worse than take the first turning on your left as you face the bus station and head straight to the Aladdin. You can eat your pastries at the shop or get them to go, or both. Pastries cost 3,500 Dr ($15) and up a kilo, and the place is usually open most of the day 10am–10pm. **The Pink Panther,** Odos Staikopoulou (no phone), has ice cream sundaes from 1,250 Dr ($5.30), and there are those who swear that this place has the best ice cream in town. Anyone wanting to test the assertion might do a comparison taste test at the Fantasia, also on Odos Staikopoulou, and then try the mango sherbet at the Napoli di Romania cafe on Akti Miaoulis—but perhaps not all in one day. It's open 10am–midnight.

Shopping
Nafplion has not escaped the invasion of T-shirt and mass-produced-souvenir shops that threatens to overwhelm Greece, but there are also some genuinely fine shops here, many on or just off Odos Spiliadou, the street immediately above Plateia Syntagma. As in most Greek towns heavily dependent on tourism, many of these shops are closed in winter.

The **Aelios** jewelry store, at 4 V. Konstantinou (☎ **0752/28-149**), sometimes has unusually distinctive rings and bracelets for both men and women from around 23,000 Dr ($97.85). The shop's owner speaks excellent English and can show you pieces done by a number of Greek jewelers doing fine work. Virtually everything on sale here is a pleasant departure from the more customary mass-produced gold jewelry on sale elsewhere in Nafplion.

In her shop near the waterfront, **Helene Papadopoulou,** 5 Odos Spiliadou (☎ **0752/25-842**), sells dolls made from brightly painted gourds and traditional weavings, both from 10,000 Dr ($42.55). Next door, her husband has a wide collection of excellent-quality Greek costume dolls from 12,000 Dr ($51), as well as some nice ceramic jewelry of Greek ships and flowers from 1,500 Dr ($6.40).

Konstantine Beselmes, 6 Athan Siokou St. (☎ **0752/27-274**), sells his own quite magical paintings of village scenes, sailing ships, idyllic landscapes, and family groups. Although new, the paintings are done on weathered boards, which gives them a pleasantly aged look. Paintings begin at 15,000 Dr ($63.85).

The **Odyssey** bookshop, Syntagma Square, has a wide selection of newspapers, magazines, and books in English, as well as a collection of startling pornographic drink coasters. This is also a good place to pick up a copy of Timothy Gregory's excellent guide to Nafplion (Lycabettus Press).

Day Trips to Tiryns & Nemea

TIRYNS   The Archeological Site of Tiryns is 3 miles outside Nafplion on the Argos road. From the moment that you see Tiryns, you'll understand why Homer called this citadel, which may have been Mycenae's port, "well walled." Tiryns stands on a rocky outcropping 87 feet high and about 330 yards long, girdled by the massive walls that so impressed Homer but didn't keep Tiryns from being destroyed around 1,200 B.C. Later Greeks thought that only the giants known as Cyclopes could have hefted the 14-ton red limestone blocks into place for the walls that archeologists still call "cyclopean." Even today Tiryns's walls stand more than 30 feet high; originally, they were twice as tall—and as much as 57 feet thick. The citadel is crowned by the palace, whose megaron (great hall) has a well-preserved circular hearth and the base of a putative throne. This room would have been gaily decorated with frescoes (the surviving frescoes are now in the National Archeological Museum in Athens). It's open daily: 8am–7pm in summer, 8am–5pm in winter. Admission is 500 Dr ($2.15).

NEMEA   Throughout antiquity, panhellenic games were held every 4 years at Oympia and Delphi and every 2 years at Isthmia, near Corinth, and at Nemea, in a gentle valley in the eastern foothills of the Arcadian mountains. Thanks to the Society for the Revival of the Nemean Games, games were held again at Nemea on June 1, 1996, and, it is hoped, will be held again in 2000. So the stadium you see is not only the place where athletes once contended, but the site of the new Nemean Games.

The **Nemea Museum,** set on an uncharacteristically Greek green lawn, is one of the most charming small museums in Greece, with helpful labels in English. When you're in the museum, be sure to take a look out of one of the large picture windows that overlook the shaded **ancient site** where the coins, vases, athletic gear, and architectural fragments on display were found. A raised stone path tactfully suggests the route from the museum to the site, passing a carefully preserved early Christian burial tomb and skirting a large Christian basilica and Hellenistic bath before arriving at the Temple of Zeus, with 3 of its 32 original Doric columns still standing.

The **stadium** is signposted across the road from the site. Athletes would have stripped down in the locker room, whose foundations are visible just outside the stadium, and then oiled their bodies with olive oil before sprinting into the stadium through the vaulted tunnel. In the stadium, spectators sprawled on earthen benches carved out of the hillside and watched the athletes take their places at the well-preserved stone starting line. In antiquity, athletes ran both naked and barefoot; contestants in the revived Nemean Games run barefoot, but wear short tunics.

The site is open year-round, Tues–Sun 8:30am–3pm. Admission is 500 Dr ($2.15) for both the museum and the ancient site, plus another 500 Dr ($2.15) for the stadium.

MYCENAE

According to Greek legend and the poet Homer, King Agamemnon of Mycenae was the most powerful leader in Greece at the time of the Trojan War. It was Agamemnon, Homer says, who in about 1250 B.C. led the Greeks from Mycenae, which he called "rich in gold," to Troy. There, the Greeks fought for 10 years to reclaim fair Helen, the wife of Agamemnon's brother Menelaus, from the Trojan prince, Paris. The German archeologist Heinrich Schliemann, who found and excavated Troy, began to excavate at Mycenae in 1874. Did Schliemann's excavations here prove that what Homer wrote was based on an actual event, not myth and legend? Scholars are suspicious, although most admit that Mycenae could have been built to order from Homer's descriptions of Mycenaean palaces.

Essentials

ARRIVING By Bus There is frequent bus service from the Peloponnese bus station (☎ **01/513-4100**) in Athens to Corinth, Argos, and Nafplion (allow 3–4 hours). From any of these places you can travel on by bus to Mycenae (allow an hour).

By Car Mycenae is 71 miles southwest of Athens and 31 miles south of Corinth. From Corinth, take the old Corinth–Argos highway south for about 30 miles and then take the left turn to Mycenae, which is about 5 miles down the road. From Nafplion, take the road out of town toward Argos. When you reach the Corinth–Argos highway, turn right and then, after about 10 miles, right again at the sign for Mycenae. If you're going to Nafplion when you leave Mycenae, try the very pleasant backroad that runs through villages and rich farmland. You'll see the sign for Nafplion on your left shortly after you leave Mycenae.

VISITOR INFORMATION The **telephone area code** for the modern village of Mycenae is 0751. You can buy stamps and change money at the **mobile post office** at the ancient site Mon–Fri 8am–2pm. This office is sometimes open on weekends and after 2pm, but don't count on it.

The Citadel & the Treasury of Atreus

As you walk uphill to Mycenae, you begin to get an idea of why people settled here as long ago as 3,000 B.C. Mycenae straddles a low bluff between two protecting mountains and is a superb natural citadel overlooking one of the richest plains in Greece.

By about 1400 B.C. Mycenae controlled not just the Plain of Argos, but much of mainland Greece, as well as Crete, many of the Aegean islands, and outposts in distant Italy and Asia Minor. Then some unknown disaster struck Mycenaean Greece; by about 1100 B.C. the Mycenaeans were on the decline. By the time of the classical era, almost all memory of the Mycenaeans had been lost, and Greeks speculated that places like Mycenae and Tiryns had been built by the Cyclopes. Only such enormous giants, people reasoned, could have moved the huge rocks used to build the ancient citadels' defense walls. You'll enter Mycenae through just such a wall, passing under the massive Lion Gate, whose two lions probably symbolized Mycenae's strength. The door itself (missing, like the lions' heads) probably was made of wood, covered with bronze for additional protection; cuttings for the door jambs and pivots are clearly visible in the lintel. Soldiers stationed in the round tower on your right would have shot arrows down at any attackers who tried to storm the citadel.

One of the most famous spots at Mycenae is immediately ahead of the Lion Gate—the so-called Grave Circle A, where Schliemann found the gold jewelry now on display at the National Museum in Athens. When Schliemann opened the tombs and found some 30 pounds of gold here, including several solid-gold face masks, he concluded that he had found the grave of Agamemnon himself. At once, Schliemann fired off a telegram to the king of Greece saying: "I have looked upon the face of Agamemnon bare." Alas, recent scholars have concluded that Schliemann was wrong, and that the kings buried here died long before Agamemnon was born.

From the grave circle, head uphill past the low remains of a number of houses. Mycenae was not merely a palace, but a small village, with its administrative buildings and homes on the slopes below the palace, which had reception rooms, bedrooms, a throne room, and a large megaron (ceremonial hall). You can see the imprint of the four columns that held up the roof in the megaron, as well as the outline of a circular altar on the floor.

If you're not claustrophobic, head to the northeast corner of the citadel and climb down the flight of stairs to have a look at Mycenae's enormous cistern. (You may find someone here selling candles, but it's a good idea to bring your own flashlight.) Along with Mycenae's great walls, this cistern, which held a water supply channeled from a spring 500 yards away, helped to make the citadel impregnable for several centuries.

There's one more thing to see before you leave Mycenae, the massive tomb known as the Treasury of Atreus, the largest of the tholos tombs found here. You'll see signs for the Treasury of Atreus on your right as you head down the modern road away from Mycenae. The Treasury of Atreus may have been built around 1300 B.C., at about the same time as the Lion Gate, in the last century of Mycenae's real greatness. This enormous tomb, with its 118-ton lintel, is 43 feet high and 47 feet wide. To build the tomb, workers first cut the 115-foot-long passageway into the hill and faced it with stone blocks. Then the tholos chamber itself was built, by placing slightly overlapping courses of stone one on top of the other until a capstone could close the final course. As you look up toward the ceiling of the tomb, you'll see why these are called "beehive tombs." Once your eyes get accustomed to the poor light, you can make out the bronze nails that once held hundreds of bronze rosettes in place in the ceiling. This tomb was robbed even in antiquity, so we'll never know what it contained, although the contents of Grave Circle A (on view at the National Museum in Athens) give an idea of what riches must have been here. If this was the family vault of Atreus, it's entirely possible that Agamemnon himself was buried here.

Accommodations

La Belle Hélène. Mycenae, 212 00 Argolis. ☎ **0751/76-225.** 8 rms (none with bath). 14,000–16,000 Dr ($59–$68) double. Rates include breakfast. Rates sometimes lower offseason. DC, V.

The real reason to stay here is to add your name in the guestbook to that of Schliemann and other luminaries. Sentiment aside, this small hotel is usually very quiet and the simple rooms are clean and comfortable. If you stay here, be sure to drive or walk up to the ancient site at night, especially if it's a full moon.

La Petite Planete. Mycenae, 212 00 Argolis. ☎ **0751/76-240.** 30 rms. TEL. 18,500 Dr ($79) double. Rates include breakfast. Rates sometimes lower off-season. AE, V.

This would be a nice place to stay even without its swimming pool, which is irresistible after a hot day's trek around Mycenae. We've usually found it quieter here than at La Belle Hélène, and friends who stayed here recently praised the restaurant and enjoyed the view over the hills from their window.

Dining

Most of the restaurants here specialize in serving up fixed-price meals to groups. You won't starve if you eat at one of these big, impersonal, roadside restaurants, but you're likely to be served a bland, lukewarm "European-style" meal of overcooked roast veal, underripe tomatoes, and, even in summer, canned vegetables. You'll have better luck trying the smaller restaurants at La Petite Planete or La Belle Hélène hotels. It's sometimes possible to avoid tour groups at the **Achilleus,** on Main Street (☎ 0751/76-027), where you can eat lunch or dinner for less than $10.

EPIDAUROS

Epidauros, dedicated to the healing god Asclepios, was one of the most famous shrines in ancient Greece. Greeks came to the shrine of Asclepios in antiquity as they go to the shrine of the Virgin on the island of Tinos today, to give thanks for good health and in the hopes of finding cures for their ailments. While at Epidauros, patients and their families could "take the waters" at any one of a number of healing springs and in the superb baths here. Visitors could also take in a performance in the theater, just as you can do today.

Essentials

ARRIVING   By Bus   Two buses a day run from the Peloponnesian bus station in Athens (☎ 01/513-4100). Buses take about 3 hours. There are three buses a day from the Nafplion bus station, off Plateia Kapodistrias (☎ 0752/27-323), to Epidauros, as well as extra buses when there are performances at the Theater of Epidauros. The trip takes about an hour.

By Car   Epidauros is 39 miles south of Corinth and 20 miles east of Nafplion. If you're coming from Athens or Corinth, turn left for Epidauros immediately after the Corinth canal and take the coast road to the Theatro (ancient theater), not to Nea Epidauvos or Palaia Epidauros. From Nafplion, follow the signs for Epidauros. If you drive to Epidauros from Nafplion for a performance, be alert; the road will be clogged with tour buses and other tourists who are driving the road for the first time.

THEATER PERFORMANCES   There are usually performances at the ancient theater June–Sept Sat–Sun. Many are given by the National Theater of Greece, some by foreign companies. For information and ticket prices, contact the **Athens Festival Box Office,** 4 Odos Stadiou (☎ **01/322-1459**). It's also possible to buy tickets at most of the travel agencies in Nafplion and at the theater itself, from 5pm on the day of a performance. The performance starts around 9pm. The ancient tragedies are usually performed either in classical or modern Greek; programs at 1,000 Dr ($4.25) usually have either a full translation or a full synopsis of the play. The excellent **Odyssey bookstore** in Nafplion has English translations of the plays being performed at Epidauros.

SPECIAL EVENTS   In 1995 the Society of the Friends of Music sponsored a **music festival** during the last two weekends of July at the recently restored 4th-century theater at Palea Epidauros, 4½ miles from Epidauros. The society hopes to hold a music festival every year at the small theater, which seats 4,000; check with the Greek National Tourist Office to see if the festival is taking place in 1997.

Exploring the Ancient Site

The **excavation museum** at the entrance to the site helps to put some flesh on the bones of the confusing remains of the Sanctuary of Asclepios. The museum has an extensive collection of architectural fragments from the sanctuary, including lovely acanthus flowers from the mysterious tholos, which you'll see when you visit the site. There are also an impressive number of the votive offerings that pilgrims dedicated on view here: The terra-cotta body parts show precisely what part of the anatomy was cured. The display of surgical implements will send you away grateful that you didn't have to go under the knife here, although hundreds of inscriptions record the gratitude of satisfied patients.

Although it's pleasant to wander through the shady **Sanctuary of Asclepios,** it's not at all easy to deceipher the scant remains here. The Asklepion had accommodations for visitors, several large bathhouses, civic buildings, a stadium and gymnasium, and several temples and shrines. The remains are so meager that you may have to take this on faith. Try to find the round **tholos,** that you'll pass about halfway into the sanctuary. The famous 4th-century B.C. architect Polykleitos, who built similar round buildings at Olympia and Delphi, was the architect here. If you wonder why the inner foundations of the tholos are so convoluted and labyrinthine, you're in good company—scholars still aren't sure what went on here, although some suspect that Asclepios's healing serpents lived in the labyrinth.

The museum and archeological site are open in summer, Mon–Fri 8am–7pm and Sat–Sun 8:30am–3:15pm; in winter, Mon–Fri 8am–5pm and Sat–Sun 8:30am–3:15pm. Admission (also covering the theater; see below) is 1,500 Dr ($6.40). There are several kiosks selling snacks and cold drinks near the ticket booth.

The Theater

If you've found the remains of the ancient sanctuary a bit of a let down, don't worry—the Theater of Epidauros is one of the most impressive sights in Greece. Probably built in the 4th century B.C., possibly by Polykleitos, the architect of the tholos, the theater seats some 14,000 spectators. Unlike so many ancient buildings, and almost everything at the Sanctuary of Asclepios, the theater was not pillaged for building blocks in antiquity. As a result, it's astonishingly well preserved; restorations have been minimal and tactful.

If you climb to the top, you can look down over the 55 rows of seats, divided into a lower section of 34 rows and an upper section with 21 rows. The upper seats were added when the original theater was enlarged in the 2nd century B.C. The theater's acoustics are famous and you'll almost certainly see someone demonstrating that a whisper can be heard all the way from the round orchestra to the topmost row of seats. Just as the stadium at Olympia brings out the sprinter in many visitors, the theater at Epidauros tempts many to step center stage and recite poetry, declaim the opening of the Gettysburg Address, or burst into song. It's always a magical moment here when a performance begins as the sun sinks behind the orchestra and the first actor steps onto the stage.

The theater can be visited during the same hours and on the same ticket as the museum and archeological site (see above).

Accommodations & Dining

Epidauros Xenia Hotel. Ligourio, Nafplias, Peloponnese. ☎ **0753/22-005.** 26 rms, 12 with bath. TEL. 17,250 Dr ($73.40) double. Rates include breakfast. Rates sometimes lower off-season.

The best place to stay overnight at Epidauros is the Epidauros Xenia Hotel at the site itself. Once everyone leaves, this is a lovely, quiet spot, in a pine grove beside the ancient site. The 26 bungalowlike units go quickly, so reserve well in advance if you plan to be here the night of a performance. The restaurant serves bland but acceptable food.

OLYMPIA

With its shady groves of pine, olive, and oak trees, the considerable remains of two temples, and the stadium where the first Olympic races were run in 776 B.C., Olympia is the most beautiful major site in the Peloponnese. When you realize that the archeological museum is one of the finest in Greece, you'll see why you can easily spend a full day or more here. The straggling modern village of Olympia (confusingly known as Ancient Olympia) is bisected by its one main street, Leoforos Kondili. The town has the usual assortment of tourist shops as well as more than a dozen hotels and restaurants.

The ancient site of Olympia lies an easily walkable 15 minutes south of the modern village, but if you have a car, you might as well drive; the road teems with tour buses and the walk is less than relaxing.

Essentials

ARRIVING   By Train   There are several trains a day from Athens to Pirgos, where you change to the train for Olympia. Information on schedules and fares is available from the **Stathmos Peloponnisou** (Railroad Station for the Peloponnese) in Athens (☎ **01/513-1601**).

By Bus   There are three buses a day to Olympia from the Peloponnesian Bus Station in Athens (☎ **01/513-4110**). There are also frequent buses from Patras to Pirgos, with a connecting service to Olympia. In Patras, **KTEL buses** leave from the intersection of Zaimi and Othonos Streets (☎ **061/273-694**).

By Car   Olympia is at least a 6-hour drive (199 miles) from Athens, whether you take the coast road that links Athens–Corinth–Patras and Olympia or head inland to Tripolis and Olympia on the new Corinth–Tripolis road. Heavy traffic in Patras (99 miles south) means that the drive from Patras to Olympia can easily take 2 hours.

VISITOR INFORMATION   The **EOT (government tourist office),** on the way to the ancient site near the south end of Leoforos Kondili, the main street (☎ **0624/23-100** or 0624/23-125), is usually open daily: 9am–10pm in summer and 11am–6pm in winter. The **Tourist Police** are at 6 Odos Ethnossinelefseos (☎ **0624/22-100**).

FAST FACTS   The **telephone area code** for Olympia is 0624. The **OTE** (telephone and telegraph office) on Odos Praxitelous is open Mon–Fri 7:30am–10pm. The **train station** is at the north end of town, one street off Leoforos Kondili. You can call for a **taxi** at 0624/22-580.

The Museums & the Ancient Site

Archeological Museum. Admission 1,200 Dr ($5.10). Summer, Mon noon–6pm, Tues–Sat 8am–5pm; winter, Mon noon–6pm, Tues–Sat 11am–5pm.

Even though you'll be eager to see the ancient site, it's a good idea to begin your visit with the museum whose collection makes clear Olympia's astonishing wealth and importance in antiquity. Every victorious city and almost every victorious athlete dedicated a bronze or marble statue here. Nothing but the best was good enough for Olympia, and many of the superb works of art found since excavations began here more than 150 years ago are on view in the museum. Most of the exhibits are displayed in galleries on either side of the main entrance and follow a chronological sequence from severe Neolithic vases to baroque Roman imperial statues. The museum's superstars are in the central galleries directly ahead of the entrance.

The monumental sculpture from the Temple of Zeus is probably the finest surviving example of archaic Greek sculpture. The sculpture from the west pediment shows the battle of the Lapiths and Centaurs raging around the magisterial figure of Apollo, god of reason. On the east pediment, Zeus oversees the chariot race between Oinomaos, king of Pisa, and Pelops, the legendary figure who wooed and won Oinomaos's daughter by the unsporting expedient of loosening his opponent's chariot pins. On either end of the room, sculptured metopes show scenes from the labors of Hercules, including the one he performed at Olympia: cleansing the Augean stables.

Just beyond the sculpture from the Temple of Zeus are the 5th-century B.C. winged victory done by the artist Paionios and the 4th-century B.C. figure of Hermes and the infant Dionysios known as the *Hermes of Praxiteles*. The *Hermes* has a room to itself—or would, if tourists didn't make a beeline to admire Hermes smiling with amused tolerance at his chubby half-brother Dionysios. If you want to impress your companions, mention casually that many scholars think that this is not an original work by Praxiteles, but a Roman copy. In addition to several cases of glorious bronze heads of snarling griffins and the lovely terracotta of a resolute Zeus carrying off the youthful Ganymede, the museum has a good deal of athletic paraphernalia from the ancient games: stone and bronze weights used for balance by long jumpers, bronze and stone discuses, and even an enormous stone with an inscription boasting that a weight lifter had raised it over his head with only one hand.

Before you leave the museum, have a look at the two excellent site models just inside the main entrance. As the models make clear, ancient Olympia was quite literally divided by a low wall into two distinct parts: the Altis or religious sanctuary, containing temples and shrines, and the civic area, with athletic and municipal buildings. Between festivals, Olympia was crowded only with its thousands of statues, but every 4 years, during the games, so many people thronged here that it was said that by the time that the games began, not even one more spectator could have wedged himself into the stadium. So if the site is very crowded when you visit, just remember that it would have been much worse in antiquity.

The Ancient Site. Admission 1,200 Dr ($5.10). Summer, Mon–Fri 7:30am–7pm, Sat–Sun 8:30am–3pm; winter, Mon–Fri 8am–5pm, Sat–Sun 8:30am–3pm.

Olympia's setting is magical—pine trees shade the little valley, dominated by the conical Hill of Kronos, that lies between the Alphios and Kladeos Rivers. The handsome temples and the famous stadium that you've come here to see, however, are not at once apparent as you enter the site. Immediately to the left are the unimpressive low walls that are all that remain of the Roman baths where athletes and spectators could enjoy hot and cold plunge baths. The considerably more impressive remains with the slender columns on your right mark the gymnasium and palestra, where athletes practiced their foot racing and boxing skills. The enormous gymnasium had one roofed track, precisely twice the length of the stadium, where athletes could practice in bad weather. Still ahead on the right are the fairly meager remains of a number of structures, including a swimming pool and the large square Leonidaion, which served as a hotel for visiting dignitaries until a Roman governor decided it would do nicely as his villa. If you want, you can continue around the outskirts of the site, identifying other civic buildings, but you'll probably want to enter the sanctuary itself.

The religious sanctuary was—and is—dominated by two temples: the good-sized Temple of Hera and the massive Temple of Zeus. The Temple of Hera with its three standing columns is the older of the two, built around 600 B.C. If you look closely, you'll see that the temple's column capitals and drums are not uniform. That's because this temple was originally built with wooden columns and as each column decayed, it was replaced; inevitably, the new columns had variations. The *Hermes of Praxiteles* was found here, buried under the mud that covered Olympia for so long, caused by the repeated flooding of the Alphios and Kladeos Rivers. The Temple of Zeus, which once had a veritable thicket of 34 stocky Doric columns, was built around 456 B.C. The entire temple—so austere and gray today—was anything but austere in antiquity. Gold, red, and blue paint was everywhere, and inside the temple stood the enormous gold-and-ivory statue of Zeus seated on an ivory-and-ebony throne. The statue was so ornate that it was considered one of the Seven Wonders of the Ancient World—and so large that people joked that if Zeus stood up, his head would go through the temple's roof. In fact, the antiquarian Philo of Byzantium suggested that Zeus had created elephants simply so that the sculptor Pheidias would have the ivory to make his statue.

Not only do we know that Pheidias made the 42-foot-tall statue, we know where he made it: The Workshop of Pheidias was on the site of the well-preserved brick building clearly visible west of the temple just outside the sanctuary. How do we know that this was Pheidias's workshop? Because a cup with "I belong to Pheidias" on it and artists' tools were found here. Between the Temples of Zeus and Hera you can make out the low foundations of a round building: this is all that remains of the shrine that Philip of Macedon, never modest, built here to pat himself on the back after conquering Greece in 338 B.C. Beyond the two temples, built up against the Hill of Kronos itself, are the curved remains of a once-elegant Roman fountain and the foundations of 11 treasuries where Greek cities stored votive offerings and money. In front of the treasuries are the low bases of a series of bronze statues of Zeus dedicated not by victorious athletes but by those caught cheating in the stadium. These statues would have been the last thing that competitors saw before they ran through the vaulted tunnel into the stadium.

Ancient tradition makes clear that the Olympic games began here in 776 B.C. and ended in A.D. 395, but is less clear on just why they were held every 4 years. According to one legend, Herakles initiated the games to celebrate completing his 12 labors, one of which took place nearby when the hero diverted the Alphios River to clean the fetid stables that King Augeas had neglected for more than a decade. The stables clean, Herakles paced off the stadium and then he ran its entire length of 600 Olympic feet (192.27 meters) without having to take a single breath.

Museum of the Olympic Games. Admission 500 Dr ($2.15). Mon–Sat 8am–3:30pm, Sun and holidays 9am–2:30pm.

When you head back to town, try to set aside half an hour to visit the Museum of the Olympic Games. Not many tourists come here and the guards are often glad to show visitors around. Displays include victors' medals, commemorative stamps, and photos of winning athletes, such as former King Constantine of Greece and the great African-American athlete Jesse Owens. There's also a photo of the bust of the founder of the modern Olympics, Baron de Coubertin. (The bust itself stands just off the main road east of the ancient site and marks the spot where de Coubertin's heart is buried.)

Shopping

Antonios Kosmopoulos's main-street bookstore, **Galerie Orphee** (☎ **0624/23-555**), with its extensive range of cassettes and CDs of Greek music, and frequent displays of contemporary art, is a pleasant contrast to Olympia's other shops, which have all too many T-shirts, museum reproductions, and machine-made rugs and embroideries sold as "genuine handmade crafts."

Accommodations

Olympia has more than 20 hotels, which means that you can almost always find a room, although if you arrive without a reservation in July or August you may not get your first choice. In the winter, many hotels are closed.

Hotel Europa. 270 65 Ancient Olympia, Peloponnese. ☎ **0624/22-650** or 0624/22-700. Fax 0624/23-166. 42 rms. A/C TV TEL. 28,750 Dr ($122.35) double. Rates include breakfast. AE, DC, MC, V.

The Europa plans to be open all year. This member of the Best Western hotel chain, a few minutes' drive out of town on a hill overlooking both the modern village and the ancient site, is clearly the best hotel in town—and one of the best in the entire Peloponnese. Most of the bedrooms overlook a large pool and garden, and several overlook the ancient site itself. The bedrooms are large, with colorful rugs, extra-firm mattresses, and sliding glass doors opening onto generous balconies. Friends who travel through the Peloponnese every summer rave about the Hotel Europa's unusual tranquillity.

Hotel Neda. Odos Praxiteles, 270 65 Ancient Olympia, Peloponnese. ☎ **0624/22-563.** Fax 0624/22-206. 43 rms. TEL. 17,500 Dr ($74.45) double. AE, V.

With a pleasant rooftop cafe, a comfortable lobby, a serviceable restaurant, and a distinctive red-and-white facade, the Neda offers good value. The double rooms, many decorated in shades of pink and rose, are large, with colorful shaggy flokaki rugs on the floor and good bedside reading lamps. Some of the double rooms have double beds, but most have twins, so specify which you want. Each room has a good-sized balcony and the bathrooms are better than those usually found in hotels in this price category, thanks to the presence of shower curtains which help you to avoid spraying the entire room. The bedrooms here are usually quieter than at hotels on the main street.

Hotel Pelops. 2 Odos Varela, 270 65 Ancient Olympia, Peloponnese. ☎ **0624/22-213.** 25 rms. TEL. 11,500 Dr ($48.95) double. EC, MC, V. Closed Nov–Feb.

The English-speaking owner, Susanna Spiliopoulou, described by many visitors here as especially helpful, makes this one of the most welcoming hotels in Olympia. There are flokaki rugs on the floors, good mattresses on the beds, and plants and vines shading the terrace.

Hotel Praxiteles. 7 Spiliopoulou, 270 65 Ancient Olympia, Peloponnese. ☎ **0624/22-592.** 10 rms. 5,750 Dr ($24.45) double. AE, EC, V.

The small, inexpensive family-run Hotel Praxiteles is the best bargain in town. Just one street back from Olympia's main street, Odos Spiliopoulou has a nice neighborhood feel, with children often playing ball in the street in front of the police station. Although the bedrooms are small and very spare, the beds are decent and the front rooms have balconies. If you want to avoid the murmurs of conversation from the Praxiteles's excellent restaurant on the sidewalk below the balconies, ask for a room at the back (and hope that the neighborhood dogs don't bark too much).

Dining

There are almost as many restaurants as hotels in Olympia. The ones on and just off the main street with large signs in English and German tend to have indifferent food and service, although it's possible to get good snacks of yogurt or tiropites (cheese pies) in most of the cafes.

Taverna Ambrosia. Behind the train station. ☎ **0624/23-414.** Main courses 1,150–2,875 Dr ($4.90–$12.25). AE, MC, V. Daily 7–11pm and some weekends for lunch. GREEK.

This large restaurant with a pleasant outside veranda continues to attract locals although it does a brisk business with tour groups. You'll find the usual grilled chops and souvlakia here, but the vegetable dishes are unusually good, as is the lamb stew with lots of garlic and oregano.

Taverna Kladeos. Behind the train station. ☎ **0624/23-322.** Main courses 1,000–1,725 Dr ($4.25–$7.35). EC, MC, V. Daily 7–11pm. GREEK.

The charming Kladeos, with the best food in town, is at the end of the little paved road that runs steeply downhill past the Ambrosia restaurant. You may not be the only foreigner, but you'll probably find lots of locals here. In good weather, tables are set up under canvas awnings and roofs made of rushes. If you sit in the hillside, you'll be serenaded by the frogs that live beside the river. Rather than offering an inflexible menu, the Kladeos varies its menu according to what's in season. In summer, the lightly grilled green peppers, zucchini, and eggplant are especially delicious. The house wine, a light rosé, is heavenly. If you want to buy a bottle to take with you, give your empty water bottle to your waiter and ask him to fill it with krassi (wine).

Taverna Praxiteles. In the Hotel Praxiteles, 7 Odos Spiliopoulou. ☎ **0624/23-570** or 0624/22-592. Main courses 700–2,300 Dr ($2.95–$9.80). AE, EC, V. Daily for lunch and dinner. GREEK.

The reputation of the Hotel Praxiteles' excellent and reasonably priced restaurant has spread rapidly and it's packed almost every evening, first with foreigners, eating un-fashionably early for Greece, and then with locals, who start showing up around 10pm. Although the entrees are very good, especially the rabbit stew with onions (stifado), it's easy to make an entire meal out of the delicious and varied appetizers. A large plate of mezes (appetizers) is only 1,500 Dr ($6.40) and may include octopus, eggplant salad, taramasalada and Russian salad, meatballs stuffed with zucchini, fried cheese, and a handful of olives. In good weather, tables are outside on the sidewalk; for the rest of the year, meals are in the pine-paneled dining room.

3 The Cyclades

The Cyclades ("Circling Islands"), so called because they were once thought to orbit the sacred island of Delos, are the best known and most popular of the Greek islands. Most appear as barren rock piles jutting out of the clear Aegean Sea, with picturesque harbors and hills topped with villages of asymmetrical sugar-white houses. They're especially delightful to visit by ferry, cruise ship, or yacht. And each individual island has its own unique attractions and identity.

Of the islands discussed here, **Tinos,** often referred to as the "Lourdes of Greece," is the most important destination for religious pilgrimage for Greeks. **Mykonos** is famous for its excellent beaches, sophisticated amenities, and swinging social life; but be warned that it's expensive and reservations are imperative in the summer. **Ios** is the party capital of the Aegean, if not the Mediterranean, and in summer is strictly for the young and resilient. **Santorini (Thira)** is the spectacular remains of an ancient volcanic eruption, and a thrill to visit, though it's among the most expensive islands. **Sifnos** is close enough to Pireaus to be popular with Athenians, but it retains its quiet charm. **Paros** has an established nightlife and excellent windsurfing, though it remains less intense and expensive. For more detailed information on the Cyclades, consult *Frommer's Greece,* 1st Edition.

The Cyclades are best visited in the spring (Apr to early June) or fall (Sept–Oct), as they're most crowded and expensive in the high season (July–Aug). They're easily reached from Athens, and, for the most part, conveniently interconnected. (There are also regular connections with Crete, as well as connections with other Greek islands, including the Dodecanese and northeast Aegean islands.)

ONLY IN THE CYCLADES

Making a Pilgrimage to Panayia Evangelistria   Heralded as the "Lourdes of Greece," this church on Tinos is one of the most important religious destinations in the country. "Our Lady of Good Tidings" is home to an icon believed to have miraculous powers.

Lounging at Paradise Beach on Mykonos   Sure, it's crowded, and often noisy; but the island's most famous beach is remarkably pristine, and the water still sparklingly clear. Enjoy the view—whether of the tranquil Aegean or the nude sunbathers lined up like french fries on the sand. After all, you're on Mykonos, where an exuberant, party-all-night attitude is de rigueur.

Taking in the View from the Rim of Santorini's Caldera   In a region brimming with spectacular vistas, none other is quite so stunning. Climb to the edge of hilltop Fira and gaze down the cliff into a vast underwater crater. More than 3,500 years ago this volcano erupted, wiping out life on the island before it sank into the sea. Many scientists believe that this is the site of the lost colony of Atlantis.

GETTING TO THE CYCLADES

If you have travel connections in Athens you should plan on spending your last night there, especially during those times of the year when winds are likely to interfere with sea travel, or make a flight reservation early and reconfirm it.

BY AIR   Olympic Airways (☎ **01/926-7593** in Athens; or consult a travel agent) has service from Athens to Mykonos (7 flights daily, 10 daily in high season), Paros (5 flights daily, 10 daily in high season), and Santorini (4 flights daily, 6 daily in high season); service between Mykonos and Thessaloniki (three times a week in summer), Iraklio, Crete (twice a week), and Rhodes (three times a week); and service between Santorini and Thessaloniki (three times a week), Iraklio, Crete (three times a week), and Rhodes (three times a week). There are, of course, an increasing number of charter flights from all over Europe into the various islands.

BY SEA   Sea travel is frequently affected by the winds. In July the *meltemi* arrive, often playing havoc with the seas and hydrofoil schedules. The larger ferries still run—though if you're prone to seasickness, take precautions. In the winter the strong north *vorias* make sea travel virtually impossible.

Ferries leave daily from Piraeus and Rafina, the major port east of Athens; contact the **Piraeus Port Authority** (☎ 01/451-1311) or the **Rafina Port Police** (☎ 0294/22-300) for schedules. It sometimes takes an hour for the 17-mile bus ride from Athens to Rafina (the most convenient port to Tinos, Mykonos, and sometimes to Paros), but you save about an hour of sailing time and about 20% on the fare; buses leave every 30 minutes 6am–10pm from 29 Mavromateon St. (☎ 01/821-0872), near Areos Park north of the Archeology Museum. **Ilio Lines** (☎ 01/422-4772 in Athens or 0294/22-888 in Rafina) offers regular hydrofoil service from Rafina.

In summer there's regular ferry and hydrofoil service to Iraklio, Crete. There are also ferry connections three to four times a week in the summer between Paros and Samos, Ikaria, Karpathos, and Rhodes; several times a week between Mykonos and Kos and Rhodes; twice a week between Mykonos and Skyros, Skiathos, and Thessaloniki; and two or three times a week between Syros and the Dodecanese.

GETTING AROUND THE CYCLADES

There's frequent and extensive ferry service between most of the islands. Schedules can be erratic, and service diminishes suddenly at the end of the season. Smaller excursion vessels are easily affected by high winds. To further complicate matters, a line will sometimes have only one agent selling tickets or limit the number of tickets available to an agency, giving other agents little incentive to tout their service. You may want to visit several agents or inquire at the port authority. (For specifics, see "Arriving/Departing" under "Essentials" for each island.)

The easiest way to island-hop is aboard a chartered yacht cruise; you don't have to worry about ferry connections, hotel reservations, and most meals. **Viking Star Cruises,** 1 Artemidos St., Glyfada, 166 74 Athens (☎ **01/898-0729;** fax 01/894-0952; e-mail vikings@forum.ars.net.gr or bjgh44a@prodigy.com) offers 7-day

The Cyclades

ATTICA

Aegean

ÁNDROS
Gávrio
Bátsi

Sea

KÉA
Gyáros
Kéa

TÍNOS
Koúmaros
Falatados **1**
Tínos

SÝROS
Áno Sýros
Ano Sýros
Ermoúpolis
Possidón

MÝKONOS **2**
Áyios
Stéphanos
Platís Yialós

DÉLOS

Kythnos
KÝTHNOS

Serfopoúla

SÉRIFOS
Sérifos
Livádi

Náxos
(Hóra)
3
Náoussa
Parikía **4**
Aliki

Apóllonas
5
Kóronos
Ay. Anna
Ay. Prokópios

Donoússa
Donoússa

SÍFNOS
Artemóna
Kástro
Kamáres
Apollonía
Platís Yialós
Antíparos
PÁROS

NÁXOS
Koufoníssi
Káros

Iráklia

AMORGÓS
Lefkés

Mílos
Adámas
MÍLOS

Yialós
Hóra
ÍOS

Folégandros

SANTORÍNI (THÍRA)
Ia
Fíra **6**
Kamári
7
Embório
Périssa

Anáfi

3-0759

GREECE
Athens ★
The
Cyclades

Akrotíri **7**
Kamári Beach **6**
Kolymbíthres Beach **3**
Panayía
    Ekatontapylianí **4**

Panayía
    Evanyelístria **1**
Panayía Paraportianí
    Church **2**
Temple of Apollo **5**

Ferry Route

cruises beginning every Friday, Apr to early Nov, with stops on Tinos, Ios, Santorini, Paros, Naxos, Mykonos, and Delos. Last-minute discount fares are occasionally available.

For more information on cruises, contact **Intercruise Ltd.** (☎ 800/668-7475 in Canada), the **Greek National Tourist Organization** (☎ 0171/734-5997 in London), and the **Greek Island Cruise Center** (☎ 800/342-3030 in the U.S.).

TINOS

Tinos is the most important place of religious pilgrimage in Greece, just 87 nautical miles southeast of Piraeus, and yet it's one of the least commercial of the Cyclades and a joy to visit. Home to the famous church of Panayia Evangelistria, where the miraculous icon that excites so much religious interest is enshrined, Tinos also has an attractive port town (also called Tinos), a lovely green landscape with scores of white Venetian dovecotes (for which the island is also famous), some beautiful beaches, and a friendly, hospitable population.

Note: Unless you have firm hotel reservations, you shouldn't plan an overnight visit to Tinos on summer weekends or during important religious holidays, especially March 25 (Feast of the Annunciation) and August 15 (Feast of the Assumption)—though a summer night under the stars wouldn't be too high a price to pay for such an experience.

ESSENTIALS

ARRIVING/DEPARTING   By Sea   There are several ferries daily from Piraeus and three daily from Rafina; **schedules** should be confirmed with Tourist Information in Athens (☎ 143), the Piraeus Port Authority (☎ 01/451-1311), or in Rafina (☎ 0294/25-200). **Ilio Lines** (☎ 01/422-4772 in Athens or 0294/22-888 in Rafina) has hydrofoil service from Rafina. There are connections several times daily with nearby Andros, Mykonos, and Syros, and several daily excursions to Mykonos and Delos for about 10,000 Dr ($42.55).

There are two piers in Tinos harbor, the newer one 600 yards northwest of the main one; be sure to find out from which your ship will depart. The **port authority** can be reached at 0283/22-348.

VISITOR INFORMATION   There's no official information center on the island, but there are several helpful travel agents along the waterfront. **Tinos Mariner** (☎ **0283/23-193**) has information and a good map of the island. The **Nicholas Information Center,** 24 Evangelistria St. (☎ **0283/24-142;** fax 0283/24-049), the main market street to the left and perpendicular to the port, open 6:30am–midnight, has information, ferry tickets, and rooms.

FAST FACTS   The **banks** are on the waterfront. The **Tourist Police** (☎ 0283/22-255) have an office opposite the bus station on the harbor, but if it's not manned during your visit you can find the **town police** (☎ 0283/22-255) by turning right from the ferry quay, then left. The **telephone office** (**OTE**), open 8am–midnight, is on Megaloharis Avenue, the main street leading up to the Church of Panayia Evangelistria, at Lazarou Dochou Street. The **post office** is at the southeast end of the waterfront. The **first-aid center** can be reached at 0283/22-210.

GETTING AROUND   The **bus station** is on the harbor; check at the KTEL office there for the schedule (which is erratic) and rates. The **taxi stand** is also nearby on the harbor. There are several shops renting **mopeds,** from about 4,000 Dr ($17) a day; **Nicholas** (☎ 0283/24-142) and **Moto Mike** (☎ 0283/23-304) are reliable. **Cars** can be rented from about 15,500 Dr ($66) a day with insurance.

WHAT TO SEE & DO

The **Church of Panayia Evangelistria** ("Our Lady of Good Tidings"), the "Lourdes of Greece," draws thousands of pilgrims every year who seek the aid of a miraculous icon enshrined there. In 1822 a nun named Pelayia had a dream that an icon was buried on a nearby farm. She summoned her neighbors to help excavate, and they discovered the foundation of a Byzantine church, where a workman found a gold icon, said to be the work of St. Luke. Work was begun immediately on the elegant neoclassical church that can be seen today.

Almost any day of the year you can see people, particularly elderly women, with padded arms and knees, crawling from the port up the street to the church in supplication, usually, it's said, to ask for intercession for a loved one. Grand marble stairs lead up into the church itself; hundreds of lamps overhead light a truly fantastic array of gold, silver, precious jewels, and thousands of flickering candles. If you haven't yet attended an Orthodox service and experienced its resonance and mystery, you might wait for one. The church and its galleries are open daily: 8am–8pm in summer and noon–6pm in winter. To enter, men must wear long pants and shirts with sleeves, and women must wear skirts and sleeves.

The town of Tinos is a pleasant place for a ramble, with a **flea market** area behind the port, up the street from Ferry Boat Naias office. Besides a huge variety of candles and religious paraphernalia, you'll find local embroidery, weavings, and the delicious local nougat. Several ceramics shops on the waterfront—**Margarita, Bernardo, Manina**—have interesting pottery, jewelry, and copperware at moderate prices.

Harris Prassas Ostria-Tinos, 20 Evangelistrias St. (☎ **0283/23-893;** fax 0283/24-568), is recommended for his fine collection of jewelry and religious objects. Harris is friendly and informative, and he accepts credit cards.

Those interested in authentic hand-painted icons should find the small shop of **Maria Vryoni** (take the first left from the port off the street up to the church, and it's the second shop on the left). Maria spends at least a week on each of her works of art, so they aren't cheap, costing up to 50,000 Dr ($212) for a large one, but they are superb, and she accepts credit cards.

The famous **Venetian dovecotes,** many dating from the 17th century, are scattered throughout the island. You can see several, as well as the **Temple of Poseidon and Amphitrite,** by taking the coastal road 1 1/4 miles west of town to **Kionia** ("Columns"), a pleasant 30-minute hike past the Hotel Aigli.

Some of the island's best beaches are at **Kolimbithres,** where there's a taverna and some rooms to let. But beach enthusiasts may want to head east of town. The first beach, about 1 1/4 miles out, is busy **Ayios Fokas,** which has the very nice little **Golden Beach Hotel** (☎ **0283/22-579**), with a lovely garden and clean, comfortable doubles from about 10,500 Dr ($44.70). There is bus service (usually four times a day) 5 miles east to the resort of **Porto,** which has two beaches and several hotel complexes but little in the way of eateries, so you may want to bring a picnic. If it's crowded, walk back southwest to **Xeres,** which is less developed.

ACCOMMODATIONS

If you avoid the religious holidays and summer weekends, you'll have no trouble finding a room. People will offer you their rooms, more politely than elsewhere, at the landing. **O Yannis,** next to the Hotel Oceanis on Gizi Street (☎ **0283/22-515**), has large, homey, high-ceilinged rooms with clean shared facilities for about 5,000 Dr ($21.25) for a double. Stratis Keladitis, at the **Nicholas Information Center,** 24 Evangelistrias St. (☎ **0283/24-142**), has plain rooms upstairs for about

4,800 Dr ($20.40) for a double with shared facilities, as well as friendly advice and inexpensive moped rental.

Avra Hotel. Tinos town, 842 00 Tinos. ☎ **0283/22-242.** 14 rms. 12,300 Dr ($52.35) double. No credit cards. Turn right from the ferry quay and walk southeast on the waterfront.

This century-old neoclassical hotel has simple, spacious, high-ceilinged rooms. Its quaint plant-filled tiled courtyard is a pleasant retreat.

⑤ Hotel Eleana. Ierarchon Sq., Tinos town, 842 00 Tinos. ☎ **0283/22-561.** 17 rms. 8,600 Dr ($36.60) double. V. Turn right from the ferry quay, then left up the street to the right of the Hotel Posidonios; it's about 400 yards up on the right.

Tinos's best-value hotel doesn't have harbor views, of course, but the rooms are large, comfortable, clean, and quiet. The friendly, hospitable management more than makes up for a lack of proficiency in English.

DINING

Tinos has a number of good restaurants, probably because most of their customers are other Greeks, who won't settle for second-rate food. As in most Greek ports, you should generally avoid harborfront joints; the food is often inferior and more expensive, and the service can be rushed.

Lefteris. Harborfront, Tinos town. ☎ **0283/23-013.** Main courses 800–2,600 Dr ($3.40–$11.05). No credit cards. Daily 11am–midnight. GREEK.

This is an exception to the harborfront rule: Look for a blue sign on the harbor over an arched entrance that leads to a large courtyard decorated with fish plaques. The menu is large and varied; the grilled sea bass, veal stifado, and dolmades (stuffed grape leaves in lemon sauce) are particularly good. There's plenty of room for dancing, and the waiters often demonstrate and urge diners to join them.

⑤ O Kipos (The Garden). Tinos town. ☎ **0283/22-838.** Main courses 900–2,400 Dr ($3.85–$10.20). No credit cards. Daily noon–midnight. Take the first street to the right of the Posidonion Hotel and wander inland through the quiet residential area, about four lanes, until you see the bright lights of this taverna. GREEK.

At this small, friendly taverna, the cooking is typical down-home Greek, with the usual dishes, including tasty moussaka and tender souvlaki. You can have a complete meal with good retsina (home-brewed wine) for less than 3,000 Dr ($12.75).

✪ Peristerionas (Dovecote). 12 Paksimadi Fraiskou St., Tinos town. ☎ **0283/23-425.** Main courses 1,600–2,400 Dr ($6.80–$10.20). No credit cards. Daily noon–3pm and 7–11:30pm. GREEK.

On a small lane uphill behind the Lido Hotel, this restaurant, decorated like one on the island's famous dovecotes, has outdoor tables filling the walkway. It serves excellent grilled meats and fish, and delicious marathotiganites, vegetable fritters with onions and dill.

TINOS AFTER DARK

As you surely already suspect, there's not an abundance of nightlife on Tinos, but there is a small enclave of music bars off the left (west) of the port, including **Argonautis,** the **Sibylla Bar,** and **George's Place,** which features Greek dancing.

MYKONOS

Jet-setty Mykonos, 96 nautical miles southeast of Pireaus and 81 nautical miles southeast of Rafina, is one of the smaller of the Cyclades, and yet the busiest—a permanent population of 15,000 hosts an average of 800,000 visitors annually. It's an arid, rocky island, with excellent beaches, attractive architecture, numerous but often expensive accommodations, good restaurants, chic shopping, and wild nightlife. Though it continues to attract hordes of international visitors, it somehow manages to retain its charm and self-respect. *Note:* Don't plan a stay on Mykonos without reservations in the high season, unless you enjoy sleeping outdoors.

ESSENTIALS

ARRIVING/DEPARTING   By Air   Olympic Airways has 7 flights daily (10 in high season) between Athens and Mykonos; 1 flight daily between Mykonos and Iraklio (Crete), Rhodes, and Santorini; and 3 flights a week between Mykonos and Hios, Lesvos, and Samos. It's difficult to get a seat on any of these flights, so make reservations early and reconfirm them at the Olympic office in Athens (☎ 01/961-6161) or Mykonos (☎ 0289/22-490).

By Sea   From Piraeus, the **Ventouris Lines** (☎ 01/482-5815) has departures at least once daily, usually at 8am, with a second on summer afternoons; check schedules in Athens by calling 171. From Rafina, **Strintzis Lines** has daily ferry service; schedules can be checked with the port police (☎ 0294/25-200). There are daily ferry connections between Mykonos and Andros, Paros, Syros, and Tinos; five to seven times a week with Ios; four times a week with Iraklio, Crete; several times a week with Kos and Rhodes; and twice weekly with Ikaria, Samos, Skiathos, Skyros, and Thessaloniki. **Ilio Lines** (☎ 01/422-4772 in Athens or 0294/22-888 in Rafina) has daily hydrofoil service to Mykonos from Rafina.

Check each travel agent's current schedule, as most ferry tickets are not interchangeable. **Sea & Sky Travel,** on Taxi Square (☎ 0289/22-853; fax 0289/24-753), represents the Strintzis, Ilio and Agapitos lines, changes money, and offers excursions to Delos. The **Veronis Agency,** also on Taxi Square (☎ 0289/22-687; fax 0289/23-763), offers information, safekeeping of baggage, and other services.

Hydrofoil (catamaran) service to Crete, Ios, Paros, and Santorini is often irregular. For information, call the **Port Authority** in Piraeus (☎ 01/451-1311), Rafina (☎ 0294/23-300), or Mykonos (☎ 0289/22-218).

VISITOR INFORMATION   The **Mykonos Tourist Office** (☎ 0289/23-990) is on the west side of the port near the excursion boats to Delos. Look for a copy of the free *Mykonos Summertime* magazine.

LAYOUT   The streets of **Mykonos town,** which locals call **Hora,** were designed purposely to confuse pirates, so your own confusion will be understandable. (*Hora* means "chief town," and islanders usually use it when speaking of an island capital rather than using the name of the island.) As you get off the ferry you can see the main square south across the harbor beyond the small town beach and a cluster of buildings; we refer to it as **Taxi Square,** though it's officially called **Platia Mando Mavroyenous,** after a local heroine. Here you'll find several travel agents, kiosks, snack bars, and of course the town's taxi stand. You might want to buy a map from one of the kiosks; the one published by Stamatis Bozinakis, at 400 Dr ($1.70), is particularly good.

The "main" street, **Matoyanni,** leads south off Taxi Square behind the church; it's narrow, but you can hardly miss it for the bars, boutiques, and restaurants. Several "blocks" along it you'll find a "major" cross street, **Kaloyera,** and by turning right you'll find several of the hotels and restaurants we recommend.

GETTING AROUND   One of Hora's greatest assets is the government decree that made Mykonos an architectural landmark and prohibited motorized traffic from its streets. The only way to get around town is to walk. Much of the rest of the island is served by a good transportation system.

By Bus   Mykonos has one of the best organized bus systems in the Greek islands; the buses run frequently, on schedule, and cost 200–800 Dr (85¢–$3.40) one-way. There are two bus stations in Hora: the **north station,** near the middle of the harbor below the Leto Hotel; and the **south station,** about a 10-minute walk from the harbor, near the Olympic Airways office (follow the helpful blue signs). Schedules are posted, though subject to change.

By Boat   Excursion boats to Delos depart every day from the west side of the harbor near the tourist office at 9am. (For more information, see "An Excursion to Delos," below, or consult a travel agent; guided tours are available.) Caïques to Super Paradise, Agrari, and Elia depart from the town harbor every morning, weather permitting. Caïques to Paradise, Super Paradise, Agrari, and Elia leave from Platis Yialos every morning, weather permitting. (Caïque service is almost continuous during the high season, when they also depart from Ornos Bay.)

By Car & Moped   Rental cars and Jeeps are available from travel agents for about 22,500 Dr ($95.75) per day, including full insurance, during the high season, and substantially less at other times if you bargain. Mopeds can be a fun way to get around if you know how to handle one properly and can negotiate the sometimes treacherous roads. They're available from shops near both bus stations; the north one usually has a better selection than the south one. *Note:* If you park in town or in a no-parking area, the police will remove your license plates, and you—not the rental office—will have to find the police station and pay a steep fine to get them back.

By Taxi   Getting a taxi in Hora is easy; walk to Taxi (Mavro) Square, near the statue, and get on line; there's a notice board that gives rates for each destination for both high and low seasons. You can also phone (☎ 0289/22-400, or 0289/23-700 for late-hours and out-of-town service). You'll be charged the fare from Hora to your pickup point plus the fare to your destination, so before calling try to find an empty taxi returning to Hora or flag one down along the road.

FAST FACTS: HORA

Banks   The Commercial Bank and the National Bank of Greece are conveniently located on the harbor a couple of blocks west of Taxi Square, both open Mon–Fri 8am–2pm and 6–8:30pm. The National Bank is also open Sat 9am–12:30pm and 5:30–8:30pm and Sun 5:30–8:30pm, but for currency exchange only. Traveler's checks can also be cashed at the post office, as well as at many travel agents and hotels, at less than bank rates.

Laundry   The Apollon Laundry is at 17 Mavroyenous St. (☎ 0289/22-496), near Taxi Square. A self-service launderette is on Ayion Anaryiron Steet at Scarpa, behind the Church of Paraportiani.

Medical Treatment   The Mykonos Health Center (☎ 0289/23-944) handles minor medical complaints. The hospital (☎ 0289/23-994) offers 24-hour emergency service and is open for general visits daily 9am–1pm and 5–10pm.

Police   The **Tourist Police** office is on the west side of the port near the the ferries to Delos (☎ 0289/22-482). The **local police** office is behind the grammar school (☎ 0289/22-235).

Post Office   The post office is on the east side of the harbor near the Port Police, open Mon–Fri 7:30am–2pm.

Telephones   The OTE office is on the east side of the harbor beyond the Hotel Leto (☎ 0289/22-499), open daily 7:30am–10pm.

WHAT TO SEE & DO

Beyond the excursion boats to Delos and the tourist office, near the northwest corner you'll find the **Folk Art Museum,** which contains old artifacts and a re-created kitchen and bedroom with a big four-poster; it's open Mon–Sat 4–8pm and Sun 5–8pm. Beyond it is the old Venetian **Kastro** and the most famous little church on the island, **Panayia Paraportiani** ("Our Lady of the Port"), a whitewashed asymmetrical joining of four smaller chapels.

Beyond this church is the quarter known as **Little Venice,** officially called **Alefkanda,** a neighborhood of mansions built right on the water. Many have been converted into fashionable bars prized for their sunset views. Along **Ayion Anaryiron** you'll find some of the island's best shopping for art and crafts. The famous windmills of **Kato Myli** crown the hill above and can be easily reached. If you'd like to further acquaint yourself with the **Tria Pigadia** ("Three Wells"), continue on up the "main" street, Matoyanni, past Kaloyera and turn right on Enoplon Dinameon. Local legend says that if a virgin drinks from all three of the wells she is sure to find a husband—but today she's more likely to contract a disease.

We don't want to be unduly negative about **shopping** in Hora, especially as it's such a prominent possibility and the prices are sometimes lower than they are in similar boutiques in Athens. Our chief complaint is that local sales techniques are high-pressure, state-of-the-art sharp. If you'll be visiting less expensive islands, such as Sifnos, you should postpone purchasing leather goods, ceramics, and textiles—little of which is actually manufactured on Mykonos.

The one commodity Mykonos can boast of is fine **jewelry**—not at bargain prices of course, but skillfully handcrafted in a variety of designs, some of them unique. The best known is **Ilias Lalaounis,** 14 Polykandrioti St. (☎ **0289/22-444**), near the taxi station, which has an international reputation, especially in classical, Byzantine, and natural motifs. **Delos Dolphins,** Matoyanni at Enoplon Dimameon (☎ **0289/ 22-765**), specializes in copies of museum pieces. **Mykonos Gold,** on Ayios Efthimios, in Little Venice (☎ **0289/22-649**), specializes in traditional Mykonian designs. **Vildiridis,** at 12 Matoyanni St. (☎ **0289/23-245**), has designs based on ancient jewelry as well as the very latest.

THE BEACHES Take a little time to ask around, as conditions change quickly on Mykonos, and then catch the bus or a caïque to the beach of your choice. For those who can't wait to hit the beach, the closest one to Hora is **Megali Ammos** ("Big Sand") about a 10-minute walk south of town. Don't be surprised if it's crowded, and don't expect to see topless bathing. Another better but crowded one is 2½ miles farther north at **Ayios Stephanos,** a major resort center with water sports.

Platis Yialos is your best bet because, though it's likely to be crowded, the bus runs every 15 minutes 8am–8pm, then every 30 minutes until midnight during the summer; from there, catch a caïque to the more distant beaches of Paradise, Super Paradise, Agrari, and Elia.

It's only a few little semiprivate beaches farther to **Paradise,** the island's most famous (and original nude) beach, which has regular bus as well as caïque service. It remains remarkably beautiful, despite the crowds and activity, with especially clear water, and it's still where "the beautiful people" seek each other out.

Super Paradise (Plindri) is accessible only by a very poor road, footpath, or caïque, so it's less crowded. It's still predominantly gay and nude, but clothed sunbathing by heterosexuals is tolerated. Farther east across the little peninsula is **Agrari,** a lovely cove sheltered by lush foliage, with a good little taverna.

Elia, a 45-minute caïque ride from Platis Yialos, is one of the island's best and largest beaches. It's usually one of the least crowded, though bus service from the north station will probably soon put an end to that. If it gets too crowded, head back west to Agrari.

The next major beach, **Kalo Livadi** ("Good Pasture"), a beautiful beach in an idyllic farming valley, is accessible by a scramble over the peninsula east from Elia and by bus from the north station in the summer; there's even a nice restaurant.

The last resort area on the southern coast accessible by bus from the north station is at **Kalafati,** a fishing village that was once the port for the ancient citadel of Mykonos. It's now dominated by the large Aphrodite Beach Hotel complex. Several miles farther east, accessible by a fairly good road from Kalafati, is **Lia,** which has fine sand, clear water, bamboo wind breaks, and a small taverna.

ACCOMMODATIONS

If you arrive by ferry, you'll be met by a throng of people hawking rooms, but most of these are up the hill from Hora and not especially pleasant. Accept one for one night only if you don't have a reservation and you're too exhausted for a lengthy hotel search.

Many hotels are fully booked in advance by tour groups or regular clientele, so reserve at least 1–3 months in advance. It's worth repeating that *Mykonos is a much easier and more pleasant place to visit in the spring or fall.* Hotel rates are sometimes nearly half the quoted high-season rate in April, May, and October.

If you want to save time and effort, contact the **Mykonos Accommmodations Center (MAC),** Enoplon Dinameon at Malamatenias (in Tria Pigadia), 846 00 Mykonos (☎ **0289/23-160** or 0289/23-408; fax 0289/24-137). It has a helpful multilingual staff who will correspond, talk by phone, or meet with you to determine the best accommodation for your budget. The charge is 15% of the rental or a 5,000-Dr ($21.30) minimum. You can also contact the parent company, **Accommodation Centers of Greece,** 7 Voulis St., 105 62 Athens (☎ **01/322-0000** or 01/322-3400; fax 0289/24-137).

In & Around Hora

There are a number of **pensions** and **rooms-to-let** in and around town, many of them larger, more comfortable, and with better views than the older hotels. Most of them don't serve breakfast, and some of them are quite a hike up the hill and not in the most fashionable neighborhoods. Try the two we list below first. If the **tourist office** (☎ **0289/23-900**) is open, check with them to see what's available.

Hotel Matina. 3 Fournakion St., Hora, 846 00 Mykonos. ☎ **0289/22-387** or 0289/24-501. 14 rms. 30,750 Dr ($130.90) double. Rates include breakfast. No credit cards.

This small hotel is inside a large garden that makes it especially quiet for its central location. The rooms are small but clean, modern, and comfortable.

Hotel Philippi. 32 Kaloyera St., Hora, 846 00 Mykonos. ☎ **0289/22-294** or 0289/22-295. 12 rms. 19,900 Dr ($84.70) double. No credit cards.

Each room in this homey little hotel is unique, so you may want to check yours out before accepting it. The owner tends a lush garden that often provides flowers for her son's restaurant, the elegant Philippi's, which can be reached through the garden.

K Hotels. P.O. Box 64, 846 00 Mykonos. ☎ **0289/23-435** or 0289/23-431. Fax 0289/ 23-455. 135 rms. A/C. 38,500 Dr ($163.95) double. Rates include breakfast. AE, EC, MC, V.

The four K Hotels (Kalypso, Kohili, Korali, and Kyma) form a complex just off the south beach road. Clean, modern, air-conditioned rooms are stacked on two levels to give views of the sea, hills, pool, or tennis courts. Each building has a small bar and breakfast lounge, and there's a common restaurant.

Kouros Apartment Hotel. Tagou, 846 00 Mykonos. ☎ **0289/25-381** or 0289/25-383. Fax 0289/25-379. 20 apts, 5 suites. TEL TV. 34,000 Dr ($144.70) apt for two; 54,500 Dr ($231.80) suite. Rates include full American breakfast. Children 11 and under stay in parents' unit for half price; infants under 2 stay free. AE, DC, EC, MC, V. Head north just outside town; it's above the road to Ayios Stephanos.

This new apartment hotel has spacious rooms, all with kitchenettes, large modern bathrooms, and large balconies with sea views. Its pool has fresh water, and the staff is friendly. Its cut rates for kids makes this a good place for families.

Maria and Mike Mitropia. Laka Sq., Hora, 846 00 Mykonos. ☎ **0289/23-528.** 20 rms, 13 with shower only. 15,000 Dr ($63.85) double without bath, 17,200 Dr ($73.20) double with shower only. Rates include breakfast. V.

Maria and Mike have tidy, comfortable rooms above Mike's locksmith shop in a good central location on Laka Square opposite the Mykonos Market. Write or call to reserve one of their quiet, good-value rooms.

⑤ Pension Stelios. 9 Apollonos St., Hora, 846 00 Mykonos. ☎ **0289/24-641.** 12 rms (all with shower). 21,500 Dr ($91.50) double. Rates include breakfast. No credit cards. Head near ferry pier on the northeast end of harbor; it's on the hill above the OTE office (take the broad stone steps above the road).

This place is conveniently located, especially for those interested in those destinations reached from the north bus stop, including the far east coast beaches. The rooms are clean and modern, with twin beds and balconies with good views.

Around the Island

There are hotels clustered around many of the more popular beaches on the island, but most people prefer to stay in town and commute to the beaches. Those who prefer the more serene beach scene can consider these suggestions:

There are private studios and simple pensions at both **Paradise** and **Super Paradise** beaches, but rooms are almost impossible to get, and prices more than double in July and August. Contact **MAC** (☎ 0289/23-160) or, for Super Paradise, **GATS Travel** (☎ 0289/22-404) for information on the rooms they represent. The tavernas at each beach may also have suggestions.

At **Kalafati,** the **Paradise Aphrodite Hotel** (☎ 0289/71-367), has a large pool, two restaurants, and 150 rooms, which are a good value in May, June, and Oct, when a double costs about 25,000 Dr ($106.40).

AT COSTA ILIOS   This village over a small cove on Ornos Bay is one of the most beautiful spots on the island, with its own beach, swimming pool, children's pool, and tennis court. Private homes, in the traditional style, of course, with accommodations for two to six people, with twice-weekly maid service, can be rented by the week for 248,000–375,000 Dr ($1,055–$1,595). Contact **LEMA,** 1 Odos Makras Stoas, 185 31 Piraeus (☎ **01/417-5988** or 01/417-6741; fax 01/417-9310); or **Maria Koulalia,** Costa Ilios, 846 00 Mykonos (☎ **0289/24-522**).

AT PLATIS YIALOS   This sandy, crescent-shaped beach is just a 15-minute bus or a half-hour walk from Hora, and it's the caïque stop for shuttles to Paradise, Super Paradise, Agrari, and Elia beaches. There are several excellent hotels, some very similarly named.

At the **۞ Hotel Petassos Bay,** Platis Yialos, 846 00 Mykonos (☎ **0289/23-737;** fax 0289/24-101), the 21 rooms—all with air-conditioning, minibars, and telephones—are large and comfortable and rent for 34,400 Dr ($146.40) double. Each has a balcony overlooking the beach which is less than 40 yards away. The hotel has a good-sized pool and sun deck, a Jacuzzi, gym, and sauna, and offers free round-trip transportation from the harbor or airport, safety boxes, and laundry service. The new seaside restaurant has the best view in town and a large wine list, and serves a big buffet breakfast. The gracious family that owns this hotel and their friendly multi-lingual staff win the star. The same family also owns the larger **Hotel Petassos Beach** next door and the **Petassos Town Hotel** in Hora.

The **Hotel Petinos,** Platis Yialos, 846 00 Mykonos (☎ **0289/22-127;** fax 0289/23-680), has 66 good, clean, attractive rooms with air-conditioning, telephones, TVs, and large balconies. The charge is 30,500 Dr ($129.80) double, including breakfast. The owners also have the smaller, slightly more expensive **Nissaki Hotel** up the hill, as well as the more luxurious **Petinos Beach Hotel,** which has a pool and doubles for 54,500 Dr ($231.90).

AT AYIOS STEPHANOS   The popular resort of Ayios Stephanos, about 2¹/₂ miles north of Hora, has a number of hotels, including the **Hotel Artemis** (☎ **0289/22-345**), near the beach and bus stop, with 23 rooms with bath for 21,000 Dr ($89.35), breakfast included; the small **Hotel Mina** (☎ **0289/23-024**), uphill behind the Artemis, with 15 doubles with bath for 13,500 Dr ($57.50); and the **Hotel Panorama** (☎ **0289/22-337**), about 80 yards from the beach, with 27 rooms with bath for 19,400 Dr ($82.40).

CAMPING   **Paradise Camping,** at Paradise Beach (☎ **0289/22-852;** fax 0289/24-350), charges 2,400 Dr ($10.20) per person, and 1,500 Dr ($6.40) for a tent. Campers get the use of showers, a bar, restaurant, minimarket, and transportation to and from the port and town. Rooms and bungalows are also available. MasterCard and Visa are accepted. A couple of miles west at Paranga Beach, **Paranga Beach Camping** (☎ **0289/24-578**) is a newer and nicer facility that offers all Paradise does and more—including cooking and laundry facilities. The fee is 2,400 Dr ($10.20) per person, and 1,500 Dr ($6.40) for a tent.

DINING

Mykonos has a number of excellent restaurants and plenty of fast food. There are several grocery stores where you can pick up snacks and picnic supplies. As usual, the harborside joints are mostly expensive and mediocre. One of the best places for a snack is practically a landmark—the **Alexis Snack Bar** on Taxi Square, which is open all hours and features a salad bar, as well as good inexpensive gyros, burgers, other snacks, and refreshments. The **Andreas Pouloudis Bakery,** 3 Florou Zuganeli St. (☎ **0289/22-304**), off Taxi Square in the little lane behind the gold store, has good cheese, spinach, and zucchini pies, as well as other baked treats. The more refined **Hibiscus Croissanterie,** 38 Kaloyera St. (☎ **0289/24-899**), near the Hotel Philippi, a good place for a light breakfast, has a large variety of croissants, good quiche Lorraine, and other authentic delights.

Ⓢ Niko's Taverna. Off the west end of harbor behind the town hall. No phone. Main courses 1,000–3,200 Dr ($4.25–$9.85); fresh fish 3,000 Dr ($12.75) for 300 grams. No credit cards. Daily noon–11pm. Turn left before the small quay and you'll find it on the left. GREEK.

This bustling little taverna has tables on both sides of the lane, and it's always busy with locals and tourists. The menu is standard taverna fare, with a little variety, inexpensive for Mykonos, and the staff is friendly and energetic, if often rushed.

Philippi. Off Matoyanni St. ☎ **0289/22-294.** Reservations recommended July–Aug. Main courses 2,200–5,000 Dr ($9.35–$21.25). AE, MC, V. Daily 7pm–1am. Walk up the "main street," past Kaloyera, and you'll find it on the right. GREEK/CONTINENTAL.

This restaurant in a quiet garden is one of the island's most special dining experiences. Its atmosphere is especially romantic. The menu includes French classics, curry, and superbly prepared traditional Greek dishes. The wine list is also impressive.

Sesame Kitchen. Tria Pigadia ("Three Wells") Sq. ☎ **0289/24-710.** Main courses 1,500–3,200 Dr ($6.40–$13.60). V. Daily 7pm–12:30am. Walk up the "main street," turn right on Enoplon Dinameon, and it's on the right next to the Naval Museum. GREEK/INTERNATIONAL/VEGETARIAN.

This small health-conscious taverna offers spinach, vegetable, cheese, and chicken pies baked fresh daily. There's a large variety of salads, brown rice, and soya dishes, including a vegetable moussaka, and lightly grilled and seasoned meat dishes.

To Steki Manthos. Tourlos Beach. ☎ **0289/23-435.** Main courses 1,400–3,600 Dr ($5.95–$15.30). No credit cards. Daily 9:30am–3pm and 7pm–1am. Drive, take the bus (to the Yephiraki stop), or walk north toward Ayios Stephanos. INTERNATIONAL.

This excellent place is well worth the 15-minute hike. It has a large and varied menu, a gifted chef, and a fine view of the sea and the nearby cruise-ship pier.

MYKONOS AFTER DARK

Mykonos has the liveliest, most abundant, and most chameleonlike nightlife in the Aegean. Don't be surprised if the places we suggest have closed, moved, or changed their name or image.

Catch the sunset in one of the sophisticated bars in Little Venice. The **Kastro** (☎ 0289/23-070), near the Paraportiani Church, is famous for classical music and frozen daiquiris. If you find it too crowded or tame, sashay on along to the **Caprice,** which also has a seaside perch and rocks a little harder, or across the street to **Diva.** The **Montparnasse** (☎ 0289/23-719), on the same lane, is cozier, with classical music and Toulouse-Lautrec posters. The **Veranda** (☎ 0289/23-290), in an old mansion overlooking the water with a good view of the windmills, is as relaxing as its name implies.

If all this just isn't quite up to your speed, you should probably hit "Main Street," starting near the harbor with **Pierro's,** which rocks all night long to American and European music. The **Anchor** plays blues, jazz, and classic rock for its 30-something clients. **Argo** (☎ 0289/24-674) is considered especially hip. **Stavros Irish Bar,** behind the town hall (☎ 0289/23-867), is still among the wildest places on the island. The **Windmill Disco** draws a younger crowd more interested in actually getting to know each other before anything significant happens. And if you'd like to sample some Greek music and dancing, **Thalami,** a small club underneath the town hall (☎ 0289/23-291), may have room for you to experience something very nearly authentic.

The **City Club** has a nightly transvestite show, and maybe we saw part of it. Who can be sure on Mykonos? The **Factory,** near the windmills, is the place for gay striptease.

AN EXCURSION TO THE ISLAND OF DELOS

The ancient Greeks considered this small island the holiest of sanctuaries—the place where, according to myth, Leto gave birth to Artemis and Apollo. Though it has suffered much theft, pillaging, and wanton destruction over the last two millennia, it's still one of the most remarkable archeological preserves in the world. Just as in ancient times people were not allowed to die or be born on the sacred island, today they are not allowed to spend the night, and the site can be visited only between the hours of 8:30am and 3pm.

ARRIVING/DEPARTING   Delos can be visited by sea only. Most people visit on excursion boats from nearby Mykonos, though there are excursions from other neighboring islands, and Delos is a prominent stop for cruise ships and yachts. From Mykonos, organized guided and unguided excursions leave Tues–Sun from the west end of the harbor; the trip takes about 40 minutes and costs about 2,750 Dr ($11.70) round-trip for transportation alone. **Yiannakis Tours** (☎ **0289/22-089**) offers guided tours for 8,500 Dr ($36.15) that depart at 9 or 10am and return at 12:30 or 2pm.

Note: We recommend the earliest possible departure, especially in the summer, when the afternoon heat gets intense and the crowds get worse. Sturdy shoes and water are necessary; a hat or cap and food are advised. (There's a cafe near the museum, but the prices are high and the quality is poor.)

What to See & Do

The 3 hours allotted by most excursion boats should be enough for all except the most avid archeology enthusiasts to explore the site. To the left (north) of the new jetty where your boat will dock is the **Sacred Harbor,** now too silted in for use, where pilgrims, merchants, and sailors from throughout the Mediterranean used to land.

Entrance to the site costs 1,500 Dr ($6.40) (unless it was included in your tour), and at the ticket kiosk you'll see a number of site plans and picture guides for sale. If you're on your own and have the energy, you may want to head up to **Mount Kythnos,** the highest point on the island, for an overview of the site and a fine view of the neighboring Cyclades.

Nearest the jetty is the **Agora of the Competialists,** built in the 2nd century B.C., where Roman citizens, mostly former slaves, worshipped the minor "crossroad" deities associated with the Greek god Hermes, patron of travelers and commerce. From the far left corner of this "square," the **Sacred Way,** once lined with statues and votive monuments, leads north toward the **Sanctuary of Apollo,** which was in ancient times crowded with temples, altars, statues, and votive offerings.

The island reached its economic and political peak during the Hellenistic and Roman eras; the scattered remains of theaters, reservoirs, statuary, and residential buildings attest to its prominence. Near the new harbor in the **House of Cleopatra,** headless statues eloquently express the sad centuries of abuse and neglect since the island fell from grace and became the domain of archeologists, tourists, guides, and lizards.

IOS

One of the Mediterranean's premier party islands is 107 nautical miles southeast of Piraeus, midway between Paros and Santorini. In the summer most people over 25 will find it tiresomely unrestrained, but it remains an attractive island with a particularly handsome hilltop Hora.

Some locals have worked very hard in recent years to save their island from party animals. There are still a few problems: Theft is still common; accept the portside travel agents' offer of free luggage storage and safes for your valuables. Female travelers should exercise caution—sexual assault is not unheard of. Everyone should be aware that *bomba* (illegally brewed booze) is still sometimes served on Ios, so be careful in bars where the prices seem to be too good and your fellow drinkers are getting too merry too fast. *Above all, never accept a "free" drink, unless you're fond of waking up with a raging hangover.* Overcrowding in the summer exacerbates the local water shortage and can lead to toilet overload (with the resulting powerful stench).

ESSENTIALS

ARRIVING/DEPARTING   By Sea   There is one ferry daily (more frequently in the summer) from Piraeus; service is irregular and by several carriers, so check the schedules in Athens (☎ 171 or 01/451-1311) or with the Ios Port Police (☎ 0286/91-264). **Ilio Lines** (☎ 01/422-4772 in Athens or 0294/22-888 in Rafina) has hydrofoil service daily except Saturday from Rafina. There are daily (several times daily in the summer) ferry connections with Mykonos, Paros, and Santorini, as well as daily hydrofoil connections with the same islands in the summer. There are ferry connections twice a week with Sifnos.

VISITOR INFORMATION   The helpful **Ios Tourist Information Office** (☎ **0286/91-029**) operates an office on the port in summer, daily 7am–2am, and a main office near the bus stop in Hora (☎ **0286/91-028**), open daily 6am–2am in summer; they reserve rooms and hotels, sell tickets for all boat lines, and will help you make a collect phone call. Ferry schedules are posted. The most knowledgeable and helpful travel agency is **Acteon Travel,** the local American Express representative, on the port square and at Milopotas Beach (☎ **0286/91-343** or 0286/91-318; fax 0286/91-088), usually open until 10:30pm, which can assist you with information and maps, and in making calls, changing money, finding accommodations, booking tickets, and storing luggage.

FAST FACTS   The **police station** (☎ 0286/91-22) is across from the bus stop in Hora. The **post office**, open Mon–Fri 8am–2pm, is a couple of blocks south of the main square and church. The **telephone center** (**OTE**) is farther south, off the road to Milopotas Beach, up from the police station; collect calls can be booked Mon–Fri 7:30am–1pm, though the OTE is open until 10pm in summer. For **medical emergencies** call 0286/91-227; there's a doctor in Hora (☎ 0286/91-545). There are three **banks** near the main square, open Mon–Fri 8am–2:30pm, with extended hours in summer.

GETTING AROUND   There's good **bus service** between the port of Yialos, Hora, and Milopotas Beach approximately every half hour 8am–midnight for 180 Dr (80¢). You can walk the same route, though the 30-minute climb up to Hora along the stepped pedestrian route can be exhausting under the hot sun. The walk down is pleasant, but be careful at night—the path is poorly lit. Travel agents also offer private bus tours. **Kritikakis Tours** (☎ **0286/91-3950**) has a boat trip to Maganari Beach twice daily in July and August for about 2,250 Dr ($10) round-trip.

   Motorbikes and **cars** are also available, though they're not an especially good idea on an island where drunk drivers are all too common and the roads are rough and steep. **Rent A Reliable Car,** on the south side of the port (☎ **0286/91-047**), has mopeds from about 5,000 Dr ($21.30) a day, including a tankful of gas, a helmet (which you should accept and wear), and third-party insurance only (if you damage the bike, you pay).

WHAT TO SEE & DO

Yialos is a busy but fairly pleasant port with tourist services, good accommodations, a good grocery store, and a variety of eating establishments. The **town beach,** a 5-minute stroll west of the harbor, is surprisingly pleasant but often crowded. A 20-minute hike over the headland beyond it will take you to **Koumbara Beach,** which is smaller, usually less crowded, and predominantly nude, with an okay taverna.

   Most young revelers will head immediately up to the hill to **Hora** (Ios town), which is party headquarters at night but still one of the Cyclades' more charming whitewashed capitals. Parts of the ancient walls and a Venetian fortress built in 1400 can still be seen, though most people's attention is attracted by the clubs, fashion boutiques, and jewelry shops that spring up.

Nine out of 10 visitors never make it any farther than **Milopotamos Beach,** half a mile southeast, which is usually shortened to **Milopotas** and almost universally considered the best beach in the Cyclades. Though it's constantly crowded, local efforts to keep the beach and water clean seem to be successful.

Ayios Theodotis Beach, which is mainly nudist, is on the east coast and can be reached by bus from Yialos and Hora only in the summer. The south-coast beach at **Manganari** is a more developed resort, popular with serious over-all tanners, which is best reached by excursion caïques from Yialos that depart about 10am and return late in the afternoon. It's also accessible by a rather rough road south from Milopotas. The new **Manganari Bungalow Resort** (☎ **0286/91-200**) has some fairly luxurious accommodations, a restaurant, and a nightclub.

ACCOMMODATIONS

Ios is mobbed during high season, but if you simply *must* see for yourself, reservations are imperative. If you arrive without one, listen to the offers made to you on arrival at the port. Travel agents and the police can also help you find a room. The police have a complete list of accommodations, with official prices, and will help you if you think you're being overcharged.

Acteon Hotel. Yialos, 84 001 Ios. ☎ **0286/91-343.** Fax 0286/91-088. 15 rms. 9,800 Dr ($41.70) double. AE, MC, V.

Conveniently located above the helpful Acteon Travel, the rooms are clean and reasonably priced, a bargain for last-minute arrivals. The late-night ferries and nearby cafes may prove too noisy for light sleepers.

Aphroditi Hotel. Hora, 84 001 Ios. ☎ **0286/91-546.** 12 rms. 12,800 Dr ($54.50) double. No credit cards.

The island's only year-round hotel is on the west side of Hora, on the hill opposite the big church. The rooms are clean and modern, with marble floors.

Francesco's. Hora, 84 001 Ios. ☎ **0286/91-223.** 35 rms, 30 with bath (shower). 9,800 Dr ($43.55) double with bath.

Francesco has renovated the "last" house above Hora, turning a 300-year-old mansion into a charming collection of rooms with a bar and several gathering spaces, some with splendid views. The rooms are modern, clean, and comfortable, far enough above the "jungle" for a modicum of quiet.

Golden Sun. Yialos–Hora road, 84 001 Ios. ☎ **0286/91-110.** 17 rms. 10,800 Dr ($48) double. V.

John and Koula Kladis recently moved back home from New Jersey and built this handsome place 300 yards up from the port on the pedestrian path. The rooms are large, comfortable, and especially clean. It's far enough above the port and off the road for quiet and only a 10-minute walk down from Hora, for those who want to enjoy the nightlife, then get some sleep.

Hotel Mare-Monte. Ormos, 84 001 Ios. ☎ **0286/91-564.** 30 rms. 19,500 Dr ($86.65) double. Rates include breakfast. V.

One of the best conventional hotels is on the town beach, left (south) from the harbor. The rooms are large and clean, with balconies and sea views. The breakfast lounge is especially pleasant.

At Milopotas Beach

Milopotas Beach is an increasingly popular place to stay, and new hotels are springing up like mushrooms. There are two excellent campgrounds. **Far Out Camping** (☎ **0286/91-468**), probably the best in Greece, has an air-conditioned restaurant and bar, a minimarket, kitchen facilities, handicapped-access toilets, a swimming pool, water-sports facilities, and an athletic center with regulation tennis, volleyball, basketball, and squash courts—plus free transfer from the port. Waste water is treated by a state-of-the-art system and recycled to trees and shrubs, which beautify and cool. Rates are 1,400 Dr ($6.20) per person plus 400 Dr ($1.80) per tent, and 4,500 Dr ($20) per person in comfortable bungalows. **Stars** (☎ **0286/91-302**), near the beach, offers a restaurant, snack bar, disco, bar, minimarket, showers, and lockers for 1,500 Dr ($6.40) per person and 600 Dr ($2.65) per tent. Both places take Amex, MasterCard, and Visa.

✪ **Far Out Hotel.** Milopotas, 84 001 Ios. ☎ **0286/91-446,** or 0286/91-560 in winter. 45 rms (with shower). TEL. 20,800 Dr ($92.45) double. AE, MC, V.

The name comes from the once-popular expression of enthusiastic approval, not the location, which is only 5 minutes above the beach. There's a good pool, a friendly and helpful staff, and free transportation to and from the port. The rooms are handsomely furnished, quite luxurious for Ios, all with sea views.

DINING

Ios isn't famous for good food, but prices are generally reasonable because eateries must try to compete with the grocery stores and bakeries where most tourists buy their food. At Milopotas Beach we recommend **Drakos Taverna**—no. 1 at the north end of the beach (open 9am–midnight) and no. 2 at the south end (open 11am–midnight), where you'll find fresh fish and grilled meat for about 3,000–3,500 Dr ($13.35–$15.55) per person.

Enigma Cafe-Bar. Yialos. ☎ **0286/91-047.** Main courses 900–2,300 Dr ($4–$10.20); breakfast 800–1,700 Dr ($3.55–$7.55). No credit cards. Daily 7am–1am. Head to the far right of the central square. FAST FOOD.

There's plenty of fast food on the port, but the best selection and quality is at this attractive cafe, which becomes a lively bar in the evenings. The selection of drinks is among the best on the island.

The Mills Taverna. Hora. ☎ **0286/91-284.** Main courses 1,000–3,000 Dr ($4.45–$13.35). No credit cards. Daily 6pm–midnight. GREEK.

Climb to the highest point in town, opposite the windmills, to find classic Greek food at its best. The village salad is made with misithra or xino cheese, a delicious alternative to the usual feta. The pork souvlaki with ripe tomatoes is tender and savory, and the stuffed eggplant is excellent.

The Nest. Hora. No phone. Main courses 700–1,700 Dr ($3.10–$7.55). No credit cards. Daily 12:20–3:30pm and 5pm–midnight. Walk northeast of the main square; it's across from the pharmacy. GREEK.

This unpretentious budget place consistently wins the approval of locals and tourists. You'll find big portions of well-prepared typical Greek fare with a few Italian dishes.

Ouzeri 33. Yialos. No phone. Main courses 1,000–2,800 Dr ($4.45–$12.45). No credit cards. Turn left (south) from the harbor and it's before the town beach. SEAFOOD.

According to locals, this homely and somewhat erratic place serves the best seafood on the island.

IOS AFTER DARK

Ios often seems like one big all-night party. Wander the labyrinth of Hora's older village—you won't have to go inside to learn what kind of music a place is playing. The last time we were there **Taboo,** the **Blue Note,** and **John's Electric,** all on or near the main square (difficult to say because of the roiling crowd), were joining in a cacaphony that defies description. One of the hottest spots in town was **Sweet Irish Dream**—have we forgotten to say that Ios is often said to be an acronym for Ireland Over Seas? The **Ios Club,** at the top of town, was once again operational and playing classical music until dusk; later it becomes a disco.

On the road to Milopotas, the **Scorpion** is one of the oldest nightclubs on the island, and the **Slammer Bar** has plenty of loud music and heavy action. The beach itself is often one all-night party. Down in Yialos things are a bit more sedate, but the **Enigma** plays good music and serves a wide variety of drinks, and the **Frog Club** is jumping. The **Marina Bar,** on the beach, plays Greek music.

SANTORINI (THIRA)

Santorini (Thira), one of the most southerly and the most spectacular of the Cyclades, lies 126 nautical miles southeast of Piraeus. Evidence suggests that the island may have been home to the lost colony of Atlantis. Thousands of individual and group tourists sail into the port of Athenios—into the huge caldera left by the eruption of a titanic volcano over 3,600 years ago. They spend a few nights, wandering through the bustling capital of Fira, visiting the premier archeological site at Akrotiri, seeing the sunset at Ia, and maybe swimming at one of the island's black-sand beaches.

ESSENTIALS

ARRIVING/DEPARTING   By Air   Olympic Airways has several (six in the high season) daily flights between Athens and the airport at Monolithos, which also receives European charters. There are also daily connections with Mykonos, three or four times a week with Rhodes, two or three times a week with Iraklion, Crete, and even three times a week during the high season with Thessaloniki. For schedule information and reservations, check with the **Olympic Airways** office on Ayiou Athanassiou Street (☎ **0286/22-493,** or 01/961-6161 in Athens).

By Sea   There is **ferry** service at least twice daily from Piraeus by several companies; the trip takes 10–12 hours, but it's relaxing and a good opportunity to see most of the rest of the Cyclades. There are ferry connections several times a day with Ios, Mykonos, and Paros. Check the schedules with Tourist Information in Athens (☎ 171) or the Port Authority in Piraeus (☎ 01/451-1311) or Santorini (☎ 0286/22-239). There are almost daily **excursion boats** from Iraklio, Crete, for about 5,000 Dr ($21.25), but because this is an an open-sea route the trip can be an ordeal in bad weather.

The high-speed hydrofoil *Nearchos* connects Santorini with Ios, Paros, Mykonos, and Iraklio, Crete, three times weekly in low season, almost daily in high season, if the winds aren't too strong. Contact a travel agent for schedule information. Most ferry tickets can be purchased at **Nomikos Travel** (☎ **0286/23-660**) with offices in Fira, Karterados, and Perissa.

VISITOR INFORMATION   There is no official government tourist office, but there are a number of helpful travel agencies. We recommend **Kamari Tours,** 2 blocks south of the main square on the right (☎ **0286/22-666;** fax 0286/ 22-971), which offers day trips to most of the island's sites and can help you find a room and rent a moped; **Damigos Tours,** on the main square (☎ **0286/22-504;**

fax 0286/22-266), the first established in Fira, which offers excellent guided tours at slightly lower prices; and **Nomikos Tours** (☎ **0286/23-660;** fax 0286/23-666), which has three helpful offices in Fira.

GETTING AROUND   By Bus   Santorini has very good bus service. The island's central **bus station** is just south of the main square in Fira. Schedules are posted on the wall of the office above it; most routes are serviced every half hour 7am–11pm in the summer, less frequently off-season.

By Car   Most travel agents will be able to help you rent a car. You might find that a local company such as **Zeus** (☎ **0286/24-013**) will offer better prices, though the quality might be a bit lower. Of the better-known agencies, we recommend **Budget Rent-A-Car,** a block below the bus-stop square in Fira (☎ **0286/22-900;** fax 0286/ 22-887), where a four-seat Fiat Panda should cost about 19,500 Dr ($82.95) a day, with unlimited mileage.

By Moped   The roads on the island are notoriously treacherous, narrow, and winding, and local drivers have little respect for them, so there are a number of serious moped accidents and several fatalities every year. If you're determined to use two-wheeled transportation, expect to pay about 3,000–6,000 Dr ($12.75–$25.55) per day, depending on the size and season.

By Taxi   The **taxi station** is just south of the main square (☎ **0286/22-555**), though in high season you should book ahead by phone. The drivers are better organized here than elsewhere, but prices are standard from point to point. If you call for a taxi outside Fira, you're required to pay the fare from there to your pickup point, though you can sometimes find one that has dropped off a passenger.

FAST FACTS: FIRA

American Express   The X-Ray Kilo Travel Service, on the main square (☎ 0286/ 22-624; fax 0286/23-600), is the American Express representative on Santorini.

Banks   The National Bank (open Mon–Fri 8am–2pm) is a block south from the main square on the right near the taxi station. Many travel agents also change money; most are open daily 8am–9:30pm.

Hospital   The small Health Clinic is on the southeast edge of town on Ayiou Athanassiou Street (☎ 0286/22-237), to the left after the children's playground.

Police   The police station is on I. Dekigala Street (☎ 0286/22-649), several blocks south of the main square, on the left. The port police can be reached at 0286/ 22-239.

Post Office   The post office (☎ 0286/22-238; fax 0286/22-698), open Mon–Fri 8am–1pm, is up to the right from the bus station.

Telephones   The telephone center (OTE) is just off Ypapantis Street ("Gold Street"), up from the post office.

WHAT TO SEE & DO

The island's west coast is a sheer, crescent-shaped cliff with geologic layers of brick-red, charcoal, gray, pink, and pale green. It overlooks the **caldera,** the 6-mile-wide crater of the volcano that erupted here in 1647 B.C. The eruption buried the Minoan city of Akrotiri, the ruins of which were unearthed in the 1860s. The island was named Thira in the 10th century B.C. in honor of a Spartan invader, though Venetian crusaders later gave it the name most of us know it by, Santorini (after Saint Irene, the island's patron saint, who died here in A.D. 304).

   Fira is the island's hilltop capital and shopping mecca. If you want to head straight for the famous view, just climb the hill and it will be waiting for you along **Ypapantis**

Street ("Gold Street"); the shopping is to the right, and the **Cathedral of Panayia Ypapantis** is to the left. If you're interested in fine jewelry, the prices are just a little higher than they are in Athens, but the selection is fantastic. **Porphyra,** in the Fabrica Shopping Center near the cathedral (☎ **0286/22-981**), has some impressive work. Santorini's best-known jeweler is probably **Kostas Antoniou,** on Ayiou Ioannou Street (☎ **0286/22-633**), north of the cable-car station. And there are plenty of shops between the two.

The pretty village of **Pirgos** ("Tower") is the oldest and highest settlement on the island, worth a visit for its charming churches and the ruins of old houses that cling to the ruins of the Venetian castle. **Ia** is the most beautiful and pleasantly unconventional village on the island, if not in the whole Cyclades, and world famous for its spectacular sunsets (head for the ruined **Lontza Castle** for the best view).

The **beaches** on Santorini are not the best. **Monolithos,** near the end of the road to the airport, has a small beach and a couple of tavernas. **Kamari,** a little over halfway down the coast, has the best beach on the island, and it's also the best developed beach, lined its entire length by hotels, tavernas, restaurants, shops, and clubs. On the way to Kamari from Fira you can stop at **Canava Roussos** (☎ **0286/31-278**) to sample their reasonably priced wines. Though the black pebbled beach at Kamari is often overcrowded, the resort itself remains quite pleasant, especially at night.

Near Kamari are the ruins of **Ancient Thira,** first inhabited by the Dorians in the 9th century B.C., though most of the buildings date from the Hellenistic era when the site was occupied by Ptolemaic forces. It's open Tues–Sat 9am–2:30pm and Sun and holidays 9am–1pm. You can get there by taxi or various excursions from Fira, including an ascent by mule, or you can hike—but if you do, wear sturdy shoes and bring food and water.

Last and most impressive is the archeological site of **Akrotiri,** near the southwestern end of the crescent, which has given the world a fascinating look at daily Minoan life. Akrotiri can be reached by public bus or private bus tour; **Damigos Tours,** on the main square (☎ **0286/22-504**), has expert and entertaining guides. Admission costs 1,500 Dr ($6.40), and the site is open daily 8:30am–3pm, but because the excavation is protected by a greenhouselike roof it gets quite hot by midday, so go as early as possible. You can stop at the **Boutari winery** (☎ **0286/81-011**) afterward to sample some of this excellent company's fare.

ACCOMMODATIONS

Santorini is packed in July and August, so if you plan a summer visit, make a reservation with a deposit at least 2 months in advance or be prepared to accept pot luck. Don't accept rooms offered at the port unless you're exhausted and don't care how remote the village is that you wake up in in the morning. If you come between April and mid-June or in September or October, when the island is less crowded and far more pleasant, the rates can be nearly half the high-season rates we quote.

Hotel Anemones. Ia, 847 02 Santorini. ☎ 0286/71-220. 10 rms. 12,500 Dr ($53.20) double. No credit cards.

Here you'll get comfortable, modern rooms at a good price, and a superb view from the breakfast room.

Hotel Finikia. Finikia, 847 02 Santorini. ☎ 0286/71-373, or 01/654-7944 in Athens. Fax 0286/71-338. 15 rms. 17,500 Dr ($74.45) double. MC, V.

This new complex in the traditional cubic style just east of Ia has a good pool. Each room has its own personality and its own small front patio garden.

S Loucas Hotel. Fira, 847 00 Santorini. ☎ **0286/22-480** or 0286/22-680. Fax 0286/24-882. 20 rms. A/C TV TEL. 25,600 Dr ($108.95) double. Rates include breakfast. MC, V.

This is one of the oldest and best hotels on the caldera, with barrel-ceilinged "caves" built to prevent collapse during an earthquake. All rooms have been newly renovated, some enlarged and furnished with handsome new lively blue furniture, with shared patios overlooking the caldera. It's an excellent value for the location, amenities, and view.

Matina Hotel. Kamari Beach, 847 00 Santorini. ☎ **0286/31-491.** Fax 0286/31-860. 27 rms. 19,450 Dr ($82.75) double in the annex (without breakfast); 24,500 Dr ($104.25) double in the main hotel (with breakfast). AE, EC, MC, V.

The Matina is a thoroughly modern hotel a 2-minute walk from the beach. If it's booked, ask about the nearby annex, Pension Matina.

Pension Blue Sky. Fira, 847 00 Santorini. ☎ **0286/23-400.** 25 rms. 20,750 Dr ($88.30) double. Walk down past the Pelican Hotel northeast off the main square, turn left at the supermarket, take the next right, and it's about 100 yards down on the right.

This good new hotel just below town has a swimming pool. If they're full, ask about the Pension Soula across the street.

Rooms Hesperides. Kamari, 847 00 Santorini. ☎ **0286/31-185.** 17 rms. 12,500 Dr ($53.20) double. No credit cards.

Little English is spoken at this neat, modern pension in the middle of the pistachio orchard across from the Akis Hotel in town, but the owners are very friendly and hospitable. Excavations around the pension have revealed buried Byzantine ruins.

Camping

Kamari Camping (☎ **0286/32-452** or 0286/31-453) is an attractive facility 800 yards from the beach with 590 sites for 2,000 Dr ($8.50) per person, a tourist information center, restaurant, cafeteria, minimarket, laundry, hot showers, public telephone, and bus service. There's an excellent campsite at **Camping Santorini** (☎ **0286/22-944**), south of Fira.

DINING

In Fira, generally the closer you are to the cable car, the steeper the prices and the lower the quality. The better restaurants on Gold Street are nearer the cathedral: **Alexandria, Aris, Meridiana, Selene,** and **Sphinx.**

Agiris Taverna. Kamari village. ☎ **0286/31-795.** Main courses 1,100–4,000 Dr ($5.10–$13.60). V. Daily 6pm–midnight. GREEK.

The best Greek food is in the village opposite the main church. This old family-run taverna depends on a loyal local clientele, so the quality of the authentic food must be kept high. Stuffed chicken is one of the delicious specialties.

Aris Restaurant. Ayiou Mina St., Fira. ☎ **0286/22-840.** Main courses 1,250–3,000 Dr ($5.30–$12.75). MC, V. Daily noon–1am. GREEK/INTERNATIONAL.

This excellent restaurant is on the lower pedestrian street, south of the donkey path down to Skala, below the Loucas Hotel. The chef was formerly at the Athens Hilton, and though the dishes are mainly Greek, the cooking is more updated and refined. The mezedes are delicious, especially the saganaki made with graviera cheese, and the dish-baked moussaka is superb. Try Aris Ziras's own white house wine.

Barbara's Cafe-Brasserie. In the Fabrica Shopping Center, Fira. Breakfast 600–1,500 Dr ($2.55–$6.40); sandwiches 750–1,500 Dr ($3.20–$6.40). No credit cards. Daily 9am–1am. INTERNATIONAL.

One of the best places for breakfast or a light lunch is up from the bus station toward the cathedral. After 7pm it becomes one of the least expensive bars in town, with beer for 500 Dr ($2.15) and wine by the glass for 600 Dr ($2.55).

✪ **Camille Stephani.** Kamari Beach. ☎ **0286/31-716.** Reservations recommended July–Sept. Main courses 2,250–5,000 Dr ($9.55–$21.25). AE, DC, MC, V. Daily 1–4pm and 6:30pm–midnight. GREEK/INTERNATIONAL.

Even if you're not staying at Kamari, this excellent more formal restaurant on the north end of the beach, 500 yards from the bus stop, will make the trip worthwhile, and you can take a moonlight stroll along the beach afterward. The special is a tender beef filet with green pepper in madeira sauce.

Katina Fish-Taverna. Port of Ia. ☎ **0286/71-280.** Main courses 1,250–3,500 Dr ($5.30–$14.90). No credit cards. Daily 11am–1am. SEAFOOD.

One of the best places to eat in Ia isn't in town but rather down in the port of Ammoudi, which is best reached by donkey. Katina Pagoni is considered one of the very best local cooks, and the setting beside the glittering Aegean is very romantic.

✪ **Meridiana Restaurant Bar.** In the Fabrica Shopping Center, Ypapantis St., Fira. ☎ **0286/23-427.** Reservations recommended for dinner in summer. Main courses 2,800–8,000 Dr ($11.90–$34.05). AE, MC, V. Daily 11am–3pm and 7pm–1am. INTERNATIONAL.

This excellent restaurant on the second story of the Fabrica Shopping Center on Gold Street near the cathedral has views of both the caldera and the town and island. The emphasis is on the food, which is meticulously prepared with little oil and salt so that the subtle flavors of the distinctive spices can come through. The desserts are also excellent.

🅢 **Naoussa Restaurant.** In the Lagouder Shopping Center, Fira. ☎ **0286/24-869.** Main courses 450–1,250 Dr ($1.90–$5.30). V. Daily noon–midnight. GREEK/INTERNATIONAL.

This friendly family-run place is above the shopping lane above the main street north of the central square toward the cable car station. The menu isn't large, but it includes quite a variety, including a Mexican salad, five kinds of spaghetti, shrimp flambé, souvlaki oriental, chicken américaine, and mixed grill, all in generous portions.

SANTORINI AFTER DARK

Most people will want to start the evening with a drink on the caldera watching the sunset. **Franco's** (☎ 0286/22-881) is still the most famous place for this magic hour, but drinks are expensive. **Archipelago** (☎ 0286/23-673) and the **Canava Cafe** (☎ 0286/22-565) also have good views, but for more reasonable prices and the same fantastic view continue on down below the Loucas Hotel to the **Renaissance Bar** (☎ 0286/22-880).

Most of the action is north and west of the main square. Underneath the square, the **Kirathira Bar** plays jazz at a level that permits conversation. The **Town Club** appeals to clean-cut rockers, while the **Two Brothers** pulls in the biggest, chummiest crowd on the island. For Greek music find the **Apocalypse Club,** or **Bar 33** for bouzouki. Discos come and go; follow your ears to find them. The **Koo Club** is the biggest, and **Enigma** is still popular with those interested in good music.

In Ia, **Melissa's Piano Bar** is an excellent place to station yourself for the sunset, and a good place for an interesting light meal. **Zorba's** is another good cliffside pub. Kamari has its share of bars. The **Yellow Donkey Disco** (☎ 0286/31-462) is popular with younger partiers, and the more sophisticated usually seek the chic **Valentino's,** near the bus stop.

SIFNOS

Sifnos, 93 nautical miles southeast of Piraeus, is the most beautiful of the western Cyclades. It's a favorite destination for Greeks who want to escape foreign tourists on the other islands, but it's still very crowded in July and August. It's full of charm, tranquillity, well-tended fields, good restaurants, and easy-going people, both locals and visitors.

ESSENTIALS

ARRIVING/DEPARTING   There's at least one boat daily from Piraeus, in addition to daily (twice daily in summer) connections to the other western Cyclades, Serifos and Milos, and less frequently to Kimolos and Kythnos. There are ferry connections four times a week with Santorini; three times a week with Folegandros, Ios, and Sikinos; and once a week with Andros, Crete, Mykonos, Paros, Rafina, Syros, and Tinos. There's also a once-weekly connection with the Dodecannese islands of Karpathos, Kassos, Rhodes, and Symi. Contact the Port Authority in Piraeus (☎ 143 or 01/451-1131) or in Sifnos (☎ 0284/31-617) for information.

VISITOR INFORMATION   Your first stop should be the excellent **Aegean Thesaurus Travel and Tourism** office on the port (☎ 0284/31-804) or **Siphanto Travel** (☎ 0284/32-034; fax 0284/31-024), where you can book a room, buy ferry tickets, rent a car or motorbike, arrange excursions, and leave your luggage.

FAST FACTS   Tourist services are centered around the main square, **Platia Iroon** ("Heroes Square") in Apollonia. The **post office** (☎ 0284/31-329) is open Mon–Fri 8am–3pm, plus Sat–Sun 9am–1:30pm in summer. The **National Bank** (☎ 0284/31-237) is open Mon–Thurs 8am–2pm and Fri 8am–1:30pm. The **telephone center (OTE),** just down the vehicle road, is open daily 8am–3pm, and in summer also 5–10pm. (The news kiosk on the square has a metered phone for after-hours calls.) The **police station** (☎ 0284/31-210) is just east of the square, and a **first-aid station** is nearby; for **medical emergencies,** phone 0284/31-315.

GETTING AROUND   Getting around Sifnos is one of its pleasures—many visitors come for the wonderful hiking and mountain trails. We don't think a car or moped is necessary, but **cars** can be rented at **FS** (☎ 0284/31-795) and **Aegean Thesaurus** (☎ 0284/31-145) in Apollonia, or in Kamares at **Siphanto Travel** (☎ 0284/32-034) or **Sifnos Car** (☎ 0284/31-793). Apollonia has a few moped dealers; try **Yoni's** (☎ 0284/31-155) on the main square or **Easy Rider** (☎ 0284/31-001) on the road circling the village.

By Bus   Apollonia's Heroes Square is the central **bus stop** for the island. The bus system is fairly efficient; they run regularly to and from the port at Kamares, north to Artemonas, east to Kastro, and south to Faros and Platis Yialos.

By Taxi   Apollonia's Heroes Square is also the main taxi stand, though there aren't many of them on the island.

WHAT TO SEE & DO

Kamares, on the west coast, is the island's port and will be most visitors' introduction to Sifnos. The town beach is the focal point of most people's day, but don't miss the shops, many of which are filled with the island's best-known contemporary product, ceramics. One of the most interesting is the ceramics workshop of **Antonis Kalogirou,** on the main harborside lane (☎ **0284/31-651**).

Most people, however, will hop on the first bus up to **Apollonia,** the capital, which is of course sometimes called Hora. The 3-mile drive between Kamares and Apollonia reveals the island's agricultural heart. Small Cycladic farmhouses are scattered throughout, most sporting geraniums, hibiscus, or apricot trees.

Apollonia's **Heroes' Square** (Platia Iroon), site of a monument to Sifnos's World War II veterans, is the transportation hub of the island where its vehicle roads converge. From it, gently sloped, winding pedestrian paths of flagstone and marble lead through this beautiful village. Along the village's only car route are a few shops, a few small markets with island maps, a restaurant or two, and the island's hangout, Lakis Kafeneion.

Faros is a small resort on the east coast with some good budget accommodations and tavernas, a reliable base if you don't find a room elswhere. **Apokofto** has a good long sand beach, and nude bathing is permitted at nearby **Fasolou.**

Platis Yialos is the biggest and southernmost of the west-coast beaches. It's a long stretch of fine tan sand lining a shallow cove that's perfect for swimming laps, and is a great place for families, particularly in late May, June, and September when the sea is warm but calm.

ACCOMMODATIONS

Many young Athenians vacation on Sifnos, particularly on summer weekends, and it can be very difficult to find a room. If you plan to be in Kamares during high season, for example, be sure to make reservations by May. **Aegean Thesaurus** (☎ and fax **0284/32-190**) can place two in a room in a private house with your own bathroom, in a studio with a kitchenette, or in other accommodations ranging up to a stylish villa. If you want to rough it, try **Community Camping** (☎ **0284/31-786**). It's just 600 yards from the beach and charges 750 Dr ($3.20) per person, with free showers for guests.

Hotel Anthoussa. Apollonia, 840 03 Sifnos. ☎ **0284/31-431.** 7 rms. 12,000 Dr ($51.05) double. MC, V.

This hotel is above the excellent and popular Yerontopoulos cafe-pâtisserie, on the right past Heroes Square. Although the streetside rooms offer wonderful views over the hills, they overlook the late-night sweet-tooth crowd and in high season can only be recommended to night owls. The back rooms are quieter and overlook a beautiful bower of bougainvillea.

Hotel Benakis. Platis Yialos, 840 03 Sifnos. ☎ **0284/32-221.** 24 rms. 18,400 Dr ($78.30) double. Rates include breakfast. No credit cards.

This small hotel with a lovely sea view from its perch on the main road is run by the friendly, helpful Benakis family. The rooms are spotless, quiet, and comfortable.

Hotel Boulis. Kamares, 840 03 Sifnos. ☎ **0284/32-122,** or 0284/31-640 in winter. Fax 0284/32-381. 45 rms. TEL. 12,250 Dr ($52.15) double. Rates include breakfast. AE.

This recently built hotel is right on the port's beach and has many amenities, including large, carpeted rooms with beach-view balconies and a spacious marble-floored reception.

Hotel Kamari. Kamares, 840 03 Sifnos. ☎ **0284/31-709.** Fax 0284/31-709. 18 rms. TEL. 11,250 Dr ($47.90) double. AE, MC, V.

This is a clean, attractive lodging with balconied rooms at the quiet end of town, where the road and beach meet. The friendly and attentive management also offers car rental and transfer to other villages by minibus. They also manage the Hotel Stavros, on the harborfront.

✪ **Hotel Platis Yialos.** Platis Yialos, 840 03 Sifnos. ☎ **0284/31-324,** or 0831/22-626 in winter. Fax 0284/31-325, or 0831/55-049 in winter. 26 rms. A/C TEL. 31,750 Dr ($135.10) double. Rates include breakfast. No credit cards.

The island's best hotel is ideally situated overlooking the beach on the west side of the cove. A recent renovation has added large private patios to the ground-floor rooms, modern bathrooms, and decorative ceramics, painted tiles, and small paintings. The Platis Yialos's flagstone sun deck extends from the beach to a dive platform at the end of the cove, with a bar and restaurant sharing the same Aegean views.

✪ **Hotel Sifnos.** Apollonia, 840 03 Sifnos. ☎ **0284/31-624.** 9 rms. 12,000 Dr ($51.05) double. AE, EC, MC, V.

The best hotel in the village is southeast of the main square, on the pedestrians-only street to the cathedral. The hotel's owner, Helen Diareme, and her son Apostolos will do their best to make your stay comfortable. The Sifnos is open year-round and is the most traditional choice in terms of island architecture.

DINING

Apostoli's Koutouki Taverna. Apollonia. ☎ **0284/31-186.** Main courses 1,250–3,200 Dr ($5.30–$13.60). No credit cards. Daily noon–midnight. GREEK.

There are several tavernas in Apollonia, but this one on the main pedestrian street is the best for Greek food, though the service is usually leisurely. All the vegetable dishes, most made from locally grown produce, are delicious.

Captain Andreas. Kamares. ☎ **0284/32-356.** Main courses 1,000–1,600 Dr ($4.25–$6.80); fish 2,500–16,000 Dr ($10.65–$68.10) per kilo. No credit cards. Daily 1–5pm and 7:30pm–12:30am. SEAFOOD.

The favorite place for seafood has tables right on the town beach. Andreas the fisherman serves the catch of the day, usually simply cooked but terrific.

Pothotas Taverna (O Simos). Kamares. No phone. Main courses 800–2,000 Dr ($3.40–$8.50). No credit cards. Daily 11am–midnight. GREEK.

This unobtrusive portside place has a basic Greek menu, but everything is well prepared. The bread brought to your table is sprinkled with sesame seeds, and the village salad is made with locally aged mizithra cheese. The fish is fresh and not expensive; the individually baked pots of moussaka are delicious.

Sifnos Cafe-Restaurant. Apollonia. ☎ **0284/31-624.** Main courses 1,000–2,800 Dr ($4.25–$11.90). AE, EC, MC, V. Daily 8am–midnight. GREEK.

You'll find the best all-around place to eat in Apollonia just a little farther along the main pedestrian street toward the cathedral. Breakfast includes fresh fruit juice and your choice of a dozen coffees. Choose from a variety of snacks, light meals, and desserts during the day. Or have ouzo and mezedes for a mellow sunset.

Sofia Restaurant. Platis Yialas. ☎ **0284/31-890.** Main courses 800–2,800 Dr ($3.40–$11.90). No credit cards. Daily 9pm–1am. GREEK.

At the east end of the beach is the best restaurant for Greek peasant fare, popular for its outdoor terrace and large wine list. For many in Apollonia, the casual seaside ambience warrants an evening outing.

✪ **To Liotrivi (Manganas).** Artemona. ☎ **0284/32-051.** Main courses 900–3,200 Dr ($3.85–$13.60). No credit cards. Daily noon–midnight. GREEK.

The island's favorite taverna is in the pretty village of Artemona, just over a mile walk from Apollonia. Taste for yourself why the Sifnians consider Yannis Yiorgoulis one of their best cooks. Try his delectable *kaparosalata* (minced caper leaves and onion salad), *povithokeftedes* (croquettes of ground chickpeas), or *ambelofasoula* (crisp local black-eyed peas in the pod). The beef filet with potatoes baked in foil is a mouth-watering delight.

SIFNOS AFTER DARK

In Apollonia, the **Argo Bar, Botzi,** and **Volto** on the main pedestrian street are good for the latest European and American pop. In summertime the large **Dolphin Pub** becomes a lively and elegant nightspot, closing in mid-September. Even if you're sleeping in Apollonia, consider the cab fare to Kamares for a special evening. At sunset you can seek relative tranquillity near the beach at the picturesque **Old Captain's Bar.** Later, the **Mobilize Dance Club** and the moreelegant **Follie-Follie,** right on the beach, start cranking up the volume to become seaside discos.

PAROS

Geographically near the center of the archipelago, 91 nautical miles southeast of Piraeus, Paros, one of the largest and most fertile of the Cyclades, has become its transportation hub. Thousands of visitors, including many tour groups, have slightly diminished the island's considerable charm. But it remains remarkably attractive, and rivals even Mykonos for good beaches and surpasses it for windsurfing conditions. Parikia, its lively capital, has an enticing agora (market area), the remains of a Venetian castle, and the finest Byzantine cathedral in Greece. The island also has the pretty fishing village of Naoussa, which has become a major resort center.

ESSENTIALS

ARRIVING/DEPARTING   By Air   Olympic Airlines has 5 flights daily (10 in summer) between Athens and Paros. For schedule information and reservations call 01/961-6161 in Athens or 0284/21-900 in Parikia.

By Sea   The main port, **Parikia,** has ferry service from Piraeus at least once daily (a 6-hour trip), and four times daily in the summer. Confirm schedules with tourist information in Athens (☎ 171 or 01/451-1311). **Strintzi Lines** (☎ 01/422-5000 in Athens) and **Ventouris Ferries** (☎ 01/482-8901 in Athens) have service three or four times a week from Piraeus via Syros. **Ilio Lines** (☎ 01/422-4772 in Athens) has hydrofoil service almost daily from Rafina.

Daily ferry service from Parikia links Paros with Ios, Mykonos, Santorini (Thira), and Tinos. Daily excursion tours link Parikia and Naoussa (the north-coast port) with Mykonos. Call the **port authority** (☎ 0284/21-240) or check each travel agent's current schedule, as most ferry tickets are not interchangeable.

VISITOR INFORMATION   The **Paros Information Bureau** is inside the windmill on the harbor (☎ **0284/22-079**). It's open June–Sept, daily 9am–11pm; the staff speaks English and French, provides local schedules, and changes traveler's checks.

GETTING AROUND   Parikia is best enjoyed by simply strolling about and getting pleasantly lost. Naoussa can also be enjoyed on foot.

By Bicycle   Paros's rolling fertile hills make it well suited to exploration by bike, though some of the pebble-and-dirt roads will require strong tires. **Mountain Bike Club Paros,** just off the waterfront (☎ **0284/23-778**), offers organized tours as well as such essentials as a helmet, insurance, repair kits, and water bottles.

By Bus   The **bus station** in Parikia is on the waterfront (☎ **0284/21-233**), left from the windmill. There's hourly public bus service between Parikia and Naoussa.

The other public buses from Parikia run hourly. Schedules are posted at the stations, or you can call.

By Car   There are several agencies along the waterfront, and except in July and August you should be able to bargain. **Rent-A-Car Acropolis,** left from the windmill on the waterfront (☎ **0284/21-830**), has wildly painted dune buggies or Suzuki Jeeps. Purchasing full insurance is recommended. **Budget Rent-a-Car,** also on the waterfront (☎ **0284/22-320**), is another good choice.

By Moped   There are several moped dealers along the waterfront. Make sure the cycle is in proper condition before you accept it, and be careful on pebble-and-dirt surfaces.

By Taxi   Taxis can be booked (☎ 0284/21-500) or hailed at the windmill taxi stand. If you're coming off the ferry with lots of luggage and a hotel reservation in Naoussa, it's worth the 2,000 Dr ($8.50) to take a taxi directly there.

FAST FACTS: PARIKIA

Banks   There are three banks on Mavroyenous Square (to the right behind the windmill), open Mon–Fri 8am–2pm, and also evenings and Sat in high season.

Medical Clinic   The new private Medical Center of Paros (☎ 0284/24-410) is left (west) of the central square, across from the post office, a block off the port, in Parikia. The public Parikia Health Clinic (☎ 0284/22-500) is down the road from the Ekantopyliani Church.

Police   The police station is on the central square (☎ 100 or 0284/23-333). The **Tourist Police** are behind the windmill on the port (☎ 0284/21-673). In Marpissa, call 41-202; in Naoussa, 51-202.

Post Office   The post office is left of the windmill along the waterfront road, on the right-hand side (☎ 0284/21-236), open Mon–Fri 7:30am–2pm, with extended hours July–Aug. It offers fax service at 0284/22-449.

Telephones   The telephone center (OTE) is to the right of the windmill, open 7:30am–midnight. (If the front door is closed, go around to the back—wind direction determines which door is open.)

WHAT TO SEE & DO

Parikia, site of the ancient capital, is the main port and largest town on the island. Its best-known landmark is the squat, whitewashed **windmill** just off the main pier. Behind the windmill to the right is the long, irregular **Mavroyenous Square,** which contains the town's banks, travel agents, several hotels, restaurants, and various stores. Follow the main street through the square and between the banks to reach the town's picturesque **agora** (market) section, home to clothing boutiques, handcraft shops, and food markets.

The heart of the old town is the **Kastro** (Venetian castle) neighborhood. The 13th-century fortress was built from marble taken from the ancient temples to Apollo and Demeter, and is now incorporated into local housing. Parikia's most famous sight, the beautiful 6th-century **Cathedral of Panayia Ekatondapyliani** ("Our Lady of a Hundred Doors"), was founded by St. Helen, mother of the first Byzantine emperor Constantine, in gratitude for the shelter the port had given during a storm. You can visit the church daily 8am–1pm and 5–8pm; admission is free.

Until recently **Naoussa** was a fishing village with simple white houses in a labyrinth of narrow streets, but it's now a growing resort center with good restaurants, trendy bars, and sophisticated boutiques. Most of the new building has concentrated along the nearby beaches, so the town retains much of its charm. There are a number of good beaches within walking distance of town, or you can catch a caïque to the more distant ones.

OUTDOOR ACTIVITIES   The free booklet *Paros Windsurfing Guide* has a good small map of the island, maps of several beaches, and useful information, and is especially recommended to those interested in water sports. The free *Summer Paros/Antiparos* also has a map of the island, a fairly good map of Parikia, and information.

There are beaches north along Parikia Bay, but beach seekers will probably want to head east to Naoussa Bay. One of the island's best and most famous beaches, picturesque **Kolymbithres,** is an hour's walk or a 10-minute moped ride west from Naoussa, where smooth giant rocks divide the golden sand beach into little coves. There are several tavernas nearby.

North of Kolymbithres, by the Ayios Ioannis Church, is **Monastery Beach,** with some nudism, and the **Monasteri Club,** a bar-restaurant with music and beach service. Most of the other beaches west of Naoussa are overcrowded because of all the new hotels. **Santa Maria Beach** is one of the most beautiful on the island. It has particularly clear water, shallow dunes (rare in Greece) of fine sand along the irregular coastline, and some of the best windsurfing. The nearby **Santa Maria Surf Club** provides windsailing gear and lessons.

Chrissi Akti ("Golden Beach"), half a mile of fine golden sand, is generally considered the best beach on the island, and the windiest. It has become a major windsurfing center. Two windsurfing clubs, the **Sunwind BIC Center** (☎ 2084/42-384) and **Force Seven** (☎ 0284/41-789), give lessons for beginners and advanced surfers. The beach also has a few tavernas, rooms to let, hotels, and a disco.

ACCOMMODATIONS

Most hotels now require reservations for July and August, and these should be made at least a month in advance. The gauntlet of room hawkers that meets you at the port gets increasingly daunting. If it's high season, you don't have a reservation, and you're exhausted, you might consider taking one—but don't commit for more than 1 night. The **Hotelliers Association of Paros** (☎ **0284/24-555** or 0284/24-556) has an information and reservation office at the entrance of Mavroyenous Square, behind the windmill and to the right.

✪ **Hotel Argonauta.** Agora, Parikia, 844 00 Paros. ☎ **0284/21-440.** Fax 0284/23-422. 15 rms (all with shower). TEL. 14,000 Dr ($59.55) double. Rates include breakfast. EC, MC, V. Head to the far end of Mavroyenous Square, behind the Emboriki (Commercial) Bank.

This charming and comfortable hotel is far enough from the center of excitement to be refreshingly quiet. The rooms are modern and well equipped with a few traditional touches, built around an inner second-floor courtyard. The owners, Soula and Dimitri Ghikas, make their spacious and attractive lobby feel like home.

Hotel Asterias. Parikia, 844 00 Paros. ☎ **0284/21-797** or 0284/22-171. Fax 0284/22-172. 36 rms (all with shower). TEL. 16,100 Dr ($68.50) double. AC, EC, MC, V.

This Cycladic-style hotel with a flowering garden out front is the closest to Livadi beach, and one of the best in the area. The spacious rooms have wooden shuttered doors that open onto balconies, all with sea views.

Hotel Fotilia. Naoussa, 844 01 Paros. ☎ **0284/51-480.** Fax 0284/51-189. 14 rms. TEL. 22,500 Dr ($95.75) double. Rates include breakfast. Climb to the top of the steps at the end of town and to the left of the church you'll see a restored windmill behind a stone archway.

The companionable Michael Leondaris will probably meet you with a cup of coffee or a glass of wine. The rooms are spacious and furnished in an elegant country style, with crisp blue-and-white curtains that open to balconies that overlook the old harbor and bay.

Ⓢ Kalypso Hotel. Ayii Anaryiri Beach, 844 01 Paros. ☎ **0284/51-488.** Fax 0284/51-607. 40 rms. 20,600 Dr ($87.65) double. Rates include breakfast. AC, MC, V.

This very nice, traditional-style seaside hotel east of town is built around a cobblestone courtyard, though many of the outer rooms have balconies with views of the sea. The spacious upper-floor rooms are reached by an ornately carved wooden mezzanine that overlooks Kalypso's bar.

Lily Apartments. Naoussa, 844 01 Paros. ☎ **0284/51-377,** or 01/958-9314 in Athens. Fax 0284/51-716, or 01/958-9314 in Athens. 17 apts. TEL. 16,500 Dr ($70.20) apt for two. EC, MC, V.

Lily Ananiadou has our favorite apartments: simple, pleasantly modern, fully equipped—with kitchens, telephones, and balconies overlooking dry, scrub-brush hills.

Pension Vangelistra. Parikia, 844 00 Paros. ☎ **0284/21-482.** 6 rms, 2 apts. 10,500 Dr ($46.70) double; 11,900 Dr ($50.65) apt. No credit cards.

Call Yorgos and Voula Maounis and one of their friendly English-speaking kids will help you find this cozy and attractive lodging in a quiet neighborhood. The rooms are spotless, all with balconies, and the flower-covered terrace brightens the whole street.

At the Beaches

Near the parking lot for Chrissi Akti, the **Golden Beach Hotel** (☎ **0284/41-194;** fax 0284/41-195) has 35 rooms with beach views; doubles go for 13,800 Dr ($58.70). A 10-minute walk from Kolymbithres is the excellent **Hotel Kouros** (☎ **0284/51-565;** fax 0284/51-000), with 55 spacious, full-amenity rooms and a freshwater pool in quiet, beautifully landscaped grounds a hundred yards from the beach, with doubles for 18,750 Dr ($79.75). **Santa Maria Camping** (☎ **0284/ 52-490;** fax 0284/51-937) has the best campsite on the island, with two restaurants, a bar, a swimming pool, minimarket, laundry, bungalows, water sports, and 50 hot showers; the fee is 1,250 ($5.30) per person, with tent sites free. **Camping Naoussa,** about 60 yards from the beach (☎ **0284/51-595**), has hot showers, a kitchen, and clothes and dishwashing, and charges 1,250 Dr ($5.30) per person; tent sites are free and tents can be rented for 800 Dr ($3.40).

DINING

Naoussa's main square has plenty of casual eating establishments. The **Naoussa Pâtisserie,** on the east side of the square, has delicious cheese pies, pastries, biscuits, and espresso.

Ⓢ Aligaria Restaurant. Platia Aligari, Parikia. ☎ **0284/22-026.** Main courses 1,250–2,300 Dr ($5.30–$9.80). EC, MC, V. Daily noon–3:30pm and 6:30pm–midnight. Turn left off Mavroyenous Square behind the Hotel Kontes. GREEK.

This is a charming little place with green trim and white lace curtains. Owner Elizabeth Nikolousou is an excellent cook, who prepares specialties, such as a light zucchini pie, that disappear early. Even her standards, like stuffed tomatoes, are special, and her servings are generous. She also has a good selection of Greek wines.

Barbarossa Ouzeri. On the waterfront, Naoussa. ☎ **0284/51-391.** Mezedes 500–1,200 Dr ($2.10–$5.10). No credit cards. Daily 7:30–11:30pm. SNACKS.

This authentic *ouzeri* is right on the port. Old, wind-burned fishermen sit for hours nursing their milky ouzo in water and their miniportions of grilled octopus and olives. If you haven't partaken of this experience yet, this is the place to try it.

Hibiscus Cafe. Platia Valentza, Parikia. ☎ **0284/21-849.** Main courses 1,000–2,000 Dr ($4.25–$8.50). No credit cards. Daily noon–midnight. Walk down the harborfront about 100 yards south (right) of the port. GREEK/PIZZA.

This is one of the few casual yet stylish places on the *paralia*. It's inexpensive, with sea-view tables, a wide selection of snacks, and brick-oven pizza.

✪ **Lalula.** Naoussa. ☎ **0284/51-547.** Resrevations recommended July–Aug. Main courses 1,800–3,300 Dr ($7.65–$14). No credit cards. Daily 7–11:45pm. Take a left at the post office; it's across from the Minoa Hotel. GREEK/MEDITERRANEAN/VEGETARIAN.

A gifted German restaurateur is responsible for the delicious and distinctive food, subdued decor, and interesting but unobtrusive music. There's a lovely little garden in the back. The cooking is lighter than typical Greek cuisine; the menu depends upon what's fresh at the market. Regular items include vegetable quiche, sweet-and-sour chicken with rice and ginger chutney, and fish steamed in herbs.

Levantis Restaurant. Market St., Parikia. ☎ **0284/23-613.** Reservations recommended July–Aug. Main courses 1,850–3,000 Dr ($7.85–$12.75). AE, DC, EC, MC, V. Wed–Mon 7pm–2am. GREEK/EASTERN MEDITERRANEAN.

Dinner is served under grapevines that some of the older citizens remember being there when they were young. Vivacious Mariana is happy to recommend her favorite of the day, and her husband, Nikolas, offers a friendly glass of wine. The fish can be disappointing, but the Eastern specialties are excellent.

Poseidon Grill. Livadi Beach, Parikia. ☎ **0284/22-667.** Main courses 1,000–2,000 Dr ($4.25–$8.50). No credit cards. Daily 8am–midnight. Head near the town beach, across from the Stella Hotel. GREEK.

This somewhat fancier taverna has a wide range of vegetable entrees and excellent fish. Share swordfish, grilled calamari, some mezedes, salad, and a bottle of Nissiotissa wine.

PAROS AFTER DARK

Warning: Several places will offer very cheap drinks or "buy one, get one free"—usually locally brewed alcohol the locals call *bomba.* Beware: It's illegal, and it makes one intoxicated quickly and very sick afterward.

Just behind the windmill is a local landmark, the **Port Cafe,** a basic *kafenio* lit by bare incandescent bulbs and filled day and night with tourists waiting for a ferry, bus, taxi, or fellow traveler. The **Pebbles Bar** plays classical music at sunset for those who want to start their evening in a mellow mood.

The **Saloon d'Or,** south of the port (☎ **0284/22-176**), is the most popular place for inexpensive drinks. If you're not in the mood to party, the **Pirate Bar,** in the agora, is a tastefully decorated bar that plays mellow jazz, blues, and classical music with slightly more expensive drinks. For partiers, there's the nearby **Rendezvous,** with pretty good rock music. **Black Bart's,** midway on the harbor (☎ **0284/21-802**), is a good place for loud music and boisterous big drinkers. The outdoor **Cine Rex,** on the right off the road to Pounda (☎ **0284/21-676**), has two features, often in English.

In **Naoussa,** the hot spot is still **Banana Moon,** about a 10-minute walk up the main street. For relaxing, a local friend recommends the **Sofrano Bar,** on the harbor. There's also an outdoor movie theater, **Makis Cinema** (☎ **0284/21-676**), which often shows action films in English.

Hungary 9

by Joseph Lieber

The dramatic political changes of 1989 have irreversibly altered Hungary. Budapest, awakened after its long slumber behind the Iron Curtain, is now one of Europe's hottest travel destinations. Poised between East and West, both geographically and culturally, Budapest is at the center of the region's cultural rebirth.

1 Budapest

Budapest came of age as a city in the 19th century, at the start of which the two towns of Buda and Pest were little more than provincial outposts on the Danube. The dawning of a modern Hungarian identity spawned the neoclassical development of the city. Later in the century the rise of the eclectic style coincided with the great post-1867 boom, creating most of the historic inner city. Indeed, Budapest, despite its Roman ruins and reconstructed medieval castle district, is very much a *fin-de-siècle* city, with its characteristic coffeehouse and music hall culture. The decades after World War I were not kind to Hungary's charming capital, and until recently Budapest's turn-of-the-century glory seemed irretrievably lost. How fitting it is, then, that Budapest's post–Cold War renaissance comes when it does: The city will once again attract visitors from far and wide as a new century turns.

Notwithstanding the collapse of the Iron Curtain and the westernization of Budapest, the city retains an exotic feeling seldom experienced in the better-known capitals of Europe. Take a turn off any of the city's main boulevards and you'll quickly find yourself in a quiet residential neighborhood, where the scent of a hearty *gulyás* wafts from a kitchen window or cigarette smoke fogs the cavelike entryway of the corner pub.

ONLY IN BUDAPEST

Spending a Night at the Opera   For the price of a baseball ticket back home, you can sit in the royal box, once the preserve of Habsburg monarchs.

Shopping the Market Halls   Built at the turn of the century, Budapest's vintage market halls continue to be home to lively commerce in fruits and vegetables.

Budapest Attractions & Accommodations

Amusement Park **21**
Buda Palace **14**
Budapest History
  Museum **15**
Chain Bridge **12**
City Park **23**
Dohány Synagogue **37**
Ethnographical Museum **27**
Ferenc Liszt Memorial
  Museum **29**
Fisherman's Bastion **8**
Gellért Hill **17**
Great Circus **20**
Heroes' Square **25**
Hungarian National
  Gallery **11**
Hungarian National
  Museum **38**
Hungarian State Opera
  House **28**
Inner City Parish Church **35**
Ludwig Museum and
  Contemporary
  Historical Museum **10**
Matthias Church **9**
Medieval Jewish Prayer
  House **6**
Museum of Applied Arts **39**
Museum of Commerce
  and Catering **7**
Museum of Fine Arts **24**
Museum of the History
  of Warfare **5**
Museum of Music History **4**
National Jewish Museum **36**
Parliament **26**
Post Office Museum **31**
Postal Stamp Museum **30**
St. Stephen's Church **32**
Semmelweis Museum
  of Medical History **16**
Tomb of Gül Baba **1**
Transport Museum **22**
Zoo **19**

INFORMATION
Tourinform **34**

SPA BATHING
Gellért Baths **18**
Király Baths **2**

TRANSPORTATION HUBS
Erzsébet tér Bus Station **33**
HÉV Suburban Rail Station **3**
Vigadó tér Boat Station **13**

ACCOMMODATIONS:
Alba Hotel Budapest **3**
Charles Apartments **4**
Délibáb **9**
Family Hotel **10**
Fórum Hotel **5**
Hilton Hotel **1**
King's Hotel **6**
Medosz **8**
Nemzeti **7**
Victoria **2**

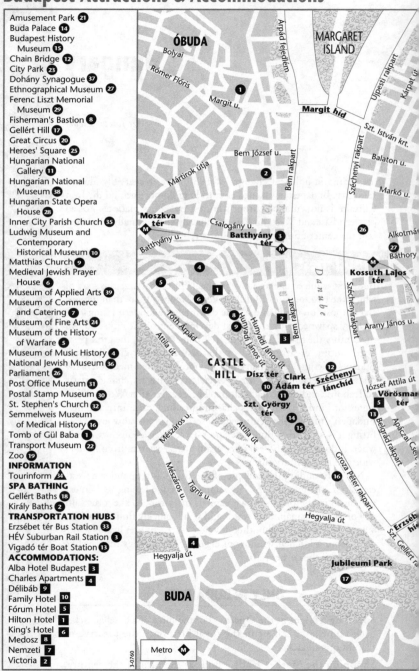

538

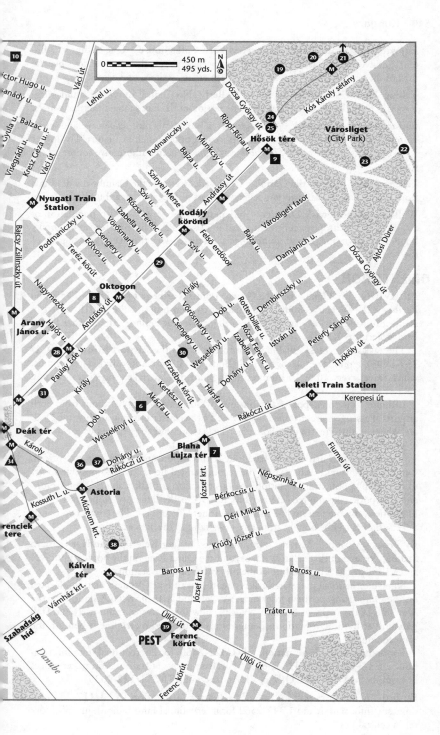

0 |■■■■■| 450 m
                495 yds.

N

10

Víctor Hugo u.
Csanády u.
Gyula u.
Viségradi u.
Kresz Géza u.
Balzac u.
Váci út
Lehel u.
Váci út

Nyugati Train Station

Bajcsy Zsilinszky út
Podmaniczky u.
Teréz körút
Eötvös u.
Csengery u.
Vörösmarty u.
Izabella u.
Rózsa Ferenc u.
Szív u.
Szinyei Merse
Podmaniczky u.
Bajza u.
Munkácsy u.
Rippl-Rónai u.
Dózsa György út

19
20
21
M

24
25
M
9

Hősök tére

Városliget (City Park)

22
23

Kós Károly sétány

Andrássy út
M

Kodály körönd

Felső erdősor
Szív u.
Bajza u.
Városligeti fasor
Damjanich u.
Dózsa György út
Ajtósi Dürer

Nagymező u.
Andrássy út
Teréz körút

Oktogon
8
M

Arany János u.
M

Hajós u.
Paulay Ede u.
Király
28
31
M

Király
Vörösmarty u.
Csengery u.
Dob u.
Rottenbiller u.
Dembinszky u.
Rózsa Ferenc u.
Izabella u.
István út
Péterfy Sándor
Thököly út

29

30
Wesselényi u.
Dohány u.
Erzsébet körút
Kertész u.
Akácfa u.
Hársfa u.

6

Dob u.
Wesselényi u.

Deák tér
M
M
Károly
34

36 **37** Dohány u.
Rákóczi út

Blaha Lujza tér M **7**

Keleti Train Station
M
Kerepesi út

Rákóczi út
József krt.
Népszínház u.
Fiumei út

Kossuth L. u.
Astoria M
Múzeum krt.
Bérkocsis u.
Déri Miksa u.
Krúdy József u.

Ferenciek tere
M

38

Kálvin tér
M
Baross u.
József krt.
Baross u.

Vámház krt.
Práter u.

Szabadság híd
Üllői út
39
M
Ferenc körút

PEST

Ferenc körút
Üllői út

Danube

539

Enjoying Coffee and Pastry at the New York Coffeehouse   One of the city's finest art nouveau interiors, the New York has been serving coffee and pastries since the turn of the century, when it was *the* place for artists, writers, and actors.

Taking Thermal Baths at the Hotel Gellért   No Central European could imagine a trip to Budapest without at least one session in the city's fabled thermal waters.

Eating Dinner at Gundel   Although this is Budapest's most expensive and fanciest restaurant, you can dine here for the price of a casual lunch in Vienna. The owner is George Lang, whose book *The Cuisine of Hungary* is an authoritative source on the subject.

Taking a Boat Ride on the Danube   The wide stretch of the Danube divides Buda from Pest; a boat ride affords you a view of most of the city's great buildings.

Walking in the Jewish District   Budapest has the largest Jewish population of any city on the European continent, outside Russia. Pest's historic Jewish neighborhood, run-down but relatively unchanged, resonates with the magic and tragedy of the past.

ORIENTATION

ARRIVING   **By Plane**   Budapest's two airports, **Ferihegy I** (☎ 1/157-7155) and **Ferihegy II** (☎ 1/157-8000), are adjacent to each other in the XVIII district in southeastern Pest. Malév and Lufthansa flights land at Ferihegy II; all other flights land at Ferihegy I.

The easiest and most reliable way into the city is the **Airport Minibus** (☎ 1/157-8993), a public service of the LRI (Budapest Airport Authority). The minibus, which leaves every 10 or 15 minutes throughout the day, takes you directly to any address in the city.

LRI also runs an **Airport-Centrum** bus, which leaves every half hour from both airports. Passengers are dropped off at Pest's Erzsébet tér bus station, just off Deák tér, where all three metro lines converge. Tickets are sold aboard the bus for the 30- to 40-minute trip.

The private **taxi** drivers who hang out at the airport are notoriously overpriced. Our advice is to take only taxis of the recommended fleets. It's also possible to get to the city by public transportation; the bus to metro trip takes about 1 hour. From either airport, take the red-lettered **bus no. 93** to the last stop, Kőbánya-Kispest. From there, the Blue metro line runs to the Inner City of Pest. The cost is two transit tickets; tickets can be bought from any newsstand in the airport.

By Train   Most international trains pull into bustling **Keleti pályaudvar** (Eastern Station), located in Pest's Baross tér, beyond the Outer Ring on the border of the VII and VIII districts. The Red line of the metro is below the station.

Some international trains arrive at **Nyugati pályaudvar** (Western Station), located on the Outer Ring, at the border of the V, VI, and XIII districts. A station for the Blue line of the metro is beneath Nyugati. Few international trains arrive at **Déli pályaudvar** (Southern Station); the terminus of the Red metro line is beneath the train station.

For domestic train information, call **1/322-7860;** for international train information, call **1/342-9150** or **1/122-8035.** Purchase tickets at train station ticket offices or from the **MÁV Service Office,** VI. Andrássy út 35 (☎ **1/122-9035**).

By Bus   Most buses pull into the **Erzsébet tér bus station** (☎ 1/117-2345 for domestic information and 1/117-2562 for international information), just off Deák tér in central Pest.

By Car   The border crossings from Austria and Slovakia are generally hassle-free. You may be requested to present your driver's license, vehicle registration, and proof of insurance (the number plate and symbol indicating country of origin are acceptable proof). Hungary doesn't require the International Driver's License. Cars entering Hungary are required to have a decal indicating country of registration, a first-aid kit, and an emergency triangle.

By Hydrofoil   Two companies, the Hungarian **MAHART** and the Austrian **Donau Dampfschiffarts Gesellschaft (DDSG),** operate hydrofoils on the Danube between Vienna and Budapest in the spring and summer. Book your tickets well in advance. In Vienna, contact MAHART, Karlsplatz 26. (☎ 1/512-36-18); DDSG, the more expensive line, can be contacted at Handelskai 265 (☎ 1/26-65-36). The Budapest office of **MAHART** is at V. Belgrád rakpart (☎ **1/118-1223** or 1/118-1704). Boats and hydrofoils from Vienna arrive at the **Belgrád rakpart** (☎ **1/118-1704**), on the Pest side of the Danube.

VISITOR INFORMATION   The city's best information source is **Tourinform** (☎ **1/117-9800**), centrally located at V. Sütő u. 2, just off Deák tér (reached by all three metro lines) in Pest, open daily 8am–8pm. The staff speaks English.

CITY LAYOUT   The city of Budapest came into being in 1873, the result of a union of three separate cities: **Buda, Pest,** and **Óbuda.** Budapest, like Hungary itself, is defined by the **River Danube (Duna),** along which many of the city's historic sites are found. Eight bridges connect the two banks, including five in the city center.

On the right bank of the Danube lies Pest, the capital's commercial and administrative center. Central Pest is that part of the city between the Danube and the semicircular **Outer Ring** boulevard (Nagykörút), stretches of which are called by the names of former monarchs: Ferenc, József, Erzsébet, Teréz, and Szent István. The Outer Ring begins at the Pest side of the Petőfi Bridge in the south and wraps itself around the center, ending at the Margit Bridge in the north. Several of Pest's busiest squares are found along the Outer Ring, and Pest's major east–west avenues bisect it at these squares.

Central Pest is further defined by the **Inner Ring (Kiskörút),** which lies within the Outer Ring. It starts at Szabadság híd (Freedom Bridge) in the south and is alternately named Vámház körút, Múzeum körút, Károly körút, Bajcsy-Zsilinszky út, and József Attila utca before ending at the Chain Bridge. Inside this ring is the **Belváros,** the historic Inner City of Pest.

Váci utca is a popular pedestrian shopping street between the Inner Ring and the Danube. It spills into Vörösmarty tér, one of the area's best-known squares. The **Dunakorzó** (Danube Promenade), a popular evening strolling place, runs along the river in Pest, between the Chain Bridge and the Erzsébet Bridge. The historic Jewish district of Pest is in the **Erzsébetváros,** between the two ring boulevards.

Margaret Island (Margit-sziget) is in the middle of the Danube. Accessible via the Margaret Bridge or Árpád Bridge, it's a popular park without vehicular traffic.

On the left bank of the Danube is Buda; to its north, beyond the city center, lies Óbuda. Buda is as hilly as Pest is flat. **Castle Hill** is widely considered the most beautiful part of Budapest. A number of steep paths, staircases, and small streets go up to Castle Hill, but no major roads do. The easiest access is from Clark Ádám tér (at the head of the Chain Bridge) by funicular, or from Várfok utca (near Moszkva tér) by foot or bus. Castle Hill consists of the royal palace itself, home to numerous museums, and the so-called **Castle District,** a lovely neighborhood of small, winding streets, centered around the gothic Matthias Church.

Below Castle Hill, along the Danube, is a long, narrow neighborhood known as the **Watertown** (Víziváros).

Central Buda is a collection of mostly low-lying neighborhoods below Castle Hill. The main square of central Buda is Moszkva tér, just north of Castle Hill. Beyond Central Buda, mainly to the east, are the **Buda Hills.**

Óbuda is on the left bank of the Danube, north of Buda. Although the greater part of Óbuda is modern and drab, it features a beautiful old city center and impressive Roman ruins.

Budapest is divided into 22 districts, called *kerülets* (abbreviated as *ker.*). A Roman numeral followed by a period precedes every written address in Budapest, signifying the kerület; for example, XII. Csörsz utca 9 is in the 12th kerület. Because many street names are repeated in different parts of the city, it's very important to know which kerület a certain address is in.

GETTING AROUND   Budapest has an extensive, efficient, and inexpensive public transportation system. The system's biggest disadvantage is that except for 17 well-traveled bus and tram routes, all forms of transport shut down for the night at around 11:30pm; certain areas of the city, most notably the Buda Hills, are beyond the reach of the limited night service, so you'll have to take a taxi.

All forms of public transportation in Budapest require the self-validation of prepurchased tickets (*jegy*); you can buy them at metro ticket windows, newspaper kiosks, and the occasional tobacco shop. It's a good idea to stock up; for 600 Ft ($4), you can get a 20-pack (ask for a *huszos csomag*).

Day passes (*napijegy*) cost 280 Ft ($1.90) and are valid until midnight of the day of purchase. Buy them from metro ticket windows; the clerk validates the pass at the time of purchase. A 3-day *turistajegy* costs 560 Ft ($3.75), and a weekly pass costs 750 Ft ($5).

Inspectors frequently come around checking for valid tickets, particularly in the metro stations. On-the-spot fines (400 Ft/$2.70) are assessed to fare-dodgers.

All public transport operates on rough schedules, posted at bus and tram shelters and in metro stations. The Budapest Transport Authority (BKV térkép) produces a more detailed transportation map, available at most metro ticket windows for 65 Ft (45¢).

By Metro   The metro is clean and efficient, with trains running every 3 to 5 minutes from about 4:30am until about 11:30pm. The three lines are universally known by color—Yellow, Red, and Blue. Officially they have numbers as well (1, 2, and 3 respectively), but all signs are color coded. All three lines converge at Deák tér, the only point where any meet.

The **Yellow (1) line** is the oldest metro on the European continent. The Yellow line runs from Vörösmarty tér in the heart of central Pest, out the length of Andrássy út, past the Városliget (City Park), ending at Mexikói út. Tickets for the Yellow line are self-validated on the train itself.

The **Red (2) and Blue (3) lines** are modern metros. The Red line runs from eastern Pest, through the center, and across the Danube to Déli Station. The Blue line runs from southeastern Pest, through the center, and out to northern Pest. Tickets should be validated at automatic boxes before you descend the escalator. When changing lines at Deák tér, you're required to validate another ticket at the orange validating machines in the hallways between lines.

Metro tickets are good for 1 hour for any distance along the line you're riding.

Budapest Metro

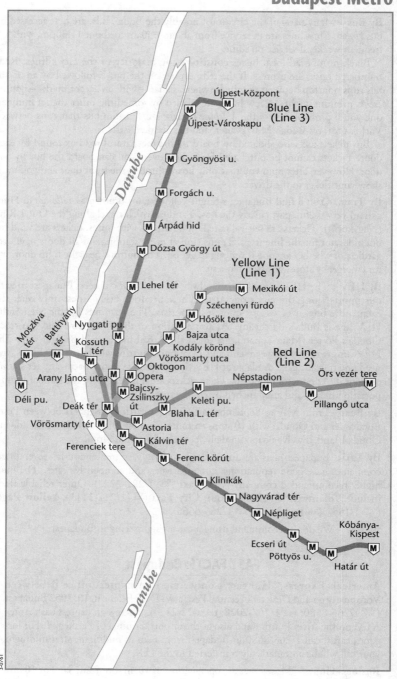

Újpest-Központ

Blue Line
(Line 3)

Újpest-Városkapu

Gyöngyösi u.

Forgách u.

Árpád hid

Dózsa György út

Yellow Line
(Line 1)

Lehel tér

Mexikói út

Széchenyi fürdő

Hősök tere

Bajza utca

Moszkva tér

Bathyány tér

Nyugati pu.

Kossuth L. tér

Kodály körönd

Vörösmarty utca

Oktogon

Red Line
(Line 2)

Arany János utca

Opera

Népstadion

Örs vezér tere

Déli pu.

Bajcsy-Zsilinszky út

Keleti pu.

Pillangó utca

Deák tér

Blaha L. tér

Vörösmarty tér

Astoria

Ferenciek tere

Kálvin tér

Ferenc körút

Klinikák

Nagyvárad tér

Népliget

Kőbánya-Kispest

Ecseri út

Pöttyös u.

Határ út

Danube

3-0761

By Bus Many parts of the city, most notably the Buda Hills, are best accessed by bus (*busz*). Most lines are in service from about 4:30am to about 11:30pm, with less frequent weekend service on some.

Black-numbered local buses constitute the majority of the city's lines. Red-numbered buses are express. If the red number on the bus is followed by an *E*, the bus runs nonstop between terminals (whereas an *É*—with an accent mark—signifies *észak,* meaning night). A few buses are labeled by something other than a number; one you'll probably use is the *Várbusz* (Palace Bus), a minibus that runs between Várfok utca, off Buda's Moszkva tér, and the Castle District.

Bus tickets are self-validated on board by the mechanical red box found by each door. Tickets cannot be purchased from the driver. You can board the bus by any door. However, after 8pm you may only board through the front door and you must show your ticket to the driver.

By Tram You'll find Budapest's bright-yellow trams (known as *villamos* in Hungarian) very useful, particularly the nos. 4 and 6, which travel along the Outer Ring (Nagykörút). Tickets are self-validated on board. As with buses, tickets are valid for one ride, not for the line itself. Trams stop at every station, and all doors open, regardless of whether anyone is waiting to get on. The buttons near the tram doors are for emergency stops, not stop requests.

By HÉV The HÉV is a suburban railway network that connects Budapest to various points along the city's outskirts. There are four HÉV lines; only one, the Szentendre line, is of serious interest to tourists. The terminus for the Szentendre HÉV line is Buda's Batthyány tér, also a station of the Red metro line. To reach Óbuda's Fő tér (Main Square), get off at the Árpád híd (Árpád Bridge) stop. The HÉV runs regularly between 4am and 11:30pm. For trips within the city limits, you need one transit ticket, available at HÉV ticket windows at the Batthyány tér station or from the conductor on board. These tickets are different from the standard transportation tickets and are punched by conductors on board.

By Boat From May to September a BKV boat carries passengers between Pest's Boráros tér and Óbuda, with 10 stops en route—in Pest, Buda, Margaret Island, and Óbuda Island. Twelve boats run daily, between 10am and 4pm.

By Taxi Budapest taxis are unregulated, so fares vary tremendously. Several fleet companies have good reputations, honest drivers, and competitive rates. The most highly recommended company is **Fő Taxi** (☎ 1/222-2222). Other reliable fleets include **Volántaxi** (☎ 1/166-6666), **City Taxi** (☎ 1/211-1111), **Yellow Pages** (☎ 1/155-5000), and **6x6** (☎ 1/266-6666).

By Car We don't recommend using a car for sightseeing in Budapest.

FAST FACTS: Budapest

American Express Hungary's only American Express office is between Vörösmarty tér and Deák tér in central Pest, at V. Deák Ferenc u. 10, 1052 Budapest (☎ 1/266-8680; fax 1/267-2028; telex 22-2124). There's an express cash Amex ATM on the street in front and also at the airport terminal of Ferihegy I. For lost Amex cards, call 1/266-8680 in Budapest from 8am to midnight; after midnight your call will be automatically transferred to the U.K.

Business Hours Most stores are open Mon–Fri 10am–6pm and Sat 9 or 10am–1 to 2pm. Many shops close for an hour at lunchtime, and only stores in central tourist areas are open Sunday. Many shops and restaurants close for 2 weeks in Aug. Banks are usually open Mon–Thurs 8am–3pm, Fri 8am–1pm.

Currency   The basic unit of currency is the **Forint (Ft)**. There are 100 **fillérs** (almost worthless and soon to be taken out of circulation) in a Forint. Coins come in denominations of 10, 20, and 50 fillérs; and 1, 2, 5, 10, 20, 100, and 200 Ft. Newly issued coins, without the symbols of the previous regime, are now in use. Banknotes come in denominations of 50, 100, 500, 1,000, and 5,000 Ft. The rate of exchange used in this chapter is $1 = 150 Ft.

Currency Exchange   The best rates for cash or traveler's checks are obtained at banks. Exchange booths are located throughout the city center, in train stations, and in most hotels. Automatic exchange machines that accept foreign cash and spit out Hungarian Forints operate around the clock, but do not accept denominations over $20. Technically, you're allowed to reexchange into hard currency up to half the amount of Forints you originally purchased. This is sometimes harder in practice than in theory; keep all exchange receipts and return to the bank or to the exchange booth used originally.

Doctors & Dentists   IMS, a private outpatient clinic at XIII. Váci út 202 (☎ 1/129-8423), has English-speaking doctors; take the Blue metro line (Gyöngyös utca). Személyi Orvosi Szolgálat, I. Csalogány u. 4/D (☎ 1/118-8288), is another private medical clinic where English and other foreign languages are spoken. Many luxury hotels also have a staff or private doctor with rented office space. For further options, ask at Tourinform.

Drugstores   The Hungarian word is *gyógyszertár* or *patika*. Generally, pharmacies carry only prescription drugs. Hotel drugstores are just shops with soap, perfume, aspirin, and other nonprescription items. There are a number of 24-hour pharmacies in the city—every pharmacy posts the address of the nearest one in its window.

Embassies   The **Australian** embassy is at VI. Délibáb u. 30 (☎ 1/201-8899); the **Canadian** embassy, at XII. Budakeszi út 32 (☎ 1/275-1200); the **United Kingdom** embassy at V. Harmincad u. 6 (☎ 1/266-2888); and the **U.S.** embassy at V. Szabadság tér 12 (☎ 1/267-4400). New Zealand and Ireland have no representation in Hungary.

Emergencies   Police (☎ 07), fire (☎ 05), and ambulance (☎ 04). To reach the 24-hour English-speaking emergency service, dial 1/118-8212.

Eyeglasses   *Optika* is the Hungarian name for an optometrist's shop. The word for eyeglasses is *szemüveg*.

Hospitals   See "Doctors & Dentists" above.

Lost Property   The BKV (Budapest Transportation Authority) lost-and-found office is at VII. Akácfa u. 18 (☎ 1/322-6613). For items lost at Ferihegy I, call 1/295-3480; for Ferihegy II, call 1/157-8301 or 1/157-8108. For items lost on a train or in a train station, call 1/129-8037. For items lost on an intercity bus (not on a local BKV bus), call 1/118-2122.

Luggage Storage   You can leave luggage at all three major railroad stations. At Keleti the office is near the head of Track 5, and at Nyugati, alongside Track 10; both are open 24 hours. There are also self-storage lockers in Keleti and Nyugati stations; get a key to the locker from the left-luggage office. Déli Station has a new locker system in operation in the main ticket-purchasing area; the lockers are very large and directions for use are provided by a multilingual computer. The Erzsébet tér bus station, near Deák tér in central Pest, has a left-luggage office, open Mon–Thurs 6am–7pm, Fri 6am–9pm, Sat–Sun 6am–6pm.

Post Office   The Magyar Posta, Petőfi Sándor u. 17–19, not far from Deák tér (all metro lines), is the city's main post office, open Mon–Fri 8am–8pm, Sat 8am–3pm. There are 24-hour post offices near Keleti and Nyugati stations.

Taxes   Taxes are included in all restaurant prices, hotel rates, and shop purchases. A 25% value-added tax (VAT) is added to all car rentals.

ACCOMMODATIONS

Budapest's hotels range from beautiful, historic turn-of-the-century gems to drab, utilitarian establishments typical of the city's socialist period. Hotel prices are some of the lowest of any major European city. However, Budapest still is a city without enough guest beds, particularly in summer.

When booking, if you want a room with a double bed, be sure to request one; otherwise you'll get a room with two twin beds. Single rooms are generally available, as are extra beds or cots. Hungarian hotels use the word *apartment* to describe the kind of room we call a *suite* (that is, connected rooms, without a kitchen). In these listings, we have called a suite a suite, so to speak.

ACCOMMODATIONS AGENCIES   Most accommodations agencies can secure private room rentals, help reserve hotel and pension rooms, and book you into a youth hostel. The most established agencies are the former state-owned travel agents: Ibusz, Cooptourist, MÁV Tours, and Budapest Tourist. There are agencies in both airports, all three major train stations, throughout central Pest, and along the main roads into Budapest. The main **Ibusz reservations office,** at Petőfi tér 1 (☎ **1/118-5707** or 1/118-4842; fax 1/117-9099), near the Intercontinental Hotel, a short walk from Deák tér, is open 24 hours.

⊘ PRIVATE ROOMS   When you book a private room you get a room in someone's apartment; usually you share the bathroom. Breakfast is usually offered for a fee (300–500 Ft/$2–$3.35). You may also have limited kitchen privileges (ask in advance).

You can book rooms through accommodation agencies. Rooms usually cost 2,000–4,000 Ft ($13.40–$26.80), plus 2% tax. Most agencies add a 30% surcharge (to the first night only) for stays of less than 4 nights.

THE INNER CITY & CENTRAL PEST

Very Expensive

Fórum Hotel. V. Apáczai Csere J. u. 12–14, 1052 Budapest. ☎ **1/117-8088**. Fax 1/117-9808. 400 rms, 8 suites. A/C MINIBAR TV TEL. DM 320–420 ($214–$281) double; DM 500–700 ($335–$469) suite. Breakfast DM 15–25 ($10–$16.75) extra. AE, CB, EC, JCB, MC, V. Parking: 1,300 Ft ($8.70) per day. Metro: Deák tér (all lines).

Built in 1981, the Fórum has some 285 rooms overlooking the Danube, with spectacular views of the Chain Bridge and Castle Hill. The rooms are plush and luxurious, without the depressing, claustrophobic feeling found in some of Budapest's modern hotels. Windows are soundproof. No-smoking rooms and rooms equipped for travelers with disabilities are available. Services include 24-hour room service, laundry, and babysitting. Facilities include a business center, barbershop, hairdresser, drugstore, fitness center, swimming pool, sauna, massage, solarium, and conference rooms.

Expensive

○ Hotel Nemzeti. VIII. József krt. 4, 1088 Budapest. ☎ **1/133-9160** or 1/133-9169. Fax 1/114-0019. 76 rms. MINIBAR TV TEL. DM 160 ($107) double. Rates include breakfast. Rates 40% lower in low season. AE, DC, MC, V. Parking: 600 Ft ($4) in neighborhood garage. Metro: Blaha Lujza tér (Red line).

The turn-of-the-century Hotel Nemzeti, just off Blaha Lujza Square, underwent a 1987 restoration that returned much of its original art nouveau splendor. Ask for a room that faces the interior courtyard. This is perhaps Pest's most handsome and historic hotel, though it lacks the luxuries of the more modern hotels. Room service and laundry are available, plus car rental.

Moderate

○ King's Hotel. VII. Nagydiófa u. 25–27. ☎ and fax **1/267-9324.** 95 rms, 5 suites. TV TEL. $60–$80 double; $120 suite. AE. Free parking on street.

In summer 1995 the King's Hotel opened in a beautifully renovated and restored *fin-de-siècle* building in the Jewish district. Despite the somewhat unappealing modern furnishings, the rooms retain a 19th-century atmosphere, many with small balconies overlooking the quiet residential street.

Inexpensive

⊝ Hotel Medosz. VI. Jókai tér 9, 1061 Budapest. ☎ **1/153-1700** or 1/153-1434. Fax 1/132-4316. 70 rms. TV. DM 68 ($46) double. Rates include breakfast. Rates 15% lower in low season. No credit cards. Parking difficult in neighborhood. Metro: Oktogon (Yellow line).

The Medosz was formerly a trade-union hotel for agricultural workers. Its location on sleepy Jókai tér, in the heart of Pest's theater district, is as good as it gets off the river in central Pest. Although the hotel has not been renovated since privatization (and the staff has yet to learn to smile), it remains a great value given its location.

JUST BEYOND CENTRAL PEST

Expensive

Family Hotel. XIII. Ipoly u. 8/b, 1133 Budapest. ☎ **1/120-1284.** Fax 1/129-1620. 10 rms, 3 suites. A/C MINIBAR TV TEL. DM 180 ($121) double; DM 240 ($161) suite. Rates include breakfast. Rates 10%–15% lower in low season. AE, DC, EC, JCB, MC, V. Free parking. Trolleybus: 79 from Keleti pu. to Ipoly utca.

This charming little place is two blocks from the Danube in a quiet neighborhood just north of the Inner City of Pest. The suites—all duplexes—are among the city's nicest rooms, with skylights over the upstairs bedrooms and enormous floor-to-ceiling windows. Room service is available. Facilities include sauna, massage, hairdresser, and a conference room.

Inexpensive

⊝ Hotel Délibáb. VI. Délibáb u. 35, 1062 Budapest. ☎ **1/342-9301** or 1/122-8763. Fax 1/342-8153. 34 rms. TV TEL. 6,000–8,600 Ft ($40–$58) double. Rates include breakfast. No credit cards. Parking difficult in neighborhood. Metro: Hősök tere (Yellow line).

The Hotel Délibáb enjoys a wonderful location across the street from Heroes' Square and City Park, in an exclusive Pest neighborhood that's home to most of the city's embassies. The spacious rooms have hardwood floors; the fixtures are old, but everything works and is clean.

CENTRAL BUDA & THE CASTLE DISTRICT

Very Expensive

○ Hilton Hotel. I. Hess András tér 1–3, 1014 Budapest. ☎ **1/175-1000.** Fax 1/175-0882. 323 rms and suites. A/C MINIBAR TV TEL. DM 390–460 ($261–$308) double; DM 530–720

($355–$482) suite. Children stay free in parents' room. Breakfast DM 29 ($19.45) extra. AE, CB, DC, EC, MC, V. Parking: DM 29 ($19.45) in garage. Bus: "Várbusz" from Moszkva tér, 16 from Deák tér, or 116 from Március 15 tér. Funicular: From Clark Ádám tér.

The only hotel in Buda's elegant Castle District, the Hilton is widely considered the city's finest hotel. Its location, next door to Matthias Church and the Fisherman's Bastion, is spectacular. The hotel's design incorporates both the ruins of a 13th-century Dominican church (the church tower rises above the hotel) and the baroque facade of a 17th-century Jesuit college (the hotel's main entrance). The ruins were carefully restored during the hotel's construction in 1977, and the results are magnificent. The more expensive rooms have views over the Danube, with a full Pest skyline; rooms on the hotel's other side overlook the delightful streets of the Castle District. Services include room service, baby-sitting, plus a Malév desk and Ibusz desk. Facilities include a business center, conference rooms, doctor/dentist on call, laundry, newsstand, free airport minibus, beauty salon, antiques shop, florist, photo shop, and souvenir shop.

Expensive

Alba Hotel Budapest. I. Apor Péter u. 3, 1011 Budapest. ☎ **1/175-9244.** Fax 1/175-9899. 95 rms. MINIBAR TV TEL. DM 200 ($134) double. Rates include breakfast. Rates 20% lower in low season. AE, DC, EC, MC, V. Parking: DM 22 ($14.75) per day. Many buses run to Clark Ádám tér, including no. 16 from Deák tér.

Opened in 1990, the Alba Hotel Budapest belongs to a Swiss chain, and the Swiss influence is pervasive—from the buffet breakfast to the antiseptically clean rooms. The hotel is nestled in a tiny cobblestoned alley directly beneath Buda Castle. It has seven floors, but only rooms on the top floor have views; the two best are 706, which has a castle view, and 707, which overlooks Matthias Church. Other seventh-floor rooms offer a pleasing vista of red Buda rooftops. Room service and laundry are available, plus there are conference rooms and car rental.

✪ Hotel Victoria. I. Bem rakpart 11, 1011 Budapest. ☎ **1/201-8644.** Fax 1/201-5816. 27 rms. A/C MINIBAR TV TEL. DM 195 ($131) double; DM 350 ($235) suite. Rates include breakfast. Rates 25% lower in low season. AE, DC, EC, MC, V. Free parking in garage. Tram: 19 from Batthyány tér to the first stop.

The Hotel Victoria is separated from Buda's Danube bank only by the busy road that runs alongside the river. It's situated in a narrow building, with only three rooms on each of its nine floors. This design makes two-thirds of the rooms corner rooms with large double windows providing great views over the river to Pest's skyline beyond. The somewhat smaller middle rooms also have windows facing the river. Unfortunately, noise from the busy road beneath your window may disturb your rest. The hotel is just minutes by foot from both Batthyány tér and Clark Ádám tér, with dozens of metro, tram, and bus connections. There's 24-hour room service, plus a safe, laundry, and car rental. Facilities include a bar, sauna, mini–business center, conference rooms, and beauty salon.

Moderate

⊗ Charles Apartments. I. Hegyalja út 23, 1016 Budapest. ☎ **1/201-1796.** Fax 1/212-2584. 26 apts. TV TEL. $50–$55 apt for one or two; $64 apt for three. Rates 10%–15% lower in low season. No credit cards. Parking: 400 Ft ($2.70) per day. Bus: 78 from Keleti pu. to Mészáros utca.

This is one of the better housing deals in Budapest. Owner Károly Szombati has bought up 22 apartments in a single apartment building in a dull but convenient Buda neighborhood (near the large luxury Hotel Novotel), in addition to four apartments in nearby buildings. These average Budapest flats in average residential buildings all have full bathrooms and kitchens. Hegyalja is a very busy street, but only two apartments face it; the rest are in the interior or on the building's side. A park nearby has tennis courts and a track, and next door is a grocery store.

THE BUDA HILLS

Moderate

Gizella Panzió. XII. Arató u. 42/b, 1121 Budapest. ☎ and fax **1/182-0324.** 8 rms, 6 suites. MINIBAR TV TEL. $60 double; $80 suite. AE, MC. Free parking. Tram: 59 from Moszkva tér to the last stop.

This charming pension is a 10-minute walk from the nearest tram station. Built on the side of a hill, it has a lovely view and a series of terraced gardens leading down to the swimming pool. The pension also features a sauna, solarium, fitness room, and bar.

Hotel Tanne. XII. Esze Tamás u. 6, 2092 Budapest. ☎ **1/176-6144** or 1/138-6520. Fax 1/138-6942. 40 rms, 2 suites. MINIBAR TV TEL. DM 90–100 ($60–$67) double; DM 130–160 ($87–$107) suite. Rates include breakfast. Rates 20% lower in low season. AE, DC, EC, MC, V. Free parking in hotel lot. Bus: 22 Red or Black from Moszkva tér to Szanatórium utca.

Every room is different in the Hotel Tanne; half have been recently refurbished in light, cheerful colors. All rooms are comfortable and the bathrooms are spacious. A few top-floor rooms feature skylights. The neighborhood, near the Budapest city line, has a village-like flavor and is near numerous hiking trails. A very direct bus line makes the hotel quickly accessible from the city center.

✪ Vadvirág Panzió. II. Nagybányai út 18, 1025 Budapest. ☎ and fax **1/176-4292.** 12 rms, 2 suites. TV TEL. DM 85–120 ($57–$80) double; DM 140–150 ($94–$101) suite. Rates include breakfast. No credit cards. Parking: DM 8 ($5.40) per day in private garage. Bus: 5 from Március 15 tér or Moszkva tér to Pasaréti tér (the last stop).

A 10-minute walk from the bus stop, the Vadvirág (its name means wildflower) is in a gorgeous part of the Buda Hills, surrounded by sloping gardens and terraces. Inside, the hallways are decorated with prints by the Hungarian-born op artist Victor Vasarely. Room 2—a small suite with a balcony—is the best in the house. There's a sauna (DM 15/$10 per hour) and a small restaurant with plenty of outdoor seating.

DINING

In most restaurants, you'll have to initiate the paying and tipping ritual. The bill is usually written out on the spot for you. If you think the bill is incorrect, don't be embarrassed to call it into question; waiters readily correct the bill when challenged. After handing over the bill, in all but the fanciest, most Westernized restaurants, the waiter will stand there waiting patiently for payment. The tip (generally about 10%) should be included in the amount you give him. State the full amount you are paying (bill plus tip) and the waiter will give you change on the spot. Hungarians never leave tips on the table.

THE INNER CITY & CENTRAL PEST

Very Expensive

Légrádi Testvérek. V. Magyar u. 23. ☎ **1/118-6804.** Reservations highly recommended. Main courses 1,200–2,000 Ft ($8.05–$13.40). AE. Mon–Fri 6pm–1am. Metro: Kalvin tér (Blue line). HUNGARIAN.

A very small (nine tables) and inconspicuously marked restaurant on a sleepy side street, Légrádi Brothers is one of Budapest's most elegant and formal eateries. The food is served on Herend china, the cutlery is sterling, and an excellent string trio livens the atmosphere with its repertoire of Hungarian classics. The chicken paprika served with cheese dumplings and seasoned with fresh dill and the veal cavellier are equally sumptuous.

Expensive

Amadeus. V. Apáczai Csere János u. 13 (behind the Forum Hotel). ☎ **1/118-4677.** Reservations recommended for dinner. Main courses 1,100–2,300 Ft ($7.40–$15.40). No credit cards. Mon–Fri noon–midnight, Sat–Sun 6pm–midnight. Metro: Deák tér (all lines). CONTINENTAL.

The menu, scribbled in chalk above the grill, features unusually tasty nouvelle fare. The grill turns out steaks, burgers, chicken breast, and scampi. From the salad case you can design your own (by pointing), choosing from sumptuous grilled peppers in garlic and olive oil, slices of grilled eggplant, steamed spinach, and fresh tomatoes in balsamic vinegar, to name just a few; it's fine to order salad only. Every meal is served with garlic bread.

Moderate

⑤ Fészek. VII. Kertész u. 36. ☎ **1/322-6043.** Reservations recommended. Main courses 460–820 Ft ($3.10–$5.50); fixed-price meals 790 Ft ($5.30). AE. Daily noon–1am. Tram: 4 or 6 to Király utca. HUNGARIAN.

Wild game and freshwater fish dishes are the house specialties. You'll find a large, quiet interior garden, offering an outdoor dining experience without equal in the busy center of Pest. Be sure to reserve ahead of time since Fészek is always crowded.

Inexpensive

Csarnok-Vendéglő. V. Hold u. 11. ☎ **1/269-4906.** Soup 75–135 Ft (50¢–90¢); main courses 280–950 Ft ($1.90–$6.35); fixed-price meals 280–320 ($1.90–$2.15). MC. Mon–Sat 9am–midnight, Sun noon–10pm. Metro: Arany János (Blue line). HUNGARIAN.

On a quiet street in the Inner City, the Csarnok Vendéglő is notable for its uniformly low prices. The menu (in English translation) features typical Hungarian fare, heavy on meat dishes. Outdoor seating is available on the sidewalk, but sit inside for the full effect.

○ Kádár Étkezde. VII. Klauzál tér 9. ☎ **1/121-3622.** Main courses 260–360 Ft ($1.75–$2.40). No credit cards. Tues–Sat 11:30am–3:30pm. Metro: Astoria (Red line) or Deák tér (all lines). HUNGARIAN.

By 11:45am, Uncle Kádár's, in the heart of the historic Jewish district, is filled with a steady stream of lunchtime regulars—from paint-spattered workers to elderly Jewish couples. Uncle Kádár, a neighborhood legend, personally greets them as they file in. It's no more than a lunchroom, but it has a great atmosphere. Table sharing is the norm.

○ Semiramis. V. Alkotmány u. 20. ☎ **1/111-7627.** Main courses 400–650 Ft ($2.70–$4.35). No credit cards. Mon–Sat noon–9pm. Metro: Kossuth tér (Red line). MIDDLE EASTERN.

A block away from Parliament, this little eatery is best suited for lunch since it tends to run out of the more popular dishes by evening. Seating is primarily upstairs. The waiters are friendly, and all speak English. Vegetarians can easily build a meal out of several appetizers; try the yogurt-cucumber salad (yogurtos saláta) and the fül (a zesty garlic and fava bean dish).

JUST BEYOND CENTRAL PEST

Very Expensive

Gundel. XIV. Állatkerti út 2. ☎ **1/321-3550.** Reservations highly recommended. Main courses 1,900–3,000 Ft ($12.75–$20.10). AE, DC, EC, MC, V. Daily noon–4pm and 7pm–midnight. Metro: Hősök tere (Yellow line). HUNGARIAN/INTERNATIONAL.

Budapest's fanciest and most famous restaurant, Gundel was reopened in 1992 by the well-known Hungarian-born restaurateur George Lang, owner of New York's Café des Artistes. He has spared no effort in attempting to re-create the original splendor for which Gundel, founded in 1894, achieved its international reputation. Lamb and wild-game entrees are house specialties. Gundel has perhaps the most extensive wine list in town. For a less expensive meal, consider dining at Bagolyvár, the less fancy "home-style" restaurant next door, also owned by Lang.

Moderate

🟢 **Bagolyvár.** XIV. Állatkerti út 2. ☎ 1/321-3550. Reservations recommended. Main courses 540–1,700 Ft ($3.60–$11.40). AE, MC, V. Daily noon–11pm. Metro: Hósök tere (Yellow line). HUNGARIAN.

Bagolyvár (Owl Palace) offers something unique to the budget traveler—a taste of Gundel, Budapest's most famous (and most expensive) restaurant, at budget prices. The Bagolyvár menu is limited to half a dozen main courses (supplemented by daily specials). The food is carefully prepared and presented. You can dine outdoors in the restaurant's garden.

CENTRAL BUDA

Expensive

⭕ **Kacsa Vendéglő.** I. Fő u. 75. ☎ 1/201-9992. Reservations recommended. Main courses 1,170–2,000 Ft ($7.85–$13.40). AE, DC, EC, MC, V. Daily 6pm–1am. Metro: Batthyány tér (Red line). HUNGARIAN.

Kacsa (which means "duck") is located on the main street of Watertown, the Buda neighborhood between Castle Hill and the Danube. Here you'll find an intimate dining atmosphere that's elegant and understated. The service, however, is overly attentive and ceremonious. The menu is replete with Hungarian specialties.

Moderate

Aranyszarvas. I. Szarvas tér 1. ☎ 1/175-6451. Reservations recommended. Main courses 480–810 Ft ($3.20–$5.40). AE, CB, DC, EC, JCB, MC, V. June–Aug daily noon–midnight; Sept–May daily 6pm–midnight. Bus: A number of buses serve Döbrentei tér, including 8 from Március 15 tér. HUNGARIAN.

The Golden Stag is located just beneath and to the south of Castle Hill. On pleasant nights, you can dine on the outdoor terrace. As the name and decor suggest, this restaurant serves wild game, and the menu lists reasonably priced dishes, such as hunter's saddle of hare, Serbian wild boar, and venison stew.

Horgásztanya Vendéglő. I. Fő u. 29. ☎ 1/212-3780. Main courses 430–1,300 Ft ($2.90–$8.70). No credit cards. Daily noon–11pm. Metro: Battyhány tér (Red line). HUNGARIAN.

Just a short block from the Danube, in Buda's Watertown (Víziváros), the Horgásztanya Vendéglő is a family-style fish restaurant; some nonfish dishes are available, too. The decor is traditional Hungarian.

THE BUDA HILLS

Moderate

Nánsci Néni Vendéglője. II. Ördögárok út 80. ☎ 1/176-5809. Reservations recommended for dinner. Main courses 460–800 Ft ($3.10–$5.35). AE, CB, DC, EC, JCB, MC, V. Daily noon–midnight. Tram no. 56 from Moszkva tér to the last stop, then change to bus no. 63 to Széchenyi utca. HUNGARIAN.

Decorated with photographs of turn-of-the-century Budapest, this popular restaurant is located high in the Buda Hills. There's outdoor garden dining in the summer, with live accordion music at night. The menu features typical Hungarian dishes prepared with care.

⑤ Szép Ilona. II. Budakeszi út 1–3. ☎ **1/275-1392.** Main courses 550–1,200 Ft ($3.70–$8.05). No credit cards. Daily 11:30am–10pm. Bus: 158 from Moszkva tér (departs from Csaba utca, at the top of the stairs, by the little Várbusz). HUNGARIAN.

This cheerful, unassuming restaurant serves a mostly local clientele. There's a good selection of Hungarian specialties; try the borjúpaprikás galuskával (veal paprika with dumplings). There's a small sidewalk-side garden for summer dining. The Szép Ilona is located in a pleasant Buda neighborhood; after your meal, stroll through the tree-lined streets.

NORTHERN BUDA & ÓBUDA
Expensive
❶ Kis Buda Gyöngye. III. Kenyeres u. 34. ☎ **1/168-6402.** Reservations highly recommended. Main courses 820–2,000 Ft ($5.50–$13.40); fish dishes to 2,700 Ft ($18.10). AE. Daily noon–midnight. Closed Sun mid-May to the end of Aug. Tram: 17 from Margit híd (Buda side). HUNGARIAN.

On a quiet side street in a residential Óbuda neighborhood, Kis Buda Gyöngye (Little Pearl of Buda) is a favorite of Hungarians and tourists alike. This lively establishment features an interior garden, which sits in the shade of a wonderful old gnarly tree. An eccentric violin player entertains diners. The standard Hungarian fare is painstakingly prepared. Consider the goose plate, a rich combination platter including roast goose leg, goose cracklings, and goose liver.

Sipos Halászkert. III. Fő tér 6. ☎ **1/188-8745.** Reservations recommended. Main courses 750–1,580 Ft ($5–$10.60). 10% service charge added to the bill. AE, CB, DC, EC, JCB, MC, V. Daily noon–midnight. Train: Suburban HÉV line to Árpád híd. HUNGARIAN/SEAFOOD.

In its own handsome building on Óbuda's dignified main square, the restaurant consists of several rooms with a comfortable air of worn elegance. The menu specializes in Hungarian seafood dishes.

COFFEEHOUSES
Imperial Budapest, like Vienna, was famous for its coffeehouse culture. Literary movements and political circles alike were identified in large part by which coffeehouse they met in. You can still go to several classic coffeehouses, all of which offer delicious pastries, coffee, and more in an atmosphere of luxurious splendor. Table sharing is common.

The best are **Gerbeaud's,** in the Inner City at V. Vörösmarty tér 7 (☎ 1/118-1311); **❶ Művész Kávéház,** across the street from the Opera House at VI. Andrássy út 29 (☎ 1/112-4606); the **New York Kávéház,** on the Outer Ring at VII. Erzsébet krt. 9–11 (☎ 1/122-3849)—but avoid the overpriced and mediocre dinners here; and **❶ Ruszwurm Cukrászda,** in the Castle District at I. Szentháromság u. 7 (☎ 1/175-5284).

ATTRACTIONS
SIGHTSEEING SUGGESTIONS
If You Have 1 Day Spend a few hours in the morning exploring the Inner City and central Pest. Stroll along the Danube as far as the neo-gothic Parliament Building, noting along the way the Chain Bridge. In the afternoon, visit the major sites of Castle Hill and explore the cobblestone streets of the Castle District.

If You Have 2 Days Save the castle for the second day, and on the first day in the afternoon, head for Buda's Gellért Hotel and have a dip in its spa waters. Then hike up the stairs of Gellért Hill to see an unparalleled panorama of the city. Devote most of the second day to the Castle District and the sites of Castle Hill, and visit some of the smaller museums. Head back to Pest to see Heroes' Square and City Park, and in the evening stroll the length of grand Andrássu út back to the center of Pest.

If You Have 3 Days or More   On Day 3, take a boat up the Danube to visit Sztendre, a charming riverside town. On the fourth and fifth days, visit some of the central sites you may have missed, and after lunch cross the Chain Bridge to Watertown, to explore Buda's historic riverside neighborhood. See St. Anne's Church, the Capuchin Church, and the Király Baths. Check out Pest's authentic indoor markets, and visit Margaret Island.

THE TOP ATTRACTIONS

In Pest

Néprajzi Múzeum (Ethnographical Museum). V. Kossuth tér 12. ☎ **1/132-6340.** Admission 80 Ft (55¢). Tues–Sun 10am–6pm. Metro: Kossuth tér (Red line).

Directly across Kossuth tér from the House of Parliament, the vast Ethnographical Museum features an ornate interior equal to that of the Opera House. A ceiling fresco of Justitia, the goddess of justice, by the well-known artist Károly Lotz, dominates the lobby. Concentrate on the items from Hungarian ethnography.

☉ Nemzeti Múzeum (Hungarian National Museum). VIII. Múzeum krt. 14. ☎ **1/138-2122.** Admission 60 Ft (40¢). Tues–Sun 10am–6pm. Metro: Kálvin tér (Blue line).

The Hungarian National Museum, an enormous neoclassical structure built in 1837–47, played a major role in the beginning of the Hungarian Revolution of 1848–49; on its wide steps on March 15, 1848, the poet Sándor Petőfi and other young radicals are said to have exhorted the people of Pest to revolt against the Habsburgs. The museum's main attraction is the crown of St. Stephen (King Stephen ruled 1000–38), ceremoniously returned by Secretary of State Cyrus Vance to Hungary in 1978 from the United States, where it had been stored since the end of World War II. Out of respect, visitors must put slippers on over their shoes when entering the room where the crown is displayed.

In Buda

Budapesti Történeti Múzeum (Budapest History Museum). I. In Buda Palace, Wing E, on Castle Hill. ☎ **1/175-7533.** Admission 100 Ft (70¢); temporary exhibits up to 200 Ft ($1.35) each; free Wed. Guided tours in English for 400 Ft ($2.70) available upon request. Mar–Oct Tues–Sun 10am–6pm; Nov–Feb Wed–Mon 10am–4pm. Bus: Várbusz from Moszkva tér, 106 from Deák tér, or 116 from Március 15 tér to Castle Hill. Funicular: From Clark Ádám tér to Castle Hill.

This museum, also known as the Castle Museum, is the best place to get a sense of the once-great medieval Buda. It's probably worth splurging for a guided tour; even though the museum's descriptions are written in English, the history of the palace's repeated construction and destruction is so arcane that it's difficult to understand what you're really seeing.

☉ Nemzeti Galéria (Hungarian National Gallery). I. In Buda Palace, Wings B, C, and D, on Castle Hill. ☎ **1/175-7533.** Admission 100 Ft (70¢); free Sat. Guided tours in English for 800 Ft ($5.35). Mar–Oct Tues–Sun 10am–6pm; Nov–Feb Tues–Sun 10am–4pm. Bus: Várbusz from Moszkva tér, 106 from Deák tér, or 116 from Március 15 tér to Castle Hill. Funicular: From Clark Ádám tér to Castle Hill.

Few people outside Hungary are familiar with even the country's best-known artists. Nevertheless, Hungary has produced some fine artists, particularly in the late 19th century, and this is *the* place to view their work. The giants of the time are the brilliant, moody Mihály Munkácsy; László Paál, a painter of village scenes; Károly Ferenczy, a master of light; and Pál Szinyei Merse, the plein-air artist and contemporary of the early French impressionists.

MORE ATTRACTIONS

☼ Vidám Park (Amusement Park). XIV. Állatkerti krt. 14–16. ☎ 1/343-0996. Admission 50 Ft (35¢) adults, 20 Ft (15¢) children. Rides have individual charges, 60–140 Ft (40¢–95¢). Daily 10am–7pm (some rides closed in winter). Metro: Széchenyi fürdő (Yellow line).

Budapest's amusement park is a marvelous example of the city's faded splendor, and is much frequented by Hungarian families. Two rides in particular are not to be missed. The delightfully rickety old **Merry-Go-Round (*Körhinta*)**, constructed almost entirely of wood, was clearly once a thing of great beauty. The ornate horses face out from the center, like the spokes of a wheel. The rider must actively pump to keep the horse rocking. There is no music, but as the apparatus spins round and round it creaks mightily. The **Ferris wheel (*Óriáskerék*)** is also wonderful, although it has little in common with the rambunctious Ferris wheels of the modern age. A gangly, pale-yellow structure, it rotates at a liltingly slow pace, lifting you high into the sky for a remarkable view.

Nagy Cirkusz (Great Circus). XIV. Állatkerti krt. 7. ☎ 1/343-9630. Tickets 220–460 Ft ($1.50–$3.10). Metro: Hősök tere or Széchenyi fürdő (Yellow line).

Okay, it's not the Big Apple Circus or the Cirque de Soleil, but kids love it anyway. Actually, Budapest has a long circus tradition, though most Hungarian circus stars opt for the more glamorous and financially rewarding circus life abroad. The box office is open from 10am–7pm. Performances are held year-round Wednesday through Sunday, although the schedule may be abbreviated in winter.

Historic Buildings

☼ Magyar Állami Operaház (Hungarian State Opera House). VI. Andrássy út 22. ☎ 1/153-0170. Admission (only on guided tours) 400 Ft ($2.70). Tours given daily at 3 and 4pm. Metro: Opera (Yellow line).

Completed in 1884, Budapest's Opera House boasts a fantastically ornate interior featuring frescoes by two of the best-known Hungarian artists of the day, Bertalan Székely and Károly Lotz. Home to both the State Opera and the State Ballet, the Opera House has a rich and evocative history.

Parliament. V. Kossuth tér. ☎ 1/268-4437. Admission (by guided tour only): 45-minute tour, 400 Ft ($2.70); 2-hour Ibusz tour (see "Organized Tours"), 1,200 Ft ($8.05). Jan–Oct, English-language tours given Wed and Fri at 10am and 2pm, Sat–Sun at 12:30pm; Nov–Dec, Fri at 10am and 2pm. (Purchase tickets at Gate X and enter at Gate XII; it's best to reserve a space ahead of time, but you may be able to join a tour if you show up at the meeting point.) Closed when Parliament is in session. Metro: Kossuth tér (Red line).

Budapest's great Parliament building, an eclectic design that mixes the predominant neo-gothic style with a neo-Renaissance dome, was completed in 1902. Standing proudly on the Danube bank, visible from almost any riverside vantage point, it has from the outset been one of Budapest's symbols, though until 1989 a democratically elected government had convened here exactly once (just after World War II, before the communist takeover).

Churches & Synagogues

☼ Dohány Synagogue. VII. Dohány u. 2–8. ☎ 1/342-8949. Admission by donation. Officially open Sun–Fri 10am–2pm, though hours have been erratic during the restoration. Metro: Astoria (Red line) or Deák tér (all lines).

Built in 1859, this is the largest synagogue in Europe and the world's second-largest synagogue. Budapest's Jewish community still uses it. The architecture has striking Moorish elements; the interior is vast and ornate, with two balconies, and the unusual presence of an organ. The synagogue has a rich but tragic history. There is a Jewish museum next door.

Belvárosi Plébániatemplom (Inner City Parish Church). V. Március 15 tér. ☎ **1/ 118-3108.** Free admission. Daily 9am–11pm. Metro: Ferenciek tere (Blue line).

The Inner City Parish Church, standing flush against the Erzsébet Bridge in Pest, is one of the city's great architectural monuments. The 12th-century romanesque church first built on this spot was constructed inside the remains of the walls of the Roman fortress of Contra-Aquincum. In the early 14th century a gothic church was built, and this medieval church, with numerous additions and reconstructions reflecting the architectural trends of the time, stands today.

Bazilika (St. Stephen's Church). V. Szent István tér 33. ☎ **1/117-2859.** Church, free; tower, 100 Ft (70¢) adults, 50 Ft (35¢) students. Church, Mon–Sat 6am–7pm, Sun 6am–8:30pm; tower, daily 10am–5:30pm; treasury, daily 9am–5pm; Szent Jobb Chapel, Mon–Sat 9am–5pm, Sun 1–5pm. Metro: Arany János utca (Blue line) or Bajcsy-Zsilinszky út (Yellow line).

The largest church in the country, the Basilica took over 50 years to build (the collapse of the dome in 1868 caused significant delay). It was finally completed in 1906, but during its long construction Pest had undergone radical growth; strangely, while the front of the church dominates sleepy Szent István tér, the rear faces out onto the far busier Inner Ring boulevard. Inside the church, in the Chapel of the Holy Right (Szent Jobb Kápolna), you can see Hungarian Catholicism's most cherished—and bizarre—holy relic: the preserved right hand of Hungary's first Christian king, Stephen.

✪ Mátyás Templom (Matthias Church). I. Szentháromság tér 2. ☎ **1/116-1543.** Church, free; exhibition rooms beneath the altar, 50 Ft (35¢). Daily 9am–7pm. Bus: Várbusz from Moszkva tér, 106 from Deák tér, or 116 from Március 15 tér to Castle Hill. Funicular: From Clark Ádám tér to Castle Hill.

Officially named the Church of Our Lady, the symbol of Buda's Castle District is popularly known as Matthias Church after the 15th-century king who was twice married here. Although the structure dates to the mid-13th century, like other old churches in Budapest it has an interesting history of destruction and reconstruction, always being refashioned in the architectural style of the time.

A Spectacular View

Gellért Hegy (Gellért Hill), towering 230m (750 ft.) above the Danube, offers the single best panorama of the city. The hill is named after the Italian Bishop Gellért who assisted Hungary's first Christian king, Stephen I, in converting the Magyars. Gellért became a martyr when he was rolled in a barrel to his death from the side of the hill on which his enormous statue now stands. On top of Gellért Hill you'll find the **Liberation Monument,** built in 1947 to commemorate the Red Army's liberation of Budapest from Nazi occupation. Also atop Gellért Hill is the **Citadella,** built by the Austrians shortly after they crushed the Hungarian War of Independence of 1848–49. To get here, take bus no. 27 from Móricz Zsigmond körtér.

PARKS & GARDENS

Popular **Margaret Island (Margit-sziget)** has been a public park since 1908. The long, narrow island, connected to both Buda and Pest via the Margaret and Árpád bridges, is barred to most vehicular traffic. Facilities on the island include the

Palatinus Strand open-air baths (see "Thermal Baths" below), which draw upon the famous thermal waters under Margaret Island; the Alfréd Hajós Sport Pool; and the Open Air Theater. Sunbathers line the steep embankments along the river and bicycles are available for rent. Despite all this, Margaret Island is a quiet, tranquil place. Margaret Island is best reached by bus no. 26 from Nyugati tér, which runs the length of the island, or tram no. 4 or 6, which stops at the entrance to the island midway across the Margaret Bridge. (*Warning:* These are popular lines for pickpockets.)

City Park (Városliget) is an equally popular place to spend a summer day. Heroes' Square, at the end of Andrássy út, is the most logical starting point for a walk in City Park. The lake behind the square is used for boating in summer and ice skating in winter. The park's Zoo Boulevard (Állatkerti körút), the favorite street of generations of Hungarian children, is where the zoo, the circus, and the amusement park are all found. Gundel, Budapest's most famous restaurant, is also here, as are the Széchenyi Baths. The Yellow metro line makes stops at Hősök tere (Heroes' Square), at the edge of the park, and Széchenyi Fürdő, in the middle of it.

THERMAL BATHS

The baths of Budapest have a long and proud history, stretching back to Roman times. Under Turkish occupation the culture of the baths flourished, and several still-functioning bathhouses—Király, Rudas, and Rac—are among the architectural relics of the Turkish period. In the late 19th and early 20th centuries, Budapest's "golden age," several fabulous bathhouses were built: the extravagant eclectic Széchenyi Baths in City Park, the splendid art nouveau Gellért Baths, and the solid neoclassical Lukács Baths. All are still in use.

Because thermal bathing is an activity shaped by ritual, and because bathhouse employees tend to be unfriendly relics of the old system, many foreigners find a trip to the baths confusing at first. The most baffling step may well be the ticket window with its endless list of prices for different facilities and services, often without English translations: *uszoda,* pool; *termál,* thermal pool; *fürdő,* bath; *gozfürdő,* steam bath, massage, and sauna. Towel rental is *törülköző* or *lepedo.* An entry ticket generally entitles you to a free locker in the locker room (*öltözo*); you can usually opt to pay an additional fee for a private cabin (*kabin*).

Budapest's most spectacular bathhouse, the **Gellért Baths** are located in Buda's Hotel Gellért, at XI. Kelenhegyi út 4 (☎ 1/166-6166). Enter the baths through the side entrance. The unisex indoor pool is exquisite, with marble columns, majolica tiles, and stone lion heads spouting water. The segregated Turkish-style thermal baths, one off to each side of the pool through badly marked doors, are also glorious though in need of restoration. The outdoor roof pool attracts great attention for 10 minutes every hour on the hour when the artificial wave machine is turned on.

Admission to the thermal bath costs 250 Ft ($1.70); 15-minute massage is 250 Ft ($1.70) plus tip. Lockers are free; a cabin can be rented for 150 Ft ($1). Admission to all services costs 600 Ft ($4) for adults and 200 Ft ($1.35) for children. Prices are posted in English. The thermal baths are open all year, daily 6am–7pm (last entry 6pm). Take tram no. 47 or 49 from Deák tér to Szent Gellért tér.

In the middle of Margaret Island is the **Palatinus Strand,** Budapest's best located *strand* (literally "beach," but better translated as "outdoor pool complex"), at XIII. Margit-sziget (☎ 1/112-3069). There are three thermal pools—a vast swimming pool, a smaller artificial wave pool, a water slide—segregated nude sunbathing decks, and large, grassy grounds. The waters of the thermal pools are as relaxing as at any of the bathhouses, but the experience here is not as memorable as it is at the older bathhouses.

The single admission price for all pools is 200 Ft ($1.35) for adults and 110 Ft (75¢) for children; half price Mon–Fri after 4pm. Open May–Sept daily 8am–7pm (last entry at 6pm). Take bus no. 26 from Nyugati pu.; beware of pickpockets on the bus!

ORGANIZED TOURS

Ibusz (☎ 1/118-1139 or 1/118-1043) offers 18 different boat and bus tours, ranging from basic city tours to special folklore-oriented tours. Bus tours leave from the Erzsébet tér bus station, near Deák tér; boat tours leave from the Vigadó tér landing. There's also a free hotel pickup service 30 minutes before departure time.

Legenda, Fraknó utca 4 (☎ 1/117-2203), a private company founded in 1990, offers boat tours on the Danube. A majority of the city's grand sights can be seen from the river. Tours run from mid-April to mid-Oct; all boats leave from the Vigadó tér port, Pier 6 or 7. Tickets are available through most major hotels, at the dock, or through the Legenda office.

SHOPPING

Shoppers throng the pedestrian-only stretch of **Váci utca,** from the rear of Kossuth Lajos utca to the wide, stately Vörösmarty tér, the center of Pest. Váci utca, and the pedestrian streets bisecting it, are lined with shops. Boutiques, not visible from the street, fill the courtyards. The **Castle District** in Buda, with many folk-art boutiques and galleries, is another popular area for souvenir hunters.

While Hungarians enjoy window-shopping in these two neighborhoods, they do their serious shopping elsewhere. The most popular street is Pest's **Outer Ring** (Nagykörút); another bustling shopping street is Pest's **Kossuth Lajos utca,** off the Erzsébet Bridge, and its continuation **Rákóczi út,** which extends all the way out to Keleti Station. In Buda, Hungarians frequent the Buda Skála department store near **Móricz Zsigmond körtér.**

In addition to the two new shopping malls—**Fortuna Department Store,** Váci u. 16, and **Made in World Centre,** Váci u. 30—there are plenty of places to shop for clothes along the central pedestrian streets. Here are some less-touristy suggestions: ♦ **Joker Applied Arts,** VII. Akácfa u. 5/a (☎ 1/141-4281), with handmade goods by local artisans; **Kaláka Design Studio,** V. Haris köz 2 (☎ 1/118-3313), with clothing by ultra-hip Hungarian designers; ♦ **Manu-Art,** VI. Bajcsy-Zsilinszky köz 3 (☎ 1/132-0298). Metro: Arany János (Blue line), with handcrafted originals by local student artisans.

For department stores, there's the ever-crowded **Skála Metro,** at Nyugati tér across from Nyugati Station, or the equally popular **Buda Skála,** on Október 23 utca, near Móricz Zsigmond körtér. On Váci utca is the **Fortuna Department Store.**

Except for a few specialty shops we recommend, the stores of the state-owned **Folkart Háziipar** should be your main source of Hungary's justly famous folk items. Almost everything is handmade—from tablecloths to miniature dolls, from ceramic dishes to vests. The main store, **Folkart Centrum,** is at V. Váci u. 14 (☎ 1/118-5840), and there are eight other Folkart stores with similar offerings at similar prices, but they're closed Sunday.

One outstanding private shop on Váci utca is ♦ **Vali Folklor,** in the courtyard of Váci u. 23 (☎ 1/118-6495). Filled with authentic folk items, the store has great traditional women's clothing. **Holló Folkart Gallery,** at V. Vitkovics Mihály u. 12 (☎ 1/117-8103), is an unusual gallery selling handcrafted reproductions of original folk-art pieces from various regions of the country.

There are five vintage market halls (*vásárcsarnok*) in Budapest. These vast cavernous spaces, all wonders of steel and glass, were built in the 1890s in the ambitious grandiose style of the time. Three are still in use as markets and provide a measure of local color you won't find in the grocery store. Hungarian produce is exceptional. The **Központi Vásárcsarnok** (Central Market Hall), on IX. Vámház körút, is the largest and most spectacular market hall. Located on the Inner Ring (Kiskörút), on the Pest side of the Szabadság Bridge, this trilevel hall has been impeccably reconstructed; it reopened for business in 1995. Other vintage market halls include the **Belvárosi Vásárcsarnok** (Inner City Market Hall), on V. Hold utca, behind Szabadság tér in central Pest, and the **Józsefváros Vásárcsarnok,** on VIII. Rákóczi tér.

If you're looking for Hungarian folk music, stop by **Hungaroton Hanglemezszalon,** V. Vörösmarty tér 1 (☎ 1/138-2810), for the city's best selection. And Budapest's musical crowd frequents **Liszt Ferenc Zeneműboltja (Ferenc Liszt Music Shop),** VI. Andrássy út 45 (☎ 1/322-4091).

You'll find the world-renowned hand-painted Herend porcelain, first produced in 1826, at the **Herend Shop,** V. József nádor tér 11 (☎ 1/117-2622). This shop has the widest Herend selection in the capital, but unfortunately it can't arrange shipping. If Herend porcelain isn't within your price range, the delightfully casual pottery you can find at ❸ **Herend Village Pottery,** II. Bem rakpart 37 (☎ 1/156-7899), might be just the thing. And delightfully gaudy Zsolnay porcelain from the southern city of Pécs is Hungary's second-most celebrated brand of porcelain; you'll find it at **Zsolnay Márkabolt,** V. Kígyó u. 4 (☎ 1/118-3712).

BUDAPEST AFTER DARK

The most complete schedule of mainstream performing arts is found in the free bimonthly **Koncert Kalendárium,** available at the Central Philharmonic Ticket Office in Vörösmarty tér. The **Budapest Sun,** one of two English-language weeklies, also has a comprehensive events calendar.

For opera, ballet, theater, and concert tickets, you're better off going to one of the commission-free state-run ticket offices than to the individual box offices. For **classical performances,** go to the National Philharmonic Ticket Office (Filharmónia Nemzeti Jegyiroda), V. Vörösmarty tér 1 (☎ 1/117-6222). For **theater and operetta,** go to the Central Theater Ticket Office (Színházak Központi Jegyiroda), VI. Andrássy út 18 (☎ 1/112-0000); a second branch is at II. Moszkva tér 3 (☎ 1/135-9136). For **opera and ballet,** go to the Hungarian State Opera Ticket Office (Magyar Állami Opera Jegyiroda), VI. Andrássy út 20 (entrance inside the courtyard) (☎ 1/132-7914). For events in the **Budapest Spring Festival,** go to the Festival Ticket Service, V. Szomory Dezső tér (just across from Tourinform) (☎ 1/118-9570). For **rock concert** tickets, try Music Mix, V. Váci u. 33 (☎ 1/138-2237 or 1/117-7736).

THE PERFORMING ARTS

Completed in 1884, the **Magyar Állami Operaház (Hungarian State Opera House),** VI. Andrássy út 22 (☎ 1/153-0170), is Budapest's most famous performance hall and a tourist attraction in its own right. Hungarians adore opera, and a large percentage of seats are sold on a subscription basis; buy your tickets a few days ahead if you have the chance. The season runs from mid-September–mid-June, although there are also about a dozen performances (both opera and ballet) in the Summer Festival, in July or August.

Zeneakadémia (Ferenc Liszt Academy of Music). VI. Liszt Ferenc tér 8. ☎ **1/341-4788** or 1/342-0179.

The Great Hall (Nagyterem) of the Academy of Music is Budapest's premier music hall. The Academy was built in the art nouveau style of the early 20th century. The acoustics in the Great Hall are said to be the best of any hall in the city. Unfortunately, it is generally not used in the summer months; the smaller Kisterem, also a fine hall, is used then. A weekly schedule is posted outside the Király utca entrance to the Academy.

MUSIC FOR A SUMMER EVENING

During the summer, you'll find several special venues for classical music. Tickets for all such performances are available at the **Central Philharmonic Ticket Office,** V. Vörösmarty tér 1 (☎ 1/117-6222).

The historic outdoor **Dominican Courtyard,** inside the Castle District's Hilton Hotel, I. Hess András tér 1–3 (☎ 1/175-1000), is the site for a series of classical recitals during the summer; schedules vary. The Castle District's beautiful **Matthias Church** (Mátyás Templom), just nexy door at I. Szentháromság tér 2, holds a regular Friday-night series of organ concerts (7:30pm) June–Sept. Concerts start at 7:30pm. Tickets can be purchased before the performance at the church entry. Take the Várbusz from Moszkva tér, bus no. 16 from Deák tér, or bus no. 116 from Március 15 tér to Castle Hill.

Organ concerts are also held Monday evenings at 7pm during July and August at **St. Stephen's Church (Basilica),** Hungary's largest church, V. Szent István tér 33 (☎ 1/117-2859). Tickets can be purchased before the performance at the church entry. Take the metro to Arany János utca (Blue line) or Bajcsy-Zsilinszky út (Yellow line).

THE CLUB SCENE

The club scene in Budapest has found fertile ground since the political changes of 1989, so much so, in fact, that clubs come in and out of fashion overnight. A few, however, like Tilos az Á and Made Inn Mine, have shown a solid staying power over the past 5 or 6 years. Check the *Budapest Sun* and *Budapest Week* for up-to-the-minute club listings.

Made Inn Mine. VI. Andrássy út 112. ☎ **1/111-3437.** Cover 300 Ft ($2). Metro: Bajza utca (Yellow line).

This popular club shares the building of the Young Artists' Club (FMK), another rock-music club, but the two establishments are completely different. The air-conditioned Made Inn has a subterranean cavelike atmosphere. Wednesday night features a funk dance party. For some reason, Thursday night is *the* night to be here. Open daily 8pm–5am.

Morrison's Music Pub. VI. Révay u. 25. ☎ **1/269-4060.** Metro: Opera (Yellow line).

A 20-something crowd fills this cozy pub every night of the week. There's a small dance floor and an eclectic variety of loud live music.

Piaf. VI. Nagymező u. 25. ☎ **1/112-3823.** Cover 200 Ft ($1.35). Metro: Oktogon (Yellow line).

In the heart of Budapest's theater district, Piaf is a classy French-style nightclub, with red velvet chairs and a candlelit atmosphere. There's live piano music, and drinks are pricy. Open daily 10pm–6am.

Ⓢ Picasso Point Pub. VI. Hajós u. 31. No phone. Cover 150 Ft ($1). Metro: Opera (Yellow line). Tram: 4 or 6.

Live jazz, folk, rock, or world music is featured three times a week in this funky ramshackle establishment. Avoid ordering food (terrible and overpriced) or coffee (even worse than the food). Come for the beer and the offbeat atmosphere.

❂ **Tilos Az Á.** VIII. Mikszáth Kálmán tér 2. ☎ **1/118-0684.** Cover usually 200 Ft ($1.35). Metro: Kálvin tér (Blue line).

With a cult following from the day it opened, just after the political changes, Tilos has become the standard against which all other Budapest clubs are measured. The name is taken from the Hungarian version of the broken NO TRESPASSING sign on Piglet's door in *Winnie-the-Pooh*. Originally a small, smoky, counterculture hangout, it has evolved over the years into a larger, equally smoky, slightly more mainstream place with live music. Open varied hours, but stays open very late.

BARS

A dark, friendly cellar bar, **Big Mambo,** VIII. Mária u. 48 (☎ 1/134-4277), caters to a bohemian ex-pat and Hungarian clientele. The beer is cheap, as is the pizza. Open daily 5pm–4am.

One in a chain of popular English pubs, the ❂ **John Bull Pub,** VI. Lövölde tér 3 (☎ 1/268-0617), has occasional live music (Irish, folk, country), but no cover charge. Open daily from noon to midnight. There are other John Bull Pubs in Budapest at V. Podmaniczky tér 4 (☎ 1/269-3116), XII. Maros u. 28 (☎ 1/156-3565), and elsewhere.

The ⊛ **Tokaji Borbár (Tokaj Wine Bar),** V. Andrássy út 20 (no phone), is a casual, unpretentious place to sample delicious, fruity whites of the famous Tokaj region. Open Mon–Sat 9am–9pm.

HUNGARIAN DANCE HOUSES

Recent years have seen the growth of an urban-centered folk revival movement known as the *táncház* (dance house). This interactive evening of folk music and folk dancing, held in community centers around town, is one of the best cultural experiences you can have in Hungary. The format usually consists of about an hour of dance-step instruction followed by several hours of dancing accompanied by a live band, which might include some of Hungary's best folk musicians, in an authentic, casual atmosphere.

The leading Hungarian folk band Muzsikás hosts a táncház every Tuesday (Sept–May only) at 5:30pm (150 Ft/$1) at the ❂ **FMH Cultural House (Szakszervezetek Fővárosi Művelődési Háza),** XI. Fehérvári út 47 (☎ 1/203-3868). It also has a year-round weekly Balkan táncház held on Wednesday at 7pm (150 Ft/$1). Tram no. 47 from Deák tér gets you there.

The **First District Cultural Center,** at I. Bem rakpart 6 (☎ 1/201-0324), hosts the Téka (another well-known folk band) táncház every Friday at 7pm, September to May (200 Ft/$1.35). The First District Cultural Center is near Clark Ádám tér, which is served by a large number of buses and trams, including bus no. 16 from Deák tér.

DAY TRIPS TO THE DANUBE BEND

The delightful towns along the Bend—**Szentendre, Esztergom,** and **Vác**—are easy day trips from Budapest. The great natural beauty of the area, where steep forested hills loom over the river, makes it a welcome departure for the city-weary.

ESSENTIALS

GETTING THERE **By Boat** From Apr–Sept **boats** run between Budapest and the towns of the Danube Bend. All boats leave Budapest's Vigadó tér boat landing,

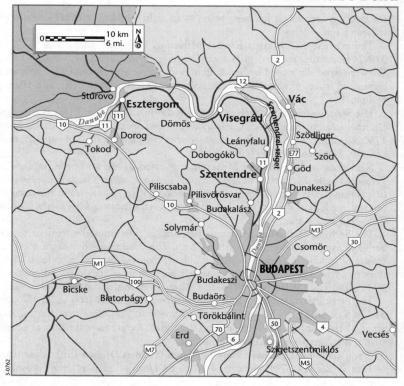

stopping to pick up passengers 5 minutes later at Buda's Batthyány tér landing, before continuing up the river. Schedules and towns served are complicated, so contact **MAHART**, the state shipping company, at the Vigadó tér landing (☎ **1/ 118-1223**) for information. A round-trip costs 540 Ft ($3.60) to Szentendre, 650 Ft ($4.35) to Vác, and 760 Ft ($5.10) to Esztergom, with discounts for children. The trip from Budapest takes 1¹/₂ hours to Szentendre, 2¹/₂ hours to Vác, and 4 hours to Esztergom.

MAHART also runs a much faster **hydrofoil** nonstop between Budapest's Vigadó tér and Esztergom, late May–early Sept, Sat, Sun, and holidays only; from the end of June it also runs Fri. It departs Budapest for Esztergom at 9:20am, arriving at 10:30am; it returns from Esztergom at 4:30pm, arriving in Budapest at 5:40pm.

By Train   The HÉV suburban railroad connects Budapest's Batthyány tér with Szentendre, a 45-minute trip; trains leave daily, year-round, every 20 minutes or so from 4am to 11:30pm. Ten daily trains make the run between Budapest's Nyugati Station and Esztergom, a 1¹/₄-hour trip. Tickets cost 288 Ft ($1.90) in first class and 192 Ft ($1.30) in second class. Frequent trains depart Budapest's Nyugati Station for the 1-hour trip to Vác; tickets cost 180 Ft ($1.20) in first class and 120 Ft (80¢) in second class.

SZENTENDRE   Peopled in medieval times by Serbian settlers, Szentendre (pronouned *Sen*-ten-dreh), 21km (13 miles) north of Budapest, counts half a dozen Serbian churches among its rich collection of historical buildings. Since the turn of the century, Szentendre has been home to an artist's colony, and has a wealth of museums and galleries.

The expansive ✪ **Margit Kovács Museum,** Vastagh György u. 1 (☎ 26/ 310-244), features the work of Hungary's leading ceramic artist, who died in 1977. We were especially moved by her sculptures of elderly women and by her folk art–influenced friezes of village life. Admission 120 Ft (80¢); open Tues–Sun 10am–5:30pm.

The **Blagovestenska Church** at Fő tér 4 is the only one of the Serbian Orthodox churches in Szentendre you can be fairly sure to find open. The church, dating from 1752, was built on the site of an earlier wooden church from the Serbian migration of 1690. Admission is 30 Ft (20¢).

Next door is the **Ferenczy Museum,** dedicated to the art of the prodigious Ferenczy family. Featured is Károly Ferenczy, one of Hungary's leading impressionists. Works of his children Noémi (tapestry maker), Valer (painter), and Beni (sculptor and medallion maker) are also on display. Admission is 60 Ft (40¢); open Tues–Sun 10am–4pm.

The **Serbian Orthodox Museum,** Patriarka u. 5, is housed next door to the Serbian Orthodox church just north of Fő tér. This collection—one of the most extensive of its kind in predominantly Catholic Hungary—features exceptional 16th-through 19th-century icons, liturgical vessels, and Ottoman-era scrolls. Admission is 30 Ft (20¢); open in summer, Wed–Sun 10am–4pm; winter, Sat–Sun 10am–4pm.

The main information office is **Tourinform,** at Dumtsa Jenő u. 22 (☎ 26/ 317-965 or 26/317-966), open Mon–Fri 9am–5pm, Sat–Sun 9am–2pm. If you arrive by train or bus, you'll come upon this office as you follow the flow of pedestrian traffic into town on Kossuth Lajos utca.

If you get hungry, **Aranysárkány Vendéglő (Golden Dragon Inn),** Alkotmány u. 1/a (☎ 26/311-670), just east of Fő tér on Hunyadi utca, is always crowded, sometimes with lots of locals. You can choose from such enticing offerings as alpine lamb, roast leg of goose, quail, and venison ragoût. Vegetarians can order the vegetable plate. Various beers are on draft.

If you walk directly south from Fő tér, you'll find ✪ **Régimodi,** Fűtő u. 3 (☎ 26/ 311-105). This elegant restaurant in a former private home serves Hungarian specialties, with an emphasis on game dishes. The wild-boar stew in red wine is particularly sumptuous.

ESZTERGOM   Formerly a Roman settlement, Esztergom (pronounced *Ess*-tair-gum), 46km (29 miles) northwest of Budapest, was the seat of the Hungarian kingdom for 300 years. Hungary's first king, István I (Stephen I), crowned by the pope in A.D. 1000, converted Hungary to Catholicism, and Esztergom became the country's center of the early church. Though its glory days are far behind it, the quiet town remains today the seat of the archbishop-primate—the "Hungarian Rome."

The massive, neoclassical **Esztergom Cathedral** on Castle Hill, Esztergom's most popular attraction and one of Hungary's most impressive buildings, was built in the last century to replace the cathedral ruined during the Turkish occupation. The cathedral **Treasury** (*Kincstár*) contains a stunning array of ecclesiastical jewels and gold works. Since Cardinal Mindszenty's body was moved to the **crypt** in 1991 (he died in exile in 1975), it has been a place of pilgrimage for Hungarians. The **cupola** has, as far as church towers go, one of the scarier ascents. You're rewarded at the top with unparalleled views of Esztergom and the surrounding Hungarian and Slovak countryside. Admission to the treasury is 75 Ft (50¢); cupola, 28 Ft (20¢). The cathedral is open in summer daily 7am–7pm; winter, daily 7am–5pm; the crypt, daily 9am–5pm; the treasury, daily 9am–4:30pm (closed Jan); the cupola, daily 9am–5pm.

It's definitely worth taking a break from the crowds at the cathedral and taking a stroll through the quiet, cobblestoned streets of Esztergom's Víziváros (Watertown). There you'll find the **Keresztény Múzeum (Christian Museum),** Mindszenty tér 2 (☎ **33/313-880**), in the neoclassical former primate's palace, which houses Hungary's largest collection of religious art and the largest collection of medieval art outside the National Gallery. Admission is 70 Ft (45¢). Open Tues–Sun 10am–5:30pm.

For information, stop by **Gran Tours,** centrally located at Széchenyi tér 25 (☎ **33/313-756**), open Mon–Fri 8am–4pm, Sat 8am–noon.

The food at the recently remodeled and enlarged ✪ **Szalma Csárda,** located at Nagy-Duna sétány 2 (☎ **33/315-336**), is absolutely first-rate, with everything made to order and served piping hot. The excellent house soups (110–230 Ft/75¢–$1.55)—fish soup (halászlé), goulash (gulyásleves), and bean soup (babgulyás)—constitute meals in themselves.

VÁC Largely overlooked by tourists, who generally neglect the flatter east bank of the Danube Bend, Vác (pronounced *Vahts*), 34km (21 miles) north of Budapest, is a quietly charming baroque town, with a historic core dating from the early 18th century. The town's elegant, well-maintained squares and its sleepy Danube-side parks exude an unmistakable charm.

Wander around the historic Inner City and its four main squares and admire the baroque architecture. **Március 15 tér** is the town's central square. Here you'll find the Town Hall (Városház), with its intricate wrought-iron gate; the Fehérek Church, with its elegant facade dominating the square's southern end; and a row of baroque houses across from the Town Hall. Nearby **Szentháromság tér** features an elaborate Plague Column and the Piarist Church, whose church bell is the favorite of locals. Lush beds of roses ring large, empty **Konstantin tér.** Old-fashioned street lamps line the walkways. The Bishop's Cathedral, one of Hungary's earliest (1765–77) examples of neoclassical architecture, dominates Konstantin tér. **Géza király tér,** the center of medieval Vác, was the site of the former fortress and cathedral. Now you can see the baroque Franciscan church here.

For information go to **Tourinform,** at Dr. Csányi László krt. 45 (☎ **27/316-160**), open daily 9am–5pm. **Halászkert Étterem,** at Liszt Ferenc sétány 9 (☎ **27/315-985**), is a large outdoor garden restaurant set right on the Danube Promenade at the northern end of the Inner City. The extensive menu features a number of fish specialties (the restaurant's name means "fish garden").

2 Lake Balaton

Lake Balaton may not be the Mediterranean, but don't tell that to the Hungarians. Somehow over the years they have managed to create their own Central European hybrid variety of a Mediterranean culture—an easygoing atmosphere of sun, water, music, wine, and fruit—along the shores of their long, shallow, milky-white lake, Europe's largest at 80 km (50 miles) long and 15 km (10 miles) wide at its broadest stretch.

ESSENTIALS

ARRIVING By Train From Budapest, trains to the various towns along the lake depart from Déli Station. The local trains are interminably slow, so try to get on an express.

By Car If you're driving from Budapest, take the M-7 motorway south through Székesfehérvár until you hit the lake. Route 71 circles the lake.

By Boat Passenger boat travel on Lake Balaton lets you travel across the lake as well as between towns on the same shore. It's both extensive and cheap, but considerably slower than surface transportation. All major towns have a dock with departures and arrivals. Children 3 and under travel free, and those 13 and under get half-price tickets. A single ferry (*komp*) running between Tihany and Szántód lets you transport a car across the width of the lake.

VISITOR INFORMATION All boat and ferry information is available from the **MAHART** office in Siófok (☎ **84/310-050**). Local tourist offices along the lake also have schedules and other information.

STAYING AROUND THE LAKE

Throughout the long summer, swimmers, windsurfers, sailboats, kayaks, and cruisers fill the warm and silky-smooth lake; people cast their reels for pike, play tennis, ride horses, and hike in the hills.

The south shore towns are as flat as Pest; walk 10 minutes from the lake and you're in farm country. The air here is still and quiet; in summer, the sun hangs heavily in the sky. Teenagers, students, and young travelers tend to congregate in the hedonistic towns of the south shore. Here, huge 1970s-style beachside hotels are filled to capacity all summer long, and disco music pulsates into the early-morning hours.

On the more graceful north shore, little villages are neatly tucked away in the rolling countryside, where the grapes of the popular Balaton wines ripen in the strong southern sun. Traveling from Budapest, the northern shore of the lake at first appears every bit as built up and crowded as the southern shore. Beyond Balatonfüred, this impression begins to fade. You'll discover the Tihany Peninsula, a protected area whose 12 square kilometers (4³/₄ square miles) jut out into the lake like a knob. Stop for a swim—or the night—in a small town like Szigliget. Moving westward along the coast, you can make forays inland into the rolling hills of the Balaton wine country. The city of Keszthély, sitting at the lake's western edge, marks the end of its northern shore.

If you stay for more than a day, anywhere you go on the lake, SZOBA KIADÓ signs (or their German equivalent, ZIMMER FREI) beckon you to stop and spend the night in a private home. Because hotel prices are unusually high in the Balaton region, and because just about every local family rents out a room or two in summer, we especially recommend private rooms. You can reserve a room through a local tourist office or you can just look for the SZOBA KIADÓ signs that decorate most front gates in the region. When you take a room without using a tourist agency as the intermediary, prices are generally negotiable. In the height of the season, you shouldn't have to pay more than $30 for a double room within reasonable proximity of the lake.

VESZPRÉM

On your way to Lake Balaton, you may want to make a stop in this charming town. Just 10 miles from Lake Balaton, Veszprém (pronounced *Vess*-praym), 116km (72 miles) southwest of Budapest, surely ranks as one of Hungary's most vibrant small cities, and is often used as a starting point for trips to that popular resort area. In Veszprém you'll find a harmonious mix of old and new: A delightfully self-contained and well-preserved 18th-century baroque Castle District spills effortlessly into a typically modern city center, itself distinguished by lively wide-open pedestrian-only plazas.

Five daily trains depart Budapest's Déli Station for Veszprém, a 1³/₄-hour trip. First-class tickets cost 648 Ft ($4.35); second-class tickets, 432 Ft ($2.90).

The two best information sources are **Balatontourist,** at Kossuth u. 21 (☎ **88/ 429-630;** fax 88/427-062), open Mon–Fri 8:30am–5pm (until 4pm off-season), Sat 9am–noon; and **Ibusz,** at Kossuth u. 6 (☎ **88/426-492** or 88/427-604), open Mon– Fri 8am–4pm, Sat 8am–noon.

Most of Veszprém's main sights are clustered along Vár utca, the street that runs the length of the city's small but lovely Castle District.

Housed inside the 18th-century canon's house, the **Exhibition of Religious Art,** Vár u. 35, has a fine collection of religious (Roman Catholic) art. Admission is 20 Ft (15¢); open daily 9am–5pm.

At Vár u. 16, the vaulted **Gizella Chapel,** named for King Stephen's wife, was unearthed during the construction of the adjoining Bishop's Palace in the 18th century. Today it houses a modest collection of ecclesiastical art, but is best known for the 13th-century frescoes that, in various states of restoration, decorate its walls. Admission is 10 Ft (7¢); open daily 9am–5pm.

For a wonderful view of the surrounding Bakony region, climb up the steps to the narrow observation deck at the top of the ✪ **Fire Tower,** at Óváros tér. Though the foundations of the tower are medieval, the structure itself was built in the early 19th century. Enter via the courtyard of Vár u. 17, behind Óváros tér. Admission is 80 Ft (55¢); open daily 10am–6pm.

Dining

For fast food, try **Mackó Cukrászda,** at Kossuth u. 6 (a few doors down from Ibusz). This stand-up eatery, which is somewhat grungy yet always bustling, is popular with young locals. Pizza, hot dogs, french fries, fried chicken, and various sweets are served. A meal here will put you back about 300 Ft ($2) tops. **Magyaros Étterem,** housed in the same structure, is an authentic *önkiszólgáló* (self-service cafeteria). You'll find the restaurant behind the Nike store; go up the winding staircase inside the building. Magyaros serves up extremely cheap traditional fare for lunch.

You can get lunch or dinner at **Óváros Vendéglő (Old City Guest House),** at Szabadság tér 14, a typical Hungarian restaurant with a large outdoor terrace. The food is nothing special, but prices are reasonable. Steer clear of the salad bar—the vegetables are all pickled.

For something more upscale, ✪ **Villa Medici Étterem,** next to the zoo at Kittenberger u. 11 (☎ **88/321-273**), is *the* place. Reputedly one of Hungary's best restaurants, it's also more expensive. Villa Medici serves Hungarian and continental cuisine only at lunchtime.

THE TIHANY PENINSULA

The Tihany (pronounced *Tee*-hine) Peninsula is a protected area, and building is heavily restricted. Consequently, it maintains a rustic charm that's unusual in the Balaton region. The peninsula also features a lush, protected interior, accessible by a trail from Tihany Village, with several little inland lakes as well as a lookout tower offering views over the Balaton.

The rail line that circles Lake Balaton does not serve the Tihany Peninsula. The nearest railway station is in Aszófő, about 3 miles from Tihany Village. A local bus comes to Tihany from the nearby town of Balatonfüred. You can also go by ferry from Szántód or Balatonföldvár, or by boat from Balatonfüred.

Visitor information is available at **Balatontourist,** Kossuth u. 20 (☎ and fax **86/ 348-519**), open March–Oct Mon–Fri 8am–4:30pm, Sat 8am–12:30pm.

The 18th-century baroque ✪ **Abbey Church** is Tihany Village's main attraction. A resident monk carved the exquisite wooden altar and pulpit in the 18th century.

The frescoes in the church are by three of Hungary's better-known 19th-century painters: Károly Lotz, Bertalan Székely, and Lajos Deák-Ébner.

Next door to the Abbey Church is the **Tihany Museum,** housed in an 18th-century baroque structure like the church. The museum features exhibitions on the surrounding region's history and culture. You pay a single entry fee of 80 Ft (55¢) for both church and museum. Both are open daily: 9am–5:30pm in summer, 10am–3pm off-season.

SZIGLIGET

Halfway between Tihany and Keszthély is the scenic little village of Szigliget (pronounced *Sig*-lee-get). The village is marked by the fantastic ruins of the 13th-century ✪ **Szigliget Castle,** which stand above it on **Várhegy** (Castle Hill). In the days of the Turkish invasions, the Hungarian Balaton fleet, protected by the high castle, called Szigliget its home. You can hike up to the ruins for a splendid view of the lake and the surrounding countryside; look for the path behind the white 18th-century church that stands on the highest spot in the village.

Better yet, if you're in the mood for hiking, take a local bus from Szigliget to the nondescript nearby village of **Hegymagas,** about 3 miles to the north along the Szigliget–Tapolca bus route. The town's name means "Tall Hill," and from here you can hike up onto **Szent György-hegy (St. George Hill).** This marvelous vineyard-covered hill has several hiking trails, the most strenuous of which goes up and over the rocky summit.

KESZTHÉLY

At the western edge of Lake Balaton, Keszthély (pronounced *Kest*-hay), 117 miles southwest of Budapest, is one the largest towns on the lake. Though Keszthély was largely destroyed during the Turkish wars, the town was rebuilt in the 18th century by the Festetics family, an aristocratic family who made Keszthély their home through World War II.

Stop in at **Tourinform,** at Kossuth u. 28 (☎ and fax **83/314-144**), open in summer, Mon–Fri 9am–6pm, Sat 9am–1pm; off-season, Mon–Fri 8am–4pm, Sat 9am–1pm. For private-room bookings, try **Zalatours,** at Fő tér 1 (☎ **83/312-560**), or **Ibusz,** at Széchenyi u. 1–3 (☎ **83/312-951**).

The highlight of a visit to Keszthély is the splendid ✪ **Festetics Mansion,** at Szabadsag u. 1 (☎ **83/315-039**), the baroque 18th-century home (with its 19th-century additions) for generations of the Festetics family. Part of the mansion is now open as a museum, the main attraction of which is the ornate library. The museum also features hunting gear and trophies of a bygone era. The museum is open in summer, daily 10am–6pm (closed Mon in off-season). Admission for foreigners is 300 Ft ($2).

The mansion's lovely concert hall is the site of **classical music concerts** almost every night throughout the summer (just on Mon night off-season). Concerts usually start at 8pm; tickets, at 300 Ft ($2) apiece, are available at the door or earlier in the day at the museum cashier. Another part of the mansion has in the past—and may again—served as a hotel.

The center of Keszthély's summer scene, just like that of every other settlement on Lake Balaton, is down by the water on the "strand." Keszthély's **beachfront** is dominated by several large hotels. Regardless of whether or not you're a guest, you can rent windsurfers, boats, and other water-related equipment from these hotels.

An Excursion to the Thermal Lake in Hévíz

If you find the water of Lake Balaton warm, just wait until you jump into the lake at Hévíz (pronounced *Hay*-veez), a town about 5 miles northwest of Keszthély. You can easily reach Hévíz by bus from Keszthély. Buses depart every half hour or so from the bus station (conveniently stopping to pick up passengers in front of the church on Főtér).

This is Europe's largest thermal lake (and the second largest in the world). The lake's water temperature seldom dips below 85–90°F even in the bitterest spell of winter. Consequently, people swim in the lake year-round. Hévíz has been one of Hungary's leading spa resorts for over 100 years, and it retains some of the 19th-century character that's more typical of the spas in the Czech Republic than of those in Hungary.

While the lakeside area is suitable for ambling, no visit to Hévíz would be complete without a swim. A wooden causeway leads into the center of the lake where a gaudy wood-and-glass structure houses locker rooms and the requisite services, including massage, float rental, and a snack bar.

10 Ireland

by Richard Jones

reland today is a country on the move. Increasingly prosperous, Euro-pean, and defined by its youthful population, it is undergoing rapid change. But you'll still find the traditional warm welcome and gracious hospitality, and even hordes of visitors can't spoil Kerry's legendary beauty.

1 Dublin

On Ireland's east coast overlooking the Irish Sea, Dublin is bisected by the River Liffey and sheltered on three sides by a crescent of mountains. Compact and easily walkable, Dublin harmoniously blends past and present in its narrow cobblestone lanes and wide one-way streets, medieval cathedrals and open-air markets, 18th-century town houses and multistory shopping centers, horse-drawn liveries and double-decker buses.

Over a million people live in the Dublin area—in one generation it has leapt from town to metropolis. Once the second city of the British empire, Dublin again is full of aspirations and ideas and attitude. But it's still a city where conviviality is the norm, and the visitor is welcomed.

ONLY IN DUBLIN

Viewing the *Book of Kells* This amazing 8th-century, meticulously illuminated version of the Four Gospels is housed at Trinity College.

Enjoying Dublin's Georgian Landmarks Dublin is still filled with classic Georgian architecture: Merrion and Fitzwilliam Squares, wide Georgian streets and parks lined by rows of restored brick-fronted town houses; the Custom House, with a long classical facade overlooking the River Liffey; and Leinster House, on Merrion square, which served as a model for the design of the White House.

Discovering Dublin's Literary Heritage Make a visit to the Dublin Writers Museum to learn about Dublin's great writers, with books galore, exhibits, paintings, sculptures, and memorabilia. Also visit the martello tower where Joyce lived, described in *Ulysses*.

Exploring Dublin Castle Once the seat of the British government in Ireland, the ancient castle boasts a 13th-century tower, a

19th-century chapel, elaborate ceremonial state apartments, and a medieval under-croft with excavations going back to Viking times.

Spending an Afternoon in Phoenix Park   Wander down the quiet lanes and walk-ways, and visit the zoo, one of the oldest in Europe.

Going to the Theater   Dublin has two major theaters, the legendary Abbey The-ater for which Sean O'Casey wrote his plays, now the National Theater of Ireland, and the renowned Gate, known worldwide for its distinguished productions.

Spending an Evening in Dublin's Traditional Pubs   Dublin is full of traditional Irish pubs, where you can have a few pints, some fine conversation, and listen to tra-ditional Irish music, which is experiencing a major revival.

ORIENTATION

ARRIVING   By Plane   The **Dublin International Airport** (☎ 01/837-9900) is located 7 miles north of the city center. Dublin Bus (☎ 01/873-4222) provides express coach service from the airport into the city's central bus station, Busarus, on Store Street. Service runs daily 7:30am–10:30pm, with departures every 20 to 30 minutes. The one-way fare is £2.50 ($4) for adults and £1.25 ($2) for children 11 and under.

Taxi fares, depending on your destination, average £10–£13 ($16–$20.80). Taxis are lined up at a first-come, first-served taxi stand outside the arrivals terminal.

By Ferry   Passenger/car-ferries from Britain arrive at the **Dublin Ferryport** (☎ 01/874-3293), on the eastern end of the North Docks, and at the **Dun Laoghaire Ferryport** (☎ 01/280-1905), about 10 miles south of city center. There is bus and taxi service from both ports.

By Train   Irish Rail (☎ 01/836-6222) operates daily train service into Dublin from Belfast in Northern Ireland and all major cities in the Irish Republic. Trains from the south, west, and southwest arrive at **Heuston Station,** Kingsbridge, off St. John's Road; from the north and northwest at **Connolly Station,** Amiens Street; and from the southeast at **Pearse Station,** Westland Row, Tara Street.

By Bus   Bus Eireann (☎ 01/836-6111) operates daily express coach and local bus services from all major cities and towns in Ireland into Dublin's central bus station, Busaras, on Store Street.

By Car   If you're arriving by car from other parts of Ireland or via car-ferry from Britain, all main roads lead into the heart of Dublin and are well signposted to City Centre. If you're staying on the north side of the River Liffey, follow the signs for North Ring; if you're staying on the south side of the river, follow the signs for South Ring.

VISITOR INFORMATION   Dublin Tourism operates year-round walk-in visi-tor offices on Suffolk Street, Dublin 2 (☎ 01/605-7797). Other offices are at Dublin Airport in the arrivals hall; at the ferry dock in Dun Laoghaire; and at 18 Eustace St., Temple Bar (☎ 01/671-5717). Hours vary for each location, depending on the month, but the offices are generally open Mon–Fri 9am–6pm and Sat 9am–1pm, though the information desk at the airport is open daily 8am–6pm.

CITY LAYOUT   Compared with other European capitals, Dublin is a relatively small metropolis and easy to get to know. The downtown core of the city, identified in Gaelic on bus destination signs as AN LAR (the Center), is shaped somewhat like a pie, with the River Liffey cutting across the middle from east to west. The top half of the pie, or north side of the city, is rimmed in a semicircular sweep by the Royal

Dublin Attractions & Accommodations

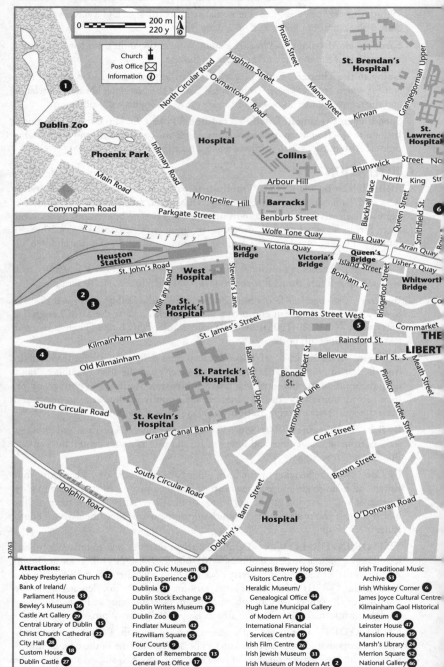

Attractions:

Abbey Presbyterian Church 12
Bank of Ireland/
  Parliament House 33
Bewley's Museum 36
Castle Art Gallery 29
Central Library of Dublin 15
Christ Church Cathedral 22
City Hall 28
Custom House 18
Dublin Castle 27

Dublin Civic Museum 38
Dublin Experience 34
Dublinia 21
Dublin Stock Exchange 32
Dublin Writers Museum 12
Dublin Zoo 1
Findlater Museum 42
Fitzwilliam Square 55
Four Courts 9
Garden of Remembrance 13
General Post Office 17

Guinness Brewery Hop Store/
  Visitors Centre 5
Heraldic Museum/
  Genealogical Office 44
Hugh Lane Municipal Gallery
  of Modern Art 11
International Financial
  Services Centre 19
Irish Film Centre 26
Irish Jewish Museum 31
Irish Museum of Modern Art 2

Irish Traditional Music
  Archive 53
Irish Whiskey Corner 6
James Joyce Cultural Centre
Kilmainham Gaol Historical
  Museum 4
Leinster House 47
Mansion House 39
Marsh's Library 24
Merrion Square 52
National Gallery 46

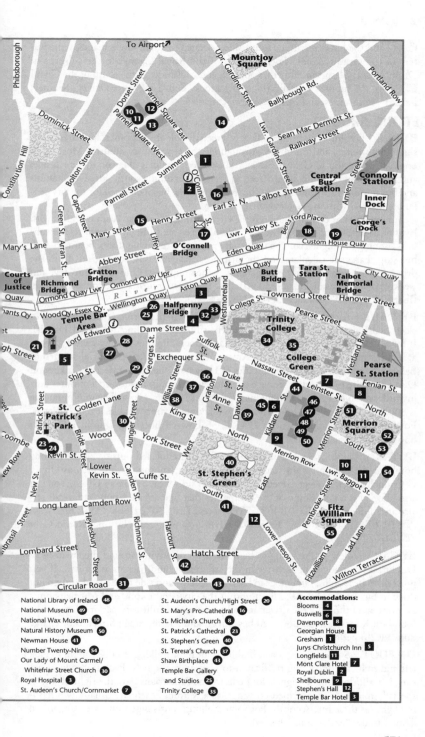

National Library of Ireland 48
National Museum 49
National Wax Museum 10
Natural History Museum 50
Newman House 41
Number Twenty-Nine 54
Our Lady of Mount Carmel/
    Whitefriar Street Church 30
Royal Hospital 3
St. Audeon's Church/Cornmarket 7

St. Audeon's Church/High Street 20
St. Mary's Pro-Cathedral 16
St. Michan's Church 8
St. Patrick's Cathedral 23
St. Stephen's Green 40
St. Teresa's Church 17
Shaw Birthplace 43
Temple Bar Gallery
    and Studios 25
Trinity College 35

Accommodations:
Blooms 4
Buswells 6
Davenport 8
Georgian House 10
Gresham 1
Jurys Christchurch Inn 5
Longfields 11
Mont Clare Hotel 7
Royal Dublin 2
Shelbourne 9
Stephen's Hall 12
Temple Bar Hotel 3

Canal; and the bottom half, or south side, is edged in a half-circle shape by the waters of the Grand Canal. To the north of the Royal Canal are the suburbs of Drumcondra, Glasnevin, Howth, Clontarf, and Malahide; to the south of the Grand Canal are the suburbs of Ballsbridge, Blackrock, Dun Laoghaire, Dalkey, Killiney, Rathgar, Rathmines, and other residential areas.

GETTING AROUND

BY BUS   Dublin Bus operates a fleet of green double-decker buses, high-frequency single-deck buses, and minibuses throughout the city and its suburbs. Most buses originate on or near O'Connell Street, Abbey Street, or Eden Quay on the north side; and from Aston Quay, College Street, or Fleet Street on the south side. Destinations and bus numbers are posted above the front windows; buses destined for the city center are marked with the Gaelic words "An Lar."

Bus service runs daily throughout the city, starting at 6am (at 10am on Sun), with last bus at 11:30pm; Fri–Sat there's a Nitelink service from city center to the suburbs running midnight–3am. Schedules are posted on revolving notice boards at each bus stop. Fares are calculated on the distances traveled. Buy your tickets from the driver as you enter the bus; exact change is not required. One-day, four-day, and weekly passes are available at reduced rates. For more information, contact **Dublin Bus,** 59 Upper O'Connell St. (☎ **01/873-4222**).

BY DART   Although Dublin has no subway in the strict sense, there is an electrified-train rapid-transit system, known as DART (Dublin Area Rapid Transit). It travels mostly at ground level or on elevated tracks, linking the city-center stations at Tara Street, Pearse Street, and Amiens Street with the residential suburb of Ballsbridge and the seaside communities of Howth on the north side and Dalkey and Dun Laoghaire to the south. Service operates every 15 minutes (every 5 minutes during rush hours) Mon–Sat 7am–midnight and Sun 9:30am–11pm. The minimum fare is 80p ($1.20). One-day, four-day, and weekly passes are available at reduced rates. For further information, contact **DART,** 35 Lower Abbey St., Dublin 1 (☎ **01/ 836-6222**).

BY TAXI   Dublin taxis line up at ranks. Ranks are located outside all the leading hotels, at the bus and train stations, and on prime thoroughfares, such as Upper O'Connell Street, College Green, and the north side of St. Stephen's Green. You can also phone for a taxi. Some of the companies that operate a 24-hour radio-call service are All Fives Taxi (☎ 01/455-5555), Access Taxis (☎ 01/668-3333), Blue Cabs (☎ 01/676 1111), Co-op Taxis (☎ 01/676-6666), and National Radio Cabs (☎ 01/677-2222).

BY CAR   Unless you're going to be doing a lot of driving around the environs of Dublin, it's not advisable to drive in the city center, and parking is limited. If you must drive in Dublin, remember to keep to the left-hand side of the road and do not drive in bus lanes. The speed limit within the city is 30 m.p.h. and seat belts must be worn at all times by the driver and all passengers. Multistory parking lots can be found on Kildare Street, Lower Abbey Street, and Marlborough Street; they charge 80p ($1.20) per hour.

ON FOOT   Small and compact, Dublin is ideal for walking. But be careful to look left and right for oncoming traffic and to obey traffic signals. Each traffic light has timed "walk/don't walk" signals for pedestrians. Pedestrians have the right of way at specially marked, zebra-striped crossings; as a warning, there are usually two flashing lights at these intersections. For some walking-tour suggestions, see "Organized Tours" under "Attractions," below).

FAST FACTS: Dublin

American Express　The American Express office is opposite Trinity College, just off College Green, at 116 Grafton St., Dublin 2 (☎ 01/677-2874). It's open Mon–Fri 9am–5pm and Sat 9am–noon; the foreign exchange operates Mon–Sat 9am–5pm and Sun 11am–4pm. In an emergency, traveler's checks can be reported lost or stolen by dialing 800/626-0000.

Baby-sitters　With advance notice, most hotels and guesthouses will arrange for baby-sitting.

Business Hours　Most **banks** are open Mon–Wed and Fri 10am–12:30pm and 1:30–3pm, and Thurs 10am–12:30pm and 1:30–5pm. Most **business offices** are open Mon–Fri 9am–5pm. Stores and **shops** are open Mon–Wed and Fri–Sat 9am–5:30pm and Thurs 9am–8pm. Some bookshops and tourist-oriented stores are also open Sun 11am or noon–4 or 5pm. During peak season (May–Sept) many gift and souvenir shops are open Sunday hours.

Currency　The basic unit of currency is the **punt, or Irish pound (£).** The punt is divided into 100 **pence (p).** There are 1p, 2p, 5p, 10p, 20p, and 50p coins, and punt notes and coins of 5, 10, 20, 50, and 100 punts. At press time $1 = 62p (or £1 = $1.60), and this was the rate of exchange used in this chapter.

Currency Exchange　Currency-exchange services, signposted as a bureau de change, are in all banks and at many branches of the Irish post office system, known as An Post. A bureau de change operates daily during flight arrival and departure times at Dublin airport; a foreign currency note-exchanger machine is also available on a 24-hour basis in the main arrivals hall. Many hotels and travel agencies offer bureau de change services, although the best rate of exchange is usually given at banks.

Dentists/Doctors　For dental emergencies, contact the Irish Dental Council, 57 Merrion Sq. (☎ 01/676-2226 or 01/676-2069). For medical emergencies, most hotels and guesthouses will contact a house doctor for you. You can also ask for a recommendation from the Irish Medical Organization, 10 Fitzwilliam Place (☎ 01/676-7273).

Drugstores　Centrally located drugstores, known locally as pharmacies or chemist shops, include Crowley's Pharmacy at 25 Nassau St. (☎ 01/676-6261) and 6 Lower Baggot St. (☎ 01/678-5612); Hamilton Long and Co., 5 Lower O'Connell St. (☎ 01/874-3352); and Smith's Pharmacy, 50 Grafton St. (☎ 01/677-9288).

Embassies/Consulates　The Embassy of the **United States** is at 42 Elgin Rd., Ballsbridge, Dublin 4 (☎ 01/668-8777); the Embassy of **Canada,** 65/68 St. Stephen's Green, Dublin 2 (☎ 01/478/1988); the Embassy of the **United Kingdom,** 33 Merrion Rd., Dublin 4 (☎ 01/269-5211); and the Embassy of **Australia,** Fitzwilton House, Wilton Terrace, Dublin 2 (☎ 01/676-1517).

Emergencies　For the Garda (police), fire, or other emergencies, dial 999.

Eyeglasses　For 1-hour service on glasses or contact lenses, try Specsavers, Unit 9, GPO Arcade, Henry Street (☎ 01/872-8155).

Hospitals　For emergency care, two of the most modern health-care facilities are St. Vincent's Hospital, Elm Park (☎ 01/269-4533), on the south side of the city; and Beaumont Hospital, Beaumont (☎ 01/837-7755), on the north side.

Laundry/Dry Cleaning　Most hotels provide same-day or next-day laundry and/or dry-cleaning services. Two centrally located choices are Craft Cleaners,

12 Upper Baggot St. (☎ 01/668-8198), and Grafton Cleaners, 32 S. William St. (☎ 01/679-4409).

Libraries   The National Library of Ireland is on Kildare Street (☎ 01/661-8811); Dublin's Central Library, is at the ILAC Centre, Henry Street (☎ 01/873-4333).

Lost Property   Most hotels have a lost-property service, usually under the aegis of the housekeeping department. For items lost in public places, contact Garda (police) headquarters, Harcourt Square (☎ 01/873-2222).

Newspapers/Magazines   The three morning Irish dailies are the *Irish Times* (except Sunday), *Irish Independent,* and *Irish Press.* In the afternoon, two tabloids, the *Evening Herald* and *Evening Press* hit the stands. There are also two weeklies, *The Sunday World* and *The Sunday Tribune.* The leading magazine for upcoming events and happenings is *In Dublin,* published every 2 weeks.

Photographic Needs   For photographic equipment, supplies, and repairs, visit the Camera Exchange, 63 S. Great George's St. (☎ 01/478-4125), or City Cameras, 23A Dawson St. (☎ 01/676-2891). For fast developing, try the Camera Centre, 56 Grafton St., or One Hour Photo, 5 St. Stephen's Green.

Police   Dial 999 in an emergency. The metropolitan headquarters for the Dublin Garda Siochana is at Harcourt Square (☎ 01/873-2222).

Post Office   The General Post Office (GPO) is located on O'Connell Street (☎ 01/872-8888), open Mon–Sat 8am–8pm and Sun and holidays 10:30am–6pm. Branch offices, identified by the sign OIFIG AN POST / POST OFFICE, are open Mon–Sat 8am–5:30pm or 6pm.

Radio/TV   RTE (Radiotelefis Eireann) is the national broadcasting authority and controls two TV channels and three radio stations. There are several privately owned local stations, and BBC television and radio broadcasts can be picked up.

Shoe Repairs   Two reliable shops in mid-city are O'Connell's Shoe Repair, 3 Upper Baggot St. (no phone), and Rapid Shoe Repair, Sackville Place, off Lower O'Connell Street (no phone).

Telephone   There's a local and international phone center at the General Post Office on O'Connell Street. A local call costs 20p (30¢). Pay phones accept a variety of coins or a phone card (available at post offices). For information on finding a telephone number, dial 1190.

Weather   Call 01/842-5555.

Yellow Pages   The classified section of the Dublin telephone book is called the Golden Pages.

ACCOMMODATIONS

In general, rates for Dublin hotels don't vary with the seasons as they do in the Irish countryside. Some hotels do charge slightly higher prices during special events, such as the Dublin Horse Show. For the best deals, try to reserve a room in Dublin over a weekend, and ask if there's a reduction or a weekend package in effect. Some Dublin hotels cut their rates by as much as 50% on Friday and Saturday nights, when business traffic is low.

HISTORIC OLD CITY & TEMPLE BAR/TRINITY COLLEGE AREA
Moderate
Blooms. Anglesea St., Dublin 2. ☎ **800/44-UTELL** in the U.S., or 01/671-5622. Fax 01/671-5997. 86 rms. £138.74 ($222) double. AE, DC, MC, V. Rates include full Irish breakfast and

service charge. Parking available. DART: Tara Street Station. Bus: 21A, 46A, 46B, 51B, 51C, 68, 69, or 86.

Lovers of Irish literature will feel at home at Blooms. Named after Leopold Bloom, a character in James Joyce's *Ulysses*, this hotel is in the heart of Dublin, near Trinity College and on the edge of the artsy Temple Bar district. The bedrooms are modern and functional, with useful extras like garment presses and hair dryers. The hotel has concierge service, 24-hour room service, and valet/laundry service. The formal restaurant is the Bia restaurant, or for more casual fare, try the Anglesea Bar. Late-night entertainment is available in the basement-level nightclub, known simply as M.

Temple Bar Hotel. Fleet St., Temple Bar, Dublin 2. ☎ **800/44-UTELL** in the U.S., or 01/677-3333. Fax 01/677-3088. 108 rms. TV TEL. £95–£130 ($152–$208) double. MC, V. Rates include full Irish breakfast. No service charge. DART: Tara Street Station. Bus: 78A or 78B.

If you want to be in the heart of the action in the Temple Bar district, then this is a prime place to stay. Opened in the summer of 1993, this five-story hotel was created from a row of town houses, preserving the Georgian brick-front facade and the Victorian mansard roof. The guest rooms are modern with traditional furnishings, including amenities such as a garment press, towel warmer, hair dryer, and tea/coffeemaker. Facilities include a skylit garden-style restaurant, the Terrace Cafe, and an Old Dublin–theme pub, Buskers.

Inexpensive

⑤ Jurys Christchurch Inn. Christchurch Place, Dublin 8. ☎ **800/44-UTELL** in the U.S., or 01/475-0111. Fax 01/475-0488. 183 rms. A/C TV TEL. £49 ($78.40) single, double, or triple. AE, CB, DC, MC, V. No service charge. Continental breakfast £4.50 ($6.75) extra; full Irish breakfast £6 ($9) extra. Bus: 21A, 50, 50A, 78, 78A, 78B.

Situated across from Christ Church Cathedral, this brand-new four-story hotel was designed in keeping with the area's Georgian/Victorian architecture. Geared to the cost-conscious traveler, it's the first of its kind in the city's historic district, offering quality hotel lodgings at guesthouse prices. The bedrooms, decorated with contemporary furnishings, can accommodate up to three adults or two adults and two children—all for the same price. Facilities include a moderately priced restaurant, a pub lounge, and an adjacent multistory parking area.

ST. STEPHEN'S GREEN/GRAFTON STREET AREA

Very Expensive

❂ Shelbourne. 27 St. Stephen's Green, Dublin 2. ☎ **800/225-5843** in the U.S., or 01/676-6471. Fax 01/661-6006. 164 rms. MINIBAR TV TEL. £159–£182 ($254.40–$291.20) double. AE, CB, DC, MC, V. Breakfast £14 ($21) extra. Service charge 15%. DART: Pearse Station. Bus: 10, 11A, 11B, 13, or 20B.

With a fanciful redbrick and white-trimmed facade enhanced by wrought-iron railings and window boxes brimming with flowers, this grand six-story hostelry stands out on the north side of St. Stephen's Green. Built in 1824, it has played a significant role in Irish history (the new nation's constitution was signed here in Room 112 in 1921), and it has often been host to international leaders, screen stars, and literary figures. The public areas, replete with glowing fireplaces, Waterford chandeliers, and original art, are popular rendezvous spots for Dubliners. The guest rooms vary in size, but all offer up-to-date comforts and are furnished with antique and period pieces; the front units overlook St. Stephen's Green.

Expensive

Stephen's Hall. 14–17 Lower Leeson St., Earlsfort Terrace, Dublin 2. ☎ **800/223-6510** in the U.S., or 01/661-0585. Fax 01/661-0606. 37 suites. TV TEL. £140 ($224) one-bedroom suite;

£180 ($288) two-bedroom suite; £210 ($336) penthouse/town-house suite. AE, DC, MC, V. No service charge. DART: Pearse Station. Bus: 14A, 11A, 11B, 13, 46A, 46B, or 86.

On the southeast corner of St. Stephen's Green, with a gracious Georgian exterior and entranceway, this is Dublin's first all-suite hotel. It's ideal for visitors who plan an extended stay or want to entertain. Furnished in a contemporary motif, each suite contains a hallway, sitting room, dining area, kitchen, bathroom, and one or two bedrooms. The luxury penthouse suites on the upper floors offer city views, while the ground-level town-house suites have private entrances.

Moderate

Buswells. 25 Molesworth St., Dublin 2. ☎ **800/473-9527** in the U.S., or 01/676-4013 or 01/661-3888. Fax 01/676-2090. 60 rms. TV TEL. £140 ($235.20) double. AE, DC, MC, V. Rates include full breakfast. No service charge. DART: Pearse Station. Bus: 10, 11A, 11B, 13, or 20B.

Situated on a quiet street 2 blocks from Trinity College, and opposite the National Museum, Library, and Art Gallery and Leinster House, this vintage four-story hotel has long been a meeting point for artists, poets, scholars, and politicians. Originally two Georgian town houses (dating back to 1736), it was launched as a hotel in 1928 and has been managed by three generations of the Duff family. The public rooms have period furniture, intricate plasterwork, Wedgwood flourishes, old prints, and memorabilia. All the bedrooms have been updated in a contemporary decor and Victorian touches, plus added amenities of tea/coffeemakers and hair dryers. Facilities include a restaurant, two bars, concierge, and room service.

Inexpensive

⊛ Georgian House. 20 Lower Baggot St., Dublin 2. ☎ **01/661-8832.** Fax 01/661-8834. 33 rms. TV TEL. £78–£140 ($124.80–$224) double. AE, DC, MC, V. Rates include full breakfast. Service charge 10%. DART: Pearse Station. Bus: 10.

Located less than 2 blocks from St. Stephen's Green, this four-story, 200-year-old brick town house sits in the heart of Georgian Dublin, within walking distance of most major attractions. The bedrooms are smallish, but offer all the essentials as well as a colorful decor with pine furniture. As at most small hotels in landmark buildings there is no elevator, but there is an enclosed parking area at the rear, and a restaurant specializing in seafood, the Ante Room, in the basement, and a lively in-house pub, Maguire's.

FITZWILLIAM/MERRION SQUARE AREA

Expensive

Davenport Hotel. Merrion Sq., Dublin 2. ☎ **800/44-UTELL** in the U.S., or 01/661-6800. Fax 01/661-5663. 120 rms. A/C TV TEL. £180–£220 ($288–$352) double. AE, DC, MC, V. Rates include full Irish breakfast and service charge. DART: Pearse Station. Bus: 5, 7A, 8, or 62.

The hotel building incorporates the neoclassical facade of Merrion Hall, an 1863 church. Inside is an impressive domed entranceway, with a six-story atrium lobby of marble flooring and plaster moldings, encircled by classic Georgian windows and pillars. The guest rooms, in a new section, have traditional furnishings, orthopedic beds, textured wall coverings, quilted floral bedspreads and matching drapes, and brass accoutrements. There are three telephone lines in each room plus a computer data line, work desk, personal safe, garment press, tea/coffee welcome tray, mirrored closet, and hair dryer. It's a sister hotel to the Mont Clare, which is across the street and shares valet car parking arrangements.

Expensive

Mont Clare Hotel. Merrion Sq., Clare St., Dublin 2. ☎ **800/44-UTELL** in the U.S., or 01/661-6799. Fax 01/661-5663. 74 rms. AC MINIBAR TV TEL. £100–£190 ($160–$304) double.

AE, DC, MC, V. Rates include full Irish breakfast and service charge. DART: Pearse Station. Bus: 5, 7A, 8, or 62.

Overlooking the northwest corner of Merrion Square, this vintage six-story brick-faced hotel has a typically Georgian facade, matched tastefully inside by period furnishings of dark woods and polished brass. The guest rooms, decked out in contemporary style, offer every up-to-date amenity including hair dryer, tea/coffeemaker, and garment press. In honor of Ireland's great writers, the main restaurant, Goldsmith's, has a literary theme. There's also a traditional lounge bar.

Moderate

Longfields. 9/10 Lower Fitzwilliam St., Dublin 2. ☎ **800/223-1588** in the U.S., or 01/676-1367. Fax 01/676-1542. 26 rms. MINIBAR TV TEL. £88–£112 ($140.80–$179.20) double. AE, DC, MC, V. Rates include full breakfast. No service charge. DART: Pearse Station. Bus: 10.

Created from two 18th-century Georgian town houses, this smart little hotel combines Georgian decor with reproduction period furnishings of dark woods and brass trim. The bedrooms offer such extras as clock radios and hair dryers. Facilities include a restaurant with bar, room service, and foreign-currency exchange, but no parking lot.

BALLSBRIDGE/EMBASSY ROW AREA

Expensive

✪ **Berkeley Court.** Lansdowne Rd., Ballsbridge, Dublin 4. ☎ **800/42-DOYLE**, 800/223-6800, or 800/44-UTELL in the U.S., or 01/660-1711. Fax 01/661-7238. 197 rms, 10 suites. TV TEL. £159–£175 ($254.40–$280) double; £250–£450 ($400–$720) suite. AE, CB, DC, MC, V. Service charge 15%. DART: Lansdowne Road Station. Bus: 5, 7A, 8, 46, 63, or 84.

The flagship of the Irish-owned Doyle Hotel group and the first Irish member of Leading Hotels of the World, the Berkeley Court is nestled in a residential area near the American Embassy on well-tended grounds that were once part of the Botanic Gardens of University College. A favorite haunt of diplomats and international business leaders, the hotel is known for its posh lobby decorated with fine antiques, original paintings, mirrored columns, and Irish-made carpets and furnishings. The guest rooms, which aim to convey an air of elegance, have designer fabrics, semi-canopy beds, dark woods, and bathrooms fitted with marble accoutrements.

✪ **Jurys Hotel.** Pembroke Rd., Ballsbridge, Dublin 4. ☎ **800/843-3311** in the U.S., or 01/660-5000. Fax 01/660-5540. 390 rms. TV TEL. £142 ($227.20) double in the main hotel, £191 ($305.60) double in the Towers wing. AE, DC, MC, V. Towers wing rates include continental breakfast. Service charge 12.5%. DART: Lansdowne Road Station. Bus: 6, 7, 8, 18, 45, 46, or 84.

Setting a progressive tone in a city steeped in tradition, this unusual hotel welcomes guests to a three-story skylit-atrium lobby with a marble and teak decor. Situated on its own grounds opposite the American Embassy, this sprawling property is actually two interconnected hotels—a modern eight-story high-rise and a new 100-unit tower with its own check-in desk, separate elevators, and private entrance, as well as full access to all the main hotel's amenities. The guest rooms in the main wing, recently refurbished, have dark-wood furnishings, brass trim, and designer fabrics. The Towers section, a first for the Irish capital, is an exclusive wing of oversize concierge-style rooms with bay windows. Each unit has computer-card key access, stocked minibar, three telephone lines, well-lit work area with desk, reclining chairs, tile and marble bathrooms, walk-in closets, and either a king- or queen-size bed. Decors vary, from contemporary light woods with floral fabrics to dark tones with Far Eastern motifs.

Moderate

☯ Ariel House. 52 Lansdowne Rd., Ballsbridge, Dublin 4. ☎ **01/668-5512.** Fax 01/ 668-5845. 28 rms. TV TEL. £50–£150 ($80–$240) double. MC, V. Rates include full Irish breakfast and service charge. DART: Lansdowne Road Station. Bus: 5, 7A, 8, 46, 63, or 84.

As Dublin guesthouses go, this one is the benchmark, opened over 25 years ago by Dublin-born and San Francisco–trained hotelier Michael O'Brien. With a historic mid–19th-century mansion as its core, it has been expanded and enhanced continually over the years. Guests are welcome to relax in the drawing room, rich in Victorian style, with Waterford glass chandeliers, an open fireplace, and delicately carved cornices. The bedrooms are individually decorated, with period furniture and real Irish linens, as well as modern extras such as a hair dryer, garment press, and iron/ ironing board. Facilities include a conservatory-style dining room that serves breakfast, morning coffee, and afternoon tea; a wine bar; and a private parking area.

Ⓢ Burlington. Upper Leeson St., Dublin 4. ☎ **800/223-0888** or 800/44-DOYLE in the U.S., or 01/660-5222. Fax 01/660-8496. 477 rms. TV TEL. £165.46–£174 ($264.75–$278.40) double. AE, CB, DC, MC, V. Rates include full Irish breakfast and service charge. Bus: 10 or 18.

A favorite headquarters for conventions, meetings, conferences, and group tours, this is the largest hotel in Ireland. Situated a block south of the Grand Canal in a fashionable residential section within walking distance of St. Stephen's Green, it's a modern, crisply furnished seven-story property, constantly being refurbished. The bedrooms are outfitted with brass-bound oak furniture and designer fabrics. The good proportion of connecting units are ideal for families.

☯ Doyle Tara. Merrion Rd., Dublin 4. ☎ **800/42-DOYLE** in the U.S., or 01/269-4666. Fax 01/269-1027. 100 rms. TV TEL. £94–£115 ($150.40–$184) double. AE, CB, DC, MC, V. Service charge 15%. DART: Booterstown Station. Bus: 5, 7, 7A, or 8.

Positioned along the coast road between downtown Dublin and the ferryport of Dun Laoghaire, this modern seven-story hotel offers wide-windowed views of Dublin Bay, just 10 minutes from the city center in a residential area. It's an ideal place for car renters, as there's ample parking space; and for those who prefer to use public transport, it's within easy walking distance of major bus routes and a DART station. The guest rooms, with every modern convenience, have attractive Irish-made furnishings.

Inexpensive

Glenveagh Town House. 31 Northumberland Rd., Ballsbridge, Dublin 4. ☎ **01/668-4612.** Fax 01/668-4559. 11 rms. TV TEL. £50–£81 ($80–$130) double. AE, MC, V. No service charge. DART: Lansdowne Road Station. Bus: 5, 7, 7A, 8, or 45.

Fashioned into a guesthouse by the Cunningham family, this converted three-story Georgian residence is situated south of the Grand Canal on a quiet, tree-lined street. It offers a homey atmosphere with a glowing fireplace in the sitting room, high ceilings, and tall windows bedecked with floral drapery. The guest rooms are decorated with light woods, lots of frilly pastel fabrics, and all the modern conveniences. There is a private parking area.

Mount Herbert. 7 Herbert Rd., Ballsbridge, Dublin 4. ☎ **01/668-4321.** Fax 01/660-7077. 155 rms. TV TEL. £63–£79 ($100.80–$126.40) double. AE, DC, MC, V. No service charge. DART: Lansdowne Road Station. Bus: 5, 7, 7A, 8, 46, 63, or 84.

Although technically classified as a guesthouse, this much-expanded three-story property is more like a small hotel. Originally the family home of Lord Robinson, it's a gracious residence set in its own grounds and gardens in a residential neighborhood near the DART station and major bus routes. Operated by the Loughran family, it offers bedrooms of various vintages and sizes, but all have standard amenities including garment presses. Facilities include a restaurant, wine bar, sauna, indoor solarium, gift shop, and guest parking area.

O'CONNELL STREET AREA

Expensive

Gresham. 23 Upper O'Connell St., Dublin 1. ☎ **800/44-UTELL** in the U.S., or 01/874-6881. Fax 01/878-7175. 202 rms, 6 suites. TV TEL. £158–£225 ($252.80–$360) double. AE, CB, DC, MC, V. Rates include full Irish breakfast and service charge. DART: Connolly Station. Bus: 40A, 40B, 40C, or 51A.

Centrally located on the city's main business thoroughfare, this Regency-style hotel is one of Ireland's oldest (1817) and best-known lodging establishments. Although much of the tourist trade in Dublin has shifted south of the River Liffey in recent years, the Gresham is still synonymous with stylish Irish hospitality and provides easy access to the Abbey and Gate Theatres and other northside attractions. The lobby and public areas are a panorama of marble floors, molded plasterwork, and crystal chandeliers. With high ceilings and individual decors, the guest rooms vary in size and style, with soft lighting, tile bathrooms, and period furniture, including padded headboards and armoires. One-of-a-kind luxury terrace suites grace the upper front floors.

Moderate

Royal Dublin. 40 Upper O'Connell St., Dublin 1. ☎ **800/528-1234** in the U.S., or 01/873-3666. Fax 01/873-3120. 120 rms. TV TEL. £94–£114 ($117–$177) double. AE, DC, MC, V. Rates include full Irish breakfast and service charge. DART: Connolly Station. Bus: 36A, 40A, 40B, 40C, or 51A.

Romantically floodlit at night, this modern five-story hotel is positioned near Parnell Square at the north end of Dublin's main thoroughfare, within walking distance of all the main theaters and northside attractions. It combines a contemporary skylit lobby full of art deco overtones with adjacent lounge areas that were part of an original building, dating back to 1752, that have high Georgian ceilings, ornate cornices, crystal chandeliers, gilt-edged mirrors, and open fireplaces. The bedrooms are strictly modern with light woods and three-sided full-length windows that extend over the busy street below. The corridors are extremely well lit, with individual lights at each doorway.

DINING

HISTORIC OLD CITY/LIBERTIES AREA

Expensive

Lord Edward. 23 Christ Church Place. ☎ **01/454-2420.** Reservations required. Main courses £12.95–£17.95 ($20.70–$28.70). AE, DC, MC, V. Mon–Fri noon–2:45pm and 5–10:45pm, Sat 5–10:45pm. Bus: 21A, 50, 50A, 78, 78A, or 78B. SEAFOOD.

Established in 1890, this cozy upstairs dining room claims to be Dublin's oldest seafood restaurant. A dozen different preparations of sole (including au gratin and Véronique) are served, as are seven variations of prawns (from Thermidor to provençal), and fresh lobster is prepared au naturel or in sauces, plus fresh fish from salmon and sea trout to plaice and turbot—grilled, fried, or poached. Vegetarian dishes are also available. At lunchtime, light snacks and simpler fare are served in the bar.

Inexpensive

Leo Burdock's. 2 Werburgh St. ☎ **01/454-0306.** Reservations not accepted. £2.50–£3.50 ($4–$5.60). No credit cards. Mon–Fri 12:30–11pm, Sat 2–11pm. Bus: 21A, 50, 50A, 78, 78A, or 78B. FISH & CHIPS.

Established in 1913, this is a quintessential Dublin takeaway fish-and-chips shop. Situated at the corner of Castle and Werburgh Streets, it's a stone's throw from Christ Church Cathedral and other Old City landmarks. Types of fish vary from ray and cod to whiting, but they're always fresh, light, and flaky, and the chips are said to be among the crispest in town. There's no seating at the shop, but you can sit on a nearby bench or stroll down to the park at St. Patrick's Cathedral.

TEMPLE BAR/TRINITY COLLEGE AREA

Expensive

Les Frères Jacques. 74 Dame St. ☎ **01/679-4555.** Reservations recommended. Main courses £16–£20 ($25.60–$32); fixed-price lunch £13.50 ($21.60). AE, DC, MC, V. Mon–Fri 12:30–2:30pm and 7–10:30pm, Sat 7–11pm. Bus: 50, 50A, 54, 56, or 77. FRENCH.

Well situated between Crampton Court and Sycamore Street opposite Dublin Castle, this restaurant brings a touch of haute cuisine to the lower edge of the trendy Temple Bar district. The menu offers such creative entrees as filet of beef in red-wine and bone-marrow sauce, duck suprême on a sweet-corn pancake in tangy ginger sauce, rosette of spring lamb in meat juice sabayon and tomato coulis with crispy potato straws, and veal on rainbow pasta with garlic-and-basil sauce.

Moderate

Eammon Doran, Licensed Vintner. 3A Crown Alley. ☎ **01/679-9114.** Reservations recommended for dinner. Main courses £4.95–£10.95 ($7.90–$17.50) at lunch, £7.95–£15.15 ($12.70–$24.80) at dinner. AE, DC, MC, V. Daily 11am–2:30am. IRISH/AMERICAN.

A little bit of New York City can be found in Temple Bar at this huge two-story pub/restaurant with a melting-pot decor—it serves a New York–style brunch on weekends. It's a branch of a long-established midtown Manhattan eatery, both of which are named for Eammon Doran, an Irish-born entrepreneur who flies back and forth across the Atlantic to tend to his business interests. Restaurant specialties include Gaelic steak, steak-and-kidney pie, shepherd's pie, chicken pot pie, fish and chips, and braised lamb stew. Universal favorites—roast duck flambé, rack of lamb, and chateaubriand—are offered, along with a good selection of fresh seafood, pastas, sandwiches, salads, and omelets. The downstairs level is a venue for traditional music and plays.

Inexpensive

Elephant & Castle. 18 Temple Bar. ☎ **01/679-3121.** Reservations not necessary. Main courses £5.50–£8.95 ($8.80–$14.30) at lunch, £6.50–£12.50 ($10.40–$20) at dinner. AE, DC, MC, V. Sun–Thurs 11:30am–11:30pm, Fri–Sat 11:30am–midnight. DART: Tara Street Station. Bus: 21A, 46A, 46B, 51B, 51C, 68, 69, or 86. CALIFORNIAN/INTERNATIONAL.

Located in the heart of the Temple Bar district, this is an informal and fun restaurant, a favorite with kids, with simple pine-wood tables and benches and a decor blending modern art with statues of elephants and cartoon figures. The menu is eclectic, made up of exotic salads and multi-ingredient omelets, as well as sesame chicken with spinach and cucumber; fettuccine with shrimp, sun-dried tomatoes, and saffron; and a house-special Elephant burger with curried sour cream, bacon, scallions, cheddar, and tomato.

Gallagher's Boxty House. 20–21 Temple Bar. ☎ **01/677-2762.** Reservations recommended. Main courses £2.95–£4.50 ($4.70–$7.20) at lunch, £5.95–£9.95 ($9.50–$15.90) at dinner. MC, V. Daily noon–11:30pm. DART: Tara Street Station. Bus: 21A, 46A, 46B, 51B, 51C, 68, 69, or 86. TRADITIONAL IRISH.

Although native Irish cooking is sometimes hard to find in Dublin restaurants, here is one spot that keeps traditions alive, with a particular emphasis on Irish stew, bacon and cabbage, and a dish called boxty. Boxty is an Irish potato pancake grilled and rolled with various fillings such as beef, lamb, chicken, fish or combinations like bacon and cabbage. Besides all types of boxty, salmon, and steaks, there are hearty sandwiches served on open wedges of brown bread at lunchtime.

ST. STEPHEN'S GREEN/GRAFTON STREET AREA

Expensive

✪ **The Commons.** 85–86 St. Stephen's Green. ☎ **01/475-2597** or 01/478-0530. Reservations required. Fixed-price menu £18 ($28.80) at lunch, £32 or £42 ($51.20 or $67.20) at dinner. AE, MC, V. Mon–Fri 12:30–2:15pm and 7–10pm, Sat 7–10pm. DART: Pearse Station. Bus: 62 or 14A. CONTINENTAL.

On the south side of St. Stephen's Green, this Michelin-starred restaurant occupies the basement level of Newman House, the historic seat of Ireland's major university and comprised of two elegant town houses dating back to 1740. The interior of the dining rooms is a blend of Georgian architecture, cloister-style arches, and original contemporary artworks. For an apéritif in fine weather, there's a lovely stone courtyard terrace surrounded by a garden. The inventive menu changes daily, and might offer pan-fried tuna with red wine, quail breasts with wild-mushroom timbale honey sauce, or tournedos of beef in chive and madeira juice.

✪ **Cooke's Cafe.** 14 S. William St. ☎ **01/679-0536.** Reservations required. Main courses £9.75–£16 ($15.60–$25.60) at lunch, £11.95–£16.95 ($19.10–$27.10) at dinner. AE, DC, MC, V. Mon–Fri 9am–midnight, Sat–Sun noon–3pm and 6pm–midnight. DART: Tara Street Station. Bus: 16A, 19A, 22A, 55, or 83. CALIFORNIA/MEDITERRANEAN.

Reservations for this popular and fashionable restaurant should be made as far in advance as possible. It's located 2 blocks from Grafton Street opposite the Powerscourt Townhouse Center. Owner-chef Johnny Cooke's decor is dominated by an open kitchen; there's also seating outdoors with antique tables and chairs originally from Brighton Pier. Specialties include dry-aged filet of beef grilled with field mushrooms; grilled duck with pancetta, marsala-balsamic sauce, and wilted endive; angel-hair pasta with clams, cockles, chili, and tomato; whole lobster with fines herbs butter; and Dover sole with capers and croutons.

Moderate

⑤ **Cafe Caruso.** 47 S. William St. ☎ **01/677-0708.** Reservations recommended. Main courses £6.95–£12.50 ($10.45–$18.75). AE, DC, MC, V. Mon–Sat 6pm–12:15am, Sun 6–11:15pm. Bus: 16A, 19A, 22A, 55, or 83. ITALIAN/INTERNATIONAL.

Skylit and plant-filled, this festive and airy eatery is just 2 blocks from St. Stephen's Green or Grafton Street. As its name implies, it brings a touch of Italy and beyond to this corner of the city. The menu features a variety of freshly made pastas as well such dishes as pork marsala and osso buco. In addition, the choices often include steaks, seafood, lamb kidneys, chicken Kiev, rack of lamb, and traditional Irish stew. A resident pianist supplies background music in the mostly classical or blues genres.

Trocadero. 3 St. Andrew St. ☎ **01/677-5545.** Reservations recommended. Main courses £7.95–£12.95 ($12.70–$20.70). AE, DC, MC, V. Mon–Sat 6pm–12:15am, Sun 6–11:15pm. DART: Tara Street Station. Bus: 16A, 19A, 22A, 55, or 83. INTERNATIONAL.

In many ways the Troc is the Sardi's of Dublin, and has been for almost 20 years. Located close to the Andrews Lane and other theaters, it's a favorite gathering spot for theater-goers, performers, and press, particularly because it serves food after the theaters let out. Before- and after-theater specials are also offered. As might be expected, the decor is theatrical too, with subdued lighting, banquette seating and close-knit tables, and photos of entertainers on the walls. Steaks are a specialty, but the menu also offers rack of lamb, daily fish specials, pastas, and traditional dishes such as Irish stew or corned beef and cabbage with parsley sauce, as well as chicken Dijon, Kiev, or stuffed with cream cheese and chives.

Inexpensive

○ Bewley's Cafe. 78/79 Grafton St. ☎ **01/677-6761.** Reservations not required. All items £1.65–£5 ($2.65–$8). AE, DC, MC, V. Mon–Wed 7:30am–1am, Thurs–Sat 8am–2am, Sun 9:30am–10pm. DART: Pearse Station. Bus: 15A, 15B, 15C, 46, 55, 63, or 83. IRISH.

This three-story landmark was founded in 1840 by a Quaker named Joshua Bewley. It has a traditional decor of high ceilings, stained-glass windows, and dark woods. The busy coffee shop-cum-restaurant serves breakfast and light meals, but it's best known for its dozens of freshly brewed coffees and teas, accompanied by home-baked scones, pastries, or sticky buns. Other items on the menu range from soups and salads to sandwiches and quiches. There's a choice of self-service or waitress/waiter service, depending on which floor you choose.

There are several branches throughout Dublin, including 11/12 Westmoreland St. (☎ 01/677-6761) and 13 S. Great George's St. (☎ 01/679-2078).

Ⓢ St. Teresa's Courtyard. Clarendon St. ☎ **01/671-8466** or 01/671-8127. Reservations not required. All items £1–£2.50 ($1.60–$4). No credit cards. Mon–Sat 10:30am–4pm. DART: Tara Street Station. Bus: 16, 16A, 19, 19A, 22A, 55, or 83. IRISH/SELF-SERVICE.

Situated in the cobblestone courtyard of early 19th-century St. Teresa's Church, this serene little dining room is one of a handful of new eateries inconspicuously springing up in historic or ecclesiastical surroundings. With high ceilings and an old-world decor, it's a welcome contrast to the bustle of Grafton Street a block away. The menu changes daily but usually includes homemade soups, sandwiches, salads, quiches, lasagnes, sausage rolls, hot scones, and other baked goods.

FITZWILLIAM/MERRION SQUARE AREA

Expensive

✪ Dobbins Wine Bistro. 15 Stephen's Lane (off Upper Mount St.). ☎ **01/676-4679** and 01/676-4670. Reservations recommended. Main courses £12.95–£19.95 ($20.70–$31.90); fixed-price lunch £14.95 ($23.90). AE, DC, MC, V. Mon 12:30–3pm, Tues–Fri 12:30–3pm and 8pm–midnight, Sat 8pm–midnight. DART: Pearse Station. Bus: 5, 7A, 8, 46, or 84. IRISH/CONTINENTAL.

Almost hidden in a lane between Upper and Lower Mount Streets a block east of Merrion Square, this friendly enclave is a haven for inventive cuisine. The menu changes often, but usually includes such items as duckling with orange and port sauce; steamed paupiette of black sole with salmon, crab, and prawn filling; fresh prawns in garlic butter; pan-fried veal kidneys in pastry; rack of lamb with a mint crust; and filet of beef topped with crispy herb breadcrumbs with a shallot and madeira sauce. You'll have a choice of sitting in the bistro, with checkered tablecloths and sawdust on the floor, or in the tropical patio, with an all-weather sliding glass roof.

✪ Patrick Guilbaud. 46 James Place, off Lower Baggot St. ☎ **01/676-4192.** Reservations required. Main courses £17–£21 ($27.20–$33.60); fixed-price lunch £17 ($27.20). AE, DC, MC, V. Tues–Sat 12:30–2pm and 7:30–10:15pm. DART: Pearse Station. Bus: 10. NOUVELLE FRENCH.

Tucked in a lane behind a Bank of Ireland building, this modern skylit restaurant could easily be overlooked except for its glowing Michelin-star reputation for fine food and artful service. The menu features such dishes as casserole of black sole and prawns, steamed salmon with orange-and-grapefruit sauce, filet of spring lamb with parsley sauce and herb salad, and breast of guinea fowl with madeira sauce and potato crust.

Moderate

⑤ The Lane Gallery. 55 Pembroke Lane (off Pembroke St.). ☎ **01/661-1829.** Reservations recommended. Main courses £9.95–£13.50 ($15.90–$21.60); fixed-price lunch £5.95 ($9.50). MC, V. Mon 12:30–2:30pm, Tues–Fri 12:30–2:30pm and 7:30–11pm, Sat 7:30–11pm. DART: Pearse Station. Bus: 10. FRENCH.

An ever-changing display of works by local artists is the focal point of this restaurant, tucked in a lane between Baggot Street and Fitzwilliam Square, near the Focus Theatre. The decor compliments the art with skylight or candlelight, whitewashed brick walls, and pastel linens. The menu is equally artistic, with choices such as filet of beef with smoked-bacon and black-pepper sauce, prawns in chive-and-ginger sauce, salmon on a bed of leeks with spinach-butter sauce, roast brace of quail with white and black pudding and whiskey sauce, or breast of chicken stuffed with walnut mousse. There's live piano music most evenings from 9pm. The lunch and dinner specials offer great value.

Inexpensive

Grays. 109D Lower Baggot St. ☎ **01/676-0676.** Reservations not required. All items £2–£5.95 ($3.20–$9.50). MC, V. Mon–Fri 7:30am–4pm. DART: Pearse Station. Bus: 10. INTERNATIONAL/ SELF-SERVICE.

A popular self-service eatery, this cozy converted mews has choir benches, caned chairs, and lots of hanging plants, on both ground and upstairs levels, and an outdoor courtyard for dining in fine weather. The menu choices concentrate on sandwiches and salads made to order, as well as pastas, quiches, curries, and casseroles.

BALLSBRIDGE/EMBASSY ROW AREA

Very Expensive

✪ Le Coq Hardi. 35 Pembroke Rd., Ballsbridge. ☎ **01/668-9070.** Reservations required. Main courses £16–£25 ($16.15–$37.50); fixed-price lunch £18 ($22.45) for full menu, £10 ($22.45) for one course and coffee. AE, CB, MC, V. Mon–Fri 12:30–2:30pm and 7–10:45pm, Sat 7–10:45pm. DART: Lansdowne Road Station. Bus: 18, 46, 63, or 84. FRENCH.

They say that this is the only place in Dublin where Rolls-Royces vie nightly for parking places. Located on the corner of Wellington Road in a Georgian town house setting close to the American Embassy, this plush 50-seat restaurant has no trouble drawing a well-heeled local and international business clientele. Chef John Howard has garnered many an award by offering such specialties as Dover sole stuffed with prawns, darne of Irish wild salmon on fresh spinach leaves, filet of hake roasted on green cabbage and bacon with Pernod-butter sauce, filet of prime beef in beef marrow and beaujolais-wine sauce with wild mushrooms, and steaks flamed in Irish whiskey. The 700-bin wine cellar boasts a complete collection of Château Mouton Rothschild, dating from 1945 to the present.

Expensive

Lobster Pot. 9 Ballsbridge Terrace, Ballsbridge. ☎ **01/668-0025.** Reservations required. Main courses £9–£14 ($14.40–$22.40) at lunch, £10.95–£17.95 ($17.50–$28.70) at dinner. AE, DC, MC, V. Mon–Fri 12:30–2:30pm and 6:30–10:30pm, Sat 6:30–10:30pm. DART: Lansdowne Road Station. Bus: 5, 7, 7A, 8, 46, 63, or 84. SEAFOOD.

This upstairs restaurant is known, of course, for its lobster dishes. Other menu choices range from coquilles St-Jacques, prawns mornay, prawns sautéed in garlic butter, and monkfish Thermidor to tableside preparations of steak Diane, pepper steak, and steak tartare.

Moderate

✪ Roly's Bistro. 7 Ballsbridge Terrace. ☎ **01/668-2611.** Reservations required. Main courses £7.50–£12.95 ($12–$20.70); fixed-price lunch £9.50 ($14.25). AE, DC, MC, V. Mon–Sat noon–3pm and 6–10pm, Sun noon–3pm (brunch) and 6–9:30pm. DART: Lansdowne Road Station. Bus: 6, 7, 8, 18, 45, 46, or 84. IRISH/INTERNATIONAL.

This popular place, in a trendy location between the American Embassy and the Royal Dublin Society, is presided over by genial and astute host Roly Saul and master chef Colin O'Daly, who prepares excellent and imaginative food. The main dining rooms, with a bright and airy decor and lots of windows, can be noisy with the din of a full house; but the nonsmoking section has a quiet enclave of booths laid out in an *Orient Express* style. The bistro serves roast breast of duck with vanilla-and-apricot sauce, sautéed monkfish with apple and dates in honey-spiced sauce, filet of pork stuffed with eggplant and wrapped in bacon, seafood bake (salmon, haddock, cod, and clams in shellfish sauce), and a vegetarian dish of tomato, zucchini, and black olives with basil and rosemary in pastry.

Inexpensive

Ⓢ Da Vincenzo. 133 Upper Leeson St. ☎ **01/660-9906.** Reservations recommended. Main courses £6.50–£12.25 ($10.40–$19.60); fixed-price lunch £6.95 ($11.10). AE, MC, V. Mon–Fri 12:30pm–midnight, Sat 1pm–midnight, Sun 1–10pm. Bus: 10, 11A, 11B, 46A, or 46B. ITALIAN.

This informal and friendly owner-run bistro offers ground-level and upstairs seating amid a casual decor of glowing brick fireplaces, pine walls, modern-art posters, blue and white pottery, and a busy open kitchen. Pizza with a light pita-style dough is a specialty here, cooked in a wood-burning oven. Other entrees range from pastas such as tagliatelle, lasagne, canelloni, spaghetti, and fettuccine to veal and beef dishes, including an organically produced filet steak.

O'CONNELL STREET AREA

Moderate

✪ Chapter One. 18/19 Parnell Sq. ☎ **01/873-2266** or 01/873-2281. Reservations recommended. Main courses £9.50–£14 ($15.20–$22.40); fixed-price lunch £10 ($16). AE, MC, V. Tues–Fri noon–2:30pm and 6–11pm, Sat–Sun 6–11pm. DART: Connolly Station. Bus: 10, 11, 11A, 11B, 12, 13, 14, 16, 16A, 19, 19A, 22, 22A, or 36. IRISH.

A literary theme prevails at this restaurant, housed in the basement of the Dublin Writers Museum, just north of Parnell Square. The layout is spread over three rooms and alcoves, all accentuated by stained-glass windows and literary memorabilia. The catering staff, affiliated with the Old Dublin Restaurant, have added a few Scandinavian influences. Main courses include filet of salmon on a bed of avocado with smoked tomato vinaigrette; black sole with citrus fruit and dill/cucumber-cream sauce; pot-roasted breast of chicken with onions, sage, garlic, and peapods; roast half duck with apricot sauce; and a selection of fish with garlic, mango, fennel, cucumber, and tomato salad.

Inexpensive

Ⓢ 101 Talbot. 101 Talbot St. (near Marlborough St.). ☎ **01/874-5011.** Reservations recommended. Main courses £3.25–£5.50 ($5.20–$8.80) at lunch, £7.90–£9.90 ($12.65–$15.85) at dinner. AE, DC, MC, V. Mon 10am–3pm, Tues–Sat 10am–11pm. DART: Connolly Station. Bus: 27A, 31A, 311B, 32A, 32B, 42B, 42C, 43, or 44A. INTERNATIONAL/VEGETARIAN.

This second-floor shopfront restaurant features light and healthy foods, with a strong emphasis on vegetarian dishes. The setting is bright and casual, with contemporary Irish art on display, big windows, ash-topped tables, and newspapers to read. Entrees include medaillons of pork with brandy-and-mustard sauce, spanikopita (Greek spinach and feta cheese pie), parsnips stuffed with brazil nuts and vegetables in red-pepper sauce, and various pastas. The lunch menu changes daily, the dinner menu weekly. Espresso and cappuccino are available, and there's a full bar. It's convenient to the Abbey Theatre.

The Winding Stair. 40 Lower Ormond Quay. ☎ **01/873-3292.** Reservations not necessary. All items £1–£4.50 ($1.60–$7.20). MC, V. Mon–Wed and Fri–Sat 10am–6pm, Thurs 10am–2pm, Sun 1–5pm. Bus: 70 or 80. IRISH/SELF-SERVICE.

Retreat from the bustle of the north side's busy quays at this cafe-cum-bookshop. Classical music plays gently in the background, and there are three floors, each chock full of used books, connected by a winding 18th-century staircase. A cage-style elevator serves those who prefer not to climb stairs. Tall windows provide expansive views of the Ha'penny Bridge and River Liffey. The food is simple and healthy—sandwiches made with additive-free meats or fruits such as banana and honey, organic salads, homemade soups, and natural juices.

ATTRACTIONS
SIGHTSEEING SUGGESTIONS

If You Have 1 Day   Start at the beginning—Dublin's medieval quarter, the area around Christ Church and St. Patrick's Cathedral. Tour these great churches and then walk the cobblestone streets and inspect the nearby old city walls at High Street. From Old Dublin, take a turn eastward and see Dublin Castle and then Trinity College with the famous *Book of Kells.* Cross over the River Liffey to O'Connell Street, Dublin's main thoroughfare. Walk up this wide street, passing the landmark General Post Office (GPO), to Parnell Square and the picturesque Garden of Remembrance. If time permits, visit the Dublin Writers' Museum, and then hop on a double-decker bus heading to the south bank of the Liffey for a visit to St. Stephen's Green for a relaxing stroll amid the greenery. Cap the day with a show at the Abbey Theatre and maybe a drink or two at a nearby pub.

If You Have 2 Days   On your second day, take a Dublin Bus city sightseeing tour to give you an overview of the city—you'll see all the local downtown landmarks, plus some of the leading sites on the edge of the city such as the Guinness Brewery, the Royal Hospital, and Phoenix Park. In the afternoon, head for Grafton Street for some shopping. If time allows, stroll around Merrion or Fitzwilliam Squares to give you a sampling of the best of Dublin's Georgian architecture.

If You Have 3 Days   Make day 3 a day for Dublin's artistic and cultural attractions—visit the National Museum and National Gallery, the Guinness Hop Store or a special-interest museum, such as the Writers' Museum, or the Museum of Childhood. Save time for a walk around Temple Bar, the city's Left Bank district, lined with art galleries and film studios, interesting secondhand shops, and casual eateries.

If You Have 4 Days   On day 4, take a ride aboard DART, Dublin's rapid-transit system, to the suburbs, either southward to Dun Laoghaire or Dalkey, or northward to Howth. The DART routes follow the rim of Dublin Bay in both directions, so you'll enjoy a scenic ride and get to spend some time in an Irish coastal village.

THE TOP ATTRACTIONS

✪ **Trinity College and the *Book of Kells*.** College Green. ☎ **01/677-2941.** Admission £3.50 ($5.60) adults, £3 ($4.80) students and seniors, free for children 11 and under. Mon–Sat 9:30am–5pm, Sun noon–4:30pm. DART: Tara Street Station. Bus: 5, 7A, 8, 15A, 15B, 15C, 46, 55, 62, 63, 83, or 84.

The oldest university in Ireland, Trinity was founded in 1592 by Elizabeth I. It sits in the heart of the city on a 40-acre site just south of the River Liffey, with cobblestone squares, gardens, a picturesque quadrangle, and buildings dating from the 17th century. The college is best known as the home of the *Book of Kells,* an 8th-century version of the Four Gospels with elaborate scripting and illumination. This famous treasure and other early Christian manuscripts are on permanent view for the public in the Colonnades, an exhibition area located on the ground floor of the Old Library.

✪ **National Museum.** Kildare St. and Merrion Row. ☎ **01/661-8811.** Free admission. Tues–Sat 10am–5pm, Sun 2–5pm. DART: Pearse Station. Bus: 7, 7A, 8, 10, 11, or 13.

This important museum reflects Ireland's heritage from 2000 B.C. to the present. It's the home of many of the country's greatest historical finds, including the Ardagh Chalice, Tara Brooch, and Cross of Cong. Other highlights range from the artifacts from the Wood Quay excavations of the Old Dublin Settlements to an extensive exhibition of Irish gold ornaments from the Bronze Age.

✪ **Dublin Castle.** Palace St. (off Dame St.). ☎ **01/679-3713.** Admission £2 ($3.20) adults, £1 ($1.60) for seniors, students, and children 11 and under. Mon–Fri 10am–12:15pm and 2–5pm, Sat–Sun 2–5pm. Guided tours given every 20–25 minutes. Bus: 54, 50, 50A, 56A, or 77.

Built between 1208 and 1220, this complex represents some of the oldest surviving architecture in the city, and was the center of British power in Ireland for more than 7 centuries until it was taken over by the new Irish government in 1922. Highlights include the 13th-century Record Tower; the State Apartments, once the residence of English viceroys; and the Chapel Royal, a 19th-century gothic building with particularly fine plaster decoration and carved oak gallery fronts and fittings. The newest developments are the Undercroft, an excavated site on the grounds where an early Viking fortress stood, and the Treasury, built between 1712 and 1715, believed to be the oldest surviving purpose-built office building in Ireland. It houses a visitor center in its vaulted basement, which also serves as an entrance to the medieval undercroft.

✪ **Dublin Writers Museum.** 18/19 Parnell Sq. N. ☎ **01/872-2077.** Admission £2.75 ($4.40) adults, £2.35 ($3.75) seniors and students, £1.15 ($1.85) children 11 and under, £7.50 ($12) families. Daily 10am–5pm. Closed Mon Sept–May. DART: Connolly Station. Bus: 10, 11, 11A, 11B, 12, 13, 14, 16, 16A, 19, 19A, 22, 22A, or 36.

As a city known for its literary contributions to the world, Dublin has embraced this new museum with open arms. Housed in two restored 18th-century buildings, the exhibits focus on Ireland's many great writers including Dublin's three Nobel Prize winners—George Bernard Shaw, William Butler Yeats, and Samuel Beckett—and a host of others from Jonathan Swift and Oscar Wilde to Sean O'Casey, James Joyce, and Brendan Behan.

Christ Church Cathedral. Christ Church Place. ☎ **01/677-8099.** Admission: suggested donation £1 ($1.60) adults. Daily 10am–5pm. Closed Dec 26. Bus: 21A, 50, 50A, 78, 78A, or 78B.

Standing on a ridge above the site of the original Norse town, the cathedral was founded in 1038, although the present building dates from around 1172, with substantial renovations from 1871 and 1878. Inside you'll find a monument to Strongbow, the ruler who had the cathedral built. Make sure to look back from the altar and note the leaning wall of Dublin, which has been out of perpendicular by some 18 inches since 1562. The crypt has remained unchanged since the 13th century and is one of the largest medieval crypts in either Britain or Ireland.

✪ St. Patrick's Cathedral. Patrick's Close, Patrick St. ☎ **01/475-4817.** Admission: suggested donation £1.20 ($1.90) adults, 60p ($1) students. Apr–Oct, Mon–Fri 9am–6pm, Sat 9am–5pm, Sun 10am–4:30pm; Nov–Mar, Mon–Fri 9am–6pm, Sat 9am–4pm, Sun 10:30am–4:30pm. Bus: 50, 50A, 54, 54A, or 56A.

It's said that St. Patrick baptized converts on the site and consequently a church has stood here since A.D. 450, making it the oldest Christian site in Dublin. The present cathedral dates from 1190, but because of a fire and a rebuilding in the 14th century, not much remains from the foundation days. It's mainly early English in style, with a square medieval tower that houses the largest ringing peal bells in Ireland, an 18th-century spire, and a 300-foot-long interior, making it the longest church in Ireland. The national cathedral of the Church of Ireland (Anglican), St. Patrick's is closely associated with Jonathan Swift, who was dean here from 1713 to 1745 and whose tomb lies in the south aisle.

MORE ATTRACTIONS

✪ Dublinia. Christ Church Place (at High St.). ☎ **01/679-4611.** Admission £4 ($6.40) adults, £3 ($4.80) for children, students, and seniors, £10 ($16) family. Daily 10am–5pm. Bus: 21A, 50, 50A, 78, 78A, or 78B.

What was Dublin like in medieval times? Here is a historically accurate presentation of the city from 1170 to 1540, re-created through a series of theme exhibits, spectacles, and experiences. Highlights include an illuminated Medieval Maze, complete with visual effects, background sounds, and aromas, that lead you on a journey through time from the first arrival of the Anglo-Normans in 1170 to the closure of the monasteries in the 1530s. The next segment depicts everyday life in medieval Dublin. The finale takes you to the Great Hall for a 360° wrap-up portrait of the city via a 12-minute cyclorama-style audio-visual.

Guinness Hop Store Gallery. Crane St. (off Thomas St.). ☎ **01/453-6700,** ext 5155. Admission £2 ($3.20) adults, £1.50 ($2.40) seniors and students, 50p (80¢) children 11 and under. Mon–Fri 10am–4pm. Bus 21A, 78, or 78A.

The Guinness brewery is one of Dublin's most important institutions. Though the brewery itself is not open for tours, at the brewery museum you can learn all about the famous black stout that has been brewed in Dublin since 1769. There's also a tasting room (to which children under 12 are not admitted).

Hugh Lane Municipal Gallery of Modern Art. Parnell Sq. ☎ **01/874-1903.** Free admission but donations accepted. Tues–Fri 9:30am–6pm, Sat 9:30am–5pm, Sun 11am–5pm. DART: Connolly Station. Bus: 10, 11, 11A, 11B, 12, 13, 14, 16, 16A, 19, 19A, 22, 22A, or 36.

Housed in a finely restored 18th-century building, this gallery is named after Hugh Lane, an Irish art connoisseur who willed his collection (including works by Courbet, Manet, Monet, and Corot) to be shared between the government of Ireland and the National Gallery of London. With the Lane collection as its nucleus, this gallery also contains post-impressionist paintings, sculptures by Rodin, stained glass, and works by modern Irish artists.

✪ Irish Film Centre. 6 Eustace St. ☎ **01/679-5744,** or 01/679-3477 for the cinema box office. Admission: Institute, free; cinemas, £2.50–£4 ($4–$6.40); *Flashback,* £2 ($3.20) adults, £1.50 ($2.40) seniors and students. Institute, Mon–Sat 10am–11:30pm, Sun 11am–11:30pm; cinemas, daily 2–11:30pm (cinema box office, daily 2–9pm); *Flashback,* Wed–Sun at noon. Bus: 21A, 78A, or 78B.

As a city with great dramatic and theatrical traditions and as a setting for many films, Dublin is a natural for a film institute. Opened in 1993, this center has become a focal point for Dublin's artsy Temple Bar district. It houses two film theaters, the

Irish Film Archive, a library, a film-theme bookshop and restaurant/bar, and eight film-related organizations. In summer there are showings of *Flashback,* a history of Irish film in the past century. There's also a very good cafe/restaurant.

National Gallery. Merrion Sq. W. ☎ **01/661-5133.** Free admission. Mon–Wed and Fri–Sat 10am–5:30pm, Thurs 10am–8:30pm, Sun 2–5pm. Guided tours given Sat at 3pm and Sun at 2:30, 3:15, and 4pm. DART: Pearse Station. Bus: 5, 7, 7A, 8, 10, 44, 47, 48A, or 62.

Established by an Act of Parliament in 1854, this gallery first opened its doors in 1864, with just over 100 paintings. Today the collection has more than 2,400 paintings. The museum also has drawings, watercolors, and sculpture, representing every major European school. There's also an extensive grouping of Irish work.

Museum of Childhood. The Palms, 20 Palmerston Park, Rathmines. ☎ **01/497-3223.** Admission £1 ($1.60) adults, 75p ($1.20) children 11 and under. July–Aug, Wed and Sun 2–5:30pm; Sept and Nov–June, Sun 2–5:30pm. Bus: 13 or 14.

This museum specializes in dolls and dollhouses of all nations, from 1730 to 1940. Among the unique items on display are dollhouses that belonged to Empress Elizabeth of Austria and Daphne du Maurier. In addition, there are antique toys, rocking horses, and doll carriages.

PARKS & ZOOS

✪ **Phoenix Park,** Parkgate Street (☎ **01/677-0095**), is Dublin's playground, the largest urban enclosed park in Europe, with a circumference of 7 miles and a total area of 1,760 acres. Opened in 1747, it also contains the home of the Irish president and the U.S. ambassador to Ireland. Situated 2 miles west of the city center, it's traversed by a network of roads, quiet pedestrian walkways, and nature trails, and informally landscaped with ornamental gardens and broad expanses of grassland separated by avenues of trees. Livestock graze peacefully on pasturelands and deer roam the forested areas.

The **Dublin Zoo** (☎ **01/677-1425**), also located here, was established in 1830 and is the third-oldest zoo in the world (after London and Paris). The 30-acre zoo provides a naturally landscaped habitat for more than 235 species of wild animals and tropical birds. Highlights for youngsters include the Children's Pets' Corner and a train ride around the zoo. Admission is £5.50 ($8.25) for adults, £2.75 ($4.15) for children 11 and under and seniors. Open Mon–Sat 9:30am–6pm and Sun 11am–6pm. Bus: 10, 25, or 26.

ORGANIZED TOURS

BUS TOURS For the standard see-it-all-in-under-3-hours bus tour of Dublin, climb aboard the **Dublin Bus** open-deck sightseeing coach. Tours leave from the Dublin Bus office at 59 Upper O'Connell St. (☎ **01/873-4222**), Mar–Nov, daily at 10:15am and 2:15pm; and Dec–Mar, Tues and Fri–Sat at 10:15am. You can purchase your ticket at the office or on the bus: £9 ($14.40) for adults and £4.50 ($7.20) for children.

There's another similar bus tour operated Apr–Sept in conjunction with the walking-tour Heritage Trail booklets. Tickets for the Heritage Tour cost £5 ($8) for adults and £2.50 ($4) for children. Tickets are good for 1 day and allow you to get on and off at various convenient stops.

WALKING TOURS Small and compact, Dublin lends itself to walking tours. You can set out with a map on your own, but you can also consider a self-guided or an escorted group tour.

The **Dublin Tourism Office,** Suffolk Street (☎ **01/605-7797**), has mapped out and signposted four different Tourist Trails: Old Dublin City, Georgian Heritage, Cultural Heritage, and Rock 'n' Stroll/Music Theme. For each separate trail there's a handy booklet that maps out the route and provides a commentary about each place along the trail. The booklets cost £1 ($1.60) each; the Rock 'n' Stroll booklet costs £1.95 ($3.10).

Several firms offer tours led by knowledgeable local guides. Tour times and charges vary, but most last about 2 hours and cost £4–£6 ($6.40–$9.60) per person. **Discover Dublin Tours** (☎ 01/478-0191) offers a musical pub crawl led by two professional musicians. **Dublin Footsteps** (☎ 01/496-0641 or 01/845-0722) offer tours focussing on medieval, literary, 18th-century, or other city-center sites. The **Dublin Literary Pub Crawl** (☎ 01/454-0228) departs evenings from the Duke Street Pub, Duke Street. **Historical Walking Tours** (☎ 01/845-0241) depart from the front gates of Trinity College. The **Original Ghost Walk of Dublin** (☎ 01/626-3175) sets off Wed–Sun at 8pm from outside the Dublin Tourist Office, Suffolk Street. **Trinity College Walking Tours** (☎ 01/679-4291) depart from the front sqaure of Trinity College.

HORSE-DRAWN CARRIAGE TOURS   **Dublin Horse-Drawn Carriage Tours,** St. Stephen's Green (☎ **01/453-8888** or 01/821-6463), cost £5–£30 ($8–$48) for two to five passengers, depending on the duration of ride, given Apr–Oct, daily and nightly, depending on weather. To arrange a ride, consult with one of the drivers stationed with carriages at the Grafton Street side of St. Stephen's Green. Rides can also be booked by phone in advance.

SPORTS & OUTDOOR ACTIVITIES

SPECTATOR SPORTS   Ireland's national games, **hurling** and **Gaelic football,** are played every weekend throughout the summer at various local fields, culminating in September with the All-Ireland Finals, an Irish version of the Super Bowl. For schedules and admission charges, contact the **Gaelic Athletic Association,** Croke Park, Jones Road, Dublin 3 (☎ **01/836-3222**).

Dublin's racing fans gather at **Leopardstown Race Course,** off Stillorgan Road (N11), Foxrock, Dublin 18 (☎ **01/289-3607**), 6 miles south of the city center. This is a modern facility with all-weather glass-enclosed spectator stands. Races are scheduled throughout the year, two or three times a month, on weekdays or weekends.

The **Kerrygold Dublin Horse Show,** Royal Dublin Society (RDS), Merrion Road, Ballsbridge (☎ **01/668-0645**), is a famous internatioal event that takes place in August.

OUTDOOR ACTIVITIES   **Beaches**   On the outskirts of Dublin are beaches that offer safe swimming and sandy strands and can all be reached via city buses heading northward: Dollymount, $3\frac{1}{2}$ miles; Sutton, 7 miles; Howth, 9 miles; and Portmarnock and Malahide, each 10 miles away. The southern suburb of Dun Laoghaire, 7 miles away, offers a beach at Sandycove, and a long bayfront promenade, ideal for strolling.

Golf   Leading 18-hole courses in the Dublin area are the **Elm Park Golf Club,** Nutley Lane (☎ 01/269-3438); the **Portmarnock Golf Club,** Portmarnock, Co. Dublin (☎ 01/846-2968); and the **Royal Dublin Golf Club,** Bull Island, Dollymount (☎ 01/833-6346), a top course which has often been compared to St. Andrews in layout, and has hosted several Irish Open tournaments.

Horseback Riding   Almost a dozen riding stables are within easy reach. Prices average about £10 ($16) an hour, with or without instruction. Nearest to downtown are the **Calliaghstown Riding Centre,** Calliaghstown, Rathcoole, Co. Dublin (☎ 01/458-9236); the **Carrickmines Equestrian Centre,** Glenamuck Road, Foxrock, Dublin 18 (☎ 01/295-5990); and the **Malahide Riding School,** Ivy Grangge, Malahide, Co. Dublin (☎ 01/846-3622).

Walking The walk **from Bray to Greystones** along the rocky promontory of Bray Head is a great excursion, with beautiful views back toward Killiney Bay, Dalkey Island, and Howth. Bray, the southern terminus of the DART line, is readily accessible from Dublin. Follow the beachside promenade south through town; at the outskirts of the town the promenade turns left and up, beginning the ascent of Bray Head. Shortly after the beginning of this ascent a trail branches to the left—this is the cliffside walk, which continues another 3¹/₂ miles along the coast to Greystones. From the center of Greystones there's a train that will take you back to Bray. This is an easy walk, about 2 hours one-way.

SHOPPING

In general, Dublin shops are open Mon–Sat 9 or 9:30am–5:30 or 6pm, with late hours Thurs to 8pm. In tourist season, many shops also post Sunday hours.

If you're looking for a souvenir reflecting Irish art, try **M. Kennedy & Sons Ltd.,** 12 Harcourt St. (☎ 01/475-1749). This interesting shop has books on Irish artists, all types of artist's supplies, and an excellent art gallery on the upstairs level.

For books, go to ✪ **Eason & Son Ltd.,** 40–42 Lower O'Connell St. (☎ 01/873-3811), with a comprehensive selection of books and maps about Dublin and Ireland.

✪ **Hodges Figgis,** 56/58 Dawson St. (☎ 01/677-4754), is a three-story landmark store with great charm and browse appeal. There are particularly good sections on Irish literature, Celtic studies, and folklore.

China Showrooms, 32/33 Abbey St. (☎ 01/878-6211), is a one-stop source of fine china such as Belleek, Aynsley, Royal Doulton, and hand-cut crystal from Waterford, Tipperary, and Tyrone. The **Dublin Crystal Glass Company,** Brookfield Terrace, Carysfort Avenue, Blackrock (☎ 01/288-7932), is Dublin's own distinctive hand-cut crystal business, founded in 1764 and revived in 1968. Visitors are welcome to browse in the factory shop and to see the glass being made and engraved.

The ✪ **Powerscourt Townhouse Centre,** 59 S. William St. (☎ 01/679-4144), is a four-story complex with more than 60 boutiques, craft shops, art galleries, snackeries, wine bars, and restaurants. The wares include all kinds of crafts, antiques, paintings, prints, and hand-dipped chocolates and Farmhouse cheeses.

✪ **Cleo,** 18 Kildare St.(☎ 01/676-1421), is the shop for the Joyce family's designer ready-to-wear clothing in a rainbow of vibrant tweed colors. **Pat Crowley,** 3 Molesworth Place (☎ 01/661-5580), is known for her exclusive line of tweeds and couture evening wear. Men shouldn't miss ✪ **Kevin and Howlin,** 31 Nassau St. (☎ 01/677-0257), a shop that has specialized in men's tweed garments for over 50 years. There's also a selection of sweaters, scarves, vests, and hats. ✪ **Louis Copeland,** 39–41 Capel St. (☎ 01/872-1600), is known for high-quality work in made-to-measure and ready-to-wear men's suits, coats, and shirts. There are also branches at 30 Pembroke St. and 18 Wicklow St.

Irish design from the 5th to the 15th century has been the inspiration for much of the craft work at **Fergus O'Farrell Workshop,** 62 Dawson St. (☎ 01/677-0862). ✪ **The Irish Times Collection,** 10–16 D'Olier St. (☎ 01/671-8446), features Irish-made crafts, many of which are commissioned by the newspaper for special offers to its readers.

Heraldic Artists, 3 Nassau St. (☎ **01/679-7020**), has been known for helping visitors locate their family roots for over 20 years. In addition to tracing surnames, it also sells all the usual heraldic items, from parchments and mahogany wall plaques to crests, scrolls, and books on researching ancestry.

The **Blarney Woolen Mills,** 21–23 Nassau St. (☎ **01/671-0068**), known for its competitive prices, stocks a wide range of woolen knitwear made at its home base in Blarney, as well as crystal, china, pottery, and souvenirs. The **Dublin Woolen Mills,** 41 Lower Ormond Quay (☎ **01/677-0301**), is on the north side of the River Liffey next to the Ha'penny Bridge, a leading source of Aran hand-knit sweaters as well as vests, hats, jackets, and tweeds. The **Sheepskin Shop,** 20 Wicklow St. (☎ **01/ 671-9585**), is a good place to find sheepskin jackets and hats, as well as suede coats and lambskin wear.

If you want a cashmere sweater, go to ✪ **Monaghan's,** 15/17 Grafton Arcade, Grafton Street (☎ **01/677-0823**), which has the best selection of colors, sizes, and styles for both men and women anywhere in Ireland. It's also located at 4/5 Royal Hibernian Way, off Dawson Street (☎ 01/679-4451).

Tutty's Handmade Shoes Ltd., 59 S. William St. (☎ **01/679-6566**), on the top floor of the Powerscourt Townhouse Centre, is a tiny shop specializing in made-to-measure shoes and boots, crafted from the finest leathers.

Just in case it rains, **H. Johnston,** 11 Wicklow St. (☎ **01/677-1249**), is the place for durable umbrellas. And if you're looking for an Irish blackthorn stick, otherwise known as a shillelagh, this spot has been specializing in them for more than 110 years.

MARKETS At the **Blackrock Market,** 19a Main St., Blackrock (☎ **01/ 283-3522**), more than 60 vendors sell a wide variety of old and new goods at great prices in this indoor/outdoor setting; open Sat 11am–5:30pm and Sun noon–5:30pm.

The ✪ **Mother Redcaps Market,** Back Lane, off High Street (☎ **01/454-4655**), is one of Dublin's best, an enclosed market in the heart of Old Dublin. The various stalls offer everything from antiques and used books and coins to silver, handcrafts, music tapes, furniture, and even a fortune teller! It's worth a trip here just to sample the farm-made cheeses, baked goods, and jams at the Ryefield Foods stall.

DUBLIN AFTER DARK

The best way to find out what's going on is to ask for current calendar listings at the Dublin Tourism Office, Suffolk Street (☎ 01/605-7797), or consult the entertainment/leisure pages of the *Irish Times* and other daily newspapers. The tourist office and most hotels distribute copies of the biweekly *Dublin Event Guide,* a free newspaper listing entertainment and theater programs.

THE PERFORMING ARTS
Concert & Performance Halls
The **National Concert Hall,** Earlsfort Terrace (☎ **01/671-1533**), a 1,200-seat hall, is the home of the Concert Orchestra of Ireland and the Irish Chamber Orchestra.

The Point, East Link Bridge, North Wall Quay (☎ **01/836-3633**), is Ireland's newest and largest concert venue, attracting top Broadway-caliber shows and international stars.

The **City Arts Centre,** 23–25 Moss St., at City Quay (☎ **01/677-0643**), opened in 1989, is an affiliate of Trans Europe Halles, the European network of independent arts centers. It presents a varied program, from local drama groups, theatrical discussions, and readings by local writers to touring companies from abroad.

The **Gaiety Theatre,** South King Street (☎ **01/677-1717**), is a fine 19th-century venue, where the Dublin Grand Opera Society performs its spring (Apr) and winter (Dec) seasons. The **Olympia,** 72 Dame St. (☎ **01/677-7744**), a Victorian music hall theater, presents an eclectic schedule of variety shows, operettas, and concerts, and features live bands for the late-night crowd.

Theater

⭐ **Abbey Theatre.** Lower Abbey St. ☎ **01/878-7222.** Tickets £8–£14 ($12.80–$22.40).

For over 90 years the Abbey has been the national theater of Ireland and home of the world-famed Abbey Players. The original theater, destroyed in a 1951 fire, was replaced in 1966 by the current modern 600-seat building. The box office is open Mon–Sat 10:30am–7pm.

Andrews Lane Theatre. 12/16 Andrews Lane. ☎ **01/679-5720.** Tickets £6–£12 ($9.60–$19.20).

This showplace consists of a 220-seat main theater, which presents contemporary work from home and abroad, and a 76-seat studio geared for experimental productions. The box office is open Mon–Sat 10:30am–7pm.

The Gate. 1 Cavendish Row. ☎ **01/874-4045.** Tickets £10–£12 ($16–$19.20).

Situated just north of O'Connell Street off Parnell Square in a restored 370-seat theater, this company was founded in 1928 by Hilton Edwards and Michael MacLiammoir to provide a showing for a broad range of plays. Though less well known to visitors than the Abbey, this is probably Ireland's most distinguished theater. The box office is open Mon–Sat 10am–7pm.

Dinner Shows with Traditional Music

At the **Abbey Tavern**, Abbey Road, Howth, Co. Dublin (☎ **01/839-0307**), a complete four-course meal is accompanied by authentic Irish ballad music, with its blend of fiddles, pipes, tin whistles, and spoons. Tickets for dinner and entertainment are £23–£28 ($36.80–$44.80); entertainment only, £3 ($4.80).

Doyle's Irish Cabaret, Upper Leeson Street (☎ **01/660-5222,** ext. 1162), takes place in the ballroom of the Hotel Burlington, featuring some of Ireland's top performers in a program of Irish music, dancing, ballad singing, and storytelling. Shows are May–Oct, Mon–Sat with dinner at 7pm and the show at 8pm. Tickets for dinner and the show are £30.90 ($49.45); for the show with two drinks, £19.50 ($31.20).

Jury's Irish Cabaret, Pembroke Road, Ballsbridge (☎ **01/660-5000**), is Ireland's longest-running show (over 30 years). It offers a mix of traditional Irish music and Broadway classics, set dancing, humorous monologues, and audience participation. Shows take place May–Oct, Tues–Sun with dinner at 7:15pm and the show at 8pm. Tickets for dinner and the show are £31.50 ($50.40); for the show with two drinks, £19 ($30.40).

Traditional Irish Entertainment

⭐ **Culturlann Na heireann.** 32 Belgrave Sq., Monkstown. ☎ **01/280-0295.** Tickets: Ceilis, £4 ($6.40); informal music sessions, £1.50 ($2.40); stage shows, £5 ($8).

This is the home of Comhaltas Ceoltoiri Eireann, an Irish cultural organization that has been the prime mover in encouraging the renewal of Irish traditional music. An authentic fully costumed show featuring traditional music, song, and dance is staged June–Sept, Sat–Thurs 9–10:30pm. No reservations are necessary. Year-round, ceili dances are performed Fri 9:30pm–12:30am; informal music sessions, Fri–Sat 9:30–11:30pm.

CLUBS & DISCOS

The club scene in Dublin is complex and volatile. The night scene in the "in" places is definitely young. Many of the most sizzling spots have a "strict" or "unfriendly" door policy, admitting only those who look and feel right for the scene inside. Most trendy clubs have DJs and not live music, and the genre of current choice is rave.

Average cover charges range from nominal to £8 ($12.80), and most clubs open between 10pm and 11pm and go on to 2pm or later. Trendy clubs include **The Kitchen,** 6/8 Wellington Quay (☎ 01/677-6178), housed in the basement of the Clarence Hotel in the heart of the Temple Bar district, partly owned by the rock group U2. **Lillie's Bordello,** 45 Nassau St. (☎ 01/679-9204), a private club, open to members and nonmembers, has a stylish and self-consciously decadent ambience with a mix of music 7 days a week. **POD,** Harcourt Street (☎ 01/478-0166), is as loud as it is dazzling to behold. **Rí-Rá,** 1 Exchequer St. (☎ 01/677-4835), has a more friendly door policy.

Another set of clubs have friendly door policies and people of most any age are likely to feel comfortable. These include **Annabel's,** in the Burlington Hotel, Upper Leeson Street (☎ 01/660-5222), which welcomes a mix of tourists and locals; **Club M,** Anglesea Street (☎ 01/671-5622); **Buck Whaley's,** Lower Leeson Street (☎ 01/676-1755); **Court,** in the Harcourt Hotel, Harcourt Street (☎ 01/478-3677); and **Rumours,** in the Gresham Hotel, O'Connell Street (☎ 01/874-1635).

The principal live-music places are **Whelans,** 25 Wexford St. (☎ 01/478-0766); **Eammon Doran's,** 3A Crown Alley, Temple Bar (☎ 01/679-9114); and **Mean Fiddler,** 26 Wexford St. (☎ 01/475-8555).

PUBS

Conversation & Atmosphere

✪ **Brazen Head.** 20 Lower Bridge St. ☎ **01/679-5186.**

This brass-filled and lantern-lit pub claims to be the city's oldest—and with good reason, considering that it was licensed in 1661 and occupies the site of an earlier tavern dating from 1198. On the south bank of the River Liffey, it's at the end of a cobblestone courtyard and was once the meeting place of Irish freedom fighters such as Robert Emmet and Wolfe Tone.

Davy Byrnes. 21 Duke St. (just off Grafton St.). ☎ **01/677-5217.**

Referred to as a "moral pub" by James Joyce in *Ulysses,* this imbibers' landmark has drawn poets, writers, and lovers of literature ever since. Davy Byrnes first opened the doors in 1873; he presided here for more than 50 years and visitors today can still see his likeness on one of the turn-of-the-century murals hanging over the bar.

Flannery's Temple Bar. 48 Temple Bar. ☎ **01/677-3807.**

In the heart of the trendy Temple Bar district on the corner of Temple Lane, this small three-room pub was established in 1840. The decor is an interesting mix of crackling fireplaces, globe ceiling lights, old pictures on the walls, and shelves filled with local memorabilia.

✪ **John M. Keating.** 14 Mary St. ☎ **01/873-1567.**

Situated north of the Liffey at the corner of Jervis Street, this bilevel pub is known for its old-world decor, from its marble-top bar and spiral staircase to the upstairs loft.

The Long Hall. 51 S. Great George's St. ☎ **01/475-1590.**

Tucked into a busy commercial street, this is one of the city's most photographed pubs, with a beautiful Victorian decor of filigree-edged mirrors, polished dark woods, and traditional snugs. The hand-carved bar is said to be the longest counter in the city.

✪ **W. Ryan.** 28 Parkgate St. ☎ **01/677-6097.**

Three generations of the Ryan family have contributed to the success of this public house, located on the north side of the Liffey near Phoenix Park. The pub has such fine features as the metal ceiling and domed skylight, beveled mirrors, etched glass, brass lamp holders, a mahogany bar, and four old-style snugs.

Traditional/Folk Music

An Beal Brocht. 58 Charlemont St. (off Harcourt St. at Albert Place W.). ☎ **01/475-5614.** No cover.

Located between St. Stephen's Green and the Grand Canal, this cozy vintage pub offers a varied program of Irish traditional music on most nights and Sun 12:30–2pm.

Barry Fitzgeralds. 90–92 Marlborough St. ☎ **01/874-0685.** No cover.

Named for the Abbey actor who became a Hollywood movie star, this place has a theatrical atmosphere, with lots of thespian memorabilia lining the walls and alcoves. It offers live traditional music on Friday night and Sunday afternoon, and karaoke on Saturday. Music usually starts at 8:45pm.

✪ **Kitty O'Shea's.** 23–25 Upper Grand Canal St. ☎ **01/660-9965.** No cover.

Situated just south of the Grand Canal, this pub is named after the sweetheart of 19th-century Irish statesman Charles Stewart Parnell. The decor reflects the Parnell era, with ornate oak paneling, stained-glass windows, old political posters, cozy alcoves, and brass railings. Traditional Irish music is on tap every night.

Mother Redcaps Tavern. Back Lane. ☎ **01/453-3960.** Cover: none, except for concerts £5–£6 ($8–$9.60).

A former shoe factory in the heart of the Liberties section of the city, this large two-story pub exudes an old Dublin atmosphere, with eclectic mahogany and stripped pine furnishings, and walls lined with old paintings and newspaper clippings. On Sunday there's usually a midday session of traditional Irish music, with everyone invited to bring an instrument and join in. On many nights there's also traditional music on an informal basis or in a concert setting upstairs.

O'Donoghue's. 5 Merrion Row. ☎ **01/661-4303.** No cover.

Tucked between St. Stephen's Green and Merrion Street, this smoke-filled enclave is widely heralded as the granddaddy of traditional music pubs. At almost any time of the day or night a spontaneous session is likely to erupt.

Oliver St. John Gogarty. 57/58 Fleet St. ☎ **01/671-1822.** No cover.

Situated in the heart of Temple Bar and named for one of Ireland's literary greats, this pub has an inviting old-world atmosphere, with shelves of empty bottles, stacks of dusty books, a horseshoe-shaped bar, and old barrels for seats. There are traditional music sessions Sat 3:30–7pm, Sun 12:30–3pm, and every night 9–11pm.

Slattery's. 129–130 Capel St. ☎ **01/872-7971.** Cover: none for Irish-music sessions, £3–£4 ($4.80–$6.40) cover for rock or blues.

Located on the north side of the Liffey, this pub has a classic facade and an interior of brass trim, dark wood, gas lamps, and church pew benches. On Sunday at 12:30 and 2pm it's a focal point for traditional Irish music and ballads, with as many as 20 musicians playing in an informal session in the main bar. Rock and blues music is featured in the upstairs lounge Wed–Sun 9–11:30pm.

DAY TRIPS FROM DUBLIN

THE JOYCE TOWER   Sitting on the edge of Dublin Bay about 6 miles south of the city center, this 40-foot granite monument is one of a series of martello towers built in 1804 to withstand a threatened invasion by Napoleon. The tower's greatest claim to fame, however, is that it was inhabited in 1904 by James Joyce, as the guest of Oliver Gogarty, who had rented the tower from the army for an annual fee of £8 ($12). Joyce made the tower the setting for the first chapter of his famous novel *Ulysses* and it has been known as "Joyce's Tower" ever since. Its collection of Joycean memorabilia includes letters, documents, first and rare editions, personal possessions, and photographs.

The tower can be reached by taking the DART to Sandycove Station or taking bus no. 8. Admission is £2 ($3.20) for adults, £1.60 ($2.56) for seniors, students, and children, and £6 ($9.60) for a family; it's open Apr–Oct, Mon–Sat 10am–1pm and 2–5pm and Sun 2–6pm. Call 01/280-9265 for more information.

۞ MALAHIDE CASTLE   One of Dublin's most historic castles, Malahide Castle (☎ **01/845-2337**) is about 8 miles north of Dublin. Founded in the 12th century by Richard Talbot and occupied by his descendants until 1973, it has been fully restored. The interior is the setting for a comprehensive collection of Irish furniture, dating from the 17th through the 19th century, and the walls are lined with Irish historical portraits and tableaux on loan from the National Gallery. The furnishings and art reflect life in and near the house over the past 8 centuries.

After touring the house, you can explore the 250-acre estate, which includes 20 acres of prized gardens with more than 5,000 species of plants and flowers.

Admission to the castle is £2.85 ($4.55) for adults, £2.30 ($3.70) for seniors and students, £1.50 ($2.40) for children 11 and under, and £7.75 ($12.40) for a family; the gardens are free. The castle is open Apr–Oct, Mon–Fri 10am–5pm, Sat 11am–6pm, and Sun 11:30am–6pm; Nov–Mar, Mon–Fri 10am–5pm and Sat–Sun 2–5pm. The gardens are open May–Sept, daily 2–5pm. The castle is closed for tours 12:45–2pm, although the restaurant remains open. Bus: 42.

The Malahide grounds also contain the **Fry Model Railway Museum** (☎ **01/845-2758**), an exhibit of rare handmade models of more than 300 Irish trains, from the introduction of rail to the present. A combination ticket with the castle is available.

2 Kerry & the Dingle Peninsula

Not only does County Kerry shelter Ireland's number one scenic attraction, the Killarney area, it also possesses the highest mountain peaks in the country, Macgillycuddy's Reeks and Mount Brandon. "The Kingdom," as it's sometimes called, is also home to Ireland's two most heralded touring routes, the Ring of Kerry and the Dingle Peninsula.

On Ireland's extreme southwest coast, County Kerry extends into the Atlantic with a rugged coastline dominated by two finger-shaped peninsulas. Warmed by the Gulf Stream, the county has a mild climate, in places subtropical, with temperatures averaging 40°–45°F in winter and 55°–65°F in the summer. It has been said that Kerry doesn't have a climate—just weather. This means that you can have a beautifully sunny morning and then suddenly a storm front blows in off the Atlantic and a very wet afternoon sets in. But it's this changeable weather that makes Kerry so varied and such a delight to explore. Learn to go with the weather and to change your plans at short notice, if needs be, and the scenic rewards will be well worth it.

GETTING TO COUNTRY KERRY **By Plane** Aer Lingus offers daily direct flights from Dublin into **Kerry County Airport,** Farranfore, Co. Kerry (☎ **066/64-644**), about 10 miles north of Killarney and 15 miles south of Tralee.

By Car Roads leading into Kerry include N21 and N23 from Limerick, N22 from Cork, N72 from Mallow, and N70 from West Cork.

ONLY IN KERRY

Enjoying Killarney's Natural Beauty Killarney National Park, a 25,000-acre expanse of natural lakeland and mountain scenery, is one of world's most beautiful spots. Hike to the Gap of Dunloe, and then take a boat across Killarney's lakes, set amid craggy mountains.

Touring the Ring of Kerry and the Dingle Peninsula Ireland's highest mountains contrast with spectacular views of dramatic coastline on both these panoramic routes. Drive around the Ring of Kerry, but tour the Dingle Peninsula by bicycle.

Exploring Ireland's Archeological Heritage Recalling Ireland's rich cultural past as preserver of learning and scholarship are Skellig Michael, a 6th-century monastic settlement; Gallarus Oratory, one of Ireland's best-preserved early Christian buildings; and the ruins of St. Brendan's House, where the saint reputedly set out to discover America long before Columbus.

Shopping for Crafts County Kerry has many local craftspeople, who produce wonderful weaving, leatherwork, and the distinctive colored Kerry glass in Killorglin.

Spending an Evening in a Pub Most of of Kerry's pubs have traditional music evenings, especially in Killarney and Dingle. Irish music is played every night in any pub in Dingle, sometimes with step dancing.

KILLARNEY TOWN

Killarney is a relatively small town with a population of around 7,000 people. The town is very walkable, though the streets are usually crowded with tourists, especially in summer. The busiest section of town is at the southern tip of Main Street, where it meets East Avenue Road. Here the road curves and heads southward out to Muckross Road and the entrance to Killarney National Park.

ESSENTIALS

ARRIVING **By Train** Irish Rail offers daily service from most major Irish cities, arriving at **Killarney Railway Station,** Railway Road, off East Avenue Road (☎ **064/31-067**).

By Bus Bus Eireann operates regularly scheduled bus service from all parts of Ireland. The **bus station** is adjacent to the train station at Railway Road, off East Avenue Road, Killarney (☎ **064/34-777**).

VISITOR INFORMATION The **Killarney Tourist Office** is located in the Town Hall, Church Place, off Main Street (☎ **064/31-633**). It's open Mon–Sat: in June 9:15am–6pm, July–Aug 9:15am–8pm, and Sept–May 9:30am–5pm. It offers many useful booklets and can also book accommodations for you. The area code for most Killarney phone numbers is 064. *Killarney,* a quarterly magazine available at hotels and guesthouses, contains helpful and up-to-date information for visitors.

GETTING AROUND The town is so small and compact that it's best traversed on foot. **Taxis** line up at the rank on College Square (☎ 064/31-331), or you can phone for a taxi from Dero's Taxi Service (☎ 064/31-251).

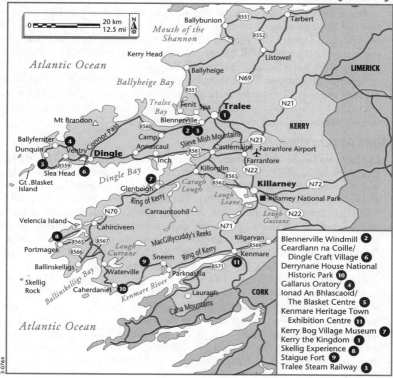

County Kerry

Blennerville Windmill **2**
Ceardlann na Coille/
  Dingle Craft Village **6**
Derrynane House National
  Historic Park **10**
Gallarus Oratory **4**
Ionad An Bhlascaoid/
  The Blasket Centre **5**
Kenmare Heritage Town
  Exhibition Centre **11**
Kerry Bog Village Museum **7**
Kerry the Kingdom **1**
Skellig Experience **8**
Staigue Fort **9**
Tralee Steam Railway **3**

You can drive to Killarney National Park, or go by **jaunting car**. The horse-drawn jaunting cars line up at Kenmare Place, offering rides to Killarney National Park sites and other scenic areas. See "Sightseeing Tours," below.

✪ KILLARNEY NATIONAL PARK

This is Killarney's centerpiece, a 25,000-acre area of unsurpassed natural beauty, including three legendary lakes, the Lower Lake or Lough Leane, the Middle Lake or Muckross Lake, and the Upper Lake. A myriad of waterfalls, rivers, islands, valleys, mountains, bogs, and woodlands add to the wonderment. Four signposted walking and nature trails wend their way along the lakeshore.

No automobiles are allowed inside the park, so touring is best done on foot or by bicycle, pony, or jaunting car.

Access is available from several points along Kenmare Road (N71); the main entrance is at Muckross House, where there's a visitor center featuring background exhibits on the park and a 15-minute audiovisual film, *Killarney: A Special Place.* Admission is free, and the park is open year-round during daylight hours.

VIEWS & VISTAS The journey through the ✪ **Gap of Dunloe,** amid mountains and lakes, is a must. The dirt-track route passes a kaleidoscope of craggy rocks, massive cliffs, meandering streams, and deep valleys. Make sure to stop by the second lake (known locally as "Echo Lake") and shout at the top of your voice. Farther on, Serpent Lake is where St. Patrick supposedly drowned the last snake in Ireland. To this day the lake has no fish. The road through the gap ends at Upper Lake. The track makes an interesting hike or bicycle trip. You can also drive to Kate Kearney's Cottage and hire a jaunting car or a pony, or take one of the daily sightseeing tours (see below). From Upper Lake, you can make the return trip by water, as a boat glides you across the three lakes of Killarney and then pulls ashore at Ross Castle, where a jaunting car or bus will take you back to Killarney.

Aghadoe Heights, on Tralee Road (off N22) is a spectacular viewing point over the lakes and town. To your left is the ruin of the 13th-century Castle of Parkvonear, erected by Norman invaders and well worth a visit. In the nearby churchyard are the remains of a stone church and round tower dating from 1027.

MORE ATTRACTIONS

✪ **Muckross House and Gardens,** on Kenmare Road (N71; ☎ **064/31-440**), is the focal point of the Middle lake. The gracious ivy-covered, Elizabethan-style residence with its colorful and well-tended gardens was built by Henry Arthur Herbert in 1843 and visited by Queen Victoria in 1861. The house is now a folk museum, and the cellars have been converted into craft shops where local artisans demonstrate the traditional trades of bookbinding, weaving, and pottery making. The adjacent gardens are known for their fine collection of rhododendrons and azaleas. Admission is £3.30 ($5.30) for adults, £2.20 ($3.50) for seniors, and £1.50 ($2.40) for children. It's open July–Aug, daily 9am–7pm; Sept–June, daily 9am–6pm.

Ross Castle, on Ross Road, off Kenmare Road (N71; ☎ **064/35-851**), was built in the 14th century by the O'Donoghue chieftains, and was the last significant stronghold in Ireland to fall to Cromwell's armies. All that remains today is a tower house, surrounded by a fortified bawn with rounded turrets. The castle offers a magnificent view of the lakes and islands from its top, but access is by guided tour only. Admission is £2 ($3.20) for adults, £1.50 ($2.40) for seniors, and £1 ($1.60) for children. It's open June–Aug, daily 9am–6pm; and Mar–May and Sept–Oct, daily 10:30am–5pm.

If you like caves, **Crag Cave,** off Limerick Road (N21; ☎ **064/41-244**), a limestone cave thought to be over a million years old, is one of the longest in Ireland and contains some of the largest stalactites in Europe. By guided tour only, admission is £3 ($4.80) for adults, £2.50 ($4) for seniors and students, £1.50 ($2.40) for children 7 and over. It's open July–Aug, daily 10am–7pm; and Mar 17–June and Sept–Oct, daily 10am–6pm.

SIGHTSEEING TOURS

BUS TOURS   Dero's Tours, 7 Main St. (☎ **064/31-251** or 064/31-567), offers Killarney Highlights, a 3-hour tour that takes you to Killarney's lakes, Aghadoe, the Gap of Dunloe, Ross Castle, Muckross House, and Torc Waterfall. Tours are given May–Sept, daily at 10am and 2pm; the cost is £7.50 ($12). **Castlelough Tours,** 7 High St. (☎ **064/32-496** or 064/31-115), offers a 3¹/₂-hour Lakeland Tour that visits Muckross House and Gardens and includes a tour of the lakes by Killarney Waterbus. Tours are given May–Sept, daily at 10:30am and 2pm, and cost £10 ($16).

**JAUNTING-CAR TOURS   There's no better way to explore the national park than in one of these lightweight, horse-drawn carts. You're driven by a jarvey who gives you a running narrative as you go, and exchanges banter with other jarveys passed en route. The rates are set and carefully monitered by the Killarney Urban District Council, based on four people and running £5–£8 ($8–$12.80) per person. To arrange for a jaunting-car trip, go to the places where cars and drivers line up: at

Kenmare Place in town, the first entrance to Killarney National Park on Muckross Road, the Muckross Abbey entrance to the park, Muckross House, or Kate Kearney's Cottage. If you need assistance or guidlines on prices, the tourist office will help you.

Gap of Dunloe excursions are offered by Castlelough Tours and Dero's Tours (see above); Corcoran's Tours, Kilcummin (☎ 064/43-151); and O'Donoghue's Tours, 3 High St. (☎ 064/31-068). A tour will cost about £20–£25 ($32–$40).

BOAT TOURS   There's nothing quite like being in a boat on the lakes of Killarney. Two companies offer regular boating excursions with full commentary. **M.V. *Pride of the Lakes* Tours,** Scotts Gardens (☎ **064/32-638**), has sailings in an enclosed waterbus from the pier at Ross Castle, Apr–Oct, daily at 11am and 12:30, 2:30, 4, and 5:15pm. The trip lasts just over an hour and reservations are suggested. Adults pay £5 ($8); children are charged £2.50 ($4). **M.V. *Lily of Killarney* Tours,** 3 High St. (☎ **064/31-068**), also departing from Ross Castle pier, sails Apr–Oct, daily at 10:30am, noon, and 1:45, 3:15, 4:30, and 5:45pm. The cruise lasts about an hour, and again reservations are recommended. The charge is £5 ($8) for adults and £2.50 ($4) for children.

Abbey Boating Trips, Ross Castle (☎ **064/34-010**), takes you by open motorboat onto the lakes; this trip's highlight is a visit to Innisfallen Island, where you can see the 6th-century abbey ruins. Fares begin at £4 ($6.40) per person, based on four people.

OUTDOOR ACTIVITIES

BICYCLING   The Killarney National Park with its many lakeside and forest pathways is a paradise for bikers. Rental charges average around £6 ($9.60) per day or £30 ($40) per week. Bicycles can be rented from **Killarney Rent-a-Bike,** Old Market Lane, off High Street (☎ 064/32-578); the **O'Neill Cycle Shop,** 6 Plunkett St. (☎ 064/31-970); or **O'Sullivan's Bike Shop,** Pawn Office Lane, off High Street (☎ 064/31-282). Most shops are open all year, daily 9am–6pm, with extended hours to 8 or 9pm in the summer.

FISHING   Fishing for salmon and brown trout is a big attraction in Killarney's unpolluted lakes and rivers. Brown trout fishing is free on the lakes, but a permit is necessary for the Rivers Flesk and Laune. Permits and licenses can be obtained at the **Fishery Office** at Knockreer Estate Office, New Street (☎ **064/31-246**).

For tackle, bait, rod rental, and other gear, as well as permits and licenses, try **O'Neill's Fishing Tackle Shop,** 6 Plunkett St. (☎ 064/31-970). This shop also arranges the rental of boats and guides. Gear and tackle can also be purchased from **Handy Stores,** Kenmare Place (☎ 064/31-188), and **Angler's Paradise,** Loreto Road (☎ 064/33-818).

HORSEBACK RIDING   Many trails in the Killarney area are suitable for horseback riding (English tack). The cost of hiring a horse runs £8–£12 ($12.80–$19.20) per hour. You can rent at **Killarney Riding Stables,** R562, Ballydowney (☎ 064/31-686); **O'Donovan's Farm,** Mangerton Road, Muckross (☎ 064/32-238); and **Rocklands Stables,** Rockfield, Tralee Road (☎ 064/32-592). Lessons and week-long trail rides are available.

WALKING   Leaflets with maps for the four nature trails in Killarney National park are available at the park's visitor center. There are also regularly scheduled organized walks by **Kerry Country Rambles,** 5 Tracks and Trails, 53 High St. (☎ 064/35-277), priced from £12 ($19.20) per person per day. The duration varies from a day to a weekend or a full week.

Shopping

Shopping hours are normally Mon–Sat 9am–6pm, but May–Sept most shops stay open to 9 or 10pm.

The ✪ **Kerry Glass Studio and Visitor Centre,** Killorglin Road, Fossa (☎ **064/44-666**), is the studio that produces Killarney's distinctive colored glass. Visitors are welcome to watch—and photograph—the craftspeople firing, blowing, and adding color to the glass. The center includes a factory shop.

The **Blarney Woolen Mills,** 10 Main St. (☎ **064/33-222**), has everything from hand-knit or hand-loomed Irish-made sweaters to tweeds, crystal, china, pottery, and souvenirs. **Quill's Woolen Market,** 1 High St. (☎ **064/32-277**), is one of the best shops in town for hand-knit sweaters of all kinds, as well as tweeds, mohair, and sheepskins.

Serendipity, 15 College St. (☎ **064/31-056**), is a place for souvenirs, such as copper leprechauns mounted on aged bogwood and ceramic sheep and goats.

Accommodations

Expensive

Aghadoe Heights Hotel. Off Tralee Rd. (N22), Aghadoe, Killarney, Co. Kerry. ☎ **800/44-UTELL** in the U.S., or 064/31-766. Fax 064/31-345. 60 units. TV TEL. £120–£175 ($192–$280) double; £175–£225 ($280–$360) suite. AE, DC, MC, V. Rates include full breakfast. No service charge.

Offering panoramic views, overlooking the lakes and mountains, this modern two-story hotel is a luxury hotel with elegant bedrooms fitted in mahogany, cherrywood, or ash, with coordinated fabrics and furnishings and deep carpets. Each guest room sports floor-to-ceiling windows providing stunning views. The rooftop restaurant is Frederick's, and facilities include an indoor heated swimming pool with a waterfall, Jacuzzi, sauna, steam pool, and solarium.

Moderate

Castlerosse. Killorglin Rd., Killarney, Co. Kerry. ☎ **800/528-1234** in the U.S., or 064/31-114. Fax 064/31-031. 65 rms. TV TEL. £76–£102 ($121.60–$163.20) double. AE, DC, MC, V. Rates include full Irish breakfast and service charge. Closed Dec–Feb.

With an idyllic setting between the Lower Lake and the surrounding mountains, this modern, ranch-style inn is 2 miles from the center of town. The guest rooms offer contemporary furnishings and views of the lake. Facilities include a restaurant, lounge, gym, sauna, two tennis courts, putting green, walking paths, and jogging trails, and it's next to Killarney's two golf courses.

Europe. Off Killorglin Rd., Fossa, Killarney, Co. Kerry. ☎ **800/221-1074** in the U.S., or 064/31-900. Fax 064/32-118. 205 rms. TV TEL. £76–£102 ($121.60–$163.20) double. AE, DC, MC, V. Rates include full Irish breakfast and service charge. Closed Dec–Feb.

In a picturesque setting, right on the shores of the Lower Lake 3 miles west of town, this modern five-story hotel is adjacent to Killarney's golf courses and surrounded by stunning vistas of mountain peaks. The public areas are spacious, open, and filled with antiques; the guest rooms offer contemporary furnishings enhanced by lakeside views. Most of the bedrooms have private balconies. Guests can dine in the aptly named Panorama Restaurant. There's an Olympic-size swimming pool, saunas, a gym, and a hairdresing salon. Boating and fishing can be arranged, and the hotel has its own stables, with Haflinger horses.

✪ **Killeen House.** Aghadoe, Killarney, Co. Kerry. ☎ **064/31-711.** Fax 064/31-811. 15 rms. TV TEL. £80–£110 ($128–$176) double. AE, DC, MC, V. Rates include full breakfast. Service charge 10%.

Dating back to 1838 and overlooking Killarney's lakes, this rambling country manor house is surrounded by mature gardens in a quiet residential area, about 2 miles northwest of town. The bedrooms vary in size and decor, and feature semi-orthopedic beds. The public areas include an intimate 24-seat restaurant and a fireside lounge.

✪ **Muckross Park.** Muckross Rd., Killarney, Co. Kerry. ☎ **064/31-938.** Fax 064/31-938. 27 rms. TV TEL. £80–£120 ($128–$192) double. AE, DC, MC, V. Rates include full breakfast. No service charge. Closed Dec to mid-Mar.

Located just off the main road, about 2 miles outside town opposite Muckross House, this fairly new hotel is furnished in an old-world, country-house style with paneled walls and open fireplaces. The guest rooms vary in style and decor, and have period furniture, including some semi-canopy beds, plus modern amenities such as garment presses and hair dryers.

Inexpensive

Kathleen's Country House. Madam's Height, Tralee Rd. (N22), Killarney, Co. Kerry. ☎ **064/ 32-810.** Fax 064/32-340. 16 rms. TV TEL. £45–£75 ($72–$120) double. AE, MC, V. Rates include full breakfast. No service charge. Closed early Nov to mid-Mar.

Of the many guesthouses in this area, this one really does stand out. It's a two-story contemporary house, with many picture windows. The enthusiastic and efficient hostess, Kathleen O'Regan, has also outfitted all the bedrooms with orthopedic beds, hair dryers, tea/coffeemakers, and cheerful furnishings.

A Holiday House

Hillock House. Off Tralee Rd. (N22), Aghadoe, Killarney, Co. Kerry ☎ **064/36-199.** Holiday home for six. TV TEL. £550–£700 ($880–$1,134) per week. Sat–Sat only. AE, MC, V.

If you wish to spend a full week based in the Killarney area, this holiday home is ideal. Overlooking the lakes, this modern house offers a fully equipped kitchen with dishwasher, washing machine, and dryer. The house also has an indoor, heated swimming pool and sauna.

DINING

Expensive

Gaby's. 27 High St. ☎ **064/32-519.** Main courses £4–£6 ($6.40–$9.60) at lunch, £11.50– £26 ($18.40–$41.60) at dinner. MC, V. Mon 6–10pm, Tues–Sat 12:30–2:30pm and 6–10pm. SEAFOOD.

A mecca for lovers of fresh seafood, this restaurant is known for its succulent lobster, cooked every which way. Other dishes include smoked mackerel pâté, sole, salmon, and brill. The Kerry shellfish platter is a feast of prawns, scallops, mussels, lobster, and oysters. Be warned, though, that vegetables are extra and can run up the bill.

Moderate

Foley's. 23 High St. ☎ **064/31-217.** Reservations recommended for dinner. Main courses £8.80–£14.50 ($14.10–$23.20). AE, DC, MC, V. Daily 12:30–3pm and 5–10pm. Closed Dec 22–27. IRISH.

A Georgian country-home atmosphere prevails at this heart-of-town restaurant. The ever-changing menu features lobster, Dingle Bay scallops mornay, rainbow trout, and fresh wild salmon. If seafood is not to your taste, there's pheasant in port wine, duck in blackcurrant sauce, and Kerry mountain lamb. Don't pass up the home-baked brown-bread scones that accompany each meal.

Inexpensive

✪ **Bricin.** 26 High St. ☎ **064/34-902.** Reservations suggested for dinner. Main courses £6.90– £12.50 ($11.05–$20); snacks £1.50–£5 ($2.40–$8). MC, V. Mon–Sat 10am–10pm, Sun 6–10pm. IRISH.

Upstairs in one of Killarney's oldest buildings, this eatery sports original stone walls, pine furniture, and turf-burning fireplaces. Extremely popular are the Kerry boxty dishes (potato pancakes with fillings that can include chicken, seafood, curried lamb, or vegetables). The menu also includes fresh seafood, pastas, and chicken Bricin—breast of chicken in redcurrant and raspberry sauce.

✪ **Robertino's** . 9 High St. ☎ **064/34-966.** Reservations recommended. Main courses £6–£15 ($9.60–$24). MC, V. Daily 6–10:30pm. ITALIAN.

Step through the wrought-iron gates of this restaurant and experience the ambience of Italy, with a Mediterranean decor and operatic arias playing in the background. There are five dining areas, including a "green zone" for nonsmokers. The menu offers such dishes as veal saltimbocca and roast rib of lamb flamed in marsala-wine sauce, as well as a variety of local seafood and homemade pastas.

KILLARNEY AFTER DARK

The **Killarney Manor Banquet,** Loreto Road, Killarney (☎ 064/31-551), is a five-course dinner, served 19th-century style in an 1840 stone-faced mansion on a hillside overlooking the panorama of Killarney, complete with a full program of entertainment.

PUBS Convivial conversation is the attraction at **Buckley's,** 2 College St. (☎ 064/31-037). Live music is performed Apr–Sept, Mon–Tues and Fri at 9:30pm. **Danny Mann,** 97 New St. (☎ 064/31-640), is known for its traditional music, and attracts locals and visitors. The music usually starts at around 9pm. **Molly Darcy's,** Muckross Village, Muckross Road (☎ 064/31-938), across the road from Muckross House, is one of Killarney's best traditional pubs, with a picturesque thatched roof, stone walls, oak-beamed ceiling, and open fireplaces. There's set dancing on Sunday evenings.

THE RING OF KERRY

The Ring of Kerry is Ireland's most popular scenic drive, a 110-mile circle of seacoast, mountain, and lakeland vistas. The drive can take anywhere from 4 or 5 hours to a whole day or several days. The recommendation is that you go at a leisurely pace, stopping frequently to admire the stunning scenery and overnighting in the Waterville area. There are organized tours, but these really don't allow you to do justice to the scenery.

ESSENTIALS

MAKING THE DRIVE By Bus If you must go by bus, **Bus Eireann** (☎ 064/34-777) provides limited daily service from Killarney to Caherciveen, Waterville, Kenmare, and other towns on the Ring of Kerry.

By Car This is by far the best way to get around the Ring. For the most part the route follows N70.

VISITOR INFORMATION For year-round information, stop in at the **Killarney Tourist Office,** Town Hall, Main Street, Killarney (☎ 064/31-633), before you begin your drive. In summer, June–Sept, **The Barracks Tourist Office,** Caherciveen (☎ 066/72-589), is open; and May–Sept, the **Kenmare Tourist Office,** Market Square, Kenmare (☎ 064/41-233), is open. Most telephone numbers on the Ring of Kerry use the 064 or 066 code.

EXPLORING THE RING

The Ring of Kerry can be explored in either direction, but the most popular route is counterclockwise. It's worth noting that the farther you get along the road, the more the signs tend to be in Gaelic only. Since the maps are all in English this can be somewhat confusing. Careful study of the maps is suggested when exploring away from N20. You can purchase from the tourist office an Ordnance Survey map (sheet 83) at a cost of £4.10 ($6.55), which gives names in both English and Gaelic.

Leave Killarney and follow the signs for Killorglin. Be sure to make the detour to visit **Ballymalis Castle.** Probably built by the Ferris family at the end of the 16th century, this ruin is typical of the tower houses built by wealthy landlords to protect their households from unwelcome intruders. Climbing the narrow, winding staircase, you're rewarded with splendid views over mountains, rivers, and fields. Backtrack to the main road and continue.

When you arrive in **Killorglin,** you may wish to stop and walk around this spot, known far and wide for its annual mid-August horse, sheep, and cattle fair. It's official name is Puck Fair—the locals capture a wild goat from the mountains and enthrone it in the center of town as a sign to begin unrestricted merrymaking, though not necessarily for the goat.

Continuing on N70, follow the signs for Glenbeigh, with views of Ireland's tallest Mountain, **Carrantuohill** (3,414 ft.) to your left. Open bogland is a constant companion on this stretch. It provides local residents with fuel—they dig peat, or turf, to burn in their fireplaces. On your right before arrival in Glenbeigh is the **Kerry Bog Village Museum** (☎ **066/69-184**), where a cluster of thatched cottages illustrates Kerry life in the early 1800s. As you explore the blacksmith's forge, the turf cutters' house, and the laborer's cottage, the smell of burning peat hangs heavy in the air. The village is also home to the Kerry Bog pony, a breed that has been saved from extinction and is now unique to this museum.

The next town on the Ring is **Glenbeigh,** a palm tree–lined fishing resort with a lovely duney beach called Rossbeigh Strand. You may wish to stop here, or continue, with the first sightings of the Atlantic appearing away to your right. The views on the next section are breathtaking, although the drive can be a bit hair-raising since the road twists and winds around the cliffs. There's a gorgeous view down over Kells Bay, best viewed from the road, rather than making the drive down to it. The route now moves inland with mountains to your right and a patchwork of fields in many shades of green to your left.

On arrival at **Cahersiveen,** follow the signs right for the two forts, reached along a scenic though narrow road. You need to park a little way past the first fort, **Cahergeal,** and walk back along a rough track. The fort is made from gray stones and boulders piled one on top of the other. Staircases and walkways snake their way up and around ramparts, and the view across the bay is magical. The second fort can be reached along a narrow road to the right a little farther along. This is **Leacanabuaile Fort** and is one of the few stone forts to have been excavated. The objects found suggest that the fort was in use until the 9th or 10th century. The castle that can be seen from both forts is Ballycarbery and isn't really worth a visit, being best viewed from the distance.

Return to Cahersiveen and rejoin N70, then follow the signs right marked VALENTIA VIA FERRY. **Valentia** can also be reached by road, following the signs for Port Magee farther along N70, but the ferry crossing saves a good deal of time and costs just £3 ($4.80) for the car. Valentia Island is 7 miles long, one of the most westerly points in Europe, and has the distinction of being the place from which the first telegraph cable was laid across the Atlantic, in 1866.

Once ashore at Knightstown, follow the signs for **Glanleam Gardens,** Glanleam House (☎ **066/76-176**). Created over 150 years ago by the Knights of Kerry, the gardens are justly famous for a unique collection of southern hemisphere plants. Broad walks weave through junglelike plantings of South American palms, Australian tree ferns, bananas, giant groves of bamboo, and rust-colored myrtles from Chile.

Leaving the gardens, follow the signs for Portmagee, stopping on the outskirts to visit **The Skellig Experience,** Skellig Heritage Centre (☎ **066/76-306**). This attraction blends right in with the terrain, with a stark, stone facade, framed by grassy mounds. The center presents a detailed look at the bird and plant life of the Valentia area. In particular it gives the story of the **Skellig rocks**—Skellig Michael and Little Skellig—two rocky islands sitting off the coast in the Atlantic. In the 6th century Skellig Michael, the larger of the two, became home to a group of monks who founded a monastery that survived for more than 600 years. Today the other Skellig is one of the largest breeding grounds for the gannet in Western Europe.

It's well worth making the 8-mile sea journey to the Skelligs, if only to climb the "stairway to Heaven," leading to the remains of the monastic settlement where you can marvel at the lifestyle of the monks who once lived here. Thanks to the degree to which the place has been preserved, little imagination is needed to picture those early years of Irish Christianity. **Tours** can be arranged by Des Lavelle (☎ 066/76-124) or Michael O'Sullivan (☎ 066/74-233). Admission to the Skellig Experience is £3 ($4.50) for adults, £2.70 ($4.30) for students and seniors, £1.50 ($2.40) for children 11 and under; open May–June and Sept, daily 10am–7pm, and July–Aug, daily 9:30am–7pm.

In the 18th century Valentia harbor was famous as a refuge for smugglers and privateers; tradition has it that John Paul Jones, the Scottish-born American naval officer in the War of Independence, anchored here frequently.

The route now continues into **Portmagee** and on through the **Coomanaspig Pass,** with dramatic views across St. Finan's Bay. This remote Irish-speaking area is an outpost of Gaelic culture and has an Irish college to which children come in the summer months to learn their native language. Continue through the glen, passing miles of golden, sandy beaches, and upon arrival at Ballinskelligs, follow the road around the bay to **Waterville.** An overnight at this idyllic spot is highly recommended. There are many excellent restaurants, and from 9pm on, almost every bar on the seafront comes alive with the singing of traditional Irish songs. Walt Disney holidayed here in the 1940s and in the early 1970s Waterville became a favored holiday retreat of Charlie Chaplin.

Leaving Waterville, continue along N70. If time allows (you'll need a good 50 minutes), take the first left turn, signposted CLUB MED (yes, you'll pass their only branch in Ireland) and enjoy a spectacular drive along the shores of **Lough Currane.** This is a very narrow and little-used road, but the dramatic views are well worth the effort. To your left, the dark waters of the lough and the towering ruggedness of the purple mountains suddenly give way to a patchwork of green fields. Take your time and take it all in. The road ends at a cottage, where you'll need to turn around and backtrack to N70.

Continuing on N70 through the Coomakista Pass, you arrive at another viewpoint at the crest of the road, sited by a statue of the Virgin Mary looking down onto the mouth of the Kenmare River and back along the pass to Waterville.

The next village is Caherdaniel, where a right turn leads to **Derrynane House** (☎ 066/75-113), the home, for most of his life, of Daniel O'Connell, the liberator. The house is now a museum dedicated to his struggle, with documents, maps, and memorabilia. Nature trails twist and turn through the 320-acre grounds and an explanatory booklet is available.

Return to N70 and continue on, arriving at the signs left for the **Staigue Fort,** possibly dating from around 1000 B.C. Forts such as this, with massive stone walls, were built as centers for communal refuge. As it nestles between the hills and mountains, the views down over the tree tops across the bay and estuary are magnificent.

Back on N70, you arrive at the pretty and colorful village of **Sneem,** its houses painted in vibrant shades of blue, pink, yellow, and purple. There's a memorial commemorating General de Gaulle's visit in 1969, and don't miss, to the right of the Catholic church, *The Way the Fairies Went,* a creation by James Scanlon, with four pyramid-shaped natural-stone structures with stained-glass panels.

Once through Sneem, you have a choice. You can continue on the Ring to Kenmare, a route that's pretty but at times tedious and uneventful. Or for a truly awe-inspiring scenic drive, follow the signs left to Killarney, on a route that takes you through the mountains. At every twist and turn of the road, a spectacular new vista opens out before you—a patchwork quilt of fields in 40 shades of green, surrounded on all sides by the moody, purple mountains, and babbling brooks that trickle into dark roadside lakes. Arriving at Molls Gap, turn right for a visit to **Kenmare,** an enchanting place originally called Neidin, meaning "Little Nest." Well laid out and immaculately maintained by its proud residents (population 1,200), Kenmare more than rivals Killarney as a base for County Kerry sightseeing.

However, our last section of the Ring and the grand finale beckons. Backtrack to Molls Gap and then follow the signs for Killarney. Soon you're crossing the boundary of the national park and every viewpoint is well worth the time it takes to stop and gaze across the Lakes of Killarney. Most popular is **Ladies View,** so called because of the pleasure expressed by Queen Victoria's ladies in waiting when they visited this picturesque spot in 1861. Farther on, don't miss the **Torc Waterfall,** signposted from the road and located in a peaceful woodland setting. From here it's a short distance to Muckross House and then back to Killarney.

ACCOMMODATIONS AROUND THE RING

Expensive

✪ **Glanleam House.** Glanleam, Valentia Island, Co. Kerry. ☎ **066/76-176.** Fax 066/76-108. 6 rms. TV TEL. £110 ($176) double. MC, V. Rates include full breakfast. Reduced rates for stays of 2 nights or more.

One of my favorite Ring of Kerry hideaways, Glanleam House dates back to the 1830s and is located amid lush, subtropical gardens that sweep down to the Atlantic. The interior is palatial, with huge chandeliers, an enormous guests' dining table, and numerous antiques. The large en suite bedrooms are luxuriosly furnished, and several of the bathrooms have gold fittings and sunken baths. Guests are made to feel very much at home by the hotel's German-born owner, Mrs. Meta Kreissig.

Parknasilla Hotel. Ring of Kerry Rd. (N70), Parknasilla, Co. Kerry. ☎ **800/44-UTELL** in the U.S., or 064/45-122. Fax 064/45-323. 84 rms. TV TEL. £104–£124 ($166.40–$198.40) double. AE, DC, MC, V. Service charge 12.5%. Closed Jan to mid-Mar.

Facing one of the loveliest seascape settings in Ireland, this château-style hotel is set amid 300 acres of lush, subtropical palm trees and flowering shrubs. George Bernard Shaw stayed here and was inspired to write much of his play *Saint Joan.* The hotel has a private nine-hole golf course, a heated indoor saltwater swimming pool, saunas, and tennis courts, and offers riding, fishing, and boating. The bedrooms are individually furnished, and most look out onto broad vistas of the Kenmare River and the Atlantic.

Moderate

Butler Arms. Waterville, Co. Kerry. ☎ **800/447-7462** in the U.S., or 066/74-144. Fax 066/74-520. 31 rms. TV TEL. £80–£99 ($128–$158.40) double. AE, DC, MC, V. Rates include full breakfast. No service charge. Closed Nov–Mar.

In the early 1970s this grand old inn became a favored retreat of Charlie Chaplin. It's run by the third generation of the Huggard family. The guest rooms are functional and pleasant, and the public rooms, with open turf fireplaces, have an old-world charm. Facilities include a full-service restaurant, sun lounge, tennis court, and free salmon and trout fishing on Lough Currane.

Dromquinna Manor Country House. Blackwater Bridge P.O., off Ring of Kerry Rd., Kenmare, Co. Kerry. ☎ **064/41-657.** Fax 064/41-791. 26 rms, 1 tree house. TV TEL. £55–£100 ($88–$160) double; £100–£150 ($160–$240) tree house. AE, DC, MC, V. Rates include full breakfast. No service charge.

This Victorian-style hotel dates back to 1850 and is situated amid 42 acres of woodland with three-quarters of a mile of sheltered, south-facing sea frontage. It retains an old-world ambience and offers log fires, original oak paneling, and ornate ceilings. Each bedroom has an individual theme, from modern furnishings to Victorian-style four-poster beds. It also has the only tree-house accommodation in the British Isles, with two bedrooms, a bathroom, and a large balcony, securely perched 15 feet up on the top of a tree.

Inexpensive

Derrynane Hotel. Off Ring of Kerry Rd. (N71), Caherdaniel, Co. Kerry. ☎ **800/528-1234** in the U.S., or 066/75-136. Fax 066/75-160. 75 rms. TV TEL. £56–£66 ($89.60–$105.60) double. AE, DC, MC, V. Service charge 10%. Closed Nov–Mar.

This contemporary-style three-story hotel is located between Waterville and Sneem and set amid beautiful beaches, hills, and the nearby Derrynane National Historic Park. The guest rooms are standard, but greatly enhanced by superb views from every window. The public areas include a restaurant and lounge and a heated outdoor swimming pool.

✪ **Lakelands Farm Guesthouse.** Lake Rd., Waterville, Co. Kerry. ☎ **066/74-303.** £25 ($40) per person double. MC, V. Rates include full breakfast.

On the picturesque shores of Lough Currane this dormer-style country house is owned and operated by Ann and Frank Donnelly. It offers attractively furnished en suite bedrooms and breathtaking views of the lake with the rugged, purple mountains towering above. Ann cooks good, wholesome fare, while good angling and shooting is assured by Frank, who has a thorough knowledge of the local waters and countryside.

DINING

The Blue Bull. South Sq., Sneem. ☎ **064/45-382.** Main courses £8.95–£13.95 ($14.30–$22.30). AE, DC, MC, V. Daily 6–10pm. Closed Jan–Feb. SEAFOOD/INTERNATIONAL.

A blue straw bull's head rests over the doorway of this old pub/restaurant. Each of the three small rooms has an open fireplace and walls lined with old prints. The menu offers dishes such as salmon hollandaise, smoked salmon in white-wine sauce, Valencia scallops in brandy, chicken stuffed with prawns, steaks, and Irish stew.

The Huntsman. The Strand, Waterville. ☎ **066/74-124.** Main courses £7.95–£16.95 ($12.70–$27.10); lunch/bar food items £2.50–£10 ($4–$16). AE, DC, MC, V. May–Sept, daily noon–4pm and 6–10pm; Apr and Oct, Wed–Sun noon–4pm and 6–10pm. Closed Nov–Mar. INTERNATIONAL.

It's worth a trip to Waterville just to dine at this contemporary restaurant on the shores of Ballinskelligs Bay. Owner/chef Raymond Hunt takes the time to circulate and chat with diners, offering suggestions as to the extensive menu, which uses only the freshest local catch and produce. Skellig lobster fresh from the tank and Kenmare Bay scampi are among the seafood dishes, while meat dishes include rack of lamb, seasonal pheasant, and rabbit, duck, and Irish stew.

✪ **Lime Tree.** Shelbourne Rd., Kenmare. ☎ **064/42-225.** Reservations recommended. Main courses £8.95–£14.50 ($14.30–$23.20). MC, V. Daily 6:30–10pm. Closed Nov–Mar. IRISH.

Innovative cuisine is the focus at this landmark renovated schoolhouse. The decor includes a skylit gallery and stone walls lined with paintings by local artists. The menu offers such dishes as breast of chicken with apple-rosemary marmalade, charcoal-grilled filet of beef with home-style horseradish mustard, and monkfish tail with warm herb vinaigrette.

Packie's. Henry St., Kenmare. ☎ **064/41-508.** Main courses £7.90–£15.70 ($12.65–$25.10). MC, V. Mon–Sat 5:30–10pm. Closed mid-Nov to Easter. IRISH.

This pretty, informal, bistro-style restaurant has colorful window boxes outside and a slate floor with dark oak furniture inside. Chef/owner Maura Foley uses herbs from her own garden to enhance such dishes as roast rack of lamb, gratin of crab and prawns, pasta breast of chicken, and dover sole.

SHOPPING IN KENMARE

The Green Note, 18 Henry St. (☎ **064/41-212**), is a traditional Irish-music store selling banjos, harps, and tin whistles. You can also purchase a bodhran, the Irish hand drum, at an attractive price. The shop also sells colorful pottery as well as knitwear.

Nostalgia Linen and Lace, 27 Henry St. (☎ **064/41-389**), specializes in Irish linens and sells lace by the meter. **Suede-Knits,** 29 Henry St. (☎ **064/42-068**), has an amazing choice of suede items, hand-knitted Arran sweaters, cottons, and woolens. All garments are their own designs and any size can be made to order.

TRALEE

Tralee, with its population of 22,000, is the County Kerry's chief town and the gateway to the Dingle Peninsula. A busy, bustling, and not particularly attractive place, its greatest claim to fame is that it was the inspiration for the song "The Rose of Tralee," composed by local resident William Mulninock more than 100 years ago. Consequently, Tralee is now the setting for the Rose of Tralee festival, the country's largest annual festival, held in August. It's also the permanent home of the National Folk Theatre of Ireland, Siamsa Tire.

ESSENTIALS

ARRIVING   By Train   The **Tralee Railway Station** is on John Jo Sheehy Road (☎ **066/23-522**).

By Bus   The **Bus Eierann Depot** is on John Jo Sheehy Road, near the train station (☎ **066/23-566**).

VISITOR INFORMATION   The **Tralee Tourist Office,** in Ashe Memorial Hall, Denny Street, Tralee (☎ **066/21-288**), is open all year, Mon–Fri 9am–6pm and Sat 9am–1pm, with extended hours in the summer. The area code for most of the numbers in the area is 066.

WHAT TO SEE & DO

Kerry the Kingdom, in Ashe Memorial Hall, Denny Street (☎ 066/27-777), offers an in-depth look at 7,000 years of life in Kerry. A 10-minute video presents the sea and landscapes, and there's a theme park–style ride through a re-creation of Tralee during the Middle Ages. The Kerry County Museum has exhibits on music, history, legends, and archeology. Admission is £3.90 ($6.25) for adults and £2.20 ($3.50) for children. Open Mar–Oct, daily 10am–6pm; Nov–Dec, daily 2–5pm; closed Jan–Feb.

The restored ✪ **Tralee Steam Railway** (☎ 066/28-888) offers 2-mile narrated scenic trips from Tralee's Ballyard Station to Blennerville. It uses equipment that was once part of the Tralee & Dingle Light Railway, one of the world's most famous narrow-gauge railways. Trains run on the hour from Tralee and on the half hour from Blennerville, and the trip costs £2.50 ($4) for adults and £1.50 ($2.40) for children. It operates Apr–Sept daily; closed on the second Mon each month for maintenance.

ACCOMMODATIONS

Abbey Gate Hotel. Main St., Tralee, Co. Kerry. ☎ **066/29-888.** Fax 066/29-821. 100 rms. TV TEL. £60–£75 ($96–$120) double. AE, DC, MC, V.

At this modern three-story hotel located in the center of Tralee, the bedrooms are spacious and tastefully decorated and the guest areas are modern and functional.

Ballygarry House. Killarney Rd., Leebrook, Tralee, Co. Kerry. ☎ **066/21-233.** Fax 066/27-630. 16 rms. TV TEL. £50–£60 ($80–$96) double. AE, MC, V. Rates include full breakfast. Service charge 10%.

This country inn is on the edge of a residential neighborhood about a mile from the town center. The public areas have a distinctly equestrian feel, with pictures of prize-winning thoroughbreds and horse brasses. The bedrooms vary in size and are individually decorated. Amenities include the Monarchs Restaurant and an old-world–style lounge bar.

Ballyseede Castle Hotel. Killarney Rd., Tralee, Co. Kerry. ☎ **800/223-5695** in the U.S., or 066/35-799. Fax 066/25-287. 12 rms. £55–£113 ($88–$180.80) double. MC, V. Rates include full breakfast. Service charge 12.5%.

This turreted four-story castle was once the chief garrison of the legendary Fitzgeralds, the earls of Desmond. The lobby has Doric columns and a hand-carved oak staircase, decorated with cornices of ornamental plasterwork. The two drawing rooms are warmed by marble fireplaces. Residents can feel like royalty in the elegant bedrooms, a feeling that's reiterated in the Regency restaurant with its huge oil paintings and fabric-lined walls. It goes without saying that the castle is haunted.

DINING

Finnigans Basement Restaurant. 17 Denny St. ☎ **066/27-610.** Reservations suggested. Main courses £7.95–£13.95 ($12.70–$22.30). MC, V. Daily 6–10:30pm. INTERNATIONAL.

This extremely atmospheric basement restaurant is very popular with locals. Stone walls, dark-wood tables, and candlelight combine with a menu that includes monkfish, salmon, steaks, and curries.

The Tilley Lamp. 14 Princes St. ☎ **066/21-300.** Reservations recommended. Main courses £3.25–£5.95 ($5.20–$9.50) at lunch, £8.95–£12.50 ($14.30–$20) at dinner. Daily 12:30–2:30pm and 6:30–10pm. INTERNATIONAL.

This homey basement restaurant is known for its innovative cooking. Specialties include kebab of beef, lamb, and chicken; filet of duck with strawberry and green-pepper sauce; charcoal-grilled filet of lamb; and seafood and vegetarian dishes.

TRALEE AFTER DARK

Tralee pubs can be a little crowded and impersonal. **Paddy Macs,** The Mall (☎ **066/ 21-572**), is an exception. From the delightful flowers in the hanging baskets outside to the dark-wood interior, the pub exudes atmosphere. Conversation is lighthearted and the regulars are extremely friendly.

THE DINGLE PENINSULA

While the Dingle Peninsula is an ideal drive, it also makes a fine bicycling tour. Dingle village is a delightful place to stay (see below) while exploring the peninsula.

The best route to the Dingle Peninsula is to follow the camp road (N86) from Tralee. Three miles to the west you'll pass the **Blennerville Windmill** (☎ **066/ 21-064**). This is the largest working windmill in Ireland and was built in 1850. After years of neglect it was recently restored and now produces 5 tons of whole-meal flour per week. The visitors complex has an emigration exhibition center, craft workshops, and a cafe. Admission is £2.50 ($4) for adults, £2 ($3.20) for seniors and students, £1.50 ($2.40) for children over 5; open Apr–Oct, Mon–Sat 10am–6pm and Sun 11am–6pm.

The route continues with delightful vistas over Tralee Bay, passing through the town of Camp. From here on the road hugs the shore with vistas of **Brandon Mountain,** Ireland's second highest. Follow the signs for the **Connor Pass,** a spectacular drive through the mountains that reaches a height of 1,500 feet. Rising steeply, the often very narrow road passes through a landscape of rocky mountain slopes, dark lakes, and cliffs. On a clear day the views of Tralee and Brandon Bays are superb. Be sure to stop at the viewpoint when you reach the top of the pass. The final descent offers views over Dingle Bay and an enticing glimpse of Dingle itself (see below).

From Dingle, follow the signs for Slea Head Drive, a route that will take you on a spectacular, often rugged trip, returning eventually to Dingle. The **Beehive Huts** that stand to the right of the road past Ventry are worth a stop. These unmortared, prehistoric cells or huts owe their shape to the ancient method of construction known as drystone corbelling, in which the circular walls are constructed of overlapping stones and curve gradually inward until they can be covered with a capstone at the top.

Also worth a visit is the **Dunbeg Fort,** situated on an oceanside site with beautiful sea views. A viewpoint at Slea Head overlooks a mountainous curve at the end of the peninsula; it's been the setting for many a picture postcard and sea-splashed landscape painting. You also have a view of the seven Blasket Islands, sitting out in the Atlantic. Until the 1953 the largest of these, Great Blasket, was still inhabited. Great Blasket was once an outpost of Irish civilization and nurtured a small band of Irish-language writers. The **Blasket Centre,** on the westerly tip of the Dingle Peninsula near Dunquin (☎ **066/56-371**), has a series of displays, exhibits, and a video presentation that celebrate the cultural and literary traditions of the Blaskets. Admission is £2 ($3.20) for adults, £1.50 ($2.40) for seniors, and £1 ($1.60) for children and students; open Easter–Sept, daily 10am–6pm.

The route now continues to Ballyferriter, a largely Gaelic-speaking village. From here you head east and follow the signs to the **Gallarus Oratory,** one of the best-preserved early Christian church buildings in Ireland. Constructed of unmortered stone and shaped like an upturned boat, it's still watertight even after a thousand years.

Continue to follow the signs marked SLEA HEAD DRIVE to arrive at the **Kilmalkedar Church,** dating from the 12th century. Inside the ruined church is an abcedarium stone, with the Latin alphabet crudely carved, a relic of a 7th-century school and probably the oldest-surviving Irish relic of Roman script. Don't miss the 15th-century ruins of **St. Brendan's House,** hidden among the bushes a little way past the church, once a substantial priests' dwelling.

Continue on the road and turn right, following the signs to Brandon Creek. It was from here, in the 6th century, that St. Brendan reputedly set out for the Islands of Paradise in the Western Ocean, a 7-year voyage that led him, it has been claimed, to discover America. The life of the saint and the story of his voyage, *Navigation Sancti Brendai Abbatis,* was written in the 9th century. The Latin narrative was popular reading in medieval Europe and the inspiration for many voyagers and explorers, including Christopher Columbus.

Backtrack to Slea Head Drive and follow it on a picturesque route back to Dingle. From here take R561 eastward along Dingle Bay, through the villages of Lispole and Annascaul to Inch, one of Dingle's most beautiful seascapes, a 4-mile stretch of sandy beach, with distant views of the Ring of Kerry and Killarney. From here you can return to Camp or Tralee or continue to Castlemaine (where the Wild Colonial Boy was born) and onward to Limerick or other parts of Kerry and Cork.

DINGLE TOWN

With a charter dating back many centuries, Dingle was Kerry's principal harbor in medieval times. Even though it's just a small town (pop. 1,500), Dingle has more fine restaurants than many of Ireland's major cities, and is known for the traditional Irish music in its pubs.

WHAT TO SEE & DO

Just west of the Dingle Marina is **Ceardlann Na Coille** (☎ **066/51-797**), a cluster of traditional cottages in a circular craft village. Each craft worker produces and sells his or her own wares, which include knitwear, leather goods, hand-weaving, and wood turning. It's open daily 10am–6pm.

In 1984 Fungie, an adult male bottlenosed dolphin, swam solo into the waters of Dingle harbor. Since then a whole industry has grown up around him. **Fungie the Dolphin Tours** (☎ **066/51-967**) will ferry you out to find him (if there's no sighting, you don't pay). Fungie happily swims alongside the boats, although his enthusiasm has abated slightly in recent years. More adventurous visitors can swim with him on a dolphin encounter, arranged by **Seventh Wave,** Slea Head Road (☎ **066/51-548**). Fares for the 1-hour boat trip are £5 ($8) for adults and £2.50 ($4) for children 11 and under. Dolphin encounters, including wetsuit rental, run £9–£14 ($14.40–$22.40).

Organized Tours

Local experts lead 2- to 3-hour archeological tours, visiting four or five monuments from the Stone Age to medieval times. Contact **Sciuird Tours,** Holy Ground (☎ **066/76-306**).

Guided nature walks over Dingle's less-traveled paths are offered by **Celtic Nature Expeditions,** at the Old Stone House, Claddaun (☎ 066/59-882). **Moran's Slea Head Tours,** Moran's Garage, Mail Road (☎ 066/51-129), offers a narrated 3-hour coach tour covering all the highlights of the peninsula and stopping at some great view points.

Outdoor Activities

BICYCLING   Rentals begin at £5 ($8) per day or £25 ($40) per week. Contact **Foxy John's Hardware Store,** Main Street (☎ 066/51-316). Mountain bikes can be rented at The Mountain Man, Strand Street, Dingle for £6 ($9.60) per day or £30 ($48) per week.

HORSEBACK RIDING   Contact **Milltown House Stables** (☎ 066/52-018) or **Thompson's Horse Riding Centre,** Dunquin (☎ 066/56-144).

SAILING   Sailing in the beautiful waters of Dingle Bay is a great way to enjoy the coastline. Skippered sailing trips are offered by **John Doyle,** 3 John St. (☎ **066/51-174**). The price is £60 ($96) for half a day and £120 ($192) for a full day, for up to four people. Advance booking is required.

WALKING   The Dingle Way begins in Tralee and circles the peninsula, covering 95 miles of gorgeous mountain and coastal landscape. The most rugged section is along Brandon Head, where the trail passes between Mount Brandon and the ocean; the views are tremendous, but the walk is long (about 15 miles/9 hours) and strenuous, and should only be attempted when the sky is clear. The section between Dunquin and Ballyferriter (15 miles) follows an especially lovely stretch of coast. For more information see *The Dingle Way Map Guide*, available in local tourist offices and shops.

ACCOMMODATIONS

Bambury's Guest House. Mail Rd., Dingle, Co. Kerry. ☎ **066/51-244.** Fax 066/51-786. 12 rms. TV TEL. £26–£40 ($41.60–$64) double. MC, V. Rates include full breakfast. No service charge. Closed Jan 1–12.

A lovely two-story pink-toned guesthouse stands out as you enter Dingle from the east. The guest rooms are bright and contemporary, with lovely views of the town and bay.

Doyle's Town House. 5 John St., Dingle, Co. Kerry. ☎ **800/223-6510** in the U.S., or 066/51-174. Fax 066/51-816. 12 rms. TV TEL. £66 ($105.60) double. DC, MC, V. Rates include full breakfast. Service charge 10%. Closed mid-Nov to mid-Mar.

This old-world guesthouse is just a few minutes' walk away from Dingle's main street. It has a lovely Victorian fireplace in the main sitting room area and many of the antique furnishings date back 250 years or more. Period pieces and country pine predominate in the bedrooms, although the fixtures and fittings are modern and include semi-orthopedic beds. Some back rooms face a garden with mountain vistas in the background.

✪ Milltown House. Dingle, Co. Kerry. ☎ **066/51-372.** Fax 066/51-095. 10 rms. TV TEL. £34–£50 ($54.40–$80). MC, V. Rates include full breakfast. Closed Jan–Mar 15.

You couldn't wish for a more picturesque Dingle setting than this bayside haven. A narrow road leads to it and, once inside, you'll see why much of their business is repeat. The guest rooms are tastefully and individually furnished, several offering bay windows that gaze out onto a bay and harbor panorama. The public areas include a peaceful lounge with an open fire and a bright, airy conservatory. The owners, John and Angela Gill, go out of their way to leave you wanting for nothing. A four-course evening meal is offered with a full wine list. There are also on-site stables for riding and trekking.

DINING

✪ Doyle's Seafood Bar. 4 John St. ☎ **066/51-174.** Reservations required. Main courses £10.90–£16 ($17.45–$25.60). DC, MC, V. Mon–Sat 6–10pm. Closed mid-Nov to mid-Mar. SEAFOOD.

Owned by John and Steela Doyle, this excellent restaurant has won international acclaim and is the benchmark of all Dingle's eateries. The atmosphere is homey with stone walls and floors, sugan chairs, and old Dingle sketches. All the ingredients come from the sea, the Doyles' own garden, or nearby farms. Specialties include the Doyles' own smoked salmon, baked filet of lemon sole with prawn sauce, hot poached lobster, and a signature platter of seafood (sole, salmon, lobster, oysters, and crab claws).

Lord Baker. Main St. ☎ **066/51-277.** Reservations recommended. Main courses £10–£20 ($16–$32); bar food £2–£10 ($3.20–$16). AE, MC, V. Daily 11:30am–2:30pm and 6–10pm. Closed Christmas. IRISH/SEAFOOD.

Named after a 19th-century Dingle poet and politician, this restaurant is part of what's reputedly the oldest pub in Dingle. The decor includes a stone fireplace and cozy alcoves. The menu offers bar food such as seafood salads, soups, and sandwiches, while full dinner specialties include sole stuffed with smoked salmon, lobster Thermidor, black sole on the bone, and rack of lamb.

Old Smokehouse. Main St. ☎ **066/51-147.** Reservations not necessary. All items £1.50–£8 ($2.40–$12.80). MC, V. Apr–May, Wed–Mon noon–6pm; June–Oct, daily noon–10pm; Nov–Jan 15, daily noon–6pm. INTERNATIONAL.

Situated in the heart of town beside a flowing stream, this cottage restaurant offers a country-kitchen decor, plus an outdoor patio for alfresco dining when the weather's good. The menu ranges from freshly made salads and seafood sandwiches to hot dishes such as chicken Kiev, beef lasagne, and deep-fried cod.

Whelan's. Main St. ☎ **066/51-622.** Reservations recommended. Main courses £9.75–£13.55 ($15.60–$21.70). Daily 6–9:30pm. IRISH.

This is *the* place for good, old-fashioned Irish stew. The menu also includes flaming Gaelic steak and beef Stroganoff, plus seafood mixed grills and seafood pancakes. It has a cottagelike interior, with stone walls trimmed in dark-wood wainscotting, lanterns, and hand-woven tablecloths.

SHOPPING

Brian De Staic, The Wood (☎ **066/51-298**), is considered by many to be Ireland's leading goldsmith. His workshop is just west of the Dingle Pier. He specializes in unusual Irish jewelry, handcrafted and engraved with the letters of the Ogham alphabet, an ancient Irish form of writing dating back to the 3rd century.

At **Holden Leathergoods / Sparan Sioda (The Silk Purse),** Main Street (☎ **066/51-896**), Jackie and Conor Holden offer beautiful handcrafted leather handbags lined with suede and silk pockets as well as duffle and travel bags and brief cases.

Lispeth Mulcahy / The Weavers Shop, Green Street (☎ **066/51-688**), is one of Ireland's leading weavers. Lispeth creates fabrics and tapestries inspired by seasonal changes in the Irish land- and seascapes. Pure Irish wool, linen/cotton, and alpaca are used in the weaving of wall hangings and tapestries, as well as scarves, shawls, and knee rugs.

DINGLE AFTER DARK

At night virtually every pub in Dingle offers live music from 9pm on.

An Droichead Beag / The Small Bridge. Lower Main St. ☎ **066/51-723.**

One of Dingle's most atmospheric pubs, it has a dark, cavernous interior that's filled with banter and laughter. Traditional Irish music takes place every night at 9pm. But be warned: It's popular, so get there early if you want a seat.

Dick Mack's "Haberdashery." Green St. ☎ **066/51-070.**

Although Richard "Dick" Mack died a few years ago, his family keeps up the traditions of this unique pub where Dick handcrafted leather boots, belts, and other items in between pub chores. Corridors lined with old pictures and mugs lead into tiny snug bars where locals and visitors stand around sipping stout and exchanging jokes and gossip. It's a favorite pub with celebrities such as Robert Mitchum, Timothy Dalton, and Paul Simon, whose names are now commemorated with stars on the sidewalk outside the pub.

Kruger's Guest House and Bar. Ballinaraha, Dunquin. ☎ **066/56-127.**

Deep in the outer reaches of the Dingle Peninsula, this pub is a social center of the Irish-speaking district. This pub is an entertainment hub, with nightly performances of the "sean-nos" Irish singing (an old, unaccompanied style), plus traditional music and step dancing on weekends. The unusual name comes from its former owner, Muiris "Kruger" Kavanagh, a local man who was known as a fighter at school, nicknamed "Kruger" after a famous Boer leader. He emigrated to the United States where he worked at a number of jobs, including being the P.R. man for the Schubert Theaters. After 16 years he returned to Dunquin and opened this pub, to which he then drew his great circle of friends from the entertainment fields.

11 Italy

by Darwin Porter & Danforth Prince

Italy is a feast for the senses and the intellect. Any mention of Italy calls up visions of Pompeii, the Renaissance, and Italy's rich treasury of art and architecture. But some of the country's best experiences can involve the simple act of living in the Italian style, eating the regional cuisines, and enjoying the countryside.

1 Rome

The city of Rome is simultaneously strident, romantic, and sensual. And although the romantic poets would probably be horrified at today's traffic, pollution, overcrowding, crime, political discontent, and the barely controlled chaos of modern Rome, the city endures and thrives in a way that is called "eternal."

Some of the gearing up for the Jubilee Year/Roma 2000 celebration may affect your visit to Rome—especially when you find more pedestrian zones created (making traffic problems even more unbearable than usual) or you wonder why the Spanish Steps are torn up or why you can't go into the Colosseum. Bear in mind that other special restrictions and more monument restoration may interfere with your sightseeing agenda. But it's all for the jubilee, known as "the big event."

ONLY IN ROME

Walking Through Ancient Rome   There exists a vast, almost unified archeological park cut through the center of Rome—all the way from the Rome of the Caesars to Via Appia Antica. You can wander at will through the very streets where Julius Caesar's carriage once rolled or (much later) that of Lucrezia Borgia. A slice of history unfolds at every turn—an ancient fountain, a long-forgotten statue, the ruins of a temple dedicated to some long-faded cult. The Roman Forum and the Palatine Hill are the most rewarding targets for your archeological probe, but the glory of Rome is hardly confined to these dusty fields.

Strolling at Sunset in the Pincio Gardens   Above the landmark Piazza del Popolo, this terraced and lushly planted hillside is the most romantic place for a twilight walk. A dusty orange-rose glow often colors the sky, giving an aura to the park's umbrella pines and broad avenues. The ancient Romans turned this hill into gardens, but today's look came from the design of Giuseppe Valadier in the 1800s. The main square, Piazzale Napoleone I, proffers a spectacular city view that stretches from the Janiculum to Monte Mario. The Egyptian-style obelisk you see was erected by Hadrian on the tomb of his great love, Antinous, a beautiful male slave who died prematurely.

Hanging Out at the Pantheon   The world's best-preserved ancient monument at Piazza della Rotunda is now a hot spot—especially at night. Find a cafe table on the square and observe what a young Fellini should be recording on film. First a Roman temple to "all the gods," then a church since the Middle Ages, this behemoth, built on the foundations of Agrippa's temple, has become a symbol of Rome itself.

Wandering Through Campo de' Fiori at Mid-morning   In an incomparable setting of medieval houses, this is the liveliest fruit and vegetable market in Rome. It's best viewed after 9am Monday to Saturday—by 1pm the stalls are closing down. We come here every day we're in Rome for a lively view of local life that no other place seems to match. Often you'll spot your favorite trattoria chef bargaining for the best and freshest produce—from fresh cherries to the perfect vine-ripened tomato. Once a meadow, this "field of flora" sprawls across a site fronting the Pompey Theater.

Touring the Janiculum   On the Trastevere side of the river, where in 1849 Garibaldi held off the attacking French troops, the Janiculum Hill was always strategic in Rome's defense. Today a walk in this park at the top of the hill is a much-needed retreat from the traffic-filled and often hot streets of Trastevere. Filled with monuments to Garibaldi and his brave men, the hill is no longer peppered with monasteries as it was in the Middle Ages. The best view is from the Villa Lante, a Renaissance summer residence.

Spending a Day on the Appian Way   Dating from 312 B.C., the Appian Way once traversed the whole peninsula of Italy, the road on which Roman legions marched to Brindisi and their conquests in the East. One of its darkest moments was the crucifixion of the rebellious slave army of Spartacus in 71 B.C., when bodies lined the road from Rome to Capua. Fashionable Romans were buried here, and early Christians dug catacombs to flee their persecutors. Begin at the Tomb of Cecilia Metella and proceed up Via Appia Antica past a series of tombs and monuments, including the Tomb of Marcus Servilius. You can go all the way to the Church of Domine Quo Vadis.

Listening to Music in the Churches   Concerts in the churches are advertised all over Rome. The top professionals such as Plácido Domingo and Luciano Pavarotti play at the "big name" churches, but don't overlook those smaller, hard-to-find ones—some of the best music we've ever heard has been by up-and-coming musicians getting their start in little-known churches. By decree of Pope John Paul II music in the churches must be sacred, no pop music allowed.

Visiting the Campidoglio at Night   There is no more splendid place to be at night than Piazza del Campidoglio, where Michelangelo designed both the geometric paving and the building facades. A broad flight of steps, the Cordonata, takes you up to this panoramic site, citadel of ancient Rome from which traitors to the empire were once tossed to their deaths. Home during the day to the Capitoline museums, it feels different at night when it's dramatically lit, the measured Renaissance facades glowing like jewel boxes. The views of the brilliantly lit Forum and Palatine Hill at night are worth the long trek up those stairs.

ORIENTATION

ARRIVING   By Plane   Chances are that you'll arrive in Italy at Rome's **Leonardo da Vinci International Airport** (☎ **06/65951** or 06/65953640 for information), popularly known as Fiumicino, 18¹/₂ miles from the city center. Domestic flights arrive at one terminal, international ones at the other. (If you're flying by charter, you might arrive at Ciampino Airport.)

To get into the city, there's a shuttle service directly from Fiumicino to the main train station, Stazione Termini. Upon leaving Customs, follow the signs marked TRENI. Trains go back and forth between the airport and the rail station daily 7am–10pm. A one-way ticket costs 13,000L ($8.30). Trains arrive at Track 22 at Stazione Termini. A local train, costing 7,000L ($4.50), also runs between the airport and Tiburtina Station, from which you can go the rest of the way to Rome's Termini by subway line B (go down the stairs at the back of the train), costing another 1,000L (65¢), but this is an inconvenient connection.

Taxis from Fiumicino are expensive—70,000L ($44.80) and up.

Should you arrive on a charter flight at **Ciampino airport** (☎ **06/794961**), take a COTRAL bus, departing every 30 minutes or so, which will deliver you to the Anagnina stop of Metropolitana Line A. At Anagnina you can take Linea A to the Stazione Termini, the rail station in the heart of Rome, where your final connections can be made. The trip takes about 45 minutes, and costs 2,000L ($1.30).

By Train   Trains arrive in the center of old Rome at the **Stazione Termini,** Piazza dei Cinquecento (☎ **06/4775**), the train and subway transportation hub for the city. Many hotels lie near the station, and you can walk to your hotel if you don't have too much luggage. Otherwise, an array of taxi, bus, and subway lines awaits you.

If you're taking the Metropolitana (Rome's subway network), follow the illuminated M sign in red that points the way. To catch a bus, go straight through the outer hall of the Termini and enter the sprawling bus lot of Piazza dei Cinquecento. Taxis are also found here.

By Bus   Arrivals are at the **Stazione Termini** (see "By Train," above). Information on buses is dispensed at a booth operated by ATAC, the city bus company, at Piazza dei Cinquecento (☎ **06/46951** or 06/4695444 for bus information), open daily 7:30am–7:30pm.

By Car   From the north the main access route is **A1 (Autostrada del Sole),** cutting through Milan and Florence, or you can take the coastal route, SSI Aurelia, from Genoa. If you're driving north from Naples, you take the southern lap of the **Autostrada del Sole (A2).** All these autostrade join with the **Grande Raccordo Anulare,** a ring road that encircles Rome, channeling traffic into the congested city.

VISITOR INFORMATION   Tourist information is available at the **Ente Provinciale per il Turismo,** Via Parigi 5, 00185 Roma (☎ **06/48899200**), open Mon–Sat 8:15am–7pm, but the information dispensed here is meager. There's another information bureau at the Stazione Termini (☎ **06/4871270**), open daily 8:15am–7:15pm.

CITY LAYOUT   The drive into the city from the airport is rather uneventful until you pass through the city wall, the still remarkably intact **Great Aurelian Wall,** started in A.D. 271 to calm Rome's barbarian jitters. Suddenly, ruins of imperial baths loom on one side and great monuments can be seen in the middle of blocks.

The Stazione Termini, the modern railroad station, faces a huge piazza, **Piazza dei Cinquecento,** named after 500 Italians who died heroically in a 19th-century battle in Africa.

Most of the old city and its monuments lie on the east side of the **Fiume Tevere (Tiber River),** which meanders between 19th-century stone embankments. However, several important monuments are on the other side: **St. Peter's Basilica** and the **Vatican,** the **Castel Sant' Angelo** (formerly the tomb of the emperor Hadrian), and the colorful section of town known as **Trastevere.** The bulk of ancient, Renaissance, and baroque Rome lies across the Tiber from St. Peter's on the same side as the Stazione Termini. The city's various quarters are linked by large boulevards (large at least in some places) that have mostly been laid out since the late 19th century.

Starting from the **Victor Emmanuel monument,** a highly controversial pile of snow-white Brescian marble, there's a street running practically due north to **Piazza del Popolo** and the city wall. This is **Via del Corso,** one of Rome's main streets—noisy, congested, always crowded with buses and shoppers, called simply "the Corso." Again from the Victor Emmanuel monument, the major artery going west (and ultimately across the Tiber to St. Peter's) is **Corso Vittorio Emanuele.** To go in the other direction, toward the Colosseum, you take **Via dei Fori Imperiali,** named for the excavated ruins of the imperial forums that flank this avenue. Yet another central conduit is **Via Nazionale,** running from **Piazza della Repubblica (also called Piazza Esedra)** and ending near the Victor Emmanuel monument at **Piazza Venezia,** which lies in front of it. The final lap of Via Nazionale is called **Via Quattro Novembre.**

GETTING AROUND

Much of the inner core of Rome is traffic-free—so you'll need to walk whether you like it or not. However, walking in many parts of the city is hazardous and uncomfortable, because of overcrowded streets, heavy traffic, and very narrow sidewalks.

BY SUBWAY The **Metropolitana,** or **Metro** for short, is the fastest means of transportation in Rome. It has two underground lines: Line A goes from Via Ottaviano, near St. Peter's, to Anagnina, stopping at Piazzale Flaminio (near Piazza del Popolo), Piazza Vittorio Emanuele, and Piazza San Giovanni in Laterano. Line B connects the Rebibbia district with Via Laurentina, stopping at Via Cavour, Piazza Bologna, Stazione Termini, the Colosseum, Circus Maximus, the Pyramid of C. Cestius, St. Paul's Outside the Walls, the Magliana, and the E.U.R. A big red letter M indicates the subway entrance. The fare is 1,500L (95¢).

Tickets are available from vending machines at all stations. These machines accept 50L, 100L, and 200L coins. Ticket booklets are available at *tabacchi* (tobacco) shops and in some terminals. Some machines change 1,000L (65¢) notes into coins.

BY BUS/TRAM Roman buses are operated by **ATAC (Azienda Tramvie e Autobus del Commune di Roma),** Via Volturno 65 (☎ 06/46954444 for information). For only 1,500L (95¢) you can ride to most parts of Rome on quite good bus service. The ticket is valid for 1¼ hours, and you can get on many buses during that time period, using the same ticket. At the Stazione Termini, you can purchase a special tourist bus pass, which costs 6,000L ($3.85) for 1 day or 24,000L ($15.35) for a week. The tourist pass is also valid on the subway—but never ride the trains when the Romans are going to or from work or you'll be mashed flatter than fettuccine.

BY TAXI Don't count on hailing a taxi on the street or even getting one at a stand. If you're going out, have your hotel call one. At a restaurant, ask the waiter or cashier to dial for you. If you want to call yourself, try one of these numbers: 6645, 3570, or 4994. The meter begins at 6,400L ($4.10) for the first 3 kilometers, then 300L (20¢) per kilometer. On Sunday a 5,000L ($3.20) supplement is assessed, plus

Rome Metro

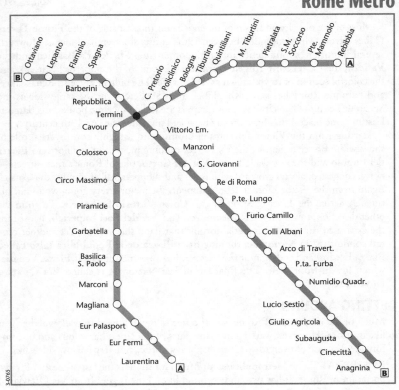

another 2,000L ($1.30) supplement from 10pm to 7am. There's yet another 500L (30¢) supplement for every suitcase. The driver will expect a 10% tip.

BY CAR   You can rent a car from **Hertz,** near the parking lot of the Villa Borghese, Via Vittorio Veneto 156 (☎ 06/3216831); **Budget,** Via Ludovisi 60 (☎ 06/4820966); or the local Italian company **Maggiore,** Via di Tor Cervara 225 (☎ 06/229351).

BY BICYCLE, MOTORSCOOTER & MOTORCYCLE   You can rent mopeds at **St. Peter Moto Renting & Selling,** Via di Porto Castello 43 (☎ **06/68804608**), open Mon–Sat 9am–7pm. Rates range upward from 40,000L ($25.60) per day. Take the Metro to Ottaviano. You can also rent mopeds from **Happy Rent,** conveniently located at Piazza Esquilino 8H (☎ **06/4818185**), 300 yards from the Termini station. Most mopeds cost 40,000L ($25.60) per hour or 60,000L ($38.40) for the day.

You can also rent bicycles at many places throughout Rome. Ask at your hotel for the nearest rental location, or else go to **I Bike Rome,** Via Vittorio Veneto 156 (☎ **06/3225240**), which rents bicycles from the underground parking garage at the Villa Borghese. Most bikes cost 5,000L ($3.20) per hour or 13,000L ($8.30) per day.

FAST FACTS: Rome

American Express   The offices are at Piazza di Spagna 38 (☎ 06/67641). The travel service and tour desk are open Mon–Fri 9am–5:30pm and Sat 9am–12:30pm

(May–Oct, the travel desk is also open Sat 2–2:30pm), and the financial and mail services are open Mon–Fri 9am–5pm and Sat 9am–noon.

Baby-sitters   Most hotel desks in Rome will help you secure a baby-sitter. Or you can call Agenzia Intermediati, Via Bramante 13 (☎ 06/5747444), or ARCI, Via dei Mille 23 (☎ 06/4958877).

Business Hours   In general, banks are open Mon–Fri 8:30am–1:30pm and 3–4pm. Most stores are open year-round Mon–Sat 9am–1pm and 3:30 or 4pm–7:30 or 8pm.

Currency   The Italian unit of currency is the lira, almost always used in the plural form, **lire** (abbreviated as "L" in this guide). The lowest unit of currency these days is the silver 50-lira coin. There is also a silver 100-lira piece, a gold 200-lira coin, and a combination of silver-and-gold 500-lira coin. Notes come in 1,000, 2,000, 5,000, 10,000, 50,000, 100,000, and 200,000 lire. The rate of exchange used in this chapter was $1 = 1,563L, or 1L = .00064¢

Dentist   For an English-speaking dentist, call the U.S. Embassy in Rome, Via Vittorio Veneto (☎ 06/46741). There's also the 24-hour G. Eastman Dental Hospital, Viale Regina Elena 287 (☎ 06/4453228).

Doctor   Call the U.S. Embassy (see "Dentist," above), which will provide a list of English-speaking doctors. All big hospitals in Rome have a 24-hour first-aid service (go to the emergency room). You'll find English-speaking doctors at the Rome American Hospital, Via Emilio Longoni 69 (☎ 06/22551).

Drugstores   A reliable pharmacy is Farmacia Internazionale, Piazza Barberini 49 (☎ 06/6794680), open day and night. Most pharmacies are open 8:30am–1pm and 4–7:30pm. In general, pharmacies follow a rotation system so that several are always open on Sunday.

Embassies/Consulates   The Embassy of the **United States,** Via Vittorio Veneto 121 (☎ 06/46741), is open Mon–Fri 8:30am–noon and 2–4pm. Consular and passport services for **Canada,** Via Zara 30 (☎ 06/445981), are open Mon–Fri 10am–12:30pm. The office of the **United Kingdom,** Via XX Settembre 80A (☎ 06/4825441), is open Mon–Fri 9:15am–1:30pm. The Embassy of **Australia,** Via Alessandria 215 (☎ 06/852721), is open Mon–Thurs 8:30am–12:30pm and 1:30–5:30pm and Fri 8:30am–1:15pm. The **New Zealand** office, Via Zara 28 (☎ 06/4402928), is open Mon–Fri 8:30am–12:45pm and 1:45–5pm. In case of emergency, embassies have a 24-hour referral service.

Emergencies   The police "hotline" number is **212121**. Usually, however, dial **112** for the police, to report a fire, or summon an ambulance.

Eyeglasses   Try Vasari, Piazza della Repubblica 61 (☎ 06/4882240), which lies adjacent to the Grand Hotel.

Lost Property   You might check at Ogetti Rinvenuti, Via Nicolò Bettoni 1 (☎ 06/5816040), open Mon–Fri 8:30am–4pm and Sat 8:30–11:30am. A branch at the Stazione Termini off Track 1 (☎ 06/47301) is open daily 8am–noon and 2–8pm.

Post Office   The central post office, on Piazza San Silvestro, behind the Rinascente department store on Piazza Colonna (☎ 06/6771), is open Mon–Fri 8:30am–7:50pm for mail service, to 1:50pm for money service. Both are open Sun 8:30am–noon.

Safety   Purse snatching is commonplace in Rome. Young men on Vespas or whatever ride through the city looking for victims. To avoid trouble, stay away from the curb and hold on tightly to your purse. Don't lay anything valuable on tables or chairs where it can be grabbed up easily. Gypsy children are a particular menace. You'll often virtually have to fight them off, if they completely surround you. They'll often approach you with pieces of cardboard hiding their stealing hands.

Taxes A value-added tax (called IVA in Italy) is added to all consumer products and most services, including restaurants and hotels.

ACCOMMODATIONS
NEAR STAZIONE TERMINI
Very Expensive

✪ **Le Grand Hotel.** Via Vittorio Emanuele Orlando 3, 00185 Roma. ☎ **800/221-2340** in the U.S., 800/955-2442 in Canada, or 06/4709. Fax 06/4747307. 134 rms, 36 suites. A/C MINIBAR TV TEL. 530,000–580,000L ($339.20–$371.20) double; from 900,000L ($576) suite. AE, DC, MC, V. Parking 35,000–40,000L ($22.40–$25.60). Metro: Piazza della Repubblica.

When inaugurated in 1894, Le Grand struck a note of grandeur it has tried to maintain ever since. Today its location near the railway station—once highly desirable—no longer is. Only a few minutes from Via Vittorio Veneto, the Grand looks like a large late Renaissance palace, its five-floor facade covered with carved loggias, lintels, quoins, and cornices. Inside, the floors are covered with marble and oriental rugs. The spacious bedrooms are conservatively decorated with matching curtains and carpets, and equipped with dressing room and fully tiled bath. Every room is different, although some are less grand than you might expect from entering the impressive lobby. Le Restaurant is the hotel's more formal dining room, where you can arrange for dietetic or kosher meals with advance notice.

Moderate

Medici. Via Flavia 96, 00187 Roma. ☎ **06/4827319.** Fax 06/4740767. 68 rms. MINIBAR TV TEL. 200,000L ($128) double. Rates include breakfast. AE, DC, MC, V. Air-conditioning 20,000L ($12.80) extra. Parking 28,000–35,000L ($17.90–$22.40). Metro: Piazza della Repubblica.

Quite a comedown from the Grand, the Medici, built in 1906, is still a substantial hotel that has easy access to the railway terminal and the shops along Via XX Settembre. Many of its better rooms overlook an inner patio garden, with Roman columns and benches. The traditional furnishings include lots of antiques, and the bedrooms are a generous size.

Inexpensive

Aberdeen Hotel. Via Firenze 48, 00184 Roma. ☎ **06/4823920.** Fax 06/4821092. 26 rms. A/C MINIBAR TV TEL. 230,000L ($147.20) double. Rates include breakfast. AE, DC, MC, V. Metro: Stazione Termini.

This completely renovated 26-room hotel near the Rome Opera House is centrally located for most landmarks and for rail and bus connections at the main station. It's located in front of the Ministry of Defense, a rather quiet and fairly safe area of Rome. The rooms, furnished with an uninspired modern styling, have amenities such as hair dryer and radio. Only a breakfast buffet is served.

Hotel Pavia. Via Gaeta 83, 00185 Roma. ☎ **06/483801.** Fax 06/4819090. 50 rms. A/C MINIBAR TV TEL. 130,000–190,000L ($83.20–$121.60) double. Rates include breakfast. AE, DC, MC, V. Parking 12,000–20,000L ($7.70–$12.80). Metro: Stazione Termini.

The Hotel Pavia is a popular choice on this quiet street near the gardens of the Baths of Diocletian and the railway station. Established in the 1980s, it occupies a much-renovated century-old building. The front rooms tend to be noisy, but that's the curse of all Termini hotels. Nevertheless, the rooms are comfortable and fairly attractive.

⑤ Hotel Venezia. Via Varese 18, 00185 Roma. ☎ **06/4457101.** Fax 06/4957687. 61 rms. A/C MINIBAR TV TEL. 235,000L ($150.40) double; 320,000L ($204.80) triple. AE, DC, MC, V. Rates include breakfast. Parking 30,000L ($19.20). Metro: Stazione Termini.

The location is good—3 blocks from the railroad station, in a part-business, part-residential area dotted with a few old villas and palm trees. The Venezia was totally renovated in 1991, which transformed it into a good-looking and cheerful hostelry, with a charming collection of public rooms. Some bedrooms are furnished with furniture in the 17th-century style, although some are beginning to look shop-worn, while other pieces are contemporary. All units have Murano chandeliers, and all are air-conditioned, but only from July to September.

NEAR VIA VENETO & PIAZZA BARBERINI
Very Expensive
✪ Hotel Eden. Via Ludovisi 49, 00187 Roma. ☎ **800/225-5843** in the U.S., or 06/478121. Fax 06/4821584. 101 rms, 11 suites. A/C MINIBAR TV TEL. 600,000–700,000L ($384–$448) double; from 1,300,000L ($832) suite. AE, DC, MC, V. Parking 40,000L ($25.60).

During the heyday of this ornate five-story hotel, Hemingway, Maria Callas, Ingrid Bergman, Fellini—all the big names—checked in here. In 1994 it reopened after a 2-year (and $20 million) radical renovation that enhanced its original fin de siècle grandeur and added the modern amenities to justify its five-star status. Its hilltop position guarantees a panoramic city view from most bedrooms that guests consider worth the rather high expense. These contain marble-sheethed bathrooms, and a plushly configured allegiance to the decor of the late 19th century. Understated elegance is the rule. On the premises are a gym and health club, a piano bar, and a glamorous restaurant, La Terrazza.

Expensive
Victoria Roma. Via Campania 41, 00187 Roma. ☎ **06/473931.** Fax 06/4871890. 108 rms. A/C MINIBAR TV TEL. 350,000L ($224) double. Rates include breakfast. AE, DC, MC, V. Parking 30,000–40,000L ($19.20–$25.60). Metro: Piazza Barberini. Bus: 52, 53, 490, 495, or 910.

Its chic *la dolce vita* glory days have passed by, but this hotel still keeps abreast of changing times and is frequently renewed. Its location right off Via Veneto remains one of its most desirable assets. The lounges and living rooms retain a country-house decor, and the recently refurbished bedrooms are well furnished and maintained. Meals can be taken à la carte in the elegant grill room, which serves the best of Italian and French cuisine. There's also a roof garden.

Moderate
Alexandra. Via Vittorio Veneto 18, 00187 Roma. ☎ **06/4881943.** Fax 06/4871804. 39 rms, 6 suites. A/C MINIBAR TV TEL. 260,000L ($166.40) double; 360,000L ($230.40) suite. Rates include breakfast. AE, DC, MC, V. Parking 35,000L ($22.40). Metro: Piazza Barberini. Bus: 52, 53, 56, 58, 95, or 586.

Here's where you can stay on Via Veneto without going broke. Set behind the dignified stone facade of what was originally a 19th-century private mansion, this hotel offers clean, comfortable accommodations filled with antique furniture and modern conveniences. The rooms facing the front are exposed to the roaring traffic and animated street life of Via Veneto; those in back are quieter but with less of a view. Breakfast is the only meal served. The breakfast room is especially appealing: Inspired by an Italian garden, it was designed by the noted architect Paolo Portoghesi.

Rome Accommodations

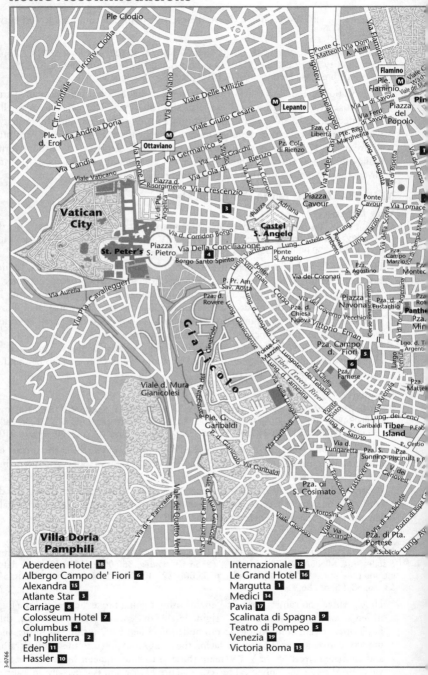

Aberdeen Hotel **18**
Albergo Campo de' Fiori **6**
Alexandra **15**
Atlante Star **3**
Carriage **8**
Colosseum Hotel **7**
Columbus **4**
d' Inghliterra **2**
Eden **11**
Hassler **10**

Internazionale **12**
Le Grand Hotel **16**
Margutta **1**
Medici **14**
Pavia **17**
Scalinata di Spagna **9**
Teatro di Pompeo **5**
Venezia **19**
Victoria Roma **13**

3-0766

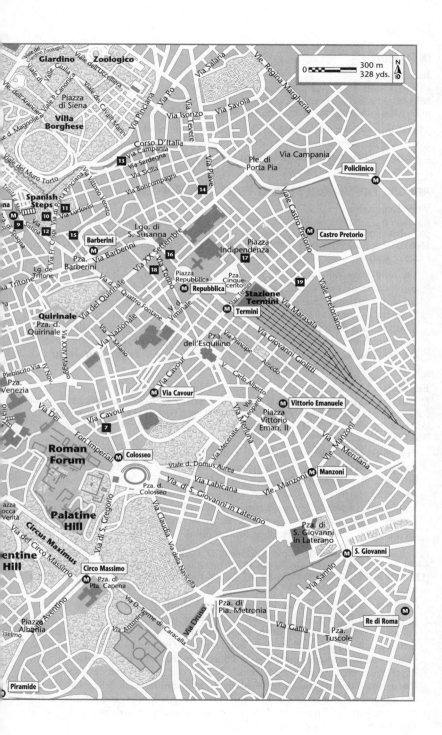

IN PARIOLI

Inexpensive

⑤ Hotel delle Muse. Via Tommaso Salvini 18, 00197 Roma. ☎ **06/8088333.** Fax 06/8085749. 61 rms. TV TEL. 160,000–180,000L ($102.40–$115.20) double; 220,000L ($140.80) triple. Rates include buffet breakfast. AE, DC, MC, V. Bus: 4. Tram: 19.

This three-star establishment, which is a half mile north of the Villa Borghese, is a winning but unheralded choice. Most rooms have been renovated but remain rather spartan and minimalist. In the summer the hotel operates a restaurant in the garden. A bar is open 24 hours a day.

AROUND THE SPANISH STEPS & PIAZZA DEL POPOLO

Very Expensive

Hassler. Piazza Trinità dei Monti 6, 00187 Roma. ☎ **800/223-6800** in the U.S., or 06/699340. Fax 06/6789991. 85 rms, 15 suites. A/C MINIBAR TV TEL. 650,000–950,000L ($416–$608) double; from 1,550,000L ($992) suite. AE, DC, MC, V. Parking 40,000L ($25.60). Metro: Piazza di Spagna.

The only deluxe hotel in this old part of Rome, it uses the Spanish Steps as its grand entrance. The crown worn by the Hassler is a bit tarnished these days; the hostelry has such a mystique that it prospers and endures in spite of overpriced rooms. The bedrooms, some of which are small, have a personalized look—oriental rugs, tasteful draperies at the French windows, brocade furnishings, comfortable beds, and (the nicest touch of all) bowls of fresh flowers. Some rooms have balconies with views of the city. The Hassler Roof Restaurant, on the top floor, is a favorite with visitors and Romans alike for its fine cuisine and view.

Expensive

✪ Hotel d'Inghilterra. Via Bocca di Leone 14, 00187 Roma. ☎ **06/69981.** Fax 06/69922243. 102 rms, 12 suites. A/C MINIBAR TV TEL. 496,000L ($317.45) double; 599,000L ($383.35) triple; 840,000L ($537.60) suite. Rates include breakfast. AE, DC, MC, V. Metro: Piazza di Spagna.

The Hotel d'Inghilterra nostalgically holds onto its traditions and heritage, even though it has been completely renovated. Rome's most fashionable small hotel, the bedrooms have mostly old pieces—gilt and much marble, along with mahogany chests and glittery mirrors, as well as modern conveniences. The preferred bedrooms are higher up, opening onto a tile terrace, with a balustrade and a railing covered with flowering vines and plants. Some, however, are just too small. The hotel's restaurant, the Roman Garden, serves excellent Roman dishes.

✪ Scalinata di Spagna. Piazza Trinità dei Monti 17, 00187 Roma. ☎ **06/6793006.** Fax 06/69940598. 15 rms, 1 suite. A/C MINIBAR TV TEL. 380,000L ($243.20) double; 480,000L ($307.20) triple; 650,000L ($416) suite. AE, MC, V. Parking 35,000L ($22.40). Metro: Piazza di Spagna.

This hotel near the Spanish Steps seems to be climbing up and up the ladder—possibly it will reach four-star status and increase its prices in the lifetime of this edition. It's right at the top of the steps, directly across the small piazza from the deluxe Hassler. This delightful little building—only two floors are visible from the outside—is painted mustard-yellow and burgundy-red and is nestled between much larger structures. The decor varies radically from one room to the next; some have low, beamed ceilings and ancient-looking wood furniture, while others have loftier ceilings and more average appointments. Everything is spotless and pleasing to the eye. In season, breakfast is served on the roof-garden terrace with its sweeping view of the dome of St. Peter's across the Tiber.

Moderate

Carriage. Via della Carrozze 36, 00187 Roma. ☎ **06/6990124.** Fax 06/6788279. 24 rms, 2 suites. A/C MINIBAR TV TEL. 295,000L ($188.80) double; 380,000L ($243.20) triple; from 380,000L ($243.20) suite. Rates include breakfast. AE, DC, MC, V. Metro: Piazza di Spagna.

The 18th-century facade of this hotel covers some charming, although small, accommodations (if you reserve, ask for one of the two rooftop bedrooms). Antiques have been used tastefully, even in the bedrooms with their matching bedcovers and draperies. Each bedroom has a radio and other amenities. Head for the Renaissance-style salon that's called an American bar or the roof garden.

Hotel Internazionale. Via Sistina 79, 00187 Roma. ☎ **06/69941823.** Fax 06/6784764. 42 rms, 2 suites. A/C MINIBAR TV TEL. 295,000L ($188.80) double; 600,000L ($384) suite. Rates include breakfast. AE, MC, V. Parking 35,000L ($22.40). Bus: 60, 61, 62, or 492 from Stazione Termini.

Half a block from the top of the Spanish Steps on Via Sistina, this albergo has operated since 1870. It's a combination of the antique and the modern—wingback chairs and coffered ceilings charm the bedrooms, contrasting with contemporary built-in pieces. Accommodations facing the narrow Via Sistina have double windows to cut down the noise.

Inexpensive

Hotel Margutta. Via Laurina 34, 00187 Roma. ☎ **06/3223674.** Fax 06/3200395. 21 rms. 147,000L ($94.10) double; 190,000L ($121.60) triple. Rates include breakfast. AE, DC, MC, V. Metro: Flaminio. Bus: 95, 119, 490, or 495.

The Hotel Margutta, on a cobblestone street near Piazza del Popolo, offers attractively decorated rooms and a helpful staff. The hotel is housed in a two-centuries-old building. Off the paneled, black stone-floored lobby is a simple breakfast room with framed lithographs. The best rooms are on the top floor. Two of these share a terrace, and another larger bedroom has a private terrace. Management always reserves the right to charge a 20% to 35% supplement for these accommodations. The hotel is not air-conditioned, nor does it have room phones or TVs.

NEAR CAMPO DE' FIORI

Moderate

Ⓢ **Teatro di Pompeo.** Largo del Pallaro 8, 00186 Roma. ☎ **06/68300170.** Fax 06/68805531. 12 rms. A/C TV TEL. 250,000L ($160) double. Rates include breakfast. AE, DC, MC, V. Bus: 46, 62, or 64.

Built on the top of the ruins of the Theater of Pompey, which dates from about 55 B.C., this small charmer lies near the spot where Julius Caesar met his final fate. Intimate and refined, it's on a quiet piazzetta near the Palazzo Farnese and Campo de' Fiori. The bedrooms, all doubles, are decorated in an old-fashioned Italian style with hand-painted tiles. The beamed ceilings date from the days of Michelangelo. There's no restaurant, but breakfast is served. English is spoken.

Inexpensive

Ⓢ **Albergo Campo de' Fiori.** Via del Biscione 6, 00186 Roma. ☎ **06/68806865.** Fax 06/6876003. 27 rms, 9 with shower and toilet, 4 with shower only; 1 honeymoon suite. 130,000L ($83.20) double without bath, 160,000L ($102.40) double with shower only, 190,000L ($121.60) double with bath, honeymoon suite; 160,000L ($105.60) triple without bath, 190,000L ($121.60) triple with shower only, 240,000L ($153.60) triple with bath. Rates include breakfast. MC, V. Bus: 64 from Stazione Termini to Museo di Roma; then arm yourself with a good map for the walk to this place.

This seems to be everybody's favorite budget hideaway. Lying in the historic center of Rome in a market area, this cozy, narrow six-story hotel offers rustic rooms, many quite tiny and sparsely adorned, others with a lot of character. The best of them have been restored and are on the first floor. Yours might have a ceiling of clouds and blue skies along with mirrored walls. The best accommodation is the honeymoon retreat on the sixth floor, with a canopied king-size bed. But honeymooners beware: There's no elevator.

NEAR VATICAN CITY
Expensive
✪ **Hotel Atlante Star.** Via Vitelleschi 34, 00193 Roma. ☎ **06/6873233.** Fax 06/6872300. 80 rms, 10 suites. A/C MINIBAR TV TEL. 490,000L ($313.60) double; 580,000L ($371.20) suite. Rates include breakfast. AE, DC, MC, V. Parking 40,000L ($25.60). Metro: Ottaviano. Bus: 23, 64, 81, or 492. Tram: 19 or 30.

The Atlante Star is a first-class hotel a short distance from St. Peter's Basilica and the Vatican. The tastefully renovated lobby is covered with dark marble, chrome trim, and lots of exposed wood, while the upper floors give the impression of being inside a luxuriously appointed ocean liner. Even the door handles are art deco inspired. These doors open into small but posh accommodations outfitted with all the modern comforts. A royal suite features a Jacuzzi. The hotel has the most striking views of St. Peter's of any hotel in Rome. The restaurant, Les Etoiles, is an elegant roof-garden choice at night, offering a 360° panoramic view of Rome, with an illuminated St. Peter's in the background.

Hotel Columbus. Via della Conciliazione 33, 00193 Roma. ☎ **06/6865435.** Fax 06/6865435. 105 rms, 4 suites. A/C MINIBAR TV TEL. 270,000L ($172.80) double; 380,000L ($243.20) suite. Rates include breakfast. AE, DC, MC, V. Free parking. Bus: 64.

In an impressive 15th-century palace, the Hotel Columbus is a few minutes' walk from St. Peter's. It was once the private home of a wealthy cardinal who later became Pope Julius II and had Michelangelo paint the Sistine Chapel. The building looks much as it must have done those long centuries ago—a severe, time-stained facade, small windows, and heavy wooden doors leading from the street to the colonnades and arches of the inner courtyard. The bedrooms are considerably simpler than the tiled and tapestried salons. All accommodations are spacious; a few are enormous and still have such original details as decorated wood ceilings and frescoed walls.

NEAR ANCIENT ROME
Inexpensive
Colosseum Hotel. Via Sforza 10, 00184 Roma. ☎ **06/4827228.** Fax 06/4827285. 50 rms. TEL TV. 220,000L ($140.80) double. Rates include breakfast. AE, DC, MC, V. Air-conditioning 20,000L ($12.80) extra. Parking 30,000L ($19.20). Metro: Cavour. Bus: 11, 27, or 81.

Not far from the Santa Maria Maggiore Basilica, the Colosseum offers baronial living on a miniature scale; in excellent taste, it reflects the best in Italy's design heritage. The white-walled bedrooms are furnished with well-conceived antique reproductions (beds of heavy carved wood, dark-paneled wardrobes, leatherwood chairs). The drawing room, with its long refectory table, white walls, red tiles, and provincial armchairs, invites lingering.

DINING
NEAR STAZIONE TERMINI
Moderate
Massimo d'Azeglio. Via Cavour 18. ☎ **06/4814101.** Reservations recommended. Main courses 22,000–32,000L ($14.10–$20.50); fixed-price menu 35,000–45,000L ($22.40–$28.80). AE, DC, MC, V. Mon–Sat 12:30–3pm and 7–11pm. Metro: Stazione Termini. ROMAN.

The Massimo d'Azeglio, in a hotel but with a separate entrance, has dispensed Roman cuisine since 1875. The classic cuisine is traditional Italian with some innovation. The bollito (boiled meats and vegetables served with a fruity mustard sauce) has always reigned supreme. Many habitués prefer to start with a succulent pasta dish, or else risotto with mushrooms and salad. Delectable main dishes include grilled squid with turnip tops and a mixed grill of Tyrrhenian fish. Some bottles in the wine cellar date back to the 1800s.

⑤ Scoglio di Frisio. Via Merulana 256. ☎ **06/4872765.** Reservations recommended. Main courses 16,000–30,000L ($10.25–$19.20); fixed-price menu 24,000L ($15.35) at lunch, 62,000–90,000L ($39.70–$57.60) at dinner. AE, DC, MC, V. Mon–Fri 12:30–3pm and 7:30–11pm, Sat–Sun 7:30–11pm. Bus: 714 from Stazione Termini. NEAPOLITAN.

South of the Stazione Termini, Scoglio di Frisio is the choice *suprême* to introduce yourself to the Neapolitan kitchen. While here, you should get reacquainted with pizza ("pizza pie" is redundant)—this is the the genuine article. At night, you can begin with a plate-size Neapolitan pizza (crunchy, oozy, and excellent) with clams and mussels. After a medley of stuffed vegetables and antipasti, you may then settle for chicken cacciatore or hunter's style, or veal scaloppine. Scoglio di Frisio also has entertainment, so it makes for an inexpensive night on the town.

Inexpensive
Trimani Wine Bar. Via Cernaia 37b. ☎ **06/4469630.** Fixed-price lunch 26,000L ($16.65); salads and light platters 12,000–19,000L ($7.70–$12.15). AE, DC, MC, V. Mon–Sat 11:30am–3pm and 5:30pm–midnight. Closed several weeks in Aug. Metro: Piazza della Repubblica or Castro Pretorio. CONTINENTAL.

Specifically conceived as a tasting center for French and Italian wines, spumantis, and liqueurs, this elegant wine bar lies at the edge of a historic district where vehicular traffic is partially restricted. Amid an award-winning postmodern interior decor inspired by classical Rome, you'll find comfortable seating, occasional live music, and a staff devoted to pressurizing half-full bottles of wine between pours. Menu items are inspired by the cuisine of stylish Parisian bistros, and might include vegetarian pastas (in summer), herb-laden bean soups (fagiole), slices of quiche, Hungarian goulash, gazpacho, and platters of French and Italian cheeses and pâtés.

IN PARIOLI
Very Expensive
✪ Relais Le Jardin. In the Hotel Lord Byron, Via G. de Notaris 5. ☎ **06/3613041.** Reservations required. Main courses 45,000–53,000L ($28.80–$33.90). AE, DC, MC, V. Mon–Sat 1–3pm and 8–10:30pm. Closed Aug. Bus: 26 or 52. ITALIAN.

For both a traditional and creative cuisine in an elegant setting, the Relais Le Jardin is the place to go. A chichi crowd with demanding palates patronize it nightly. Inside one of Rome's most elite small hotels, the restaurant sports a decor that's almost aggressively lighthearted. A member of Relais Gourmands, the establishment serves a frequently changing array of dishes that vary by season. The pasta and soups are among the best in town—the tonnarelli pasta with asparagus and smoked ham served with concassé tomatoes is terrific. The chef can take a dish once served only to the "plebs" in Roman days—bean soup with clams—and make it elegantly refined. For your main course you face such selections as roast loin of lamb with artichoke romana or grilled beef sirloin with hot chicory and sautéed potatoes.

Moderate
Al Ceppo. Via Panama 2. ☎ **06/8419696.** Reservations recommended. Main courses 18,000–25,000L ($11.50–$16). AE, DC, MC, V. Tues–Sun 12:30–3pm and 8–11pm. Closed the last 3 weeks of Aug. Bus: 4, 52, or 53. ROMAN.

This restaurant's somewhat hidden location (although it's only 2 blocks from the Villa Borghese, near Piazza Ungheria) means that the clientele is likely to be Roman rather than foreign. At this longtime and enduring favorite, the cuisine is as good as it ever was in its heyday. "The Log" (its name in English) features an open fireplace where the chef prepares lamb chops, liver, and bacon to charcoal perfection. The beefsteak, which hails from Tuscany, is also succulent. Other dishes include linguine monteconero (made with clams and fresh tomatoes), and a savory version of spaghetti with pepperoni, fresh basil, and pecorini cheese.

NEAR VIA VENETO & PIAZZA BARBERINI
Very Expensive

✪ **Sans Souci**. Via Sicilia 20. ☎ **06/4821814.** Reservations required. Main courses 36,000–58,000L ($23.05–$37.10). AE, DC, MC, V. Tues–Sun 8pm–1am. Closed Aug 10–30. Metro: Piazza Barberini. Bus: 52, 53, 95, 490, or 495. FRENCH.

The Sans Souci may no longer be the best restaurant in Rome—at least Michelin no longer awards its stars. Admittedly, the cuisine is better at the Relais Le Jardin. But for glitz and glamour, the nostalgia for the nights of *la dolce vita,* nothing quite matches the overly decorated Sans Souci. It serves good food to those on the see-and-be-seen circuit, and might be your best bet for spotting a movie star. The menu is ever changing, as "new creations" are devised. You might begin with a terrine of goose liver with truffles, a special creation of the chef, or escalopes of foie gras and black truffles in salad. The fish soup, according to one Rome restaurant critic, is "a legend to experience." The soufflés are also popular, including artichoke, asparagus, or spinach, and the risottos are also prepared for two.

Moderate

Girarrosto Toscano. Via Campania 29. ☎ **06/4823835.** Reservations required. Main courses 20,000–50,000L ($12.80–$32). AE, DC, MC, V. Thurs–Tues 12:30–3pm and 7:30–11:30pm. Bus: 90B, 95, 490, or 495. TUSCAN.

Girarrosto Toscano, facing the walls of the Borghese Gardens, draws a coterie of guests from Via Veneto haunts, which means that you may have to wait. Under vaulted ceilings in a cellar setting, fine Tuscan specialties are served. Begin with an enormous selection of antipasti: succulent little meatballs, vine-ripened melon with prosciutto, mozzarella, and especially delicious Tuscan salami. You're then given a choice of pasta. Priced according to weight, the bistecca alla fiorentina—grilled steak seasoned with oil, salt, and pepper—is the best item to order, although it's expensive. Oysters and fresh fish from the Adriatic are also served every day.

Inexpensive

Césarina. Via Piemonte 109. ☎ **06/4880828.** Reservations recommended. Main courses 16,000–25,000L ($10.25–$16). AE, DC, MC, V. Mon–Sat 12:30–3pm and 7:30–11pm. Bus: 52, 53, 56, 58, or 95. EMILIANA-ROMAGNOLA/ROMAN.

This restaurant has grown since it was originally established by a well-meaning matriarch, Césarina Masi. Although she died in the mid-1980s, the restaurant perpetuates her culinary traditions in a newer manifestation of the original corner-in-the-wall. Today with three dining rooms and more than 200 seats, the restaurant serves excellent versions of bollito misto (an array of well-seasoned boiled meats), rolled from table to table on a trolley; and a misto Césarina—three kinds of pasta, each handmade and served with a different sauce. Equally appealing is the saltimbocca and the cotoletta alla bolognese, a veal cutlet baked with ham and cheese.

Colline Emiliane. Via Avignonesi 22. ☎ **06/4817538.** Reservations required. Main courses 16,000–25,000L ($10.25–$16). MC, V. Sat–Thurs 12:45–2:45pm and 7:45–10:45pm. Closed Aug. Metro: Piazza Barberini. EMILIANA-ROMAGNOLA.

The Colline Emiliane, a small restaurant right off Piazza Barberini, serves *classica cucina bolognese.* It's a family-run place where everybody helps out. The owner is the cook and his wife makes the pasta, which, incidentally, is about the best you'll encounter in Rome. The house specialty is an inspired tortellini alla panna (cream sauce) with truffles. All pastas are excellent and handmade. To start your meal, we suggest culatello di Zibello, a delicacy from a small town near Parma that's known for having the finest prosciutto in the world. Main courses include braciola di maiale—boneless rolled pork cutlets that have been stuffed with ham and cheese, breaded, and sautéed. Bollito misto (mixed boiled meats) is another specialty.

NEAR THE SPANISH STEPS & PIAZZA DEL POPOLO
Expensive

✪ **El Toulà.** Via della Lupa 29B. ☎ **06/6873498.** Reservations required for dinner. Main courses 50,000L ($32); fixed-price menu 100,000L ($64). AE, DC, MC, V. Mon 8–11pm, Tues– Sat 1–3pm and 8–11pm. Closed Aug. Bus: 81, 90, 90b, 628, or 913. ROMAN/VENETIAN.

El Toulà offers quintessential Roman haute cuisine with a creative flair in an elegant setting of vaulted ceilings and large archways. Guests stop in the charming bar to order a drink while deciding on their food selections from the impressive menu, which changes every month. In honor of the restaurant's Venetian origins, one section of the menu is devoted exclusively to culinary specialties of that city. Items include Venice's classic dish, fegato (liver) alla Veneziana, along with calamari stuffed with vegetables, bigoli pasta in squid ink, and another Venetian classic, broetto, a fish soup made with monkfish and clams. El Toulà usually isn't crowded at lunchtime.

Moderate

Dal Bolognese. Piazza del Popolo 1–2. ☎ **06/3611426.** Reservations required. Main courses 20,000–26,000L ($12.80–$16.65); fixed-price menu 60,000L ($38.40). AE, MC, V. Tues–Sun 12:30–3pm and 8:15–1am. Closed 20 days in Aug. Metro: Flaminio. BOLOGNESE.

If *La Dolce Vita* were being filmed now, this restaurant would be used as a backdrop, its patrons photographed in their latest Fendi drag. It's one of those rare dining spots that's not only chic, but noted for its food as well. Young actors, shapely models, artists from nearby Via Margutta, even industrialists on an off-the-record evening on the town show up here. To begin your repast, we suggest a misto de pasta—four forms of pasta, each flavored with a different sauce, arranged on the same plate. For your main course, specialties include lasagne verde, tagliatelle alla bolognese, and a most recommendable cotolette alla bolognese.

Inexpensive

Otello alla Concordia. Via della Croce 81. ☎ **06/6791178.** Main courses 13,000–36,000L ($8.30–$23.05); fixed-price menu 36,000L ($23.05). AE, DC, MC, V. Mon–Sat 12:30–3pm and 7:30–11pm. Closed 2 weeks in Feb. Metro: Piazza di Spagna. ROMAN.

On a side street amid the glamorous boutiques near the northern edge of the Spanish Steps, this is a popular and consistently reliable restaurant. Diners enter from a stone corridor that leads from the street into a dignified building, the Palazzo Povero, choosing a table (space permitting) in either an arbor-covered courtyard or in a cramped but convivial series of inner dining rooms. The spaghetti alle vongole veraci (spaghetti with clams) is excellent, as are breast of turkey with mushrooms, Roman-style saltimbocca abbacchio arrosto (roasted baby lamb), and a selection of grilled or sautéed fish dishes.

Ristorante Nino. Via Borgognona 11. ☎ **06/6795676.** Reservations recommended. Main courses 20,000–30,000L ($12.80–$19.20). AE, DC, MC, V. Mon–Sat 12:30–3pm and 7:30– 11pm. Closed Aug. Metro: Piazza di Spagna. TUSCAN.

The Ristorante Nino, off Via Condotti a short walk from the Spanish Steps, is a tavern mecca for writers, artists, and an occasional model from one of the nearby high-fashion houses. Nino's enjoys deserved acclaim for its Tuscan dishes. The hearty cooking is completely unpretentious. The restaurant is particularly known for its steaks, shipped in from Florence and charcoal broiled—and these are priced according to weight. Cannelloni Nino is one of the chef's specialties.

Ristorante Ranieri. Via Mario de' Fiori 26. ☎ **06/6791592.** Reservations required. Main courses 22,000–32,000L ($14.10–$20.50). AE, DC, MC, V. Mon–Sat 12:30–3pm and 7:30–11pm. Metro: Piazza di Spagna. INTERNATIONAL/ITALIAN.

The Ristorante Ranieri, off Via Condotti, is well into its second century (it was founded in 1843). Neapolitan-born Giuseppe Ranieri, for whom the restaurant is named, was the chef to Queen Victoria. The Ranieri still maintains its Victorian trappings; nothing ever seems to change here. Many dishes on the menu reflect the restaurant's ties with royalty—veal cutlet l'Impériale, tournedos Enrico IV, and mignonettes of veal à la Regina Victoria, served with asparagus and mushrooms, a dish that was actually created some time in the 19th century for the queen herself.

NEAR CAMPO DE' FIORI & THE JEWISH GHETTO
Expensive

Il Drappo. Vicolo del Malpasso 9. ☎ **06/6877365.** Reservations required. Main courses 20,000–25,000L ($12.80–$16); fixed-price menu (including Sardinian wine) 60,000L ($38.40). AE, MC, V. Mon–Sat 8pm–midnight. Closed 2 weeks in Aug. Bus: 46, 62, or 64. SARDINIAN.

Il Drappo, on a hard-to-find, narrow street off a square near the Tiber, is operated by a woman known to her habitués only as "Valentina." The facade is graced with a modernized trompe-l'oeil painting above the stone entrance, flanked with potted plants. Inside, you'll have your choice of two tastefully decorated dining rooms. Fixed-price dinners may include a wafer-thin appetizer called carte di musica (sheet-music paper), topped with tomatoes, green peppers, parsley, and olive oil, followed by fresh spring lamb in season, or a changing selection of strongly flavored regional specialties that are otherwise difficult to find in Rome.

Moderate

Vecchia Roma. Via della Tribuna di Campitelli 18. ☎ **06/6864604.** Reservations recommended. Main courses 22,000–25,000L ($14.10–$16). AE, DC. Thurs–Tues 1–3:30pm and 8–11:30pm. Closed 10 days in Aug. Bus: 64, 90, 90b, 97, or 774. ITALIAN.

Vecchia Roma is a charming, moderately priced trattoria in the heart of the ghetto (a short walk from Michelangelo's Campidoglio). Head toward the Theater of Marcellus, but turn right at the synagogue. The room in the back, with a bas-relief, is more popular. The owners are known for their selection of fresh seafood. The minestrone of the day is made with fresh vegetables. An interesting selection of antipasti is always presented, including salmon and a vegetable antipasto. The pastas and risottos are also excellent, including linguine alla marinara with scampi. A "green" risotto with porcini mushrooms is invariably good. Lamb is a specialty of the chef.

Inexpensive

Da Giggetto. Via del Portico d'Ottavia 21–22. ☎ **06/6861105.** Reservations recommended. Main courses 18,000–24,000L ($11.50–$15.35). AE, DC, MC, V. Tues–Sun 12:30–3pm and 7:30–11pm. Closed Aug 1–15. Bus: 62, 64, 75, 90, or 170. ROMAN.

Da Giggetto, in the old ghetto, is a short walk from the Theater of Marcellus. Not only is it right next to these ruins, but old Roman columns extend practically to its doorway. The Romans flock to this bustling trattoria for their special traditional dishes. None is more typical than carciofi alla giudia, the baby-tender fried artichokes—thistles to make you whistle with delight. This is a true delicacy! The cheese concoction, mozzarella in carrozza, is another delight. Yet another specialty is zucchini flowers stuffed with mozzarella and anchovies, or sample fettuccine alla matriciana, shrimp sautéed in garlic and olive oil.

NEAR PIAZZA NAVONA & THE PANTHEON

Moderate

Alfredo alla Scrofa. Via della Scrofa 104. ☎ **06/68806163.** Reservations recommended. Main courses 18,000–26,000L ($11.50–$16.65); fixed-price menu 45,000L ($28.80). AE, DC, MC, V. Wed–Mon 12:30–3pm and 7:30–11:30pm. Metro: Piazza di Spagna. ROMAN/INTERNATIONAL.

This restaurant maintains a visitors' autograph book that reads like a retrospective of 20th-century history. Gold-framed photographs of famous visitors hang on the walls. The restaurant aggressively trades on its fame of yesterday—believe it or not, it was once virtually mandatory to dine here when visiting Rome. Many first-time visitors order the maestose fettuccine al triplo burro, where waiters make choreography out of whipping butter and cheese on rolling carts at tableside. The main-course specialties include filetto di tacchino dorato (breast of turkey, sautéed in batter and covered with thin slices of Piedmontese white truffles), filet mignon Casanova (prepared with red wine, pepper, and foie gras), and roasted lamb with potatoes in the Roman style.

Passetto. Via Zanardelli 14. ☎ **06/68806569.** Reservations recommended. Main courses 24,000–40,000L ($15.35–$25.60). AE, DC, MC, V. Daily noon–3pm and 7pm–midnight. Bus: 70, 87, or 90. ROMAN/ITALIAN.

Passetto, dramatically positioned at the north end of the landmark Piazza Navona, has drawn patrons for 142 years. Regrettably, its location and success have spoiled it somewhat and service is a bit rude. The surroundings are stylish—three rooms, one with frosted-glass–cylinder chandeliers. In summer, however, it's better to try one of the outside tables on the big terrace looking out on Piazza Sant'Apollinare. The pastas are exceptional, including penne alla Norma. A recommended main dish is orata al cartoccio (sea bass baked in a paper bag with tomatoes, mushrooms, capers, and white wine).

Inexpensive

L'Eau Vive. Via Monterone 85. ☎ **06/68801095.** Reservations recommended. Main courses 10,000–28,000L ($6.40–$17.90); fixed-price menus 15,000L, 22,000L, and 28,000L ($9.60, $14.10 and $17.90). AE, MC, V. Mon–Sat 12:30–2:30pm and 8–10:30pm. Closed Aug 1–20. Bus: 46, 62, 64, 78, or 492. FRENCH/INTERNATIONAL.

L'Eau Vive is run by lay missionaries who wear the dress or costumes of their native countries. The restaurant occupies the cellar and the ground floor of a 17th-century palace, and is filled with monumental paintings. In this formal atmosphere, at 10pm nightly, the waitresses sing religious hymns and "Ave Marias." Your gratuity for service will be turned over for religious purposes. Pope John Paul II used to dine here when he was still archbishop of Kraków. Specialties include hors d'oeuvres and frogs' legs. Main dishes range from guinea hen with onions and grapes in a wine sauce to couscous. Other selections include platters of charcuterie, several kinds of homemade pâté, and beefsteak in wine sauce. A smooth finish is the chocolate mousse.

NEAR VATICAN CITY

Expensive

✪ **Les Etoiles.** In the Hotel Atlante Star, Via Vitelleschi 34. ☎ **06/6893434.** Reservations required. Main courses 30,000–48,000L ($19.20–$30.70). AE, DC, MC, V. Daily 12:30–2:30pm and 7:30–11pm. Metro: Ottaviano. Bus: 23, 49, 64, 81, or 492. MEDITERRANEAN.

Les Etoiles deserves all the stars it receives—both for its cuisine and for its panoramic view of Rome. At this garden in the sky you'll have an open window over the roof-tops of Rome—a 360° view of landmarks, especially the floodlit dome of St. Peter's. In summer everyone wants a table outside, but in winter almost the same view can be seen through the picture windows. Refined Mediterranean cuisine, with perfectly balanced flavors, is served here. Dishes include quail cooked either with radicchio or in a casserole with mushrooms and herbs, artichokes stuffed with ricotta and pecorino cheese, and Venetian-style risotto with squid ink, and fish prepared either in the style of the Tyrrhenian or the Adriatic Sea.

Moderate

Il Matriciano. Via dei Gracchi 55. ☎ **06/3212327.** Reservations required, especially for dinner. Main courses 14,000–24,000L ($8.95–$15.35). AE, DC, MC, V. May–Oct, Sun–Fri 12:30–3pm and 8–11:30pm; Nov–Apr, Thurs–Tues 12:30–3pm and 8–11:30pm. Closed Aug 5–25. Metro: Ottaviano. ROMAN.

Il Matriciano is a family restaurant with a devoted following. The food is good, but it's only country fare—nothing fancy. The decor, likewise, is kept to a minimum. In summer, try to sit at a sidewalk table behind a green hedge under a shady canopy. The luncheon clientele seems to linger a long time. For openers, you might choose a zuppa di verdura or ravioli di ricotta, but we suggest the tagliolini con tartufi. From many dishes, we recommend scaloppa alla valdostana, abbacchio (baby lamb) al forno, and trippa (tripe) alla romana. The house specialty is based on that Roman favorite, matriciana sauce. Here, it's prepared with bucatini pasta and richly flavored with bacon, tomatoes, and basil.

Inexpensive

Ristorante Giardinaccio. Via Aurelia 53. ☎ **06/631367.** Reservations recommended, especially on weekends. Main courses 10,000–15,000L ($6.40–$9.60). AE, DC, MC, V. Wed–Mon 12:15–3:30pm and 7:15–11pm. Bus: 46, 62, or 98. ITALIAN/MOLISIAN.

This popular restaurant, operated by Nicolino Mancini, is only 200 yards from St. Peter's. Unusual for Rome, it offers Molisian specialties, from one of the provincial regions of southeastern Italy, and is appropriately decorated in rustic country-tavern style. Flaming grills provide succulent versions of perfectly done quail, goat, and other dishes, but perhaps the mutton goulash would be more adventurous. Many pastas are featured, including taconelle, a homemade pasta with lamb sauce. Vegetarians and others will like the large self-service selection of antipasti.

IN TRASTEVERE

Expensive

Alberto Ciarla. Piazza San Cosimato 40. ☎ **06/5818668.** Reservations required, especially on weekends. Main courses 24,000–45,000L ($15.35–$28.80); fixed-price menu 80,000–90,000L ($51.20–$57.60). AE, DC, MC, V. Mon–Sat 8:30pm–12:30am. Closed 1 week in Jan and 1 week in Aug. Bus: 44, 75, 170, 280, or 718. SEAFOOD.

Alberto Ciarla is the best and most expensive restaurant in Trastevere. Some critics still consider it one of Rome's finest, although it's not as chic as it was in the late 1980s, and Michelin no longer awards a star. In a 1890 building in an obscure corner of an enormous square, a dramatically modern decor plays shades of brilliant light against patches of shadow for a result that a Renaissance artist might have called chiaroscuro. It serves some of the most elegant fish dishes in the city. Specialties include a handful of ancient recipes subtly improved by Signor Ciarla, such as soup of pasta and beans with seafood. Original dishes include a delectable salmon Marcel Trompier with lobster sauce, as well as well-flavored sushi, a full array of shellfish, and filet of sea bass prepared in at least three different ways, including an award-winning version with almonds.

Moderate

La Cisterna. Via della Cisterna 13. ☎ **06/5812543.** Reservations recommended. Main courses 16,000–30,000L ($10.25–$19.20). AE, DC, MC, V. Mon–Sat 7pm–midnight. Bus: 44, 75, 170, 280, or 710. ROMAN.

La Cisterna lies deep in the heart of Trastevere. For more than half a century it has been run by the Simmi family, who are genuinely interested in serving only the best as well as providing a good time for all guests. The cistern in the name comes from an ancient Roman well discovered in the cellar. No one's ever awarded any stars to this place—and food critics probably never will—but if you like traditional cookery based on the best of regional produce, then come here. In summer you can inspect the antipasti—a mixed selection of hors d'oeuvres—right out on the street before going in. House specialties include Roman-style suckling lamb (abbacchio), rigatoni a l'amatriciana (with diced bacon, olive oil, garlic, tomatoes, red peppers, and onions), and fresh fish—especially sea bass baked with herbs.

ATTRACTIONS

Rome is studded with ancient monuments that silently evoke its history as one of the greatest centers of Western civilization—once all roads led to Rome with good reason. It became the first cosmopolitan city in Europe, importing everything from slaves and gladiators to great art from the far corners of the empire. With all its carnage and mismanagement, it left a legacy of law and order and an uncanny lesson in how to conquer enemies by absorbing their cultures. But ancient Rome is only part of the spectacle. The Vatican also made the city a center of the world in art as well as religion. And although Vatican architects rifled much of the glory of the past for their projects, they also created the great Renaissance treasures we come to see today.

SIGHTSEEING SUGGESTIONS

If You Have 1 Day   Rome wasn't built in a day and you aren't likely to see it in a day either, but make the most of your limited time. You'll basically have to decide on the legacy of imperial Rome—the Roman Forum, the Imperial Forum, and the Colosseum—or else St. Peter's and the Vatican. Walk along the Spanish Steps at sunset. At night go to Piazza del Campidoglio for a fantastic view of the Forum below. Have a nightcap on Via Veneto, which, although past its prime, is still a lure for the first-time visitor. Toss a coin in the Trevi fountain and promise yourself a return visit.

If You Have 2 Days   If you elected to see the Roman Forum and the Colosseum and your first day, then spend the second day exploring St. Peter's and the Vatican Museums (or vice versa). Have dinner in a restaurant in Trastevere.

If You Have 3 Days   In the morning go to the Pantheon in the heart of Old Rome, then, after lunch, try to explore the Castel Sant'Angelo and the Etruscan Museum. Have dinner at a restaurant on Piazza Navona.

If You Have 5 Days   On day 4 head for the environs, notably Tivoli, where you can see the Villa d'Este and Hadrian's Villa. On day 5 explore the ruins of Ostia Antica, return to Rome for lunch, and visit the Capitoline Museum and Basilica di San Giovanni in Laterano in the afternoon.

Rome Major & Outlying Attractions

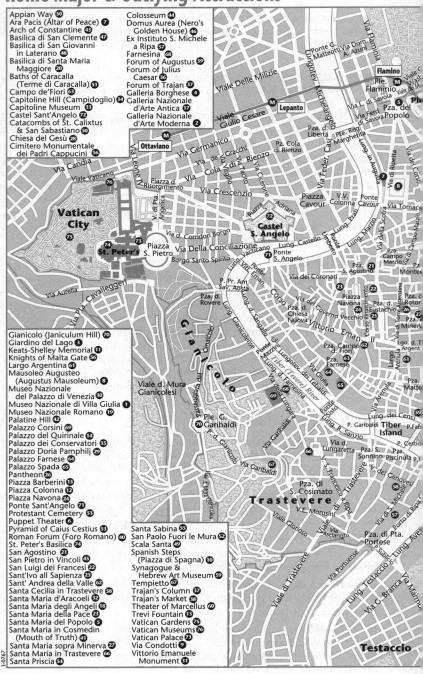

3-0761

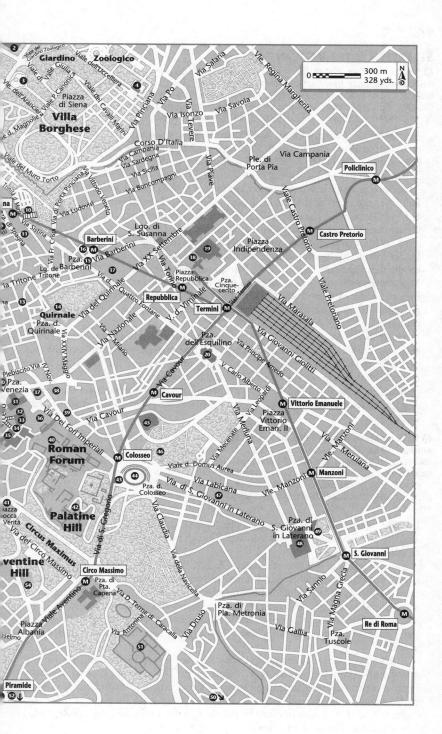

ST. PETER'S & THE VATICAN

✪ **Basilica di San Pietro (St. Peter's Basilica).** Piazza San Pietro. ☎ **06/69884466.** Basilica and grottoes, free; stairs to dome and roof, 5,000L ($3.20) adults, 1,000L (65¢) students; elevator to roof 6,000L ($3.85). Basilica, Apr–Aug, daily 7am–7pm; Sept–Mar, daily 7am–6pm. Grottoes, Apr–Sept, daily 7am–6pm; Oct–Mar, daily 7am–5pm. Dome, Mar–Sept, daily 8am–6pm; Oct–Feb, daily 8am–4:30pm. Bus: 23, 30, 32, 49, 51, or 64.

As you stand in Bernini's **Piazza San Pietro** (St. Peter's Square), you'll be in the arms of an ellipse; like a loving parent, the Doric-pillared colonnade reaches out to embrace the faithful. Holding 300,000 is no problem for this square.

Inside, the size of this famous church is awe-inspiring—although its dimensions (about two football fields long) are not apparent at first. St. Peter's is said to have been built over the tomb of the crucified saint. The original church was erected on the order of Constantine, but the present structure is essentially Renaissance and baroque; it showcases the talents of some of Italy's greatest artists.

In such a grand church, don't expect subtlety. But the basilica is rich in art. Under Michelangelo's dome is the celebrated **baldacchino** by Bernini. In the nave on the right (the first chapel) is the best-known piece of sculpture, the *Pietà* that Michelangelo sculpted while still in his early twenties. You can visit the sacristy and treasury, filled with jewel-studded chalices, reliquaries, and copes and the **Vatican grottoes,** with their tombs, both ancient and modern (Pope John XXII gets the most adulation).

The grandest sight is yet to come: the climb to **Michelangelo's dome,** which towers about 375 feet high. Although you can walk up the steps, we recommend the elevator for as far as it'll carry you. You can walk along the roof, for which you'll be rewarded with a panoramic view of Rome and the Vatican.

Note: To be admitted to St. Peter's, women must wear skirts that cover the knees or pants. Sleeveless tops and shorts are not allowed for either gender. You *will* be turned away.

✪ **Vatican Museums and the Sistine Chapel.** Viale Vaticano, Vatican City. ☎ **06/6982.** Admission 15,000L ($9.60) adults, 10,000L ($6.40) children, free the last Sun of each month (be ready for a crowd). Apr–June 14 and Sept–Oct, Mon–Fri 8:45am–4pm, Sat 8:45am–1pm; June 15–Aug and Nov–Mar, Mon–Sat 8:45am–1pm; also the last Sun of each month. Last admission 1 hour before closing. Closed religious holidays. Metro: Ottaviano. Bus: 19, 23, 32, 34, 49, 51, or 64. The museum entrance is a long walk around the Vatican walls from St. Peter's Square.

In 1929 the Lateran Treaty between Pope Pius XI and the Italian government created the world's smallest independent state. Though tiny, this state contains a gigantic repository of treasures.

You can follow one of four itineraries—A, B, C, or D—according to the time you have at your disposal (from 1 1/2 to 5 hours) and your special interests. You can choose from the picture gallery, which houses paintings from the 11th to the 19th century, the Egyptian collection, the Etruscan museum, Greek and Roman sculpture, and, of course, the Sistine Chapel. Consult the large panels at the entrance, then follow the letter and color of the itinerary chosen. Facilities for persons with disabilities are available.

Michelangelo labored for 4 years (1508–12) over the epic Sistine Chapel, now restored, not without controversy, to its original glory. The work was so physically taxing that it permanently damaged his eyesight. Glorifying the human body as only a sculptor could, Michelangelo painted nine panels taken from the pages of Genesis, and surrounded them with prophets and sibyls. Also don't miss the Stanze di Raphael, rooms decorated by Raphael when still a young man.

THE FORUM, THE COLOSSEUM & THE HEART OF ANCIENT ROME

✪ **Foro Romano (Roman Forum).** Via dei Fori Imperiali. ☎ **06/6990110.** Admission 12,000L ($7.70) adults, free for children 17 and under and seniors 60 and over. Mon and Wed–Sat 9am–1 hour before sunset, Tues and Sun 9am–2pm; last admission 1 hour before closing. Closed Jan 16–Feb 15. Metro: Colosseo. Bus: 27, 81, 85, 87, or 186.

The Roman Forum was built in the marshy land between the Palatine and the Capitoline Hills. It flourished as the center of Roman life in the days of the Republic, before it gradually lost prestige to the Imperial Forum. By day the columns of now-vanished temples and the stones from which long-forgotten orators spoke are mere shells. But at night, when the Forum is silent in the moonlight, it isn't difficult to imagine that Vestal Virgins still guard the sacred temple fire.

If you want the stones to have some meaning, you'll have to purchase a detailed plan, as the temples are hard to locate otherwise. The best of the lot is the handsomely adorned **Temple of Castor and Pollux,** erected in the 5th century B.C. in honor of a battle triumph. The **Temple of Faustina,** with its lovely columns and frieze (griffins and candelabra), was converted into the San Lorenzo in Miranda Church. The **Temple of the Vestal Virgins** is a popular attraction; some of the statuary, mostly headless, remains.

A long walk up from the Roman Forum leads to the **Palatine Hill,** one of the seven hills of Rome; your ticket from the Forum will admit you to this attraction (it's open the same hours). The Palatine, tradition tells us, was the spot on which the first settlers built their huts, under the direction of Romulus. In later years the hill became a patrican residential district that attracted citizens like Cicero. It's worth the climb for the panoramic, sweeping view of both the Roman and Imperial Forums, as well as the Capitoline Hill and the Colosseum. Of the ruins that remain, none is finer than the so-called **House of Livia** (the "abominable grandmother" of Robert Graves's *I, Claudius*).

When the glory that was Rome has completely overwhelmed you, you can enjoy a respite in the cooling **Farnese Gardens,** laid out in the 16th century, which incorporate some of Michelangelo's designs.

✪ **Colosseo (Colosseum).** Piazzale del Colosseo, Via dei Fori Imperiali. ☎ **06/7004261.** Admission: Street level, free; upper levels, 8,000L ($5.10). Mon–Tues and Thurs–Sat 9am–1 hour before sunset, Wed and holidays 9am–2pm. Metro: Colosseo.

In spite of the fact that it's a mere shell, the Colosseum remains the greatest architectural inheritance from ancient Rome. Vespasian ordered the construction of the elliptically shaped bowl, called the Amphitheatrum Flavium, in A.D. 72; it was inaugurated by Titus in A.D. 80 with a many-weeks-long bloody combat between gladiators and wild beasts. At its peak, the Colosseum could seat 50,000 spectators, and exotic animals—humans also—were shipped in from the far corners of the empire to satisfy jaded tastes.

Campidoglio (Capitoline Hill). Piazza del Campidoglio. Bus: 46, 89, 92, 94, or 716.

Of the Seven Hills of Rome, the Campidoglio is the most sacred—its origins stretch way back into antiquity (an Etruscan temple to Jupiter once stood on this spot). The approach to the Capitoline Hill is dramatic—climbing the long, sloping steps designed by Michelangelo. At the top is a perfectly proportioned square, Piazza del Campidoglio, also laid out by the Florentine artist.

One side of the piazza is open; the others are bounded by the Senatorium (Town Council), the statuary-filled Palazza dei Conservatori, and the Capitoline Museum (see "More Attractions," below). The Campidoglio is dramatic at night (walk around to the back for a regal view of the floodlit Roman Forum).

Castel Sant'Angelo. Lungotevere Castello 50. ☎ **06/6875036.** Admission 8,000L ($5.10) adults, free for children 17 and under and seniors 60 and over. Daily 9am–1pm. Closed second and last Tues of each month. Metro: Ottaviano. Bus: 23, 46, 49, 62, 64, 87, 98, 280, or 910.

This overpowering structure, in a landmark position on the Tiber, was originally built in the 2nd century A.D. as a tomb for the emperor Hadrian; it continued as an imperial mausoleum until the time of Caracalla. It's an imposing and grim castle with thick walls and cylindrical shape. If it looks like a fortress, it should, as that was its function in the Middle Ages. In the 14th century it became a papal residence. Its legend rests largely on its link with Pope Alexander VI, whose mistress bore him two children—Cesare and Lucrezia Borgia. Today the highlight of the castle is a trip through the Renaissance apartments with their coffered ceilings and lush decoration. Their walls have witnessed plots and intrigues that make up some of the arch-treachery of the High Renaissance.

Now an art museum, the castle halls display the history of the Roman mausoleum, along with a wide-ranging selection of ancient arms and armor. You can climb to the top terrace for another one of those dazzling views of the Eternal City.

✪ **Pantheon.** Piazza della Rotonda. ☎ **06/68300230.** Free admission. July–Sept, daily 9am–6pm; Oct–June, Mon–Sat 9am–4pm, Sun 9am–1pm. Bus: 46, 62, 64, 170, or 492 to Largo di Torre Argentina; then walk up Via di Torre Argentina or Via dei Cestari.

Of all the great buildings of ancient Rome, only the Pantheon ("All the Gods") remains intact today. It was built in 27 B.C. by Marcus Agrippa, and later reconstructed by the emperor Hadrian in the first part of the 2nd century A.D. This remarkable building is among the architectural wonders of the world because of its dome and its concept of space.

The Pantheon was once ringed with white marble statues of Roman gods in its niches. Animals were sacrificed and burned in the center, and the smoke escaped through the only means of light, an opening at the top 27 feet in diameter. Michelangelo came here to study the dome before designing the cupola of St. Peter's (whose dome is only 2 feet smaller than the Pantheon's).

THE CATACOMBS OF THE APPIAN WAY

Of all the roads that led to Rome, **Via Appia Antica**—built in 312 B.C.—was reigned the leader. It eventually stretched all the way from Rome to the seaport of Brindisi, through which trade with the colonies in Greece and the East was funneled.

Along the Appian Way the patrician Romans built great monuments above the ground, whereas Christians met in the catacombs beneath. The remains of both can be visited today. In some dank, dark grottoes (never stray too far from either your party or one of the exposed lightbulbs), you can still discover traces of early Christian art.

Of the catacombs open to the public, the Catacombs of St. Callixtus and those of St. Sebastian are the most important. Both can be reached by taking bus no. 118, which leaves from near the Colosseum close to the Metro station.

The **Catacombe di San Sebastiano** is at Via Appia Antica 136 (☎ **06/7887035**). Today the tomb of the martyr is in the basilica (church), but was originally in the catacomb under the basilica. From the reign of the emperor Valerian to the reign of Constantine, the bodies of Saint Peter and Saint Paul were hidden in this catacomb. The tunnels here, if stretched out, would reach a length of 7 miles. Admission is 8,000L ($5.10) for adults, 4,000L ($2.55) for children 6 to 15, and free for children 5 and under. Open Wed–Mon 9am–noon and 2:30–5:30pm.

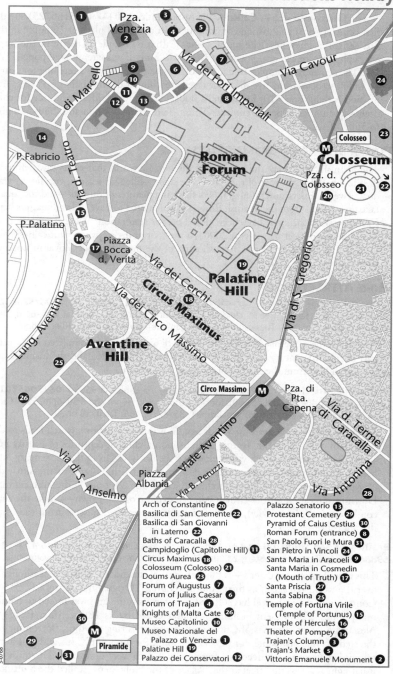

Ancient Rome & Attractions Nearby

Pza. Venezia

P. Fabricio

P. Palatino

di Marcello

Via d. Teatro

Via dei Fori Imperiali

Via Cavour

Roman Forum

Colosseo

M

Colosseum

Pza. d. Colosseo

Piazza Bocca d. Verità

Via dei Cerchi

Via dei Circo Massimo

Circus Maximus

Palatine Hill

Via di S. Gregorio

Lung. Aventino

Aventine Hill

Circo Massimo **M**

Pza. di Pta. Capena

Via d. Terme di Caracalla

Via di S. Anselmo

Piazza Albania

Viale Aventino

Via B. Peruzzi

Via Antonina

Piramide

M

Arch of Constantine 20
Basilica di San Clemente 22
Basilica di San Giovanni
  in Laterno 22
Baths of Caracalla 28
Campidoglio (Capitoline Hill) 11
Circus Maximus 18
Colosseum (Colosseo) 21
Doums Aurea 23
Forum of Augustus 7
Forum of Julius Caesar 6
Forum of Trajan 4
Knights of Malta Gate 26
Museo Capitolinio 10
Museo Nazionale del
  Palazzo di Venezia 1
Palatine Hill 19
Palazzo dei Conservatori 12

Palazzo Senatorio 13
Protestant Cemetery 29
Pyramid of Caius Cestius 30
Roman Forum (entrance) 8
San Paolo Fuori le Mura 31
San Pietro in Vincoli 24
Santa Maria in Aracoeli 9
Santa Maria in Cosmedin
  (Mouth of Truth) 17
Santa Priscia 27
Santa Sabina 25
Temple of Fortuna Virile
  (Temple of Portunus) 15
Temple of Hercules 16
Theater of Pompey 14
Trajan's Column 3
Trajan's Market 5
Vittorio Emanuele Monument 2

3-0768

↓ 31

The **Catacombs di San Callisto,** Via Appia Antica 110 (☎ **06/5136725**), are the first cemetery of the Christian community of Rome, burial place of 16 popes in the 3rd century. They bear the name of St. Callixtus, the deacon whom the pope St. Zephyrinus put in charge of them. Callixtus himself was later elected pope (217–22). The cemeterial complex is made up of a network of galleries stretching for nearly 12 miles, structured in five different levels, reaching a depth of about 65 feet. Admission is 8,000L ($5.10) for adults, 4,000L ($2.55) for children, and free for children 4 and under. Open in summer Thurs–Tues 8:30am–noon and 2:30–5:30pm, to 5pm off-season.

PIAZZA DI SPAGNA (SPANISH STEPS)

The Spanish Steps were the last part of the outside world that Keats saw before he died in a house at the foot of the stairs. The steps—filled, in season, with flower vendors, jewelry dealers, and photographers snapping pictures of tourists—and the square take their names from the Spanish Embassy, which used to have its headquarters here. In recent years the steps have been closed off for restoration. Work is underway to complete the project by the year 2000. At the foot of the steps is a nautically shaped fountain, designed by Pietro Bernini, papa of the more famous Giovanni Lorenzo Bernini.

MORE ATTRACTIONS

Terme di Caracalla (Baths of Caracalla). Via delle Terme di Caracalla 52. ☎ **06/5758626.** Admission 8,000L ($5.10), free for children 11 and under. Apr–Sept, Tues–Sat 9am–6pm, Sun–Mon 9am–1pm; Oct–Mar, Tues–Sat 9am–3pm, Sun–Mon 9am–1pm. Bus: 90 or 118.

Named for the emperor Caracalla, the Terme di Caracalla were completed in the early part of the 3rd century. The richness of decoration has faded and the lushness can only be judged from the shell of brick ruins that remain.

Basilica di San Clemente. Piazza San Clemente, Via Labicana 95. ☎ **06/70451018.** Church, free; grottoes, 2,000L ($1.30). Mon–Sat 9:30am–12:30pm and 3:30–6pm, Sun 10am–noon and 3:30–6pm. Metro: Colosseo. Bus: 81, 85, 87, or 186. Tram: 13 or 30.

From the Colosseum, head up Via di San Giovanni in Laterano, which leads to the Basilica of Saint Clement. In this church-upon-a-church, centuries of history peel away: A 4th-century church was built over a secular house from the 1st century A.D., beside which stood a pagan temple dedicated to Mithras (god of the sun); the Normans destroyed the lower church, and a new one was built in the 12th century. Down in the eerie grottoes (which you can explore on your own—unlike the catacombs on the Appian Way), you'll discover well-preserved frescoes from the 1st to the 3rd centuries A.D.

Basilica di San Giovanni in Laterano. Piazza San Giovanni in Laterano 4. ☎ **06/69886433.** Basilica, free; cloisters, 2,000L ($1.30). Daily 7am–6pm. Metro: San Giovanni.

This church—not St. Peter's—is the cathedral of the diocese of Rome. Catholics all over the world refer to it as their "mother church." Originally built in A.D. 314 by Constantine, the cathedral has suffered many vicissitudes and was forced to rebuild many times. The present building is characterized by its 18th-century facade by Alessandro Galilei (statues of Christ and the Apostles ring the top). Borromini gets the credit (some say blame) for the interior, built for Innocent X. It's said that in the misguided attempt to redecorate, frescoes by Giotto were destroyed. The most unusual sight is across the street at the "Palace of the Holy Steps," called the **Santuario della Scala Sancta,** Piazza San Giovanni in Laterano (☎ 06/70494619). It's alleged that these were the actual steps that Christ climbed when he was brought before

Pilate. These steps are supposed to be climbed only on your knees, which you're likely to see the faithful doing throughout the day.

Basilica di Santa Maria Maggiore (Saint Mary Major). Piazza Santa Maria Maggiore. ☎ **06/483194.** Free admission. Daily 7am–7pm. Metro: Stazione Termini.

This great church was originally founded by Pope Liberius in A.D. 358 but rebuilt by Pope Sixtus III in 432–440. Its campanile, erected in the 14th century, is the loftiest in the city. Much doctored in the 18th century, the church's facade is not an accurate reflection of the treasures inside. The basilica is especially noted for the 5th-century Roman mosaics in its nave, as well as for its coffered ceiling, said to have been gilded with gold brought from the New World. In the 16th century Domenico Fontana built a now-restored "Sistine Chapel." The church contains the tomb of Bernini, Italy's most important architect during the flowering of the baroque in the 17th century.

✪ Museo Capitolino and Palace of the Conservatori. Piazza del Campidoglio. ☎ **06/67102071.** Admission to both museum and palace 10,000L ($6.40). Apr–Sept, Tues 9am–1:45pm and 5–8pm, Wed–Fri 9am–1:30pm, Sat 9am–1:30pm and 8–11pm, Sun 9am–1:30pm; Oct–Mar, Tues and Sat 9am–1:45pm and 5–8pm, Wed–Fri 9am–1:30pm, Sun 9am–1:30pm. Bus: 46, 89, 92, 94, or 716.

The Capitoline Museum was built in the 17th century, based on an architectural sketch by Michelangelo. In the first room is *The Dying Gaul,* a work of majestic skill; in a special gallery all her own is *The Capitoline Venus,* who demurely covers herself—this statue (a Roman copy of the Greek original) was the symbol of feminine beauty and charm down through the centuries.

The famous statue of *Marcus Aurelius* is the only bronze equestrian statue to have survived from ancient Rome. It was retrieved from the Tiber where it had been tossed by marauding barbarians. For centuries it was thought to be a statue of Constantine the Great; this mistake protected it further, since papal Rome respected the memory of the first Christian emperor.

The **Palace of the Conservatori,** across the way, is rich in classical sculpture and paintings. One of the most notable bronzes—a work of incomparable beauty—is the *Spinario* (the little boy picking a thorn from his foot), a Greek classic that dates from the 1st century B.C. In addition, you'll find *Lupa Capitolina* (the Capitoline Wolf), a rare Etruscan bronze that may go back to the 5th century B.C. (Romulus and Remus, the legendary twins that the wolf suckled, were added at a later date.)

✪ Galleria Borghese. Piazzale del Museo Borghese, off Via Pinciano. ☎ **06/8548577.** Admission 4,000L ($2.55). Tues–Sat 9am–2pm, Sun 9am–7pm. Bus: 910 from Stazione Termini or 56 from Piazza Barberini.

Still under restoration, the gallery, housed in a handsome villa, contains a representative collection of Renaissance and baroque masters along with important Bernini sculpture. Among these is the *Conquering Venus* by Antonio Canova, Italy's greatest neoclassic sculptor. Actually, this early 19th-century work created a sensation in its day, because its model was Pauline Bonaparte Borghese, sister of Napoleon. The second floor, which normally houses the paintings, is still closed, and may be for a long time. The paintings are more or less on semipermanent display at **San Michele a Ripa,** Via di San Michele 22 (☎ 06/58431) in the Trastevere district. Admission is included in your Galleria Borghese ticket; it's open Mon–Fri 9:30am–1pm and 4–8pm and Sat 9:30am–1pm.

Galleria Nazionale d'Arte Antica. Via delle Quattro Fontane 13. ☎ **06/4814430.** Admission 8,000L ($5.10) adults, free for children 17 and under and seniors 60 and over. Tues–Sat 9am–2pm, Sun 9am–1pm. Metro: Piazza Barberini.

The Palazzo Barberini, right off Piazza Barberini, is one of Rome's most magnificent baroque palaces. It was begun by Carlo Maderno in 1627 and completed in 1633 by Bernini, whose lavishly decorated rococo apartments, called the Gallery of Decorative Art, are on view. The palace houses the Galleria Nazionale. On the first floor of the palace, a splendid array of paintings includes works that date back to the 13th and 14th centuries, notably the *Mother and Child* by Simone Martini. Art from the 15th and 16th centuries include works by Filippo Lippi, Andrea Solario, Francesco Francia, Il Sodoma (Giovanni Antonio Bazzi), and Raphael.

✪ **Museo Nazionale di Villa Giulia (Etruscan).** Piazzale di Villa Giulia 9. ☎ **06/3226571.** Admission 8,000L ($5.10) adults, free for children 17 and under and seniors 60 and over. Tues–Sat 9am–7pm, Sun 9am–1pm. Metro: Flaminio. Bus: 19, 30, 225, or 926.

A 16th-century papal palace in the Villa Borghese Gardens shelters this priceless collection of art and artifacts of the mysterious Etruscans, who predated the Romans, and of whom little is known except for their sophisticated art and design. If you have time only for the masterpieces, head for Sala 7, which has a remarkable *Apollo* from Veio from the end of the 6th century B.C. (clothed, for a change). The other two widely acclaimed pieces of statuary in this gallery are *Dea con Bambino* (a goddess with a baby) and a greatly mutilated, but still powerful, *Hercules* with a stag. In the adjoining room, Sala 8, you'll see the lions' sarcophagus from the mid–6th century B.C. which was excavated at Cerveteri, north of Rome. Finally, in Sala 9, is one of the world's most important Etruscan art treasures, the bride and bridegroom coffin from the 6th century B.C., also dug out of the tombs of Cerveteri.

ORGANIZED TOURS

One of the leading tour operators (among the zillions of possibilities) is **American Express,** Piazza di Spagna 38 (☎ **06/67641**), open Mon–Fri 9am–5:30pm and Sat 9am–12:30pm. One popular tour is a 4-hour orientation tour of Rome and the Vatican, which departs most mornings at 9:30am and costs 60,000L ($38.40) per person. Another 4-hour tour, which focuses on the Rome of antiquity (including visits to the Colosseum, the Roman Forum, the ruins of the Imperial Palace, and the Church of San Pietro in Vincoli), costs 50,000L ($32). Outside Rome, a popular excursion is a 5-hour bus tour to Tivoli, where visits are conducted of the Villa d'Este and its spectacular gardens and the ruins of the Villa Adriana, all for the price of 63,000L ($40.30) per person.

If your time in Italy is rigidly limited, you might opt for 1-day excursions to points farther afield on tours that are marketed (but not conducted) by American Express. A series of 1-day tours is offered to Pompeii, Naples, and Sorrento for 132,000L ($84.50) per person; to Florence for 162,000L ($103.70); and to Capri for 184,000L ($117.75). These trips, which include lunch, depart from Rome around 7am and return sometime after 9 or 10pm to your hotel.

SHOPPING

Many antiques at the **Galleria Coronari,** Via dei Coronari 59 (☎ **06/6869917**), are nostalgia-laden bric-a-brac small enough to fit into a suitcase, including jewelry, dolls, paintings, and ornate picture frames. There's also furniture.

Alberto di Castro, Via del Babuino 71 (☎ **06/361752**), is one of the largest dealers of antique prints and engravings in Rome, with rack after rack of depictions of Mediterranean architecture, priced between $25 and $1,000.

The upscale department store, **La Rinascente,** Piazza Colonna, Via del Corso 189 (☎ **06/6797691**), is the largest of the Italian department-store chains.

Emporio Armani, Via del Babuino 119 (☎ 06/322151), stocks moderately priced men's wear crafted by the couturier who has dressed more stage and screen stars than any other designer in Italy. The designer's more expensive line—sold at prices that are sometimes 30% less than what you'd pay in the United States—lies a short walk away, at **Giorgio Armani,** Via Condotti 77 (☎ 06/6991460). The clothing of **Renato Balestra,** Via Sistina 67 (☎ 06/6795424), attains standards of lighthearted elegance at its best. This branch carries a complete line of the latest Balestra ready-to-wear designs for women.

Salvatore Ferragamo, Via Condotti 73–74 (☎ 06/6798402), sells elegant and fabled footwear, plus women's clothing and accessories, and ties, in an atmosphere full of Italian style, but figure on a 30-minute wait outside.

Federico Buccellati, Via Condotti 31 (☎ 06/6790329), one of the best gold- and silversmiths in Italy, sells neo-Renaissance creations. The designs of the handmade jewelry and holloware recall those of Renaissance goldmaster Benvenuto Cellini.

Anatriello del Regalo, Via Frattina 123 (☎ 06/6789601), stocks new and antique silver, some of it quite unusual. The new items are made by Italian silversmiths, in designs ranging from the whimsical to the severely formal.

Cesare Diomedi Leather Goods, located in front of the Grand Hotel at Via Vittorio Emanuele Orlando 96–97 (☎ 06/4884822), offers an outstanding collection of leather goods.

At the sprawling **Porta Portese** open-air flea market of Rome, held every Sunday morning in Trastevere, every peddler from Trastevere and the surrounding Castelli Romani sets up a temporary shop. The vendors sell merchandise ranging from secondhand paintings of madonnas to pseudo-Etruscan hairpins. The flea market is near the end of Viale Trastevere (bus no. 75 to Porta Portese), then a short walk away to Via Portuense, to catch the workday Roman in an unguarded moment. By 10:30am the market is full of people. As you would at any street market, beware of pickpockets. Open Sun 7am–1pm.

ROME AFTER DARK

There are few evening diversions quite as pleasurable as a stroll past the solemn pillars of old temples or the cascading torrents of Renaissance fountains glowing under the blue-black sky. Of the **fountains,** the Naiads (Piazza della Repubblica), the Tortoises (Piazza Mattei), and, of course, the Trevi are particularly beautiful at night. The **Capitoline Hill** is magnificently lit after dark, with its measured Renaissance facades glowing like jewel boxes. Behind the Senatorial Palace is a fine view of the **Roman Forum.** If you're staying across the Tiber, **Piazza San Pietro** (in front of St. Peter's Basilica) is impressive at night without tour buses and crowds. And a combination of illuminated architecture, Renaissance fountains, and, frequently, sidewalk shows and art expositions is at **Piazza Navona.** If you're ambitious and have a good sense of direction, try exploring the streets to the west of Piazza Navona, which look like a stage set when they're lit at night.

Even if you don't speak Italian, you can generally follow the listings featured in *La Repubblica,* a leading Italian newspaper. *TrovaRoma,* a special weekly entertainment supplement—good for the coming week—is published in this paper on Thursday.

THE PERFORMING ARTS

If you're in the capital for the opera season, which usually runs from December to June, you can attend a performance at the historic **Teatro dell'Opera (Rome Opera House),** located off Via Nazionale, at Piazza Beniamino Gigli 1 (☎ 06/481601).

In the summer the venue switches to Piazza di Siena. The **Rome Opera Ballet** also performs at the Teatro dell'Opera. Look for announcements of classical concerts that take place in churches and other venues.

Roman rusticity is combined with theatrical flair at **Fantasie di Trastevere,** Via di Santa Dorotea 6 (☎ **06/5881671**), the "people's theater" where the famous actor Petrolini made his debut. Waiters dressed in regional garb serve with drama. The cuisine isn't subtle, but it's bountiful. Expect to pay 75,000–85,000L ($48–$54.40) for a full meal. Your first drink will cost 35,000L ($22.40). Some two dozen folk singers and musicians in regional costumes perform, making it a festive affair. Meals are served daily beginning at 8pm, and piano bar music is offered from 8:30 to 9:30pm, followed by the show, lasting from 9:30 to 10:30pm.

THE CLUB & MUSIC SCENE

Nightclubs

Arciliuto. Piazza Monte Vecchio 5. ☎ **06/6879419.** Cover (including one drink) 35,000L ($22.40). Closed July 20–Sept 3.

Arciliuto, reputedly the former studio of Raphael, is one of the most romantic candlelit spots in Rome. Mon–Sat 10pm–2am guests enjoy a musical salon ambience, listening to both a guitarist and a flutist. The evening's presentation also includes live Neapolitan songs, and new Italian madrigals, even current hits from Broadway or London's West End.

Folkstudio. Via Frangipane 42. ☎ **06/4871063.** Tickets 10,000–20,000L ($6.40–$12.80), plus a one-time membership fee of 5,000L ($3.20).

It prides itself on a battered and well-used venue that resembles "an old underground cantina" from the earliest days of the hippie era. The PA system and lighting aren't very sophisticated, but the ambience is refreshing and can be fun, and the musical acts manage to draw some surprisingly likable performers of old-fashioned soul music, gospel, funk, and folk and traditional music. Some kind of act is presented Tues–Sun 9:30–11pm. No drinks are served inside, as the place considers itself a concert hall rather than a nightclub. Closed July–late Sept.

La Cabala/The Blue Bar/Hostaria dell'Orso. Via dei Soldiati 25. ☎ **06/6864221.** No cover, but a 15,000–35,000L ($9.60–$22.40) one-drink minimum in the Blue Bar and La Cabala.

The setting is a 14th-century palazzo, near Piazza Navona. In the cellar, the Blue Bar is a moody but mellow enclave featuring cocktails and music from two pianists and guitarists. On the street level is a formal restaurant serving international cuisine, the Hostaria dell'Orso. One floor above street level is La Cabala, a disco that attracts a well-dressed, over-25 crowd. The restaurant serves dinner only, Mon–Sat 7:30pm–midnight. The Blue Bar and La Cabala are open Mon–Sat 10:30pm–3 or 4am.

Yes, Brazil. Via San Francesco a Ripa 103. ☎ **06/5816267.** No cover.

This is one of Rome's most animated and popular Latin American nightspots; it attracts mobs of Italians and South Americans who dip and sway to dance steps that usually manage to be some derivation of Brazil's most famous dance, the samba. There's live music every night of the week. It's open nightly 9:30pm–2am.

Jazz, Soul & Funk

Alexanderplatz. Via Ostia 9. ☎ **06/39742171.** 3-month membership 12,000L ($7.70).

You can hear jazz Mon–Sat 9pm–2am, with live music beginning at 10:15pm. A whisky goes for 10,000L ($6.40). There's also a restaurant, with a good kitchen.

Big Mama. Vicolo San Francesco a Ripa 18. ☎ **06/5812551.** Cover: none for minor shows, 20,000–30,000L ($12.80–$19.20) cover for big acts, plus a one-time 20,000L ($12.80) membership.

Big Mama is a hangout for jazz and blues musicians where you're likely to meet the up-and-coming jazz stars of tomorrow. But sometimes the big names appear as well. The club is open Mon–Sat 9pm–1:30am (closed July–Sept).

Gilda. Via Mario dei Fiori 97. ☎ **06/6784838.** Cover (including one drink) 40,000L ($25.60).

Gilda is an adventurous combination of nightclub, disco, and restaurant known for the glamorous acts it books. The artistic direction assures first-class shows, a well-run restaurant, and disco music played between the live musical acts. The restaurant and pizzeria open at 9:30pm and occasionally present shows. The nightclub, opening at midnight, presents music of the 1960s as well as modern recordings. The club stays open until 4am.

Gay Clubs

Angelo Azzuro. Via Cardinal Merry del Val 13. ☎ **06/5800472.** Cover (including an obligatory first drink) 10,000L ($6.40) Fri and Sun, 20,000L ($12.80) Sat.

This gay "hot spot," deep in the heart of Trastevere, is open Fri–Sun 11pm–4am. No food is served, nor is live music presented. Men dance with men to recorded music, and women are also invited to patronize the club. Friday is for women only.

The Hangar. Via in Selci 69. ☎ **06/4881397.** No cover.

This is the premier gay bar in Rome, on one of the city's oldest streets, adjacent to the Roman Forum. Each of the establishment's two bars contains its own independent sound system. Women are welcome any night except Monday, when videos and entertainment for gay men are featured. The busiest nights are Saturday, Sunday, and Monday, when as many as 500 clients cram inside. Open Wed–Mon 10:30pm–2:30am (closed 3 weeks in Aug).

Joli Coeur. Via Sirte 5. ☎ **06/86215827.** Cover (including the first drink) 10,000L ($6.40).

Open only Sat–Sun 10:30pm–2am, this bar caters mainly to gay women. Saturday night is reserved for women only, although Sunday the crowd can be mixed.

L'Alibi. Via Monte Testaccio 44. ☎ **06/5743448.** Cover 10,000L ($6.40) Thurs, 12,000L ($7.70) Wed and Fri–Sun.

L'Alibi, in the Testaccio sector, away from the heart of Rome, is a year-round venue on many a gay man's agenda. The crowd, however, tends to be mixed, both Roman and international, straight and gay, male and female. One room is devoted to dancing. Open Wed–Sun 11pm–5am. Take bus no. 20N or 30N from Largo Argentina near the Piramide.

THE BAR & CAFE SCENE

The **Caffè de Paris,** Via Vittorio Veneto 90 (☎ **06/4885284**), rises and falls in popularity depending on the decade. In the 1950s it was a haven for the fashionable and now it's a popular restaurant in summer where you can sit at the counter along a bar or select a table inside. If the weather's right, the tables spill right out onto the sidewalk and the passing crowd walks through the maze. A cup of coffee costs 6,000L ($3.85) if you sit outside, but only 1,200L (75¢) if you stand at the bar. Open Thurs–Tues 8am–1am.

The **Canova Café,** Piazza del Popolo (☎ **06/3612231**), has a sidewalk terrace for pedestrian-watching, plus a snack bar, a restaurant, and a wine shop inside. In summer you'll have access to a courtyard with ivy-covered walls. Expect to spend 1,300L

(85¢) for coffee at the stand-up bar; if ordered at a table, coffee costs 5,300L ($3.40). Food is served daily noon–3:30pm and 7–11pm, but the bar is open daily 7am–midnight or 1am.

The **Caffè Sant'Eustachio,** Piazza Sant'Eustachio 82 (☎ **06/6861309**), one of the city's most celebrated espresso shops, is on a small square near the Pantheon, where the water supply comes from a source outside Rome, which the emperor Augustus funneled into the city with an aqueduct in 19 B.C. Rome's most experienced espresso judges claim that the water plays an important part in the coffee's flavor, although steam forced through ground Brazilian coffee roasted on the premises has an important effect as well. Stand-up coffee at this well-known place costs 1,400L (90¢); if you sit, you'll pay 3,000L ($1.90). Open Tues–Fri and Sun 8:30am–1am, until 1:30am on Sat.

Since 1760, **Antico Caffè Greco,** Via Condotti 86 (☎ **06/6791700**), has been Rome's poshest and most fashionable coffee bar. Attired in the trappings of the turn of the century, it has for years enjoyed a reputation as the gathering place of the literati. In the front is a wooden bar, and beyond that a series of small salons, decorated in a 19th-century style. You sit at marble-top tables of Napoleonic design, against a backdrop of gold or red damask, romantic paintings, and antique mirrors. Cappuccino costs 8,000L ($5.10). Open Mon–Sat 8am–9pm (closed 10 days in Aug).

DAY TRIPS FROM ROME

TIVOLI   Tivoli, known as Tibur to the ancient Romans, was the playground of emperors. Today its reputation continues unabated: It's the most popular half-day jaunt from Rome.

The town of Tivoli is 20 miles east of Rome on Via Tiburtina—about an hour's drive with traffic. You can also take public transportation: Take Metro Linea B to the end of the line, the Rebibbia station; after exiting the station, take an Acotral bus the rest of the way to Tivoli; buses generally depart about every 20 minutes during the day.

While the ✪ **Villa d'Este,** Piazza Trento, Viale delle Centro Fontane (☎ **0774/312070**), is just a dank Renaissance palace with second-rate paintings that's hardly worth the trek from Rome, its gardens—designed by Pirro Ligorio—dim the luster of Versailles. Visitors descend the cypress-studded slope to the bottom, and on their way are rewarded with everything from lilies to gargoyles spouting water, torrential streams, and waterfalls. The loveliest fountain—on this there is some agreement—is the **Fontana del'Ovato,** designed by Ligorio. But nearby is the most spectacular achievement—the **hydraulic organ fountain,** dazzling visitors with its water jets in front of a baroque chapel, with four maidens who look tipsy. The best walk is along the promenade, which has 100 spraying fountains. When the water jets are set at full power, admission is 8,000L ($5.10) for adults, 5,000L ($3.20) at other times, and always free for those 17 and under and seniors 60 and over. Open Nov–Jan, daily 9am–4pm; Feb, daily 9am–5pm; Mar and Oct, daily 9am–5:30pm; Apr and Sept, daily 9am–6:30pm; and May–Aug, daily 9am–6:45pm.

Whereas the Villa d'Este dazzles with artificial glamour, the **Villa Gregoriana,** Largo Sant'Angelo (☎ **0774/334522**), relies more on nature. The gardens were built by Pope Gregory XVI in the 19th century. At one point on the circuitous walk carved along a slope, visitors stand and look out onto Tivoli's most panoramic waterfall (Aniene). The trek to the bottom on the banks of the Anio is studded with grottoes and balconies that open onto the chasm. From one belvedere there's an exciting

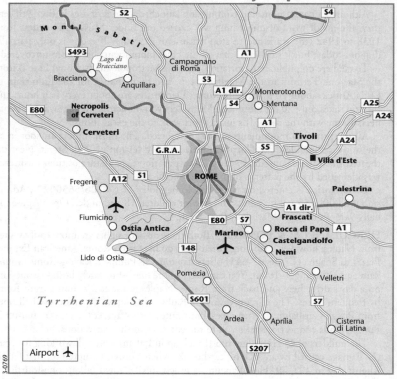

3-0769

Airport ✈

view of the Temple of Vesta on the hill. Admission is 2,500L ($1.60). Open daily 9am–1 hour before sunset.

Of all the Roman emperors dedicated to *la dolce vita,* the globe-trotting Hadrian spent the last 3 years of his life in the grandest style. Less than 4 miles from Tivoli he built his great estate—the ✪ **Villa Adriana (Hadrian's Villa),** Via di Villa Adriana (☎ **0774/530203**)—and filled acre after acre with some of the architectural wonders he'd seen on his many trips. Hadrian directed the construction of much more than a villa—a self-contained world for a vast royal entourage, the guards required to protect them, and the hundreds of servants needed to bathe them, feed them, and satisfy their libidos. On the estate were theaters, baths, temples, fountains, gardens, and canals bordered with statuary. For a glimpse of what the villa once was, see the plastic reconstruction at the entrance. Admission is 8,000L ($5.10) for adults, free for those 17 and under and seniors 60 and over. Open daily 9am–sunset (about 6:30pm in summer, 4pm Nov–Mar).

OSTIA ANTICA   This major attraction is particularly interesting to those who can't make it to Pompeii. At the mouth of the Tiber, this was the port of ancient Rome. Through it were funneled riches from the far corners of the empire. It was founded in the 4th century B.C., and became a major port and naval base primarily under two later emperors: Claudius and Trajan. A thriving, prosperous city developed, full of temples, baths, theaters, and patrician homes. Ostia Antica flourished for about eight centuries before it began eventually to wither and the wholesale business of carting off its art treasures began.

Although a papal-sponsored commission launched a series of digs in the 19th century, the major work of unearthing was carried out under Mussolini's orders from 1938 to 1942 (the work had to stop because of the war). The city is only partially dug out today, but it's believed that all the chief monuments have been uncovered.

To get here on public transportation, take the Metropolitana (subway) Line B from the Stazione Termini to the Magliana stop, and then change for the Lido train to Ostia Antica, about 16 miles from Rome. Departures are about every half hour, and the trip takes only 20 minutes. The Metro lets you off across the highway that connects Rome with the coast. It's just a short walk to the excavations.

All the principal monuments are clearly labeled. The most important spot in all the ruins is **Piazzale delle Corporazioni,** an early version of Wall Street. Near the theater, this square contained nearly 75 corporations; the nature of their businesses was identified by the patterns of preserved mosaics.

Ostia Antica is entered on Viale dei Romagnoli 717 (☎ **06/5650022**). Admission is 8,000L ($5.12) for adults and free for children 18 and under. Open Apr–Sept, daily 9am–6pm; Oct–Mar, daily 9am–5pm.

HERCULANEUM & POMPEII Both these ancient sights are more easily visited from Naples; however, many organized tours go here from Rome. American Express, Piazza di Spagna (☎ **06/67-641**) offers day tours to Pompeii, leaving Rome around 7am and returning 9–10pm. You can also explore one—but rarely both—attractions on a day's drive here and back from Rome. Naples is about 2^1/$_2$ hours from Rome by frequent trains. The Circumvesuviana Railway in Naples departs every half hour from Piazza Garibaldi; the trip takes 45 minutes each way. At the railway station in Pompeii, bus connections take you to the entrance to the excavations.

The builders of ✪ **Herculaneum** (Ercolano in Italian) were still working to repair the damage caused by an A.D. 62 earthquake when Vesuvius erupted on that fateful August day in A.D. 79. Herculaneum, a much smaller town (about one-fourth the size of Pompeii), didn't start to come to light again until 1709, when Prince Elbeuf launched the unfortunate fashion of tunneling through it for treasures. The prince was more intent on profiting from the sale of objets d'art than in uncovering a dead Roman town.

Subsequent excavations at the site, **Ufficio Scavi di Ercolano,** Corso Resina, Ercolano (☎ **081/7390963**), have been slow. Herculaneum is not completely dug out today.

All the streets and buildings of Herculaneum hold interest, especially the baths (*terme*), divided between those at the forum and those on the outskirts (Terme Suburbane, near the more elegant villas). The municipal baths, which segregated the sexes, are larger, but the ones at the edge of town are more lavishly adorned. Important private homes to see include the "House of the Bicentenary," the "House of the Wooden Cabinet," the "House of the Wooden Partition," and the "House of Poseidon (Neptune) and Amphitrite," the last containing what is the best-known mosaic discovered in the ruins. The finest example of how the aristocracy lived is provided by a visit to the "Casa dei Cervi," named the House of the Stags because of sculpture found inside.

The ruins may be visited daily 9am–1 hour before sunset. Admission is 12,000L ($7.70) for adults and free for children 17 and under and seniors 60 and over. To reach the archeological zone, take the regular train service from Naples on the Circumvesuviana Railway, a 20-minute ride leaving about every half hour from Corso Garibaldi 387; or take bus no. 255 from Piazza Municipio. Otherwise, it's a 4^1/$_2$-mile drive on the autostrada to Salerno (turn off at Ercolano).

When Vesuvius erupted in A.D. 79, Pliny the Younger, who later recorded the event, thought the end of the world had come. Lying 15 miles south of Naples, the ruined Roman city of ✪ **Pompeii** (Pompei in Italian) has been dug out from the inundation of volcanic ash and pumice stone rained on it by Vesuvius in the year A.D. 79. At the excavations, the life of 19 centuries ago is vividly experienced.

The **Ufficio Scavi di Pompei** is entered at Piazza Esedra (☎ **081/8611051**). The most elegant of the patrician villas, the **House of Vettii** has a courtyard, statuary (such as a two-faced Janus), paintings, and a black-and-red Pompeiian dining room frescoed with cupids. The second important villa, near the Porto Ercolano (Herculaneum Gate), lies outside the walls. The **House of Mysteries** (Villa dei Misteri) is reached by going out Viale alla Villa dei Misteri. What makes the villa exceptional, aside from its architectural features, are its remarkable frescoes. The **House of the Faun** (Casa del Fauno), so called because of a bronze statue of a dancing faun found there, takes up a city block and has four different dining rooms and two spacious peristyle gardens. In the center of town is the **Forum**—although rather small, it was the heart of Pompeiian life.

The excavations may be visited daily 9am–1 hour before sunset. Admission is 12,000L ($7.70) for adults and free for children 17 and under and seniors 60 and over.

2 Florence & Tuscany

No other city in Europe, with the exception of Venice, lives off its past in the way Florence does. The Renaissance began here. Florence is a bit foreboding and architecturally severe; many of its palazzi, as was the Medici style, look like fortresses. But you must remember that when these structures were built the aim was to keep foreign enemies at bay. And these facades guard treasures within, as the thousands of visitors who overrun the narrow streets know and appreciate.

Ever since the 19th century, the city has been visited by seemingly half the world—the city has impressed some hard-to-impress people, including Mark Twain, who found it overwhelmed with "tides of color that make all the sharp lines dim and faint and turn the old city to a city of dreams." Even Albert Camus, Henry James, and Stendhal were impressed.

It may appear that Florence is caught in a time warp—a Medici returning to the city from the past would have no trouble finding his way around. But Florence virtually pulsates with modern life. Students racing to and from the university quarter add vibrance to the city, and it's amusing to watch the way many local businesspeople avoid the city's impossible traffic today: They whiz by on Vespas while cars are stalled in traffic.

Florentines like to present *una bella figura* (a good appearance) to the rest of the world and are incredibly upset when that appearance is attacked, as in the case of the May 1993 bombing of the Uffizi that cost them many treasures. The entire city rallied to reopen this treasure trove of Renaissance and other works of art.

Don't miss this city, even on the most rushed of European itineraries. There's nothing like it anywhere else. Venice and Rome are too different from Florence to invite meaningful comparisons. One myth you must not believe is that Florence is becoming the Los Angeles of Italy. How did that rumor get started? Perhaps because Florentines have the highest per capita number of cellular phones in Europe. That's because they're trying to be modern and keep up with the changing world, but they also know you're coming to pay homage to their glorious past and not for their achievements of today.

Florence is an ideal base from which to explore the district of Tuscany. Though increasingly built up, Tuscany still has enough old hill towns and rolling hills studded with olives and grapevines to attract the romantic. Tuscany is the heart of Italy, and its Tuscan dialect, the speech of Dante and Petrarch, is the country's textbook Italian. Florence and Siena are the chief drawing cards, but Fiesole (right outside Florence) and Pisa also have their allure.

ONLY IN FLORENCE

Sipping Coffee on Piazza della Signoria Find a cafe table and order a cappuccino and the day is yours. This ancient center of city life is one of the world's most dramatic squares and the setting for many epic moments in Florence's history, including Savonarola's "bonfire of the vanities," in which Florentines burned such precious items as paintings to "purify" themselves. The reformer ended up getting set afire himself. Today the square is home to the Loggia dei Lanzi, with Cellini's *Perseus* holding a beheaded Medusa (at present under repair). Michelangelo's *David* on the square is a copy, however.

Checking Out Piazza del Duomo's Architectural Wonders In the heart of Florence, this is a treasure of Renaissance architecture, dominated by the Duomo, the Cathedral of Santa Maria del Fiore. Capped by Brunelleschi's dome—an amazing architectural feat—the Duomo dominates the skyline. Visitors also flock here to see the neighboring bell tower, one of the most beautiful in all of Italy, and the Baptistry across the way with its famous doors, jewels among Italian Renaissance sculpture.

Shopping for Gold on the Ponte Vecchio The oldest of Florence's bridges is flanked by jewelry stores and will carry you across the Arno to the left bank. The shops peddle exquisite jewelry at an unprecedented rate. Many of the great artists of Florence began as goldsmiths, including Ghiberti and Donatello and ending with Cellini. The Corridoio Vasariano runs the length of the Ponte Vecchio—built by Vasari in just 5 months. Stand on the bridge at sunset, when it becomes a stream of molten gold itself.

Escaping to Fiesole This ancient town is on a hill overlooking Florence and offers the greatest panoramic views of the city of the Renaissance and the Arno Valley. Founded by the Etruscans as early as the 7th century B.C., it lures you to its Piazza Mino da Fiesole, the center of local life. The air is always fresh and clean here and you don't have to visit any special sights—just enjoy Fiesole for itself.

Staring in Awe at Michelangelo's *David* The world's most reproduced statue resides at the Galleria dell'Accademia. The artist's study of the male anatomy has been hailed as "flawless," though Michelangelo had hardly turned 26 when he began the 4-year project. The statue has never met with universal approval and has been the subject of cruel jeers and even rotten egg attacks over the years—one historian called David "an awkward overgrown actor at one of our minor theaters, without his clothes." But most art lovers view David as an enduring legacy of the ideals of the High Renaissance.

Spending a Day at the Uffizi When the last grand duchess of the Medici family died, she bequeathed to the people of Tuscany a wealth of Renaissance and classical art. The paintings and sculpture had been accumulated over three centuries that witnessed the height of the Renaissance. It's waiting for you today in a palace from the 16th century that Vasari designed for Cosimo I. Everyone has his or her favorites—ours is Botticelli's *Allegory of Spring* or *Primavera.* It's a gem, often called a symphony because you can listen to it. The three graces, in lyrical composition, form the painting's chief claim to greatness.

ORIENTATION

ARRIVING   By Plane   If you're flying from New York, the best air connection is Rome, where you can board a domestic flight to the **Galileo Galilei Airport** at Pisa (☎ **050/500707**), 58 miles west of Florence. You can then take an express train to Florence in an hour. There's also a small domestic airport, **Amerigo Vespucci,** on Via del Termine, near A11 (☎ **055/373498**), 3¹/₂ miles northwest of Florence, a 15-minute drive. This airport can be reached by city bus service available on the ATAF line (no. 62), departing from the main Santa Maria Novella rail terminal. Domestic air service is provided by **Alitalia** at Lungarno degli Acciaiuoli 10–12 in Florence (☎ **055/27881**).

By Train   If you're coming north from Rome, count on a 2- to 3-hour trip, depending on your connection. The **Santa Maria Novella rail station,** in Piazza della Stazione, adjoins Piazza di Santa Maria Novella. For railway information, call **055/288785.** Some trains into Florence stop at the **Stazione Campo di Marte,** on the eastern side of Florence. A 24-hour bus service (no. 91) runs between the two rail terminals.

By Bus   Long-distance buses service Florence, run by **SITA,** Viale Cadorna 103–105 (☎ **055/483651**), and **Lazzi Eurolines,** Piazza della Stazione 4–6 (☎ **055/215154**). SITA connects Florence with such Tuscan hill towns as Siena, Arezzo, Pisa, and San Gimignano, and Lazzi Eurolines provides service from such cities as Rome and Naples.

By Car   Autostrada A1 connects Florence with both the north and the south of Italy. Drivers need about an hour to reach Florence from Bologna and about 3 hours from Rome in the south (or vice versa). The Tyrrhenian coast is only an hour from Florence on A11 heading west. Florence lies 172 miles north of Rome, 65 miles west of Bologna, and 185 miles south of Milan. Use a car only to get to Florence. Don't even contemplate its use once there.

VISITOR INFORMATION   Contact the **Azienda Promozione Turistica,** Via A. Manzoni 16 (☎ **055/2346284**), open Mon–Sat 8:30am–1:30pm. Another helpful office handling data about Florence and Tuscany is at Via Cavour 1R (☎ **055/290832**), open Mon–Sat 8am–1:45pm.

CITY LAYOUT   The city is split by the **Arno River,** which usually looks serene and peaceful but can turn ferocious with floodwaters on rare occasions. The major monumental and historical core lies on the north ("right") side of the river. But the "left" side (called the Oltrarno) is not devoid of attractions. Many long-time visitors frequent the left bank for its tantalizing trattoria meals; they also maintain that the shopping here is less expensive. Even the most hurried visitor will want to cross over to the left bank to see the Pitti Palace with its many art treasures and walk through the Giardini di Boboli, a series of formal gardens.

The Arno is spanned by eight bridges, of which the **Ponte Vecchio,** with jewelry stores on either side, is the most celebrated. The Ponte S. Trinità is the second most important bridge spanning the Arno. After crossing it you can continue along **Via dei Tornabuoni,** the most important right-bank shopping street. At the Ponte Vecchio you can walk, again on the right bank, along Via Por Santa Maria, which will become Calimala. This will lead you into **Piazza della Repubblica,** a commercial district known for its cafes.

Florence Attractions & Accommodations

Attractions:
Basilica di San Lorenzo 10
Basilica di Santa Croce 16
Basilica di Santa Maria
  Novella 12
Battistero San Giovanni 7
Campanile 9
Cappelle Medici 11
Casa Buonarroti 15
Casa di Dante 13
Cathedral of Santa Maria
  del Fiore (Duomo) 6
Galleria degli Uffizi 18
Galleria dell'Accademia 2
Giardini di Boboli 22
Museo Archeologico 4
Museo dell'Opera del
  Duomo 8
Museo di San Marco 1
Museo Nazionale del
  Bargello 14
Palazzo Medici-Riccardi 5
Palazzo Pitti 21
Palazzo Vecchio 17
Piazzale Michelangiolo 25
Ponte Vecchio 19
Ospedale degli
  Innocenti 3
Santa Maria
  del Carmine 24
Santa Trinita 20
Santo Spirito 23

Accommodations:
Albergo Losanna 13
Grand Hotel 7
Hermitage Hotel 9
Hotel Astoria Palazzo
  Gaddi 3
Hotel Augustus 8
Hotel Casci 15
Hotel de la Ville 4
Hotel Europa 14
Hotel Excelsior 6
Hotel Mona Lisa 11
Hotel Regency 12
Hotel Vasari 1
Romantik Hotel J and J 10
Tornabuoni Beacci 5
Villa Azalée 2

Church ✝   Post Office ✉
Information ⓘ

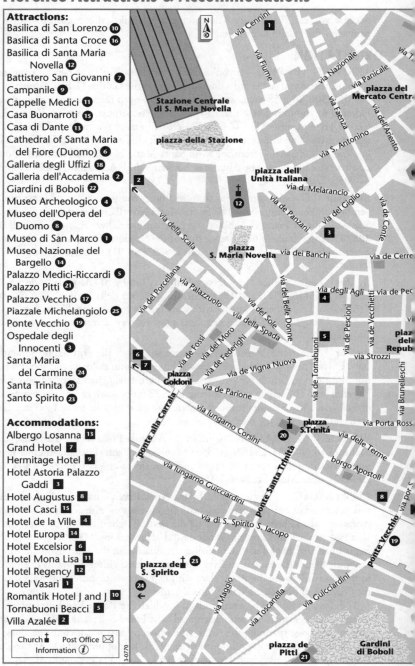

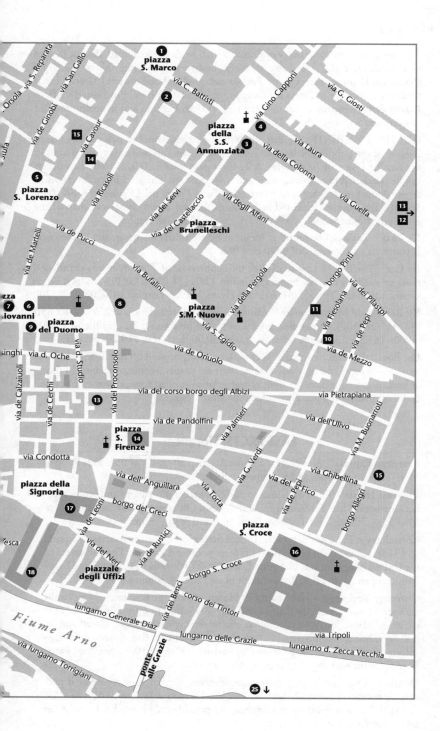

From here, you can take Via Roma, which leads directly into **Piazza di San Giovanni.** Here you'll find the baptistery and its neighboring sibling, the larger **Piazza del Duomo,** with a world-famous cathedral and bell tower by Giotto. From the far western edge of Piazza del Duomo, you can take Via del Proconsolo south to **Piazza della Signoria,** to see the landmark Palazzo Vecchio and its sculpture-filled Loggia della Signoria.

GETTING AROUND   By Bus   You must purchase your bus ticket before boarding one of the public vehicles. For 1,400L (90¢), you can ride on any public bus in the city for a total of 70 minutes. A 24-hour pass costs 5,000L ($3.20). Bus tickets can be purchased from tobacconists and news vendors. The local bus station (which serves as the terminal for ATAF city buses) is at Piazza del Duomo 57F (☎ **055/ 56501**). Bus routes are posted at bus stops, but for a comprehensive map of the Florentine bus network, go to the ATAF booth at the rail station.

By Taxi   Taxis can be found at stands at nearly all the major squares in Florence. If you need a radio taxi, call **4390** or **4798.**

By Car   You'll need a car to explore the countryside of Tuscany in any depth, and these are available at **Avis,** Borgo Ognissanti 128R (☎ 055/213629); **Budget,** Borgo Ognissanti 134R (☎ 055/287161); and **Hertz,** Via del Termine 1 (☎ 055/307370).

By Bicycle or Motorscooter   **Alinari** is near the rail station at Via Guelfa 85R (☎ 055/280500). Depending on the model of bike you rent, they'll cost 2,000–5,000L ($1.30–$3.20) per hour or 15,000–30,000L ($9.60–$19.20) per day.

On Foot   Because Florence is so compact, getting around on foot is the ideal way to do it—at times, the only way because there are so many pedestrian zones. In theory at least, pedestrians have the right of way at uncontrolled zebra crossings, but don't count on that should you encounter a speeding Vespa.

FAST FACTS: Florence

American Express   Amex is at Via Dante Alighieri 20–22R (☎ 055/50981), open Mon–Fri 9am–5:30pm and Sat 9am–12:30pm.

Business Hours   From mid-June to mid-September most shops and business offices are open Mon–Fri 9am–1pm and 4–8pm. Off-season hours, in general, are Mon 3:30–7:30pm and Tues–Sat 9am–1pm and 3:30–7:30pm.

Consulates   The Consulate of the **United States** is at Lungarno Amerigo Vespucci 46 (☎ 055/2398276), open Mon–Fri 8am–noon and 2–4pm. The Consulate of the **United Kingdom** is at Lungarno Corsini 2 (☎ 055/284133), near Piazza Santa Trinità, open Mon–Fri 9:30am–12:30pm and 2:30–4:30pm.

Currency Exchange   Local banks in Florence grant the best rates. Most banks are open Mon–Fri 8:30am–1:30pm and 2:45–3:45pm. The tourist office (see "Orientation," above) exchanges money at official rates when banks are closed and on holidays, but a commission is often charged. You can also go to the Ufficio Informazione booth at the rail station, open daily 7:30am–7:40pm. See "Fast Facts: Rome" for the exchange rate used in this chapter.

Dentists   For a list of English-speaking dentists, consult your consulate if possible or contact Tourist Medical Service, Via Lorenzo il Magnifico 59 (☎ 055/ 475411). Visits without an appointment are possible only Mon–Fri 11am–noon and 5–6pm and Sat 11am–noon.

Doctors   Contact your national consulate for a list of English-speaking physicians. You can also contact Tourist Medical Service, Via Lorenzo il Magnifico 59 (☎ 055/475411). See also "Dentists," above.

Emergencies   For fire, call 115; for an ambulance, call 055/212222; for the police, 113; and for road service, 116.

Hospitals   Call the General Hospital of Santa Maria Nuova, Piazza Santa Maria Nuova 1 (☎ 055/27581).

Lost Property   The lost-and-found office, Oggetti Smarriti, is at Via Circondaria 19 (☎ 055/367943), near the rail terminal.

Luggage Storage   This is available at the Santa Maria Novella train station, in the center of the city at Piazza della Stazione (☎ 055/278785). It's open daily 4:15am–1:45am.

Police   Dial 113 in an emergency. English-speaking foreigners who want to see and talk to the police should go to the Ufficio Stranieri station at Via Zara 2 (☎ 055/49771), where English-speaking personnel are available daily 9am–2pm.

Post Office   The Central Post Office is at Via Pellicceria 3, off Piazza della Repubblica (☎ 055/212305), open Mon–Fri 8:15am–6pm and Sat 8:15am–12:30pm. Stamps are purchased in the main post office at windows 21–22. If you want your mail sent to Italy general delivery (*fermo postal*), have it sent in care of this post office (use the 50100 Firenze postal code). Mail can be picked up at windows 23–24.

Safety   The most violent crimes are rare in Florence, where crime consists mainly of pickpockets who frequent crowded tourist centers, such as the corridors of the Uffizi Galleries. Members of group tours who cluster together are often singled out as victims. Car thefts are relatively common: Don't leave your luggage in an unguarded car, even if it's locked in the trunk. Women should be especially careful in avoiding purse snatchers, some of whom grab a purse while whizzing by on a Vespa, often knocking the woman down. Documents such as passports and extra money are better stored in the safe at your hotel.

Transit Information   For international flights from Galileo Galilei Airport, call 050/500707; for domestic flights at Peretola, call 055/30615; for rail information, dial 055/288785; for long-distance bus information, call 055/215154; and for city buses, dial 055/56501.

ACCOMMODATIONS
On Piazza Ognissanti
Very Expensive

Grand Hotel. Piazza Ognissanti 1, 50123 Firenze. ☎ **800/325-3589** in the U.S. and Canada, or 055/288781. Fax 055/217400. 90 rms, 17 suites. A/C MINIBAR TV TEL. 580,000–650,000L ($371.20–$416) double; from 1,000,000L ($640) suite. AE, DC, MC, V. Parking from 50,000L ($32). Bus: 6 or 17.

The Grand Hotel is a bastion of luxury, fronting a car-clogged Renaissance piazza across from the Excelsior. Neither the Grand nor the Excelsior, though among the top three or four hotels of Florence, has the exclusivity of the more refined Regency. A hotel of history and tradition, the Grand is known for its halls and salons. Its rooms and suites have a refined elegance, and the most desirable overlook the Arno. Each room contains silks, brocades, and real or reproduction antiques. A highlight of the hotel is the Winter Garden, an enclosed court lined with arches.

Expensive

♻ **Hotel Excelsior.** Piazza Ognissanti 3, 50123 Firenze. ☎ **800/325-3535** in the U.S. and Canada, or 055/264201. Fax 055/210278. 172 rms, 23 suites. A/C MINIBAR TV TEL. 550,000–620,000L ($352–$396.80) double; from 900,000L ($576) suite. AE, DC, MC, V. Parking 50,000L ($32). Bus: 6 or 17.

The Excelsior, on a car-filled Renaissance square in a neo-Renaissance palace, is the ultimate in luxury. Cosmpolitan and sophisticated, it has the best-trained staff in town, but in recent years more tranquil and less commercial establishments, including the Regency, have attracted away customers. But if you like glamour and glitz, stay here. The opulent rooms have 19th-century Florentine antiques and sumptuous fabrics. In these old palaces, expect the accommodations to come in a variety of configurations. Il Cestello, the hotel's deluxe restaurant, attracts an upper-crust clientele.

On or Near Piazza Massimo d'Azeglio

Expensive

♻ **Hotel Regency.** Piazza Massimo d'Azeglio 3, 50121 Firenze. ☎ **055/245247.** Fax 055/2346735. 29 rms, 5 suites. A/C MINIBAR TV TEL. 380,000–600,000L ($243.20–$384) double; from 800,000L ($512) suite. Rates include breakfast. AE, DC, MC, V. Parking 45,000L ($28.80). Bus: 6.

The Regency is for the cognoscenti, an intimate villa of taste and exclusivity. It's only a 15-minute stroll to the cathedral. This well-built old-style villa, a member of Relais & Châteaux, has its own garden across from a park in a residential area of the city. This luxurious hideaway, filled with stained glass, paneled walls, and reproduction antiques, offers exquisitely furnished rooms. The dining room, Relais le Jardin, is renowned for its *alta cucina*.

Inexpensive

Albergo Losanna. Via Vittorio Alfieri 9, 50121 Firenze. ☎ and fax **055/245840.** 10 rms, 4 with bath; 1 suite. TEL. 90,000L ($57.60) double without bath, 110,000L ($70.40) double with bath; 200,000L ($128) suite. Rates include breakfast. MC, V. Parking 30,000–35,000L ($19.20–$22.40). Bus: 6.

A good choice, the Albergo Losanna is a tiny family-run place off Viale Antonio Gramsci, between Piazzale Donatello and Piazza Massimo d'Azeglio. It offers utter simplicity and cleanliness. The rooms, all doubles, are homey and well kept, but the furnishings are simple and a bit tired.

Near the Railway Station

Expensive

Hotel Astoria Palazzo Gaddi. Via del Giglio 9, 50123 Firenze. ☎ **055/2398095.** Fax 055/214632. 90 rms, 5 suites. A/C MINIBAR TV TEL. 360,000L ($230.40) double; 450,000L ($288) suite. Rates include buffet breakfast. AE, DC, MC, V. Parking 40,000L ($25.60) nearby. Bus: 19, 22, 23, 29, or 30.

In spite of its location in a setting of cheap railroad station hotels, this is an impressive Renaissance palace. In the 17th century John Milton wrote parts of *Paradise Lost* in one of the rooms. The Astoria has been renovated and turned into a serviceable and enduring choice, with a helpful staff. From the rooms on the upper floors, you'll have a view over the terracotta rooftops. The rooms have stylish traditional furnishings for the most part; some are decorated in a more modern style.

Inexpensive

♻ **Hotel Casci.** Via Cavour 13, 50129 Firenze. ☎ **055/211686.** Fax 055/2396461. 25 rms. TV TEL. 100,000–150,000L ($64–$96) double; 135,000–200,000L ($86.40–$128) triple; 170,000–250,000L ($108.80–$160) quad. Rates include breakfast. AE, DC, MC, V. Parking 35,000–40,000L ($22.40–$25.60). Bus: 1, 6, 7, 11, or 17.

The Casci is a well-run little hotel in the historic district, 200 yards from the main rail station and 100 yards from Piazza del Duomo. The building dates from the 14th century, and some of the public rooms feature the original frescoes. The hotel is both traditional and modern, and the English-speaking reception staff is attentive. The guest rooms are comfortably furnished. Each year four or five rooms are upgraded and renovated.

Hotel Vasari. Via B. Cennini 9–11, 50123 Firenze. ☎ **055/212753.** Fax 055/294246. 30 rms. A/C MINIBAR TV TEL. 150,000–210,000L ($96–$134.40) double. Rates include breakfast. AE, DC, MC, V. Parking 15,000L ($9.60). Bus: 7 or 11.

Built in the 1840s as a private home, the Vasari was for several years the home of 19th-century French poet Alphonse de la Martine. It was a rundown two-star hotel until 1993, when its owners poured money into a renovation and upgraded it to one of the most fairly priced three-star hotels in town. Its three stories are connected by an elevator; the rooms are comfortable, albeit somewhat spartan and clean.

Villa Azalée. Viale Fratelli Rosselli 44, 50123 Firenze. ☎ **055/214242.** Fax 055/268264. 24 rms. A/C MINIBAR TV TEL. 280,000L ($179.20) double; 295,000L ($188.80) triple. Rates include buffet breakfast. AE, DC, MC, V. Parking from 30,000L ($19.20). Bus: 17.

The Villa Azalée, a handsome structure set on a street corner with a big garden, is a remake of a private home built in the 1860s and transformed into a hotel in 1964. The decorating is tasteful: tall white-paneled doors with ornate brass fittings, parquet floors, crystal chandeliers, and antiques intermixed with credible reproductions. The rooms have distinction (one boasts a flouncy canopy bed). The hotel is a 5-minute walk from the rail station. You can rent bicycles at the hotel for 5,000L ($3.20) per day.

ON OR NEAR VIA TORNABUONI
Moderate

Hotel de la Ville. Piazza Antinori 1, 50123 Firenze. ☎ **055/2381805.** Fax 055/2381809. 75 rms, 4 suites. A/C MINIBAR TV TEL. 300,000–448,000L ($192–$286.70) double; 650,000L ($416) suite. Rates include buffet breakfast. AE, DC, MC, V. Parking 40,000L ($25.60). Bus: 22, 31, 32, 36, or 37.

On the most elegant street of the historic center, close to the Arno and the rail station, this recently refurbished hotel has a loyal following among Italian business travelers. It has a conservatively contemporary appearance, with a decor that includes flowering plants, mirror-bright marble floors, and many sitting areas. The rooms are soundproof, with private safes and contemporary decors in muted colors. There's an American-style bar, a breakfast room, and a parking area reserved for guests. Laundry and baby-sitting are available.

Tornabuoni Beacci. Via Tornabuoni 3, 50123 Firenze. ☎ **055/212645.** Fax 055/283594. 29 rms. A/C MINIBAR TV TEL. 230,000–260,000L ($147.20–$166.40) double. Rates include breakfast. AE, DC, MC, V. Parking 30,000L ($19.20). Bus: 14, 31, 32, 36, or 37.

Near the Arno and Piazza S. Trinità, on the principal shopping street, the pensione occupies the top three floors of a 14th-century palazzo. The public rooms have been furnished in a tatty provincial style, with bowls of flowers, parquet floors, a formal fireplace, old paintings, murals, and rugs. The hotel was completely renovated recently, but it still bears an air of old-fashioned gentility. The roof terrace, surrounded by potted plants and flowers, is for breakfast or late-afternoon drinks. Dinner, typically Florentine and Italian dishes, is served here in summer. The view of the nearby churches, towers, and rooftops is worth experiencing. The rooms are moderately well furnished.

NEAR THE DUOMO
Moderate

Hotel Monna Lisa. Borgo Pinti 27, 50121 Firenze. ☎ **055/2479751.** Fax 055/2479755. 30 rms. A/C MINIBAR TV TEL. 400,000L ($256) double; 480,000L ($307.20) triple. Rates include breakfast. AE, DC, MC, V. Parking 20,000L ($12.80). Bus: 14 or 23.

The Hotel Monna Lisa (yes, that's the right spelling) is a privately owned Renaissance palazzo, 4 blocks east of the Duomo. On a narrow street where carts were once driven, the palace's facade is forbiddingly severe, in keeping with the style of its day. But when you enter the reception rooms, you'll find an inviting atmosphere. Most of the great old rooms overlook either an inner patio or a modest rear garden. Each of the salons is handsomely furnished, with fine antiques and oil paintings. The rooms vary greatly—some are quite large, though no two are alike.

Romantik Hotel J and J. Via di Mezzo 20, 50121 Firenze. ☎ **055/234005.** Fax 055/240282. 15 rms, 5 suites. A/C MINIBAR TV TEL. 350,000–450,000L ($224–$288) double; 500,000–575,000L ($320–$368) suite. Rates include breakfast. AE, DC, MC, V. Parking 35,000L ($22.40). Bus: 15.

This charming hotel was built in the 16th century as a monastery. A 5-minute walk from the church of Santa Croce, it underwent a massive restoration in 1990. You'll find many sitting areas throughout, including a flagstone-covered courtyard with stone columns and a salon with vaulted ceilings and several preserved ceiling frescoes. The guest rooms combine an unusual mixture of modern furniture with the monastery's original beamed ceilings. The suites usually contain sleeping lofts and, in some cases, rooftop balconies overlooking Florence's historic core.

Inexpensive

Hotel Europa. Via Cavour 14, 50129 Firenze. ☎ **055/210361.** 13 rms. TV TEL. 130,000–140,000L ($83.20–$89.60) double. Rates include breakfast. AE, DC, MC, V. Bus: 1, 6, or 17.

Two long blocks north of the Duomo, this 16th-century building has functioned as a family-run hotel since 1925. Despite the antique appearance of the simple exterior, much of the interior has been modernized with enough homey touches to remind newcomers of its ongoing administration by members of the Cassim family. All but four of the rooms overlook the back and usually open onto a view of the campanile of the Duomo. Those that face the street are noisier but benefit from double-glazing that keeps out at least some of the traffic noises.

NEAR THE PONTE VECCHIO
Moderate

Hermitage Hotel. Vicolo Marzio 1, Piazza del Pesce I, 50122 Firenze. ☎ **055/287216.** Fax 055/212208. 22 rms. AC TV TEL. 210,000–280,000L ($134.40–$179.20) double. Rates include breakfast. MC, V. Parking 30,000–40,000L ($19.20–$25.60).

The offbeat, intimate Hermitage is a charming place, with a sun terrace on the roof providing a view of much of Florence. You can take your breakfast under a leafy arbor surrounded by potted roses and geraniums. The extrememly small rooms are pleasantly furnished, many with Tuscan antiques, rich brocades, and good beds. The tiled baths are superb and contain lots of gadgets. Those rooms overlooking the Arno have the most scenic view, and they've been fitted with double-glazed windows, which reduces the traffic noise by 40%.

Hotel Augustus. Vicolo del'Oro 5, 50123 Firenze. ☎ **055/283054.** Fax 055/268557. 62 rms, 8 suites. A/C MINIBAR TV TEL. 215,000–430,000L ($137.60–$275.20) double; 260,000–520,000L ($166.40–$332.80) suite. Rates include buffet breakfast. AE, DC, MC, V. Parking 30,000–40,000L ($19.20–$25.60). Bus 7, 13, 14, 16, or 23.

The Augustus is for those who require modern comforts in an historic setting. The Ponte Vecchio is a short stroll away, as is the Uffizi. The exterior is rather pillbox modern, but the interior is light, bright, and comfortable. The expansive lounge and drinking area is like an illuminated cave. Some of the rooms open onto little private balconies with garden furniture. The decor in the rooms consists of relatively simple provincial pieces.

DINING
NEAR THE RAILWAY STATION
Moderate

✪ **Don Chisciotte.** Via Ridolfi 4R. ☎ **055/475430.** Reservations recommended. Main courses 25,000–30,000L ($16–$19.20). AE, DC, MC, V. Mon 8–10:30pm, Tues–Sat 1–2:30pm and 8–10:30pm. ITALIAN/SEAFOOD.

One floor above the street level in a Florentine palazzo, this restaurant is known for its creative cuisine and changing array of very fresh fish. Menu items are produced with a flourish from the kitchens. The cuisine is creative, based on flavors often enhanced with the boiled-down essence of an unusual assortment of fresh herbs, vegetables, and fish stocks. Examples include pink tagliatelle with shrimp, herbs, and cream sauce; risotto of broccoli and baby squid; and black ravioli colored with squid ink and stuffed with a purée of shrimp and crayfish.

Ristorante Otello. Via degli Orti Oricellari 36R. ☎ **055/216517.** Reservations recommended. Main courses 12,000–30,000L ($7.70–$19.20). AE, DC, MC, V. Daily noon–3pm and 7:30–11pm. Bus: 14, 17, 23, 28, 35, or 62. FLORENTINE.

Beside the train station, the Ristorante Otello is a long-established comfortable Florentine dining room. Its antipasto Toscano is one of the best in town, an array of appetizing hors d'oeuvres that practically becomes a meal in itself. The waiter urges you to "Mangi, mangi, mangi!" ("Eat, eat, eat!") and that's what diners do here, as the victuals at Otello have been known to stir the most lethargic of appetites. The true trencherperson goes on to order one of the succulent pasta dishes, such as spaghetti with baby clams or pappardelle with garlic sauce. The meat and poultry dishes are equally delectable, including sole meunière and veal pizzaiola with lots of garlic.

✪ **Sabatini.** Via de'Panzani 9A. ☎ **055/211559.** Reservations recommended. Main courses 25,000–38,000L ($16–$24.30). AE, DC, MC, V. Tues–Sun 12:30–2:30pm and 7:30–10:30pm. Bus: 14 or 19. FLORENTINE.

Despite its less than chic location near the rail station, Sabatini has long been extolled by Florentines and visitors alike as the finest of the restaurants characteristic of the city. To celebrate our return visit every year, we order the same main course—boiled Valdarno chicken with savory green sauce. Other main courses are delectable, especially the veal scaloppine with artichokes. Of course, you can always order a good sole meunière and the classic beefsteak Florentine.

Inexpensive

Le Fonticine. Via Nazionale 79R. ☎ **055/282106.** Reservations recommended for dinner. Main courses 15,000–25,000L ($9.60–$16). AE, DC, MC, V. Tues–Sat noon–3pm and 7:30–10:30pm. Closed Jan 1–15 and Aug. Bus: 19. TUSCAN/BOLOGNESE.

Le Fonticine used to be part of a convent until owner Silvano Bruci converted both it and its adjoining garden into one of the most hospitable restaurants in Florence. The richly decorated interior contains the second passion of Signor Bruci's life, his collection of original modern paintings. The first passion, as a meal here reveals, is the cuisine he and his wife produce from recipes she collected from her childhood in Bologna. The food, served in copious portions, is both traditional and delectable. Begin with a platter of fresh antipasti, then follow with samplings of three of the most excellent pasta dishes of the day. This might be followed by veal scaloppine.

NEAR PIAZZA SANTA MARIA NOVELLA

Moderate

I Quattro Amici. Via degli Orti Oricellari 29. ☎ **055/215413.** Reservations recommended. Main courses 43,000–70,000L ($27.50–$44.80). AE, DC, MC, V. Daily noon–3pm and 7–10:30pm. Bus: All buses to the train station. SEAFOOD.

Opened in 1990 by four Tuscan entrepreneurs, this restaurant occupies the street level of a modern building near the rail station. Amid a vaguely neoclassical decor, the place serves endless quantities of fish. Specialties include such dishes as pasta with fish sauce and fragments of sausage, fish soup, fried shrimp and squid in the style of Livorno, and grilled, stewed, or baked versions of all the bounty of the Mediterranean. The roast sea bass and roast snapper, flavored with Mediterranean herbs, are among the finest dishes.

Inexpensive

⑤ Sostanza. Via del Porcellana 25R. ☎ **055/212691.** Reservations recommended. Main courses 14,000–28,000L ($8.95–$17.90). No credit cards. Mon–Fri noon–2:10pm and 7:30–9:30pm. Closed Aug and 2 weeks at Christmas. Bus: All buses to the station. FLORENTINE.

Sostanza is a tucked-away little trattoria where working people have gone for years to get excellent, reasonably priced food. It's the city's oldest and most revered trattoria. The small dining room has crowded family tables. The rear kitchen is open, its secrets exposed to diners. Specialties include breaded chicken breast and a succulent T-bone steak. You might also want to try tripe the Florentine way—cut into strips and baked in a casserole with tomatoes, onions, and Parmesan.

⑤ Trattoria Antellesi. Via Faenza 9R. ☎ **055/216990.** Reservations recommended. Main courses 15,000–22,000L ($9.60–$14.10). AE, DC, MC, V. Mon–Sat noon–3pm and 7–10:30pm. Bus: All buses to the station. TUSCAN.

On the ground floor of a 15th-century historic monument, a few steps from the Medici Chapel, this restaurant is devoted almost exclusively to Tuscan recipes that've stood the test of time. Owned by the Italian-American team of Enrico Verrecchia and his Arizona-born wife, Janice, the restaurant prepares at least seven *piatti del giorno* that change according to the availability of the ingredients. Menu items may include tagliatelle with porcini mushrooms or with braised arugula, a spicy-hot penne arrabiata, crespelle alla fiorentina (a Tuscan Renaissance cheesy spinach crêpe introduced to France by Catherine de Medici's kitchen staff), market-fresh fish (generally on Friday), and delicious Valdostana chicken.

NEAR THE DUOMO

Moderate

Trattoria Coco Lezzone. Via del Parioncino 26R. ☎ **055/287178.** Reservations accepted only for groups of 10 or more. Main courses 15,000–50,000L ($9.60–$32). No credit cards. Mon–Sat noon–2:30pm and 7–10pm. Closed last week of July to Aug and Dec 25–Jan 6. Bus: 27 or 31. FLORENTINE.

In Florentine dialect, the establishment's name refers to the sauce-stained apron of the extroverted chef who established this place more than a century ago. Today some of the heartiness of the Tuscan countryside can be purchased for the price of a meal at this duet of tile-covered rooms on a backstreet a short walk from the Duomo.

Florentine "blue bloods" wait with workers crowding in on their lunch hours for a seat at one of the long tables. Go before the rush begins if you want a seat in this bustling trattoria. The rib-sticking fare includes generous portions of boiled meats with a green sauce, pasta fagiole (beans), osso buco, tripe, and beefsteak Florentine.

NEAR PIAZZA DELLA SIGNORIA
Inexpensive
Da Ganino. Piazza dei Cimatori 4R. ☎ **055/214125.** Reservations recommended. Main courses 15,000–25,000L ($9.60–$16). AE, DC, MC, V. Mon–Sat 1–3pm and 8–11pm. Bus: All buses to the Duomo. FLORENTINE/TUSCAN.

Da Ganino is staffed with the kind of waiters who take the quality of your meal as their personal responsibility. This little-known restaurant has vaulted ceilings, glazed walls, and an array of paintings by Florentine artists. Someone will recite to you the frequently changing specialties of the day, which may include well-seasoned versions of Tuscan beans, spinach risotto, grilled veal chops, and Florentine beefsteak on the bone. The delightful tagliatelle con tartufo is the most expensive appetizer because of the truffles used.

Paoli. Via dei Tavolini 12R. ☎ **055/216215.** Reservations required. Main courses 15,000–28,000L ($9.60–$17.90); fixed-price menu 38,000L ($24.30). AE, DC, MC, V. Wed–Mon noon–2:30pm and 7–10:30pm. Closed 3 weeks in Aug. Bus: 14 or 23. TUSCAN/ITALIAN.

Paoli, between the Duomo and Piazza della Signoria, is one of Florence's finest restaurants. It turns out a host of specialties but could be recommended almost solely for its medieval-tavern atmosphere, with arches and ceramics stuck into the walls like medallions. Its pastas are homemade, and the fettuccine alla Paoli is served piping hot and full of flavor. The chef also does a superb rognoncino (kidney) trifolato and sole meunière. A recommendable side dish is piselli (garden peas) alla fiorentina.

ON THE ARNO
Expensive
Harry's Bar. Lungarno Vespucci 22R. ☎ **055/2396700.** Reservations required. Main courses 18,000–33,000L ($11.50–$21.10). AE, MC, V. Mon–Sat noon–3pm and 7–11pm. Closed 1 week in Aug and Dec 18–Jan 8. Bus: 6. ITALIAN.

Harry's Bar, in a prime position on the Arno, is an enclave of expatriate and well-heeled visiting Yankees that deserves its reputation. Patrons can order from an international menu—small but select and beautifully prepared. A specialty is risotto or tagliatelle with ham, onions, and cheese. Harry has created his own tortellini (stuffed pasta), but Harry's hamburger and his club sandwich are the most popular items. The chef also prepares about a dozen specialties every day, like breast of chicken "our way," grilled giant-size scampi, and lean broiled sirloin.

La Capannina di Sante. Piazza Ravenna, adjacent to the Ponte Giovanni da Verrazzano. ☎ **055/688345.** Reservations recommended. Main dishes 20,000–40,000L ($12.80–$25.60); fixed-price menu 90,000L ($57.60). AE, DC, MC, V. Mon–Sat 7:30pm–1am. Closed 1 week in Aug. Bus: 23. SEAFOOD.

The restaurant serves only the best and freshest seafood. On the banks of the Arno, with a river-view terrace for outdoor seating, this unpretentious restaurant has functioned in more or less the same way on and off since 1935. Its specialty is fish, which is prepared simply and healthfully, usually with olive oil or butter and Mediterranean seasonings. Examples include filets of sea bass or turbot, mixed seafood grills, and an occasional portion of veal or steak for anyone who doesn't care for fish.

NEAR THE PONTE VECCHIO
Inexpensive

⊛ **Buca dell'Orafo.** Via Volta dei Girolami 28R. ☎ **055/213619.** Main courses 10,000–30,000L ($6.40–$19.20). No credit cards. Tues–Sat 12:30–2:30pm and 7:30–10:30pm. Closed Aug and 2 weeks in Dec. Bus: 3, 6, 22, 31, or 32. FLORENTINE.

Buca dell'Orafo is a little dive (one of the many cellars or *buca*-type establishments beloved by Florentines). The trattoria is usually stuffed with its regulars, so if you want a seat, go early. Over the years the chef has made little concession to the foreign palate, turning out genuine Florentine specialties, like tripe and mixed boiled meats with a green sauce and stracotto e fagioli (beef braised in a sauce of chopped vegetables and red wine), served with beans in a tomato sauce.

NEAR SANTA CROCE
Moderate

⊛ **Cibreo.** Via dei Macci 118R. ☎ **055/2341100.** Reservations recommended in the restaurant, not accepted in the trattoria. Main courses 40,000L ($25.60) in the restaurant, 15,000L ($9.60) in the trattoria. AE, DC, MC, V accepted, but only in the restaurant. Tues–Sat 12:30–3pm and 8–11pm. Closed late July to early Sept. Bus: 6 or 14. MEDITERRANEAN.

Despite its lack of pretentions, Cibreo is one of the largest eateries in the neighborhood. From a small and impossibly old-fashioned kitchen, it prepares food for a restaurant, a less formal tavern-style trattoria, and a cafe-bar across the surging traffic of the street. The kitchens are noteworthy for not containing a grill and not serving pastas. They specialize in foodstuffs cooked in a wood-burning oven and cold marinated dishes (especially vegetables) that presumably taste better when prepared a day or several hours in advance. Menu items include a sformato (a soufflé made from potatoes and ricotta, served with Parmesan and tomato sauce) and a flan of Parmesan, veal tongue, and artichokes.

La Baraonda. Via Ghibellina 67R. ☎ **055/2341171.** Reservations recommended. Main courses 20,000L ($12.80). AE, DC. Mon 8–10:30pm, Tues–Sat 1–2:30pm and 8–10:30pm. Bus: 14. TUSCAN.

About 80% of the clientele of this bustling trattoria are local residents, many of them merchants and hotel employees from the surrounding neighborhood. Small, gregarious, and well choreographed, the restaurant serves Tuscan cuisine flavored with seasonally available local ingredients. Examples are a changing array of sformato di verdure (vegetable soufflés made from, among other ingredients, artichokes or whatever else is in season), risotto with fresh greens, pennette with broccoli, and a savory version of meatloaf (polpettone in umido) made with veal and fresh tomatoes.

AT PIAZZA ANTINORI
Moderate

Buca Lapi. Via del Trebbio 1R. ☎ **055/213768.** Reservations required for dinner. Main courses 22,000–35,000L ($14.10–$22.40). AE, DC, MC, V. Mon 7:30–10:30pm, Tues–Sat 12:30–2:30pm and 7:30–10:30pm. Closed 2 weeks in Aug. Bus: 22. TUSCAN.

Buca Lapi, a cellar restaurant, is big on glamour, good food, and the enthusiasm of fellow diners. Its decor alone—under the Palazzo Antinori—makes it fun: Vaulted ceilings are covered with travel posters from all over the world. There's a long table of interesting fruits, desserts, and vegetables. The cooks know how to turn out the most classic dishes of the Tuscan kitchen with superb finesse. Specialties include pâté, cannelloni, scampi giganti alla girglia (a super-size shrimp), and bistecca alla fiorentina (local beefsteak). In season, the fagioli toscani all'olio (Tuscan beans in the native olive oil) are a delicacy.

ACROSS THE ARNO
Inexpensive
Mamma Gina. Borgo Sant'Jacopo 37R. ☎ **055/2396009.** Reservations required for dinner. Main courses 17,000–25,000L ($10.90–$16). AE, DC, MC, V. Mon–Sat noon–2:30pm and 7–10pm. Closed Aug 7–21. Bus: 6. TUSCAN.

Mamma Gina is a rustic left-bank restaurant that's a winner for fine foods prepared in the traditional bustling manner. This restaurant is named after its founding matriarch (Mamma Gina), whose legend has continued despite her death in the 1980s. This exceptional trattoria, well worth the trek across the Ponte Vecchio, is a center for hearty Tuscan fare. The menu items are rich, savory, and tied to the seasons and include such dishes as cannelloni Mamma Gina (stuffed with a purée of minced meats, spices, and vegetables), tagliolini with artichoke hearts or mushrooms and whatever else is in season at the time, and chicken breast "Mamma Gina," baked in the northern Italian style with prosciutto and Emmenthaler cheese.

ATTRACTIONS

Florence was the fountainhead of the Renaissance, the city of Dante and Boccaccio. Characteristically, it was the city of Machiavelli and, uncharacteristically, of Savonarola. For 3 centuries it was dominated by the Medici family, patrons of the arts and masters of assassination. But it's chiefly through its artists that we know of the apogee of the Renaissance: Ghiberti, Fra Angelico, Donatello, Brunelleschi, Botticelli, and the incomparable Leonardo and Michelangelo.

Piazza della Signoria, though never completed, is one of the most beautiful in Italy. On the square is the Fountain of Neptune, the sea god surrounded by creatures from the deep, as well as frisky satyrs and nymphs. Near the fountain is the spot where Savonarola walked his last mile. This zealous monk was a fire-and-brimstone reformer who rivaled Dante in conjuring up the punishment hell would inflict on sinners. For centuries Michelangelo's *David* stood in this piazza, but it was moved to the Academy Gallery in the 19th century. The work you see here today is an inferior copy.

On the piazza, the 14th-century **Loggia della Signoria** (sometimes called the Loggia dei Lanzi) is a gallery of sculpture that often depicts fierce, violent scenes. The best piece is a rare work by Benvenuto Cellini, the goldsmith and tell-all autobiographer. Critics have said that his exquisite but ungentlemanly *Perseus,* who holds the severed head of Medusa, is the most significant Florentine sculpture since Michelangelo's *Night* and *Day.* (At present, the sculpture is undergoing repairs and is covered over.)

For a view of the wonders of Florence below and Fiesole above, climb aboard bus no. 13 from the central station and head for **Piazzale Michelangiolo,** a 19th-century belvedere with a view seen in many a Renaissance painting. It's best at dusk, when the purple-fringed Tuscan hills form a frame for Giotto's bell tower, Brunelleschi's dome, and the towering stones sticking up from the Palazzo Vecchio. Another copy of Michelangelo's *David* dominates the square.

SIGHTSEEING SUGGESTIONS

If You Have 1 Day   You'll have to accept the inevitable—you can see only a fraction of Florence's three-star attractions. Go to the Uffizi Galleries as soon as they open and concentrate only on some of the masterpieces. Before 1:30pm, visit the Accademia to see Michelangelo's *David* . . . at least that. Have lunch on Piazza della Signoria, dominated by the Palazzo Vecchio, and admire the statues in the Loggia della Signoria. After lunch, visit the Duomo and Baptistery, then pay a late-afternoon call at the open-air straw market, the Mercanto San Lorenzo, before crossing the Ponte Vecchio at sunset. Finish a very busy day with a hearty Tuscan dinner in one of Florence's many bucas (cellar restaurants).

If You Have 2 Days   Spend your first day as above. On day 2, return to the Uffizi for a more thorough look at Italy's most important museum. In the afternoon, visit the Pitti Palace, on the other side of the Arno, and wander through the Galleria Palatina, with its 16th- and 17th-century masterpieces, including 11 works by Raphael. Then stroll through the adjoining Boboli Gardens. At sunset, go again to the Duomo and the Baptistery for a much better look.

If You Have 3 Days   Spend your first two days as above. In the morning of day 3, visit the Palazzo Vecchio on Piazza della Signoria, then walk nearby to the Palazzo del Bargello, which contains the most important works of Tuscan and Florentine sculpture from the Renaissance. After lunch, visit the Museo dell'Opera del Duomo, with its sculptural masterpieces from the Duomo, including Donatello's *Mary Magdalene*.

If You Have 5 Days   Spend days 1–3 as above. On day 4, continue your exploration of Renaissance masterpieces by visiting the Medici Chapels, with Michelangelo's tomb for Lorenzo de Medici, including the figures of *Dawn* and *Dusk*. Later in the morning, go to the Museo di San Marco, a small museum that's a monument to the work of Fra Angelico. Before it closes at 6:30pm, call at the Basilica di Santa Croce, with its two restored chapels by Giotto. On day 5, leave Florence, as fascinating as it is, and head south to yet another fascinating art city, Siena, the most important of the Tuscan hill towns.

THE TOP MUSEUMS

✪ **Galleria degli Uffizi.** Piazzale degli Uffizi 6. ☎ **055/23886512.** Admission 12,000L ($7.70). Tues–Sat 9am–7pm, Sun and holidays 9am–1pm (last entrance 45 minutes before closing). Bus: 14 or 15.

This is one of the world's outstanding museums, and Italy's finest collection of art, and to see and absorb all the paintings would take at least two weeks. The Uffizi is nicely grouped into periods or schools to show the progress of Italian and European art. The first room begins with classical sculpture. A special treasure is a work by Masaccio, who died at an early age but is credited as the father of modern painting. In his madonnas and bambini you can see the beginnings of the use of perspective. The Botticelli rooms contain his finest works, including what's commonly called "Venus on the Half Shell." This supreme conception of life— *The Birth of Venus*—especially packs 'em in. In another room you'll see Leonardo da Vinci's unfinished but brilliant *Adoration of the Magi* and Verrocchio's *Baptism of Christ,* not a very important painting but noted because Leonardo painted one of the angels when he was 14. Also in this salon hangs Leonardo's *Annunciation.*

In the rooms that follow are works by Perugino, Dürer, Mantegna, Bellini, Giorgione, and Correggio. Finally, you can view Michelangelo's *Holy Family,* as well as Raphael's *Madonna of the Goldfinch,* plus his portraits of Julius II and Leo X. There is also what might be dubbed the Titian salon, which has two of his interpretations of Venus (one depicted with Cupid).

✪ **Galleria dell'Accademia.** Via Ricasoll 60. ☎ **055/2388609.** Admission 12,000L ($7.70). Tues–Sat 8:30am–7pm, Sun 8:30am–2pm. Bus: 1, 6, 10, 11, 17, 20, or 25.

This museum contains Michelangelo's colossal *David,* unveiled in 1504, which overshadows everything else. In the connecting picture gallery is a collection of Tuscan masters, such as Botticelli, and Umbrian works by Perugino (teacher of Raphael).

⊙ **Palazzo Pitti and the Giardini di Boboli (Boboli Gardens).** Piazza de'Pitti. ☎ **055/2388611.** Palatina, 12,000L ($7.70); Modern Art Gallery, 8,000L ($5.10); Argenti, 8,000L ($5); Boboli Gardens, 4,000L ($2.55). Palace museums, Tues–Sat 9am–7pm. Boboli Gardens, June–Sept, daily 8:30am–7:30pm; Apr–May and Oct, daily 8:30am–6:30pm; Nov–Mar, daily 9am–4:30pm. Ticket office closes an hour before the gardens. Bus: 3 or 15.

The Palatine Gallery, on the left bank (a 5-minute walk from the Ponte Vecchio), houses one of Europe's great art collections, with masterpieces hung one on top of the other, as in the days of the Enlightenment. If for no other reason, come here for the Raphaels. In the Sala di Saturno, look to the left of the entrance wall to see Raphael's *Madonna of the Canopy.* On the third wall near the door is the greatest Pitti prize, Raphael's *Madonna of the Chair,* his best-known interpretation of the Virgin, and what is probably one of the six most celebrated paintings in all Europe. The Pitti, built in the mid–15th century (Brunelleschi was the original architect), was once the residence of the powerful Medici family.

There are actually several museums in this complex, including the most important, the **Galleria Palatina,** a repository of old masters. Other museums are the **Appartamenti Reali,** which the Medici family once called home; the **Museo degli Argenti,** 16 rooms devoted to displays of the "loot" acquired by the Medici dukes; the **Coach and Carriage Museum;** the **Galleria d'Arte Moderna;** the **Museo della Porcellane** (porcelain); and the **Galleria del Costume.**

Behind the Pitti Palace are the **Boboli Gardens,** Piazza de'Pitti 1 (☎ **055/218741**), through which the Medici romped. The gardens were laid out by Triboli, a great landscape artist, in the 16th century. The Boboli is ever-popular for a promenade or an idyllic interlude in a pleasant setting. The gardens are filled with fountains and statuary, such as a Giambologna *Venus* in the "Grotto" of Buontalenti. You can climb to the top of the Fortezza di Belvedere for a dazzling city view.

⊙ **Cappelle Medicee (Medici Chapel).** Piazza Madonna degli Aldobrandini 6. ☎ **055/23885.** Admission 10,000L ($6.40). Tues–Sat 9am–2pm, Sun 9am–1pm. Bus: 1, 6, 11, 17, 19, or 23.

The Medici tombs are adjacent to the Basilica of San Lorenzo (see "Other Churches," below). You enter the tombs, housing the "blue-blooded" Medici, in back of the church by going around to Piazza di Madonna degli Aldobrandini. The "New Sacristy" was designed by Michelangelo. Working from 1521 to 1534, he created the Medici tomb in a style that foreshadowed the baroque. Lorenzo the Magnificent—a ruler who seemed to embody the qualities of the Renaissance itself—was buried near Michelangelo's uncompleted *Madonna and Child* group, a simple monument that evokes a promise unfulfilled. Ironically, the finest groups of sculpture were reserved for two Medici "clan" members, who (in the words of Mary McCarthy) "would better have been forgotten." They're represented by Michelangelo as armored, idealized princes. The other two figures on Lorenzo's tomb are most often called *Dawn* and *Dusk,* with morning represented as woman and evening as man. The best-known figures—Michelangelo at his most powerful—are *Night* and *Day* at the feet of Giuliano, the duke of Nemours. *Night* is chiseled as a woman in troubled sleep; *Day* is a man of strength awakening to a foreboding world.

⊙ **Museo Nazionale del Bargello.** Via del Proconsolo 4. ☎ **055/2388606.** Admission 8,000L ($5.10). Tues–Sat 9am–2pm; 2nd and 4th Sun of the month 9am–2pm, 1st and 3rd Mon of the month 9am–2pm. Bus: 14.

The National Museum, a short walk from Piazza della Signoria, is a 13th-century fortress palace whose dark underground chambers once resounded with the cries of the tortured. Today it's a vast repository of some of the most important Renaissance sculpture, including works by Michelangelo and Donatello.

Here you'll see another Michelangelo *David* (referred to in the past as *Apollo*), chiseled perhaps 25 to 30 years after the statuesque figure in the Academy Gallery. The Bargello *David* is totally different—even effete when compared to its stronger brother. Among the more significant sculptures is Giambologna's *Winged Mercury*. The Bargello displays two versions of Donatello's *John the Baptist*—one emaciated, the other a younger and much kinder edition. Look for at least one more notable work, another *David*—this one by Andrea del Verrocchio, one of the finest of the 15th-century sculptors. The Bargello contains a large number of terra-cottas by the della Robbia clan.

Museo di San Marco. Piazza San Marco 1. ☎ **055/2388608.** Admission 8,000L ($5.10). Tues–Sat 9am–2pm, Sun 9am–2pm. Closed 1st and 3rd Sun of the month, and 2nd and 4th Mon of the month. Bus: 1, 6, 7, 10, 11, 17, or 20.

This state museum is a handsome Renaissance palace whose cell walls are decorated with frescoes by the mystical Fra Angelico, one of Europe's greatest 15th-century painters. In the days of Cosimo dei Medici, San Marco was built by Michelozzo as a Dominican convent. It originally contained bleak, bare cells, which Angelico and his students then brightened considerably with some of the most important works of this pious artist of Fiesole, who portrayed recognizable landscapes in vivid colors. One of his better-known paintings here is *The Last Judgment,* which depicts people with angels on the left dancing in a circle and lordly saints towering overhead. On the second floor—at the top of the hall—is Angelico's masterpiece, *The Annunciation.*

THE DUOMO, CAMPANILE & BAPTISTERY

☉ Cattedrale di Santa Maria del Fiore (Duomo). Piazza del Duomo. ☎ **055/294514.** Cathedral, free; excavations 3,000L ($1.90); cupola 8,000L ($5.10). Cathedral, daily 10am–5pm; excavations, Mon–Sat 9:30am–5pm; cupola, Mon–Fri 9am–6pm, Sat 8:30am–5pm. Bus: 1, 6, 11, 17, 19, or 23.

The Duomo, graced by Brunelleschi's dome, is the crowning glory of Florence. But don't rush inside too quickly, as the view of the exterior, with its geometrically patterned bands of white, pink, and green marble, is, along with the dome, the best feature. One of the world's largest churches, the Duomo represents the flowering of the "Florentine Gothic" style. Begun in 1296, it was finally consecrated in 1436, yet finishing touches on the facade were applied as late as the 19th century. The cathedral was designed by Arnolfo di Cambio in the late 13th century.

Inside, the overall effect of the cathedral is bleak, except when you stand under the cupola, frescoed in part by Vasari. Some of the stained-glass windows in the dome were based on designs by Donatello (Brunelleschi's friend) and Ghiberti (Brunelleschi's rival). If you resisted scaling Giotto's bell tower (below), you may want to climb Brunelleschi's ribbed dome. The view is well worth the trek.

☉ Campanile (Giotto's Bell Tower). Piazza del Duomo. ☎ **055/215380.** Admission 8,000L ($5.10). Mid-Mar to Sept, daily 9am–7:30pm; Oct to mid-Mar, daily 9am–5:30pm. Bus: 1, 6, 11, 17, 19, or 23.

Giotto left to posterity the most beautiful bell tower, or campanile, in Europe, rhythmic in line and form. He designed the campanile in the last 2 or 3 years of his life and died before its completion. The final work was admirably carried out by Andrea Pisano, one of the greatest gothic sculptors in Italy (see his bronze doors on the nearby Baptistery). The 274-foot tower, a "Tuscanized" gothic, with bands of colored marble, can be scaled for a panorama of the sienna-colored city. The view will surely rank among your most memorable—it encompasses the enveloping hills and Medici villas.

☉ Battistero San Giovanni (Baptistery). Piazza S. Giovanni. ☎ **055/215380.** Admission 3,000L ($1.90). Mon–Sat 1:30–6pm, Sun 9am–1:30pm. Bus: 1, 6, 11, 17, 19, or 23.

Named after the city's patron saint, Giovanni (John the Baptist), the present octagonal Battistero dates from the 11th and 12th centuries. The oldest structure in Florence, the baptistery is a highly original interpretation of the romanesque style, with its bands of pink, white, and green marble. Visitors from all over the world come to gape at its three sets of bronze doors. The east door is a copy; the other two are originals. In his work on two sets of doors, Lorenzo Ghiberti reached the pinnacle of his artistry in *quattrocento* Florence. The gilt panels—representing scenes from the New Testament, including the *Annunciation,* the *Adoration,* and Christ debating the elders in the temple—make up a flowing, rhythmic narration in bronze.

After his long labor, the Florentines gratefully gave Ghiberti the task of sculpting the east doors (directly opposite the entrance to the Duomo). Upon seeing the doors, Michelangelo is said to have exclaimed, "The Gateway to Paradise!"

OTHER CHURCHES

Basilica di Santa Croce. Piazza Santa Croce 16. ☎ **055/244619.** Church, free; cloisters and church museum, 4,000L ($2.55) adults, 1,000L (65¢) children. Church, daily 8am–12.30pm and 3–6:30pm. Museum and cloisters, Mar–Sept, Thurs–Tues 10am–12:30pm and 2:30–6:30pm; Oct–Feb, daily 10am–12:30pm and 3–5pm. Bus: 13, 14, or 19.

The Pantheon of Florence, this church shelters the tombs of everyone from Michelangelo to Machiavelli, from Dante (he was actually buried at Ravenna) to Galileo. Santa Croce was the church of the Franciscans, said to have been designed by Arnolfo di Cambio. In the right nave (first tomb) is the Vasari-executed monument to Michelangelo, whose body was smuggled back to his native Florence from its original burial place in Rome. The Trecento frescoes are reason enough for visiting Santa Croce—especially those by Giotto to the right of the main chapel.

Basilica di San Lorenzo. Piazza San Lorenzo. ☎ **055/216634.** Free admission. Library, Mon–Sat 9am–1pm; study room, Mon–Sat 8am–2pm. Bus: 1, 6, 11, or 17.

This is Brunelleschi's 15th-century Renaissance church, where the Medici used to attend services from their nearby palace on Via Larga, now Via Camillo Cavour. Most visitors flock to see Michelangelo's "New Sacristy" with his *Night* and *Day* (see the Medici Chapels under "The Top Museums," above), but Brunelleschi's handiwork deserves some time, too. Built in the style of a Latin cross, the church is distinguished by harmonious grays and rows of Corinthian columns.

The **Biblioteca Medicea Laurenziana** (☎ 055/210760) is entered separately at Piazza San Lorenzo 9 and was designed by Michelangelo to shelter the expanding library of the Medici. Beautiful in design and concept, and approached by exquisite stairs, the library is filled with some of Italy's greatest manuscripts—many of which are handsomely illustrated.

Basilica di Santa Maria Novella. Piazza Santa Maria Novella. ☎ **055/215918.** Church, free; Spanish Chapel and cloisters, 5,000L ($3.20). Church, Mon–Fri 7–11:30am and 3:30–6pm, Sat 10–11:30am and 3:30–5pm, Sun 3:30–5pm; Spanish Chapel and cloisters, Mon–Thurs and Sat 9am–2pm, Sun 8am–1pm.

Near the railway station is one of Florence's most distinguished churches, begun in 1278 for the Dominicans. Its geometric facade, with bands of white and green marble, was designed in the late 15th century by Leon Battista Alberti, an aristocrat and true Renaissance man. The church borrows from and harmonizes the romanesque, gothic, and Renaissance styles.

In the left nave as you enter (the third large painting) is the great Masaccio's *Trinity,* a curious work that has the architectural form of a Renaissance stage setting, but whose figures—in perfect perspective—are like actors in a Greek tragedy. Head straight up the left nave to the Gondi Chapel for a look at Brunelleschi's wooden *Christ on the Cross*, which is said to have been carved to compete with Donatello's same subject in Santa Croce.

PALACES

Palazzo Vecchio. Piazza della Signoria. ☎ **055/2768325.** Admission 10,000L ($6.40). Mon–Wed and Fri–Sat 9am–7pm, Sun 8am–1pm. Ticket office closes 1 hour before palace. Bus: 13, 14, or 23.

The secular "Old Palace" is without doubt the most famous and imposing palace in Florence. It dates from the closing years of the 13th century. Its remarkable architectural feature is its 308-foot tower, an engineering feat that required supreme skill. Once home to the Medici, the Palazzo Vecchio (also called the Palazzo della Signoria) is occupied today by city employees, but much of it is open to the public.

The 16th-century "Hall of the 500" (Dei Cinquecento), the most outstanding part of the palace, is filled with Vasari & Co. frescoes as well as sculpture. As you enter the hall, look for Michelangelo's *Victory*. Later you can stroll through the rest of the palace, through its apartments and main halls. You can also visit the private apartments of Eleanor of Toledo, wife of Cosimo I, and a chapel that was begun in 1540 and frescoed by Bronzino.

Palazzo Medici-Riccardi. Via Camillo Cavour 1. ☎ **055/2760360.** Admission 6,000L ($3.85). Mon–Tues and Thurs–Sat 9am–1pm and 3–6pm, Sun 9am–1pm. Bus: 1, 6, 11, 14, or 23.

This palace, a short walk from the Duomo, was the home of Cosimo dei Medici before he took his household to the Palazzo della Signoria. Built by palace architect Michelozzo in the mid–15th century, the brown stone building was also the scene, at times, of the court of Lorenzo the Magnificent. Art lovers visit today chiefly to see the mid–15th-century frescoes by Benozzo Gozzoli in the Medici Chapel. Gozzoli's frescoes, which depict the *Journey of the Magi*, form his masterpiece—in fact, they're a hallmark in Renaissance painting in that they abandoned ecclesiastical themes to celebrate emerging man (he peopled his work with the Medici, the artist's master Fra Angelico, and even himself).

OTHER MUSEUMS

Museo Archeologico. Via della Colonna 38. ☎ **055/23575.** Admission 8,000L ($5.10). Tues–Sat 9am–2pm, Sun 9am–1pm. Bus: 6, 31, or 32.

The Archeological Museum, a short walk from Piazza della SS. Annunziata, houses one of Europe's most outstanding Egyptian and Etruscan collections. Its Egyptian mummies and sarcophagi are on the first floor, along with some of the better-known Etruscan works. Pause to look at the lid to the coffin of a fat Etruscan. Three bronze Etruscan masterpieces are among the rarest objets d'art of these relatively unknown people; one is the Chimera, a lion with a goat sticking out of its back.

Museo dell'Opera del Duomo. Piazza del Duomo 9. ☎ **055/215380.** Admission 8,000L ($5.10). Apr–Oct, Mon–Sat 9am–6:50pm; Nov–Mar, Mon–Sat 9am–5:20pm. Bus: 1, 6, 11, 14, 19, or 23.

The Museo dell'Opera del Duomo, across the street but facing the apse of Santa Maria del Fiore, is beloved by connoisseurs of Renaissance sculptural works. It shelters the sculpture removed from the campanile and the Duomo. A major attraction of this museum is the unfinished *Pietà* by Michelangelo, which is in the middle of the stairs. It was carved between 1548 and 1555 when the artist was in his seventies.

A good reason for visiting the museum is to see the marble choirs—*cantorie*—of Donatello and Luca della Robbia (the works face each other, and are in the first room you enter after climbing the stairs). The Luca della Robbia choir is more restrained, but it still "praises the Lord" in marble—with clashing cymbals and sounding brass that constitute a reaffirmation of life.

SHOPPING

Skilled craftsmanship and traditional design unchanged since the days of the Medici have made Florence a destination for serious shoppers. Florence is noted for its hand-tooled **leather goods** and its various **straw merchandise,** as well as superbly crafted **silver jewelry.** Its reputation for fashionable custom-made clothes is no longer what it was, having lost its position of supremacy to Milan.

The **Bottega San Felice,** Via Maggio 39R (☎ **055/215479**), offers many intriguing antiques from the 19th century, sometimes in the style known as "Charles X," but also sells more modern pieces. Many art deco items are for sale, as are many Biedermeier pieces. Open Mon 4–7:30pm and Tues–Sat 9am–1pm and 4–7:30pm. The **Galleria Masini,** Piazza Goldoni 6R (☎ **055/294000**), was opened in 1870, making it the oldest art gallery in Florence. The selection of modern and contemporary paintings by top artists is extensive, representing the work of more than 500 Italian painters. Even if you're not a collector, this is a good place to select a picture that'll be a lasting reminder of your visit to Italy—you can take it home duty-free. Open Mon 3–7pm and Tues–Sat 9am–1pm and 3–7pm; closed 2 weeks in Aug.

In the commercial center of town near the Duomo, **Romano,** Piazza della Repubblica (☎ **055/2396890**), is a glamorous clothing store for both women and men. The owners commissioned a curving stairwell to be constructed under the high, ornate ceiling. But even more exciting are their well-stocked leather and suede goods, along with an assortment of dresses, shoes, and handbags, many at very high prices if you're willing to pay for quality. Open Mon 3:30–7:30pm and Tues–Sat 9:30am–1pm and 3:30–7:30pm.

The **Balatresi Gift Shop,** Lungarno Acciaiuoli 22R (☎ **055/287851**), is presided over by Umberto and Giovanna Balatresi, who've stocked the shop with treasures. Among them are Florentine mosaics created for them by Maestro Metello Montelatici, who is arguably one of the greatest mosaicists alive. The store also sells original ceramic figurines by the sculptor Giannitrapani and a fine selection of hand-carved alabaster, enamel ware, and Tuscan glass. Open Tues–Sat 9am–8pm. **Aurum,** Lungarno Corsini 16R (☎ **055/284259**), sells contemporary 18-karat-gold jewelry. Many pieces are modern, based on designs created exclusively for this store. Others are reproductions of Etruscan designs. Open Mon–Sat 9:30am–7:30pm.

Bojola, Via dei Rondinelli 25R (☎ **055/211155**), is a leading name in leather. Sergio Bojola has distinguished himself in Florence by his selections for many types and tastes, in both synthetic materials and beautiful leathers. Hundreds of customers are always enthusiastic about the variety of items found here, which reflect first-class quality and craftsmanship. Open Apr–Oct, Mon–Fri 9am–7:30pm and Sat 9am–3:30pm; Nov–Mar, Mon 3:30–7:30pm and Tues–Sat 9am–7:30pm.

After checking into a hotel, the most intrepid shoppers head for **Piazza del Mercato Nuovo (the Straw Market),** called Il Porcellino by the Italians because of the bronze statue of a reclining wild boar there (it's a copy of the one in the Uffizi). Tourists pet its snout (which is well worn) for good luck. The market stands in the monumental heart of Florence, an easy stroll from the Palazzo Vecchio. It sells not only straw items but also leather goods, along with typical Florentine merchandise—frames, trays, hand-embroidery, table linens, and hand-sprayed and -painted boxes in traditional designs. Open Mon–Sat 9am–7pm.

FLORENCE AFTER DARK

For theatrical and concert listings, pick up a free copy of *Welcome to Florence,* available at the tourist office. This helpful publication contains information on recitals, concerts, theatrical productions, and other cultural presentations that are offered in Florence at the time of your visit.

Many cultural presentations are performed in churches. These might include open-air concerts in the cloisters of the Badia Fiesolana in Fiesole (the hill town above Florence) or at the Ospedale degli Innocenti, the foundling "hospital of the innocents" on summer evenings only.

THE PERFORMING ARTS

Teatro Comunale di Firenze/Maggio Musicale Fiorentino. Corso Italia 16. ☎ **055/211158.** Tickets, 30,000–180,000L ($19.20–$115.20) for opera, 25,000–180,000L ($16–$115.20) for concerts.

This is the main theater in Florence, with an opera, concert, and ballet season presented Sept–Apr. The short opera season usually lasts mid-Dec–mid-Jan. This theater is also the major venue for the Maggio Musicale festival of opera, ballet, concerts, and recitals, lasting from late April to July. Its maestro is Zubin Mehta. The box office is open Tues–Fri 11am–5:30pm and Sat 9am–1pm.

Teatro della Pergola. Via della Pergola 18. ☎ **055/2479651.** Tickets 11,500–70,000L ($7.35–$44.80).

You'll have to understand Italian to appreciate most of the plays presented here. Plays are performed year-round except during the Maggio Musicale, when the theater becomes the setting for the many musical presentations of the festival. Performances are Tues–Sat at 8:45pm.

MUSIC & DANCE CLUBS

The Red Garter. Via de' Benci 33R. ☎ **055/2344904.** No cover.

Perhaps nothing could be more unexpected in this city of Donatello and Michelangelo than a club called the Red Garter, right off Piazza Santa Croce. The American Prohibition era lives on—in fact, it has been exported. Visitors to the Red Garter can hear a variety of music, from rock to bluegrass. The club is open Mon–Thurs 8:30pm–1am and Fri–Sun 9pm–1:30am. "Happy Hour" is every evening to 9:30pm.

Space Electronic. Via Palazzuolo 37. ☎ **055/293082.** Cover (including one drink) 25,000L ($16).

This is the only dance club in Florence with karaoke. On the ground floor, you can have a quiet drink singing or listening to karaoke. The decor consists of gigantic carnival heads, wall-to-wall mirrors, and an imitation space capsule that goes back and forth across the dance floor. If karaoke doesn't thrill you, head to the new ground-floor pub that's stocked with an ample supply of imported beers. On the upper level is a large dance floor with a wide choice of music, and the best sound-and-light show in town. The disco opens nightly at 10pm (usually going to 2:30am or later, depending on business).

BARS

The **Donatello Bar,** on the ground floor of the Hotel Excelsior, Piazza Ognissanti 3 (☎ **055/264201**), is the city's most elegant watering hole. Named in honor of the great Renaissance artist, this bar and its adjoining restaurant, Il Cestello, attract well-heeled international visitors along with the Florentine elite. The ambience is enlivened by a marble fountain and works of art. Piano music is featured daily 7pm–1am and the bar is open daily 11am–1:30am.

After an initial success in Rome, the Irish pub **Fiddler's Elbow,** Piazza Santa Maria Novella 7R (☎ **055/21506**), located near the rail station, has now invaded the city of Donatello and Michelangelo. The pub is open daily 3pm–12:30am.

CAFES

Café Rivoire, Piazza della Signoria 4R (☎ **055/214412**), offers a classy and amusing old-world ambience with a direct view of the statues of one of our favorite squares. You can sit at one of the metal tables set up on the flagstones outside or at one of the tables in a choice of inner rooms filled with marble detailing and unusual oil renderings of the piazza. If you don't want to sit at all, try the mahogany and green-marble bar, where many colorful characters talk, flirt, or gossip. The cafe is noted for its hot chocolate. It's open Tues–Sun 8am–midnight.

Behind three Tuscan arches on a fashionable shopping street in the center of the old city, **Giacosa,** Via Tornabuoni 83R (☎ **055/2396226**), has a warmly paneled interior, a lavish display of pastries and sandwiches, and a reputation as the birthplace of the Negroni, a drink that's a combination of gin, Campari, and red vermouth. Ice cream, for which the cafe is famous, runs 6,000–10,000L ($3.85–$6.40). A Negroni costs 7,500L ($4.80) at a counter or 12,000L ($7.70) at a table. The cafe is open Mon–Sat 7:30am–8:30pm.

Gilli, Piazza della Repubblica 39R (☎ **055/213896**), the oldest and most beautiful cafe in Florence, a few minutes' walk from the Duomo, was founded in 1733. You can sit at a small, brightly lit table near the bar or retreat to an intricately paneled pair of rooms to the side and enjoy the flattering light from the Venetian-glass chandeliers. A cappuccino costs 5,000L ($3.20) at a table or 1,700L ($1.10) if you stand at the bar. The cafe is open Mar 16–Nov 14, Wed–Mon 7:30am–1am; Nov 15–Mar 15, Wed–Fri 7:30am–9pm and Sat–Mon 7:30am–1am.

The waiters at **Giubbe Rosse,** Piazza della Repubblica 13R (☎ **055/212280**), still wear the red coats as they did when it was founded in 1888. Originally a beerhall, it's now an elegant cafe/bar/restaurant filled with turn-of-the-century chandeliers and polished granite floors. You can enjoy a drink or cup of coffee, which costs 5,000L ($3.20) at one of the small tables near the zinc-top bar.

GAY CLUBS

Florence's leading gay bar, **Crisco,** Via S. Egidio 43R (☎ **055/2480580**), caters only to men. Its 18th-century building contains a bar and a dance floor. Classified as a *club privato,* but open to the public, its hours are Sun–Mon and Wed–Thurs 10:30pm–3:30am, Fri–Sat 10:30pm–5 or 6am. The cover is 12,000–16,000L ($7.70–$10.25), depending on the night of the week.

Tuscany's community of gay men considers a visit to the **Santanassa Bar,** Via del Pandolfini 26 (☎ **055/243356**), a standard Saturday-night staple. In summer, the crowd's international, looking like a cross-section of all the nations of Europe. There's a crowded bar on street level, sometimes with a live piano player. On Friday and Saturday the cellar is transformed into a disco. It's open Sun–Thurs 10pm–4am and Fri–Sat 10pm–6am. The bar is open year-round; the disco, only Sept–June. Cover (including the first drink) is 12,000L ($7.70) Sun–Thurs or 15,000–20,000L ($9.60–$12.80) Fri–Sat.

TUSCANY: TOURS & DAY TRIPS

TOURING TUSCANY **C.I.T.,** at the corner of Piazza della Stazione and Piazza dell'Unità (☎ **055/21-09-64**), offers organized tours to the Chianti region and other Tuscan cities and small towns. If you love to walk or bike, **I Bike Italy** (☎ **055/ 23-42-371** weekdays or 0368/45-92-23 weekends) books guided bike rides through the countryside from March to November. **Country Walks in Italy** can be booked with the same outfit year-round. If you want to see Italy as did the Romans and the Renaissance condottieri, you can book a horseback trek through **Equitour** (☎ 800/545-00191 in the U.S.); see "Outdoor and Adventure Vacations" in the introduction for details.

FIESOLE This town—once an Etruscan settlement—is the most popular outing from Florence. Bus no. 7, which leaves from Piazza San Marco, brings you here in 25 minutes and gives you a panoramic view along the way. You'll pass fountains, statuary, and gardens strung out over the hills like a scrambled jigsaw puzzle.

Exploring Fiesole You won't find anything as dazzling here as the Renaissance treasures of Florence—the charms of Fiesole are more subtle. Fortunately, all major sights branch out within walking distance of the main piazza, beginning with the **Cattedrale di San Romolo.** Dating from A.D. 1000, it was much altered during the Renaissance. In the Salutati Chapel are important sculptural works by Mino da Fiesole. It's open daily 7:30am–noon and 4–7pm.

The ecclesiastical **Bandini Museum,** Via Dupre (☎ 055/59477; bus: 7), around to the side of the Duomo, belongs to the Fiesole Cathedral Chapter. On the ground floor are della Robbia terra-cotta works, as well as art by Michelangelo and Nino Pisano. Admission is 6,000L ($3.85) for adults and 3,000L ($1.90) for children 17 and under and seniors to and over. Open daily 9am–6pm.

The hardest task you'll have in Fiesole is to take the steep goat-climb up to the **Museo Missionario Francescano Fiesole,** Via San Francesco 13 (☎ 055/59175; bus: 7). You can visit the Franciscan church, built in the Gothic style in the first years of the 1400s. The church was consecrated in 1516. Inside are many paintings by well-known Florentine artists. In the basement of the church is the ethnological museum. Begun in 1906, the collection has a large section of Chinese artifacts, including ancient bronzes. An Etruscan-Roman section contains some 330 archeological pieces and an Egyptian section also has numerous objects. Admission is free (donation expected). Open Mon–Fri 9am–noon and 3–6pm and Sat 3–6pm.

On the site of the **Teatro Romano e Museo Civico,** Via Portigiani 1 (☎ 055/59477; bus: 7), is the major surviving evidence that Fiesole was an Etruscan city 6 centuries before Christ, then later a Roman town. In the 1st century B.C. a theater was built, the restored remains of which you can see today. Near the theater are the skeletonlike ruins of the baths, which may have been built at the same time. The Etruscan-Roman museum contains many interesting finds that date from the days when Fiesole—not Florence—was supreme (a guide is on hand to show you through). Admission is 5,000L ($3.20) for adults and 3,000L ($1.90) for children 6–16 and seniors 60 and over. Open Mon–Fri 9am–6pm and Wed–Sun 9am–6pm.

Dining The **Trattoria le Cave di Maiano,** Via delle Cave 16 (☎ 055/59133; bus: 7), is at Maiano, a 15-minute ride east from the heart of Florence and a short distance south of Fiesole. The rustically decorated trattoria is a garden restaurant, with stone tables and large, sheltering trees, which create a setting for the excellent cooking. Inside, the restaurant is in the tavern style, with a beamed ceiling. For a main course, there's golden grilled chicken or savory herb-flavored roast lamb. For side dishes, we suggest fried polenta, Tuscan beans, or fried potatoes. Reservations are required. Open Mon 7–11:30pm and Tues–Sun noon–3pm and 7–11:30pm; closed Aug 10–20.

SIENA In Rome you see classicism and the baroque; in Florence, the Renaissance; but in the walled city of Siena you stand solidly planted in the Middle Ages. On three sienna-colored hills in the center of Tuscany, Sena Vetus lies in chianti country, 21 miles south of Florence. Preserving its original character more markedly than any other Italian city, it's even today a showplace of the Italian gothic.

Had Siena continued to expand and change after reaching the zenith of its power in the 14th century, chances are it would be markedly different today, influenced by the rising tides of the Renaissance and the baroque (represented here only to a small degree). But Siena retained its uniqueness (certain Sienese painters were still showing the influence of Byzantium in the late 15th century).

Trains arrive hourly from both Florence and Pisa, and **TRA-IN,** Piazza San Domenico 1 (☎ **0577/204245**), in Siena, offers bus service to all of Tuscany, with air-conditioned coaches. The one-way cost between Florence and Siena is 10,000L ($6.40) per person. Motorists can head south from Florence along the Firenze–Siena autostrada, a superhighway linking the cities, going through Poggibonsi.

The **tourist information office** is at Piazza del Campo 56 (☎ **0577/280551**), open Mon–Sat 8:30am–7:30pm and Sun 8:30am–2pm.

Exploring Siena   Start in the heart of Siena, the shell-shaped **Piazza del Campo,** described by Montaigne as "the finest of any city in the world." Pause to enjoy the Fonte Gaia, with embellishments by Jacopo della Quercia (the present sculptured works are reproductions; the badly beaten original ones are found in the town hall).

The **Palazzo Pubblico,** Piazza del Campo (☎ **0577/292263**), dates from 1288–1309 and is filled with important artworks by some of the leaders in the Sienese school of painting and sculpture. This collection is the Museo Civico. Upstairs in the museum is the Sala della Pace, frescoed from 1337 to 1339 by Ambrogio Lorenzetti; the allegorical frescoes show the idealized effects of good government and bad government. Admission is 6,000L ($3.85) for adults and 3,000L ($1.90) for students and seniors 65 and over. Open Nov 6–Feb, daily 9:30am–1:30pm; Mar–Nov 5, Mon–Sat 9am–7pm and Sun and holidays 9am–1:30pm.

At Piazza del Duomo, southeast of Piazza del Campo, stands the architectural fantasy of ✪ **Il Duomo** (☎ **0577/283048**). With its colored bands of marble, the Sienese cathedral is an original and exciting building, erected in the romanesque and Italian gothic styles during the 12th century. The dramatic facade—designed in part by Giovanni Pisano—dates from the 13th century, as does the romanesque bell tower.

The zebralike interior, with its black and white stripes, is equally stunning. The floor consists of various embedded works of art, many of which are roped off to preserve the richness in design, depicting both biblical and mythological subjects. Numerous artists worked on the floor, notably Domenico Beccafumi.

The octagonal 13th-century pulpit is by Niccolo Pisano (Giovanni's father), who was one of the most significant Italian sculptors before the dawn of the Renaissance (see his pulpit in the Baptistery at Pisa). The Siena pulpit is his masterpiece; it reveals in relief such scenes as the slaughter of the innocents and the Crucifixion. Admission is free. Open Mar 17–Oct, daily 7:30am–7:30pm; Nov–Mar 16, daily 7:30am–1:30pm and 2:30pm–sunset.

The facade of the **Battistero,** Piazza San Giovanni (☎ **0577/283048**), dates from the 14th century. In the center of the interior is the baptismal font by Jacopo della Quercia, which contains some bas-reliefs by Donatello and Ghiberti. Admission is 3,000L ($1.90). Open Mar 16–Sept, daily 9am–7:30pm; Oct, daily 9am–6pm; Nov–Mar 15, daily 10am–1pm and 2:30–5pm; closed Jan 1 and Dec 25.

Housed in the 14th-century Palazzo Buonsignori, near Piazza del Campo, the **Pinacoteca Nazionale (Picture Gallery),** Via San Pietro 29 (☎ **0577/281161**), contains a collection of the Sienese school of painting, which once rivaled that of Florence. Displayed are some of the giants of the pre-Renaissance. Most of the paintings cover the period from the late 12th to the mid–16th century. The principal treasures are on the second floor, where you'll contemplate the artistry of Duccio in the early salons. The gallery is rich in the art of the two Lorenzetti brothers, Ambrogio and Pietro, who painted in the 14th century. Ambrogio is represented by an *Annunciation* and a *Crucifix,* but one of his most celebrated works is an almond-eyed *Madonna and Bambino* surrounded by saints and angels. Pietro's most important entry is an altarpiece— *The Madonna of the Carmine*—made for a church in Siena in 1329. Simone Martini's *Madonna and Child* is damaged but one of the best-known paintings here. Admission is 8,000L ($5.10) for adults; free for children 17 and under and seniors 60 and over. Open Apr–Oct, Tues–Sat 9am–7pm and Sun 8am–1pm; Nov–Mar, Tues–Sun 8:30am–1:30pm.

Dining The beautiful **Al Marsili (Ristorante Enoteca Gallo Nero),** Via del Castoro 3 (☎ **0577/47154**), the best in Siena, stands between the Duomo and Via della Città in a neighborhood packed with medieval and Renaissance buildings. You dine beneath crisscrossed ceiling vaults whose russet-colored brickwork was designed centuries ago. Specialties of the chef include roast boar with tomatoes and herbs, ribollita (a savory vegetable soup in the Sienese style), spaghetti with a sauce of seasonal mushrooms, and veal scaloppine with tarragon and tomato sauce. Reservations are recommended. Open Tues–Sun 12:30–2:30pm and 7:30–10:30pm.

PISA Few buildings in the world have captured imaginations as much as the Leaning Tower of Pisa. It's one of the most instantly recognizable buildings in the Western world. Visitors are drawn to it as a symbol of the fragility of people—or at least the fragility of their work. The Leaning Tower is a landmark powerful enough to entice visitors to call at Pisa, and once here, they find many other sights to explore as well.

Trains link Pisa and Florence every 30 minutes. Trip time is 1 hour, and a one-way fare is 7,200L ($4.60). There's frequent bus service to Florence operated by APT (call 050/505511 in Pisa for more information and schedules). From Florence, motorists take the autostrada west (A11) to the intersection (A12) going south to Pisa.

The **tourist information office** is at Piazza del Duomo 3 (☎ **050/560464**), open daily 8am–8pm.

Exploring Pisa In the Middle Ages, Pisa reached the apex of its power as a maritime republic before it eventually fell to its rivals, Florence and Genoa. Its greatest legacy remains at **Piazza del Duomo,** which D'Annunzio labeled Piazza dei Miracoli (miracles). Here you'll find an ensemble of the top three attractions—original "Pisanromanesque" buildings, including the Duomo, the Baptistery, and the Leaning Tower itself.

Construction of the ✪ **Leaning Tower,** an eight-story campanile, began in 1174 by Bonanno, and a persistent legend is that the architect deliberately intended the bell tower to lean (that claim is undocumented). Another legend is that Galileo let objects of different weights fall from the tower, then timed their descent to prove his theories on bodies in motion.

Unfortunately, the tower is in serious danger of collapse. The government is taking various measures to keep it from falling, including clamping five rings of half-inch steel cable around its lower stones and pouring tons of lead around its base to keep it stabilized. The tower is said to be floating on a sandy base of water-soaked clay; it leans at least 14 feet from perpendicular. If it stood up straight, the tower would measure about 180 feet tall. In 1990 the government suspended visits inside the tower. In years gone by one of the major attractions in Europe was to climb the Tower of Pisa—taking all 294 steps.

Siena

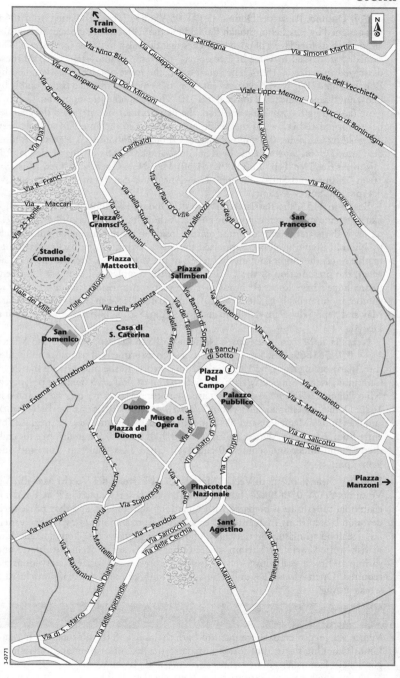

Train Station

Via Sardegna

Via Simone Martini

Via Nino Bixio

Via Giuseppe Mazzini

Via di Campansi

Via Don Minzoni

Viale dell' Vecchietta

Via di Camollia

Viale Lippo Memmi

V. Duccio di Boninsegna

Via Diaz

Via Garibaldi

Via Simone Martini

Via R. Franci

Via del Pian d'Ovile

Via Baldassarre Peruzzi

Via   Maccari

Via della Stufa Secca

Via Vallerozzi

Via degli Orti

San Francesco

Piazza Gramsci

Via dei Montanini

Via 25 Aprile

Stadio Comunale

Piazza Matteotti

Piazza Salimbeni

Via Banchi di Sopra

Via Refenero

Viale dei Mille

Viale Curtatone

Via della Sapienza

Via dei Termini

Via S. Bandini

San Domenico

Casa di S. Caterina

Via delle Terme

Via Banchi di Sotto

Via Esterna di Fontebranda

Piazza Del Campo

Via Pantaneto

Duomo

Via di Città

Palazzo Pubblico

Via S. Martina

Piazza del Duomo

Museo d. Opera

Via Casato di sotto

Via G. Dupré

Via di Salicotto

Via del Sole

Piazza Manzoni

V. d. Fosso d. S. Ansano

Via Stalloreggi

Via S. Pietro

Pinacoteca Nazionale

Via Mascagni

Via T. Pendola

Sant' Agostino

Via E. Bastianini

P. Buio-P. Mantellini

Via Sarrocchi

Via delle Cerchia

Via di Fontanella

Via di S. Marco

V. Della Diana

Via delle Sperandie

Via Mattioli

✪ **Il Duomo,** Piazza del Duomo 17 (☎ **050/560547; bus: 1**), dating from 1063, was designed by Buschetto, though Rainaldo in the 13th century erected the unusual facade with its four layers of open-air arches that diminish in size as they ascend. The cathedral is marked by three bronze doors—rhythmic in line—that replaced those destroyed in a fire in 1596. The south door, the most notable, was designed by Bonanno in 1180. In the restored interior, the chief art treasure is the pulpit by Giovanni Pisano, which was finished in 1310. There are other treasures, too: Galileo's lamp (according to unreliable tradition, the Pisa-born astronomer used the chandelier to formulate his laws of the pendulum), mosaics in the apse said to have been designed by Cimabue, the tomb of Henry VII of Luxembourg, *St. Agnes* by Andrea del Sarto, *Descent from the Cross* by Il Sodoma, and a Crucifix by Giambologna. Admission is free Dec–Feb but 2,000L ($1.30) Mar–Nov. Open May–Oct, Mon–Sat 10am–7:40pm and Sun 1–7:40pm; Nov–Apr, Mon–Sat 10am–12:45pm and 3–4:45pm and Sun 3–4:45pm.

Begun in 1153, the **Battistero,** Piazza del Duomo (☎ **050/560547; bus: 1**), is like a romanesque crown capped by gothic. Although it's most beautiful on the exterior, with its arches and columns, venture inside to see the hexagonal pulpit made by Niccolò Pisano in 1260. Supported by pillars resting on the backs of a trio of marble lions, the pulpit contains bas-reliefs of the Crucifixion, the Adoration of the Magi, the presentation of the Christ child at the temple, and the Last Judgment (many angels have lost their heads over the years). Admission (including entry to another monument) is 10,000L ($6.40). Open daily: Dec–Feb, 9am–4:40pm; Mar–May and Sept–Nov, 9am–5:40pm; and June–Aug, 8am–7:40pm. Closed Jan 1 and Dec 31.

Near Piazza Mazzini, the **Museo Nazionale di San Matteo,** Piazzetta San Matteo 1 (☎ **050/541865; bus: 5 or 7**), contains a good assortment of paintings and sculpture, many dating from the 13th to the 16th century. In the museum are statues by Giovanni Pisano; Simone Martini's *Madonna and Child with Saints,* a polyptych; Nino Pisano's *Madonna de Latte,* a marble sculpture; Masaccio's *St. Paul,* painted in 1426; Domenico Ghirlandaio's two *Madonna and Saints* depictions; works by Strozzi and Alessandro Magnasco; and old copies of works by Jan and Pieter Brueghel. You enter from Piazza San Matteo. Admission is 8,000L ($5.10) for adults, free for children 17 and under and seniors 60 and over. Open Tues–Sat 9am–7pm and Sun 9am–1pm.

Dining Near Piazzetta di Vecchi Macelli, ✪ **Al Ristoro dei Vecchi Macelli,** Via Volturno 49 (☎ **050/20424; bus: 1, 3, or 4**), is the best restaurant in Pisa. Residents claim that the cuisine is prepared with something akin to love, and they prove their devotion by returning frequently. After selecting from a choice of two dozen varieties of seafood antipasti, you can enjoy a homemade pasta with scallops and zucchini or fish-stuffed ravioli in shrimp sauce. Other dishes are gnocchi with pesto and shrimp and roast veal with a velvety truffle-flavored cream sauce. Reservations are required. Open Mon–Tues and Thurs–Sat noon–3pm and 8–10:30pm; closed 2 weeks in Aug.

3 Venice

Venice is a preposterous monument to both the folly and the obstinacy of humankind. It shouldn't exist, but it does, much to the delight of thousands of tourists, gondoliers, lacemakers, hoteliers, restaurateurs, and glassblowers.

Fleeing the barbarians centuries ago, Venetians left drydock and drifted out to a flotilla of "uninhabitable" islands in the lagoon. Survival was difficult enough, but no Venetian has ever settled for mere survival. The remote ancestors of today's inhabitants created the world's most beautiful and unusual city.

However, it's sinking at a rate of about 2¹/₂ inches per decade, and it's estimated that one-third of the city's art will have deteriorated hopelessly within the next decades, if action isn't taken to save it. Clearly, Venice is in peril, under assault by uncontrolled tides, pollution, atmospheric acid, and old age. Efforts are being made to address these problems, but it's possible that to your children or their children, Venice may become a legend from the past.

The city is virtually selling its past to the world, even more aggressively than Florence, successfully, if you observe the literal hoardes that clog the streets and squares. Everybody who's been here leaves complaining of the prices, which are celestial. This is one of the most enchantingly evocative cities on earth, but you must pay a price for all this beauty. In the sultry heat of the Adriatic in summer, the canals become a smelly stew. Steamy, overcrowded July and August are the worst times to visit; May and June and September and October are much more ideal.

Still, Venice endures. And for however long it lasts, the Venice of today is still a magical city that is like no other.

ONLY IN VENICE

Viewing Giorgione's _Tempest_ at the Accademia　One of the world's most famous paintings, the _Tempest_ depicts a baby suckling from the breast of its mother, while a man with a staff looks on. What might've emerged as a simple pastoral scene on the easel of a lesser artist comes forth as a picture of exceptional beauty. Summer lightning pierces the sky, but the tempest seems to be in the background—far away from the figures in the foreground, who are menaced without knowing it. In a city filled with art, no painting has captured our endless fascination as much as this one.

Wandering the Narrow Streets of Dorsoduro　This southernmost section of the historic district is the least populated of Venice's six _sestieri_ (quarters), filled with old homes and half-forgotten churches. Its major attractions are the Gallerie dell'Accademia and the Guggenheim Foundation. Dorsoduro's heyday came in the 19th century, when it was the most fashionable area in which to live. Its most famous church is La Salute, whose first stone was laid in 1631. The Zattere is a broad quay built after 1516 and is one of Venice's favorite promenades. Cafes, trattorie, and pensiones abound in the area.

Hanging Out on Piazza San Marco　Called "the drawing room of Europe" by Napoleon, this piazza has been the heart of Venetian life for more than a thousand years. It's the address of St. Mark's Basilica and the campanile (bell tower). Around the corner is the Palazzo Ducale (Doge's Palace), with its Bridge of Sighs. Though the square has become a gaudy tourist belt filled with fanfare, sitting on the square at a cafe table as a string quartet plays "As Time Goes By" is still one of the highlights of Europe.

Spending a Day at the Lido　This slim, sandy island cradles the Venetian lagoon. Italy's most fashionable bathing resort, it's 7¹/₂ miles long and about half a mile wide, though reaching 2¹/₂ miles at its broadest point. The Lido's discovery came back in the mid-1800s when Musset, Byron, and Shelley, among others, sang its praises. Today few traces of that past remain. It has some of the most fashionable and expensive hotels in Venice along its Lido Promenade, but there are cheaper ones as well. The best way to get around is by bike or tandem, which you can rent on the

Venice Attractions & Accommodations

Attractions:

Accademia **9**
Arsenale **22**
Basilica di San Giorgio Maggiore **23**
Basilica di San Marco **1**
Basilica di Santa Maria Gloriosa
    dei Frari **12**
Bridge of Sighs **18**
Campanile di San Marco **3**
Ca' d'Oro **14**
Ca' Rezzonico **10**
Chiesa di San Zaccaria **20**
Chiesa Madonna dell'Orto **16**
Collezione Peggy Guggenheim **8**
Museo Civico Correr **6**
Museo Comunita Ebraica **15**
Museo Storico Navale **21**
Palazzo delle Prigioni **19**
Palazzo Ducale **4**
Piazza San Marco **5**
Ponte di Rialto **13**
Santa Maria della Salute **7**
Santi Giovanni e Paolo Basilica **17**
Scuola di San Rocco **11**
Torre dell'Orologio **2**

Accommodations:

American Hotal **4**
Boston Hotel **9**
Giorgione **11**
Gritti Palace **6**
Hotel Carpaccio **1**
Hotel Casanova **8**
Hotel Cipriani **5**
Hotel Concordia **10**
Hotel la Fenice et Des Artistes **7**
Hotel San Cassiano Ca'Favretto **12**
Locanda Montin **3**
Pensione Accademia **2**

Church ✝

Stae

Ca' Pesaro

12

Palazzo
Fontana

Ca' d'Oro **14**

Strada Nuova

Palazzo
Sagredo

Santi Apostoli

Campo SS
Apostoli **11**

Palazzo
Michiel
d.Colonne

Canal Grande

Pescaria

C. del Campanile

Calle D. Botteri

Fond. delle Prigioni

Ca' da Mosto

Rio di

S.M. dei
Miracoli

Palazzo
Sanudo

S. Giovanni
Crisostomo

17

Rio di S. Marina

San Giovanni
Elemosinario

San Giacomo
di Rialto

Palazzo del
Dieci Savi **13**

Campo S.
Aponal

Fondaco
die Tedeschi

Ponte
di Rialto

Pal.
Dona

Palazzo
Priuli

Campo
S. Maria
Formosa

San
Silvestro

Riva del Vin

S. Silvestro

Rialto

Riva del Ferro

San
Bartolomeo

C. Stagneri

Santa Maria
della Fava

Palazzo
Dolfin-Manin

Merc. S. Salvador

Palazzo
Bembo

Riva del Carbon

Pal.
Dandolo

San
Salvatore

Palazzo
Querini-
Stampalia

Palazzo
Loredan

C. del Teatro

Merc. S. Salvatore

C. Cuerra

Pal. Grimari

San Luca

Campo
S. Luca

Calle Fabbri

C. Specchieri

C. Rimedio

San
Benedetto

C. dei Fuseri

Campo
Manin

C. Coldoni

10

Palazzo
Trevisan-
Cappello

Larga S. Marco

Canonica

C. Mandola

Pal. Contarini
del Bovolo

9

Pal. Patriarcale **1**

Sant
Apollonia

Campo
S. Angelo

Ateneo
Veneto

8 Bacino
Orseolo

2

Basilica di
San Marco

San
Apollonia

7

Campo
S. Fantin

Pisc di Frezzeria

Frezzeria

C. dell'Ascension

Piazza
San Marco

5

3

4 Palazzo
Ducale

18

19

Teatro
La Fenice

Rio delle Veste

6

Piazzetta

S.S. Moisè

San
Moisè

C. Vallaresso

Giardinetti
Reali

Molo

Area of
Inset →

zzo Corner
Grande)

Campo S.M.
Zobenigo

6

S.M. del
Giglio

Palazzi
Contarini

C. Larga XXII Marzo

San Marco
Vallaresso

San Marco
Giardinetti

Riva Degli Schiavoni

20

Pal.
Venier
dei
Leoni

8

Palazzo
Dario

Punta della
Dogana

13

Cl. de la Pietà

Cl. del Dose

Cl. del Forno

Cp. de
l'Arsenal

22

Santa Maria
della Salute

San
Gregorio

7

Dogana
al Mare

Seminario
Patriarcale

23 **5**

Riva

degli Schiavoni

P. de la
Ca' di Dio

21

To San Giorgio
Maggiore

Bacino San Marco

spot at Via Zara and Gran Viale. The Lido is different architecturally from Venice. Here everything seems to be Liberty style or neo-gothic or neo-Byzantine.

Exploring Torcello, the Gem of the Lagoon   Lying 6½ miles northeast of Venice, Torcello is called "the mother of Venice," having been settled between the 9th and the 17th century. Once it was the most populous of the islands in the lagoon, but since the 18th century it has been nearly deserted. If you ever hope to find solitude in Venice, you'll find it here. A ghost of its former life, it was once a flourishing island until it degenerated into a malarial swamp after the 14th century. It's visited chiefly today by those wishing to see the Cattedrale di Torcello with stunning Byzantine mosaics and to lunch at the Locanda Cipriani.

Riding in a Gondola   In *Death in Venice,* Thomas Mann wrote: "Is there anyone but must repress a secret thrill, on arriving in Venice for the first time—or returning thither after long absence—and stepping into a Venetian gondola? That singular conveyance, come down unchanged from ballad times, black as nothing else on earth except a coffin—what pictures it calls up of lawless, silent adventures in the plashing night; or even more, what visions of death itself, the bier and solemn rites and last soundless voyage!" It's estimated that in the heyday of the Renaissance there were some 15,000 gondolas afloat in Venice. What a sight it must have been, like a giant festive regatta. Now there are only about 350 gondolas, mostly serving tourists.

ORIENTATION

ARRIVING   All roads lead not necessarily to Rome but, in this case, to the docks of mainland Venice. The arrival scene at the unattractive Piazzale Roma is filled with nervous expectation, and even the most veteran traveler can become confused. Whether you arrive by train, bus, car, or airport limousine, there's one common denominator—everyone walks to the nearby docks to select a method of transport to his or her hotel. The cheapest way is by vaporetto, the more expensive by gondola or motor launch.

By Plane   You can now fly from North America to Venice via Rome on Alitalia. You'll land at Mestre, with its **Marco Polo Aeroporto** (☎ **041/5415491**). Boats depart directly from the airport, taking you to a terminal near Piazza San Marco.

It's less expensive to take a bus from the airport, a trip of less than 5 miles. Cross the Ponte della Libertà to the Stazione di Santa Lucia, Venice's rail station. You'll be at Piazzale Roma, where you can make transportation connections to most parts of Venice, including the Lido. It's at this point that first-time visitors encounter the Canal Grande (Grand Canal), a channel leading to the Canale di San Marco, which heads directly to the Adriatic.

By Train   Trains pull into the **Stazione di Santa Lucia,** at Piazzale Roma. Travel time by train from Rome is about 5¼ hours; from Milan, 3½ hours; from Florence, 4 hours; and from Bologna, 2 hours. For information about rail connections, call 041/715555. The best and least expensive way to get from the station to the rest of town is to take a vaporetto, which departs near the main entrance to the station.

By Bus   Buses arrive from points on the mainland of Italy at Piazzale Roma. For information about schedules, call the office of ACTV at Piazzale Roma (☎ **041/5287886**). If you're coming from a distant city in Italy, it's better to take the train.

By Car   Venice has autostrada links with the rest of Italy, with direct routes from such cities as Trieste (driving time: 1½ hours), Milan (driving time: 3 hours), and Bologna (driving time: 2 hours). Bologna is 94 miles southwest of Venice; Milan, 165 miles west of Venice; and Trieste, 97 miles east. Rome is 327 miles to the southwest.

If you arrive by car, there are several multitiered parking areas at the terminus where the roads end and the canals begin. One of the most visible is the **Garage San Marco,** Piazzale Roma (☎ 041/5235101), near the vaporetto, gondola, and motorlaunch docks. You'll be charged 30,000–45,000L ($19.20–$28.80) per day, maybe more, depending on the size of your car.

VISITOR INFORMATION You can get information at the **Azienda di Promozione Turistica,** Palazzetto Selva-Giardinetti Reali (Molo S. Marco) (☎ 041/5226356). It's open Mon–Sat 9:40am–3:30pm.

CITY LAYOUT Venice, 2½ miles from the Italian mainland and 1¼ miles from the Adriatic, is an archipelago of some 117 islands. Most visitors, however, concern themselves only with Piazza San Marco and its vicinity. In fact, the entire city has only one piazza: San Marco. Venice is divided into six quarters that locals call *sestieri.* These include the most frequented, San Marco, but also Santa Croce, San Paolo, Castello, Cannaregio, and Dorsoduro, the last of which has been compared to New York's Greenwich Village.

Many of the so-called streets of Venice are actually **canals,** 150 in all. A canal is called a *rio,* and a total of 400 bridges span these canals. If Venice has a main street, it's the **Grand Canal,** which is spanned by three bridges: the Rialto, the Academy Bridge, and the stone Railway Bridge (the last dating from the 20th century). The canal splits Venice into two unequal parts.

South of the section called Dorsoduro, which is south of the Grand Canal, is the **Canale della Giudecca,** a major channel separating Dorsoduro from the large island of La Giudecca. At the point where the Canale della Giudecca meets the Canale di San Marco, you'll spot the little **Isola di San Giorgio Maggiore,** with a church by Palladio. The most visited islands in the lagoon, aside from the **Lido,** are **Murano, Burano,** and **Torcello.**

Once you land and explore Piazza San Marco and its satellite, Piazzetta San Marco, you can head down **Riva degli Schiavoni,** with its deluxe and first-class hotels, or follow the signs along the **Mercerie,** the major shopping artery, which leads to the Rialto, site of the market area.

Maps & Finding an Address The system of addresses in Venice is so confusing it's probably known only to the postman. The best thing to do is to arm yourself with a good map, such as the **Falk** map of Venice, which is pocket size and available in many kiosks and bookstores.

GETTING AROUND

BY VAPORETTO The motorboats, or *vaporetti,* of Venice provide inexpensive and frequent, if not always fast, transportation in this canal-riddled city. An *accelerato* is a vessel that makes every stop and a *diretto* makes only express stops. The average fare is 4,000L ($2.55). In summer the vaporetti are often fiercely crowded. Pick up a map of the system from the tourist office. There is frequent service daily 7am–midnight, then hourly midnight–7am.

Visitors to Venice may avail themselves of a 24-hour 15,000L ($9.60) *biglietto turistico* (tourist ticket), which allows them to travel all day long on any of the many routes of the city's boat services. This all-inclusive ticket is a bargain, as is the 3-day ticket allowing travel for 30,000L ($19.20).

ON FOOT This is the only way to explore Venice unless you plan to see it from a boat on the Grand Canal. Everybody walks in Venice—there's no other way.

BY WATER TAXI / MOTOR LAUNCH The city's many private motor launches are called *taxi acquei.* You may or may not have the cabin of one of these sleek vessels to yourself, since the captains fill their boats with as many passengers as the law allows before taking off. The price of a transit by water taxi from Piazzale Roma (the road and rail terminus) to Piazza San Marco begins at 80,000L ($51.20) for one to six passengers. You can also call for a taxi acquei—try **Cooperativa San Marco** at **041/5222303.**

BY GONDOLA   When riding in a gondola, two major agreements have to be reached: the price of the ride and the length of the trip. Gondola rides are best taken at high tide. The official rate is 80,000L ($51.20), but virtually no one pays that amount. Two major stations at which you can hire gondolas are Piazza San Marco (☎ **041/5200685**) and the Ponte Rialto (☎ **041/5224904**).

FAST FACTS: Venice

American Express   The office of American Express is at San Marco 1471 (☎ 041/5200844), in the San Marco area. City tours and mail handling can be obtained here. The office is open May–Oct, Mon–Sat 8am–8pm for currency exchange and 9am–5:30pm for all other transactions; Nov–Apr, Mon–Fri 9am–5:30pm and Sat 9am–12:30pm.

Consulates   There's no U.S. consulate in Venice; the closest is in Milan, at Via Prìncipe Amedeo 2 (☎ 02/290351). The British consulate is at Dorsoduro 1051 (☎ 041/5227207), open Mon–Fri 10am–noon and 2–3pm.

Currency   See "Fast Facts: Rome" in section 1.

Currency Exchange   There are many banks in Venice where you can exchange money. For example, try the Deutsch Bank SPA, San Marco 2216 (☎ 041/5207024). Many travelers find that Guetta, San Marco 1289 (☎ 041/5208711), offers the best rates in Venice.

Dentist/Doctor   Your best bet is to have your hotel call and set up an appointment with an English-speaking dentist or doctor. The American Express office and the British Consulate also have a list.

Drugstores   If you need a drugstore in the middle of the night, call 192 for information about which one is open. Pharmacies take turns staying open late. A well-recommended, centrally located one is the International Pharmacy, Via XXII Marzo 2067 (☎ 041/5222311).

Emergencies   Emergency phone numbers are 113 for the police, 523-0000 for an ambulance, and 522-2222 to report a fire.

Hospitals   Get in touch with the Civili Riuniti di Venezia, Campo Santi Giovanni e Paolo (☎ 041/260711).

Lost Property   The central office for recovering lost property is the Ufficio Oggetti Rinvenuti, an annex to the Municipio (town hall) at San Marco 4134 (☎ 041/2708225), on Calle Piscopia o Loredan, lying off Rive del Carbon on the Grand Canal. Open Mon, Wed, and Fri 9:30am–12:30pm.

Luggage Storage/Lockers   These services are available at the main rail station, Stazione di Santa Lucia, at Piazzale Roma (☎ 041/715555).

Post Office   The main post office is at Fondaco dei Tedeschi (☎ 041/2717111), in the vicinity of the Rialto Bridge. It's open Mon–Sat 8:15am–7pm.

Safety   The curse of Venice is the pickpocket. Violent crime is rare, but because of the overcrowding on vaporetti and even on the small, narrow streets, it's easy to pick pockets. Purse snatchings are commonplace as well. A purse snatcher seemingly darts out of nowhere, grabs a purse, and in seconds seems to have disappeared down some narrow, dark alley. Secure your valuables, and if your hotel has such amenities, keep them locked in a safe there when not needed.

Transit Information   For flights, call 041/5415491; for rail information, 041/715555; and for bus schedules, 041/5287886.

ACCOMMODATIONS
On Isola della Giudecca
Very Expensive

✪ Cipriani. Isola della Giudecca 10, 30133 Venezia. ☎ **800/992-5055** in the U.S., or 041/5207744. Fax 041/5207745. 76 rms, 28 suites. A/C MINIBAR TV TEL. 850,000–1,200,000L ($544–$768) double; from 1,850,000L ($1,184) suite. Rates include breakfast. AE, DC, MC, V. Closed Nov–Mar. Vaporetto: Zitelle.

Isolated, security-conscious, and elegant, the Cipriani occupies a 16th-century cloister on the residential island of Giudecca. This refined, tranquil, and sybaritic resort hotel was established in 1958 by the late Giuseppe Cipriani, the founder of Harry's Bar and the one real-life character in Hemingway's Venetian novel. The guest rooms have different amenities—ranging from tasteful contemporary to an antique design—but all have splendid views. Lunch is served at Il Gabbiano, either indoors or on terraces overlooking the water. More formal meals are served at night in the Restaurant. There's an Olympic-size pool with filtered salt water, tennis courts, a sauna, and a fitness center.

Near Piazza San Marco
Expensive

Hotel Concordia. Calle Larga San Marco 367, 30124 Venezia. ☎ **041/5206866.** Fax 041/5206775. 55 rms. A/C MINIBAR TV TEL. 260,000–510,000L ($166.40–$326.40) double. Rates include breakfast. AE, DC, MC, V. Vaporetto: San Marco.

The Concordia is the only hotel in Venice containing some rooms that look out over St. Mark's Square. Completely renovated and awarded four stars, the hotel is housed in a russet-colored building with stone-trimmed windows. A series of gold-plated marble steps takes you to the lobby, where you'll find a comfortable bar area, good service, and elevators to whisk you to the labyrinthine corridors. All the guest rooms—often filled with leisure groups—are decorated in a Venetian antique style and contain an electronic safe and hair dryer in addition to other amenities. Light meals and Italian snacks are available in the bar.

Moderate

Hotel Carpaccio. San Tomà 2765, 30125 Venezia. ☎ **041/5235946.** Fax 041/5242134. 18 rms. MINIBAR TEL. 280,000L ($179.20) double. Rates include breakfast. MC, V. Closed mid-Nov to Mid-Mar. Vaporetto: San Tomà.

Don't be put off by the narrow, winding alleys leading up to the wrought-iron entrance of this second-class hotel—the building was meant to be approached by gondola. Once you're inside, you'll realize that your location in the heart of the oldest part of the city justifies your confusing arrival. This building used to be the Palazzo Barbarigo della Terrazza, and part of it is still reserved for private apartments. The hotel maintains tasteful and spacious rooms filled with serviceable furniture. The salon is decorated with gracious pieces, marble floors, and a big arched window whose exterior is crowned with a bearded head of stone looking, along with you, over the Grand Canal.

Hotel Casanova. Frezzeria 1284, 30124 Venezia. ☎ **041/5206855.** Fax 041/5206413. 43 rms, 3 suites. A/C MINIBAR TV TEL. 340,000L ($217.60) double; 420,000L ($268.80) triple; 445,000L ($284.80) suite. Rates include breakfast. AE, DC, MC, V. Vaporetto: San Marco.

The Hotel Casanova, a few steps from Piazza San Marco, is without much character. Public areas have a collection of church art and benches from old monasteries that sit on flagstone floors near oil portraits. Modernized rooms have contemporary furnishings and are missing the charm of the public areas, though generally well maintained. The accommodations vary considerably in size—some are quite small. The most intriguing are found on the top floor, with exposed brick walls and sloping beamed ceilings.

Hotel la Fenice et des Artistes. Campiello de la Fenice 1936, 30124 Venezia. ☎ **041/5232333.** Fax 041/5203721. 65 rms, 4 suites. TV TEL. 310,000L ($198.40) double; from 420,000L ($268.80) suite. Rates include breakfast. AE, DC, MC, V. Vaporetto: San Marco.

This hotel offers widely varying accommodations in two connected buildings, each at least 100 years old. One building is rather romantic yet time worn, with an architecturally rich staircase leading to the overly decorated rooms. Your satin-lined room may have an inlaid desk and a wardrobe painted in the Venetian manner to match a baroque bed frame. The carpets might be thin, however, and the fabrics aging. Chambers in the other building are far less glamorous. The older of the two has no elevator, and while the newer has an elevator, its modern rooms have conservative, rather sterile furniture.

Hotel San Cassiano Ca'Favretto. Calle della Rosa 2232, 30135 Venezia. ☎ **041/5241768.** Fax 041/721033. 36 rms. A/C MINIBAR TV TEL. 170,000–327,000L ($108.80–$209.30) double. Rates include breakfast. AE, DC, MC, V. Vaporetto: San Stae.

The San Cassiano Ca'Favretto was once the studio of 19th-century painter Giacomo Favretto. The views from the hotel's gondola pier and from the dining room's four-arched porch encompass the lacy facade of the Ca' d'Oro, sometimes considered the most beautiful building in Venice. The hotel was constructed in the 14th century as a palace. The present owner has worked closely with Venetian authorities to preserve the original details, which include a 20-foot beamed ceiling in the entrance area. Fifteen of the conservatively decorated rooms overlook one of two canals, and many are filled with antiques or high-quality reproductions.

Inexpensive

Boston Hotel. Ponte dei Dai 848, 30124 Venezia. ☎ **041/5287665.** Fax 041/5226628. 42 rms. TEL. 110,000–240,000L ($70.40–$153.60) double. Rates include breakfast. AE, DC, MC, V. Closed Nov–Feb. Vaporetto: San Marco.

The Boston Hotel, run by Mario and Adriana Bernardi, is a whisper away from St. Mark's. The hotel was named after an uncle who left to seek his fortune in Boston and never returned. The little living rooms combine old and new, containing many antiques and Venetian ceilings. For the skinny guest, there's a tiny self-operated elevator and a postage-stamp–size street entrance. Most of the rooms with parquet floors have built-in features, snugly designed beds, chests, and wardrobes. Fortunately, several have tiny balconies opening onto canals. Some rooms are air-conditioned and a TV is available upon request.

Giorgione. SS. Apostoli 4586, 30131 Venezia. ☎ **041/5225810.** Fax 041/5239092. 70 rms, 8 suites. A/C MINIBAR TV TEL. 270,000–300,000L ($172.80–$192) double; 350,000–390,000L ($224–$249.60) suite. Rates include breakfast. AE, DC, MC, V. Vaporetto: Ca' d'Oro.

In spite of modernization here the decor is traditionally Venetian. The lounges and public rooms are equipped with fine furnishings and decorative accessories. Likewise, the comfortable as well as stylish guest rooms are designed to coddle you. The hotel also has a typical Venetian garden. It's rated second class by the government, but the Giorgione maintains higher standards than many of the first-class establishments. Breakfast is the only meal served.

NEAR THE ACCADEMIA
Moderate

⑤ American Hotel. Campo San Vio 628, 30123 Venezia. ☎ **041/5204733.** Fax 041/5204048. 29 rms. A/C MINIBAR TV TEL. 310,000L ($198.40) double; 370,000L ($236.80) triple. Rates include breakfast. AE, DC, MC, V. Vaporetto: Accademia.

Set on a small waterway, the American Hotel (there's nothing American about it) occupies an ochre building across the Grand Canal from the most heavily touristed areas. It's one of your best budget bets. The modest lobby is filled with murals, warm colors, and antiques, and the location is perfect for anyone wanting to avoid the crowds that descend in summer. The rooms are comfortably furnished in a Venetian style, but they vary in size; some of the smaller ones are a bit cramped. On the second floor is a beautiful terrace where guests relax over drinks. Many rooms with a private terrace face the canal.

Inexpensive

⑤ Locanda Montin. Fondamenta di Borgo 1147, in Dorsoduro, 31000 Venezia. ☎ **041/5227151.** Fax 041/5200255. 12 rms, 5 with bath. 75,000L ($48) double without bath, 85,000L ($54.40) double with bath. AE, DC, MC, V. Vaporetto: Accademia.

The well-recommended Locanda Montin is an old-fashioned Venetian inn whose adjoining restaurant is one of the most loved in the area. The hotel is in the Dorsoduro section, across the Grand Canal from the most popular tourist zones. It's officially listed as a fourth-class hotel, but the accommodations are considerably larger and better than that rating suggests. Reservations are virtually mandatory, because of the reputation of this locanda. Marked only by a small carriage lamp etched with the name of the establishment extending over the pavement, the inn is a little difficult to locate but worth the search.

⑤ Pensione Accademia. Fondamenta Bollani 1058, in Dorsoduro, 30123 Venezia. ☎ **041/5237846.** Fax 041/5239152. 29 rms. 225,000L ($144) double. Rates include breakfast. AE, DC, MC, V. Vaporetto: Accademia.

This is the most patrician of the pensioni, in a villa whose garden extends into the angle created by the junction of two canals. Iron fences, twisting vines, and neoclassical sculpture are a part of the setting, as are gothic-style paneling, Venetian chandeliers, and Victorian-era furniture. There's an upstairs sitting room with two large windows and a formal rose garden that's visible from the breakfast room. The rooms are spacious and decorated with original 19th-century furniture. Some of the rooms are air-conditioned and most have been renovated. This was the fictional residence of Katharine Hepburn's character in the film *Summertime*.

ON CAMPO MARIA DEL GIGLIO
Very Expensive

✪ Gritti Palace. Campo Santa Maria del Giglio 2467, 30124 Venezia. ☎ **800/221-2340** in the U.S., 800/955-2442 in Canada, or 041/794611. Fax 041/5200942. 96 rms, 10 suites. A/C MINIBAR TV TEL. 660,000–760,000L ($422.40–$486.40) double; from 1,600,000L ($1,024) suite. AE, DC, MC, V. Vaporetto: Santa Maria del Giglio.

The Gritti Palace, in a stately setting on the Grand Canal, is the renovated four-story palazzo of the 15th-century doge Andrea Gritti. It's a bit starchy, but is topped only by the Cipriani as the prestige address. There's something of a museum aura to the place. "Our home in Venice" to Ernest Hemingway, it has for years drawn a clientele of theatrical, literary, political, and royal figures. The range and variety of the rooms seem almost limitless, from elaborate suites to relatively small singles. But in every case the stamp of glamour is evident. Antiques are often used in both the guest rooms and the public rooms. For a splurge, ask for Hemingway's old suite or the Doge Suite, once occupied by Somerset Maugham.

DINING
NEAR PIAZZA SAN MARCO & LA FENICE
Expensive

✪ **Antico Martini.** San Marco 1983, Campo San Fantin. ☎ **041/5224121.** Reservations required. Main courses 32,000–50,000L ($20.50–$32); fixed-price menu 40,000–55,000L ($25.60–$35.20) at lunch, 72,000–98,000L ($46.10–$62.70) at dinner. AE, DC, MC, V. Wed 7–11:30pm, Thurs–Mon noon–2:30pm and 7–11:30pm. Vaporetto: San Marco or Santa Maria del Giglio. VENETIAN/INTERNATIONAL.

As the city's leading restaurant, the Antico Martini elevates Venetian cuisine to its highest level. The walls are paneled, elaborate chandeliers glitter overhead, and gilt-framed oil paintings adorn the walls. The courtyard is favored in summer. An excellent beginning to your meal is the risotto di frutti di mare, creamy Venetian style with plenty of fresh seafood. For a main dish, try the fegato alla veneziana, which is tender liver fried with onions and served with polenta, a yellow cornmeal mush praised by Goldoni. The chefs are better at regional dishes than they are with those of the international kitchen.

Harry's Bar. Calle Vallaresso 1323. ☎ **041/5285777.** Reservations required. Main courses 75,000–85,000L ($48–$54.40). AE, DC, MC, V. Daily 10:30am–11pm. Vaporetto: San Marco. VENETIAN.

Harry's Bar serves the best food in Venice, though Quadri and the Antico Martini have more elegant atmospheres. Its fame was spread by Ernest Hemingway. A. E. Hotchner, in *Papa Hemingway*, quoted the writer as saying, "We can't eat straight hamburger in a Renaissance palazzo on the Grand Canal." So he ordered a 5-pound "tin of beluga caviar" to, as he said, "take the curse off it." Hemingway would probably skip the place today, and the prices would come as a shock even to him. You can have your choice of dining in the bar downstairs or the room with a view upstairs. We recommend the Venetian fish soup, followed by scampi Thermidor with rice pilaf or seafood ravioli, and topped off by chocolate mousse. The food is relatively simple, but fresh ingredients are used and cooked only a short time to ensure their flavors.

Quadri. Piazza San Marco 120–124. ☎ **041/5289299.** Reservations required. Main courses 39,000–57,000L ($24.95–$36.50). AE, DC, MC, V. Tues–Sun noon–2:30pm and 7–10:30pm. Vaporetto: San Marco. INTERNATIONAL.

One of Europe's famous restaurants, the deluxe Quadri is on the second floor, overlooking the "living room" of Venice. The setting is one of gilt and rosy velvet, evoking the world of its former patrons, Marcel Proust and Stendhal. Many diners come here just for the setting and are often surprised when they're treated to a high-quality cuisine and impeccable service. You pay for all this nostalgia, however. The Venetian cuisine has been acclaimed (at least by one food critic) as "befitting a doge," though we doubt if those old doges ate as well. Even the classic Venetian sautéed liver seems to taste better here. The chef is likely to tempt you with such dishes as octopus in fresh tomato sauce, salt codfish with polenta, or sea bass with crab sauce.

Moderate

Da Ivo. Calle dei Fuseri 1809. ☎ **041/5285004.** Reservations required. Main courses 35,000–50,000L ($22.40–$32). AE, DC, MC, V. Mon–Sat noon–2:40pm and 7pm–midnight. Closed Jan 6–31. Vaporetto: San Marco. TUSCAN/VENETIAN.

Da Ivo has such a faithful clientele that you'll think at first you're in a semiprivate club. The rustic atmosphere is both cozy and relaxing, with candles on the well-set tables. Homesick Florentines go here for fine Tuscan cookery; regional Venetian dishes are also served. In season, game, according to an ancient tradition, is cooked over an open charcoal grill. On one cold day our hearts and plates were warmed when we ordered homemade tagliatelli. It came with slivers of tartufi bianchi, the pungent white truffle from the Piedmont district that's unforgettable to the palate, spread over it. Dishes change according to the season and the availability of ingredients.

Ristorante à la Vecia Cavana. Rio Terà SS. Apostoli 4624. ☎ **041/5287106.** Main courses 20,000–40,000L ($12.80–$25.60); fixed-price menu 30,000L ($19.20). AE, DC, MC, V. Fri–Wed noon–2:30pm and 7:30–10:30pm. Vaporetto: Ca' d'Oro. SEAFOOD.

This restaurant is off the tourist circuit and well worth the trek through the winding streets to find it. When you enter, you'll be greeted with brick arches, stone columns, terra-cotta floors, framed modern paintings, and a photograph of 19th-century fishermen relaxing after a day's work. It's an appropriate introduction to a menu that specializes in seafood, including a mixed grill from the Adriatic, fresh sole, three types of risotto (each prepared with seafood), and spicy zuppa di pesce (fish soup). Another specialty is antipasti di pesce Cavana, which includes an assortment of just about every sea creature.

Taverna la Fenice. Campiello de la Fenice 1938. ☎ **041/5223856.** Reservations required. Main courses 18,000–28,000L ($11.50–$17.90). AE, DC, MC, V. June–Aug, daily noon–2:30pm and 7–10:30pm; Sept–May, Mon 7–10:30pm, Tues–Sat noon–2:30pm and 7–10:30pm. Closed 2nd week in Jan. Vaporetto: San Marco. ITALIAN/VENETIAN.

Opened in 1907, when Venetians were flocking in record numbers to hear the *bel canto* performances in the opera house nearby, this restaurant is one of Venice's most romantic dining spots. The interior is suitably elegant, but the preferred spot in clement weather is out beneath a canopy, a few steps from the burned Teatro La Fenice, where Stravinski introduced works that included *The Rake's Progress.* The service is smooth and efficient. You might enjoy risotto with scampi and arugula, freshly made tagliatelle with cream and exotic mushrooms, or John Dory filets with artichokes.

Trattoria La Colomba. San Marco-Piscina-Frezzeria 1665. ☎ **041/5221175.** Reservations recommended. Main courses 25,000–60,000L ($16–$38.40). AE, DC, MC, V. Daily noon–3pm and 7–11pm. Closed Wed June 16–Aug and Nov 16–Apr 14. Vaporetto: San Marco or Rialto. VENETIAN/INTERNATIONAL.

This is one of the most distinctive and popular trattorie in town, with a history going back at least a century and a by-now legendary association with some of Venice's leading painters. In 1985 a $2-million restoration improved the infrastructure, making it a more attractive foil for the dozens of modern paintings that hang on its walls. Menu items are likely to include at least five daily specials based exclusively on the time-honored cuisine of Venice. Otherwise, you can order risotto di funghi del Montello (risotto with mushrooms from the local hills of Montello) or baccalà alla vicentina (milk-simmered dry cod seasoned with onions, anchovies, and cinnamon, then served with polenta).

Inexpensive

§ **Nuova Rivetta.** Castello 4625, Campo San Filippo. ☎ **041/5287302.** Reservations required. Main courses 15,000–35,000L ($9.60–$22.40). AE, MC, V. Tues–Sun 10am–10pm. Closed July 23–Aug 20. Vaporetto: San Zaccaria. SEAFOOD.

The Nuova Rivetta is an old-fashioned Venetian trattoria where you eat well without having to pay a lot. The restaurant stands in the monumental heart of the old city. Many find it best for lunch during a stroll around Venice. The most representative dish to order is frittura di pesce, a mixed fish fry from the Adriatic, which includes squid or various other "sea creatures" that turned up at the market that day. Other specialties are gnocchi stuffed with Adriatic spider crab, pasticcho of fish (a main course), and spaghetti flavored with squid ink.

Ristorante al Mondo Novo. Salizzada di San Lio, Castello 5409. ☎ **041/5200698.** Reservations recommended. Main courses 15,000–24,000L ($9.60–$15.35); fixed-price menus 22,000–30,000L ($14.10–$19.20). AE, MC, V. Tues–Sun 11am–3pm and 7pm–midnight (last order). Vaporetto: Rialto or San Marco. VENETIAN/SEAFOOD.

In a very old Venetian villa built during the Renaissance, this well-established restaurant offers professional service, a kindly staff, and a willingness to remain open later than many of its nearby competitors. Menu items include a wide array of seafood, prepared succulently as frittura misto dell' Adriatico or charcoal grilled. Other items include an array of such pastas as maccaroni alla verdura (with fresh vegetables and greens), an antipasti of fresh fish, and filets of beef with pepper sauce and rissole potatoes.

Ristorante da Raffaele. Calle Larga XXII Marzo 2347 (Fondamenta delle Ostreghe). ☎ **041/5232317.** Reservations recommended. Main courses 22,000–35,000L ($14.10–$22.40). AE, DC, MC, V. Fri–Wed noon–3pm and 7–10:30pm. Closed Dec 10 to mid-Feb. Vaporetto: San Marco or Santa Maria del Giglio. ITALIAN/VENETIAN.

This place, a 5-minute walk from Piazza San Marco and a minute from the Grand Canal, has long been a favorite canalside stop. It's often overrun with tourists, but the veteran kitchen staff holds up well. The restaurant offers the kind of charm and special atmosphere that are unique to the city. The huge inner sanctum has a high-beamed ceiling, 17th- to 19th-century pistols and sabers, exposed brick, wrought-iron chandeliers, a massive fireplace, and hundreds of copper pots. The food is excellent, beginning with a choice of tasty antipasti or well-prepared pastas. Seafood specialties include scampi, squid, or a platter of deep-fried fish from the Adriatic. The grilled meats are also succulent and can be followed by rich, tempting desserts.

Vini da Arturo. Calle degli Assassini 3656. ☎ **041/5286974.** Reservations recommended. Main courses 25,000–40,000L ($16–$25.60). No credit cards. Mon–Sat noon–2:30pm and 7–10:30pm. Closed Aug. Vaporetto: San Marco or Rialto. VENETIAN.

Vini da Arturo attracts many devoted regulars, including artists and writers. Here you get some of the most delectable local cooking—and not just the standard cliché Venetian dishes, and not seafood, which may be unique for a Venetian restaurant. Instead of ordering plain pasta, try a tantalizing dish called spaghetti alla Gorgonzola. The beef is also good, especially when prepared with a cream sauce flavored with mustard and freshly ground pepper. The salads are made with crisp, fresh ingredients, often in unusual combinations. The place is small and contains only seven tables; it's between the Fenice Opera House and St. Mark's Square.

EAST OF PIAZZA SAN MARCO
Moderate
Arcimboldo. Castello, Calle dei Furiani 3219. ☎ **041/5286569.** Reservations recommended. Main courses 22,000–38,000L ($14.10–$24.30); fixed-price menu 40,000L ($25.60). AE, DC, MC, V. Wed–Mon 7:30pm–midnight. Vaporetto: Arsenale or San Zaccaria. VENETIAN/ITALIAN.

At the corner on which sits the Scuola di San Giorgio degli Schiavoni (containing Carpaccio's celebrated cycle of paintings), turn onto a little street and follow a narrow footpath leading deep into Venice's oldest quarter. At the end of the street you'll stumble on Arcimboldo, one of the city's most charming restaurants. It overlooks a canal and is named for Giuseppe Arcimboldo, a famous 16th-century painter who worked at the Hapsburg court making fantastical portraits of fruits and vegetables. Reproductions of his work line the walls. The romantic decor is a fitting backdrop for the traditional Venetian fare served here. Both old and modern dishes are prepared with the excellent fruits and vegetables grown on the neighboring islands. You can enjoy Venetian-style antipasti, excellent pasta dishes, fish, risotto, and the pick of poultry and meat.

NEAR THE RIALTO
Moderate

"Al graspo de ua". Calle dei Bombaseri 5093. ☎ **041/5200150.** Reservations required. Main courses 25,000–35,000L ($16–$22.40). AE, DC, MC, V. Wed–Sun noon–3pm and 8–11pm. Closed Jan 2–17. Vaporetto: Rialto. SEAFOOD/VENETIAN.

"Al graspo de ua" is one bunch of grapes you'll want to pluck. For that special meal, it's a winner. Decorated in the old taverna style, it offers several air-conditioned dining rooms. One has a beamed ceiling, hung with garlic and copper bric-a-brac. Among the best fish restaurants in Venice, this place has been patronized by such celebs as Elizabeth Taylor, Jeanne Moreau, and even Giorgio de Chirico. You can help yourself to all the hors d'oeuvres you want—known on the menu as "self-service mammoth." The wonderful gran fritto dell'Adriatico is a mixed treat of deep-fried fish from the Adriatic.

Poste Vechie. Pescheria Rialto 1608. ☎ **041/721822.** Reservations recommended. Main courses 20,000–35,000L ($12.80–$22.40). AE, DC, MC, V. Wed–Mon noon–3:30pm and 7–10:30pm. Vaporetto: Rialto. SEAFOOD.

This is one of Venice's most charming restaurants, near the Rialto fish market and connected to the rest of the city with a small, privately owned bridge. It was established in the early 1500s as the local post office—food was served to the mail carriers to fortify them for their deliveries. Today it's one of the oldest restaurants in town, with a pair of intimate dining rooms and a verdant courtyard. Menu items include a super-fresh array of fish from the nearby markets; a salad of shellfish and exotic mushrooms; a spicy soup of Adriatic fish; tagliolini flavored with squid ink, crabmeat, and fish sauce; and the restaurant's pièce de résistance, seppi (cuttlefish) à la veneziana with polenta. If you don't like fish, calf's liver or veal shank with ham and cheese are also well prepared. The desserts come rolling to your table on a trolley and are usually delicious.

Inexpensive

Restaurant da Bruno. Castello, Calle del Paradiso 5731. ☎ **041/5221480.** Main courses 12,000–20,000L ($7.70–$12.80); fixed-price menu 23,000L ($14.70). AE, DC, MC, V. Wed–Mon noon–3pm and 7–11pm. Closed 1 week in Jan. Vaporetto: San Marco or Rialto. VENETIAN.

The Restaurant da Bruno is like a country tavern in the center of Venice. On a narrow street about halfway between the Rialto Bridge and Piazza San Marco, the restaurant attracts its crowds by grilling meats on an open-hearth fire. Get your antipasti at the counter and watch your prosciutto being prepared—paper-thin slices of spicy flavored ham wrapped around breadsticks (grissini). In the right season, da Bruno does some of the finest game specialty dishes in Venice. If it's featured, try capriolo (roebuck) or fagiano (pheasant). Another great dish is veal scaloppine with wild mushrooms.

⑤ Rosticceria San Bartolomeo. Calle della Bissa, San Marco 5424. ☎ **041/5223569.** Main courses 15,000–22,000L ($9.60–$14.10); fixed-price menus 26,000–27,000L ($16.65–$17.30). AE, MC, V. Tues–Sun 10am–2:30pm and 5–9pm. Vaporetto: Rialto. VENETIAN.

The Rosticceria San Bartolomeo is Venice's most frequented fast-food eatery and has long been a haven for budget travelers. Downstairs is a tavola calda where you can eat standing up, but upstairs is a restaurant with waiter service. Typical dishes include baccalà alla vicentina (codfish simmered in herbs and milk), deep-fried mozzarella (which the Italians call in carrozza), and seppi con polenta (cuttlefish in its own ink sauce, with a cornmeal mush). Everything can be washed down with typical Veneto wine.

⑤ Trattoria Madonna. Calle de la Madonna 594. ☎ **041/5223824.** Reservations recommended but not always accepted. Main courses 5,000–20,000L ($3.20–$12.80). AE, MC, V. Thurs–Tues noon–3pm and 7:15–10pm. Closed Jan 7–Feb 7 and Aug 1–15. Vaporetto: Rialto. VENETIAN.

This restaurant was opened in 1954 in a 300-year-old building of historic distinction. Named after *another* famous Madonna, it's one of the most popular and characteristic trattorie of Venice, specializing in traditional recipes and an array of grilled fresh fish. A suitable beginning may be the antipasto frutti di mare. Pastas, polentas, risottos, meats (including *fegato alla veneziana,* liver with onions), and many kinds of irreproachably fresh fish are widely available.

IN THE DORSODURO

Inexpensive

⑤ La Furatola. Calle Lunga San Barnaba 2870A. ☎ **041/5208594.** Reservations recommended for dinner. Main courses 20,000–30,000L ($12.80–$19.20). No credit cards. Fri–Tues noon–2:30pm and 7–9:30pm. Closed July–Aug. Vaporetto: Ca' Rezzonico or Accademia. SEAFOOD.

La Furatola (an old Venetian word meaning "restaurant") is very much a Dorsoduro neighborhood hangout, but it has captured the imagination of local foodies. It's in a 300-year-old building, along a narrow flagstone-paved street that you'll need a good map and a lot of patience to find. Perhaps you'll have lunch here after a visit to the Church of San Rocco, only a short distance away. The specialty is fish brought to your table in a wicker basket so you can judge its size and freshness by its bright eyes and red gills. A display of seafood antipasti is set out near the entrance. A standout is the baby octopus boiled and eaten with a drop of red-wine vinegar.

✪ Locanda Montin. Fondamenta di Borgo 1147. ☎ **041/5227151.** Reservations recommended. Main courses 12,000–30,000L ($7.70–$19.20). AE, DC, MC, V. Tues 12:30–2:30pm, Thurs–Mon 12:30–2:30pm and 7:30–9:30pm. Vaporetto: Accademia. INTERNATIONAL/ITALIAN.

Since it opened just after World War II, famous patrons have included Ezra Pound, Jackson Pollock, Mark Rothko, and many of the assorted artist friends of the late Peggy Guggenheim. The inn is owned and run by the Carretins, who have covered the walls with paintings donated by or purchased from their many friends and diners. Today the arbor-covered garden courtyard of this 17th-century building is filled with regulars, many of whom allow their favorite waiter to select most of their dishes. The frequently changing menu includes a variety of salads, grilled meats, and fish caught in the Adriatic.

ATTRACTIONS

Ahead, we'll explore the city's great art and architecture. But, unlike Florence, Venice would reward you with treasures even if you never ducked inside a museum or church. In the city on the islands, the frame eternally competes with the picture inside. "For all its vanity and villainy," wrote Lewis Mumford, "life touched some of its highest moments in Venice."

SIGHTSEEING SUGGESTIONS

If You Have 1 Day   Get up early and watch the sun rise over Piazza San Marco, as the city wakes up. The pigeons will already be here to greet you. Have an early-morning cappuccino on the square, then visit the Basilica of San Marco and the Palazzo Ducale later. Ride the Grand Canal in a gondola 2 hours before sunset and spend the rest of the evening wandering the narrow streets of this strangely unreal and most fascinating of the cities of Europe. Apologize to yourself for such a short visit and promise to return.

If You Have 2 Days   Spend your first day as above. On day 2 it's time for more concentrated sightseeing. Begin at Piazza San Marco (viewing it should be a daily ritual, regardless of how many days you have in Venice), then head for the major museum, the Accademia, in the morning. In the afternoon, visit the Collezione Peggy Guggenheim (modern art) and perhaps the Ca' d'Oro and Ca' Rezzonico.

If You Have 3 Days   Spend your first 2 days as above. Begin day 3 by having a cappuccino on Piazza San Marco, then inspect the Campanile di San Marco. Later in the morning visit the Museo Correr. In the afternoon, go to the Scuola Grande di San Rocco to see the works of Tintoretto. Spend the rest of the day strolling the streets of Venice and ducking into shops that capture your imagination. Even if you get lost, you'll eventually return to a familiar landmark, and you can't help but see the signs pointing you back to Piazza San Marco. Have dinner in one of the most typical of Venetian trattorias, such as Locanda Montin.

If You Have 5 Days   Spend days 1 to 3 as above. On day 4 plan to visit the islands of the lagoon, including Murano, Burano, and Torcello. All three can be covered (at least briefly) on 1 busy day. On day 5, relax, wander around the streets, and take in some of the many attractions you may have missed.

THE GRAND CANAL

Peoria may have its Main Street, Paris its Champs-Elysées—but Venice, for uniqueness, tops them all with its ✪ **Canal Grande (Grand Canal).** Lined with palazzi—many in elegant Venetian-gothic style—this great road of water is today filled with vaporetti, motorboats, and gondolas. Along the canal the boat moorings are like peppermint sticks. It begins at Piazzetta San Marco on one side and Longhena's Salute Church on the opposite bank. At midpoint it's spanned by the Rialto Bridge. Eventually the canal winds its serpentine course to the railway station. We can guarantee that there's not a dull sight en route.

THE BASILICA, DOGES' PALACE & CAMPANILE

✪ **Piazza San Marco (St. Mark's Square)** was the heartbeat of La Serenissima (the Serene Republic) in the heyday of its glory as a seafaring state, the crystallization of its dreams and aspirations. If you have only 1 day for Venice, you need not leave the square, as the city's major attractions, such as the Basilica of St. Mark and the Doges' Palace, are centered here or nearby. Thanks to Napoleon, the square was unified architecturally. The emperor added the Fabbrica Nuova, thus bridging the Old and New Procuratie. Flanked with medieval-looking palaces, Sansovino's Library, elegant shops and colonnades, the square is now finished—unlike Piazza della Signoria in Florence.

If Piazza San Marco is the drawing room of Europe, then its satellite, **Piazzetta San Marco,** is the antechamber. Hedged in by the Doges' Palace, Sansovino's Library, and a side of St. Mark's Basilica, the tiny square faces the Grand Canal. One of the two tall granite columns is surmounted by a winged lion, which represents St. Mark. The other is topped by a statue of a man taming a dragon, supposedly the dethroned patron saint Theodore. Both columns came from the East in the 12th century.

✪ Basilica di San Marco. Piazza San Marco. ☎ **041/5225205.** Admission: Basilica, baptistery, free; treasury, 3,000L ($1.90); presbytery, 3,000L ($1.90); Marciano Museum, 3,000L ($1.90). Basilica, baptistery, and presbytery, Apr–Sept, Mon–Sat 9:30am–5:30pm, Sun 2–5:30pm; Oct–Mar, Mon–Sat 9:30am–5pm, Sun 1:30–4:30pm. Treasury, Mon–Sat 9:30am–5pm, Sun 2–5pm. Marciano Museum, Apr–Sept, Mon–Sat 10am–5:30pm, Sun 2–4:30pm; Oct–Mar, Mon–Sat 10am–4:45pm, Sun 2–4:30pm. *Warning:* Visitors must wear appropriate clothing and remain silent during their visit. Photography is forbidden. Vaporetto: San Marco.

The so-called Church of Gold dominates Piazza San Marco. This is one of the world's greatest and most richly embellished churches. In fact, it looks as if it had been moved intact from Istanbul. The basilica is a conglomeration of styles, yet it's particularly indebted to Byzantium. It incorporates other schools of design, such as romanesque and gothic, with freewheeling abandon. Like Venice, it's adorned with booty from every corner of the city's once far-flung mercantile empire—capitals from Sicily, columns from Alexandria, porphyry from Syria, sculpture from Constantinople. The basilica is capped by a dome that—like a spider plant—sends off shoots, in this case a quartet of smaller-scale cupolas. Spanning the facade is a loggia, surmounted by replicas of the four famous St. Mark's horses—the *Triumphal Quadriga*.

To the right is the **baptistery,** dominated by the Sansovino-inspired baptismal font, upon which John the Baptist is ready to pour water. If you look back at the aperture over the entryway, you can see a mosaic, the dance of Salome in front of Herod and his court. Wearing a star-studded russet-red dress and three white fox tails, Salome dances under a platter holding John's head. Her glassy face is that of a Madonna, not an enchantress. After touring the baptistery, proceed up the right nave to the doorway to the **treasury** (*tesoro*). The entrance to the **presbytery** is nearby. On the high altar, the alleged sarcophagus of St. Mark rests under a green marble blanket and is held up by four sculptured alabaster Corinthian columns. The Byzantine-style **Pala d'Oro,** from Constantinople, is the rarest treasure at St. Mark's—made of gold and studded with precious stones.

On leaving the basilica, head up the stairs in the atrium for the **Marciano Museum** and the Loggia dei Cavalli. The star attraction of the museum is the world-famous Quadriga, four horses looted from Constantinople by Venetian crusaders in the sack of that city in 1204. This is the only quadriga (a quartet of horses yoked together) to have survived from the classical era.

✪ Palazzo Ducale. Piazzetta San Marco. ☎ **041/5224951.** Admission 10,000L ($6.40). Easter–Oct, daily 9am–6pm; Nov–Easter, daily 9am–4pm. Vaporetto: San Marco.

You enter the Palace of the Doges through the magnificent 15th-century Porta della Carta on the piazzetta. It's somewhat like a frosty birthday cake in pinkish red marble and white Istrian stone. The Venetian-gothic palazzo—with all the architectural intricacies of a doily—gleams in the tremulous Venetian light. The grandest civic structure in Italy, it dates back to 1309, though a fire in 1577 destroyed much of the original.

After climbing the Sansovino stairway of gold, proceed to the Anti-Collegio salon, which houses the palace's greatest artworks—notably Veronese's *Rape of Europa,* to the far left on the right wall. Tintoretto is well represented with his *Three Graces* and *Bacchus and Ariadne.* Some critics consider the latter his supreme achievement.

Now trek downstairs through the once-private apartments of the doges to the grand Maggior Consiglio, with its allegorical *Triumph of Venice* on the ceiling, painted by Veronese. What makes the room outstanding, however, is Tintoretto's *Paradise,* over the Grand Council chamber—said to be the largest oil painting in the world.

Reenter the Maggior Consiglio and follow the arrows on their trail across the **Bridge of Sighs,** linking the Doges' Palace with the Palazzo delle Prigioni, where the cell blocks are found, the ones that lodged the prisoners who felt the quick justice of the Terrible Ten. The "sighs" in the bridge's name stemmed from the sad laments of the numerous victims led across it to certain torture and possible death.

Campanile di San Marco. Piazza San Marco. ☎ **041/5224064.** Admission 6,000L ($3.85). May–Oct, daily 9am–8pm; Nov–Apr, daily 9:30am–3:45pm. Vaporetto: San Marco.

One summer night back in 1902, the bell tower of the Basilica of St. Mark on Piazza San Marco, which was suffering from years of rheumatism in the damp Venetian climate, gave out a warning sound that sent the fashionable crowd scurrying from the Florian Caffè in a dash for their lives. But the campanile gracefully waited until the next morning—July 14—before it tumbled into the piazza. The Venetians rebuilt their belfry, and it's now safe to ascend. A modern elevator takes you up for a pigeon's view of the city. It's a particularly good vantage point for viewing the cupolas of St. Mark's Basilica.

MUSEUMS

✪ **Accademia.** Campo della Carità, Dorsoduro. ☎ **041/5222247.** Admission 12,000L ($7.70) adults, free for children 17 and under and seniors 60 and over. Mon–Sat 9am–7pm, Sun 9am–2pm. Vaporetto: Accademia.

The pomp and circumstance, the glory that was Venice, lives on in this remarkable collection of paintings spanning the 14th to the 18th century. The hallmark of the Venetian school is color and more color. From Giorgione to Veronese, from Titian to Tintoretto, with a Carpaccio cycle thrown in, the Accademia has samples—often their best—of its most famous sons.

You'll first see works by such 14th-century artists as Paolo and Lorenzo Veneziano, who bridged the gap from Byzantine art to gothic (see the latter's *Annunciation*). Next, you'll view Giovanni Bellini's *Madonna and Saint* (poor Sebastian, not another arrow), and Carpaccio's fascinating yet gruesome work of mass crucifixion. Two of the most important works with secular themes are Mantegna's armored *St. George,* with the dragon slain at his feet, and Hans Memling's 15th-century portrait of a young man. Giorgione's *Tempest* is the most famous painting at the Accademia.

✪ **Collezione Peggy Guggenheim.** Ca' Venier dei Leoni, Dorsoduro 701, calle San Cristoforo. ☎ **041/5206288.** Admission 10,000L ($6.40) adults, 5,000L ($3.20) students and children 16 and under. Wed–Mon 11am–6pm. Vaporetto: Accademia.

This is one of the most comprehensive and brilliant modern-art collections in the Western world, and it reveals the foresight and critical judgment of its founder. The collection is housed in an unfinished palazzo, the former home of Peggy Guggenheim, who died in 1979. In the tradition of her family, Guggenheim was a lifelong patron of contemporary painters and sculptors. As her private collection increased, she decided to find a larger showcase and selected Venice. Displayed here are works not only by Pollock and Ernst but also by Picasso (see his cubist *The Poet* of

1911), Duchamp, Chagall, Mondrian, Brancusi, Delvaux, and Dalí, plus a garden of modern sculpture that includes works by Giacometti.

Ca' d'Oro. Cannaregio 3931–3932, Ca' d'Oro. ☎ **041/5238790.** Admission 4,000L ($2.55). Daily 9am–1:30pm. Closed Jan 1, May 1, and Dec 25. Vaporetto: Ca' d'Oro.

This is one of the most handsomely embellished palaces along the Grand Canal. Although it contains the important Galleria Giorgio Franchetti, the House of Gold (so named because its facade was once gilded) competes with its own paintings. Built in the first part of the 15th century in the ogival style, it has a lacy look. Baron Franchetti, who restored the palace and filled it with his collection of paintings, sculpture, and furniture, presented it to Italy during World War I. In a special niche reserved for the masterpiece of the Franchetti collection is Andrea Mantegna's icy-cold *St. Sebastian,* the central figure of which is riddled with what must be a record number of arrows.

Museo Civico Correr. In the Procuratie Nuove, Piazza San Marco. ☎ **041/5525625.** Admission 8,000L ($5.10) adults, 5,000L ($3.20) children 12–18, free for children 11 and under. June–Aug, Thurs–Mon 10am–5pm; Sept–May, Thurs–Mon 10am–4pm. Vaporetto: San Marco.

This museum traces the development of Venetian painting from the 14th to the 16th century. On the second floor are the red and maroon robes once worn by the doges, plus some fabulous street lanterns. There's also an illustrated copy of *Marco Polo in Tartaria.* You can see Cosmé Tura's *La Pietà,* a miniature of renown from the genius in the Ferrara School. This is one of his more gruesome works. It depicts a bony, gnarled Christ sprawled on the lap of the Madonna. Farther on, search out a Schiavone *Madonna and Child* (no. 545), our candidate for ugliest bambino ever depicted on canvas (no wonder the mother looks askance). One of the most important rooms at the Correr is filled with three masterpieces: *La Pietà* by Antonello da Messina, *The Crucifixion* by the Flemish painter Hugo van der Goes, and *Madonna and Child* by Dieric Bouts, who depicted the baby suckling his mother in a sensual manner. The star attraction of the Correr is the Bellini salon, which includes works by founding padre Jacopo and his son, Gentile. But the real master of the household was the other son, Giovanni.

Ca' Rezzonico. Fondamenta Rezzonico, Dorsoduro. ☎ **041/2410100.** Admission 8,000L ($5.10) adults, 5,000L ($3.20) children 12–18, free for children 11 and under. Sat–Thurs 10am–4pm. Vaporetto: Ca' Rezzonico.

This 17th- and 18th-century palace along the Grand Canal is where Robert Browning set up his bachelor headquarters. Pope Clement XIII also stayed here. It's a virtual treasure house, known for its baroque paintings and furniture. You first enter the Grand Ballroom with its allegorical ceiling, then proceed through lavishly embellished rooms with Venetian chandeliers, brocaded walls, portraits of patricians, tapestries, gilded furnishings, and touches of chinoiserie. At the end of the first walk is the Throne Room, with its allegorical ceilings by Giovanni Battista Tiepolo.

Upstairs you'll find a survey of 18th-century Venetian art. As you enter the main room from downstairs, head for the first salon on your right (facing the canal), which contains the best works of all, paintings from the brush of Pietro Longhi. His most famous work, *The Lady and the Hairdresser,* is the first canvas to the right on the entrance wall.

THE SCUOLE

✪ **Scuola di San Rocco.** Campo San Rocco, San Polo. ☎ **041/5234864.** Admission 8,000L ($5.10) adults, 2,500L ($1.60) children. Mar 28–Nov 2, daily 9am–5:30pm; Nov 3–Mar 27, Mon–Fri 10am–1pm, Sat–Sun 10am–4pm. Closed Easter and Dec 25–Jan 1. Vaporetto: San

Tomà; from the station, walk straight onto Ramo Mondoler, which becomes Larga Prima; then take Salizzada San Rocco, which opens into Campo San Rocco.

Of Venice's *scuole* (in the Renaissance, centers used by social and religious organizations affiliated with the local parish), none is as richly embellished as the Scuola di San Rocco, filled with epic canvases by Tintoretto. By clever trick, he won the competition to decorate the darkly illuminated early 16th-century building. He began painting in 1564 and the work stretched on till his powers as an artist waned. The paintings sweep across the upper and lower halls, mesmerizing the viewer with a kind of passion play. In the grand hallway they depict New Testament scenes, devoted largely to episodes in the life of Mary (the *Flight into Egypt* is among the best). In the top gallery are works illustrating scenes from the Old and the New Testament, the most renowned being those devoted to the life of Christ. In a separate room is what's considered Tintoretto's masterpiece—a mammoth *Crucifixion*, one of the world's most celebrated paintings.

Scuola di San Giorgio degli Schiavoni. Calle Furiani, Castello. ☎ **041/5228828.** Admission 5,000L ($3.20). Apr–Oct, Tues–Sat 9:30am–12:30pm and 3:30–6:30pm, Sun 9:30am–12:30pm; Nov–Mar, Tues–Sat 10am–12:30pm and 3–6pm, Sun 10am–12:30pm. Vaporetto: San Zaccaria.

At the St. Antonino Bridge (Fondamenta dei Furlani) is the second important scuola to visit in Venice. Between 1502 and 1509, Vittore Carpaccio painted a pictorial cycle here of exceptional merit and interest. Of enduring fame are his works of St. George and the dragon—these are our favorite pieces of art in all of Venice and certainly the most delightful. For example, in one frame St. George charges the dragon on a field littered with half-eaten bodies and skulls. Gruesome? Not at all. Any moment you expect the director to call "Cut!"

ORGANIZED TOURS

Daily at 9:10am, **American Express,** San Marco 1471 (☎ **041/5200844**), offers a 2-hour guided tour of the city, costing 33,000L ($21.10). Sights include St. Mark's Square, the basilica, the Doges' Palace, the prison, the bell tower, and in some cases a demonstration of the art of Venetian glassblowing. Daily between 3 and 5pm a 2-hour guided tour incorporates visits to the exteriors of several palaces along Campo San Benetto and other sights of the city. The tour eventually crosses the Grand Canal to visit the Church of Santa Maria dei Frari (which contains the *Assumption* by Titian). The tour continues by gondola down the canal to visit the Ca' d'Oro and ends at the Rialto Bridge. The cost of the afternoon tour is 35,000L ($22.40). A combined purchase of the morning and afternoon tour is just 60,000L ($38.40).

The Evening Serenade Tour, at 50,000L ($32) per person, allows a nocturnal view of Venice accompanied by the sound of singing musicians in gondolas. From May to October there are two daily departures, at 7 and 8pm, leaving from Campo Santa Maria del Giglio. Five to six occupants fit in each gondola as a singer and a handful of musicians perform throughout the Venetian evening. The experience lasts 50 minutes.

SHOPPING

Laboratorio Artigiano Maschere, Castello 6657, Barbaria delle Tole (☎ **041/5223110;** vaporetto: Rialto), is one of the best places to purchase carnival masks handcrafted in papier-mâché or leather. The masks carry names and symbols, the best known being the birdlike luck bringer, called *Buonaventura* in Italian. Masks are sold all over Venice, but this well-established store has a particularly good selection, including masks of commedia dell'arte characters. Open Mon 10–11:30am, Tues–Fri 10am–1pm and 3–7pm, and Sat 10am–1pm and 3–5pm.

Il Papiro, Campo San Maurizio 2764 (☎ **041/5223055;** vaporetto: Accademia), is mainly noted for its stationery supplies, but it also carries and sells many textures and colors of writing paper and cards. In addition to hand-printed paper, it sells any number of easy-to-pack gift items, which include wooden animals and copybooks. Open Mon 3:30–7:30pm, Tues–Sat 9:30am–7:30pm, and Sun 10am–6pm.

At **Pauly & Co.,** San Marco, Ponte Consorzi (☎ **041/5209899;** vaporetto: San Zaccaria), you can wander through 21 salons, enjoy an exhibition of artistic glassware, and later see a furnace in full action. There's no catalog offered; Pauly's production, which is mainly made to order, consists of continually renewed patterns, subject to change and alteration based on customer desire. Open Easter–Oct, daily 10am–7pm; off-season, Mon–Sat 10am–1pm and 3–7pm. **Venini,** Piazzetta Leoncini 314, San Marco (☎ **041/5224045;** vaporetto: San Zaccaria), has won collector fans all over the globe for its Venetian art glass. It sells lamps, bottles, and vases, but not ordinary ones. Many are works of art, representing the best of Venetian craftsmanship in design and manufacture. Their best-known glass has a distinctive swirl pattern in several colors, which is called a *venature.* Open Mon 3:30–7:30pm and Tues–Sat 9am–7:30pm.

For serious lace purchases, **Jesurum,** Mercerie del Capitello, San Marco 4857 (☎ **041/5206177;** vaporetto: San Zaccaria), is the best place. This elegant shop, a center of noted lacemakers and fashion creators, has been in a 12th-century church since 1868. You'll find Venetian hand- or machine-made lace and embroidery on table, bed, and bath linens; and hand-printed bathing suits. The quality and originality are guaranteed, and special orders are accepted. Open Mon–Sat 9:30am–7:30pm and Sun 10am–1pm and 2–7pm.

Bottega Veneta, Calle Vallaresso 1337, San Marco (☎ **041/5228489;** vaporetto: San Marco), is primarily known for its woven leather bags. These bags are sold elsewhere too, but the cost is said to be less at the company's flagship outlet in Venice. In addition, the shop sells shoes for men and women, suitcases, belts, and everything made of leather. There's also an array of high-fashion accessories. Open Mon 3–6:30pm, Tues–Sat 9:30am–1pm and 3–6:30pm, and Sun 11am–1pm and 2–6pm; closed Sun Jan–Feb and Oct–Nov.

If you're seeking some bargain-basement buys, head not for any basement but to one of the little shops that line the **Rialto Bridge.** The shops there branch out to encompass fruit and vegetable markets as well. The Rialto isn't the Ponte Vecchio in Florence, but, for what it offers, it isn't bad, particularly if your lire are running short. You'll find a wide assortment of merchandise here, from angora sweaters to leather gloves. Quality is likely to vary, so plunge in with the utmost discrimination.

VENICE AFTER DARK

The tourist office distributes a free pamphlet (part in English, part in Italian), called *Un Ospite di Venezia.* A section of this useful publication lists events, including any music and opera or theatrical presentations, along with art exhibitions and local special events. It's the best guide to "what's happening" at the time of your visit to Venice.

In addition, classical concerts are often featured using various churches, such as the Chiesa di Vivaldi, as a venue. To see if any **church concerts** are being presented at the time of your visit, call **041/5208722** for information.

THE PERFORMING ARTS

In January 1996, Venetians mourned their major venue for the performing arts, as a dramatic fire left the fabled **La Fenice** at Campo San Fantin a blackened shell and a smoldering ruin. The Italian government has pledged $12.5 million for the reconstruction of the theater, one of the most beautiful in Italy.

The **Teatro Goldoni,** Calle Goldoni, near Campo San Luca (☎ 041/5207583), close to the Ponte Rialto in the San Marco district, honors Carlo Goldoni (1707–93), the most prolific—critics say the best—of Italian playwrights. The theater presents a changing repertoire of productions, often plays in Italian, but musical presentations as well. The box office is open Mon–Sat 10am–1pm and 4:30–7pm. Tickets are 20,000–40,000L ($12.80–$25.60).

A NIGHTCLUB

Near the Accademia, the kasbahlike **El Souk,** Calle Contarini Corfu 1056A (☎ 041/5200371; vaporetto: Accademia), continues year after year to swim in the otherwise shallow sea of Venetian nightlife. It's run somewhat like a private club, but everybody is welcome, provided they're dressed properly. The crowd is often young, and recorded music prevails. It's open Thurs–Tues 10pm–4am, but the action usually doesn't begin until after midnight. Cover (including the first drink) is 15,000L ($9.60) Sun–Tues and Thurs–Fri and 20,000L ($12.80) Sat.

BARS

The single most famous of all the watering holes of Ernest Hemingway, **Harry's Bar,** Calle Vallaresso 1323 (☎ 041/5285777; vaporetto: San Marco), is known for inventing its own drinks and exporting them around the world. It's also said that carpaccio, the delicate raw-beef dish, was also invented here. Devotees say that Harry's makes the best Bellini of any bar in the world. A libation costs 16,000L ($10.25), though many oldtime visitors still prefer a vodka martini at 12,000L ($7.70). In Venice, this bar is a tradition and landmark, not quite as famous as the Basilica di San Marco, but almost. Open Tues–Sun 10:30am–11pm.

Martini Scala Club, Campo San Fantin 1980 (☎ 041/5224121; vaporetto: San Marco or Santa Maria del Giglio), is an elegant restaurant with a piano bar and has functioned as some kind of an inn, in one manifestation or another, since 1724. You can enjoy its food and wine until 2am—it's the only kitchen in Venice that stays open late. After 10pm you can come here to enjoy the piano bar. The restaurant is open year-round, Wed–Mon 7pm–2am. Meals average 75,000L ($48). The bar is open Wed–Mon 10pm–3am.

CAFES

Venice's most famous cafe is the ✪ **Caffè Florian,** Piazza San Marco 56–59 (☎ 041/5285338; vaporetto: San Marco). It was built in 1720 and remains romantically and elegantly decorated—pure Venetian salons with red plush banquettes, elaborate murals under glass, and art-nouveau lighting and lamps. Open Thurs–Tues 9am–midnight.

The ✪ **Quadri,** Piazza San Marco 120–124 (☎ 041/5289299; vaporetto: San Marco), stands on the opposite side of the square from the Florian. Founded in 1638, it's elegantly decorated in an antique style. Wagner used to drop in for a drink when he was working on *Tristan und Isolde*. Open July–Sept, daily 9am–midnight; Oct–June, Tues–Sun 9am–midnight.

CASINOS

If you want to risk your luck and your lire, you can take a vaporetto ride on the Casino Express, which leaves from the stops at the rail station, Piazzale Roma, and Piazzetta San Marco and delivers you to the landing dock of the **Casino Municipale,** Lungomare G. Marconi 4, Lido (☎ 041/5297111). Admission is 18,000L ($11.50), and bring your passport. The building itself is foreboding, almost as if it could've been inspired by Mussolini-era architects. However, the action gets hotter once you step inside. At the casino, you can play blackjack, roulette, baccarat, or whatever. You can also dine, drink at the bar, or enjoy a floor show. Open June–Sept, daily 4pm–2:30am.

From October to May the casino action moves to the **Vendramin-Calergi Palace,** Cannaregio 2040, Strada Nuova (☎ **041/5297111;** vaporetto, San Marcuola). Incidentally, in 1883 Wagner died in this house, which opens onto the Grand Canal. Open daily 3pm–2:30am. Admission is 18,000L ($11.50).

DAY TRIPS FROM VENICE

MURANO   On this island **glassblowers** have for centuries performed oral gymnastics to turn out those fantastic chandeliers that Victorian ladies used to prize so highly. They also produce heavily ornamented glasses so ruby red or so indigo blue you can't tell if you're drinking blackberry juice or pure wood grain. Happily, the glassblowers are still plying their trade, though increasing competition (notably from Sweden) has compelled a greater degree of sophistication in design. You can combine a tour of Murano with a trip along the lagoon. To reach it, take vaporetto no. 5 at Riva degli Schiavoni, a short walk from Piazzetta San Marco. The boat docks at the landing platform at Murano where—lo and behold—the first furnace awaits conveniently. It's best to go Mon–Fri 10am–noon if you want to see some glassblowing action.

BURANO   Burano became world famous as a center of **lacemaking,** a craft that reached its pinnacle in the 18th century (recall Venetian point?). If you can spare a morning to visit this island you'll be rewarded with a charming little fishing village far removed in spirit from the grandeur of Venice, but lying half an hour away by ferry. Boats leave from Fondamente Nuove, overlooking the Venetian graveyard (which is well worth the trip all on its own). Take vaporetto no. 5 from Riva degli Schiavoni, get off at Fondamente Nuove, and catch a separate boat, Line 12, marked Burano.

Once at Burano, you'll discover that the houses of the islanders come in varied colors—sienna, robin's-egg or cobalt blue, barn-red, butterscotch, grass green. The **Scuola Merietti** stands in the center of the fishing village on Piazza Baldassare Galuppi. The Burano School of Lace was founded in 1872 as part of a resurgence movement aimed at restoring the age-old craft that had earlier declined, giving way to such other lacemaking centers as Chantilly and Bruges. By going up to the second floor you can see the lacemakers, mostly young women, at painstaking work and can purchase hand-embroidered or handmade-lace items.

After visiting the lace school, you can walk across the square to the **Duomo** and its leaning campanile (inside, look for the *Crucifixion* by Tiepolo). However, do so at once, because the bell tower is leaning so precariously it looks as if it may topple at any moment.

TORCELLO   Of all the islands of the lagoon, Torcello—the so-called Mother of Venice—offers the most charm. If Burano is behind the times, Torcello is positively antediluvian. You can follow in the footsteps of Hemingway and stroll across a grassy meadow, traverse an ancient stone bridge, and step back into that time when the Venetians first fled from invading barbarians to create a city of Neptune in the lagoon. To reach Torcello, take vaporetto no. 12 from Fondamenta Nuova on Murano. The trip takes about 45 minutes.

The **Cattedrale di Torcello,** also called the Church of Santa Maria Assunta Isola di Torcello (☎ **041/730084**), was founded in A.D. 639 and was subsequently rebuilt.

It stands in a lonely, grassy meadow beside a campanile dating from the 11th century. It's visited chiefly because of its Byzantine mosaics. Clutching her child, the weeping Madonna in the apse is a magnificent sight, whereas on the opposite wall is a powerful *Last Judgment.* It's open daily: Apr–Oct 10am–12:30pm and 2:30–6:30pm; Nov–Mar 10am–12:30pm and 2:30–5pm. Admission is 1,500L (95¢).

✪ **THE LIDO**   Near the turn of the century the Lido began to blossom into a fashionable beachfront resort, complete with deluxe hotels and its Casino Municipale.

The Lido today is past its heyday. The fashionable and chic of the world still patronize the Excelsior Palace and the Hotel des Bains, but the beach strip is overtouristed and opens onto polluted waters. It's not just the beaches around Venice that are polluted—the entire Adriatic is reputedly polluted. For swimming, guests use the pools of their hotels. They can, however, still enjoy the sands along the Lido. Try the Lungomare G. d'Annunzio Public Bathing Beach at the end of the Gran Viale (Piazzale Ettore Sorger), a long stroll from the vaporetto stop. You can book cabins—called *camerini*—and enjoy the sand. Rates change seasonally.

To reach the Lido, take vaporetto no. 6 (the ride takes about 15 minutes). The boat departs from a landing stage near the Doges' Palace.

Accommodations   The ✪ **Excelsior Palace,** Lungomare Marconi 41, 30126 Venezia Lido (☎ **800/325-3535** in the U.S. and Canada, or 041/5260201; fax 041/5267276; vaporetto: Lido, then bus A, B, or C), is a monument to *la dolce vita* and did much to make the Lido fashionable. Today it is the Lido's most luxurious hotel. Rooms range in style and amenities from cozy singles to suites. Most of the social life takes place around the angular pool or on the flowered terraces leading up to the cabanas on the sandy beach. All guest rooms (some big enough for tennis games) have been modernized, often with vivid colors that look like reminders of summer, regardless of the season. On the premises is one of the most elegant dining rooms of the Adriatic, the Tropicana. Rates (including breakfast) are 530,000–620,000L ($339.20–$396.80) for a double and 1,460,000L ($934.40) and up for a suite. AE, DC, MC, and V are accepted. Closed Nov–Mar 15.

The ✪ **Hotel des Bains,** Lungomare Marconi 17, 30126 Venezia Lido (☎ **800/325-3535** in the U.S. and Canada, or 041/5265921; fax 041/5260113; vaporetto, Lido, then bus A, B, or C), was built in the grand era of European resort hotels. It has its own wooded park and private beach with individual cabanas along with a kind of confectionary facade from the turn of the century. Thomas Mann stayed here several times before making it the setting for *Death in Venice,* and later it was used as a set for the film of the same name. The hotel has fairly large, well-furnished rooms. Many resort-type amenities are offered, including tennis courts, a large pool, a private pier, and a park. Rates are 320,000–405,000L ($204.80–$259.20) for a double; suites begin at 660,000L ($422.40). AE, DC, MC, and V are accepted. Closed Nov–Mar.

12

The Netherlands

by George McDonald

It's surprising how many people today still think of Amsterdam as caught in some rose-tinted timewarp of free love, free drugs, free everything. The heady heyday of the 1960s and 1970s—if it ever really existed to the extent legend and the soft-focus afterglow of memory would have us believe—has given way to 1990s realities. A tour of the burgeoning suburban business zones, whose modern architecture is light years away from golden age gables, is evidence enough of Amsterdam's new priorities, but Amsterdam also remains a vibrant, living museum.

Amsterdam

The city government has worked assiduously to transform Amsterdam into a cosmopolitan international business center—and there seems little doubt that it's succeeding. Fortunately, it's not succeeding all the way. Amsterdam is still different. Its citizens, bubbling along happily in their multiracial melting pot, are not so easily poured into the restrictive molds dictated by trade and industry. Free thinking and free living not only still have their place but are the watchwords by which Amsterdam lives its collective life. Don't kid yourself, though. The free living is fueled not so much by clouds of hashish smoke as by the affluence generated by a successful economy.

Nearly 7,000 of Amsterdam's historic 17th-century buildings and hundreds of its graceful bridges are listed with the Dutch government and permanently protected from alteration, destruction, and the ugliness of most modern urban development. Amsterdam is proud of its history and wants the world to see and sense its greatest era, the 17th-century golden age. But it's also brimming with contemporary life, in a thoroughly modern golden age that you'll see, feel, and experience all around you.

ONLY IN AMSTERDAM

Cruising the Canals   Hop aboard a glass-topped canal boat for a cruise through Amsterdam's beautiful canals and the best possible view of all those gabled golden age merchants' houses and the many picturesque bridges, including the famous Skinny Bridge over the Amstel. A canal-boat cruise is undoubtedly the best way to see old Amsterdam and its busy harbor.

Admiring Rembrandt Stand in front of Rembrandt's *The Night Watch* at the Rijksmuseum, and then go on to explore the 200-plus rooms display works by Dutch and other European masters.

Visiting van Goghs Visit the outstanding Vincent van Gogh Museum, where you can trace the artistic and psychological development of this great impressionist. Then head next door to the always-challenging Stedelijk Museum of Modern Art.

Remembering Anne Frank Spend a reflective moment in the tragic world of Anne Frank, amid the surroundings of her World War II hideaway, now the Anne Frankhuis, where she wrote her famous diary.

Visiting the Flower Centers There's nothing like the burst of bloom come spring millions of bulbs in bloom make the greatest flower show on earth. Narcissi, daffodils and hyacinths, bluebells, crocuses, lilies, amaryllis, and of course, tulips carpet the ground in a blaze of color, in the park, the greenhouses, and along the paths and in the neighboring fields.

Biking Around Town Rent a bicycle and join the flow of cyclists for one of the classic Amsterdam experiences—only go carefully.

Listening to Classical Music If you want to hear how classical music sounds in one of the most acoustically perfect halls in the world, take in a concert by the Royal Concertgebouw orchestra at the Concertgebouw.

Strolling the Red Light District Stroll through the Red Light District, to examine the quaint gabled architecture along its narrow canals. Oh, yes, and you might also notice certain ladies watching the world go by through their red-fringed windows.

Spending an Evening in a Brown Cafe Spend a leisurely evening in a brown cafe, the traditional kind of Amsterdam watering hole. Even if you're not a beer lover, an evening in an atmospheric brown cafe will give you a peek into Amsterdam's everyday life, and you'll feel the centuries of conviviality the minute you walk in the door.

ORIENTATION

ARRIVING By Plane The Amsterdam airport, **Schiphol** (☎ **06/350-340-50** for flight information), is served by the Dutch national carrier KLM, by United Airlines and Northwest Airlines, and by most other major international carriers. You emerge from baggage retrieval into Schiphol Plaza, a combined arrivals hall, railway station, and shopping mall.

The KLM hotel shuttle bus operates between the airport and the city center on a circular route directly serving 16 top hotels, with stops close to many others. The one-way fare is Dfl 17.50 ($10.50); no reservations are needed and buses leave from in front of Schiphol Plaza every 20 minutes from 7am to 6pm and every 30 minutes from 6 to 9:30pm.

Trains leave from Schiphol Station, downstairs from Schiphol Plaza, for Amsterdam's Centraal Station. Departures range from one per hour at night to six per hour at peak times. The fare is Dfl 6 ($3.60) one-way and the trip takes about 20 minutes. Other stations—Amsterdam Zuid (South) and RAI—are also served, so be sure to check which one is best (including any tram or bus connection) for your hotel.

From the airport to the city center, taxis charge about Dfl 60 ($36).

By Train International trains arrive at Amsterdam's **Centraal Station** from Brussels, Paris (including the new Thalys high-speed train), and several German cities, as well as from more distant locations in eastern Europe, Switzerland, and Italy, and

Amsterdam Attractions & Accommodations

Attractions:

Amsterdam Historisch Museum **9**

Anne Frankhuis **2**

The Begijnhof **10**

Centraal Station **18**

Dam Square **5**

Floating Flower Market **12**

Koninklijk Paleis (Royal Palace) **7**

Leidseplein **14**

Madame Tussaud's Wax Museum **8**

Muntplein **11**

Museum van Loon **13**

Museum Willet-Holthuysen **25**

Musiektheater **24**

Netherlands Theater Institute **1**

Nieuwe Kerk **4**

Oude Kerk **21**

"Our Lord in the Attic" (Amstelkring Museum) **20**

Red Light District **22**

Rijksmuseum **15**

St. Nicolaas Church **19**

Stedelijk Museum of Modern Art **17**

Vincent van Gogh Museum **16**

Westerkerk **3**

World War II Memorial **6**

Zuiderkerk **23**

Accommodations:

American Hotel **6**

Amstel Botel **13**

Amstel Hotel **9**

Canal House Hotel **3**

Grand Hotel Krasnapolsky **4**

Hôtel de l'Europe **12**

Jan Luyken **8**

Piet Hein **7**

Pulitzer **1**

Seven Bridges **10**

Toren **2**

Rembrandt Karena Hotel **5**

Schiller Hotel **11**

3-0773

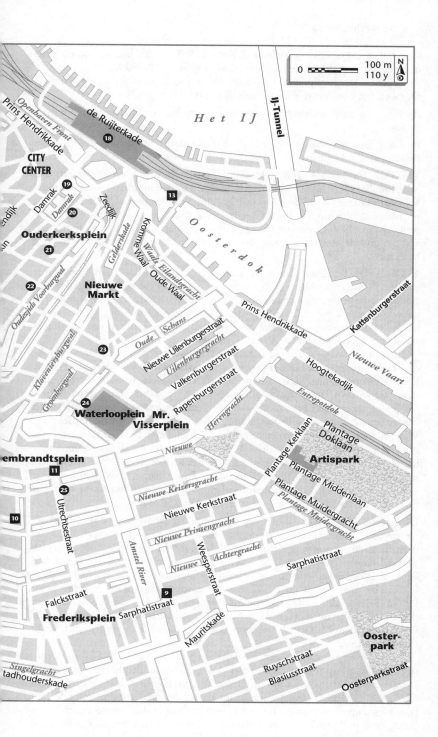

from towns and cities all over Holland. For schedule and fare information on travel in Holland call **06/9292,** and for international trains call **06/9296.**

To get to your hotel, take a tram from the stops in front of the station building. Or take a taxi from the taxi stand that's also in front of the station.

By Bus   International coaches arrive at the main bus terminal opposite Centraal Station.

By Car   European expressways E19, E35, E231, and E22 reach Amsterdam from Belgium and/or Germany.

VISITOR INFORMATION   Holland Tourist Information has an office in Schiphol Plaza at Schiphol Airport. Amsterdam's tourist information organization, **VVV Amsterdam** (☎ **06/340-340-66**), has offices inside Centraal Station beside the reservations office, outside the station at Stationsplein 10, at Leidseplein 1, and at Stadionplein. VVV Amsterdam will help you with almost any question about the city, and can provide brochures, maps, and more. There are separate desks for reserving hotel rooms.

CITY LAYOUT   Amsterdam center is small enough that its residents think of it as a village. However, as villages go, it can be confusing until you get the hang of it. The concentric rings of **major canals** are its defining characteristic, along with several important squares that act as focal points. It's perfectly possible to think that you're headed in one direction along the canal ring only to find out that you're going in exactly the opposite direction. A map is essential.

There are six major squares in Amsterdam that will be "hubs" of your visit to the city. **Dam Square** is the heart of the city, encircled by the Royal Palace, the Nieuwe Kerk, department stores, hotels, and restaurants. **Leidseplein,** with the streets around it, is Amsterdam's Times Square, glittering with restaurants, cafes, nightclubs, discos, performance centers, and movie theaters. **Rembrandtplein** is Amsterdam's other Times Square, bustling with restaurants, cafes, and a casino. **Museumplein** and **Waterlooplein** are the cultural hubs, with the Rijksmuseum, the Concertgebouw, the van Gogh Museum, and the Stedelijk Museum of Modern Art all in and around the former, and the Muziektheater (plus a superb flea market) at the latter. **Muntplein** is a transportation hub, identified by the Munt Tower, dating from 1620.

The VVV offices have several maps and guides available, including the small but detailed VVV Amsterdam map, which sells for Dfl 3.50 ($2.10).

GETTING AROUND   There are 11 public transport fare zones in greater Amsterdam, although tourists rarely travel beyond the city center zone 5700 (Centrum). Make sure your **tickets** are validated for the number of zones you plan to travel through. Several types of tickets are valid on buses, trams, the metro, and light rail. A day ticket, valid for the entire day of purchase and also the night following, can be bought from any bus or tram driver, conductor, or ticket dispenser for Dfl 12 ($7.20). Also available are tickets ranging from 2-day to 8-day validity with prices from Dfl 16 to 38.50 ($9.60 to $23.10), but these have to be purchased at the GVB/Amsterdam Municipal Transport ticket booths on Stationsplein in front of Centraal Station.

A single-journey ticket (an *enkeltje*) costs Dfl 3 to 7.50 ($1.80 to $4.50) depending on how many zones you'll travel through. For multiple journeys, buy a *strippenkaart,* or strip card, from the driver. You can buy an eight-strip card for Dfl 12 ($7.20), then use the validating machine aboard the tram each time you ride until you've used up all your strips. It's easy to use: Just fold at the line and punch in (on buses, the driver cancels the strips). Better-value strip cards are available at train and metro station ticket counters, the GVB ticket office in front of Centraal Station, post offices, and many news vendors, where you pay Dfl 11 ($6.60) for a card with 15 strips or Dfl 32.25 ($19.35) for 45 strips. (After the end of 1996, add a 2% increase per annum.)

Validated cards can be used for any number of transfers between lines and modes of transport, within 1 hour of the time stamped on them at validation and within the paid-for number of zones. The fare system is based on canceling one strip more than the number of zones you travel within—that is, two strips for one zone, three strips for two zones, and so on.

By Metro & Light Rail   Amsterdam has two subway lines and three light rail (sneltram) lines to bring people in from the suburbs.

By Bus & Tram   An extensive bus network complements 16 tram routes, 10 of which begin and end at Centraal Station. Most bus/tram shelters have maps that show the entire system. A detailed map is available from the VVV or the office of GVB/ Amsterdam Municipal Transport, Stationsplein, or call transportation information (☎ 06/9292 Mon–Sat 7am–10pm, Sun 8am–10pm).

By Taxi   Officially, you can't simply hail a cab, but more and more often they will stop if you do. Otherwise, you must call **Taxi Centrale** (☎ 020/677-77-77) or find a taxi stand sprinkled around the city, generally near the luxury hotels and at major squares such as Dam Square, Centraal Station, Spui, Rembrandtplein, Westermarkt, and Leidseplein. Taxis are metered, and fares—which *include* the tip—begin at Dfl 5 ($3) when you get in and run up at the rate of Dfl 2.85 ($1.70) per kilometer. For a **water taxi,** call **020/622-21-81.**

By Car   Don't rent a car to get around Amsterdam—you'll regret both the expense and the hassle. The city is a jumble of one-way streets, narrow bridges, and no-parking zones.

Outside the city, driving is another story. You may well want to rent a car for a foray into the Dutch countryside. Call Avis, Nassaukade 380 (☎ 020/683-60-61); Budget, Overtoom 121 (☎ 020/612-60-66); or Hertz, Overtoom 333 (☎ 020/612-24-41).

By Bicycle   Follow the Dutch example and cycle: Rent a bike while you're in Amsterdam. Sunday, when the city is quiet, is a particularly good day to pedal through the parks and to practice riding on cobblestones and dealing with trams before venturing forth into the fray of an Amsterdam rush hour. Bike-rental rates average Dfl 10 ($6) per day or Dfl 55 ($33) per week, with a deposit required. You can rent bikes from **Mac Bike,** Nieuwe Uilenburgerstraat 116 (☎ 06/620-09-85); **Mac Bike Too,** Marnixstraat 220 (☎ 06/626-69-64); and **Bike City,** Bloemgracht 70 (☎ 06/626-37-21).

By Water Bicycle   Rent a water bicycle to pedal along the canals; they seat two or four and cost Dfl 25 ($15) for a 1-hour jaunt for two; a four-passenger water bicycle is Dfl 10.50 ($6.30) per person per hour. Moorings are at Centraal Station, Leidseplein, Westerkerk near the Anne Frankhuis, Stadhouderskade, between the Rijksmuseum and the Heineken Brewery Museum, and at Toronto Bridge on the Keizersgracht, near Leidsestraat.

FAST FACTS: Amsterdam

American Express   Offices in Amsterdam are at Damrak 66 (☎ 020/ 520-77-77) and Van Baerlestraat 39 (☎ 020/671-41-41).

Baby-sitters   Ask your hotel manager or desk clerk.

Business Hours   Banks are open Mon–Fri 9am–4 or 5pm (some remain open until 7pm Thurs eve).

Currency   Holland's basic monetary unit is the guilder, yet you'll see it written as Dutch florins (abbreviated "f.," "fl.," or "Dfl."); since this is a holdover from the past, just ignore the written symbol and read all prices as guilders. There are 100 Dutch cents to a guilder. The rate of exchange used in this chapter was $1 = Dfl. 1.70, or Dfl. 1 = 58¢.

Currency Exchange   Change your money at the VVV Tourist Office, or if you carry American Express traveler's checks, at American Express, Damrak 66 (☎ 020/520-77-77), open Mon–Fri 9am–5pm, where there's no commission charge. Other fair-dealing options are the GWK exchanges at Schiphol airport and Centraal Station, which also handle money transfers via Western Union.

Doctors & Dentists   Contact the Central Medical Service (☎ 06/350-320-42).

Drugstores   In Holland pharmacies are called *apotheek*. Try Apotheek Hans at Museumplein (☎ 020/333-96-51). All pharmacies have the name of an all-night pharmacy posted in the shop.

Embassies/Consulates   The Consulate of the **United States** is at Museumplein 19 (☎ 020/664-56-61); the American Embassy is located at Lange Voorhout 102, Den Haag (☎ 070/310-92-09). The Consulate-General of the **United Kingdom** is at Koningslaan 44 (☎ 020/676-43-43).

Emergencies   In an emergency, dial **06-11** for the police, to report a fire, or to summon an ambulance.

Post Office   The main post office/PTT is at Singel 250–256, behind the Royal Palace at Dam Square, at the corner of Radhuisstraat (☎ 020/556-33-11), open Mon–Fri 9am–6pm and Sat 9am–1pm.

Taxes   Citizens from outside the European Union can shop tax free. The shops that offer tax-free shopping will advertise with a sign in the window, and they will provide you with the form you need to recover the value-added tax (VAT) when you leave the country.

ACCOMMODATIONS

Most Amsterdam hotels, whatever their cost, are spotlessly clean and tidily furnished, and in many cases they've been recently renovated or redecorated. An advance reservation is always advised. Or contact the free hotel-booking service of the Dutch hotel industry: **NRC/Netherlands Reservations Centre,** P.O. Box 404, 2260 AK Leidschendam (☎ **070/320-25-00;** fax 070/320-26-11).

If you arrive in Amsterdam without a reservation, the **VVV Tourist Office** outside Centraal Station will help you for the moderate charge of Dfl 5 ($3) per person.

VERY EXPENSIVE

✪ **American Hotel.** Leidsekade 97, 1017 PN Amsterdam. ☎ **020/624-53-22.** Fax 020/625-32-36. 188 rms. MINIBAR TV TEL. Dfl 425–525 ($255–$315) double. AE, DC, MC, V.

One of the most fascinating buildings on Amsterdam's long list of monuments is the art nouveau, neo-gothic, castlelike American Hotel, which has been both a prominent landmark and a popular meeting place for Amsterdammers since the turn of the century. The location, beside Leidseplein, is one of the best in town. In the famous Café Américain you can relax in magnificent art deco surroundings. There's 24-hour room service, plus dry cleaning available. Facilities include a gift shop and fitness center.

Amstel. Professor Tulpplein 1, 1018 GX Amsterdam. ☎ **020/622-60-60.** Fax 020/622-58-08. 79 suites. A/C MINIBAR TV TEL. Dfl 1,000–1,600 ($600–$961) suite for two. AE, DC, EC, MC, V.

The grande dame of Dutch hotels since its 1867 opening, this is where royalty and superstars sleep. The hotel looks as if it belongs in Paris, with its mansard roof and wrought-iron window guards, while, inside, the rooms have all the elegance of an English country home. The hotel has been completely refurbished. Each of the luxurious suites has a VCR and stereo sound system (for which the guests are given their favorite compact discs). The marble bathrooms have a separate toilet and shower. La Rive is the Amstel's famous, top-flight restaurant. The breakfast, lunch, and dinner menus are à la carte. The new Brasserie bar has a more informal atmosphere. There's 24-hour room service, plus valet laundry and limousine service (on request). Facilities include a fully equipped health center, with professional masseurs, a personal trainer, and beauty specialists at guests' disposal.

Grand Hotel Krasnapolsky. Dam 9, 1012 JS Amsterdam. ☎ **020/554-91-11.** Fax 020/622-86-07. 429 rms, 18 suites/apts. A/C MINIBAR TV TEL. Dfl 405–575 ($243–$345) double; Dfl 575–1,300 ($243–$781) suite/apt. Rates include breakfast. Children 5 and under stay free in parents' room; children 6–12 are charged half price. AE, DC, EC, MC, V. Parking Dfl 4 ($2.40) per hour.

One of Amsterdam's landmark hotels, the Krasnapolsky faces the Royal Palace. It began life as the Wintertuin ("Winter Garden") restaurant, where Victorian ladies and gentlemen sipped wine and nibbled pancakes beneath the hanging plants and lofty skylight ceiling—and today the restaurant still dominates the hotel's ground floor. The sizes and shapes of the rooms at the "Kras" vary, with some tastefully converted into individually decorated mini-apartments. The Brasserie Reflet specializes in French cuisine, while the restaurants Edo and Kyo maintain high standards of Japanese cuisine, plus there's 24-hour room service. Facilities include a business center.

Hôtel de l'Europe. Nieuwe Doelenstraat 2–8, 1012 CP Amsterdam. ☎ **020/623-48-36.** Fax 020/624-29-62. 101 rms and suites. A/C MINIBAR TV TEL. Dfl 515–650 ($309–$390) double; Dfl 845–1,370 ($507–$822) suite. Rates include continental breakfast. AE, EC, MC, V.

Built in 1895, the Hôtel de l'Europe has a grand style and a sense of ease. The guest rooms and baths are spacious and bright, furnished with classic good taste. Some rooms have minibalconies overlooking the river, and all boast marble bathrooms. The Restaurant Excelsior serves breakfast, lunch, and dinner daily. In the Restaurant Le Relais you'll find less formal surroundings for light lunches or dinners. Le Bar and La Terrasse (summer only) serve drinks and hors d'oeuvres daily 11am–1am. There's room service. Facilities include an indoor pool, sauna, health club, and massage.

EXPENSIVE

✪ **Pulitzer.** Prinsengracht 315–331, 1016 HX Amsterdam. ☎ **020/523-52-35.** Fax 020/627-67-53. 220 rms, 10 suites. MINIBAR TV TEL. Dfl 455–540 ($273–$324) double; Dfl 1,075 ($646) suite. Additional person Dfl 90 ($54) extra. AE, DC, MC, V. Valet parking Dfl 42.50 ($25.50) per day.

A real prize-winner, the Pulitzer was built within the walls of 24 canal houses, most of which are between 200 and 400 years old and adjoin one another, side by side and garden to garden. From the outside the Pulitzer blends inconspicuously with its neighborhood. You walk between two houses to enter the lobby or climb the steps of a former merchant's house to enter the ever-crowded and cheerful bar. The rooms are spacious and modern. Expansion and redecoration has made the Pulitzer quite chic, and some rooms contain elaborate bathrooms done entirely in gray marble. On the premises are a restaurant, bar, and coffee shop. Services include 24-hour room service, photo developing, and laundry.

Schiller. Rembrandtplein 26–36, 1017 CV Amsterdam. ☎ **020/623-16-60.** Fax 020/ 624-00-98. 92 rms. TV TEL. Dfl 315 ($189) double. Rates include breakfast. AE, DC, MC, V.

The Schiller was built by a painter of the same name during the 1890s. Bright and cheerful, the rooms have been totally renovated, refurnished, and reappointed with such thoughtful amenities as pants presses and, in specially designated ladies' rooms, coffeemakers and wall-mounted hair dryers. Perhaps the happiest outcome of the revitalization of the Schiller is the new life it brings to the hotel's gracious oak-paneled dining room and to the Schiller Café.

MODERATE

Ⓢ **Acacia.** Lindengracht 251, 1015 KH Amsterdam. ☎ **020/622-14-60.** Fax 020/638-07-48. 14 rms, 2 studios, 2 houseboats. TV TEL. Dfl 125 ($75) double; Dfl 155 ($93) houseboat double. Rates include breakfast. MC, V. Bus: 18 to Nieuwe Willemsstraat.

Not located on one of the major canals, but in the Jordaan and facing a small canal, just a block from the Prinsengracht, the Acacia is a clean, well-kept hotel run by Hans and Marlene van Vliet, a friendly young couple who have worked hard to make their hotel feel like a home away from home. The rooms are simple but clean and comfortable. Their two houseboats add a nice touch and are moored nearby on the Lijnbaansgracht.

Canal House Hotel. Keizersgracht 148, 1015 CX Amsterdam. ☎ **020/622-51-82.** Fax 020/ 624-13-17. 26 rms. TEL. Dfl 225–265 ($135–$159) double. Rates include breakfast. AE, DC, EC, V.

A contemporary approach to reestablishing the elegant canal-house atmosphere has been taken by the American owner of the Canal House Hotel. This small hotel below Raadhuisstraat is in three adjoining houses that date from 1630; they were gutted and rebuilt to provide private baths and then were filled with antiques, quilts, and Chinese rugs. Fortunately, it's blessed with an elevator, plus a manageable staircase, and overlooking the back garden is a magnificently elegant breakfast room that seems to have been untouched since the 17th century.

Jan Luyken. Jan Luykenstraat 54–58, 1071 CS Amsterdam. ☎ **020/573-07-30.** Fax 020/ 676-38-41. 63 rms. MINIBAR TV TEL. Dfl 330–435 ($198–$261) double. Rates include breakfast. Children 3 and under stay free in parents' room. Additional person Dfl 85 ($51) extra; children 4–12 are charged half price. AE, DC, EC, V.

One block from the Vincent van Gogh Museum and from the elegant P. C. Hooftstraat shopping street, the Jan Luyken is best described as a small hotel with many of the amenities and facilities of a big hotel. It maintains a balance between sophisticated facilities and an intimate and personalized approach appropriate to a residential neighborhood. The owners are proud of the atmosphere they've created, and are constantly improving the hotel's look.

Rembrandt Karena. Herengracht 225, 1016 BJ Amsterdam. ☎ **020/622-17-27.** Fax 020/ 625-06-30. 111 rms. TV TEL. Dfl 295 ($177) standard double; Dfl 400 ($240) executive room. Children 14 and under stay free in parents' room. Additional person Dfl 70 ($42) extra. AE, DC, MC, V. Parking at nearby lot.

Following the example of the Hotel Pulitzer, the British-owned Rembrandt Karena was built anew within old walls. In this case the structures are a wide 18th-century building on one canal above Raadhuistraat and four small 16th-century houses directly behind on the Singel canal. The look of the place is best described as basic, but the rooms tend to be large and fully equipped; some still have old fireplaces with elegant wood or marble mantels. And as you walk around, occasionally you see an old beam or pass through a former foyer on the way to your room.

✪ Seven Bridges. Reguliersgracht 31, 1017 LK Amsterdam. ☎ **020/623-13-29.** 11 rms, 6 with bath. Dfl 130–210 ($78–$126) double. Rates include full breakfast. AE, MC, V.

The owners, Pierre Keulers and Gunter Glaner, have transformed the Seven Bridges into one of Amsterdam's true gems. Each room is individually decorated with antique furnishings and posters of impressionist art. The biggest room, sleeping four, is on the second floor, and it has a huge bathroom with wood paneling, double sinks, a fair-sized shower, and a separate area for the lavatory. There are some attic rooms with sloped ceilings and exposed wood beams, plus big, bright basement rooms done almost entirely in white. Their latest update includes handmade Italian drapes, hand-painted tiles, and wood-tiled floors.

✪ Wiechmann. Prinsengracht 328–330, 1016 HX Amsterdam. ☎ **020/626-33-21.** Fax 020/626-89-62. 40 rms. TV TEL. Dfl 195–250 ($117–$150) double. Rates include breakfast. No credit cards.

It takes only a moment to feel at home in the antique-adorned lobby of the Amsterdam Wiechmann. Owned for a number of years by American T. Boddy and his Dutch wife, Nicky, the Wiechmann is a comfortable, casual sort of place. Like a good wine, it just gets better with age. Besides, the location is one of the best you'll find in this or any price range. The furnishings are elegant, and oriental rugs grace many of the floors in the public spaces. The higher-priced doubles have antique furnishings and TVs, and many have a view of the two canals. The breakfast room has hardwood floors, greenery, and white linen cloths on the tables. There's a lounge and bar.

INEXPENSIVE

Amstel Botel. Oosterdokskade 2–4, 1011 AE Amsterdam. ☎ **020/626-42-47.** Fax 020/639-19-52. 176 cabins (352 beds). TV TEL. Dfl 139 ($83) double. Rates include buffet breakfast. AE, MC, V. Free parking.

This is a boat-hotel moored 250 yards away from Centraal Station (turn left out of Centraal Station, pass the bike rental, and you'll see it floating in front of you). Aboard you'll find 176 cabins spread over four decks connected by elevator. The botel, built in 1993, has become popular because of its central location and reasonable comfort at reasonable rates.

⑤ Casa Cara. Emmastraat 24, 1075 HV Amsterdam. ☎ **020/662-31-35.** Fax 020/676-81-19. 9 rms, 6 with bath (shower). TEL. Dfl 75 ($45) double without bath, Dfl 105 ($63) double with bath. Rates include breakfast. No credit cards. Tram: 2 or 16 from Centraal Station to Emmastraat.

Gradually and faithfully trying to meet the demands of the 1990s traveler, the Casa Cara, near Vondelpark, is a simple but well-crafted conversion of a residential house in a neighborhood with deep front lawns. The hotel offers two large rooms with private shower and toilet on each floor, plus a trio of bathless rooms that, as a result, have the hall facilities almost to themselves.

Piet Hein. Vossiusstraat 52–53, 1071 AK Amsterdam. ☎ **020/662-72-05.** Fax 020/662-15-26. 36 rms. TV TEL. Dfl 115–185 ($69–$111) double. Rates include breakfast. AE, DC, MC, V. Tram: 2 or 5 from Centraal Station to Paulus Potterstraat.

Facing Vondelpark, near the most important museums, the appealing Piet Hein is one of the best-kept establishments in town. It's located in a dream villa and named after a Dutch folktale hero. The rooms are spacious and well furnished, and the staff is charming and professional. Half the rooms overlook the park, and two second-floor double rooms feature semicircular balconies. The lower-priced rooms are in the annex behind the hotel. The honeymoon suite has a waterbed and whirlpool.

Prinsenhof. Prinsengracht 810, 1017 SL Amsterdam. ☎ **020/623-17-72.** Fax 020/638-33-68. 10 rms, 4 with bath (tub or shower). TEL. Dfl 125 ($75) double without bath, Dfl 165 ($99) double with bath. Rates include breakfast. MC, V. Tram: 4 to Prinsengracht.

Located near the Amstel River, the Prinsenhof is a modernized canal house. Most guest rooms are large, with beamed ceilings. The front rooms look out onto the Prinsengracht, where colorful small houseboats are docked. Breakfast is served in an attractive blue-and-white dining room. A pulley hauls your bags to the upper floors as there's no elevator.

Toren. Keizersgracht 164, 1015 CZ Amsterdam. ☎ **020/622-63-52.** Fax 020/626-97-05. 43 rms. TV TEL. Dfl 150–245 ($90–$147) double. Rates include breakfast. AE, DC, MC, V.

The Toren sprawls over two buildings, separated by neighboring houses. With so many rooms, it's a better bet than most canal-house hotels during the tourist seasons in Amsterdam. Clean, attractive, and well maintained, the Toren promises private facilities with every room, although in a few cases that means a private bath located off the public hall (with your own private key).

⑤ Van de Kasteelen. Frans van Mierisstraat 34, 1071 RT Amsterdam. ☎ **020/679-89-95.** 12 rms, none with bath. Dfl 80 ($48) double. No credit cards.

On a relatively quiet side street just off Van Baerlestraat and not far from the Concertgebouw, this hotel is run by an elderly Indonesian couple who give a gracious welcome to their guests. The rooms are spartan but clean, and the price ensures that there's no lack of demand. A simple breakfast is served in the lounge, where there's also a television that guests can watch in the evening.

DINING

As a trading city, a gateway city, and one that positively revels in its melting-pot character, Amsterdam has absorbed culinary influences from far, wide, and yonder, and rustled them up to its own collective satisfaction. Just about any international cuisine can be found on the city's restaurant roster.

In general, with the exception of late-night restaurants, kitchens in Amsterdam take their last dinner orders at 10 or 11pm. Note that restaurants with outside terraces are always in big demand on pleasant summer evenings and reservations for such places are either essential or not possible.

One way to combat escalating dinner tabs is to take advantage of the tourist menu and, usually even better, the *dagschotel* (dish of the day) offered by many restaurants. An old budget standby, the official Dutch Tourist Menu, has been discontinued.

EXPENSIVE

De Kersentuin. In the Garden Hotel, Dijsselhofplantsoen 7. ☎ **020/664-21-21.** Reservations recommended. Fixed-price menu Dfl 50 ($30) for two courses, Dfl 60 ($36.05) for three courses; à la carte up to Dfl 125 ($75.05). AE, DC, EC, MC, V. Mon–Sat from 6pm. INTERNATIONAL.

All cherry red and gleaming brass, the "Cherry Orchard" has floor-to-ceiling windows looking onto the residential street outside, and semiscreened interior windows looking into the glimmering kitchen inside. From nouvelle cuisine and a strictly French approach to cooking, they have progressed to their own unique culinary concept, based on regional recipes from around the world, using fresh ingredients from Dutch waters and farmlands. A sample is a terrine of lightly smoked guinea fowl in aspic with armagnac prunes.

Dorrius. In the Holiday Inn Crowne Plaza, Nieuwe Zijds Voorburgwal 5. ☎ **020/620-05-00.** Reservations recommended. Three-course meal Dfl 78 ($46.85). AE, DC, EC, V. Daily noon–11pm. DUTCH.

Housed in adjoining canal houses, Dorrius is one of Amsterdam's most elegant dining rooms. The traditional feeling of the beamed ceilings and black-and-white marble floor is updated by coral-pink linens and a spacious arrangement of tables and fixtures. The bounty of the Dutch waters is the raison d'être of this fine restaurant. Perhaps the most unique and sensible idea here, however, is the Trolley Specialties—each night beginning at 6pm a trolley is presented with various meat, game, and poultry choices to be carved at the table and served with vegetables, a potato, and sauce.

D'Vijff Vlieghen. Spuistraat 294–302. ☎ **020/624-83-69.** Reservations recommended. Fixed-price menu Dfl 57.50 ($34.55) for three courses Dfl 72.50–300 ($43.55–$180.20) for four courses. DC, EC, MC, V. Daily 5:30pm–midnight. DUTCH.

This is one of the most famous restaurants in Amsterdam. Occupying five canal houses, it's a kind of Dutch cuisine theme park for tourists and out-of-towners, and the food is authentic, though not many Amsterdammers seem persuaded. The blessing of this popular place is that, once seated in one of the dining rooms, you never realize how large the restaurant is. You can enjoy cutlets of wild boar from the Royal Estates with a stuffed apple, veal steak with prunes and apple, or smoked filet of turkey with mashed cranberry from the island of Terschelling. Another specialty is the traditional Flemish dish, waterzooï.

't Swarte Schaep. Korte Leidsedwarsstraat 24 (at Leidseplein). ☎ **020/622-30-21.** Reservations recommended. Three-course meal Dfl 75–140 ($45.05–$84.10). AE, DC, EC, V. Daily noon–11pm. DUTCH.

Located in a house that dates from 1687, this restaurant still seems like an old Dutch home. You climb a steep flight of tiled steps to reach the second-floor dining room, where the beams and ceiling panels are dark with age. It's a cozy, almost crowded place made both fragrant and inviting by the fresh flowers on every table and those that spill from the polished brass buckets hanging from the ceiling beams. The "Black Sheep" is well known for its wine list and its crêpes Suzette. Taking a peek at the menu choices, you might find sole meunière with asparagus or grilled salmon with fresh thyme.

MODERATE

✪ **Bodega Keyzer.** Van Baerlestraat 96. ☎ **020/671-14-41.** Reservations recommended. Three-course meal Dfl 60 ($36.05); à la carte up to Dfl 125 ($75.05). AE, DC, EC, MC, V. Mon–Sat 9pm–midnight. CONTINENTAL.

Whether or not you attend a concert at the Concertgebouw, you may want to plan a visit to its next-door neighbor, the Bodega Keyzer. An Amsterdam landmark since 1903, the Keyzer has enjoyed a colorful joint heritage with the world-famous concert hall. There's an elegance here that is a combination of traditional dark-and-dusky decor and highly starched pink linens. The menu leans heavily to fish from Dutch waters and, in season, to game specialties, such as hare and venison.

Café Américain. In the American Hotel, Leidsekade 97. ☎ **020/624-53-22.** Reservations recommended. Three-course meal Dfl 45–85 ($27–$51.05). AE, DC, MC, V. Daily 7am–1am. CONTINENTAL.

You'll dine here in a lofty room that's a national monument of Dutch Jugendstijl and original art deco. Mata Hari held her wedding reception here in her pre-espionage days, and since its 1897 opening the place has been a haven for Dutch and international artists, writers, dancers, and actors. Leaded windows, newspaper-littered reading tables, bargello-patterned velvet upholstery, frosted-glass chandeliers from the 1920s, and tall carved columns are all part of the dusky sit-and-chat atmosphere.

De Oesterbar. Leidseplein 10. ☎ **020/623-29-88.** Reservations recommended. Main meal Dfl 45–63 ($27–$37.85). AE, DC, MC, V. Daily noon–midnight. SEAFOOD.

More than 50 years old, De Oesterbar is the best-known and most popular fish restaurant in Amsterdam. The decor is a delight: all white tiles with fish tanks bubbling at your elbows on the street level, and Victorian brocades and etched glass in the more formal dining room upstairs. The menu is a directory of the variety of fish available in Holland and the variety of ways they can be prepared, but includes a few meat selections (tournedos or veal) for those who don't like fish or seafood. Selections include sole Danoise with tiny North Sea shrimp, sole Véronique with muscadet grapes, stewed eel in wine sauce, and the assorted fish plate of turbot, halibut, and fresh salmon.

⑤ De Prins. Prinsengracht 124. ☎ **020/624-93-82.** Reservations recommended. Dish of the day Dfl 19.50 ($11.70); specials Dfl 23.50 and 27.50 ($14.10 and $16.50). AE, DC, MC, V. Daily 10am–10pm. DUTCH/FRENCH.

This companionable sort of restaurant, with brown cafe style, serves food you'd expect at a much more expensive place. It therefore generates both loyalty and popularity among its clientele, and its relatively few tables fill up quickly. It's a quiet neighborhood restaurant—nothing fancy or trendy, but quite appealing, housed in a 17th-century canal house, with the bar on a slightly lower level than the restaurant. De Prins offers an unbeatable price-to-quality ratio for typically Dutch/French menu items, and long may it continue to do so.

⑤ Haesje Claes. Spuistraat 273–275. ☎ **020/624-99-98.** Reservations recommended. Three-course meal Dfl 35–75 ($21–$45.05). AE, DC, EC, V. Daily noon–midnight. DUTCH.

If you're yearning for a cozy Old Dutch environment and hearty Dutch food at moderate prices, go to Haesje Claes. It's an inviting place with lots of nooks and crannies; brocaded benches and traditional Dutch hanging lamps with fringed covers give an intimate and comfortable feeling to the tables. The straightforward menu ranges from omelets to tournedos.

Kantjil en de Tiger. Spuistraat 291. ☎ **020/620-09-94.** Reservations not required. Main courses Dfl 25–95 ($15–$57.05). AE, DC, MC, V. Daily 4:30–11pm. JAVANESE/INDONESIAN.

The two best-sellers in this very popular large restaurant are nasi goreng Kantjil (fried rice with pork kebabs, stewed beef, pickled cucumbers, and mixed vegetables) and the 20-item rijsttafel for two. Other choices include stewed chicken in soja sauce, tofu omelet, shrimp with coconut dressing, Indonesian pumpkin, and mixed steamed vegetables with peanut-butter sauce. Finish off your meal with the multilayered cinnamon cake or the coffee with ginger liqueur and whipped cream.

✪ Kort. Amstelveld 12. ☎ **020/626-11-99.** Reservations recommended (required for dining on the terrace on a warm summer evening). Main courses Dfl 25–40 ($15–$24); three-course menu Dfl 60 ($36.05). AE, DC, MC, V. Wed–Mon 11am–midnight. CONTINENTAL.

This is one of the few restaurants that accepts reservations for evening dining outdoors in good weather—a time when such facilities fill up instantly. On the edge of a canal and a wide, open square, the tree-shaded terrace is far enough away from traffic to be unaffected by the nuisance. Service is friendly, and the food, which includes several excellent vegetarian dishes such as grilled goat's cheese with spinach and salad, is very good. Look also for the red mullet specialty. Dining indoors is also recommended, in an atmospheric room with fancier table sets than outside.

Le Relais. In the Hôtel de l'Europe, Nieuwe Doelenstraat 2–8 (at Muntplein). ☎ **020/623-48-36.** Reservations recommended for dinner. From Dfl 22.50 ($13.50) à la carte; fixed-price menu Dfl 49.50 ($29.75). AE, DC, MC, V. Daily noon–midnight. FRENCH/CONTINENTAL.

This restaurant on the ground floor of the Hôtel de l'Europe is moderately priced. Start with the beef carpaccio or a cold lobster and follow with leg of lamb in honey and thyme. Cap it off with cassata ice cream or coconut cake. Lighter luncheon dishes include a tuna sandwich with a salad as well as curried chicken soup. For open-air dining with a view of the canal and the Muntplein choose La Terrasse.

Schiller. In the Schiller Crest Hotel, Rembrandtplein 26–36. ☎ **020/623-16-60.** Reservations recommended. Three-course meal Dfl 35–45 ($21–$27). AE, DC, MC, V. Daily noon–10:30pm. CONTINENTAL.

Beamed and paneled in well-aged oak and graced with etched-glass panels and stained-glass skylights, this 100-plus-year-old landmark is a splendid sight indeed. A particularly amusing little dining room is called the *spreukenzaal,* or "sayings rooms," because it's adorned with homey little mottos in five languages that are painted on the paneling in gold leaf. Among dishes on the traditional menu you'll find everything from stewed eel and potato-and-cabbage casserole to T-bone steak, roast leg of lamb with mint sauce, and spaghetti bolognese.

INEXPENSIVE

Café de Jaren. Nieuwe Doelenstraat 20–22. ☎ **020/625-57-71.** Reservations not required. Main courses Dfl 7.50–25 ($4.50–$15); fixed-price meal Dfl 20 ($12) at lunch, Dfl 28 ($16.80) at dinner. No credit cards. Daily 10am–1am. DUTCH/CONTINENTAL.

One of the city's largest cafes, the Café de Jaren has 300 seats inside and 150 more out on the terrace. Many students lunch here. The building originally served as a bank and so, besides being spacious, has unusually high ceilings. You can enjoy everything from a cup of coffee or a glass of jenever (a very potent Dutch gin) to spaghetti bolognese and rib-eye steak.

Café Luxembourg. Spuistraat 24. ☎ **020/620-62-64.** Reservations not required. Snacks from Dfl 10 ($6). EC, V. Mon–Thurs 9am–1am, Fri–Sat 9am–2am. INTERNATIONAL.

The Café Luxembourg attracts all kinds of people because it offers amazingly large portions of food at reasonable prices. Soups, sandwiches, and such dishes as meat loaf are available. It's a relaxing place where people are encouraged to linger and read one of the many international newspapers that are available. In summer there's sidewalk dining.

Café-Restaurant Blincker. St. Barberenstraat 7. ☎ **020/627-19-38.** Reservations recommended. Main courses Dfl 10–30 ($6–$18). AE, DC, MC, V. Mon–Sat 4pm–1am. CONTINENTAL.

This intimate restaurant in the Frascati Theater building, on a small side street off Rokin, attracts actors, journalists, artists, and other assorted bohemians. At night the place is jammed with people who cluster around the bar. To find the Café Blincker, turn into Nesstraat from Dam Square, then turn left after the Frascati Theater.

⑤ Het Station. On Platform 1 of Centraal Station. ☎ **020/627-33-06.** Reservations not accepted. Dish of the day Dfl 11.75 ($7.05). No credit cards. Mon–Sat 7am–10pm, Sun 8am–10pm. DUTCH.

For a little bit of elegance with your budget meal, try the Centraal Station restaurant, at Platform 1, a self-service spot in a lofty wood-paneled chamber with chandeliers. Each month there's a different special plate offered here at a rock-bottom price, but if you're expecting a boring choice, you should know that trout, jugged hare, and coq au vin have found their way onto plates in the recent past, always with salad, vegetable, and other appropriate accompaniments.

Keuken van 1870. Spuistraat 4. ☎ **020/624-89-65.** Reservations not accepted. Main courses Dfl 8.50–16.50 ($5.10–$9.90). AE, DC, EC, V. Mon–Fri 12:30–8pm, Sat–Sun 4–9pm. DUTCH.

The Keuken van 1870, near the Amsterdam Sonesta Hotel, is said to be one of the cheapest places to eat in Amsterdam. It also must surely be the plainest place to eat: There's absolutely no attempt at decor here, meals are served cafeteria style, tables are bare, and dishes are plain—but the food is good. Pork chops, fish, and chicken—all accompanied by vegetables and potatoes—are some of the main courses available on the menu.

Rose's Cantina. Reguliersdwarsstraat 38–40. ☎ **020/625-97-97.** Reservations recommended. Main courses Dfl 18.50–32.50 ($11.10–$19.50). AE, DC, MC, V. Daily 5–11pm. MEXICAN.

To attract English-speaking guests, Rose's Cantina advertises typical American favorites like hamburgers and meatballs, although the decor and most of the cuisine are Mexican inspired. A meal starting with tortilla chips and salsa, followed by a *prato mixto* or fried galinhas (roast chicken with fries and red peppers), and washed down with a Mexican beer will cost you less than Dfl 50 ($30). The tables are oak, the service is decent, and the atmosphere is Latin American. Just be careful of waiting times that can easily run into hours at peak times, while you sit at the bar and, like as not, down one margarita after another. Rose's is near the Flower Market.

ATTRACTIONS

The **Amsterdam Culture & Leisure Pass** is a sound investment if you plan to do a lot of paid-for sightseeing. Its 28 coupons allow free entry into some top museums, a free canal cruise and diamond factory tour, and discounts on many other attractions and purchases. The pass costs Dfl 29.50 ($17.70) and is available from any of the city's VVV offices and from Holland Tourist Information at Schiphol Plaza.

SIGHTSEEING SUGGESTIONS

If You Have 1 Day   Explore the historic center in the morning, taking a look at Dam Square and the Royal Palace and other principal squares. In the afternoon, visit the Rijksmuseum to see the Rembrandts. In the evening, go to a traditional restaurant, or opt for a rijsttafel, and end your day by dropping into a brown cafe.

If You Have 2 Days   On day 2 pay a visit to the Anne Frank house in the morning. In the afternoon, take in the Vincent van Gogh Museum, or the Stedelijk Museum of Modern Art. Relax over coffee at the Hotel American, with its stunning art nouveau interior. In the evening, attend a concert at the Concertgebouw.

If You Have 3 Days   On day 3, take a cruise on the canals and admire their retinue of gabled merchants' houses and the almost 1,200 bridges the canals are even more special after dark, when the glow of street and house lights shimmers on the water. Investigate some of Amsterdam's markets, especially the Albert Cuyp street market and the floating Flower Market on the Singel Canal. Take a walk in the Red Light District, and lest this brings you too close to perdition, salvation is close at hand in the main churches—Nieuwe Kerk, Wester Kerk, and Oude Kerk—and the Portuguese Synagogue.

If you have 4 or 5 Days On day 4, take a trip outside Amsterdam—if it's April or May go to the flower centers; otherwise visit the art city of Haarlem and see the organ Mozart played on, or go to Delft, home of the famous blue-and-white ware. On the fifth day, visit some of the museums you may have missed, take a walk in the Vondelpark, and shop for gifts in the Kalverstraat area.

THE TOP ATTRACTIONS

✪ **Anne Frankhuis.** Prinsengracht 263 (just below Westermarkt). ☎ **020/556-71-00.** Admission Dfl 10 ($6) adults, Dfl 5 ($3) children 10–17. June–Aug, Mon–Sat 9am–7pm, Sun and holidays 10am–7pm; Sept–May, Mon–Sat 9am–5pm, Sun and holidays 10am–5pm. Tram: 13, 14, or 17 to Westermarkt; then walk past the Westerkerk along the canal.

No one should miss seeing and experiencing this house, where eight people from three separate families lived together in nearly total silence for more than 2 years during World War II. The hiding place Otto Frank found for his family and some friends kept them all safe until, tragically close to the end of the war, it was discovered and raided by the Nazi occupation forces. It was here that the famous diary was written. The rooms are still as bare as they were when Anne's father returned, the only survivor of the eight *onderduikers* (divers or hiders)—and nothing has been changed.

✪ **Rijksmuseum.** Stadhouderskade 42 (at Museumplein). ☎ **06/889-812-12.** Admission Dfl 12.50 ($7.50) adults, Dfl 5 ($3) children 6–18. Daily 10am–5pm. Tram: 2 or 5 to Hobbemastraat, or 6, 7, or 10 to Spiegelgracht. Bus: 26, 65, or 66 to Museumplein.

In Amsterdam, you'll see the architectural legacy of Holland's 17th-century golden age all around you. For the artistic lowdown, head for the neo-gothic Rijksmuseum, opened in 1885. It contains the world's largest collection of paintings by the Dutch masters, including the most famous: Rembrandt's 1642 *The Night Watch*. Rembrandt, van Ruysdael, van Heemskerck, Frans Hals, Paulus Potter, Jan Steen, Vermeer, de Hooch, Terborch, and Gerard Dou are all represented, as are Fra Angelico, Tiepolo, Goya, Rubens, van Dyck, and later Dutch artists of the Hague school and the Amsterdam impressionist movement; plus prints and sculpture, furniture, Asian and Islamic art, china and porcelain, trinkets and glassware, armaments and ship models, 17th-century dollhouses, costumes, screens, badges, and laces.

✪ **Vincent van Gogh Museum.** Paulus Potterstraat 7–11 (at Museumplein). ☎ **020/570-52-00.** Admission Dfl 10 ($6) adults, Dfl 5 ($3) aged 18 and under. Daily 10am–5pm. Tram: 2 or 5 to Paulus Potterstraat, or no. 16 to Museumplein-Concertgebouw. Bus: 26, 65, or 66 to Museumplein.

Nearly every painting, sketch, print, etching, and illustrated piece of correspondence that Vincent van Gogh ever produced has been housed here in its own three-story museum in Amsterdam. You can see more than 200 paintings displayed simply and in a straightforward chronological order. The second floor displays a progression of 18 paintings produced during the 2-year period when van Gogh lived in the south of France, generally considered to be the high point of his career. This symphony of colors and color contrasts includes *Gauguin's Chair, The Yellow House, Self-portrait with Pipe and Straw Hat, Vincent's Bedroom at Arles, Wheatfield with Reaper, Bugler of the Zouave Regiment,* and one of the most famous paintings of modern times, *Still Life Vase with Fourteen Sunflowers,* best known simply as *Sunflowers.*

Canals & Canalside Houses

Taking a canal-boat cruise is the undoubtedly the best way to see old Amsterdam and its surprisingly large and busy harbor. A typical canal-boat itinerary will include Centraal Station, the Harlemmersluis floodgates, the Cat Boat (a houseboat—one of around 2,400 houseboats—with a permanent population of as many as 150 wayward felines), and both the narrowest building in the city and one of the largest houses still in use as a single-family residence. Plus, you'll see the official residence of the burgomaster (mayor) of Amsterdam, the "Golden Bend" of the Herengracht (traditionally the best address in the city), many picturesque bridges (including the famous Skinny Bridge over the Amstel), and the Amsterdam Drydocks.

Trips last approximately 1 hour and leave at regular intervals from *rondvaart* (canal circuit) piers in key locations around town. The majority of launches, however, are docked along Damrak or Prins Hendrikkade near Centraal Station and on the Rokin near Muntplein and near Leidseplein; they leave every 45 minutes in winter (10am–4pm), every 15 to 30 minutes during the summer season (9am–9:30pm). The average fare is Dfl 10 to 15 ($6 to $9) for adults, Dfl 8 to 10 ($4.80 to $6) for children 4 to 13.

Major operators of canal-boat cruises are Amsterdam Canal Cruises (☎ 020/626-56-36), Holland International (☎ 020/622-77-88), Rederij Plas (☎ 020/624-54-06), Meyers Rondvaarten (☎ 020/623-42-08), Rederij Boekel (☎ 020/612-99-05), Rederij Hof van Holland (☎ 020/623-71-22), Rederij P. Kooij (☎ 020/623-38-10), Rederij Noord-Zuid (☎ 020/679-13-70), Rederij Lovers (☎ 020/622-21-81), and Rederij Wisman (☎ 020/638-03-38).

MORE ATTRACTIONS

✪ **Artis Zoo.** Plantage Kerklaan 38–40. ☎ **020/523-34-00.** Admission (including zoo, children's farm, planetarium, and zoological museum) Dfl 21 ($12.60) adults, Dfl 13.50 ($8.10) children 10 and under. Daily 9am–5pm.

Established in 1838, this is the oldest zoo in the Netherlands, housing more than 6,000 animals. Also on the property are a planetarium, an aquarium, and a geological and zoological museum. There's also a children's farm.

Red Light District (Walletjes). Tram: 9 or 14 to Mr. Visserplein. Metro: Waterlooplein.

This warren of streets around Oudezijds Achterburgwal and Oudezijds Voorburgwal by the Oude Kerk is on most people's sightseeing agenda—however, a visit to this area is not for everyone, and if you do choose to go you need to exercise some caution because the area is a center of crime, vice, and drugs. Stick to the crowded streets, and be wary of pickpockets. Do not take photographs unless you want to lose your camera or have it broken.

Still, it's extraordinary to view the prostitutes in leather and lace sitting in their storefronts with their radios and TVs blaring as they knit or adjust their makeup, waiting patiently for customers. It seems to reflect the Dutch pragmatism: If you can't stop the oldest trade in the world, you can at least confine it to a particular area and impose health and other regulations on it.

Historic Buildings & Monuments

Koninklijk Paleis (Royal Palace). Dam Sq. ☎ **020/624-86-98.** Admission Dfl 5 ($3) adults, Dfl 3 ($1.80) children 12 and under. Two weeks at Easter, mid-June to the first week in Sept, and the second week in Oct, daily 12:30–5pm; other times, Tues–Thurs 1–4pm. Tram: 1, 2, 4, 5, 9, 13, 14, 16, 17, 24, 25 to Dam Square, or the Dam Square stop on the Nieuwe Zijds Voorburgwal.

If you visit Amsterdam in summer, you can see the inside of the impressive 17th-century Royal Palace. For the first 153 years of its existence, this was Amsterdam's town hall. Its first use as a palace occurred during the 5-year French rule of the city by Napoleon in the early 19th century, when the French emperor's brother, Louis Bonaparte, was king of Holland. Since the return to the throne of the Dutch House of Orange, this has been the official palace of the reigning king or queen of the

Netherlands; few, however, have used it for more than an occasional reception or official ceremony.

Begijnhof. Spui. No phone. Free admission. Daily until sunset. Tram: 1, 2, or 5 to Spui; then walk east 1 block, turn left on the Gedempte Begijnensloot, and the main gate of the Begijnhof is on the left, halfway along the block.

The Begijnhof is a beautifully atmospheric cloister of small homes around a garden courtyard that makes a perfect escape from the city's bustle. It was an almshouse for pious lay women—the *begijns*—who were involved in religious and charitable work for the nunnery. All but the Begijnhof's tiny 17th- and 18th-century houses surrounding a small 14th-century courtyard still house the city's elderly poor.

Museums & Galleries

☼ Amsterdams Historisch Museum. Kalverstraat 92. ☎ **020/523-18-22.** Admission Dfl 8 ($4.80) adults, Dfl 4 ($2.40) children 6–16. Mon–Fri 10am–5pm, Sat–Sun 11am–5pm. Tram: 1, 2, 4, 5, 9, 14, 16, 24, or 25 to Spui. At Dam Square, walk along Kalverstraat; the museum is on the right, just past St. Luciensteeg.

Few cities in the world have gone to as much trouble and expense as Amsterdam to display and explain their history. The Amsterdams Historisch (Historical) Museum, housed in the huge, beautifully restored 17th-century buildings of the former city orphanage, is an attractive and fascinating place to visit that will give you a better understanding of everything you see when you go out to explore the city on your own. Gallery by gallery, century by century, you see how a small fishing village became a major world power; you also see many of the famous paintings by the "Dutch masters" in the context of their time and place in history. Located next to the Begijnhof, the museum has three courtyards and a civic-guard gallery.

☼ Scheepvaartmuseum (Maritime Museum). Kattenburgerplein 1. ☎ **020/523-22-22.** Admission Dfl 12.50 ($7.50) adults, Dfl 8 ($4.80) children 16 and under. Mon–Sat 10am–5pm, Sun and holidays noon–5pm. Closed Mon mid-Sept to mid-June. Bus: 22 or 28 from Centraal Station to Kattenburgerplein; the museum is on the left.

Housed in a former rigging house of the Amsterdam Admiralty, the Maritime Museum overlooks busy Amsterdam harbor. Here you'll see room after room of ships and ship models, seascapes, and old maps, including a 15th-century Ptolemaic atlas and a sumptuously bound edition of the *Great Atlas, or Description of the World*, produced over a lifetime by Jan Blaeu, who was the stay-at-home master cartographer of Holland's golden age. Among the important papers on display are several pertaining to the Dutch colonies of Nieuwe Amsterdam (New York City) and Nieuwe Nederland (New York State), including a receipt for the land that now surrounds the New York state capital at Albany. A full-size replica of the Dutch East Indiaman *Amsterdam*, which foundered off Hastings in 1749 on her maiden voyage to the fabled Spice Islands (Indonesia), is tied up at the museum's wharf.

Museum Het Rembrandthuis. Jodenbreestraat 4–6 (near Waterlooplein). ☎ **020/638-46-68.** Admission Dfl 5 ($3) adults, Dfl 3.50 ($2.10) children. Mon–Sat 10am–5pm, Sun and holidays 1–5pm. Tram: 9 or 14 to Mr. Visserplein. Metro: Waterlooplein; then walk west 1 block and the museum is on the left just before the canal.

Rembrandt was forced to leave his home because of bankruptcy in 1658. Thanks to an inventory made for his creditors, his house has been faithfully restored to the way it looked when he lived and worked here. His printing press is back in place, and more than 260 of his etchings now hang on the walls, including self-portraits, landscapes, and several that relate to the traditionally Jewish character of the neighborhood, such as the portrait of Rabbi Menassah ben Israel, who lived across the street.

○ **Stedelijk Museum of Modern Art.** Paulus Potterstraat 13 (at Museumplein). ☎ **020/ 573-27-37.** Admission Dfl 8 ($4.80) adults, Dfl 4 ($2.40) children 7–16. Apr–Sept, daily 11am– 7pm; Oct–Mar, daily 11am–5pm. Tram: 2 or 5 to Paulus Potterstraat, or 16 to Museumplein-Concertgebouw. Bus: 26, 65, or 66 to Museumplein.

This is the contemporary art museum of Amsterdam and the place to see the works of such modern Dutch painters as Karel Appel, Willem de Kooning, and Piet Mondrian; there are also works by French artists Chagall, Cézanne, Picasso, Renoir, Monet, and Manet, as well as those by Americans Calder, Oldenburg, Rosenquist, and Warhol. The Stedelijk centers its collection around the following schools of modern art: De Stijl Cobra, and post-Cobra painting, nouveau réalisme, pop art, color-field painting, zero and minimal art, and conceptual art.

○ **Tropenmuseum.** Linnaeusstraat 2 (at Mauritskade). ☎ **020/568-82-15.** Admission Dfl 10 ($6) adults, Dfl 5 ($3) children 18 and under. Mon–Fri 10am–5pm, Sat–Sun and holidays noon–5pm. Tram: 9 to Mauritskade.

The Tropical Museum, of the Royal Tropical Institute, is devoted to the study of the cultures and cultural problems of tropical areas around the world. Its most interesting exhibits are the walk-through model villages that capture the daily life of such places as India and Indonesia (minus the inhabitants); the displays of tools and techniques used to produce batik, the distinctively dyed Indonesian fabrics; and the displays of the tools, instruments, and ornaments that clutter a tropical residence. A section of the museum is reserved just for kids. Called the **Kindermuseum TM Junior** (phone 020/568-83-00 for information), it's open only to children 6 to 12 (one adult per child is allowed).

○ **Joods Historisch Museum (Jewish Historical Museum).** Jonas Daniël Meijerplein 2–4 (near Waterlooplein). ☎ **020/626-99-45.** Admission Dfl 7 ($4.20) adults, Dfl 3.50 ($2.10) children 10–16. Daily 11am–5pm. Tram: 9 or 14 to Waterlooplein; then walk past the Portuguese Synagogue.

In 1987 the Jewish Historical Museum opened in the restored Ashkenazi Synagogue complex. Through its objects, photographs, artworks, and interactive displays, it was designed to tell three complex, intertwining stories: the stories of Jewish identity, Jewish religion and culture, and Jewish history in the Netherlands. Leave time to appreciate the beauty and size of the buildings themselves, which include the oldest public synagogue in Europe. It's important to note that this is a museum for everyone— Jewish or otherwise—that presents the community through both good times and bad times and provides insights into the Jewish way of life over the centuries.

Churches & a Synagogue

Amsterdam's history can be traced through its many churches and synagogues. The most important are the **Nieuwe Kerk,** on Dam Square; the 17th-century **Westerkerk,** on the Prinsengracht at Westermarkt, which has the tallest and most beautiful tower in Amsterdam and is the burial place of Rembrandt; the **Oude Kerk,** at Oudekerksplein on Oude Zijds Voorburgwal, which dates from the 14th century and is surrounded by small almshouses; and the 17th-century **Portuguese Synagogue,** where attendance at services is by advance appointment (call 020/624-53-51).

Diamond-Cutting Demonstrations

Although this will probably just be one lone polisher working at a small wheel set up in the back of a jewelry store or in the lobby of a factory building, you can still get an idea of how a diamond is cut and polished. You'll see signs all over town for diamond-cutting demonstrations.

The major diamond factories and showrooms in Amsterdam are the **Amsterdam Diamond Center,** Rokin 1, just off Dam Square (☎ 020/624-57-87); **Coster Diamonds,** Paulus Potterstraat 2–6, near the Rijksmuseum (☎ 020/676-22-22); **Gassan Diamonds,** Nieuwe Uilenbuergerstraat 173–175 (☎ 020/622-53-33); **Holshuijsen Stoeltie,** Wagenstraat 13–17 (☎ 020/623-76-01); **Van Moppes Diamonds,** Albert Cuypstraat 2–6, at the daily street market (☎ 020/676-12-42); and **Reuter Diamonds,** Kalverstraat 165 or Singel 526 (☎ 020/623-35-00).

ORGANIZED TOURS

A 3-hour **bus tour** costs Dfl 28 to Dfl 42 ($16.80 to $25.20); children are charged half price. Major companies offering these and other bus sightseeing trips are Holland International Excursions, Damrak 90 (☎ 020/551-28-00); Keytours, Dam Sq. 19 (☎ 020/624-73-04); and Lindbergh Excursions, Damrak 26 (☎ 020/622-27-66).

A clever way of using all that water, and a great time-saver for anyone in a hurry, the **Museum Boat,** Stationsplein 8 (☎ **020/622-21-81**), motors between major museums close to the canals and harbor and provides every bit as good a view of the city as a regular canal-boat cruise. Stops are made every 30 minutes at seven key spots, providing access to 16 museums. The fare, which is for the whole day and includes a discount on museum admissions, is Dfl 22 ($13.20) for adults and Dfl 18 ($10.80) for children 13 and under (after 1pm, Dfl 15/$9).

SHOPPING

Regular **shopping hours** are Mon 11am–6pm, Tues–Wed and Fri 9am–6pm, Thurs 9am–9pm, and Sat 9am–5pm. As a visitor living outside the European Union, you're entitled to a **refund of the VAT** (value-added tax) you pay on your purchases in Holland. Ask stores about this for big-ticket items.

Best buys include special items that the Dutch produce to perfection, or had produced to perfection in the past and now retail as antiques—Delftware, pewter, crystal, and old-fashioned clocks—or commodities in which they have significantly cornered a market, like diamonds. If cost is an important consideration, remember that the Dutch also have inexpensive specialties, such as cheese, flower bulbs, and chocolate.

For jewelry, trendy clothing, or athletic gear, try the department stores on Dam Square, plus the shops on Kalverstraat and Leidsestraat. For fashion, antiques, and art, shop on Van Baerlestraat, P. C. Hooftstraat, and Nieuwe Spiegelstraat. For fashion boutiques and funky little specialty shops, or a good browse through a flea market or secondhand store, Reestraat, Hartenstraat, Wolvenstraat, and Runstraat are particularly good choices.

For more than 30 years, **A van der Meer,** P. C. Hooftstraat 112 (☎ **020/662-19-36**), has been a landmark amid the fashionable shops of P. C. Hooftstraat and a quiet place to enjoy a beautiful collection of antique maps, prints, and engravings, including 17th- and 18th-century Dutch world maps.

✪ **Kunst- & Antiekcentrum de Looier,** Elandsgracht 109 (☎ **020/624-90-38**), is a big indoor antiques market that spreads through several old warehouses along the canals in the Jordaan. Individual dealers rent small stalls and corners to show their best wares: antique jewelry, prints, and engravings.

The ✪ **ABK Gallery for Sculpture,** Zeilmakersstraat 15 (☎ **020/625-63-32**), is a cooperative gallery for Amsterdam sculptors. Call before you head out, since it's open only by appointment Thurs–Sun noon–6pm. Got a favorite cartoon character? ✪ **Animation Art,** Borenstraat 39 (☎ **020/627-76-00**), has original drawings and cel paintings of all kinds of cartoons.

P. G. C. Hajenius, Rokin 92–96 (☎ 020/623-74-94), has been the leading purveyor of cigars and smoking articles since 1826. Cigars are the house specialty, and there's a room full of Havanas, too. Hajenius also sells the long, uniquely Dutch, handmade clay pipes you see in the old paintings (a good gift idea), as well as ceramic pipes.

Folke & Meltzer, P. C. Hooftstraat 65–69 (☎ 020/664-23-11), is the best one-stop shop you'll find for authentic Delft Blue and Makkumware, as well as Hummel figurines, Leerdam crystal, and a world of other fine china, porcelain, silver, glass, or crystal products.

Unless you simply have to have the brand-name articles, you can save considerably on your hand-painted pottery, and also have the fun of seeing the product made, at **Heinen,** Prinsengracht 440, just off Leidesestraat (☎ 020/627-82-99).

Amsterdam's best-known department store, and the one with the best variety of goods, is **De Bijenkorf,** Dam 1 (☎ 020/621-80-80). Ongoing expansion and renovation is gradually changing this once-frumpy little dry-goods emporium into Amsterdam's answer to New York's Bloomingdale's.

Hema, Reguliersbreestraat 10 (☎ 020/624-65-06), has all the merchandise you'd expect to find in a Woolworth store in the United States. If you can't figure out where to find it, your best bet is to look here. **Vroom & Dreesman,** Kalverstraat 201–221 and 212–224 (☎ 020/622-01-71), is a no-nonsense sort of store with a wide range of middle-of-the-road goods and prices and services to match.

Opened in 1743, **Jacob Hooy & Co.,** Kloveniersburgwal 12 (☎ 020/624-30-41), is a wonderland of fragrant smells that offers more than 500 different herbs and spices, and 30 different teas, sold loose, by weight. Everything is stored in wooden drawers and wooden barrels with the names of the contents hand-scripted in gold, and across the counter are fishbowl jars in racks containing 30 or more different types of *dropjes* (drops or lozenges).

Specializing in coffee as well as tea, ✪ **H. Keijzer,** Prinsengracht 180 (☎ 020/624-08-23), was founded in 1839.

The counter display at **Patisserie Pompadour,** Huidenstraat 12 (☎ 020/623-95-54), is amazing—close to 50 luscious pastries that can be enjoyed in this exquisite Louis XVI tearoom.

The distillery **H. P. de Vreng en Zonen,** Nieuwendijk 75 (☎ 020/624-45-81), creates Dutch liqueurs and gins according to the old-fashioned methods, sans additives. Try the traditional Old Amsterdam jenever or some of the more flamboyantly colored liquids, like the brilliant green Pruimpje prik in.

At the ✪ **Albert Cuyp Markt,** Albert Cuypstraat, you'll find all different types of foods, clothing, flowers, and plants, as well as textiles. The market houses 350 different stalls and is held 6 days a week. And every Friday there's a book market held on the Spui, with about 25 different booths offering secondhand books.

At the ✪ **Floating Flower Market,** on the Singel at Muntplein, a row of barges is permanently parked to sell fresh-cut flowers, bright- and healthy-looking plants, ready-to-travel packets of tulip bulbs, and all the necessary accessories of home gardening. Buying at the Singel flower market is an Amsterdam ritual.

The **Sunday Art Market,** at Thorbeckeplein, runs from March to December. Local artists come and show their wares, putting them on display for sale. You'll find sculptures, paintings, jewelry, and mixed-media pieces.

The ✪ **Waterlooplein Flea Market,** at Waterlooplein, is the classic market of Amsterdam. You'll find everything and anything here. On Sunday in the summer (late May to Sept), the junk goes away for a day and the antiques and books come in.

AMSTERDAM AFTER DARK

There's a strong jazz tradition, as well as a thriving club and dance-bar scene, but the dance clubs may seem quiet and small compared to those in New York or Los Angeles. However, the brown cafes—the typical Amsterdam pubs—have never been better, the ballet and opera seasons never more fully subscribed. The music clubs can be good fun, and the little cabarets and dusty theaters along the canals also can be counted on for English-language shows on a regular basis.

Your best source of information on all the nightlife and cultural possibilities of Amsterdam is a publication called *What's On in Amsterdam,* VVV Amsterdam's official program, published every 3 weeks. Many hotels have copies available for guests, or you can easily get one at the VVV tourist information office.

THE PERFORMING ARTS

Music in Amsterdam is focused around one world-famous orchestra—the **Royal Concertgebouw Orchestra**—based in the Concertgebouw, Concertgebouwplein 2–6 (☎ 020/671-83-45), one of the world's most acoustically perfect concert halls. Throughout both the musical season (Sept–May) and the annual Holland Festival (June–July), the world's greatest orchestras, ensembles, conductors, and soloists regularly travel to Amsterdam to perform. Concerts and recitals are performed in the Grote Zaal, or Great Hall, or in a smaller recital hall, the Kleine Zaal, or Little Hall.

From September to March, the **Netherlands Opera Society** produces classics at the Muziektheater, Waterlooplein 22 (☎ 020/625-54-55).

Also performing at the Muziektheater are two dance companies. The **Dutch National Ballet** (☎ 020/625-54-55) is becoming increasingly popular. The **Netherlands Dance Theater** (☎ 020/625-54-55) is one of the best in Holland. Artistic director and choreographer Jirí Kylián has enjoyed great success during his long tenure. Dance performances are also occasionally held at the **Felix Meritis theater,** Keizersgracht 324, below Leidsestraat (☎ 020/626-23-21).

Theater

Amsterdammers speak English so well that Broadway road shows and English-language touring companies (such as the Young Vic company) often make Amsterdam a stop on their European itineraries. Broadway and London musicals also come to Amsterdam from time to time.

Look for touring shows on the schedule at the **Royal Théâtre Carré,** Amstel 115–125 (☎ 020/622-52-25), but get your tickets as far in advance as possible—the hot shows sell out quickly. Another theater is the **Melkweg,** Lijnbaansgracht 234a (☎ 020/624-17-77)—it had been a dairy factory.

Located near Leidseplein, **Lido,** Max Euweplein 64 (☎ 020/622-52-25), offers a dinner show Thurs–Sat evenings (and also Wed in summer). Before the show you can choose from among three different dinner menus. The restaurant opens at 6:30pm, and dinner begins at 7pm.

THE CLUB & MUSIC SCENE

While some international artists perform at **Théâter Carré,** Amstel 115–125 (☎ 020/622-52-25), most of the truly big names are booked into the Feijenoord Stadium or the Ahoy Congress Hall, both of which are in Rotterdam. In future, more performers will probably appear at the new Amsterdam Arena stadium.

Alto Jazz Café. Korte Leidsedwarsstraat 115. ☎ 020/626-32-49. No cover.

There's a regular crowd and a regular quartet that plays jazz nightly in this small, comfortable cafe. Open Sun–Thurs 9pm–3am, Fri–Sat 9pm–4am.

Bimhuis. Oudeschans 73–77. ☎ **020/623-13-61.** No cover Mon–Wed, Dfl 15–25 ($9–$15) Thurs–Sun.

Near the harbor, this theater regularly features European and American artists. The atmosphere is relaxed and serious about jazz. It offers a regular schedule of concerts, with the cafe opening at 8pm and concerts beginning about an hour later, until midnight or 1pm.

Dance Clubs

As long as your attire and behavior suit the sensibilities of the management, you shouldn't have any problems getting past the bouncer. Drinks can be expensive— a beer or Coke averages Dfl 10 ($6), and a whisky or cocktail, Dfl 15 ($9)—but you can nurse one drink along while you dance your feet off, or down a quick beer if the crowd or the music mix is not your style.

Melkweg, Lijnbaansgracht 234a (☎ **020/624-17-77**), is a multipurpose venue that also houses a club. You must pay for a temporary membership, which is Dfl 4 ($2.40), plus a cover of Dfl 7.50 to 25 ($4.50 to $15).

Paradiso, Weteringschans 6–8 (☎ **020/623-73-48**), is located in an old church, and presents an eclectic variety of music, mostly Latin and African. You might not want to go in initially, but the inside is bright, and you might catch some great acts before they become really famous. It isn't open every day, but hours are usually 8pm– 2am. Cover ranges from Dfl 7.50 to 30 ($4.50 to $18).

At the **Roxy,** Singel 465–467 (☎ **020/620-03-54**), one of the hippest, trendiest places in Amsterdam, the membership policy is extremely strict, so it might be difficult for you to get in. Some nights, however, the rules for admittance are dropped and anyone can enter. Cover is Dfl 8 to 15 ($4.80 to $9). Open Wed–Thurs and Sun 11pm–4am, Fri–Sat 11pm–5am.

Brown Cafes

You haven't really tasted Dutch beer until you've tasted it in a real *bruine kroeg,* or brown cafe, amid the unpolished environment of a place where pouring another beer is much more important than dusting off the back bottles on the bar. Even if you're not a beer lover, venturing into a brown cafe in Amsterdam will give you a peek into the everyday life of the city. You'll find brown cafes on almost every corner in the old neighborhoods. There will be no mistaking you've found the right place once you're inside; the smoky, mustard brownness of the interior is unique to an Amsterdam brown cafe, the result of years—no, centuries—of thick smoke and heated conversation. You'll feel the centuries of conviviality the minute you walk in the door of a really old, really *brown* brown cafe, and indeed some have been on their corners since Rembrandt's time. The best of them are on the Prinsengracht, below Westermarkt, at Dam Square, at Leidseplein, on Spui, or with a bit of looking, on tiny streets between the canals.

The **Café Chris,** Bloemstraat 42 (☎ **020/624-59-42**), is said to be the place where the builders of Westerkerk were paid every week or two. It opened in 1624 and has been going strong ever since. There are a lot of curious old features to this bar that keep drawing people year after year, including the flushing system of the toilet in the bathroom—it flushes from outside the door.

Not too many people know about the **Café de Druif,** Rapenburg 83 (☎ **020/ 624-45-30**). De Druif ("The Grape") is located on the waterfront, and is mainly frequented by friendly locals. The bar's mythology has it that the Dutch naval hero, Piet Heyn, was a frequent patron—quite a feat, considering that the bar opened in 1631 and Heyn died in 1629.

It's often standing room only at the **Café Hoppe,** Spuistraat 18–20 (☎ **020/ 623-78-49**)—the crowds sometimes even overflow out onto the street. It seems that, quite by accident, the Hoppe has become a tourist attraction. Locals love this spot, which dates from 1670, and often stop on their way home for a drink. It's worth stopping by just to see it.

Opened in 1629, the **Café Karpershoek,** Martelaarsgracht 2 (☎ **020/624-78-86**), was a favorite hangout of sailors and seamen. As it was in the 17th century, the floor is covered with sand.

Opened by Pieter Hoppe in 1786 as a liquor distillery and tasting house, the **Café 't Smalle,** Egelantiersgracht 12 (☎ **020/623-96-17**), is a wonderfully cozy spot in which you're highly unlikely to get a seat, or even *see* one. If you really want the brown cafe experience, you should at least try to stop in.

In a medieval alley, **In de Wildeman,** Kolksteeg 3 (☎ **020/638-23-48**), a wood-paneled tavern lit by brass, is loaded with atmosphere. The tile floor and rows of bottles and jars behind the counters are remnants from its earlier days, when it functioned as a pharmacy. Today it serves 150 kinds of beer.

DAY TRIPS FROM AMSTERDAM

HAARLEM Haarlem is a city of music and art just 12 miles west of Amsterdam. If you have only 1 day to travel beyond Amsterdam, spend it in this charming town, which is the home of two of Holland's finest museums.

Haarlem is only an hour from Amsterdam by train, and there is a train every hour, leaving from Central Station. It can also be reached by frequent buses. If you go by car, take route A16.

Haarlem is where Frans Hals, Jacob van Ruysdael, and Pieter Saenredam were living and painting their famous portraits, landscapes, and church interiors while Rembrandt was living and working in Amsterdam. It's also a city to which both Handel and Mozart made special visits just to play the magnificent organ of the **Church of St. Bavo,** also known as Grote Kerk, Oude Groenmarkt 23. Look for the tombstone of painter Frans Hals, and for a cannonball that has been imbedded in the wall ever since it came flying through a window during the siege of Haarlem in 1572–73. And, of course, don't miss seeing the famous **Christian Muller Organ,** built in 1738. You can hear it at one of the free concerts given on Tues and Thurs Apr–Oct. It has 5,068 pipes and is nearly 98 feet tall. The woodwork was done by Jan van Logteren. Mozart played the organ in 1766 when he was just 10 years old. St. Bavo's is open Mon–Sat 10am–4pm.

From St. Bavo's, it's an easy walk to the oldest and perhaps the most unusual museum in Holland, the **Teylers Museum,** Spaarne 16 (☎ **023/531-90-10**). It contains a curious collection of displays: drawings by Michelangelo, Raphael, and Rembrandt; fossils, minerals, and skeletons; instruments of physics and an odd assortment of inventions, including the largest electrostatic generator in the world (1784) and a 19th-century radarscope. Open Tues–Sat 10am–5pm and Sun noon–5pm. Admission is Dfl 7.50 ($4.50) for adults, Dfl 5 ($3) for seniors, Dfl 3.50 ($2.10) for children 5 to 15.

Saving the best for last, visit the **Frans Halsmuseum,** Groot Heiligeland 62 (☎ **023/516-42-00**), where the galleries are the halls and furnished chambers of a former pensioners' home and the famous paintings by the masters of the Haarlem school hang in settings that look like the 17th-century homes they were intended to adorn. Open Mon–Sat 11am–5pm and Sun 1–5pm. Admission is Dfl 6.50 ($3.90) for adults, Dfl 3 ($1.80) for children 10 to 18, and free for children 9 and under.

DELFT Yes, this is the city of the famous blue-and-white earthenware. And, yes, you can visit the factory of De Porceleyne Fles as long as you realize it's only a visit to a showroom and not the painting studios and other workrooms. But don't let Delftware be your only reason to visit Delft. Not only is this one of the prettiest small cities in Holland, but also Delft is important as a cradle of the Dutch Republic and the traditional burial place of the royal family. Plus, it was the birthplace—and inspiration—of the 17th-century master of light and subtle emotion, the painter Jan Vermeer. Delft remains a quiet and intimate little town, with flowers in its flower boxes and linden trees bending over its gracious canals.

For bus information, call 020/651-27-93. Delft can be reached by train and is also a short drive away.

The house where Vermeer was born, lived, and painted is long gone from Delft, as are his paintings. Instead, you can visit the **Oude Kerk,** at Roland Holstlaan 753, where he's buried; open Apr–Oct, Mon–Sat 10am–5pm. Also, you might want to visit the **Nieuwe Kerk,** on Markt near the VVV office, where Prince William of Orange and all other members of the House of Oranje-Nassau are buried. Open Mon–Sat 11am–5pm; its tower is open May–Sept, Tues–Sat 10am–4:30pm.

The **Prinsenhof Museum,** Sint-Agathaplein 1 (☎ **015/260-23-58**), on the nearby Oude Delft canal, is where William I of Orange (William the Silent) lived and had his headquarters in the years during which he helped found the Dutch Republic. It's also where he was assassinated in 1584 (you can still see the musket-ball holes in the stairwell). Today, however, the Prinsenhof is a museum of paintings, tapestries, silverware, and pottery. Open Tues–Sat 10am–5pm and Sun 1–5pm (also Mon 1–5pm June–Aug).

In the same neighborhood you can also see a fine collection of old Delft tiles displayed in the wood-paneled setting of a 19th-century mansion museum called **Lambert van Meerten,** located at Oude Delft 199 and open Tues–Sat 10am–5pm and Sun 1–5pm. Or to see brand-new Delftware, and a demonstration of the art of hand-painting Delftware, visit the showroom of **De Porceleyne Fles,** Rotterdamseweg 196 (☎ **015/256-92-14**), open Apr–Oct, Mon–Sat 9am–5pm and Sun 9:30am–4pm; Nov–Mar, Mon–Sat 9am–5pm. Admission is free.

THE FLOWER CENTERS Flowers at their peak and the **Keukenhof Gardens at Lisse** (☎ **025/465-555**) both have short but glorious seasons, and you'll never forget a visit to this meandering 70-acre wooded park in the heart of the bulb-producing region, planted each fall by the major Dutch growers. Come spring, the bulbs burst forth and produce millions (seven million at last count) of tulips and narcissi, daffodils and hyacinths, bluebells, crocuses, lilies, amaryllis, and much more. The blaze of color is everywhere in the park and in the greenhouses, beside the brooks and shady ponds, along the paths and in the neighboring fields, in neat little plots and helter-skelter on the lawns. By its own report it's the greatest flower show on earth.

The park is open late from March to late May, daily 8am–7:30pm. There are special train-bus connections via Haarlem and the nearby town of Leiden. Admission is Dfl 17 ($10.20) for adults, Dfl 15 ($9) for seniors, and Dfl 8.50 ($5.10) for children 4 to 12.

Flowers are also a year-round business that nets more than a billion guilders a year at the **Aalsmeer Flower Auction** (☎ **0297/332-185** or 0297/334-567), held in the lakeside community of Aalsmeer, near Schiphol Airport. Every year, three billion flowers and 400 million plants are sold, coming from 8,000 nurseries. Get there early to see the biggest array of flowers in the distribution rooms and to have as much time as possible to watch the computerized auctioning process—it works basically like the old *Beat the Clock* TV show: The first one to press the button gets the posies.

In keeping with a Dutch auctioneering philosophy that demands quick handling for perishable goods, the bidding on flowers goes from high to low instead of proceeding in the usual manner of bidding up. There are 13 mammoth bidding clocks that are numbered from 100 to 1. As the bunches of tulips or daffodils go by the stand on carts, they are auctioned in a matter of seconds, with the first bid—which is the first bid to stop the clock as it works down from 100 to 1—as the only bid. Whether or not it's really for the sake of the freshness of the flowers, the Aalsmeer Flower Auction is smart Dutch business.

The auction is held Mon–Fri 7:30–11am; bus no. 172 will take you there from Centraal Station. The entrance fee is Dfl 5 ($3) per person, free for children 11 and under.

13

Norway

by Darwin Porter & Danforth Prince

Norway is a land of tradition, as exemplified by its rustic stave churches and folk dances stepped to the airs of a fiddler. But Norway is also modern, a technologically advanced nation that's rich in petroleum and hydroelectric energy. Norwegians also enjoy a well-developed public system of social insurance, comprising old-age pensions, health insurance, unemployment insurance, and rehabilitation assistance.

One of the last great natural frontiers of the world, Norway invites exploration, with its steep and jagged fjords, salmon-teeming rivers, glaciers, mountains, and meadows. In winter, the shimmering aurora borealis beckons; in summer, the midnight sun burns.

Oslo, Bergen & the Fjords

Our tour begins in the Norwegian capital of Oslo and continues west to the capital of the fjord district, Bergen. Then we discuss the many options for exploring the spectacular fjords.

ONLY IN OSLO

Experiencing Life on the Water   In summer, head for the harbor, where boats wait to take you sightseeing, fishing, or to the beaches.

Hanging Out in Students' Grove   Summer is short in Oslo, and it's savored. Late-night drinkers sit in open-air beer gardens, enjoying the pale nights that have no end.

Enjoying Fresh Shrimp off the Boats   In Oslo, head for the harbor in front of the Rådhuset and buy a bag of freshly caught and cooked shrimp from a shrimp fisher. Get a beer at an Aker Brygge cafe and shell and eat your shrimp along the harbor.

Listening to the Street Musicians   Hundreds of musicians flock to Oslo in summer. You can enjoy their music along Karl Johans Gate and at the Marketplace.

Taking the Ferry to Bygdøy   The Bygdøy peninsula is a treasure trove of Viking ships, Thor Heyerdahl's *Kon-Tiki,* seafood buffets, a sailboat harbor, bathing beaches, and a folk museum with old farmsteads, houses, and often folk dancing.

OSLO

Today Oslo is one of the 10 largest capitals in the world in sheer area, if not in urban buildup. After World War II, Oslo grew to 175 square miles. The city is one of the most heavily forested on earth and fewer than half a million Norwegians live and work here.

One of the oldest Scandinavian capital cities, founded in the mid-11th century, Oslo has never been a mainstream tourist site. But the city is a culturally rich capital with many diversions, enough to fill at least 3 or 4 busy days. It's also the center for many easy excursions along the Oslofjord or to towns and villages in its environs, both north and south.

In recent years Oslo has grown from what even the Scandinavians viewed as a Nordic backwater to one of Europe's happening cities. Restaurants, nightclubs, cafes, shopping complexes, and other venues keep on opening. A kind of Nordic joie de vivre permeates the city. But the only drawback is that all this fun is expensive, as Oslo ranks as one of Europe's most expensive cities.

ESSENTIALS

ARRIVING   By Plane   Most arrivals are at **Fornebu** (☎ **67-59-33-40**) at Snaroya, 5¹/₂ miles from Oslo. Fornebu services both domestic and international flights of SAS and other intra-European airlines, including British Airways and Icelandair.

SAS operates a bus service from both terminals to the Sentralstasjon and other points in Oslo every 15 minutes. The fare is 35Kr ($5.40) to and from Fornebu.

By Train   Trains from the Continent and from Sweden or Copenhagen pull into **Oslo Sentralstasjon,** Jernbanetorget 1 at the beginning of Karl Johans Gate (☎ **81-50-08-88** for train information), in the city center. The station is open daily 7am–11pm. From the Central Station, you can catch trains heading for Bergen and all other rail links in Norway. You can also take trams to all major parts of Oslo.

By Car   If you're driving from mainland Europe, the fastest way to reach Oslo is to take the car-ferry from Frederikshavn (Denmark). You can also take a car-ferry from Copenhagen or drive from Copenhagen by crossing over to Helsingborg (Sweden) from Helsingør (Denmark). Once at Helsingborg, take E6 north all the way to Stockholm. If you're driving from Stockholm to Oslo, take E18 west all the way. Once you near the outskirts of Oslo from any direction, follow the signs into the Sentrum (center city).

By Ferry   Ferries from Europe arrive at the Oslo port, a 15-minute walk (or a short taxi ride) from the center. From Denmark, ferries depart for Oslo from Copenhagen, Hirtshals, and Frederikshavn. From Strømstad (Sweden), there's a daily crossing in summer to Sandefjord (Norway), which takes 2¹/₂ hours; from Sandefjord, it's an easy drive or train ride north to Oslo.

VISITOR INFORMATION   The **Tourist Information Office,** Vestbaneplassen 1, N-0250 Oslo (☎ **22-83-00-50**), is open Dec–Jan, Mon–Fri 9am–4pm; Feb–Apr and Oct–Nov, Mon–Sat 9am–4pm; May and Sept, Mon–Sat 9am–6pm; June, daily 9am–6pm; and July–Aug, daily 9am–8pm. Free maps, brochures, sightseeing tickets, and guide services are available.

There's also an **information office** at the Oslo Sentralstasjon (Central Station), Jernbanetorget 1, at the beginning of Karl Johans Gate (☎ **82-06-01-00**), open daily 8am–11pm.

Oslo Attractions & Accommodations

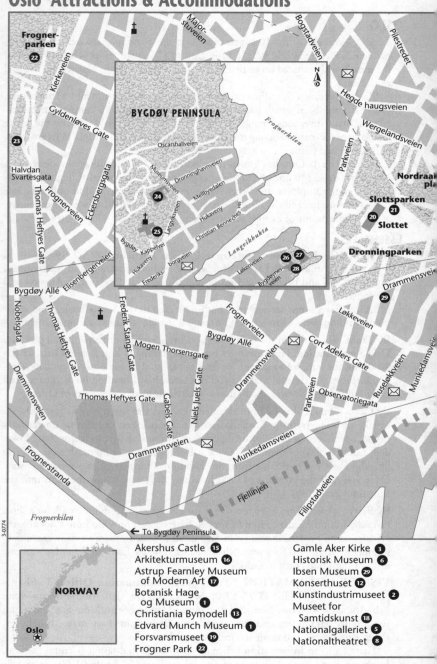

Akershus Castle **15**
Arkitekturmuseum **16**
Astrup Fearnley Museum
   of Modern Art **17**
Botanisk Hage
   og Museum **1**
Christiania Bymodell **13**
Edvard Munch Museum **1**
Forsvarsmuseet **19**
Frogner Park **22**

Gamle Aker Kirke **3**
Historisk Museum **6**
Ibsen Museum **29**
Konserthuset **12**
Kunstindustrimuseet **2**
Museet for
   Samtidskunst **18**
Nationalgalleriet **5**
Nationaltheatret **8**

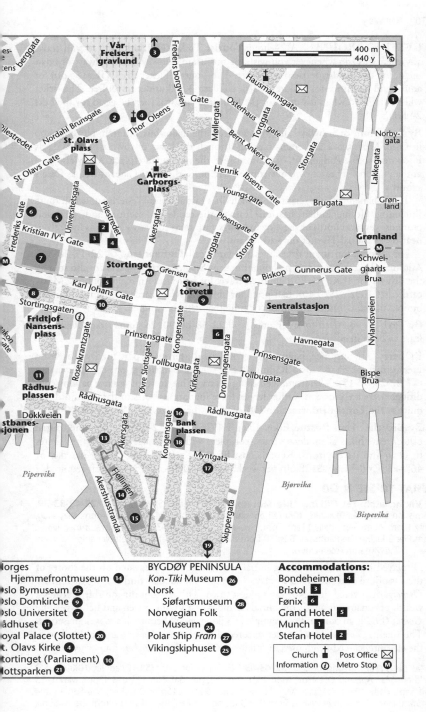

Vår Frelsers gravlund

Fredens borgveien

Hausmannsgate

Fredens Gate

Østerhaus gate

Nordahl Brungate

Thor Olsens

Møllergata

Torggata

Storgata

Norby-gata

St. Olavs plass

Lakkegata

St. Olavs Gate

Arne-Garborgs-plass

Henrik Ibsens Gate

Youngs gate

Berndt Ankers Gate

Frederiks Gate

Kristian IV's Gate

Universitetsgata

Pilestredet

Akersgata

Ploensgate

Torggata

Storgata

Brugata

Grøn-land

Grønland

Schwei-gaards Brua

Stortinget

Grensen

Stor-torvet

Biskop Gunnerus Gate

Karl Johans Gate

Stortingsgaten

Fridtjof-Nansens-plass

Sentralstasjon

Rosenkrantzgate

Prinsensgate

Kongensgate

Dronningensgata

Havnegata

Prinsensgate

Nylandsveien

Rådhus-plassen

Rådhusgata

Øvre Slottsgate

Tollbugata

Kirkegata

Tollbugata

Rådhusgata

Bispe Brua

Dokkveien

stbanes-sjonen

Akersgata

Kongensgate

Bank plassen

Myntgata

Pipervika

Fjellinjen

Akershusstranda

Skippergata

Bjørvika

Bispevika

lorges	**BYGDØY PENINSULA**	**Accommodations:**
Hjemmefrontmuseum ⑭	*Kon-Tiki* Museum ㉖	Bondeheimen ☐4
›slo Bymuseum ㉓	Norsk	Bristol ☐3
›slo Domkirche ⑨	Sjøfartsmuseum ㉘	Fønix ☐6
›slo Universitet ⑦	Norwegian Folk	Grand Hotel ☐5
ådhuset ⑪	Museum ㉔	Munch ☐1
oyal Palace (Slottet) ⑳	Polar Ship *Fram* ㉗	Stefan Hotel ☐2
t. Olavs Kirke ④	Vikingskiphuset ㉕	
tortinget (Parliament) ⑩		
lottsparken ㉑		

Church ✝	Post Office ✉
Information ⓘ	Metro Stop Ⓜ

GETTING AROUND A 24-hour **Tourist Ticket (Turistkort)** lets you travel anywhere in Oslo whenever you wish, by bus, tram, subway, local railway, or boat, including the Bygdøy ferries in summer. The Tourist Ticket costs 35Kr ($5.40) for adults and half price for children 4–15; children 3 and under travel free. The ticket will be stamped when it's used for the first time and will then be good for the next 24 hours.

By Bus, Tram & Subway Jernbanetorget is the major bus and tram terminal stop in Oslo. Most buses and trams passing through the heart of town stop at Wessels Plass, next to the Parliament, or at Stortorget, the main marketplace. Many also stop at the National Theater or University Square on Karl Johans Gate, as well as Oslo's suburbs.

The T-banen (subway) has four branch lines east and the Western Suburban route (including Holmenkollen) has four lines to the residential sections and recreation grounds west and north of the city. Subways and trains to Oslo's environs leave from near the National Theater on Karl Johans Gate.

For information about timetables and fares, call **Trafikanten** (☎ **22-17-70-30**). Automated machines cancel prebought tickets. Single-journey tickets are also sold by the drivers for 18Kr ($2.75); children travel for half fare. An eight-coupon "Maxi" card costs 100Kr ($15.40), half price for children. Maxi cards can be used for unlimited transfers within 1 hour of the time the ticket is stamped.

By Taxi If you need to order a taxi, call **22-38-80-90,** 24 hours a day. Reserve at least an hour in advance.

By Ferry In summer, beginning in mid-April, ferries depart for Bygdøy from Pier 3 in front of the Oslo Rådhuset. For schedule information, call **Båtservice** (☎ **22-20-07-15**). We recommend using a ferry or bus to Bygdøy since parking conditions there are crowded. Other ferries leave for various parts of the Oslofjord; inquire at the **Tourist Information Office** at Vestbaneplassen 1 (☎ **22-83-00-50**).

By Bicycle **Den Rustne Eike,** Enga 2 (☎ **22-83-72-31**), behind the tourist office, rents bikes at moderate rates, complete with free maps of interesting routes in Oslo and its environs. Rentals cost 85–135Kr ($13.10–$20.80) per day or 465–835Kr ($71.60–$128.60) per week, with a 1,000Kr ($154) deposit required.

WHAT TO SEE & DO

✪ Vikingskiphuset (Viking Ship Museum). Huk Aveny 35, Bygdøy. ☎ **22-43-83-79.** Admission 30Kr ($4.60) adults, 10Kr ($1.55) children. Apr and Oct, daily 11am–4pm; May–Aug, daily 10am–6pm; Sept, daily 11am–5pm; Nov–Mar, daily 11am–3pm. Ferry: In summer, leaves from Pier 3 facing the Rådhuset. Bus: 30 from the National Theater to the polar ship *Fram* and the *Kon-Tiki* Museum (see below).

Displayed here are three Viking burial vessels that were excavated on the shores of the Oslofjord and preserved in clay. The most spectacular find is the 9th-century *Oseberg,* discovered near Norway's oldest town. This 64-foot dragon ship features a wealth of ornaments and is the burial chamber of a Viking queen and her slave. The *Gokstad* find is an outstanding example of Viking vessels because it's so well preserved. The smaller *Tune* ship was never restored. Look for the *Oseberg* animal-head post, the elegantly carved sleigh used by Viking royalty, and the *Oseberg* four-wheeled cart.

Polar Ship *Fram.* Bygdøynes. ☎ **22-43-83-70.** Admission 20Kr ($3.10) adults, 10Kr ($1.55) children. Mar–Apr and Oct–Nov, Mon–Fri 11am–2:45pm, Sat–Sun 11am–3:45pm; May 1–15 and Sept, daily 10am–4:45pm; May 16–Aug, daily 9am–5:45pm; Dec–Feb, Sat–Sun 11am–3:45pm. Ferry: In summer, leaves from Pier 3 facing the Rådhuset. Bus: 30 from the National Theater.

A long walk from the Viking ships, the Frammuseet contains the sturdy polar exploration ship *Fram*, which Fridtjof Nansen sailed across the Arctic (1893–96). The vessel was later used by famed Norwegian explorer Roald Amundsen, the first man to reach the South Pole (1911).

***Kon-Tiki* Museum.** Bygdøynesveien 36. ☎ **22-43-80-50.** Admission 25Kr ($3.85) adults, 10Kr ($1.55) children. Apr–May and Sept, daily 10:30am–5pm; June–Aug, daily 9:30am–5:45pm; Oct–Mar, daily 10:30am–4pm. Ferry: In summer, leaves from Pier 3 facing the Rådhuset. Bus: 30 from the National Theater.

The *Kon-Tiki* is the world-famed balsa-log raft that the young Norwegian scientist Thor Heyerdahl and his five comrades sailed in for 4,300 miles in 1947—all the way from Callao, Peru, to Raroia, Polynesia. Besides the raft, there are other exhibits from Heyerdahl's subsequent visit to Easter Island: casts of stone giants and small originals, a facsimile of the whale shark, and an Easter Island family cave, with a collection of sacred lava figurines hoarded in secret underground passages by inhabitants of that island.

Norsk Sjøfartsmuseum (Norwegian Maritime Museum). Bygdøynesveien 37. ☎ **22-43-82-40.** Admission (museum and boat hall) 20Kr ($3.10) adults, 10Kr ($1.55) children. May–Sept, daily 10am–7pm; Oct–Apr, Mon–Sat 10:30am–4pm, Sun 10:30am–5pm. Ferry: In summer, leaves from Pier 3 facing the Rådhuset. Bus: 30 from the National Theater.

This museum chronicles the maritime history and culture of Norway, complete with a ship's deck with helm and chart house. There's also a three-deck-high section of the passenger steamer *Sandnaes*. The Boat Hall features a fine collection of original small craft. The fully restored polar vessel *Gjoa*, used by Roald Amundsen in his search for America's Northwest Passage, is also on display. The three-masted schooner *Svanen* (Swan) is moored at the museum.

☺ Norwegian Folk Museum. Museumsveien 10. ☎ **22-12-37-00.** Admission 50Kr ($7.70) adults, 10Kr ($1.55) children 16 and under. May and Sept, daily 10am–5pm; June–Aug, daily 9am–6pm; Oct–Apr, Mon–Sat 11am–3pm, Sun 11am–4pm. Ferry: In summer, leaves from Pier 3, near the Rådhuset. Bus: 30 from the National Theater.

From all over Norway, 140 original buildings have been transported and reassembled on 35 acres on the Bygdøy peninsula. This open-air folk museum, one of the oldest of its kind, includes a number of medieval buildings, such as the Raulandstua, one of the oldest wooden dwellings still standing in Norway, and a stave church from about 1200. The rural buildings are grouped together by region of origin, while the urban houses have been laid out in the form of an old town.

☺ Vigeland Sculpture Park. Frogner Park, Nobelsgata 32. ☎ **22-44-23-06.** Park, free; museum, 20Kr ($3.10) adults, 10Kr ($1.55) children. Park, daily 24 hours. Museum, May–Sept, Tues–Sat 10am–6pm, Sun noon–7pm; Oct–Apr, Tues–Sat noon–4pm, Sun noon–6pm. Tram: 12 or 15. Bus: 20.

The lifetime work of Gustav Vigeland, Norway's greatest sculptor, is displayed in the 75-acre Frogner Park in western Oslo. Nearly 211 sculptures in granite, bronze, and iron can be admired. See in particular his four granite columns, symbolizing the fight between humanity and evil (a dragon, the embodiment of evil, embraces a woman). The angry boy is the most photographed statue in the park, but the really celebrated work is the 52-foot-high monolith, composed of 121 figures of colossal size—all carved into one piece of stone.

☺ Edvard Munch Museum. Tøyengate 53. ☎ **22-67-37-74.** Admission 40Kr ($6.15) adults, 15Kr ($2.30) children. June to mid-Sept, daily 10am–6pm; mid-Sept to May, Tues–Wed and Fri–Sat 10am–4pm, Thurs and Sun 10am–6pm. T-banen: Tøyen. Bus: 20.

Devoted exclusively to the works of Edvard Munch (1863–1944), the leading painter of Scandinavia, the exhibit, Munch's gift to the city, traces his work from early realism to his latter-day expressionism. The collection comprises 1,100 paintings, some 4,500 drawings, around 18,000 prints, numerous graphic plates, six sculptures, and important documentary material.

Akershus Castle. Festnings-Plassen. ☎ **22-41-25-21.** Admission 20Kr ($3.10) adults, 10Kr ($1.55) children. Apr 15–30 and Sept 16–Oct, Sun 12:30–4pm; May–Sept 15, Mon–Sat 10am–4pm, Sun 12:30–4pm. Closed Nov–Apr 14. Guided tours Mon–Sat at 11am, 1pm, and 3pm; Sun at 1 and 3pm. Tram: 1, 2, or 10.

One of the oldest historical monuments in Oslo, Akershus Castle was built in 1300 by King Haakon V Magnusson. It was a fortress and a royal residence for several centuries. A fire in 1527 devastated the northern wing, and the castle was rebuilt and transformed into a royal Renaissance palace under the Danish-Norwegian king, Christian IV. Now it's used by the Norwegian government for state occasions.

Attractions Nearby

Tryvannstårnet (Lookout Tower). Voksenkollen. ☎ **22-14-67-11.** Admission 30Kr ($4.60) adults, 15Kr ($2.30) children. May and Sept, daily 10am–5pm; June, daily 10am–7pm; July, daily 9am–10pm; Aug, daily 9am–8pm; Oct–Apr, Mon–Fri 10am–3pm, Sat–Sun 11am–4pm. T-banen: Holmenkollen SST Line 15 from near the National Theater to Voksenkollen, a 30-minute ride; then an uphill 15-minute walk.

The loftiest lookout tower in Scandinavia—the gallery is approximately 1,900 feet above sea level—offers a view of the Oslofjord with Sweden to the east. A walk down the hill takes you back to Frognerseteren. You can take another 20-minute walk down the hill to the Holmenkollen ski jump, the site of the 1952 Olympic competitions as well as the Holmenkollen Ski Festival, when skiers compete in downhill, slalom, giant slalom, cross-country ski races, and jumping.

۞ Henie-Onstad Kunstsenter (Henie-Onstad Art Center). Høkvikodden, Baerum. ☎ **67-54-30-50.** Admission 40Kr ($6.15) adults, 20Kr ($3.10) children 16 and under. June–Aug, Mon 11am–5pm, Tues–Fri 9am–9pm, Sat–Sun 11am–7pm; Sept–May, Sat–Mon 11am–5pm, Tues 9am–9pm. Bus: 151, 152, 251, or 261 to Høvikodden.

On a site beside the Oslofjord 7 miles west of Oslo, ex-movie star and skating champion Sonja Henie and her husband, Niels Onstad, a shipping tycoon, opened a museum to display their art collection. This especially good 20th-century collection includes some 1,800 works by Munch, Picasso, Matisse, Léger, Bonnard, and Miró. Ms. Henie's Trophy Room is impressive with 600 trophies and medals, including three Olympic gold medals—she was the star at the 1936 competition—and 10 world skating championships.

Organized Tours

H. M. Kristiansens Automobilbyrå, Hegdehaugsveien 4 (☎ **22-20-82-06**), known as H.M.K. tours, has been showing visitors around Oslo for more than a century. In July and August the agency offers a full-day Oslo sightseeing tour, leaving daily at 10am and returning at 4:15pm. It costs 350Kr ($53.90) for adults and 180Kr ($27.70) for children—not including lunch. A half-day highlight tour leaves at 10am and costs 190Kr ($29.25) for adults, 100Kr ($15.40) for children. Tours leave from the Norway information center, Vestbaneplassen 1; you should arrive 15 minutes before departure. Authorized guides speak English.

Shopping

Near the marketplace and the cathedral, **Den Norske Husflidsforening,** Møllergata 4 (☎ **22-42-10-75**)—Husfliden, as it's called—is the display and retail center for the Norwegian Association of Home Arts and Crafts, founded in 1891. Today it's almost eight times larger than any of its competitors, with two floors displaying the very finest of Norwegian design in ceramics, glassware, furniture, and woodworking. You can also purchase souvenirs, gifts, textiles, rugs, knotted Rya rugs, embroidery, wrought iron, and fabrics by the yard. Goods are shipped all over the world.

Norway's largest department store, **Steen & Strøm,** Kongensgate 23 (☎ **22-00-40-00**), is a treasure house of hundreds of Nordic items—from the ground-floor souvenir shop to the sales departments on the top floors. Look for hand-knit sweaters and caps, hand-painted wooden dishes reflecting traditional Norwegian art, and pewter dinner plates made from old molds.

Heimen Husflid, Rosenkrantzgate 8 (☎ 22-41-40-50), about a block from Karl Johans Gate, carries folk costumes, antiques, and reproductions. You'll have more than three dozen different *bunads* (styles) to choose from, including different regions of Norway, both north and south. Hand-knit sweaters in traditional Norwegian patterns are a special item, as are pewter and brass items.

Established more than a century ago, the outstanding Norwegian jeweler **David-Andersen,** Karl Johans Gate 20 (☎ 22-41-69-55), distributes enameled demitasse spoons and sterling-silver bracelets with enamel, available in many stunning colors such as turquoise and dark blue. The multicolored butterfly pins are also popular. David-Andersen's collection of Saga silver is inspired by traditional features in Norwegian folklore and by Viking designs.

William Schmidt, Karl Johans Gate 41 (☎ 22-42-02-88), established in 1853, is a leading purveyor of unique souvenirs, including pewter items (everything from Viking ships to beer goblets), Norwegian dolls in national costumes, wood carvings (the troll collection is the most outstanding in Oslo), and sealskin items such as moccasins and handbags. The shop specializes in hand-knit cardigans, pullovers, gloves, and caps; sweaters are made from moth-proofed 100% Norwegian wool.

ACCOMMODATIONS

Very Expensive

✪ **Grand Hotel.** Karl Johans Gate 31, N-0159 Oslo 1. ☎ **800/223-5652** in the U.S., or 22-42-93-90. Fax 22-42-12-25. 287 rms, 40 suites. MINIBAR TV TEL. Summer, 1,090Kr ($167.85) double; 2,050–10,000Kr ($315.70–$1,540) suite. Winter, 1,875Kr ($288.75) double; 2,675–10,000Kr ($411.95–$1,540) suite. Rates include buffet breakfast. AE, DC, MC, V. Parking 120Kr ($18.50). T-banen: Stortinget.

Norway's leading hotel, located on the wide boulevard that leads to the Royal Palace, is a stone-walled building from 1874, with mansard gables and copper tower. Dramatically renovated in 1996, the bedrooms are either in the 19th-century core or in one of the tasteful modern additions. The newer rooms contain plush facilities and electronic amenities, and the older ones have been completely modernized as well to offer luxurious comfort. Some rooms have air-conditioning. The hotel has several restaurants, serving both international and Scandinavian food. The Palmen, the Julius Fritzner, and the Grand Café offer live entertainment. The Grand Café is the most famous in Oslo. Facilities include an indoor swimming pool, sauna, and solarium.

Expensive

Bristol. Kristian IV's Gate 7, N-0164 Oslo 1. ☎ **22-82-60-00.** Fax 22-82-60-01. 141 rms, 4 suites. A/C MINIBAR TV TEL. June 21–Aug 4, 1,050Kr ($161.70) double. Aug 5–June 20, 1,595Kr ($245.65) double Mon–Thurs, 850Kr ($130.90) double Fri–Sun. Year-round, 2,950Kr ($454.30) suite. Rates include breakfast. AE, DC, MC, V. Parking 130Kr ($20). T-banen: Stortinget.

In the heart of the city, on a side street north of Karl Johans Gate, this 1920s-era hotel is warm, inviting, and luxurious. The Moorish-inspired lobby, with its Winter

Garden and Library Bar, sets the elegant tone. The bedrooms are homelike and comfortable, most often furnished in light Nordic pastels, although the bathrooms need an overhaul. Many thoughtful amenities are installed. The Bristol has several drinking and dining venues, including the intimate Bristol Grill.

Moderate

Ⓢ Bondeheimen. Rosenkrantzgate 8, N-0159 Oslo 1. ☎ **800/528-1234** in the U.S. and Canada, or 22-42-95-30. Fax 22-41-94-37. 76 rms. MINIBAR TV TEL. July, 710Kr ($109.35) double. Aug–June, 990Kr ($152.45) double Mon–Thurs, 710Kr ($109.35) double Fri–Sun. Rates include breakfast. AE, DC, MC, V. Tram: 7 or 11.

In the city center, only a short block from the Students' Grove at Karl Johans Gate, the Bondeheimen was built in 1913 by a cooperative of farmers and students to provide inexpensive, clean, and safe accommodations when they visited Oslo from the countryside. Although small, the rooms are comfortably furnished, often with Norwegian pine pieces, and no-smoking rooms are available. There's an inexpensive Kaffistova on the premises.

Stefan Hotel. Rosenkrantzgate 1, N-0159 Oslo 1. ☎ **22-42-92-50.** Fax 22-33-70-22. 138 rms. A/C MINIBAR TV TEL. 895Kr ($137.85) double Mon–Thurs, 695Kr ($107.05) double Fri–Sun. Rates include breakfast. AE, DC, MC, V. Parking 125Kr ($19.25). Tram: 11, 17, or 18.

This clean and comfortable hotel boasts an excellent location in the city center. Built in 1952, it has been modernized and much improved since then, with a partial renovation in 1996. The bedrooms are well furnished and maintained. Two bedrooms have facilities for travelers with disabilities. At lunch guests can enjoy selections from a Norwegian cold-table buffet.

Inexpensive

Ⓢ Fønix. Dronningensgate 19, N-0154 Oslo 1. ☎ **22-42-59-57.** Fax 22-33-12-10. 64 rms, 20 with bath. TEL. 500Kr ($77) double without bath, 675–750Kr ($103.95–$115.50) double with bath. Rates include breakfast. AE, DC, MC, V. T-banen: Jernbanetorget.

A 3-minute walk from the Central Station, the Hotel Fønix offers great value. Though constructed in 1924, the hotel has been frequently redecorated, and some sections were renovated in 1995. Breakfast is served in its restaurant, Kristine, furnished with turn-of-the-century oak dining suites.

Ⓢ Munch. Munchsgaten 5, N-0130 Oslo 1. ☎ **22-42-42-75.** Fax 22-20-64-69. 180 rms. MINIBAR TV TEL. 685–785Kr ($105.50–$120.90) double Mon–Thurs, 560–785Kr ($86.25–$120.90) double Fri–Sun. Rates include breakfast. AE, DC, MC, V. Parking 100Kr ($15.40). T-banen: Stortinget. Tram: 7 or 11. Bus: 37.

Five minutes north of Karl Johans Gate is this good one-star hotel that's really like a bed-and-breakfast. Built in 1983, this solid, nine-floor hotel offers comfortably furnished, well-maintained, and functional bedrooms, decorated with reproductions of Edvard Munch paintings. There's no bar or restaurant, but the surrounding neighborhood is well supplied.

DINING
Very Expensive

Ⓒ Bagatelle. Bygdøy Allé 3. ☎ **22-44-63-97.** Reservations required. Main courses 280–320Kr ($43.10–$49.30); fixed-price menu 410Kr ($63.15) for three courses, 660Kr ($101.65) for five courses (fish), 780Kr ($120.10) for seven courses. AE, DC, MC, V. Mon–Sat 6–10:30pm. Bus: 30, 31, 45, 72, or 73. FRENCH.

This contemporary, informal French restaurant in the west end is widely regarded as the premier dining choice in Oslo. In 1982 it introduced a light, modern cuisine, based on market-fresh ingredients. Fish and seafood are featured, but the menu changes daily, depending on the market and the whim of its owner and chef, Eyvind Hellstrøm. Fish dishes include the catch of the day, as well as other selections such as smoked and steamed halibut with a caviar-cream sauce and sole steamed in seaweed. Other main dishes are roast rabbit flavored with basil (served for two people) and loin of veal with sage. Another dish for two is rack of lamb with ratatouille.

✪ **D'Artagnan.** Øvre Slottsgate 16. ☎ **22-41-50-62.** Reservations required. Main courses 245–285Kr ($37.75–$43.90); five-course fixed-price menu 595Kr ($91.65). AE, DC, MC, V. Mon–Fri (also Sat Oct–Christmas) 6–11pm. Closed July–Aug 5 and Dec 22–Jan 3. Bus: 27, 29, 30, 41, or 61. FRENCH.

Named after one of the three musketeers, a childhood hero of the restaurant's owner, Freddie Nielson, D'Artagnan is one of Oslo's most elegant and upscale restaurants. Amid flickering candles and bouquets of flowers, you'll enjoy menu items that change with the seasons. Dishes might include a salad of king crab from Finnmark with avocados and grapefruit segments, foie gras of duck with a caramelized port-wine sauce, grilled breast of honey-glazed duck with raspberry vinaigrette, and one of the most unusual dishes of all—pieces of wild lamb shot in the mountains of central Norway, served with a herb-flavored mustard sauce.

Expensive

Blom. Karl Johans Gate 41B. ☎ **22-42-73-00.** Reservations required. Main courses 182–230Kr ($28.05–$35.40); fixed-price menu 200Kr ($30.80) at lunch, 385Kr ($59.30) at dinner. AE, DC, MC, V. Mon–Fri 11am–2:30pm and 5pm–midnight, Sat 3pm–midnight. T-banen: Stortinget. NORWEGIAN/INTERNATIONAL.

A cultural and architectural landmark, Charles Chaplin, Henrik Ibsen, and Edvard Munch dined here. (They are commemorated by heraldic plaques depicting important symbols of their careers.) The food is tasty and well prepared. At dinner, dishes might include marinated filet of reindeer with a morel-cream sauce, lamb cutlet with lamb médaillons in a Dijon mustard and rosemary sauce, and a host of fresh fish dishes. The wine list is one of the most complete in Oslo.

D. S. Louise. Stranden 3 (in Aker Brygge). ☎ **22-83-00-60.** Reservations recommended. Main courses 163–235Kr ($25.10–$36.20); three-course fixed-price menu 284–326Kr ($43.75–$50.20). AE, DC, MC, V. Mon–Sat 11:30am–11pm, Sun 11:30am–10pm. Bus: 27. NORWEGIAN.

This is judged the best restaurant in the harborfront shopping-and-dining complex, Aker Brygge. On the street level, it takes its name from a 19th-century Norwegian steamboat. The chef prepares such tasty specialties as braised hare with brussels sprouts and stewed mushrooms and cranberries, and a "cold symphony" of shrimp, salmon, hare, roast beef, potato salad, and cheese. It's a meal unto itself. A house specialty is the Brygge Tallerken—fried horsemeat with stewed mushrooms.

Moderate

✪ **Grand Café.** In the Grand Hotel, Karl Johans Gate 31. ☎ **22-42-93-90.** Reservations recommended. Main courses 172–266Kr ($26.50–$40.95). AE, DC, MC, V. Mon–Sat 11am–midnight, Sun noon–midnight. T-banen: Stortinget. NORWEGIAN.

This is the grand old cafe of Oslo, steeped in legend and tradition. Ibsen, who used to patronize the Grand Café, enjoying whale steaks, is depicted, along with Edvard Munch and many others, in a large mural. You can order anything from a napoleon with coffee to a full meal. Dishes include fried stingray, standard veal and beef dishes, reindeer steaks, and elk stew.

3 Brødre. Øvre Slottsgate 14. ☎ **22-42-39-00.** Main courses 170–194Kr ($26.20–$29.90). AE, DC, MC, V. Kaelleren, Mon–Sat 5–11pm. (Street-level bar, Mon–Sat 8:30am–11pm; piano bar, Mon–Sat 8:30pm–4am.) Bus: 27, 29, or 30. NORWEGIAN.

"Three Brothers" is named after the glove manufacturers who once occupied the building. The street level is devoted to a bustling bar. The Kaelleren, downstairs, serves soup as an appetizer, followed by cheese and meat fondues. Or you might begin with Norwegian salmon tartare or snails, and follow with an almond-and-garlic gratinée. For a main course, try the fried catfish with prawns, mussels, red peppers, and capers, or beefsteak with béarnaise sauce. The upstairs has been turned into a piano bar.

Inexpensive

⑤ Engebret Café. Bankplassen 1. ☎ **22-33-66-94.** Reservations recommended. Main courses 164–222Kr ($25.25–$34.20); smørbrød 40–65Kr ($6.15–$10). AE, DC, MC, V. Mon–Sat 11am–midnight. Bus: 27, 29, or 30. NORWEGIAN.

An enduring Oslovian favorite since 1857, this restaurant is housed in two joined landmark buildings directly north of Akershus Castle. It has an old-fashioned atmosphere and good food. From 2:30 to 6pm, a *dagens menu* (daily menu) is good value. You get one course, perhaps Norwegian shark in a butter sauce, plus coffee. During lunch, a tempting selection of open-face sandwiches (smørbrød) is available. The menu grows more elaborate in the evening when you might begin with a terrine of game with blackberry/port-wine sauce or Engebret's fish soup. You can then order such dishes as red wild boar with whortleberry sauce, salmon Christiana, or Engebret's big fishpot.

⑤ Gamla Rådhus (Old Town Hall). Nedre Slottsgate 1. ☎ **22-42-01-07.** Reservations recommended. Main courses 118–220Kr ($18.15–$33.90); open-face sandwiches at lunch 45–65Kr ($6.95–$10). AE, DC, MC, V. Mon–Fri 11am–11pm, Sat 5–11pm. (Kroen Bar, Mon–Sat 3pm–midnight.) Bus: 27, 29, 30, 41, or 61. NORWEGIAN.

The oldest restaurant in Oslo, the Gamla Rådhus is located in what in 1641 was Oslo's Town Hall. At noon you can sit in the spacious dining room and choose from an array of open-face sandwiches. A la carte dinner selections can be made from a varied menu including fresh fish, game, and Norwegian specialties.

OSLO AFTER DARK

To find out what's happening when you're visiting, pick up *What's On in Oslo,* which details concerts and theaters and other useful information.

Theater, ballet, and opera tickets are sold at various box offices and also at **Billettsentralen,** Karl Johans Gate 35 (☎ **81-03-31-33;** from outside Norway, call 75-12-41-20 for ticket information). Tickets to most sports and cultural events can now be purchased via computer linkup to any post office in the city, so when you buy a stamp you can also buy a voucher for a ticket to the ballet, theater, or hockey game.

The Performing Arts

Two blocks from the National Theater, the **Oslo Konserthus,** Munkedamsveien 14 (☎ **22-83-32-00**), is the home of the widely acclaimed Oslo Philharmonic. Performances are given autumn to spring, on Thursday and Friday.

The 1931 building, originally a movie theater, at Storgaten 23, was adapted for better acoustics and dedicated in 1959 to the **Den Norske Opera (Norwegian National Opera)** (☎ **22-42-94-75**). It's also the leading venue for ballet.

Summer Cultural Entertainment

Det Norske Folkloreshowet (Norwegian Folklore Show) performs from July to early September at the Oslo Konserthus, Munkedamsveien 15 (☎ **22-83-32-00;** or 22-83-45-10 for reservations). The 1-hour performances are Monday and Thursday at 8:30pm.

The **Norwegian Folk Museum,** on Bygdøy, often presents folk-dance performances by its own ensemble on summer Sunday afternoons at the museum's open-air theater (see *What's On in Oslo* for details). Admission is free, as the performance is included in the museum's entrance price. Take the ferry from Pier 3 near the Rådhuset.

The Club & Music Scene

A labyrinth of hallways, dance areas, and bars, **Humla,** Universitetsgata 26 (☎ 22-42-44-20), is one of Oslo's busiest nightlife emporiums, with three restaurants, four bars, and endless visual distractions. **John's Bar,** thanks to its murals, pays tribute to a 19th-century folk legend about a Norwegian and two Swedes who set off together to see the world. The **Exit Disco,** which doesn't open its doors until midnight Fri–Sat, is four floors above the street; cover is 50Kr ($7.70). A beer in John's Bar will cost around 33Kr ($5.10); in the Exit Disco, 39Kr ($6). The Humla Restaurant is open Tues–Sat 8pm–3:30am; John's Bar, Wed–Mon 8pm–12:30am; the Exit Disco, Fri–Sat midnight–6am.

Smuget, Rosenkrantzgate 22 (☎ 22-42-52-62), is the most talked-about nightlife emporium in the city, with long lines forming for admission, especially on weekends. It's in a 19th-century building that originally functioned as the district's post office, in back of the Grand Hotel. On the premises are a restaurant offering Thai, Chinese, Norwegian, Italian, and American food; an active dance floor with music; and a stage where live bands (sometimes two a night on weekends) are imported from throughout Europe and the world. The complex is open Mon–Sat, with a cover of 20–70Kr ($3.10–$10.80). Food is served Mon–Sat 8pm–2:30am; live music is played 11:15pm–3am; and disco music is switched on at 10pm till very late. Half liters of beer cost 42Kr ($6.45); meals run 100–400Kr ($15.40–$61.60).

With a capacity of 1,200 patrons, the **Rockefeller Music Hall,** Torggata 16 (☎ 22-20-32-32), is one of the largest establishments of its kind in Oslo, calling itself both a concert hall and a club. It sits one floor above street level in a 1910 building, originally a public bath. Almost every night live concerts are presented, everything from reggae to rock to jazz. On nights when no concert is given, films are shown on a wide screen. Most of the crowd seems in the 18–37 age bracket. Cover runs 60–300Kr ($9.25–$46.20). It's usually open Sun–Thurs 8pm–2:30am and Fri–Sat 9pm–3:30am. Show time is about an hour after the doors open. A beer costs 32–45Kr ($4.95–$6.95); snacks, 25–70Kr ($3.85–$10.80).

DAY TRIPS FROM OSLO

The best 1-day excursion from Oslo includes visits to Frederikstad and Tønsberg, which gives you a chance to explore the scenic highlights of the Oslofjord. A trip to Fredrikstad, in Østfold on the east bank of the Oslofjord, can easily be combined in 1 day with a visit to the port of Tønsberg on the west bank, by crossing over on the ferry from Moss to Horten, then heading south.

To reach the first stop, Fredrikstad, take E6 south from Oslo toward Moss. Continue past Moss until you reach the juction of Route 110, which is signposted south of Fredrikstad.

FREDRIKSTAD   In recent years Fredrikstad, 60 miles south of Oslo, has become a major tourist center, thanks to its Old Town and 17th-century fortress. Across the river on the west is a modern industrial section, and although a bridge links the two sections, the best way to reach Old Town is by ferry, which costs 5Kr (75¢). The departure point is about 4 blocks from the Fredrikstad railroad station—simply follow the crowd out the main door of the station, make an obvious left turn, and continue down to the shore of the river. It's also possible to travel between the two areas by bus (no. 360 or 362), although most pedestrians opt for the ferry.

Fredrikstad was founded in 1567 as a market place at the mouth of the River Glomma. **Gamlebyen** (Old Town) became a fortress in 1663 and continued in that role until 1903, boasting some 200 guns in its heyday. It still serves as a military camp. The main guardroom and old convict prison are now at the **Fredrikstad Museum,** Gamleslaveri (☎ **69-32-09-01**), open May–Sept, Mon–Fri 11am–5pm and Sat–Sun noon–5pm. Admission is 30Kr ($4.60) for adults, 10Kr ($1.55) for children.

Outside the gates of Old Town is **Kongsten Fort,** on what was first called Gallows Hill, an execution site. When Fredrikstad Fortress was built, it was provisionally fortified in 1677, becoming known as Svenskeskremme (Swede Scarer). Today's Kongsten Fort was subsequently built there, with 20 cannons, underground chambers, passages, and countermines.

Since Fredrikstad's heyday as a trading port and merchant base, Old Town has attracted craftspeople and artisans, many of whom create their products in some of Old Town's historic houses and barns. Many of these glassblowers, ceramic artists, and silversmiths choose not to display or sell their products at their studios, preferring instead to leave the sales aspect to local shops. Although other outlets exist, one of the better emporiums of the town's artistic trove is **Plus,** Kirkegatan 28 (☎ **69-32-06-78**).

En Route to Tønsberg   You can drive back north from Fredrikstad to the town of Moss, where you can take a ferry to Horten. Once at Horten, signs will point the way south for the short drive to Tønsberg.

TØNSBERG   Bordering the western bank of the Oslofjord, Tønsberg, 64 miles south of Oslo, is Norway's oldest town. It's divided into a historic area, filled with old clapboard-sided houses, and the commercial center, where the marketplace is located.

Tønsberg was founded a year before King Harald Fairhair united parts of the country in 872, and this Viking town became a royal coronation site. Svend Foyn, who invented modern whaling and seal hunting, was born here.

Slottsfjellet, a huge hill fortress directly ahead of the train station, is touted as "the Acropolis of Norway." But it has only some meager ruins, and people mostly come here for the view from the lookout tower. Built in 1888, the **Slottsfjelltårnet** (☎ **33-31-18-72**) is open May 18–June 23, Mon–Fri 10am–3pm; June 24–Aug 18, daily 11am–6pm; Aug 19–Sept 15, Sat–Sun noon–5pm; and Sept 16–29, Sat–Sun noon–3pm. Admission is 10Kr ($1.55) for adults, 5Kr (75¢) for children.

Nordbyen is the old and scenic part of town, with well-preserved houses. **Haugar** cemetery, at Møllebakken, is right in the town center, with the Viking graves of King Harald's sons, Olav and Sigrød.

Sem Church, Hageveien 32 (☎ **33-38-03-29**), the oldest in Vestfold, was built of stone in the romanesque style around 1100. It's open Tues–Fri 9am–2pm; inquire at the vestry. Admission is free.

You should also see **Fjerdingen,** a street of charming restored houses near the mountain farmstead. Tønsberg was also a Hanseatic town during the Middle Ages, and some houses have been redone in typical Hanseatic style.

In the **Vestfold Folk Museum,** Frammannsveien 30 (☎ **33-31-29-19**), there are many Viking and whaling treasures. One of the chief sights is the skeleton of a blue whale, the largest animal the world has ever known (sometimes weighing 150 tons). There's also a real Viking ship displayed, the *Klastad* from Tjolling, built about A.D. 800. Admission is 20Kr ($3.10) for adults, 5Kr (75¢) for children. It's open mid-May to mid-Sept, Mon–Sat 10am–5pm and Sun and holidays noon–5pm; mid-Sept to mid-May, Mon–Fri 10am–2pm.

BERGEN

In western Norway the landscape takes on an awesome beauty, with iridescent glaciers, deep fjords that slash into rugged, snowcapped mountains, roaring waterfalls, and secluded valleys that lie at the end of corkscrew-twisting roads. From Bergen the most beautiful fjords to visit are the **Hardanger** (best at blossom time, May and early June), to the south; the **Sogne,** Norway's longest fjord, immediately to the north; and the **Nordfjord,** north of that. A popular excursion on the Nordfjord takes visitors from Loen to Olden along rivers and lakes to the Brixdal Glacier.

If you have time, on the Hardangerfjord you can stop over at one of the fjord resorts, such as Ulvik or Lofthus. From many vantage points it's possible to see the Folgefonn Glacier, Norway's second-largest ice field, which spans more than 100 square miles.

Bergen, with its many sightseeing attractions, good hotels, boardinghouses, and restaurants, and its excellent boat, rail, and coach connections, makes it the best center in the fjord district. This ancient city looms large in Viking sagas. Until the 14th century it was the seat of the medieval kingdom of Norway. The Hanseatic merchants established a major trading post here, holding sway until the 18th century.

ESSENTIALS

ARRIVING   By Plane   The **Bergen Airport** at Flesland, 12 miles south of the city, offers frequent flights to such larger cities as Copenhagen and London, through which most international flights are routed. In addition, dozens of direct flights leave here for nearly every medium-sized city in Norway through such airlines as **SAS** (☎ 55-99-75-90) and **Braathens S.A.F.E.** (☎ 55-99-82-50).

Frequent airport bus service makes a circuit from the airport to the SAS Royal Hotel, Braathens SAFE's office at the Hotel Norge, and the city bus station. Buses depart every 20 minutes Mon–Fri and every 30 minutes Sat–Sun. The one-way fare is 40Kr ($6.15).

By Train   Day and night trains arrive from Oslo and stations en route. For information, call **55-96-60-00.** The trip from Oslo can take 6–8¹/₂ hours.

By Bus   Express buses travel to Bergen from Oslo in 11 hours.

VISITOR INFORMATION   For information, maps, and brochures about Bergen and its environs, **Tourist Information,** Bryggen 7 (☎ 55-32-14-80), is open May–Sept, Mon–Sat 8:30am–9pm and Sun 10am–7pm; and Oct–Apr, Mon–Sat 9am–4pm. Tourist Information will also help you find accommodations, exchange foreign currency, and cash traveler's checks when banks are closed. In addition, you can purchase tickets for city sightseeing or for tours of the fjords.

GETTING AROUND   To cut costs, purchase the **Bergen Card,** giving you free bus transport and usually free museum entrance throughout Bergen, plus discounts on car rentals, parking, and some cultural and leisure activities. Ask at Tourist Information. A 24-hour card costs 120Kr ($18.50) for adults, 55Kr ($8.45) for children 3–15. A 48-hour card costs 190Kr ($29.25) for adults, 80Kr ($12.30) for children 3–15. Children 2 and under generally travel or enter free.

By Bus   The **Central Bus Station** (Bystasjonen), Strømgaten 8 (☎ 55-32-67-80), is the terminal for all buses serving the Bergen and the Hardanger area, as well as the airport bus. The station has luggage storage, shops, and a restaurant. A network of yellow-sided **city buses** (☎ 55-28-13-30 for information) also serves the city center.

By Taxi   Taxis are readily available at the airport, or call **55-99-70-00.** A ride to the center costs 235Kr ($36.20). Sightseeing by taxi costs about 275Kr ($42.35) per hour.

WHAT TO SEE & DO

In addition to the sights below, take a stroll around **Bryggen.** This row of Hanseatic timbered houses, rebuilt along the waterfront after the disastrous fire of 1702, is what remains of medieval Bergen. The northern half burned to the ground as late as 1955. Bryggen has been incorporated into UNESCO's World Heritage List as one of the world's most significant cultural and historical re-creations of a medieval settlement, skillfully blending with the surroundings of modern Bergen. It's a center for arts and crafts, where painters, weavers, and craftspeople have their workshops. As you stroll along, you'll see that some workshops are open to the public.

✪ **Det Hanseatiske Museum.** Finnegårdsgaten 1A, Bryggen. ☎ **55-31-41-89.** Admission May–Sept, 35Kr ($5.40) adults, free for children; Oct–Apr, 20Kr ($3.10) adults, free for children. June–Aug, daily 9am–5pm; Sept–May, daily 11am–2pm. Bus: 1, 5, or 9.

In one of the best-preserved wooden buildings at Bryggen, this museum illustrates Bergen's commercial life on the wharf centuries ago. German merchants, representatives of the Hanseatic League centered in Lübeck, lived in these medieval houses built in long rows up from the harbor. With dried cod, grain, and salt as articles of exchange, fishers from northern Norway met German merchants during the busy summer season. The museum is furnished with authentic articles dating from 1704.

Mariakirke (St. Mary's Church). Dreggen. ☎ **55-31-59-60.** Admission May 18–Sept 9, 10Kr ($1.55) adults, free for children; Sept 10–May 17, free for everyone. May 18–Sept 9, Mon–Fri 11am–4pm; Sept 10–May 17, Tues–Fri noon–1:30pm. Bus: 1, 5, or 9.

The oldest building in Bergen (its exact date is unknown, but perhaps from the mid–12th century) is this romanesque church, one of the most beautiful in Norway. Its altar is the oldest ornament in the church, and there's a baroque pulpit, donated by Hanseatic merchants, with carved figures depicting everything from Chastity to Naked Truth. Church-music concerts are given May to August several nights a week.

Fløibanen. Vetrlidsalm 23A. ☎ **55-31-48-00.** Round-trip ticket 30Kr ($4.60) adults, 14Kr ($2.15) children. May 25–Aug, Mon–Fri 7:30am–midnight, Sat 8am–midnight, Sun 9am–midnight; Sept–May 24, Mon–Thurs 7:30am–11pm, Fri 7:30am–11:30pm, Sat 8am–11:30pm, Sun 9am–11pm. Bus: 6.

A short walk from the fish market is the station where the funicular heads up to Fløien, the most famous of Bergen's seven hills. At 1,050 feet, the view of the city, the neighboring hills, and the harbor is worth every øre.

Gamle Bergen. Elsesro, Sandviken. ☎ **55-25-78-50.** Admission 40Kr ($6.15) adults, 20Kr ($3.10) children and students. Houses, mid-May to Aug, guided tours daily every hour 11am–5pm. Park and restaurant, daily noon–10pm. Bus: 1 or 9 from the city center, leaving every 10 minutes.

At Elsesro and Sandviken is a collection of houses from the 18th and 19th centuries set in a park. Old Town is complete with streets, an open square, and narrow alleyways. Some of the interiors are exceptional, including a merchant's living room in the typical style of the 1870s—with padded sofas, heavy curtains, potted plants—a perfect setting for Ibsen's *A Doll's House.*

✪ **Troldhaugen (Troll's Hill).** Troldhaugveien 65, Hop. ☎ **55-91-17-91.** Admission 40Kr ($6.15) adults, 15Kr ($2.30) children. Apr 21–Sept, daily 9am–5:30pm; Oct–Nov, Mon–Fri 10am–2pm, Sat–Sun 10am–4pm; Jan–Apr 20, Mon–Fri 10am–2pm. Closed Dec. Bus: Hop-bound buses leave from the bus station at Bergen (Platforms 18–20); once the bus lets you off, turn right, walk about 200 yards, turn left at Hopsvegen, and from there just follow the signs to Troldhaugen, a 20- to 30-minute walk.

This Victorian house, in beautiful rural surroundings at Hop, near Bergen, was the summer villa of composer Edvard Grieg. The house still contains Grieg's own furniture, paintings, and other mementos. His Steinway grand piano is frequently used at concerts given in the house during the annual Bergen festival, as well as at Troldhaugen's own summer concerts. Grieg and his wife, Nina, are buried in a cliff grotto on the estate. At his cottage by the sea, he composed many of his famous works.

Organized Tours

A 1-hour **tram tour** uses the city tram lines and specially designed red-sided tramcars equipped with multilingual headsets. The tour departs every hour on the hour from Bryggen and costs 60Kr ($9.25) for adults, 30Kr ($4.60) for children. It operates May–Sept, daily 10am–7pm.

The most popular and most highly recommended **bus tour** of Bergen is still the 3-hour city tour, which departs daily at 10am and covers all major sightseeing attractions. These include Troldhaugen and Old Bergen. It also runs May–Sept and costs 180Kr ($27.70) for adults, 90Kr ($13.85) for children. For information and tickets for either tour, contact the tourist office at Bryggen 7 (☎ **55-32-14-80**).

Shopping

Despite its role as Bergen's leading department store, **Sundt & Co.,** Torgalmenningen (☎ **55-38-80-20**), faces stiff competition from such newer emporiums as **Galleriet,** Torgalmenningen 8 (☎ **55-32-45-50**), the most important shopping complex in the Bergen area, with 70 different stores offering tax-free shopping.

You'll find the widest selection of national handcrafts at **Husfliden I Bergen,** Vågsalmenningen 3 (☎ **55-31-78-70**)—the finest handmade knitwear from the western district, along with woodwork, brass, pewterware, and national costumes.

The leading outlet for glassware and ceramics, **Prydkunst-Hjertholm,** Olav Kyrres Gate 7 (☎ **55-31-70-27**), purchases much of its merchandise directly from the studios of artisans who turn out quality goods not only in glass and ceramics, but also in pewter, wood, and textiles. Gift articles and souvenirs are also sold.

ACCOMMODATIONS

Expensive

✪ **Hotel Norge.** Ole Bulls Plass 2–4, N-5001 Bergen. ☎ **800/223-5652** in the U.S. and Canada, or 55-21-01-00. Fax 55-21-02-99. 347 rms, 12 suites. A/C MINIBAR TV TEL. June 25–Aug 18, 900Kr ($138.60) double; 1,600–2,500Kr ($246.40–$385) suite. Aug 19–June 24, 1,325Kr ($204.05) double; 2,500Kr ($385) suite. Rates include breakfast. Children 11 and under stay free in parents' room. DC, MC, V. Parking 100Kr ($15.40). Bus: 2, 3, or 4.

In the city center, near Torgalmenningen, the Norge has been a Bergen tradition since 1885. Some rooms have oversize bathtubs big enough for two, while other units open onto private balconies overlooking the flower-ringed borders of a nearby park. The hotel offers the widest array of drinking and dining establishments in Bergen, including its gourmet restaurant, Grillen, and Ole Bull, an informal place for lunch and light meals. Facilities include a swimming pool, solarium, sauna, Jacuzzi, gym, and garage.

✪ **Radisson SAS Royal Hotel.** Bryggen, N-5000 Bergen. ☎ **800/221-2350** in the U.S., or 55-31-80-00. Fax 55-32-48-08. 273 rms, 5 suites. A/C MINIBAR TV TEL. May–Sept and Fri–Sun year-round, 995Kr ($153.25) double. Oct–Apr, Mon–Thurs, 1,575Kr ($242.55) double.

Year-round, 2,200–2,600Kr ($338.80–$400.40) suite. Rates include breakfast. AE, DC, MC, V. Parking 85Kr ($13.10). Bus: 1, 5, or 9.

Opened in 1982, this hotel stands on ancient ground, having been built on the fire-ravaged site of old warehouses that stood here since 1170. Houses along Bryggen (The Quay) were reconstructed in the old style and Radisson maintains the architectural spirit in preserving this excellent hotel. The hotel is completely modernized with what are the finest services and amenities in Bergen. The bedrooms are beautifully maintained, each with lithographs and comfortably upholstered furniture. Sixty rooms are reserved for nonsmokers. The hotel attracts mainly commercial clients in winter. Guests can dine in the hotel's gourmet restaurant, Statsraaden. Facilities include an indoor swimming pool, sauna, health club, and garage.

Moderate

Ⓢ **Hotell Hordaheimen.** C. Sundtsgate 18, N-5004 Bergen. ☎ **55-23-23-20.** Fax 55-23-49-50. 64 rms, 5 junior suites. TV TEL. May 15–Sept 15, 790Kr ($121.65) double. Sept 16–May 14, 995Kr ($153.25) double Mon–Thurs, 650Kr ($100.10) double Fri–Sun. Year-round, 870Kr ($134) junior suite. Rates include breakfast. AE, DC, MC, V. Bus: 1, 5, or 9.

Operated by the Bondeungdomslaget i Bergen, an association that sponsors cultural and folklore programs, the hotel has long been a Bergen base for many young people from nearby districts. School and civic groups traveling together sometimes fill up nearly all the rooms. The hotel was built at the turn of the century, but renovated in stages between 1989 and 1995. The lounge and dining rooms have been tastefully designed and coordinated, and the bedrooms—simple and utilitarian—are immaculate. Accommodations contain minibars, but no alcohol is stocked.

Rosenkrantz. Rosenkrantzgate 7, N-5003 Bergen. ☎ **55-31-50-00.** Fax 55-31-14-76. 129 rms. MINIBAR TV TEL. May 15–Sept 15, 710Kr ($109.35) double. Sept 16–May 14, 990Kr ($152.45) double Sun–Thurs, 680Kr ($104.70) double Fri–Sat. Rates include breakfast. AE, DC, MC, V. Parking 60Kr ($9.25). Bus: 1, 5, or 9.

This 1921 hotel stands near Bryggen in the city center, a simple, unpretentious choice. The lobby, floored in white marble, leads to a comfortable dining room and bar. The rooms are pleasantly furnished and equipped with modern amenities, including hair dryers. Sixty-four rooms are reserved for nonsmokers. Facilities include a TV lounge, a piano bar, a restaurant (Harmoni), and a nightclub (Rubinen) with live music. Next door to the hotel is a covered parking garage.

Inexpensive

Ⓢ **Fagerheim Pensjonat.** Kalvedalsveien 49A, N-5018 Bergen. ☎ **55-31-01-72.** 20 rms, none with bath. 360Kr ($55.45) double. Additional bed 100Kr ($15.40) extra. MC, V. Free parking. Bus: 2, 4, 7, or 11 from the post office.

This attractively old-fashioned 1900 hillside house lies about a 15-minute walk from the town center. A few of the homelike bedrooms have small kitchens. Most accommodations have a view of the water and city. A garden surrounds the house.

Ⓢ **Romantik Hotel Park.** Harald Hårfagresgaten 35 and Parkveien 22, N-5000 Bergen. ☎ **55-32-09-60.** Fax 55-31-03-34. 40 rms. TV TEL. 750Kr ($115.50) double. Rates include breakfast. AE, V. Free parking. Bus: 11.

Located in an attractive university area near Grieghall and Nygård Park, this converted 1890 town house has traditionally furnished rooms. Because of the popularity of this place, in summer the hotel uses a neighboring building (furnished in the same style as the hotel) to handle overflow guests. In summer, reserve well in advance. The Park is a 10-minute walk from the train and bus stations.

DINING

Banco Rotto. Vågsalmenningen 14–22. ☎ **55-32-75-20.** Reservations required. Main courses 129–229Kr ($19.85–$35.25); lunch platters 60–110Kr ($9.25–$16.95). AE, DC, MC, V. Restaurant, Fri–Sat 8pm–2am; pub, Mon–Sat 6pm–1am. Bus: 1, 5, or 9. NORWEGIAN.

One of the town's most unusual restaurants is in the fortresslike premises of what was originally built in 1875 as a bank. High-ceilinged, and decorated with hints of the rococo splendor of the gilded age, it contains two pubs (accessible through separate entrances), a bar, a restaurant, and a dance floor where live bands perform Fri–Sat beginning at 10pm. Dinners are elaborate, with dishes like grilled filets of beef with pepper sauce. A luxurious bar adjoins the restaurant.

✪ Fiskekroen. Zacchariasbrygge 50. ☎ **55-55-96-60.** Reservations required. Main courses 185–226Kr ($28.50–$34.80). AE, DC, MC, V. May–Aug, Mon–Sat noon–11pm, Sun 1–10pm; Sept–Apr, Mon–Sat 4–11pm. Bus: 1, 5, or 9. FISH/GAME.

One of the smallest (36 seats) and most exclusive restaurants in Bergen, this fish-and-game dining room occupies rustically elegant premises in the historic (and rebuilt) Zacchariasbrygge harborfront complex. You can watch the goings-on in a bubbling aquarium or enjoy the panoramic view of the harbor. Menu specialties change with the seasons and might include a delectable symphony of fish (salmon, wolffish, and anglerfish in a lobster sauce), fried filet of reindeer with green-pepper gravy, and several different preparations of venison.

Holberg-Stuen. Torgalmenningen 6. ☎ **55-31-80-15.** Main courses 148–179Kr ($22.80–$27.55). AE, DC, MC, V. Tues–Sat 11am–11:30pm, Sun–Mon 1–10:30pm. Bus: 1, 5, or 9. NORWEGIAN.

One floor above street level, this restaurant was established in 1927 midway between the harborfront and Ole Bulls Plass. It was named in honor of 18th-century writer Ludvig Holberg. The setting is much like a tavern, with beamed ceilings, an open log fire, leaded-glass casement windows, and lots of exposed wood. Well-prepared menu items include filets of fish in white-wine sauce with prawns, mushrooms, and asparagus; and many different versions of meat, some of them grilled.

BERGEN AFTER DARK

Opened in mid-1978, the modern **Grieg Hall (Grieghallen),** Lars Hillesgate 3A (☎ 55-21-61-50), is Bergen's monumental showcase for music, drama, and a host of other cultural events. The stage can accommodate an entire grand opera production, and the main foyer will comfortably seat 1,500 guests for lunch or dinner. The Bergen Symphony Orchestra, founded in 1765, performs here Aug–May on Thurs at 7:30pm and often on Sat at 12:30pm.

Norway's oldest theater performs Sept–June at the **Den National Scene,** Engen 1 (☎ 55-90-17-88). Its repertoire consists of classical Norwegian and international drama and contemporary plays, as well as visiting productions of opera and ballet.

In summer, the **Bergen Folklore dancing troupe** (☎ 55-31-67-10), arranges a folklore program at the Bryggens Museum June–Aug on Tues and Thurs at 9pm. The 1-hour program consists of traditional folk dances and music from rural Norway. Tickets are on sale at the tourist information center or at the door.

The Club & Music Scene

Rubinen, Rosenkrantzgate 7 (☎ 51-31-74-70), is one of Bergen's most popular nightclubs, attracting an over-35 crowd of mostly married couples. It plays all kinds of danceable and drinkable music, including country western and rock 'n' roll. Drinks cost about 45Kr ($6.95); cover is 50Kr ($7.70). It's open Tues–Sun 8pm–3am.

The Night Spot, in the Hotel Norge, Ole Bulls Plass 2–4 (☎ 55-21-01-00), offers a well-engineered sound system, a plush interior, and a 30-something crowd. Drinks start at 60Kr ($9.25); cover is 50Kr ($7.70). It's open Fri–Sat 9pm–3am.

EXPLORING THE FJORDS

From both Oslo and Bergen, the fjords of Norway can be explored by ship and car or by a scenic train ride. Here are the details.

BY CAR FROM OSLO

The mountain drive from Oslo to Bergen is filled with dramatic scenery. However, since the country is split by mountains, there's no direct road. You have your choice of the southern or northern route. The **southern route,** E76, goes through mountain passes until the junction with Route 47; then head north to the ferry crossing at Kinsarvik that goes across the fjords to E16 leading west to Bergen. The **northern route** is via Highway 7, going through the resort of Geilo, to the junction with Route 47; then heads south to Kinsarvik. After crossing on the ferry, you arrive at E16. Head west to reach Bergen.

BY CAR FROM BERGEN

Bergen is the best departure point for trips to the fjords: To the south lies the famous Hardangerfjord and to the north the Sognefjord, cutting 111 miles inland. We've outlined a driving tour of the fjords, starting in Bergen and heading east on Route 7 to Ulvik, a distance of 93 miles.

Ulvik

Ulvik is that rarity—an unspoiled resort—lying like a fist at the end of an arm of the Hardangerfjord that's surrounded in summer by misty peaks and fruit farms. The village's 1858 church is attractively decorated in the style of the region. It's open June–Aug, daily 9am–5pm, with concerts presented.

From Ulvik, you can explore the Eidfjord district, which is the northern tip of the Hardangerfjord, home to some 1,000 people and a paradise for hikers. Anglers are attracted to the area because of its mountain trout.

The district contains nearly one-quarter of ✪ **Hardangervidda National Park,** which is on Europe's largest high-mountain plateau. It's home to 20,000 wild reindeer. Well-marked hiking trails connect a series of 15 tourist huts.

Several canyons, including the renowned **Måbø Valley,** lead down from the plateau to the fjords. Here you'll see the famous 550-foot Voringfoss waterfall; the Valurefoss in Hjømo Valley has a free fall of almost 800 feet.

Part of the 1,000-year-old road across Norway, traversing the Måbø Valley, has been restored for hardy hikers.

EN ROUTE TO VOSS   From Ulvik, take Highway 20 to Route 13. Follow Route 13 to Voss, 25 miles west of Ulvik and 63 miles east of Bergen.

Voss

Between the Sogne and Hardanger fjords, Voss is a famous year-round resort, also known for its folklore. It was the birthplace of football hero Knute Rockne. Maybe the trolls don't strike fear into the hearts of farm children anymore, but they're still called out of hiding to give visitors a little fun.

Voss is a natural base for exploring the two largest fjords in Norway, the Sognefjord to the north and the Hardangerfjord to the south. In and around Voss are glaciers, mountains, fjords, waterfalls, orchards, rivers, and lakes.

Oslo to Bergen & Along the Fjords

A ride on the **Hangursbanen cable car** (☎ 56-51-12-12) offers panoramic views of Voss and the environs. The hardy take the cable car up, then spend the rest of the afternoon strolling down the mountain. A round-trip ride costs 50Kr ($7.70) for adults, 25Kr ($3.85) for children 8–16, free for children 7 and under. The cable-car entrance is on a hillside that's a 10-minute walk north of the center. It's open in summer and winter, but is closed during May and Sept–Nov.

Built in 1277, the **Vangskyrkje,** Vangsgata 3 (☎ 56-51-22-78), with a timbered tower, contains a striking Renaissance pulpit, a stone altar and triptych, fine wood carvings, and a painted ceiling. It's a 5-minute walk east of the railroad station. We recommend that you call in advance to reserve an English-speaking guide. Admission is 10Kr ($1.55) for adults, 5Kr (75¢) for children, free for children 6 and under. The church is open June–Aug, daily 9am–5pm.

The **Voss Folkemuseum,** Mølster (☎ 56-51-15-11), is a collection of authentically furnished houses that shows what early farm life was like. Lying half a mile north of Voss on a hillside overlooking the town, the museum consists of more than a dozen farmhouses and other buildings, ranging in age from the 1500s to around 1870. Admission is 25Kr ($3.85) for adults, free for children. It's open May and Sept, daily 10am–5pm; June–Aug, daily 10am–7pm; and Oct–Apr, Mon–Fri 10am–3pm and Sun noon–3pm.

About a mile west of Voss in Finne, **Finnesloftet** (☎ 56-51-11-00) is one of Norway's oldest timbered houses, dating from the mid-13th century. It's a 15-minute walk west of the railway station. Admission is 25Kr ($3.85) for adults, 10Kr ($1.55) for children. It's open June 15–Aug 15, daily 10am–4pm.

AN EXCURSION TO THE SOGNEFJORD   If you have time, you may want to visit the Sognefjord district, the largest of all Norwegian fjords. From Voss the northern route leads to **Vik.** The scenery is beautiful and the road goes along for miles across a desolate tableland at 3,000 feet above sea level. The lakes on a summer day appear green, and on the distant slopes is snow.

In Vik, see the stave church, one of the most attractive in Norway; then take the road to **Vangsnes,** where you can make ferry connections across the Sognefjord to Balestrand or Dragsvik. Once across, take Route 5 north. The highway is steep, bringing you through rolling countryside with waterfalls until you reach **Viksdalen,** about 40 miles from Dragsvik.

EN ROUTE TO BALESTRAND   From Voss, continue north on Route 13 to Vangsnes and board a car-ferry for the short crossing northwest to Balestrand, 56 miles north of Voss and 130 miles northeast of Bergen.

Balestrand

Long known for its arts and crafts, Balestrand lies on the northern rim of the Sognefjord, at the junction of the Vetlefjord, the Esefjord, and the Fjaerlandsfjord.

Kaiser Wilhelm II, a frequent visitor to Balestrand, presented the district with two statues of old Norse heroes, King Bele and Fridtjof the Bold, standing in the center. Another sight in town is the English church of **St. Olav** in Balestrand, a tiny wooden building, dating from 1897.

You can explore by setting out in nearly any direction, on scenic country lanes with little traffic, or a wide choice of marked trails and upland farm tracks. A touring map may be purchased at the **tourist office** in the town center (☎ 57-69-12-55). There's good sea fishing, as well as lake and river trout fishing. Fishing tackle, rowboats, and bicycles can all be rented in the area.

EN ROUTE TO FLÅM   From Balestrand, follow Route 55 east along the Sognefjord, crossing the fjord via ferry at Dragsvik and by bridge at Sogndal. At

Sogndal, drive east to Kaupanger, where you'll cross the Ardalsfjord by ferry, south to Revsnes. In Revsnes, pick up Route 11 heading southeast. Drive east until you connect with a secondary road heading southwest through Kvigno and Aurland. When you arrive in Aurland, take Route 601 southwest to the town of Flåm, 60 miles southeast of Balestrand and 103 miles east of Bergen.

Flåm

Flåm (pronounced "Flawm") lies on the Aurlandsfjord, a tip of the more famous Sognefjord. In the village you can visit the old church dating from 1667, with painted walls done in typical Norwegian country style.

Flåm is an excellent starting point for excursions by car or boat to other well-known centers on the Sognefjord, Europe's longest and deepest fjord. Worth exploring are two of the wildest and most beautiful fingers of the Sognefjord: Næroyfjord and Aurlandfjord. Ask at the **tourist office,** near the rail station (☎ **57-63-21-06**), about a summer-only cruise from Flåm, where you can experience the dramatic scenery of both of these fjords. From Flåm by boat, you can disembark either in Gudvangen or Aurland and continue to tour by coach. Alternatively, you can return to Flåm by train.

There are also a number of easy walks in the Flåm district. The tourist office has a map detailing these walks.

BY SHIP/TOUR FROM OSLO

Departing from Pier 3 in front of the Oslo Rådhuset (City Hall), **Båtservice Sightseeing,** Rådhusbrygge 3, Rådhusplassen (☎ **22-20-07-15**), offers a 50-minute mini-cruise boat tour, with a view of the harbor and the city, including the ancient fortess of Akershus and the islands in the inner part of the Oslofjord. Cruises depart mid-May to late Aug, on the hour daily 11am–8pm (limited sailing at the season's beginning and end). Adults pay 70Kr ($10.80); children, 35Kr ($5.40).

If you have more time, take the 2-hour fjord cruise through the maze of islands and narrow sounds in the fjord. Departures are May–Sept, daily at 10:30am and 1, 3:30, and 5:45pm; the cost is 135Kr ($20.80) for adults, 67Kr ($10.30) for children.

An evening fjord cruise, including a maritime buffet, also at the Lanternen, leaves late June–Aug, daily at 3:30 and 5:45pm. The 3$^1/_2$-hour cruise costs 295Kr ($45.45) for adults, 120Kr ($18.50) for children.

BY SHIP/TOUR FROM BERGEN

Norway's longest fjord, the Sognefjord, can be crossed by express steamer to **Gudvangen.** From Gudvangen, passengers go to Voss (see above), and from Voss a train runs back to Bergen. That's but one of several alternatives for visiting this world-famous fjord. You can go by boat, bus, and then train for 495Kr ($76.25) round-trip. Details about the various possibilities are available from Tourist Information in Bergen.

If you have more than a day to see the fjords in the environs of Bergen, you can take the grandest fjord cruise in the world, a **coastal steamer** going all the way to the North Cape and beyond. The coastal steamers are elegantly appointed ships that travel along the western coast of Norway from Bergen to Kirkenes, carrying passengers and cargo to 34 ports along the Norwegian coast. Eleven ships in all make the journey year-round. The ships sail through Norway's more obscure fjords, providing panoramic scenery and numerous opportunities for adventure. Along the way, sightseeing excursions to the surrounding mountains and glaciers are offered, as well as sails on smaller vessels through some of the more obscure fjords.

The chief operator for these coastal cruises is the **Bergen Line,** 405 Park Ave., New York, NY 10022 (☎ **800/323-7436** or 212/319-1300). Tours may be booked heading north from Bergen, south from Kirkenes, or round-trip. The 7-day northbound journey costs $799–$1,858 per person, including meals and taxes. Visitors opting for the southbound trip from Kirkenes pay $660–$1,573. The round-trip voyage lasts 12 days and costs $1,195–$2,855 per person.

BY SCENIC TRAIN RIDE FROM OSLO

One of the great train rides of Europe is the **Bergensbanen** (☎ **55-96-60-60** for schedule information), with five daily departures from Oslo, plus an additional train on Sunday. The most popular routing is Oslo to Bergen, although you can also take the train from Bergen to Oslo, depending on where you land in Norway. There are those (and we are among them) who claim that this is the most scenic and beautiful train ride in the world. Departures are from Oslo S station, and the trip takes 7$^1/_2$–8$^1/_2$ hours. You cut across some of the most panoramic fjord and mountain scenery in Europe.

BY SCENIC TRAIN RIDE FROM BERGEN

If you land in Bergen instead of Oslo, consider a train ride to Oslo, the most scenic and panoramic rail journey in Europe (see above). If your time is more limited, you can take a brief train ride from Bergen that will cover the most breathtaking part of the journey.

The most exciting rail journey in Norway is a 12-hour tour from Bergen, encompassing two arms of the Sognefjord. The single aspect of this journey—and the reason most passengers take the ride—is the 12-mile route from Myrdal to Flåm (see above). An electric train "drops" 2,900 feet, past seemingly endless waterfalls.

In June, July, and Aug, the tour leaves from the Bergen railroad station daily at 7:33am and 8:50am, and Mon–Fri at 11:48am. Guests may have lunch at Flåm, then board a river steamer for Gudvangen, where they hop on a bus to Voss, then a train back to Bergen. The round-trip fare, excluding meals, is 450Kr ($69.30) for adults, 225Kr ($34.65) for children. Holders of Eurail or Scandinavian Rail Passes get a reduction. For more information, contact the Bergen tourist office (☎ 55-32-14-80).

Portugal 14

by Darwin Porter & Danforth Prince

Lisbon presides over a country that has the fastest-growing economy in Europe, much of it fueled by investments that have poured in since Portugal joined the EU.

1 Lisbon & Environs

The Lisbon of today has blossomed into a cosmopolitan city. Sophistication is in the air, and Europe's smallest capital is no longer a backwater at the far corner of Iberia.

Sections along the Avenida da Liberdade, the main street of Lisbon, at times evoke Paris in miniature. Just as in Paris, sidewalk portrait painters will sketch your likeness, artisans will offer you jewelry claiming it's gold (when you both know it isn't), and vendors peddle handcrafts—from embroidery to leatherwork—right on the streets. The formerly clogged streets of the Baixa have in some cases been closed to traffic, and cobblestone pedestrian malls have been created.

Some 1.6 million people now call Lisbon home, and many Lisboetas (Lisbonites), having drifted in from the far corners of the world, don't even speak Portuguese. It's beset with construction pains—many of its old structures are simply falling apart and either must be restored or replaced.

Consider an off-season visit, especially in the spring or fall, when the city is at its most glorious weatherwise, before the hot and humid days of July and August descend. The city isn't infested with visitors then, and you can wander about and take in its attractions without fear of being trampled underfoot.

ONLY IN LISBON

Getting Lost in the Alfama Maze The houses are so close together in the Alfama that in many places it's impossible to stretch your arms to their full length. From the smallest houses, streamers of laundry protrude. The fishwives make early-morning appearances on their iron balconies to water their pots of geraniums. In the street markets, you can wander in a maze of stacks of brightly colored vegetables from the country, bananas from Madeira, pineapples from the Azores, and fish from the sea. Armies of cats protect the street from rats. Occasionally, a black-shawled old woman, stooping over a brazier grilling sardines in front of her house, will toss one of these felines a fish head.

Going on the Trail of Fado in the Bairro Alto   Fado, an authentic Portuguese musical genre, means "fate" or "destiny." Its sad lament to lost love and glory is heard nightly in the little houses of the Bairro Alto. Women swathed in black (called *fadistas,* as are male fado singers) are accompanied by 12-stringed guitars. Listening to these melancholy songs is the quintessential Lisbon experience.

Shopping for Handcrafts   The shopping in Lisbon is irresistible. Artisans from all over the country display their finest wares in its capital: ceramics, embroidery (from both the Azores and Madeira), silver, elegant porcelain, gleaming crystal, *azulejos* (tiles), hand-woven rugs, and hand-knit sweaters.

Spending an Afternoon in Sintra   Some savvy travelers claim that after visiting Sintra, the rest of Europe seems like a footnote. Follow in the footsteps of Portuguese kings and queens of yesteryear and head for Byron's "glorious Eden." Byron was not alone in proclaiming the village of Sintra as "perhaps the most delightful in Europe." Even the sometimes skeptical Spanish proclaim: "To see the world and yet leave Sintra out / Is, verily, to go blindfold about."

Witnessing Relics of a Vanished Empire at Belém   At Belém, where the River Tagus (Tejo in Portuguese) meets the sea, the Portuguese caravels that charted the areas unknown to the Western world were launched on their missions: Vasco da Gama to India, Ferdinand Magellan to circumnavigate the globe, and Bartolomeu Dias to round the Cape of Good Hope. Belém flourished as riches poured back into Portugal. Great monuments, including the Belém Tower and Jerónimos Monastery, were built and embellished in the Manueline style. Much of the district's character still remains, including those monuments to former glory.

Shopping on Market Day   The big market of Ribeira Nova is as close as you can get to the heart of Lisbon. Near the Cais do Sodré, where trains are boarded for the Costa do Sol, an enormous roof shelters a collection of stalls offering the produce used in Lisbon's fine restaurants. Foodstuffs are brought in each morning in wicker baskets bulging with oversize carrots, cabbages big enough for shrubbery, and stalks of bananas. Some of the freshly plucked produce arrives by donkey, some by truck, some balanced on the heads of Lisboan women in Mediterranean fashion. "Seeing-eye" fishing boats (believed to have been based on Phoenician designs), dock at dawn with their catch. Soon the *varinas,* balancing wicker baskets of the fresh catch on their heads, climb the cobbled streets of the Alfama or the Bairro Alto to sell fish from door to door.

ORIENTATION

ARRIVING   By Plane   Both foreign and domestic flights land at Lisbon's **Portela Airport** (☎ 01/841-37-00), located about 4 miles north of the city. From the airport, a small yellow-sided Airbus—identified locally as bus route no. 91—carries passengers at 20-minute intervals from the airport into the center of town. Charging 430$ ($2.85) per person each way, the bus stops at several key places, including points along the key hotel thoroughfare Avenida da Liberdade, before stopping at Cais do Sodre. Buses operate daily 7am–9pm. A less expensive, but less efficient, option involves catching municipal bus no. 44 or 45, which navigates at half-hour intervals between the airport and central Lisbon. This bus follows a route similar to that of the Airbus for a one-way fare of 150$ ($1), but it makes an interminable number of local stops. You can also take a taxi; the average fare into central Lisbon is 2,000$ ($13.20), plus a surcharge of 300$ ($2) per piece of luggage.

Lisbon Attractions & Accommodations

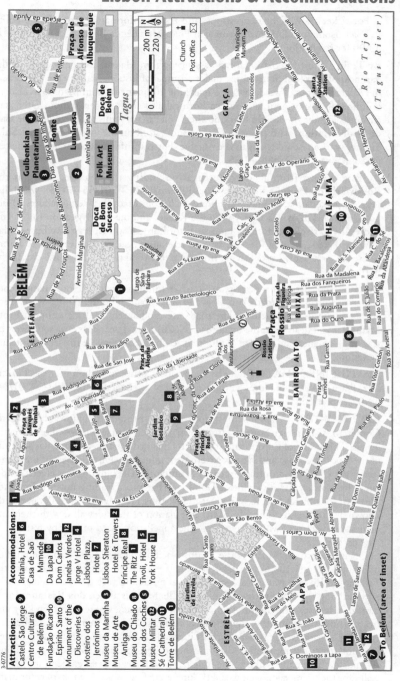

Attractions:

Castelo São Jorge 9
Centro Cultural de Belém 2
Fundação Ricardo Espírito Santo 10
Monument of the Discoveries 6
Mosteiro dos Jerónimos 4
Museu da Marinha 3
Museu de Arte Antiga 7
Museu do Chiado 8
Museu dos Coches 5
Museu Militar 12
Sé (Cathedral) 11
Torre de Belém 1

Accommodations:

Britania, Hotel 6
Casa de Saõ Mamede 9
Da Lapa 10
Dom Carlos 3
Janelas Verdes 12
Jorge V Hotel 4
Lisboa Plaza, Hotel 7
Lisboa Sheraton Hotel & Towers 2
Príncipe Real 8
The Ritz 1
Tivoli, Hotel 5
York House 11

3-0776

For ticket sales, flight reservations, and tourist information, contact the polite Lisboa personnel of **TAP Air Portugal** at Praça Marquês de Pombal 3A (☎ **01/841-69-90** for reservations).

By Train   Most international rail passengers from Madrid and Paris arrive at the **Santa Apolónia Rail Station,** the major terminal of Lisbon, lying by the Tagus near the Alfama district. Two daily trains make the 10-hour run from Madrid to Lisbon. Rail lines from northern and eastern Portugal also arrive at this station. Other rail terminals include the **Rossio Station,** where you can get trains to Sintra, and the **Cais do Sodré Station,** with trains to Cascais and Estoril on the Costa do Sol. At **Sul e Sueste,** you can board trains to the Algarve. For **rail information** at any of the terminals above, call **01/888-40-25.**

By Bus   Buses from all over Portugal, including the Algarve, arrive at the **Rodoviária da Estremadura,** Av. Casal Ribeiro 18B (☎ **01/55-77-15**), which lies near Praça Saldanha, about a 30-minute walk from Praça dos Restauradores. Buses no. 1, 21, and 32 will deliver you to the Rossio, and bus no. 1 goes on to Cais do Sodré, if you're checked into a hotel at Estoril or Cascais. At least five buses a day leave for Faro, capital of the Algarve, and five buses head north every day to Porto. There are eight daily buses leaving from here to Coimbra, the university city in the north.

By Car   International motorists must arrive through Spain, the only nation connected to Portugal via road. You'll have to cross Spanish border points, which usually poses no great difficulty. The roads are moderately well maintained. From Madrid, if you head west, the main road (N620) from Tordesillas goes southwest by way of Salamanca and Ciudad Rodrigo to reach the Portuguese frontier at Fuentes de Onoro.

VISITOR INFORMATION   The main tourist office in Lisbon is at the **Palácio Foz,** Praça dos Restauradores, at the Baixa end of Avenida da Liberdade (☎ **01/34-63-07**), open daily 9am–8pm.

CITY LAYOUT   Lisbon is best approached through its gateway, **Praça do Comércio (Commerce Square,** also known as **Black Horse Square**), bordering the Tagus. This is one of Europe's most perfectly planned squares, and today it's the site of the Stock Exchange and various government ministries. Directly west of the square stands the City Hall, fronting **Praça do Município.** The building was erected in the late 19th century by the architect Domingos Parente. Heading north from Black Horse or Commerce Square, you enter the bustling Praça Dom Pedro IV, popularly known as the **Rossio.** The "drunken" undulation of the sidewalks, with their arabesques of black and white, have led to the appellation, used mainly by tourists, of "the dizzy praça."

Opening onto the Rossio is the Teatro Nacional Dona Maria II, a freestanding building whose facade has been preserved. If you arrive by train, you'll enter the **Estação do Rossio,** whose exuberant Manueline architecture is worth seeing.

Separating the Rossio from Avenida da Liberdade is **Praça dos Restauradores,** named in honor of the Restoration, when the Portuguese chose their own king and freed themselves from 60 years of Spanish rule. The event is marked by an obelisk.

Lisbon's main avenue is **Avenida da Liberdade** (Avenue of Liberty), a handsomely laid out street dating from 1880 and once called the "antechamber of Lisbon." Avenida da Liberdade is like a mile-long park, with shade trees, gardens, and center walks for the promenading crowds. Flanking it are fine shops, headquarters for many major airlines, travel agents, coffeehouses with sidewalk tables, and hotels, including the Tivoli.

At the top of the avenue is **Praça Marquês de Pombal,** with a statue erected in honor of Pombal, the 18th-century prime minister credited with Lisbon's reconstruction in the aftermath of the 1755 earthquake.

Proceeding north, you'll enter **Parque Eduardo VII,** named in honor of the son of Queen Victoria, who paid a state visit to Lisbon. In the park is the Estufa Fria, a greenhouse well worth a visit.

GETTING AROUND   Tickets valid for 4 or 7 days of travel on all the city's trams, the Metro, buses, funicular, and the Santa Justa Elevator cost 1,500$ or 2,200$ ($9.90 or $14.50), respectively. These discount passes may be purchased at the **Santa Justa Elevator,** just south of Rossio Square, daily 8am–8pm.

By Metro   Lisbon's Metro stations are designated by large M signs, and the subway system has 24 stations. A single ticket costs 70$ (45¢) per ride if you purchase it from a vending machine or 75$ (50¢) if you purchase it from a toll booth. You can purchase 10 tickets at one time for 500$ ($3.30) at a toll booth or 475$ ($3.15) at a vending machine.

By Bus & Tram   These are among the cheapest in Europe. The trolley cars— **eléctricos**—make the steep run up to the Bairro Alto and are usually painted a rich Roman gold. The **double-decker buses,** on the other hand, come from London. You pay a flat fare of 150$ ($1) on a bus if you buy the ticket from the driver. The transportation system within the city limits is divided into zones ranging from one to five. Your fare depends on how many zones you traverse. You can purchase a book of 10 tickets (*módulos*) for 685$ ($4.50). Buses and eléctricos run daily 6am–1am.

By Electric Train   Lisbon is connected to all the towns and villages along the Portuguese Riviera by a smooth-running, modern electric train system. You can board the train at the waterfront **Cais do Sodré Station** in Lisbon and head up the coast all the way to Cascais. Only one class of seat is offered, and the rides are cheap and generally comfortable. Sintra cannot be reached by the electric train. You must go to the **Estação do Rossio** station, opening onto Praça Dom Pedro IV, or the Rossio, where frequent connections can be made. The one-way fare is one class only. On the Lisbon–Cascais, Lisbon–Estoril, and Lisbon–Sintra run, the one-way fare is 170$ ($1.10) per person.

By Taxi   The taxis usually are diesel-engine Mercedes, charging a basic fare of 250$ ($1.65) for the first 480 yards. Most fares in the city average 600$ ($3.95), with 20% additional at night (10pm–6am). The driver is allowed by law to tack on another 50% to your bill if your luggage weighs more than 66 pounds. Portuguese tip about 20% of an already modest fare. For a **Radio Taxi,** call 01/815-50-61 or 01/793-27-56.

By Car   Car-rental kiosks are found at the airport as well as in the city center. These include **Avis,** Rua da Glória 14 (☎ 01/346-26-76); **Hertz,** Av. 5 de Outubro 10 (☎ 01/353-28-94); and **Europcar,** Av. António Augusto de Aguiar 24 (☎ 01/353-67-57).

FAST FACTS: Lisbon

American Express   This agency is represented by Top Tours, Av. Duque de Loulé 108 (☎ 01/315-58-85), open Mon–Fri 9:30am–1pm and 2:30–6:30pm.

Baby-sitters   Most first-class hotels can provide baby-sitters from lists the concierge keeps. At small establishments, the sitter is likely to be a relative of the proprietor. Rates are low. You need to request a baby-sitter early in the day.

Business Hours Typically, **shops** are open Mon–Fri 9am–1pm and 3–7pm (though some now stay open through lunch) and Sat 9am–1pm; some are also open Saturday afternoon. **Banks** are open Mon–Fri 8:30am–3pm; some offer a foreign-exchange service Mon–Sat 6–11pm.

Currency The Portuguese currency unit is the **escudo,** written 1$00. Fractions of an escudo (centavos) follow the "$"; for example, 100 escudos is written "100$00." Coins are minted in 50 centavos and 1, 5, 10, 20, 50, 100, and 200 escudos. Notes are printed in 500, 1,000, 2,000, 5,000, and 10,000 escudos. The exchange rate used in this chapter was $1 = 167 escudos, or 1 escudo = .006¢.

Dentists/Doctors Contact Centro de Medicina Dentaria, Calçada Bento da Rocha Cabral (☎ 01/388-41-91), where some dentists speak English. Virtually every hotel in Lisbon maintains a list of doctors and dentists who can be called upon in emergencies.

Drugstores A central and well-stocked one is Farmácia Azevedo, Praça Dom Pedro IV, Rossio (☎ 01/342-74-78). Pharmacies that are closed post a notice indicating the nearest one that's open.

Embassies/Consulates The Embassy of the **United States,** on Avenida das Forças Armadas (☎ 01/726-66-00), is open Mon–Fri 8am–noon and 1:30–4pm. The Embassy of the **United Kingdom** is at Rua São Domingos a Lapa 37 (☎ 01/396-11-91), open Mon–Fri 9am–1pm and 2:30–5:30pm, with the British Consulate at Rua de Estrela 4 (☎ 01/395-40-82), open Mon–Fri 10am–noon and 3–4:30pm. The Embassy of **Canada,** at Av. da Liberdade 144–56, third floor (☎ 01/347-48-92), is open Mon–Fri 8:30am–5pm. The Embassy of **Australia,** at Av. da Liberdade 244, third floor (☎ 01/52-33-50), is open Mon–Thurs 9am–12:30pm and 1:30–5pm and Fri 9am–12:20pm.

Emergencies To call the **police** or an **ambulance** in Lisbon, call 115. In case of **fire,** call 01/32-22-22.

Eyeglasses One of the city's best-recommended eyeglass shops is Oculista das Avenidas, Avenida Marquês de Tomar 71A (☎ 01/796-42-97).

Hospitals In case of a medical emergency, ask at your hotel or call your embassy and ask the staff there to recommend an English-speaking physician; or try the **British Hospital,** Rua Saraiva de Carvalho 49 (☎ 01/395-50-67), where the telephone operator, staff, and doctors all speak English.

Lost Property Go in person (don't call) to the municipal Governo Civil, which is next to the San Carlos Opera House and is open Mon–Sat 9am–noon and 2–6pm. For items lost on public transportation, inquire at Secção de Achados da PSP, Olivais Sul, Praça Cidade Salazar Lote 180 (☎ 01/853-54-03), open Mon–Fri 9am–noon and 2–6pm.

Luggage Storage/Lockers These can be found at the Santa Apolónia station, located by the river near the Alfama. Lockers cost 390$–850$ ($2.55–$5.60) for up to 48 hours.

Photographic Needs A convenient place to develop film or buy photo-related equipment is Instanta, an American-style chain with 10 branches in Lisbon. One of the most centrally located is at Rua Garrett 40 (☎ 01/346-65-40; Metro: Rossio), open Mon–Fri 9am–7pm and Sat 9am–1pm.

Post Office The general post office is on Praça do Comércio (☎ 01/346-32-31), open Mon–Fri 9am–7pm.

ACCOMMODATIONS
IN THE CENTER
Very Expensive

○ Da Lapa. Rua do Pau de Bandeira 4, 1200 Lisboa. ☎ **01/395-00-05.** Fax 01/395-06-65. 94 rms, 8 suites. A/C MINIBAR TV TEL. 35,000$–41,000$ ($231–$270.60) double; from 49,000$ ($323.40) suite. AE, DC, MC, V. Bus: 27.

We never thought we'd see a hotel replace the Ritz as the premier address in Lisbon, but Da Lapa has done just that. Its lushly manicured gardens (huge by urban standards) lie close to the Tagus, south of the city center. All but about 20 of the accommodations are in a six-story modern wing. The guest rooms contain amply proportioned marble surfaces, reproductions of French and English furniture, and a classic design inspired by a late 18th-century model. The public areas have multicolored ceiling frescoes and richly patterned marble floors laid out in sometimes startling geometric patterns. The Restaurant Embaixada is one of Lisbon's most elegant choices. Facilities include an outdoor pool.

Hotel Lisboa Plaza. Travessa do Salitre 7, Av. da Liberdade, 1250 Lisboa. ☎ **800/528-1234** in the U.S., or 01/346-39-22. Fax 01/347-16-30. 112 rms, 6 suites. A/C MINIBAR TV TEL. 19,000$–27,000$ ($125.40–$178.20) double; from 29,000$ ($191.40) suite. Rates include buffet breakfast. Children 11 and under stay free in parents' room. AE, DC, MC, V. Parking 2,300$ ($15.20) nearby. Metro: Avenida. Bus: 1, 2, 36, or 44.

This family-owned and -operated four-star hotel in the heart of the city is a charmer. It has many appealing art nouveau touches, including the facade. When the hotel was completely overhauled in 1988, a well-known Portuguese designer decorated it in a contemporary classic style; modern amenities were added. The guest rooms—with well-stocked marble baths, hair dryers, and in-house videos—are well styled and comfortable, and renovation is ongoing here. Try for a room in the rear, looking out over the botanical gardens. Through an art nouveau entrance you approach the Quinta d'Avenida Restaurant, which specializes in a traditional Portuguese cuisine.

○ Hotel Tivoli. Av. da Liberdade 185, 1298 Lisboa Codex. ☎ **01/383-01-81.** Fax 01/357-94-61. 297 rms, 30 suites. A/C MINIBAR TV TEL. 24,000$ ($158.40) double; from 40,000$ ($264) suite. Rates include continental breakfast. AE, DC, MC, V. Parking 1,600$ ($10.55). Metro: Avenida. Bus: 1, 2, 9, or 32.

The Hotel Tivoli has enticing features, including the only hotel pool in central Lisbon. A much-needed renovation in 1992 made the hotel sparkle once again. Located right on the main boulevard of Lisbon, it has extensive facilities. Best of all, its prices are not extravagant, considering the amenities. The guest rooms contain a mixture of modern and traditionally styled furniture; the largest and best rooms face the front, although those in the rear are quieter. Not all the rooms are standardized: Some are better appointed and more spacious than others. The wood-paneled O Zodíaco restaurant serves a buffet for both lunch and dinner. The top-floor O Terraço offers a view of Lisbon as well as à la carte meals. Facilities include access to the Tivoli Club, surrounded by a lovely garden, with a pool that can be heated when necessary, tennis court, and a solarium.

○ Inter-Continental Ritz. Rua Rodrigo da Fonseca 88, 1200 Lisboa. ☎ **800/327-0200** in the U.S., or 01/383-20-20. Fax 01/383-17-83. 310 rms, 40 suites. A/C MINIBAR TV TEL. 38,000$–46,000$ ($250.80–$303.60) double; from 80,000$ ($528) suite. AE, DC, MC, V. Free parking. Metro: Rotunda. Bus: 2 or 12.

The Ritz was built by the dictator Salazar in the late 1950s. Now operated by Inter-Continental Hotels, although some critics view all its ostentation as "fading fifties," the hotel is valiantly struggling to adjust to modern tastes. Its suites boast slender mahogany canopied beds with fringed swags, marquetry desks, satinwood dressing tables with tip mirrors, and plush carpeting. Some of the soundproof modern rooms have terraces opening onto Edward VII Park; each boasts a marble bath with a double basin. The least desirable rooms are the even-numbered ones facing the street. The main dining room, Veranda, is dignified and pleasant, and from May to October you can take meals out onto the attractive Veranda Terrace.

Lisboa Sheraton Hotel & Towers. Rua Latino Coelho 1, 1097 Lisboa. ☎ **800/325-3535** in the U.S., or 01/357-57-57. Fax 01/354-71-64. 384 rms, 7 suites. A/C MINIBAR TV TEL. 32,000$–52,000$ ($211.20–$343.20) double; from 80,000$ ($528) suite. AE, DC, MC, V. Parking 1,900$ ($12.55). Bus: 1, 2, 9, or 32.

The 25-floor skyscraper lies at a traffic-clogged intersection a bit removed from the center of the action, a few blocks north of Praça Marquês de Pombal. The impressive pink marble lobby features chandeliers and fancy carpeting. Individual rooms don't match the grandeur of the public rooms, but they are generally spacious. The understated decor includes thick wool carpeting, print fabrics, and traditional (if a bit chunky) wood furniture. Marble baths are a highlight, and the most desirable rooms are in the tower, opening onto views of the longest bridge in Europe. The hotel's three star restaurants include the glamour choice, the Alfama Grill. A rooftop bar features live music nightly, and there's also an outdoor pool, plus a health club.

Moderate

Britania. Rua Rodrigues Sampaio 17, 1100 Lisboa. ☎ **01/315-50-16.** Fax 01/315-50-21. 30 rms. A/C MINIBAR TV TEL. 14,900$ ($101.30) double. Rates include American buffet breakfast. AE, DC, MC, V. Metro: Avenida da Liberdade.

In its own way, the Britania is one of Lisbon's most traditional and refreshingly conservative hotels, designed by the well-known Portuguese architect Cassiano Branco in 1944. Located about a block from Avenida da Liberdade, it boasts a distinguished clientele, who return repeatedly, and an old-fashioned, almost courtly, staff. In 1995 the hotel was refurbished, making the pastel-colored bedrooms on all five of its floors more comfortable.

⑤ Dom Carlos. Av. Duque de Loulé 121, 1050 Lisboa. ☎ **01/353-90-71.** Fax 01/352-07-28. 76 rms. A/C MINIBAR TV TEL. 15,500$ ($102.30) double; 17,000$ ($112.20) triple. Rates include buffet breakfast. AE, DC, MC, V. Metro: Rotunda. Bus: 1, 36, 44, or 45.

Just off Praça Marquês de Pombal, the Dom Carlos faces its own triangular park dedicated to the partially blind Camilo Castelo Branco, a 19th-century "eternity poet." The curvy facade is all glass, giving guests an outdoorsy feeling reinforced by green trees and beds of orange and red canna. The hotel was completely renovated in early 1994. The guest rooms are paneled in reddish Portuguese wood; even so, they're rather uninspired and functional. The reason to stay here is economy: the Dom Carlos charges only a fraction of what its more expensive neighborhood rivals get.

✪ Janelas Verdes. Rua das Janelas Verdes 47, 1200 Lisboa. ☎ **01/396-81-43.** Fax 01/396-81-44. 17 rms. TV TEL. 18,500$–28,500$ ($122.10–$188.10) double. Rates include American buffet breakfast. AE, DC, MC, V. Bus: 27, 40, 49, 54, or 60.

Owned by the proprietors of the Lisboa Plaza (see above), this aristocratic 18th-century mansion was the home of the late Portuguese novelist Eça de Queiros. It's near the Museum of Ancient Art. The large, luxurious, and marvelously restored rooms have abundant closet space and generous tile baths. The predominantly red lounge is evocative of turn-of-the-century Lisbon. The hotel's major drawback is its somewhat-remote location on a mildly unsavory residential street.

Príncipe Real. Rua de Alegria 53, 1200 Lisboa. ☎ **01/346-01-16.** Fax 01/342-21-04. 24 rms. A/C MINIBAR TV TEL. 13,500$–15,500$ ($89.10–$102.30) double. Rates include continental breakfast. AE, DC, MC, V. Metro: Restauradores. Bus: 2, 44, or 45.

This modern five-story hotel, which houses the overflow from the Ritz (see above), is reached after a long, steep climb from Avenida da Liberdade and lies in the vicinity of the botanical gardens. Selectivity and care are shown in the individualized guest rooms, which are small but tasteful. The beds, reproductions of fine antiques, have excellent mattresses. Each room is a color-coordinated blend of floral fabrics. The hotel's restaurant opens onto panoramic views of Lisbon and serves excellent Portuguese cuisine.

✪ York House. Rua das Janelas Verdes 32, 1200 Lisboa. ☎ **01/396-24-35.** Fax 01/397-27-93. 34 rms. TV TEL. 20,900$–27,500$ ($137.95–$181.50) double. Rates include continental breakfast. AE, DC, MC, V. Free parking on street. Bus: 27, 40, 49, or 60.

York House mixes the drama of the past with modern convenience. Once a 16th-century convent, it lies outside the center of traffic-filled Lisbon, almost opposite the Museum of Ancient Art. York House was tastefully furnished by one of the most distinguished Lisbon designers. All guest rooms, which come in various sizes, have antique beds, soft mattresses, and 18th- and 19th-century bric-a-brac.

Inexpensive

Casa de São Mamede. Rua da Escola Politécnica 159, 1200 Lisboa. ☎ **01/396-31-66.** Fax 01/395-18-96. 28 rms. TEL. 10,500$ ($69.30) double. Rates include continental breakfast. No credit cards. Tram: 24. Bus: 9, 22, or 49.

Built in the 1800s as a private villa for the count of Coruche, this place, located behind the Botanical Gardens, was transformed into a hotel in 1945. Today it's managed by the Marquês family. Breakfast is served in a sunny second-floor dining room decorated with antique yellow-and-blue tiles. Although renovated, the rooms retain an aura of their original high-ceilinged, slightly dowdy, somewhat frayed charm. The location is about midpoint between Avenida da Liberdade and the Amoreiras shopping center.

Jorge V Hotel. Rua Mouzinho da Silveira 3, 1200 Lisboa. ☎ **01/356-25-25.** Fax 01/315-03-19. 43 rms, 6 suites. A/C TV TEL. 10,750$ ($70.95) double; 12,850$ ($84.80) suite. Rates include continental breakfast. AE, DC, MC, V. Free parking on street. Metro: Avenida or Rotunda.

The Jorge V is a neat little hotel with a 1960s design. This inexpensive place to stay boasts a choice location a block off noisy Avenida da Liberdade. Its facade contains rows of cellular balconies, roomy enough for guests to have breakfast or afternoon "coolers." A tiny elevator takes guests to a variety of aging rooms, which aren't generous in size but are comfortable in a compact way; all have small tile baths.

Residência Nazareth. Av. António Augusto de Aguiar 25, 1000 Lisboa. ☎ **051/354-20-16.** Fax 01/356-08-36. 32 rms. A/C MINIBAR TV TEL. 7,500$ ($49.50) double. Rates include continental breakfast. AE, DC, MC, V. Metro: São Sebastião. Bus: 31, 41, or 46.

You'll recognize this establishment by its dusty-pink facade and the windows, some of which are surrounded with decorative arches raised in low relief. Take an elevator to the fourth-floor landing, where, far from the beauticians, hair stylists, and offices below, there's a medieval vaulting you might find in a romanticized version of a Portuguese fortress. The distressed plaster and the wrought-iron lanterns are obvious facsimiles. Even the spacious bar/TV lounge looks like a vaulted cellar. Some guest rooms, which are very basic, contain platforms, requiring guests to step up or down to the bath or to the comfortable bed. A little refurbishing is in order here.

IN THE GRAÇA DISTRICT
Moderate

⑤ **Hotel Albergaria da Senhora do Monte.** Calçada do Monte 39, 1100 Lisboa. ☎ **01/886-60-02.** Fax 01/887-77-83. 28 rms, 4 suites. A/C TV TEL. 17,000$–24,000$ ($112.20–$158.40) double; 22,500$–27,500$ ($148.50–$181.50) suite. Rates include continental breakfast. AE, DC, MC, V. Metro: Socorro. Tram: 28. Bus: 12, 17, or 35.

This little hilltop hotel has a unique character, and was completely renovated in 1995. It's perched near a belvedere, the Miradouro Senhora do Monte, in the Graça district, where there's a memorable nighttime view of the city, the Castle of St. George, and the Tagus. Built originally as an apartment house, the hotel has been converted into a clublike establishment. The intimate living room features large tufted sofas and oversize tables and lamps. Multilevel corridors lead to the excellent guest rooms, all of which have verandas. The rooms reveal a decorator's touch, especially the gilt-edged door panels, the grass-cloth walls, and the tile baths with bronze fixtures.

DINING
IN THE CENTER
Very Expensive

✪ **Gambrinus.** Rua das Portas de Santo Antão 25. ☎ **01/342-14-66.** Reservations required. Main courses 3,600$–4,600$ ($23.75–$30.35). AE, MC, V. Daily noon–1:30am. Metro: Rossio. SEAFOOD.

One of Lisbon's premier restaurants since 1936, Gambrinus is the finest choice for fish and shellfish. It's in the congested heart of the city, off the Rossio near the rail station on a little square behind the National Theater. Have your meal in the severely macho dining room with leather chairs under a cathedral-beamed ceiling, or select a little table beside a fireplace on the raised end of the room. Gambrinus offers a diversified à la carte menu accompanied by specialties of the day. The most expensive items are shrimp and lobster dishes. However, you might prefer conch with shellfish Thermidor or sea bass minhota. If you don't fancy fish and like your dishes spicy *hot*, ask for chicken piri-piri.

Restaurant Aviz. In the Centre Comerciale Amoreiras, Av. Eng. Duarte Pacheco. ☎ **01/385-18-88.** Reservations required. Main courses 34,000$–10,000$ ($26.40–$66). AE, DC, MC, V. Mon–Fri 12:30–4pm and 7:30–10:30pm, Sat 7:30–10:30pm. Closed Aug. Bus: 15. PORTUGUESE/INTERNATIONAL.

This bastion of upper-class conservatism used to welcome an ongoing roster of celebrities and aristocrats. In the mid-1990s the restaurant took the almost heretical step of moving from premises it had occupied since its long-ago origins into the glistening interior of the capital's showcase shopping center. Here, one floor above street level, against dignified black-painted walls, management moved the chandeliers, mirrors, oil paintings, and culinary awards it garnered during its long history in a not altogether successful attempt to duplicate the legendary aura of the original premises. The food remains as stylish and elegant as before, and might include superb versions of smoked swordfish or chicken Kiev, several versions of pâté (salmon, country style, and a type liberally infused with champagne), fettuccine with pesto, a succulent chateaubriand with béarnaise, or roast goat in the Portuguese style.

Expensive

António Clara. Av. da República 38. ☎ **01/796-63-80.** Reservations required. Jackets required for men. Main courses 2,500$–3,200$ ($16.50–$21.10). AE, DC, MC, V. Mon–Sat noon–4pm and 7–11:30pm. Metro: Entre Campos or Campo Pequeño. PORTUGUESE/INTERNATIONAL.

Even if it weren't one of the capital's best restaurants, this exquisitely crafted turn-of-the-century art nouveau villa would still be famous as the former home of one of Portugal's most revered architects. It was built in 1890 by Miguel Ventura Terra (1866–1918), whose photograph hangs amid polished antiques and gilded mirrors. The villa's angled, tiled wings seem to embrace visitors as they approach the vaguely Moorish facade. Meals include such specialties as smoked swordfish, paella for two, chateaubriand béarnaise, codfish Margarida da Praça, and beef Wellington. These dishes may be familiar, but only the highest quality of ingredients go into them.

✪ Casa da Comida. Travessa de Amoireiras 1. ☎ **01/388-53-76.** Reservations required. Main courses 3,000$–5,000$ ($19.80–$33). AE, DC, MC, V. Mon–Fri 1–3pm and 8–11pm, Sat 8–11pm. Metro: Rotunda. PORTUGUESE/FRENCH.

The Casa da Comida, off Rua Alexandre Herculano, is touted by local gourmets as having some of the finest food in Lisbon. You'll find the food good and the atmosphere pleasant. The dining room is handsomely decorated. The bar is done in period style, and there's a charming walled garden. Specialties include roast kid with herbs, a medley of shellfish Casa da Comida, and faisão à convento de Alcântara (stewed pheasant covered with caviar). An excellent selection of wines is available from the cellar. The food is often more imaginative here than at some of the other top-rated choices such as Aviz.

Clara. Campo dos Mártires da Pátria 49. ☎ **01/885-30-53.** Reservations required. Main courses 3,100$–4,600$ ($20.45–$30.35). AE, DC, MC, V. Mon–Sat noon–3:30pm and 7pm–midnight. Closed Aug 1–15. Metro: Avenida da Liberdade. PORTUGUESE/INTERNATIONAL.

In a hillside location amid decaying villas and city squares, this green-tile house contains an elegant restaurant. During lunch, you might prefer to sit near the garden terrace's plants and fountain. At night, an indoor seat—perhaps near the large marble fireplace—is more appealing. A piano plays softly at dinner. Specialties include tournedos Clara, stuffed rabbit with red-wine sauce, codfish Clara, filet of sole with orange, and pheasant with grapes. Again, as in so many top-rated Lisbon restaurants, these dishes aren't creative or innovative in any way, but they're often prepared flawlessly.

Escorial. Rua das Portas de Santo Antão 47. ☎ **01/346-37-58.** Reservations recommended. Main courses 2,250$–3,500$ ($14.85–$23.10). AE, DC, MC, V. Daily noon–4pm and 7pm–midnight. Metro: Rossio. INTERNATIONAL.

Near Praça dos Restauradores, this Spanish-owned establishment combines classic Spanish dishes with an inviting ambience. The dining-room walls are paneled in rosewood, with frosted-globe lighting. A menu is printed in English (always look for the course of the day). You might enjoy a sampling of Portuguese oysters or squid on a skewer. A selection of the chef's specialties might include barbecued baby goat, beef Stroganoff, or partridge casserole. In spite of its neighborhood, which grows increasingly sleazy at night, Escorial has stood the test of time in Lisbon and has remained an enduring though not incredibly innovative favorite.

Restaurante Tavares. Rua da Misericórdia 37. ☎ **01/342-11-12.** Reservations required. Main courses 1,600$–4,200$ ($10.55–$27.70); fixed-price menu 6,000$ ($39.60) at lunch, 8,000$ ($52.80) at dinner. AE, DC, MC, V. Mon–Fri 12:30–3pm and 8–10:30pm, Sun 8–10:30pm. Bus: 15. PORTUGUESE/CONTINENTAL.

Tavares, the oldest restaurant in Lisbon, remains a nostalgic favorite. It still serves competently prepared food with flawless service. One of the capital's more glittering settings, it's beginning to show a little wear and tear. White- and gold-paneled walls, three chandeliers, and Louis XV armchairs keep the spirit of the 18th century intact.

Your meal might begin with crêpes de marisco. A main-course selection might be sole in champagne, stuffed crab Tavares style, clams Bulhao Pato, or tournedos Grand Duc. Many continental dishes are scattered throughout the menu, including the classic scallops of veal viennoise. The restaurant nearly always serves such basic Portuguese dishes as sardines and salted codfish.

Sua Excelência. Rua do Conde 34. ☎ **01/60-36-14.** Reservations required. Main courses 2,500$–3,900$ ($16.50–$25.75). AE, MC, V. Mon–Tues and Thurs–Fri 1–3pm and 8–10:30pm, Sun 8–10:30pm. Closed Sept. Bus: 27 or 49. ANGOLAN/PORTUGUESE.

Sua Excelência is the creation of Francisco Queiroz, who has created an atmosphere somewhat like a fashionable drawing room, with colorful tables placed in an intimate Portuguese provincial decor, cooled by the terracotta floor and high, painted ceiling. Some dishes served are uncommon in Portugal, such as Angolan chicken Moamba. Specialties include prawns piri-piri (not unreasonably hot), lulas a moda da casa (squid stewed in white wine, crème fraîche, and cognac), what Queiroz proclaims as the "best smoked swordfish in Portugal," and clams cooked at least five ways. One unusual specialty is "little jacks," a small fish eaten whole, served with a well-flavored "paste" made from 2-day-old bread. The restaurant is just a block up the hill from the entrance to the National Art Gallery.

Moderate

⭕ **A Gôndola.** Av. de Berna 64. ☎ **01/797-15-52.** Reservations required. Main courses 1,800$–3,200$ ($11.90–$21.10). V. Mon–Fri 12:30–3pm and 7:30–10pm, Sat 12:30–3pm. Metro: Praça de Espanha. Bus: 31 or 46. ITALIAN/PORTUGUESE.

A Gôndola—Lisbon's "Little Italy"—serves what are among the finest Italian specialties in town. It offers indoor dining as well as alfresco meals in the courtyard. Although the decor isn't inspired, the food makes up for it. A full dinner is quite a buy considering what you get. A first-course selection might be Chaves ham with melon and figs, followed by filet of sole meunière or grilled sardines with pimientos. This is followed by yet another course, ravioli or cannelloni Roman style or veal cutlet milanese. The banquet is topped off by fruit or dessert.

⑤ **António Oliveira.** Rua Tomás Ribiero 63. ☎ **01/353-87-80.** Main courses 2,500$–3,600$ ($16.50–$23.75); fixed-price menu 3,000$ ($19.80). V. Daily noon–4pm and 7–10:30pm. Metro: Picoas. Bus: 30, 36, or 38. PORTUGUESE/INTERNATIONAL.

This place was created especially for Portuguese businesspeople who want a relaxing ambience and good food. A corner establishment, just a bit away from the din of central traffic, it's a refreshing oasis with blue-and-white glazed earthenware tiles and a free-form blue ceiling. Fish dishes, garnished with vegetables, include filets with tomato sauce and baked sole. Polvo à lagareira (octopus with broiled potatoes, olive oil, and garlic) is a specialty. From among the fowl and meat dishes, try the frango na prata (chicken broiled in foil with potatoes) or pork with clams Alentejana style. The owner-manager recommends his açorda de marisco, a stewlike breaded shellfish-and-egg dish that's a treat.

Bachus. Largo da Trindade 8–9. ☎ **01/342-28-28.** Reservations recommended. Main courses 1,600$–3,600$ ($10.55–$23.75). AE, DC, MC, V. Daily noon–1am. Bus: 15. INTERNATIONAL.

Amusing murals cover the wood-paneled facade of this restaurant; inside, the decor is elaborate and sophisticated. The ambience is a mixture of a private salon in a Russian palace, a turn-of-the-century English club, and a stylized Manhattan bistro. A brass staircase winds around a column of illuminated glass to the dining room. Specialties change frequently, depending on the market availability of their ingredients. Full meals might include mixed grill Bachus, chateaubriand with béarnaise, mountain goat, beef Stroganoff, shrimp Bachus, or other daily specials. The chef has a conservative approach to his cuisine, and perhaps because of this, he reportedly rarely gets any complaints. The wine list is extensive.

⑤ Bonjardim. Travessa de Santo Antão 10. ☎ **01/342-74-24.** Main courses 1,100$–2,200$ ($7.25–$14.50). DC, MC, V. Daily noon–11pm. Metro: Restauradores. PORTUGUESE.

Owner/manager Manuel Castanheira caters mostly to families, providing wholesome meals at good prices. The restaurant, one of the most popular in town, is just east of Avenida da Liberdade near the grimy Praça dos Restauradores. In the main restaurant, the second-floor air-conditioned dining room is designed in rustic Portuguese style, with a beamed ceiling and a tile mural depicting farm creatures. The street-floor dining room, with an adjoining bar for before-meal drinks, has walls of decorative tiles. During your dinner, the aroma of fat chickens roasting to a golden brown on the charcoal spit can only persuade you to try one. An order of this house specialty, called frango no espeto, is adequate for two, with a side dish of french fries. The cook also bakes hake in the Portuguese style; an alternative dish is pork fried with clams.

✪ Conventual. Praça das Flores 45. ☎ **01/60-91-96.** Reservations required. Main courses 1,900$–3,200$ ($12.55–$21.10); fixed-price menu 4,500$ ($29.70). AE, DC, MC, V. Mon–Fri 12:30–3:30pm and 7:30–11:30pm, Sat 7:30–11:30pm. Closed Aug. Metro: Avenida de Liberdade. Bus: 100. PORTUGUESE.

In many ways this is one of our favorite Lisbon restaurants, because of the taste and sensitivity of its gracious owner, Dina Marquês. Many of its admirers (who include the prime minister of Portugal) rank it as the best place to dine in Lisbon today, even though its prices are about a quarter less than at many of its competitors. Once inside, you'll be treated to a display of old panels from baroque churches, religious statues, and bric-a-brac from Mrs. Marquês's private collection. The owner invented many of the delectably flavored recipes: creamy coriander soup, stewed partridge in port, duck in rich champagne sauce, grilled monkfish in herb-flavored cream sauce, osso buco, and frogs' legs in buttery garlic.

Restaurant 33. Rua Alexandre Herculano 33A. ☎ **01/354-60-79.** Reservations recommended. Main courses 2,250$–3,550$ ($14.85–$23.45); fixed-price menu 4,800$ ($31.70). AE, DC, MC, V. Mon–Fri 12:30–3pm and 8–10pm, Sat 8–10pm. Metro: Rotunda. Tram: 20 or 25. Bus: 6 or 9. PORTUGUESE/INTERNATIONAL.

Restaurant 33 is a treasure. Decorated in a style evocative of an English hunting lodge, it lies near many recommended hotels, including the Ritz. Specialties include shellfish rice served in a crab shell, smoked salmon or lobster Tour d'Argent, and peppersteak. One reader from New Rochelle, New York, described her meal here as "flawless." Large portions, tasty stews, and strong-flavored ingredients characterize the food. You can enjoy a glass of port in the small bar at the entrance and enjoy the pianist who performs during dinner.

Sancho. Travessa da Glória 14. ☎ **01/346-97-80.** Reservations recommended. Main courses 1,100$–2,500$ ($7.25–$16.50). AE, MC, V. Mon–Sat noon–3pm and 7–10:30pm. Metro: Avenida de Liberdade. PORTUGUESE/INTERNATIONAL.

Sancho is a cozy rustic-style restaurant just off Avenida da Liberdade, close to Praça dos Restauradores. The decor is classic Iberian, with a beamed ceiling, fireplace, leather-and-wood chairs, and stuccoed walls. Fish gratinée soup is a traditional way to begin. Shellfish, always expensive, is the specialty. Main dishes might include the chef's special hake or pan-broiled Portuguese steak. If your palate is fireproof, order churrasco de cabrito (goat) au piri-piri. For dessert, sample the crêpes Suzette or perhaps chocolate mousse. This is a longtime local favorite, and the recipes never change.

Inexpensive

The Big Apple. Av. Elias Garcia 19B. ☎ **01/797-55-75.** Burgers 800$–1,000$ ($5.30–$6.60); steaks 1,200$–2,000$ ($7.90–$13.20). AE, DC, MC, V. Daily noon–3pm and 7–11pm. Metro: Campo Pequeño. AMERICAN.

Dozens of tongue-in-cheek accessories adorn the walls and menu of this American-style eatery on a tree-lined boulevard in a residential neighborhood. You'll find a Texan's map of the United States (in which Amarillo appears just south of the Canadian border) and a red, white, and blue checkerboard awning out front. It's simple, pleasant, and clean. There are 18 variations of hamburgers to choose from, many a meal in themselves. You can also select five kinds of dinner crêpes or five kinds of temptingly sweet dessert crêpes.

Cervejaria Brilhante. Rua das Portas de Santo Antão 105. ☎ **01/346-14-07.** Main courses 1,200$–3,200$ ($7.90–$21.10); tourist menu 1,830$ ($12.10). AE, DC, MC, V. Daily noon–midnight. Metro: Rossio. Bus: 1, 2, 36, 44, or 45. SEAFOOD.

Lisboans from every walk of life stop here for a stein of beer and mariscos (seafood). Opposite the Coliseu, the tavern is decorated with stone arches, wood-paneled walls, and pictorial tiles of sea life. You can dine either at the bar or at marble tables. The front window is packed with an appetizing array of king crabs, oysters, lobsters, baby clams, shrimp, even barnacles. The price changes every day, depending on the market, and you pay by the kilo. This is hearty, robust eating. It's a challenge here to attract a waiter's attention.

Cervejaria Ribadoura. Av. da Liberdade 155. ☎ **01/354-94-11.** Main courses 1,200$–3,300$ ($7.90–$21.80). AE, DC, MC, V. Daily noon–1:30am. Metro: Avenida. Bus: 1, 2, 44, or 45. SEAFOOD.

The Cervejaria Ribadoura is one of the typical shellfish-and-beer eateries in central Lisbon, located midway along the city's major boulevard at the corner of Rua do Salitre. The decor is simple; the emphasis is on the fish. Try the bacalhau (codfish) à Bras. You can dine lightly as well, particularly at lunch, on such plates as shrimp omelet. Many diners often follow fish with a meat dish. However, only those who've been trained for at least 25 years on the most mouth-wilting Indian curries should try the sautéed pork cutlets with piri-piri, made with red-hot peppers from Angola.

Cervejaria Trindade. Rua Nova de Trindade 20B. ☎ **01/342-35-06.** Main courses 1,100$–2,500$ ($7.25–$16.50); tourist menu 2,300$ ($15.20). AE, DC, MC, V. Daily 9am–1:30am. Metro: Rossio. Tram: 24. Bus: 15, 20, or 100. PORTUGUESE.

The Cervejaria Trindade is a combination German beerhall and Portuguese tavern. In operation since 1836, it's the oldest tavern in Lisbon. Surrounded by walls tiled with Portuguese scenes, you can order tasty little steaks and heaps of crisp french-fried potatoes. Many Portuguese prefer bife na frigideira—steak with mustard sauce and a fried egg, served in a clay frying pan. The tavern features shellfish, which come from private fish ponds, and the house specialties are ameijoas (clams) à Trindade and giant prawns.

IN THE CHIADO DISTRICT

Expensive

Tágide. Largo da Académia Nacional de Belas Artes 18–20. ☎ **01/342-07-20.** Reservations required. Main courses 2,900$–3,800$ ($19.15–$25.10); fixed-price menu 7,000$ ($46.20). AE, DC, MC, V. Mon–Fri 12:30–2:30pm and 7:30–10:30pm, Sat 7:30–10:30pm. Metro: Chiado. Tram: 20. Bus: 15. PORTUGUESE/INTERNATIONAL.

Tágide has had a prestigious past—once the town house of a diplomat, then a major nightclub, it's now one of Lisbon's leading restaurants. It's located up from the docks, atop a steep hill overlooking the old part of Lisbon and the Tagus. The dining room has windows that look down on the ships moored in the port. Specialties include suprême of halibut with coriander, pork with clams and coriander, and grilled baby goat with herbs. Habitués from the world of Lisbon finance and government, including the president of Portugal, are given preferential seating and treatment.

IN THE ALCÂNTARA
Expensive

Café Alcântara. Rua Maria Holstein 15. ☎ **01/362-12-26.** Reservations recommended. Main courses 2,500$–6,000$ ($16.50–$39.60). AE, DC, MC, V. Daily 8pm–1am. Bus: 32 and 42. FRENCH/PORTUGUESE.

One of Lisbon's most fun, worthwhile, and internationally hip dining-and-entertainment complexes, it attracts a mixed straight/gay crowd. A 600-year-old warehouse for storing timber, today the vast building has forest-green and bordeaux walls, exposed marble, ceiling fans, burgeoning plants, and simple wooden tables and chairs. Menu items include rillettes of salmon, fresh fish, lacquered duck, steak tartare, and a Portuguese platter of the day, which might include fried bacalhau (codfish) or a hearty feijoada inspired by the traditions of Trás-os-Montes.

COFFEEHOUSES

A Brasileira. Rua Garrett 120. ☎ **01/346-95-41.** Sandwiches 240$–500$ ($1.60-$3.30); pastries 100$ (65¢). No credit cards. Daily 7:30am–2pm. Metro: Rossio. SANDWICHES/PASTRIES.

One of the oldest coffeehouses in Lisbon, A Brasileira lies in the Chiado district. Behind an art nouveau facade, the 19th-century emporium was once a gathering place of Lisbon literati. Guests sit at small tables on chairs made of tooled leather, amid mirrored walls and marble pilasters. A statue of the great Portuguese poet Fernando Pessoa sits on a chair side by side with the customers.

ATTRACTIONS

If your time is limited, then you should explore the National Coach Museum, the Jerónimos Monastery, and the Alfama and the Castle of St. George. At least two art museums merit attention: the Museu Nacional de Art Antiga and the Museu Calouste Gulbenkian.

SIGHTSEEING SUGGESTIONS

If You Have 1 Day   This is just enough time to take a walking tour of the Alfama, the most interesting district of Lisbon. Visit the 12th-century Sé (cathedral), and take in a view of the city and the River Tagus from the Santa Luzia Belvedere. Climb up to the Castelo São Jorge (St. George's Castle). Take a taxi or bus to Belém to see the Mosteiro dos Jerónimos (Jerónimos Monastery) and the Torre de Belém. While at Belém, explore the Museu Nacional dos Coches (National Coach Museum).

If You Have 2 Days   On your second day, head for Sintra, the single most visited sight in the environs of Lisbon—Byron called it "glorious Eden." You can spend the day here, exploring the castle and other palaces in the stunning area. Try at least to visit the Palácio Nacional de Sintra and the Palácio Nacional da Pena. Return to Lisbon for a night at a fado cafe.

If You Have 3 Days   Spend the morning of your third day at the Museu Calouste Gulbenkian, one of Europe's artistic treasure troves. Have lunch at a *típico* restaurant in the Bairro Alto. In the afternoon see the Fundação Ricardo Esprito Santo (Museum of Decorative Art) and the Museu Nacional de Art Antiga (National Museum of Ancient Art). At the day's end, wander through Parque Eduardo VII.

If You Have 5 Days   On your fourth day, take an excursion from Lisbon (perhaps an organized tour) to visit the fishing village of Nazaré and the walled city of Óbidos. Those interested in Roman Catholic sights might also want to go to the shrine at Fátima, although it would be hectic to see this on the same day. On the final day, slow your pace a bit with a morning at the beach at Estoril on Portugal's Costa do Sol. Then continue along the coast to Cascais for lunch. After lunch, wander around this old fishing village now turned into a major resort. Go to Guincho, 4 miles along the coast from Cascais, which is near the westernmost point on the European continent and has panoramic views.

THE TOP ATTRACTIONS

✪ The Alfama

The Lisbon of bygone days lives on in the Alfama, the most typical quarter of the city. The wall built by the Visigoths and incorporated into some of the old houses is mute testimony to its ancient past. In East Lisbon, the Alfama was the Saracen sector centuries before its conquest by the Christians. Some of the buildings were spared from the devastating 1755 earthquake, and the Alfama has retained much of its original charm—narrow cobblestone streets, cages of canaries chirping in the afternoon sun, strings of garlic and pepper inviting you inside *típico* taverns, old street markets, and charming balconies.

One of the best views is from the belvedere of **Largo das Portas do Sol,** near the Museum of Decorative Art. It's a balcony opening onto the sea, overlooking the typical houses as they sweep down to the Tagus. One of the oldest churches is **Santo Estevão** (St. Stephen), at Largo de Santo Estevão. It was originally constructed in the 13th century; the present marble structure dates from the 18th century. Also of medieval origin is the **Church of São Miguel** (St. Michael), at Largo de São Miguel, deep in the Alfama on a palm tree–shaded square. **Rua da Judiaria** (Street of the Jews) is another reminder of the past. It was settled largely by Jewish refugees fleeing Spain to escape the Inquisition.

✪ **Castelo São Jorge (Saint George's Castle).** Rua Costa do Castelo. ☎ **01/887-17-22.** Free admission. Apr–Sept, daily 9am–9pm; Oct–Mar, daily 9am–7pm. Bus: 37.

Believed to have predated the Romans, the hilltop was used as a fortress to guard the Tagus and its settlement below. Beginning in the 5th century A.D., the site was a Visigothic fortification; it fell in the early 8th century to the Saracens. Many of the walls that are still standing were erected during the centuries of Moorish domination. The Moors were in control until 1147, the year that Afonso Henríques, the country's first king, chased them out and extended his kingdom south. Even before Lisbon was made the capital of the newly emerging nation, the site was used as a royal palace. For what is the finest view of the Tagus and the Alfama, walk the esplanades and climb the ramparts of the old castle. The castle is named in commemoration of an Anglo-Portuguese pact dating from as early as 1371. Inside the castle grounds you can stroll through a setting of olive, pine, and cork trees, all graced by the appearance of swans and rare white peacocks.

Cathedral (Sé). Largo da Sé. ☎ **01/886-67-52.** Cathedral, free; sacristy, 400$ ($2.65). Daily 9am–5pm. Tram: 28 (Graça). Bus: 37.

Characterized by twin towers flanking its entrance, the Sé represents an architectural wedding of romanesque and gothic. The facade is severe enough to resemble a medieval fortress. When the city was captured early in the 12th century by Christian Crusaders, led by Portugal's first king, Afonso Henríques, the Sé then became the first church in Lisbon. It was damaged in the earthquakes of 1344 and 1755.

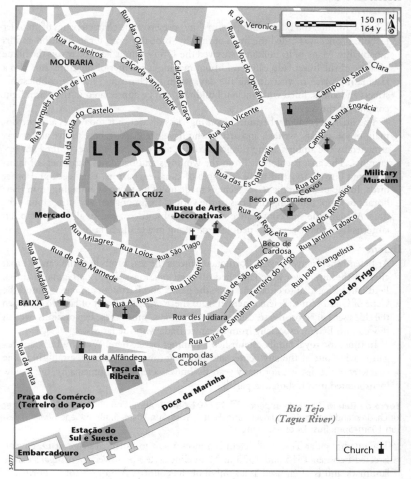

Inside the rough exterior are many treasures, including the font where St. Anthony of Padua is said to have been christened in 1195. A visit to the sacristy and cloister requires a guide. The cloister, built in the 14th century by King Dinis, is of ogival construction, with garlands, a romanesque wrought-iron grille, and tombs with inscription stones. In the sacristy are housed marbles, relics, valuable images, and pieces of ecclesiastical treasure from the 15th and 16th centuries.

Museu Antoniano. Largo de Santo António de Sé. ☎ **01/868-04-47.** Admission 160$ ($1.05). Tues–Sun 10am–1pm and 1–6pm. Metro: Rossio. Bus: 37. Tram: 28 or 28B.

St. Anthony of Padua, an itinerant Franciscan monk who became the patron saint of Portugal, was born in 1195 in a house that once stood here. The original church was destroyed by the 1755 earthquake, and the present building was designed by Mateus Vicente in the 18th century. In the crypt, a guide will show you the spot where the saint was allegedly born. He is buried in Padua, Italy. The devout come to this little church to light candles under his picture. He is known as a protector of young brides and also has a special connection with the children of Lisbon.

The Bairro Alto

Like the Alfama, the Bairro Alto (Upper City) preserves the characteristics of an older Lisbon. It once was called the heart of the city, probably both for its location and its inhabitants. Many of its buildings survived the 1755 earthquake. Today it is the home of some of the finest fado cafes in Lisbon, making it a center of nightlife. It is also a fascinating place to visit during the day, when its charming, narrow cobblestone streets and alleys, lined with ancient buildings, can be appreciated in the warm light coming off the sea.

The quarter gradually became a working-class district, but today it is also the domain of journalists, writers, and artists who have been drawn here to live and work, attracted by the ambience and the good cuisine and reasonable prices of the local restaurants. The area is colorful. From the windows and balconies, streamers of laundry hang out to dry, and there are cages of canaries, parrots, parakeets, and other birds. In the morning the street scene is made up of housewives emerging from their homes to shop, following the cries of the varinas (fishmongers) and other food vendors. At night the area comes alive with fado clubs, discos, and small bars, Victorian lanterns light the streets, and people stroll along in a leisurely fashion.

Belém

At Belém, the Tagus (*Tejo* in Portuguese) meets the sea. From here the caravels that charted the unknown were launched on their missions: Vasco da Gama to India, Ferdinand Magellan to circumnavigate the globe, and Bartolomeu Dias to round the Cape of Good Hope. Belém emerged from the *Restelo,* the point of land from which the ships set sail across the so-called Sea of Darkness. From these explorations, wealth flowed into Belém, especially from the spice trade with the far east.

In time, the royal family established a summer palace here. Wealthy Lisboans began moving out of the city center and building town houses here, establishing the character of the district. For many years Belém was a separate municipality, but is now incorporated into Lisbon as a parish.

Torre de Belém. Praça do Imperio. ☎ **01/301-68-92.** Admission 400$ ($2.65) adults, free for children and seniors 65 and over. June–Sept 3, Tues–Sun 10am–6:30pm; Sept 4–May, Tues–Sun 10am–5pm. Bus: 14 or 43. Tram: 15.

The quadrangular Tower of Belém is a monument to Portugal's Age of Discovery. Erected between 1515 and 1520 in Manueline style, the tower is Portugal's classic landmark and is often used as a symbol of the country. A monument to Portugal's great military and naval past, the tower stands on or near the spot where the caravels once set out across the sea. Its architect, Francisco de Arruda, blended gothic and Moorish elements, using such architectural details as twisting ropes carved of stone. The coat-of-arms of Manuel I rests above the loggia, and balconies grace three sides of the monument. Along the balustrade of the loggias, stone crosses symbolize the Portuguese Crusaders.

Padrão dos Descobrimentos (Memorial to the Discoveries). Praça da Boa Esperança. ☎ **01/301-62-20.** Free admission. Tues–Sun 9:30am–6:45pm. Bus: 27, 28, 43, or 49. Tram: 15 or 17.

Like the prow of a caravel from the Age of Discovery, this memorial stands on the Tagus, looking as if it's ready at any moment to strike out across the Sea of Darkness. Memorable explorers, chiefly Vasco da Gama, are immortalized in stone along the ramps. At the point where the two ramps meet stands a representation of Henry the Navigator, whose genius opened up new worlds. The memorial was unveiled in 1960, and one of the stone figures is that of a kneeling Philippa of Lancaster, Henry's

English mother. Other figures in the frieze symbolize Crusaders, navigators, monks, cartographers, and cosmographers.

✪ **Mosteiro dos Jerónimos (Jerónimos Monastery).** Praça do Império. ☎ **01/362-00-34.** Church, free. Cloisters, June–Sept, 400$ ($2.65); Oct–May, 250$ ($1.65); free for children and seniors 65 and over. June–Sept, Tues–Sun 10am–5pm; Oct–May, 10am–1pm and 2:50–5pm. Bus: 14 or 42. Tram: 15.

In an expansive mood of celebration, Manuel I, the Fortunate, ordered this monastery built in 1502 to commemorate Vasco da Gama's voyage to India and to give thanks to the Virgin Mary for its success. Manueline, the style of architecture to which the king contributed his name, combines flamboyant gothic and Moorish influences with elements of the nascent Renaissance in Portugal. The great 1755 earthquake damaged the monastery, and extensive restoration, some of it ill-conceived, was carried out.

The church interior is divided into a trio of naves, noted for their fragile-looking pillars. Some of the ceilings, like those in the monks' refectory, have a ribbed barrel vault. The "palm tree" in the sacristy is also exceptional.

Museu de Marinha (Maritime Museum). Praça do Império. ☎ **01/362-00-19.** June 15–Sept, 400$ ($2.65) adults, 200$ ($1.30) children; Oct–June 14, 300$ ($2) adults, 150$ ($1) children. Tues–Sun 10am–6pm. Bus: 29, 43, or 49. Tram: 15 or 17.

The pageant and the glory that characterized Portugal's domination of the high seas is evoked for posterity in the Maritime Museum, one of the most important in Europe. Appropriately, it's installed in the west wing of the Mosteiro dos Jerónimos. These royal galleys re-create an age of opulence that never feared excess. Dragon heads drip with gilt, and sea monsters coil with abandon.

The museum contains hundreds of models, from 15th-century sailing ships to 20th-century warships. In a special room is a model of the queen's stateroom on the royal yacht of Carlos I, the Bragança king who was assassinated at Praça do Comércio in 1908.

✪ **Museu Nacional dos Coches (National Coach Museum).** Praça Afonso de Albuquerque. ☎ **01/363-80-22.** June–Sept, 400$ ($2.65); Oct–May, 250$ ($1.65). Tues–Sun 10am–6pm. Closed holidays. Bus: 14 or 43. Tram: 15.

Visited by more tourists than any other attraction in Lisbon, the National Coach Museum is the finest of its type in the world. The coaches stand in a former 18th-century riding academy connected to the Belém Royal Palace; most date from the 17th to the 19th century. Of interest is a trio of opulently gilded baroque carriages once used by the Portuguese ambassador to the Vatican at the time of Pope Clement XI (1716). Also displayed is a 17th-century coach in which the Spanish Hapsburg king, Phillip II, journeyed from Madrid to Lisbon to see his new possession.

Museu de Arte Popular (Folk Art Museum). Av. de Brasília. ☎ **01/301-12-82.** 300$ ($2), free for children 9 and under. Tues–Sun 10am–12:30pm and 2–5pm. Closed holidays. Bus: 14 or 40.

This is the most dramatic exhibition of the folk arts and customs of the Portuguese. The walls of the building are painted by contemporary artists, including Carlos Botelho, Eduardo Anahory, Estrêla Faria, Manuel Lapa, Paulo Ferreira, and Tomás de Melo. The 1948 establishment of the Folk Art Museum was a result of a campaign for ethnic revival directed by António Ferro. The collections—including ceramics, furniture, wickerwork, clothes, farm implements, and painting—are displayed in five rooms that correspond more or less to the provinces, each of which maintains its own distinct personality.

MORE ATTRACTIONS

⭘ **Museu Nacional de Arte Antiga (National Museum of Ancient Art).** Jardim 9 de Abril. ☎ **01/396-41-51.** Admission 500$ ($3.30) adults, 250$ ($1.65) students, free for children 13 and under. Tues–Sun 10am–1pm and 2–5pm. Tram: Alcântara. Bus: 27, 40, 49, or 60.

The National Museum of Ancient Art occupies two connected buildings: a 17th-century palace and an added edifice that was built on the site of the old Carmelite Convent of Santo Alberto.

The museum has many notable paintings, including the famous polyptych from St. Vincent's monastery attributed to Nuno Gonçalves between 1460 and 1470. Outstanding works are Hieronymus Bosch's triptych *The Temptation of St. Anthony;* Hans Memling's *Mother and Child;* Albrecht Dürer's *St. Jerome;* and paintings by Velázquez, Zurbarán, Poussin, and Courbet. Paintings from the 15th through the 19th century trace the development of Portuguese art. The museum also exhibits a remarkable collection of gold- and silversmiths' work.

⭐ **Museu Calouste Gulbenkian.** Av. de Berna 45A. ☎ **01/795-02-41.** Admission 500$ ($3.30), free for children 9 and under and for seniors 65 and over, free for everyone on Sun. June–Sept, Tues–Wed, Fri, and Sun 10am–5pm; Thurs and Sat 2–7:30pm. Metro: Sebastião or Palhava. Tram: 24. Bus: 16, 18, 26, 31, 42, 46, or 56.

Opened in 1969, this museum, part of the Fundação Calouste Gulbenkian, houses what one critic called "one of the world's finest private art collections." It was deeded by the Armenian oil tycoon Calouste Gulbenkian, who died in 1955.

The collection covers Egyptian, Greek, and Roman antiquities; a remarkable set of Islamic art, and vases, prints, and lacquerwork from China and Japan. The European displays include medieval illuminated manuscripts and ivories, 15th- to 19th-century painting and sculpture, important collections of 18th-century French decorative works, French impressionist painting, and Lalique jewelry and glassware. Notable are Gulbenkian's two Rembrandts, Rubens's *Portrait of Hélène Fourment,* and *Portrait of Madame Claude Monet* by Pierre-Auguste Renoir.

ORGANIZED TOURS

Three tour operators run bus tours through Lisbon. Prices and the tours available at all three are remarkably similar. Tickets are sold at the reception desks of virtually every hotel in Lisbon, and buses often stop at prominent hotels to pick up passengers. Buses also depart from the upper end of Avenida Sidonio País, in the Parque Eduardo VII.

The most popular tour is a 3-hour City Tour of Lisbon, that includes stops at St. George's Castle and Belém. The tour departs daily at 9:30am and 2:30pm, and costs 4,900$ ($32.35) per person. You can also take a tour of some of Lisbon's far-flung, and richly historic, suburbs—Mafra, Sintra, and Estoril. This half-day excursion, which includes lunch, costs 12,900$ ($85.15) per person and departs daily at 9:30am.

SHOPPING

Baixa, between the Rossio and the River Tagus, is a major shopping area. Rua do Ouro (Street of Gold), Rua da Prata, and Rua Augusta are Lisbon's three principal shopping streets. Another major upscale shopping artery is Rua Garrett, in the Chiado; to reach the area, you can take the Santa Justa elevator near the Rossio.

The most unusual buys in Lisbon are *Asulejos,* the decorated glazed tiles that are sought by collectors, and pottery from all over Portugal. Pottery with brightly colored roosters from Barcelos is legendary. Blue-and-white pottery is made in Coimbra.

Our favorites come from Caldas da Rainha, including yellow-and-green dishes in the shape of vegetables, fruit, and animals. Vila Real is known for its black pottery, and polychrome pottery comes from Aceiro. The red-clay pots from the Alentejo region are based on designs that go back to the Etruscans.

One of the very best buys in Portugal is gold. Gold is strictly regulated by the government, which requires jewelers to put a minimum of $19^1/4$ karats in the jewelry they sell. Filigree jewelry, made of fine gold or silver wire, is an art that dates back to ancient times.

Along both sides of narrow **Rua de S. José** are treasure troves of shops packed with antiques from all over the world. **Rua Dom Pedro V** is another street of antiques shops; our personal favorite is **Solar** at no. 68–70 (☎ **01/346-55-22**), stocked with antique tiles salvaged from some of Portugal's historic buildings and manor houses.

Near the Ritz Hotel, the **Galleria Sesimbra,** Rua Castilho 77 (☎ **01/387-02-91**), is a top art gallery, mainly displaying Portugese artists.

✪ **Casa Quintão,** Rua do Alecrim, 115 (☎ **01/346-58-37**), is the showcase for Arraiolos carpets. Rugs sold here are priced by the square foot, according to the density of the stitching. Casa Quintão can reproduce intricate oriental or medieval designs in rugs or tapestries as well as create any customized pattern. The shop, dating from 1880, also sells materials and gives instructions on how to make your own carpets and tapestry-covered pillows.

✪ **Vista Alegre,** Largo do Chiado 18 (☎ **01/347-54-81**), turns out some of the finest porcelain dinner services in the country, along with objets d'art and limited editions for collectors and a range of practical day-to-day tableware.

For something typically Portuguese, try **Casa das Cortiças,** Rua da Escola Politécnica 4–6 (☎ **01/342-58-58**). "Mr. Cork," the original owner, became somewhat of a legend in Lisbon for offering "everything conceivable" that could be made of cork, of which Portugal controls a hefty part of the world market. He's long gone now, but the store carries on.

Situated in the same building as the Hotel Avenida Palace, **Casa Bordados da Madeira,** Rua 1 de Dezembro 135–139 (☎ **01/342-14-47**), offers handmade embroideries from Madeira, Viana, and Lixa e Prado. If you wish to place an order, the staff will mail it to you. And the specialty of **Casa Regional da Ilha Verde,** Rua Paiva de Andrade 4 (☎ **01/342-59-74**), is handmade items, especially embroideries from the Azores—that's why it's called the "Regional House of the Green Island." You can get some good buys here. **Madeira House,** Rua Augusta 131–135 (☎ **01/342-68-13**), specializes in regional, high-quality cottons, linens, and gift items.

If you're looking for fado recordings, **Valentim de Carvalho,** Rossio 57 (☎ **01/342-58-95**), is the largest outlet in Portugal for records and tapes, with a staggering collection of fado music. If an artist ever was even remotely known for his or her fado sounds, chances are high that this store will have it in at least one version, and sometimes in several.

At the **Feira da Ladra,** you can experience the fun of haggling for bargains at an open-air street market. The vendors peddle their wares on Tuesday and Saturday. About a 5-minute walk from the waterfront in the Alfama district, the market sits behind the Maritime Museum, adjoining the Pantheon of São Vicente. Start your browsing at Campo de Santa Clara. Portable stalls and individual displays are lined up on this hilly street with its tree-lined center.

Well on its way to being a century old, the **Joalharia do Carmo,** Rua do Carmo 87B (☎ **01/342-42-00**), is one of the best shops in Lisbon for gold filigree work. **W. A. Sarmento,** Rua Áurea 251 (☎ **01/342-67-74**), are the most distinguished silver- and goldsmiths in Portugal, specializing in lacy filigree jewelry, including charm bracelets.

Founded in 1741 in the Chiado district, ✪ **Sant'Anna,** Rua do Alecrim 95–97 (☎ **01/342-25-37**), is Portugal's leading ceramic center, famous for its *azulejos* (glazed tiles). The showroom is on Rua do Alecrim, but you can also visit the factory at Calçada da Boa Hora 96; however, you must telephone ahead to make an appointment at 01/363-31-17.

LISBON AFTER DARK

Consult *What's On in Lisbon,* available at most newsstands, for the latest listings. The local newspaper, *Diário de Notícias,* also carries cultural listings, but in Portuguese. No special discount tickets are offered, except that students get 50% off on tickets purchased for the national theater.

THE PERFORMING ARTS

The **Teatro Nacional de São Carlos,** Rua Serpa Pinto 9 (☎ **01/346-59-14**), attracts opera and ballet aficionados from all over Europe. Top companies from around the world perform at this 18th-century theater. The season begins in mid-September and extends through July.

From October to June, concerts, recitals, and occasionally ballet are performed at the **Museu da Fundação Calouste Gulbenkian,** Av. de Berna 45 (☎ **01/793-51-31**); sometimes there are also jazz concerts. There are also chamber-music and symphony concerts and ballet presented at the **Teatro Municipal de São Luís,** Rua António Maria Cardoso 40 (☎ **01/342-71-72**).

FADO CLUBS

Fado is Portugal's most vivid art form; no visit to Lisbon is complete without at least one night in one of the taverns where this traditional music is heard. Fado is typically sung by women, called *fadistas,* accompanied by guitar and viola. The songs express the mood of romantic longing and sadness, *saudade,* the country's sense of nostalgia for the past.

Adega Machado. Rua do Norte 91. ☎ **01/346-00-95.** Cover (including two drinks) 2,500$ ($16.50).

This spot has passed the test of time and is still one of Portugal's favored fado clubs. Alternating with the fadistas are folk dancers whirling, clapping, and singing their native songs in colorful costumes. Dinner is à la carte, and the cuisine is mostly Portuguese, with a number of regional dishes. Dining starts at 8pm, and the doors don't close until 2am. The first show starts at 9:15pm. Open daily (closed Mon Nov–Mar).

A Severa. Rua das Gaveas 51. ☎ **01/346-40-06.** Cover (including two drinks) 3,500$ ($23.10). Bus: 58.

Every night top fadistas sing, both male and female, alternating with folk dancers. In a niche you'll spot a statue honoring the club's namesake, Maria Severa, the legendary 19th-century Gypsy fadista who made fado famous. The kitchen turns out regional dishes based on recipes from the north of Portugal. Open Fri–Wed 8pm–3:30am.

Lisboa a Noite. Rua das Gaveas 69. ☎ **01/346-85-57.** Cover (including two drinks) 2,750$ ($18.15). Tram: 20 or 24. Bus: 15 or 100.

Try to catch the tempestuous Fernanda Maria, the club's owner, when she's about to make her first appearance of the evening. The 17th-century-style setting is rustic yet luxurious (this Bairro Alto club was once a stable). In the rear is an open kitchen and charcoal grill. Open Mon–Sat 8pm–3am; shows begin at 9:30pm.

Parreirinha da Alfama. Beco do Espirito Santo 1. ☎ **01/886-82-09.** Cover (credited toward drinks) 2,000$ ($13.20). Tram: 5. Bus: 105.

Seemingly every fadista worth her shawl has sung at this old-time cafe, just a minute's walk from the docks of the Alfama. It's fado and fado only here, not folk dancing. Open daily 8:30pm–2:30am. In the first part of the program, fadistas get all the popular songs out of the way, then settle in to their more classic favorites.

PORT-WINE TASTING

Solar do Vinho do Porto. Rua de São Pedro de Alcântara 45. ☎ **01/347-57-07.** Bus: 15 or 100.

A bar devoted exclusively to the drinking and enjoyment of port in all its known types, Solar lies near the Bairro Alto and its fado clubs. You enter what appears to be a private living room that offers a relaxing atmosphere enhanced by an open stone fireplace. Owned and sponsored by the Port Wine Institute, Solar displays many artifacts related to the industry. But the real reason for dropping in here during the day is for its *lista de vinhos*—there are nearly 150 wines from which to choose. Solar is about 50 feet from the upper terminus of the Gloria funicular.

A glass of wine costs 150$–1,900$ ($1–$12.55). AE, MC, V. It's open Mon–Fri 10am–11:30pm, Sat 11am–10:30pm.

DANCE CLUBS

The Bar of the Café Alcântara/Disco Alcântara Mar. Rua Maria Luisa Holstein 15. ☎ **01/363-71-76.** Cover 6,000$ ($39.60) for nondiners, 2,000$ ($13.20) for patrons of the Café Alcântara. Bus: 57 or 90.

Although the sophisticated restaurant draws many visitors (see above), many people come here for its bar and its dance club. The bar is long and curvy, with the accessories you might have expected in a railway car pulling into turn-of-the-century Paris. Draft beer in both the bar and the dance club begins at 500$ ($3.30); imported whisky costs 900$ ($5.95) and up.

The entertainment continues for anyone adventurous enough to cross an interior footbridge into the Disco Alcântara Mar, an all-green, high-tech enclave of American disco music and energetic night owls. The bar is open nightly 8pm–3 or 4am; the dance club, Wed–Sun midnight–8am.

The Garage. Rua João de Oliveira Miguéns 38 and 40, Alcântara. ☎ **01/395-59-77.** Cover (including two beers or one whisky) 1,000$–5,500$ ($6.60–$36.30). Bus: 32 or 37.

Set one floor above street level in a dingy-looking and rather old riverside warehouse, above the Restaurant Paraiso, this club caters to a dance-a-mania crowd of young Europeans who appreciate the House and (you guessed it) Garage-style music that's preferred by the DJs. The disco is open Tues and Fri–Sat midnight–6am. Other nights it's a venue for live concerts by rock 'n' roll and punk-rock artists from Britain, the United States, and Iberia.

Kremlin. Escadinhas da Praia 5. ☎ **01/395-71-01.** Cover 1,000$ ($6.60). Bus: 27, 32, or 49. Tram: 15.

Kremlin, the most energetic and iconoclastic of Lisbon's discos, welcomes a very hip crowd of techno-music lovers. The decor changes about once a month. Beer costs 600$ ($3.95); a whisky with soda goes for 1,000$ ($6.60). Open Tues (rock 'n' roll night) and Thurs–Sat ("house" music).

THE BAR SCENE

In addition to being a restaurant, **Bachus,** Largo da Trindade 9 (☎ 01/342-28-28), offers one of the capital's most convivial watering spots. In a setting filled with oriental carpets, fine hardwoods, bronze statues, intimate lighting, and very polite uniformed waiters, you can hobnob with some of the most glamorous people in Lisbon. Late-night candlelit suppers are served in the bar.

A Polynesian bar might seem out of context in Lisbon, but its concept is all the rage in Iberia these days. **Bora-Bora,** Rua da Madalena 201 (☎ 01/887-20-43), serves imaginative variations on fruited, flaming, and rum-laced drinks. The couches are comfortable and inviting.

The **Panorama Bar,** in the Lisboa Sheraton Hotel, Rua Latino Coelho 1 (☎ 01/357-57-57), occupies the top floor of one of Portugal's tallest buildings, the 30-story Lisboa Sheraton. The view features the old and new cities of Lisbon, the mighty Tagus, and many towns on the river's far bank. Amid a decor of chiseled stone and stained glass, a polite uniformed staff will serve you.

A longtime favorite of journalists, politicians, and foreign actors, the once-innovative **Procópio Bar,** Alto de San Francisco 21A (☎ 01/385-28-51), has become a tried-and-true staple among Lisbon's watering holes. It might easily become your favorite bar—if you can find it. It lies just off Rua de João Penha, which itself lies off the landmark Praça das Amoreiras. It's closed Aug 13–Sept 1.

Gay & Lesbian Bars

Since the collapse of Salazar and the new openness of Lisbon nightlife, at least eight gay bars have sprung up in the district known as Príncipe Real.

In the narrow streets of the Bairro Alto, **Memorial,** Rua Gustavo de Matos Sequeira 42 (☎ 01/396-88-91), is a "household word" for dozens of lesbians, who consider it one of the premier networking sites for gay women in Portugal. This small and rather cramped disco with ample bar space welcomes newcomers. There's an occasional round of live entertainment; otherwise, the place is low-key and unpretentious.

Agua No Bico Bar, Rua de São Marçal 170 (☎ 01/347-28-30), is the premier bar in a neighborhood known for many gay bars. This dark pink watering hole is lined with movie posters and filled mainly with men. You won't see any sign out in front—instead, there's a discreet brass plaque set on a steeply sloping street lined with dignified 18th-century villas. Recorded music plays in a format that might remind you—because of its lack of a dance floor—of an English pub.

DAY TRIPS FROM LISBON

The environs of Lisbon are so intriguing that many fail to see the capital itself, lured by Guincho (near the westernmost point in continental Europe), the Mouth of Hell, and Lord Byron's "glorious Eden" at Sintra. A day could be spent drinking in the wonders of the pretty pink rococo palace at Queluz, or enjoying seafood at the Atlantic beach resort of Cascais.

COSTA DO SOL: THE PORTUGUESE RIVIERA   The chief magnet is the Costa do Sol, the string of beach resorts, such as Estoril and Cascais, that form the Portuguese Riviera on the northern bank of the mouth of the Tagus. If you arrive in Lisbon when the sun is shining and the air is balmy, you should consider heading for this cabana-studded shoreline. So near to Lisbon is Estoril that it's easy to dart in and out of the capital to see the sights or visit the fado clubs, while you spend your nights in a hotel by the sea. An inexpensive electric train leaving from the Cais do Sodré in Lisbon makes the trip frequently throughout the day and evening, ending its run in Cascais.

The Riviera is a microcosm of Portugal. Ride out on the train, even if you don't plan to stay there. Along the way you'll pass pastel-washed houses, with red-tile roofs and facades of antique blue and white tiles; miles of modern apartment dwellings; rows of canna, pines, mimosa, and eucalyptus; swimming pools; and in the background, green hills studded with villas, chalets, and new homes. The sun coast is sometimes known as A Costa dos Reis, "the coast of kings," because of all the deposed royalty who have settled there—everybody from exiled kings to pretenders, marquesses from Italy, princesses from Russia, and baronesses from Germany.

Estoril   The first stop here is 15 miles west of Lisbon. This chic resort has long basked in its reputation as a playground of monarchs.

The **Parque Estoril**, in the town center, is a well-manicured piece of landscaping, a subtropical setting with plants swaying in the breeze. At night, when it's floodlit, guests go for a stroll. The palm trees studding the grounds have prompted many to call it "a corner of Africa." At the top of the park sits the **casino,** offering not only gambling but also international floor shows, dancing, and movies.

Across the railroad tracks is the beach, where some of Europe's most fashionable women sun themselves on the peppermint-striped canvas chairs along the Tamariz Esplanade. The atmosphere is cosmopolitan and the beach sandy, unlike the pebbly strand at Nice. If you don't want to swim in the polluted ocean, you can check in at an oceanfront pool for a plunge instead.

Cascais   Just 4 miles west of Estoril and 19 miles west of Lisbon, Cascais has more of a Portuguese atmosphere than Estoril, even though it has been increasingly overbuilt. That Cascais is growing is an understatement: It's leapfrogging! Apartment houses, new hotels, and the finest restaurants along the Costa do Sol draw a never-ending stream of visitors every year.

However, the life of the simple fisher folk still goes on. Auctions, called *lotas,* at which the latest catch is sold, still take place on the main square, although a modern hotel has sprouted up in the background. In the small harbor, rainbow-colored fishing boats must share space with pleasure craft owned by an international set that flocks to Cascais from early spring until autumn.

The most popular excursion outside Cascais is to ✪ **Boca de Inferno** (Mouth of Hell). Reached by heading out the highway to Guincho, then turning left toward the sea, the Boca deserves its ferocious reputation. At their peak, thundering waves sweep in with such power and fury they long ago carved a wide hole, or *boca,* in the cliffs. However, if you should arrive when the sea is calm, you'll wonder why it's called a cauldron. The Mouth of Hell can be a windswept roar if you don't stumble over too many souvenir hawkers.

The three sandy beaches at Cascais are almost as overcrowded as those at Estoril, and the waters here are less polluted, but contaminated nonetheless. Hotel swimming pools remain the safer choice. Although there's a dangerous undertow for swimming, the best beach—at least from the standpoint of lying on the sands—is Praia do Guincho, around Cabo da Roca, right outside Cascais. The beach is duned and mostly uncrowded, and is relatively pollution free. The continental winds make it a favorite for surfers.

Queluz   At the Estação Rossio in Lisbon, take the Sintra line train 9 miles northwest of Lisbon to Queluz. Trains depart every 15 minutes, and the trip takes half an hour. After getting off at Queluz, take a left turn and follow the signs for half a mile to the **Palácio de Queluz,** Largo do Palácio (☎ **01/435-00-39**), a brilliant example of the rococo in Portugal. Pedro III ordered its construction in 1747, and the work dragged on until 1787. What you see now is not exactly what it was in the 18th century. Queluz suffered a lot during the French invasions, and almost all its belongings were transported to Brazil with the royal family. A 1934 fire destroyed a great deal of Queluz, but tasteful and sensitive reconstruction has restored the lighthearted aura of the 18th century. Inside, you can wander through the queen's dressing room, lined with painted panels depicting a children's romp; through the Don Quixote Chamber (Dom Pedro was born here and returned from Brazil to die in the same bed); through the Music Room, complete with a French grande pianoforte and an 18th-century English harpsichord; and through the mirrored throne room adorned with crystal chandeliers. Festooning the palace are all the eclectic props of the rococo era including the inevitable chinoiserie panels. The palace is open Wed–Mon (except holidays) 10am–1pm and 2–5pm. Admission is 470$ ($3.10) June–Sept, 260$ ($1.70) Oct–May; free for children, and free for everyone on Sunday morning.

Sintra Sintra, 18 miles northwest of Lisbon, is a 45-minute train ride from the Estação Rossio at the Rossio in Lisbon. Lord Byron called it a "glorious Eden," and so it remains. Visitors flock here not only to absorb the town's beauty and scenic setting, but also to visit two major sights.

The ✪ **Palácio Nacional de Sintra,** Largo da Rainha D. Amélia (☎ 01/923-41-18), was a royal palace until 1910. Much of the palace was constructed in the days of the first Manuel, the Fortunate. The palace opens onto the central town square. Outside, two conical chimney towers form the most distinctive landmark on the Sintra skyline. The Swan Room was a favorite of João I, one of the founding kings, father of Henry the Navigator and husband of Philippa of Lancaster. The Room of the Sirens or Mermaids is one of the most elegant in the palace. In the Heraldic or Stag Room, coats-of-arms of aristocratic Portuguese families and hunting scenes are depicted. The palace is rich in paintings and Iberian and Flemish tapestries. But it's at its best when you wander into a tree- and plant-shaded patio and listen to the water of a fountain. Admission is 475$ ($3.15) June–Sept, 260$ ($1.70) Oct–May. The palace is open Thurs–Tues 10am–1pm and 2–5pm.

Towering over Sintra, the **Palácio Nacional da Pena,** Estrada de Pena (☎ 01/923-02-27), sits on a plateau about 1,500 feet above sea level. At the top the castle is a soaring agglomeration of towers, cupolas, and battlemented walls. Crossing over a drawbridge, you'll enter the palace proper, whose last royal occupant was Queen Amélia in 1910. Pena has remained much as Amélia left it, which is part of its fascination; it emerges as a rare record of European royal life in the halcyon days preceding World War I. Admission is 475$ ($3.15) June–Sept, 260$ ($1.70) Oct–May; free for children 9 and under. It's open Tues–Fri 10am–5pm and Sat–Sun 10am–1pm and 2–5pm.

2 The Algarve

The maritime province of the Algarve, often called the "garden of Portugal," is the southwesternmost part of Europe. Its coastline stretches 100 miles—all the way from Henry the Navigator's Cape St. Vincent to the border town of Vila Real de Santo António, fronting Spain. The varied coastline contains sluggish estuaries, sheltered lagoons, low-lying areas where the cluck of the marsh hen can be heard, long sandy spits, and promontories jutting out into the white-capped aquamarine foam.

Called Al-Gharb by the Moors, the land south of the *serras* (hills) of Monchique and Caldeirão remains a spectacular anomaly that seems more like a transplanted section of the North African coastline. The winter temperature averages around 60°F, increasing to an average of 74°F in summer. The countryside abounds in vegetation: almonds, lemons, oranges, carobs, pomegranates, and figs.

Many Moorish and even Roman ruins remain. In the character of its fret-cut chimneys, mosquelike cupolas, and cubist houses, a distinct oriental flavor prevails. Phoenicians, Greeks, Romans, Visigoths, Moors, and Christians all touched this land. However, much of the historic flavor is gone forever, swallowed by a sea of dreary high-rise apartment blocks surrounding most towns.

Many former fishing villages—now summer resorts—dot the Algarvian coast: Carvoeiro, Albufeira, Olhão, Portimão. The sea is still the source of life, as it always has been. The marketplaces in the Algarvian villages sell esparto mats, copperwork, pottery, and almond and fig sweets that are sometimes shaped like birds and fish.

Our tour stretches along the coast, beginning at Lagos, which is 164 miles south of Lisbon and 21 miles east of the most southwestern point of Sagres. From Sagres the road to Lagos (N125) generally has little traffic, unlike the rest of the Algarve.

ONLY IN THE ALGARVE

Seeing the Almond Blossoms of the Algarve   There's no more dramatic sight in Portugal than the burgeoning white almond blossoms that bloom and blanket the Algarve in late January and early February. Legend says that a vizier who married a Nordic princess ordered the trees planted to remind his homesick bride of the snow-covered hills and valleys of her native land.

Experiencing Algarvian Beach Life   The coast is dotted with literally hundreds of beaches—the finest in Portugal. The best cove beaches are at Lagos, especially Praia Dona Ana, and at Albufeira. Praia da Rocha, a creamy-yellow beach, has become the most popular seaside resort in the Algarve, and Praia dos Três Irmãos offers 9 miles of burnished sand lying 3 miles southwest of Portimão.

Visiting Sagres   This is Portugal's southwesternmost point. Once at Sagres, a dramatic promontory, Cabo de São Vicente, lies but 4 miles away, forming a rugged landscape. Ancients believed it was the meeting place of the gods, and Prince Henry the Navigator established a school of geography and navigation here.

Golfing in the Algarve   Since around 1965 vast stretches of terrain have been bulldozed, landscaped, irrigated, and reconfigured into golf courses that stretch like strands in a necklace all along the coast. Many are associated with real-estate developments or major resorts, such as the 2,000-acre Quinta del Lago, where retirement villas nestle amid vegetation at the edges of the fairways. Most are open to qualified golfers who inquire in advance about tee times.

Seeking Out the Famous Chimneys   If you never thought that chimneys could excite you, you haven't seen the ones on the Algarve. The best parade of these chimneys is at Loulé, $9^1/_2$ miles north of Faro. From many of the houses and cottages here, these fret-cut plaster towers rise. They resemble fine lacework or filigree in stone; others are delicately contrived as forms of snow crystals blown against glass.

Discovering the Whitewashed Fishing Villages   Not many fishing villages remain, but of those that do, our favorite is Praia do Carvoeiro, 3 miles south of the wine-rich town of Lagoa. Now an expatriate colony, it offers a sandy beach nestled between two rock masses, creating a solarium. The shadows of the cliffs are cooling, the seas calm. East of the beach on a steep slope is a belvedere with a panoramic view. Nearby, you can explore Algar Seco, a collection of huge reddish stones carved by the sea into interesting shapes, plus a number of sea caves, often underwater. The local fishers will take you out in their boats.

LAGOS

Lagos, known to the Lusitanians and Romans as Locobriga and to the Moors as Zawaia, became a private, experimental shipyard of caravels during the time of Henry the Navigator. Edged by the Costa do Ouro (Golden Coast), the Bay of Sagres at one point in its epic history was big enough to allow 407 warships to maneuver with ease. An ancient port city (one historian traced its origins back to the Carthaginians 3 centuries before the birth of Christ), Lagos was well known by the sailors of Admiral Nelson's fleet.

Actually, not that much has changed since Nelson's day. The reasons to go to Lagos are to enjoy the pleasures of table and beach. In winter the almond blossoms match the whitecaps on the water and the climate is often warm enough for sunbathing. In town, the flea market sprawls through narrow streets, the vendors selling rattan baskets, earthenware pottery, fruits, vegetables, crude furniture, cutlery, knitted shawls, and leather boots.

Less than a mile down the coast, the hustle and bustle of market day is forgotten as the rocky headland of the Ponta da Piedade (Point of Piety) appears. This spot is the most beautiful on the entire coast. Amid the colorful cliffs and secret grottoes carved by the waves are the most flamboyant examples of Manueline architecture.

ESSENTIALS

ARRIVING   By Ferry & Train   From Lisbon, take the ferryboat at Praça do Comércio across the Tagus to Barreiro. There, connections to Lagos can be made on the Southern Line Railway. Five trains per day arrive from Lisbon, taking 6¹/₂ hours.

By Bus   Eight buses a day make the run between Lisbon and Lagos, taking 5 hours.

VISITOR INFORMATION   The **Lagos Tourist Office** is at Largo Marquês de Pombal (☎ **082/76-30-31**), open daily 9:30am–7pm.

WHAT TO SEE & DO

Igreja de Santo António (Church of St. Anthony). Rua Silva Lopes. Free admission. Daily 9am–5pm.

Just off the waterfront sits the 18th-century Church of St. Anthony. Decorating the altar are some of Portugal's most notable rococo gilt carvings. Begun in the 17th century, they were damaged in the 1755 earthquake but subsequently restored. What you see today represents the work of many artisans—at times, each of them apparently pursuing a different theme.

Museu Municipal Dr. José Formosinho (Municipal Museum). Rua General Alberto Carlos Silveira. ☎ **082/76-23-01.** Admission 200$ ($1.30). Tues–Sun 9:30am–12:30pm and 2–5pm. Closed holidays.

This museum contains replicas of the fret-cut chimneys of the Algarve, three-dimensional cork carvings, 16th-century vestments, ceramics, 17th-century embroidery, ecclesiastical sculpture, a painting gallery, weapons, minerals, and a numismatic collection. An oddity is a sort of believe-it-or-not section displaying, among other things, an eight-legged calf. In the archeological wing are Neolithic artifacts, along with Roman mosaics found at Boca do Rio near Budens, fragments of statuary and columns, and other remains of antiquity from excavations along the Algarve.

Antigo Mercado de Escravos (Old Customs House). Praça Infante Dom Henríques. Free admission. Open for viewing at any time.

The Algarve

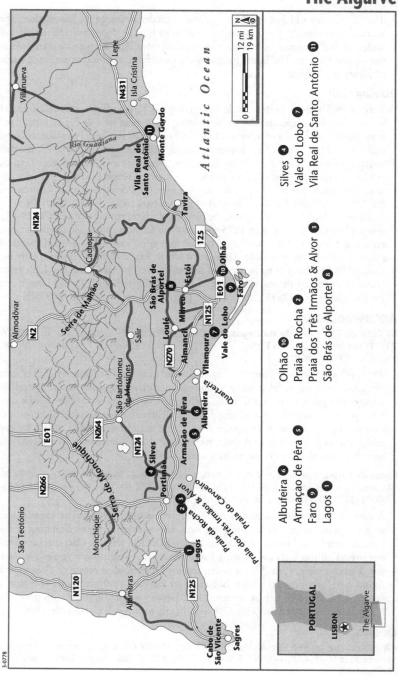

Albufeira **6**
Armação de Pêra **5**
Faro **9**
Lagos **1**

Olhão **10**
Praia da Rocha **2**
Praia dos Três Irmãos & Alvor **3**
São Brás de Alportel **8**

Silves **4**
Vale do Lobo **7**
Vila Real de Santo António **11**

The Old Customs House stands as a painful reminder of the Age of Exploration. The arcaded slave market, the only one of its kind in Europe, looks peaceful today, but under its four romanesque arches captives taken from their homelands were sold to the highest bidders. The house opens onto a peaceful square dominated by a statue of Henry the Navigator.

Playing Golf

Parque da Floresta, Budens, Vale do Poco, 8650 Vila do Bispo (☎ **082/65333**), is one of the few important Algarvian courses. It's 9 miles west of Lagos, just inland from the fishing hamlet of Salema. Designed by Spanish architect Pepe Gancedo and built as the centerpiece of a complex of holiday villas inaugurated in 1987, it offers sweeping views. Some shots must be driven over vineyards; others, over ravines, creeks, and gardens. Critics of the course have cited its rough grading and rocky terrain. The clubhouse offers a panoramic view over the Portuguese coast. Greens fees are 7,500$ ($49.50) for 18 holes; a set of golf clubs rents for 3,000$ ($19.80).

Some $2^1/_2$ miles west of Lagos is the par-71 **Palmares** course (☎ **082/76-29-61**), designed by Frank Pennink in 1975 with many differences in altitude. Some fairways require driving a ball across railroad tracks, over small ravines, or around groves of palms. Its landscaping is more evocative of North Africa than of Europe, partly because of its hundreds of palm, fig, and almond trees. The view from the 17th green is said to be among the most dramatic of any golf course on the Algarve. Greens fees for 18 holes are 7,700$ ($50.80); a set of golf clubs rents for 3,000$ ($19.80).

ACCOMMODATIONS

Ⓢ **Casa de São Gonçalo da Lagos.** Rua Cândido dos Reis 73, 8600 Lagos. ☎ **082/76-21-71.** Fax 082/76-39-27. 13 rms. TEL. 9,000$–12,000$ ($59.40–$79.20) double. AE, DC, MC, V. Closed Nov–Mar.

This pink villa, with its fancy iron balconies, dates to the 18th century. At the core of Lagos, the antiques-filled home is almost an undiscovered gem. Most of the public lounges and guest rooms turn, in the Iberian fashion, to the inward peace of a sun-filled patio. All furnishings are individualized: delicate hand-embroidered linens, period mahogany tables, silver candlesticks, chests with brass handles, inlaid tip-top tables, fine ornate beds from Angola, even crystal chandeliers. Street-level rooms can be very noisy. Modern amenities have been added.

Hotel de Lagos. Rua Nova da Aldeia 1, 8600 Lagos. ☎ **082/76-99-67.** Fax 082/76-99-20. 315 rms, 11 suites. MINIBAR TV TEL. 11,000$–19,000$ ($72.60–$125.40) double; 18,000$–27,000$ ($118.80–$178.20) suite. AE, DC, MC, V.

A 20th-century castle of Moorish and Portuguese design, the Hotel de Lagos has its own ramparts and moats (a swimming pool and a paddling pool). Standing at the eastern side of the old town, far removed from the beach, this first-class hotel is spread out over 3 hilltop acres overlooking Lagos; no matter which room you're assigned, you'll have a view, even if it's a courtyard with semitropical greenery. Some guest rooms have ground-level patios, but most are on the upper six floors; you have a choice of standard or deluxe rooms. The 31-room wing, complete with pool and health club, was added in 1989. The hotel has its own beach club a mile away.

DINING

Alpendre. Rua António Barbosa Viana 17. ☎ **082/76-27-05.** Reservations recommended. Main courses 900$–4,000$ ($5.95–$26.40). AE, DC, MC, V. Daily noon–11pm. Closed Nov. PORTUGUESE.

Alpendre offers one of the most elaborate and sophisticated menus along the Algarve, but, considering the lackluster competition, that's not saying too much. The food is tasty, but portions aren't large. Service tends to be slow, so don't come here if you're rushed. House specialties include peppersteak and filet of sole that's sautéed in butter, flambéed with cognac, and served with a sauce of cream, orange and lemon juices, vermouth, and seasonings known only to the chef.

PRAIA DA ROCHA

En route to Praia da Rocha, off N125 between Lagos and Portimão, 11 miles away, you'll find several good beaches and rocky coves, particularly at Praia dos Três Irmãos and Alvor. But the most popular seaside resort on the Algarve is the creamy-yellow beach of Praia da Rocha. At the outbreak of World War II there were only two small hotels on the Red Coast, but nowadays Praia da Rocha is booming, as many have been enchanted by the spell cast by its shoreline and climate.

It's named the Beach of the Rock because of its beautiful sculptural rock formations. At the end of the mussel-encrusted cliff, where the Arcade flows into the sea, are the ruins of the **Fort of St. Catarina,** whose location offers many views of Portimão's satellite, Ferragudo, and of the bay.

To reach Praia da Rocha from Portimão, you can catch a bus for the 1 1/2-mile trip south.

PLAYING GOLF

Vale de Pint / Quinta do Gramacho, Praia do Carvoeiro (☎ **082/34-09-00**), are twin par-71 courses, sharing a common clubhouse and staff. They're set amid a landscape of tawny-colored rocks and arid hillocks. Both of them route their players through groves of twisted olive, almond, carob, and fig trees. Views from the fairways, designed in 1992 by Californian Ronald Fream, sweep over the low masses of the Monchique mountains, close to the beach resort of Carvoeiro. Experts cite the layout of these two courses as one of the most varied set of challenges in the competitive world of Portuguese golf. Clusters of bunkers, barrier walls composed of beige-colored rocks assembled without mortar, and abrupt changes in elevation make the course complicated. On the premises are two recently opened golf academies, one of which is a branch of the David Ledbetter group, where 50-minute lessons range from 6,500$–12,500$ ($42.90–$82.50). Greens fees at either course are 9,000$ ($59.40) for 18 holes, 5,000$ ($33) for 9 holes; a set of clubs rents for 2,500$– 5,000$ ($16.50–$33), depending on how many holes you play.

ACCOMMODATIONS

✪ **Algarve Hotel.** Av. Tomás Cabreira, Praia da Rocha, 8500 Portimão. ☎ **082/41-50-01.** Fax 082/41-59-99. 198 rms, 16 suites. A/C MINIBAR TV TEL. 18,000$–39,000$ ($118.80– $257.40) double; 30,000$–69,000$ ($198–$455.40) suite. AE, DC, MC, V.

The resort's leading hotel is strictly for those who love glitter and don't object to the prices, which are much too high. With a vast staff at your beck and call, you'll be ensconced in luxury in an elongated block of rooms poised securely on the top ledge of a cliff. The main lounge is like a sultan's palace: gold-velvet chairs, oriental rugs, brass-and-teak screens, and deep sofas. Guest rooms have white walls, colored ceilings, intricate tile floors, mirrored entryways, balconies with garden furniture, and baths with separate showers. Portuguese chefs, with French backgrounds, provide gourmet meals on the à la carte menu served in either the Grill Azul or Das Amendoeiros. Facilities include a huge kidney-shaped heated pool (plus another pool for children), two tennis courts at the beach, a sun deck cantilevered over the cliff, and a sauna. In 1996 the hotel opened a casino.

Residencial Sol. Av. Tomás Cabreira 10, Praia da Rocha, 8500 Portimão. ☎ **082/24071.** Fax 082/41-71-99. 27 rms, 2 suites. TEL. Summer, 7,000$–7,8000$ ($46.20–$514.80) double;

8,500$ ($56.10) suite. Off-season, 4,000$–4,800$ ($26.40–$31.70) double; 6,800$ ($44.90) suite. Rates include breakfast. AE, DC, MC, V.

The painted concrete facade of this establishment appears somewhat bleak, in part because of its location near the noisy main street. In this case, however, appearances are deceiving, since the guest rooms offer some of the cleanest, most unpretentious, most attractive accommodations in town. Each unit is designed for two. The rooms in back are quieter, but the terrace-dotted front units look across the traffic toward a bougainvillea-filled park.

DINING

Bamboo Garden. In the Edifício Lamego, Loja (Shop) 1, Av. Tomás Cabreira. ☎ **082/83083.** Reservations recommended. Main courses 820$–1,950$ ($5.40–$12.85). AE, DC, MC, V. Daily noon–3pm and 6pm–midnight. CHINESE.

The Bamboo Garden, which has a classic Asian decor, has the best Chinese food along the coast. In air-conditioned comfort, diners can select from a large menu that includes everything from squid chop suey to prawns with hot sauce. You might prefer fried duck with soybean sauce or chicken with almonds from the Algarve. It doesn't equal restaurants in London or Paris, but it's a reliable haven when you've overdosed on Portuguese codfish.

PRAIA DOS TRÊS IRMÃOS & ALVOR

Portimão, the "Beach of the Three Brothers" has been discovered by skin divers who explore its undersea grottoes and shoreside cave.

Its neighbor is the whitewashed fishing village of **Alvor,** where Portuguese and Moorish arts and traditions have mingled since the Arabs gave up their 500 years of occupation. Alvor was a favorite coastal haunt of João II. The **Casino de Alvor,** with roulette, blackjack, and craps, is modest in size compared to the one at Estoril. A restaurant features good food and a nightly floor show at 11pm and 1am. From Portimão, you can reach either Praia dos Três Irmãos and Alvor by public buses that run frequently throughout the day.

PLAYING GOLF

Penina, Apartado 146 (☎ **082/41-54-15**), lies outside Portimão, farther west than many of the other great golf courses of the Algarve. Completed in 1966, it was one of the first golf courses here and the universally acknowledged masterpiece of British designer Sir Henry Cotton. It occupies what was once a network of marshy rice paddies, on level terrain that critics said was unsuited for anything except wetlands. The solution involved planting groves of eucalyptus (350,000 trees in all), which grew quickly in the muddy soil, eventually drying it out enough to bulldoze dozens of water traps and a labyrinth of fairways and greens. The course wraps itself around a luxury hotel (the Penina). Greens fees are 10,500$ ($69.30) for 18 holes; a set of golf clubs rents for 4,000$ ($26.40).

ACCOMMODATIONS

✪ **Alvor Praia.** Praia dos Três Irmãos, Alvor, 8500 Portimão. ☎ **082/45-89-00.** Fax 082/45-89-99. 182 rms, 17 suites. A/C MINIBAR TV TEL. Summer, 35,000$–47,500$ ($231–$313.50) double; from 62,000$ ($409.20) suite. Off-season, 13,100$–17,600$ ($86.45–$116.15) double; from 29,500$ ($194.70) suite. Rates include breakfast. AE, DC, MC, V.

This citadel of hedonism is so self-contained you may never stray from the premises. On a landscaped crest, the luxury hotel has many of its guest rooms and public rooms exposed to the ocean view, the gardens, and the free-form Olympic-size pool. Accommodations are decorated in a classically modern style; most contain oversize beds, long desk-and-chest combinations, and well-designed baths with double basins and lots of towels. Many rooms have private balconies where you can eat breakfast with a view of the Bay of Lagos. Rooms to avoid are those in the rear with so-so views, small balconies, and Murphy beds. The bilevel main dining room boasts three glass walls so every guest has an ocean view. The Grill Maisonette is your best bet. Facilities include a health club and an outdoor pool.

Le Meridien Penina Golf & Resort. Montes de Alvor, 8502 Portimão. ☎ **082/41-54-15.** Fax 082/41-50-00. 179 rms, 17 suites. A/C MINIBAR TV TEL. 26,000$–36,000$ ($171.60–$237.60) double; from 39,000$ ($257.40) suite. Children 3–13 stay free in parents' room. AE, DC, MC, V.

The first deluxe hotel on the Algarve was the Penina Golf & Resort, located between Portimão and Lagos. It's a major sporting mecca. Most guest rooms contain picture windows and honeycomb balconies, with views of the course and pool or vistas of the Monchique hills. The standard rooms are furnished pleasantly, combining traditional pieces with Portuguese provincial spool beds. All rooms are spacious and contain good-sized beds; the so-called attic rooms have the most charm, with French doors opening onto terraces. Guests can dine at any of the five on-site restaurants. Facilities include three championship golf courses (the 18-hole, the 9-hole Academy, and the 9-hole Resort), a private beach with its own snack bar and changing cabins reached by shuttle bus, a swimming pool, and six floodlit hard tennis courts.

DINING

Restaurante O Búzio. Aldeamento da Prainha, Praia dos Três Irmãos. ☎ **082/45-87-72.** Reservations required. Main courses 1,200$–2,750$ ($7.90–$18.15); fixed-price dinner 3,300$ ($21.80). AE, DC, MC, V. Daily noon–4pm and 7–10:30pm. INTERNATIONAL.

Restaurante O Búzio stands at the end of a road encircling a resort development dotted with exotic shrubbery. Lunch and dinner are served in separate locations. Lunch is offered on a shaded hillock overlooking a landscaped pool. For an entrance fee you can spend the rest of the day on its grassy lawns beside its waters. The real draw of the place, however, is after dark. Your dinner might include fish soup, carré de borrego Serra da Estrêla (grantinée of roast carré of lamb with garlic, butter, and mustard), Italian pasta dishes, boiled or grilled fish of the day, or pepper steak.

SILVES

To reach Silves from Portimão, take N125 east for 5 miles to Lagoa, a market town. This is the junction with the road (124) leading 4 1/2 miles north to Silves.

When you pass through the Moorish-inspired entrance of this hillside town, you'll quickly realize that Silves is unlike other Algarve towns and villages. It lives in the past, recalling its heyday when it was known as Xelb, the seat of Muslim culture in the south before it fell to the crusaders. Christian warriors and earthquakes have been rough on Silves.

EXPLORING SILVES

The red-sandstone **Castle of Silves,** crowning the hilltop, may date back to the 9th century. From its ramparts you can look down on the saffron-mossed tile roofs of the village houses, and on the narrow cobbled streets where roosters strut and scrappy dogs sleep peacefully in the doorways. Once the blood of the Muslims, staging their last stand in Silves, "flowed like red wine," as one Portuguese historian wrote, and the cries and screams of women and children resounded over the walls. Inside the walls, the government has planted a flower garden, adorning it with golden chrysanthemums and scarlet poinsettias. In the fortress, water rushes through a huge cistern and a deep well made of sandstone. Below are dungeon chambers and labyrinthine tunnels where the last of the Moors hid out before the crusaders found them and sent them to their deaths.

The 13th-century former **cathedral of Silves** (now a church), down below, was built in the gothic style. You can wander through its aisles and nave, noting the beauty in their simplicity. Both the chancel and the transept date from a later period, having been built in the flamboyant gothic style. The Christian architects who originally constructed it may have torn down an old mosque. Many of the tombs contained here are believed to have been the graves of crusaders who took the town in 1244. The structure is one of the most outstanding religious monuments in the Algarve.

DINING

Ladeira. Ladeira de São Pedro 1. ☎ **082/44-28-70.** Main courses 1,000$–1,500$ ($6.60–$9.90); tourist menu 1,400$ ($9.25). No credit cards. Mon–Sat noon–3pm and 6–10pm. PORTUGUESE.

This rustic restaurant is known to virtually everyone in its neighborhood on the western outskirts of Silves. It features grilled fish, home-cooking, and regional specialties. Steak Ladeira and mixed-fish cataplana (a local stew) are specials. In season, game such as partridge or rabbit is often served.

ARMAÇÃO DE PÊRA

From Silves, head 9 miles southeast along N125 and follow the signs to Alcantarilha, where you'll see the first signs pointing to Armação de Pêra, 5 miles away. The resort can also be reached by bus from Lisbon, a trip of about 4 hours, or by train to the village of Alcantarilha.

Squat fishers' cottages make up the core of this ancient village. It rests almost at water's edge on a curvy bay that comes near its Golden Beach, one of the largest along Portugal's southern coast. In the direction of Portimão are rolling low ridges, toward Albufeira's rosy cliffs. Because Armação de Pêra has such a fine beach, it has almost become engulfed in a sea of high-rise buildings, which have virtually eliminated its once rather charming character.

Once Armação de Pêra was utilized by the Phoenicians as a trading post and stopping-off point for cruises around Cape St. Vincent. Near the center of the village is a wide beach where fishing boats are drawn up on the sand when a fish auction (*lota*) is held.

While at the resort, you may want to walk out to **Nossa Senhora da Rocha** (Our Lady of the Rock), a romanesque chapel on a 95-foot-high stone that sticks out into the ocean like the prow of a boat. Underneath are the cathedral-size **sea grottos** (*furnas*). Unique in the Algarve, the sea caves are entered through a series of arches that frame the sky and ocean from the inside. In their galleries and vaults, where pigeons nest, the splashing and cooing reverberate in the upper stalactite-studded chambers.

The **tourist office,** on Avenida Marginal (☎ **082/32-13-94**), open Mon–Fri 9:30am–12:30pm and 2–5:30pm and Sat 9:30am–12:30pm, can provide advice about how to visit these sea caves. But basically all you need to do is walk down to any local beach and negotiate with a group of fishers to take you to the caves. There is no formal tour operator for this. A 2-hour excursion generally costs 2,000$ ($13.20) per person.

ACCOMMODATIONS

Hotel Viking. Praia da Nossa Senhora da Rocha, 8365 Armação de Pera. ☎ **082/31-48-76.** Fax 082/31-48-52. 96 rms, 90 suites. A/C MINIBAR TV TEL. Apr–Oct, 30,000$ ($198) double; 37,000$ ($244.20) suite. Nov–Mar, 10,000$ ($66) double; 12,800$ ($84.50) suite. Rates include breakfast. AE, DC, MC, V.

Set about a mile southwest of the resort, with many signs directing you, this hotel rises in a mass of gray stone and buff-colored concrete between two spits of land jutting into the sea. The hotel has comfortably contemporary bedrooms with wall-to-wall carpeting, marble-sheathed bathrooms, and private balconies angled toward a view of the sea. Drinking and dining choices include an English pub, a large cocktail bar leading into an enormous dining room, and a snack bar. There's also a replica of a 19th-century cafe set in a courtyard that's sheltered from the gusty wind of the Algarve. Facilities include tennis courts, a water sports staff, and a pair of clifftop swimming pools.

DINING

Panorama Sol Grill. Alporchinos. ☎ **082/31-24-24.** Reservations recommended. Main courses 700$–2,500$ ($4.60–$16.50). No credit cards. Daily noon–3pm and 6–10:30pm. PORTUGUESE/INTERNATIONAL.

Set on the road west of town leading to the Hotel Viking, this restaurant occupies a 150-year-old building that has been enlarged many times. The first seating you see is on an outdoor, walled-in terrace, but if you continue to climb past an outdoor grill to the top of the stairs, you'll find a baronial dining hall with its own stone fireplace and a relatively dignified ambience. The catch of the day, as well as an array of meats, is usually displayed in a refrigerated case as a testament to their freshness. Menu choices might include sea bass, fresh asparagus, giant prawns with garlic, and several preparations of beef, veal, and pork.

Santola. Largo 25 de Abril. ☎ **082/31-23-32.** Reservations recommended. Main courses 950$–5,800$ ($6.25–$38.30). AE, MC, V. Daily noon–3pm and 6:30–11pm. PORTUGUESE/SEAFOOD.

This popular restaurant was thriving back when Armação de Pêra was only a sleepy fishing village. "The Crab" specializes in very fresh fish dishes that always seem to focus with justifiable pride on a succulent version of cataplana, a local stew concocted with onions, tomatoes, shellfish, and fish. Other worthy choices include filets of hake in white sauce with mushrooms and shrimp, sea bass or monkfish in garlic sauce, and grilled swordfish. Grilled meats such as steak and filets of pork supplement the menu, and in wintertime a blazing fireplace alleviates the chilly dampness of the Algarvian winds.

ALBUFEIRA

The cliffside town of Albufeira, formerly a fishing village, is the St-Tropez of the Algarve. The lazy life, sunshine, and beaches make it a haven for young people and artists, although the old-timers still regard the invasion that began in the late 1960s with some ambivalence. Some residents open the doors of their cottages to those seeking a place to stay. Travelers without the money often sleep in tents on the cliff or under the sky.

The big, bustling resort retains characteristics more closely associated with a North African seaside community. Its streets are steep and the villas are staggered up and down the hillside. Albufeira rises above a sickle-shaped beach that shines in the bright sunlight. A rocky, grottoed bluff separates the strip used by the sunbathers from the working beach, where brightly painted fishing boats are drawn up on the sand. Beach access is through a passageway tunneled through the rock.

ESSENTIALS

ARRIVING   By Train   Trains connect Albufeira with Faro (see below), which has good connections to and from Lisbon. The train station lies 4 miles from the center, but frequent buses run back and forth from the station to the resort every 30 minutes.

By Bus   Buses run between Albufeira and Faro every hour; the trip takes 1 hour. Seven buses per day link Portimão with Albufeira, also a 1-hour trip.

By Car   Continue east from Armação de Pêra for 8¹/₂ miles along N125.

VISITOR INFORMATION   The **Tourist Information Office** is on Rua 5 de Outubro (☎ 089/51-21-44), open daily 9:30am–7pm.

ACCOMMODATIONS

Estalagem do Cerro. Rua Samora Barros, 8200 Albufeira. ☎ **089/58-61-91.** Fax 089/58-61-94. 95 rms. A/C TV TEL. Summer, 14,000$ ($92.40) double. Off-season, 11,000$ ($72.60) double. Rates include breakfast. AE, DC, MC, V.

The Estalagem do Cerro captures Algarvian charm yet doesn't neglect modern amenities. This "Inn of the Craggy Hill" is located ¹/₂ mile east of the center at the top of a hill overlooking Albufeira's bay, about a 10-minute walk down to the beach. An older, regional-style building has been recently renovated, but its character has been maintained, and it's joined to a modern structure in a similar Moorish style. The tastefully furnished guest rooms have verandas overlooking the sea, pool, or garden. A panoramic dining room provides good meals. On most nights, guests can dance to disco music, and fado and folklore shows are also presented. The inn has an outdoor heated pool in a garden setting.

Hotel Montechoro. Av. Dr. Francisco Sá Carneiro, Montechoro (Apartado 928), 8201 Albufeira. ☎ **089/58-94-23.** Fax 089/58-99-47. 302 rms, 40 suites. A/C TV TEL. Summer, 19,500$ ($128.70) double. Off-season, 13,000$ ($85.80) double. Rates include continental breakfast. AE, DC, MC, V.

This is the largest, and one of the best-accessorized, hotels in and around Albufeira, a four-star resort set in the vacation-oriented suburb of Montechoro, about a mile northeast of Albufeira's center. Bulky and angular, it evokes a holiday hotel in North Africa, but is large enough that you might get lost in its many facilities. The bedrooms are outfitted in a modern and somewhat streamlined style, opening onto views of the sunbaked surrounding countryside. The hotel's only drawback involves its lack of a beach adjacent to its grounds, although management supplies frequent minivans to both Oura Beach, about a mile away, and the bar-packed center of Albufeira. Dining choices include the Restaurant Montechoro and the more formal Grill das Amendoeiras, on the hotel's panoramic fifth floor. Facilities include two pools, eight professional tennis courts, two squash courts, a sauna, and a gymnasium.

DINING

O Cabaz da Praia. Praça Miguel Bombarda 7. ☎ **089/51-21-37.** Reservations recommended. Main courses 2,200$–3,800$ ($14.50–$25.10). AE, MC, V. Fri–Wed noon–2:30pm and 6:30–11pm. FRENCH/PORTUGUESE.

The 30-year old "Beach Basket," near the Hotel Sol e Mar, sits on a colorful little square near the Church of São Sebastião, which is now a museum. In a former fisher's cottage, the restaurant has an inviting ambience and good food. With its large, sheltered terrace, it offers diners a view over the main Albufeira beach. Main courses, including such favorites as cassoulet of seafood, salade océane, and papillotte of salmon, are served with fresh vegetables. The restaurant is renowned for its lemon meringue pie.

VALE DO LOBO

Almancil, 8 miles west of Faro and east along N125 from Albufeira, is a small market town of little tourist interest, yet is a center for two of the most exclusive tourist developments along the Algarve: Vale do Lobo, lying 4 miles southeast of Almancil, and Quinta do Lago, lying 6 miles southeast of town. Both are a golfer's paradise.

GOLF GALORE

The name **Vale do Lobo** (Valley of the Wolf) suggests some forlorn spot set amid bleak terrain. Hardly likely! The Vale, about a 20-minute drive from the Faro Airport, is the site of a golf course (☎ **089/39-44-44**) designed by Henry Cotton, the British champion. It contains a trio of 9-hole courses: the Green (par 35), the Orange (par 36), and the Yellow (par 36). They're played consecutively to produce 9-hole or 18-hole combinations. A fourth 9-hole course (the Blue) is envisioned for 1997. Many of its runs stretch over rocks and arid hills, often within view of olive and almond groves, the blue Atlantic, and the high-rise hotels of nearby Vilamoura and Quarteira. Some of the long shots (especially of the Yellow) require driving golf balls over two ravines, where variable winds and bunkers that have been called "ravenous" make this course particularly difficult. Greens fees are 12,000$ ($79.20) for 18 holes; a set of golf clubs rents for 3,000$ ($19.80). In addition, the tennis center here is among the best in Europe.

Since its opening in 1991, **Vila Sol,** Alto do Semino (☎ **089/30-21-44**), has been judged as having the best fairways and the boldest and most inventive contours of any golf course in the Algarve. Designed by English architect Donald Steel, it's part of a 362-acre residential estate. Great care was taken in allowing the terrain's natural contours to determine the layout of the fairways and greens. Despite its relative youth, Vila Sol was selected as host to the Portuguese Open 2 years in a row (1992 and 1993). Golfers especially praise the configuration of holes 6, 7, and 8, which collectively manage to funnel golf balls around and over ponds, creek beds, and pine groves in nerve-racking order. Its greens are impeccable. Par is 72. Greens fees for 18 holes are 13,500$ ($89.10); a set of golf clubs rents for 4,000$ ($26.40).

Vilamoura I, II, and III, Lusotur S.A. Club de Golf, Vilamoura (☎ **089/32-15-62**), have a layout and texture that's the most English of southern Portugal's golf courses, designed beginning in 1969 by the English architect Frank Pennink. The oldest and most verdant of the three, Vilamoura I (sometimes known as the "Old Course" in ways that mimic the ancient traditions of St. Andrews in Scotland) is lined with verdant stretches of trees and the need for accurate drives to avoid losing your ball in the forests that rise on either side of the fairways. The newest of the trio (Vilamoura III) was opened in the early 1990s and has begun to gain favor with golfers. All three of the sites are within a 10-minute drive of one another, but Vilamoura I has had a history of being closed for long and sometimes unpredictable periods of many months at a time. Greens fees, depending on the time of day and the course, range from 9,000$–12,000$ ($59.40–$79.20); golf clubs rent for 3,500$ ($23.10). Vilamoura I is a par-73 course; Vilamoura II and III are both par-72.

Quinta do Lago also has superb facilities and is one of the most elegant "tourist estates" on the Algarve. This pine-covered beachfront property has been the retreat of everybody from movie stars to European presidents. The resort's 27 superb holes of golf are also a potent lure.

Of the four golf courses that undulate across the massive Quinta do Lago development, the par-72 **São Lourenço** (San Lorenzo) (☎ **089/39-65-22**) is the most interesting and challenging. Set at the edge of the grassy wetlands of the Rio Formosa Nature Reserve, home to millions of waterfowl, it opened in 1988. Its contours were crafted by American golf designers William (Rocky) Roquemore and Joe Lee. Its most panoramic hole is the sixth; its most frustrating, the eighth. Many long drives, especially those aimed at the 17th and 18th holes, soar over the waters of a saltwater lagoon. Greens fees for 18 holes are 15,000$ ($99); a set of golf clubs rents for 4,000$ ($26.40).

Quinta do Lago (☎ **089/39-47-82**), the namesake course of the massive development, is actually composed of four 9-hole golf courses identified as A, B, C (designed in 1974 by American William Mitchell), and D (designed by American Joe Lee in 1989). Together they comprise more than 600 acres of sandy terrain that abuts the Rio Formosa Wildlife Sanctuary. Very few long drives here are over open water; instead, the fairways undulate through cork forests, groves of pine trees, and terrain with sometimes abrupt changes in elevation. Golfers can combine any of the course's four quadrants into different 18-hole combinations, all of which are par 72. Greens fees for 18 holes run 12,000$ ($79.20); a set of golf clubs rents for 4,250$ ($28.05).

Pinheiros Altos, Quinta do Lago (☎ **089/39-43-40**), is one of the most deceptive golf courses on the Algarve, with contours that even professional golfers cite as being far more difficult than appear at first glance. Abutting the wetland refuge of the Rio Formosa National Park, its 250 acres of terrain, designed by U.S. architect Ronald Fream, are dotted with umbrella pines and with dozens of small lakes at 9 of the course's 18 holes. Carts navigate their way around the terrain on cobble-covered paths whose construction techniques have changed very little in hundreds of years. Its par is 73. Greens fees are 12,000$ ($79.20) for 18 holes; a set of golf clubs rents for 4,000$ ($26.40).

ACCOMMODATIONS

✪ **Hotel Dona Filipa.** Vale de Lobo, 8136 Almancil. ☎ **089/39-41-41.** Fax 089/39-42-88. 147 rms, 9 junior suites, 6 deluxe suites. A/C MINIBAR TV TEL. 43,000$ ($283.80) double; 66,000$ ($435.60) junior suite; 95,000$ ($627) deluxe suite. AE, DC, MC, V.

A citadel of ostentatious living, the Dona Filipa is a deluxe golf hotel with impressive grounds that embrace 450 acres of rugged coastline. The hotel's exterior is comparatively uninspired, but a greater dimension was brought to the interior by Duarte Pinto Coelho, who installed green-silk banquettes, marble fireplaces, Portuguese ceramic lamps, and old prints over baroque-style love seats. The well-furnished guest rooms have balconies. The hotel includes a grill restaurant serving an à la carte menu and, by the pool, a coffee shop that serves lunch. Facilities include three tennis courts, a pool, and free greens fees at the São Lorenço Golf Course.

✪ **Quinta do Lago.** Quinta do Lago, 8135 Almancil. ☎ **800/223-6800** in the U.S., or 089/ 39-66-66. Fax 089/39-63-93. 132 rms, 9 suites. A/C MINIBAR TV TEL. 35,100$–61,300$ ($231.65–$404.60) double; from 75,000$ ($495) suite. AE, DC, MC, V.

A pocket of the high life since 1986, Quinta do Lago is a sprawling 1,600-acre estate beside the Rio Formosa estuary. The contemporary buildings in Mediterranean style rise three to six floors. The guest rooms are generally spacious, with tile or marble baths, and balconies open onto views of the estuary. The Navegadores is for both adults and children who prefer an informal grill room overlooking a pool. Facilities include a riding center, one of the best in southern Europe; a 27-hole golf course, designed by American William F. Mitchell, among the top six in Europe; tennis courts; indoor and outdoor pools; and a health club.

DINING

Casa Velha. Quinta do Lago. ☎ **089/39-49-83.** Reservations recommended. Main courses 2,500$–3,800$ ($16.50–$25.10). AE, MC, V. Mon–Sat 7–10:30pm. FRENCH.

Casa Velha is an excellent dining choice that's not part of the massive nearby Quinta do Lago resort. It overlooks the resort's lake from a century-old farmhouse. The menu is French, with a scattering of Portuguese and international dishes as well. Specialties include a salad of chicken livers and gizzards with leeks and vinaigrette, and roasted duck en service (the staff presents different parts of the bird throughout the meal, beginning with the thighs en confit and ending with the breast en magret). Other choices include carefully flavored preparations of sea bass, délices of sole, and rack or saddle of lamb persillé.

FARO

Once loved by the Romans and later by the Moors, Faro is the main city of the Algarve. Since Afonso III drove out the Moors for the last time in 1266, Faro has been Portuguese. On its outskirts an international jet airport brings in thousands of visitors every summer. The airport has done more than anything else to speed tourism not only to Faro but to the entire Algarve.

ESSENTIALS

ARRIVING   By Plane   You can fly to Faro from Lisbon in 30 minutes. For **flight information,** call **089/80-02-00.** You can take bus no. 16, 17, or 18 to the railway station in Faro. The bus operates daily 7:10am–7:56pm, leaving every 45 minutes.

By Train   Trains arrive from Lisbon six times a day. The trip takes 5 hours. For rail information in Faro, call the **train station** at Largo Estação (☎ **089/82-26-53**).

By Bus   Buses arrive seven times a day from Lisbon after a 7-hour journey. The **bus station** is on Avenida da República (☎ **089/80-37-92**).

By Car   After leaving Vale do Lobo, continue east along N125 directly into Faro.

VISITOR INFORMATION   The **Tourist Office** is at Rua da Misericórdia 8–12 (☎ **089/80-36-04**), open daily 9:30am–7pm. You can pick up a copy of *The Algarve Guide to Walks,* which will direct you to area nature trails.

WHAT TO SEE & DO

The most bizarre attraction in Faro is the **Capela d'Ossos** (Chapel of Bones), entered via a courtyard from the rear of the Igreja (Church) de Nossa Senhora do Monte do Carmo do Faro, on Largo do Carmo. Erected in the 19th century, this chapel is completely lined with the skulls and bones of human skeletons, an extraordinarily ossicular rococo. In all, it's estimated that there are 1,245 human skulls. It's open daily 10am–1pm and 3–5pm. Entrance is free.

Other religious monuments include the old **Sé** (cathedral), Largo da Sé, built in the gothic and Renaissance styles (originally a Muslim mosque stood on this site); and the **Igreja de São Francisco,** Largo de São Francisco, with panels of glazed earthenware tiles in milk white and Dutch blue depicting the life of the patron saint.

But most visitors don't come to Faro to look at churches. Rather, they take the harbor ferry to the wide white-sand beaches called the **Praia de Faro,** on an islet. The ride is available only in summer. The beach is also connected to the mainland by bridge, a distance of about 3¹/₂ miles from the town center. Once here, you can waterski and fish or just rent a deck chair and umbrella and lounge in the sun.

ACCOMMODATIONS

Casa de Lumena. Praça Alexandre Herculano 27, 8000 Faro. ☎ **089/80-19-90.** Fax 089/80-40-19. 12 rms. TEL. Summer, 7,500$–10,000$ ($49.50–$66) double. Winter, 5,500$–7,500$ ($36.30–$49.50) double. Rates include breakfast. AE, DC, MC, V.

The Casa de Lumena is an English-run *pensão* (bed-and-breakfast) on a square shaded by jacaranda trees. The Lumena offers central heating and renovated and upgraded accommodations, some with TVs. The rooms are of different shapes and furnished in part with pieces inherited with the casa. Throughout are antiques, carved chests, satinwood tables, painted dressers, and armoires. At its bar/restaurant, the Grapevine, the Anglophile community often meets at lunchtime. The restaurant serves a Mexican cuisine.

Eva. Av. da República, 8000 Faro. ☎ **089/80-33-54.** Fax 089/80-23-04. 138 rms, 12 suites. A/C TEL. 15,000$–22,000$ ($99–$145.20) double; from 23,000$ ($151.80) suite. AE, DC, MC, V.

The Eva dominates the harbor like a fortress. This modern eight-story hotel occupies an entire side of the yacht-clogged harbor. The hotel was beginning to look worn and tired, but a recent rejuvenation has perked it up. There are direct sea views from most guest rooms, which are furnished in a restrained, even austere, style; some contain minibars. The better rooms open onto the water with large balconies. The Eva's best features are its penthouse restaurant and rooftop pool.

DINING

Dois Irmãos. Largo do Terreiro do Bispo 13–15. ☎ **089/82-33-37.** Reservations required. Main courses 1,000$–3,800$ ($6.60–$25.10); fixed-price menu 1,500$ ($9.90). AE, MC, V. Daily noon–3pm and 6pm–midnight. PORTUGUESE.

This popular Portuguese bistro, founded in 1925, has a no-nonsense atmosphere, yet it has its devotees. The menu is as modest as the establishment and its prices, but you get a good choice of fresh fish and shellfish dishes. Ignore the paper napkins and concentrate on the fine kettle of fish placed before you. Clams in savory sauce is a favorite, and sole is regularly featured—but, of course, everything depends on the catch of the day. Service is slow and amiable, and no one seems in a hurry.

⑤ Restaurante Cidade Velha. Rua Domingos Guieiro 19. ☎ **089/27145.** Main courses 1,300$–1,500$ ($8.60–$9.90). AE, DC, V. Mon–Fri 12:30–2:30pm and 7:30–11:30pm, Sat 7:30–11:30pm. PORTUGUESE/INTERNATIONAL.

The leading restaurant in town is the Cidade Velha, which used to be one of the best-located private homes in Faro; today it serves as a very charming culinary hideaway. You'll find it behind the cathedral, with thick stone walls that were built at least 250 years ago. Your meal will be served in one of a pair of rooms, each with a vaulted brick ceiling. Full meals might include such items as crab cakes or smoked swordfish with horseradish sauce, followed by roast rack of lamb with rosemary and mint sauce or roast duck with apricot sauce.

DAY TRIPS FROM FARO

OLHÃO   Olhão, described as the living re-creation of a Georges Braque collage, is the famous cubist town of the Algarve, so long beloved by painters. In its heart, white blocks stacked one upon the other, with flat red-tile roofs and exterior stairways on the stark walls, evoke the aura of the casbahs of North African cities. But let us not paint too romantic a portrait. Many readers have found it disappointing—dirty, dusty, too commercial.

If you do go here, try to attend the fish market near the waterfront when a *lota* (auction) is under way. Olhão is also known for its bullfights of the sea, in which fishermen wrestle with struggling tuna trapped in nets and headed for the smelly warehouses along the harbor.

For the best view, climb **Cabeça Hill,** its grottos punctured with stalagmites and stalactites, or perhaps **St. Micheal's Mount,** offering a panorama of the casbahlike Barreta. Finally, for what is perhaps one of the most idyllic beaches on the Algarve, take a 10-minute motorboat ride to the **Ilha de Armona,** a nautical mile away. Olhão is 6¹/₂ miles west of Faro, and is reached by going east on N125.

SÃO BRAS DE ALPORTEL   Traveling north from Faro for 12¹/₂ miles, you'll pass through groves of figs, almonds, and oranges, through pine woods where resin collects in wooden cups on the tree trunks. At the end of the run, you'll come upon isolated São Bras de Alportel, one of the most charming and least-known spots on the Algarve.

Far from the crowded beaches, it attracts those wanting pure air, peace, and quiet—a bucolic setting filled with flowers pushing through nutmeg-colored soil. Northeast of Loulé, this whitewashed, tile-roofed town rarely gets lively except on market days. Like its neighbor, Faro, it's noted for its perforated plaster chimneys. Lying at the foot of the Serra do Caldeirão, the whole area has been called one vast garden.

Regrettably, one of the reasons to visit—to dine or stay at the government-run pousada, Poudada de São Brás—is closed for a long-enduring renovation. The **tourist office** at Rua Dr. Evaristo Gago 1 (☎ **089/84-22-11**) can provide details about where to tour and dine in the general area. It's open Mon–Fri 9:30am–12:30pm and 2–5:30pm and on Sat 9:30am–noon.

VILA REAL DE SANTO ANTÓNIO

Twenty years after the marquês de Pombal rebuilt Lisbon, which had been destroyed in the great 1755 earthquake, he sent architects and builders to Vila Real de Santo António, where they reestablished the frontier town on the bank opposite Spain. It took only 5 months to build the town. Pombal's motivation was jealousy of Spain. Much has changed, of course, although Praça de Pombal remains. An obelisk stands in the center of the square, which is paved with inlays of black-and-white tiles radiating like rays of the sun and is filled with orange trees. Separated from its Iberian neighbor by the Guadiana River, Vila Real de Santo António offers a car-ferry between Portugal and Ayamonte, Spain.

ESSENTIALS

ARRIVING   By Train   Eleven trains per day arrive from Faro, taking 2¹/₂ hours. Four trains arrive from Lagos, taking 4¹/₂ hours.

By Bus   It's better to take the bus from Faro to Vila Real. Five *espressos* per day arrive from Faro, taking 1 hour. Eight buses arrive from Lagos (a 4-hour trip), and four buses a day pull in from Lisbon (a 7¹/₂-hour trip).

By Car   From Faro, take N125 for 53 miles east to reach our final destination, at the Spanish frontier.

VISITOR INFORMATION   The **tourist office,** on Avenida Infante Henrique (☎ **081/44495**), is open Mon–Fri 9am–5pm and Sat 9am–12:30pm.

EXPLORING VILA REAL

A long esplanade, **Avenida da República,** lines the river, and from its northern extremity you can view the Spanish town across the way. Gaily painted **horse-drawn carriages** take you sightseeing past the shipyards and the lighthouse.

A short drive north on the road to Mertola will take you to the gull-gray castle-fortress of **Castro Marim.** This formidable structure is a legacy of the old border wars between Spain and Portugal. The ramparts and walls watch Spain across the river. Afonso III, who expelled the Moors from this region, founded the original fortress, which was razed by the 1755 earthquake. Inside the walls are the ruins of the Church of São Tiago, dedicated to St. James.

Directly southwest of Vila Real is the emerging resort of **Monte Gordo,** which has the greatest concentration of hotels in the eastern Algarve after Faro. Monte Gordo is the last in a long line of Algarvian resorts; it lies 2 miles southwest of the frontier town of Vila Real de Santo António at the mouth of the Guadiana River. Its wide beach, one of the finest along the southern coast of Portugal, is backed by pine-studded lowlands.

Sadly, this was once a sleepy little fishing village. Nowadays, young men tend to work in the hotels instead of on the sea, fishing for tips instead of tunny. Monte Gordo has succumbed to high-rises; it often attracts Spaniards from across the border. It has many good hotels, and a number of Europeans use it as their place in the Algarvian sun.

ACCOMMODATIONS

In Vila Real

Hotel Apolo. Av. dos Bombeiros Portugueses, 8900 Vila Real de Santo António. ☎ **081/51-24-48.** Fax 081/51-24-50. 42 rms. A/C TV TEL. Summer, 12,000$ ($79.20) double. Winter, 6,000$ ($39.60) double. AE, DC, MC, V.

The Hotel Apolo, built in the mid-1980s, lies on the western edge of town as you enter Vila Real from Monte Gordo or Faro. Near the beach and the river, it attracts vacationers as well as travelers who don't want to cross the Spanish border at night. The hotel is a marginal choice, with a spacious marble-floored lobby leading into a large bar scattered with comfortable sofas and flooded with sunlight. Each of the simply furnished guest rooms has a private balcony.

✪ **Hotel Guadiana.** Av. da República 94, 8900 Vila Real de Santo António. ☎ **081/51-14-82.** Fax 081/51-14-78. 37 rms, 5 suites. A/C TV TEL. 12,500$ ($82.50) double; from 21,000$ ($138.60) suite. AE, DC, MC, V. Free parking.

This is the best hotel in town (which isn't saying a lot), installed in a mansion classified as a historic national monument. Close to the river and the Spanish border, it's ideally located for exploring the town, less than a mile from Santo António beach and near the beach attractions of Monte Gordo as well. A three-star hotel, the restored building retains an aura of Portuguese tradition. Azulejos (decorated tiles) line some of the walls. The guest rooms are traditional and old-fashioned in decor, but have the modern amenities, such as air-conditioning. There's a cozy bar, and only breakfast is served.

In Monte Gordo

Hotel Alcázar. Rua de Ceuta, Monte Gordo, 8900 Vila Real de Santo António. ☎ **081/51-21-84.** Fax 081/51-22-42. 50 rms, 50 suites. Summer, 17,000$ ($112.20) double; 24,000$ ($158.40) suite. Off-season, 7,000$ ($46.20) double; 15,000$ ($99) suite. Rates include breakfast. AE, DC, MC, V.

The Hotel Alcázar is the best in town, and was last renovated in 1994. A free-form pool is built on terraces into the retaining walls that shelter it from the wind and extend the hot-weather season late into autumn. The interior design is a vaguely Arab-style series of repetitive arches and vaults crafted from distressed concrete. Each rather austere unit contains its own sun terrace and a radio. The basement disco has night-time entertainment in summer. An alluring spot is under the soaring ceiling of the in-house restaurant, where formal meals—rather standard fare—are served.

Hotel dos Navegadores. Monte Gordo, 8900 Vila Real de Santo António. ☎ **081/51-24-90.** Fax 081/51-28-72. 338 rms, 6 suites. A/C TEL. Summer, 13,300$–15,400$ ($87.80–$101.65) double; 17,500$–23,000$ ($115.50–$151.80) suite. Off-season, 9,300$ ($61.40) double; 12,500$ ($82.50) suite. AE, DC, MC, V.

It's popular with vacationing Portuguese and British families, who congregate under the dome covering the atrium's swimming pool. Public rooms are clean and functional, and about ³/₄ of the standardized guest rooms have private balconies. The beach is only a 5-minute walk away. There are dull boutiques in a corridor near the pool, along with a hairdresser and a coffee shop. The hotel restaurant, offering dinner only, serves Portuguese and international dishes.

Hotel Vasco Da Gama. Av. Infante D. Henríque, Monte Gordo, 8900 Vila Real de Santo António. ☎ **081/51-13-21.** Fax 081/51-16-22. 163 rms. TV TEL. 16,300$–19,700$ ($107.60–$130) double. AE, DC, MC, V.

The entrepreneurs here know what their northern guests seek—lots of sunbathing and swimming. Although this 1960s hotel enjoys a position on a long, wide sandy beach, it also offers an Olympic pool with a high-dive board and nearly an acre of flagstoned sun terrace. All the spartan guest rooms are furnished conservatively, and glass doors open onto balconies. Inside there's an oceanfront dining room.

Dining

Edmundo. Av. da República 55. ☎ **081/44689.** Reservations recommended. Main courses 1,450$–1,900$ ($9.55–$12.55); tourist menu 1,500$ ($9.90). AE, MC, V. Mon–Sat noon–3pm and 7–10pm, Sun 7–10pm. PORTUGUESE.

Edmundo has long been known in the Algarve, attracting Spaniards who often visit just for the day. It overlooks the river and Spain across the water—try to get a sidewalk table. The people who run this place are friendly and are proud of their repertoire of local cuisine, especially fresh fish. You might begin with shrimp cocktail, then follow with fried sole, crayfish, or sautéed red mullet. You can also order such meat dishes as lamb cutlets and veal filet.

15 Scotland

by Darwin Porter & Danforth Prince

Whether you go to Scotland to search out your ancestors, play golf, enjoy the gorgeous scenery, or attend the Edinburgh Festival, you'll find a country permeated with history, legend, and romance.

1 Edinburgh & Environs

Edinburgh has been called one of Europe's fairest cities, "the Athens of the North." You can decide for yourself whether that is appropriate. Edinburgh is filled with historical and literary associations—John Knox, Mary Queen of Scots, Robert Louis Stevenson, Sir Arthur Conan Doyle, Alexander Graham Bell, Sir Walter Scott, and Bonnie Prince Charlie are all part of its past, and you can walk in their footsteps and explore sights associated with them.

The city has become famous as the scene of the ever-growing international Edinburgh Festival with its action-packed list of cultural events. It's the second most visited city in Britain after London, a "white-collar" city in contrast to such industrialized bastions as Aberdeen or Glasgow. Even though the Scottish Parliament was long ago (1707) transferred to London, the government in Edinburgh still maintains a firm grip on politics. The most radical of officials in Edinburgh advocate a clean break with England and a *Braveheart* reassertion of Scottish autonomy—the film played here to cheering houses. An event to gladden the hearts of all Scots as well as the separatists was the 1996 return to Scotland of an important symbol, the Stone of Scone, that had rested for centuries in Westminster Abbey and is now at home in Edinburgh Castle.

ONLY IN EDINBURGH

Contemplating Edinburgh from Arthur's Seat   At 823 feet (reached by a climb up Holyrood Park), you'll visit the Highlands in miniature. The view from here has been called "magical." Scots congregate here to await the summer solstice.

Visiting Dean Village   About 100 feet below the level of the rest of the city, Dean Village is an 800-year-old grain-milling town on the Water of Leith. Go here to soak up local color from its woodland walk along the river. Exotic denizens of nearby Stockbridge village amuse with their zany makeup and dress.

Shopping Along Princes Street   This is Edinburgh's main street, the local equivalent of New York's Fifth Avenue. Flower-filled gardens stretch along the street's south side. You can make selections from the country's finest merchandise—from kilts to Scottish crystal.

Downing a Pint in an Edinburgh Pub   The city is famous for its pubs. Sampling a pint of McEwan's real ale or Tennent's lager is a chance to soak up the special atmosphere of Edinburgh, following an age-old tradition set by such figures as Robert Louis Stevenson and Arthur Conan Doyle when they were students at the University of Edinburgh in the 1870s.

Discovering Old Town   This is where Edinburgh began. Its "backbone" is the Royal Mile, a medieval thoroughfare stretching for about a mile from Edinburgh Castle running downhill to the Palace of Holyroodhouse. English author Daniel Defoe thought that this is "perhaps the largest, longest, and finest street for buildings and number of inhabitants in the world."

Wandering the Streets of New Town   Lying below Old Town, New Town burst into full bloom between 1766 and 1840, one of the largest Georgian developments in the world. It takes in most of the northern half of the heart of the city, made up of a network of squares, streets, terraces, and "circuses," which reach from Haymarket in the west to Abbeyhill toward the east.

ORIENTATION

ARRIVING   By Plane   Edinburgh is about an hour's flying time from London, 393 miles to the south. **Edinburgh Airport** (☎ **0131/3443136** for flight information) lies 10 miles northwest of the center. Flights from within the British Isles and Europe come here; international flights go to Glasgow's airport. A double-decker Airlink bus makes the trip between the airport and the city center every 30 minutes, letting you off near Waverley Bridge, between Old Town and New Town; the one-way fare is £3.20 ($5.10). A taxi into the city costs £15 ($24) or more, depending on traffic.

By Train   Fast, efficient, air-conditioned InterCity trains with restaurant and bar service link London with Edinburgh. Trains from London's King's Cross Station arrive in Edinburgh at **Waverley Station,** at the east end of Princes Street (☎ **0131/5562451,** or 0171/2782477 in London, for rail information). Trains depart London every hour or so, taking 4 to 5½ hours. An overnight sleeper requires reservations. Taxis and buses are found right outside the station in Edinburgh.

By Bus   The least expensive way to go from London to Edinburgh is by bus, but it's an 8½-hour journey. The fare is about £20.50 ($32.80) one way or £25.50 ($40.80) round-trip. National Express coaches depart from London's Victoria Coach Station, delivering you to Edinburgh's **St. Andrew Square Bus Station,** St. Andrew Square (☎ **990/505050** in Edinburgh).

By Car   Edinburgh lies 46 miles east of Glasgow and 105 miles north of Newcastle-upon-Tyne in England. There is no express motorway linking London and Edinburgh. The M-1 motorway from London takes you part of the way north, but you'll have to come into Edinburgh along secondary roads: A-68 or A-7 from the southeast, A-1 from the east, or A-702 from the north. Highway A-71 or A-8 comes in from the west, A-8 connecting with M-8 just west of Edinburgh; A-90 comes down from the north over the Forth Road Bridge.

VISITOR INFORMATION   The **Edinburgh & Scotland Information Centre,** Waverley Shopping Centre, 3 Princes St. (☎ **0131/5571700**), can give you

Edinburgh Attractions & Accommodations

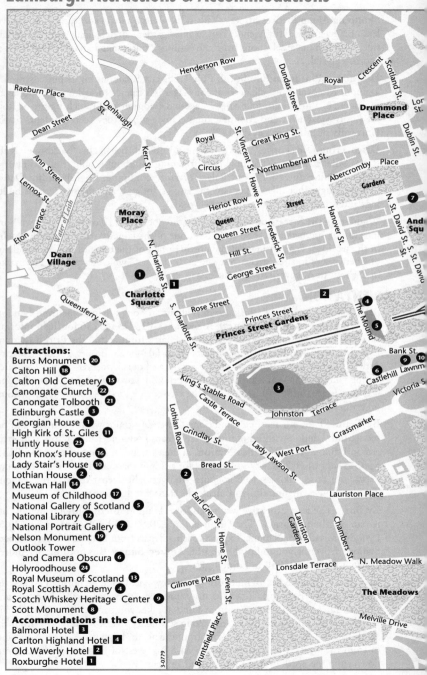

Attractions:
Burns Monument 20
Calton Hill 18
Calton Old Cemetery 15
Canongate Church 22
Canongate Tolbooth 21
Edinburgh Castle 3
Georgian House 1
High Kirk of St. Giles 11
Huntly House 23
John Knox's House 16
Lady Stair's House 10
Lothian House 2
McEwan Hall 14
Museum of Childhood 17
National Gallery of Scotland 5
National Library 12
National Portrait Gallery 7
Nelson Monument 19
Outlook Tower
 and Camera Obscura 6
Holyroodhouse 24
Royal Museum of Scotland 13
Royal Scottish Academy 4
Scotch Whiskey Heritage Center 9
Scott Monument 8
Accommodations in the Center:
Balmoral Hotel 3
Carlton Highland Hotel 4
Old Waverly Hotel 2
Roxburghe Hotel 1

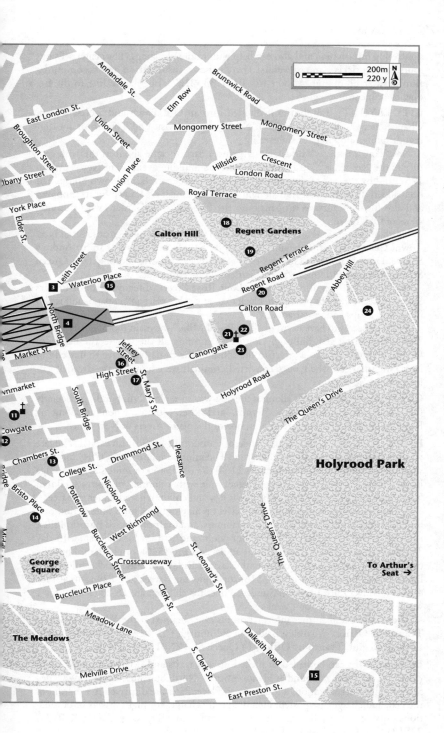

795

sightseeing information and also can help with finding lodgings. The center sells bus tours, theater tickets, and souvenirs. There's also an **information and accommodation desk** at Edinburgh Airport (☎ **0131/3332167**), open according to the frequency of incoming flights.

CITY LAYOUT Edinburgh is divided into an **Old Town** and a **New Town.** Chances are, you'll find lodgings in New Town and visit Old Town only for dining, drinking, shopping, or sightseeing.

New Town, with its world-famous **Princes Street,** came about in the 18th century in the "golden age" of Edinburgh. The first building went up in New Town in 1767, and by the end of the century, classical squares, streets, and town houses had been added. Princes Street runs straight for about a mile; it's known for its shopping and also for its beauty, as it opens onto the Princes Street Gardens with stunning views of Old Town.

North of Princes Street, and running parallel to it, is the second great street of New Town, **George Street.** It begins at Charlotte Square and runs east to St. Andrew Square. Directly north of George Street is another impressive thoroughfare, **Queen Street,** opening onto Queen Street Gardens on its north side.

In Edinburgh, you also hear a lot about **Rose Street,** directly north of Princes Street. It has more pubs per square block than any other place in Scotland, and is also filled with shops and restaurants.

Everyone seems to have heard of **"The Royal Mile,"** the main thoroughfare of Old Town, beginning at Edinburgh Castle and running all the way to the Palace of Holyroodhouse. A famous street to the south of the castle (you have to descend to it) is **Grassmarket,** where once convicted criminals were hung on the dreaded gallows that stood here.

GETTING AROUND Walking is the best way to explore Edinburgh, particularly Old Town with its narrow lanes, "wynds," and closes. Most attractions are along the Royal Mile, along Princes Street, or in one of the major streets of New Town.

By Bus This will be your chief method of transport in the Scottish capital. The fare you pay depends on the distance you ride. The minimum fare is 45p (70¢) for three stages or less, and the maximum fare is £1.90 ($3.05) for 44 or more stages. (A stage is not a stop; it's a distance of about a half mile with a number of stops.) Children 5 to 15 are charged 45p (70¢) to 80p ($1.30), and children 4 and under ride free.

A **TouristCard** includes unlimited travel on all city buses for a time period of 2 to 7 days, special discounts at certain restaurants, and tours of selected historical sites. A 2-day TouristCard costs £10 ($16) for adults and £5 ($8) for children; a 13-day TouristCard goes for £17.50 ($28) for adults and £10 ($16) for children. For daily commuters or for diehard Scottish enthusiasts, a **RidaCard** season ticket allows unlimited travel on all buses at £10 ($16) for adults for 1 week and £29 ($46.40) for 4 weeks. Travel must begin on Sunday. Prices for children are £6.20 ($9.90) for 1 week, £15.90 ($25.45) for 4 weeks.

These tickets and further information may be obtained at the **Waverley Bridge Transport Office,** Waverley Bridge in Edinburgh (☎ **0131/5544494**), or the **Lothian Region Transport Office,** 14 Queen St. (☎ **0131/2204111**).

By Taxi Cabs can be hailed or picked up at a taxi stand. Meters begin at £1.10 ($1.75). Taxi ranks are found at Hanover Street, North St. Andrew Street, Waverley Station, Haymarket Station, and Lauriston Place. Fares are displayed in the front of the taxi, and charges are posted, including extra charges for night drivers or destinations outside the city limits. You can also call a taxi: Try **City Cabs** (☎ **0131/ 2281211**) or **Central Radio Taxis** (☎ **0131/2292468**).

By Car   Car rentals are relatively expensive, and driving in Edinburgh is a tricky business. It's a warren of one-way streets, with parking spots at a premium. However, a car is convenient for touring in the countryside. Most companies will accept your U.S. or Canadian driver's license, provided you have held it for more than a year and are over 21.

By Bicycle   You can rent bikes by the day or by the week from a number of outfits. Nevertheless, bicycling is not a good idea for most visitors because the city is constructed on a series of high ridges and terraces.

You may, however, want to rent a bike for exploring the flatter countryside. Try **Bike Trax-Cycle Hire,** 13 Lochrin Place (☎ **0131/2286333**), off Home Street in Tollcross, near the Cameo Cinema. Depending on the type of bike, charges range from £8 to £15 ($12.80 to $24) per day. A deposit of £50 to £100 ($80 to $160) is imposed. The shop is open Mon–Sat 10am–5:30pm, and June–Aug also Sun 10am–noon and 5–7pm.

FAST FACTS: Edinburgh

American Express   The office is at 139 Princes St. (☎ 0131/2257881), five blocks from Waverley Station, open Mon–Fri 9am–5:30pm, Sat 9am–4pm.

Babysitters   The most reliable service is Bountsfield Helping Hands, 45 Barclay Place (☎ 0131/2281382).

Business Hours   In Edinburgh, **banks** are usually open Mon–Thurs 9:30am–12:30pm and 1:30–3:30pm, Fri 9:30am–4:30pm. **Shops** are generally open Mon–Sat 9am–5:30 or 6pm, Thurs until 7:30pm.

Currency   The basic unit of currency is the **pound sterling** (£), which is divided into 100 **pence** (p). There are 1p, 2p, 10p, 20p, 50p, and £1 coins; banknotes are issued in £1, £5, £10, £20, and £50. The exchange rate used in this chapter was $1 = 62.5p, or £1 = $1.60.

Currency Exchange   There's a bureau de change of the Clydesdale Bank at Hanover Street and at Waverley Market.

Dentists   Go to the Dental Surgery School, 37 Chambers St. (☎ 0131/5364900), open Mon–Fri 9am–3pm.

Doctors   In a medical emergency, you can seek help from the Edinburgh Royal Infirmary, 1 Lauriston Place (☎ 0131/5361000). Medical attention is available 24 hours.

Drugstores   There are no 24-hour drugstores (called "chemists" or "pharmacies") in Edinburgh. The major drugstore is Boots, 48 Shandwick Place (☎ 0131/2256757), open Mon–Sat 8am–9pm, Sun 10am–5pm.

Embassies/Consulates   The Consulate of the **United States** is at 3 Regent Terrace (☎ 0131/5568315), which is an extension of Princes Street beyond Nelson's Monument. The Consulate of **Australia** is in Hobart House, 80 Hanover St. (☎ 0131/2266271). Visitors from Canada and New Zealand should contact their High Commissions in London.

Emergencies   Call 999 in an emergency to summon the police, an ambulance, or firefighters.

Eyeglasses   Your best bet is Boots Opticians, 101–103 Princes St. (☎ 0131/2256397), open Mon–Sat 9am–6pm (Thurs until 7:30pm).

Hospital   The best and most convenient is the Edinburgh Royal Infirmary, 1 Lauriston Place (☎ 0131/5361000).

Lost Property   If you've lost property (or had it stolen), go to Police Headquarters on Fettes Avenue (☎ 0131/3113131).

Luggage Storage/Lockers   You can store luggage at Waverley Station, at Waverley Bridge (☎ 0131/484950), open daily 7am–11pm.

Photographic Needs   Edinburgh Cameras, 55 Lothian Rd. (☎ 0131/2294416), is open Mon–Sat 9am–5:30pm.

Post Office   The Edinburgh Branch Post Office, St. James's Centre (☎ 0131/5560478), is open Mon–Fri 9am–5:30pm, Sat 8:30am–6pm.

Taxes   A 17.5% value-added tax (known as VAT) is added to all goods and services in Edinburgh, as elsewhere in Britain. There are no special city taxes.

ACCOMMODATIONS
IN THE CENTER
Very Expensive
✪ **Balmoral Hotel.** Princes St., Edinburgh, Lothian EH2 2EQ. ☎ **800/225-5843** in the U.S. or 0131/5562414. Fax 0131/5578740. 189 rms, 22 suites. A/C MINIBAR TV TEL. £165 ($264) double; £250–£600 ($400–$960) suite. AE, DC, MC, V. Parking £10 ($15). Bus: 4, 15, or 44.

This legendary establishment was originally opened in 1902 as the largest, grandest, and most impressive hotel in the north of Britain. In the 1980s its massive premises were sometimes in limbo between investment groups. It reopened in 1991 after an expenditure of $35 million under a new name, the Balmoral. Its soaring clock tower is a city landmark. Furnished with reproduction pieces, the bedrooms are distinguished, conservative, and rather large, a graceful reminder of Edwardian sprawl with a contemporary twist. The hotel's most elegant eatery is the Grill Room. Facilities include a large and well-equipped health club with Jacuzzi, sauna, exercise equipment, and a pool.

Caledonian Hotel. Princes St., Edinburgh, Lothian EH1 2AB. ☎ **0131/4599988.** Fax 0131/2256632. 216 rms, 23 suites. MINIBAR TV TEL. £170–£290 ($272–$464) double; from £300 ($480) suite. Children 15 and under stay free in parents' room. AE, DC, MC, V. Bus: 4, 15, or 44.

"The Caley" is Edinburgh's most visible hotel, with commanding views over Edinburgh Castle and the Princes Street Gardens. Dumfriesshire stone—a form of deep-red sandstone used in its construction—was used in only three other buildings in town. Renovated in 1996, the hotel remains one of the city's landmarks. The pastel-colored public rooms are reminiscent of an age of Edwardian splendor, and the bedrooms are conservatively but individually styled with reproduction furniture, and often exceptionally spacious. The fifth-floor rooms are the smallest. For the price, however, the Balmoral (see above), its major competitor, remains a better deal, as the Caledonian lacks leisure facilities. Among the hotel eateries, the best food and the most formal meals are served in the Pompadour Restaurant.

Expensive
Carlton Highland Hotel. 19 North Bridge, Edinburgh, Lothian EH1 1SD. ☎ **0131/5567277.** Fax 0131/5562691. 197 rms, 4 suites. MINIBAR TV TEL. £170 ($272) double; from £260 ($416) suite. Rates include breakfast. Children 14 and under stay free in parents' room. AE, DC, MC, V. Bus: 4, 15, or 44.

The Victorian turrets, Flemish-style gables, and severe gray stonework of this hotel rise imposingly from a street corner on the Royal Mile, a few steps from Waverley

Station. The interior was converted into a bright and airy milieu of hardwood paneling, pastel colors, and modern conveniences. Each bedroom has a kind of Scandinavian simplicity, with matching tartan draperies and spreads, and such amenities as coffeemakers, hair dryers, and trouser presses. Baths tend to be quite small. The hotel's restaurant, Quills, is designed like a private 19th-century library, and offers an international and Scottish regional menu. Facilities include an exercise room with a swimming pool, solarium, whirlpool, sauna, two squash courts, and an aerobics studio.

Channings Hotel. South Learmonth Gardens, Edinburgh, Lothian EH4 1EZ. ☎ **0131/ 3152226.** Fax 0131/3329631. 48 rms. TV TEL. £120–£150 ($192–$240) double. Rates include breakfast. Children 14 and under stay free in parents' room. AE, DC, MC, V. Bus: 18, 19, 41, or 81.

Seven blocks north of Dean Village, in a tranquil residential area that's a 5-minute drive from the city center, this is one of Edinburgh's leading town house hotels. Five Edwardian terrace houses were combined to create this privately owned hotel. It maintains the atmosphere of a Scottish country house, with oak paneling, ornate fireplaces, molded ceilings, and antiques. The bedrooms are outfitted in a modern style. The front rooms get the view, but the accommodations in back are quieter. Standard rooms are a bit cheaper, but much smaller. The most desirable units are labeled "Executive," and these often have bay windows with wingback chairs. In the downstairs bar and brasserie, a Scottish/French cuisine is served.

Old Waverley Hotel. 43 Princes St., Edinburgh, Lothian EH2 2BY. ☎ **0131/5564648.** Fax 0131/5576316. 66 rms. TV TEL. £144 ($230.40) double. AE, DC, MC, V. Bus: 4, 15, or 44.

Opposite Waverley Station, the Old Waverley Hotel goes back to 1848, a seven-floor structure originally built to celebrate the then-newfangled railroads, and patronized by a wide-ranging clientele: families, business travelers, couples, students. About half the rooms are being refurbished, and more renovations are continuing (but not during the busy summer tourist season). The lounges on the second floor have been given a contemporary look. Some rooms look onto Princes Street and, at night, the floodlit castle. Rooms have trouser presses and hair dryers. A good carvery-style restaurant serves à la carte and table d'hôte meals.

Roxburghe Hotel. 38 Charlotte Sq., Edinburgh, Lothian EH2 4HG. ☎ **0131/2253921.** Fax 0131/2202518. 75 rms, 2 suites. A/C TV TEL. £125 ($200) double; £180 ($288) suite. Rates include breakfast. Children 13 and under stay free in parents' room. AE, DC, MC, V. Parking £8 ($12.80). Bus: 3, 21, 26, 31, or 85.

A stately Adam four-story town house of dove-gray stone on a tree-filled square, the hotel is a short walk from Princes Street, and stands at a corner of noisy George Street. The atmosphere is traditional, as reflected in the drawing room with its ornate ceiling and woodwork, antique furnishings, and tall arched windows opening toward the park. All the bedrooms, reached by elevator, have clock radios, trouser presses, and tea- and coffeemakers, plus sewing kits, shower caps, and foam baths, as well as fruit baskets. The units, renovated in 1993, are handsomely traditional with Adam-style paneling. Some rooms are small and very modestly furnished.

♦ Sheraton Grand Hotel. 1 Festival Sq., Edinburgh, Lothian EH3 9SR. ☎ **800/325-3535** in the U.S. and Canada, or 0131/2299131. Fax 0131/2284510. 261 rms, 17 suites. A/C MINIBAR TV TEL. £190 ($304) double; from £270 ($432) suite. Children 16 and under stay free in parents' room. AE, DC, MC, V. Bus: 4, 15, or 44.

Town leaders still praise the development of a former railway siding, a short walk from Princes Street, into a six-story postmodern structure that houses a glamorous hotel and office complex. The hotel is elegantly appointed, with soaring public rooms. The spacious, well-upholstered rooms offer double glazing on the windows, and easy contact with a team of concierges. The hotel offers two restaurants: The Terrace, with castle views, a brasserie-style restaurant with a conservatory atmosphere where chefs prepare specialties before you; and the Grill Room, small and intimate with traditional warm wood paneling, providing the best of Scottish produce. A leisure center offers a swimming pool (too small for lap swimming), whirlpool, sauna, and fully equipped gym.

Moderate

17 Abercromby Place. 17 Abercromby Place, Edinburgh, Lothian EH3 6LB. ☎ **0131/5578036.** Fax 0131/5583453. 9 rms. TV TEL. £80 ($128) double. Rates include breakfast. MC, V.

Eirlys Lloyd runs this fine B&B address, just a 5-minute walk north of Princes Street. Although designed by a less-well-known architect, the five-story gray stone terrace house was the home in the 1820s of William Playfair, who designed many of Edinburgh's most visible landmarks, including the Royal Scottish Academy, and Surgeon Hall on the campus of the Royal College of Surgeons. Two rooms are in what was originally conceived as a Mews House, but which today is connected architecturally to the main house. Evening meals can be arranged.

ⓈSibbet House. 26 Northumberland St., Edinburgh, Lothian EH3 6LS. ☎ **0131/5561078.** Fax 0131/5579445. 5 rms, 1 suite, 2 apts. TV TEL. £60 ($96) double; from £80 ($128) suite or apt. Rates include breakfast. MC, V. Bus: 13, 23, or 27.

Set on a residential terrace a 10-minute walk from Princes Street, this sandstone-fronted, three-story Georgian house is the cheerful domain of James Sibbet and his French-born wife, Aurora, who do everything they can to distinguish their family home from "just another hotel." If asked, James (proud of his Lowland Scottish origins) will play the bagpipes. There's a drawing room/salon where, if requested, drinks are served, and an ambience that never wavers from the homelike. The bedrooms are furnished in part with antiques (one has a four-poster bed).

Inexpensive

ⓈA Haven. 180 Ferry Rd., Edinburgh, Midlothian EH6 4NS. ☎ **0131/5546559.** Fax 0131/5545252. 12 rms. TV TEL. £54–£80 ($86.40–$128) double. Rates include breakfast. AE, MC, V. Bus: 1, 6, 7, 11, 14, 25, or 69.

This is a semidetached gray stone four-story Victorian house, built in 1862, within a 15-minute walk or a 5-minute bus ride north of the rail station. The rooms are substantially furnished with traditional pieces; all have been refurbished. Some rooms in back overlook the Firth of Forth, and those in the front open onto views of Arthur's Seat. Moira and Ronnie Murdock extend a Scottish welcome in this family-type place, and often advise guests about sightseeing. They have a licensed bar, but the only meal served is breakfast.

ⓈGreenside Hotel. 9 Royal Terrace, Edinburgh, Midlothian EH7 5AB. ☎ **0131/5570022.** Fax 0131/5570022. 14 rms. £55 ($88) double. Rates include breakfast. AE, DC, MC, V. Bus: 4, 15, or 44.

A four-floor Georgian house originally built in 1786, the Greenside is furnished with a number of antique pieces to give it the right spirit. There are singles, doubles, twins, and three family rooms, all centrally heated and all with private bath. The rooms, refurbished in 1995, open onto views of a private garden or the Firth of Forth. There's a color TV set in the lounge, where coffee and tea are available all day. Four-course Scottish dinners can be arranged.

27 Heriot Row. 27 Heriot Row, Edinburgh, Lothian EH3 6EN. ☎ **0131/2259474.** Fax 0131/2201699. 6 rms. TV TEL. £80 ($128) double. Rates include breakfast. MC, V.

At least part of the draw of this 18th-century Georgian rowhouse derives from a decor that many visitors liken to a fashion magazine illustration. Andrea and Gene Targett-Adams are the likable owners, whose accommodation has won several awards from the Scottish Tourist Board. Guests enjoy use of a private sitting room on the second floor. You'll find high ceilings, elaborate cove moldings, and many elegant touches that make this a truly desirable B&B. Only breakfast is served.

WEST OF THE CENTER
Moderate

Ellersly Country House Hotel. 4 Ellersly Rd., Edinburgh, Lothian EH12 6HZ. ☎ **0131/3376888.** Fax 0131/3132543. 57 rms, 5 suites. TV TEL. £115 ($184) double; £135 ($216) suite. AE, DC, MC, V. Take A-8 2¹/₂ miles west of the city center.

Standing in walled gardens, this three-story Edwardian country house has been said to offer the "privacy of a home." It's in a dignified west-end residential section near the Murrayfield rugby grounds, about a 5-minute ride from the center, and is one of Edinburgh's best moderately priced hotels. The well-equipped bedrooms are in either the main house or a less desirable annex. The rooms vary in size. After a refurbishment, the hotel is better than ever, and service is first class. The hotel possesses a well-stocked wine cellar and offers good-tasting Scottish and French meals. A fitness center is nearby.

DINING
IN THE CENTER—NEW TOWN
Expensive

✪ **L'Auberge.** 56 St. Mary's St. ☎ **0131/5565888.** Reservations required. Main courses £21.50 ($34.40); fixed-price lunch £13 ($20.80); fixed-price dinner £23.50 ($37.60). AE, DC, MC, V. Daily 12:15–2pm and 7–9:30pm. Bus: 1, 6, 34, or 35. FRENCH.

L'Auberge, just off the Royal Mile, between Cowgate and Canongate, is ranked among the top three or four restaurants in Edinburgh. It uses the finest of Scottish ingredients in its classic French cuisine, which is backed up by a carefully chosen wine list. Service is the most polished in town. Game and fish are specialties, and each dish—whether from the moors, loch, or sea—is individually prepared. Some main dishes taste as if you've been transported to the Périgord region of France. The menu changes frequently but has included confit of duck in a Madeira wine sauce with mushrooms, Scottish salmon in a Provençal vinaigrette sauce, and grilled shark with butter sauce.

✪ **The Atrium.** 10 Cambridge St. (beneath Saltire Ct.). ☎ **0131/2288882.** Reservations recommended. Main courses £8.50–£11.50 ($13.60–$18.40) at lunch, £11.50–£16.50 ($18.40–$26.40) at dinner. AE, MC, V. Mon–Fri noon–2:30pm and 6–10:30pm, Sat 6–10:30pm. Closed for 1 week at Christmas. MODERN MEDITERRANEAN.

This is the most frequently analyzed, most frequently discussed, and most frequently emulated restaurant in Edinburgh. Some 60 diners enjoy flickering oil lamps and a decor of rusted metal, etched glass, and dark colors. Menu items change with the inspiration of chef Andrew Radford and his manager, James Sankey, but might include a *ciabatta* of leeks, mozzarella, and sun-dried tomatoes; a pastry tart of seared scallops with frisée lettuce and pesto sauce; or a combination platter of roast duck with smoked venison and salsa-infused couscous.

✪ **Grill Room.** In the Balmoral Hotel, 1 Princes St. ☎ **0131/5562414.** Reservations recommended. Main courses £9.50–£23 ($15.20–$36.80); fixed-price lunch £19.95 ($31.90);

fixed-price five-course dinner £29.50 ($47.20). AE, DC, MC, V. Mon–Fri noon–2:30pm and 7–10:30pm. SCOTTISH/CONTINENTAL.

This, the premier restaurant in the Balmoral Hotel, is an intimate, crimson-colored enclave one floor below the reception area. The walls are studded with Scottish memorabilia in patterns just informal enough to be sporting and just formal enough to be very, very elegant. This is very much the grand-style hotel dining room, and it offers good food if you don't mind paying such high tabs. From the North Sea comes turbot flavored with rosemary. Angus beef is used in abundance, or perhaps the River Tay salmon with rhubarb sauce will interest you.

✪ **Pompadour Room.** In the Caledonian Hotel, Princes St. ☎ **0131/4599988.** Reservations required. Jacket and tie required. Main courses £19–£25 ($30.40–$40); fixed-price dinner without wine £45 ($72). AE, DC, MC, V. Mon–Fri 12:30–2pm, Tues–Sat 7–10:15pm. Bus: 3, 4, 21, 22, or 26. SCOTTISH/FRENCH.

The Pompadour Room, on the mezzanine floor of the famous hotel, serves fine Scottish and French cuisine. The restaurant has been refurbished, with gray wall panels interspersed with panels of floral-patterned silk in a sort of Louis XV decor—after all, the restaurant is named for his mistress. The chef blends *cuisine moderne* with traditional menus in this intimate, luxurious place. The à la carte menu features fresh produce from both local and French markets—dishes such as goose liver with wild mushrooms, fillet of lamb with spinach and rosemary, and charlotte of marinated salmon filled with seafood. There is a no-smoking area. The wine list is lethal in price and strangely absent of bottles from the New World.

Moderate
Alp Horn Restaurant. 167 Rose St. ☎ **0131/2254787.** Reservations recommended. Main courses £5.75–£11.25 ($9.20–$18). AE, DC, MC, V. Mon–Sat noon–2pm and 6:30–10pm. Bus: 31 or 33. SWISS/SCOTTISH.

The Alp Horn Restaurant, just off Charlotte Square in an antique stone building on a street long famous for its pubs, provides a meal that's like a vacation in Switzerland. The wooden door opens to reveal decor in the Swiss chalet style. As you'd expect, the menu offers air-dried meats (Grisons style), several fondues, venison in season, and a version of rösti, the famous potato dish of Switzerland. Fresh Scottish fish is also served. All this might be capped off with a slice of apfelstrudel, made on the premises. Nonsmokers get a room to themselves.

Cosmo Ristorante. 58A N. Castle St. ☎ **0131/2266743.** Reservations required. Main courses £12–£16 ($19.20–$25.60); fixed-price lunch £15.90 ($25.45). AE, MC, V. Mon–Fri 12:30–2:15pm; Mon–Sat 8–10:45pm. Bus: 31 or 33. ITALIAN.

Courtesy, efficiency, and good cookery are featured here. In season you can ask for mussels as an appetizer, and the soups and pastas are always reliable. Saltimbocca is a specialty, and the kitchen is known for its light-handed Italian-inspired preparations of Italian fish. The cassata siciliana is well made and not unbearably sweet. This is not the greatest Italian dining in the U.K., but dishes seem to have survived reasonably well this far north of the Mediterranean.

Henderson's Salad Table. 94 Hanover St. ☎ **0131/2252131.** Main courses £3–£3.60 ($4.80–$5.75). AE, MC, V. Mon–Sat 8am–11pm. Bus: 23 or 27. VEGETARIAN.

This is a Shangri-La for health-food lovers. At this self-service place, you can pick and choose eggs, carrots, grapes, nuts, yogurt, cheese, potatoes, cabbage, watercress—you name it. Hot dishes such as peppers stuffed with rice and pimiento are served on request, and a new twist on the national dish of Scotland—vegetarian haggis—is usually available. The homemade desserts include a fresh-fruit salad or a cake with double-whipped cream and chocolate sauce. Henderson's is furnished with pinewood tables (often shared) and chairs. The wine cellar offers 30 wines. Live music, ranging from classical to jazz to folk, is played every evening.

Ⓢ Indian Cavalry Club. 3 Atholl Place. ☎ **0131/2283282.** Reservations required. Main courses £6.50–£11 ($10.40–$17.60); two-course buffet lunch £7.95 ($12.70); five-course table d'hôte dinner £16 ($25.30). AE, DC, MC, V. Daily noon–2pm and 5:30–11:30pm. Bus: 3, 21, 23, or 26. INDIAN.

Vegetarians flock here to enjoy the elegant atmosphere that evokes the British heyday in India. Along with the classic and tandoori food items, many dishes are based on recipes from Nepal or Burma. Much of the cuisine is steamed. The restaurant with its various areas, including the ground-floor Officers' Mess and the marquee-style Club Tent downstairs, is many cuts above the ordinary curry houses of Edinburgh.

Oyster Bar. 17 W. Register St. ☎ **0131/5564124.** Reservations recommended year-round, but essential during the festival. Main courses £13.20–£15.50 ($21.10–$24.80); three-course Sun brunch £12.50–£17.50 ($20–$28). MC, V. Mon–Sat noon–2pm and 7–10:15pm, Sun 12:30–2:30pm (brunch) and 7–10:15pm. Bus: 10 or 16. SEAFOOD/GAME.

Its physical plant is one of the most dramatic in Edinburgh, thanks to its richly ornate Victorian bar and its soaring windows inset with stained-glass depictions of 19th-century Scotsmen in full Highland dress. This intimate and quiet corner specializes, as its name implies, in seafood, plus game dishes. You might like the salmon with mussels, shrimp with Camembert and white wine, or oak-smoked haddock poached in cream and topped with spinach. The Oyster Bar is also the town's best and most interesting venue for a Sunday brunch.

Szechuan House. 12–14 Leamington Terrace. ☎ **0131/2294655.** Main courses £5.25–£10 ($8.40–$16). AE, MC, V. Tues–Sun 5:30pm–midnight. Bus: 27. SZECHUAN.

You don't come here for elegant trappings, but you get zesty, chili-hot platters of poultry and fish, especially chicken, duck, and prawns. You might begin with either "bang-bang" chicken or fishhead soup, and follow with diced chicken with chili or fried squid family style. Vegetarians can also dine happily. The cookery is classic and authentic, as the chef comes from Szechuan province, and has brought his bag of spices with him to tempt the haggis-and-neeps crowd, who might—just might—have once rather fearfully added a half teaspoon of curry into some mutton stew.

In the Center—Old Town
Moderate

Jackson's Restaurant. 209 High St., Royal Mile. ☎ **0131/2251793.** Reservations recommended. Main courses £13.50–£17 ($21.60–$27.20). AE, MC, V. Mon–Fri noon–2pm and 6:30–10:30pm, Sat–Sun noon–2pm and 6–11pm. Bus: 35. SCOTTISH/FRENCH.

Serving a cuisine described as "Scottish with a French flair," this bustling and popular restaurant is in the austere but cozy stone cellar of a 300-year-old building. You select from a "Taste of Scotland" menu featuring local ingredients. The charming staff might help you translate such items as "beasties of the glen" (a poetic designation for haggis with a whisky-cream sauce), noisettes of venison served in a blackberry, red currant, and port wine sauce, and "kilted salmon pan-fried in a green ginger and whisky sauce." The menu items sound so cute you might think it's a tourist trap, but it isn't.

Ⓢ Pierre Victoire. 10 Victoria St. ☎ **0131/2251721.** Reservations required. Main courses £4.90–£9 ($7.85–$14.40); fixed-price lunch £4.90 ($7.75). MC, V. Daily noon–3pm and 6–11pm (also open Sun during the Edinburgh Festival). Bus: 14, 23, or 33. FRENCH.

This was the original model for a series of franchise copies, each named Pierre Victoire, that have sprouted up in recent years in six other areas of Edinburgh. Many residents still prefer the original to the newer versions. It's an ideal, if chaotic, stop-over if you're antique shopping and climbing Victoria Street. It's also one of the most popular evening gathering places as it keeps long hours. Wine specials are posted on the chalkboard. In a bistro setting with crowded tables, you can order grilled mussels in garlic with Pernod butter, salmon with ginger, or roast pheasant with Cassis. Vegetarians are also welcome.

Witchery by the Castle. Castlehill, Royal Mile. ☎ **0131/2255613.** Reservations recommended. Main courses £14–£21.50 ($22.40–$34.40); fixed-price two-course lunch £12.95 ($20.70). AE, DC, MC, V. Daily 6–11:30pm. Bus: 1, 34, or 35. SCOTTISH.

This place bills itself as the "oldest, most haunted" restaurant in town, and the Hellfire Club was supposed to have met here during the Middle Ages. The building has been linked with witchcraft since the period between 1470 and 1722 when more than 1,000 people were burned alive on Castlehill. One of the victims is alleged to haunt the Witchery. She is known as Old Mother Long Nose, once a practitioner of herbal medicine, and a model of her sits by the entrance. James Thomson, the owner, uses his creative flair as a chef to make the restaurant a member of the "Taste of Scotland" program for unfussy Scottish food and hospitality. Menus change seasonally and might include Skye prawns or Tay salmon. Angus steak is a specialty. Vegetarian dishes are also offered.

Inexpensive
Baked Potato Shop. 56 Cockburn St. ☎ **0131/2257572.** Reservations not accepted. Food items 50p–£3 (80¢–$4.80). No credit cards. Daily 10am–9pm. Bus: 5. VEGETARIAN/WHOLE FOOD.

This is the least expensive restaurant in a very glamorous neighborhood, and it attracts mobs of office workers every day, who often carry their food away for consumption on one of the many outdoor seating areas scattered in the vicinity of the Royal Mile and High Street. Place your order at the countertop and it will be served in ecology-conscious recycled cardboard containers by the staff clad in T-shirts and aprons. Only free-range eggs, whole foods, and vegetarian cheeses are used.

SOUTH OF THE CENTER
Moderate
✪ **Kelly's.** 46 W. Richmond St. ☎ **0131/6683847.** Reservations recommended. Fixed-price three-course dinner £23 ($36.80). AE, MC, V. Wed–Sat 7–10pm. Closed Oct. Bus: 2, 12, or 21. MODERN BRITISH/MODERN FRENCH.

Catering to a dinner-only crowd of barristers, artists, financiers, and employees of the nearby university, this stylish restaurant is a 20-minute walk south of the center in a residential neighborhood. The place offers an intimate setting lined with flowers, light antique oak furniture, watercolors, and unusual ceramics. Focusing on fresh ingredients and vaguely inspired by the culinary techniques of the late British culinary authority Robert Carrier, the menu includes such dishes as galantine of duck with Cumberland sauce; a parcel of turbot with a seafood mousse, a timbale of leeks and lemons, and a dill-flavored *beurre-blanc* sauce; and a platter containing both loin of lamb and breast of pigeon bound together with port-flavored cranberries.

LEITH
In the northern regions of Edinburgh, Leith is the old port town, opening onto the Firth of Forth. Once it was a city in its own right until it (and its harbor facilities) were slowly absorbed into Edinburgh.

Expensive

Vintners Room. The Vaults, 87 Giles St., Leith. ☎ **0131/5546767.** Reservations recommended. Main courses £14–£17 ($22.40–$27.20); fixed-price lunch (in wine bar only) £9–£12 ($14.40–$19.20). AE, MC, V. Mon–Sat noon–2:30pm and 7–10:30pm. Closed for 2 weeks at Christmas. Bus: 7 or 10. FRENCH/SCOTTISH.

This stone-fronted building was originally constructed around 1650 as a warehouse for the barrels of bordeaux (claret) and port that came in from Europe's mainland. Near the entrance, beneath a venerable ceiling of oaken beams, a wine bar serves platters and drinks beside a large stone fireplace. Most diners, however, head for the small but elegant dining room, illuminated by flickering candles. Here, elaborate Italianate plasterwork decorates a room that functioned 300 years ago as the site of wine auctions. A robust cuisine includes seafood salad with mango mayonnaise, a terrine of smoked salmon and rabbit, or loin of pork with mustard sauce.

ATTRACTIONS
SIGHTSEEING SUGGESTIONS

If You Have 1 Day   Visit Edinburgh Castle as soon as it opens in the morning, then walk the Royal Mile to the Palace of Holyroodhouse, former abode of Mary, Queen of Scots. Look out over the city from the vantage point of Arthur's Seat, and stroll through Princes Street Gardens, capping your day with a walk along the major shopping thoroughfare, Princes Street.

If You Have 2 Days   In the morning of your second day, head for Old Town again, but this time explore its narrow streets, "wynds," and closes, and visit John Knox House, the High Kirk of St. Giles, and the small museums. After lunch, climb the Scott Monument for a good view of Old Town and the Princes Street Gardens. Spend the rest of the afternoon exploring the National Gallery of Scotland.

If You Have 3 Days   Spend day 3 getting acquainted with the major attractions of New Town, including the Royal Museum of Scotland, National Portrait Gallery, Georgian House, and Royal Botanic Garden.

If You Have 5 Days   On the fourth day, take a trip west to Stirling Castle and see some of the dramatic scenery of the Trossachs. On the fifth day you'll feel like a native, so seek out some of the city's minor but interesting attractions, such as the Camera Obscura, the Scotch Whisky Heritage Centre, and Dean Village. If time remains, cap your day with a visit to the Edinburgh Zoo.

THE ROYAL MILE

The Royal Mile stretches from Edinburgh Castle all the way to the Palace of Holyroodhouse. Walking along, you'll see some of the most interesting old structures in Edinburgh, with their turrets, gables, and towering chimneys. Take bus no. 1, 6, 23, 27, 30, 34, or 36 to reach it.

Inside the **High Kirk of St. Giles** on High Street (☎ **0131/2259442**), one outstanding feature is its Thistle Chapel, designed by Sir Robert Lorimer, housing beautiful stalls and notable heraldic stained-glass windows. The church is open Mon–Sat 9am–5pm, Sun 1–5pm. Of course, you're welcome to join in the cathedral's services on Sunday conducted at various times from 7am–9pm. A group of cathedral guides is available at all times to conduct guided tours. Admission is free, except for the 50p (80¢) charge to visit Thistle Chapel.

The **Writer's Museum** lies in a close off Lawnmarket (☎ **0131/5294901,** ext. 6593). It was built in 1622 by a prominent merchant burgess and was once known as Lady Stair's House, taking its name from a former owner, Elizabeth, the dowager countess of Stair. Today it's a treasure house of portraits, relics, and manuscripts relating to three of Scotland's greatest men of letters—Robert Burns, Sir Walter Scott, and Robert Louis Stevenson. It's open Mon–Sat 10am–5pm (until 6pm June–Sept). Admission is free.

The **Museum of Childhood,** 42 High St. (☎ **0131/5294142**), stands just opposite John Knox's House, the first museum in the world of its kind. Contents of its four floors range from antique toys to games to exhibits on health, education, and costumes. Because of the youthful clientele it naturally attracts, it ranks as the "noisiest museum in the world." It's open June–Sept Mon–Sat 10am–5:30pm (until 5pm the rest of the year), and also from 2–5pm Sun during the Edinburgh Festival. Admission is free.

Farther down the street at 43–45 High St. is the **John Knox House** (☎ **0131/5569579**), with a history going back to the late 15th century. Even if you're not interested in the reformer who founded the Scottish Presbyterian church, you may want to visit his house, as it is characteristic of the "lands" that used to flank the Royal Mile. All of them are gone now, except Knox's house, with its timbered gallery. Inside, you'll see the tempera ceiling in the Oak Room, along with exhibitions of Knox memorabilia. The house is open Mon–Sat 10am–4:30pm; admission is £1.75 ($2.80) for adults, 75p ($1.20) for children.

Continue along Canongate toward the Palace of Holyroodhouse. At 163 Canongate stands one of the handsomest buildings along the Royal Mile. **Canongate Tolbooth** was constructed in 1591 and was once the courthouse, prison, and center of municipal affairs for the burgh of Canongate.

Across the street at 142 Canongate is **Huntly House** (☎ **0131/5294143**), an example of a restored 16th-century mansion. Now it's Edinburgh's principal museum of local history. You can stroll through period rooms and reconstructions Mon–Sat 10am–5pm (until 6pm June–Sept), and during the festival also Sun 2–5pm. Admission is free.

At 354 Castlehill, Royal Mile, the **Scotch Whisky Heritage Center** (☎ **0131/2200441**) is privately funded by a conglomeration of Scotland's biggest whisky distillers. It highlights the economic effect of whisky on both Scotland and the world and illuminates the centuries-old traditions associated with whisky making, showing the exact science and art form of distilling. There's a 7-minute audiovisual show, and an electric car ride moves past 13 theatrical sets showing historic moments in the whisky industry. Prebooked groups of eight people or more, for a supplemental £15 ($24), can experience a tutored whisky tasting where four different malts are offered. Otherwise, admission is £4.20 ($6.70) for adults, £3 ($4.80) for senior citizens, £2 ($3.20) for children 5 to 17, free for children 4 and under. Open year-round 10am–5pm.

THE HISTORIC SITES

✪ **Edinburgh Castle.** Castlehill. ☎ **0131/2259846.** Admission £5.50 ($8.80) adults, £1.50 ($2.40) children 15 and under. Apr–Sept daily 9:30am–5:15pm; Oct–Mar daily 9:30am–4:15pm. Bus: 1, 2, 6, or 35.

It's believed that the ancient city grew up on the seat of the dead volcano, Castle Rock. Early history is vague, although it is known that in the 11th century Malcolm III (Canmore) and his Saxon queen, later venerated as St. Margaret, founded a castle on this spot. The only fragment left of their original castle—in fact the oldest structure in Edinburgh—is **St. Margaret's Chapel,** built in the Norman style, the oblong structure dating principally from the 12th century.

Inside the castle you can visit the **State Apartments,** particularly Queen Mary's Bedroom, where Mary Queen of Scots gave birth to James VI of Scotland (later James I of England). The highlight is the Crown Chamber, which houses the Honours of

Scotland (Scottish Crown Jewels), used at the coronation of James VI, along with the scepter and the sword of state of Scotland.

You can also view the Stone of Scone or "Stone of Destiny," on which Scottish kings had been crowned since time immemorial, now returned to its rightful home in Scotland, where it was welcomed with much pomp and circumstance in November 1996. Edward I of England had carried the stone off to Westminster Abbey in 1296, where it rested under the British coronation chair, and the Scots have been trying to get it back ever since.

✪ Palace of Holyroodhouse. Canongate, at the eastern end of the Royal Mile. ☎ **0131/ 5561096.** Admission £3.75 ($6) adults, £2.75 ($4.40) children under 17. Daily 9:30am–5:15pm. Closed last 2 weeks in May and 3 weeks in late June–early July (dates vary). Bus: 1 or 6.

This palace was built adjacent to an Augustinian abbey established by David I in the 12th century. The nave, now in ruins, remains today. James IV founded the palace nearby in the early part of the 16th century, but only the north tower is left. Much of what you see today was ordered built by Charles II.

In the old wing the most dramatic incident in the history of Holyroodhouse occurred when Mary Queen of Scots was in residence. Her Italian secretary, David Rizzio, was murdered (with 56 stab wounds) in the audience chamber by Mary's husband, Lord Darnley, and his accomplices. The palace suffered long periods of neglect, although it basked in glory at the ball thrown by Bonnie Prince Charlie in the mid-18th century. The present queen and Prince Philip live at Holyroodhouse whenever they visit Edinburgh. When they're not in residence, the palace is open to visitors.

MORE ATTRACTIONS

Scott Monument. In the East Princes Street Gardens. ☎ **0131/5294068.** Admission £1.50 ($2.40). Apr–Sept Mon–Sat 9am–6pm; Oct–Mar Mon–Sat 9am–3pm. Bus: 1 or 6.

The gothic-inspired Scott Monument is the most famous landmark of Edinburgh, completed in the mid-19th century. Sir Walter Scott's heroes are carved as small figures in the monument, and you can climb to the top, provided that it's open, following a major renovation (check with the tourist office). West Princes Street Gardens has the first-ever Floral Clock, which was constructed in 1904.

✪ National Gallery of Scotland. 2 The Mound. ☎ **0131/5568921.** Free admission. Mon–Sat 10am–5pm, Sun 2–5pm (during the festival, Mon–Sat 10am–6pm, Sun 11am–6pm). Bus: 3, 21, or 26.

This museum is located in the center of Princes Street Gardens. The gallery is small as national galleries go, but the collection was chosen with great care and has been expanded considerably by bequests, gifts, and loans. The duke of Sutherland lent the museum some paintings, including two Raphaels, Titian's two Diana canvases and his Venus rising from the sea, and the *Seven Sacraments,* a work of the great 17th-century Frenchman Nicolas Poussin. The Spanish masters are represented as well.

You can also see excellent examples of English painting: Gainsborough's *The Hon. Mrs. Graham* and Constable's *Dedham Vale,* along with works by Turner, Reynolds, and Hogarth. Naturally, the work of Scottish painters is prominent.

Camera Obscura. Castlehill. ☎ **0131/2263709.** Admission £3.40 ($5.45) adults, £2.20 ($3.50) seniors, £2.75 ($4.40) students, £1.75 ($2.80) children. Apr–Oct daily 9:30am–6pm; Nov–Mar daily 10am–5pm. Bus: 1 or 6.

It's at the top of the Outlook Tower and offers a panoramic view of the surrounding city. Trained guides point out the landmarks and talk about Edinburgh's fascinating history. In addition, there are several entertaining exhibitions, all with an optical theme, and a well-stocked shop selling books, crafts, and compact discs.

Royal Observatory Visitor Centre. Blackford Hill. ☎ **0131/6688405.** Admission £2 ($3.20) adults; £1.25 ($2) children 5–16, students, and seniors; free for children 4 and under. Apr–Sept daily 10am–5pm; Oct–Mar Sat 10am–5pm, Sun 2–5pm. Bus: 41 or 42.

This place shows the works of the Scottish National Observatory at home and abroad, featuring the finest images of astronomical objects, Scotland's largest telescope, and antique instruments. There's also a panoramic view of the city from the balcony. An exhibit, *The Universe,* uses photographs, videos, computers, and models to take you on a cosmic whirlwind tour from the beginning of time to the farthest depths of space in a couple of hours.

Royal Museum of Scotland. Queen St. or Chambers St. ☎ **0131/2257534.** Free admission, except for some temporary exhibitions. Mon–Sat 10am–5pm, Sun noon–5pm.

Two long-established museums, the Royal Scottish Museum and the National Museum of Antiquities, were combined in 1985 to form a single institution, although until a projected date of 1998, they will remain in separate buildings. Displays at both museums range through the decorative arts, ethnography, natural history, geology, archeology, technology, and science.

The Chambers Street building near the Royal Mile, begun in 1861, is a fine example of Victorian architecture and houses international collections in the arts and sciences. The Findlay Building, on Queen Street, opened in 1890, contains collections of Scottish artifacts from prehistoric times to the present.

✪ **Scottish National Gallery of Modern Art.** Belford Rd. ☎ **0131/5568921.** Free admission, except for some temporary exhibitions. Mon–Sat 10am–5pm, Sun 2–5pm. Bus: 13.

In 1984 Scotland's national collection of 20th-century art moved into a gallery converted from a former school building dated 1828. It's set in 12 acres of grounds just a 15-minute walk from the west end of Princes Street. The collection is international in scope and quality in spite of its modest size.

Major sculptures sited outside the building include pieces by Henry Moore and Barbara Hepworth. Inside, the collection ranges from a fauve Derain and cubist Braque and Picasso to recent works by Paolozzi. There's a strong representation of English and Scottish art, and highlights of the collection include works by artists from Europe and America, notably Matisse, Miró, Kirchner, Kokoschka, Ernst, Ben Nicholson, Nevelson, Balthus, Lichtenstein, Kitaj, Hockney, and many others.

Scottish National Portrait Gallery. 1 Queen St. ☎ **0131/2257534.** Free admission, except for some temporary exhibitions. Mon–Sat 10am–5pm, Sun 2–5pm. Bus: 18, 20, or 41.

Housed in a red stone Victorian gothic building by Rowand Anderson, this portrait gallery gives you a chance to see what the famous people of Scottish history looked like. The portraits, several by Ramsay and Raeburn, include everybody from Mary Queen of Scots to Sir Walter Scott, from Flora Macdonald to Ramsay Macdonald.

Dean Village

The village is one of the most photographed sights in the city. Set in a valley about 100 feet below the level of the rest of Edinburgh, it is full of nostalgic charm. A few minutes from the West End, it's located at the end of Bell's Brae, off Queensferry Street, on the Water of Leith. The settlement dates from the 12th century, and the fame of Dean Village grew as a result of its being a grain-milling center. You can enjoy a celebrated view by looking downstream under the high arches of Dean Bridge, designed by Telford in 1833. It's customary to walk along the water in the direction of St. Bernard's Well.

GARDENS

Gardeners and nature lovers in general will be attracted to **Royal Botanic Garden,** Inverleith Row (☎ **0131/5527171**), open May–Aug daily 10am–8pm; Mar–Apr and Sept–Oct daily 10am–6pm; Nov–Feb daily 10am–4pm. Main areas of interest are the Exhibition Plant Houses, Inverleith House, Exhibition Hall, Alpine House, the Demonstration Garden, the Heath Garden, and many others.

The Exhibition Plant Houses range from displays of the fern forests of the southern hemisphere, to desert succulents of arid areas. It's open year-round daily 9am to 1 hour before sunset.

ORGANIZED TOURS

If you want a quick introduction to the principal attractions in and around Edinburgh, consider one or more of the tours offered by **Lothian Region Transport,** 14 Queen St. (☎ **0131/5544494**). You won't find a cheaper way to hit the highlights. The coaches (buses) leave from Waverley Bridge, near the Scott Monument. The tours start in April and run through late October. A curtailed winter program is also offered.

You can see most of the major sights of Edinburgh, including the Royal Mile, Holyrood Castle, Princes Street, and Edinburgh Castle, by double-deck motorcoach for £5 ($8) for adults and £1.50 ($2.40) for children. This ticket is valid all day on any LRT Edinburgh Classic Tour bus, which allows passengers to get on and off at any of the 15 stops along its routes. Buses start from the Waverley Railway Station every day beginning at 9:10am, departing every 15 minutes in summer and about every 30 minutes in winter, then embark on a touristic circuit of Edinburgh, which— if you remain on the bus without ever getting off—will take about 2 hours. Guided commentary is offered along the way.

LRT also operates half-day and full-day motorcoach excursions throughout the various regions of Scotland. White-sided buses identified by their black trim depart from the Waverley Station for "Highland Splendour Tours" to such places as Loch Lomond, Loch Katrine, the Trossachs, St. Andrews, the Isle of Arran, and selected sights in Braemar and Deeside. Their prices, depending on the distance they travel from Edinburgh and their duration, range from £8 to £24 ($12.80 to $38.40) per person, and, in some cases, include lunch. Itineraries vary with the day of the week.

Tickets for any of these tours can be bought at LRT offices at Waverley Bridge, or at 27 Hanover St., or at the tourist information center in Waverley Market. Advance reservations are a good idea for the half-day and full-day tours. For more information, call **0131/5556363,** 24 hours a day.

SHOPPING

For beautiful wall hangings, you can make your own brass rubbings or buy them ready-made from the **Scottish Stone and Brass Rubbing Centre,** Trinity Apse, Chalmers Close, near the Royal Mile (☎ **0131/5564364**). You can visit the center's collection of replicas molded from ancient Pictish stones, rare Scottish brasses, and medieval church brasses.

One of about 30 such shops through the United Kingdom, **Millshop,** 134C Princes St. (☎ **0131/2252319**), sells knitwear, skirts, giftware, and travel rugs. You can purchase some good Scottish woolens here. Most of the merchandise is made in Britain.

The **Edinburgh Crystal** factory, Eastfield, Penicuik (☎ **01968/675128**), lies about 10 miles south of Edinburgh, just off A-701 to Peebles; take bus 62, 64, 65, 81, or 87. It's devoted entirely to handmade crystal glassware, and you can take tours to watch glassmakers at work Mon–Fri 9am–3:30pm. At the Visitor Centre is a factory shop where the world's largest collection of Edinburgh crystal is on view and on sale. You can find inexpensively priced factory seconds.

The two best department stores in Edinburgh are **Debenham's,** 109–112 Princes St. (☎ **0131/2251320**), and **Jenners,** 48 Princes St. (☎ **0131/2252442**). Both stock Scottish and international merchandise.

Looking for a knitted memento? Moira-Anne Leask, owner of the **Shetland Connection,** 491 Lawnmarket (☎ **0131/2253525**), promotes the skills of the Shetland knitter, and her shop is packed with sweaters, hats, and gloves in colorful Fairisle designs. She also offers hand-knitted mohair, Arran, and Icelandic sweaters. Her oldest knitter is 88 years old. Items range from fine-ply cobweb shawls to chunky ski sweaters handcrafted by skilled knitters in top-quality wool.

The **Clan Tartan Centre,** 70–74 Bangor Rd., Leith (☎ **0131/5535100**), is one of the leading specialists in Edinburgh, regardless of which clan you claim as your own. If you want help in identifying a particular tartan, the staff at this shop will assist you. There's also the **James Pringle Woolen Mill,** 70–74 Bangor Rd., Leith (☎ **0131/5535161**), which produces a large variety of top-quality wool items, including a range of Scottish knitwear—cashmere sweaters, tartan and tweed ties, travel rugs, tweed hats, tam o'shanters. In addition, the mill has the only Clan Tartan Centre in Scotland, where more than 2,500 sets and trade designs are accessible through their research facilities.

If you've ever suspected that you might be Scottish, **Tartan Gift Shops,** 54 High St. (☎ **0131/5583187**), has a chart indicating the place of origin (in Scotland) of your family name. You'll then be faced with a bewildering array of hunt and dress tartans for your personal use. The high-quality wool is sold by the yard as well as in the form of kilts for both men and women.

EDINBURGH AFTER DARK

Ask for a free copy of *What's On in Edinburgh* at the Tourist Information Office at Waverley Market. This pocket-size pamphlet, published monthly, lists all the major happenings around town. Even better is the magazine, *The List,* published biweekly, which you can buy at the Tourist Information Office.

✪ EDINBURGH FESTIVAL

The highlight of Edinburgh's year—some would say the only time when the real Edinburgh emerges—comes in the last weeks of August during the **Edinburgh International Festival.** Since 1947 the festival has attracted artists and companies of the highest international standard in all fields of the arts, including music, opera, dance, theater, exhibition, poetry, and prose, and "Auld Reekie" takes on a cosmopolitan air.

During the festival, one of the most exciting spectacles is the Military Tattoo on the floodlit esplanade in front of Edinburgh Castle, high on its rock above the city. Vast audiences watch the precision marching of Scottish regiments and military units from all parts of the world, and of course the stirring skirl of the bagpipes and the swirl of the kilt.

Less predictable in quality but greater in quantity is the **Edinburgh Festival Fringe,** an opportunity for anybody—professional or nonprofessional, an individual, a group of friends, or a whole company of performers—to put on a show wherever they can find an empty stage or street corner. Late-night reviews, outrageous and irreverent contemporary drama, university theater presentations, maybe even a full-length opera—Edinburgh gives them all free rein. As if that weren't enough,

Edinburgh has a **Film Festival,** a **Jazz Festival,** a **Television Festival,** and a **Book Festival** (every second year) at the same time.

Ticket prices vary from £5 ($8) up to about £45 ($72) a seat. Information can be obtained at **Edinburgh International Festival,** 21 Market St., Edinburgh EH1 1BW (☎ **0131/2264001**), open Mon–Fri 9:30am–5:30pm.

Other sources of information include **Edinburgh Festival Fringe,** 180 High St., Edinburgh EH1 1BW (☎ **0131/2265257**); **Edinburgh Book Festival,** 137 Dundee St., Edinburgh EH11 1BG (☎ **0131/2285444**); **Edinburgh Film Festival,** 88 Lothian Rd., Edinburgh EH3 9BZ (☎ **0131/2284051**); and **Edinburgh Military Tattoo,** 32 Market St., Edinburgh EH1 1QB (☎ **0131/2251188**).

THEATER

Edinburgh has a lively theater scene. In 1994, the ✪ **Edinburgh Festival Theatre,** 13–29 Nicolson St. (☎ **0131/6621112** for administration, 0131/5296000 for tickets during nonfestival times, 0131/2255756 for tickets during the Edinburgh Festival), opened in time for some aspects of the Edinburgh Festival. Set on the eastern edge of Edinburgh, near the old campus of the University of Edinburgh, it has since been called "Britain's *de facto* Dance House" because of its sprung floor, its enormous stage (the largest in Britain), and its suitability for opera presentations of all kinds.

Another major theater is the **King's Theatre,** 2 Leven St. (☎ **0131/2204349**), a 1,600-seat Victorian theater offering a wide repertoire of classical entertainment, including ballet, opera, and West End productions. The **Netherbow Arts Centre,** 43 High St. (☎ **0131/5569579**), has been called "informal," but productions here are often experimental and delightful—new Scottish theater at its best. Ask about lunchtime performances.

The resident company of **Royal Lyceum Theatre,** Grindlay Street (☎ **0131/2299697**), also has an enviable reputation; its presentations range from Shakespeare to new Scottish playwrights. The **Traverse Theatre,** Cambridge Street (☎ **0131/2281404**), is one of the few theaters in Britain funded solely to present new plays by British writers and first translations into English of international works. In a modern location, it now offers two theaters under one roof: Traverse 1, with a seating capacity of 250, and Traverse 2, with a smaller capacity of 100.

BALLET, OPERA & CLASSICAL MUSIC

The **Scottish Ballet** and the **Scottish Opera** perform at the **Playhouse Theatre,** 18–22 Greenside Place (☎ **0131/5572590**), which, with 3,100 seats, is the town's largest theater. The **Scottish Chamber Orchestra** makes its home at the **Queen's Hall,** Clerk St. (☎ **0131/6682019**), also a major venue for the Edinburgh International Festival.

The **Royal Scottish Orchestra** plays at **Usher Hall,** Lothian Rd., near Princes Street (☎ **0131/2288616**), Edinburgh's chief venue for orchestral and choral music.

FOLK MUSIC & CEILIDHS

Folk music is presented in many clubs and pubs in Edinburgh, but these strolling players tend to be somewhat erratic or irregular in their appearances. It's best to read notices in pubs and talk to the tourist office to see where the ceilidh will be on the night of your visit.

The Edinburgh Folk Club offers performances on stage at the **Pleasance Cabaret Bar,** 60 The Pleasance (☎ **0131/6521471**), every Wednesday at 8pm. Cover is £4 ($6.40) for adults and £3 ($4.80) for seniors and students (free for children 15 and under).

Some hotels regularly feature traditional Scottish music in the evenings. You might check with the **Carlton Highland Hotel** on North Bridge (☎ **0131/5567277**) or the **George Hotel** on George Street (☎ **0131/2251251**). **Jamie's Scottish Evening** is presented at the King James Hotel on Leith Street (☎ **0131/5560111**) Tues–Sun at 7pm.

A WEE DRAM FOR FANS OF MALT WHISKY

It requires a bit of an effort to reach it (take bus no. 60 from Princes Street to Leith), but for fans of malt whisky, the **Scotch Malt Whisky Society** has been called "The Top of the Whisky Pyramid" by distillery-industry magazines in Britain. It's on the second floor of a 16th-century warehouse at 87 Giles St., Leith (☎ **0131/5543451**), originally designed to store bordeaux and port wines from France and Portugal. All you can order are single-malt whiskies, served neat, usually in a dram (unless you want yours watered down with branch water) and selected from a staggering choice of whiskies from more than 100 distilleries throughout Scotland.

A DANCE CLUB & JAZZ BAR

Century 2000, 31 Lothian Rd. (☎ **0131/2297670**), is the largest disco in Edinburgh as well as one of the most popular. The under-25 crowd flocks here in droves. But it's open only 2 nights a week: Fri–Sat 10pm–4am (no admission after 2am). Cover is £6 ($9.60).

Every night the **Malt Shovel,** 11–15 Cockburn St. (☎ **0131/2256843**), dispenses lots of real ales and single-malt whiskies to a neighborhood clientele, but every Tuesday its live bands draw in a bigger-than-average crowd. Live jazz and traditional Scottish music are featured.

PUBS & BARS

Because it's located on a shop-lined street below the Royal Mile, the **Black Bull,** 12 Grassmarket (☎ **0131/2256636**), is often overlooked by visitors. You can take a shortcut on foot from Edinburgh Castle by descending a steep flight of stone steps, or window-shop along the streets. The pub is decorated like a scarlet version of a Victorian railway car. Of course, the head of a black bull is a focal point. The place jumps at night to the recorded music of whatever group is hot at the time.

Edinburgh's most famous pub—✪ **Café Royal Circle Bar,** 17 W. Register St. (☎ **0131/5561884**)—is a long-enduring favorite. One part is now occupied by the Oyster Bar of the Café Royal, but life in the Circle Bar continues at its old pace. The opulent trappings of the Victorian era are still to be seen. Go up to the serving counter, which stands like an island in a sea of drinkers, and place your order.

Established in 1806, **Deacon Brodie's Tavern,** 435 Lawnmarket (☎ **0131/ 2256531**), is the neighborhood pub along the Royal Mile. It perpetuates the memory of Deacon Brodie, good citizen by day, robber by night. The tavern and wine cellars contain a restaurant and lounge bar.

GAY BARS & CLUBS

Casekudas, 22 Greenside Place (☎ **0131/5581270**), is Edinburgh's best-known gay venue for drinking. As one local wag put it, "Casekudas answers that eternal question of what's under the kilt." There's a cafe downstairs and a weekend disco upstairs.

In a very large once-private duplex apartment a 7-minute walk north of Princes Street, **Laughing Duck,** 24 Howe St. (☎ **0131/2256711**), attracts a very mixed crowd of gay men, as well as a scattering of women. Music videos play, and the music goes on and on. Every Tuesday night the scene is devoted to karaoke performances by members of the audience. Every other Wednesday is "Lady Samantha's Night," when gay women take over. (Every alternate Wednesday gay bingo parties are held upstairs.)

DAY TRIPS FROM EDINBURGH

LINLITHGOW In this royal burgh, a county town in West Lothian, 18 miles west of Edinburgh, Mary Queen of Scots was born. Buses and trains arrive daily from Edinburgh. The ride takes only 20 to 25 minutes.

The roofless ✪ **Linlithgow Palace** (☎ **01506/842896**), birthplace of Mary Queen of Scots in 1542, can still be explored today, even if it's but a shell of its former self. The queen's suite was in the north quarter, but was rebuilt for the homecoming of James VI (James I of Great Britain) in 1620. The palace burned to the ground in 1746. The Great Hall is on the first floor, and a small display shows some of the more interesting architectural relics. The ruined palace is half a mile from Linlithgow Station. Admission is £2 ($3.20) for adults, £1.25 ($2) for seniors, 75p ($1.20) for children. Open Apr–Sept Mon–Sat 9:30am–6:30pm, Sun 2–6pm; Oct–Mar Mon–Sat 9:30am–4:30pm, Sun 2–4pm.

South of the palace stands the medieval kirk of **St. Michael's Parish Church** (☎ **01506/842188**), open daily 10am–4:30pm. It's been where many a Scottish monarch has worshiped since its consecration in 1242. Despite being ravaged by the disciples of John Knox and transformed into a stable by Cromwell, it's one of Scotland's best examples of a parish church.

Set in the midst of beautifully landscaped grounds laid out along the lines of Versailles, **Hopetoun House** lies near the Forth Road Bridge at South Queensferry, 10 miles from Edinburgh. This is Scotland's greatest Adam mansion, and a fine example of 18th-century architecture. The splendid reception rooms are filled with 18th-century furniture, paintings, statuary, and other artworks. From a rooftop viewing platform you see a panoramic view of the Firth of Forth. You can take the nature trail, explore the deer parks, investigate the Stables Museum, or stroll through the formal gardens, all on the grounds. The house (☎ **0131/3312451**) is 2 miles from the Forth Road Bridge near South Queensferry, off A-904. Admission is £4.20 ($6.70) for adults, £3.50 ($5.60) for seniors, £2.10 ($3.35) for children; family ticket (for up to six) £11.50 ($18.40). Open Easter weekend to Sept daily 10am–4:45pm.

NORTH BERWICK This royal burgh, created in the 14th century, was once an important Scottish port. In East Lothian, 24 miles east from Edinburgh, it is today a holiday resort popular with the Scots. Visitors are drawn to its golf courses, beach sands, and harbor life on the Firth of Forth. You can climb the rocky shoreline or enjoy the heated outdoor swimming pool in July and August.

By train on a direct rail line from Edinburgh, the trip takes 30 minutes. There is also bus service to North Berwick from Edinburgh, taking 1¼ hours.

At the **information centre,** Quality Street (☎ **01620/892197**), you can pick up information on boat trips to the offshore islands, including **Bass Rock,** a volcanic island that is a breeding ground for about 10,000 gannets.

Some 2 miles east of North Berwick, and 25 miles east of Edinburgh on A-198, stand the ruins of the 14th-century diked and rose-colored **Tantallon Castle** (☎ **01620/892727**). This was the ancient stronghold of the Douglases until its defeat by Cromwell's forces in 1650. Overlooking the Firth of Forth, the castle ruins still are formidable, with a square, five-story central tower and a dovecote, plus the shell of its east tower, a D-shaped structure with a wall from the central tower. Open Apr–Sept Mon–Sat 9:30am–6pm, Sun 2:30–6pm; Oct–March Mon–Wed and Sat 9:30am–4pm, Thurs 9:30am–noon, Sun 2–4pm. Admission is £2 ($3.20) for adults, £1.25 ($2) for seniors, and 75p ($1.20) for children.

DIRLETON This little town, a preservation village, vies for the title of "prettiest village in Scotland." The town plan, drafted in the early 16th century, is essentially unchanged today. Dirleton has two greens shaped like triangles, with a pub opposite Dirleton Castle, placed at right angles to a group of cottages. It's on the Edinburgh–North Berwick road (A-198). North Berwick (see above) is 5 miles to the east and Edinburgh 19 miles to the west.

A rose-tinted 13th-century castle with surrounding gardens, once the seat of the wealthy Anglo-Norman de Vaux family, **Dirleton Castle** (☎ **01620/850330**) looks like a fairy-tale fortification, with its towers, arched entries, and oak ramp. Ruins of the Great Hall and kitchen can be seen, as well as what's left of the lord's chamber where the de Vaux family lived. The 16th-century main gate has a hole through which boiling tar or water could be poured to discourage unwanted visitors. The castle's country garden and bowling green are still in use. Admission is £2 ($3.20) for adults, £1.25 ($2) for seniors, 75p ($1.20) for children. Open Apr–Sept Mon–Sat 9:30am–6pm, Sun 2–6pm; Oct–Mar Mon–Sat 9:30am–4pm, Sun 2–4pm.

2 Tayside & Grampian

Tayside and Grampian in northeast Scotland, two history-rich sections, offer a vast array of sightseeing, even though they're relatively small areas. Tayside, for example, is about 85 miles, east to west, and some 60 miles south to north. The two regions share the North Sea coast between the Firth of Tay in the south and the Firth of Moray farther north. The so-called Highland Line separating the Lowlands in the south from the Highlands in the north crosses both regions. The Grampians, the highest mountain range in Scotland, are to the west of this line.

Carved out of the old counties of Perth and Angus, **Tayside** is named for its major river, the 119-mile-long Tay. The region is easy to explore. Its tributaries and dozens of lochs and Highland streams are among the best salmon and trout waters in Europe. One of the loveliest regions of Scotland, Tayside is filled with heather-clad Highland hills, long blue lochs under tree-clad banks, and miles and miles of walking trails. Perth and Dundee are among the six leading cities of Scotland. Tayside provided the backdrop for many novels by Sir Walter Scott, including *The Fair Maid of Perth, Waverley,* and *The Abbot.* Its golf courses are world famous, ranging from the trio of 18-hole courses at Gleneagles to the open championship links at Carnoustie.

The **Grampian region** has Aberdeen, Scotland's third-largest city, and Braemar, site of the most famous of the Highland gatherings. The queen herself comes here for holidays to stay at Balmoral Castle, her private residence, a tradition dating back to the days of Queen Victoria and her consort, Prince Albert. As you journey on the scenic roads of Scotland's northeast, you'll pass heather-covered moorland and peaty lochs, wood glens and salmon-filled rivers, granite-stone villages and ancient castles, and fishing harbors as well as North Sea beach resorts.

After exploring Edinburgh, you can tour Tayside and Grampian. Perth, 44 miles north of Edinburgh, makes the best "gateway" to the region. To reach it from Edinburgh, take A-90 northwest and go across the Forth Road Bridge, continuing north along M-90.

PERTH

From its majestic position on the Tay, the ancient city of Perth was the capital of Scotland until the middle of the 15th century. Here the Highlands meet the Lowlands.

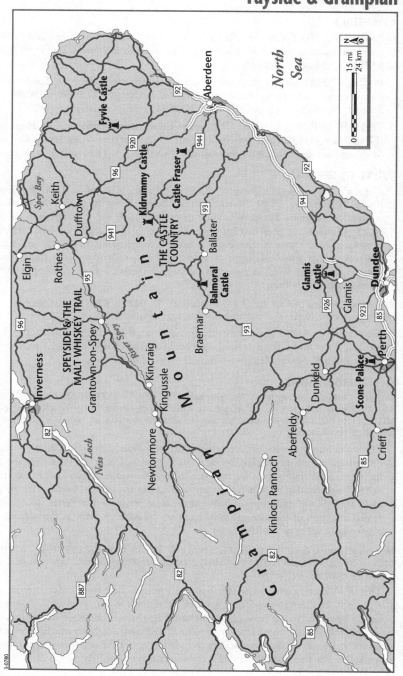

North
Sea

N

15 mi

24 km

0

Aberdeen

92

92

94

Fyvie Castle

920

Kidrummy Castle

944

Castle Fraser

96

Keith

Spey Bay

Dufftown

941

Ballater

93

Elgin

Rothes

95

THE CASTLE COUNTRY

Balmoral Castle

Dundee

96

SPEYSIDE & THE MALT WHISKEY TRAIL

River Spey

Grantown-on-Spey

Kincraig

Braemar

93

Glamis Castle

Glamis

923

85

926

Perth

Inverness

Kingussie

Scone Palace

82

Newtonmore

Mountains

Dunkeld

85

Loch Ness

Aberfeldy

Crieff

Kinloch Rannoch

82

887

82

Grampian

85

3-0780

815

ESSENTIALS

ARRIVING   By Train   ScotRail provides service between Edinburgh and Perth, with continuing service to Dundee. Trip time to Perth is 2 hours. Phone **01738/637117** for 24-hour information.

By Bus   Edinburgh and Perth are connected by frequent bus service. For bus information and schedules, check with National Exchange (☎ **0990/808080**) or Strathtay Scottish Omnibuses (☎ **01382/228345**) for information.

VISITOR INFORMATION   The **tourist information center** is at 45 High St. (☎ **01738/638353**). Hours are Apr 12–Sept 8 Mon–Sat 9am–8pm; Sept 9–Oct 27 Mon–Sat 9am–6pm and Sun noon–6pm; and Oct 28–Apr 11 Mon–Sat 9am–5pm.

WHAT TO SEE & DO

The main sightseeing attraction of "the fair city" is the **Kirk of St. John the Baptist,** 31 St. John St. (☎ **01738/622241**); it's believed that the original foundation is from Pictish times. The present choir dates from 1440 and the nave from 1490. In 1559 John Knox preached his famous sermon here attacking idolatry, which caused a turbulent wave of iconoclasm to sweep across the land. In its wake, religious artifacts, stained glass, and organs were destroyed all over Scotland. The church was restored as a World War I memorial in the mid-1920s. Apr 1–Oct 30, it's open daily 10am–noon and 2–4pm.

Branklyn Garden. Dundee Rd. (A-85), in Branklyn. ☎ **01738/625535.** Admission £2.10 ($3.40) adults, £1.40 ($2.25) children. Mar–Oct daily 9:30am–sunset.

Once the finest 2 acres of private garden in Scotland, the garden now belongs to the National Trust for Scotland. It has a superb collection of rhododendrons, alpines, and herbaceous and peat-garden plants from all over the world.

ACCOMMODATIONS

Dupplin Castle. Near Aberdalgie, Perth, Perthshire PH2 0PY. ☎ **01738/623224.** Fax 01738/444140. 6 rms. TEL. £125 ($200) per person. Rates include dinner, all drinks, and breakfast. MC, V. From Perth follow the main highway to Glasgow, turning left onto B-9112 toward Aberdalgie and Forteviot.

This modern, severely dignified mansion with sandstone mullions was built in 1968 by well-known architect Schomber Scott to replace the last of the three castles that had once risen proudly from the site. The last of these was visited by Queen Victoria in 1842. Surrounded by 30 acres of forest and spectacular gardens (some of its specimens are 250 years old), the site is one of the most beautiful near Perth. Rooms are rented in a spirit of elegance and good manners. Views from many of the bedrooms overlook the valley of the River Earn.

Hunting Tower. Crieff Rd., Perth, Perthshire PH1 3JT. ☎ **01738/583771.** Fax 01738/583777. 25 rms. MINIBAR TV TEL. £90 ($144) double. Rates include Scottish breakfast. AE, DC, MC, V. Drive 2 miles west on A-85.

This late-Victorian country house, about a 10-minute drive from the city center, is set in 3¹/₂ acres of well-manicured gardens. Taste and concern went into its decoration. The public rooms have fine wood paneling; the bedrooms are distinguished, although they range from rather large to small and compact. Such amenities as hair dryers, radios, and trouser presses are included; seven of the accommodations have spa baths. The fine Scottish cuisine is reason enough to stay here.

✪ **Parklands Hotel & Restaurant.** 1 St. Leonard's Bank, Perth, Perthshire PH2 8EB. ☎ **01738/622451.** Fax 01738/622046. 14 rms. TV TEL. £95–£125 ($152–$200) double. Rates include Scottish breakfast. AE, DC, MC, V. Free parking.

Luxuriously overhauled, this is a country-house hotel in the middle of the city, with beautifully decorated bedrooms, filled with wood paneling and cornices, overlooking the South Inch Park. All the rooms are spacious and contain teamakers and hair dryers. Light traditional fare is served in country-house style.

DINING

Littlejohn's. 24 St. John's St. ☎ **01738/639999.** Main courses £3.95–£11.95 ($6.35–$19.15). AE, DC, MC, V. Daily 10am–11pm. INTERNATIONAL.

Set on one of Perth's busiest commercial streets, behind a century-old facade, this restaurant has one large dining room with old-fashioned wood paneling, antique signs, and lots of Scottish charm. Despite the conservative nature of the setting, the food offerings are eclectic, including such items as pizzas, pastas, Mexican tortillas, burgers, steaks, and an occasional lobster dish.

Number Thirty Three. 33 George St. ☎ **01738/633771.** Reservations required. Main courses £10.85–£14.90 ($17.40–$23.85). AE, MC, V. Tues–Sat 12:30–2:30pm and 6:30–9:30pm. Closed Dec 25–26, Jan 1–2, and the last 2 weeks at the end of Jan and the first week in Feb. SEAFOOD.

Acclaimed as the finest dining choice in Perth, this restaurant is the creation of Gavin Billingshurt. Many patrons come here just to enjoy the treats from the oyster bar. In the art deco dining room beyond, you can sample such dishes as grilled salmon seasoned with thyme with a julienne of spring vegetables. Be prepared to put all thoughts of diets aside to enjoy the restaurant's most famous dessert, sticky toffee pudding with butterscotch sauce. Since the restaurant is small, with only seven tables, reservations are vital.

A DAY TRIP TO SCONE

Old Scone, 2 miles from Perth on the River Tay, was the ancient capital of the Picts. On a lump of granite called the "Stone of Destiny" the early Scottish monarchs were enthroned. In 1296 Edward I, the "Hammer of the Scots," moved it to Westminster Abbey, and for hundreds of years it rested under the chair on which British monarchs were crowned. The Scots have always bitterly resented this theft, and at last it has been returned to Scotland, to find a permanent home in Edinburgh Castle (see the introduction to section 1), where it can be viewed by the public.

The seat of the earls of Mansfield and birthplace of David Douglas of fir-tree fame, **Scone Palace,** along A-93 (☎ **01738/552300**), was largely rebuilt in 1802, incorporating the old palace of 1580. Inside is an impressive collection of French furniture, china, ivories, and 16th-century needlework, including bed hangings executed by Mary Queen of Scots. A fine collection of rare conifers is found on the grounds in the Pinetum. Rhododendrons and azaleas grow profusely in the gardens and woodlands around the palace. To reach the palace, head 2 miles northeast of Perth on A-93. The site is open from Good Friday to mid-Oct only, daily 9:30am–5pm. Admission is £5 ($7.30) for adults, £2.80 ($4.50) for children, including entrance to both house and grounds.

Accommodation & Dining

✪ **Murrayshall House Hotel.** New Scone, Perthshire PH2 7PH. ☎ **01738/551171.** Fax 01738/552595. 26 rms. TV TEL. £140 ($225) double. Rates include Scottish breakfast. AE, DC, MC, V. Take A-94, 1¹/₂ miles east of New Scone.

The Murrayshall is an elegant country-house hotel and restaurant set in 300 acres of parkland. It was completely refurbished in 1987 and reopened as one of the showpieces of Perthshire. The Victorian mansion offers its own 18-hole, par-73 golf course, interspersed with trees, water hazards, and white-sand bunkers. The hotel is traditionally styled, in both its public rooms and its bedrooms. The hotel offers the finest dining in the area.

GLENEAGLES

This famous golfing center and sports complex is on a moor between Strath Earn and Strath Allan. Gleneagles has **four 18-hole golf courses,** open only to residents of the Gleneagles hotel: King's Course, the longest one; Queen's Course, next in length; Prince's Course, shortest of all; and Glendevon, the newest of the quartet, built in 1980. They're among the best in Scotland, and the sports complex is one of the best equipped in Europe. Gleneagles is on A-9, about halfway between Perth and Stirling, a short distance from the village of Auchterarder. It lies 55 miles from Edinburgh and 45 miles from Glasgow.

Accommodations & Dining

✪ **Auchterarder House.** Auchterarder, Perthshire PH3 1DZ. ☎ **01764/663646.** Fax 01764/ 662939. 9 rms, 6 suites. TV TEL. £150–£160 ($240–$260) double; £225 ($360) suite. Rates include Scottish breakfast. AE, DC, MC, V.

Auchterarder House, 1 mile from Gleneagles, sits in its own grounds off B-8062 between Auchterarder and Crieff. A fine example of 1830s architecture and construction in the Scots Jacobean style, the mansion house has been completely restored and the interior refurbished to a high standard of luxury by its present owners. The house has elegant public rooms and comfortable bedrooms, all with amenities calculated to please a discerning clientele. At lunch or dinner in the Victorian dining room or in the library, you can choose from a French or British menu.

✪ **Gleneagles Hotel.** Auchterarder, Perthshire PH3 1NF. ☎ **01764/662231.** Fax 01764/ 662134. 234 rms, 18 suites. MINIBAR TV TEL. £230–£355 ($370–$570) double; from £350 ($560) suite. Rates include Scottish breakfast. AE, DC, MC, V. Take A-9, 1¹/₂ miles southwest of Auchterarder.

Gleneagles Hotel stands in its own 830-acre estate. Built in isolated grandeur in 1924, it was then the only five-star hotel in Scotland. The hotel's legendary golf course is its main attraction. The course is open only to residents of Gleneagles, who pay £60 ($100) per person to play the course's famous 18 holes.

Service and decor are among the finest in the country. Each of the luxurious bedrooms contains elegant furnishings and offers views of hills and glens of the surrounding countryside. The chef uses fresh Scottish and French produce, cooked in a light style while still incorporating traditional flair and imagination. Service is impeccable. The hotel's country club, enclosed in a glass dome to provide a year-round tropical climate, offers members and hotel guests use of a swimming pool, whirlpool, Turkish bath, saunas, plunge pool, and children's pool.

CRIEFF

From Perth, head west on A-85 for 18 miles to Crieff. At the edge of the Perthshire Highlands, with good fishing and golf, Crieff makes a pleasant stopover. This small burgh was the seat of the court of the earls of Strathearn until 1747. The gallows in its marketplace was once used to execute Highland cattle rustlers.

You can take a "day trail" into **Strathearn,** the valley of the River Earn, the very center of Scotland. Highland mountains meet gentle Lowland slopes, and moorland mingles with rich green pastures. North of Crieff, the road to Aberfeldy passes through the narrow pass of the **Sma' Glen,** a famous beauty spot, with hills rising on either side to 2,000 feet.

ESSENTIALS

ARRIVING   By Train   There is no direct service. The nearest rail stations are at Gleneagles, 9 miles away, and at Perth, 18 miles away (see above).

By Bus   Once you arrive in Perth, you'll find regular connecting bus service hourly during the day. However, the bus service from Gleneagles is too poor to recommend.

VISITOR INFORMATION   The year-round **tourist information office** is on High Street (☎ **01764/652578**); hours are Mon–Sat 9am–7pm and Sun 11am–6pm.

WHAT TO SEE & DO

Glenturret Distillery Ltd. Hwy. A-85, Glenturret. ☎ **01764/652424.** Guided tours £2.90 ($4.65) adults, £1.70 ($2.75) students 12–17, free for children 11 and under. Mar–Dec Mon–Sat 9:30am–6pm, Sun noon–6pm; Jan–Feb Mon–Fri 11:30am–4pm. Closed Jan 1–2 and Dec 25–26. Take A-85 toward Comrie; three-quarters of a mile from Crieff, turn right at the cross-roads; the distillery is a quarter mile up the road.

Scotland's oldest distillery, Glenturret was established in 1775 on the banks of the River Turret. Visitors can see the milling of malt, mashing, fermentation, distillation, and cask filling, followed by a free "wee dram" dispensed at the end of the tour. Guided tours leave every 10 minutes and take about 25 minutes. The Glenturret Heritage Centre incorporates a 100-seat audiovisual theater and an Exhibition Display Museum. The presentation lasts about 20 minutes.

Drummond Castle. Grimsthorpe, Crieff. ☎ **01764/681257.** Admission £3 ($4.80) adults, £1.50 ($2.40) children. May–Oct daily 2–6pm. Closed Nov–Apr. Take A-822 for 3 miles south of Crieff.

The gardens of Drummond Castle, first laid out in the early 17th century by John Drummond, second earl of Perth, are among the finest formal gardens in Europe. Don't miss the panoramic view from the upper terrace, overlooking an example of an early Victorian parterre in the form of St. Andrew's Cross. The multifaceted sundial by John Mylne, master mason to Charles I, has been the centerpiece since 1630.

Playing Golf

Crieff Golf Club (☎ **01764/652909**) has two courses—both are set in Perthshire with panoramic views and excellent facilities. The most challenging is the 18-hole Fern Tower, a par-71 course with three par-5 holes. The Dornock is a 32-par, 9-hole course with three par-3 holes. It's not quite as difficult as the Fern Tower, but a test nonetheless. Greens fees for the Fern Tower are £18 ($28.80) per round Mon–Fri, and £25 ($40) on weekends. Greens fees for the Dornock are £8 ($12.80) for 9 holes and £12 ($19.20) for 18 holes during the week and £12 ($19.20) for 9 holes and £15 ($24) for 18 holes on weekends. Carts cost £15 ($24.15) per round. No blue jeans are allowed, and all shirts must have collars.

ACCOMMODATIONS & DINING

Murraypark Hotel. Connaught Terrace, Crieff, Perthshire PH7 3DJ. ☎ **01764/653731.** Fax 01764/655311. 21 rms. TV TEL. £75 ($120) double. Rates include Scottish breakfast. AE, DC, MC, V.

This stone-fronted house lies in a residential neighborhood about a 10-minute walk from Crieff's center. In 1993 a new wing was opened, enlarging the public rooms and the number of simply furnished guest accommodations. The restaurant's cuisine is based on Scottish, French, and international inspirations.

ABERFELDY

The "Birks o' Aberfeldy" are among the beauty spots made famous by the poet Robert Burns. Once a Pictish center, this small town makes a fine base for touring Perthshire's glens and lochs. Loch Tay lies 6 miles to the west; Glen Lyon, 15 miles west; and Kinloch Rannoch, 18 miles northwest. In the town's shops are good buys in tweeds and tartans, plus other items of Highland dress.

ESSENTIALS

ARRIVING   By Train   There is no direct service into Aberfeldy. You can take a train to either Perth (see above) or Pitlochry, then continue the rest of the way by bus.

By Bus   Approximately 10 buses a day from Perth and Pitlochry make the journey to Aberfeldy (no connections Sun). Buses from Perth sometimes come through Pitlochry first.

By Car   From Crieff, take A-822 on a winding road north to Aberfeldy.

VISITOR INFORMATION   The **tourist information office** is at The Square (☎ **01887/820276**). Hours are Apr–June Mon–Sat 9:30am–5:30pm and Sun 11am–4pm; July 1–Sept 8 Mon–Sat 9am–7pm and Sun 11am–6pm; Sept 9–Oct 27 Mon–Sat 9:30am–5:30pm and Sun 11am–4pm; Oct 28–Mar Mon–Fri 9:30am–5pm and Sat 9:30am–1:30pm.

PLAYING GOLF

Aberfeldy Golf Club, at Aberfeldy (☎ **01887/820535**), is a pleasant flatland course located on the banks of the River Tay. It is an 18-hole par 68 that is viewed as a "challenge" by the local pro. The River Tay comes in to play on several holes, and if you're not careful, you'll be making trips back to the Pro Shop for more golf balls. Greens fees are £14 ($22.40) for 18 holes, and cart fees are £1.50 ($2.40) per round (pull carts).

ACCOMMODATIONS & DINING

Farleyer House Hotel. Hwy. B-846, Aberfeldy, Perthshire PH15 2JE. ☎ **01887/820332.** Fax 01887/829430. 10 rms, 1 suite. TV TEL. £170–£210 ($275–$340) double; £190 ($305) suite. Rates include Scottish breakfast. AE, MC, V. Take B-846 for 2 miles west of Aberfeldy.

A tranquil oasis, this Scottish hotel of character stands on 70 acres of grounds in the Tay Valley. Dating from the 1500s but much restored and altered over the years, it entertains guests as if they were in a private home. The public rooms are immaculate and beautifully furnished, and the bedrooms are well maintained and comfortable. The internationally renowned Menzies Restaurant offers a fixed-price menu of five courses changed daily.

DUNKELD

A cathedral town, Dunkeld lies in a thickly wooded valley of the Tay River at the edge of the Perthshire Highlands. Once a major ecclesiastical center, it's one of the seats of ancient Scottish history and an important center of the Celtic church.

ESSENTIALS

ARRIVING   By Train   Trains from Perth arrive every 2 hours at Dunkeld Station, which is actually in the neighboring town of Birnam.

By Bus   Pitlochry-bound buses leaving from Perth make a stopover in Dunkeld, letting you off at the Dunkeld Car Park.

By Car   From Aberfeldy, take the A-827 east until you reach the junction of A-9 heading south to Dunkeld.

VISITOR INFORMATION   A **tourist information office** is at The Cross (☎ **01350/727688**). It's open Apr–June Mon–Sat 9:30am–5:30pm and Sun 11am–4pm; July 1–Sept 8 Mon–Sat 9am–7:30pm and Sun 11am–7pm; Sept 9–Oct 27 Mon–Sat 9:30am–5:30pm and Sun 11am–4pm; Oct 28–Dec Mon–Sat 9:30am–1:30pm (closed Jan–Mar).

WHAT TO SEE & DO

Founded in A.D. 815, the **Cathedral of Dunkeld** was converted from a church to a cathedral in 1127 by David I. It stands on Cathedral Street in a scenic setting along the River Tay. The 14th and 15th centuries witnessed subsequent additions. The cathedral was first restored in 1815, and traces of the 12th-century structure clearly remain today. It can be visited Apr–Sept daily 9:30am–6pm; Oct–Mar Mon–Sat 9:30am–4pm and Sun 2–4pm. Admission is free.

The National Trust for Scotland has restored many of the old houses and shops around the marketplace and cathedral that had fallen into decay. The trust owns 20 houses on High Street and Cathedral Street as well. Many of these houses were constructed in the closing years of the 17th century after the rebuilding of the town following the Battle of Dunkeld. The Trust runs the **Ell Shop,** The Cross (☎ **01350/727460**), open Easter weekend to May and Sept–Dec 22 Mon–Sat 10am–4:30pm; June–Aug Mon–Sat 10am–5:30pm and Sun 1:30–5:30pm.

The **Scottish Horse Museum,** The Cross, has exhibits tracing the history of the Scottish Horse Yeomanry, a cavalry force first raised in 1900. Open Mon–Wed 10am–5pm; admission by voluntary donation.

Shakespeare fans may want to seek out the oak and sycamore in front of the destroyed Birnam House, a mile to the south. This was believed to be a remnant of the **Birnam Wood** in *Macbeth;* you may recall, Macbeth could be defeated only when Birnam Wood came to Dunsinane.

The Hermitage, lying off A-9 about 2 miles west of Dunkeld, was called a "folly" when it was constructed in 1758 above the wooded gorge of the River Braan. Today it makes for one of the most scenic woodland walks in the area.

Playing Golf

Dunkeld & Birnam, at Dunkeld (☎ **01350/727524**), is touted as the best in the area. The 18-hole course is not too long, but can be quite difficult to play. It's edged in many areas with brachen, and many a golfer has had to take a drop (along with the mandatory extra stroke) instead of searching for their errant ball. There are sweeping views of the surrounding environs. Greens fees: Mon–Fri £11 ($17.60) for 18 holes or £22 ($20.80) for a day ticket (2 rounds); Sat–Sun £16 ($25.60) for 18 holes or £22 ($35.20) for a day ticket. There are no electric carts; pull carts are available for £2 ($3.20) per round. There is no official dress code, although if the starter feels you are not dressed "appropriately" you will be asked to "smarten up" the next time you play the course.

ACCOMMODATIONS & DINING

✪ **Kinnaird.** Kinnaird, Kinnaird Estate, Dunkeld, Perthshire PH8 0LB. ☎ **01796/482440.** Fax 01796/482289. 8 rms, 1 suite. TV TEL. £200–£240 ($320–$384) double; £275 ($440) suite. Rates include Scottish breakfast. No children under 12 accepted. AE, MC, V.

On a 9,000-acre private estate, this is a small hotel of great warmth, charm, and comfort. Built in 1770 as a hunting lodge, the house has been restored to its previous grandeur. All the beautifully furnished bedrooms have king-size beds, private baths, and views. Some rooms overlook the valley of the River Tay, and others open onto gardens and woodlands. Kinnaird House Restaurant brings a high-caliber cuisine to the area. The chef cooks in the modern, post-nouvelle British and continental style, depending on fresh ingredients, with changing menus based on the season. Sporting facilities on the estate include salmon and trout fishing, roe stalking, and shooting for pheasant, grouse, and duck.

✪ **Stakis Dunkeld House Resort Hotel.** Dunkeld, Perthshire PH8 0HX. ☎ **01350/727771.** Fax 01350/728924. 83 rms, 3 suites. MINIBAR TV TEL. £112 ($179.20) double; £184 ($294.40) suite. Rates include Scottish breakfast. AE, DC, MC, V.

The hotel offers the quiet dignity of life in a Scottish country house. It's ranked as one of the leading leisure and sports hotels in the area. On the banks of the Tay, the surrounding grounds—280 acres in all—make a parklike setting. The house is beautifully kept, and the accommodations come in a wide range of styles, space, and furnishings. The hotel, extensively restored and expanded by the Stakis chain, now offers first-class bedrooms. Its restaurant is one of the finest in the area, paying homage to its "Taste of Scotland" dishes. Salmon and trout fishing are possible right on the grounds, and facilities include an indooor swimming pool and all-weather tennis courts.

DUNDEE & GLAMIS CASTLE

This royal burgh and old seaport is an industrial city on the north shore of the Firth of Tay. When steamers took over the whaling industry from sailing vessels, Dundee became the leading home port for the ships from the 1860s until World War I. Long known for its jute and flax operations, we think today of the rich Dundee fruitcakes and Dundee marmalades and jams. This was also the home of the man who invented stick-on postage stamps, James Chalmers.

Spanning the Firth of Tay is the **Tay Railway Bridge,** opened in 1888. Constructed over the tidal estuary, the bridge is some 2 miles long, one of the longest in Europe. There's also a road bridge 1 1/4 miles long, with four traffic lanes and a walkway in the center.

ESSENTIALS

ARRIVING   By Train   ScotRail offers frequent service between Perth, Dundee, and Aberdeen. Phone **01345/212282** in Perth for schedules and departure times.

By Bus   National Express buses offer frequent bus service from Edinburgh and Glasgow. In Edinburgh phone **0990/400400** for information.

By Car   The fastest way to reach Dundee is to cut south back to Perth along A-9 and link up with the A-972 going east.

VISITOR INFORMATION   The **tourist information office** is at 4 City Square (☎ **01382/227723**). Hours are Mon–Fri 9am–5pm and Sat 9:30am–1:30am.

WHAT TO SEE & DO

For a panoramic view of Dundee, the Tay bridges across to Fife, and mountains to the north go to **Dundee Law,** a 572-foot hill a mile north of the city. The hill is an ancient volcanic plug.

HMS Frigate *Unicorn.* Victoria Dock. ☎ **01382/200900.** Admission £2 ($3.20) adults, £1.50 ($2.40) children. Daily 10am–5pm. Bus: 6, 23, or 78.

This 46-gun ship of war commissioned in 1824 by the Royal Navy, now the oldest British-built ship afloat, has been restored and visitors can explore all four decks: the quarterdeck with 32-pound cannonades, the gun deck with its battery of 18-pound cannons and the captain's quarters, the berth deck with officers' cabins and crews' hammocks, and the orlop deck and hold. Various displays portraying life in the sailing navy and the history of the *Unicorn* make this a rewarding visit.

Broughty Castle. Castle Green, Broughty Ferry. ☎ **01382/776121.** Free admission. July–Sept Mon–Thurs and Sat 11am–1pm and 2–5pm, Sun 2–5pm; Oct–June Mon–Thurs 10am–1pm and 2–5pm. Bus: 7, 9, 11, or 24.

This 15th-century estuary fort lies about 4 miles east of the city center on the seafront, at Broughty Ferry, a little fishing hamlet and once the terminus for ferries crossing the Firth of Tay before the bridges were built. Besieged by the English in the 16th century, and attacked by Cromwell's army under General Monk in the 17th, it was eventually restored as part of Britain's coastal defenses in 1861. Its gun battery was dismantled in 1956, and it's now a museum with displays on local history, arms and armor, and Dundee's whaling story. The observation area at the top of the castle provides fine views of the Tay estuary and northeast Fife.

Playing Golf

Caird Park, at Dundee (☎ **01382/434706**), is an 18-hole, par-72 course that presents most golfers with an average challenge. The course is quite flat, but there are more than a few bunkers to navigate. There is also a restaurant and bar on the premises (functioning as the famed 19th hole). Greens fees are £13.30 ($21.30) for 18 holes, or £22 ($35.20) for a day ticket. No carts of any sort are allowed on the course, and there is no particular dress code.

ACCOMMODATIONS

Invercarse Hotel. 371 Perth Rd., Dundee, Angus DD2 1PG. ☎ **01382/669231.** Fax 01382/644112. 32 rms. TV TEL. £80 ($128) double. Rates include Scottish breakfast. AE, MC, V.

In landscaped gardens overlooking the River Tay, this privately owned hotel lies 3 miles west of the heart of Dundee. Many prefer it for its fresh air, tranquil location, and Victorian country-house aura. The guest rooms open onto views across the Tay to the hills of the Kingdom of Fife. Accommodations come in a variety of sizes, but all are well maintained and furnished, often with pieces crafted from light-grained wood. Guests enjoy drinks in the bar, furnished in red leather, later ordering a continental or Scottish cuisine.

Stakis Earl Grey Hotel. Earl Grey Place, Dundee, Angus DD1 4DE. ☎ **01382/229271.** Fax 01382/200072. 102 rms, 2 suites. TV TEL. £115 ($184) double; £170 ($272) suite. AE, DC, MC, V. Free parking. Bus: 1A, 1B, or 20.

This chain hotel helped rejuvenate the once-seedy waterfront of Dundee. Built in a severe modern style, it takes its name from a famous English tea, which most often accompanies marmalade and Dundee fruitcakes, the city's two most famous products. Some of the well-furnished bedrooms overlook the Firth, the river, or the Tay Bridge. Guests can dine at Juliana's Table Restaurant, featuring buffet-style meals along with table d'hôte lunches and dinners. Facilities include a heated indoor swimming pool, exercise equipment, sauna, and whirlpool.

DINING

Jahangir Tandoori. 1 Sessions St. (at the corner of Hawk Hill). ☎ **01382/202022.** Reservations recommended. Main courses £6.50–£15 ($10.40–$24). AE, MC, V. Daily 5pm–midnight. INDIAN.

Built around an indoor fish pond in a dining room draped with the soft folds of an embroidered tent, this is one of the most exotic restaurants in the region. Meals are prepared with fresh ingredients and cover the gamut of recipes from both north and south India. Some preparations are slow-cooked in clay pots (tandoori) and seasoned to the degree of spiciness you prefer. Both meat and meatless dishes are available, and the staff is polite and discreet.

A Day Trip to Glamis

The little village of Glamis (pronounced without the "i") grew up around **Glamis Castle,** Estate Office, Glamis (☎ **01307/840242**). Next to Balmoral Castle, visitors to Scotland most want to see Glamis Castle for its link with the crown. For six centuries it has been connected to members of the British royal family. The Queen Mother was brought up here; and Princess Margaret was born here, becoming the first royal princess born in Scotland in three centuries. The present owner is the queen's great-nephew. The castle contains Duncan's Hall, supposedly the setting for Shakespeare's *Macbeth,* who was thane of Glamis.

The present Glamis Castle dates from the early 15th century, but there are records of a castle having been in existence in the 11th century. Glamis Castle has been in the possession of the Lyon family since 1372. It contains some fine plaster ceilings, furniture, and paintings.

The castle is open to the public, with access to the Royal Apartments and many other rooms, and the fine gardens, early April–Oct daily 10:30am–5:30pm; closed Nov–Mar. Admission to the castle and gardens is £4.70 ($7.55) adults, £2.60 ($4.20) children. If you wish to visit the grounds only, the charge is £2.20 ($3.55) adults, £1.10 ($1.80) children. Buses run between Dundee and Glamis.

Accommodations

Castleton House. Eassie by Glamis, Forfar, Tayside DD8 1SJ. ☎ **01307/840340.** Fax 01307/ 840506. 6 rms. TV TEL. £130 ($208) double. Children stay free in parents' room. Rates include Scottish breakfast. AE, DC, MC, V. Drive 3 miles west of Glamis on A-94.

This Victorian hotel has been restored with love and care by its owners, Maureen and William Little. In cool weather you're greeted by welcoming coal fires in both the bar and public lounge, and a youthful staff that's the most considerate we've encountered in the area. Bedrooms of various sizes are furnished with reproduction antiques. Chef William Little features a set luncheon and a fixed-price dinner. The menu changes daily but is based on the freshest produce in any given season.

Dining

Strathomore Arms. Glamis. ☎ **01307/840248.** Reservations recommended. Main courses £4.95–£11.75 ($7.95–$18.80); fixed-price menu £18.75 ($30). AE, MC, V. Daily noon–9pm. FRENCH/SCOTTISH.

Try this place near the castle for one of the best lunches in the area. You might begin with a freshly made soup of the day or Cheddar-filled mushrooms wrapped in bacon and grilled. Grilled lamb cutlets are regularly featured, as is poached sole with prawns and mushrooms in a light curry sauce. You might also try fillet of Angus beef in a whisky sauce.

BRAEMAR

In the heart of some of Grampian's most beautiful scenery, Braemar is not only known for its own castle but it also makes a good center from which to explore Balmoral Castle (see "Ballater & Balmoral Castle," later in this chapter). In this Highland village, set against a massive backdrop of hills covered with heather in summer, Clunie Water joins the River Dee. The massive **Cairn Toul** towers over Braemar, reaching a height of 4,241 feet.

ESSENTIALS

ARRIVING **By Train** Take the train to Aberdeen, then continue the rest of the way by bus.

By Bus Regular buses run daily from Aberdeen west to Braemar. The bus station in Aberdeen is on Guild Street (call **01224/212266** for information about schedules), beside the train station.

By Car To reach Braemar from Dundee, return west to Perth, then head north along A-93, following the signs into Braemar.

VISITOR INFORMATION The summer-only **Braemar Tourist Office** is in The Mews, Mar Road (☎ **013397/41600**). Hours are July–Aug daily 9:30am–7pm; Sept–June, daily 9:30am–5:30pm.

SPECIAL EVENTS The spectacular **Royal Highland Gathering** takes place annually the first Saturday in September in the Princess Royal and Duke of Fife Memorial Park. The queen herself often attends the gathering. These ancient games are thought to have been originated by King Malcolm Canmore. That chieftain ruled much of Scotland at the time of the Norman conquest of England, and he selected his hardiest warriors from all the clans for a "keen and fair contest."

The secretary of the Balmoral Highland Society (☎ **013397/55377**) can also reserve tickets. Braemar is overrun with visitors during the gathering—anyone thinking of attending would be wise to reserve accommodations anywhere within a 20-mile radius of Braemar not later than early April.

WHAT TO SEE & DO

If you're a royal family watcher, you might be able to spot members of the family, even the queen, at **Crathie Church,** 9 miles east of Braemar on A-93 (☎ **013397/422208**), where they attend Sunday services when in residence. Services are at 11:30am; otherwise the church is open to view Apr–Oct Mon–Sat 9:30am–5:30pm and Sun2–5:30pm.

Nature lovers may want to drive to the **Linn of Dee,** 6 miles west of Braemar, a narrow chasm on the River Dee, which is a local beauty spot. Other beauty spots include Glen Muick, Loch Muick, and Lochnagar. A **Scottish Wildlife Trust Visitor Centre,** reached by a minor road, is located in this Highland glen, off the South Deeside road. An access road joins B-976 at a point 16 miles east of Braemar. The tourist office (see above) will give you a map pinpointing these beauty spots.

✪ **Braemar Castle.** On the Aberdeen–Ballater–Perth Rd. (A-93). ☎ **013397/41219.** Admission £2 ($3.20) adults, £1 ($1.60) children. May–Oct 15 Sat–Thurs 10am–6pm. Closed Nov–Good Friday. Take A-93 half a mile northeast of Braemar.

This romantic 17th-century castle is a fully furnished private residence of architectural grace, scenic charm, and historical interest. The castle has barrel-vaulted ceilings and an underground prison and is known for its remarkable star-shaped defensive curtain wall.

Playing Golf

Braemar Golf Course, at Braemar (☎ **013397/41618**), is the highest golf course in the country. The green of the second hole is 1,250 feet above sea level—this is the trickiest hole on the course. Pro golf commentator Peter Alliss has deemed it "the hardest par 4 in all of Scotland." Set on a plateau, the hole is bordered on the right by the River Clunie and lined on the left by rough. Greens fees are as follows: Mon–Fri £12 ($19.20) for 18 holes and £16 ($25.60) for a day ticket; Sat and Sun £15 ($24) for 18 holes and £20 ($32) for a day ticket. Pull carts can be rented for £1.50

($2.40) per round and sets of clubs can be borrowed for £5 ($8) per day. The only dress code is "be reasonable."

ACCOMMODATIONS & DINING

Braemar Lodge Hotel. Glenshee Rd., Braemar, Aberdeenshire AB35 5YQ. ☎ and fax **013397/41627.** 6 rms. TV. £72 ($115.20) double. Rates include Scottish breakfast. MC, V. Closed Nov–Easter. Bus: 201.

This hotel, popular with skiers at the nearby Glenshee slopes, is set on 2 acres of grounds at the head of Glen Clunie. The bedrooms have a strikingly modern decor. Dinner, served in the restaurant from 7pm, includes "Taste of Scotland" dishes on the à la carte menu. Lunch is not served. The food is excellent. A typical dinner might begin with smoked venison, followed with fennel and green pepper soup, then noisettes of Scottish lamb grilled with fresh rosemary for a main course. The hotel is on the road to the Glenshee ski slopes, near the cottage where Robert Louis Stevenson wrote *Treasure Island*.

Invercauld Arms Hotel. Braemar, Aberdeenshire AB35 5YR. ☎ **013397/41605.** Fax 013397/41428. 68 rms. £102 ($163.20) double. Rates include Scottish breakfast. AE, DC, MC, V. Bus: 201.

The Invercauld Arms Hotel is an old granite building of which the original part dates back to the 18th century. In cool weather there's a roaring log fire on the hearth. You can go hill walking and see deer, golden eagles, and other wildlife. Fishing and, in winter, skiing are other pursuits in the nearby area. The bedrooms are comfortably furnished, but rather uninspired. In the pub close by you'll meet the "ghillies" and "stalkers" and then return to the Scottish and international fare served at the hotel, with fresh Dee salmon, Aberdeen Angus beef, venison, and grouse.

BALLATER & BALMORAL CASTLE

Ballater is a holiday resort center on the Dee River, with the Grampian Mountains in the background. The town still centers around its Station Square, where the royal family used to be photographed as they arrived to spend holidays. The railway is now closed.

ESSENTIALS

ARRIVING   By Train   Go to Aberdeen and continue the rest of the way by connecting bus.

By Bus   Regular buses run daily from Aberdeen west to Ballater. The bus station in Aberdeen is on Guild Street (☎ **01224/212266** for information about schedules), beside the train station. Bus no. 201 from Braemar runs to Ballater.

By Car   Go east along A-93.

VISITOR INFORMATION   The summer-only **tourist information office** is at Station Square (☎ **013397/55306**). Hours are July–Aug daily 10am–1pm and 2–6pm; Sept–Oct and May–June Mon–Sat 10am–1pm and 2–5pm, Sun 1–5pm; closed Nov–Apr.

THE CASTLE

✪ **Balmoral Castle.** Balmoral, Ballater. ☎ **013397/42334.** Admission £3 ($4.80) adults, £2.50 ($4) senior citizens, free for children 15 and under. May–July Mon–Sat 10am–5pm. Crathie bus from Aberdeen to the Crathie station; Balmoral Castle is signposted from there (a quarter-mile walk).

"This dear paradise" is how Queen Victoria described Balmoral Castle, rebuilt in the Scottish baronial style by her beloved Albert and completed in 1855. Today Balmoral,

8 miles west of Ballater, is still a private residence of the British sovereign. Its principal feature is a 100-foot tower. On the grounds are many memorials to the royal family. In addition to the gardens there are country walks, pony trekking, souvenir shops, and a refreshment room. Of the actual castle, only the ballroom is open to the public. It houses an exhibition of pictures, porcelain, and works of art.

Playing Golf

Ballater Golf Club, at Ballater (☎ **013397/55567**), is one of the more scenic courses in the area. Set in a bowl of mountains and situated on the banks of the River Dee, this is a 5,638-yard, par-67 course. Greens fees are as follows: Mon–Fri £17 ($27.20) for 18 holes or £26 ($41.60) for a day ticket; Sat–Sun £20 ($32) for 18 holes or £30 ($48) for a day ticket. There are no carts for hire. Dress is smart but casual.

ACCOMMODATIONS

Craigendarroch Hotel and Country Club. Braemar Rd., Ballater, Aberdeenshire AB35 5XA. ☎ **013397/55858.** Fax 013397/55447. 49 rms, 6 suites. TV TEL. £129 ($206.40) double; £199 ($318.40) suite. Rates include Scottish breakfast. AE, DC, MC, V.

The hotel, built in the Scottish baronial style, is set amid old trees on a 28-acre estate. Modern 20th-century comfort has been added, but the owners have tried to maintain a 19th-century aura. The public rooms include a regal oaken staircase and a large sitting room. The fair-size bedrooms open onto views of the village of Ballater and the River Dee. The accommodations are furnished in an individual style and have such amenities as hair dryers, trouser presses, private baths (with showers), and small refrigerators (not minibars). The public facilities are luxurious, especially the study with oak paneling, a log fire, and book-lined shelves. Facilities include the Leisure Club with a spa pool, two swimming pools, a sauna, and a solarium.

✪ **Monaltrie Hotel.** 5 Bridge Sq., Ballater, Aberdeenshire AB35 5QJ. ☎ **013397/55417.** Fax 013397/55180. 25 rms. TV TEL. £60 ($96) double. Rates include Scottish breakfast. AE, DC, MC, V.

This hotel, the first in the region, was built in 1835 of Aberdeen granite to accommodate the clients of a now-defunct spa. Today it bustles with a contemporary clientele who come for the live music in its pub and for the savory food served in its two restaurants. The more unusual of the two is a Thai restaurant, which serves dinner only, Thurs–Tues 7–10pm. Each of the bedrooms contains an unobtrusive monochromatic decor and comfortable beds.

DINING

Green Inn. 9 Victoria Rd., Ballater, Aberdeenshire AB35 5QQ. ☎ **013397/55701.** Reservations required. Main courses £12.75–£16.50 ($20.40–$26.40); fixed-price lunch £8.50–£10.50 ($13.60–$16.80). MC, V. Mon–Sat 7–9:30pm, Sun 12:30–1:30pm and 7–9:30pm. Closed the first week in Jan and 2 weeks in Oct. SCOTTISH.

In the heart of town, this establishment was once a temperance hotel. Now the pink-granite inn is one of the finest dining rooms in town, especially for traditional Scottish dishes. The chef places emphasis on local produce, including home-grown vegetables when available. In season, loin of venison is served with a bramble sauce, and you can always count on fresh salmon and the best of Angus beef.

Three very simply furnished double bedrooms are rented here, all with private baths (with shower) and TV. B&B costs £44.50 ($70.30) per person.

✪ **Oaks Restaurant.** In the Craigendarroch Hotel & Country Club, Braemar Rd. ☎ **013397/ 55858.** Reservations strongly recommended. Fixed-price Sun lunch £14 ($22.40); fixed-price four-course dinner £27 ($43.20). AE, DC, MC, V. Mon–Sat 7–10:30pm, Sun 12:30–2:30pm and 7–10:30pm. BRITISH.

The most glamorous restaurant in the region, the Oaks is in the century-old mansion that was originally built by the "marmalade kings" of Britain, the Keiller family. (The company's marmalade is still a household word throughout the U.K.) This is the most upscale of the three restaurants in a resort complex that includes hotel rooms, time-share villas, and access to a nearby golf course. Specialties include fillets of beef and veal on a bed of parsnips with red-wine sauce, wild duck with assorted sweetbreads in a chive dressing, poached lobster with tomato ravioli, or pan-fried rack of lamb with rosemary, watercress, poppyseed, and sesame-seed dressing.

THE CASTLE COUNTRY

The city of Aberdeen, Scotland's "third city," is bordered by fine sandy beaches (if you're a polar bear) and is filled with buildings constructed largely of pink and gray granite. The harbor in this seaport is one of the largest fishing ports in the country, and Aberdeen is the capital of the oil workers of six North Sea oilfields. However, far more interesting to visitors with limited time is the array of 40 inhabited castles on the periphery of the city, which has earned the area the title of "castle country," all lying within a 40-mile radius of Aberdeen. Since time is limited for most motorists, we've spotlighted only the most intriguing.

Castle Fraser. Sauchen, near Kemnay. ☎ **01330/833463.** Admission £3.60 ($5.75) adults, £2.40 ($3.85) children, free for children 4 and under. Apr and Oct Sat–Sun 2–5:30pm; May–June daily 1:30–5:30pm; July–Aug daily 11am–5:30pm; Sept daily 2–5:30pm. Closed Nov–Mar. Head 3 miles south of Kemnay, 16 miles west of Aberdeen, off A-944.

One of the most impressive of the fortresslike castles of Mar, Castle Fraser stands in a 25-acre parkland setting. The sixth laird, Michael Fraser, began the structure in 1575, and his son finished it in 1636. Its Great Hall is spectacular, and you can wander around the grounds, which include an 18th-century walled garden.

Kildrummy Castle. Hwy. A-97, Kildrummy. ☎ **019755/71331.** Admission £1.50 ($2.40) adults, 75p ($1.20) children. Apr–Sept Mon–Sat 9:30am–6pm, Sun 2–6pm; Oct–Nov Mon–Sat 9:30am–4pm, Sun 2–4pm. Closed Dec–Mar. Take A-944 for 35 miles west of Aberdeen; it's signposted off A-97, 10 miles west of Alford.

The ruins of the ancient seat of the earls of Mar, this is the most extensive example of a 13th-century castle in Scotland. You can see the four round towers, the hall, and the chapel from the original structure. The great gatehouse and other remains date from the 16th century. The castle played a major role in Scottish history up to 1715, when it was dismantled.

✪ Fyvie Castle. Fyvie, on the Aberdeen–Banff road. ☎ **01651/891266.** Admission £4 ($6.40) adults, £2.70 ($4.30) children. Apr–June daily 1:30–5:30pm; July–Aug daily 11am–5:30pm; Sept daily 1:30–5:30pm; Oct Sat–Sun 1:30–5:30pm. Closed Nov–Mar. Take A947 for 23 miles northwest of Aberdeen.

The National Trust for Scotland opened this castle to the public in 1986. The oldest part, dating from the 13th century, is the grandest existing example of Scottish baronial architecture. There are five towers, named after Fyvie's five families—the Prestons, Melddrums, Setons, Gordons, and Leiths—who lived here over five centuries. Originally built in a royal hunting forest, Fyvie means "deer hill" in Gaelic. The interior, created by the first Lord Leith of Fyvie, a steel magnate, reflects the opulence of the Edwardian era. His collections contain arms and armor, 16th-century tapestries, and important artworks by Raeburn, Gainsborough, and Romney. The castle is rich in ghosts, curses, and legends.

SPEYSIDE & THE MALT WHISKY TRAIL

Much of the region covered in this section is in the Moray district, on the southern shore of the Moray Firth, a great inlet cutting into the northeastern coast of Scotland. The district stretches in a triangular shape south from the coast to the wild heart of the Cairngorm Mountains near Aviemore. It's a land steeped in history, as its many castles, battle sites, and ancient monuments testify. It's also very sports oriented, attracting not only fishers but also golfers. Golfers can purchase a 5-day ticket from tourist information centers that will allow them to play at more than 11 courses in the area.

One of the best of these courses is **Boat of Garten,** Speyside (☎ **01479/831282**). If you're up for a nice stroll, you've come to the right place. There are no carts allowed on the almost 6,000-yard venue. Relatively difficult, the course is dotted with many bunkers and wooded areas. Greens fees are Mon–Fri £15 ($24) per day, and Sat–Sun £20 ($32) per day. Dress is reasonable, although blue jeans are not acceptable.

The valley of the second-largest river in Scotland, the Spey, lies north and south of Aviemore. It's a land of great natural beauty. A journey north through Speyside will take you toward the Malt Whisky Trail. The Spey is born in the Highlands above Loch Laggan, which lies 40 miles south of Inverness. Little more than a creek at its inception, it gains in force, fed by the many "burns" that drain water from the surrounding hills. It's one of Scotland's great rivers for salmon fishing, and it runs between the towering Cairngorms on the east and the Monadhliath Mountains on the west. Its major center is Grantown-on-Spey.

The major tourist attraction is the **Malt Whisky Trail,** 70 miles long, running through the glens of Speyside. Here distilleries, many of which can be visited, are known for their production of *uisge beatha* or "water of life." Whisky (note the spelling without the e) is its more familiar name.

Half the malt distilleries in the country lie along the River Spey and its tributaries. Here peat smoke and Highland water are used to turn out single-malt (unblended) whisky. There are five malt distilleries in the area: Glenlivet, Glenfiddich, Glenfarclas, Strathisla, and Tamdhu. Allow about an hour each to visit them.

The best way to reach Speyside from Aberdeen is to take A-96 northwest signposted Elgin. If you're traveling north on the A-9 road from Perth and Pitlochry, your first stop might be at Dalwhinnie, which has the highest whisky distillery in the world at 1,888 feet. It's not in the Spey Valley but is at the northeastern end of Loch Ericht, with views of lochs and forests.

GLENLIVET

To reach your first distillery on the designated Malt Whisky Trail, you leave Grantown-on-Spey (see below) and head east along A-95 until you come to the junction with B-9008. Go south along this route and you can't miss it. The location of the **Glenlivet Reception Centre** (☎ **01542/783220**) is 10 miles north of the nearest town, Tomintoul. Near the River Livet, a Spey tributary, this distillery is one of the most famous in Scotland, and it's open to visitors Easter–Oct Mon–Sat 10am–4pm (July–Aug until 7pm).

Back on A-95, you can visit the **Glenfarclas Distillery** at Ballindalloch (☎ **01807/500245**), one of the few malt-whisky distilleries that's still independent of the giants. Founded in 1836, Glenfarclas is managed by the fifth generation of the Grant family. It's open all year, Mon–Fri 9am–4:30pm; June–Sept, also Sat 10am–4pm. There's a small craft shop, and each visitor is offered a dram of Glenfarclas Malt Whisky.

Accommodations

⊙ **Minmore House Hotel.** Glenlivet, Ballindalloch, Banffshire AB3 9DB. ☎ **01807/590378.** Fax 01807/590472. 10 rms. £70 ($112) double. Half board £50 ($80) per person, 50% discount for children 5–14 in parents' room. MC, V. Closed Nov–Mar.

Standing on 7 acres of private grounds adjacent to the Glenlivet Distillery, this impressive country house was the home of the owners before becoming a hotel. The hotel operators have elegantly furnished their drawing room, which opens onto views of the Ladder Hills and an outdoor swimming pool. The well-furnished bedrooms have tea/coffeemakers, and drinks can be enjoyed in the oak-paneled lounge bar, which has an open log fire on chilly nights. The Scottish food is excellent, served in a Regency-style dining room with mahogany tables and matching chairs.

DUFFTOWN

James Duff, the fourth earl of Fife, founded this town in 1817. The four main streets of town converge at the battlemented **clock tower,** which is also the tourist information center. A center of the whisky-distilling industry, Dufftown is surrounded by seven malt distilleries. The family-owned **Glenfiddich Distillery** is on A-941, half a mile north of Dufftown (☎ **01340/820000**). It's open all year, Mon–Fri 9:30am–4:30pm, and in addition, Easter to mid-Oct Sat 9:30am–4:30pm and Sun noon–4:30pm. Guides in kilts show visitors around the plant and explain the process of distilling. A film of the history of distilling is also shown. At the finish of the tour, you're given a dram of malt whisky. The tour is free. There's a souvenir shop. The first whisky was produced on Christmas Day back in 1887.

Other sights include **Balvenie Castle,** along A-941 (☎ **01340/820121**), the ruins of a moated stronghold from the 14th century on the south side of the Glenfiddich Distillery. During her northern campaign against the earl of Huntly, Mary Queen of Scots spent 2 nights here. It's open Apr–Nov Mon–Sat 9:30am–6:30pm and Sun 2–6pm. Admission is £1.20 ($1.90) for adults and 75p ($1.20) for children 15 and under.

The **Mortlach Parish Church** in Dufftown is one of the oldest places of Christian worship in the country. It's reputed to have been founded in 566 by St. Moluag. A Pictish cross stands in the graveyard. The present church was reconstructed in 1931 and incorporates portions of an older building.

Dining

⊙ **Taste of Speyside.** 10 Balvenie St. ☎ **01340/820860.** Reservations recommended in the evening. Main courses £8.60–£13 ($13.75–$20.80); fixed-price dinners £10.40–£12.50 ($16.65–$20). AE, MC, V. Daily 11am–5:30pm and 6–9pm. Closed Nov–Feb. SCOTTISH.

True to its name, this restaurant in the town center, just off the main square, avidly promotes a Speyside cuisine as well as Speyside malt whiskies, and in the bar you can buy the product of each of Speyside's 46 distilleries. A platter including a slice of smoked salmon, smoked venison, smoked trout, pâté flavored with malt whisky, locally made cheese (cow or goat), salads, and homemade oat cakes is offered at noon and at night. Nourishing soup is made fresh daily and is served with homemade bread. There's also a choice of meat pies, including venison with red wine and herbs or rabbit. For dessert, try Scotch Mist, which contains fresh cream, malt whisky, and crumbled meringue.

KEITH

Keith, 11 miles northwest of Huntly, grew up because of its strategic location, where the main road and rail routes between Inverness and Aberdeen cross the River Isla. It has an ancient history, but owes its present look to the "town planning" of the late

18th and early 19th centuries. Today it's a major stopover along the Malt Whisky Trail.

The oldest operating distillery in the Scottish Highlands, the **Strathisla Distillery,** on Seafield Avenue (☎ **01542/783044**), was established in 1786. It offers guided tours Easter–Sept Mon–Fri 9am–4:30pm.

There's also a fine woolen mill in the town, **G. & G. Kynoch,** Isla Bank Mills, Bradsord Road (☎ **01924/465982**), which has been in business since 1788 producing high-quality tweeds and woolens. The mill shop is open daily from 8:30am to 4:15pm, and mill tours are conducted on Tuesday and Thursday at 2:30pm.

Accommodations & Dining

Royal Hotel. Church Rd., Keith, Banffshire AB5 5BQ. ☎ **015422/882528.** Fax 01542/88601. 16 rms (3 with bath). £33 ($52.80) double without bath, £42 ($67.20) double with bath. Rates include Scottish breakfast. AE, MC, V.

In addition to being a cozy and comfortable hotel, this stone establishment a quarter mile north of town beside A-96 serves as the village pub and social center. Built in 1883, it has probably welcomed the grandparents and parents of virtually every longtime resident of Keith. A handful of the more expensive bedrooms contain TV sets and tea-making facilities. On the premises is a restaurant; inexpensive platters are served as bar snacks in the lounge.

ROTHES

A Speyside town with five distilleries, Rothes is just to the south of the Glen of Rothes, 62 miles northwest of Aberdeen. Founded in 1766, the town lies between Ben Aigan and Conerock Hill. A little settlement, the basis of the town today, grew up around **Rothes Castle,** ancient stronghold of the Leslie family, who lived here until 1622. Only a single massive wall of the castle remains.

Among the several distilleries launched by the Grant family is the **Glen Grant Distillery** (☎ **01340/831413**), opened in the mid-19th century. It's located right outside town (signposted from the center) and can be visited mid-Apr to Sept Mon–Fri 10am–4pm. A visitor reception center offers guided tours. Admission is £2.50 ($4), which includes a tour of both the gardens and distillery, plus a £2 ($3.20) voucher applied against one of the large bottles of whisky on sale here.

Accommodations & Dining

Rothes Glen Hotel. Rothes, Morayshire AB38 7AH. ☎ **01340/831254.** Fax 01340/831566. 16 rms. TV TEL. £90 ($144) double. Rates include Scottish breakfast. MC, V. Take A-941 and drive 3 miles north of Rothes.

The old turreted house was designed by the architect who built Balmoral. It's surrounded by about 40 acres of fields with grazing Highland cattle. This historic building retains many of its original pieces of furniture. The dining room is paneled in wood, and good wholesome meals are served in true Scottish tradition. A fixed-price four-course dinner is offered.

NEWTONMORE

This Highland resort in Speyside is a good center for the Grampian and Monadhliath mountains, and it offers excellent fishing, golf, pony trekking, and hill walking. A track from the village climbs past the Calder River to Loch Dubh and the massive **Carn Ban** (3,087 ft.), where eagles fly. **Castle Cluny,** ancient seat of the MacPherson chiefs, is 6 miles west of Newtonmore.

You may want to stop and have a look at **Clan Macpherson House & Museum,** Main St. (☎ **01540/673332**). Displayed are clan relics and memorials, including the Black Chanter and Green Banner as well as a "charmed sword," and the broken fiddle of the freebooter, James MacPherson—a Scottish Robin Hood. Relics associated with Bonnie Prince Charlie are also here. An annual clan rally is held in August. Admission is free, but donations are accepted. It's open Mon–Sat 10am–5:30pm, Sun 2:30–5:30pm.

Accommodations

Balavil Hotel. Main St., Newtonmore, Inverness-shire PH20 1AY. ☎ **01540/673220.** Fax 01540/673773. 50 rms. £60 ($96) double. Rates include traditional Highland breakfast. MC, V. Closed the first 2 weeks in Dec.

This hotel, located in the center of town, is owned by the Coyle family. The bedrooms are comfortably furnished and decorated in muted pastel colors. There is a dining room where guests can enjoy traditional Highland fare. Rates include membership to the Balavil Splash Club, which features a pool and sauna.

KINGUSSIE

Your next stop along the Spey might be at the little summer holiday resort and winter ski center of Kingussie (it's pronounced "King-*you*-see"), just off A-9, the capital of Badenoch, a district known as "the drowned land" because the Spey can flood the valley when the snows of a severe winter melt in the spring.

Kingussie practically adjoins Newtonmore (see above), for it lies directly northeast along A-86. The location is 117 miles northwest of Edinburgh, 41 miles south of Inverness, and 11 miles southwest of Aviemore.

A **tourist information center** is on King Street (☎ **01540/661297**), open only May 22–Sept 22 Mon–Sat 10am–1pm and 2–6pm, Sun 10am–1pm and 2–5pm.

What to See & Do

Highland Folk Museum. Duke St. ☎ **01540/661307.** Admission £2.70 ($4.30) adults, £1.60 ($2.55) children and senior citizens. Apr–Oct Mon–Sat 10am–6pm, Sun 2–6pm; Nov–Mar Mon–Fri 10am–3pm.

This is the first folk museum established in Scotland (1934), and its collections are based on the life of the Highlanders. You'll see domestic, agricultural, and industrial items. Open-air exhibits are a turf kailyard (kitchen garden), a Lewis "black house," and old vehicles and carts. Traditional events such as spinning, music-making, and handcraft fairs are held throughout the summer.

Accommodations

🟢 **Homewood Lodge.** Newtonmore Rd., Kingussie, Inverness-shire PH21 1HD. ☎ **01540/661507.** 6 rms. £11.50–£18.50 ($18.40–$29.60) per person. Rates include Scottish breakfast. No credit cards.

One of the best B&Bs in the area, this small Highland house offers large, simply furnished rooms for either two travelers or families. Set on a half acre of garden and woodland, the house has a sitting room with an open fire and TV. Good traditional local fare is served in the evening when reservations are a must, and summer barbecues are also offered. Children are welcome.

Osprey Hotel. Ruthven Rd. (at High St.), Kingussie, Inverness-shire PH21 1EN. ☎ and fax **01540/661510.** 8 rms. £42–£47 ($67.20–$75.20) double. Rates include half board. AE, MC, V. Closed Nov 1–14.

This 1895 Victorian structure, 300 yards from the rail station, is a convenient place to stay, with comfortable although very plain bedrooms, all with hot and cold running water, central heating, electric blankets, and electric fires. The hotel has a licensed bar, residents' lounge, and a TV lounge. Baby-sitting and baby-listening service is provided, and laundry and ironing facilities are available. The place is known for its pure, fresh, 100% homemade food. Prime Scottish meats are served; in summer, salmon and trout from local rivers are offered either fresh or peat-smoked.

Dining

✪ **The Cross.** Tweed Mill Brae, off the Ardbroilach road, Kingussie, Inverness-shire PH21 1TC. ☎ **01540/661166.** Fax 01540/661080. Reservations recommended. Fixed-price five-course dinner £35 ($56). MC, V. Wed–Mon 7–9pm. Closed Dec–Feb. SCOTTISH.

This chic restaurant comes as a surprise: In an out-of-the-way setting in a remote Highland village, it serves superlative meals that involve theater as much as they do fine food. The restaurant stands on 4 acres, with the Gynack Burn running through the grounds. The main building of the complex is an old tweed mill, and the restaurant has an open-beam ceiling and French doors leading out onto a terrace over the water's edge where al fresco dinners are served. Specialties depend on the availability of produce in the local markets and might include venison Francatelli, wild pigeon with grapes, or Highland lamb with sorrel.

Nine rooms are rented in a new building. Each room is different in size and style—for example, two rooms have canopied beds, and another has a balcony overlooking the mill pond. Doubles, including half board, cost £170 ($272). Personal service and attention to detail go into the running of this place, operated by Ruth and Tony Hadley, and Ruth's cooking has put it on the gastronomic map of Scotland.

KINCRAIG

Kincraig enjoys a scenic spot at the northern end of Loch Insh, overlooking the Spey Valley to the west and the Cairngorm Mountains to the east. From Kingussie, continue northeast along A-9 (the route north to Aviemore) to reach Kincraig.

Near Kincraig, the most notable sight is the **Highland Wildlife Park** (☎ **01540/ 651270**), a natural area of parkland with a collection of wildlife, some of which is extinct elsewhere in Scotland. Herds of European bison, red deer, shaggy Highland cattle, wild horses, St. Kilda Soay sheep, and roe deer range the park.

In enclosures are wolves, polecats, wildcats, beavers, badgers, and pine martens. Protected birds to see are golden eagles and several species of grouse—of special interest is the capercaillie ("horse of the woods"), a large Eurasian grouse that's a native of Scotland's pine forests. There's a visitor center with a gift shop, cafe, and exhibition areas. Ample parking and a picnic site are also available.

The park is open daily 10am–4pm. Admission is £6 ($9.60) to £17 ($27.20) per day, depending on the number of occupants.

GRANTOWN-ON-SPEY

This holiday resort, with its gray granite buildings, is 34 miles southeast of Inverness, in a wooded valley from which it commands views of the Cairngorm Mountains. It's a key center of winter sports in Scotland. Fishers are also attracted to this setting, because the Spey is renowned for its salmon. One of Scotland's many 18th-century planned towns, it was founded on a heather-covered moor in 1765 by Sir James Grant of Grant and became the seat of that ancient family. The town was famous in the 19th century as a Highland tourist center.

From a base here, you can explore the valleys of the Don and Dee, the Cairngorms, and Culloden Moor, scene of the historic battle in 1746, when Bonnie Prince Charlie and his army were defeated.

A **tourist information office** is on High Street (☎ **01479/872773**), open in summer only, Mon–Fri 9am–6pm and Sun 10am–5pm.

Accommodations

Garth Hotel. The Square, Castle Rd., Grantown-on-Spey, Morayshire PH26 3HN. ☎ **01479/ 872836.** Fax 01479/872116. 18 rms. TV TEL. £80 ($128) double. Half board £56 ($89.60) per person. AE, MC, V.

The elegant, comfortable Garth stands on 4 acres of grounds beside the town square. Guests enjoy the use of a spacious upstairs lounge, whose high ceilings, wood-burning stove, and vine-covered veranda make it an attractive place for morning coffee or afternoon tea. This pleasant hotel features comfortable and handsomely furnished bedrooms, with all the necessary amenities. Extensive and selective meals favor "Taste of Scotland" dishes, with emphasis on fresh local produce, including seafood, salmon, venison, game, and beef.

✪ **Tulchan Lodge.** Advie, Grantown-on-Spey, Morayshire PH26 3PW. ☎ **01807/510200.** Fax 01807/510234. 13 rms (all with bath). TEL. £350–£400 ($560–$640) double. Rates include full board. No credit cards. Closed Feb–Mar. Drive 9 miles northeast of Grantown on B-9102.

Tulchan Lodge, built in 1906 to serve as the 23,000-acre Tulchan Estate's fishing and shooting lodge, is a place for both sports-oriented visitors and travelers who want to experience a place designed with the elegance required by Edward VII, who came here for sports. The lodge has panoramic views of the Spey Valley. Each of the bedrooms is different in size and furnishings. Tulchan Lodge is open from April to January. In the two elegant dining rooms, Scottish and international dishes are served, with particular attention to Scottish beef, lamb, game, and fresh local seafood. The vegetables are grown in the lodge's garden. Only full-board residents are accepted. Facilities include a tennis court, nature trails, and a golf course nearby.

Dining

Craggan Mill. Hwy. A-95 three-quarters of a mile south of Grantown-on-Spey. ☎ **01479/ 2288.** Reservations recommended. Main courses £6.95–£12.95 ($11.10–$20.70). MC, V. June– Sept daily noon–2pm and 6–10pm; Oct–May Tues–Sun 7–10pm. BRITISH/ITALIAN.

This licensed restaurant and lounge bar, a 10-minute walk south of the town center, is housed in a restored ruined granite mill whose waterwheel is still visible. The owners offer British or Italian cuisine at attractive prices. Therefore your appetizer might be smoked trout in deference to Scotland, or ravioli, inspired by sunny Italy. Main courses might be breast of chicken with cream or chicken cacciatore, followed by a dessert of rum-raisin ice cream or peach Melba. You've probably had better versions of all the dishes offered here, but what you get isn't bad. A good selection of Italian wines is also offered.

Spain 16

by Darwin Porter & Danforth Prince

Today's Spain is a vital and exciting place. This land of sun-drenched beaches, terraced vineyards, sleepy villages, and jeweled Moorish palaces is undergoing a remarkable cultural renaissance known as *la movida*. Gone are the conditions that drove Picasso away to another country. Today contemporary art, literature, the cinema, and fashion are constantly finding new and original expression, and cafes and bars hum with animated discussion about politics, society, and Spain's new-found prosperity.

1 Madrid

Madrid lies landlocked on a windswept and often arid plain, beneath a sky that has been described as Velázquez blue. Certain poets have even labeled Madrid the "gateway to the skies." It's populated by adopted sons and daughters from virtually every region of Spain, adding to its cosmopolitan gloss. Despite its influence as the cultural beacon of the Spanish-speaking world and its quintessentially Spanish nature, the city lacks such all-important Iberian features as a beach, an ancient castle and cathedral, and an archbishop. To compensate for this lack, the always-practical Madrileños long ago learned to substitute long strolls through the city's verdant parks and along its *paseos*. They built an elegant palace and erected countless churches, many with baroque ornamentation and gilt. As for an archbishop, Madrileños are content with falling under the jurisdiction of the archbishop in nearby Toledo.

Artists and writers gravitate to the newly revitalized Madrid and its fertile artistic climate. The legendary propensity of Spaniards to celebrate their nightlife is observed with something approaching passion; Madrileños stay awake till the wee hours, congregating in the very early morning over hot chocolate and *churros* (fried fingerlike doughnuts). But despite the city's many pleasures, Madrileños recognize that their city is also a place for work, evidenced by the spate of emerging industries, services, and products.

ONLY IN MADRID

Spending an Afternoon at the Bullfights The art of bullfighting is more closely associated with the temperament and passions of the land than any other pastime in Iberia. Detractors cite the sport as cruel, bloody, violent, hot, and savage. Aficionados view bullfighting as a microcosm of death, catharsis, and rebirth and defend it as one of the most evocative and memorable events in Spain. Head for the *plaza de toros* (bullring) in Madrid. You'll find feverish crowds, the ballet of the *bandilleros*, the thundering fury of the bull, the arrogance of the matador—all leading to "death in the afternoon."

Visiting the Prado   It's "the world's supreme art museum," at least to a Spaniard, or "one of the world's supreme art museums" to anyone else, ranking up there with the Louvre. The Prado is the artistic repository of some 4,000 universal masterpieces, many of them acquired by Spanish kings. The wealth of Spanish painters is staggering—everything from Goya's *Naked Maja* to the celebrated *Las Meninas* by Velázquez (our favorite). Masterpiece after masterpiece unfolds before your eyes. It would take a lifetime to savor the Prado's wonders.

Feasting on Tapas in the Tascas   This is reason enough to go to Madrid. Spanish tapas are so good that their once-secret recipes have been broadcast around the world, but they always taste better here. The *tapeo* is the equivalent of the pub crawl in London. Tapas bars (*tascas*) are the quintessential Madrileño experience. Originally tapas were cured ham or chorizo (spicy sausage). Today they're likely to include everything from *gambas* (deep-fried shrimp) to stuffed peppers. To go native, try lamb's sweetbreads or bull's testicles. These dazzling spreads will fortify you until the 10pm fashionable dining hour. The best streets for your tasca crawl are Ventura de la Vega, the area around Plaza de Santa Ana or Plaza de Santa Bárbara, Cava Baja, or Calle de Cuchilleros.

Shopping the Rastro   This is Madrid's flea market, a tradition dating back 500 years. Savvy shoppers arrive before 7am every Sunday to beat the rush and to be the first to bid on the best merchandise. The teeming place doesn't really get going until about 9am, and then it's shoulder-to-shoulder stretching down Calle Ribera de Curtidores. Real or fake antiques, secondhand clothing, porno films, Franco-era furniture, paintings (endless copies of Velázquez), bullfight posters, old books, religious relics, and plenty of plain junk are sold here. Women who have lost their purse to a mugger the day before often report that they can find it here for resale—after it's been thoroughly emptied, of course.

Experiencing La Movida   Meaning in very rough translation the "shift" or "movement," la movida characterizes post-Franco life as Madrileños threw off the yoke of repression. One Madrid commentator defined la movida this way: "Instead of patronizing prostitutes the way they did back in the whore-or-madonna days, some men are now dating transvestites or transsexuals as part of their new-found liberation." La movida is about doing what was only recently regarded as "unthinkable." La movida is best seen after dark, when the town just starts to wake up at midnight. The liveliest areas to see la movida are Chueca, Huertas, Malasaña, and the big clubs around Calle Arenal.

ORIENTATION

ARRIVING   By Plane   Nine miles east of the city center, **Barajas** (☎ 91/ 305-83-43 for airport information), Madrid's international airport, has two terminals—one international, the other domestic. A conveyor belt connects the two.

Air-conditioned yellow airport buses take you from the arrivals terminal to the bus depot under Plaza de Colón. You can also get off at stops along the way, provided that your baggage isn't stored in the hold. The fare is 325 ptas. ($2.60), and the buses leave every 15 minutes, either to or from the airport.

If you go into town by taxi, expect to pay 2,500 ptas. ($20) and up, plus surcharges for the trip to/from the airport and for baggage handling. If you take an unmetered limousine, negotiate the price in advance.

By Train Madrid has three major railway stations: **Atocha,** Avenida Ciudad de Barcelona (Metro: Atocha RENFE), for trains to Lisbon, Toledo, Andalusia, and Extremadura; **Chamartín,** in the northern suburbs at Augustín de Foxá (Metro: Chamartín), for trains to and from Barcelona, Asturias, Cantabria, Castille-León, the Basque country, Aragón, Catalonia, Levante (Valencia), Murcia, and the French frontier; and **Estación Príncipe Pío** or Norte, Po. del Rey 30 (Metro: Norte), for trains to and from northwest Spain (Salamanca and Galicia). For information about connections from any of these stations, call **RENFE,** Spanish State Railways (☎ **91/ 328-90-20** daily 7am–11pm). For tickets, go to the principal office of RENFE, Alcalá 44 (Metro: Banco de España), open Mon–Fri 9am–8pm.

By Bus Madrid has at least eight major bus terminals, including the large **Estación Sur de Autobuses,** Calle Canarias 17 (☎ **91/468-45-11;** Metro, Palos de la Frontera). Most buses pass through this station.

By Car The following are the major highways into Madrid, with information on driving distances to the city: Rte. NI from Irún, 315 miles; NII from Barcelona, 389 miles; NIII from Valencia, 217 miles; NIV from Cádiz, 388 miles; NV from Badajoz, 254 miles; and NVI from Galicia, 374 miles.

VISITOR INFORMATION The most convenient **tourist office** is on the ground floor of the 40-story Torre de Madrid, Plaza de España (☎ **91/541-23-25;** Metro: Plaza de España); it's open Mon–Fri 9am–7pm and Sat 9:30am–1:30pm. Ask for a street map of the next town on your itinerary, especially if you're driving.

CITY LAYOUT In modern Spain all roads and rail and phone lines lead to Madrid. The capital has outgrown all previous boundaries and is branching out in all directions.

Every new arrival must find the **Gran Vía,** which cuts a winding pathway across the city beginning at **Plaza de España,** where you'll find one of Europe's tallest skyscrapers, the Edificio España. On this principal avenue is the largest concentration of shops, hotels, restaurants, and movie houses. **Calle de Serrano** is a runner-up.

South of the avenue lies the **Puerta del Sol.** All road distances in Spain are measured from this square. However, its significance has declined, and today it's a prime hunting ground for pickpockets and purse snatchers. Here **Calle de Alcalá** begins and runs for 2$^1/_2$ miles.

Plaza Mayor is the heart of Old Madrid, an attraction in itself with its mix of French and Georgian architecture. (Again, be wary, especially late at night.) Pedestrians pass under the arches of the huge square onto the narrow streets of the old town, where you can find some of the capital's most intriguing restaurants and tascas.

The area south of Plaza Mayor—known as **barrios bajos**—merits exploration. The narrow cobblestone streets are lined with 16th- and 17th-century architecture. Directly south of the plaza is the **Arco de Cuchilleros,** a street packed with markets, restaurants, flamenco clubs, and taverns.

The Gran Vía ends at Calle de Alcalá, and at this juncture lies **Plaza de la Cibeles,** with its fountain to Cybele, "the mother of the gods," and what has become known as "the cathedral of post offices." From Cibeles, the wide **Paseo de Recoletos** begins a short run to **Plaza de Colón.** From this latter square rolls the serpentine **Paseo de la Castellana,** flanked by expensive shops, apartment buildings, luxury hotels, and foreign embassies.

Back at Cibeles again: Heading south is **Paseo del Prado,** where you'll find Spain's major attraction, the Museo del Prado, as well as the Jardín Botánica (Botanical Garden). The paseo also leads to the Atocha Rail Station. To the west of the garden lies the **Parque del Retiro,** once reserved for royalty, with restaurants, nightclubs, a rose garden, and two lakes.

GETTING AROUND

Getting around Madrid isn't easy, because everything is spread out. Even many Madrileño taxi drivers, often new arrivals from some foreign country, are unfamiliar with their own city once they're off the main boulevards.

ON FOOT   This is the perfect way to see Madrid, especially the ancient narrow streets of the old town. If you're going to another district (and chances are that your hotel will be outside the old town), you can take the bus or Metro. For such a large city, Madrid can be covered amazingly well on foot, because so much of what will interest a visitor lies in various clusters.

BY SUBWAY (METRO)   The Metro system is easy to learn. The central converging point is the Puerta del Sol, and the fare is 130 ptas. ($1.05) for a one-way trip. The Metro operates daily 6am–1:30am. Avoid rush hours. For information, call **91/ 552-49-00.** You can save money on public transportation by purchasing a 10-trip ticket known as a *bonos*—for the Metro it costs 645 ptas. ($5.15).

BY BUS   A bus network also services the city and suburbs, with routes clearly shown at each stop on a schematic diagram. Buses are fast and efficient because they travel along special lanes. Both red and yellow buses charge 130 ptas. ($1.05) per ride.

For 645 ptas. ($5.15) you can purchase a 10-trip ticket (but without transfers) for Madrid's bus system. It's sold at **Empresa Municipal de Transportes,** Plaza de la Cibeles (☎ **91/401-99-00**), where you can also purchase a guide to the bus routes. The office is open daily 8am–8:30pm.

BY TAXI   Even though cab fares have risen recently, they're still reasonable. When you flag down a taxi, the meter should register 170 ptas. ($1.35); for every kilometer thereafter, the fare increases by 50–75 ptas. (40¢–60¢). A supplement is charged for trips to the rail station or the bullring, as well as on Sundays and holidays. The ride to Barajas Airport carries a 325-pta. ($2.60) surcharge and there's a 160-pta. ($1.30) supplement for trips from the rail stations. In addition, there's a 150-pta. ($1.20) supplement on Sundays and holidays, plus a 150-pta. ($1.10) supplement at night. It's customary to tip at least 10% of the fare. To call a taxi, dial **91/445-90-08** or 91/447-51-80.

BY CAR   Driving is a nightmare and potentially dangerous in congested Madrid—it always feels like rush hour. Should you want to rent a car in Madrid to tour the environs, you'll have several choices. In addition to its office at Barajas Airport (☎ **91/305-42-73**), **Avis** has a main office downtown at Gran Vía 60 (☎ **91/348-03-48**). **Hertz,** too, has an office at Barajas Airport (☎ **91/305-84-52**) and another in the heart of Madrid in the Edificio España, Gran Vía 88 (☎ **91/542-58-05**). **Budget Rent-a-Car** maintains its headquarters at Gran Vía 49 (☎ **91/401-12-54**).

BY BICYCLE   Ever wonder why you see so few people riding bicycles in Madrid? Those who tried were overcome by the traffic pollution. It's better to walk.

FAST FACTS: Madrid

American Express   For your mail or banking needs, you can go to the American Express office at the corner of Marqués de Cubas and Plaza de las Cortes 2, across

Madrid Metro

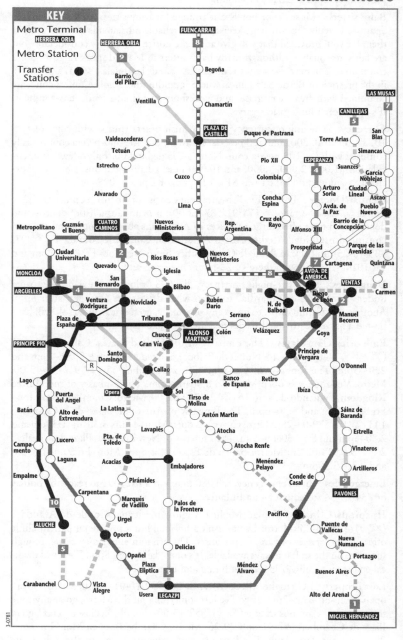

the street from the Palace Hotel (☎ 91/322-55-00; Metro: Gran Vía). Open Mon–Fri 9am–5:30pm and Sat 9am–noon.

Baby-sitters   Most major hotels can arrange for baby-sitters, called *canguros* in Spanish. Usually the concierge keeps a list of reliable nursemaids and will contact them for you, provided that you give adequate notice. Rates vary considerably but are fairly reasonable. Although many baby-sitters in Madrid speak English, don't count on it. You may also want to contact La Casa de la Abuela (☎ 91/574-3094), in the prestigious Barrio Salamanca, where "grandmother's house" offers childcare combined with creative exercises and workshops in a child-friendly environment. It's open year-round; prices vary.

Currency   The unit of currency is the Spanish **peseta (pta.),** with coins of 1, 5, 10, 25, 50, 100, 200, and 500 pesetas. Be aware that the 500-peseta coin is easily confused with the 100-peseta coin. Notes are issued in 500 (only a few left in circulation), 1,000, 2,000, 5,000, and 10,000-peseta denominations. The rate of exchange used in this chapter was $1 = 125 pta., or 1 pta. = .008¢.

Dentist/Doctor   For an English-speaking dentist or doctor, contact the U.S. Embassy, Calle Serrano 75 (☎ 91/587-22-00); it maintains a list of dentists and doctors who have offered their services to Americans abroad. For dental services, consult also Unidad Médica Anglo-Americana, Conde de Arandá 1 (☎ 91/435-18-23), in back of Plaza de Colón; office hours are Mon–Fri 9am–8pm and Sat 10am–1pm, though there's a 24-hour answering service.

Drugstores   For a late-night pharmacy, dial 098 or look in the daily newspaper under "Farmacias de Guardia" to learn what drugstores are open after 8pm. Another way to find out is to go to any pharmacy, even if it's closed—it will have posted a list of nearby pharmacies that are open late that day.

Embassies/Consulates   The Embassy of the **United States,** Calle Serrano 75 (☎ 91/577-40-00; Metro, Núñez de Balboa), is open Mon–Fri 9:30am–1pm and 2:30–5pm. The Embassy of **Canada,** Núñez de Balboa 35 (☎ 91/431-43-00; Metro: Velázquez), is open Mon–Fri 8:30am–5pm. The Embassy of the **United Kingdom,** Fernando el Santo 16 (☎ 91/319-02-00; Metro: Colón), is open Mon–Fri 9am–2pm and 3:30–6pm. The Embassy of **Australia,** Paseo de la Castellana 143 (☎ 91/579-04-28; Metro: Cuzco), is open Mon–Thurs 8:30am–1:30pm and 2:30–5pm and Fri 8:30am–2pm. The Embassy of **New Zealand,** Plaza de la Lealtad 2 (☎ 91/523-02-26; Metro: Banco de España), is open Mon–Fri 9am–1:30pm and 2:30–5:30pm.

Emergencies   In an emergency, call 080 to report a **fire,** 091 to reach the **police,** or 734-25-54 to request an **ambulance.**

Hospitals/Clinics   Unidad Médica Anglo-Americana, Conde de Arandá 1 (☎ 91/435-18-23; Metro: Usera), isn't a hospital but a private outpatient clinic offering the services of various specialists. This isn't an emergency clinic, though someone on the staff is always available. It's open daily 9am–8pm. For a real medical emergency, call 91/734-25-54 for an ambulance.

Lost Property   Go to the office at Alcántra 26 (☎ 91/401-31-00; Metro: Goya), open Mon–Fri 8am–2pm. If you've lost something on the Metro, go at any time to the Cuatro Caminos station (☎ 91/552-49-00). For objects lost in a taxi, go to Plaza de Chamberí (☎ 91/448-79-26; Metro: Chamberí), open Mon–Fri 9am–2pm and Sat 9am–1pm. For items lost anywhere else, go to the Palacio de Comunicaciones at Plaza de la Cibeles (☎ 91/532-93-52; Metro: Banco de España), open Mon–Fri 9am–2pm and Sat 9am–1pm. Don't call—show up in person.

Luggage Storage/Lockers   These can be found at both the Atocha and Chamartín railway terminals, as well as the major bus station at the Estación Sur de Autobuses, Calle Canarias 17 (☎ 91/468-45-11; Metro: Palos de la Frontera). Storage is also provided at the air terminal underneath Plaza de Colón.

Police   In an emergency, dial 091.

Post Office   If you don't want to receive your mail at your hotel or the American Express office, direct it to *Lista de Correos* at the central post office in Madrid. To pick up mail, go to the window marked LISTA, where you'll be asked to show your passport. Madrid's central office is in "the cathedral of the post offices" at Plaza de la Cibeles (☎ 91/536-01-11).

Safety   Because of an increasing crime rate in Madrid, the U.S. Embassy has warned visitors to leave their valuables in a hotel safe or other secure place when going out. Your passport may be needed, however, as the police often stop foreigners for identification checks. The embassy advises that you carry only enough cash for the day's needs. Purse snatching is common, and the criminals often work in pairs, grabbing purses from pedestrians, cyclists, and even cars.

Taxes   There are no special city taxes for tourists.

Telephone   For long-distance calls, especially transatlantic ones, it may be best to go to the main phone exchange, Locutorio Gran Vía, at Gran Vía 30, or Locutorio Recoletos, at Paseo de Recoletos 37–41. You may not be lucky enough to find an English-speaking operator, but you can fill out a simple form that will facilitate the placement of a call.

Transit Information   For Metro information, call 91/552-49-00.

ACCOMMODATIONS
NEAR PLAZA DE LAS CORTES
Very Expensive

Palace. Plaza de las Cortes 7, 28014 Madrid. ☎ **800/325-3535** in the U.S., 800/325-3589 in Canada, or 91/429-75-51. Fax 91/429-86-55. 424 rms, 31 suites. A/C MINIBAR TV TEL. 40,000–46,000 ptas. ($320–$368) double; from 75,000 ptas. ($600) suite. AE, DC, MC, V. Parking 2,300 ptas. ($18.40). Metro: Banco de España.

The Palace, an ornate Victorian "wedding cake" covering a city block, faces the Prado and Neptune Fountain, within walking distance of the main shopping center. architecturally, the Palace captures the elegant pre–World War I grand hotel style. However, it doesn't achieve the snob appeal of its sibling, the Ritz (under the same management). The rooms are conservative and traditional, boasting plenty of space and large baths with lots of amenities. As was the style when the hotel was built, the accommodations vary widely, with the best rooms on the fourth, fifth, and sixth floors. The elegant dining choice is La Cupola, serving Italian specialties along with some of the more famous dishes of the Spanish cuisine.

Inexpensive

⑤ Hostal Cervantes. Cervantes 34, 28014 Madrid. ☎ **91/429-27-45.** 12 rms. 6,000 ptas. ($48) double. No credit cards. Metro: Banco de España.

One of Madrid's most pleasant family-run hotels, the Cervantes has been widely appreciated by our readers for years. You'll take a tiny birdcage-style elevator to the immaculately maintained second floor of this stone-and-brick building. Each accommodation contains a bed and spartan furniture. No breakfast is served, but the owners, the Alfonsos, will direct you to a nearby cafe. The establishment is convenient to the Prado, Retiro Park, and the older sections of Madrid.

Madrid Accommodations

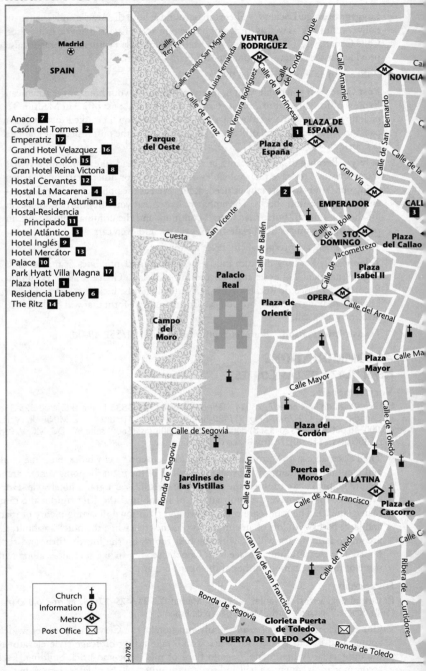

Anaco **7**
Casón del Tormes **2**
Emperatriz **17**
Grand Hotel Velazquez **16**
Gran Hotel Colón **15**
Gran Hotel Reina Victoria **8**
Hostal Cervantes **12**
Hostal La Macarena **4**
Hostal La Perla Asturiana **5**
Hostal-Residencia
  Principado **11**
Hotel Atlántico **3**
Hotel Inglés **9**
Hotel Mercátor **13**
Palace **10**
Park Hyatt Villa Magna **17**
Plaza Hotel **1**
Residencia Liabeny **6**
The Ritz **14**

Church †
Information ⓘ
Metro Ⓜ
Post Office ✉

NEAR PLAZA DE ESPAÑA

Expensive

Plaza Hotel. Plaza de España 8, 28013 Madrid. ☎ **91/547-12-00.** Fax 91/548-23-89. 231 rms, 75 suites. A/C MINIBAR TV TEL. 21,200 ptas. ($169.60) double; from 25,600 ptas. ($204.80) suite. AE, DC, MC, V. Parking 2,500 ptas. ($20). Metro: Plaza de España.

Atop a city garage, the Plaza, built in 1953, could be called the Waldorf-Astoria of Spain. A massive rose-and-white structure, it soars to a central 26-story tower. It's a landmark visible for miles around and one of the tallest skyscrapers in Europe. Once one of the best hotels in Spain, the Plaza has declined in recent years in spite of a 1992 renovation. The hotel's accommodations include both conventional doubles and luxurious suites, each of which contains a sitting room and abundant amenities. The furniture is usually of a standard modern style, in harmonized colors. The quieter rooms are on the upper floors.

Inexpensive

Ⓢ **Casón del Tormes.** Calle del Río 7, 28013 Madrid. ☎ **91/541-97-46.** Fax 91/541-18-52. 63 rms. A/C TV TEL. 12,000 ptas. ($96) double; 15,300 ptas. ($122.40) triple. MC, V. Parking 1,200 ptas. ($9.60). Metro: Plaza de España.

The attractive three-star Casón del Tormes is around the corner from the Royal Palace and Plaza de España. Set behind a four-story red-brick facade with stone-trimmed windows, it overlooks a quiet one-way street. The long, narrow lobby contains vertical wooden paneling, a marble floor, and a bar opening into a separate room. The guest rooms have a certain harmony of color and coordination of furnishings, and each is individually styled. They're not spectacular but are generally roomy and comfortable.

ON OR NEAR THE GRAN VÍA

Moderate

Hotel Atlántico. Gran Vía 38, 28013 Madrid. ☎ **800/528-1234** in the U.S. and Canada, or 91/522-64-80. Fax 91/531-02-10. 80 rms. A/C MINIBAR TV TEL. 13,305 ptas. ($106.45) double. Rates include breakfast. AE, DC, MC, V. Metro: Gran Vía.

Refurbished in stages between the late 1980s and 1994, this hotel occupies five floors of a grand turn-of-the-century building on a corner of one of Madrid's most impressive avenues. It has relatively unadorned but well-maintained rooms that have been insulated against noise, and are rather small. The hotel contains an English-inspired bar serving drinks and snacks near the reception area that's open 24 hours a day. Don't judge the hotel by its bleak check-in area or shabby third-floor lounge.

Residencia Liabeny. Salud 3, 28013 Madrid. ☎ **91/531-90-00.** Fax 91/532-74-21. 224 rms. A/C MINIBAR TV TEL. 9,600–14,000 ptas. ($76.80–$112) double; 16,000–21,000 ptas. ($128–$168) triple. AE, MC, V. Parking 1,400 ptas. ($11.20). Metro: Puerta del Sol, Callao, or Gran Vía.

This hotel, behind an austere stone-sheathed facade, is in a prime location midway between the tourist highlights of the Gran Vía and the Puerta del Sol. Named after the original owner, it contains seven floors of comfortable, contemporary rooms that, even though newly redecorated, are a bit too pristine for our tastes. The cocktail bar is more warming, but in a "macho" style, and the dining room is strictly for convenience. A coffee shop is also on the premises, and good laundry service and personalized attention from the staff add to the allure of the place.

Inexpensive

Anaco. Tres Cruces 3, 28013 Madrid. ☎ **91/522-46-04.** Fax 91/531-64-84. 39 rms. A/C TV TEL. 8,500–9,500 ptas. ($72–$76) double; 10,500–12,000 ptas. ($84–$96) triple. AE, DC, MC, V. Metro: Gran Vía, Callao, or Puerta del Sol.

Modest yet modern, the Anaco is just off the main shopping thoroughfare, the Gran Vía. Opening onto a tree-shaded plaza, it attracts those seeking a resting place that features contemporary appurtenances and cleanliness. The rooms are compact, with built-in headboards, reading lamps, and lounge chairs. A useful tip: Ask for one of the five terraced rooms on the top floor, which rent at no extra charge. The hotel has a bar/cafeteria/restaurant open daily.

NEAR THE PUERTA DEL SOL

Expensive

Gran Hotel Reina Victoria. Plaza de Santa Ana 14, 28012 Madrid. ☎ **91/531-45-00.** Fax 91/522-03-07. 197 rms, 4 suites. A/C MINIBAR TV TEL. 21,900 ptas. ($175.20) double; from 55,100 ptas. ($440.80) suite (includes breakfast). AE, DC, MC, V. Parking 1,700 ptas. ($13.60). Metro: Tirso de Molina or Puerta del Sol.

Since a recent renovation and upgrading by Spain's Tryp Hotel Group, this hotel is less staid and more impressive than ever. The hotel boasts an ornate and eclectic stone facade that the Spanish government protects as a historic monument. Though it's in a congested and noisy neighborhood in the center of town, the Reina Victoria opens onto its own sloping plaza, rich in tradition as a meeting place of intellectuals during the 17th century. Each room contains sound-resistant insulation, a safe, and a private bath with many amenities. The lobby bar, Manuel González Manolete, displays bullfighting memorabilia, and there's a good in-house restaurant, El Ruedo.

Inexpensive

Ⓢ **Hostal la Macarena.** Cava de San Miguel 8, 28005 Madrid. ☎ **91/365-92-21.** Fax 91/364-27-57. 18 rms. TEL. 6,000 ptas. ($48) double; 7,500 ptas. ($60) triple; 8,000 ptas. ($64) quad. MC, V. Metro: Puerta del Sol, Ópera, or La Latina.

Known for its reasonable prices and praised by readers for the warmth of its reception, this unpretentious, clean hostal is run by the Ricardo González family. Its 19th-century facade, accented with belle époque patterns, offers an ornate contrast to the chiseled simplicity of the ancient buildings facing it. The location is one of the hostal's assets: It's on a street (an admittedly noisy one) immediately behind Plaza Mayor, near one of the best clusters of tascas in Madrid. Windows facing the street have double panes.

Hostal la Perla Asturiana. Plaza de Santa Cruz 3, 28012 Madrid. ☎ **91/366-46-00.** Fax 91/366-46-08. 33 rms. TV TEL. 4,900 ptas. ($39.20) double; 7,000 ptas. ($56) triple. AE, DC, MC, V. Metro: Puerta del Sol.

Ideal for those who want to stay in the heart of Old Madrid (1 block off Plaza Mayor and 2 blocks from the Puerta del Sol), this small family-run establishment has a courteous staff member at the desk 24 hours a day for security and convenience. You can socialize in the small, comfortable lobby that's adjacent to the reception desk. The rooms are clean but simple and often cramped, with fresh towels supplied daily. Many inexpensive restaurants and tapas bars are nearby. No breakfast is served.

Ⓢ **Hostal-Residencia Principado.** Zorrilla 7, 28014 Madrid. ☎ **91/429-81-87.** 15 rms. TV. 5,800 ptas. ($46.40) double. AE, MC, V. Metro: Sevilla or Banco de España. Bus: 5, 9, or 53.

The two-star Principado is a real find. Located in a well-kept town house, it's run by a gracious owner who keeps everything clean and inviting. New tiles, attractive bedspreads, and curtains give the rooms a fresh look. Safety boxes are provided. For breakfast, you can go to a nearby cafe.

⑤ Hotel Inglés. Calle Echegaray 8, 28014 Madrid. ☎ **91/429-65-51.** Fax 91/420-24-23. 50 rms, 8 suites. TV TEL. 10,000 ptas. ($80) double; 13,600 ptas. ($108.80) suite. AE, DC, MC, V. Parking 1,200 ptas. ($9.60). Metro: Puerta del Sol or Sevilla.

On a central street lined with tascas, the hotel operates its own 24-hour cafeteria. It's more modern and impersonal than it was when Virginia Woolf made it her address in Madrid. Behind its red-brick facade you'll find unpretentious and contemporary rooms, all well maintained. The comfortable armchairs in the TV lounge are likely to be filled with avid soccer fans. The lobby is air-conditioned, though the guest rooms aren't. Guests who open their windows at night are likely to hear noise from the enclosed courtyard, so light sleepers beware.

NEAR ATOCHA STATION
Moderate

Hotel Mercátor. Calle Atocha 123, 28012 Madrid. ☎ **91/429-05-00.** Fax 91/369-12-52. 89 rms, 3 suites. MINIBAR TV TEL. 11,350 ptas. ($90.80) double; 12,750 ptas. ($102) suite. AE, DC, MC, V. Parking 1,320 ptas. ($10.55). Metro: Atocha or Antón Martín.

Only a 3-minute walk from the Prado, Centro de Arte Reina Sofía, and Thyssen-Bornemisza Museum, the Mercátor draws a clientele seeking a good hotel—orderly, well run, and clean, with enough comforts and conveniences to please the weary traveler. The public rooms are simple, in a vaguely modern minimalism. Some of the guest rooms are more inviting than others, especially those with desks and armchairs. Twenty-one units are air-conditioned. It has a bar and cafeteria serving light meals, such as *platos combinados* (combination plates).

NEAR RETIRO & SALAMANCA
Very Expensive

✪ Park Hyatt Villa Magna. Paseo de la Castellana 22, 28046 Madrid. ☎ **800/223-1234** in the U.S. and Canada, or 91/587-12-34. Fax 91/431-22-86. 164 rms, 18 suites. A/C MINIBAR TV TEL. 42,000 ptas. ($336) double; from 78,000 ptas. ($624) suite. AE, DC, MC, V. Two-night weekend packages available for 40,000 ptas. ($320) double. Parking 2,000 ptas. ($16). Metro: Rubén Darío.

One of Europe's finest hotels, the nine-story Park Hyatt is set behind a bank of pines and laurels on the city's most fashionable boulevard. Today it's an even finer choice than the Palace and is matched in luxury, ambience, and tranquillity only by the Ritz. Its facade of rose-colored granite has contemporary lines; in contrast, its interior recaptures the style of Carlos IV, with paneled walls, marble floors, and fresh flowers. This luxury palace offers plush but dignified rooms decorated in Louis XVI, English Regency, or Italian provincial style. The Berceo serves international food in a glamorous setting. The hotel is known for its summer terraces, set in gardens.

✪ Ritz. Plaza de la Lealtad 5, 28014 Madrid. ☎ **800/225-5843** in the U.S. and Canada, or 91/521-28-57. Fax 91/532-87-76. 158 rms, 24 suites. A/C MINIBAR TV TEL. 52,000–63,500 ptas. ($416–$508) double; from 92,500 ptas. ($740) suite. AE, DC, MC, V. Parking 2,000 ptas. ($16). Metro: Banco de España.

This is Spain's most famous hotel and Madrid's most prestigious address, encased in a turn-of-the-century shell of soaring ceilings and graceful columns. Billions of pesetas have been spent on renovations since the British-based Forte chain acquired it in the 1980s. The result is a bastion of glamour. The Ritz was built at the command of Alfonso XIII, with the aid of César Ritz, in 1908. The rooms contain fresh flowers, well-accessorized marble baths, and TVs with video movies and satellite reception. The chefs present an international menu featuring a paella that's Madrid's most elaborate.

Expensive

Emperatriz. López de Hoyos 4, 28006 Madrid. ☎ **91/563-80-88.** Fax 91/563-98-04. 153 rms, 5 suites. A/C MINIBAR TV TEL. 24,000 ptas. ($192) double; 60,000 ptas. ($480) suite. AE, DC, MC, V. Parking 1,500 ptas. ($12) nearby. Metro: Rubén Darío.

This hotel is just off the wide Paseo de Castellana, only a short walk from some of Madrid's most deluxe hotels, but it charges relatively reasonable rates. Built in the 1970s, it was last renovated in 1995, though the guest rooms (classically styled and comfortable, with both traditional and modern furniture) remain much finer than the dowdy public rooms. If one is available, ask for a seventh-floor room, where you'll get a private terrace at no extra charge.

Grand Hotel Velázquez. Calle de Velázquez 62, 28001 Madrid. ☎ **91/575-28-00.** Fax 91/575-28-09. 71 rms, 75 suites. A/C MINIBAR TV TEL. 21,970 ptas. ($175.75) double; from 29,160 ptas. ($233.30) suite. AE, DC, MC, V. Parking 1,700 ptas. ($13.60). Metro: Retiro.

On an affluent residential street near the center of town, this hotel has an art deco facade and a 1940s interior filled with well-upholstered furniture and richly grained paneling. Several public rooms lead off a central oval area; one of them includes a bar area. As in many hotels of its era, the rooms vary; some are large enough for entertaining, with a small but separate sitting area for reading or watching TV. This is one of the most attractive medium-size hotels in Madrid, with plenty of comfort and convenience.

Moderate

Gran Hotel Colón. Pez Volador 11, 28007 Madrid. ☎ **91/573-59-00.** Fax 91/573-08-09. 380 rms. A/C MINIBAR TV TEL. 17,600 ptas. ($140.80) double. AE, DC, MC, V. Parking 1,500 ptas. ($12). Metro: Sainz de Baranda.

West of Retiro Park, the Gran Hotel Colón is a few minutes from the city center by subway. It offers comfortable yet moderately priced accommodations. More than half the rooms have private balconies, and all contain comfortably traditional furniture, much of it built-in. Other assets include two dining rooms, a covered garage, and Bingo games.

DINING
NEAR PLAZA DE LAS CORTES

Expensive

El Espejo. Paseo de Recoletos 31. ☎ **91/308-23-47.** Reservations required. *Menú del día* 2,750 ptas. ($22). AE, DC, MC, V. Sun–Fri 1–4pm and 9pm–1am, Sat 9pm–1am. Metro: Banco de España or Colón. Bus: 27. INTERNATIONAL.

Here you'll find good-tasting food and one of the most perfectly crafted art nouveau decors in Madrid. If the weather is good, you can choose one of the outdoor tables, served by uniformed waiters who carry food across the busy street to a green area flanked with trees and strolling pedestrians. There's a charming cafe/bar. Menu items include grouper ragoût with clams, steak tartare, guinea fowl with Armagnac, and lean duck meat with pineapple.

Inexpensive

La Trucha. Manuel Fernández González 3. ☎ **91/429-58-33.** Reservations recommended. Main courses 1,200–3,200 ptas. ($9.60–$25.60); *menú del día* 2,800 ptas. ($22.40). AE, MC, V. Mon–Sat 2:30–4pm and 7:30pm–midnight. Metro: Sevilla. SPANISH/SEAFOOD.

With its Andalusian tavern ambience, La Trucha boasts a street-level bar and a small dining room—the arched ceiling and whitewashed walls festive with hanging braids of garlic, dried peppers, and onions; on the lower level the is a second bustling area. The specialty is fish, and there's a complete à la carte menu including trucha (trout), verbenas de abumados (literally, a "street party" of smoked delicacies), a stew called fabada ("glorious"; made with beans, Galician ham, black sausage, and smoked bacon), and comida casera rabo de toro (home-style oxtail). No one should miss nibbling on the tapas variadas in the bar.

NEAR PLAZA DE ESPAÑA

Expensive

Bajamar. Gran Vía 78. ☎ **91/559-59-03.** Reservations recommended. Main courses 1,850–4,500 ptas. ($14.80–$36). AE, DC, MC, V. Daily 1–4pm and 8pm–midnight. Metro: Plaza de España. SEAFOOD.

Bajamar is one of the best fish houses in Spain. Both fish and shellfish are shipped in fresh daily by air, the prices depending on what the market charges. Lobster, king crab, prawns, soft-shell crabs, and the like are all priced according to weight. There's a large array of reasonably priced dishes as well. The setting is contemporary and attractive, with smooth professional service. For an appetizer, we recommend half a dozen giant oysters or rover crayfish. The special seafood soup is a meal in itself. Some of the more recommendable main courses are turbot Gallego style, the special seafood paella, and baby squid cooked in its own ink.

Moderate

Las Cuevas del Duque. Princesa 16. ☎ **91/559-50-37.** Reservations required. Main courses 1,875–3,000 ptas. ($15–$24). AE, DC, MC, V. Mon–Fri 1–4pm and 8pm–midnight, Sat–Sun 8pm–midnight. Metro: Ventura Rodríguez. Bus: 1, 2, or 42. SPANISH.

In front of the duke of Alba's palace, a short walk from Plaza de España, is Las Cuevas del Duque, with an underground bar and a 20-table mesón serving simple Spanish fare like roast suckling pig, sirloin, tiny grilled lamb cutlets, and a few seafood dishes, including hake in garlic sauce or sole cooked in cider. In fair weather a few tables are set out beside a tiny triangular garden. Other tables line the Calle de la Princesa side and make an enjoyable roost for an afternoon drink.

ON OR NEAR THE GRAN VÍA

Moderate

Arce. Augusto Figueroa 32. ☎ **91/522-59-13.** Reservations recommended. Main courses 2,500–3,500 ptas. ($20–$28). AE, DC, MC, V. Mon–Fri 1:30–4pm and 9pm–midnight, Sat 9pm–midnight. Closed the week before Easter and Aug 15–31. Metro: Colón. BASQUE.

Arce has brought some of the best modern interpretations of Basque cuisine to Madrid, thanks to the enthusiasm of owner/chef Iñaki Camba and his wife, Theresa. In a comfortably decorated dining room, you can enjoy simple preparations, where the natural flavors are designed to dominate your taste buds. Examples include a salad of fresh scallops, an oven-baked casserole of fresh boletus mushrooms with few seasonings other than the woodsy taste of the original ingredients, unusual preparations of hake, and seasonal variations of such game dishes as pheasant and woodcock.

El Mentidero de la Villa. Santo Tomé 6. ☎ **91/308-12-85.** Reservations required. Main courses 1,950–2,400 ptas. ($15.60–$19.20). AE, DC, MC, V. Mon–Fri 1:30–4pm and 9pm–midnight, Sat 9pm–midnight. Closed the last 2 weeks of Aug. Metro: Alonso Martínez, Colón, or Gran Vía. Bus: 37. SPANISH/FRENCH.

This "Gossip Shop" is certainly a multicultural experience. The owner describes the cuisine as "modern Spanish with Japanese influence; the cooking technique is French." The result is usually a graceful achievement, as each ingredient in every dish manages to retain its natural flavor. The kitchen prepares such adventuresome dishes as veal liver in sage sauce, a version of spring rolls filled with fresh shrimp and leeks, filet steak with a sauce of mustard and brown sugar, medaillons of venison with purées of chestnut and celery, and such desserts as sherry trifle.

NEAR THE PUERTA DEL SOL
Expensive
Lhardy. Carrera de San Jerónimo 8. ☎ **91/521-33-85.** Reservations recommended in the upstairs dining room. Main courses 1,900–5,000 ptas. ($15.20–$40). AE, DC, MC, V. Mon–Sat 1–3:30pm and 9–11:30pm. Closed Aug. Metro: Puerta del Sol. SPANISH/INTERNATIONAL.

Lhardy has been a Madrileño legend since it opened in 1839 as a gathering place for the city's literati and political leaders. Its street level contains what might be the most elegant snack bar in Spain. In a dignified setting of marble and varnished hardwoods, cups of steaming consommé are dispensed from silver samovars into delicate porcelain cups. The real culinary skill of the place, however, is visible on Lhardy's second floor, where you'll find a formal restaurant decorated in the ornate style of Isabel Segunda. Specialties are fresh fish, tripe in a garlicky tomato-and-onion/wine sauce, and cocido, the chick-pea stew of Madrid, made with sausage, pork, and vegetables. Soufflé sorpresa (baked Alaska) is the dessert specialty.

Platerías Comedor. Plaza de Santa Ana 11. ☎ **91/429-70-48.** Reservations recommended. Main courses 1,000–5,000 ptas. ($8–$40). AE, DC, MC, V. Mon–Fri 2:30–4pm and 9pm–midnight, Sat 9pm–midnight. Metro: Puerta del Sol. SPANISH.

One of the most charming dining rooms in Madrid, Platerías Comedor has richly brocaded walls evocative of 19th-century Spain. Despite the busy socializing on the plaza outside, this serene oasis makes few concessions to the new generation in its food, decor, or formally attired waiters. Specialties are beans with clams, stuffed partridge with cabbage and sausage, magret of duckling with pomegranates, duck liver with white grapes, veal stew with snails and mushrooms, and guinea hen with figs and plumbs. You might follow with passionfruit sorbet.

Moderate
Café de Oriente. Plaza de Oriente 2. ☎ **91/541-39-74.** Reservations recommended (in restaurant only). Cafe, tapas 850 ptas. ($6.80); coffee 650 ptas. ($5.20). Restaurant, main courses 1,700–3,950 ptas. ($13.60–$31.60). AE, DC, MC, V. Daily 1–4pm and 9pm–1:30am. Metro: Ópera. FRENCH/SPANISH.

The Oriente is a cafe/restaurant complex. The cafe tables on the terrace have a spectacular view of the Royal Palace and Teatro Real. The dining rooms (Castilian upstairs, French Basque downstairs) are frequented by royalty and diplomats. Typical of the refined cuisine are vichyssoise, fresh vegetable flan, and many savory meat and fresh-fish offerings; the service is excellent. The cafe is decorated in turn-of-the-century style, with banquettes and regal paneling, as befits its location.

Casa Paco. Plaza de la Puerta Cerrada 11. ☎ **91/366-31-66.** Reservations required. Main courses 1,100–3,800 ptas. ($8.80–$30.40); fixed-price menu 3,300 ptas. ($26.40). DC. Mon–Sat 1:30–4pm and 8:30pm–midnight. Closed Aug. Metro: Puerta del Sol, Ópera, or La Latina. Bus: 3, 21, or 65. STEAK.

Madrileños defiantly name Casa Paco, beside Plaza Mayor in the old town, when someone has the "nerve" to put down Spanish steaks. They know that here you can get the thickest, juiciest steaks in Spain, priced according to weight. Señor Paco was the first in Madrid to sear steaks in boiling oil before serving them on plates so hot that the almost-raw meat continues to cook, preserving the natural juices. The two-story restaurant offers three dining rooms for which reservations are imperative— otherwise, you face a long wait. Casa Paco isn't just a steak house. You can start with a fish soup and proceed to a dish such as grilled sole, lamb, or Casa Paco cocido, the famous chick-pea/meat soup of Madrid.

Inexpensive

Casa Alberto. Huertas 18. ☎ **91/429-93-56.** Reservations recommended. Main courses 650– 2,250 ptas. ($5.20–$18). AE, V. Tues–Sat 1–4pm and 8:30pm–midnight, Sun 1–4pm. Metro: Antón Martín. CASTILIAN.

One of the oldest tascas in the neighborhood, Casa Alberto is on the street level of the house where Miguel de Cervantes lived briefly in 1614 and contains an appeal- ing mixture of bullfighting memorabilia, engravings, and reproductions of old mas- ter paintings. Tapas are continually replenished from platters on the bartop, but there's also a sit-down dining area for more substantial meals. Specialties include fried squid, shellfish in vinaigrette sauce, chorizo (sausage) in cider sauce, and several ver- sions of baked or roasted lamb.

Hylogui. Ventura de la Vega 3. ☎ **91/429-73-57.** Reservations recommended. Main courses 1,000–2,200 ptas. ($8–$17.60); fixed-price menu 1,400–1,700 ptas. ($11,20–$13.60). AE, MC, V. Mon–Sat 1–4:30pm and 9pm–midnight, Sun 1–4:30pm. Metro: Sevilla. SPANISH.

Hylogui, a local legend, is one of the largest dining rooms along Ventura de la Vega, but there are many arches and nooks for privacy. One globe-trotting American wrote enthusiastically that he took all his Madrid meals here, finding the soup pleasant and rich, the flan soothing, and the regional wine dry. The food is old-fashioned Span- ish homestyle cooking.

NEAR RETIRO & SALAMANCA

Very Expensive

Horcher. Alfonso XII 6. ☎ **91/532-35-96.** Reservations required. Jackets and ties required for men. Main courses 3,400–8,000 ptas. ($27.20–$64). AE, DC, MC, V. Mon–Fri 1:30–4pm and 8:30pm–midnight, Sat 8:30pm–midnight. Metro: Retiro. GERMAN/INTERNATIONAL.

Horcher originated in Berlin in 1904. Prompted by a tip from a high-ranking Ger- man officer that Germany was losing the war, Herr Horcher moved his restaurant to Madrid in 1943. The restaurant has continued its grand European traditions, including excellent service, ever since. You might try the skate or shrimp tartar or the distinctive warm hake salad. The venison stew in green pepper with orange peel and the crayfish with parsley and cucumber are the type of elegant fare served with impeccable style; you can sample game dishes like wild boar or roast wild duck in autumn. Other main courses include veal scaloppine in tarragon and sea bass with saffron.

✪ **La Gamella.** Alfonso XII 4. ☎ **91/532-45-09.** Reservations required. Main courses 2,300– 4,200 ptas. ($18.40–$33.60). AE, DC, MC, V. Mon–Fri 1:30–4pm and 9pm–midnight, Sat 9pm–midnight. Closed 2 weeks around Easter and 2 weeks in Aug. Metro: Retiro. Bus: 19. CALIFORNIAN/CASTILIAN.

In 1988 La Gamella's Illinois-born owner, former choreographer Dick Stephens, moved his restaurant into this 19th-century building where Spanish philosopher Ortega y Gasset was born. The legendary Horcher is across the street, but the food here is better. The design and decor invite you to relax in russet-colored high- ceilinged warmth. Mr. Stephens has prepared his delicate and light-textured specialties for the king and queen of Spain. Typical menu items are ceviche of Mediterranean fish, sliced duck liver in truffle sauce, duck breast with peppers, and an array of well-prepared desserts, among which is an all-American cheesecake. Traditional Spanish dishes such as chicken with garlic have been added to the menu, plus what has been called "the only edible hamburger in Madrid."

Expensive

Alkalde. Jorge Juan 10. ☎ **91/576-33-59.** Reservations required. Main courses 1,550–5,600 ptas. ($12.40–$44.80); fixed-price menu from 4,750 ptas. ($38). AE, DC, MC, V. Daily 1–4:30pm and 8:30pm–midnight. Closed Sat–Sun July–Aug. Metro: Retiro or Serrano. Bus: 8, 20, 21, or 53. BASQUE/INTERNATIONAL.

Alkalde serves top-quality Spanish food in an old tavern setting decorated like a Basque inn, with beamed ceilings and hams hanging from the rafters. Upstairs is a large *típico* tavern; downstairs is a maze of stone-sided cellars that are pleasantly cool in summer. Basque cookery is the best in Spain, and Alkalde honors that tradition nobly. You might begin with the cream-of-crabmeat soup, followed by gambas à la plancha (grilled shrimp) or cigalas (crayfish). Other well-recommended dishes are mero salsa verde (brill in a green sauce), trout Alkalde, stuffed peppers, and chicken steak.

✪ El Amparo. Callejón de Puígcerdá 8 (at the corner of Jorge Juan). ☎ **91/431-64-56.** Reservations required. Main courses 3,000–4,000 ptas. ($24–$32); fixed-price menu 9,500 ptas. ($76). AE, MC, V. Mon–Fri 1:30–3:30pm and 9:30–11:30pm, Sat 9:30–11:30pm. Closed the week before Easter and Aug. Metro: Goya. Bus: 21 or 53. BASQUE.

Behind the cascading vines on its facade, this is one of Madrid's most elegant gastronomic enclaves. A sloping skylight floods the interior with sun by day; at night, pinpoints of light from the high-tech hanging lanterns create intimate shadows. A battalion of polite uniformed waiters serves well-prepared nouvelle-cuisine versions of cold marinated salmon with tomato sorbet, bisque of shellfish with Armagnac, ravioli stuffed with seafood, a platter of steamed fish of the day, and steamed hake with pepper sauce.

✪ Viridiana. Juan de Mena 14. ☎ **91/523-44-78.** Reservations recommended. Main courses 3,000–4,000 ptas. ($24–$32). AE, MC, V. Mon–Sat 1:30–4pm and 9pm–midnight. Closed Aug and 1 week at Easter. Metro: Banco. INTERNATIONAL.

Praised as one of Madrid's up-and-coming new restaurants, Viridiana is known for the creative imagination of chef and part-owner Abraham García. Menu specialties are usually contemporary adaptations of traditional recipes and change frequently according to the availability of the ingredients. Examples are a salad of exotic lettuces with smoked salmon, guinea fowl stuffed with herbs and wild mushrooms, baby squid with curry served on a bed of lentils, and roast lamb in puff pastry with fresh basil.

Inexpensive

Gran Café de Gijón. Paseo de Recoletos 21. ☎ **91/521-54-25.** Reservations needed for restaurant. Main courses 3,000–5,000 ptas. ($24–$40); fixed-price menu 1,500 ptas. ($12). MC, V. Sun–Fri 9am–1:30am, Sat 9am–2am. Metro: Banco de España, Colón, or Recoletos. SPANISH.

Each European capital has a coffeehouse that traditionally attracts the literati—in Madrid it's the Gijón, which opened in 1888. Artists and writers still patronize this venerated old cafe; many spend hours over one cup of coffee. Hemingway made the place famous for Americans. Gijón has open windows looking out onto the wide paseo, as well as a large terrace for sun worshipers and bird-watchers. Along one side is a stand-up bar and on the lower level is a restaurant. The cookery is the "way it used to be" in Madrid.

CHAMBERÍ
Very Expensive

☉ Jockey. Amador de los Ríos 6. ☎ **91/319-24-35.** Reservations required. Main courses 2,000–5,000 ptas. ($16–$40). AE, DC, MC, V. Mon–Sat 1–4pm and 9–11:30pm. Closed Aug. Metro: Colón. INTERNATIONAL.

For decades this was Spain's premier restaurant, though competition is severe today. At any rate, it's the favorite of international celebrities, and some of the more faithful patrons look on it as their private club. Wood-paneled walls and colored linen provide warmth. Against the paneling are a dozen prints of horses mounted by jockeys—hence the name of the place. The chef prides himself on coming up with new and creative dishes. Try his goose-liver terrine or slices of Jabugo ham. His cold melon soup with shrimp is soothing on a hot day, especially when followed by grill-roasted young pigeon from Talavera cooked in its own juice or sole filets with figs in chardonnay. Stuffed small chicken Jockey style is a specialty.

☉ Las Cuatro Estaciones. General Ibéñez Ibero 5. ☎ **91/553-63-05.** Reservations required. Main courses 1,500–5,000 ptas. ($12–$40); fixed-price dinner 4,500 ptas. ($36). AE, DC, MC, V. Mon–Fri 1:30–4pm and 9pm–midnight, Sat 9–11:30pm. Closed Aug. Metro: Guzmán el Bueno. MEDITERRANEAN.

Praised by gastronomes and horticulturists, Las Cuatro Estaciones has become a neck-and-neck rival with the prestigious Jockey. In addition to superb food, the establishment prides itself on the masses of flowers that change with the season, plus a modern and softly inviting decor. Representative specialties are petite marmite of fish and shellfish, imaginative preparations of salmon, a salad of eels, fresh asparagus and mushrooms in puff pastry with parsley-butter sauce, and a three-fish platter with fines herbes.

Inexpensive
Foster's Hollywood. Magallanes 1. ☎ **91/448-91-65.** Main courses 600–1,000 ptas. ($4.80–$8). AE, DC, MC, V. Sun–Thurs 1pm–midnight, Fri–Sat 1pm–2am. Metro: Quevedo. AMERICAN.

When Foster's opened in 1971, it was not only the first American restaurant in Spain, it was one of the first in Europe. It has now grown to 15 restaurants in Madrid alone. A popular hangout for both locals and visiting Yanks, it offers a choice of dining venues, ranging from "classical club American" to studios, the latter evoking a working movie studio with props. Its varied menu includes Tex-Mex selections, ribs, steaks, sandwiches, freshly made salads, and, as its signature product, hamburgers grilled over natural charcoal in many variations.

OFF PLAZA MAYOR
Moderate
☉ Sobrino de Botín. Calle de Cuchilleros 17. ☎ **91/366-42-17.** Reservations required. Main courses 800–3,000 ptas. ($6.40–$24); fixed-price menu 3,700 ptas. ($29.60). AE, DC, MC, V. Daily 1–4pm and 8pm–midnight. Metro: La Latina or Ópera. SPANISH.

Ernest Hemingway made Sobrino de Botín famous—in the final pages of *The Sun Also Rises,* Jake invites Lady Brett there for the Segovian specialty of roast suckling pig, washed down with Rioja Alta. By merely entering its portals you step back to 1725, the year the restaurant was founded. You'll see an open kitchen with a charcoal hearth, hanging copper pots, an 18th-century tile oven for roasting the suckling pig, and a big pot of regional soup whose aroma wafts across the room. The other house specialty is roast Segovian lamb. You can wash down your meal with Valdepeñas or Aragón wine, or even sangría.

ATTRACTIONS

Madrid has changed drastically in recent years. No longer is it fair to say that it has only the Prado, and after you see that you should head for Toledo or El Escorial. As you'll discover, Madrid has something to amuse and delight everyone.

SIGHTSEEING SUGGESTIONS

If You Have 1 Day   If you have just arrived in Spain after a long flight, don't tackle too much on this day. Spend the morning at the Prado, one of the world's great art museums, arriving when it opens at 9am (remember, it's closed Monday). Have lunch and then visit the Palacio Real (Royal Palace). Have an early dinner near Plaza Mayor.

If You Have 2 Days   Spend day 1 as above. On Day 2 take a trip to Toledo, where you can visit El Greco's House and Museum, the Santa Cruz Museum, the Church of Santo Tomé, and the Alcázar. Return to Madrid in the evening.

If You Have 3 Days   Follow the above suggestions for days 1 and 2. On your third day take a 1-hour train ride to the Monastery of San Lorenzo de El Escorial, in the foothills of the Sierra de Guadarrama. Return to Madrid in the evening.

If You Have 5 Days   Follow the above for days 1–3. Day 4 would be very busy indeed if you visited the Thyssen-Bornemisza Museum in the morning, strolled around Madrid's medieval area, and visited the Museo Nacional Centro de Arte Reina Sofía in the late afternoon or early evening (it closes at 9pm most nights). Here you can see Picasso's *Guernica* plus other great art of the 20th century. Have dinner once again at one of the many restaurants off Plaza Mayor. On Day 5 take a trip to Toledo in New Castile.

THE TOP MUSEUMS

✪ **Museo del Prado.** Paseo del Prado. ☎ **91/420-28-36.** Admission 450 ptas. ($3.60). Tues–Sat 9am–7pm, Sun and holidays 9am–2pm. Closed Jan 1, Good Fri, May 1, and Dec 25. Metro: Banco de España or Atocha. Bus: 10, 14, 27, 34, 37, or 45.

With more than 7,000 paintings, the Prado is one of the most important repositories of art in the world. It began as a royal collection and was enhanced by the Hapsburgs. In paintings of the Spanish school the Prado has no equal, so on your first visit, concentrate on the Spanish masters—Velázquez, Goya, and El Greco. Most major works are on the first floor.

The Prado is a treasure trove of the work of El Greco (1524–1614), the Crete-born artist who lived much of his life in Toledo. You'll also find a splendid array of works by the incomparable Diego Velázquez (1599–1660); the museum's most famous painting is his *Las Meninas,* a triumph in the use of light. The Prado also contains an outstanding collection of the work of Hieronymus Bosch (1450?–1516), the Flemish genius; his best-known work, *The Garden of Earthly Delights,* is here. Francisco de Goya (1746–1828) ranks along with Velázquez and El Greco in the trio of great Spanish artists. Hanging here are his unflattering portraits of his patron, Charles IV, and his family, as well as the *Clothed Maja* and the *Naked Maja.*

✪ **Thyssen-Bornemisza Museum.** Palacio de Villahermosa, Paseo del Prado 8. ☎ **91/369-01-51.** Admission 650 ptas. ($5.20). Tues–Sun 10am–7pm. Metro: Banco de España. Bus: 1, 2, 5, 9, 10, 14, 15, 20, 27, 34, 45, 51, 52, 53, 74, 146, or 150.

An almost unrivaled private collection was amassed over a period of about 60 years by the Thyssen-Bornemisza family, scions of a shipping/banking/mining fortune. When it went on the market, Spain acquired it for $350 million. To house the collection, an 18th-century building adjacent to the Prado, the Villahermosa Palace, was retrofitted and the rooms arranged numerically so that by following the order of the

Madrid Attractions

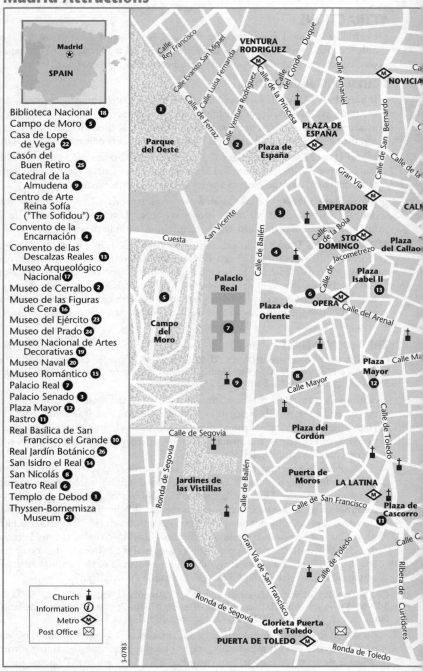

Biblioteca Nacional **18**
Campo de Moro **5**
Casa de Lope de Vega **22**
Casón del Buen Retiro **25**
Catedral de la Almudena **9**
Centro de Arte Reina Sofía ("The Sofidou") **27**
Convento de la Encarnación **4**
Convento de las Descalzas Reales **13**
Museo Arqueológico Nacional **17**
Museo de Cerralbo **2**
Museo de las Figuras de Cera **16**
Museo del Ejército **23**
Museo del Prado **24**
Museo Nacional de Artes Decorativas **19**
Museo Naval **20**
Museo Romántico **15**
Palacio Real **7**
Palacio Senado **3**
Plaza Mayor **12**
Rastro **11**
Real Basílica de San Francisco el Grande **10**
Real Jardín Botánico **26**
San Isidro el Real **14**
San Nicolás **8**
Teatro Real **6**
Templo de Debod **1**
Thyssen-Bornemisza Museum **21**

Church †
Information ⓘ
Metro Ⓜ
Post Office ✉

3-0783

855

various rooms (nos. 1–48, spread over three floors) a logical sequence of European painting can be followed from the 13th through the 20th century. The nucleus of the collection consists of 700 world-class paintings. They include works by El Greco, Velázquez, Dürer, Rembrandt, Watteau, Canaletto, Caravaggio, Frans Hals, Hans Memling, and Goya.

✪ **Museo Nacional Centro de Arte Reina Sofía.** Santa Isabel 52. ☎ **91/467-50-62.** Admission 450 ptas. ($3.60). Mon and Wed–Sat 10am–9pm, Sun 10am–2:30pm. Metro: Atocha. Bus: 6, 14, 26, 27, 32, 45, 57, or C.

Madrid's "MoMA" is Spain's greatest repository of 20th-century art. The museum is a high-ceilinged showplace named after the Greek-born wife of Spain's present king. One of Europe's largest museums, it was designated as "the ugliest building in Spain" by Catalán architect Oriol Bohigas. Special emphasis is paid to the great artists of contemporary Spain: Juan Gris, Dalí, and Miró. Picasso's masterpiece, *Guernica,* now rests here after a long and troubling history of traveling. This antiwar piece immortalizes the blanket bombing by the German Luftwaffe for Franco during the Spanish Civil War of the village of Guernica, cradle of the Basque nation.

✪ **Palacio Real (Royal Palace).** Plaza de Oriente, Calle de Bailén 2. ☎ **91/542-00-59.** Admission 900 ptas. ($7.20). Mon–Sat 9am–6pm, Sun 9am–3pm. Metro: Ópera or Plaza de España.

This huge palace was begun in 1738 on the site of the Madrid Alcázar, which burned in 1734. Some of its 2,000 rooms are open to the public, though others are still used for state business. The guided tour includes the Reception Room, the State Apartments, the Armory, and the Royal Pharmacy. The rooms are literally stuffed with art treasures and antiques—salon after salon of monumental grandeur, with no apologies for the damask, mosaics, stucco, Tiepolo ceilings, gilt and bronze, chandeliers, and paintings. In the Armory you'll see a fine collection of weaponry.

More Attractions

Museo de la Real Academia de Bellas Artes de San Fernando (Fine Arts Museum). Alcalá 13. ☎ **91/522-14-91.** Tues–Fri 200 ptas. ($1.60), free for children and seniors 60 and over; Sat–Sun free for everyone. Tues–Fri 9am–7pm, Sat–Mon 9am–2:30pm. Metro: Puerta del Sol or Sevilla. Bus: 15, 20, 51, 52, 53, or 150.

An easy stroll from the Puerta del Sol, the Fine Arts Museum is located in the restored and remodeled 17th-century baroque palace of Juan de Goyeneche. The collection—more than 1,500 paintings and 570 sculptures, ranging from the 16th century to the present—was started in 1752 during the reign of Fernando VI (1746–59). It emphasizes works by Spanish, Flemish, and Italian artists. Masterpieces by El Greco, Rubens, Velázquez, Zurbarán, Ribera, Cano, Coello, Murillo, Goya, and Sorolla are here.

Panteón de Goya (Goya's Tomb). Glorieta de San António de la Florida. ☎ **91/542-07-22.** Admission 300 ptas. ($2.40). Tues–Fri 10am–2pm and 4–8pm, Sat–Sun 10am–2pm. Metro: Norte. Bus: 41, 46, 75, or C.

In a remote part of town beyond the North Station lies Goya's tomb, containing one of his masterpieces—an elaborately beautiful fresco depicting the miracles of St. Anthony on the dome and cupola of the little hermitage of San António de la Florida. This has been called Goya's Sistine Chapel. Already deaf when he began the painting, Goya labored from dawn to dusk for 16 weeks, painting with sponges rather than brushes. By depicting common street life—stone masons, prostitutes, and beggars—Goya raised the ire of the nobility. However, when Carlos IV viewed it and approved, the formerly "outrageous" painting was deemed acceptable.

○ **Museo Lázaro Galdiano.** Serrano 122. ☎ **91/561-60-84.** Admission 300 ptas. ($2.40). Tues–Sun 10am–2pm. Closed holidays and Aug. Metro: Avenida de América. Bus: 9, 16, 19, 51, or 89.

This well-preserved 19th-century mansion bulges with artworks of all kinds. You can take the elevator to the top floor and work your way down. There are 15th-century hand-woven vestments, swords and daggers, royal seals, 16th-century crystal from Limoges, Byzantine jewelry, Italian bronzes from ancient times to the Renaissance, and medieval armor. There are works by El Greco, Velázquez, Zurbarán, Ribera, Murillo, and Valdés-Leal, and Tiepolo and Guardi, and a section is devoted to works by the English artists Reynolds, Gainsborough, and Constable.

○ **Monasterio de las Descalzas Reales.** Plaza de las Descalzas Reales. ☎ **91/542-00-59.** Admission 650 ptas. ($5.20) adults, 350 ptas. ($2.80) children. Tues–Thurs and Sat 10:30am–12:30pm and 4–5:30pm, Fri 10:30am–12:30pm, Sun 11am–1:30pm. Bus: 1, 2, 5, 20, 46, 52, 53, 74, M1, M2, M3, or M5. From Plaza del Callao, off Gran Vía, walk down Postigo de San Martín to Plaza de las Descalzas Reales; the convent is on the left.

In the mid–16th century, aristocratic women came to this convent to take the veil. Each of them brought a dowry, making this one of the richest convents in the land. But by the mid–20th century the convent sheltered mostly poor women. Although it contained a priceless collection of art treasures, the sisters were forbidden to auction anything; in fact, they were literally starving. The state intervened and the pope granted special dispensation to open the convent as a museum.

In the Reliquary are the noblewomen's dowries, one of which is said to include bits of wood from the Cross; another, some bones of St. Sebastian. The most valuable painting is Titian's *Caesar's Money.* The Flemish Hall shelters other fine works, including paintings by Hans de Beken and Breughel the Elder, and tapestries based on Rubens's cartoons.

PARKS & GARDENS

The **Casa de Campo,** the former royal hunting grounds, is composed of miles of parkland lying south of the Royal Palace across the Manzanares River. You can see the gate through which the kings rode out of the palace grounds—either on horseback or in carriages—on their way to the park. The Casa de Campo has a variety of trees and a lake, usually filled with rowers. You can have drinks and light refreshments around the water or go swimming in a municipally operated pool. The Casa de Campo can be visited daily 8am–9pm. Take the Metro to the Lago or Batán stop.

Retiro Park, originally a playground for the Spanish monarchs and their guests, extends over 350 acres. The huge palaces that once stood here were destroyed in the early 19th century and only the former dance hall, Casón del Buen Retiro (housing the modern works of the Prado), and the building containing the Army Museum remain. The park boasts numerous fountains and statues, plus a large lake. There are also two exposition centers, the Velásquez and Crystal Palaces (built to honor the Philippines in 1887) and a lakeside monument, erected in 1922 in honor of Alfonso XII. In summer the rose gardens are worth a visit, and you'll find several places where you can have inexpensive snacks and drinks. The park is open daily 24 hours, but it's safest during the day (7am–8:30pm). Take the Metro to the Retiro stop.

Across Calle de Alfonso XII, at the southwest corner of Retiro Park, is the **Real Jardín Botánico (Botanical Garden).** Founded in the 18th century, the garden contains more than 100 species of trees and 3,000 types of plants. Also on the premises are an exhibition hall and a library specializing in botany. The park is open daily 10am–8pm; admission is 200 ptas. ($1.60). Take the Metro to the Atocha stop or take bus no. 10, 14, 19, 32, or 45.

ORGANIZED TOURS

One of Spain's largest tour operators is **Pullmantours,** Plaza de Oriente 8 (☎ 91/541-18-07). Regardless of its destination or duration, virtually every tour departs from the Pullmantour terminal at that address. Half-day tours of Madrid include an artistic tour at 4,950 ptas. ($39.60) per person, which provides entrance to a selection of the city's museums, and a panoramic half-day tour for 2,750 ptas. ($22).

Southward treks to Toledo are the most popular full-day excursions. They cost 7,650 ptas. ($61.20). These tours (including lunch) depart daily at 8:30am from the above-mentioned departure point, last all day, and include ample opportunities for wandering at will through the city's narrow streets. You can take an abbreviated morning tour of Toledo, without stopping for lunch, for 5,000 ptas. ($40).

Another popular tour stops briefly in Toledo and continues on to visit both the monastery at El Escorial and the Valley of the Fallen (Valle de los Caídos) before returning the same day to Madrid. With lunch included, this all-day excursion costs 10,700 ptas. ($85.60).

Other worthwhile full-day tours include visits to Segovia and the Bourbon dynasty's 18th-century palace of La Granja, costing 6,200 ptas. ($49.60) without lunch and 9,400 ptas. ($75.20) with lunch. A half-day tour of Aranjuez and Chinchón, without lunch, costs 5,900 ptas. ($47.20).

SHOPPING

Tirso de Molina, the 17th-century playwright, called Madrid "a shop stocked with every kind of merchandise," and it's true—its estimated 50,000 stores sell everything from high-fashion clothing to flamenco guitars to art and ceramics.

Galería Kreisler, Hermosilla 6 (☎ 91/431-42-64; Metro: Serrano; bus, 27, 45, or 150), specializes in figurative and contemporary paintings, sculptures, and graphics. Open Mon–Sat 10:30am–2pm and 5–9pm; closed Aug and Sat afternoon July 15–Sept 15.

Antigua Casa Talavera, Isabel la Católica 2 (☎ 91/547-34-17; Metro: Santo Domingo; bus: 1, 2, 46, 70, 75, or 148), the "first house of Spanish ceramics," has wares that include a sampling of regional styles from every major area of Spain. Sangría pitchers, dinnerware, tea sets, plates, and vases are all handmade. Inside one of the showrooms is an interesting selection of tiles painted with scenes from bullfights, dances, and folklore. Open Mon–Fri 10am–1:30pm and 5–8pm and Sat 10am–1:30pm.

El Arco de los Cuchilleros Artesanía de Hoy, Plaza Mayor 9 (basement level) (☎ 91/365-26-80; Metro: Puerta del Sol), is devoted to unusual craft items from throughout Spain. The merchandise is one-of-a-kind, and in most cases contemporary, and includes a changing array of pottery, leather, textiles, wood carvings, glassware, wickerwork, papier-mâché, and silver jewelry. It's open Mon–Sat: Jan–Sept 11am–8pm and Oct–Dec 11am–9pm.

Lasarte, Gran Vía 44 (☎ 91/521-49-22; Metro: Callao), is an imposing outlet for Lladró porcelain, devoted almost exclusively to its distribution. The staff can usually tell you about new designs and releases the Lladró company is planning for the near future. Open Mon–Fri 9:30–8pm and Sat 10am–8pm.

El Corte Inglés, Preciados 3 (☎ 91/532-18-00; Metro: Puerta del Sol), the flagship of the largest department-store chain in Madrid, sells Spanish handcrafts and also glamorous fashion articles, such as Pierre Balmain designs, for about a third less than in most European capitals. Open Mon–Sat 10am–9pm. Spain's top designers are represented in the marble-sheathed concourse below the Palace Hotel called the **Galería del Prado,** Plaza de las Cortes 7 (Metro: Banco de España or Atocha). You'll always find a good assortment of fashions, Spanish leather goods, cosmetics, perfumes, and jewelry. You can also eat and drink in the complex. The entrance to the gallery is in front of the hotel, facing the broad tree-lined Paseo del Prado across from the Prado itself. Open Mon–Sat 10am–9pm.

Since 1846, **Loewe,** Gran Vía 8 (☎ **91/522-68-15;** Metro: Banco de España), has been Spain's most elegant leather store. Its designers have always kept abreast of changing tastes and styles, but the inventory still retains a timeless chic. The store sells luggage, handbags, and jackets for men and women (in leather or suede). Open Mon–Sat 9:30am–8pm.

Perfumería Padilla, Preciados 17 (☎ **91/522-66-83;** Metro: Puerta del Sol), sells a large assortment of Spanish and international scents for women. There's also a branch at Calle del Carmen 78 (same phone). Both branches are open Mon–Sat 10am–8:30pm.

Foremost among the flea markets is **El Rastro,** Plaza Cascorro and Ribera de Curtidores (Metro: La Latina; bus: 3 or 17). El Rastro occupies a roughly triangular district of streets and plazas a few minutes' walk south of Plaza Mayor. This market will delight anyone attracted to a mishmash of fascinating junk interspersed with bric-a-brac and paintings. But thieves are rampant here (hustling more than just antiques), so secure your wallet carefully, be alert, and proceed with caution. Open Tues–Sun 9:30am–1:30pm and 5–8pm.

MADRID AFTER DARK

In summer Madrid becomes a virtual free festival because the city sponsors a series of plays, concerts, and films. Pick up a copy of the *Guía del Ocio* (available at most newsstands) for listings of these events. This guide also provides information about occasional discounts for commercial events, such as the concerts that are given in Madrid's parks. Also check the program of the Fundación Juan March, Calle Castello 77 (☎ **91/435-42-40;** Metro: Núñez de Balboa), which frequently stages free concerts.

Flamenco in Madrid is geared mainly to tourists with fat wallets, and nightclubs are expensive. But since Madrid is preeminently a city of song and dance, you can often be entertained at very little cost—in fact, for the price of a glass of wine or beer, if you sit at a bar with live entertainment.

Tickets to dramatic and musical events usually range from 700–3,000 ptas. ($5.60–$24), with discounts of up to 50% granted on certain days (usually Wednesday and early performances on Sunday). In the event your choice is sold out, you may be able to get tickets (with a considerable markup) at **Localidades Galicia,** Plaza del Carmen (☎ **91/531-27-32;** Metro: Puerta del Sol). This agency also markets tickets to bullfights and sports events. It's open Tues–Sat 9:30am–1:30pm and 4:30–7:30pm and Sun 9:30am–1:30pm.

THE PERFORMING ARTS

For those who speak Spanish, the **Compañía Nacional de Nuevas Tendencias Escénicas** is an avant-garde troupe that performs new—and often controversial—works by undiscovered writers. On the other hand, the **Compañía Nacional de Teatro Clásico,** as its name suggests, is devoted to the Spanish classics, including works by the ever-popular Lope de Vega or Tirso de Molina.

Among dance companies, the **Ballet Nacional de España** is devoted exclusively to Spanish dance, and its performances are always well attended. The national ballet company of the country is the **Ballet Lírico Nacional.** Also look for performances by choreographer Nacho Duato's **Compañía Nacional de Danza.**

World-renowned flamenco sensation António Canales and his troup, **Ballet Flamenco António Canales,** offer high-energy, spirited performances. Productions are centered around Canales's impassioned *Torero*—his interpretation of a bullfighter and the physical and emotional struggles within the man. For tickets and information, call 91/401-28-25.

Classical Music

Madrid's opera company is the **Teatro de la Ópera,** and its symphony orchestra is the outstanding **Orquesta Sinfónica de Madrid.**

Auditorio Nacional de Música. Príncipe de Vergara 146. ☎ **91/337-01-00.** Tickets 1,000–6,000 ptas. ($8–$48). Metro: Cruz del Rayo.

This hall is the ultramodern home of both the **National Orchestra of Spain,** which pays particular attention to the music of Spanish composers, and the **National Chorus of Spain.** Just north of Madrid's Salamanca district, it ranks as a major addition to the competitive circles of classical music in Europe.

Auditorio del Real Conservatorio de Música. Plaza de Isabel II. ☎ **91/337-01-00.** Tickets 1,500–7,500 ptas. ($12–$60). Metro: Ópera.

This is one of the home bases of the **Spanish Philharmonic Orchestra,** which presents its concerts between September and May. The auditorium also presents concerts by chamber-music ensembles visiting from abroad. Containing only about 400 seats, the hall is sometimes sold out long in advance, especially for such famous names as Plácido Domingo.

Flamenco

Café de Chinitas. Torija 7. ☎ **91/559-51-35**. Dinner and show 8,500 ptas. ($68); show and one drink 3,900 ptas. ($31.20). Metro: Santo Domingo. Bus: 1 or 2.

One of the best flamenco clubs in town, the Café de Chinitas is one floor above street level in a 19th-century building midway between the Ópera and the Gran Vía. It features an array of (usually) Gypsy-born flamenco artists from Madrid, Barcelona, and Andalusia, whose acts and performers change about once a month. You can arrange for dinner before the show. Open Mon–Sat, with dinner served 9–11pm and the show lasting 10:30pm–2am. Reservations are recommended.

Casa Patas. Calle Cañizares 10. ☎ **91/369-04-96.** Admission 1,500–2,000 ptas. ($12–$16). Metro: Tirso de Molina.

Following an upswing in interest in flamenco that followed a period of declining interest in the 1980s, this club is now one of the best places to see "true" flamenco as opposed to the more tourist-oriented version. It's also a bar/restaurant, with space reserved in the rear for flamenco. Shows are presented midnight Thurs–Sat and during Madrid's major fiesta month of May. The club is open daily 9pm–5am.

CABARET

Café del Foro. Calle San Andres 38. ☎ **91/445-37-52.** Free admission (but cover might be imposed for a specially booked act). Metro: Bilboa. Bus: 40, 147, 149, or N19.

This oldtime favorite in the Malasaña district has in the mid-1990s become one of the most fashionable places in Madrid to hang out after dark. Patronizing the club are members of the literati along with a large student clientele. You never know exactly what the program for the evening will be, though live music of some sort generally starts at 11:30pm. Cabaret is often featured, along with live merengue and salsa. Open daily 7pm–2am.

Scala Melía Castilla. Calle Capitán Haya 43 (entrance at Rosario Pino 7). ☎ **91/571-44-11.** Dinner and show, 9,550 ptas. ($76.40); show and one drink, 5,100 ptas. ($40.80). Metro: Cuzco.

Madrid's most famous dinner show is a major Las Vegas–style spectacle. The program is varied—you might see international or Spanish ballet, magic acts, ice skaters, whatever. Most definitely you'll be entertained by a live orchestra. It's open Mon–Sat 8:30pm–3am. Dinner is served beginning at 9pm; the show is presented at 10:30pm. Reservations are needed.

JAZZ

Café Central. Plaza del Angel 10. ☎ **91/369-41-43.** Cover 800 ptas. ($6.40) Mon, 1,000 ptas. ($8) Tues–Sun—but prices vary depending on show. Metro: Antón Martín.

Off Plaza de Santa Ana, the Café Central has a vaguely art deco interior, with an unusual series of stained-glass windows. Many of the patrons read newspapers and talk at the marble-top tables during the day, but the ambience is far more animated during the nightly jazz sessions. Open Sun–Thurs 1:30pm–2:30am and Fri–Sat 1:30pm–3:30am; live jazz is offered daily 10pm–midnight.

Clamores. Albuquerque 14. ☎ **91/445-79-38.** Cover: none Sun–Mon, 500–800 ptas. ($4–$6.40) Tues–Sat, depending on the act. Metro: Bilbao.

With dozens of small tables and a huge bar in its dark and smoky interior, Clamores is the largest and one of the most popular jazz clubs in Madrid. It has thrived because of its changing offerings of American and Spanish jazz bands that have appeared here. The place is open daily 6pm–3am or so, but jazz is presented only Tues–Sat. Tues–Thurs, performances are at 11pm and again at 1am; Sat performances begin at 11:30pm, with an additional show at 1:30am. There are no live performances Sun–Mon nights.

DANCE CLUBS

Near the Puerta del Sol, **Joy Eslava,** Arenal 1 (☎ **91/366-37-33;** Metro: Puerta del Sol), has survived the passing fashions of Madrileño nightlife with more style than many of its competitors. Virtually everyone in Madrid is likely to show up here, from traveling salespeople in town from Düsseldorf to the young and restless members of the Madrileño *Movida.* Open nightly 11:30pm–dawn. Entrance is 1,500 ptas. ($12), including the first drink.

Kapital, Atocha 125 (☎ **91/420-29-06;** Metro: Antón Martín), is the most sprawling, labyrinthine, and multicultural dance club in Madrid at the moment. In what was formerly a theater, it contains seven levels, each with a different ambience. Open Thurs–Sun 11:30pm–5:30am. Entrance is 1,000–1,500 ptas. ($8–$12), including the first drink. Catering to crowds of all ages, **Long Play,** Plaza Vásquez de Mella 2 (☎ **91/531-01-11;** Metro: Gran Vía), manages to combine recorded music with long stretches of bars, comfortable tables and chairs, and a crowd that seemingly has absolutely nothing to do except dance, dance, dance. Live bands sometimes appear. Open Tues–Sun 7pm–3am. Admission is 1,000 ptas. ($8), including the first drink.

PUBS & BARS

Bar Cock, De la Reina 16 (☎ **91/532-28-26;** Metro: Gran Vía), attracts some of the most visible artists, actors, models, and filmmakers in Madrid, among them award-winning Spanish director Pedro Almódovar. The name comes from the word *cocktail,* or so they say. The decoration is elaborately unique, in contrast to the hip clientele. Open daily 7pm–3am; closed Dec 24–31.

Beloved by Hemingway, who had quite a few drinks here, **Chicote,** Gran Vía 12 (☎ **91/532-67-37;** Metro: Gran Vía), is Madrid's most famous cocktail bar. It's a classic, with the same 1930s interior design it had when the foreign press sat out the Civil War here. Even the seats are original. Long a favorite of artists and writers, the bar became a haven for prostitutes in the late Franco era. No more. It's back in the limelight again, a sophisticated and much frequented rendezvous. Open daily 11am–3am.

The 1847 construction of the **Palacio Gaviria,** Calle del Arenal 9 (☎ **91/526-60-69;** Metro: Puerta del Sol or Ópera), was heralded as the architectural triumph of one of the era's most flamboyant aristocrats, the marqués de Gaviria. Famous as one of the paramours of Isabel II, he outfitted his palace with the ornate jumble of neoclassical and baroque styles that later became known as Isabelino. In 1993, after extensive renovations, the building was opened to the public as a concert hall for the occasional presentation of classical music and as a late-night cocktail bar. Ten high-ceilinged rooms now function as richly decorated multipurpose areas for guests to wander in. Thurs–Sat are usually dance nights, everything from the tango to the waltz. Cabaret is usually featured on other nights. Open Mon–Fri 10:30pm–3am and Sat–Sun 10:30pm–5am. Cover is 1,500 ptas. ($12), including the first drink.

GAY & LESBIAN CLUBS & CAFES

Black and White, Gravina, at the corner of Libertad (☎ **91/531-11-41;** Metro: Chueca), is Madrid's major gay bar, located in the center of the Chueca district. A guard will open the door to a large room—painted, as you might expect, black and white. There's a dance club in the basement, but the street-level bar is the premier gathering spot, featuring drag shows Thurs–Sun, male striptease, and videos. Old movies are shown against one wall. Open Mon–Fri 8pm–4am and Sat–Sun 8pm–5am.

Looking to experience the gay cafe life in Madrid? Head for **Plaza de Chueca** (Metro: Chueca), where no fewer than four gay cafes line the square's edges and where something approaching a gay living room (with goodly numbers of lesbians as well) is created every evening from 8pm to early the next morning.

Open daily 3pm–3am, both **Café Figueroa,** Calle Augusto Figueroa 17 (☎ **91/521-1673**), and **Café Aquarella,** Calle Gravina 10 (☎ **91/570-6907**), have elevated gay table-hopping to a fine art. A diverse clientele, includs both gay men and lesbians. Metro: Chueca.

CAVE CRAWLING

To capture a peculiar Madrid joie de vivre, visit some *mesones* and *cuevas,* many found in the *barrios bajos.* From Plaza Mayor, walk down Arco de Cuchilleros until you find a Gypsy-like cave that fits your fancy.

The bartenders at the **Mesón del Champiñón,** Cava de San Miguel 17 (no phone; Metro: Puerta del Sol or Ópera), keep a brimming bucket of sangría behind the long stand-up bar as a thirst quencher for the crowd. The name of the establishment in English is mushroom, and that's exactly what you'll see depicted in various sizes along sections of the vaulted ceilings. A more appetizing way to experience a champiñón is to order a *ración* (serving) of grilled, stuffed, and salted mushrooms, served with toothpicks. Open daily 6pm–2am. Our favorite cueva in the area, the **Mesón de la Guitarra,** Cava de San Miguel 13 (☎ **91/559-95-31;** Metro: Puerta del Sol or Ópera), is loud and exciting any night of the week, and it's as warmly earthy as anything you'll find in Madrid. The decor combines terracotta floors, antique brick walls, hundreds of sangría pitchers clustered above the bar, murals of gluttons, old rifles, and faded bullfighting posters. Like most things in Madrid, the place doesn't get rolling until around 10:30pm. Open daily 7pm–1:30am.

DAY TRIPS FROM MADRID

TOLEDO   If you have only 1 day for an excursion outside Madrid, go to Toledo, 42 miles to the southwest, a place made special by its blending of Arab, Jewish, Christian, and even Roman and Visigothic elements. Declared a national landmark, the city that inspired El Greco in the 16th century has remained relatively unchanged in parts of its central core. You can still stroll through streets barely wide enough for a man and his donkey—much less an automobile.

RENFE trains run here frequently every day. Those departing Madrid's Atocha Rail Station for Toledo run daily 7am–8:25pm; those leaving Toledo for Madrid run daily 7am–9pm. Travel time is approximately 2 hours. For train information in Madrid call **91/468-45-11**; in Toledo call **925/22-30-99.**

Bus transit between Madrid and Toledo is faster and more convenient than travel by train. Buses, operated by several companies, the largest of which include Continental and Galiano, depart from Madrid's South Bus Station (Estacíon Sur de Autobuses), Canarias 17 (☎ **91/527-29-61** for information, or 91/23-24-25 for the ticket office), every day 6:30am–10pm. Buses depart at 30-minute intervals throughout the day.

Motorists exit Madrid via Cibeles (Paseo del Prado) and take N401 south.

The **tourist information office** is at Puerta de Bisagra (☎ **925/22-08-43**), open Mon–Fri 9am–2pm and 4–6pm, Sat 9am–3pm and 4–7pm, and Sun 9am–3pm.

Exploring Toledo   Ranked among the greatest of gothic structures, the ✪ **cathedral,** Arcos de Palacio (☎ **925/22-22-41**; bus: 5 or 6), actually reflects a variety of styles because of the more than $2^1/_2$ centuries that went into its construction, from 1226 to 1493. The portals have witnessed many historic events, including the proclamation of Joanna the Mad and her husband, Philip the Handsome, as heirs to the throne of Spain. Among its art treasures, the *transparente* stands out—a wall of marble and florid baroque alabaster sculpture overlooked for years because the cathedral was too poorly lit. Sculptor Narciso Tomé cut a hole in the ceiling, much to the consternation of Toledans, and now light touches the high-rising angels, a *Last Supper* in alabaster, and a Virgin in ascension. The 16th-century Capilla Mozárabe, containing works by Juan de Borgona, is another curiosity of the cathedral. The Treasure Room has a 500-pound 15th-century gilded monstrance—allegedly made with gold brought back from the New World by Columbus—that's still carried through the streets of Toledo during the feast of Corpus Christi. Admission to the cathedral is free; admission to the Treasure Room is 500 ptas. ($4). Open daily 10:30am–1pm and 3:30–6pm (to 7pm in summer).

The **Alcázar,** Calle General Moscardó 4, near Plaza de Zocodover (☎ **925/ 22-30-38**; bus: 5 or 6), at the eastern edge of the old city, dominates the Toledo skyline. It became famous at the beginning of the Spanish Civil War when it underwent a 70-day siege that almost destroyed it. Today it has been rebuilt and turned into an army museum, housing such exhibits as a plastic model of what the fortress looked like after the Civil War, electronic equipment used during the siege, and photographs taken during the height of the battle. A walking tour gives a realistic simulation of the siege. Admission is 125 ptas. ($1), free for children 9 and under. Open Tues–Sun 10am–1:30pm and 4–5:30pm (to 6:30pm July–Sept).

Today a museum of art and sculpture, the ✪ **Museo de Santa Cruz,** Miguel de Cervantes 3 (☎ **925/22-10-36**; bus: 5 or 6), was originally a 16th-century Spanish Renaissance hospice, founded by Cardinal Mendoza—"the third king of Spain"—

who helped Ferdinand and Isabella gain the throne. The facade is almost more spectacular than any of the exhibits inside. It's a stunning architectural achievement in the classical plateresque style. The major artistic treasure inside is El Greco's *The Assumption of the Virgin,* his last known work. Paintings by Goya and Ribera are also on display. Admission is 200 ptas. ($1.60), free for children. Open Mon 10am–2pm and 4–6:30pm, Tues–Sat 10am–6:30pm, and Sun 10am–2pm. To get here, pass beneath the granite archway on the eastern edge of Plaza de Zocodover and walk about 1 block.

SAN LORENZO DE EL ESCORIAL   The second most important excursion from Madrid is the austere Royal Monastery of San Lorenzo de El Escorial, 30 miles to the west. Philip II ordered the construction of this rectangular granite-and-slate monster in 1563, 2 years after he moved his capital to Madrid. Once the haunt of aristocratic Spaniards, El Escorial is now a resort where hotels and restaurants flourish in summer, as hundreds flock here to escape the heat of the capital.

More than two dozen trains depart daily from Madrid's Atocha, Nuevos Ministerios, and Chamartín train stations. During summer extra coaches are added.

The Office of Empresa Herranz, Calle Reina Victoria 3 in El Escorial (☎ **91/890-41-22** or 91/890-41-25), runs some 40 buses per day back and forth between Madrid and El Escorial; on Sunday service is curtailed to 10 buses. Trip time is 1 hour, and a round-trip fare is 720 ptas. ($5.75).

Motorists can follow NVI (marked on some maps as A6) from the northwest perimeter of Madrid toward Lugo, La Coruña, and San Lorenzo de El Escorial. After about half an hour, fork left onto C505 toward San Lorenzo. Driving time from Madrid is about an hour.

The **tourist information office** is at Floridablanca 10 (☎ **91/890-15-54**), open Mon–Fri 10am–2pm and 3–5pm and Sat 10am–2pm.

Exploring the Monastery   The huge granite fortress of the ✪ **Real Monasterio de San Lorenzo de El Escorial,** Calle San Lorenzo de El Escorial 1 (☎ **91/890-59-02**), houses a wealth of paintings and tapestries and serves as a burial place for Spanish kings. Foreboding both inside and out because of its sheer size and institutional look, El Escorial took 21 years to complete. Philip II, who collected many of the paintings exhibited here in the New Museums, didn't appreciate El Greco and favored Titian. But you'll still find El Greco's *The Martyrdom of St. Maurice,* rescued from storage, and his *St. Peter.* Other superb works are Titian's *Last Supper* and Velázquez's *The Tunic of Joseph.* The Royal Library houses a priceless collection of 60,000 volumes—one of the most significant in the world. The displays range from the handwriting of St. Teresa of Ávila to medieval instructions on playing chess.

You can also visit the Philip II Apartments; these are strictly monastic, and Philip called them the "cell for my humble self" in this "palace for God." The Apartments of the Bourbon Kings are lavishly decorated, in contrast to Philip's preference for the ascetic. They're closed at present for restoration; check locally to see when they'll reopen.

A comprehensive ticket costs 850 ptas. ($6.80) for adults and 350 ptas. ($2.80) for children. Open Tues–Sun: Apr–Sept 10am–6pm and Oct–Mar 10pm–5pm.

SEGOVIA   Less commercial than Toledo, Segovia, 54 miles northwest of Madrid, typifies the glory of Old Castile. Wherever you look, you'll see reminders of a golden era—whether it's the most spectacular Alcázar on the Iberian Peninsula or the well-preserved still-functioning Roman aqueduct. Segovia lies on the slope of the Guadarrama Mountains, where the Eresma and Clamores Rivers converge. This ancient city stands in the center of the most castle-rich part of Castile. Isabella was proclaimed queen of Castile here in 1474.

Nine trains leave Madrid's Chamartín Rail Station every day and arrive 2 hours later at the station in Segovia, on Paseo Obispo Quesada (☎ **921/42-07-74**), a 20-minute walk southeast of the town center. Bus no. 3 departs every quarter hour for Plaza Mayor.

Buses arrive and depart from the Estacionamiento Municipal de Autobuses, Paseo de Ezequile González 10 (☎ **921/43-30-10**), near the corner of Avenida Fernández Ladreda and the steeply sloping Paseo Conde de Sepúlveda. There are 10–15 buses a day to and from Madrid (which depart from Paseo de la Florida 11; Metro: Norte).

Motorists can take NVI (on some maps it's known as A6) or the Autopista del Nordeste northwest from Madrid, toward León and Lugo. At the junction with Rte. 110 (signposted Segovia), turn northeast.

The **tourist information office** is at Plaza Mayor 10 (☎ **921/46-03-34**), open daily 10am–2pm and 5–8pm.

Exploring Segovia   You'll view ✪ **El Alcázar,** Plaza de la Reina Victoria Eugenia (☎ **921/43-01-76;** bus: 3), first from below, at the junction of the Clamores and Eresma Rivers. It's on the west side of Segovia, and you may not spot it when you first enter the city. But that's part of the surprise. The castle dates back to the 12th century, and royal romance is associated with it. Isabella first met Ferdinand here, and today you can see a facsimile of her dank bedroom. Walk the battlements of this once-impregnable castle, from which its occupants hurled down boiling oil onto the enemy below. Brave the hazardous stairs of the tower, built by Isabella's father as a prison, for a panoramic view of Segovia. Admission is 375 ptas. ($3) for adults, 175 ptas. ($1.40) for children 8–14, and free for children 7 and under. Open daily: Apr–Sept 10am–7pm and Oct–Mar 10am–6pm. Take either Calle Vallejo, Calle de Velarde, Calle de Daoiz, or Paseo de Ronda.

The ✪ **Roman aqueduct,** Plaza del Azoguejo, an architectural marvel built by the Romans more than 2,000 years ago, is still used to carry water. Constructed of mortarless granite, it consists of 118 arches, and in one two-tiered section it soars 95 feet to its highest point. The Spanish call it El Puente. It spans Plaza del Azoguejo, the old market square, stretching nearly 800 yards. When the Moors took Segovia in 1072, they destroyed 36 arches, which were rebuilt under Ferdinand and Isabella in 1484.

Built between 1515 and 1558, the ✪ **Cabildo Catedral de Segovia,** Plaza de la Catedral, Marqués del Arco (☎ **921/43-53-25**), is the last gothic cathedral built in Spain. Fronting historic Plaza Mayor, it stands on the spot where Isabella I was proclaimed queen of Castile. Affectionately called La Dama de las Catedrales, it contains numerous treasures, such as the Blessed Sacrament Chapel (created by the flamboyant Churriguera), stained-glass windows, elaborately carved choir stalls, and 16th- and 17th-century paintings, including a reredos portraying the deposition of Christ from the cross by Juan de Juni. Admission to the cathedral is free; admission to the cloisters, museum, and chapel room is 250 ptas. ($2) for adults and 50 ptas. (40¢) for children. Open daily: spring and summer 9am–7pm and off-season 9:30am–1pm and 3–6pm.

2 Barcelona & Environs

Hardworking Barcelona enjoys the most diversified and prosperous economy of any region in Spain. Its roster of natives and long-time residents—Antoni Gaudí, Pablo Picasso, Salvador Dalí, Joan Miró, and opera star Montserrat Caballé—have helped define Catalán culture.

Barcelona Attractions & Accommodations

BARCELONA

Attractions:
Casa Amatller ④
Casa de L'Ardiaca ⑬
Casa Batlló ③
Casa Lleó Morera ⑤
Casa Milà ①
Castell de Montjuïc ⑨
Castell de Tres Dragons ⑱
Catedral ⑭
Fundació Joan Miró ⑧
Gran Teatre del Liceu ⑫
Museu d'Art Modern ㉑
Museu Frederic Marés ⑮
Museu Geològie ⑲
Museu Marítim ⑩
Museu Nacional d'Art
   de Catalunya ⑦
Museu Picasso ⑰
Museu Tèxtil i
   d'Indumentària ⑯
Palau Güell ⑪
Parc de la Ciutadella ⑳
Parc Zoologic ㉒
Poble Espanyol ⑥
Sagrada Familia ②

Accommodations:
Claris ④
Colón ⑫
Condes de Barcelona ③
Hespería ①
Hostal Levante ⑬
Hostal Neutral ⑤
Le Meridien Barcelona ⑨
Lleó ⑦
Mesón Castilla ⑧
Montecarlo ⑩
Regencia Colón ⑪
Ritz ⑥
Wilson ②

3-0784

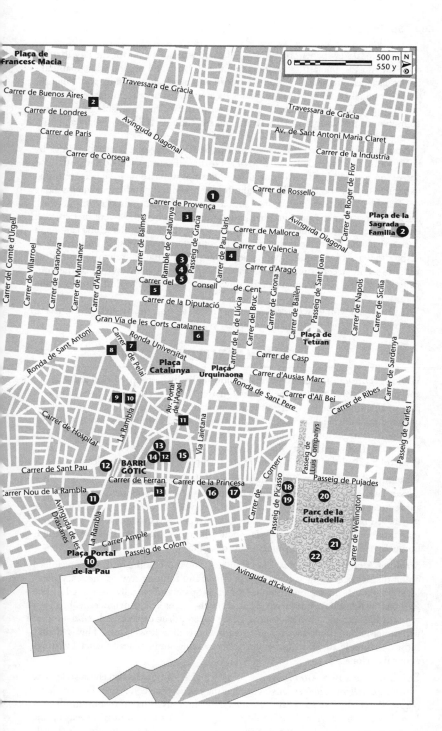

As one local newspaper critic put it, "If there were an award for the city that has done the most in the last few years to rebuild, reclaim, and expand while maintaining its elegance and charm, Barcelona would win hands down" in its post-Olympic years. Residual benefits from the games have included a roster of impressive new hotels, top-notch sporting facilities, a glittering new airport capable of funneling 18 million annual visitors into Catalonia, and a proud role as Spain's literary and publishing headquarters.

Known as the savviest business center in Spain, Barcelona boasts buildings by I. M. Pei, Arata Isozaki, Richard Meier, Norman Foster, Victorio Gregotti, and native son Ricardo Bofill. Miles of grimy industrial waterfronts have been returned to clean and sandy beaches. Flower stalls, bird cages, and decorative pavements along Les Rambles have been rejuvenated, and a state-of-the-art transportation network carries visitors past monuments that look better than when they were first erected. Unlike either of its landlocked competitors, Seville or Madrid, Barcelona can—and does—welcome the newest phenomena in tourism, the cruise-ship industry. And despite the city's burgeoning population (and the regrettable growth in both drug addiction and street crime), access to the city is easier than ever since the construction of ring roads has alleviated downtown traffic congestion, also lowering pollution.

If you decide you love Barcelona, you won't be alone—nearly 40% of tourists to Spain go to Catalonia, and many are repeat visitors.

ONLY IN BARCELONA

Walking Through the Barri Gòtic   Following in the footsteps of Dalí and Picasso, you can wander for hours in the Gothic Quarter. You'll get lost, of course, but that's part of the amusement. There's more here than a great cathedral, as you get acquainted with the neighborhood of Joan Miró, who was born in this barrio. Gurgling fountains, vintage stores, wall-to-wall cobblestones, and literary cafes like Els Quatre Gats make it all worthwhile. Stop in at Sala Parés, Spain's oldest art gallery at Carrer Petritxol 5 (☎ 93/318-70-20), one of the birthplaces of Catalán modernism.

Watching the Sardana   Catalonia's national dance is performed at noon at Plaça de San Jaume, in front of the cathedral. Nothing is more folkloric than this. This is a true street dance played out against the backdrop of a *cobla* (brass band). This dance may have originated on one of the Greek islands and was brought here by sailors. It may even have come from Sardinia—hence its name. But Cataláns have made it uniquely their own regardless of its point of origin.

Strolling Along Les Rambles   Les Rambles cuts through the heart of Barcelona'a oldest district beginning at Plaça de Catalunya and running toward the sea. A tree-lined boulevard, it's the most famous street in Spain and is really composed of five Ramblas or Rambles (either term is correct). The street is very democratic, bringing together buskers, shopowners, tourists, drag queens, drug dealers, and *putas*—mixed with hotels, cafes, porno houses, newsstands, and endless flower stalls. This is Spain's most charismatic street, its late-night scene evoking some of Jean Genet's writings about Barcelona.

Drinking Cava in a *Xampanyería*   Enjoy a glass of bubbly Barcelona style. The wines are excellent, and Cataláns swear that their *cavas* taste better than French champagne. After the Franco years, *xampanyerías* literally burst into bloom all over Barcelona, many staying open until the early hours of the morning, dispensing the Barcelona version of champagne. You can select *brut* or *brut nature* (brut is slightly sweeter). Try any of these popular brands: Mestres, Parxet, Torello, Recaredo, Gramona, or Mont-Marçal.

Exploring the Museu Picasso   Examine the evolution of a genius from the age of 14. One of Barcelona's most popular attractions, housed in three gothic mansions, this museum spans the artist's multifaceted career, taking in the Blue Period, cubism, and beyond. Of special interest is the Barcelona section from the years 1895–97, when he lived in the Catalán capital. You can even see Picasso the copyist (he re-created Velázquez's famous portrait of Philip IV) and can meet his family, especially his aunt, *Retrato de la Tipa Pepa* (Portrait of Aunt Pepa). Two rooms are devoted to the fabled *Les Meninas,* a series Picasso produced in Cannes in 1957 as a tribute to Velázquez's most famous painting (now in Madrid's Prado).

Going Gaga over Gaudí   No architect in Europe was as fantastical as Antoni Gaudí y Cornet. The city of Barcelona is studded with modernist architectural gems of this extrordinary artist—in fact, UNESCO lists all his creations as World Trust Properties. No two buildings of this eccentric genius are alike—he conceived the buildings as "visions." A recluse and celibate bachelor, he lived out his own fantasy. Nothing is more stunning than his Templo Expiatorio de la Sagrada Familia, Barcelona's best-known landmark, a church on which Gaudí labored for the last 43 years of his life before he was run over by a tram in 1926. It was never completed. If it's ever finished, "The Sacred Family" will be Europe's largest church.

ORIENTATION

ARRIVING   By Plane   In the post-Olympic world, most transatlantic passengers are obliged to change aircraft in Madrid before continuing on to Barcelona. The only exception is **TWA** (☎ **800/892-4141**), which maintains nonstop transatlantic service to Barcelona from New York. Within Spain, by far the most likely carrier is **Iberia** (☎ **800/772-4642**), which offers a string of peak-hour shuttle flights at 15-minute intervals between Madrid and Barcelona. Service from Madrid to Barcelona at less congested times of the day averages around one flight every 30–40 minutes.

The **Aeropuerto de Barcelona,** 08820 Prat de Llobregat (☎ **93/298-38-38**), lies 7¹/₂ miles southwest of the city. A train runs between the airport and Barcelona's Estació Central de Barcelona-Sants daily 6:14am–10:44pm (10:14pm is the last city departure, 6:14am the first airport departure). The 21-minute trip costs 290 ptas. ($2.30) Mon–Fri or 335 ptas. ($2.70) Sat–Sun. If your hotel lies near Plaça de Catalunya, you might opt for an Aerobús that runs daily every 15 minutes 5:30am–10pm. The fare is 435 ptas. ($3.50). A taxi from the airport into central Barcelona will cost about 2,000–2,500 ptas. ($16–$20).

By Train   A train called *Barcelona Talgo* provides rail service between Paris and Barcelona in 11¹/₂ hours. For many other connections from the mainland of Europe, it'll be necessary to change trains at Port Bou. Most trains issue seat and sleeper reservations.

Trains departing from the **Estació de Franca,** Avenida Marqués de l'Argentera, cover long distances in Spain as well as international routes. There are express night trains to Paris, Zurich, Milan, and Geneva. All the international routes served by the state-owned RENFE rail company use the Estació de Franca, including some of its most luxurious express trains, such as the *Pau Casals* and *Talgo Catalán*. From this station you can book tickets to the major cities: Madrid (five *talgos,* 7 hours; three *rápidos,* 10 hours), Seville (two per day, 10¹/₂ hours), and Valencia (11 per day, 4 hours). For general **RENFE information,** call **93/490-02-02.**

By Bus Bus travel to Barcelona is possible but not popular—it's slow. **Enatcar,** Estació del Nord (☎ **93/245-25-28**), operates five buses per day to Madrid (trip time: 8 hours) and 10 buses per day to Valencia (trip time: 4¹/₂ hours). A one-way ticket to Madrid costs 2,690 ptas. ($21.50); a one-way ticket to Valencia is 2,650 ptas. ($21.20).

By Car From France (the usual road approach to Barcelona), the major access route is at the eastern end of the Pyrenees. You have a choice of the express highway (E15) or the more scenic coastal road. From France, it's possible to approach Barcelona via Toulouse. Cross the border into Spain at Puigcerdá (frontier stations are there), near the principality of Andorra. From there, take N152 to Barcelona. From Madrid, take N2 to Zaragoza, then A2 to El Vendrell, followed by A7 to Barcelona.

VISITOR INFORMATION A conveniently located tourist office is the **Patronat de Turisme,** Gran Vía de les Corts Catalanes 658 (☎ **93/301-74-43;** Metro: Urquinaona or Plaça de Catalunya), open Mon–Sat 9am–7pm.

CITY LAYOUT **Plaça de Catalunya** (Plaza de Cataluña in Spanish) is the city's heart; the world-famous Rambles (Ramblas in Spanish) are its arteries. Les Rambles begin at Plaça Portal de la Pau, with its 164-foot-high monument to Columbus and a panoramic view of the port, and stretch north to Plaça de Catalunya, with its fountains and trees.

At the end of Les Rambles is the **Barri Xinés** (Barrio Chino in Spanish, Chinese Quarter in English), which has enjoyed notoriety as a haven of prostitution and drugs. Still a dangerous district, it's best viewed during the day, if at all. Off Les Rambles is **Plaça Reial** (Plaza Real in Spanish), Barcelona's most harmoniously proportioned square.

The major wide boulevards are **Avinguda** (Avenida in Spanish) **Diagonal** and **Passeig de Colom** and the elegant shopping street **Passeig de Gràcia** (Paseo de Gracia in Spanish). A short walk from Les Rambles will take you to the 1990s-developed **Passeig del Moll de la Fusta,** a waterfront promenade with some of the finest (but not the cheapest) restaurants in Barcelona. To the east is the old port of the city, **La Barceloneta,** from the 18th century.

The **Barri Gòtic** (Barrio Gótico in Spanish, Gothic Quarter in English) lies to the east of Les Rambles. This is the site of the city's oldest buildings, including the cathedral. North of Plaça de Catalunya, the **Eixample** unfolds. An area of wide boulevards, in contrast to the Gothic Quarter, it contains two major roads leading out of Barcelona, Avinguda Diagonal and Gran Vía de les Corts Catalanes. Another major area, **Gràcia,** lies north of the Eixample. **Montjuïc,** one of the mountains of Barcelona, begins at Plaça d'Espanya, a traffic rotary. This was the setting for the 1992 Summer Olympic Games and is today the site of Vila Olimpica. The other mountain is **Tibidabo,** in the northwest, offering views of the city and the Mediterranean and boasting an amusement park.

GETTING AROUND

To save money on public transport, buy one of the transportation cards, each valid for 10 trips: **Tarjeta T-1,** costing 650 ptas. ($5.20), is good for the Metro, bus, Montjuïc funicular, and Tramvía Blau, which runs from Passeig de Sant Gervasi / Avinguda del Tibidabo to the bottom part of the funicular to Tibidabo; **Tarjeta T-2,** for 625 ptas. ($5), is valid on everything but the bus.

Passes (*abonos temporales*) are available at the office of **Transports Metropolita de Barcelona,** Plaça de Catalunya, open Mon–Fri 8am–7pm and Sat 8am–1pm.

Barcelona Metro

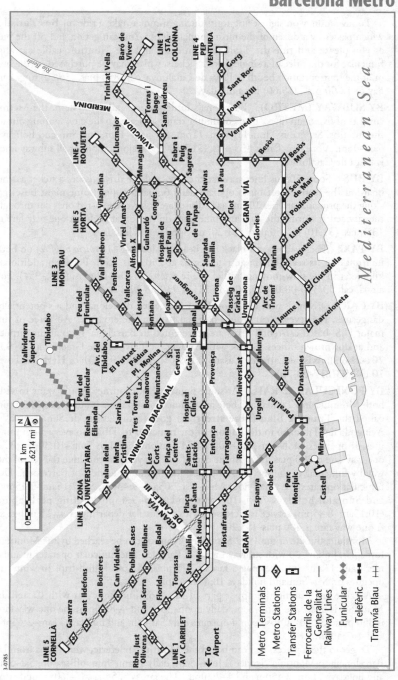

To save money on sightseeing tours during summer, take a ride on **Bus Turistic,** which passes by a dozen of the most popular sights. You can get on and off the bus as you please and ride the Tibidabo funicular and the Montjuïc cable car and funicular for the price of a single ticket. Tickets, which may be purchased on the bus or at the transportation booth at Plaça de Catalunya, cost 850 ptas. ($6.80) for a half day or 1,200 ptas. ($9.60) for a full day.

BY SUBWAY (METRO)   Barcelona's underground railway system, the Metro, consists of five main lines. Two commuter trains also service the city, fanning out to the suburbs. Service is Mon–Fri 5am–11pm, Sat 5am–1am, and Sun and holidays 6am–1am. A one-way fare is 135 ptas. ($1.10). The major station for all subway lines is Plaça de Catalunya.

BY BUS   Some 50 bus lines traverse the city, and the driver issues a ticket as you board at the front. Most buses operate daily 6:30am–10pm; some night buses go along the principal arteries 10pm–4am. Buses are color-coded—red ones cut through the city center during the day, and blue ones do the job at night. A one-way fare is 135 ptas. ($1.10) or 150 ptas. ($1.20) on Sunday and holidays.

BY TAXI   Each yellow-and-black taxi bears the letters SP (*servicio público*) on both its front and its rear. The basic rate begins at 250 ptas. ($2). For each additional kilometer in the slow-moving traffic, you're assessed 110–118 ptas. (90¢–95¢). For a taxi, call 93/330-08-04, 93/300-38-11, or 93/358-11-11.

BY CAR   Driving is next to impossible in congested Barcelona, and it's potentially dangerous. However, a car would be ideal to tour the environs. All three of the major U.S.-based car-rental firms are represented in Barcelona, both at the airport and at downtown offices. Check with **Budget,** at Travesera de Gràcia 71 (☎ **93/ 201-21-99**); **Avis,** at Carrer de Casanova 209 (☎ **93/209-95-33**); or **Hertz,** at Tuset 10 (☎ **93/217-80-76**).

BY FUNICULAR & RAIL   At some point in your journey, you'll want to visit both Montjuïc and Tibidabo. There are various links to these mountaintops. A train called the **Tramvía Blau (blue streetcar)** goes from Passeig de Sant Gervasi / Avinguda del Tibidabo to the bottom of the funicular to Tibidabo every 3–15 minutes. It operates Mon–Sat 7am–10pm and Sun and holidays 7am–10:30pm. The one-way fare is 250 ptas. ($2). At the end of the run you can continue the rest of the way by funicular to the top, at 1,600 feet, for a panoramic view of Barcelona. The funicular operates every half hour Mon–Fri 7:05am–9:43pm, Sat 7:15am–9:45pm, and Sun and holidays 7:15–10:15am and 8:45–9:45pm; during peak hours (10:15am–8:45pm) service is increased, with a funicular departing every 15 minutes. A one-way fare is 400 ptas. ($3.20).

Montjuïc, the site of the 1992 Summer Olympics, can be reached by the Montjuïc funicular, linking up with subway Line 3 at Paral.lel. The funicular operates in summer daily 11am–8m, charging a fare of 325 ptas. ($2.60) round-trip. In winter it operates on Sat–Sun and holidays 10:45am–2pm.

A **cable car** linking the upper part of the Montjuïc funicular with Castell de Montjuïc is in service June–Sept, daily noon–3pm and 4–8:30pm; the one-way fare is 350 ptas. ($2.80). Off-season it operates only Sat–Sun and holidays 11am–2:45pm and 4–7:30pm.

To get to these places, you can board the **Montjuïc telèferic,** which runs from La Barceloneta to Montjuïc. Service is June–Sept, daily 11am–9pm; off-season, Sat–Sun and holidays 11am–2:45pm and 4–7:30pm. The fare is 575 ptas. ($4.60) round-trip, 375 ptas. ($3) one-way.

FAST FACTS: Barcelona

American Express The American Express office is at Passeig de Gràcia 101 (☎ 93/217-00-70; Metro: Diagonal), near the corner of Carrer del Rosselló. It's open Mon–Fri 9:30am–6pm and Sat 10am–noon.

Consulates The Consulate of the **United States,** at Reina Elisenda 23 (☎ 93/280-22-27; train: Reina Elisenda), is open Mon–Fri 9am–12:30pm and 3–5pm. The Consulate of **Canada,** Travessera de les Corts 265 (☎ 93/410-66-99; Metro: Plaça Molina), is open Mon–Fri 9am–2pm and 3–5:30pm. The Consulate of the **United Kingdom,** Av. Diagonal 477 (☎ 93/419-90-44; Metro: Hospital Clínic), is open Mon–Fri 9am–2pm and 4–5pm. The Consulate of **Australia** is at Gran Via Carlos III 98, 9th floor (☎ 93/330-04-96; Metro: María Cristina), open Mon–Fri 10am–noon.

Currency See "Fast Facts: Madrid."

Currency Exchange Most banks will exchange currency Mon–Fri 8:30am–2pm and Sat 8:30am–1pm. A major *oficina de cambio* (exchange office) is operated at the Estació Central de Barcelona-Sants, the principal rail station; it's open Mon–Sat 8:30am–10pm and Sun 8:30am–2pm and 4:30–10pm.

Dentist Call Clinica Dental Beonadex, Paseo Bona Nova 69, 3rd floor (☎ 93/418-44-33), for an appointment. It's open Mon 4–9pm and Tues–Fri 8am–3pm.

Drugstores The most central one is Farmacía Manuel Nadal i Casas, Rambla de Canaletes 121 (☎ 93/317-49-42; Metro: Plaça de Catalunya), open Mon–Fri 9am–1:30pm and 4:30–8pm and Sat 9am–1:30pm. After hours, various pharmacies take turns staying open at night. Pharmacies not open post the names and addresses of pharmacies in the area that are open.

Emergencies In an emergency, phone 080 to report a **fire,** 092 to call the **police,** and 061 to request an **ambulance.**

Hospitals Barcelona has many hospitals and clinics, including Hospital Clínic, and Hospital de la Santa Creu i Sant Pau, at the intersection of Carrer Cartagena and Carrer Sant Antoni Maria Claret (☎ 93/291-90-00; Metro: Hospital de Sant Pau).

Lost Property To recover lost property, go to Objects Perduts, Carrer Ciutat 9 (☎ 93/402-31-61; Metro: Jaume I), Mon–Fri 9:30am–1:30pm. If you've lost property on public transport, contact the office in the Metro station at Plaça de Catalunya (☎ 93/318-52-93).

Luggage Storage/Lockers The train station, Estació Central de Barcelona-Sants (☎ 93/491-44-31), has lockers for 400–600 ptas. ($3.20–$4.80) per day. You can obtain locker space daily 7am–11pm.

Post Office The main post office is at Plaça d'Antoni López (☎ 93/318-38-31; Metro: Jaume I). It's open Mon–Fri 8am–10pm and Sat 8am–8pm.

Safety Be particularly careful with cameras, purses, and wallets, all favorite targets of thieves and pickpockets in Barcelona—particularly on the world-famous Rambles. The southern part of Les Rambles, near the waterfront, is the most dangerous section, especially at night. Proceed with caution.

Transit Information For general RENFE (train) information, dial 93/490-02-02. For airport information, call 93/298-38-38.

ACCOMMODATIONS
CIUTAT VELLA (OLD CITY)
Very Expensive
✪ Le Meridien Barcelona. Rambles 111, 08002 Barcelona. ☎ **800/543-4300** in the U.S. or 93/318-62-00. Fax 93/301-77-76. 200 rms, 8 suites. A/C MINIBAR TV TEL. 29,000–38,000 ptas. ($232–$304) double; from 48,000 ptas. ($384) suite. AE, DC, MC, V. Metro: Liceu or Plaça de Catalunya.

This is the finest hotel in the old town. It's superior in both amenities and comfort to its closest rival in the old town: the Colón. In 1991 the French-owned Meridien chain took over. Le Meridien is a medley of artful pastels and tasteful decorating, and its guest rooms are spacious and comfortable, with such amenities as extra-large beds, heated bathroom floors, 18 TV channels, three in-house videos, hair dryers, and two phones; all rooms have double-glazed windows.

Expensive
Hotel Colón. Av. de la Catedral 7, 08002 Barcelona. ☎ **800/845-0636** in the U.S. or 93/301-14-04. Fax 93/317-29-15. 136 rms, 11 suites. A/C MINIBAR TV TEL. 20,500–32,500 ptas. ($164–$260) double; from 37,000 ptas. ($296) suite. AE, DC, MC, V. Bus: 16, 17, 19, or 45.

Blessed with the most dramatic location in Barcelona, opposite the cathedral's main entrance, this hotel boasts a neoclassical facade with carved pilasters and ornamental wrought-iron balustrades. Inside you'll find conservative and slightly old-fashioned public rooms, a helpful staff, and guest rooms filled with comfortable furniture and (despite recent renovations) an appealingly dowdy kind of charm. Though lacking views, the rooms in back are quieter. The sixth-floor rooms with balconies overlooking the square are the most desirable. Some lower rooms are dark. The hotel maintains two well-recommended restaurants, the Grill (continental specialties) and the Carabela (Catalán specialties).

Moderate
Hotel Lleó. Pelal 22–24, 08001 Barcelona. ☎ **93/318-13-12.** Fax 93/412-26-57. 76 rms. A/C MINIBAR TV TEL. 12,000 ptas. ($96) double. AE, DC, MC, V. Parking 2,000 ptas. ($16) nearby. Metro: Plaça de Catalunya or Plaça de la Universitat.

Solid, well run, and conservative, this hotel occupies the premises of an 1840s building on a busy commercial street in one of the most central neighborhoods. Completely renovated in 1992 in time for the Olympics, it offers streamlined and comfortable rooms, each with a lock-box and functional furniture. There's a restaurant on one of the upper floors. For the price, this is a good standard choice, but not a lot more.

⑤ Hotel Regencia Colón. Carrer Sagristans 13–17, 08002 Barcelona. ☎ **93/318-98-58.** Fax 93/317-28-22. 55 rms. A/C MINIBAR TV TEL. 15,500 ptas. ($124) double; 19,000 ptas. ($152) triple. Rates include breakfast. AE, DC, MC, V. Metro: Jaume 1 or Urquinaona.

This stately stone six-story building stands behind the more prestigious, superior, and expensive Hotel Colón—both are in the shadow of the cathedral. The formal lobby seems a bit dour, but the well-maintained rooms are comfortable and often roomy, albeit worn. The rooms are insulated against sound, and 40 of them have full tub baths, the remainder with shower. Considering the prices charged and what you get, the hotel is a good value for Barcelona.

Inexpensive
⑤ Hostal Levante. Baïxada de Sant Miguel 2, 08002 Barcelona. ☎ **93/317-95-65.** 38 rms, 7 with bath. 3,500 ptas. ($28) double without bath, 4,500 ptas. ($36) double with bath. No credit cards. Metro: Liceu or Jaume 1.

This is one of the nicest and most reasonably priced places to stay in Barcelona. In a quiet, imposing building more than two centuries old, it stands just a short distance from Plaça de Sant Jaume, in the center of the Barri Gòtic. The units are clean and comfortable, and there's central heating. The staff speaks English. No meals are served.

⊘ Hostal Neutral. Rambla de Catalunya 42, 08007 Barcelona. ☎ **93/487-63-90.** Fax 93/487-40-28. 35 rms. TEL. 3,950–4,950 ptas. ($31.60–$39.60) double; 4,725–6,210 ptas. ($37.80–$49.70) triple. MC, V. Metro: Aragón.

An older pension but very recommendable, this hostal has a reputation for cleanliness and efficiency. As the name suggests, the small rooms here are neutral but comfortable nevertheless, though furnished with a medley of odds and ends. Colorful antique floor tiling brightens some of the high-ceilinged rooms. Breakfast is served in a salon with a coffered ceiling, and there's a large TV room nearby.

✪ Mesón Castilla. Valldoncella 5, 08002 Barcelona. ☎ **93/318-21-82.** Fax 93/412-40-20. 56 rms. A/C TEL. 9,500 ptas. ($76) double. AE, DC, MC, V. Parking 1,500 ptas. ($12). Metro: Plaça de Catalunya or Plaça de la Universitat.

This two-star hotel, a former apartment building, has a Castilian facade, with a wealth of art nouveau detailing. Owned/operated by the Spanish hotel chain HUSA, the Castilla is clean, charming, and well maintained. Its nearest rival is the Regencia Colón, to which it is comparable in atmosphere and government ratings. The rooms are comfortable—the beds have ornate Catalán-style headboards—and some open onto large terraces.

Montecarlo. Ramble dels Estudis 124, 08002 Barcelona. ☎ **93/412-04-04.** Fax 93/318-73-23. 76 rms. A/C MINIBAR TV TEL. Mon–Thurs, 12,000 ptas. ($96) double; 15,000 ptas. ($120) triple. Fri–Sun, 10,000 ptas. ($80) double; 12,700 ptas. ($101.60) triple. AE, DC, MC, V. Parking 1,900 ptas. ($15.20). Metro: Plaça de Catalunya.

This hotel, beside the wide and sloping promenade of Les Rambles, was built around 200 years ago as an opulent private home. In the 1930s it was transformed into the comfortably unpretentious hotel you'll find today. Each of the rooms is efficiently decorated, most renovated around 1989. Double-glazed windows help keep out some of the noise. The public areas include some of the building's original accessories, with carved doors, a baronial fireplace, and crystal chandeliers.

SUR DIAGONAL

Very Expensive

Barcelona Hilton. Av. Diagonal 589, 08014 Barcelona. ☎ **800/445-8667** in the U.S. and Canada or 93/419-22-33. Fax 93/405-25-73. 275 rms, 15 suites. A/C MINIBAR TV TEL. 32,000 ptas. ($256) double; from 40,000 ptas. ($320) suite. AE, DC, MC, V. Parking 2,900 ptas. ($23.20). Metro: María Cristina.

This five-star property is opposite gates to the fairgrounds of Barcelona (beyond that, to the Olympic Stadium). This is a huge seven-floor corner structure, with a massive tower placed on top. However, it lacks the glamour of the Claris and the Ritz. The lobby is sleek with lots of marble, and the public lounges are furnished with black leather and velvet chairs. Most rooms are rather large and finely equipped. The furnishings are Hilton-standardized, but with amenities such as private safes. The Restaurant Cristal Garden serves well-prepared international and Spanish menus in a relaxed but polished setting. The hotel maintains a cooperative relationship with a health club half a mile away.

✪ Claris. Carrer de Pau Claris 150, 08009 Barcelona. ☎ **800/888-4747** in the U.S. or 93/487-62-62. Fax 93/487-87-36. 121 rms, 38 suites. A/C MINIBAR TV TEL. Mon–Thurs,

31,850 ptas. ($254.80) double; from 35,100 ptas. ($280.80) suite. Fri–Sun (including breakfast), 17,800 ptas. ($142.40) double; from 22,800 ptas. ($182.40) suite. AE, DC, MC, V. Parking 1,750 ptas. ($14). Metro: Passeig de Gràcia.

One of the most unusual hotels in Barcelona, the postmodern Claris is the only five-star grand luxe hotel in the city center. It incorporated vast quantities of teak, marble, steel, and glass with the historically important facade of the landmark 19th-century Verdruna Palace. It opened in 1992, in time for the Olympics, in a seven-story format that includes a pool and garden on its roof, a mini-museum of Egyptian antiquities on its second floor, and two restaurants, one of which specializes in different brands of caviar. Each of the guest rooms is painted an iconoclastic blue-violet and incorporates unusual art objects with state-of-the-art electronic accessories.

○ **Hotel Ritz.** Gran Via de les Corts Catalanes 668, 08010 Barcelona. ☎ **800/223-1230** in the U.S. or 93/318-52-00. Fax 93/318-01-48. 155 rms, 6 suites. A/C MINIBAR TV TEL. 43,000–52,000 ptas. ($344–$416) double; from 126,000 ptas. ($1,008) suite. AE, DC, MC, V. Parking 3,000 ptas. ($24). Metro: Passeig de Gràcia.

Acknowledged as Barcelona's finest, most prestigious, and most architecturally distinguished hotel, the Ritz was built in art deco style in 1919. Richly remodeled during the late 1980s, it has welcomed more millionaires, celebrities, and aristocrats than any other hotel in northeastern Spain. One of the finest features is its cream-and-gilt neoclassical lobby, whose marble floors and potted palms are flooded with light from an overhead glass canopy and where afternoon tea is served to the strains of a string quartet. The guest rooms are as formal and richly furnished, sometimes with Regency furniture and baths accented with mosaics and tubs inspired by those in ancient Rome. The elegant Restaurant Diana serves French and Catalán cuisine amid soaring ceilings and crystal chandeliers.

○ **Rey Juan Carlos I.** Av. Diagonal 661, 08028 Barcelona. ☎ **800/448-8355** in the U.S. or 93/448-08-08. Fax 93/448-06-07. 375 rms, 37 suites. A/C MINIBAR TV TEL. Mon–Thurs, 37,000 ptas. ($296) double; 63,000 ptas. ($504) suite. Fri–Sun, 16,200 ptas. ($129.60) double; 44,000 ptas. ($352) suite. AE, DC, MC, V. Free parking for guests, 2,500 ptas. ($20) per day for others. Metro: Palau Real.

Named for the Spanish king, who attended its opening and who has visited it several times since, this is the only five-star choice that competes against the Ritz and the Claris. Opened in 1992, it rises 17 stories from a position at the northern end of the Diagonal, in a neighborhood known for corporate headquarters and banks. The design includes a soaring inner atrium, at one end of which a bank of glass-sided elevators glide silently up and down. The guest rooms contain many electronic extras, comfortable furnishings, and (in many cases) views out over Barcelona to the sea. The hotel's elegant restaurant is panoramic Chez Vous, with impeccable service and French/Catalán meals. Facilities include a pool, health club, and jogging track.

Expensive

○ **Hotel Condes de Barcelona.** Passeig de Gràcia 73–75, 08008 Barcelona. ☎ **93/488-22-00.** Fax 93/488-06-14. 181 rms, 2 suites. A/C MINIBAR TV TEL. 19,000 ptas. ($152) double; from 25,000 ptas. ($200) suite. AE, DC, MC, V. Metro: Passeig de Gràcia.

This four-star hotel is one of Barcelona's most glamorous. Business was so good that it opened a 74-room extension, which regrettably lacks the elan of the original. It boasts a unique neomedieval facade, influenced by Gaudí's modernist movement. During recent renovation, hints of high-tech furnishings were added, but everything else has the original opulence. The curved lobby-level bar and its adjacent restaurant add a touch of art deco. All the comfortable salmon-, green-, or peach-colored guest rooms contain marble baths and soundproof windows. Some are beginning to show post-Olympic wear and tear. The hotel has an outdoor pool.

Moderate

✪ **Hotel Astoria.** París 203, 08036 Barcelona. ☎ **93/209-83-11.** Fax 93/202-30-08. 114 rms. A/C MINIBAR TV TEL. 8,000–16,200 ptas. ($64–$129.60) double. AE, DC, MC, V. Metro: Diagonal.

One of our favorites, the Astoria has an art deco facade that makes it appear older than it is. The high ceilings, geometric designs, and brass-studded detailings in the public rooms could be Moorish or Andalusian. Each of the comfortable guest rooms is soundproofed; half have been renovated with slick international louvered closets and glistening white paint. The more old-fashioned rooms have warm textures of exposed cedar and elegant modern accessories.

Hotel Derby / Hotel Gran Derby. Loreto 21–25 and Loreto 28, 08029 Barcelona. ☎ **93/ 322-32-15.** Fax 93/410-08-62. 111 rms, 43 suites. A/C MINIBAR TV TEL. 9,000–17,350 ptas. ($72–$138.80) double; 11,500–17,850 ptas. ($92–$142.80) suite. AE, DC, MC, V. Parking 1,800 ptas. ($14.40). Metro: Hospital Clínic.

In two separate buildings, these twin hotels are in a tranquil neighborhood about 2 blocks south of the busy intersection of Avinguda Diagonal and Avinguda Sarría. The Derby offers conventional rooms and the Gran Derby (across the street) contains the suites, many of which have small balconies overlooking a flowered courtyard. (All drinking, dining, and entertainment facilities are in the Derby.) A team of English-inspired designers have imported a British aesthetic, and the pleasing results include well-oiled hardwood panels, soft lighting, and comfortably upholstered armchairs. Guest rooms and suites are less British in feel, outfitted with simple furniture in a variety of decorative styles, each comfortable and quiet.

NORTE DIAGONAL

Moderate

Hotel Hespería. Los Vergós 20, 08017 Barcelona. ☎ **93/204-55-51.** Fax 93/204-43-92. 139 rms. A/C MINIBAR TV TEL. 14,500 ptas. ($116) double Mon–Thurs, 9,500 ptas. ($76) double Fri–Sun. AE, DC, MC, V. Parking 1,450 ptas. ($11.60). Metro: Tres Torres.

This hotel, on the northern edge of the city, a 12-minute taxi ride from the center, is surrounded by the verdant gardens of one of Barcelona's most pleasant residential neighborhoods. Built in the late 1980s, it was renovated before the 1992 Olympics. You'll pass a Japanese rock garden to reach the stone-floored reception area, with its adjacent bar. Sunlight floods the monochromatic interiors of the rooms. The uniformed staff offers fine service. A restaurant on the premises serves a regional cuisine.

Inexpensive

Hotel Wilson. Av. Diagonal 568, 08021 Barcelona. ☎ **93/209-25-11.** Fax 93/200-83-70. 51 rms, 6 suites. A/C MINIBAR TV TEL. 12,000 ptas. ($96) double; from 21,500 ptas. ($172) suite. AE, DC, MC, V. Metro: Diagonal.

In a neighborhood rich with architectural curiosities, this comfortable hotel is a member of the nationwide HUSA chain. The small lobby isn't indicative of the rest of the building, which on the second floor opens into a large sunny coffee shop / bar / TV lounge. The guest rooms are well kept. Laundry services are provided.

VILA OLÍMPICA

Expensive

Hotel Arts. Carrer de la Marina 19–21, 08005 Barcelona. ☎ **800/241-3333** in the U.S. or 93/221-10-00. Fax 93/221-10-70. 397 rms, 56 suites. A/C MINIBAR TV TEL. Mon–Thurs, 25,000–26,000 ptas. ($200–$208) double; from 30,000 ptas. ($240) suite. Fri–Sun, 20,000 ptas. ($160) double; from 30,000 ptas. ($240) suite. AE, DC, MC, V. Parking 2,500 ptas. ($20). Metro: Ciutadella–Vila Olímpica.

This hotel, managed by the luxury-conscious Ritz-Carlton chain, occupies 33 floors of one of Spain's tallest buildings, a 44-floor postmodern tower. The location is about $1^1/_2$ miles southwest of Barcelona's historic core, adjacent to the sea and the Olympic Village. Its decor is contemporary and elegant, including a lobby sheathed in slabs of soft gray and yellow marble and guest rooms outfitted in pastel yellow or blue. Views from the rooms sweep out over the skyline and the Mediterranean. Three restaurants include the Newport Room, which pays homage to new American cuisine and the seafaring pleasures of New England. Facilities include a fitness center and an outdoor pool.

DINING
CIUTAT VELLA (OLD CITY)
Expensive

✪ **Agut d'Avignon.** Trinitat 3. ☎ **93/302-60-34.** Reservations required. Main courses 1,800–4,200 ptas. ($14.40–$33.60). AE, MC, V. Daily 1–3:30pm and 9–11:30pm. Metro: Jaume I or Liceu. CATALÁN.

One of our favorite restaurants in Barcelona is near Plaça Reial, in a tiny alleyway (the cross street is Calle d'Avinyó 8). The restaurant explosion here has toppled Agut d'Avignon from its once stellar position, but it's still going strong. A small 19th-century vestibule leads to the multilevel dining area that has two balconies and a main hall and is evocative of a hunting lodge. Specialties—all prepared according to traditional recipes—are likely to include acorn-squash soup served in its shell, fisherman soup with garlic toast, haddock stuffed with shellfish, and duck with figs.

Casa Leopoldo. Carrer Sant Rafael 24. ☎ **93/441-30-14.** Reservations required. Main courses 1,800–8,500 ptas. ($14.40–$68). AE, DC, MC, V. Tues–Sat 1–4pm and 9–11pm, Sun 1–4pm. Closed Aug. Metro: Liceu. SEAFOOD.

An excursion through the seedy streets of the Barri Xinés is part of the experience of coming to this restaurant. At night, though, it's safer to come by taxi. This colorful restaurant has some of the freshest seafood in town and caters to a loyal clientele. There's a popular stand-up tapas bar in front, then two dining rooms, one slightly more formal than the other. Specialties include eel with shrimp, barnacles, cuttlefish, seafood soup with shellfish, and deep-fried inch-long eels.

Quo Vadis. Carme 7. ☎ **93/302-40-72.** Reservations recommended. Main courses 1,650–3,500 ptas. ($13.20–$28); *menú del día* 3,750 ptas. ($30). AE, DC, MC, V. Mon–Sat 1:15–4pm and 8:30–11:30pm. Metro: Liceu. SPANISH/CONTINENTAL.

Elegant and impeccable, this is one of the finest restaurants in Barcelona, in a century-old building near the open stalls of the Boquería food market. Seating is in any of four dining rooms, each decorated with exposed paneling and a veneer of conservative charm. Personalized culinary creations include a ragoût of seasonal mushrooms, fried goose liver with prunes, and a wide variety of fish, grilled or (in some cases) flambéed.

Moderate

Brasserie Flo. Jonqueras 10. ☎ **93/319-31-02.** Reservations recommended. Main courses 1,800–3,600 ptas. ($14.40–$28.80); fixed-price menu 3,090 ptas. ($24.70). AE, DC, MC, V. Mon–Thurs 1–4pm and 8:30pm–midnight, Fri–Sun 1–4pm and 8:30pm–1am. Metro: Urquinaona. FRENCH/INTERNATIONAL.

The art deco dining room here has been compared to one on a turn-of-the-century transatlantic steamer—it's spacious, palm-filled, comfortable, and air-conditioned. Installed in a handsomely restored warehouse, it's as close as Barcelona gets to offering a brasserie you might find in Alsace. You could begin with fresh foie gras. The specialty is a large plate of choucroute (sauerkraut) served with a steamed hamhock. Also good are the shrimp in garlic, salmon tartare with vodka, and stuffed sole with spinach. These dishes are solid, satisfying, and filling.

⊗ Can Culleretes. Quintana 5. ☎ **93/317-64-85.** Reservations recommended. Main courses 850–1,900 ptas. ($6.80–$15.20). DC, V. Tues–Sat 1:30–4pm and 9–11pm, Sun 1:30–4pm. Closed 3 weeks in July. Metro: Liceu. Bus: 14 or 59. CATALÁN.

Founded in 1786 as a *pastelería* (pastry shop) in the Barri Gòtic, this oldest of Barcelona restaurants still retains many architectural features. All three dining rooms are decorated in Catalán style, with tile dadoes and wrought-iron chandeliers. The well-prepared food features authentic dishes of northeastern Spain, including sole Roman style, zarzuela à la marinara (shellfish medley), canalones (cannelloni), and paella. Oct–Jan special game dishes are available, including perdiz (partridge).

Egipte. Carrer Jerusalem 3. ☎ **93/317-74-80.** Reservations recommended. Main courses 1,200–2,400 ptas. ($9.60–$19.20); fixed-price menu 950–3,000 ptas. ($7.60–$24). AE, DC, MC, V. Mon–Sat 1–4pm and 8pm–midnight. Metro: Liceu. CATALÁN/SPANISH.

A favorite among locals, this tiny place, behind the central marketplace, is lively day and night. The excellent menu includes spinach vol-au-vent (traditionally served with an egg on top), lengua de ternera (tongue), and berengeras (stuffed eggplant), a chef's specialty. The local favorite is codfish in cream sauce. The ingredients are fresh and the price is right. Expect hearty market food and a total lack of pretension.

Els Quatre Gats. Montsió 3. ☎ **93/302-41-40.** Reservations required Sat–Sun. Main courses 1,200–2,800 ptas. ($9.60–$22.40); fixed-price menu 1,800 ptas. ($14.40). AE, MC, V. Restaurant, Mon–Sat 1–4pm and 9pm–midnight; café, daily 8am–2am. Metro: Plaça de Catalunya. CATALÁN.

A Barcelona legend since 1897, the Four Cats was the favorite of Picasso and other artists. In their heyday, their works decorated the walls of this fin-de-siècle cafe on a narrow cobblestone street near the cathedral. This small, dark beer hall was a base for the modernism movement and played a major role in the intellectual and bohemian life of the city. Today a *tertulia* (clublike) bar in the heart of the Barri Gòtic, it was restored but retains its fine old look. The good food is prepared in an unpretentious style of Catalán cooking called *cuina de mercat* (based on whatever looked fresh at the market that day). The constantly changing menu reflects the seasons.

⊗ Los Caracoles. Escudellers 14. ☎ **93/302-31-85.** Reservations required. Main courses 1,500–3,600 ptas. ($12–$28.80). AE, DC, MC, V. Daily 1pm–midnight. Metro: Drassanes. CATALÁN/SPANISH.

Set in a labyrinth of narrow cobblestone streets, Los Caracoles is the port's most colorful restaurant—and it has been since 1835. It has won acclaim for its spit-roasted chicken and its namesake, snails. A long angular bar is up front, with a bilevel restaurant in back. You can watch the busy preparations in the kitchen, where dried herbs, smoked ham shanks, and garlic bouquets hang from the ceiling. In summer tables are placed outside. The excellent food features all sorts of Spanish and Catalán specialties. Although a number-one tourist stop, it's not a tourist trap but delivers the same aromatic and robust food it always did.

Inexpensive

Biocenter. Pintor Fortuny 25. ☎ **93/301-45-83.** Main courses 900–1,000 ptas. ($7.20–$8); fixed-price menu 1,075 ptas. ($8.60). No credit cards. Mon–Sat 1–5pm. (Bar, Mon–Sat 9am–11pm.) Metro: Plaça de Catalunya. VEGETARIAN.

This is Barcelona's largest and best-known vegetarian restaurant, the creation of Catalán-born entrepreneur Pep Cañameras. Meals are served in two ground-floor dining rooms, whose walls are decorated with the paintings and artworks of the owner and his colleagues. There's a salad bar, an array of vegetarian casseroles, such soups as gazpacho and lentil, and a changing selection of seasonal vegetables.

Ⓢ **Garduña.** Morera 17–19. ☎ **93/302-43-23.** Reservations recommended. Main courses 1,200–2,800 ptas. ($9.60–$22.40); fixed-price menu 975–1,375 ptas. ($7.80–$11). AE, MC, V. Mon–Sat 1–4pm and 8pm–midnight, Sun 1–4pm. Metro: Liceu. CATALÁN.

This is the most famous restaurant in La Bouquería, the covered food market. Battered and somewhat ramshackle, it nonetheless enjoys a fashionable reputation among actors, sculptors, writers, and painters who appreciate a blue-collar atmosphere. Because of its position near the back of the market, you'll pass endless rows of fresh produce, cheese, and meats that whet your appetite before you reach it. You can dine downstairs, near a crowded bar, or a bit more formally upstairs. The food is ultra-fresh and might include "hors d'oeuvres of the sea," canalones (cannelloni) Rossini, grilled hake with herbs, seafood rice, filet steak with green peppercorns, or zarzuela of fresh fish.

Ⓢ **Nou Celler.** Princesa 16. ☎ **93/310-47-73.** Reservations required. Main courses 600–1,800 ptas. ($4.80–$14.40). MC, V. Sun–Fri 8am–midnight. Closed June 15–July 15. Metro: Jaume I. CATALÁN/SPANISH.

Near the Museu Picasso, this establishment is perfect for either a bodega-type meal or a cup of coffee. Country artifacts hang from the beamed ceiling and plaster walls. The back entrance, at Barra de Ferro 3, is at the quieter end of the place, where dozens of original artworks are arranged into a collage. The dining room offers such "Franco-era" food as fish soup, Catalán soup, zarzuela (a medley of seafood), paella, and hake.

Ⓢ **Pitarra.** Avinyó 56. ☎ **93/301-16-47.** Reservations required. Main courses 950–2,000 ptas. ($7.60–$16); fixed-price lunch 1,100 ptas. ($8.80). AE, DC, MC, V. Mon–Sat 1–4pm and 8:30–11pm. Metro: Liceu. CATALÁN.

This restaurant in the Barri Gòtic was named after the 19th-century Catalán playwright who lived and wrote his plays and poetry in the back room. Try the grilled fish chowder or Catalán salad, followed by grilled salmon or squid Málaga style. Valencian paella is another specialty. The cuisine doesn't even pretend to be imaginative but adheres to time-tested recipes—"the type of food we ate when growing up," in the words of one diner.

SUR DIAGONAL

Very Expensive

Beltxenea. Mallorca 275. ☎ **93/215-30-24.** Reservations recommended. Main courses 2,500–5,500 ptas. ($20–$44); *menú degustación* 6,900 ptas. ($55.20). AE, DC, MC, V. Mon–Fri 1:30–4pm and 8:30–11:30pm, Sat 8:30–11:30pm. Closed 2 weeks in Aug. Metro: Passeig de Gràcia. BASQUE.

In a late-19th-century modernist apartment building, this restaurant celebrates the nuances and subtleties of Basque cuisine. Since the Basques are noted as the finest chefs in Spain, the cuisine is grand indeed, and the restaurant is also one of the most elegantly and comfortably furnished in Barcelona. Save a visit for that special night—it's worth the money. The cuisine reflects the inspiration of the chef and the availability of ingredients. Examples are hake served either fried with garlic or garnished with clams and served with fish broth. Roast lamb, grilled rabbit, and pheasant are well prepared and succulent, as are the desserts. Summer dining is possible out in the formal garden.

✪ **Ca l'Isidre.** Les Flors 12. ☎ **93/441-11-39.** Reservations required. Main courses 2,200–3,800 ptas. ($17.60–$30.40). AE, MC, V. Mon–Sat 1:30–4pm and 8:30–11:30pm. Closed Aug. Metro: Paral.lel. CATALÁN.

In spite of its seedy location, this is the most sophisticated Catalán bistro in Barcelona, drawing such patrons as King Juan Carlos and Queen Sofía, who probably arrived by cab to protect their royal noggings from muggers. Isidre Gironés, helped by his wife, Montserrat, is known for his market-fresh Catalonian cuisine. Flowers decorate the restaurant, along with artwork, and the array of food is beautifully prepared and served. Try spider crabs and shrimp, a gourmand salad with foie gras, sweetbreads with port and flap mushrooms, or carpaccio of veal Harry's Bar style.

Expensive

✪ **Jaume de Provença.** Provença 88. ☎ **93/430-00-29.** Reservations recommended. Main courses 1,950–3,000 ptas. ($15.60–$24). AE, DC, MC, V. Tues–Sat Sun 1–4pm and 9–11:30pm, Sun 1–4pm. Closed Easter week and Aug. Metro: Estació-Sants. CATALÁN/FRENCH.

A few steps from the Estació Central de Barcelona-Sants rail station at the western end of the Eixample, this is a cozy and personalized restaurant with a country-rustic decor. It's the only restaurant on the Diagonal that serves food to equal La Dama. Named after owner/chef Jaume Bargués, it serves modern interpretations of traditional Catalán and southern French cuisine. Examples are a gratin of clams with spinach, small packets of foie gras and truffles, pig's trotters with plums and truffles, and crabmeat lasagne.

✪ **La Dama.** Av. Diagonal 423. ☎ **93/202-06-86.** Reservations required. Main courses 1,800–4,000 ptas. ($14.40–$32); fixed-price menu 4,750–7,500 ptas. ($38–$60). AE, DC, MC, V. Daily 1–4pm and 8:30–11:30pm. Metro: Provença. CATALÁN/INTERNATIONAL.

This is one of the few Barcelona restaurants that deserves—and gets—a Michelin star. Located one floor above street level in one of the grand iconoclastic 19th-century buildings for which Barcelona is famous, this stylish and well-managed restaurant serves a clientele of local residents and civic dignitaries with impeccable taste. You'll take an art nouveau elevator (or the sinuous stairs) up one flight to reach the dining room. Specialties may include roast filet of goat, salmon steak served with vinegar derived from cava and onions, an abundant seasonal platter of autumn mushrooms, and succulent preparations of lamb, fish and shellfish, beef, and veal. The building that contains the restaurant, designed by modernist architect Manuel Sayrach, is three blocks west of the intersection of Avinguda Diagonal and Passeig de Gràcia.

Inexpensive

Ca La María. Tallers 76. ☎ **93/318-89-93.** Reservations recommended Sat–Sun. Main courses 925–1,550 ptas. ($7.40–$12.40). AE, DC, MC, V. Tues–Sat 1:30–4pm and 8:30–11pm, Sun–Mon 1:30–4pm. Metro: Plaça de la Universitat. CATALÁN.

This small blue- and green-tiled bistro (only 18 tables) is on a quiet square opposite a Byzantine-style church near Plaça de la Universitat. Look for the constantly changing daily specials. This isn't a place for haute cuisine. A bit battered, the restaurant serves endearingly homelike food—provided you grew up in a family of Catalán cooks. These dishes, despite their simple origins, are often surprisingly tasty, as exemplified by baby squid with onions and tomatoes or angler fish with burnt garlic.

NORTE DIAGONAL

Very Expensive

✪ **Botafumiero.** Gran de Gràcia 81. ☎ **93/218-42-30.** Reservations recommended for dining rooms, not necessary for meals at the bar. Main courses 2,500–5,800 ptas. ($20–$46.40); fixed-price menu 8,000–9,000 ptas. ($64–$72). AE, DC, MC, V. Mon–Sat 1pm–1am, Sun 1–5pm. Metro: Enrique Cuiraga. SEAFOOD.

Although the competition is severe, this *restaurante marisquería* (seafood restaurant) consistently serves Barcelona's finest seafood. Much of the allure of this place comes from the attention to detail paid by the white-jacketed staff. You can dine at the bar, or at the rear, where you'll find a series of attractive dining rooms with light-grained panels, white napery, polished brass, and paintings by Galician artists. Menu items include seafood prepared ultra-fresh. The establishment prides itself on its fresh- and saltwater fish, clams, mussels, lobster, crayfish, scallops, and several varieties of crustaceans that you may never have seen before. Stored live in holding tanks or enormous crates near the restaurant's entrance, many of the creatures are flown in daily from Galicia, home of owner Moncho Neira.

✪ **Neichel.** Pedralbes 16. ☎ **93/203-84-08.** Reservations required. Main courses 2,300–3,800 ptas. ($18.40–$30.40). AE, DC, MC, V. Mon–Sat 1–4pm and 8:30–11pm. Closed Aug and holidays. Metro: Palau Reial or María Christina. FRENCH.

Owned/operated by Alsatian-born Jean Louis Neichel, who has been called "the most brilliant ambassador French cuisine has ever had in Spain," this restaurant serves patrons whose credentials might best be described as stratospheric. Outfitted in cool tones of gray and pastel, with its main decoration derived from a bank of windows opening onto greenery, Neichel is almost obsessively concerned with gastronomy—the savory presentation of some of the most talked-about preparations of seafood, fowl, and sweets in Spain. Your meal might include a "mosaic" of foie gras with vegetables, strips of salmon marinated in sesame and served with escabeche sauce, or a prize-winning terrine of seacrab floating on a lavishly decorated bed of cold seafood sauce.

ATTRACTIONS

Spain's second-largest city is also its most cosmopolitan and avant-garde. Barcelona is filled with landmark buildings and world-class museums offering many sightseeing opportunities. These include Antoni Gaudí's Sagrada Familia, the Museu Picasso, Barcelona's gothic cathedral, and Les Rambles, the famous tree-lined promenade cutting through the heart of the old quarter.

Sightseeing Suggestions

If You Have 1 Day Spend the morning walking through and exploring the Barri Gòtic. In the afternoon visit Antoni Gaudí's unfinished masterpiece, La Sagrada Familia, before returning to the heart of the city for a walk down Les Rambles. To cap your day, take the funicular to the fountains at Montjuïc or go to the top of Tibidabo for a panoramic view of Barcelona and its harbor.

If You Have 2 Days On day 2 visit the Museu Picasso. Then stroll through the surrounding district, the Barri de la Ribera, which is filled with Renaissance mansions. Follow this with a ride to the top of the Columbus Monument for a panoramic view of the harborfront. Have a seafood lunch at La Barcelonata, and in the afternoon stroll up Les Rambles again. Explore Montjuïc and visit the Museu d'Art de Catalunya if time remains. End the day with a meal at Los Caracoles, the most famous restaurant in the old city, just off Les Rambles.

If You Have 3 Days On day 3, make a pilgrimage to the monastery of Montserrat to see the venerated Black Virgin and a host of artistic and scenic attractions. Try to time your visit to hear the 50-member boys' choir.

If You Have 5 Days On day 4 take a morning walk along the harbor front, or in the modernist Eixample (Ensanche) section of Barcelona, the planned urban expansion area from 1860. Have lunch on the pier at a restaurant called Moll de la Fusta.

In the afternoon visit Montjuïc again to tour the Fundació Joan Miró and walk through the Poble Espanyol, a miniature village created for the 1929 World's Fair. On day 5 take another excursion from the city. If you're interested in history, visit the former Roman city of Tarragona to the south. If you want to unwind on a beach, head south to Sitges.

THE TOP CHURCHES

✪ **La Sagrada Familia.** Mallorca 401. ☎ **93/455-02-47.** Church, 750 ptas. ($6), including a 12-minute video about Gaudí's religious and secular works; elevator to the top (about 200 ft.), 200 ptas. ($1.60). June–Aug, daily 9am–9pm; May and Sept, daily 9am–8pm; Mar–Apr and Oct, daily 9am–7pm; Nov–Feb, daily 9am–6pm. Metro: Sagrada Familia.

Gaudí's incomplete masterpiece is one of the more idiosyncratic artworks of Spain—if you have time to see only one Catalán landmark, make it this one. Begun in 1882 and still incomplete at Gaudí's death in 1926, this incredible church—the Temple of the Holy Family—is a bizarre wonder. The languid, amorphous structure embodies the essence of Gaudí's style, which some have described as art nouveau run rampant. Work continues on the structure but without any sure idea of what Gaudí intended, so disagreements are constant. Some predict that the church will be completed in the mid–21st century.

✪ **Catedral de Barcelona.** Plaça de la Seu. ☎ **93/315-15-54.** Cathedral, free; museum, 100 ptas. (80¢). Cathedral, daily 8am–1:30pm and 4–7:30pm; museum, Mon–Sat 9:30am–noon; cloister museum, daily 10am–1pm. Metro: Jaume I.

Barcelona's cathedral is a celebrated example of Catalonian gothic. Except for the 19th-century west facade, the basilica was begun at the end of the 13th century and completed in the mid–15th century. The three naves, cleaned and illuminated, have splendid gothic details. With its large bell towers, blending of medieval and Renaissance styles, beautiful cloister, high altar, side chapels, sculptured choir, and gothic arches, it ranks as one of Spain's most impressive cathedrals. The cloister, illuminated on Saturday and fiesta days, contains a museum of medieval art.

THE TOP MUSEUMS

✪ **Museu Picasso.** Montcada 15–19. ☎ **93/319-63-10.** Admission 500 ptas. ($4) adults, 250 ptas. ($2) students, free for children 17 and under. Tues–Sat 10am–8pm, Sun 10am–3pm. Metro: Jaume I.

Two converted palaces on a medieval street have been turned into a museum housing works by Pablo Picasso, who donated some 2,500 of his paintings, engravings, and drawings to the museum in 1970. Picasso was particularly fond of Barcelona, where he spent much of his formative youth. In fact, some of the paintings were done when Picasso was 9. One portrait, from 1896, depicts his stern aunt, Tía Pepa. Another, completed at the turn of the century when Picasso was 16, depicts *Science and Charity* (his father was the model for the doctor). Many of the works, especially the early paintings, show the artist's debt to van Gogh, El Greco, and Rembrandt; a famous series, *Las Meninas* (1957), is said to "impersonate" the work of Velázquez. From his Blue Period, the *La Vie* drawings are perhaps the most interesting.

Museu Nacional d'Art de Catalunya. In the Palau Nacional, Parc de Montjuïc. ☎ **93/423-71-99.** Admission charge depends on the exhibit. Tues–Wed and Fri–Sat 10am–7pm, Thurs 10am–9pm, Sun 10am–2:30pm. Metro: Plaça de Espanya.

This museum is the major depository of Catalán art, a treasure trove of this important region of the world. The National Art Museum of Catalunya is the most important center for romanesque art. More than 100 pieces, including sculptures, icons, and frescoes, are on display. The highlight of the museum is the collection of murals from various romanesque churches.

Fundació Joan Miró. Plaça de Neptú, Parc de Montjuïc. ☎ **93/329-19-08.** Admission 600 ptas. ($4.80) adults, free for children 9 and under. June–Sept, Tues–Wed and Fri–Sat 10am–8pm, Thurs 10am–9:30pm, Sun 10:30am–2:30pm; Oct–May, Tues–Wed and Fri–Sat 11am–7pm, Thurs 11am–9:30pm, Sun 10:30am–2:30pm. Bus: 61 from Plaça d'Espanya.

Born in 1893, Joan Miró went on to become one of Spain's greatest painters, known for his whimsical abstract forms and brilliant colors. Some 10,000 works by this Catalán surrealist, including paintings, graphics, and sculptures, have been collected here. The building has been greatly expanded in recent years, following the design of Catalán architect Josep Lluís Sert, a close friend of Miró's. An exhibition in a modern wing charts (in a variety of media) Miró's complete artistic evolution from his first drawings at the age of 8 to his last works.

A NEIGHBORHOOD TO EXPLORE

The ✪ **Barri Gòtic** is Barcelona's old aristocratic quarter, parts of which have survived from the Middle Ages. Spend at least 2 or 3 hours exploring its narrow streets and squares. Start by walking up Carrer del Carme, east of Les Rambles. A nighttime stroll takes on added drama, but exercise extreme caution. The buildings, for the most part, are austere and sober, the cathedral being the crowning achievement. Roman ruins and the vestiges of 3rd-century walls add further interest. This area is intricately detailed and filled with many attractions that are easy to miss.

OTHER MUSEUMS

Museu Frederic Marès / Museu Sentimental. Plaça de Sant Iù 5–6. ☎ **93/310-58-00.** Admission (to both museums) 300 ptas. ($2.40), free for children 15 and under. Tues–Sat 10am–5pm, Sun 10am–2pm. Metro: Jaume I. Bus: 17, 19, or 45.

One of the biggest repositories of medieval sculpture in the region is the Frederic Marès Museum, just behind the cathedral. It's housed in an ancient palace whose interior courtyards, chiseled stone, and soaring ceilings are impressive in their own right, an ideal setting for the hundreds of polychrome sculptures. The sculpture section dates from pre-Roman times to the 20th century. Also housed here is the Museu Sentimental, a collection of everyday items that help to illustrate life in Barcelona during the past 2 centuries.

Museu Marítim. Av. de las Drassanes. ☎ **93/318-32-45.** Admission 600 ptas. ($4.80), free for children 14 and under. Tues–Sun 10am–7pm. Closed holidays. Metro: Drassanes. Bus: 14, 18, 36, 38, or 57.

In the formal Royal Shipyards of the Drassanes Reials, this 13th-century civil gothic complex was used for the construction of ships for the Catalano-Aragonese rulers. The most outstanding exhibition here is a reconstruction of *La Galería Real* of Don Juan of Austria, a lavish royal galley. Another special exhibit features a map by Gabriel de Vallseca that was owned by explorer Amerigo Vespucci.

Museu de la Ciència. Teodor Roviralta 55. ☎ **93/212-60-50.** Admission (museum and planetarium) 725 ptas. ($5.80) adults, 650 ptas. ($5.20) children 16 and under. Tues–Sun 10am–8pm. Bus: 17, 22, 58, or 73.

The Museu de la Ciència's modern design and hands-on activities have made it a major cultural attraction. You can touch, listen, watch, and participate in a variety of hands-on exhibits. From the beauty of life in the sea to the magic of holograms, the museum offers a world of science to discover. Watch the world turn beneath the Foucault pendulum, ride on a human gyroscope, hear a friend whisper from 20 yards away, feel an earthquake, or use the tools of a scientist to examine intricate life forms with microscopes and video cameras.

Fundació Antoni Tàpies. Aragó 255. ☎ **93/487-03-15.** Admission 500 ptas. ($4) adults, 250 ptas. ($2) children 10–18, free for children 9 and under. Tues–Sun 11am–8pm. Metro: Passeig de Gràcia.

When it opened in 1990, this became Barcelona's third museum devoted to the work of a single artist. In 1984 Catalán artist Antoni Tàpies set up the foundation bearing his name, and the city of Barcelona donated an ideal site near the Passeig de Gràcia in Eixample. One of Barcelona's landmark buildings, the brick-and-iron structure was built between 1881 and 1884 by that exponent of Catalán modernism, Lluís Domènech i Montaner. The core of the museum is a collection of works by Tàpies (most contributed by the artist), covering the stages of his career as it evolved into abstract expressionism.

Museu d'Art Modern. Plaça d'Armes, Parc de la Ciutadella. ☎ **93/319-57-28.** Admission 300 ptas. ($2.40) adults, 200 ptas. ($1.60) students and seniors 65 and over, free for children 16 and under. Tues–Sat 10am–7pm, Sun 10am–2pm. Closed Jan 1 and Dec 25. Metro: Arc de Triomf. Bus: 14, 16, 17, 39, or 40.

This museum shares a wing of the Palau de la Ciutadella with the Catalonian Parliament. Constructed in the 1700s, it once formed part of Barcelona's defenses as an arsenal. Its collection of art focuses on the early 20th century and features the work of Catalán artists, including Martí Alsina, Vayreda, Casas, Fortuny, and Rusiñol. The collection also encompasses modernist furniture, including designs by architect Puig i Cadafalch.

MORE ATTRACTIONS

Poble Espanyol. Marqués de Comilias, Parc de Montjuïc. ☎ **93/325-78-66.** Village, 950 ptas. ($7.60), free for children 6 and under; audiovisual hall, 400 ptas. ($3.20), free for children 6 and under. Mon 9am–8pm, Tues–Thurs 9am–2pm, Fri–Sat 9am–3pm, Sun 9am–2pm. Metro: Plaça de Espanya; then the free red double-decker bus.

In this re-created Spanish village, built for the 1929 World's Fair, various regional architectural styles are reproduced. There are 115 life-size reproductions of buildings and monuments, ranging from the 10th to the 20th century. The center of the village has an outdoor cafe where you can have drinks. Shops sell crafts from all the provinces, and in some of them you can see artists at work, printing fabric or blowing glass. The village has 14 restaurants of varying styles, a dance club, and eight musical bars.

Monument à Colom. Portal de la Pau. ☎ **93/302-52-34.** Admission 225 ptas. ($1.80) adults, 125 ptas. ($1) children 4–12, free for children 3 and under. June–Sept 24, daily 9am–9pm; Sept 25–May, Mon–Fri 10am–1:30pm and 3:30–6:30pm, Sat–Sun and holidays 10am–6:30pm. Closed Jan 1, Jan 6, and Dec 25–26. Metro: Drassanes.

This monument to Christopher Columbus was erected at Barcelona's harborfront on the occasion of the Universal Exhibition of 1888. It's divided into three parts: a plinth with bronze bas-reliefs depicting the principal feats of Columbus; the base of the column, consisting of an eight-sided polygon; the column itself, rising 167 feet; and finally a 25-foot-high bronze statue of Columbus himself by Rafael Ataché. Inside the iron column, an elevator ascends to the mirador, where a panoramic view of Barcelona and its harbor unfolds.

PARKS & GARDENS

Parc Güell (☎ **93/424-38-09**) was begun by Gaudí as a real-estate venture for a wealthy friend, Count Eusebi Güell, a well-known Catalán industrialist, but it was never completed. Only two houses were constructed, but it makes for an interesting excursion nonetheless. The city took over the property in 1926 and turned it into a public park. It's open May–Sept, daily 10am–9pm; Oct–Apr, daily 10am–6pm. Admission is free. To reach the park, take bus no. 24, 25, 31, or 74.

Another attraction, **Tibidabo Mountain,** offers the finest panoramic view of Barcelona. A funicular takes you up 1,600 feet to the summit. The funicular runs daily 7:15am–9:45pm and costs 400 ptas. ($3.20) each way. The ideal time to visit this summit north of the port (the culminations of the Sierra de Collcerola) is at sunset, as the city lights come on. An amusement park—with Ferris wheels swinging over Barcelona—has been opened here. There's also a church in this carnival-like setting called Sacred Heart, plus restaurants and mountaintop hotels. From Plaça de Catalunya, take a bus to Avinguda del Tibidabo, where you can board a special bus that will transport you to the funicular. You can hop aboard and scale the mountain.

In the south of the city, the mountain park of **Montjuïc** (Montjuch in Spanish) has splashing fountains, gardens, outdoor restaurants, and museums. The re-created village, the Poble Espanyol, and the Joan Miró Foundation are also in the park. There are many walks and vantage points for viewing the Barcelona skyline.

ORGANIZED TOURS

Pullmantur, Gran Via de les Corts Catalanes 635 (☎ **93/317-12-97**), offers a morning tour departing from the terminal at the above address at 9:30am, taking in the cathedral, the Gothic Quarter, the Rambles, the monument to Columbus, and the Spanish Village and the Olympic Stadium. It costs 4,180 ptas. ($33.45). An afternoon tour leaves at 3:30pm, with visits to some of the most outstanding buildings in the Eixample, including Gaudí's Sagrada Familia, Parc Güell, and a stop at the Picasso Museum. This tour costs 4,190 ptas. ($33.50). Pullmantur also offers several excursions into the environs. The daily tour of the monastery of Montserrat departs at 9:30am and returns to the city at 2:30pm. Tours include a visit to the Royal Basilica to view the famous sculpture of the Black Virgin. The tour returns to Barcelona to the harbor, where passengers have the option to remain for the afternoon. Tours cost 5,300 ptas. ($42.40).

Another company that offers tours of Barcelona and the surrounding countryside is **Juliatours** (☎ **93/317-64-54**). Itineraries are similar to those above, with similar prices. One, the Visita Ciudad Artistica, offers a tour of Barcelona focusing on the city's artistic significance. Tours pass many of Gaudí's brilliant buildings, including the Casa Lleó Morera, Casa Milá (La Perdrera), and La Sagrada Familia. Also included are visits to the Museu Picasso or Museu d'Art Modern, depending on the day of your tour. Tours cost 4,180 ptas. ($33.45) and leave at 3:30pm and return at 6:30pm.

SHOPPING

Works from the romanesque period to Picasso are found in one of the finest antiques stores in Barcelona, **Artur Ramón Anticuario,** Carrer de la Palla 25 (☎ **93/302-59-70;** Metro: Jaume I). A three-level emporium with high ceilings and a medieval kind of grace, it's set on a narrow flagstone-covered street near Plaza del Pi. Prices are high, as you'd expect. Open Mon–Sat 10am–1:30pm and 5–8pm.

In business since 1840, **Sala Parés,** Petritxol 5 (☎ **93/318-70-20;** Metro: Plaça de Catalunya), is the city's finest art gallery. Paintings are displayed in a two-story amphitheater; exhibitions of the most avant-garde art in Barcelona change about every 3 weeks. Open Mon–Sat 10:30am–2pm and 4:30–8:30pm and Sun 11am–2pm.

At **Art Picasso,** Tapineria 10 (☎ **93/310-49-57;** Metro: Jaume I), you can get good lithographs of works by Picasso, Miró, and Dalí, as well as T-shirts with the designs of these masters. Tiles sold here often carry their provocatively painted scenes. Open Mon–Sat 9:30am–8pm and Sun 9:30am–3pm.

El Corte Inglés, Plaça de Catalunya 14 (☎ **93/302-12-12;** Metro: Plaça de Catalunya), is Spain's largest and most glamorous department-store chain. The store sells everything from Spanish handcrafts to high-fashion items to Catalán records to food. The store also has restaurants and cafes and offers a number of consumer-related services, such as a travel agent. It will arrange for the mailing of purchases back home. Open Mon–Fri 10am–9:30pm.

Designs for both women and men are sold at **Groc,** Ramble de Catalunya 100 (☎ **93/215-74-74;** Metro: Plaça de Catalunya). One of the most stylish shops in Barcelona, it's expensive but filled with high-quality apparel made from the finest of natural fibers. The men's store is downstairs, the women's store one flight up. Open Mon–Sat 10am–2pm and 4:30–8pm; closed Aug. The men's department is closed Mon 10am–2pm; the women's department, Sat 4:30–8pm.

Named after the Victorian English illustrator, **Beardsley,** Petritxol 12 (☎ **93/ 301-05-76;** Metro: Plaça de Catalunya), is on the same street where the works of Picasso and Dalí were exhibited before they became world famous. The wide array of gifts includes a little bit of everything from everywhere—dried flowers, writing supplies, silver dishes, unusual bags and purchases, and lots more. Open Mon–Fri 9:30am–1:30pm and 4:30–8pm and Sat 10am–2pm and 5–8pm.

El Encants antiques market is held every Mon, Wed, and Fri–Sat in Plaça de les Glóries Catalanes (Metro: Glóries) (no specific times—go any time during the day to survey the selection). Coins and postage stamps are traded and sold in **Plaça Reial** on Sun 10am–2pm. The location is off the southern flank of the Rambles (Metro: Drassanes). A book-and-coin market is held at the **Ronda Sant Antoní** every Sun 10am–2pm (Metro: Universitat).

At **Artesana I Coses,** Placeta de Montcada 2 (☎ **93/319-54-13;** Metro: Jaume I), you'll find pottery and porcelain from every major region of Spain. Most pieces are heavy and thick-sided—designs in use in the country for centuries. Open Mon–Sat 10:30am–2pm and 4:30–8pm. And at **Itaca,** Carrer Ferran 26 (☎ **93/ 301-30-44;** Metro: Liceu), you'll find a wide array of handmade pottery, not only from Catalonia but also from Spain, Portugal, Mexico, and Morocco. The merchandise has been selected for its basic purity, integrity, and simplicity. Open Mon–Fri 10am–2pm and 4:30–8pm and Sat 10am–2pm and 5–8:30pm.

BARCELONA AFTER DARK

Your best source of local information is a little magazine called *Guía del Ocio,* which previews "La Semana de Barcelona" (This Week in Barcelona). It's in Spanish, but most of its listings will be comprehensible. The magazine is sold at virtually every news kiosk along Les Rambles.

Culture is deeply ingrained in the Catalán soul. The performing arts are strong here—some, in fact, take place on the street, especially along Les Rambles. Crowds will often gather around a singer or mime.

THE PERFORMING ARTS

Companyia Flotats. Teatre Poliorama, Rambla dels Estudis 115. ☎ **93/317-75-99.** Tickets 1,500–2,500 ptas. ($12–$20). Closed Aug. Metro: Liceu.

Theater in Barcelona is presented in the Catalán language, but those who speak the language or are fluent in Spanish will enjoy a performance of this leading company, directed by Josep María Flotats, an actor/director who was trained in such theaters in Paris as the Théâtre de la Villa and the Comédie-Française. He founded his own company in Barcelona, where he presents both classic and contemporary plays.

Mercat de Los Flors. Lleida 59. ☎ **93/426-18-75.** Tickets 1,100–2,500 ptas. ($8.80–$20). Metro: Plaça de Espanya.

Housed in a building constructed for the 1929 International Exhibition at Montjuïc is this other major Catalán theater. Peter Brook used it for a 1983 presentation of *Carmen*. Innovators in drama, dance, and music are showcased here, as are modern dance companies from Europe, including troupes from Italy and France. The 999-seat house also has a restaurant overlooking the rooftops of the city.

Palau de la Música Catalán. Sant Francest de Paula 2. ☎ **93/268-10-00.** Ticket prices depend on the presentation.

In a city of architectural highlights, this one stands out. In 1908 Lluís Domènech i Montaner, a Catalán architect, designed this structure, including stained glass, ceramics, statuary, and ornate lamps. It stands today—restored—as a classic example of modernism. Concerts and leading recitals are presented here. The box office is open Mon–Fri 10am–9pm and Sat 3–9pm.

FLAMENCO

Tablao de Carmen. Poble Espanyol de Montjuïc. ☎ **93/325-68-95.** Dinner and show, 7,500 ptas. ($60); show and one drink, 4,000 ptas. ($32). Metro: Plaça de Espanya; then the free red double-decker bus.

This club provides a highly rated flamenco cabaret in the re-created village. You can go early and explore the village if you wish and even have dinner here. The club is open Tues–Sun 8pm–midnight or later. During the week they sometimes close around 1am, often staying open until 2 or 3am on weekends (everything depends on business). The first show is always at 9:30pm, and second show Tues–Thurs and Sun at 11:30pm and on Fri and Sat at midnight. Reservations are encouraged.

Tablao Flamenco Cordobés. Les Rambles 35. ☎ **93/317-66-53.** Dinner and show; 7,500 ptas. ($60); show and one drink, 4,000 ptas. ($32). Metro: Drassanes.

At the southern end of Les Rambles, you'll hear the strum of the guitar, the sound of hands clapping rhythmically, and the haunting sound of the flamenco, a tradition here since 1968. Head upstairs to an Andalusian-style room where performances take place with the traditional *cuadro flamenco*—singers, dancers, and guitarist. Cordobés is said to be the best showcase for flamenco in Barcelona. Nov–Mar (except for 1 week in Dec), the show with dinner begins at 8:30pm, and the show without dinner at 10pm. Apr–Oct and Dec 25–31, four shows are offered nightly with dinner, at 8pm and 9:45pm; without dinner at 9:30pm and 11:15pm. Reservations are required. Closed in Jan.

A CABARET

Bodega Bohemia. Lancaster 2. ☎ **93/302-50-61.** Metro: Liceu.

This cabaret extraordinaire, off Les Rambles, is a Barcelona institution. The Bodega Bohemia rates as high camp—a talent showcase for theatrical personalities whose joints aren't so flexible but who perform with bracing dignity. Curiously, most audiences fill up with young people, who cheer, boo, catcall, and scream with laughter—and the old-timers on stage love it. In all, it's an incredible entertainment bargain if your tastes lean slightly to the bizarre. The street outside is none too safe; take a taxi right to the door. Open daily 11pm–4am.

DANCE CLUBS

Barcelona's version of New York's ill-fated and long-defunct Studio 54, **Estudio 54,** Av. del Paral.lel 64 (☎ **93/329-54-54;** Metro: Paral.lel), continues to rattle and roll with a slightly faded version of the same energy as its namesake. It lies on the opposite side of the Barri Xinés from Les Rambles. Inside, you'll find a creative array of lighting effects and an energetic dance floor. The place is at its most appealing Thurs–Sat 11:30pm–5am. Cover is 1,200 ptas. ($9.60).

The chic atmosphere of **Up and Down,** Numancia Diagonal 179 (☎ 93/280-29-22; Metro: Sants Estació), attracts the elite of Barcelona, spanning a generation gap. The more mature patrons, specifically the black-tie/postopera crowd, head for the upstairs section, leaving the downstairs to the loud music and "flaming youth." Every critic who comes here comments on the sassy antics of the waiters, whose theatricality is part of the carnival-like atmosphere pervading. The restaurant is open Mon–Sat 10pm–2am, serving meals costing 4,500 ptas. ($36) and up. The dance club is open Tues–Sat 12:30am–5am or 6:30am, depending on business. Cover, including the first drink, is 2,000 ptas. ($16).

PUBS & BARS

Facing a rural-looking square, **El Born,** Passeig del Born 26 (☎ 93/319-53-33; Metro: Jaume I), is a cleverly converted fish store. There are a few tables near the front, but our preferred spot is the inner room, with rattan furniture, ceramic jugs, books, and modern paintings. Music here could be anything from Louis Armstrong to classic rock. Dinner can also be had at the upstairs buffet. Open Mon–Sat 7:30am–2:30am.

Cocktail Bar Boadas, Tallers 1 (☎ 93/318-95-92; Metro: Plaça de Catalunya), intimate and conservative, is usually filled with regulars. It lies near the top of Les Rambles. Many visitors use this place for a before-dinner drink and snack before wandering to one of the district's many restaurants. You can choose among a wide array of Caribbean rums, Russian vodkas, and English gins—the skilled bartenders know how to mix them all. The place is especially well known for its daiquiris. Open daily noon–2am.

At **Nick Havanna,** Roselló 208 (☎ 93/237-54-05; Metro: Diagonal), the soaring ceiling is supported by vaguely ecclesiastical concrete columns, off which radiate four arms like a high-tech cathedral. There's a serpentine-shaped curve of two bars upholstered in black-and-white cowhide, plus a bank of at least 30 video scenes. Some women have admitted to detouring to the men's room for a view of the famous mirrored waterfall cascading into the urinal. This has become one of Barcelona's most talked-about and most frequented watering holes. It's hip and happening—so dress accordingly and go late. Open daily 11pm–5:30am. There's no cover Sun–Thurs; on Fri–Sat, including the first drink, it's 900 ptas. ($7.20).

Otto Zutz Club, Carrer Lincoln 15 (☎ 93/238-07-22; Metro: Passeig de Gràcia or Fontana), is the last word in hip and a magnet for the city's artists and nightcrawlers. Facetiously named after a German optician and the recipient of millions of pesetas worth of interior drama, it sits behind an angular facade that reminds some visitors of a monument to some mid–20th-century megalomaniac. On the uppermost floor, a high-tech restaurant serves supper-club food. Don't even think of showing up here before midnight. Open Tues–Sat 11pm–6am. Cover is 2,000 ptas. ($16).

GAY & LESBIAN CLUBS

Gay residents of Barcelona refer to **Chaps,** Av. Diagonal 365 (☎ 93/215-53-65; Metro: Diagonal), a saloon-style watering hole, as Catalonia's premier leather bar. However, the dress code usually steers more toward boots and jeans than leather and chains. Set behind a pair of swinging doors evocative of the old American West, Chaps contains two bar areas and is open daily 7pm–3am.

Behind a pair of unmarked doors, in a neighborhood of art nouveau buildings, **Martin's Disco,** Passeig de Gràcia 130 (☎ **93/218-71-67;** Metro: Passeig de Gràcia), is one of the more popular gay dance clubs in Barcelona. In a series of all-black rooms, you'll wander through a landscape of men's erotic art, upended oil drums (used as cocktail tables), and the disembodied front-end chassis of yellow cars set amid the angular surfaces of the drinking and dancing areas. Another bar supplies drinks to a large room where films are shown. Open daily midnight–6am. Cover, including the first drink, is 1,000 ptas. ($8).

DAY TRIPS FROM BARCELONA

PENEDÉS WINERIES From the Penedés wineries comes the famous *cava* (Catalán champagne), which you can sample in Barcelona's champagne bars. You can see where this wine originates by driving 25 miles from Barcelona via highway A2, Exit 27. There are also daily trains to Sant Sadurní d'Anoia, home to 66 cava firms. Trains depart from Barcelona-Sants.

The firm best equipped to receive visitors is **Codorniu** (☎ **93/818-32-32),** the largest producer of cava—some 40 million bottles a year. Your best bet is to visit Codorniu by car because public transportation is unreliable. Tours are presented in English and take 1 1/2 hours; they visit some of the 10 miles of underground cellars by electric cart. Take a sweater, even on a hot day. The tour ends with a cava tasting. Tours are conducted Mon–Fri at 8am, 12:30pm, and 3:45pm. Call for more information. Codorniu is closed in August.

SITGES One of the most frequented resorts of southern Europe, Sitges, 25 miles south of Barcelona, is the brightest spot on the Costa Dorada. It's crowded in summer, mostly with affluent young northern Europeans, many of them gay. For years the resort was patronized largely by prosperous middle-class industrialists from Barcelona, but those rather staid days have gone; Sitges is as lively today as Benidorm and Torremolinos down the coast, but it's nowhere near as tacky.

Sitges has long been known as a city of culture thanks in part to resident artist/playwright/Bohemian mystic Santiago Rusiñol. The 19th-century modernist movement largely began at Sitges, and the town remained the scene of artistic encounters and demonstrations long after modernism waned. Sitges continued as a resort of artists, attracting such giants as Salvador Dalí and poet Federico García Lorca. Then the Spanish Civil War (1936–39) erased what has come to be called the "golden age" of Sitges.

RENFE runs trains from Barcelona-Sants to Sitges for the 50-minute trip. Call 93/490-02-02 in Barcelona for information about schedules. A round-trip same-day ticket costs 600 ptas. ($4.80). Four trains leave Barcelona per hour.

Sitges is a 45-minute drive from Barcelona along C246, a coastal road. An express highway, A7, opened in 1991. The coastal road is more scenic, but it can be extremely slow on weekends because of the heavy traffic, as all of Barcelona seemingly heads for the beaches.

The **tourist information office** is at Carrer Sínis Morera 1 (☎ **93/811-76-30),** open June–Sept 15, daily 9am–9pm; Sept 16–May, Mon–Fri 9am–2pm and 4–6:30pm and Sat 10am–1pm.

Exploring Sitges It's the **beaches** that attract most visitors. They have showers, bathing cabins, and stalls. Kiosks rent such items as motorboats and air cushions for fun on the water. Beaches on the eastern end and those inside the town center are the most peaceful, such as **Aiguadoiç** and **Els Balomins.** The **Playa San Sebastián, Fragata Beach,** and **"Beach of the Boats"** (under the church and next to the yacht club) are the area's family beaches. Most young people go to the **Playa de la Ribera,** in the west.

Beaches aside, Sitges has some interesting museums. Catalán artist Santiago Rusiñol combined two 16th-century cottages to make the house that contains the **Museu Cau Ferrat,** Carrer del Fonollar (☎ **93/894-03-64**). He lived and worked here and upon his death in 1931 he willed it to Sitges along with his art collection. The museum collection includes two paintings by El Greco and several small Picassos, including *The Bullfight.* A number of Rusiñol's works are also on display. Admission is 400 ptas. ($3.20) for adults, 200 ptas. ($1.60) for students, free for children 15 and under. A combination ticket granting admission to this museum and the two below is 600 ptas. ($4.80). The hours for the three museums are June 21–Sept 11, Tues–Sat 9:30am–2pm and 4–8pm and Sun 9:30am–2pm; Sept 12–June 20, Tues–Fri 9:30am–2pm and 4–6pm, Sat 9:30am–2pm and 4–8pm, and Sun 9:30am–2pm.

Opened by the king and queen of Spain, the **Museu Maricel,** Carrer del Fonallar (☎ **93/894-03-64**), contains art donated by Dr. Jesús Pérez Rosales. The palace, owned by American Charles Deering when it was built right after World War I, is in two parts connected by a small bridge. The museum has a good collection of gothic and Romantic paintings and sculptures, as well as many fine Catalán ceramics. There are also three noteworthy works by Rebull and an allegorical painting of World War I by Sert. Admission is 300 ptas. ($2.40) for adults, 150 ptas. ($1.20) for students, free for children 15 and under. Admission is included in the combination ticket (above). For museum hours, see above.

The **Museu Romàntic ("Can Llopis"),** Sant Gaudenci 1 (☎ **93/894-29-69**), re-creates the daily life of a Sitges landowning family in the 18th and 19th centuries. The family rooms, furniture, and household objects are most interesting. You'll also find wine cellars and an important collection of antique dolls (upstairs). Admission is 300 ptas. ($2.40) for adults, 150 ptas. ($1.20) for students, and free for children 15 and under. Admission is included in the combination ticket (above). For museum hours, see above.

MONTSERRAT   Lying 35 miles northwest of Barcelona, Montserrat is one of the most popular day excursions, though it's too overcrowded for Sunday visits. The winds blow cold at Montserrat. Even in summer, take along warm sweaters, jackets, or coats. In winter, thermal underwear might not be a bad idea.

The best and most exciting way to go is via the Catalán railway—Ferrocarrils de la Generalitat de Catalunya (Manresa line), with five trains a day leaving from Plaça de Espanya in Barcelona. The central office is at Plaça de Catalunya 1 (☎ **93/205-15-15**). The train connects with an aerial cableway (Aeri de Montserrat), included in the rail passage. Expect to spend 1,635 ptas. ($13.10), including the funicular. Motorists can take N2 southwest of Barcelona toward Tarragona, turning west at the junction with N11. The signposts and exit to Montserrat will be on your right. From the main road, it's 9 miles to the monastery through dramatic Catalán scenery, with eerie rock formations.

The **tourist information office** is at Plaça de la Creu (☎ **93/835-02-51**), open daily 10am–1:45pm and 3–5:30pm.

Exploring Montserrat   Sitting atop a 4,000-foot mountain 7 miles long and 3½ miles wide, Montserrat is one of the most important pilgrimage spots in Spain. Thousands travel here every year to see and touch the 12th-century statue of **La Moreneta (The Black Virgin),** the patron saint of Catalonia. The 50-member ✪ **Escolanía** (boys' choir) is one of Europe's oldest and most renowned, dating from the 13th century. At 1pm daily you can hear them singing "Salve Regina" and the "Virolai" (hymn of Montserrat) in the Nostra Senyora de Montserrat. The basilica is open daily 8–10:30am and noon–6:30pm. Admission is free. To view the Black Virgin (12th- or 13th-century) statue, enter the church through a side door to the right. At Plaça de Santa María you can also visit the **Museu de Montserrat** (☎ **93/835-02-51**), known for its collection of ecclesiastical paintings, including works by Caravaggio and El Greco. Charging 400 ptas. ($3.20) admission, the museum is open daily 10:30am–2pm and 3–6pm.

The 9-minute funicular ride to the 4,119-foot-high peak, Sant Jeroni, operates about every 20 minutes Apr–Oct, daily 10am–6:40pm. The cost is 700 ptas. ($5.60) round-trip. From the top, you'll see not only all Catalonia but also the Pyrenees and the islands of Majorca and Ibiza.

3 Andalusia & the Costa del Sol

This once-great stronghold of Muslim Spain is rich in history and tradition, contain- ing some of the country's most celebrated sightseeing treasures: the Mezquita (mosque) in Córdoba, the Alhambra in Granada, and the great gothic cathedral in Seville. Give Andalusia at least a week and you'll still have only skimmed the surface of its many offerings.

This dry, mountainous region also embraces the Costa del Sol (Málaga, Marbella, and Torremolinos are covered here), a popular beach strip of Spain. Go to the Costa del Sol for resorts, after-dark fun, and relaxation; visit Andalusia for its architectural wonders and beauty.

The mild winter climate and almost-guaranteed sunshine in summer have made the razzle-dazzle Costa del Sol shoreline a year-round attraction. It begins at the west- ern frontier harbor city of Algeciras and stretches east to the port city of Almería. Sandwiched between these points is a steep, rugged coastline, with poor-to-fair beaches, set against the Sierra Nevada. You'll find sandy coves, whitewashed houses, olive trees, lots of new apartment houses, fishing boats, golf courses, souvenir stands, fast-food outlets, and widely varied flora—both human and vegetable. From June to October the coast is mobbed, so make sure that you've nailed down a reservation.

A driving tour of Andalusia and the Costa del Sol can begin at the "gateway" city of Córdoba, 260 miles southwest of Madrid. The city lies astride NIV (E5) connect- ing Madrid with Seville.

ONLY IN ANDALUSIA

Listening to the Sound of Flamenco   It's best heard in some tavern in the old quarter of Seville, Granada, or Córdoba. But from the lowliest taberna to the posh- est nightclub, you can hear the heel clicking, foot stamping, castanet rattling, hand clapping, and sultry guitar playing aided by the tambourine. This is flamenco, its origins lying deep in Asia. But the Andalusian Gypsy has given it an original and unique style—a dance dramatizing inner conflict and pain. Performed by a great art- ist, flamenco can tear your heart out with its soulful and throaty singing.

Celebrating *Semana Santa* (Holy Week)   This is reason enough to go to Andalusia. Since the 16th century, the city's Easter processions and celebrations are the biggest and most elaborate in Spain. Solemn evening processions take place each day of the week before Easter—organized by *codafrías* (religious brotherhoods). Mem- bers of various codafrías dress as penitents in hoods, capes, and masks. Huge plat- forms (*pasos*) are carried on their shoulders, and religious statues are paraded through the streets of such cities as Seville. But it's not all solemn. Andalusians indulge in

Andalusia

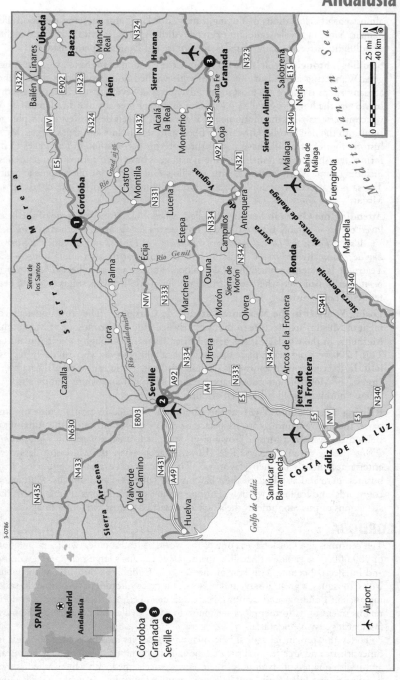

almost pagan celebrations of singing, eating, drinking, and enjoying the good life. Semana Santa in Seville segues into Feria de Abril (April Fair), with 6 days and nights of bullfights, street dancing, parades, fireworks, and flamenco performances.

Strolling Through Seville's Barrio Santa Cruz   Go in daylight to avoid the muggers. Wandering around in this area of whitewashed houses, winding streets, and artisans' shops is one of the most scenic adventures in Seville. In the Middle Ages the barrio was the home of Seville's Jewish community. Enter at Calle de Mateus Gago, which intersects with the monumental Plaza de la Virgen de los Reyes, and plunge right into the neighborhood, which is filled with restaurants and tapas places. Most historic figures of Seville have passed through this barrio, though few traces of its former Jewish heritage remain. All the synagogues have been turned into churches, including Santa Maris la Blanca, with Murillo's *Last Supper*. Murillo's home at Santa Teresa 8 is a reconstruction. Plaza de Doña Elvira is named for the character in Mozart's *Don Giovanni*.

Attending the Opera in Seville   Seville has been the setting for some of the best-loved operas—notably Bizet's *Carmen*, Donizetti's *La Favorita*, Beethoven's *Fidelio*, Verdi's *La Forza del Destino*, Mozart's *Marriage of Figaro*, and Rossini's *Barber of Seville*. Ironically, it wasn't until 1991 that Seville got its own opera house—the Teatro de la Maestranza at Núñez de Balboa. Though you may hear *The Barber of Seville* performed everywhere from Milan to New York, it always seems to sound better on its home turf.

Losing Yourself in the Mezquita-Catedral de Córdoba   The crowning achievement of Muslim architecture in the West, rivaled only by the mosque at Mecca, the Mezquita, in the words of its biggest admirers, is reason enough to visit Andalusia. This 1,200-year-old masterpiece by a series of caliphs is so vast you can easily get lost in it. In the center is an enormous Catholic cathedral. You can wander through the "forest" of Moorish horseshoe-shaped arches, all in red and white "candy stripes." There's nothing else like this in all of Europe.

Reliving *The Arabian Nights* at the Alhambra   Girded by nearly a mile of ramparts, the last remaining fortress-palace of the caliphs stands atop the Alhambra. Behind the walls is a former "royal city," straight from the pages of *The Arabian Nights*. At the core is the Casa Real (Royal Palace), where the Moorish rulers were entertained nightly by their "favorites." The sultans of yore once conducted state business here and also housed their harems and families. Fanciful halls, fountained courtyards, and scalloped windows framing picture-postcard views are just part of the attractions of this monument, the single most visited tourist attraction in Spain.

CÓRDOBA

Ten centuries ago Córdoba was one of the world's greatest cities, with a population of 900,000. The capital of Muslim Spain, it was Europe's largest city and a cultural and intellectual center. This seat of the Western Caliphate flourished, with public baths, mosques, a great library, and palaces. But greedy hordes passed through, sacking ancient buildings and carting off art treasures. Despite these assaults, Córdoba retains traces of its former glory—enough to rival Seville and Granada as the most fascinating city in Andalusia.

Today this provincial capital is known chiefly for its mosque, but it abounds in other artistic and architectural riches, especially its domestic dwellings. The old Arab and Jewish quarters are famous for their narrow streets lined with whitewashed homes boasting flower-filled patios and balconies, and it's perfectly acceptable to walk along gazing into the courtyards.

ESSENTIALS

ARRIVING   Córdoba is a railway junction for routes to the rest of Andalusia and the rest of Spain. There are about 22 *talgo* and AVE trains daily between Córdoba and Madrid (1¹/₂–2 hours). Other trains (*tranvías*) take 5–8 hours for the same trip. There are also 25 trains from Seville every day (1¹/₂ hours). The main rail station is on the town's northern periphery, at Av. de América 130, near the corner of Avenida de Cervantes. For information, call 957/49-02-02. From the bus terminal operated by Empresa Bacoma, Av. de Cervantes 22 (☎ **957/45-64-14**), a short walk south of the rail station, there are three buses per day to and from Seville (a 2-hour and 3-hour trip, respectively) and five daily buses to Jaén (3 hours). Buses arrive here from Madrid (5¹/₂ hours).

VISITOR INFORMATION   The **tourist information office** is at Calle Torrijos 10 (☎ **957/47-12-35**), open Mon–Sat 10am–7pm and Sun 10am–2pm.

DEPARTING BY CAR   Take NIV toward Seville but try to stop over in Carmona, 65 miles to the southwest. Partially surrounded by its Roman walls, this is one of the most scenic towns in all of Andalusia. You can lunch here at the parador. After lunch, continue on NIV for another 24 miles into Seville.

EXPLORING CORDOBA

Dating from the 8th century, the ✪ **Mezquita-Catedral de Córdoba,** Calle Cardenal Herrero (☎ **957/47-05-12**), was the crowning Muslim architectural achievement in the West, rivaled only by the mosque at Mecca. It's a fantastic labyrinth of red-and-white-striped pillars. To the astonishment of visitors, a cathedral sits awkwardly in the middle of the mosque, disturbing the purity of the lines. The 16th-century cathedral, a blend of many styles, is impressive in its own right, with an intricately carved ceiling and baroque choir stalls. Additional ill-conceived annexes later turned the Mezquita into an architectural oddity. Its most interesting feature is the mihrab, a domed shrine of Byzantine mosaics that once housed the Koran. After exploring the interior, stroll through the Courtyard of the Orange Trees, which has a beautiful fountain. Admission is 750 ptas. ($6) for adults and 375 ptas. ($3) for children 12 and under. Open daily: Apr–Sept 10am–7pm and Oct–Mar 10am–1:30pm and 3:30–5:30pm.

Commissioned in 1328 by Alfonso XI (the "Just"), the ✪ **Alcázar de los Reyes Cristianos** (Alcázar of the Christian Kings), Amador de los Ríos (☎ **957/42-01-51;** bus: 3 or 12), is a fine example of military architecture. Ferdinand and Isabella governed Castile from this fortress on the river as they prepared to reconquer Granada, the last Moorish stronghold in Spain. Columbus journeyed here to fill Isabella's ears with his plans for discovery. Two blocks southwest of the Mezquita, the quadrangular building is notable for powerful walls and a trio of towers—the Tower of the Lions, the Tower of Allegiance, and the Tower of the River. The Tower of the Lions contains intricately decorated ogival ceilings that are the most notable example of gothic architecture in Andalusia. The beautiful gardens (illuminated May–Sept, Tues–Sat 10pm–1am) and the Moorish baths are celebrated attractions. The Patio Morisco is a lovely spot, its pavement decorated with the arms of León and Castile. Admission is 425 ptas. ($3.40) for adults and 150 ptas. ($1.20) for children. Open May–Sept, Tues–Sat 10am–2pm and 6–8pm and Sun 10am–2pm; Oct–Apr, Tues–Sat 10am–2pm and 4:30–6:30pm and Sun 10am–2pm.

Housed in an old hospital, the **Museo de Bellas Artes de Córdoba** (Fine Arts Museum), Plazuela del Potro 1 (☎ **957/47-33-45;** bus: 3, 4, 7, or 12), contains medieval Andalusian paintings, examples of Spanish baroque art, and works by many of Spain's important 19th- and 20th-century painters, including Goya. The museum is east of the Mezquita, about a block south of the Church of St. Francis (San Francisco). Admission is 250 ptas. ($2), free for children 11 and under. Open June 15–Sept 15, Tues–Sat 10am–2pm and 6–8pm and Sun 10am–1:30pm; Sept 16–June 14, Tues–Sat 10am–2pm and 5–7pm and Sun 10am–1:30pm.

Memorabilia of great bullfights are housed in the **Museo Municipal de Arte Taurino,** Plaza de las Bulas (also called Plaza Maimónides) (☎ **957/47-20-00;** bus: 3 or 12), a 16th-century building in the Jewish Quarter, inaugurated in 1983. Its ample galleries recall Córdoba's great bullfighters with "suits of light," pictures, trophies, posters, even stuffed bulls' heads. You'll see Manolete in repose and the blood-smeared uniform of El Cordobés—both of these famous matadors came from Córdoba. Admission is 425 ptas. ($3.40), free for children 17 and under. Open May–Sept, Tues–Sat 9:30am–1:30pm and 5–8pm and Sun 9:30am–1:30pm; Oct–Apr, Tues–Sat 9:30am–1:30pm and 4–7pm and Sun 9:30am–1:30pm.

SHOPPING

The largest and most comprehensive association of craftspeople in Córdoba is **Arte Zoco,** on Calle de los Júdios (☎ **957/29-62-62**). Opened in the Jewish quarter as a business cooperative in the mid-1980s, it assembles the creative output of about a dozen artisans, whose media include leather, wood, silver, crystal, terra-cotta, and iron. About half a dozen of the artisans maintain on-premises studios, which you can visit to check out the techniques and tools they use to pursue their crafts. The center is open Mon–Fri 9:30am–8pm and Sat–Sun 9:30am–2pm. The workshops and studios of the various artisans open and close according to the whims of their occupants but are usually open Mon–Fri 10am–2pm and 5:30–8pm.

At **Meryan,** Calleja de las Flores 2 (☎ **957/47-59-02**), in a 250-year-old building you can see artisans plying their craft. Most items must be custom ordered, but there are some ready-made pieces for sale, including cigarette boxes, jewel cases, attaché cases, book and folio covers, and ottoman covers. Meryan is open Mon–Fri 9am–8pm and Sat 9am–2pm.

ACCOMMODATIONS

Very Expensive

✪ **El Conquistador Hotel.** Magistral González Francés 15, 14003 Córdoba. ☎ **957/48-11-02.** Fax 957/47-46-77. 98 rms, 3 suites. A/C TV TEL. 15,500 ptas. ($124) double; from 22,000 ptas. ($176) suite. AE, DC, MC, V. Parking 1,200 ptas. ($9.60). Bus: 12.

Built centuries ago as a private villa, this first-class hotel was tastefully renovated in 1986 into one of the most attractive in town, with triple rows of stone-trimmed windows and ornate iron balustrades. The marble-and-granite lobby opens into an interior courtyard filled with seasonal flowers, a pair of splashing fountains, and a symmetrical stone arcade. The quality, size, and comfort of the rooms—each with a black-and-white marble floor—have earned the hotel four stars from the government.

Expensive

Ⓢ **Parador Nacional de la Arruzafa.** Av. de la Arruzafa 33, 14012 Córdoba. ☎ **957/27-59-00.** Fax 957/28-04-09. 90 rms, 6 suites. A/C MINIBAR TV TEL. 15,000 ptas. ($120) double; 18,500 ptas. ($148) suite. AE, DC, MC, V. Free parking.

Lying 2¹/₂ miles outside town in the suburb of El Brillante, this parador (named after an Arab word meaning "palm grove") offers the conveniences and facilities of a luxurious resort hotel at reasonable rates. Occupying the site of a former caliphate palace, it's one of the finest paradores in Spain, with a view, a pool, and a tennis court.

The spacious rooms have been furnished with fine dark-wood pieces, and some have balconies. The restaurant serves regional specialties.

Moderate

Hotel González. Manríquez 3, 14003 Córdoba. ☎ **957/47-98-19.** Fax 957/48-61-87. 17 rms. A/C TEL. 9,750 ptas. ($78) double; 12,450 ptas. ($99.60) triple; 16,600 ptas. ($132.80) quad. Rates include breakfast. AE, DC, MC, V. Parking 1,400 ptas. ($11.20).

Within walking distance of Córdoba's major monuments, the González is clean and decent but not a lot more. The rooms are functionally furnished and comfortable. In the hotel restaurant you can sample both regional and national specialties. Readers have praised the staff's attitude. One claimed, "They solve problems like magicians, take your car to the parking lot and back, and even teach you Spanish."

Sol Gallos. Medina Azahara 7, 14005 Córdoba. ☎ **800/336-3542** in the U.S. or 957/23-55-00. Fax 957/23-16-36. 114 rms. A/C TV TEL. 9,900–10,365 ptas. ($79.20–$82.90) double; 11,900 ptas. ($95.20) triple. AE, DC, MC, V.

Half a block from a wide, tree-shaded boulevard on the western edge of town, this aging hotel stands eight floors high, crowned by an informal roof garden. The hotel is a favorite of groups and commercial travelers. The comfortable but small rooms have many extra comforts, such as balconies, and the outdoor pool is a pleasure during summer. The hotel also offers a restaurant, a drinking lounge, and a spacious lobby.

Inexpensive

Hostal el Triunfo. Corregidor Luís de la Cerda 79, 14003 Córdoba. ☎ **957/47-55-00.** Fax 957/48-68-50. 58 rms. A/C TV TEL. 5,800 ptas. ($46.40) double; 6,900 ptas. ($55.20) triple. AE, DC, MC, V. Parking 1,500 ptas. ($12). Bus: 12.

Opposite the mosque and a block from the northern bank of the Guadalquivir River is a real find—a simple hotel with a formal entrance, a pleasant, white-walled lounge, and comfortable, well-furnished rooms. Built in the late 1970s, the El Triunfo was renovated in 1992. It offers polite and efficient service. The three-floor hotel has no elevator; its only other drawback is that the bells of the Mezquita cathedral may make it difficult for one to sleep.

Hotel Riviera. Plaza de Aladreros 5, 14001 Córdoba. ☎ **957/47-30-00.** Fax 957/47-60-18. 30 rms. A/C TV TEL. 4,900–5,800 ptas. ($39.20–$46.40) double; 6,075–7,000 ptas. ($48.60–$56) triple. AE, DC.

The genial owner of this modern hotel is likely to be behind the reception desk when you arrive. His establishment—on a triangular plaza in a commercial section of town a short walk south of the train station—offers very clean "no-frills" accommodations. No meals are served, but many cafes are within walking distance.

DINING

Moderate

✪ **El Caballo Rojo.** Cardinal Herrero 28, Plaza de la Hoguera. ☎ **957/47-53-75.** Reservations required. Main courses 1,600–3,000 ptas. ($12.80–$24). AE, DC, MC, V. Daily 1–4:30pm and 8pm–midnight. Bus: 12. SPANISH.

This restaurant is the most popular in Andalusia, and except for the Almudaina it remains Córdoba's best, though often overrun by tourists. The place has a noise level matched by no other restaurant here, but the skilled waiters seem to cope with all demands. Within walking distance of the Mezquita in the old town, it's down a long open-air passage flanked with potted geraniums and vines. Try a variation on the usual gazpacho—almond-flavored broth with apple pieces. In addition to Andalusian dishes, the chef offers Sephardic and Mozarabic specialties, an example of the latter being monkfish with pine nuts, currants, carrots, and cream. Real aficionados come for the rabo de toro (stew made with the tail of an ox or a bull). The cookery is robust and flavorsome.

✪ **La Almudaina.** Plaza de los Santos Mártires 1. ☎ **957/47-43-42.** Reservations required. Main courses 1,800–2,500 ptas. ($14.40–$20); fixed-price menu 3,000–5,000 ptas. ($24–$40). AE, DC, MC, V. Mon–Sat noon–5pm and 8:30pm–midnight, Sun noon–5pm. Closed Sun July–Aug. Bus: 12. SPANISH/FRENCH.

Fronting the river in what used to be the Jewish Quarter, La Almudaina is one of the most attractive eateries in Andalusia, where you can dine in one of the lace-curtained salons or on a glass-roofed central courtyard. Specialties include salmon crêpes; a wide array of fish, such as hake with shrimp sauce; and meats, such as pork loin in wine sauce. For dessert, try the not-too-sweet chocolate crêpe. The cuisine's success is in its use of very fresh ingredients that are deftly handled by the kitchen and not over-cooked or overspiced.

Inexpensive
Restaurante Da Vinci. Plaza de los Chirinos 6. ☎ **957/47-75-17.** Reservations required. Main courses 600–1,800 ptas. ($4.80–$14.40); *menú del día* 1,600 ptas. ($12.80). V. Daily 1:30–4:30pm and 8pm–midnight. ITALIAN/INTERNATIONAL.

This ranks as one of the leading restaurants in town, though not as highly rated as those above. Both the cuisine and the decor are a blend of Andalusian, international, and Italian influences, arranged in a curious but pleasing mishmash of traditions. Menu items include a choice of roast meats (veal, pork, beefsteak, and lamb), a se-lection of pastas and salads, and many kinds of fish and seafood, especially hake, monkfish, squid, and salmon. This is standard Andalusian fare, with no innovation and little flair, but it's still good.

SEVILLE

Sometimes a city becomes famous for its beauty and romance, and Seville, the capi-tal of Andalusia, is such a place. It lies 341 miles southwest of Madrid and 135 miles northwest of Málaga. In spite of its sultry heat in summer and its many problems, such as rising unemployment and street crime, it remains one of the most charming of Spanish cities. Don Juan and Carmen—aided by Mozart and Bizet—have given Seville a romantic reputation. Because of the acclaim of *Don Giovanni* and *Carmen*, not to mention *The Barber of Seville*, debunkers have risen to challenge this reputa-tion. But if a visitor can see only two Spanish cities in a lifetime, they should be Seville and Toledo.

Unlike most Spanish cities, Seville has fared well under most of its conquerors—the Romans, Arabs, and Christians. When Spain entered its 16th-century golden age, Seville funneled gold from the New World into the rest of the country. Columbus docked here after his journey to America.

ESSENTIALS
ARRIVING From Seville's **San Pablo Airport,** Calle Almirante Lobo (☎ **95/451-53-20**), Iberia flies several times a day to and from Madrid (and elsewhere via Madrid). The airport is about 6 miles from the center of the city, along the highway leading to Carmona. Train service into Seville is now centralized into the Estación Santa Justa, Avenida Kansas City (☎ **95/454-02-02** for information and reserva-tions). Buses no. C1 and C2 at this train station take you to the bus station at Prado de San Sebastián, and bus EA runs to and from the airport. The high-speed AVE train has reduced travel time from Madrid to Seville to 2¹/₂ hours. This train makes 12 trips

daily, with a stop in Córdoba. Ten trains a day connect Seville and Córdoba; the AVE train takes 50 minutes and a *talgo* takes 1¹/₂ hours.

Most buses arrive and depart from the city's largest **bus terminal,** on the southeast edge of the old city, at Prado de San Sebastián, Calle José María Osborne 11 (☎ 95/441-71-11). Many lines also converge on Plaza de la Encarnación, on Plaza Nueva, in front of the cathedral on Avenida Constitución, and at Plaza de Armas (across the street from the old train station, Estación de Córdoba). From here, buses from several companies make frequent runs to and from Córdoba (2¹/₂ hours). For information and prices, call Alsina at 95/441-88-11.

VISITOR INFORMATION   The tourist office, **Oficina de Información del Turismo,** at Av. de la Constitución 21B (☎ **95/422-14-04**), is open Mon–Sat 9am–7pm and Sun and holidays 10am–2pm.

DEPARTING BY CAR   After Seville, the next major city of interest in Andalusia is Granada. To get there, you can drive along one of Europe's most fabled beach strips, the Costa del Sol, beginning at Marbella, the chicest enclave. Take A4 (E5) south toward Cádiz, bypassing the city by going along NIV, where you connect with N340 heading southeast. This coastal road will take you past Algeciras and Gibraltar and through the resort of Estepona until you reach Marbella.

EXPLORING SEVILLE

The largest gothic building in the world, Seville's ✪ **catedral,** Plaza del Triunfo, Avenida de la Constitución (☎ **95/421-49-71**), was designed by builders with a stated goal—that "those who come after us will take us for madmen." Construction began in the late 1400s and took centuries to complete. Built on the site of an ancient mosque, the cathedral claims to contain the remains of Columbus, with his tomb mounted on four statues.

Works of art abound, many of them architectural, such as the 15th-century stained-glass windows, the iron screens (rejas) closing off the chapels, the elaborate 15th-century choir stalls, and the gothic reredos above the main altar. Emerge into the sunlight in the Patio of Orange Trees, with its fresh citrus scents and chirping birds. Admission, including a visit to La Giralda Tower (below), is 500 ptas. ($4). The cathedral and tower are open daily 11am–5pm.

Just as Big Ben symbolizes London, ✪ **La Giralda,** Plaza del Triunfo, conjures up Seville—this Moorish tower, next to the cathedral, is the city's most famous monument. Erected as a minaret in the 12th century, it has seen later additions, such as 16th-century bells. To climb it is to take the walk of a lifetime. There are no steps—you ascend an endless ramp. If you make it to the top, you'll have a dazzling view of Seville. Entrance is through the cathedral and admission is included.

A magnificent 14th-century Mudéjar palace, the ✪ **Alcázar,** Plaza del Triunfo (☎ **95/422-71-63**), north of the cathedral, was built by Pedro the Cruel. It's the oldest royal residence in Europe still in use. From the Dolls' Court to the Maidens' Court through the domed Ambassadors' Room, it contains some of the finest work of Sevillian artisans. In many ways it evokes the Alhambra at Granada. Ferdinand and Isabella, who at one time lived in the Alcázar, welcomed Columbus here on his return from America. On the top floor, the Oratory of the Catholic Monarchs has a fine altar in polychrome tiles made by Pisano in 1504. Admission is 700 ptas. ($5.60). Open Tues–Sat 10:30am–5pm and Sun 10am–1pm.

The ✪ **Museo Provincial de Bellas Artes de Sevilla,** Plaza del Museo 9 (☎ **95/422-18-29;** bus: 21, 24, 30, or 31), a lovely old convent off Calle de Alfonso XII, houses an important Spanish art collections. A whole gallery is devoted to two paintings by El Greco, and works by Zurbarán are exhibited; however, the devoutly religious paintings of the Seville-born Murillo are the highlights. An entire wing is given over to macabre paintings by the 17th-century artist Valdés-Leál. The top floor, which displays modern paintings, is less interesting. Admission is 250 ptas. ($2), free for students. Open Tues–Sun 9am–3pm.

What was once a ghetto for Spanish Jews, who were forced out of Spain in the 15th century in the wake of the Inquisition, the ✪ **Barrio de Santa Cruz** is today Seville's most colorful district. Near the old walls of the Alcázar, winding medieval streets with names like Vida (Life) and Muerte (Death) open onto pocket-size plazas. Balconies with draping bougainvillea and potted geraniums jut out over this labyrinth, and through numerous wrought-iron gates you can glimpse patios filled with fountains and plants. To enter the Barrio Santa Cruz, turn right after leaving the Patio de Banderas exit of the Alcázar. Turn right again at Plaza de la Alianza and go down Calle Rodrigo Caro to Plaza de Doña Elvira. Use caution when strolling through the area, particularly at night; many robberies have occurred here.

The **Parque María Luisa,** dedicated to María Luisa, sister of Isabella II, was once the grounds of the Palacio de San Telmo, Avenida de Roma. Its baroque facade visible behind the deluxe Alfonso XIII Hotel, the palace today houses a seminary. The former private royal park is now open to the public. Running south along the Guadalquivir River, the park attracts those who want to take boat rides, walk along paths bordered by flowers, jog, or go bicycling. The most romantic way to traverse it is by rented horse and carriage, but this can be expensive, depending on your negotiation with the driver.

SHOPPING

Close to Seville's town hall, **Ceramics Martian,** Calle Sierpes 74 (☎ **95/421-34-13**), sells a wide array of painted tiles and ceramics, all made in or near Seville. Many of the pieces exhibit ancient geometric patterns of Andalusia. It's open Mon–Sat 10am–1:30pm and 4:30–8:30pm. Near the cathedral, **El Postigo,** Calle Arfe (☎ **95/421-39-76**), contains one of the biggest selections in town of the ceramics for which Andalusia is famous. Some of the pieces are much, much too big to fit into your suitcase; others—especially the hand-painted tiles—make charming souvenirs that can be packed with your luggage. Open Mon–Fri 10am–2pm and 5–8pm and Sat 10am–2pm.

Carmen fluttered her fan and broke hearts in ways that Andalusian maidens have done for centuries. **Casa Rubio,** Calle Sierpes 56 (☎ **95/422-68-72**), stocks a large collection of fans that range from the austere or dramatic to some of the most florid and fanciful aids to coquetry available in Spain. It's open Mon–Sat 10am–1:45pm and 5–8pm.

Artesanía Textil, Calle Sierpes 70 (☎ **95/456-28-40**), specializes in the nubbly and roughly textured textiles that reflect the earthiness of contemporary Spanish art. Weavings (some of which use linen, others the rough fibers of Spanish sheep) are the specialty here. It's open Mon–Fri 10am–2pm and 5–8pm and Sat 10am–2pm.

ACCOMMODATIONS

Very Expensive

✪ **Hotel Alfonso XIII.** San Fernando 2, 41004 Sevilla. ☎ **800/221-2340** in the U.S. and Canada or 95/422-28-50. Fax 95/421-60-33. 130 rms, 18 suites. A/C MINIBAR TV TEL. 38,000–56,000 ptas. ($304–$448) double; from 82,000 ptas. ($656) suite. AE, DC, MC, V. Parking 4,800 ptas. ($38.40).

At the southwestern corner of the gardens fronting Seville's famous Alcázar, this five-story rococo building is a legendary hotel and Seville's premier address. It reigns as a bastion of glamour. Built in the Mudéjar/Andalusian Revival style, it contains halls that glitter with hand-painted tiles, acres of marble and mahogany, antique furniture embellished with intricately embossed leather, and a floor plan and spaciousness that are nothing short of majestic. The San Fernando restaurant offers Italian/continental cuisine.

Expensive

Hotel Inglaterra. Plaza Nueva 7, 41001 Sevilla. ☎ **800/528-1234** in the U.S., or 95/422-49-70. Fax 95/456-13-36. 116 rms. A/C TV TEL. May–Mar, 17,000–22,000 ptas. ($136–$176) double. Apr, 21,000–25,000 ptas. ($168–$200) double. AE, DC, MC, V. Parking 1,500 ptas. ($12).

Opened in 1857 and since modernized into a glossy seven-story contemporary design, this eminently respectable and rather staid hotel lies a 5-minute walk southwest of the cathedral. Much of its interior is sheathed with white and gray marble, and the furnishings include ample use of Spanish leather and floral-patterned fabrics. The rooms still have old-fashioned touches of Iberian gentility. The best rooms are on the fifth floor. The sunny restaurant serves well-prepared fixed-price meals from a frequently changing international menu.

Moderate

Ⓢ **Bécquer.** Calle de los Reyes Católicos 4, 41001 Sevilla. ☎ **95/422-89-00.** Fax 95/421-44-00. 120 rms. A/C TV TEL. 11,000 ptas. ($88) double. AE, DC, MC, V. Parking 1,200 ptas. ($9.60). Bus: 21, 24, 30, or 31.

A short walk from the action of the Seville bullring (Maestranza) and only 2 blocks from the river, the Bécquer lies on a street of cafes where you can order tapas (appetizers) and drink Andalusian wine. The Museo de Bellas Artes also is nearby. The hotel occupies the site of a mansion and retains many objets d'art rescued before that building was demolished. You register in a wood-paneled lobby; rooms are all functionally furnished, well kept, and reasonably comfortable.

Hotel Doña María. Don Remondo 19, 41004 Sevilla. ☎ **95/422-49-90.** Fax 95/421-95-46. 60 rms. A/C TV TEL. Jan–Feb and July–Aug, 12,000 ptas. ($96) double. Mar–June and Sept–Dec, 16,500 ptas. ($132) double. AE, DC, MC, V. Parking 1,200 ptas. ($9.60).

Its location a few steps from the cathedral creates a dramatic view from the Doña María's rooftop terrace. Staying at this four-star four-story hotel represents a worthwhile investment, partly because of the tasteful Iberian antiques in the stone lobby and upper halls. The ornate neoclassical entry is offset with a pure-white facade and iron balconies. Amid the flowering plants on the upper floor, you'll find a pool ringed with garden-style lattices and antique wrought-iron railings. Each of the one-of-a-kind rooms is well furnished and comfortable, though some are rather small. A few have four-poster beds; others, a handful of antique reproductions.

Inexpensive

Ⓢ **Hostal Goya.** Mateus Gago 31, 41004 Sevilla. ☎ **95/421-11-70.** Fax 95/456-02-88. 20 rms, 10 with bath. May–Mar, 5,500 ptas. ($44) double without bath, 6,200 ptas. ($49.60) double with bath. Apr, 6,200 ptas. ($49.60) double without bath, 7,000 ptas. ($56) double with bath. No credit cards. Parking 1,500 ptas. ($12)

Its location in a narrow-fronted town house in the oldest part of the barrio is one of the Goya's strongest virtues. The building's gold-and-white facade, ornate iron railings, and picture-postcard demeanor are all noteworthy. The rooms are cozy and simple, without phones or TVs. Guests congregate in the marble-floored salon, where a skylight floods the couches and comfortable chairs with sun.

Residencia Murillo. Calle Lope de Rueda 7–9, 41004 Sevilla. ☎ **95/421-60-95.** Fax 95/421-96-16. 57 rms. TEL. 7,000 ptas. ($56) double; 8,500 ptas. ($68) triple. AE, DC, MC, V. Parking 1,000 ptas. ($8) nearby.

Tucked away on a narrow street in the heart of Santa Cruz, the old quarter, the Murillo (named after the artist who used to live in this district) is almost next to the Alcázar's gardens. Inside, the lounges harbor some fine architectural characteristics and antique reproductions; behind a grilled screen is a retreat for drinks. Many of the rooms we inspected were cheerless and gloomy, so have a look before checking in. Like all of Seville's hotels, the Murillo is in a noisy area.

DINING
Very Expensive
✪ **Egaña Oriza.** San Fernando 41. ☎ **95/422-72-11.** Reservations required. Main courses 2,150–3,800 ptas. ($17.20–$30.40); three-course fixed-price menu 5,000 ptas. ($40). AE, DC, MC, V. Mon–Fri 1:30–3:30pm and 9–11:30pm, Sat 9–11:30pm. (Bar, daily 9am–midnight.) Closed Aug. BASQUE/INTERNATIONAL.

In the conservatory of a restored mansion adjacent to Murillo Park is Seville's most stylish and best restaurant. It is one of the few game specialists in Andalusia—a province that's otherwise devoted to seafood. The restaurant was established by Basque-born owner/chef José Mari Egaña, who managed to combine his passion for hunting with his flair for cooking his catch. Many of the raw ingredients that go into the dishes were trapped or shot in Andalusia. Try the casserole of wild boar with cherries and raisins, quenelles of duck in a potato nest with apple purée, rice with stewed thrush, or even woodcock flamed in Spanish brandy.

Expensive
Casa Robles. Calle Alvarez Quintero 58. ☎ **95/456-32-72.** Reservations recommended. Main courses 1,200–2,200 ptas. ($9.60–$17.60); fixed-price menu 4,800–10,500 ptas. ($38.40–$84). AE, DC, MC, V. Daily 1–4:30pm and 8pm–1am. ANDALUSIAN.

This restaurant began its life as an unpretentious bar/bodega in 1954 and developed into a courteous but bustling dining hall on two floors of a building a short walk from the cathedral. Amid an all-Andalusian decor, you can enjoy such dishes as fish soup in the Andalusian style, lubina con naranjas (whitefish with Sevillana oranges), hake baked with strips of Serrano ham, and tender veal steak.

Moderate
ⓢ **Enrique Becerra.** Gamazo 2. ☎ **95/421-30-49.** Reservations recommended. Main courses 1,600–2,000 ptas. ($12.80–$16). AE, DC, MC, V. Mon–Sat 1–5pm and 8pm–midnight. ANDALUSIAN.

On our latest rounds, this restaurant off Plaza Nueva and near the cathedral provided one of our best meals. The restaurant takes its name from its owner, a smart and helpful host. A popular tapas bar and Andalusian dining spot, it offers an intimate setting and a hearty welcome. The gazpacho here is among the city's best, and the sangría is served ice cold. Specialties include hake real, sea bream Bilbaon style, and a wide range of meat and fish dishes. Many vegetarian dishes are also featured.

Inexpensive
ⓢ **Hostería del Laurel.** Plaza de los Venerables 5. ☎ **95/422-02-95.** Reservations recommended. Main courses 750–2,500 ptas. ($6–$20). AE, DC, MC, V. Daily noon–4pm and 7:30pm–midnight. ANDALUSIAN.

In one of the most charming buildings on tiny, difficult-to-find Plaza de los Venerables in the labyrinthian Barrio de Santa Cruz, this hideaway restaurant has iron-barred windows stuffed with plants. Inside, amid Andalusian tiles, beamed ceilings, and more plants, you'll enjoy good regional cooking. Many diners stop for a drink and tapas at the ground-floor bar before going into one of the dining rooms. The hostería is attached to a three-star hotel.

SEVILLE AFTER DARK

In the 1990s Seville finally got its own opera house, the **Teatro de la Maestranza,** Núñez de Balboa (☎ **95/422-65-73**), but it quickly became a premier venue for world-class operatic performances. Jazz, classical music, and even the quintessentially Spanish zarzuelas (operettas) are also performed here. The opera house can't be visited except during performances. Tickets (which vary in price, depending on the event staged) can be purchased daily 11am–2pm and 5–8pm at the box office in front of the theater.

In central Seville on the riverbank between two historic bridges, ✪ **El Patio Sevillano,** Paseo de Cristóbal Colón 11 (☎ **95/421-41-20**), is a showcase for Spanish folksong and dance, performed by exotically costumed dancers. The presentation includes a wide variety of Andalusian flamenco and songs, as well as classical pieces by composers like Falla, Albéniz, Granados, and Chueca. Mar–Oct there are three shows nightly, beginning at 7:30pm, 10pm, and 11:45pm. There are only two nightly shows Nov–Feb, beginning at 7:30 and 10pm. Admission, including one drink, is 3,500 ptas. ($28).

MARBELLA

Though it's packed with tourists, ranking just behind Torremolinos in popularity, Marbella is still the most exclusive resort along the Costa del Sol—with such bastions of posh as the Marbella Club. Despite the hordes, Marbella remains a pleasant Andalusian town at the foot of the Sierra Blanca, 50 miles east of Gibraltar and 47 miles east of Algeciras, or a distance of 373 miles south of Madrid.

Traces of the past are found in its palatial town hall, its medieval ruins, and its ancient Moorish walls. Marbella's most charming area is the **old quarter,** with narrow cobblestone streets and Arab houses, centering around Plaza de los Naranjos.

The biggest attractions in Marbella, however, are **El Fuerte** and **La Fontanilla,** the two main beaches. There are other, more secluded beaches, but you need your own transportation to get to them.

ESSENTIALS

ARRIVING   Twenty buses run between Málaga and Marbella daily, plus three buses that come in from Madrid and another three from Barcelona.

VISITOR INFORMATION   The **tourist information office** is on Glorieta de la Fontanilla (☎ **95/277-14-42**), open Apr–Oct, Mon–Fri 9:30am–9pm and Sat 10am–2pm; Nov–Mar, Mon–Fri 9:30am–8pm and Sat 10am–2pm. Another **tourist office** is on Plaza Naranjos (☎ **95/282-35-50**), keeping the same hours.

DEPARTING BY CAR   From Marbella, it's just a short drive east along E15 to Fuengirola, though traffic tends to be heavy.

ACCOMMODATIONS

Very Expensive

✪ **Marbella Club.** Bulevar Príncipe Alfonso von Hohenlohe, 29600 Marbella. ☎ **800/448-8355** in the U.S. or 95/282-22-11. Fax 95/282-98-84. 85 rms, 34 suites, 10 bungalows. A/C MINIBAR TV TEL. 25,000–55,000 ptas. ($200–$440) double; 41,000–200,000 ptas. ($328–$1,600) suite; 120,000–250,000 ptas. ($960–$2,000) bungalow. AE, DC, MC, V. Free parking.

This exclusive enclave was established in 1954, sprawling over a landscaped property that slopes from its roadside reception area down to the beach. It's composed of small, ecologically conscious clusters of garden pavilions, bungalows, and small-scale annexes (none of which is taller than two stories). The rooms have private balconies or terraces. The Marbella Club Restaurant moves from indoor shelter to an outdoor terrace according to the season. There are two pools and a beach with a lunch restaurant. Golf can be arranged nearby. Tennis courts are available within a 2-minute walk.

Expensive

✪ **Los Monteros.** Carretera de Cádiz, km 187, 29600 Marbella. ☎ **95/277-17-00.** Fax 95/282-58-46. 170 rms, 10 suites. A/C MINIBAR TV TEL. 19,600–32,000 ptas. ($156.80–$256) double; from 31,400 ptas. ($251.20) suite. Rates include breakfast. AE, DC, MC, V. Free parking.

Los Monteros, 400 yards from a beach and 4 miles east of Marbella, is one of the most tasteful resort complexes along the Costa del Sol. Between the coastal road and its own private beach, it attracts those seeking intimacy and luxury. No cavernous lounges exist here; instead, many small public rooms, Andalusian/Japanese in concept, are the style. The hotel offers various salons with open fireplaces, a library, and terraces. The guest rooms are brightly decorated, with light-colored lacquered furniture and terraces. The hotel has a bar and four restaurants on different levels that open onto flower-filled patios, gardens, and fountains. Grill El Corzo is one of the finest grill rooms along the coast. Also included are several pools, a beach club with a heated indoor pool, 10 tennis courts, and a riding club.

Moderate

Hotel El Fuerte. El Fuerte, 29600 Marbella. ☎ **95/286-15-00.** Fax 95/282-44-11. 261 rms, 2 suites. A/C MINIBAR TV TEL. 12,300–14,400 ptas. ($98.40–$115.20) double; from 30,200 ptas. ($241.60) suite. AE, DC, MC, V. Parking 650 ptas. ($5.20).

The largest and most recommendable hotel in the center of Marbella, with a balconied angular facade that's divided into two six-story towers, El Fuerte is directly on the waterfront. Built in 1957, it added a wing in 1987 and was last renovated in 1994. It caters to a sedate clientele of conservative northern Europeans and harbors a palm-fringed pool across the street from a sheltered lagoon and a wide-open beach. The hotel offers a handful of terraces, some shaded by flowering arbors.

Inexpensive

⑤ **Hostal El Castillo.** Plaza San Bernabé 2, 29600 Marbella. ☎ **95/277-17-39.** 26 rms. 3,800–4,000 ptas. ($30.40–$32) double. No credit cards.

At the foot of the castle in the narrow streets of the old town, this small hotel opens onto a minuscule triangular area used by the adjoining convent and school as a playground. There's a small, covered courtyard, and the simple second-floor rooms have only inner windows. The spartan rooms are scrubbed clean and contain white-tile baths.

DINING

Expensive

✪ **La Hacienda.** Urbanización Hacienda Las Chapas, Carretera de Cádiz, km 193. ☎ **95/283-12-67.** Reservations recommended. Main courses 2,200–3,200 ptas. ($17.60–$25.60); fixed-price menu 6,900 ptas. ($55.20). AE, DC, MC, V. Summer, daily 8:30–11:30pm; winter, Wed–Sun 1–3:30pm and 8:30–11:30pm. Closed Nov 15–Dec 20. INTERNATIONAL.

La Hacienda, a tranquil choice 8 miles east of Marbella, enjoys a reputation for serving some of the best food along the Costa del Sol. In cooler months you can dine in the rustic tavern before an open fireplace; in fair weather, meals are served on a patio partially encircled by open Romanesque arches. The chef is likely to offer foie gras with lentils, lobster croquettes (as an appetizer), and roast guinea hen with cream, minced raisins, and port. The food has a great deal of flavor, is presented with style, and is prepared with the freshest ingredients available.

Costa del Sol

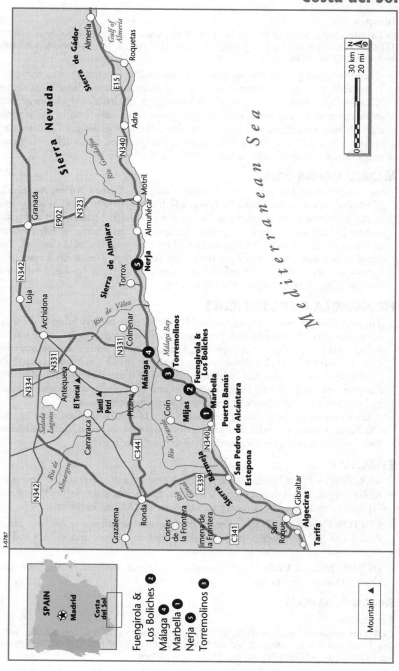

Fuengirola & Los Boliches 2
Málaga 4
Marbella 1
Nerja 5
Torremolinos 3

▲ Mountain

SPAIN
Madrid
Costa del Sol

Gulf of Almería

Mediterranean Sea

Sierra de Gádor
Sierra Nevada
Sierra de Almijara
Sierra Bermeja

Almería
Roquetas
Adra
Motril
Almuñécar
Nerja 5
Torrox
Colmenar
Torremolinos 3
Fuengirola & Los Boliches 2
Marbella 1
Puerto Banús
San Pedro de Alcántara
Estepona
Gibraltar
Algeciras
San Roque
Tarifa
Málaga 4
Málaga Bay
Mijas
Coín
Santi Petri
El Torcal ▲
Antequera
Pizarra
Carratraca
Salada Lagoon
Ronda
Grazalema
Cortes de la Frontera
Jimena de la Frontera
Granada
Loja
Archidona

Río Guadalfeo
Río de Vélez
Río Grande
Río Genal
Río de Almargen

E15
N340
E902
N342
N323
N331
N334
N340
C344
C339
C341
C339

3-0787

Inexpensive

⑤ La Tricyclette. Buitrago 14. ☎ **95/277-78-00.** Main courses 800–2,200 ptas. ($6.40–$17.60); fixed-price menu (Oct–May only) 1,800 ptas. ($14.40). AE, MC, V. Wed–Mon 7:30pm–midnight. INTERNATIONAL.

One of the more popular dining spots in Marbella, this restaurant is in a converted 18th-century home—courtyard and all—on a narrow street near Plaza de los Naranjos. Sofas in the bar area provide a living-room ambience, and a stairway leads to an intimate dining room with an open patio that's delightful in the warmer months. Start with crêpes with a soft cream-cheese filling or grilled giant prawns, then move on to a delectable main dish like roast duck in beer, filet steak with green-pepper sauce, or calves' liver cooked in sage and white wine.

MARBELLA AFTER DARK

Six miles west of Marbella, near Puerto Banús, the **Casino Nueva Andalucía Marbella,** Urbanización Nueva Andalucía (☎ **95/281-40-00**), is on the lobby level of the Andalucía Plaza Hotel. Gambling includes individual games such as French and American roulette, blackjack, punto y banco, craps, and chemin de fer. Entrance to the casino is 600 ptas. ($4.80), and you'll have to present a valid passport. You can dine before or after gambling in the Casino Restaurant. The casino is open daily 8pm–4 or 5am. La Caseta Bar offers flamenco shows at 11pm Fri–Sat. Entrance is free but drinks cost 1,800 ptas. ($14.40) and up.

FUENGIROLA & LOS BOLICHES

The twin fishing towns of Fuengirola and Los Boliches lie halfway between the more famous resorts of Marbella and Torremolinos. The distance is 20 miles west of Málaga and 64¹/₂ miles east of Algeciras. The promenade along the water stretches some 2¹/₂ miles with the less developed Los Boliches just half a mile from Fuengirola.

The towns don't have the facilities or drama of Torremolinos and Marbella. Except for two major luxury hotels, Fuengirola and Los Boliches are cheaper, though, and that has attracted a horde of budget-conscious European tourists.

On a promontory overlooking the sea, the ruins of **San Isidro Castle** can be seen. The **Santa Amalja, Carvajal,** and **Las Gaviotas beaches** are broad, clean, and sandy. Everybody goes to the big **flea market** at Fuengirola on Tuesday.

ESSENTIALS

ARRIVING From Torremolinos, take the Metro at La Nogalera station (under the RENFE sign). Trains depart every 30 minutes. Fuengirola is also on the main Costa del Sol bus route from both Algeciras in the west and Málaga in the east.

VISITOR INFORMATION The **tourist information office** is at Av. Jesús Santos Rein 6 (☎ **95/246-74-57**), open Mon–Fri 9:30am–1:30pm and 4–7pm and Sat 10am–1pm.

DEPARTING BY CAR From Fuengirola, continue northeast on the brief drive along E15 into Torremolinos.

ACCOMMODATIONS

Expensive

✪ Byblos Andaluz. Urbanización Mijas Golf, 29640 Fuengirola. ☎ **95/246-02-50.** Fax 95/247-67-83. 144 rms, 37 suites. A/C MINIBAR TV TEL. 25,000–33,500 ptas. ($200–$268) double; from 47,000 ptas. ($376) suite. AE, DC, MC, V. Free parking.

This luxurious resort is in a golf club setting 3 miles from Fuengirola and 6 miles from the beach. The grounds contain a white minaret, Moorish arches, tile-adorned walls, and an orange-tree patio inspired by the Alhambra grounds. Two 18-hole golf courses designed by Robert Trent Jones, tennis courts, spa facilities, a gym, and pools bask in the Andalusian sunshine. The health spa is in a handsome classic structure, Mijas Thalasso Palace. The rooms and suites are elegantly and individually designed and furnished in Roman, Arabic, Andalusian, and rustic styles. Private sun terraces and lavish baths add to the comfort. The dining choices include Le Nailhac, with French gastronomic offerings.

Las Pirámides. Paseo Marítimo, 29640 Fuengirola. ☎ **95/247-06-00.** Fax 95/258-32-97. 280 rms, 40 suites. A/C MINIBAR TV TEL. 13,000–17,500 ptas. ($104–$140) double; 16,000–18,500 ptas. ($128–$148) suite. Rates include breakfast. AE, MC, V. Parking 1,000 ptas. ($8).

This resort, much favored by travel groups from northern Europe, is divided into two 10-story towers capped with pyramid-shaped roofs, from which the complex takes its name. It's a citylike compound, about 50 yards from the beach, with seemingly every kind of divertissement: flamenco shows on the large patio, a cozy bar and lounge, traditionally furnished sitting rooms, a coffee shop, a poolside bar, and a gallery of boutiques and tourist facilities, such as car-rental agencies. All the rooms have slick modern styling, as well as terraces.

DINING
Moderate
Casa Vieja. Av. de Los Boliches 27, Los Boliches. ☎ **95/258-38-30.** Reservations recommended. Main courses 1,275–2,100 ptas. ($10.20–$16.80) at dinner; fixed-price three-course lunch (Sat–Sun only) 1,500 ptas. ($12). AE, MC, V. Tues–Fri 7:30–11pm, Sat–Sun 12:30–3pm and 7:30–11pm. FRENCH.

Within the thick stone walls of a cottage that was built in the 1870s for a local fisherman, this restaurant lies on the main street of Los Boliches. A flowering patio is available for outdoor dining. Menu items include a subtly flavored terrine of oxtail, fresh vegetable soup, king prawns, tournedos with béarnaise sauce, gratin of sole in puff pastry, and guinea fowl with cumin and honey-glazed turnips.

TORREMOLINOS
This Mediterranean beach resort, 9 miles west of Málaga and 76 miles east of Algeciras, is the most famous in Spain. It's a gathering place for international visitors, a melting pot of Europeans and Americans. Many relax here after a whirlwind tour of Europe—the living's easy, the people are fun, and there are no historic monuments to visit. Thus the sleepy fishing village of Torremolinos has been engulfed in a cluster of concrete-walled resort hotels. Prices are on the rise, but it nevertheless remains one of Europe's vacation bargains. The sands along the beachfront tend to be gritlike and grayish. The best beaches are **El Bajondillo** and **La Carihuela,** the latter bordering an old fishing village. All beaches here are public, but don't expect changing facilities. Although it's technically not allowed, many women go topless on the beaches.

ESSENTIALS
ARRIVING Torremolinos is served by the nearby Málaga airport. There are also frequent rail departures from the terminal at Málaga; for information, call 95/236-02-02. Buses run frequently between Málaga and Torremolinos; for information, call 95/238-24-19.

VISITOR INFORMATION The **tourist information office,** at La Nogalera 517 (☎ **95/238-01-66**), is open daily 8am–3pm.

DEPARTING BY CAR From Torremolinos, continue east along E15 for 7 miles into Málaga.

ACCOMMODATIONS

Expensive

Aloha Puerto Sol. Calle Salvador Allende 45, 29620 Torremolinos. ☎ **800/336-3542** in the U.S. or 95/238-70-66. Fax 95/238-57-01. 430 rms. A/C MINIBAR TV TEL. 11,500–17,690 ptas. ($92–$141.50) double. Rates include buffet breakfast. AE, DC, MC, V.

Heralded as one of the most modern hotels along the Costa del Sol when it was built in 1972, this now-aging hotel stands on the seashore in the suburb of El Saltillo, on the southwestern edge of Torremolinos, beside the coastal road leading to Marbella. It offers spacious rooms, each of which is defined by the hotel as a mini-suite. Each faces the sea, the Benalmádena marina, or the beach, and each contains a separate sitting area. Amid all the accessories of a resort, guests are given a choice of two restaurants and four bars. Many guests spend their days near the two pools, one of which is heated.

Don Pablo. Paseo Marítimo, 29620 Torremolinos. ☎ **95/238-38-88.** Fax 95/238-37-83. 443 rms. A/C MINIBAR TV TEL. 14,980–19,474 ptas. ($119.85–$155.80) double. Rates include buffet breakfast. AE, DC, MC, V.

One of the most desirable hotels in Torremolinos is in a modern building a minute from the beach, surrounded by its own garden and playground areas. There are two unusually shaped open-air pools, with terraces for sunbathing and refreshments, plus a large indoor pool. The surprise is the glamorous interior, which borrows heavily from Moorish palaces and medieval castle themes. The comfortably furnished rooms have sea-view terraces. The hotel has a full day-and-night entertainment program, including dancing at night to a live band.

Moderate

Hotel Las Palomas. Carmen Montes 1, 29620 Torremolinos. ☎ **95/238-50-00.** Fax 95/238-64-66. 345 rms. TEL. 6,510–13,178 ptas. ($52.10–$105.40) double. AE, DC, MC, V.

Built during Torremolinos's construction boom (1968), this well-managed hotel is one of the town's most attractive, surrounded by gardens. A 1-minute walk from the beach and a 10-minute walk south of the center of town, it has an Andalusian decor that extends into the rooms, a formal entrance, and a clientele of repeat visitors. Each room has a private balcony, a tiled bath, and furniture inspired by southern Spain. None is air-conditioned, though many guests compensate by opening windows and balcony doors to catch the sea breezes. Three pools are on site.

DINING

Moderate

ⓢ Casa Prudencio. Carmen 41, at La Carihuela. ☎ **95/238-14-52.** Reservations recommended. Main courses 950–1,800 ptas. ($7.60–$14.40); fixed-price menu 1,200 ptas. ($9.60). AE, MC, V. Daily 12:30–4:30pm and 7:30pm–midnight. Closed Dec 25–Feb 15. SEAFOOD.

Tops with locals and visitors alike, this seaside restaurant just over a mile west of the center is the oldest surviving restaurant in the fishing hamlet of Carihuela. If you want to splurge, order lubina à la sal—a huge boneless fish packed under a layer of salt, which is then broken open at your table. It makes a singular gastronomical treat. It also features gazpacho, lentils, shrimp omelets, swordfish, and shish kebab. Try the special paella for a main course, followed by strawberries with whipped cream (in late spring) for dessert. The atmosphere is cordial, and almost everyone sits together at long tables.

Ⓢ **El Gato Viudo.** La Nogalera 8. ☎ **95/238-51-29.** Main courses 700–1,850 ptas. ($5.60–$14.80). AE, DC, MC, V. Thurs–Tues 1–4pm and 6–11:30pm. SPANISH.

Simple and amiable, this old-fashioned tavern occupies the street level and cellar of a building off Calle San Miguel. It offers sidewalk seating for those who prefer it, and a tradition with local diners that dates back to its founding in 1960. The menu includes such good dishes as grilled fish; marinated hake; roasted pork, steak, and veal; calamari with spicy tomato sauce; grilled shrimp; and shellfish or fish soup. The atmosphere is informal.

TORREMOLINOS AFTER DARK

One of the major casinos along the Costa del Sol, the **Casino Torrequebrada,** Carretera de Cádiz 266, Benalmádena Costa (☎ **95/244-25-45**), is on the lobby level of the Hotel Torrequebrada. The Torrequebrada combines a nightclub/cabaret, a restaurant, and an array of tables devoted to blackjack, chemin de fer, punto y banco, and two kinds of roulette. Year-round, the nightclub offers a flamenco show presented at 11pm Thurs–Sat; in midsummer, there might be more glitz and more frequent shows (ask when you get there or call). The casino is open daily 8am–4am and the entrance fee is 600 ptas. ($4.80). Nightclub acts begin at 10:30pm (Spanish revue) and 11:30pm (Las Vegas revue); entrance is 3,800 ptas. ($30.40), which includes two drinks, admission to both shows, and admission to the casino. The restaurant is open nightly 8:30–11pm.

MÁLAGA

Málaga, 82 miles east of Algeciras, is a bustling commercial and residential center whose economy doesn't depend exclusively on tourism. Its chief attraction is the mild off-season climate—summer can be sticky. Málaga's most famous citizen is Pablo Picasso, born in 1881 at Plaza de la Merced, in the center of the city. The co-founder of cubism, who would one day paint his *Guernica* to express his horror of war, unfortunately left little of his spirit in his birthplace and only a small selection of his work.

ESSENTIALS

ARRIVING Iberia, the national airline of Spain, has frequent flights into Málaga from Madrid. To make reservations, call 800/772-4642 in the U.S. Málaga maintains good rail connections with Madrid (at least five trains a day); the trip takes around 4 hours. For rail information in Málaga, call RENFE at 95/221-31-22. Buses from all over Spain arrive at the terminal on Paseo de los Tilos, behind the RENFE office. Málaga is linked by bus to all the major cities of Spain, including Madrid (seven buses per day) and Barcelona (four per day). Trip time from Madrid is 7 hours. Call 95/235-00-61 in Málaga for bus information.

VISITOR INFORMATION The **tourist information office** is at Pasaje de Chinitas 4 (☎ **95/221-34-45**), open Mon–Fri 9am–1pm.

DEPARTING BY CAR From Málaga, N340, a curving, winding road, heads east to Nerja.

EXPLORING MÁLAGA

The remains of the ancient Moorish **Alcazaba,** Plaza de la Aduana, Alcazabilla (☎ **95/221-60-05;** bus: 4, 18, 19, or 24), are within easy walking distance of the city center, off Paseo del Parque (plenty of signs point the way up the hill). The fortress was erected in the 9th or 10th century, though there have been later additions and reconstructions. Ferdinand and Isabella stayed here when they reconquered the city. The Alcazaba now houses an archeological museum, with exhibits of cultures ranging from Greek to Phoenician to Carthaginian. Admission to the museum is 30 ptas. (25¢). The museum is open Apr–Sept, Tues–Fri 9:30am–1:30pm and 5–8pm, Sat 10am–1pm, and Sun 10am–2pm; Oct–Mar, Tues–Fri 9:30am–1:30pm and 4–7pm, Sat 10am–1pm, and Sun 10am–2pm.

The 16th-century Renaissance **cathedral,** Plaza Obispo (☎ **95/221-59-17;** bus: 14, 18, 19, or 24), in Málaga's center, was built on the site of a great mosque and suffered damage during the Civil War. But it remains vast and impressive, reflecting changing styles of interior architecture. Its most notable attributes are the richly ornamented choir stalls by Ortiz, Mena, and Michael. The cathedral has been declared a national monument. Admission is 200 ptas. ($1.60). It's open Mon–Sat 10am–12:45pm and 4–6:30pm; closed holidays.

ACCOMMODATIONS

Expensive

Parador de Málaga-Gibralfaro. Monte Gibralfaro, 29016 Málaga. ☎ **95/222-19-02.** Fax 95/222-19-04. 38 rms. A/C MINIBAR TV TEL. 15,000–24,000 ptas. ($120–$192) double. AE, DC, MC, V. Free parking.

Restored in 1994, this is one of Spain's oldest, more tradition-laden paradors. It enjoys a scenic location on a plateau near an old fortified castle, overlooking the city and the Mediterranean, with views of the bullring, mountains, and beaches. Originally a famous restaurant, the parador has been converted into a fine hotel with two dining rooms. The guest rooms, with their own entrances, have living-room areas and wide glass doors opening onto private sun terraces with garden furniture. They're tastefully decorated with modern furnishings and reproductions of Spanish antiques.

Parador Nacional del Golf. Carretera de Málaga, Torremolinos, 29080 Apartado 324, Málaga. ☎ **95/238-12-55.** Fax 95/238-09-63. 60 rms. A/C MINIBAR TV TEL. 12,000–15,000 ptas. ($96–$120) double. AE, DC, MC, V. Parking 2,400 ptas. ($19.20).

A resort hotel created by the Spanish government, this hacienda-style parador is flanked by a golf course on one side and the Mediterranean on another. It's less than 2 miles from the airport, 6¹/₂ miles from Málaga, and 2¹/₂ miles from Torremolinos. Each room has a balcony with a view of the golfing greens, the circular pool, or the water; some rooms are equipped with Jacuzzis. Long tile corridors lead to the air-conditioned public rooms—graciously furnished lounges and a restaurant.

DINING

Moderate

Café de Paris. Vélez Málaga 8. ☎ **95/222-50-43.** Reservations required. Main courses 1,800–2,500 ptas. ($14.40–$20); *menú del día* 2,500 ptas. ($20). AE, DC, MC, V. Mon–Sat 1–4pm and 8:30pm–midnight. Closed July 1–15. Bus: 13. FRENCH/SPANISH.

Málaga's best restaurant is in La Malagueta, the district surrounding the Plaza de Toros (bullring). This is the domain of proprietor/chef de cuisine José García Cortés, who has worked at many important dining rooms before carving out his own niche. Some critics have said that the cuisine is pitched too high for the taste (and budget) of the average Malagueño—particularly when it comes to caviar, game (including partridge), and foie gras, which are often featured. Much of the Cortés's cuisine has been adapted from classic French dishes to please the Andalusian palate. Menus are changed frequently, reflecting both the chef's imagination and the availability of produce. You might be served crêpes gratinées (filled with baby eels) or local white fish baked in salt (it doesn't sound good but is excellent). Meat Stroganoff is made here not with the usual cuts of beef but with ox meat.

NERJA

Nerja, 32 miles east of Málaga, is known for its good beaches and small coves, its seclusion, its narrow streets and courtyards, and its whitewashed, flat-roofed houses. Nearby is one of Spain's greatest attractions, the Cave of Nerja (below).

At the mouth of the Chillar River, Nerja gets its name from an Arabic word, *narixa,* meaning "bountiful spring." Its most dramatic spot is the **Balcón de Europa,** a palm-shaded promenade that juts out into the Mediterranean. The sea-bordering walkway was built in 1885 in honor of a visit from the Spanish king Alfonso XIII in the wake of an earthquake that had shattered part of nearby Málaga. The phrase "Balcón de Europa" is said to have been coined by the king during one of the speeches he made in Nerja praising the beauty of the panoramas around him. To reach the best beaches, head west from the Balcón and follow the shoreline.

ESSENTIALS

ARRIVING   Nerja is well serviced by buses from Málaga—at least 10 per day make the 1¹/₂-hour trip.

VISITOR INFORMATION   The **tourist information office** is at Puerta del Mar 2 (☎ 95/252-15-31), open Mon–Fri 10am–2pm and 5–7:30pm and Sat 10am–1pm.

DEPARTING BY CAR   From Nerja, E15 continues east to the little city of Motril, where you can connect with E902 heading north to Granada.

EXPLORING THE CAVE

The most popular outing from either Málaga or Nerja is to the ✪ **Cueva de Nerja** (Cave of Nerja), Carretera de Maro (☎ 95/252-95-20), which scientists believe was inhabited from 25,000 to 2,000 B.C. This prehistoric stalactite and stalagmite cave lay undiscovered until 1959, when it was found by chance by a handful of boys. When fully opened, it revealed a wealth of treasures left from the days of the cave dwellers, including Paleolithic paintings. These depict horses and deer, but as of this writing they're not open to public viewing. The archeological museum in the cave contains a number of prehistoric artifacts. You can walk through its stupendous galleries, where the ceiling soars to a height of 200 feet.

The cave is open daily 10:30am–2pm and 3:30–6pm. Admission is 500 ptas. ($4) for adults, 300 ptas. ($2.40) for children 6–12, and free for children 5 and under. Nerja Cave–bound buses leave hourly 7am–8:15pm from Muelle de Heredia in Málaga. Return buses are also hourly to 8:15pm. The journey takes about 1 hour.

ACCOMMODATIONS

Expensive

✪ **Parador Nacional de Nerja.** Calle Almuñecar 8, Playa de Burriana-Tablazo, 29780 Nerja. ☎ **95/252-00-50.** Fax 95/252-19-97. 73 rms. A/C MINIBAR TV TEL. 14,000–16,550 ptas. ($112–$132.40) double. AE, DC, MC, V. Free parking.

On the outskirts, a 5-minute walk from the center of town, this government-owned hotel takes the best of modern motel designs and blends them with a classic Spanish ambience of beamed ceilings, tile floors, and hand-loomed draperies. It's built on the edge of a cliff, around a flower-filled courtyard with a splashing fountain, and its social life centers around the large pool and tennis courts. There's a sandy beach below, reached by an elevator, plus lawns and gardens. The rooms are spacious and furnished in an understated but tasteful style. International and Spanish meals are served in the hotel restaurant.

DINING

Moderate

🟢 **Restaurant Rey Alfonso.** Paseo Balcón de Europa. ☎ **95/252-09-58.** Reservations recommended. Main courses 750–1,900 ptas. ($6–$15.20); fixed-price menu 1,000 ptas. ($8). MC, V. Thurs–Tues 11am–4pm and 7–11pm. Closed Nov. SPANISH/INTERNATIONAL.

Few visitors to the Balcón de Europa realize they're standing directly above one of the most unusual restaurants in town. You enter from the bottom of a flight of stairs that skirts the rocky base of what was designed in the late 19th century as a *miradore* (viewing station), which juts seaward as an extension of the town's main square. The restaurant's menu and interior decor don't hold many surprises, but the close-up view of the crashing waves makes dining here worthwhile. Specialties include a well-prepared paella valenciana, Cuban-style rice, five preparations of sole (from grilled to meunière), and crayfish in whisky sauce.

GRANADA

Granada, 76 miles norhteast of Málaga, is 2,200 feet above sea level. It sprawls over two main hills, the Alhambra and the Albaicín, and it's crossed by two rivers, the Genil and the Darro. The **Cuesta de Gomérez** is one of the most important streets in Granada. It climbs uphill from Plaza Nueva, the center of the modern city, to the Alhambra, Spain's major tourist attraction. This former stronghold of Moorish Spain, in the foothills of the snowcapped Sierra Nevada range, is full of romance and folk-lore. Washington Irving (*Tales of the Alhambra*) used the symbol of this city, the pomegranate (*granada*), to conjure up a spirit of romance.

ESSENTIALS

ARRIVING   Iberia flies to Granada once or twice daily from Barcelona and Madrid. Granada's **airport** (☎ 958/22-75-92 for information) lies 10 miles west of the center of town. A convenient **Iberia** ticketing office is 2 blocks east of the cathedral, at Plaza Isabel la Católica 2 (☎ 958/22-75-92). A shuttle bus departs several times daily, connecting this office with the airport.

Two trains connect Granada with Madrid's Atocha Railway Station daily (taking 6–8 hours). Many connections to the rest of Spain are funneled through the rail junction at Bobadilla, a 2-hour ride to the west. The **train station** is on Calle Dr. Jaime García Royo (☎ 958/27-12-72), at the end of Avenida Andaluces.

Most of Granada's long-distance buses arrive and depart from the **Baccona Company bus terminal,** Av. Andaluces 12 (☎ 958/28-42-51). Buses arrive from Madrid four times a day. Buses from closer destinations in Andalusia arrive at the **Alsina Graells Company bus terminal,** Camino de Ronda 97 (☎ 958/25-13-58), a small street radiating out from the larger Calle Emperatriz Eugenia. Buses arrive from Málaga about a dozen times a day, and from Seville about eight times a day.

VISITOR INFORMATION   The **tourist information office** is at Plaza de Mariana Pineda 10 (☎ 958/22-66-88), open Mon–Fri 9am–7pm and Sat. 10am–2pm.

EXPLORING GRANADA

The last remaining fortress-palace in Spain, built for the conquering caliphs of old, the ✪ **Alhambra,** Palacio de Carlos V (☎ 958/22-75-27), is a once-royal city surrounded by walls—actually a series of three palaces leading from one to the other as if part of a whole. Enter a world of *The Arabian Nights* where sultans of old conducted state business, raised their families, and were entertained by their harems.

You may be surprised by its somewhat somber exterior. You have to walk across the threshold to discover the true delights of this Moorish palace. The most-photographed part is the Court of Lions, named after its highly stylized fountain. This was the heart of the palace, the most private section. Opening onto the court are the Hall of the Two Sisters, where the "favorite" of the moment was kept, and the Gossip Room, a factory of intrigue. In the dancing room in the Hall of Kings, entertainment was provided nightly to amuse the sultan's party.

You can see the room where Washington Irving lived (in the chambers of Charles V) while he was compiling his *Tales of the Alhambra.*

Charles V may have been horrified when he saw the cathedral placed in the middle of the great mosque at Córdoba, but he's responsible for architectural meddling here, building a Renaissance palace at the Alhambra—though it's quite beautiful, it's terribly out of place. Today it houses the **Museo de las Bellas Artes en la Alhambra** (☎ **958/22-48-43**), open Mon–Sat 9am–1pm. It also shelters the **Museo Hispano-Musulman en la Alhambra** (☎ **958/22-62-79**), devoted to Hispanic-Muslim art and open Mon–Sat 9am–7:45pm.

A comprehensive ticket, including the Alhambra and the Generalife (below), is 675 ptas. ($5.40); admission to the Museo de las Bellas Artes is 200 ptas. ($1.60) and to the Museo Hispano-Musulman is 200 ptas. ($1.60). Illuminated visits are 675 ptas. ($5.40). The Alhambra is open daily: Mar–Oct 9am–7:45pm (floodlit visits daily 10pm–midnight) and Nov–Feb 9am–6pm (floodlit visits daily 8–10pm).

The sultans used to spend their summers in the ✪ **Generalife,** Alhambra, Cerro de Sol (☎ **958/22-75-27**), safely locked away with their harems. Built in the 13th century to overlook the Alhambra, the Generalife depends for its glory on its gardens and courtyards. Don't expect an Alhambra in miniature: The Generalife was always meant to be a retreat, even from the splendors of the Alhambra. For admission prices and hours, see above.

The richly ornate Spanish Renaissance ✪ **catedral,** Plaza de la Lonja, Gran Vía de Colón 5 (☎ **958/22-29-59**), with its spectacular altar, is one of the country's great architectural highlights, acclaimed for its beautiful facade and gold-and-white decor. It was begun in 1521 and completed in 1714. Behind the cathedral (entered separately) is the Flamboyant Gothic **Royal Chapel** (☎ **958/22-92-39**), where lie the remains of Isabella and Ferdinand. It was their wish to be buried in recaptured Granada, not Castile or Aragón. The coffins are remarkably tiny—a reminder of how short they must have been. Accenting the tombs is a wrought-iron grill, a masterpiece. Occupying much larger tombs are the remains of their daughter, Joanna the Mad, and her husband, Philip the Handsome. The Capilla Real abuts the cathedral's eastern edge. Admission to the cathedral is 200 ptas. ($1.60); admission to the chapel, 200 ptas. ($1.60). The cathedral and chapel are open daily 10:30am–1:30pm and 4–7pm (to 6pm in winter).

The **Albaicín,** the old Arab quarter, on one of the two main hills of Granada, doesn't belong to the city of 19th-century buildings and wide boulevards. It, and the surrounding Gypsy caves of Sacromonte, are holdovers from the past. The Albaicín once flourished as the residential section of the Moors, even after the city's reconquest, but it fell into decline when the Christians drove them out. This narrow labyrinth of crooked streets escaped the fate of much of Granada, which was torn down in the name of progress. Fortunately, it has been preserved, as have its plazas, whitewashed houses, villas, and the decaying remnants of the old city gate. Here and there you can catch a glimpse of a private patio filled with fountains and plants, a traditional elegant way of life that continues. Take bus no. 7 to Calle de Pagés.

SHOPPING

The **Alcaicería**, once the Moorish silk market, is next to the cathedral in the lower city. The narrow streets of this rebuilt village of shops are filled with vendors selling the arts and crafts of the province. The Alcaicería offers you one of Spain's most splendid assortments of tiles, castanets, and wire figures of Don Quixote chasing windmills. The jewelry found here compares favorably with the finest Toledan work. For the window shopper, in particular, it makes a pleasant stroll.

Artesanía Albaicín (Tienda Eduardo Ferrer Lucena), Calle del Agua 19 (☎ 958/27-90-56), is one of the Arab Quarter's most enduring repositories of the intricately tooled leather for which Andalusia is famous. Open daily 11am–3:30pm and 5–9:30pm.

In the Albaicín, the former Arab quarter, **Céramica Aliatar,** Plaza de Aliatar 18 (☎ 958/27-80-89), was opened in the early 1980s and ever since has been loaded with a winning assortment of Andalusian ceramics. The inventory includes water and wine pitchers, serving platters, dinner plates, and pots for the garden that are charming. Open Mon–Fri 9am–2pm and 5–8pm.

ACCOMMODATIONS

Very Expensive

✪ **Parador Nacional de San Francisco.** Alhambra, 18009 Granada. ☎ **800/343-0020** in the U.S., or 958/22-14-40. Fax 958/22-22-64. 36 rms. A/C MINIBAR TV TEL. 28,000 ptas. ($224) double. AE, DC, MC, V.

Spain's most famous parador (and the hardest to get in) is housed in an old brick building with a new annex, set on the grounds of the Alhambra. The decor is tasteful and the place evokes a lot of history and a rich Andalusian ambience. The parador itself is a former convent founded by the Catholic monarchs immediately after they conquered the city in 1492. One side of the parador opens onto its own lovely gardens and the other fronts the Alhambra. From its terrace you'll have views of the Generalife gardens and the Sacromonte caves. The rooms, generally spacious and comfortable, received their last renovation in 1992.

Expensive

Hotel Alhambra Palace. Peña Partida 2. 18009 Granada. ☎ **958/22-14-68.** Fax 958/22-64-04. 121 rms, 11 suites. A/C MINIBAR TV TEL. 18,500 ptas. ($148) double; 27,500 ptas. ($220) suite. AE, DC, MC, V. Free parking. Bus: 2.

Evoking a Moorish fortress, complete with a crenellated roofline, a crowning dome, geometric tilework, and a suggestion of a minaret, this is Granada's best known and most evocative hotel. It was built in 1910 in a sort of Mudéjar Revival style in a shady, secluded spot, midway up the slope to the Alhambra. The guest rooms don't live up to the drama of the public areas, including an *Arabian Nights* dining room and a glassed-in dining terrace. Try for a room with a balcony opening onto that view. The court rooms are less desirable because they lack double glazing and are subject to noise at night. Many rooms are spacious and comfortable, whereas others are small and need some restoration.

Moderate

Hotel Rallye. Camino de Ronda 107, 18003 Granada. ☎ **958/27-28-00.** Fax 958/27-28-62. 79 rms. A/C MINIBAR TV TEL. 14,900 ptas. ($119.20) double. AE, DC, MC, V. Parking 1,100 ptas. ($8.80). Bus: 1 or 5.

Some locals designate this as one of the best hotels in town, and a relatively good value for the price. Built as a three-star hotel in 1964, it was thoroughly upgraded into a four-star format in 1990 and today rises five light-green stories. It's a 15-minute walk from the cathedral, on the northern perimeter of Granada's urban center. The rooms are comfortable and well maintained. The in-house restaurant, the Rallye, serves very good meals.

Inexpensive

⑤ Hotel América. Real de la Alhambra 53, 18009 Granada. ☎ **958/22-74-71.** Fax 958/ 22-74-70. 13 rms, 1 suite. TEL. 10,000 ptas. ($80) double; 13,000 ptas. ($104) suite. AE, DC, MC, V. Closed Nov–Feb. Bus: 2.

Within the ancient Alhambra walls, this is one of Granada's small hotels. Walk through the covered entry of this former villa into the shady patio that's lively yet intimate, with large trees, potted plants, and ferns. Other plants cascade down the white plaster walls and entwine with the ornate grillwork. Garden chairs and tables are set out for home-cooked Spanish meals. The living room of this homey retreat is graced with a collection of regional decorative objects; some of the rooms have Andalusian reproductions.

Hotel Residencia Cóndor. Constitución 6, 18012 Granada. ☎ **958/28-37-11.** Fax 958/ 28-38-50. 104 rms. A/C TV TEL. 9,800 ptas. ($78.40) double. AE, DC, MC, V. Parking 1,200 ptas. ($9.60). Bus: 6, 8, 9, or 10.

The attractive 1987 design of this hotel helps make it one of Granada's best in its price range. It's in the center of town, a 5-minute walk from the Alhambra and the cathedral. Many of the pleasant rooms have terraces, and all have light-grained contemporary furniture. The hotel's restaurant serves both Spanish and international cuisine, and there's also a cafeteria for snacks. Room service is 24 hours a day.

DINING

Expensive

Cunini. Plaza de la Pescadería 14. ☎ **958/25-07-77.** Reservations recommended. Main courses 2,200–5,500 ptas. ($17.60–$44); fixed-price menu 5,000 ptas. ($40). AE, DC, MC, V. Tues–Sun noon–4pm and 8pm–midnight. SEAFOOD.

The array of seafood specialties offered here, perhaps a hundred selections, extends even to the tapas served at the long, stand-up bar. After a drink or two, patrons move on to the paneled ground-floor restaurant, where the cuisine reflects the whole of Spain. Meals often begin with soup, such as sopa Cunini or sopa sevillana (with ham, shrimp, and whitefish). Also popular is a deep fry of small fish called a fritura Cunini; other specialties are rice with seafood, zarzuela, smoked salmon, and grilled shrimp. Plaza de la Pescadería is adjacent to the Gran Vía de Colón, just below the cathedral.

✪ Ruta del Valleta. Carretera de la Sierra Nevada, km 5.5, Cenés de la Vega. ☎ **958/ 48-61-34.** Reservations recommended. Main courses 2,500–3,200 ptas. ($20–$25.60); fixed-price menu 4,500–5,000 ptas. ($36–$40). AE, DC, MC, V. Mon–Sat 1–4:30pm and 8pm– midnight, Sun 1–4:30pm. ANDALUSIAN/INTERNATIONAL.

Despite its origins in 1976 as an unpretentious roadhouse restaurant, this place rapidly evolved into what's usually acclaimed as the best restaurant in or around Granada. It's in the hamlet of Cenés de la Vega, about 3 1/2 miles northwest of Granada's center, and contains six dining rooms of various sizes, all decorated with a well-planned mix of English and Andalusian furniture and accessories. Menu items change with the seasons but are likely to include roast suckling pig, roasted game birds such as pheasant and partridge (often served with Rioja wine sauce), and preparations of fish and shellfish.

Moderate

Restaurante Sevilla. Calle Oficios 12. ☎ **958/22-12-23.** Reservations recommended. Main courses 900–3,000 ptas. ($7.20–$24); fixed-price menu 1,950 ptas. ($15.60). AE, DC, MC, V. Mon–Sat 1–4pm and 8–11pm, Sun 1–4pm. SPANISH/ANDALUSIAN.

Attracting a mixed crowd of all ages, the Sevilla was the favorite restaurant of such hometown boys as García Lorca and Manuel de Falla. Our most recent meal included gazpacho, Andalusian veal, and dessert (selections included caramel custard and fresh fruit). To break the gazpacho monotony, try sopa virule, made with pine nuts and chicken breasts. For a main course, we recommend the cordero à la pastoril (lamb with herbs and paprika). The best dessert is bananas flambé. You can dine inside, where it's pleasantly decorated, or on the terrace.

GRANADA AFTER DARK

The **Gypsy Caves of Sacromonte** are a tourist trap, one of the most obviously commercial and shadowy rackets in Spain. Yet visitors seem to flock to them in spite of the warnings. It's best to go on an organized tour. A visit to the caves is almost always included as part of the morning and (more frequently) afternoon city tours offered every day by such companies as **Grana Vision** (☎ **958/13-58-04**). Night tours of the caves (when they're at their most eerie, evocative, and, unfortunately, larcenous) are usually offered only to those who can assemble 10 or more people into a group. Before agreeing to a tour, negotiate the price carefully.

The best flamenco show in Granada is staged not at the caves but at **Jardines Neptuno,** Calle Arabial (☎ 958/25-11-12), nightly at 10:15pm. The acts are a bit racy, though they've been toned down. In addition to flamenco, performers attired in regional garb perform folk dances and present guitar concerts. The show takes place in a garden setting. There's a high cover charge of 3,300 ptas. ($26.40), including your first drink. It's best to take a taxi here.

Sweden | 17

by Darwin Porter & Danforth Prince

Although it was founded seven centuries ago, Stockholm didn't become Sweden's capital until the mid–17th century. Today it's the capital of a modern welfare state with a strong focus on leisure activities and access to nature only a few minutes away.

Stockholm & Environs

Stockholm (pop. 1.4 million) is built on 14 islands in Lake Mälaren, marking the beginning of an archipelago of 24,000 islands, skerries, and islets that stretches all the way to the Baltic Sea. It's a city of bridges and islands, towers and steeples, cobblestone squares and broad boulevards, Renaissance splendor and steel-and-glass skyscrapers. The medieval walls of Gamla Stan (the Old Town) no longer stand, but the winding streets have been preserved. You can even go fishing in downtown waterways, thanks to a long-ago decree from Queen Christina.

Once an ethnically homogeneous society, Stockholm has experienced a vast wave of immigration in the past several years. More than 10% of Sweden's residents are immigrants or children of immigrant parents. Most of the influx is coming from other Scandinavian countries. Because of Sweden's strong stance on human rights, the country has also become a major destination for political and social refugees from Africa and the Middle East and the former Yugoslavia.

An important aspect of Stockholm today is a growing interest in cultural activities. Over the past 20 years, locals have turned their attention to music, attendance at live concerts has grown, book sales are up, and museum attendance has greatly increased.

ONLY IN STOCKHOLM

Experiencing Skansen Be it butter churning or folk dancing, there's always something to amuse people of all ages here. Wander at will through the world's oldest open-air museum, getting a glimpse of Swedish life in the long-ago countryside on some 75 acres of parkland.

Strolling Through Gamla Stan at Night To walk the narrow cobblestone alleys of the Old Town on foot at night, with special

Stockholm Attractions & Accommodations

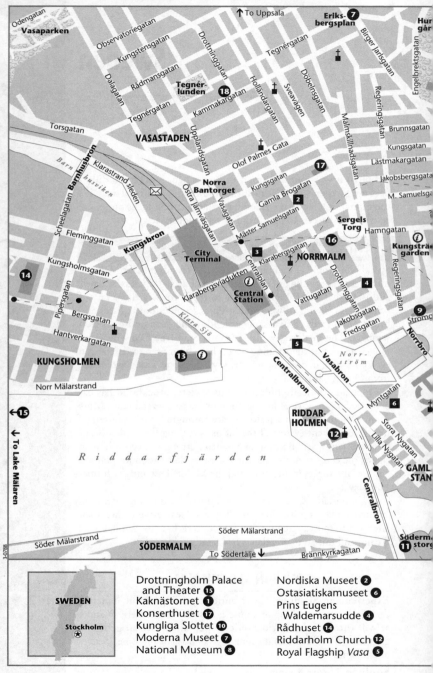

Odengatan
Vasaparken
Observatoriegatan
Kungstensgatan
Rådmansgatan
Dalagatan
Tegnérgatan
Torsgatan
Drottninggatan
Tegnér-lunden **18**
Kammakargatan
Hollandargatan
Tegnérgatan
Döbelnsgatan
Sveavägen
Birger Jarlsgatan
Engelbrektsgatan
↑ To Uppsala
Eriks-bergsplan **7**
Hur går
Regeringsgatan
Malmskillnadsgatan
Brunnsgatan
Kungsgatan
Lästmakargatan
Jakobsbergsgata
M. Samuelsga
VASASTADEN
Uppландsgatan
Olof Palmes Gata
Kungsgatan
Gamla Brogatan **2**
Norra Bantorget
Vasagatan
Barn busviken
Klarastrand sleden
Barnhusbron
Scheelegatan
Flemminggatan
Kungsbron
Kungsholmsgatan
Östra Järnvägsgatan
Klarabergsgatan
Centralplan **17**
Sergels Torg
Hamngatan
16
Kungsträd-garden
Mäster Samuelsgatan
City Terminal **3**
NORRMALM
Drottninggatan
Regeringsgatan
14
Pipersgatan
Bergsgatan
Hantverkargatan
KUNGSHOLMEN **13** (i)
Norr Mälarstrand
Klarabergsviadukten (i)
Central Station
Klara Sjö
Vattugatan
Jakobsgatan
Fredsgatan
5
Norr-ström
4
9
Strömg
Norrbro
Vasabron
Centralbron
Myntgatan
6
RIDDAR-HOLMEN **12**
Stora Nygatan
Lilla Nygatan
GAML STAN
←**15**
← To Lake Mälaren
R i d d a r f j ä r d e n
Centralbron
Söder Mälarstrand
Söder Mälarstrand
SÖDERMALM
To Södertälje ↓
Brännkyrkagatan
Söderm storg **11**

SWEDEN	Drottningholm Palace and Theater **15**	Nordiska Museet **2**
	Kaknästornet **1**	Ostasiatiskamuseet **6**
Stockholm ★	Konserthuset **17**	Prins Eugens Waldemarsudde **4**
	Kungliga Slottet **10**	Rådhuset **14**
	Moderna Museet **7**	Riddarholm Church **12**
	National Museum **8**	Royal Flagship *Vasa* **5**

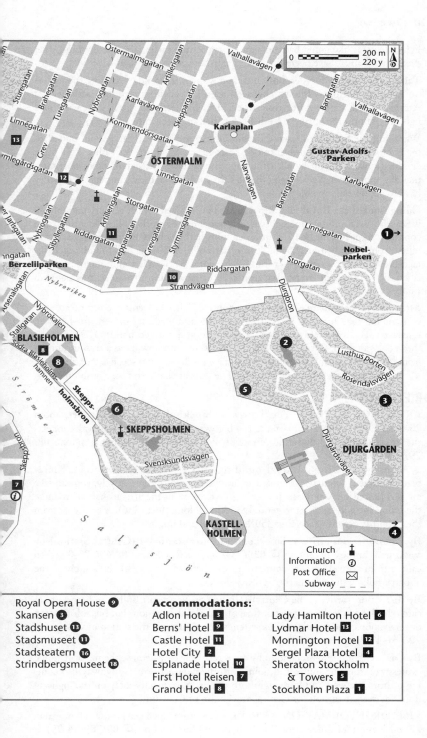

Royal Opera House **9**
Skansen **3**
Stadshuset **13**
Stadsmuseet **11**
Stadsteatern **16**
Strindbergsmuseet **18**

Accommodations:
Adlon Hotel **3**
Berns' Hotel **9**
Castle Hotel **11**
Hotel City **2**
Esplanade Hotel **10**
First Hotel Reisen **7**
Grand Hotel **8**

Lady Hamilton Hotel **6**
Lydmar Hotel **13**
Mornington Hotel **12**
Sergel Plaza Hotel **4**
Sheraton Stockholm
& Towers **5**
Stockholm Plaza **1**

light effects, is like going back in time. It takes little imagination to envision what everyday life must have been like in this "city between the bridges."

Taking the Baths Swedes, both men and women, are fond of roasting themselves on wooden platforms like chickens on a grill, then plunging into a shower of Arctic-chilled water. After this experience, bathers emerge lighthearted and lightheaded into the northern fresh air, fortified for an evening of revelry.

Watching the Summer Dawn In midsummer at 3am, you can get out of bed, as many Stockholmers do, and sit out on balconies to watch the eerie blue sky—pure, crystal, exquisite. Gradually it's bathed in peach as the early dawn of a too-short summer day approaches. Locals don't like to miss a minute of their summer, even if they have to get up early to enjoy it.

Going Aboard the Royal Flagship _Vasa_ This recovered 17th-century man-of-war is Scandinavia's number-one sightseeing attraction. The world's oldest identified and complete ship, it sank in 1628 in Stockholm harbor on its maiden voyage. It was raised from its seabed in 1961 after its discovery in 1956, the hull found largely intact. Now restored to its former (but brief) glory, the _Vasa_ is a monument to a vanished life—displaying everything from 700 original sculptures to sailor's pants in Lübeck gray.

Attending a Performance at Drottningholm This 18th-century court theater was constructed for Queen Lovisa Ulrika in 1766 as a wedding present for her son, Gustavus III. Regrettably, he was assassinated at a masked ball in 1792 and the theater wasn't used. But in 1922 it was rediscovered and now it has a season running from late May to early Sept. The original stage machinery and settings are still in use. Mozart is a perennial favorite here. Tip: The seats are hard, so take a cushion.

ORIENTATION

ARRIVING By Plane You'll arrive at **Stockholm Arlanda Airport,** about 28 miles north of Stockholm on the E-4 highway. A long covered walkway connects the international and domestic terminals. For information on flights, phone **08/797-61-00.**

A bus outside the terminal building goes to the City Terminal, Klarabergsviadukten, about a 35-minute trip, for 50Kr ($7.50). Alternatively, you can take an SAS limousine. Go to the limousine-service desk in the arrivals hall at Arlanda; the limousine will take you to central Stockholm for 240Kr ($36). A taxi to or from the airport is expensive, costing 350Kr ($52.50) and up.

By Train Trains arrive at Stockholm's **Centralstationen (Central Station)** on Vasagatan, in the city center (☎ **020/75-75-75** in Sweden, or 08/696-75-09 when calling from abroad), where connections can be made to Stockholm's subway, the T-bana. Follow the sign marked TUNNELBANA.

By Bus Buses arrive at the **Centralstationen** on Vasagatan, and from here you can catch the T-bana (subway) to your final Stockholm destination. For bus information or reservations, check with the bus system's ticket offices at the station by calling **08/700-51-47.**

By Car Getting into Stockholm by car is relatively easy because the major national expressway from the south, E-4, joins with the national express highway E-3 coming in from the west and leads right into the heart of the city. Stay on the highway until you see the turnoff for Central Stockholm or Centrum.

VISITOR INFORMATION The **Tourist Center,** Sweden House, Hamngatan 27, off Kungsträdgården (Box 7542), S-103 93 Stockholm (☎ **08/789-24-95**), is open June–Aug Mon–Fri 9am–6pm, Sat–Sun 9am–5pm; Sept–May Mon–Fri 9am–6pm, Sat–Sun 10am–3pm. Maps and other free material are available.

CITY LAYOUT   On the island of Norrmalm north of the Old Town are Stockholm's major streets, such as **Kungsgatan** (the main shopping street), **Birger Jarlsgatan,** and **Strandvägen** (leading to the Djurgården). **Stureplan,** at the junction of the major avenues Kungsgatan and Birger Jarlsgatan, is the city's commercial hub.

About 4 blocks east of the Stureplan rises **Hötorget City,** a landmark of modern urban planning that includes five 18-story skyscrapers. Its main traffic-free artery is the **Sergelgatan,** a 3-block shopper's promenade that eventually leads to the modern sculptures in the center of the Sergels Torg. About 9 blocks south of the Stureplan, at **Gustav Adolfs Torg,** are the Royal Dramatic Theater and the Royal Opera House.

A block east of the flaming torches of the Opera House is the verdant north–south stretch of **Kungsträdgården,** part avenue, part public park, which serves as a popular gathering place for students and a resting perch for shoppers. Three blocks southeast, on a famous promontory, lie the landmark Grand Hotel and the National Museum.

Kungsholmen, King's Island, is across a narrow canal from the rest of the city, a short walk west of the Central Station. It's visited chiefly by those seeking a tour of Stockholm's elegant Stadshuset (City Hall).

South of the island where Gamla Stan (Old Town) is located and separated from it by a narrow but much-navigated stretch of water is **Södermalm,** the southern district of Stockholm. Quieter than its northern counterpart, it's an important residential area with a distinctive flavor of its own.

To the east of Gamla Stan, on a large and forested island completely surrounded by the complicated waterways of Stockholm, is **Djurgården** (Deer Park). The rustically unpopulated summer pleasure ground of Stockholm, it's the site of many of its most popular attractions: the open-air museums of Skansen, the *Vasa* man-of-war, Gröna Lund's Tivoli, the Waldemarsudde estate of the "painting prince" Eugen, and the Nordic Museum.

GETTING AROUND

You can travel throughout Stockholm county by bus, local train, subway (T-bana), and tram, going from Singö in the north to Nynäshamn in the south. The routes are divided into zones, and one ticket is valid for all types of public transport in the same zone within 1 hour of when the ticket is stamped.

The basic fare for public transport (which in Stockholm means either subway, tram/streetcar, or bus) is with tickets purchased from the person in the toll booth on the subway platform, not from a vending machine. Each ticket costs 6.50Kr ($1). To travel within most of urban Stockholm, all the way to the borders of the inner city, requires only two tickets. You can transfer (or double back and return to your starting point) within 1 hour of your departure for free.

Your best transportation bet is to purchase a **tourist season ticket.** A 1-day card, costing 56Kr ($8.40), is valid for 24 hours of unlimited travel by T-bana, bus, and commuter train in Stockholm. It also includes passage on the ferry to Djurgården. Most visitors will probably want the 3-day card for 107Kr ($16.05), valid for 72 hours in both Stockholm and the adjacent county. The 3-day card is also valid for admission to Skansen, Kaknästornet, and Gröna Lund. Children under 18 pay 33Kr ($4.95), but children up to 7 can travel free with an adult. Tickets are offered at tourist-information offices, in subway stations, and at most news vendors. Call **08/600-10-00** for more information.

The **Stockholmskortet (Stockholm Card)** is a personal discount card that allows unlimited free travel by bus, subway, and local trains throughout the city and county of Stockholm (except on airport buses). You can also take a free sightseeing tour with City Sightseeing, which allows you to get on and off as often as you choose, looking at the sights according to your own schedule. These tours are available daily mid-June to mid-August. The card also allows you to take a boat trip to the Royal Palace of Drottningholm for half price. Free admission to 70 attractions is included in the package.

You can purchase the card at several places in the city, including the Tourist Center in Sweden House, HotellCentralen, the Central Station, the tourist-information desk in City Hall (in summer), the Kaknäs TV tower, SL-Center Sergels Torg (subway entrance level), and Pressbyrån newsstands. The cards are stamped with the date and time at the first point of usage. A 24-hour card costs 175Kr ($26.25). The card is valid for one adult and two children 18 and under.

BY T-BANA (SUBWAY)   Before entering the subway, passengers tell the ticket seller their destination, then purchase tickets. Subway entrances are marked with a blue T on a white background. For information about schedules, routes, and fares, phone **08/600-10-00.**

BY BUS   A bus will fill the need when the T-bana isn't convenient. The two systems have been coordinated to complement each other. Many visitors use a bus to reach Djurgården (though you can walk here), since the T-bana doesn't go here. For a list of bus routes, purchase the *SL Stockholmskartan,* sold at the Tourist Center at Sweden House, Hamngatan 27, off Kungsträdgården (☎ **08/789-24-95**).

BY CAR   For getting around Stockholm, a car isn't recommended, although you may need one if you plan to tour the environs. All the major car-rental firms are represented, including Avis at Ringvägen 90 (☎ **08/644-9980**) and Hertz at Vasagatan 2224 (☎ **08/240720**).

BY TAXI   Taxis are expensive—in fact, the most expensive in the world, with the meter starting at 23Kr ($3.45). A short ride can easily cost 75Kr ($11.25). Those that display the sign LEDIG may be hailed, or you can order one by phone. **Taxi Stockholm** (☎ **08/15-00-00** or 08/15-04-00) is one of Stockholm's larger, reputable taxi companies.

BY FERRY   Ferries from Skeppsbron in Gamla Stan (near the bridge to Södermalm) will take you to Djurgården if you don't want to go by bus or walk. They leave every 20 minutes Mon–Sat and about every 15 minutes on Sun from 9am–6pm, charging 15Kr ($2.25) for adults or 10Kr ($1.50) for seniors and young people 7 to 12; free for children under 7.

BY BICYCLE   The best place to go cycling is on Djurgården. You can rent bicycles from **Skepp o Hoj,** Djurgårdsbron (☎ **08/660-57-57**), for about 110Kr ($16.50) per day. It's open May–Aug, daily 9am–9pm.

FAST FACTS: Stockholm

American Express   American Express is at Birger Jarlsgatan 1 (☎ 08/679-78-80), open Mon–Fri 9am–5pm and Sat 10am–1pm.

Baby-sitters   Stockholm hotels maintain lists of competent baby-sitters. Nearly all of them speak English. There's no official agency; rather, it's a "word of mouth" system. Your hotel reception desk can assist you.

Bookstores   For a good selection of English-language books, including maps and touring guides, try Akademibokhandeln Almqvist & Wiksell, Mäster Samuelsgatan 32 (☎ 08/613-61-00), open Mon–Fri 9:30am–6pm and Sat 10am–3pm.

Currency   You'll pay your way in Stockholm in SwedishKr **(Kr)** or crowns (singular, **krona**), sometimes abbreviated SEK, which are divided into 100 **öre.** Bills come in denominations of 10, 20, 50, 100, and 1,000Kr. Coins are issued in 50 öre, as well as 1, 5, and 10Kr. The exchange rate used in this chapter was $1 = 6.66Kr, or 1Kr = 15¢.

Dentists   Emergency dental treatment is offered at Sct. Eriks Hospital, Fleminggatan 22 (☎ 08/654-11-17), open daily 8am–8pm. After 9pm, consult the emergency dentist on duty (☎ 08/644-92-00).

Doctors   If you need emergency medical care, check with Medical Care Information (☎ 08/644-92-00). There's also a private clinic, City Akuten, at 644 Holländargatan 3 (☎ 08/411-71-77).

Drugstores   You'll find a pharmacy open 24 hours a day in Stockholm, C. W. Scheele, Klarabergsgatan 64 (☎ 08/454-81-00).

Embassies/Consulates   The **U.S. Embassy** is at Strandvägen 101, S-115 89 Stockholm (☎ 08/783-53-00); the **British Embassy** is at Skarpögatan 6–8, S-115 27 Stockholm (☎ 08/671-90-00); the **Canadian Embassy** is at Tegelbacken 4, S-101 23 Stockholm (☎ 08/453-30-00); and the **Australian Embassy** is at Sergels Torg 12, S-103 27 Stockholm (☎ 08/613-29-00). **New Zealand** doesn't maintain an embassy in Sweden.

Emergencies   Call **112** for the police, ambulance service, or fire department.

Hospitals   Call Medical Care Information at 08/644-92-00 and an English-speaking operator will inform you of the hospital closest to you.

Lost Property   If you've lost something on the train, go to the Lost and Found office in the Central Station, lower concourse (☎ 08/762-25-50). The police also have such an office at the police station at Bergsgatan 39 (☎ 08/401-07-88). The Stockholm Transit Company (SL) keeps its recovered articles at the Rådmansgatan T-bana station (☎ 08/736-07-80), and Vaxholmsbolaget has one at Nybrokajen 2 (☎ 08/14-09-60, ext. 142).

Luggage Storage/Lockers   Facilities are available at the Central Station on Vasagatan, lower concourse (☎ 08/762-25-50). Lockers can also be rented at the ferry stations at Värtan and Tegelvikshamnen, at the Viking Line's terminal, and at the Central Station.

Post Office   The main post office is at Vasagatan 28–34 (☎ 08/781-20-00), open Mon–Fri 8am–8pm and Sat 10am–2pm. General delivery (Post Restante) pickups can be made here.

Telephone/Telex/Fax   The Telecenter, open Mon–Sat 8am–midnight, is at Skeppsbron 2 (☎ 08/780-78-90), in the Old Town behind the Royal Palace. The office at the Central Station (☎ 08/780-81-21) is open Mon–Sat 8am–9pm. Instructions in English are posted in public phone boxes, which can be found on street corners. Very few phones in Sweden are coin operated; most require the purchase of a phone card. You can obtain phone cards at most newspaper stands and tobacco shops. You can send a telegram by phoning 00-21 anytime, or from offices bearing the sign TELE or TELEBUTIK, as well as from some post offices. To send a telex or fax, go to the Telecenter.

Transit Information For information on all services, including buses and subways (Tunnelbana), even suburban trains (pendeltåg), call 08/600-10-00. Or else visit the SL Center, on the lower level of Sergels Torg. It provides info about transportation and also sells a map of the city's system, as well as tickets and special discount passes. Open in summer Mon–Thurs 9am–6pm, Fri 9am–5:30pm, Sat 9am–4pm, and Sun 10am–3pm; the rest of the year, open only Mon–Fri.

ACCOMMODATIONS

IN THE CENTER

Very Expensive

✪ Grand Hotel. Södra Blaisieholmshamnen 8, S-103 27 Stockholm. ☎ **800/223-5652** in the U.S. and Canada, or 08/679-35-00. Fax 08/611-86-86. 302 rms, 19 suites. MINIBAR TV TEL. July 4–Aug 14 and Fri–Sun year-round, 1,400–1,960Kr ($210–$294) double. Aug 15–July 3, Mon–Thurs, 2,470–3,360Kr ($370.50–$504) double. Year-round, from 6,827Kr ($1,024.05) suite. Rates include breakfast. AE, DC, MC, V. Parking 290Kr ($43.50). T-bana: Kungsträdgården. Bus: 46, 55, 62, or 76.

Opposite the Royal Palace, this hotel is grand indeed, the finest in Sweden and the choice of everybody from Sarah Bernhardt to Nobel Prize winners. Built in 1874, it has been continuously renovated, the last restoration in 1996, but its old-world style has always been maintained. The guest rooms come in all shapes and sizes, but each is elegantly appointed with traditional styling. Some contain air-conditioning. The Grand Veranda specializes in traditional food served from a buffet, and the Franska Matsalen is the hotel's gourmet restaurant.

Expensive

Berns' Hotel. Näckströmsgatan 8, S-111 47 Stockholm. ☎ **08/614-07-00.** Fax 08/611-51-75. 60 rms, 3 suites. A/C MINIBAR TV TEL. June 15–Aug, 1,250Kr ($187.50) double. Sept–June 14, Sun–Thurs, 2,190Kr ($328.50) double; Fri–Sat, 1,450Kr ($217.50) double. Year-round, from 2,990Kr ($448.50) suite. Rates include breakfast. AE, DC, MC, V. T-bana: Östermalmstorg.

During its 19th-century heyday, this was Sweden's most elegant hotel, with a lush gilded-age interior that was the setting for many a legendary rendezvous. In 1989, after years of neglect, its premises were rebuilt in their original style, with the restaurant facilities upgraded for modern tastes. Guest rooms are soundproof and comfortably isolated from the activities downstairs. Each has a satellite TV, CD player, and bath sheathed in Italian marble. The open-air terrace on the hotel's rooftop offers views over the city's historic core. The Red Room, once used as a breakfast room, is the setting and namesake of one of Strindberg's most trenchant novels, *Röda Rummet*.

Sergel Plaza. Brunkebergstorg 9, S-103 27 Stockholm. ☎ **800/THE-OMNI** in the U.S., or 08/22-66-00. Fax 08/21-50-70. 406 rms, 12 suites. A/C TV TEL. June 20–Aug 11, 995Kr ($149.25) double; 2,200Kr ($330) suite. Aug 12–June 19, 1,545–1,745Kr ($231.75–$261.75) double; 2,200Kr ($330) suite. Rates include breakfast. AE, DC, MC, V. Parking 175Kr ($26.25). T-bana: Central Station. Bus: 47, 52, or 69.

This hotel at the entrance to Drottninggatan, the main shopping street, has been improved to such an extent that today it's one of the city's leading hotels. The elegant decor includes 18th-century artwork and antiques. It's a bastion of comfort and good taste, as reflected by the beautifully decorated rooms. The Anna Rella gourmet restaurant offers both Swedish and international specialties. Facilities include saunas, solariums, and Jacuzzis.

Sheraton Stockholm & Towers. Tegelbacken 6, S-101 23 Stockholm. ☎ **800/325-3535** in the U.S. and Canada, or 08/14-26-00. Fax 08/21-70-26. 459 rms, 11 suites. A/C MINIBAR

TV TEL. Jan–June and Aug 9–Dec, Mon–Thurs, 1,950Kr ($292.50) double. July–Aug 8 and weekends year-round, 1,060Kr ($159) double. Year-round, 2,900Kr ($435) suite. Rates include breakfast. AE, DC, MC, V. Parking 160Kr ($24). T-bana: Central Station.

Sheathed with Swedish granite, this hotel rises eight stories across the street from Stockholm's City Hall (Rådhuset). Short on Swedish charm, it's excellent by chain hotel standards, attracting the business traveler. The rooms are the city's largest, decorated in blue or pink; most enjoy sweeping views over the city. The Sheraton Première Restaurant specializes in game and fish.

Moderate

Castle Hotel. Riddargatan 14, S-114 35 Stockholm. ☎ **08/679-57-00.** Fax 08/611-20-22. 48 rms, 1 suite. TV TEL. Aug–June, 1,300Kr ($195) double; July, 700Kr ($105) double. Year-round, 2,400Kr ($360) suite. Rates include breakfast. AE, DC, MC, V. T-bana: Östermalmstorg.

A short walk east of the center in an expensive neighborhood, this house was built in 1920 as a private apartment building. In the late 1980s it was renovated as a hotel. It has a gray marble floor in the lobby, and the guest rooms have gilded accents and art deco accessories to match the original construction of the building. Several times a week the hotel presents jazz evenings.

Esplanade Hotel. Strandvägen 7A, S-114 56 Stockholm. ☎ **08/663-07-40.** Fax 08/662-59-92. 32 rms, 2 suites. TV TEL. July–Aug 4 and Fri–Sat year-round, 1,095Kr ($164.25) double; 1,295Kr ($194.25) suite. Aug 5–June, Sun–Thurs, 1,500–1,800Kr ($225–$270) double; 1,900Kr ($285) suite. Rates include breakfast. AE, DC, MC, V. T-bana: Östermalmstorg. Bus: 47 or 69.

This informal hotel, next to the more expensive Diplomat, attracts diplomats from the nearby embassies and others who like its atmosphere. Constructed in 1910, it was transformed into a family-style hotel in 1954. Many rooms have minibars, and each is furnished in an old-fashioned way. Four rooms have a water view, and the English lounge has a balcony with a view of the Djurgården. Breakfast is the only meal served.

Inexpensive

Adlon Hotel. Vasagatan 42, S-111 20 Stockholm. ☎ **08/402-65-00.** Fax 08/20-86-10. 70 rms, 2 suites. TV TEL. June 20–Aug 2 and Fri–Sat year-round, 680–730Kr ($102–$109.50) double; 880Kr ($132) suite. Aug 3–June 19, Sun–Thurs, 1,025–1,180Kr ($153.75–$177) double; 1,280Kr ($192) suite. Rates include breakfast. AE, DC, MC, V. T-bana: Centralen.

This 1890s building was redesigned by brothers Axel and Hjalmar Jumlin back in the 1920s. Upgraded and improved many times since then, it lies near the Central Station and the subway and is convenient to buses to Arlanda Airport. All rooms have been renovated and are comfortably furnished, and 70% are designated for nonsmokers. A garage, charging 150Kr ($22.50), is one block away, and the hotel reception is open 24 hours.

Lydmar Hotel. Sturegatan 10, S-114 36 Stockholm. ☎ **08/22-31-60.** Fax 08/660-80-67. 61 rms, 5 suites. MINIBAR TV TEL. July–Aug 9, Mon–Thurs and Fri–Sun year-round, 1,050–1,250Kr ($157.50–$187.50) double; 2,000Kr ($300) suite. Aug 10–June, Mon–Thurs, 1,550–1,750Kr ($232.50–$262.50) double; 2,500Kr ($375) suite. Rates include buffet breakfast. AE, DC, MC, V. Parking 190Kr ($28.50). T-bana: Östermalmstorg. Bus: 41, 46, 56, or 91.

Opposite the garden of the King's Library, in what looks like an office building, the Lydmar opened in 1930 and for most of its life was known as the Eden Terrace. It offers a large dining room and a rooftop terrace where you can enjoy drinks in summer. The rooms are cozy and traditionally furnished and come in many shapes and sizes. Both Swedish and international cuisines are served in the hotel's restaurant, and there's a popular lobby bar with live jazz and soul music.

⑤ Hotel City. Slöjdgatan 7 at Hötorget, S-111 81 Stockholm. ☎ **08/723-72-00.** Fax 08/723-72-09. 292 rms. TV TEL. June 24–Aug 10, 830Kr ($124.50) double; Aug 11–June 23, 1,190Kr ($178.50) double. Rates include breakfast. AE, DC, MC, V. T-bana: Hötorget.

Clean and functional, the City is run by the Salvation Army, which works hard to make this one of the best hotels in its price bracket in Stockholm. It consists of two sections, one built as late as the 1980s. In a desirable location between two of Stockholm's biggest department stores, PUB and Åhléns, the hotel has small rooms that have been elegantly refurbished using combinations of mirrors, hardwood trim, carpeting, and tilework. Though the hotel doesn't serve alcohol of any kind, it maintains a clean but simple lunch-only restaurant.

Mornington Hotel. Nybrogatan 53, S-102 44 Stockholm. ☎ **800/528-1234** in the U.S. and Canada, or 08/663-12-40. Fax 08/662-21-79. 140 rms, 1 suite. TV TEL. June 24–Aug 10, 960Kr ($144) double; Aug 11–June 23, 1,475Kr ($221.25) double. Year-round, 1,800Kr ($270) suite. Rates include breakfast. AE, DC, MC, V. Closed Dec 23–Jan 2. Parking 150Kr ($22.50). T-bana: Östermalmstorg. Bus: 49, 54, or 62.

Proud of its image as an English-inspired hotel, this efficiently modern establishment has a concrete exterior brightened with rows of flower boxes. Most rooms (many quite small) offer a standard decor using exposed wood and pastel colors. The lobby is enhanced with a small rock garden and modern versions of Chesterfield armchairs. The hotel offers no-smoking rooms and rooms for the disabled, and its sauna and Turkish bath are free. Its Restaurant Eleonora serves international and Swedish cuisine.

Stockholm Plaza. Birger Jarlsgatan 29, S-103 95 Stockholm. ☎ **08/14-51-20.** Fax 08/10-34-92. 143 rms, 8 suites. TV TEL. June 24–Aug 12, 900Kr ($135) double; Aug 13–June 25, 1,425Kr ($213.75) double. Year-round, 2,800Kr ($420) suite. Rates include breakfast. AE, DC, MC, V. Parking 185Kr ($27.75). T-bana: Hötorget or Östermalmstorg.

Designed on a triangular lot, this is an inviting choice in the city center. Since its construction a century ago, the building has functioned as a rundown rooming house, private apartments, and offices, but in 1984 it was radically upgraded into a first-class hotel. The rooms have light, fresh interiors with many conveniences. On the premises is the elegant Plaza Grill, which serves both French and Swedish specialties. Below the restaurant, accessible from its dining room, is a stylish dance club, Penny Lane, open only to those 27 and over.

IN GAMLA STAN (OLD TOWN)

Expensive

First Hotel Reisen. Skeppsbron 12–14, S-111 30 Stockholm. ☎ **08/22-32-60.** Fax 08/20-15-59. 111 rms, 3 suites. MINIBAR TV TEL. July 18–Aug 18 and Fri–Sat year-round, 1,090Kr ($163.50) double; 2,500Kr ($375) suite. Aug 19–July 17, Sun–Thurs, 1,565–1,895Kr ($234.75–$284.25) double; 3,600Kr ($540) suite. Rates include breakfast. AE, DC, MC, V. Closed Dec 22–Jan 7. Bus: 43, 46, 55, 59, or 76.

In the Old Town, facing the water, this hotel is just three alleys from the Royal Palace. Dating from the 17th century, the three-building structure attractively combines the old and the new. The rooms are comfortably furnished in a stylish modern way, but inspired by traditional designs. The hotel's specialty restaurant, the Quarter Deck, serves a refined international and Scandinavian cuisine, and the Clipper Club specializes in grills. There's an indoor pool and a sauna, plus Jacuzzis in some suites.

Lady Hamilton Hotel. Storkyrkobrinken 5, S-111 28 Stockholm. ☎ **08/23-46-80.** Fax 08/411-11-48. 34 rms. MINIBAR TV TEL. July and Fri–Sun year-round, 1,180Kr ($177) double. Aug–June, Mon–Thurs, 1,810Kr ($271.50) double. Rates include breakfast. AE, DC, MC, V. T-bana: Gamla Stan. Bus: 48.

This hotel, a trio of interconnected buildings, stands on a quiet street surrounded by antique shops and restaurants—a very desirable location. You'll get a sense of the 1470 origins of this hotel when you use the luxurious sauna, which contains the stone-rimmed well that formerly supplied the house's water. Extra touches include antiques in the rooms, 18th-century paintings, and several carved figureheads from old sailing vessels. The ornate staircase wraps around a large model of a clipper ship suspended from the ceiling.

DINING
IN THE CENTER
Very Expensive

✪ **Operakällaren.** Operahuset, Kungsträdgården ☎ **08/676-58-00.** Reservations required. Main courses 205–295Kr ($30.75–$44.25); smörgåsbord 255Kr ($38.25); fixed-price menu 485Kr ($72.75) for three courses, 680Kr ($102) for six-course *menu gastronomique*. AE, DC, MC, V. Mon–Fri 11:30am–2pm and 5–11:30pm, Sat 11:30am–11:30pm, Sun 5–10pm. Closed July. T-bana: Kungsträdgarden. FRENCH/SWEDISH.

Opposite the Royal Palace, this is Sweden's most famous and unashamedly luxurious restaurant. Its elegant classic decor and style are reminiscent of a royal court banquet at the turn of the century. Dress formally to enjoy its impeccable service and house specialties. Many come here for the elaborate smörgåsbord; others prefer the classic Swedish dishes or modern French ones. A house specialty is the platter of northern delicacies, including everything from smoked eel to smoked reindeer along with Swedish red caviar. Salmon and game, including grouse from the northern forests, are prepared in various ways.

✪ **Paul & Norbert.** Strandvägen 9. ☎ **08/663-81-83.** Reservations required. Main courses 230–330Kr ($34.50–$49.50); eight-course *grand menu de frivolité* 970Kr ($145.50). AE, DC, MC, V. Mon–Fri noon–3pm and 5:30–10:30pm. Closed July and Dec 24–Jan 6. T-bana: Östermalmstorg. CONTINENTAL.

In a patrician residence dating from 1873, adjacent to the Hotel Diplomat, this is Stockholm's most innovative restaurant. Seating only 30, it has a vaguely art deco decor, a winter-inspired pastel color scheme, beamed ceilings, and dark paneling. Owners Paul Beck and Norbert Lang worked in many of the top restaurants of Europe before opening this establishment. Their foie gras is the finest in town. Main dishes include scampi-stuffed breast of guinea fowl, accompanied by a lentil curry sauce; grilled lamb's liver served with a fig-vinegar sauce; and juniper-marinated noisettes of reindeer in a caramelized black-currant sauce.

Expensive

✪ **Franska Matsalen (French Dining Room).** In the Grand Hotel, Södra Blasieholmshamnen 8. ☎ **08/679-35-00.** Reservations required. Main courses 175–335Kr ($26.25–$50.25); fixed-price five-course menu 625Kr ($93.75). AE, DC, MC, V. Mon–Fri 6–11pm. Closed July. T-bana: Kungsträdgården. Bus: 46, 55, 62, or 76. FRENCH.

Widely acclaimed as one of Stockholm's greatest restaurants, this elegant establishment is on the street level of the city's most deluxe hotel. The dining room is imperial, featuring an ensemble of polished mahogany, ormolu, and gilt accents—all placed under an ornate plaster ceiling. Tables on the enclosed veranda permit a view of the Royal Palace and the Old Town. Main dishes include fried lamb served with morels and leek, turbot with olives and spring onions, and rack of veal with sweetbreads and langostines.

✪ **Wedholms Fisk.** Nybrokajen 17. ☎ **08/611-78-74.** Reservations required. Main courses 230–360Kr ($34.50–$54); fixed-price lunch 130Kr ($19.50); fixed-price dinner 295Kr ($44.25). AE, DC, MC, V. Mon–Sat 5–11pm. Closed July. T-bana: Östermalmstorg. SWEDISH/FRENCH.

This is one of Stockholm's classic restaurants. Housed in an old Swedish building whose decor has been stripped down to its rustic simplicity, it has no curtains on the windows and no carpets, but displays a riveting collection of modern paintings by Swedish artists. The chef has reason to be proud of such dishes as perch poached with morels and champagne sauce; sweet pickled herring with red onion, dill, and melted butter; and grilled fillet of sole with a Dijon-flavored hollandaise.

Moderate

Bakfickan. Jakobs Torg 12. ☎ **08/676-58-09.** Reservations recommended. Main courses 72–156Kr ($10.80–$23.40). AE, DC, MC, V. July, Mon–Fri 5–11:30pm. Aug–June, Mon–Sat 11:30am–11:30pm. T-bana: Kungsträdgården. SWEDISH.

Tucked away in the back of the Operakällaren, the "Back Pocket" is a chic place to eat for a moderate price. Its food is from the same kitchen as the very glamorous Operakällaren (see above), but its prices are more bearable. Main dishes are likely to include several varieties of salmon as well as beef Rydberg (thinly sliced tenderloin). Many guests prefer to sit at the horseshoe-shaped bar, enjoying their food and drink there.

Berns' Salonger. Näckströmsgatan 8. ☎ **08/614-05-50.** Reservations recommended. Main courses 150Kr ($22.50). AE, DC, MC, V. Mon–Sat 11am–2pm and 7–11:30pm. T-bana: Östermalmstorg. SWEDISH.

Built in 1860, this "pleasure palace" was one of Stockholm's most famous restaurants and nighttime venues. It was dramatically renovated in 1989 and is now an atmospheric choice for dining, with a spectacular main hall adorned with galleries. The Red Room was frequented by August Strindberg, who described it in his novel of the same name. Each day a different Swedish specialty is featured, like fried fillet of suckling pig with fresh asparagus. You might also try calves' liver with garlic and bacon or grilled tournedos. On the premises is also a dance club (open Mon–Sat midnight–3am), charging 60Kr ($9) at the entrance. Frequent shows are staged in the adjoining theater.

⑤ Eriks Bakfica. Fredrikshovsgatan 4. ☎ **08/660-15-99.** Reservations recommended. Main courses 80–220Kr ($12–$33); three-course entrecôte dinner 275Kr ($41.25). AE, DC, MC, V. Mon–Fri 11:30am–11pm, Sat 1–11pm, Sun 3–9:30pm. Bus: 47. SWEDISH.

Though there are other restaurants here bearing the name Erik's, this one is relatively inexpensive and offers particularly good value. It features a handful of Swedish dishes from the tradition of *husmanskost* (wholesome home cooking). There's a daily choice of herring appetizers. Try the archipelago stew, a ragoût of fish flavored with tomatoes and served with garlic mayonnaise. Marinated salmon is served with hollandaise sauce, and you might also try Erik's cheeseburger with a special secret sauce.

KB Restaurant. Smålandsgatan 7. ☎ **08/679-60-32.** Reservations recommended. Main courses 136–255Kr ($20.40–$38.25); fixed-price lunch 106Kr ($15.90); fixed-price dinner 175Kr ($26.25). AE, DC, MC, V. Mon–Fri 11:30am–11:30pm, Sat 5–11:30pm. Closed June 23–Aug 7. T-bana: Östermalmstorg. SWEDISH/CONTINENTAL.

A traditional artists' rendezvous in the center of town, KB features good Swedish cookery as well as continental dishes. Fish dishes are especially recommended. You might begin with salmon trout roe and Russian caviar and follow with boiled turbot or lamb roast with stuffed zucchini in thyme-flavored bouillon. The dishes are usually accompanied by freshly baked sourdough bread.

Lisa Elmquist. Östermalms Saluhall, Nybrogatan 31. ☎ **08/660-92-32.** Reservations recommended. Main courses 100–165Kr ($15–$24.75). AE, DC, MC, V. Mon 10am–6pm, Tues–Fri 9am–6pm, Sat 9am–3pm. T-bana: Östermalmstorg. SEAFOOD.

Under the soaring roof and amid the food stalls of Stockholm's produce market (the Östermalms Saluhall), you'll find this likable cafe/oyster bar. Owned by one of the city's largest fish distributors, it serves a menu that varies according to the catch. Some people come here to order a portion of shrimp with bread and butter for 85–115Kr ($12.75–$17.25). Typical dishes are fish soup, salmon cutlets, and sautéed fillet of lemon sole.

Prinsens. Mäster Samuelsgatan 4. ☎ **08/611-13-31.** Reservations recommended. Main courses 90–189Kr ($13.50–$28.35); fixed-price lunch 79Kr ($11.85). AE, DC, MC, V. Mon–Thurs 11am–midnight, Fri 11am–1:30am, Sat 1pm–1:30am, Sun 5–11:30pm. T-bana: Östermalmstorg. SWEDISH.

A 2-minute walk from the Stureplan, this is a favorite haunt of artists and has been feeding people since 1897. Diners are seated on one of two levels, and in summer some tables are placed outside. The cuisine is fresh and flavorful and includes such traditional Swedish dishes as veal patty with homemade lingonberry preserves, sautéed fjord salmon, and roulades of beef. For dessert, try the homemade vanilla ice cream. Basically, the menu lists Swedish food prepared in a conservative French style.

Teatergrillen. Nybrogatan 3. ☎ **08/611-70-44.** Reservations recommended. Main courses 160–240Kr ($24–$36). AE, DC, MC, V. Mon–Fri 11:30am–2:30pm; Mon–Sat 5–11:30pm. Closed July. T-bana: Östermalmstorg. Bus: 46. SWEDISH/FRENCH.

For the theater buff, this restaurant decorated with theatrical memorabilia is near the Royal Dramatic Theater on Nybroplan. Many typical Swedish dishes are offered at lunch, cooked grandmother style, including fried herring with onion and potatoes, scrambled eggs with salmon, and pea soup with sausages. For dinner, try one of the roasts from the trolley, which are as good as Simpson's in the Strand in London. You can also order such elegant fare as snails braised in white wine with tarragon butter.

Inexpensive

۞ Gröna Linjen. Mäster Samuelsgatan 10. ☎ **08/611-92-96.** Buffet 69Kr ($10.35); meat dishes 55Kr ($8.25). No credit cards. Mon–Fri 10:30am–6pm (until 8pm in winter), Sat 11am–6pm. T-bana: Östermalmstorg. VEGETARIAN.

This is the oldest and best-known vegetarian restaurant in Stockholm, established in 1942 in what had functioned during the 1920s as the private apartment of the prime minister of Sweden. It lies two floors above street level and is somewhat difficult to find. Once you get there, you'll see a copious vegetarian buffet with a range of salads and three hot dishes of the day.

IN GAMLA STAN (OLD TOWN)

Very Expensive

۞ Erik's. Österlånggatan 17. ☎ **08/23-85-00.** Reservations required. Main courses 262–338Kr ($39.30–$50.70); luncheon plates 75–125Kr ($11.25–$18.75); *menu dégustation* 860Kr ($129). AE, DC, MC, V. Mon–Fri 11:30am–11pm, Sat 1–11pm. Closed July and Dec 25–Jan 1. T-bana: Gamla Stan. FRENCH.

This restaurant occupying two floors of a building from the 1600s in the Old Town has a warmly autumnal color scheme and English country-house decor. It's the best restaurant in the Old Town. You can select such appetizers as warm lobster salad with leeks, tomatillos, and lobster dressing or goose-liver terrine with truffle soufflé. The chef's specialty is fried duckling served in two courses—first the breast in cider sauce, followed by the leg in green-pepper sauce. Fish selections include the catch of the day or lobster, turbot, and halibut with a chervil-and-champagne sauce, accompanied by wild rice.

Expensive

Fem Små Hus. Nygränd 10. ☎ **08/10-87-75.** Reservations required. Main courses 175–230Kr ($26.25–$34.50). AE, DC, MC, V. Mon–Fri 11:30am–11:30pm, Sat–Sun 1–11:30pm. T-bana: Gamla Stan. SWEDISH/FRENCH.

This historic restaurant, whose cellars date from the 17th century, is furnished like the interior of a private castle, with European antiques and oil paintings. After being shown to a candlelit table somewhere in the nine rooms of the labyrinthine interior, you can order slices of fresh salmon in chablis, braised scallops with saffron sauce, terrine of duckling with goose liver and truffles, or fillet of beef with herb sauce, plus sorbets with seasonal fruits and berries.

Den Gyldene Freden. Österlånggatan 51. ☎ **08/24-97-60.** Reservations recommended. Main courses 178–235Kr ($26.70–$35.25). AE, DC, MC, V. Mon–Sat 6–11pm. Closed July 2–Aug 2. T-bana: Gamla Stan. SWEDISH.

The "Golden Peace" is said to be Stockholm's oldest tavern, opened in 1722. Its building is owned by the Swedish Academy, and members frequent the place on Thursday night. Inside, various cozy dining rooms are named for Swedish historic figures. You get good traditional Swedish cookery here, especially fresh Baltic fish and game from the forests of Sweden. Specialty main courses are baked fillet of turbot served with cèpes (flap mushrooms) and guinea fowl sautéed with dried fruit and spruce twigs (that's right).

Moderate

Cattelin Restaurant. Storkyrkobrinken 9. ☎ **08/20-18-18.** Reservations recommended. Main courses 75–189Kr ($11.25–$28.35); *dagens menu* 45Kr ($6.75). AE, DC, MC, V. Mon–Fri 11am–11pm, Sat–Sun noon–11pm. T-bana: Gamla Stan. SWEDISH.

On a historic street in Gamla Stan, this restaurant serves fish and meat in a boisterous and bustling kind of conviviality. Don't expect genteel service here—the clattering of china can at times be almost deafening, but few of the regular patrons seem to mind. Menu choices include different preparations of beef, salmon, trout, veal, and chicken, often comprising the platters of the day, which are preferred by luncheon patrons. The fixed-price lunch is served only Mon–Fri 11am–2pm.

ATTRACTIONS

Everything from the *Vasa* Ship Museum to the changing of the guard at the Royal Palace to the Gröna Tivoli amusement park will keep your interest piqued. Even just window shopping for well-designed Swedish crafts can be an enjoyable way to spend an afternoon.

SIGHTSEEING SUGGESTIONS

If You Have 1 Day   Take a ferry to Djurgården to visit the *Vasa* Ship Museum, Stockholm's most famous attraction, and to explore the open-air Skansen folk museum. In the afternoon, take a walk through Gamla Stan (Old Town) and have dinner at one of its restaurants.

If You Have 2 Days   On your first day, follow the above. On Day 2, get up early and visit the Kaknästornet TV tower for a panoramic view of Stockholm, its many islands, and the archipelago. Go to the Museum of Nordic History for insight into five centuries of life in Sweden. After lunch, visit the Millesgården of Lidingö, the sculpture garden and former home of Carl Milles.

If You Have 3 Days   For the first 2 days follow the above. Spend the third morning walking through the center of Stockholm and perhaps doing some shopping. At noon (1pm on Sunday), return to Gamla Stan to see the changing of the guard at the Royal Palace. View this French-inspired building that has been the residence of Swedish kings for more than 700 years. In the afternoon, visit the National Museum.

If You Have 5 Days For Days 1–3, follow the above. On Day 4, take one of the many tours of the Stockholm archipelago. Return to Stockholm and spend the evening at the Gröna Tivoli amusement park on Djurgården. For your last day, visit Drottningholm Palace and its 18th-century theater. In the afternoon, explore the university of the city of Uppsala, north of Stockholm, easily reached by public transportation.

THE TOP ATTRACTIONS

Even the most hurried traveler will want to see the **changing of the Royal Guard.** You can watch the parade of the military guard daily in summer and on Wednesday and Sunday in winter (on all other days you can see only the changing of the guard). The parade route on weekdays begins at Sergels Torg and proceeds along Hamngatan, Kungsträdgårdsgatan, Strömgatan, Gustav Adolfs Torg, Norrbro, Skeppsbron, and Slottsbacken. On Sunday the guard departs from the Army Museum, going along Riddargatan, Artillerigatan, Strandvägen, Hamngatan, Kungsträdgårdsgatan, Strömgatan, Gustav Adolfs Torg, Norrbro, Skeppsbron, and Slottsbacken. For information on the time of the march, ask at the Tourist Center in Sweden House. The actual changing of the guard takes place at noon Mon–Sat (at 1pm on Sun) in front of the Royal Palace in Gamla Stan.

✪ **Royal Warship Vasa.** Galärvarvet, Djurgården. ☎ **08/666-48-00.** Admission 45Kr ($6.75) adults, 30Kr ($4.50) seniors and students, 10Kr ($1.50) children 7–15; free for children under 7. June 10–Aug 20 daily 9:30am–7pm; Aug 21–June 9 Wed 10am–8pm, Thurs–Tues 10am–5pm. Closed Jan 1, May 1, and Dec 24–26 and 31. Bus: 44 or 47. Ferry from Slussen all year, from Nybroplan in summer only.

This 17th-century man-of-war is the number-one attraction in Scandinavia—and for good reason. Housed in a museum specially constructed for it at Djurgården near Skansen, the *Vasa* is the world's oldest identified and complete ship.

In 1628, on its maiden voyage and in front of thousands of horrified onlookers, the Royal Warship *Vasa* capsized and sank almost instantly to the bottom of Stockholm harbor. When it was salvaged in 1961, on board were found more than 4,000 coins, carpenters' tools, and other items of archeological interest. Best of all, 97% of the 700 original sculptures were found. Carefully restored and impregnated with preservatives, they're back aboard the ship, which looks stunning now that it once again carries grotesque faces, lion masks, fish-shaped bodies, and other carvings, some still with the original paint and gilt.

Kaknästornet (Kaknäs Television Tower). Djurgårdsbrunnsvägen. ☎ **08/667-80-30.** Admission 20Kr ($3) adults, 12Kr ($1.80) children 7–15, free for children under 7. May–Aug daily 9am–10pm; Sept–Apr daily 10am–9pm. Closed Dec 24–25. Bus: 69 from Central Station.

The tallest man-made structure in Scandinavia is in the northern district of Djurgården, a radio/television tower that stands 508 feet high. Two elevators take visitors to an observation platform, where you can see everything from the cobblestone streets of the Gamla Stan (old town) to the city's modern concrete-and-glass structures and the archipelago beyond.

✪ **Skansen.** Djurgården 49–51. ☎ **08/442-80-00.** Admission 30–55Kr ($4.50–$8.25) adults, 10Kr ($1.50) children under 15. Historic buildings, May–Aug daily 11am–5pm; Sept–Apr daily 9am–5pm. Bus: 47 from central Stockholm. Ferry from Slussen to Gröna Lund.

Often called "Old Sweden in a Nutshell," this open-air museum is on Djurgården, near Gröna Lund's Tivoli. More than 150 dwellings from Lapland to Skåne, most from the 18th and 19th centuries, have been reassembled on some 75 acres of parkland. The exhibits range from a windmill to a manor house to a complete town quarter. Browsers can explore the old workshops and see where the early book publishers, silversmiths, and pharmacists plied their trade. Handcrafts (glass blowing, for example) are demonstrated here, along with peasant crafts like weaving and churning. Folk dancing and open-air symphonic concerts are also featured.

✪ Kungliga Slottet (Royal Palace). Kungliga Husgerådskammaren. ☎ **08/402-61-30.** Apartments, 45Kr ($6.75) adults, 20Kr ($3) seniors and students, free for children under 7. Royal Armory, 40Kr ($6) adults, 30Kr ($4.50) seniors and students, 15Kr ($2.25) children, free for children under 7. Museum of Antiquities, 25Kr ($3.75) adults, 20Kr ($3) seniors and students, free for children under 7. Treasury, 40Kr ($6) adults, 25Kr ($3.75) seniors and students, free for children under 7. Apartments and treasury, Jan–May Tues–Sun noon–3pm; June–Aug daily 10am–4pm; Sept–Dec Tues–Sun noon–3pm. Museum of Antiquities, June–Aug daily noon–4pm. Royal Armory, daily 11am–4pm. T-bana: Gamla Stan. Bus: 43, 46, 55, 59, or 76.

Kungliga Slottet is one of the few official residences of a European monarch that's open to the public. The king and queen prefer to live at Drottningholm, although Kungliga Slottet remains the official address. Built in the Italian baroque style between 1691 and 1754, the palace has 608 rooms.

The **State Apartments,** with three magnificent baroque ceilings and fine tapestries, the **Bernadotte Apartment,** and the **Guest Apartment** are on view. In the cellar, the **Skattkammaren (Treasury)** (☎ **08/402-61-30**) exhibits the collection of crown jewels. The **Royal Armory,** Slottsbacken 3 (☎ **08/666-44-75**), is also housed in the cellars. You'll see coronation costumes from the 16th century, weapons, and armor. Guided tours are conducted Mon–Fri at 2pm (there's also a Sun tour for adults at 3pm and a special tour for children at 2pm).

Gustav III's collection of sculpture from the days of the Roman Empire can be viewed in the **Antikmuseum** (Museum of Antiquities) (☎ **08/402-61-30**).

✪ Drottningholm Palace and Theater. Drottningholm. ☎**08/402-62-80.** Admission: Palace, 40Kr ($6) adults, 10Kr ($1.50) children. Theater, 40Kr ($6) adults, 10Kr ($1.50) children. Chinese Pavilion, 40Kr ($6) adults, 10Kr ($1.50) children. Palace, May–Aug daily 11am–4:30pm; Sept Mon–Fri 1–3:30pm, Sat–Sun noon–3:30pm (closed Oct–Apr). Theater, May–Aug daily noon–4:30pm; Sept daily 1–3:30pm (closed Oct–Apr). Chinese Pavilion, Apr and Oct daily 1–3:30pm; May–Aug daily 11am–4:30pm; Sept Mon–Fri 1–3:30pm, Sat–Sun noon–3:30pm (closed Nov–Mar). T-bana: Brommaplan; then transfer to the Mälaröbus to Drottningholm. Ferry from the dock near the City Hall.

On an island in Lake Mälaren, **Drottningholm** (Queen's Island)—dubbed the Versailles of Sweden—lies about 7 miles from Stockholm. Drottningholm, with its courtly art, royal furnishings, and Gobelin tapestries, is surrounded by fountains and parks. The palace is the home of the royal family. Nearby is the **Drottningholm Court Theater** (☎ **08/759-04-06**), the world's best-preserved 18th-century theater, with the original stage machinery and settings still in use (see "Stockholm After Dark," below).

✪ Millesgården. Carl Milles Väg 2, Lidingö. ☎ **08/731-50-60.** Admission 50Kr ($7.50) adults, 35Kr ($5.25) seniors and students, 15Kr ($2.25) children 7–16, free for children under 7. May–Sept daily 10am–5pm; Oct–Apr Tues–Sun noon–4pm. T-bana to Ropsten and a bus from here to Torsviks torg or a train to Norsvik; there's also daily boat service from Nybroplan and Strömkajen to Millesgården June–Aug.

On the island of Lidingö, northeast of Stockholm, is Carl Milles's former villa and sculpture garden beside the sea, now a museum. Many of his best-known works are displayed here (some are copies), as are works of other artists. Milles (1875–1955), who relied heavily on mythological themes, was Sweden's most famous sculptor.

Stadshuset (Stockholm City Hall). Hantverksgatan 1. ☎ **08/785-90-74.** Admission 30Kr ($4.50) adults, free for children under 12. Tower, May–Sept daily 10am–4pm. City Hall tours (subject to change), June–Sept daily at 10am, 11am, noon, and 2pm; Oct–Apr daily at 10am and noon. T-bana to Central Station or Rådhuset. Bus: 48 or 62.

Built in what is called the "National Romantic Style," the Stockholm City Hall, on the island of Kungsholmen, is one of Europe's finest examples of modern architecture. Designed by Ragnar Ostberg, the red-brick structure is dominated by a lofty square tower 348 feet high, topped by three gilt crowns and the national coat-of-arms. The Nobel Prize banquet takes place here in the Blue Hall. About 18 million pieces of gold and colored mosaics made of special glass cover the walls, and the southern gallery contains murals by Prince Eugen, the painter prince.

Riddarholm Church. Riddarholmen. ☎ **08/789-85-00.** Admission 20Kr ($3) adults, 10Kr ($1.50) students and children. May and Sept Wed and Sat–Sun noon–3pm; June–Aug daily noon–4pm. Closed Oct–Apr. T-bana: Gamla Stan.

The second-oldest church in Stockholm is on the tiny island of Riddarholmen, next to Gamla Stan. It was founded in the 13th century as a Franciscan monastery. Almost all the royal heads of state are entombed here, except for Christina, who is buried in Rome. There are three principal royal chapels, including one—the Bernadotte wing—that belongs to the present ruling family.

National Museum (National Museum of Art). Södra Blasieholmen. ☎ **08/666-44-10.** Admission 60Kr ($9) adults, 40Kr ($6) seniors and students, free for children under 16. Tues 11am–8pm, Wed–Sun 11am–5pm. T-bana: Kungsträdgården. Bus: 46, 62, 65, or 76.

At the tip of a peninsula, a short walk from the Royal Opera House and the Grand Hotel, is Sweden's state treasure house of paintings and sculpture, one of the oldest museums in the world. The first floor is devoted to applied arts (silverware, handcrafts, porcelain, furnishings), but first-time visitors may want to head directly to the second floor where the painting collection contains works by Rembrandt and Rubens, Lucas Cranach's most amusing *Venus and Cupid,* and a rare collection of Russian icons from the Moscow School of the mid-16th century. The most important room in the gallery has one whole wall devoted to Rembrandt—*Portrait of an Old Man* and *Portrait of an Old Woman,* along with his *Kitchen Maid.*

Nordiska Museet (Nordic Museum). Djurgårdsvägen 6–16, Djurgården. ☎ **08/666-46-00.** Admission 50Kr ($7.50) adults, 20Kr ($3) children 7–15, free for children under 7. Tues–Wed and Fri–Sun 11am–5pm, Thurs 11am–8pm. Bus: 44, 47, or 69.

On the island of Djurgården, this museum houses an impressive collection of implements, costumes, and furnishings of Swedish life from the 1500s to the present. Highlights are period costumes ranging from matching garters and ties for men to purple flowerpot hats from the 1890s. In the basement is an extensive exhibit of the tools of the Swedish fishing trade, plus relics from nomadic Lapps.

MORE ATTRACTIONS

Moderna Museet (Museum of Modern Art). Birger Jarlsgatan 57. ☎ **08/666-43-63.** Admission 50Kr ($7.50) adults, 20Kr ($3) seniors and students, free for children under 17. Tues–Thurs noon–7pm, Fri–Sun noon–5pm. T-bana: Rådmansgatan. Bus: 46.

This museum focuses on contemporary works by Swedish and international artists, including kinetic sculptures. Highlights are a small but good collection of cubist art by Picasso, Braque, and Léger; Matisse's *Apollo* découpage; the famous *Enigma of William Tell* by Salvador Dalí; and works by Brancusi, Max Ernst, Giacometti, and Arp, among others.

Museum of National Antiquities. Narvavägen 13–17. ☎ **08/783-94-00.** Admission 50Kr ($7.50) adults, 30Kr ($4.50) seniors and students, 20Kr ($3) children 7–15, free for children under 7. Apr–Sept Tues–Sun 11am–5pm; Oct–Mar Tues–Sun 11am–5pm (until 8pm on Thurs). T-bana: Karlaplan or Östermalmstorg. Bus: 44, 47, or 54.

If you're interested in Swedish history, especially the Viking era, here you find the nation's finest repository of relics left by those legendary conquerors who once terrorized Europe. Many relics have been unearthed from ancient burial sites. The collection of artifacts ranges from prehistoric to medieval times, including Viking stone inscriptions and coins minted in the 10th century. The Gold Room features authentic Viking silver and gold jewelry, large ornate charms, elaborate bracelet designs found nowhere else in the world, and a unique neck collar from Färjestaden.

Prins Eugens Waldemarsudde. Prins Eugens Väg 6. ☎ **08/662-28-00.** Admission 40Kr ($6) adults, free for children. June–Aug Tues–Sun 11am–5pm (also Tues and Thurs 5–8pm); Sept–May Tues–Sun 11am–4pm. Bus: 47 to the end of the line.

This once-royal residence of the "painting prince" functions today as an art gallery and a memorial to one of the most famous royal artists in recent history, Prince Eugen (1865–1947). The youngest of King Oscar II's four children (all sons), he was credited with making innovative contributions to the techniques of Swedish landscape paintings, specializing in depictions of his favorite regions in central Sweden. Among his most visible works are the murals on the inner walls of the Stadshuset.

ORGANIZED TOURS

Stockholm Sightseeing, Skeppsbron 22 (☎ 08/24-04-70), offers many tours, the largest number in summer. The 3-hour "Royal Stockholm" tour visits the Royal Palace or the Treasury and the *Vasa* Museum, with daily departures mid-Apr to mid-Oct from Gustav Adolfs Torg by the Royal Opera House. The cost is 220Kr ($33). The quickest and least expensive tour—also the most superficial—is the regular 1-hour "City Tour," costing 85Kr ($12.75). It leaves daily, June to mid-Aug, also from Gustav Adolfs Torg. "Under the Bridges" takes 2 hours and goes through two locks and two bodies of water. Daily departures from Stromkajen, by the Grand Hotel, are mid-Apr to mid-Oct; the tour is also conducted weekends from mid-Oct to around Christmas. The cost is 130Kr ($19.50). "Sightseeing anno 1935" is in an open-topped wooden boat, with a captain in period uniform. The tour explores the Stockholm harbor for 1 hour, costing 90Kr ($13.50). Daily departures, early July to mid-Aug, are from the statue of Gustav III by the Royal Palace.

Authorized guides lead 1¹/₂-hour **walking tours of the medieval lanes of the Old Town.** These walks are conducted daily from June 1 to mid-Aug, departing from the Royal Opera House at Gustav Adolfs Torg. The cost is 75Kr ($11.25). Tickets and time of departure are available from **Stockholm Sightseeing,** Skeppsbron 22 (☎ 08/24-04-70).

SHOPPING

Blås & Knåda, Hornsgatan 26 (☎ 08/642-77-67; T-bana: Slussen), sells the products of a cooperative of 50 Swedish ceramic artists and glassmakers. Prices begin at 160Kr ($24) for a single teacup, but could rise to as much as 35,000Kr ($5,250) for museum-quality pieces. Open Tues–Fri 11am–6pm and Sat 11am–3pm.

Bone china, stoneware dinner services, and other fine table and decorative ware are made at **Keramiskt Centrum Gustavsberg** (Gustavsberg Ceramics Center) (☎ 08/570-35-658; bus: 422 or 24400), on Värmdö Island, about 13 miles east of Stockholm. A museum at the center displays historic pieces such as Parian (a kind of plaster of paris or porcelain) statues based on the work of famous Danish sculptor Torvaldsen and other artists, hand-painted vases, majolica, and willowware. There are also examples of Pyro, the first ovenware produced, dinner services made for royalty, and sculptures by modern artists. The center is open Mon–Fri 10am–5pm, Sat 10am–3pm, and Sun 11am–3pm.

In the center of Stockholm, the largest department store in Sweden is **Åhléns City,** Klarabergsgatan 50 (☎ 08/676-60-00; T-bana: T-Centralen), with a gift shop, a restaurant, and a food department that's famous. Also seek out the fine collection of home textiles and both Orrefors and Kosta crystal ware. Open Mon–Fri 10am–7pm, Sat 10am–6pm, and Sun noon–4pm. **Nordiska Kompanient,** Hamngatan 18–20 (☎ 08/762-80-00; T-bana: Kungsträdgården), NK for short, is another high-quality department store. Most of the big names in Swedish glass are displayed at NK, including Orrefors (see the Nordic Light collection) and Kosta. Swedish handcrafted items are found in the basement. Stainless steel is also a good buy in Sweden. Open Mon–Fri 10am–7pm, Sat 10am–6pm, and Sun noon–4pm. Greta Garbo got her start in the millinery department at **PUB,** Hötorget 13 (☎ 08/791-60-00; T-bana: Hötorget), a popular department store that sells middle-bracket clothing and housewares of good quality. Open Mon–Fri 10am–7pm, Sat 10am–5pm, and Sun 10am–4pm.

At **Loppmarknaden I Skärholmen (Skärholmen Shopping Center),** Skärholmen (☎ 08/710-00-60; T-bana: 13 or 23 to Skärholmen, a 20-minute ride), the biggest flea market in northern Europe, you might find a pleasing item that came from an attic in Värmland. You might indeed find *anything.* Try to go on Saturday or Sunday (the earlier the better) when the market is at its peak. Admission is 10Kr ($1.50) for adults, free for children. Open Mon–Fri 11am–6pm, Sat 9am–3pm, and Sun 10am–3pm.

Geocity, Tysta Marigången 5, Tegélbacken (☎ 08/411-11-40; T-bana: T-Centralen), offers exotic mineral crystals, jewelry, Scandinavian gems, Baltic amber, and lapidary equipment. Its staff includes two certified gemologists who'll cut and set any gem you select, as well as appraise jewelry you already own. Its inventory includes stones from Scandinavia and around the world, including Greenland, Madagascar, Siberia, and South America. Open Mon–Fri 11:30am–5:30pm and Sat 10am–2pm.

An unusual outlet, **Slottsbodarna (Royal Gift Shop),** in the south wing of the Royal Palace, Slottsbacken (☎ 08/402-60-00; T-bana: Gamla Stan), sells items related to or copied from the collections in the Royal Palace, re-created in silver, gold, brass, pewter, textiles, and glass. Every item is made in Sweden. Open July–Aug daily 10am–4pm; Sept–June Tues–Sun noon–3pm. **Svensk Hemslojd (Society for Swedish Handcrafts),** Sveavägen 44 (☎ 08/411-59-54; T-bana: Hötorget), has a wide selection of glass, pottery, gifts, and wooden and metal handcrafts, the work of some of Sweden's best artisans. You'll also see a display of hand-woven carpets, upholstery fabrics, hand-painted materials, tapestries, lace, and embroidered items. You can find beautiful yarns for weaving and embroidery. It's open Mon–Fri 10am–6pm, Sat 10am–4pm, and Sun noon–4pm.

STOCKHOLM AFTER DARK

Pick up a copy of *Stockholm This Week,* distributed at the tourist information center at Sweden House, to see what's on.

THE PERFORMING ARTS

All the major opera, theater, and concert performances begin in autumn, except for special summer festival performances. Fortunately, most of the major opera and theatrical performances are funded by the state, which keeps the ticket price reasonable.

Drottningholm Slottsteater. Drottningholm. ☎ **08/660-82-25.** Tickets 50–500Kr ($7.50–$75). T-bana: Brommaplan.

Founded by King Gustavus III in 1766, this unique theater stands on an island in Lake Mälaren, 7 miles from Stockholm. It stages operas and ballets with full 18th-century regalia, complete with period costumes and wigs. Its machinery and some 30 or more complete theater sets are still intact and are used today. The theater, a short walk from the royal residence, seats only 450 patrons, which makes tickets hard to get. Eighteenth-century music performed on antique instruments is a perennial favorite. The season is May–Sept and most performances begin at 7:30pm, lasting 2½–4 hours. To order tickets in advance, phone the number above and give your American Express card number (only American Express is accepted).

Filharmonikerna I Konserthuset (Concert Hall). Hötorget 8. ☎ **08/10-21-10** or 08/457-02-11. Tickets 80–250Kr ($12–$37.50). T-bana: Hötorget.

Home of the **Stockholm Philharmonic Orchestra,** this is the principal place to hear classical music in Sweden. The Nobel Prizes are awarded here. Constructed in 1920, the building houses two concert halls—one, seating 1,600, better suited for major orchestras; the other, seating 450, suitable for chamber music groups.

Operan (Opera House). Gustav Adolfs Torg. ☎ **08/24-82-40.** Tickets 100–300Kr ($15–$45); many tickets are discounted 10–30% for seniors and students. T-bana: Kungsträdgården.

Founded in 1773 by King Gustavus III, who was assassinated here at a masked ball, the Operan is the home of the **Royal Swedish Opera** and the **Royal Swedish Ballet.** The present building dates from 1898. Performances are traditionally given Mon–Sat at 7:30pm (closed mid-June to Aug). The box office is open Mon–Fri noon–7:30pm (closes at 6pm if no performance is scheduled) and Sat noon–3pm.

LOCAL CULTURAL ENTERTAINMENT

Skansen. Djurgården 49–51. ☎ **08/442-80-00.** Admission 30–55Kr ($4.50–$8.25) adults, 10Kr ($1.50) children 7–14, free for children under 7. Bus: 44 or 47, or Djurgården ferry lines.

Skansen arranges traditional seasonal festivities, various special events, autumn market days, and a Christmas Fair. In summer there are concerts, sing-alongs, and guest performances. Folk-dancing performances are staged June–Aug Mon–Sat at 7pm and Sun at 2:30 and 4pm. Outdoor dancing is presented with live music Mon–Fri 8:30–11:30pm, but only June–Aug.

AN AMUSEMENT PARK

Gröna Lunds Tivoli. Djurgården. ☎ **08/670-76-00.** Admission 40Kr ($6) adults, free for children under 13. Bus: 44 or 47. Djurgården ferry from Nybroplan.

Unlike its Copenhagen namesake, this is an amusement park—not a fantasyland. For those who like Coney Island–type amusements, it can be a nighttime adventure. One of the big thrills of Tivoli is to go up the revolving tower for its after-dark view of Stockholm. The park is open daily from the end of April to August, usually noon–11pm or midnight, but you'll have to call for exact hours, as they're subject to weekly changes.

A NIGHTCLUB

Café Opera. Operahuset, Kungsträdgården. ☎ **08/676-58-07.** Cover free before 11pm, 65Kr ($9.75) after midnight. T-bana: Kungsträdgården.

This cafe—Swedish beaux arts at its best—functions as a bistro, brasserie, and tearoom during the day and as one of the most crowded nightclubs in Stockholm at night. You have the best chance of getting in around noon, when a *dagens* lunch is offered for 115Kr ($17.25). This establishment isn't to be confused with the opera's main dining room, the Operakällaren, whose entrance is through a different door. Near the entrance of the cafe is a stairway leading to one of the Opera House's most beautiful corners, the clublike Operabaren (Opera Bar). Open Mon–Sat 11:30am–3am and Sun 1pm–3am.

ROCK & JAZZ CLUBS

Pub Engelen/Nightclub Kolingen. Kornhamnstorg 59B. ☎ **08/611-62-00.** Cover 50–60Kr ($7.50–$9) after 8pm to pub and nightclub; free before 8pm. T-bana: Gamla Stan.

This three-in-one combination consists of the Engelen Pub, the Restaurant Engelen, and the Nightclub Kolingen in the cellar. The restaurant, which serves some of the best steaks in town, is open Sun–Thurs 5–11:30pm and Fri–Sat 5pm–1:30am, with plates priced at 60–198Kr ($9–$29.70). Live performances, mostly Swedish groups, are offered in the pub daily 8:30pm–midnight—mostly soul, funk, and rock. The pub is open Tues–Thurs 4pm–1am, Fri–Sat 4pm–2am, and Sun 5pm–1am. In the cellar dating from the 15th century, the Nightclub Kolingen is a disco 9:30pm–3am. You have to be 23 to enter.

Stampen. Stora Nygatan 5. ☎ **08/20-57-93.** Cover 50–100Kr ($7.50–$15). T-bana: Gamla Stan.

This fun-loving pub attracts a crowd of jazz lovers in their 30s and 40s. Guests crowd in to enjoy live Dixieland, New Orleans, mainstream, and swing music from the 1920s, 1930s, and 1940s. On Tuesday it's rock from the 1950s and 1960s. A menagerie of stuffed animals and lots of old, whimsical antiques are suspended from the high ceiling. It's open on Mon 8pm–midnight, Tues 8pm–12:30am, Wed–Thurs 8pm–1am, Fri 8pm–2am, and Sat 1–5pm and 8pm–2am. In summer an outdoor veranda is open when the weather permits. The club has two stages, offering dancing upstairs and downstairs almost every night.

A DANCE CLUB

Currently, at the **Daily News,** Sverigehuset at Kungsträdgården (☎ **08/21-56-55;** T-bana: Kungsträdgården), there's a dance club and a pub in the cellar, a somewhat smaller dance floor and a bar on the street level, and a street-level restaurant serving platters of Swedish and international food. On weekends there's sometimes a line outside as patrons wait to enter a setting where dancing, drinking, and eating all flow into one high-energy labyrinth. The place is open every night from 11pm to between 4 and 5am, depending on business. The cover is 30–60Kr ($4.50–$9), depending on the night of the week.

BARS

Named after the builder of the deluxe Grand Hotel—one of the most famous in Europe—the **Cadier Bar,** Södra Blasieholmshamnen 8 (☎ **08/679-35-00;** T-bana: Kungsträdgården), enjoys a view of the harbor and Royal Palace. It's one of the most sophisticated places for a rendezvous in Stockholm. You can also enjoy light meals—open-face sandwiches and smoked salmon—at any time of day in the extension overlooking the waterfront. Open Mon–Sat noon–2am and Sun noon–12:30am; a piano player performs Mon–Sat 9:30pm–1:30am.

Café Victoria, Kungsträdgården (☎ **08/10-10-85;** T-bana: Kungsträdgården), the most central cafe, gets crowded after 9pm in winter or 7pm in summer since it attracts a diverse crowd. Many patrons come here just to drink, but if you're hungry you can have lunch or dinner in an inner section beyond the animated bar area. Open Mon–Fri 11:30am–3am, Sat noon–3am, and Sun 1pm–3am.

Since 1897 **Sturehof,** Stureplan 2 (☎ **08/679-87-50;** T-bana: Hötorget), has been one of the major venues for drinking and dining in Stockholm. In the exact center of Stockholm, this establishment has been engulfed in urban restoration and is now incorporated within a covered arcade of other restaurants and shops. It remains a pleasant refuge from the city's congestion and is popular as both an after-office bar/ restaurant. Open daily 11am–1am.

GAY CLUBS

Hus 1 Restaurant & Diskotek, Sveavägen 57 (☎ **08/31-55-33;** T-bana: Rådmansgatan), is Scandinavia's largest gay nightlife center. As a restaurant, it's open daily 7–11pm, staying open on Fri–Sat until 3am. With an elegant decor and a helpful, friendly staff, it's ideal as both a place for dinner and a venue for a drink. The menu, offering such dishes as grilled salmon and seafood stew, is reasonable in price, with main dishes costing 55–120Kr ($8.25–$18), the latter for fillet of beef.

The bar/disco is open Mon–Sat 6pm–3am, though the actual dance floor is closed Mon–Tues. Conversations are animated around the circular bar. Special events are sometimes staged, and deejays always play the latest music. Cover is free Sun–Thurs but 60Kr ($9) Fri–Sat. The first Friday of every month is reserved for women only.

DAY TRIPS FROM STOCKHOLM

SKOKLOSTER CASTLE   Skokloster, S-746 96 Sklokloster (☎ **018/38-60-77**), is a splendid 17th-century castle and one of the most interesting baroque museums in Europe. It's next to Lake Mälaren, 40 miles from Stockholm and 31 miles from Uppsala. With original interiors, the castle is noted for its rich collections of paintings, furniture, applied art, tapestries, arms, and books. Admission is 50Kr ($7.50) for adults, 40Kr ($6) for seniors, and 20Kr ($3) for students and children. Daily guided tours are conducted hourly (11am–4pm) May–Aug; in Sept, Mon–Fri at 1pm and Sat–Sun at 1, 2, and 3pm; closed off-season.

The **Skokloster Motor Museum** (☎ **018/38-61-00**), on the palace grounds, contains the largest collection of vintage automobiles and motorcycles in the country. One of the most notable cars is a 1905 8-horsepower De Dion Bouton. Unlike the castle, the museum is open all year. It costs 40Kr ($6) for adults, 10Kr ($1.50) for children 7–14, free for children under 6. Open May–Sept daily 11am–5pm; Oct–Apr Sat–Sun 11am–5pm. Take bus no. 894 from Bålsta, which has a rail link to Stockholm.

UPPSALA   The major university city of Sweden, Uppsala, 42 miles northwest of Stockholm, is the most popular destination of day-trippers from Stockholm, and for good reason. Uppsala has not only a great university but also a celebrated 15th-century cathedral. Even in the time of the Vikings, this was a religious center, the scene of animal and human sacrifices in honor of the old Norse gods, and was once the center of royalty as well. Queen Christina occasionally held court here. The church is still the seat of the archbishop, and the first Swedish university was founded here in 1477.

The town is easily reached by train in about 45 minutes from Stockholm's Central Station. Trains leave about every hour during the peak daylight hours. Boats from Stockholm to Uppsala (or vice versa) also stop at Skokloster and Sigtuna. For details, check with the tourist office in any of these towns.

The **Tourist Information Office** is at Fyris Torg 8 (☎ **018/27-48-00**), open Mon–Fri 10am–6pm and Sat 10am–3pm.

Exploring Uppsala   At the end of Drottninggatan is the **Carolina Rediviva (University Library)** (☎ **018/18-39-00;** Bus: 6, 7, or 22), with its more than 5 million volumes and 40,000 manuscripts, among them many rare works from the Middle Ages. But the one manuscript that draws visitors is in the exhibition room of the library—the *Codex Argenteus* (Silver Bible), translated into the old gothic language in the middle of the 3rd century and copied in about A.D. 525. It's the only book extant in the old gothic script. Also worth seeing is *Carta Marina*, the earliest map (1539), a fairly accurate map of Sweden and its neighboring countries. Admission is free. The Exhibition room is open June 2–17 and Aug 18–Sept 15 Sun 1–3:30pm; June 18–Aug 17 Mon–Fri 9am–5pm, Sat 10am–4pm, Sun 1–3:30pm. Closed Sept 16–June 1.

The **Linnaeus Garden and Museum,** Svartbäcksgatan 27 (☎ **018/13-65-40** for the museum, or 018/10-94-90 for the garden; walk straight from the rail station to Kungsgatan, turn right, and go for about 10 minutes to Svartbäcksgatan), former home of Swedish botanist Carl von Linné, known as Carolus Linnaeus, who developed a classification system for the world's plants and flowers, is on the spot where Uppsala University's botanical garden was restored by Linnaeus, resembling a miniature baroque garden. Linnaeus, who arranged the plants according to his sexual classification system, left detailed sketches and descriptions of the garden, which have been faithfully followed. Admission is 10Kr ($1.50) for adults and 6Kr (90¢) for children. The gardens are open May–Aug daily 9am–9pm; Sept daily 9am–7pm. The museum is open June–Aug Tues–Sun noon–4pm. Closed Oct–Apr.

The largest cathedral in Scandinavia, the twin-spired gothic ✪ **Uppsala Domkyrka,** Domkyrkoplan 5 (☎ **018/18-72-01;** bus: 1), nearly 400 feet tall, was founded in the 13th century. It was severely damaged in 1702 in a disastrous fire that swept over Uppsala, then was restored near the turn of this century. Among the regal figures buried in the crypt is Gustavus Vasa. The remains of St. Erik, patron saint of Sweden, are entombed in a silver shrine. Botanist Linnaeus and philosopher-theologian Swedenborg are also buried here. A small museum displays ecclesiastical relics of Uppsala. Admission in the cathedral is free; museum admission is 10Kr ($1.50) for adults and 5Kr (75¢) for children 7–15 (free for children 6 and under). The cathedral is open June–Aug daily 9am–5pm; Sept–May Sat–Sun 9am–6pm.

✪ **GRIPSHOLM CASTLE**   On an island in Lake Mälaren, Gripsholm Castle (☎ **0159/101-94**)—the fortress built by Gustavus Vasa in the late 1530s—is one of the best-preserved castles in Sweden, near Mariefred, an idyllic small town known for its vintage narrow-gauge railroad. The castle is 42 miles southwest of Stockholm, easily reached by driving along E-20 south. You can also take the Eskilstuna bus from Stockholm. In Stockholm, boats also leave mid-May to Sept at 10am from Stadshuset, the Klara Malarstrand Pier. The castle is a 5-minute walk from the center of Mariefred.

During the reign of the 18th-century actor-king Gustavus III a theater was built at Gripsholm, but the outstanding feature of the castle is its large collection of portrait paintings.

Even though Gripsholm was last occupied by royalty in 1864 (Charles XV), it's still a royal castle. It's open May–Aug daily 10am–4pm (9am–5pm July); Apr and Sept Tues–Sun 10am–3pm; Oct–Mar Sat–Sun noon–3pm. Admission is 40Kr ($6) for adults and 20Kr ($3) for children.

18 Switzerland

by Darwin Porter & Danforth Prince

Switzerland evokes images of towering peaks, mountain lakes, lofty pastures, and picturesque villages, but it also has a rich cultural life in cities such as sophisticated Geneva or the perfectly preserved medieval city of Bern.

1 Geneva

Geneva is in the Rhône Valley at the southwestern corner of Lake Geneva (Lac Léman in French), between the Jura Mountains and the Alps. It's the capital of the canton of Geneva, the second-smallest canton in the Swiss confederation.

Switzerland's second-largest city is the most cosmopolitan of cities. The setting is idyllic, on one of the biggest alpine lakes and within view of the glorious pinnacle of Mont Blanc. Filled with parks and promenades, the city becomes a virtual garden in summer. It's also one of the healthiest cities in the world because the prevailing north wind blows away any pollution.

The yachts bobbing in the harbor and the Rolls-Royces driving along the promenades testify to the fact that Geneva is home to some of the richest people in the world. Its state religion is said to be banking—half of the banks of Switzerland are located here.

Geneva has long held a position as a center of enlightenment and humane tolerance. Over the years it has offered a refuge to such controversial figures as Voltaire, Lenin, and its native son Jean-Jacques Rousseau. Geneva also hosted Knox and Calvin, the religious reformers, and provided a safe haven for many artists. Today the headquarters of the International Red Cross and the World Health Organization are here, and it attracts many other international organizations.

ONLY IN GENEVA

Wine Tasting in the Countryside   Winding your way through the rolling vineyards just outside Geneva makes for an enjoyable day's outing. Many of the best Swiss wines never leave the country, and grapes grow on slopes overlooking Lake Geneva and the Rhône. Pick up a brochure called "Discover Geneva and Its Vineyards" from the tourist office and set out.

Sailing Lake Geneva   The crescent-shaped lake (called Lac Léman locally) gives Geneva a resortlike ambience. In summer it's alive with activity—and you can join in the fun.

Wandering Through Old Town   Geneva's Vieille Ville has been called Europe's best-kept secret. Exploring its ancient streets brings you to art galleries, antique shops, booksellers, and tiny bistros. Follow the Grand' Rue, where Jean-Jacques Rousseau was born, and wander back into time.

Discovering Les Pâquis District   One of Geneva's most animated and elegant districts, Les Pâquis faces the harbor from the Right Bank of Lake Geneva. To reach it, head north along quai des Bergues, which leads into quai du Mont-Blanc. On your left, at the intersection of quai du Mont-Blanc and Gare Routière, stands the Brunswick Monument, the tomb of Charles II of Brunswick, who died in Geneva in 1873. Les Pâquis is a sector of cozy bistros, nightclubs, ateliers, elegant boutiques, and banks. After wandering through the district, you can tour Lake Geneva in one of the lake steamers leaving from quai du Mont-Blanc.

Seeing the Fountain & the Flower Clock   There are no two more delightful sights in all of Geneva. The Jet d'Eau, quai Gustave-Ador, is the trademark of the city. Visible for miles from Apr–Sept, it throws water 460 feet into the air above the lake. The Genevese call the fountain the *jeddo*. It dates from 1891, but was improved in 1951. Many cities have sent engineers to Geneva to study the secret workings of the fountain, though it remains a carefully guarded state secret. The fountain pumps 132 gallons of water per second into the air. The Flower Clock in the Jardin Anglais (English Garden), another Geneva landmark, lies directly off quai Général-Guisan. Its face is made of beds of flowers, and it keeps perfect time! The Jardin Anglais is at the foot of the Mont Blanc Bridge, spanning the river where the Rhône leaves Lake Geneva.

Following in the Footsteps of Rousseau   There's no more delightful spot in Geneva than the Ile Rousseau, with a statue of the philosopher sculpted by Pradier in 1834. The island, which was a stamping ground of the philosopher and the site of many of his reveries, is now home to ducks, swans, grebes, and other aquatic fowl. Situated in the middle of the Rhône, it was once a bulwark of Geneva's river defenses. Rousseau was born in Geneva on June 28, 1712. One of the controversial figures of his era, he advocated a "return to nature" to escape the corruption of civilization. His writings helped pave the way for the French Revolution, and he's the father of the Romantic movement.

ORIENTATION

ARRIVING   By Plane   The **Geneva–Cointrin Airport** (☎ 022/717-71-11), although busy, is compact and easily negotiated. To get into the center of Geneva, there's a train station linked to the air terminal with trains leaving about every 5–15 minutes from 5:39am–11:36pm for the 7-minute trip; the one-way fare is 7.40 SF ($6.15) in first class and 4.40 SF ($3.65) in second class. A taxi into town will cost 35 SF ($29.05) and up, or you can take bus no. 10 for 2.20 SF ($1.85).

By Train   Geneva's busiest, most central, and most visible CFF (Chemins de fer fédéraux) rail station is **La Gare Cornavin** (sometimes referred to as Genève–Cornavin), place Cornavin (☎ 022/157-22-22). Be careful not to confuse it with **La Gare Genève–Cointrin,** near the city's airport, which to some degree handles some of the spillover from its larger sibling. Conveniently, some trains heading off to other regions of Switzerland and the rest of Europe from Genève–Cointrin don't require transfers in Genève–Cornavin, a fact that's appreciated by many airline passengers flying to other parts of the country.

Geneva Attractions & Accommodations

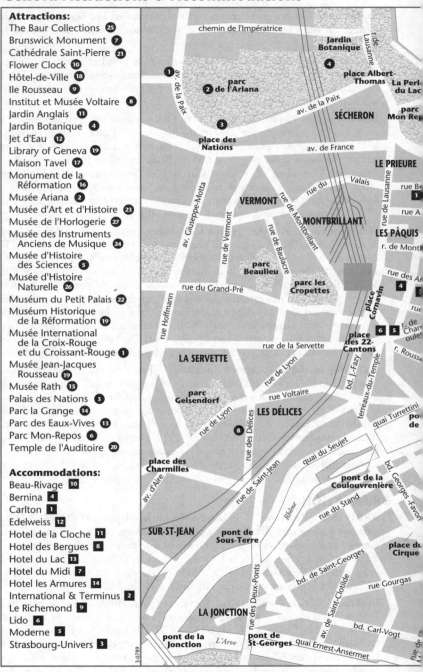

3-0789

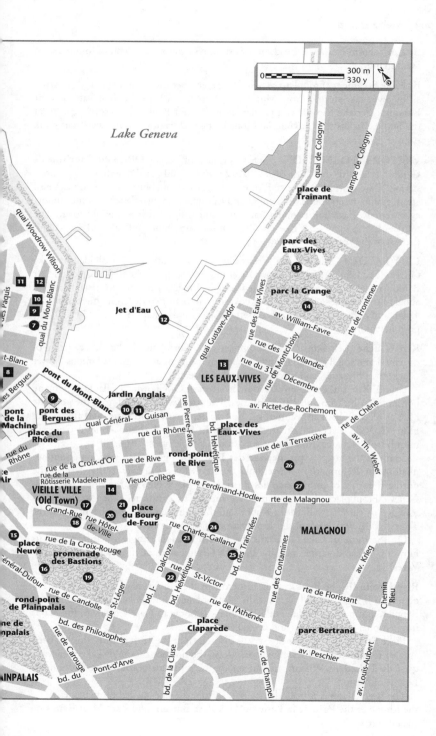

Lake Geneva

0 ——— 300 m
330 y

quai de Cologny
rampe de Cologny

place de
Traînant

parc des
Eaux-Vives
13

rte de Frontenex

parc la Grange
14

av. William-Favre

rue des Eaux-Vives

Jet d'Eau
12

quai Woodrow Wilson

quai du Mont-Blanc

11 **12**
10
9
7
es Pâquis

quai Gustave-Ador

rue des Mont-Choisy

Vollandes

rue du 31

Décembre

t-Blanc

8
es Bergues

pont du Mont-Blanc

Jardin Anglais

LES EAUX-VIVES
13

rte de Chêne

av. Th. Weber

9

**pont
de la
Machine**

**pont des
Bergues**

10 **11**
quai Général- Guisan

av. Pictet-de-Rochemont

**place du
Rhône**

rue du Rhône

rue Pierre-Fatio

bd. Helvétique

**place des
Eaux-Vives**

rue de la Terrassière

rue du
Rhône

rue de la Croix-d'Or   rue de Rive

**rond-point
de Rive**

26

e
Air

rue de la
Rôtisserie Madeleine

Vieux-Collège

rue Ferdinand-Hodler

rte de Malagnou

27

**VIEILLE VILLE
(Old Town)** **17**

14

21 **place
du Bourg-
de-Four**

rue Charles-Galland

MALAGNOU

15

Grand-Rue
18

20 rue Hôtel-
de-Ville

24

**place
Neuve**

rue de la Croix-Rouge

23

rue des Tranchées

av. Krieg

**promenade
des Bastions**

25

Dalcroze

bd. des Tranchées

rue des Contamines

énéral-Dufour

16

19

rue de Candolle

rue St-Léger

rue
St-Victor

rte de Florissant

Chemin
Rieu

**rond-point
de Plainpalais**

bd. I-

bd. Helvétique

rue de l'Athénée

22

ne de
npalais

bd. des Philosophes

**place
Claparède**

parc Bertrand

rue de Carouge

Pont-d'Arve

bd. de la Cluse

av. de Champel

av. Peschier

av. Louis-Aubert

INPALAIS

bd. du

By Car   From Lausanne, head southwest on N-1 to the very "end of southwestern Switzerland."

By Lake Steamer   From late May to late September there are frequent daily arrivals by Swiss lake steamer from Montreaux, Vevey, and Lausanne (you can use your Eurailpass for the trip). If you're staying in the Left Bank (Old Town), get off at the Jardin Anglais stop in Geneva; Mont Blanc and Pâquis are the two Right Bank stops.

VISITOR INFORMATION   Geneva's tourist office, the **Office du Tourisme de Genève,** is at 3 rue du Mont-Blanc (☎ **022/909-70-00**), at the central CFF railroad station, Gare Cornavin. The staff provides information about the city and can also arrange hotel reservations (in Geneva and throughout Switzerland), car and motorcycle rentals, excursion bookings, and an audio-guided visit to the old town. The tourist office is open June 15–Sept 15 Mon–Fri 8am–8pm and Sat–Sun 9am–6pm; the rest of the year, Mon–Sat 9am–6pm.

CITY LAYOUT   Geneva is a perfect city to explore on foot. It's divided by Lake Geneva (Lac Léman) and the Rhône River into two sections: the Right Bank and Left Bank. You may rent an audio-guided tour in English from the tourist office (see above) for 10 SF ($8.30). This tour covers more than two dozen highlights in Old Town and comes complete with cassette, player, and a map. A 50 SF ($41.50) deposit is required.

Rive Gauche (Left Bank)   This compact and colorful area is the oldest section of the city. Here you'll find Old Town, some major shopping streets, the famous Flower Clock, the university, and several important museums.

 Grand' Rue is the well-preserved main street of Old Town. It's flanked by many houses from the 15th and 18th centuries. The street winds uphill from the ponts de l'Ile; at place Bel-Air it becomes rue de la Cité, then Grand' Rue, and finally rue Hôtel-de-Ville. Eventually it reaches **place du Bourg-de-Four**—one of Geneva's most historic squares (Rousseau was born in a simple house at no. 40).

 South of this street is **promenade des Bastions,** a green-belt area with a monument to the Reformation; it overlooks the Arve River. Directly to the west, in the northern corner of promenade des Bastions, is **place Neuve,** the finest square in Geneva. From place Neuve, you can take **rue de la Corraterie,** which was once surrounded by the city wall, to the Rhône and the **ponts de l'Ile.** On this bridge is the Tour de l'Ile, what's left of the 13th-century bishops' castle.

 On the shore of Lake Geneva is the **Jardin Anglais** (English Garden) with its Flower Clock and, farther out, the **Parc La Grange** and the nearby **Parc des Eaux-Vives.**

Rive Droite (Right Bank)   You can cross to the other side of the Rhône on any of several bridges, including pont du Mont-Blanc, pont de la Machine, pont des Bergues, and ponts de l'Ile. The Right Bank is home to Gare Cornavin, the major international organizations, and several attractive parks.

 Place St-Gervais is in the St-Gervais district; since the 18th century this has been an area for jewelers and watchmakers. Along the northern shore of Lake Geneva is **quai du Président-Wilson,** named for the U.S. president who helped found the League of Nations.

 The Right Bank is surrounded by parks, from the tree-shaded promenades along the Rhône to the **Parc de la Perle du Lac, Parc Barton,** and **Parc Mon-Repos** on the outskirts.

GETTING AROUND

BY PUBLIC TRANSPORTATION   For the most part, all of Geneva's transportation lines begin at place Cornavin, in front of the main rail station. From here, you can take bus F to the Palais des Nations.

Tickets for Zone 10, covering the urban area of Geneva, are sold from automatic vending machines at each stop. These machines are coin operated or magnetic-card operated (free cards are available from Geneva public transport agencies). Tickets for other zones, including the suburbs of Geneva and France, are sold by drivers on the corresponding buses.

Four **basic tickets** are provided: (1) free transfers for 1 hour in Zone 10, with as many changes as you wish on any vehicle, for 2.20 SF ($1.85); (2) a trip limited to three stops, valid for half an hour, allowing a return trip, at a cost of 1.50 SF ($1.25); (3) free transfers for 1 1/2 hours in all zones of the network of Geneva, at a cost of 5 SF ($4.15); and (4) a ride for 1 hour in Zone 10 for children 6–12 as well as seniors (women over 62 and men over 65), at a cost of 1.50 SF ($1.25); children 5 and under ride free.

If you plan a frequent use of the system, multiuse tickets and daily cards can be purchased from agents whose addresses are listed on posts at the various stops. A wide range of these tickets is available, and often you can adapt the system to fit your needs. For example, a daily ticket for unlimited transportation in Zone 10 costs 5 SF ($4.15) for as many trips and changes as you need. It's valid from the time you stamp it up to the termination of the day's service, which is around midnight.

There's also a daily ticket costing 8.50 SF ($7.05) including transportation not only in Zone 10 but also in Zones 21, 31, and 41, taking in practically the whole network of Greater Geneva. Many worthy attractions and restaurants are in the suburbs.

These tickets and many other kinds of tickets, including combined bus/cable-car tickets to climb to the top of Mont Salève, are available from the Geneva public transport systems agencies or from official dealers.

For customer service and more information, call **022/308-34-34.**

BY TAXI   Cab fares start at 6 SF ($5), plus 2.60 SF ($2.15) for each kilometer in the city within Zone 10 and 3.50 SF ($2.90) in the countryside. The fare from the airport is about 35 SF ($29.05). No tipping is required. For a taxi, call **022/ 33-141-33** or 022/320-20-20.

BY CAR   Driving isn't recommended because parking is too difficult and the many one-way streets make navigation complicated. However, should you wish to rent a car and tour Lake Geneva, you'll find many car-rental companies represented at the airport or in the center of the city. Major offices include **Avis,** 44 rue de Lausanne (☎ 022/731-90-00); **Budget Rent-a-Car,** 37 rue de Lausanne (☎ 022/732-52-52); **Europcar,** 65 rue de Lausanne (☎ 022/731-51-50); and **Hertz,** 60 rue de Berne (☎ 022/731-12-00).

BY BICYCLE   Touring the city by bicycle isn't practical because of the steep cobblestone streets and general congestion. However, you might want to rent a bike for touring the countryside around Geneva. The major outlet for renting bikes is at the *bagages* desk at Gare Cornavin, where city bikes cost 21 SF ($17.45) per day and mountain bikes rent for 29 SF ($24.05).

Another major outlet is **Horizon Motos,** 22 rue des Pâquis (☎ **022/731-23-39**), which offers mountain bicycles for 30 SF ($24.90) per day, going up to 50 SF ($41.50) per day on Sat–Sun. Motorcycles can also be rented, beginning at 45 SF ($37.35) per day.

FAST FACTS: Geneva

American Express   The American Express office at 7 rue du Mont-Blanc (☎ 022/731-76-00), is open Mon–Fri 8:30am–5:30pm and Sat 9am–noon.

Baby-sitters   A list of agencies offering this service is available at the tourist office. Hotels will also secure an English-speaking sitter for you, or you can call Service de Placement de l'Université, 4 rue de Candolle (☎ 022/329-39-70). Call this office before 11am if you want a sitter at night.

Business Hours   Most banks are open Mon–Fri 8:30am–4:30pm (until 5:30pm Wed). Most offices are open Mon–Fri 8am–noon and 2–6pm, though this can vary. It's always best to call first.

Consulates   If you lose your passport or have other business with your home government, go to your nation's consulate: **United States,** 1–3 av. de la Paix (☎ 022/738-5095); **Australia,** 56–58 rue Moillebeau (☎ 022/734-62-00); **Canada,** 11 chemin du Pré-de-la-Bichette (☎ 022/733-90-00); **New Zealand,** 28A chemin du Petit-Saconnex (☎ 022/734-95-30); the **United Kingdom,** 37–39 rue de Vermont (☎ 022/734-38-00).

Currency   The basic unit of currency is the Swiss franc (SF), which is made up of 100 centimes. Banknotes are in denominations of 10, 20, 50, 100, 500, and 1,000 franc notes, and coin denominations are 5, 10, 20, and 50 centimes and 1, 2, and 5 francs. The rate of exchange used in this chapter was $1 = 1.28 SF, or 1 SF = 78¢.

Currency Exchange   The money exchange at Gare Cornavin 10, place Cornavin (☎ 022/715-38-11), is open daily 8:30am–4:30pm. For other financial transactions, the Société de Banque Suisse (Swiss Bank Corporation) is at 2 rue de la Confédération (☎ 022/375-75-75).

Dentists   English-speaking dentists are available at one of the *cliniques dentaires* at 5 rue Malombré (☎ 022/346-64-44), Mon–Fri 7:30am–8pm and Sat 8am–6pm.

Doctors   In a medical emergency, call 022/320-25-11; or arrange an appointment with an English-speaking doctor at the Hôpital Cantonal, 24 rue Micheli-du-Crest (☎ 022/372-3311).

Drugstores   One of Geneva's biggest drugstores, Pharmacie Principale, Confédération-Centre, rue de la Confédération (☎ 022/311-31-30), offers everything from medicine to clothing, perfumes, optical equipment, cameras, and photo supplies. It's open Mon–Fri 9am–7pm and Sat 9am–5pm.

Emergencies   In an emergency, dial 117 for the police or an ambulance. Dial 118 to report a fire.

Hospitals   You can go to the Hôpital Cantonal, 24 rue Micheli-du-Crest (☎ 022/372-3311).

Lost Property   Go to the Service cantonal des objects trouvés, 7 rue des Glacis-de-Rive (☎ 022/787-60-00), open Mon–Thurs 8am–4:30pm and Fri 8am–4pm.

Luggage Storage/Lockers   Luggage can be stored and lockers rented at the main rail station, Gare Cornavin, place Cornavin (☎ 022/715-21-11).

Post Office   A branch office of Geneva's Bureau de Poste at Gare Cornavin, 16 rue des Gares (☎ 022/739-21-11), as well as the city's main post office at 18 rue du Mont-Blanc (same phone), are both open Mon–Fri 6am–10:45pm, Sat 6am–8pm, and Sun noon–8pm.

Taxes   Geneva has no special city tax.

Telegrams/Telex/Fax   A big long-distance phone center is at the main train station, Gare Cornavin, place Cornavin, and it's open 24 hours. It's much cheaper to make your long-distance calls here than at your hotel—some Geneva hotels add a 40% surcharge to long-distance calls. Telegrams and faxes can be sent at the post office at 18 rue du Mont-Blanc (☎ 022/739-21-11), two blocks from the train station.

Transit Information   Call 022/731-64-50 for rail information, or the airport at 022/717-71-11. For bus information, call 022/308-34-34.

ACCOMMODATIONS
ON THE RIGHT BANK
Very Expensive

✪ **Hôtel Beau-Rivage.** 13 quai du Mont-Blanc, CH-1201 Genève. ☎ **022/716-66-66.** Fax 022/716-60-60. 91 rms, 6 suites. MINIBAR TV TEL. 510–720 SF ($423.30–$597.60) double; from 850 SF ($705.50) suite. AE, DC, MC, V. Parking 25 SF ($20.75). Bus: 6 or 33.

This landmark 1865 hotel receives our highest recommendation for its traditional Victorian charm and impeccable service. However, you'll pay dearly for the privilege of staying here. The hotel's most striking feature is the open five-story lobby. The guest rooms are individually furnished and frequently redecorated. Some accommodations are air-conditioned, and front rooms have views of the Right Bank. The hotel maintains two restaurants, the more elegant of which is Le Chat-Botté (Puss in Boots).

Hôtel des Bergues. 33 quai des Bergues, CH-1211 Genève. ☎ **022/731-50-50.** Fax 022/732-19-89. 119 rms, 9 suites. A/C MINIBAR TV TEL. 450–660 SF ($373.50–$547.80) double; from 1,900 SF ($1,577) suite. AE, DC, MC, V. Bus: 7.

This elegant four-story hotel—designated an historic monument—once catered to the monarchs of Europe. It has long been ranked by *Institutional Investor* as one of the world's top hotels, grandly memorable from its central position at the edge of the Rhône. The hotel and its 130-person staff are the most hospitable in Geneva. The public rooms are lavish, and the guest rooms have Directoire and Louis-Philippe furnishings, along with many other amenities. Its two restaurants and bar are highly recommended.

✪ **Le Richemond.** Jardin Brunswick, CH-1211 Genève. ☎ **022/731-14-00.** Fax 022/731-67-09. 67 rms, 31 suites. A/C MINIBAR TV TEL. 620–720 SF ($514.60–$597.60) double; from 1,100 SF ($913) suite. AE, DC, MC, V. Parking 35 SF ($29.05). Bus: 1 or 9.

Le Richemond, which counts some of the world's most prominent people among its guests, is Geneva's greatest hotel. Erected in 1875, the neoclassical building has wrought-iron balustrades and is near the lake, across from a small park. Its public rooms look like a museum, with dozens of valuable engravings and an array of furniture dating from the days of Louis XII. The guest rooms range from those opulently decorated to those with a standard international decor. Gentilhomme is among the finest dining establishments in Geneva, and Le Jardin is the most fashionable cafe in the city.

Moderate

Hôtel Carlton. 22 rue Amat, CH-1202 Genève. ☎ **022/908-68-50.** Fax 022/908-68-68. 124 rms. TV TEL. 268 SF ($222.45) double. Rates include buffet breakfast. AE, DC, MC, V. Parking 10 SF ($8.30). Bus: 4 or 44.

This hotel is about seven city blocks east of the rail station and 300 yards from the waterfront views of quai du Président-Wilson. The facade combines weathered vertical slats and smooth stones decoratively cemented into rectangular patterns beneath the modern windows. The lobby is decorated in summery tones, and the guest rooms are outfitted in tones of white with earth tones. Lunch and dinner are served in the restaurant-grill, Le Carlton, which has an international menu that includes the fresh fish of the day.

Hôtel du Midi. 1 quai des Bergues, CH-1211 Genève. ☎ **022/731-78-00.** Fax 022/731-00-20. 91 rms, 2 suites. MINIBAR TV TEL. 230 SF ($190.90) double; 450 SF ($373.50) suite for four. Rates include continental breakfast. AE, DC, MC, V. Bus: 7.

On a tree-lined square near the center of Geneva, this salmon-colored eight-story hotel reminds most visitors of an apartment building. A complete renovation in 1994 moved the reception area to the street level and added half a dozen rooms. The windows are double-glazed to keep out the noise of the city's traffic, and there's wall-to-wall carpeting in every room. The rooms contain accessories like warming racks for towels, minirefrigerators, and safes. The hotel maintains a small restaurant at street level.

Hôtel Edelweiss. 2 place de la Navigation, CH-1201 Genève. ☎ **022/731-36-58.** Fax 022/738-85-33. 39 rms. MINIBAR TV TEL. 225 SF ($186.75) double. Rates include continental breakfast. AE, DC, MC, V. Bus: 6 or 33.

This brown-and-white eight-story hotel towers above its neighbors near quai du Président-Wilson. Its rustic interior decor contrasts with its modern exterior. The rooms are cozy with pinewood furniture crafted in country-Swiss style. Built in the early 1960s, the hotel was last renovated in 1993. Its little restaurant is patronized by a lot of locals and is also inexpensively priced.

Strasbourg-Univers. 10 rue J-J-Pradier, CH-1201 Genève. ☎ **022/732-25-62.** Fax 022/738-42-08. 51 rms, 2 suites. TV TEL. 200 SF ($166) double; 400–500 SF ($332–$415) suite. Rates include continental breakfast. AE, DC, MC, V. Bus: 1 or 8.

Close to the rail station, this building was constructed around 1900, though many renovations both outside and in have kept it looking fresh. Some of the more recently renovated rooms have wooden surfaces and pastel colors; others are comfortable and traditionally conservative. About half contain a minibar. On the premises is a pleasant restaurant.

Inexpensive

☉ Hôtel Bernina. 22 place Cornavin, CH-1201 Genève. ☎ **022/731-49-50.** Fax 022/732-73-59. 80 rms (68 with bath). TV TEL. 100 SF ($83) double without bath, 150 SF ($124.50) double with bath. Rates include continental breakfast. AE, DC, MC, V. Parking 15 SF ($12.45). Bus: 6 or 33.

This six-story hotel occupies an old-fashioned building with iron balustrades and neoclassical detailing; it's across from the main rail station, a 5-minute walk from the lake. The simply furnished rooms have more space than you might expect, closets, and double glazing to keep out the traffic noise. Breakfast is the only meal served.

☉ Hôtel de la Cloche. 6 rue de la Cloche, CH-1211 Genève. ☎ **022/732-94-81.** Fax 022/738-16-12. 8 rms (3 with bath). TV TEL. 75 SF ($62.25) double without bath, 85 SF ($70.55) double with bath; 90 SF ($74.70) triple without bath; 120 SF ($99.60) quad without bath. AE, V. Bus: 1.

This small hotel, the bargain of Geneva, occupies the second floor of a 19th-century apartment building on a narrow street behind the modern bulk of the Noga Hilton. Unpretentious yet in a glamorous location, it's run by a charming elderly widow, Madame Chabbey. The building is entered using a computerized access code from the street below. The rooms are high-ceilinged, often with ornate plasterwork, elegant moldings, and simple furniture; some have views over a quiet inner courtyard and some have views over the lake. Breakfast is the only meal served.

Hôtel International & Terminus. 20 rue des Alpes, CH-1201 Genève. ☎ **022/732-80-95.** Fax 022/732-18-43. 53 rms. TV TEL. 190 SF ($157.70) double; 230 SF ($190.90) triple. Rates include continental breakfast. AE, DC, MC, V. Parking 12 SF ($9.95). Bus: 6 or 33.

This hotel lies across from the main entrance of Geneva's railway station and has been directed by three generations of the Cottier family. Built around 1900, it was radically upgraded in 1993 and 1994, with pairs of smaller rooms reconfigured into larger units and private baths or showers added. Rated three stars by the local tourist board, the hotel has a lobby that alternates Louis-style furnishings with modern pieces and guest rooms with simple accessories.

Hôtel Moderne. 1 rue de Berne, CH-1211 Genève. ☎ **022/732-81-00.** Fax 022/738-26-58. 55 rms. TV TEL. 160–170 SF ($132.80–$141.10) double. Rates include buffet breakfast. AE, DC, MC, V. Bus: 10.

Near the railroad station and the lake, this is a seven-story rectangle painted white, with a low-lying glassed-in extension containing the breakfast room. The public rooms are modern, with Nordic furniture and abstract angles and curves. Guest rooms, with soundproof windows, are predictably furnished, clean, modern, and sunny. Some are reserved for nonsmokers. Babysitting, room service, and laundry facilities are available. The hotel's restaurant serves only breakfast, but there's an Italian restaurant in the same building. The nearest parking is at the Cornavin rail station underground garage nearby.

ON THE LEFT BANK
Very Expensive

✪ **Hôtel Les Armures.** 1 rue des Puits-St-Pierre, CH-1204 Genève. ☎ **022/310-91-72.** Fax 022/310-98-46. 24 rms, 4 suites. A/C MINIBAR TV TEL. 400 SF ($332) double; 510 SF ($423.30) suite. Rates include continental breakfast. AE, DC, MC, V. Bus: 3 or 33.

This hotel, in the center of the old town, is one of the most charming in Geneva, and rooms are beautifully maintained. The 17th-century building had been used as a printing factory, and the restored public rooms reveal the original painted ceiling beams and an old blue-and-gray fresco. The lobby has oriental rugs, modern sculpture, and a suit of armor. The hotel is housed in the same building as the oldest cafe in Geneva, Les Armures.

Inexpensive

⑤ **Hôtel du Lac.** 15 rue des Eaux-Vives, CH-1207 Genève. ☎ **022/735-45-80.** 26 rms (none with bath). 80 SF ($66.40) double; 110 SF ($91.30) triple. Rates include continental breakfast. MC, V. Bus: 9 from the train station to place des Eaux-Vives.

This small budget hotel is on the Left Bank in the old city, occupying the sixth and seventh floors of an apartment building. The Swiss-Italian managers don't pretend to offer first-class service, but they make up for it with their hospitality and their ability to speak English. The rooms are simple, immaculate, and reasonably comfortable. Most have a radio, phone, and balcony. Free showers are found down the hall.

DINING
ON THE RIGHT BANK
Very Expensive

✪ **Le Chat-Botté.** In the Hôtel Beau-Rivage, 13 quai du Mont-Blanc. ☎ **022/731-65-32.** Reservations required. Main courses 25–90 SF ($20.75–$74.70); fixed-price menus 110–135 SF

($91.30–$112.05). AE, DC, MC, V. Mon–Fri noon–2pm and 7–10pm. Closed 15 days at Easter and Christmas. Bus: 1. FRENCH.

This grand restaurant is in one of the grandest hotels in Geneva. Suitably decorated with tapestries, sculpture, and rich upholsteries, with a polite staff, it serves wonderful food. If the weather is right, you can dine on the flower-bedecked terrace, overlooking the Jet d'Eau. The cuisine, though inspired by French classics, is definitely contemporary. The large selection includes fillets of red mullet vinaigrette, cutlets of salmon pan-fried with spices, and breast of chicken stuffed with vegetables. The chef's best-known dish is delicate fillet of perch from Lake Geneva, sautéed until it's golden and sometimes served with fresh fava beans.

✪ **Le Cygne.** In the Noga Hilton International, 19 quai du Mont-Blanc. ☎ **022/908-90-85.** Reservations required. Main courses 38–58 SF ($31.55–$48.15); fixed-price lunches 65–95 SF ($53.95–$78.85); fixed-price dinners 75–100 SF ($62.25–$83); all-fish menu 115 SF ($95.45); *menu dégustation* 155 SF ($128.65). AE, DC, MC, V. Daily noon–2:30pm and 7–10:30pm. Closed first 2 weeks of Jan, first 3 weeks of July. Bus: 1. FRENCH.

Among the best restaurants in Geneva, Le Cygne overlooks the harbor with the famous Jet d'Eau and, in the distance, the Alps. A refined cuisine is offered, with impeccable service. The menu changes seasonally and may offer fresh duck liver fried with grapes and sweet dessert wine, lightly sautéed scallops served with zucchini-flavored risotto and the oil of white truffles, or pigeon from the high plateaux of western France (Anjou) cooked with sesame seeds and dried fruits.

✪ **Le Neptune.** In the Hôtel du Rhône, 1 quai Turrettini. ☎ **022/731-98-31.** Reservations required. Main courses 45–55 SF ($37.35–$45.65); fixed-price lunch 65 SF ($53.95); fixed-price dinner 125 SF ($103.75). AE, DC, MC, V. Mon–Fri noon–3pm and 7pm–midnight. Bus: 6, 8, 10, or 15. SEAFOOD.

At one of Geneva's finest seafood restaurants, the decor is intimate, intensely floral, and graced with an enormous fresco at one end displaying an inside view of Neptune's kingdom. Although the menu changes, based on market conditions, you're likely to be offered such dishes as warm salad of lobster served with a confit of truffled artichokes and olive oil, fillets of John Dory with a sauce made from whipped butter and sea-urchin roe served with seafood-flavored pasta, and risotto of red snapper and stingray served with the reduced essence of squid. If you're not in the mood for fish, try rack of Scottish lamb in puff pastry with spices or gray partridge roasted en casserole with autumn herbs.

Expensive

La Mère Royaume. 9 rue des Corps-Saints. ☎ **022/732-70-08.** Reservations required. Brasserie, fixed-price meal 38–98 SF ($31.55–$81.35). Restaurant, main courses 40–70 SF ($33.20–$58.10); fixed-price menus 66–98 SF ($54.80–$81.35). AE, DC, MC, V. Mon–Fri 11:30am–2pm and 7–10pm, Sat 7–10pm. Closed July 23–Aug 15. Bus: 4, 6, or 7. FRENCH.

This is one of the oldest restaurants in town, established around the turn of the century. It's named after a heroine who in 1602 poured boiling stew over a Savoyard soldier's head and cracked his skull with the kettle. With an antecedent like that, you'd expect some of the heartiest fare in Geneva, but instead the kitchen offers delicately cooked French specialties, such as omble chevalier, a fish from Lake Geneva, and a version of trout that has been pronounced "divine." Less expensive meals are served in the informal brasserie.

Moderate

🅂 **Chez Jacky.** 9–11 rue Necker. ☎ **022/732-86-80.** Reservations required. Main courses 37–38 SF ($30.70–$31.55); business lunch 38 SF ($31.55); fixed-price menus 52 SF ($43.15),

65 SF ($53.95), and 79 SF ($65.55). AE, MC, V. Mon–Fri noon–2:30pm and 7–11pm. Closed first week of Jan and 3 weeks in Aug. Bus: 5, 13, or 44. SWISS.

This French provincial bistro should be better known, though it already attracts everyone from grandmothers to young skiers en route to Verbier. It's the domain of Jacky Gruber, an exceptional chef from Valais. There's subtlety in M. Gruber's cooking that suggests the influence of his mentor, Frédy Giradet, who some hail as the world's greatest chef. You might begin with Chinese cabbage and mussels and continue with fillet of turbot roasted with thyme or beautifully prepared pink duck on a bed of spinach with a confit of onions. Be prepared to wait for each course.

ON THE LEFT BANK
Very Expensive
Restaurant du Parc des Eaux-Vives. 82 quai Gustave-Ador. ☎ **022/735-41-40.** Reservations required. Main courses 30–65 SF ($24.90–$53.95); fixed-price lunch 78–138 SF ($64.75–$114.55); fixed-price dinner 145 SF ($120.35). AE, MC, V. Apr–Oct Tues–Sun noon–2pm, Tues–Sat 7–10pm. Nov–Mar Tues–Sat noon–2pm and 7–10pm. Bus: 2. FRENCH/SWISS.

To reach this restaurant, you'll pass through a wrought-iron gate and proceed along a winding drive that leads to the dining room of an 18th-century château owned by the city of Geneva. Excellent meals are prepared by chefs who adjust the menu seasonally but tend to concentrate on classical French cuisine. The local trout is superb; in autumn, the menu offers many game dishes. Of course, everything tastes better with truffles, including lobster salad, foie gras, and sea bass flambé with fennel.

Expensive
✪ **Le Béarn.** 4 quai de la Poste. ☎ **022/321-00-28.** Reservations required. Main courses 40–60 SF ($33.20–$49.80); fixed-price lunch 58–150 SF ($48.15–$124.50); fixed-price dinner 85–150 SF ($70.55–$124.50). AE, DC, MC, V. Mon–Fri noon–2pm; Mon–Sat 7:15–10pm. Closed mid-July to late Aug and Sat night May–Sept. Tram: 13. FRENCH.

Jean-Paul Goddard and his excellent staff have created the best restaurant in the business center of Geneva. Everything is on a small scale, as there are only 10 tables, and the service is personalized. The renovated interior contains two dining areas: one decorated in Empire style, the other with elegantly rustic accessories. The chefs prepare dishes like gazpacho of crayfish, a *papillotte* of frogs' legs with herbs "from the kitchen garden," zucchini flowers with crayfish, suprême of pigeon, and roast lamb in the style of Provence.

Moderate
Brasserie Lipp. Confédération-Centre, 8 rue de la Confédération. ☎ **022/311-10-11.** Reservations recommended. Main courses 18–40 SF ($14.95–$33.20). AE, DC, MC, V. Daily 7am–12:45am. Bus: 12. SWISS.

This bustling restaurant is named after the famous Parisian brasserie, and when you enter, especially at lunch, and see the waiters in black jackets with long white aprons rushing about, you'll think you've been transported to Paris. The impossibly long menu contains a sampling of the French repertoire of bistro dishes. Like its Parisian namesake, the Geneva Lipp specializes in several versions of charcuterie. You can also order three kinds of pot-au-feu and such classic dishes as Toulousain cassoulet with confit de canard (duckling), available in autumn and winter. The fresh oysters are among the best in the city. Tables are placed outside in summer.

La Coupole. 116 rue du Rhône. ☎ **022/735-65-44.** Reservations not required. *Plats du jour* 24–30 SF ($19.90–$24.90); fixed-price menu 36–38 SF ($29.90–$31.55). AE, DC, MC, V. Mon–Sat 7pm–2am. Bus: 6 or 9. Tram: 12. SWISS.

This is a true brasserie—far more elegant than its Parisian namesake. The place is most popular at noon, especially with shoppers and office workers. Fanciful and fun, it's dotted with grandfather clocks, a bronze *Venus*, Edwardian palms, and comfortable banquettes. The menu is limited but well selected; the *cuisine du marché* is a delight, though many patrons stick to the standard red-meat bistro specials, such as the inevitable entrecôte.

Inexpensive

Au Pied de Cochon. 4 place du Bourg-de-Four. ☎ **022/310-47-97.** Reservations recommended. Main courses 15–38 SF ($12.45–$31.55). AE, DC, MC, V. Daily noon–2:30pm and 6:30–10:30pm. Bus: 2 or 22. Tram: 12. LYONNAISE/SWISS.

Come here for hearty Lyonnaise fare if you don't mind smoke and noise. A lot of young people are attracted to this place, as well as lawyers from the Palais de Justice across the way. Artists and local workers also frequent the place. The cookery is as grandmother used to prepare it, provided she came from the Lyon area. Naturally, the namesake pieds de cochon (pigs' feet) is included on the menu, along with *petit salé* (lamb), grilled andouillettes, and tripe.

Ⓢ L'Aïoli. 6 rue Adrien-Lachenal. ☎ **022/736-79-71.** Main courses 15.50–32 SF ($12.85–$26.55); *menu gastronomique* 69 SF ($57.25). AE, DC, MC, V. Mon–Fri 10am–3pm and 6–11:30pm. Closed July 15–Aug 15. Bus: 1 or 6. Tram: 12. FRENCH.

Named after Provence's famous garlic mayonnaise, this popular neighborhood restaurant stands opposite Le Corbusier's Maison de Verre. Something of a local secret, it offers personalized service and the finest Provençal cooking in town. Owner Marius Anthoine hails from the Valais. An evening meal includes an appetizer, a first plate, a main dish, cheese, a dessert, coffee, and wine (you can spend more by ordering à la carte). Among featured dishes are lamb gigot and frogs' legs Provençal. Monsieur Anthoine makes a delectable pot-au-feu. Look for the daily specials.

Ⓢ Le Lyrique. 12 bd. du Théâtre. ☎ **022/328-00-95.** Reservations recommended. Restaurant, main courses 20–40 SF ($16.60–$33.20); fixed-price lunch 45 SF ($37.35); fixed-price dinner 50 SF ($41.50). Brasserie, main courses 18–38 SF ($14.95–$31.55); fixed-price lunch 30 SF ($24.90); fixed-price dinner 40 SF ($33.20). AE, MC, V. Mon–Fri noon–3pm and 6:30–10pm. Closed Sat–Sun except for special presentations at the Grand Théâtre de Genève. Bus: 2 or 22. SWISS.

Le Lyrique contains both a formal restaurant and a brasserie. It bustles with urban vitality and is tuned to the arts and business lives of Geneva. The brasserie, which has a terrace, is open all day but serves hot meals only during the hours above. In the brasserie, the menu might include chicken suprême with leeks, succulent steaks, or grilled sole. In the restaurant, you can order omble chevalier (the famous lake fish of Geneva), served poached, or turbot stuffed with red peppers.

Ⓢ Restaurant du Palais de Justice. 8 place du Bourg-de-Four. ☎ **022/310-42-54.** Main courses 25–37 SF ($20.75–$30.70); pizzas 15–18 SF ($12.45–$14.95); fondues 19–26 SF ($15.75–$21.60); *plat du jour* 16–17 SF ($13.30–$14.10). AE, DC, MC, V. Mon–Sat noon–2:30pm and 6:30–11pm. Bus: 2 or 22. SWISS.

A simple little place with lots of atmosphere, this restaurant is in Old Town on a colorful square, across from the Palais de Justice. It opened in the late 1950s in a historic medieval building and has thrived ever since. The building actually contains three places to eat, with the same menu for each. Small pizzas, fondues, and *plats du jour,* including an array of beef dishes, draw the crowds. The food is in the usual brasserie style, nothing special but nothing really bad either.

Ⓢ Taverne de la Madeleine. 20 rue Toutes-Ames. ☎ **022/310-60-70.** Reservations recommended. Main courses 14–22 SF ($11.60–$18.25); *plat du jour* 13 SF ($10.80). No credit cards. Mon–Fri 7:30am–6pm (last food order at 4pm), Sat 9am–3pm (last food order at 2:30pm). Bus: 2. Tram 12. SWISS.

This very good restaurant, one of the oldest in Geneva, is set against the old city wall beside the Eglise de la Madeleine. The building is a century old, and the restaurant was opened about 80 years ago. The brusquely efficient staff caters to a lunchtime business crowd. The place is operated by a philanthropic organization that forbids the consumption of alcohol (alcohol-free beer is available). You can order a variety of well-prepared dishes. Specials include four types of pasta, vegetarian sandwiches, and such hearty fare as a big plate of osso buco with *pommes frites*. The kitchen prides itself on its fillet of lake perch prepared meunière style or Vevey style with exotic mushrooms.

ATTRACTIONS

You can see most of Geneva on foot, which is the best way to familiarize yourself with the city.

SIGHTSEEING SUGGESTIONS

If You Have 1 Day   Begin the day by viewing the spectacular water fountain, the Jet d'Eau, and the Flower Clock in the Jardin Anglais. Then take a cruise of Lake Geneva on a steamer. Return in the early afternoon and explore the Left Bank's Old Town. Have dinner at a restaurant on place du Bourg-de-Four.

If You Have 2 Days   Spend the first day as above. On Day 2, visit some of the most important museums, each completely different. It'll take a full day of sightseeing to absorb the Musée d'Art et d'Histoire, the Musée International de la Croix-Rouge et du Croissant-Rouge (Red Cross Museum), and the Palais des Nations.

If You Have 3 Days   Spend the first 2 days as above. On Day 3, take a stroll along the quays of Geneva in the morning, and in the afternoon go on an organized excursion to the Alps, including Mont Blanc, for a panoramic view.

If You Have 5 Days   Spend the first 3 days as above. You can use your last days for excursions. On Day 4, while still based in Geneva, take a lake steamer to Lausanne. You'll have time to explore its old town and walk its lakeside quays at Ouchy before returning to Geneva in the evening. On Day 5, take another lake steamer, this time to Montreux; after visiting this lakeside resort, take a trip outside the town to see the Château de Chillon, immortalized by Lord Byron.

THE TOP ATTRACTIONS

In addition to the sights below, Geneva's other top attractions are the **Jet d'Eau,** the famous fountain that has virtually become the city's symbol; the **Flower Clock,** in the Jardin Anglais; and **Old Town,** the oldest part of the city.

Musée Ariana. 10 av. de la Paix. ☎ **022/418-54-50.** Free admission. Wed–Mon 10am–5pm. Bus: 5, 8, 14, F, or Z.

To the west of the Palais des Nations, the Italian Renaissance building was constructed by Gustave Revilliod, the 19th-century Genevese patron who began the collection. Today it's one of the top porcelain, glass, and pottery museums in Europe. Here you'll see Sèvres, Delft faïence, and Meissen porcelain, as well as pieces from Japan and China. It's also the headquarters of the International Academy of Ceramics.

✪ **Musée d'Art et d'Histoire (Museum of Art and History).** 2 rue Charles-Galland. ☎ **022/418-26-00.** Free admission. Tues–Sun 10am–5pm. Bus: 3 or 33.

Geneva's most important museum is between boulevard Jacques-Dalcroze and boulevard Helvétique. Displays include prehistoric relics, Greek vases, medieval stained glass, 12th-century armor, Swiss timepieces, and Flemish and Italian paintings. The Etruscan pottery and medieval furniture are both quite impressive. A 1444 altarpiece by Konrad Witz depicts the "miraculous" draught of fishes. Many galleries also contain works by such artists as Rodin, Renoir, Hodler, Vallotton, Le Corbusier, Picasso, Chagall, Corot, Monet, and Pissarro.

✪ **Musée International de la Croix-Rouge et du Croissant-Rouge (International Red Cross and Red Crescent Museum).** 17 av. de la Paix. ☎ **022/734-52-48.** Admission 8 SF ($6.65) adults, 4 SF ($3.30) students and children. Wed–Mon 10am–5pm. Bus: 8, F, V, or Z.

Here you can experience the legendary past of the Red Cross in the city where it started; it's across from the visitors' entrance to the European headquarters of the United Nations. The dramatic story from 1863 to the present is revealed through displays of rare documents and photographs, films, multiscreen slide shows, and cycloramas. You're taken from the battlefields of Europe to the plains of Africa to see the Red Cross in action. When Henry Dunant founded the Red Cross in Geneva in 1863, he needed a recognizable symbol to suggest neutrality. The Swiss flag (a white cross on a red field), with the colors reversed, ended up providing the perfect symbol for one of the world's greatest humanitarian movements.

✪ **Palais des Nations.** Parc de l'Ariana, 14 av. de la Paix. ☎ **022/907-12-34.** Admission 8 SF ($6.65) adults, 3.50 SF ($2.90) children, free for children under 6. July–Aug daily 9am–6pm; Sept–June daily 10am–noon and 2–4pm. Closed mid-Dec to Jan 1. Bus: 2, 8, 18, or F.

Surrounded by ancient trees and modern monuments, the buildings comprise the second-largest complex in Europe after Versailles. Until 1936, the League of Nations met at the Palais Wilson, when the League's headquarters were transferred to the Palais des Nations. The international organization continued minor activities through the war years until it was dissolved in 1946, just as the newly created United Nations met in San Francisco. Today the Palais des Nations is the headquarters of the United Nations in Europe. A modern wing was added in 1973.

Inside is a philatelic museum and the **League of Nations Museum,** though the building itself is the most interesting attraction. Daily tours leave from the visitors' entrance at 14 av. de la Paix, opposite the Red Cross building. For information, contact the Visitors' Service, United Nations Office, 14 av. de la Paix (☎ **022/ 907-45-39**).

OTHER MUSEUMS

Baur Collections. 8 rue Munier-Romilly. ☎ **022/346-17-29.** Admission 5 SF ($4.15) adults, free for children. Tues–Sun 2–6pm. Bus: 8.

The collections, housed in a 19th-century mansion with a garden, constitute a private exhibit of artworks from China (10th to 19th century) and Japan (17th to 20th century). On display are jade, ceramics, lacquer, ivories, and delicate sword fittings.

Maison Tavel. 6 rue du Puits-St-Pierre. ☎ **022/310-29-00.** Free admission. Tues–Sun 10am–5pm. Bus: 3, 5, 12, 17, or 23.

Built in 1303 and partially reconstructed after a fire in 1334, this is the city's oldest house and one of its newest museums. The museum exhibits historical collections from Geneva dating from the Middle Ages to the mid-19th century. The Magnin relief in the attic is outstanding, as is the copper-and-zinc model of Geneva in 1850, which is accompanied by a light-and-tape commentary. Objects of daily use are displayed in the old living quarters.

Musée de l'Horlogerie (Watch Museum). 15 route de Malagnou. ☎ **022/736-74-12.** Admission free. Wed–Mon 10am–5pm. Bus: 6 or 8. Tram: 12.

This town house chronicles the history of watches and clocks from the 16th century. It displays everything from sand timers to sundials, though most of the exhibits are concerned with Geneva's watches, usually from the 17th and 18th centuries. The enameled watches of the 19th century are particularly intriguing (many have chimes that play when you open them).

RELIGIOUS MONUMENTS

The old town, **Vieille Ville,** on the Left Bank, is dominated by the ✪ **Cathédrale St-Pierre,** Cour St-Pierre (☎ **022/311-75-75**), which was built in the 12th and 13th centuries and partially reconstructed in the 15th century. Recent excavations have disclosed that a Christian sanctuary was here as early as A.D. 400. In 1536 the people of Geneva gathered in the cloister of St-Pierre's and voted to make the cathedral Protestant. The church, which has been heavily renovated over the years, has a modern organ with 6,000 pipes. The northern tower was reconstructed at the end of the 19th century, with a metal steeple erected between the two stone towers. If you don't mind the 145 steps, you can climb to the top of the north tower for a panoramic view of the city, its lake, the Alps, and the Jura Mountains. The tower is open daily 11:30am–5:30pm. Admission is 2 SF ($1.65).

To enter the St-Pierre archeological site, called **Site Archéologique de St-Pierre,** go through the entrance in the Cour St-Pierre, at the right-hand corner of the cathedral steps. The underground passageway extends under the present cathedral and the high gothic (early 15th century) **Chapelle des Macchabées,** which adjoins the southwestern corner of the church. The chapel was restored during World War II, after having been used as a storage room following the Reformation. Excavations of the chapel have revealed baptisteries, a crypt, the foundations of several cathedrals, the bishop's palace, 4th-century mosaics, and sculptures and geological strata.

The cathedral and the chapel are open June–Sept daily 9am–7pm; Mar–May and Oct daily 9am–noon and 2–6pm; Jan–Feb and Nov–Dec daily 9am–noon and 2–3pm. There's no admission charge, though donations are welcome. The archeological site is open Tues–Sat 10am–1pm and 2–6pm; the admission is 5 SF ($4.15).

PARKS, GARDENS & SQUARES

If you walk along the quays, heading north as if to Lausanne, you'll come to some of the lushest parks in Geneva. **Parc Mon-Repos** is off avenue de France and **La Perle du Lac** is off rue de Lausanne. Directly to the right is the **Jardin Botanique** (Botanical Garden), established in 1902. It has an alpine garden, a little zoo, greenhouses, and exhibitions and can be visited free Oct–Apr daily 9:30am–5pm; May–Sept daily 8am–7:30pm.

Back at lakeside, you can take a boat to the other side, getting off at quai Gustave-Ador. From there you can explore two more lakeside parks—**Parc la Grange,** which has the most extravagant rose garden in Switzerland (especially in June), and, next to it, **Parc des Eaux-Vives.**

When you leave the Botanical Garden on the Left Bank, you can head west, along avenue de la Paix, about a mile north from pont du Mont-Blanc, to the Palais des Nations in **Parc de l'Ariana.**

ORGANIZED TOURS

A 2-hour City Tour is operated daily by **Key Tours S.A.,** 7 rue des Alpes, square du Mont-Blanc (☎ **022/731-41-40**). The tour starts from the Gare Routière, the bus station at place Dorcière, near the Key Tours office. From Nov–Mar, a tour is offered only once a day at 2pm, but from Apr–Oct two tours leave daily, at 10am and 2pm.

A bus will drive you through the city to see the monuments, landmarks, and lake promenades. In the old town you can take a walk down to the Bastions Park to the Reformation Wall. After a tour through the International Center—where you'll be shown the headquarters of the International Red Cross—the bus returns to its starting place. Adults pay 27 SF ($22.40), children 4 to 12 accompanied by an adult are charged 14 SF ($11.60), and children 3 and under go free.

SHOPPING

The city has some of the world's most famous auction houses, with sales taking place mostly in May and November. Myriad social events accompany the auctions. Moreover, the city is an important center for the world art market and hosts prominent art and antique dealers. Details and venues of sales appear in the tourist office's monthly "List of Events."

Virtually all the inventory at **Antiquorum,** 2 rue du Mont-Blanc (☎ 022/ 909-28-50), consists of antique jewelry and antique watches—a sure attraction for a city that derives so much of its income from selling timepieces. Virtually everything is sold at auction, rather than over the counter. The array includes some of the most historically important watches in the world.

The aroma of chocolate from the **Confiserie Rohr,** 3 place du Molard (☎ 022/ 311-63-03), practically pulls you in off the street. You'll find chocolate-covered truffles, "gold" bars with hazelnuts, and poubelles au chocolat (chocolate "garbage pails"). This establishment maintains another store at 42 rue du Rhône (☎ 022/ 311-68-76).

Located on place du Molard, **Bon Genie,** 34 rue du Marché (☎ 022/818-11-11), is a department store selling mostly high-fashion women's clothing. Its windows display art objects from local museums alongside designer clothes. There's also a limited selection of men's clothing. Geneva's largest department store, **Grand Passage,** 50 rue du Rhône (☎ 022/310-66-11), has just about everything under its roof: a travel bureau, an agency selling theater tickets, a hairdresser, a newspaper kiosk, a handful of boutiques, a restaurant, and a sandwich shop. **Bruno Magli,** 47 rue du Rhône (☎ 022/311-53-77), is one of the best-stocked shoe stores in Geneva, with an elegant variety of Italian shoes, purses, and accessories. This outlet of a Bologna-based chain stocks mainly women's shoes.

Opposite Mont Blanc Bridge, the chrome-and-crystal **Bucherer,** 26 quai du Général-Guisan (☎ 022/311-62-66), sells expensive watches and diamonds. The store offers such name brands as Rolex, Piaget, Baume & Mercier, Tissot, Rado, and Swatch. The carpeted third floor is filled with relatively inexpensive watches. Once you're on that floor, you'll also find a large selection of cuckoo clocks, music boxes, embroideries, and souvenirs, as well as porcelain pill boxes and other gift items.

Established over a century ago, **Langenthal,** 13 rue du Rhône (☎ 022/310-65-10), boasts an enviable reputation for good-quality merchandise and a showroom on the city's most prestigious shopping street, across from the Union des Banques Suisses. Merchandise includes napery, towels, bed linens, and "table suites," some of it embroidered by hand in the Swiss lace center of St. Gallen.

Colorful **outdoor markets,** overflowing with flowers and fruit, take place several times a week at Rive, Coutance, Carouge, and other squares. A **flea market** is held every Wednesday and Saturday on the Plaine de Plainpalais; markets for books take place on place de la Madeleine on most days during summer.

At the corner of rue de la Fontaine, **Jouets Weber (Franz Carl Weber),** 12 rue de la Croix-d'Or (☎ 022/310-42-55), is the best toy store in the city. It has all kinds of children's toys, from slide shows to cartoon characters, as well as dolls and sports equipment.

GENEVA AFTER DARK

For a preview of events at the time of your visit, pick up a copy of the monthly "List of Events" issued by the tourist office.

THE PERFORMING ARTS

Grand Théâtre de Genève. Place Neuve. ☎ **022/311-23-11.** Tickets 25–150 SF ($20.75–$124.50) for opera, 20–100 SF ($16.60–$83) for ballet

Modeled on the Paris Opéra Garnier, this building was opened in 1879. It burned down in 1951 and was subsequently rebuilt in the same style, except for the modern auditorium, which has a seating capacity of 1,488. From September to July it presents about eight operas and two ballets, as well as recitals and chamber-music concerts.

Orchestre de la Suisse Romande. ☎ **022/328-81-21.** Tickets 15–50 SF ($12.45–$41.50).

This celebrated orchestra's home is the 1,866-seat **Victoria Hall,** 14 rue du Général-Dufour. The orchestra is Geneva's most famous musical institution. For 50 years its conductor was Ernst Ansermet and, through this maestro, it was closely associated with Igor Stravinsky. The orchestra has always been noted for its interpretation of modern works, an emphasis carred on by its present incumbent, Armin Jordan.

NIGHTCLUBS & CABARETS

Griffin's Club. 36 bd. Helvétique. ☎ **022/735-12-18.** No cover.

Griffin's is the chicest club in Geneva. Technically, it's private—you may or may not get in, depending on the mood of the management at the time of your visit. Jackets are required for men. On Friday and Saturday, priority of entrance is usually given to members. The decor of the place, much of which is in a basement, is gilt and gray, with lots of live plants and large paintings in the restaurant. The restaurant serves à la carte and fixed-price meals, beginning at 120 SF ($99.60) without wine. It's open Mon–Sat 8pm–4am.

La Garçonière. 22 place Bémont. ☎ **022/310-21-61.** Cover 10 SF ($8.30).

Both straights and gays come to watch the burlesque drag act at this cramped but wordly cabaret. Two nightly shows are presented, at 11:30pm and 1:30am. Open Sun–Thurs 10pm–4am and Fri–Sat 10pm–5am.

Maxim's Cabaret. 2 rue Thalberg. ☎ **022/732-99-00.** No cover.

This is Geneva's most luxurious cabaret, with a deep-red decor, a semicircular arrangement of small tables around a half-round stage, and shows that grow progressively raunchier as the evening progresses. Three *spectacles* are presented Mon–Sat at 11:30pm and 1:30am (when the focus is on art-style dancing inspired by a mixture of jazz dance and classical ballet), and 3am, which is a striptease (topless only) that's rougher and louder than the relatively restrained earlier shows. The bar opens every night at 8:30pm, and unless you find feminine companionship among the bevy of *danseuses,* the audience is likely to consist mostly of gents.

DANCE CLUBS

In one of the downtown's most popular brasseries, La Coupole, **Le Dancing de la Coupole,** 116 rue du Rhône (☎ **022/735-65-440**), focuses most intently on retro music of the 1960s. It's open Tues–Sat 5pm–2am or so. No cover.

Velvet, 7 rue de Jeu-de-l'Arc (☎ **022/735-00-00**), presents the closest thing to an ongoing party that's carried on every night against a backdrop of disco dancing and barside flirting. The aesthetics are enhanced with two stages at opposite corners of the room where seminaked women dance, frug, boogaloo, and pose as appealingly as they can to a sometimes appreciative, sometimes blasé audience. There is likely to be a working woman or two waiting for an unaccompanied male visitor to buy her a drink; the place is very heterosexual and relatively permissive. Drinks begin at 25 SF ($20.75) each. The *artistes*—as many as 30 are employed by this place—begin their dancing at 10:30pm and continue in ongoing shifts until 4:30am. You'll find the place on the Left Bank of the commercial heart of Geneva, in the Quartier des Eaux-Vives. No cover on Sun–Thurs; Fri–Sat it's 10 SF ($8.30).

BARS

Sheathed in mahogany, brass, and dark-green upholstery, the fashionable **Bar des Bergues,** in the Hôtel des Bergues, 33 quai des Bergues (☎ **022/731-50-50**), is decorated with a carefully illustrated series of late 19th-century menus from the Cercle des Arts et des Lettres. Although most people come for only a drink or two, the establishment also serves lunches and platters from the hotel's top-notch kitchens. Ask the barman for the list of daily specials. Beginning in the early evening, there's an international array of pianists.

In the Hôtel Richemond are **Le Gentilhomme Bar** and **Bar "Le Jardin,"** Jardin Brunswick (☎ **022/731-14-00**). Although many of the clients of these bars consider them only a prelude to a meal at the hotel's elegant Restaurant Le Gentilhomme, they function as attractive and stylish options in their own right. They attract a chic crowd, ranging from U.S.-based beneficiaries of corporate mergers to Zurich bankers to glamorous women in $50,000 furs.

The fashionable **Francis Bar,** 8 bd. Helvétique (☎ **022/346-32-52**), often a venue for *le tout Genève,* becomes an attractive piano bar in the evening.

GAY CLUBS

During the day, **Le Loft,** 20 quai de Seujet (☎ **022/738-28-28**), functions as a workaday restaurant where office workers, pregnant mothers, and conservative bankers sit elbow to elbow in an unpretentious and simple setting. Every Sunday to Thursday, however, the place presents a *spectacle* within a setting similar to that of a gay disco, where the performers aren't necessarily genuine ladies. Friday and Saturday, the place becomes a full-fledged gay disco, with crowds so dense that there's no room for the performers, so no shows are presented. Cover is 6 SF ($5) Sun–Thurs and 10 SF ($8.30) Fri–Sat (includes the first drink).

Defining itself as a gay pub and decorated with the tiles and posters you'd expect to find in a station of the Parisian Métro, **Le Tube,** 3 rue de l'Université (☎ **022/ 329-82-98**), is an endlessly popular venue for meeting and mixing with a crowd of mostly gay men.

DAY TRIPS FROM GENEVA

There are many attractions in the region around Geneva. Several of the most popular places are on Lake Geneva.

MONT SALÈVE The limestone ridge of Mont Salève (House Mountain) is 4 miles south of Geneva, in France, so you'll need a passport. Its peak is at 4,000 feet. If you have a car, you can take a road that goes up the mountain, which is popular with rock climbers. Bus no. 8 will take you to Veyrier, on the French border, where there's a passport and Customs control. A 6-minute cable-car ride will take you to a height of 3,750 feet on Mont Salève. From the top you'll have a panoramic sweep of the Valley of the Arve, with Geneva and Mont Blanc in the background.

✪ **MONT-BLANC & CHAMONIX**   We highly recommend an excursion from Geneva to the high-altitude valleys and plateaux around Mont-Blanc, an outing that will require a full day. Onto the motorcoach excursion you can add a variety of supplemental cable-car and cog-railway ascents en route.

An English-speaking guide accompanies the bus tours offered by **Key Tours S.A.,** 7 rue des Alpes, place du Mont-Blanc (☎ **022/731-41-40**). A minimum of eight persons is required, though in most cases Key Tours will compile the requisite number. All participants travel by bus from Geneva to the ski resort of Chamonix for a base rate of 88 SF ($73.05). From here, at least three optional excursions can be arranged for supplements that range from 23 SF ($19.10) to 48 SF ($39.85) each. Depending on your funds, energy level, and degree of curiosity about panoramas from the high-altitude regions around Chamonix, you can participate in a gondola ascent up the side of the Aiguille du Midi, an excursion by cog railway to the base of the Mer de Glâce glacier, or an ascent by cable car to Le Brevant, a rocky belvedere 7,900 feet above sea level, a site with a view over many of the peaks of the Mont-Blanc range. The tour departs from Geneva at 8:30am and returns to the point of departure, La Gare Routière, the same day at 6pm. You must take your passport with you.

CRUISES ON LAKE GENEVA   Some travelers might appreciate a boat cruise on the calm waters of **Lac Léman,** where ringaround hills and some of the most famous vineyards in Switzerland seem to roll down to the historic waters. You can board one of the lake cruisers that, between May and September, make full circuits of the lake, stopping at many of the important resorts and towns along the way. (Stops usually include Nyon, Lausanne, Vevey, Montreux, Evian, and Thonon.) These tours are offered without guides and meals, although there's a restaurant aboard each of the boats. Tours leave from the Mont-Blanc pier every day at 9:15am and return at 8:40pm. The round-trip price is 60 SF ($49.80) for adults, 30 SF ($24.90) for children 6–16, and free for children under 6.

A less time-consuming boat tour is **Le Tour du Petit Lac,** which incorporates only the lower portion of the lake, including Nyon and Yvoire, for about half a day. Offered between late May and September, it departs from quai du Mont-Blanc at 9:15am and every afternoon at 2:30pm. The round-trip cost of this half-day tour is 30 SF ($24.90). For information about the full-day or half-day tours of Lake Geneva, call Key Tours at **022/731-41-40.**

A different tour combines a lake cruise to the **Château de Chillon** with a return by bus and train back to Geneva. Between May and September, a boat leaves from the Mont-Blanc pier daily at 9:15am, arriving in Chillon at 2:15pm. (During July and August, an additional boat departs from the Jardin Anglais pier at 10:35am, arriving in Chillon around 3:45pm.) Participants can visit the castle before taking a bus from Chillon to Montreux, then transfer to one of the hourly trains from Montreux back to Geneva. (Some visitors opt to dally in Montreux a while, perhaps remaining for lunch or dinner.) The cost for the full round-trip excursion is 55 SF ($45.65) in second class and 71 SF ($58.95) in first class. For information, call the Compagnie Generale de Navigation, Jardin Anglais (☎ **022/311-2521**).

Many other excursions are offered, including a 2³/₄-hour boat trip on the Rhône aboard the *Bâteau du Rhône,* with commentary in English. The trip takes you from Geneva to the Verbois dam and back. The group meets opposite Hotel du Rhône, quai des Moulins, Apr–Oct daily at 2:30pm and on Wed, Thurs, Sat, and Sun also at 10am. The boat trip costs 22 SF ($18.25) for adults and 15 SF ($12.45) for children 6–12; free for children under 6.

More information about boat tours is available from **Mouettes Genevoises Navigation,** 8 quai du Mont-Blanc (☎ **022/732-29-44**).

2 Bern & the Berner Oberland

Bern is one of the loveliest and oldest cities in Europe with origins going back to the 12th century. Much of its medieval architecture has remained untouched. In 1983, the United Nations declared it a world landmark. And as the capital of Switzerland, it is also a city of diplomats and the site of many international organizations and meetings.

Bern is a convenient center for exploring the lakes and peaks of the Berner Oberland —a vast recreation area only minutes from the capital, and one of the great tourist attractions of the world. It's an important center for winter sports, one of the best-equipped areas for downhill skiers, and a challenging area for hikers and mountain climbers. It sprawls between the Reuss River and Lake Geneva, with the Rhône forming its southern border. Two lakes, formed by the Aare River, are the Thun and the Brienz; the Jungfrau (13,642 feet) and the Finsteraarhorn (14,022 feet) are the highest Alpine peaks. The canton of Bern, which encompasses most of the area, is the second-largest canton in Switzerland and contains some 100 square miles of glaciers.

The best center for exploring the Berner Oberland is Interlaken, a popular summer resort. Summer and winter playgrounds are at Gstaad, Grindelwald, Kandersteg, and Mürren. You can ski in the mountains during the winter and surf, sail, and waterski on Lake Thun in the summer.

ONLY IN THE BERNER OBERLAND

Hiking in and Around Bern   After a walk through the old heart of medieval Bern (allow about $2^{1}/_{2}$ hours), you should be ready for an even greater hike in the environs of Bern. The most popular day trip is to Bern's own mountain, Gurten, 25 minutes by tram. Once here, you'll find walks in many directions and can enjoy a panorama over the Alps. But that's not all: Walks in and around Bern include 155 miles of marked rambling paths, one of the most scenic being along the banks of the Aare through the English gardens.

Bicycling Through the Berner Oberland   There are some 1,860 miles of roadway in the Berner Oberland around Bern. The tourist office here will give you a map outlining the routes, and you can rent a bicycle at the main railway station—and set off on your adventure.

Getting Around the Oberland   In this section of Switzerland, getting there is half the fun. To compensate for the region's almost impossible geography, Swiss engineers have crisscrossed the Oberland with cogwheel railways (some of them still driven by steam), aerial cableways, and sinuous mountain roads. When you tire of all this high-altitude travel, you can take more relaxing ferries across the lakes, including Thun and Brienz. Regardless of where you travel, panoramic scenery unfolds at every turn.

Taking a Rail Trip to Jungfraujoch   This will rank at the top of rail trips of a lifetime. After leaving Interlaken, you change at Kleine Scheidegg to the highest rack railway in Europe, the Jungfraubahn. From here, you have 6 miles to go, 4 of them through a tunnel carved between 1896 and 1912. You stop twice, at Eigerwand and Eismeer, to view a sea of ice from windows in the rock. The Eigerwand is at 9,400 feet, the Eismeer at 10,368 feet. When the train emerges from the tunnel, the daylight is momentarily blinding. Once here, the eerie ice world of Jungfrau awaits you.

Following the Trail of Sherlock Holmes   A 50-minute train ride from Interlaken will deliver you to Meiringen, a resort known to devotees of Holmesiana. From here, you can take an excursion to Reichenbachfall, where the rivers of the Rosenlaui valley meet. The beauty of the falls so impressed Conan Doyle that he described it in *The Final Problem,* in which the villian, Professor Moriarty, struggles with the detective before tossing him into the falls. From mid-May to mid-September, a funicular will take you to a point at 2,779 feet near terraces overlooking the water.

Skiing at Gstaad   One of the great ski resorts of the world, attracting the rich and famous, Gstaad is set against a dramatic backdrop of glaciers and peaceful alpine pastures in a district known as Saanenland, one of the most beautiful parts of Switzerland. From mountain railroads to gondolas, Gstaad is well served by public transport to take you to the skiable action, including a mountain at 6,550 feet with a vertical drop of 3,555 feet. There's even skiing in summer, and when darkness falls the après-ski life of Gstaad is legendary.

BERN

The modern mingles harmoniously with the old in this charming city. Modern buildings are discreetly designed to blend in to the historic environment. The city stands on a thumb of land that's bordered on three sides by the Aare River. Several bridges connect the old part of the city with the newer sections.

Market days in Bern—an ideal time to visit—are Tuesday and Saturday, when people from the outlying areas come to town to sell their produce and wares. If you're fortunate enough to arrive on the fourth Monday of November, you'll witness the centuries-old Zwiebelmarkt (Zibelemarit, in the local dialect), or Onion Market. This is the city's last big event before the onset of winter, as residents traditionally stock up on onions in anticipation of the first snows.

ORIENTATION

ARRIVING   By Plane   The **Bern–Belp Airport** (☎ **031/960-21-11**) is 6 miles south of the city in the town of Belpmoos. International flights arrive from London, Paris, and Nice, but transatlantic jets are not able to land here. Fortunately, it's a short hop to Bern from the international airports in Zurich and Geneva.

Taxis are very expensive, so it's better to take the shuttle bus that runs between the airport and the Bahnhof (train station); it costs 14 SF ($11.60) one way.

By Train   Bern has direct connections to the continental rail network that includes France, Italy, Germany, and the Benelux countries, even Scandinavia and Spain. The superfast TGV train connects Paris with Bern in just $4^1/_2$ hours. Bern also lies on major Swiss rail links, particularly those connecting Geneva and Zurich; each city is only 90 minutes away.

The **Bahnhof,** on Bahnhofplatz, is right in the center of town near all the major hotels. If your luggage is light, you can walk to your hotel; otherwise, take one of the taxis waiting outside the station.

For **information** about tickets and train schedules for the Swiss Federal Railways, call **031/157-22-22.** The office is open Mon–Fri 8am–7pm and Sat 8am–5pm.

VISITOR INFORMATION   The **Bern Tourist Office,** in the Bern Bahnhof, on Bahnhofplatz (☎ **031/311-66-11**), is open June–Sept daily 9am–8:30pm; Oct–May

Mon–Sat 9am–6:30pm and Sun 10am–5pm. If you need help finding a hotel room, the tourist office can make a reservation for you in the price range you select.

GETTING AROUND

BY BUS & TRAM The public transportation system, the **Stadtische Verkehrs-betriebe (SVB),** is a reliable, 48-mile network of buses and trams. Before you board, purchase a ticket from the self-service automatic machines at each stop (conductors don't sell tickets). If you're caught traveling without one, you'll be fined 50 SF ($41.50), in addition to the fare for the ride. The single fare is 1.50–2.40 SF ($1.25–$2) if you're over 25, 1.60 SF ($1.35) if you're 16–25, and 1.50 SF ($1.25) if you're under 16.

To save time, and possibly money, you can purchase a **1-day ticket** for 7.50 SF ($6.25), which entitles you to unlimited travel on the SVB network. Just get the ticket stamped at the automatic machine before you begin your first trip. One-day tickets are available at the ticket offices at Bubenbergplatz 5 (☎ **031/321-86-31**) and in the underpass of the main railroad station (☎ **031/321-86-41**), as well as at other outlets in the city.

BY TAXI You can catch a taxi at the public cab ranks, or you can call a dispatcher: the railway station (☎ **031/311-18-18**) or Weisenhausplatz (☎ **031/301-53-53**).

BY CAR Don't try to drive in the city; use your car for exploring the environs.

BY BICYCLE The Altstadt is compressed into such a small area that it's better to cover the historic district on foot rather than on a bike. Bicycles aren't allowed on the many pedestrians-only streets, anyway. However, in Greater Bern and its environs there are 248 miles of cycling paths. These are marked on a special cycling map available at the tourist office (see above). Bicycle lanes are indicated by yellow marked lanes on parts of the road network. The point of departure for most official cycling routes is Bundesplatz (Parliament Square). Special red signs will guide you through a wide variety of landscapes. For 21 SF ($17.45), bicycles are rented at the SBB Railway Station (☎ **031/220-2346**). Call the day before for a reservation.

WHAT TO SEE & DO

The **Zutgloggeturm (Clock Tower)** (Zeitglocketurm in standard German), on Kramgasse, was built in the 12th century and restored in the 16th century. Four minutes before every hour, crowds gather for the world's oldest and biggest horological puppet show. Mechanical bears, jesters, and emperors put on an animated performance. Staged since 1530, the act is one of the longest running in show business. The tower marked the west gate of Bern until 1250.

The ✪ **Bärengraben (Bear Pits),** lying on the opposite side of the river, is a deep, moon-shaped den where the bears, the mascots of Bern, have been kept since 1480. According to legend, when the duke of Zähringen established the town in 1191, he sent his hunters into the encircling woods, which were full of wild game. The duke promised to name the city after the first animal slain, which was the Bär (bear). Since then the town has been known as Bärn or Bern. Today, the bears are beloved, pampered, and fed by both residents and visitors (carrots are most appreciated). The Bear Pits lie on the opposite side of the Nydegg Bridge (Nydeggbrücke) from the rest of Altstadt. The bridge was built over one of the gorges of the Aare River; its central stone arch has a span of 180 feet and affords a sweeping view of the city from its center. Below the Bear Pits, you can visit the **Rosengarten** (Rose Gardens), from which there's a much-photographed view of the medieval sector and the river.

Bern's Altstadt

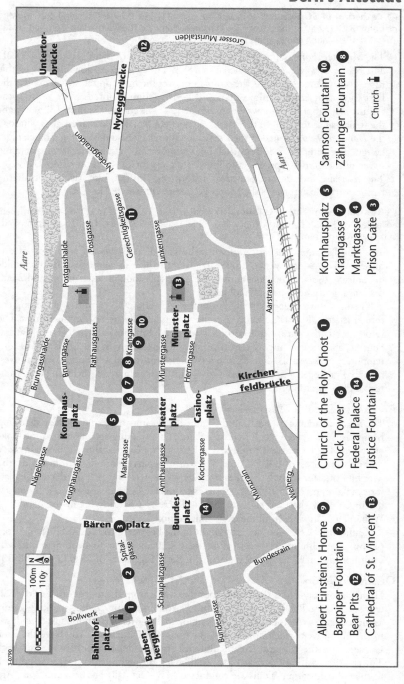

Albert Einstein's Home 9
Bagpiper Fountain 2
Bear Pits 12
Cathedral of St. Vincent 13

Church of the Holy Ghost 1
Clock Tower 6
Federal Palace 14
Justice Fountain 11

Kornhausplatz 5
Kramgasse 7
Marktgasse 4
Prison Gate 3

Samson Fountain 10
Zähringer Fountain 8

✝ ■ Church

⭘ **Cathedral of St. Vincent.** Münsterplatz. ☎ **031/311-05-72.** Cathedral, free; viewing platform, 3 SF ($2.50) adults, 1 SF (85¢) children. Summer Tues–Sun 10am–5pm; off-season Tues–Sat 10am–noon and 2–4pm. Tram: 9.

The Münster is one of the newer gothic churches in Switzerland, dating from 1421. The belfry, however, was completed in 1893. The most exceptional feature of this three-aisle, pillared basilica is the tympanum over the main portal, which depicts the Last Judgment and has more than 200 figures, some painted. Mammoth 15th-century stained-glass windows are in the chancel. The choir stalls from 1523 brought the Renaissance to Bern. In the Matter Chapel is a remarkable stained-glass window, the *Dance of Death,* created in the last year of World War I but based on a much older design. The cathedral's 300-foot-tall belfry dominates Bern and offers a panoramic sweep of the Berner Alps; to get to the viewing platform, you must climb 270 steps. The vista also includes the old town, its bridges, and the Aare River. Outside the basilica on Münsterplatz is the Moses Fountain, constructed in 1545.

⭘ **Kunstmuseum (Fine Arts Museum).** Hodlerstrasse 12. ☎ **031/311-09-44.** Permanent collection, 6 SF ($5); special exhibitions, 6–18 SF ($5–$14.95) extra. Tues 10am–9pm, Wed–Sun 10am–5pm. Tram: 3, 5, or 9.

The world's largest collection of works by Paul Klee is the star attraction of this museum. The painter was born in Switzerland in 1879, the same year that the building housing the collection was constructed. The collection includes 40 oils and 2,000 drawings, gouaches, and watercolors.

The museum's collections emphasize the 19th and 20th centuries, including the romantic artist, Hodler's allegorical paintings, and a collection of Impressionists. The important 20th-century collection has works by Kandinsky, Modigliani, Matisse, Soutine, and Picasso, and by the Surrealist and Constructivist schools as well as contemporary Swiss artists. There's also a collection of Italian 14th-century primitives, notably Fra Angelico's *Virgin and Child,* and Swiss primitives, including the "Masters of the Carnation."

An Excursion to ⭘ Mount Gurten

The most panoramic attraction in the immediate vicinity of Bern is the belvedere atop Mont Gurten. There's a children's fairyland and a walking area, as well as the lookout point. The belvedere is connected to Bern by the Gurtenbahn, a cable-train that's one of the fastest in all Europe. The train departs from a station beside the Monbijoustrasse, about 1½ miles from Bern's center. To reach the departure platform, take tram 9 (2.50 SF/$1.95 each way) to the Gurtenbahn station. If you are driving, follow the road signs to Thun. There is a parking lot in the hamlet of Wabern, a short walk from the cable-train station.

Round-trip passage on the cable-train to the belvedere costs 7.50 SF ($5.85) per person. The train operates year-round, daily 7:30am–sunset (depending on the season). For information contact Gurtenbahn Bern, Eigerplatz 3, ☎ **033/321-88-88.**

Organized Tours

Highly recommended is the 2-hour tour that leaves from the tourist office at the railway station, the Bahnhof, at Bahnhofplatz. You'll have an English-speaking guide, as the tour takes you through the city's residential quarters, past museums, and down to the Aare River, which flows below the houses of Parliament. You'll see the Rose Gardens and the late-gothic cathedral and stroll under the arcades to the Clock Tower. After visiting the Bear Pits, you'll be led through medieval streets and back to the railroad station. Tours are conducted May–Oct daily at 10am and 2pm; Apr Mon–Sat at 2pm; and Nov–Mar Sat at 2pm. The tour costs 22 SF ($18.25).

ACCOMMODATIONS

Very Expensive

⭕ **Hotel Schweizerhof.** Bahnhofplatz 11, CH-3001 Bern. ☎ **031/311-45-01.** Fax 031/312-21-79. 83 rms, 7 suites. MINIBAR TV TEL. 350–400 SF ($290.50–$332) double; from 600 SF ($498) suite. Rates include buffet breakfast. AE, DC, MC, V. Parking 25 SF ($20.75). Tram: 3, 9, or 12.

This centrally located hotel managed by the Gauer family is popular with diplomats. Built in 1859, it remains the grandest hotel in the Swiss capital. It contains many antiques and some of the best decorative art in Bern—18th-century drawing-room pieces, wall-size tapestries, and crystal chandeliers. Each room is different, but all offer comfortably upholstered chairs and sofas, with a fairly good chest, desk, or table. Some are air-conditioned. There are several formal restaurants, including the Schultheissenstube, our favorite, which offers attentive service and competitive prices.

Expensive

⭕ **Belle Époque.** Gerechtigkeitsgasse 18, CH-3001 Bern. ☎ **031/311-43-36.** Fax 031/311-39-36. 16 rms, 1 suite. MINIBAR TV TEL. 285 SF ($236.55) double; 350 SF ($290.50) suite. Rates include breakfast. AE, DC, MC, V. Bus: 12.

This medieval house in the historic heart of Bern has been gutted and renovated as a hotel, with a decor devoted to the Jugendstil, the German style of art nouveau. Each bedroom is outfitted with reproduction turn-of-the-century furniture accented with century-old artifacts, lamps, and engravings; public rooms evoke a prosperous bourgeois home during the belle époque. One of the establishment's highlights is a bar outfitted like an art and antique gallery, lined with late-19th- and early-20th-century oil paintings and filled with Jugendstil furnishings and comfortable settees.

Innere Enge. Engestrasse 54, CH-3012 Bern. ☎ **031/309-61-11.** Fax 301/309-61-12. 26 rms. TV TEL. 215 SF ($178.45) double. Rates include continental breakfast. AE, DC, MC, V. Free parking. Bus: 21 from the rail station.

When you tire of impersonal bandbox hotels, head for this choice converted inn in a building from the 1700s. Its windows open onto views of the Berner Oberland. Bedrooms are often roomy and, if the weather holds, filled with sunshine. Swiss regional and international dishes are served in the hotel restaurant. Jazz acts are booked into the Louis Armstrong Bar.

Moderate

Hotel Ambassador. Seftigenstrasse 99, CH-3007 Bern. ☎ **031/370-99-99.** Fax 031/371-41-17. 97 rms. MINIBAR TV TEL. 170–190 SF ($141.10–$157.70) double. AE, DC, MC, V. Free parking. Tram: 9.

This nine-story hotel is the tallest building in a neighborhood of older houses with red-tile roofs. Guest rooms come with a refrigerator and many have a view of the Bundeshaus. They tend to be smallish and furnished with impersonal international hotel modern, but they are well maintained. The location is about a mile from the train station, easily reached by tram. A lot of guests arrive on bicycles. Dining choices include the Restaurant Pavilion Café and the Japanese Teppan Restaurant. Facilities include a sauna, fitness center, and indoor 24-hour swimming pool.

Hotel Krebs. Genfergaasse 8, CH-3011 Bern. ☎ **031/311-49-42.** Fax 031/311-10-35. 46 rms (41 with bath). TV TEL. 145–200 SF ($120.35–$166) double with bath. Rates include buffet breakfast. AE, DC, MC, V. Tram: 3 or 9.

Fully remodeled with continuing improvements by its owners-managers, the Buri family, this three-star hotel is located near the train station. It shares its ground floor with a store. The rooms are rather Spartan but occasionally sunny, and wood paneling adds more warmth. Some of the accommodations can be converted for families. The few single rooms, without bath or shower, are among the more reasonably priced in the area. Swiss regional and continental dishes are served daily 11am–7pm in the in-house restaurant.

Inexpensive

Hospiz Zur Heimat. Gerechtigkeitsgasse 50, CH-3011 Bern. ☎ **031/311-04-36.** Fax 031/312-33-86. 45 rms (23 with bath). TEL. 96 SF ($79.70) double without bath, 128 SF ($106.25) double with bath. Rates include continental breakfast. AE, DC, MC, V. Free parking at night; day ticket 8 SF ($6.65). Tram: 12.

Set behind a gilded fountain in the old city, this hostelry is often cited as the city's affordable choice. Its architecturally intriguing facade from the 1700s is more interesting than what's inside. Once you get past the rather chilly staff, the bedrooms are generally acceptable; those with a shower have well-kept and modern bathrooms. For those without bath, the hallway plumbing is generally adequate. Consider this mainly for its hard-to-beat location in the heart of Altstadt and what in Bern is considered budget pricing. Only breakfast is served.

⑤ Hotel Goldener Schlüssel. Rathausgasse 72, CH-3011 Bern. ☎ **031/311-02-16.** Fax 031/22-56-88. 29 rms (21 with bath). TV TEL. 110 SF ($91.30) double without bath, 135 SF ($112.05) double with bath. Rates include continental breakfast. AE, MC, V. Bus: 12. Tram: 9.

In the heart of Altstadt, opening onto Rathausgasse, the building housing this little inn dates from the 13th century, when it was used as a stable. Its origins are long gone, and it's beautifully maintained today. Some of the carpeted bedrooms have wood-paneled walls. As it's fairly busy on the street outside, ask for one of the rear rooms if you want less noise. Immaculate linens on the beds and fresh tiles in the bathroom speak of good housekeeping. If you're a bargain hunter, ask for a room without a shower—the hallway plumbing is adequate. The hotel's sidewalk cafe does a thriving business throughout the summer, and the restaurant offers reasonably priced meals.

DINING

Expensive

Della Casa. Schauplatzgasse 16. ☎ **031/311-21-42.** Reservations recommended. Main courses 20–60 SF ($16.60–$49.80); fixed-price menu 21 SF ($17.45). AE, MC, V (downstairs only). Mon–Fri 11am–2pm and 6–9:30pm; Sat 9:30am–3pm. Closed upstairs level, July (downstairs dining room remains open). Tram: 3, 5, or 9. CONTINENTAL.

From under an arcade, you enter a low-ceilinged, paneled room, which is often crowded with chattering diners. For those eager to follow the latest political trends and opinions, an inner room has all the day's newspapers—indeed, the place has been called Switzerland's "unofficial Parliament headquarters." A quieter, somewhat more formal dining room is found upstairs. The menu features continental and Italian dishes, such as bollito misto (a medley of boiled meats). Two of our local favorites are the ravioli maison and the sautéed zucchini; a popular meat specialty is a filet mignon à la bordelaise with Créole rice.

Räblus. Zeughausgasse 3. ☎ **031/311-59-08.** Main courses 26–45 SF ($21.60–$37.35). AE, DC, MC, V. Mon–Sat 6pm–1am. Closed July 18–Aug 16. Tram: 3 or 9. FRENCH.

The building containing this restaurant is 200 years old, making it the oldest on its street. Centrally located, near the Clock Tower, it offers dinner guests a chance to stop for an aperitif in the ground-floor bar before proceeding upstairs to the dining room, richly paneled and filled with sculpture. The owner and chef, Peter Pulver, prepares a French cuisine with a definite Swiss/German influence. Try such dishes as a potpourri of seafood flavored with Pernod, saffron-flavored sole, citrus-flavored veal, and the old reliable tournedos Rossini and veal kidney flambé that have appeared on French menus for years.

Moderate

Ⓢ **Commerce.** Gerechtigkeitsgasse 74. ☎ **031/311-11-61.** Reservations required. Main courses 12–45 SF ($9.95–$37.35). AE, DC, MC, V. Tues–Sat noon–2pm and 6–9:30pm. Closed last 3 weeks in July to Aug 7. Tram: 12. SPANISH.

This small Spanish tavern near the Fountain of Justice (Gerechtigkeitsbrunnen) attracts many expatriate Spaniards, some of whom work at the Spanish Embassy. The decor is Iberian, and the paella is very popular, even if it isn't as authentic as that likely to be served in Valencia. The specialty is scampi prepared in several ways; we also recommend the zarzuela, a Spanish-style bouillabaisse.

Ⓢ **Goldener Schlüssel.** Rathausgasse 72. ☎ **031/311-02-16.** Reservations recommended. Main courses 19.50–31 SF ($16.20–$25.75). MC, V. Tues–Thurs 7am–11:30pm, Fri–Sat 7am–12:30am. Bus: 12. Tram: 9. SWISS.

As you dine at this very Swiss restaurant, you can relish both the food and the atmosphere. Overhead is the old planking and stonework of a 13th-century building, and all around you is the bustle of a very busy workaday restaurant. Serving wholesome food in ample portions, the restaurant is on the street level of a budget-priced hotel of the same name. Specialties include a mignon d'agneau au poivre vert (tenderloin of lamb with green-pepper sauce and corn croquettes), or schweinbratwurst mit zwiebelsauce (butter-fried sausage with onion sauce) and rösti.

Inexpensive

Gfeller am Bärenplatz. Bärenplatz. ☎ **031/311-69-44.** Main courses 11.50–25.50 SF ($9.55–$21.15); fixed-price lunch 15 SF ($12.45) Mon–Fri. No credit cards. Daily 10:30am–8pm. Closed Dec 25. Tram: 3, 5, 9, or 12. SWISS.

This place serves wholesome meals to a loyal crowd of Berner. The ground floor is divided into three dining areas. Upstairs is an American-style self-service cafeteria, with large windows opening onto a view of Bärenplatz. There's also a Swiss-style tearoom, as well as a pâtisserie buffet. The restaurant specializes in lunch and early dinners, and portions are large and filling. Try Swiss cheese pie with both Emmental and Gruyère or sauerkraut with smoked pork, bacon, and sausage.

Ratskeller. Gerechtigkeitsgasse 80. ☎ **031/311-17-71.** Reservations recommended. Main courses 17–35 SF ($14.10–$29.05); fixed-price lunch 16.50 SF ($13.70). AE, DC, MC, V. Daily 11:30am–2pm and 6–10pm. Bus: 12. SWISS.

This historic establishment has old masonry, modernized paneling, and a battalion of busy waitresses serving ample portions of food. Specialties include rack of lamb à la diable for two diners, an omelet soufflé aux fruits, veal kidneys Robert, and côte de veau in butter sauce.

BERN AFTER DARK

This Week in Bern, distributed free by the tourist office, has a list of cultural events.

The Performing Arts

The **Bern Symphony Orchestra,** one of the finest orchestras in Switzerland, is directed by the widely acclaimed Russian-born Dmitrij Kitajenko; famous guest conductors also frequently appear with the orchestra. Performances are usually at the concert facilities in the **Bern Casino,** Herrengasse 25 (☎ 031/311-42-42).

Major opera and ballet performances are usually staged in Bern's most beautiful theater, the century-old **Stadttheater,** Kornhausplatz 20 (☎ 031/311-07-77).

Plays and dance programs are presented in the **Theater am Käfigturm,** Spitalgasse 4 (☎ **031/311-6100**). Plays are usually in German, and to a lesser degree in French, but even if you don't understand those languages, you might want to attend a performance. Contemporary German-language theater is featured in the **Kleintheater,** Kramgasse 6 (☎ **031/311-30-80**). A venue offering a varying program is the **Theater am Käfigturm,** Spitalgasse 4 (☎ **031/311-61-00**).

Wine Cellars & Traditional Music

✪ **Klötzlikeller.** 62 Gerechtigkeitsgasse. ☎ **031/311-74-56.**

The oldest wine tavern in Bern is near the Gerechtigkeitsbrunnen (Fountain of Justice), the first fountain you see on your walk from the Bärengraben (Bear Pits) to the Zutgloggeturm (Clock Tower). Watch for the lantern outside an angled cellar door. The tavern, dating from 1635, is owned by the city and leased to an independent operator (by tradition, an unmarried woman). Some 20 different wines are sold by the glass, with prices ranging from 5–7.50 SF ($4.15–$6.25). The menu is changed every 6 weeks. From the traditional Berner kitchen emerge various dinner plates, reflecting regional specialties and costing 16–33 SF ($13.30–$27.40). Hours are Tues–Thurs 4pm–12:30am and Fri–Sat 4pm–1:30am.

Kornhaus Keller. Kornhausplatz 18. ☎ **031/311-11-33.**

This former grain warehouse in the Altstadt is the best-known wine cellar in the city. The symmetrical stone building, with an arcade on the ground floor, seats 462 diners in a baronial atmosphere; musical acts are often performed in the evening. A plate of smoked meats and sauerkraut is the classic dish to order. À la carte meals range from 15–45 SF ($12.45–$37.35), and the fixed-price menu goes for 60.15 SF ($49.90). Lunch is served Tues–Sat 11:30am–2:30pm and dinner Tues–Sat 5–11:30pm.

Swiss Chalet Restaurant. In the Hotel Glocke, Rathausgasse 75. ☎ **031/311-37-71.**

The dining room is brick with beamed ceilings and red-checkered tablecloths; oversize cow bells and alpine farm implements hang on the walls. Monday only, yodelers appear after the end of your meal, followed by dancing; on other nights oompah bands are featured. The kitchen is open 5pm–2am—perfect for after-theater snacks. Admission is free. Main courses are from 10 to 40 SF ($8.30–$33.20). Fondues, fish, steak, and chicken are featured; beer runs 3.20 SF ($2.65).

THE BERNER OBERLAND

The Berner Oberland is Valhalla for walkers, hikers, and skiiers. Here nature's scenery satisfies both the most ambitious adventurer and the least ambitious stroller who doesn't like strenuous exertion of any kind. It's one of the best equipped regions in the world for winter sports. More than 150 installations transport skiers to challenging downhill runs. Trails designed for walkers branch out from almost every junction. Most of these are paved and signposted, with distances posted, and estimated walking times given. Most tourist offices, including those at Interlaken (see below), will provide guidance and suggested itineraries, including those that can take you far afield in the mountains, with overnight accommodations en route.

EXPLORING THE AREA BY TRAIN & BICYCLE If you're not driving, you will find that public transportation is quite adequate for exploring the area. On most rail lines the **Regional Pass** is valid, including all mountain trains, cable cars, chairlifts, steamers on Lake Thun and Lake Brienz, as well as most postal-bus lines. The ticket also qualifies you for a 25% reduction on the Kleine Scheidegg-Eigergletscher-Jungfraujoch railway, the Mürren-Schilthorn aerial cable line, and the

The Berner Oberland

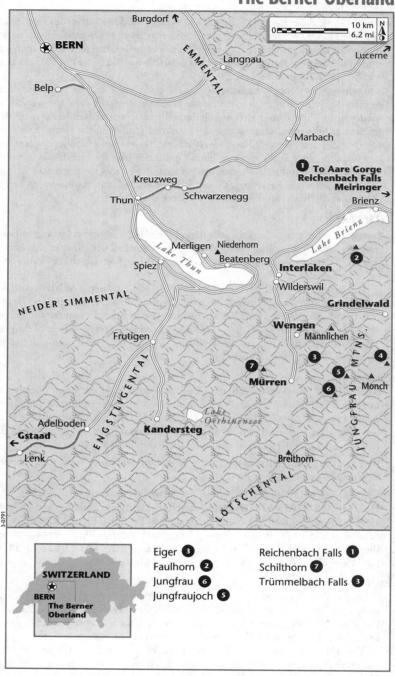

Burgdorf ↑

BERN

Belp

EMMENTAL

Langnau

Lucerne →

Marbach

Kreuzweg

Thun

Schwarzenegg

1 **To Aare Gorge**
Reichenbach Falls
Meiringer →

Brienz

Lake Thun

Merligen

Niederhorn

Beatenberg

Spiez

Lake Brienz

2

Interlaken

Wilderswil

Grindelwald

NEIDER SIMMENTAL

Frutigen

Wengen

Männlichen

JUNGFRAU MTNS.

7

Mürren

3

5

6

4

Mönch

Adelboden

Gstaad ←

Lenk

ENGSTLIGENTAL

Kandersteg

*Lake
Oeshinensee*

Breithorn

LÖTSCHENTAL

3-0791

SWITZERLAND

★
BERN
The Berner
Oberland

Eiger **3**
Faulhorn **2**
Jungfrau **6**
Jungfraujoch **5**

Reichenbach Falls **1**
Schilthorn **7**
Trümmelbach Falls **3**

bus to Grosse Scheidegg and Bussalp. The ticket, valid for 15 days, can be used for unlimited travel on 5 days of your choice and as a season ticket entitling you to any number of tickets at half fare. You can purchase your Regional Pass at any train station in the Berner Oberland. A first-class pass sells for 230 SF ($190.90), but only 190 SF ($157.70) in second class.

Cycling tours through the Berner Oberland often begin at Interlaken. Hundreds of miles of cycling paths riddle the Berner Oberland. Separate from the network of hiking paths, the bicycle routes are signposted and are marked on rental maps distributed at bike-rental agencies. Some 13 railroad stations in the Berner Oberland offer bicycle-rental services. Rates are reasonable. For example, families can rent two city bikes for the parents and a children's mountain bike for each family member under the age of 16 for an all-inclusive price of 58 SF ($48.15) per day or 220 SF ($182.60) per week. Reservations must be made at the latest in the evening before the tour at any of the railway stations providing the service.

INTERLAKEN

Interlaken is the tourist capital of the Berner Oberland. Cableways and cog railways designed for steeply inclined hills and mountains connect it with most of the region's villages. A dazzling sight is the snowy heights of the Jungfrau, which rises a short distance to the south.

The "town between the lakes" (Thun and Brienz) has been a holiday resort for more than 300 years. Although it began as a summer resort, it has developed into a year-round playground. Interlaken charges low-season prices in January and February, when smaller resorts at higher altitudes are charging their highest rates of the year. The most expensive time to visit is during midsummer, when high-altitude ski resorts often charge their lowest rates.

Essentials

ARRIVING   By Train   There are several trains daily between Zurich and Interlaken (trip time 2 hr.) and between Bern and Interlaken (40 min.). Frequent train service also connects Geneva and Interlaken (2¹/₂ hr.). Although the town has two railway stations, about 2 miles apart, Interlaken East (Ost) and Interlaken West, most of the city center lies near or around Interlaken West.

By Car   To reach Interlaken from Bern, drive south on N-6 to Spiez, then continue west on N-8 to Interlaken.

VISITOR INFORMATION   The **Tourism Organization Interlaken** is at Höheweg 37 (☎ **033/822-21-21**), in the Hotel Metropole Building, and will provide itineraries for hikers. It's open July–Aug Mon–Fri 8am–6:30pm, Sat 8am–5pm, Sun 5–7pm; in other months, Mon–Fri 8am–noon and 2–6:30pm, Sat 8am–noon. Bicycles can be rented at both rail stations, Interlaken East (☎ **033/822-21-38**) or Interlaken West (☎ **033/822-27-51**); reserve in advance.

Exploring Interlaken

What you do in Interlaken is walk. That's the best way to see everything. You can walk at random, as there are panoramic views in virtually all directions, or, if you'd like some guidance, go to the tourist office and ask for a copy of "What to Do in Interlaken." It maps out walks for both the active and the less active visitor.

The **Höheweg** covers 35 acres in the middle of town, between the west and east train stations. Once the property of Augustinian monks, it was acquired in the mid-19th century by the hotel keepers of Interlaken, who turned it into a park. As you stroll along Höhenpromenade, admire the famous view of the Jungfrau. Another beautiful sight is the **flower clock** at the Kursaal (casino). You'll also see *fiacres,* horse-drawn cabs beloved by Edwardians. The promenade is lined with hotels, cafes, and gardens.

Cross over the Aare River to **Unterseen,** built in 1280 by Berthold von Eschenbach. Here you can visit the parish church, with its late gothic tower dating from 1471. This is one of the most photographed sights in the Berner Oberland. The Mönch mountain appears on the left of the tower, the Jungfrau on the right.

Back in Interlaken, visit the **Touristik-Museum der Jungfrau-Region,** am Stadthausplatz, Obere Gasse 26 (☎ **033/22-98-39**), the first regional museum of tourism in the country, showing the development of tourism over the past two centuries. The museum is open May to mid-Oct Tues–Sun 2–5pm. Admission is 3 SF ($2.50), or 2 SF ($1.65) with a Visitor's Card.

For a sightseeing fiacre ride, go to the Westbahnhof. The half-hour round-trip tour costs 35 SF ($29.05) for one or two, plus 9 SF ($7.45) for each additional person; children 7–16 are charged half fare, and those 6 and under ride free.

Other attractions include animal parks, afternoon concerts, and the delectable pastries sold in cafes. During the summer, visitors can sit in covered grandstands and watch Schiller's version of the William Tell story. Lake steamers carry passengers across Lakes Brienz and Thun.

Expensive Accommodations

✪ **Grand Hotel Victoria-Jungfrau.** Höheweg 41, CH-3800 Interlaken. ☎ **800/874-4002** in the U.S. or 033/828-28-28. Fax 033/828-28-82. 105 rms, 66 junior suites, 28 regular and duplex suites. MINIBAR TV TEL. Summer, 520–590 SF ($431.60–$489.70) double; 620–695 SF ($514.60–$576.85) junior suite; from 860 SF ($713.80) regular and duplex suites. Winter, 390–450 SF ($323.70–$373.50) double; 510–580 SF ($423.30–$481.40) junior suite; from 800 SF ($664) regular and duplex suites. Half board 90 SF ($74.70) per person extra. Rates include buffet breakfast. AE, DC, MC, V. Parking 20 SF ($16.60).

Since 1865 this grand hotel has been one of Switzerland's most important resort properties. In a richly ornate Victorian styling, it sits in the town center at the foot of rigidly symmetrical gardens. The hotel boasts one of the best-trained staffs in the country. The most deluxe rooms open onto views of the Jungfrau. Dining choices include La Terrasse, a gourmet restaurant with a pianist and a winter garden, and Jungfraustube, a cozy rustic-style restaurant with traditional Swiss dishes and charcoal-grilled specialties. Facilities include a swimming pool, indoor and outdoor tennis courts, indoor golf center, sauna, solarium, whirlpools, steambaths, and a Health-Fitness-Beauty Center with a fitness and gymnastic room.

Hotel Bellevue. Marktgasse 59, CH-3800 Interlaken. ☎ **033/822-44-31.** Fax 033/822-92-50. 43 rms. MINIBAR TV TEL. 150–220 SF ($124.50–$182.60) double. Half-price reduction for children up to 12 sharing parents' room. Half board 34 SF ($28.20) per person extra. Rates include buffet breakfast. AE, DC, MC, V.

The Bellevue Hotel is located in a central spot and opens directly on the River Aare. It retains something of its original 1789 design as a fortified castle, and is surrounded by an English-style garden. The modernized rooms often have balconies with a view of the river and the distant mountains. Breakfast and dinner are served in the hotel's formal dining room, and guests relax in a nicely furnished salon facing the garden with its view of the Alps.

Moderate & Inexpensive Accommodations

De la Paix. Bernastrasse 24, CH-3800 Interlaken. ☎ **033/822-70-44.** Fax 033/822-87-28. 28 rms. TEL. 108–175 SF ($89.65–$145.25) double. Rates include buffet breakfast. AE, DC, MC, V. Closed Nov 10–Apr 10. Free parking.

This family-run hotel is a block away from the Westbahnhof (Interlaken West). You'll recognize it by its ornate roofline, which is gabled and tiled like a house in a Brothers Grimm fairy tale. Gillian and Georges Etterli offer a pleasant, relaxed atmosphere. The rooms are simply furnished; some have TVs.

⑤ **Hotel Beau-Site.** Seestrasee 16, CH-3800 Interlaken. ☎ **033/826-75-75.** Fax 033/826-75-85. 53 rms (42 with bath). TEL. 110 SF ($91.30) double without bath, 165–240 SF ($136.95–$199.20) double with bath. Rates include continental breakfast. AE, DC, MC, V. Free parking outside, 20 SF ($16.60) in the garage.

A short walk from the Interlaken West train station, this hotel is surrounded by spacious gardens with parasol-shaded card tables and chaise longues in the summer. Since 1943 the Ritter family has been providing a pleasant and relaxing oasis in the middle of town. The hotel has two fine restaurants, the budget-priced Stübli and the more elegant and expensive Veranda. Rooms are modern, and some open onto mountain views. Most of them have a TV and minibar.

Park-Hotel Mattenhof. Hauptstrasse, Matten, CH-3800 Interlaken. ☎ **033/821-61-21.** Fax 033/822-28-88. 85 rms. TV TEL. June–Sept and Dec 26–Jan 1, 290–370 SF ($240.70–$307.10) double. Off-season, 230–290 SF ($190.90–$240.70) double. Rates include half board. AE, DC, MC, V. Free parking. Bus: 5.

This large, old-fashioned hotel is in a secluded area at the edge of a forest 1 mile south of the center; you can reach it by heading away from the center toward Wilderswil. The exterior looks like a private castle, with its high, pointed roof, tower, loggias, and balconies. Originally a simple and sedate 19th-century pension, it adopted most of its mock-medieval look after a massive enlargement in 1906. The Bühler family offers a calm retreat, with terraces, manicured lawns, and panoramic views of the Alps. The hotel's facilities include a swimming pool, a tennis court, play areas, terraces, bars, and restaurants.

⑤ **Swiss Inn.** Général-Guisan-Strasse 23, CH-3800 Interlaken. ☎ **033/822-36-26.** Fax 033/823-23-03. 25 rms, 5 apartments. MINIBAR TV TEL. 100–160 SF ($83–$132.80) double; 110–300 SF ($91.30–$249) apartment. MC, V. Free parking.

This small Edwardian inn with balconies and gables is a good value. Mrs. Vreny Müller Lohner offers tastefully but very simply decorated one- to three-room apartments equipped with kitchenettes that accommodate two to seven guests. Children's beds or cots are available. The inn has a lounge, a sitting area with a fireplace, and a grill for barbecues in the garden. There are laundry facilities on the premises.

Dining

Il Bellini. In the Hotel Metropole, Höheweg 37. ☎ **033/821-21-51.** Reservations recommended. Main courses 20–55 SF ($16.60–$45.65). AE, DC, MC, V. Daily noon–2:30pm and 6:30–9:30pm. ITALIAN.

Some critics have praised this as one of the finest Italian restaurants in the Berner Oberland. One floor above the lobby level of the tallest hotel in Interlaken, the Metropole, it is outfitted in a graceful 19th-century rendition of pale pinks and greens. An assortment of antipasti from the buffet or a homemade minestrone is followed by such main courses as beefsteak Florentine, saltimbocca, or a small chicken flavored with fresh basil. The fish selections are limited but well chosen and can be grilled at your request.

⑤ **Gasthof Hirschen.** Hauptstrasse, Matten. ☎ **033/822-15-45.** Reservations recommended. Main courses 14–41.50 SF ($11.60–$34.45). AE, DC, MC, V. Wed–Mon 11:30am–2pm and 6–9pm. SWISS.

This hotel's restaurant offers some of the best and most reasonably priced meals in town. The menu is varied. The potato-and-mushroom soup is the finest we've ever tasted. Other appetizers include ravioli filled with crab and a homemade terrine. For a main dish, try sautéed calves' liver, fillet of beef bordelaise, broiled trout, or chateaubriand. The Hirschen operates its own farm, and many of the items it features are home-grown, including Bio-Angus beef, veal, cheese, and fresh vegetables and herbs.

Schun. Höheweg 56. ☎ **033/822-94-41.** Reservations not required. Main courses 16–36 SF ($13.30–$29.90); fixed-price menus 17.30–36 SF ($14.35–$29.90). AE, DC, MC, V. Tues–Sun 8am–11pm. SWISS.

This attractive restaurant and tearoom in the center of town has been known for its pastries since 1885. In the back, the alpine building's sunny terrace has a view of the Jungfrau and a well-kept lawn. The dining room has large windows and a Viennese ambience. A pianist provides music. The Beutler-Kropf family owns this restaurant, located near the Hotel Metropole.

✪ A Jungfraujoch Excursion

A trip to Jungfraujoch, at 11,333 feet, can be the highlight of your visit—for more than a century it has been the highest railway station in Europe. It's also one of the most expensive: A round-trip tour costs 153.20 SF ($127.15). However, families can fill out a Family Card form, available at the railway station, which allows children 16 and under to ride free. Departures are usually daily at 6:35am from the east station in Interlaken; expect to return about 6pm. To check times, contact the sales office of Jungfrau Railways, Höheweg 37 (☎ **033/828-72-33**).

Once at the Jungfraujoch terminus, you may feel a little giddy until you get used to the air. You'll find much to do in this eerie world high up Jungfrau. But take it slowly—your body metabolism will be affected and you may tire quickly.

Behind the post office is an elevator to the famed ✪ **Eispalast (Ice Palace).** Here you'll be walking within what is called "eternal ice"—caverns hewn out of the slowest-moving section of the glacier. Cut 65 feet below the glacier's surface, they were begun in 1934 by a Swiss guide and subsequently enlarged and embellished with additional sculptures by others.

After returning to the station, you can take the Sphinx Tunnel to another elevator. This one takes you up 356 feet to an observation deck called the **Sphinx Terraces,** overlooking the saddle between the Mönch and Jungfrau peaks. You can also see the Aletsch Glacier, a 14-mile river of ice—the longest in Europe. The snow melts into Lake Geneva and eventually flows into the Mediterranean.

MÜRREN

This village has a stunning location, high above the Lauterbrunnen Valley. At 5,414 feet, Mürren is the highest permanently inhabited village in the Berner Oberland. It's an exciting excursion from Interlaken in the summer and a major ski resort in the winter. Downhill skiing was developed and the slalom invented here in the 1920s. Mürren is also the birthplace of modern alpine racing.

Essentials

ARRIVING   By Train   Take the mountain railway from the Interlaken East rail station via Lauterbrunnen and Grutschalp. The trip takes an hour from Interlaken. The round-trip price of the train ride from Lauterbrunnen is 16 SF ($13.30).

By Bus   A regular postal-bus service goes once an hour from Lauterbrunnen to Stechelberg; the rest of the way you must go by cable car.

By Car   Mürren is not accessible to traffic. Drive as far as Stechelberg, the last town on the Lauterbrunnen Valley road. The cable car to Mürren costs 27 SF ($22.40) round-trip and takes about 10 minutes. Departures are every half hour.

VISITOR INFORMATION   The **Mürren Tourist Information Bureau** is at the Sportzentrum (☎ **033/55-16-16**), open Mon–Fri 9am–noon and 2–6pm, Sat and Sun 2–6pm.

Outdoor & Indoor Activities

There are 30 miles of prepared ski runs, including 16 downhills. The longest run measures 7$\frac{1}{2}$ miles. For cross-country skiers there's a 7$\frac{1}{2}$-mile track in the Lauterbrunnen Valley, 10 minutes by railway from Mürren.

The alpine **Sportzentrum (Sports Center)** (☎ **033/856-86-86**), in the middle of Mürren, is one of the finest in the Berner Oberland. The modern building has an indoor pool, lounge, snack bar, outdoor skating rink, tourist information office, and children's playroom and library. There are facilities for playing squash, outdoor tennis, and curling. Hotel owners subsidize the operation, tacking the charges onto your hotel bill. Supplemental charges include 16 SF ($13.30) per hour for tennis, 16 SF ($13.30) per 45-minute session for squash, 13 SF ($10.80) per hour for use of the sauna. The facility is usually open Mon–Fri 9am–noon and 1–6:45pm, but check locally as these times can vary.

Nearby Excursions

The famous **Mürren-Allmendhubel Cableway** leaves from the northwestern edge of Mürren. From the high destination there's a panoramic view of the Lauterbrunnen Valley as far as Wengen and Kleine Scheidegg. Between mid-June and late August the alpine meadows are covered with wildflowers. A hill walk in this region might be a highlight of your trip to Switzerland. The cable car operates daily throughout the year 8am–5pm. However, there are annual closings for maintenance in May and again in November. It costs 11.60 SF ($9.65) per person round-trip.

The most popular excursion from Mürren is a cable-car ride to the ✪ **Schilthorn,** famous for its 360° view. The panorama extends from the Jura to the Black Forest, including the Eiger, Mönch, and Jungfrau. The Schilthorn is also called "Piz Gloria" after the James Bond film *On Her Majesty's Secret Service,* partly filmed at this dramatic location. Today Piz Gloria is the name of the revolving restaurant here. The summit is the start of the world's longest downhill ski race. The cable car to Schilthorn leaves every 30 minutes. A round-trip ticket costs 55 SF ($45.65), and the journey to the top takes 20 minutes. For details, call **033/823-14-44.**

Accommodations

Hotel Alpenruh. CH-3825 Mürren. ☎ **033/855-10-55.** Fax 033/855-42-77. 26 rms. MINIBAR TV TEL. 250–300 SF ($207.50–$249) double. 50% reduction for children 12 and under sharing parents' room. Half board 30 SF ($24.90) per person. AE, DC, MC, V.

Set in the most congested (yet charming) section of the village, the Alpenruh has a plusher interior than its chalet-style facade implies. The old building was upgraded in 1986 to three-star-hotel status without sacrificing any of its small-scale charm. The rooms have pine paneling and a mix of antique and contemporary furniture.

✪ **Hotel Blumental.** CH-3825 Mürren. ☎ **033/855-36-86.** Fax 033/855-18-26. 20 rms. MINIBAR. 180–240 SF ($149.40–$199.20) double. Rates include buffet breakfast. DC, V.

Centrally located and redecorated and remodeled, this is a small chalet-type hotel, with stone masonry and wood-paneled public areas, run by the von Allmen family. It offers a cozy atmosphere inspired by the nearby mountains. The wood walls of the bedrooms contrast with new pine furnishings and attractive colors; several rooms have private balconies. The hotel also operates a French restaurant.

Hotel Eiger. CH-3825 Mürren. ☎ **033/855-13-31.** Fax 033/855-39-31. 44 rms. TV TEL. Summer, 240–280 SF ($199.20–$232.40) double. Winter, 260–340 SF ($215.80–$282.20) double. Rates include buffet breakfast. AE, DC, MC, V. Closed Easter to mid-June and mid-Sept to Christmas.

This chalet is the best-established hotel in Mürren. Public rooms are warmly decorated, and many windows have panoramic views. The bedrooms, small and cozy, are decorated in typical alpine style. The hotel has a fine restaurant and a popular après-ski bar, plus an indoor heated swimming pool with a glassed-in view of the ice and snow outside.

Dining

✪ **Eigerstübli.** In the Hotel Eiger. ☎ **033/855-13-31.** Reservations recommended. Main courses 12–45 SF ($9.95–$37.35). AE, DC, MC, V. Daily 7am–11pm. Closed Easter to mid-June and mid-Sept to Christmas. SWISS.

The best food at the resort is served here in a festive ambience. The cuisine includes fondue as well as an international range of hearty specialties well suited to the alpine heights and chill. Try, for example, roast lamb shoulder with lentils, roast breast of duck with orange sauce, or poached fillet of trout with a sauce flavored with Alpine herbs. All main dishes may be ordered with rösti.

WENGEN

The Mönch, Jungfrau, and Eiger loom above this sunny resort, built on a sheltered terrace high above the Lauterbrunnen Valley, at about 4,160 feet. Wengen (pronounced Ven-ghen) is one of the more chic and better-equipped ski and mountain resorts in the Berner Oberland. It has 30 hotels in all price categories, as well as 500 apartments and chalets for rent.

In the 1830s the International Lauberhorn Ski Race was established here. At that time, Wengen was a farm community. The British were the first to popularize the resort after World War I. Parts of the area retain their rural charm, but the main street is filled with cafes, shops, and restaurants welcoming tourists. No cars are allowed in Wengen, but the streets are still bustling with service vehicles and electric luggage carts.

Essentials

ARRIVING   By Train   Take the train (frequent service) from Interlaken East to Lauterbrunnen. From here, the journey to Wengen is by cog railway, a 15-minute trip.

By Car   Unlike Mürren, Wengen, 16 miles south of Interlaken, can be reached by car—at least for part of the trip. From Interlaken, head south in the direction of Wilderswil, following the minor signposted road to Lauterbrunnen, where there are garages or open-air spaces for parking. After that, it's cog railway the rest of the way to Wengen.

VISITOR INFORMATION   The **Wengen Tourist Information Office** (☎ **033/855-14-14**) is open Mon–Fri 8am–noon and 2–6pm, Sat 8:30am–1:30pm and 4–6pm, and Sun 4–6pm.

Outdoor Activities

The ski area around Wengen is highly developed, with straight and serpentine ski trails carved into the sides of such sloping geological formations as Männlichen,

Kleine Scheidegg, Lauberhorn, and Eigergletscher. A triumph of alpine engineering, the town and its region contain three mountain railways, two aerial cableways, one gondola, five chairlifts, nine ski lifts, and three practice lifts. You'll also find a branch of the Swiss ski school, more than 7 miles of trails for cross-country skiing, an indoor and outdoor skating rink, a curling hall, an indoor swimming pool, and a day nursery.

In the summer, the district attracts hill climbers from all over Europe. Hiking trails are well maintained and carefully marked, with dozens of unusual detours to hidden lakes and panoramas.

Excursions Nearby

In the winter, skiers take the cableway to **Männlichen,** at 7,335 feet, which opens onto a panoramic vista of the treacherous Eiger. From here, there is no direct run back to Wengen; however, skiers can enjoy an uninterrupted ski trail stretching $4^1/_2$ miles to Grindelwald.

There are many sights that can be visited up and down the Lauterbrunnen Valley from either Wengen or Grindelwald. **Trümmelbach Falls** plunges in five powerful cascades through a gorge. An elevator built through the rock leads to a series of galleries (bring a raincoat); the last stop is at a wall where the upper fall descends. The falls can be visited Apr–June and Sept–Oct daily 9am–5pm; July–Aug daily 9am–6pm; admission is 10 SF ($8.30) for adults, 4 SF ($3.30) for children 6–16. It takes about 45 minutes to reach the falls on foot. For information, call **033/ 855-32-32.** The postal bus from Lauterbrunnen departs once an hour and stops at Trümmelbach Falls; it is only 2 SF ($1.65) each way.

You might also want to visit the base of the **Staubbach Waterfall,** which plunges nearly 1,000 feet in a sheer drop over a rock wall in the valley above Lauterbrunnen. Lord Byron compared this waterfall to the "tail of the pale horse ridden by Death in the Apocalypse."

Accommodations

Ⓢ Hotel Eden. CH-3823 Wengen. ☎ **033/855-16-34.** Fax 033/855-39-50. 30 rms (6 with bath). TEL. 202–230 SF ($167.65–$190.90) double without bath, 222–250 SF ($184.25– $207.50) double with bath. Rates include breakfast. AE, DC, MC, V.

You'll find homelike comfort in this economy oasis which stands among guesthouses and private chalets above the commercial center of town. Kerstin Bucher directs a cooperative staff. Meals are served in a simple, modern room with a few frivolous touches. There's a small TV lounge and a tiny Jägerstübli, where guests mix with locals over Swiss wine and specialties.

Ⓢ Hotel Eiger. CH-3823 Wengen. ☎ **800/528-1234** in the U.S. and Canada or 033/ 855-11-31. Fax 033/855-10-30. 46 rms. TV TEL. Summer, 190 SF ($157.70) double. Winter, 270 SF ($224.10) double. Rates include breakfast. AE, DC, MC, V.

Rustic timbers cover the walls and ceilings of this attractive hotel behind the cog-railway station. Karl Fuchs and his family offer spacious, attractive rooms with balconies. A modern dining room has views of the Jungfrau massif and the Lauterbrunnen Valley. In the hotel lobby is an inviting sitting area with a fireplace, and there's also a bar reserved for hotel guests.

Hotel Regina. CH-3823 Wengen. ☎ **033/855-15-12.** Fax 033/855-15-74. 95 rms. MINIBAR TV TEL. Summer, 276–332 SF ($229.10–$275.55) double. Winter, 396–416 SF ($328.70– $345.30) double. Rates include half board. AE, DC, MC, V. Closed Oct 15–Dec 15.

A time-honored hotel, the Regina is an embellished Victorian elephant of a building with balconies and lots of charm near the cog-railway station. One of the public rooms has a baronial carved-stone fireplace; the bedrooms are comfortable and cozy. The restaurant offers a fixed-price buffet. You may also order à la carte. Le Carrousel offers dancing to disco music.

Dining

⑤ Hotel Hirschen Restaurant. ☎ 033/855-15-44. Reservations recommended. Main courses 15.50–46 SF ($12.85–$38.20); fixed-price menu 38.50–78 SF ($31.95–$64.75). DC, MC, V. Fri–Tues 11:30am–2pm, Thurs–Tues 6:30–9:15pm. Closed Apr 12–May and Sept 25–Dec 15. SWISS.

This quiet retreat at the foot of the slopes has a true alpine flavor. The rear dining room is decorated with hunting trophies, pewter, and wine racks. Johannes Abplanalp and his family offer a dinner special called *galgenspiess*—fillet of beef, veal, and pork flambéed at your table. Other dishes include fillet of breaded pork, rumpsteak Café de Paris, and fondue Bacchus, bourguignonne, or chinoise. A hearty lunch is winzerrösti—country ham, cheese, and a fried egg with homemade rösti.

GRINDELWALD

The "glacier village" of Grindelwald is set against a backdrop of the Wetterhorn and the towering north face of the Eiger. It's both a winter and a summer resort.

Grindelwald is surrounded with folkloric hamlets, swift streams, and as much alpine beauty as you're likely to find anywhere in Switzerland, and it's easier to reach from Interlaken than either Wengen or Mürren. Although at first the hiking options and cable-car networks might seem baffling, the tourist office can provide maps.

Essentials

ARRIVING   By Train   The Berner Oberland Railway (BOB) leaves from the Interlaken East station. The trip takes 35 minutes.

VISITOR INFORMATION   Grindelwald's **tourist office** is at Sportszentrum, Hauptstrasse, CH-3818 Grindelwald (☎ **033/854-12-12**), open July–Sept Mon–Fri 8am–7pm, Sat 9am–7pm, Sun 9–11am and 4–6pm. Off-season hours are Mon–Fri 8am–noon and 2–6pm, Sat 8am–noon.

Seeing the Glaciers

The town maintains a sheltered observation gallery, adjacent to the base of the **Lower Grindelwald Glacier (Untere Gletscher)** that offers a close look at the rock-strewn ravine formed by the glacier and its annual snowmelt. The half-mile gallery stretches past deeply striated rocks, which include formations of colored marble worn smooth by the glacier's powers of erosion. Don't expect a view of the actual glacier from this point, as you'll have go to a higher altitude, at least in summer, to see the actual ice. The gallery is easy to reach on foot or by car. Four yellow-sided buses labeled GLETSCHERSCHLUCHT depart from a point in front of Grindelwald's railway station four times a day for the lower glacier and points beyond. Passage to the lower glacier costs 4.80 SF ($4), each way, but since the distance from the center of Grindelwald is only about 2 miles, many hardy souls opt to trek across well-marked hiking trails instead.

A more exotic destination, farther afield from Grindelwald, is the **Blue Ice Grotto**, whose frozen mass is part of the Upper Grindelwald Glacier (Obere Gletscher). A popular destination for hillclimbers, it's a 75-minute hike (which includes navigating up an alpine staircase with 890 steps) or a 15-minute bus ride from the Lower Grindelwald Glacier. (The upper and lower glaciers are separated by rocky cliffs and flow within different valleys.) At midday the 150-foot-thick ice walls of the grotto take on an eerie blue tinge. Local guides assure visitors that although the grotto—and the glacier that contains it—are moving slowly downhill, the visitor is perfectly safe. The grotto is open daily mid-June to Oct 9am–5pm. If you don't want to make the uphill trek on foot from Grindelwald (and many visitors do), there's a yellow-sided bus that departs at hourly intervals throughout the day marked GROSSE SCHEIDEGG. One-way fares from Grindelwald to the grotto cost 5.40 SF ($4.50).

Hiking & Mountain Climbing

Grindelwald and its surroundings offer dozens of challenging paths and mountain trails that are well marked and maintained. Outdoor adventures range from an exhilarating ramble across the gentle incline of an alpine valley to a dangerous trek with ropes and pitons along the north face of Mount Eiger. The choice depends on your inclination, degree of experience, and mountaineering skills. Maps showing the region's paths, trails, and their various elevations are available at the town's tourist office.

The high-altitude plateau known as **First** (at 7,113 feet) can be reached from Grindelwald after a 30-minute ride on a six-passenger gondola ("bubble car"). The round-trip price of transport is 43 SF ($35.70). You can stop at such intermediate stations as Bort and Grindel (a site that some locals refer to as Scheckfeld) on your way to **First Mountain terminal and sun terrace.** From First, where there's a restaurant and cafe, you'll have many hiking possibilities into the neighboring Bussalp or Grosse Scheidegg area; at the end of the trails you find a site from which you can return directly to Grindelwald by bus. Also from First, an hour's brisk hike will take you to the still high-altitude walters of **Bachalpsee** (Lake Bachalp).

Faulhorn, at 8,796 feet, is a historic vantage point with a panorama of untouched alpine beauty. Near the summit is a mountain hotel, the Faulhorn Hotel, that has been here for more than 150 years (☎ **033/853-27-13**). Faulhorn is a 7-hour hike from Grindelwald. For a shorter climb, take the cable car or bus to Bussalp, the cable car to First, or the train to Schynige Platte. From any of these intermediate points, climbers can continue their treks on to Faulhorn. Hikes from Bussalp take 3 hours; from First, 2¹⁄₂ hours; and from Schynige Platte, 4 hours.

Grosse Scheidegg, at 6,434 feet, is a famous pass between the Grindelwald and Rosenlaui Valleys. You can hike here in 3 hours from Grindelwald, or you can take a 40-minute bus ride from Grindelwald to Grosse Scheidegg and begin hill walking away from the village traffic and crowds. Round-trip bus passage from Grindelwald to Grosse Scheidegg is 30 SF ($24.90) per person.

Accommodations

✪ **Grand Hotel Regina.** CH-3818 Grindelwald. ☎ **800/874-4002** in the U.S. or 033/854-54-55. Fax 033/853-47-17. 100 rms, 12 suites, 4 penthouse suites. MINIBAR TV TEL. 380 SF ($315.40) double; from 600 SF ($498) suite. AE, V. Closed Oct–Dec 18. Free parking.

Across from the Grindelwald train station, this hotel looks part rustic and part urban slick and dates from the turn of the century. It became a hotel in 1953, and is still evocative of that era's glamor. The facade of the hotel's oldest part has an imposing set of turrets with red-tile roofs. One of the salons has Victorian chairs clustered around bridge tables, with sculpture in wall niches. The bedrooms are done in various styles. There's a steel-and-glass extension housing sports facilities. Live music is performed at the hotel's disco. Both fixed-price and à la carte menus are presented in the restaurant. Facilities include an indoor and outdoor swimming pool, sauna, solarium, and two tennis courts (called "the most magnificently sited in the world").

Hotel Eiger. CH-3818 Grindelwald. ☎ **033/853-21-21.** Fax 033/853-21-01. 50 rms. TV TEL. Summer, 210–260 SF ($174.30–$215.80) double; Winter, 250–290 SF ($207.50–$240.70) double. Half board 35 SF ($29.05) per person extra. Rates include buffet breakfast. AE, DC, MC, V. Closed mid-Oct to mid-Dec. Free parking outdoors, 12 SF ($9.95) in the garage.

This hotel appears from the outside like a collection of interconnected balconies, each on a different plane, angled toward the alpine sunshine, and built of contrasting shades of white stucco and natural wood. The interior is attractive, simple, and unpretentious, with lots of warmly tinted wood, hanging lamps, and contrasting lights. The Gepsi-Bar offers live music, recently released songs, and "evergreen" (mountain) tunes. The Heller family offers a bar and restaurant, including a steakhouse. The facilities include a sauna and a steambath.

☉ Hotel Hirschen. CH-3818 Grindelwald. ☎ **033/854-54-84.** Fax 033/854-54-80. 28 rms. TV TEL. 144–214 SF ($119.50–$177.60) double. Half board 28 SF ($23.25) extra. Rates include continental breakfast. MC, V. Closed Nov–Dec 19. Free parking.

In the three-star Hirschen, the Bleuer family offers one of the resort's best values. The hotel, which has an attractive modern facade, is both comfortable and affordable. It has a respectable dining room, and a popular bowling alley in the cellar.

Dining

Il Mercato. In the Hotel Spinne. ☎ **033/853-23-41.** Reservations recommended. Main courses 26–60 SF ($21.60–$49.80); fixed-price lunch 13–17 SF ($10.80–$14.10). AE, DC, MC, V. Daily noon–2pm and 6:30–10:30pm. ITALIAN/SWISS.

The decor is elegant and alpine, with the kind of Italian touches you might expect in Italian-speaking Ticino. The dining room's visual centerpiece is a large window with a sweeping view over the mountains. During warm weather, tables are set out on the terrace. Menu items include virtually everything from the Italian repertoire, with an emphasis on cold-weather dishes from the Val d'Aosta (northern Italy's milk and cheese district). There are a tempting array of salads, pizzas, pastas, risottos, and grilled meat dishes, always with an emphasis on fresh ingredients such as you'd find in an Italian market.

✪ Restaurant Francais. In the Hotel Belvedere. ☎ **033/854-54-54.** Reservations recommended. Main courses 32–51 SF ($26.55–$42.35); fixed-price menu 49–65 SF ($40.65–$53.95). AE, DC, MC, V. Daily noon–1pm and 6:30–9pm. INTERNATIONAL.

At the best restaurant in Grindelwald, special buffets are a feature. As you listen to the soothing sounds of a live pianist, you can study the menu (which will have changed by the time of your visit). But just to give you an idea, you might be served a game terrine appetizer, roast quail in a Pinot Noir sauce, or thinly sliced bresaola carpaccio. Fish dishes might include poached fillet of turbot served on zucchini and potato rounds with a yellow-red pepper sauce. Main dishes are likely to include lamb entrecôte in a coating of peppercorns or breast of guinea fowl with red wine and prunes.

KANDERSTEG

Lying between Grindelwald and Gstaad, Kandersteg is a popular resort at one of the southern points of the Berner Oberland. It's a tranquil and lovely mountain village with rust- and orange-colored rooftops and green Swiss meadows. The summer and winter resort is spread over 2¹/₂ miles, so nothing is crowded. The village itself is at the foot of the Blumlisalp chain (12,000 ft.) and provides access to six remote alpine hamlets.

Kandersteg developed as a resting point on the road to the Gemmi Pass, which long ago linked the Valais with the Berner Oberland. The village still has many old farmhouses and a tiny church from the 16th century. It's proud of its traditions.

Essentials

ARRIVING   By Train   Kandersteg is at the northern terminus of the 9-mile-long Lotschberg Tunnel, which, ever since the beginning of World War I, has linked Bern with the Rhône Valley. The railroad that runs through the tunnel can transport cars. Trains leave every 30 minutes; no reservations are necessary. The resort is also served by the Bern–Lotschberg–Simplon railway.

By Car   Kandersteg is 27 miles southwest of Interlaken. Take N-8 east to where the Kandersteg road then heads south into the mountains. The journey from Spiez to Kandersteg along a well-built road takes only 20 minutes.

VISITOR INFORMATION   The **Kandersteg Tourist Office,** CH-3718 Kandersteg (☎ **033/675-80-80**), is open Mon–Sat 8am–noon and 2–6pm, Sun 8:30am–noon and 1:30–4:30pm.

Outdoor Activities

There's an extensive network of level footpaths and strategically located benches around Kandersteg. These paths are open year-round. In summer, qualified riders (in proper clothes) can rent horses at the local riding school.

In winter, the resort attracts cross-country skiers and downhill novices (top-speed skiers go elsewhere). It has a cable car, two chairlifts, and four ski tows; the National Nordic Ski Center offers a ski-jumping station. The 1½-mile cross-country ski trail is floodlit in the evening. Other facilities include an indoor and outdoor ice rink.

Excursions Nearby

The most popular excursion from Kandersteg is to **Oeschinensee,** or Lake Oeschinen, high above the village. The lake is surrounded by snow-covered peaks of the Blumlisalp, towering 6,000 feet above the extremely clear water. You can walk to it from the Victoria Hotel or take a chairlift, costing 16 SF ($13.30), to the Oeschinen station and walk down from that point. If you opt to walk, allow about 1½ hours, or 2 hours if you'd like to stroll. Many visitors who take the chairlift decide to hike back to Kandersteg. Be warned, however, of the steep downhill grade.

Another popular excursion is to **Klus Gorge.** Park your car at the cable station's lower platform at Stock and walk 2 miles to the gorge, which was formed by the abrasive action of the Kander River. The rushing water creates a romantic, even primeval, setting. However, you must watch your step, as the path gets very slippery in places. The spray coats the stones and pebbles and has fostered a layer of moss. There is a tunnel over the gorge. In winter the access route is dangerous and ice-bound.

Accommodations & Dining

Hotel Adler. CH-3718 Kandersteg. ☎ **033/675-80-10.** Fax 033/675-80-11. 24 rms. MINIBAR TV TEL. 210–250 SF ($174.30–$207.50) double. Rates include half board. AE, DC, MC, V. Closed Nov 22–Dec 18. Free parking.

An open fire crackling in the foyer sets the tone of this warm, cozy inn, a wood-sided chalet on the main street near the center of town. The fourth-generation owner, Andreas Fetzer, and his Finnish-born wife, Eija, offer comfortable bedrooms paneled in pinewood, a few outfitted with Jacuzzi bathtubs. Almost all accommodations open onto a private balcony. The Adler-Bar, which fills most of the ground floor, is one of the most popular après-ski hangouts in town. There's also a brasserie (the Adlerstube) as well as a relatively formal restaurant.

GSTAAD

Against a backdrop of glaciers and mountain lakes, Gstaad is a haven for the rich and famous. Built at the junction of four quiet valleys near the southern tip of the Berner

Oberland, Gstaad was once only a place to change horses on the grueling trip by carriage through the Berner Oberland. As the railroad lines developed, it grew into a resort for the wealthy who flocked to the Palace Hotel, which promised the ultimate in luxury.

The town retains much of its turn-of-the-century charm. Some first-time visitors, however, say that the resort is a bore if you can't afford to stay at the Gstaad Palace or mingle with the stars in their private chalets. Yet the town has many moderately priced hotels, taverns, and guesthouses, with an allure of their own.

Essentials

ARRIVING   By Train   Gstaad is on the local train line connecting Interlaken with Montreux and several smaller towns in central-southwest Switzerland. About a dozen trains come into Gstaad every day from both of those cities, each of which is a railway junction with good connections to the rest of Switzerland. Travel time from Montreux can be as little as 1 hour and 20 minutes; from Interlaken, about 30 minutes, sometimes with a change of train at the hamlet of Zweisimmen.

By Car   From Spiez follow Route 11 southwest to Gstaad.

VISITOR INFORMATION   The **Gstaad–Saanenland Tourist Association,** CH-3780 Gstaad (☎ **033/748-81-81**), is open Mon–Fri 8:30am–noon and 1:30–6:30pm, Sat 9am–4pm.

Skiing & Hiking

The resort is rich in entertainment and **sports facilities.** Many skiers stay in Gstaad and go to one of the nearby ski resorts in the daytime. Cable cars take passengers to altitudes of 5,000 and 10,000 feet—at the higher altitude there's skiing even in the summer. Other facilities include tennis courts, heated indoor and outdoor swimming pools, and some 200 miles of hiking trails. Many of these scenic trails are possible to walk or hike year-round (the tourist office will advise). The Gstaad International Tennis Tournament, held the second week in July, is the most important tennis event in Switzerland.

Skiers setting off from Gstaad have access to 70 lifts, mountain railroads, and gondolas. The altitude of Gstaad's highest skiable mountain is 6,550 feet, with a vertical drop of 3,555 feet. Most beginner and intermediate runs are east of the village in **Eggli,** a ski area reached by cable car. Eggli has a sunny, southern exposure. **Wispellan–Sanetch** is favored for afternoon skiing, with lots of runs down to the village. At the summit is the Glacier des Diablerets, at a height of 9,900 feet. **Wasserngrat,** reached from the south side of the resort, is another skiing area. Advanced skiers prize Wasserngrat for its powder skiing on steep slopes.

Accommodations

✪ **Palace Hotel Gstaad.** CH-3780 Gstaad. ☎ **800/223-6800** in the U.S. or 033/748-5000. Fax 033/748-5001. 72 rms, 39 suites. MINIBAR TV TEL. Winter, 760–1,100 SF ($630.80–$913) double; off-season (including summer), 480–800 SF ($398.40–$664) double. Suite from 1,300 SF ($1,079) in summer, from 1,850 SF ($1,535.50) in winter. MAP rates. AE, DC, MC, V. Closed March 24 to June 16 and mid-September to mid-December.

This landmark hotel is on a wooded hill overlooking the center of Gstaad, with mock-fortified corner towers and a neomedieval facade. It's one of the most sought-after luxury hideaways in the world, attracting corporation heads, film stars, jetsetters, and the titled. The nerve center of this chic citadel is an elegantly paneled main salon, with an eternal flame burning in the baronial stone fireplace. Radiating hallways lead to superb restaurants, bars, discos, and sports facilities. The distinguished rooms are plush and tasteful. Facilities include an indoor swimming pool with underwater sound system, fitness center, sauna, solarium, ice rink, and tennis courts.

✪ **Hostellerie Alpenrose.** Hauptstrasse, CH-3778 Schönried Gstaad. ☎ **033/744-67-67.** Fax 033/744-67-12. 21 rms. MINIBAR TV TEL. Summer, 260–440 SF ($215.80–$365.20) double. Winter, 205–470 SF ($170.15–$390.10) double. Half board 45 SF ($37.35) extra. Rates include breakfast. AE, DC, MC, V. Closed Easter–May 20 and Nov–Dec 15. Parking 15 SF ($11.70).

For those who like the charm of a small inn, this is the preferred choice, and the only Relais & Châteaux listing within 30 miles. Its soft-spoken owner, Monika von Siebenthal, is a memorable host, setting the fashionable tone of the chalet, which is famous for its restaurants. The pine-paneled rooms are exquisitely decorated with rustic furnishings, and the bedrooms are tastefully appointed.

✪ **Hotel Olden.** Hauptstrasse, CH-3780 Gstaad. ☎ **033/744-34-44.** Fax 033/744-61-64. 15 rms. MINIBAR TV TEL. Summer, 170–290 SF ($141.10–$240.70) double. Winter, 290–370 SF ($240.70–$307.10) double. Rates include continental breakfast. AE, DC, MC, V. Closed Apr–May and Nov 3–Dec 6. Parking 15 SF ($12.45).

This is a low-key and gracefully unpretentious hotel, a sort of Victorian country inn set amid a sometimes chillingly glamorous landscape. The facade is painted with regional floral designs and pithy bits of folk wisdom, with embellishments carved or painted into the stone lintels around many of the doors. Rooms are generally furnished in the typical folkloric alpine style, although the baths have been modernized. Some guests are housed in the adjacent chalet wing.

Dining

Olden Restaurant. In the Hotel Olden, Hauptstrasse. ☎ **033/744-34-44.** Reservations recommended. Main courses 32–65 SF ($26.55–$53.95). AE, DC, MC, V. Daily noon–2pm and 7:30–10pm. Closed Apr–May and Nov 3–Dec 6. MEDITERRANEAN/SWISS.

The most formal of the several dining areas in this previously recommended hotel, it attracts the latest visiting celebrity with its country charm. The menu might include smoked salmon, fresh goose-liver terrine, shrimp bisque with green peppercorns, house-style tagliatelle, raclette, medaillons of veal with a confit of lemon, or Scottish lamb.

✪ **Restaurant Chesery.** Lauenenstrasse. ☎ **033/744-24-51.** Reservations required. Main courses 45–52 SF ($37.35–$43.15); fixed-price dinner 120–138 SF ($99.60–$114.55). AE, DC, MC, V. Wed–Fri 5pm–midnight, Sat–Sun 11am–midnight. INTERNATIONAL.

At an elevation of 3,600 feet, this is one of the 10 best restaurants in Switzerland. The floors are pink marble, and the walls are polished pine. The menu changes daily, based on the freshest ingredients available. Typical dishes include a warm salad of red snapper, cassolette of flap mushrooms with a suprême of quail, fillet of beef poached with grated horseradish, and a soufflé of white cheese with the essence of fresh seasonal fruits. Piano music is played 9pm–3am.

Index

FROMMER'S COMPLETE TRAVEL GUIDES

*(Comprehensive guides to destinations around the world, with
selections in all price ranges—from deluxe to budget)*

Acapulco/Ixtapa/Zihuatenjo
Alaska
Amsterdam
Arizona
Atlanta
Australia
Austria
Bahamas
Bangkok
Barcelona, Madrid &
   Seville
Belgium, Holland &
   Luxembourg
Berlin
Bermuda
Boston
Budapest & the Best of
   Hungary
California
Canada
Cancún, Cozumel & the
   Yucatán
Caribbean
Caribbean Cruises & Ports
   of Call
Caribbean Ports of Call
Carolinas & Georgia
Chicago
Colorado
Costa Rica
Denver, Boulder &
   Colorado Springs
Dublin
England

Florida
France
Germany
Greece
Hawaii
Hong Kong
Honolulu/Waikiki/Oahu
Ireland
Italy
Jamaica & Barbados
Japan
Las Vegas
London
Los Angeles
Maryland & Delaware
Maui
Mexico
Mexico City
Miami & the Keys
Montana & Wyoming
Montréal & Québec
   City
Munich & the Bavarian
   Alps
Nashville & Memphis
Nepal
New England
New Mexico
New Orleans
New York City
Northern New England
Nova Scotia, New
   Brunswick & Prince
   Edward Island

Paris
Philadelphia & the Amish
   Country
Portugal
Prague & the Best of the
   Czech Republic
Puerto Rico
Puerto Vallarta, Manzanillo
   & Guadalajara
Rome
San Antonio & Austin
San Diego
San Francisco
Santa Fe, Taos &
   Albuquerque
Scandinavia
Scotland
Seattle & Portland
South Pacific
Spain
Switzerland
Thailand
Tokyo
Toronto
U.S.A.
Utah
Vancouver & Victoria
Vienna
Virgin Islands
Virginia
Walt Disney World &
   Orlando
Washington, D.C.
Washington & Oregon

FROMMER'S FRUGAL TRAVELER'S GUIDES

*(The grown-up guides to budget travel, offering dream vacations
at down-to-earth prices)*

Australia from $45 a Day
Berlin from $50 a Day
California from $60 a Day
Caribbean from $60 a Day
Costa Rica & Belize from
   $35 a Day
Eastern Europe from
   $30 a Day

England from $50 a Day
Europe from $50 a Day
Florida from $50 a Day
Greece from $45 a Day
Hawaii from $60 a Day
India from $40 a Day
Ireland from $45 a Day
Italy from $50 a Day

Israel from $45 a Day
London from $60 a Day
Mexico from $35 a Day
New York from $70 a Day
New Zealand from $45 a Day
Paris from $60 a Day
Washington, D.C. from
   $50 a Day

FROMMER'S PORTABLE GUIDES

(Pocket-size guides for travelers who want everything in a nutshell)

Charleston & Savannah   Las Vegas   Washington, D.C.   New Orleans   San Francisco

FROMMER'S FAMILY GUIDES

(The complete guides for successful family vacations)

California with Kids	New England with Kids	San Francisco with Kids
Los Angeles with Kids	New York City with Kids	Washington, D.C. with Kids

FROMMER'S AMERICA ON WHEELS

(Everything you need for a successful road trip, including full-color road maps and ratings for every hotel)

California & Nevada	Midwest & the Great	Northwest & the	Southwest
Florida	Lake States	Great Plains States	Texas & the South-
Mid-Atlantic	New York & the New	Southeast	Central States
	England States		

FROMMER'S WALKING TOURS

(Memorable neighborhood strolls through the world's great cities)

Berlin	Montréal & Québec City	Spain's Favorite Cities
Chicago	New York	Tokyo
England's Favorite Cities	Paris	Venice
London	San Francisco	Washington, D.C.

SPECIAL-INTEREST TITLES

Arthur Frommer's Branson!
Arthur Frommer's New World of Travel
The Civil War Trust's Official Guide to the
    Civil War Discovery Trail
Frommer's America's 100 Best-Loved State
    Parks
Frommer's Caribbean Hideaways
Frommer's Complete Hostel Vacation Guide to
    England, Scotland & Wales
Frommer's Food Lover's Companion to France
Frommer's Food Lover's Companion to Italy
Frommer's Great European Driving Tours

Frommer's National Park Guide
Outside Magazine's Adventure Guide to New
    England
Outside Magazine's Adventure Guide to
    Northern California
Places Rated Almanac
Retirement Places Rated
USA Sports Traveler's and TV Viewer's
    Golf Tournament Guide
USA Sports Minor League Baseball Book
USA Today Golf Atlas
Wonderful Weekends from NYC

FROMMER'S IRREVERENT GUIDES

(Wickedly honest guides for sophisticated travelers)

Amsterdam	Manhattan	Paris	U.S. Virgin Islands
Chicago	Miami	San Francisco	Walt Disney World
London	New Orleans	Santa Fe	Washington, D.C.

UNOFFICIAL GUIDES

(Get the unbiased truth from these candid, value-conscious guides)

Atlanta	Euro Disneyland	Mini-Mickey
Branson, Missouri	The Great Smoky & Blue	Skiing in the West
Chicago	Ridge Mountains	Walt Disney World
Cruises	Las Vegas	Walt Disney World Companion
Disneyland	Miami & the Keys	Washington, D.C.

BAEDEKER
(With four-color photographs and a free pull-out map)

Amsterdam	Florence	London	Scotland
Athens	Florida	Mexico	Singapore
Austria	Germany	New York	South Africa
Bali	Great Britain	Paris	Spain
Belgium	Greece	Portugal	Switzerland
Budapest	Greek Islands	Prague	Thailand
California	Hawaii	Provence	Tokyo
Canada	Hong Kong	Rome	Turkish Coast
Caribbean	Ireland	San Francisco	Tuscany
China	Israel	St. Petersburg	Venice
Copenhagen	Italy	Scandinavia	Vienna
Crete	Lisbon		

FROMMER'S BY NIGHT GUIDES
(The series for those who know that life begins after dark)

Amsterdam	London	Miami	Paris
Chicago	Los Angeles	New Orleans	San Francisco
Las Vegas	Manhattan		

FROMMER'S BEST BEACH VACATIONS
(The top places to sun, stroll, shop, stay, play, party, and swim, with ratings for each beach)

California	Hawaii	New England
Carolinas & Georgia	Mid-Atlantic (from New	
Florida	York to Washington, D.C.)	

FROMMER'S BED & BREAKFAST GUIDES
(Selective guides with four-color photos and full descriptions of the best inns in each region)

California	Great American Cities	New England	The Rockies
Caribbean	Hawaii	Pacific Northwest	Southwest

FROMMER'S DRIVING TOURS
(Four-color photos and detailed maps outlining spectacular scenic driving routes)

Australia	France	Italy	Spain
Austria	Germany	Scandinavia	Switzerland
Britain	Ireland	Scotland	U.S.A.
Florida			

FROMMER'S BORN TO SHOP
(The ultimate guides for travelers who love to shop)

France	Hong Kong	Mexico
Great Britain	London	New York

TRAVEL & LEISURE GUIDES
(Sophisticated pocket-size guides for discriminating travelers)

Amsterdam	Hong Kong	New York	San Francisco
Boston	London	Paris	Washington, D.C.

WHEREVER YOU TRAVEL, *H*ELP IS NEVER FAR AWAY.

From planning your trip to

providing travel assistance along

the way, American Express®

Travel Service Offices are

always there to help.

American Express Travel Service Offices are found in central locations throughout Europe.

Travel